THE CONCISE ENCYCLOPÆDIA OF ISLAM

THIRD EDITION

WITH EXTENSIVE CHRONOLOGY

THE CONCISE ENCYCLOPÆDIA OF ISLAM

THIRD EDITION

WITH EXTENSIVE CHRONOLOGY

CYRIL GLASSÉ

INTRODUCTION BY
PROFESSOR HUSTON SMITH

STACEY
INTERNATIONAL

Dedicated to Tom Stacey,
my publisher,
and all the scholars in the field of Islamic studies
who made this work possible

Photographic Acknowledgements

Ahuan Islamic Art, London ii, iii (bottom); S.M. Amin (Aramco World) xvii (bottom right); Baco Contracts Ltd/Maju Tekno Adn Bhd xii (bottom left); Ira Block (The Image Bank) x (bottom right); Maximilien Bruggmann iv, xi (bottom right), xxiii; Jusuf Buchinger xvii (top), xx (bottom), xxi (bottom); Camerapix Picture Library viii (top), xvii (bottom), xviii (bottom left); John Egan (Hutchinson Library) xxii (bottom left); Peter Fraenkel v (bottom left), ix, xvi (bottom); Cyril Glassé xx (top); IPA/TRIP v (top right), viii (right), x (top right, bottom left), xi (top, bottom left), xii (top left, bottom right); Middle East Archives i, vi, vii, xiv; Christopher Mould (NAAS Picture Library) xviii (top), xix, xxi (top); Peter Sanders (TRIP) viii (left), xxii (bottom right); Reg Seale (TRIP) xiii; Sotheby's xv (right); Tony Stone Photo Library, London xvi (top); Wim Swaan v (top left); Neil Turner (NAAS Picture Library) xxiv (5); by courtesy of the Board of Trustees of the Victoria and Albert Museum xv (left); Nik Wheeler viii (bottom right), xxii (top).

Consultant Editor J. Peter Hobson
Editors Nicholas Drake, Elizabeth Davis, and John Blackett-Ord, Charles Powell

The Concise Encyclopaedia of Islam
Stacey International
128 Kensington Church Street
London W8 4BH
Tel: +44 (0)20 7221 7166; Fax: +44 (0)20 7792 9288
E-mail: info@stacey-international.co.uk

First published 1989
Second edition 1991
Reprinted 1999
Revised edition 2001
Reprinted 2002
Third Edition 2008

Printed and bound in Singapore by Tien Wah Press

ISBN 978-1-905299-68-3

British Library Catalogue in Publication Data: A catalogue record for this book is available from the British Library

CONTENTS

AUTHOR'S PREFACE

My debt to all the scholars in Islamic studies, past and present, is so vast as to be incalculable. Without their painstaking, and dedicated labors of research and translation it would have been impossible to present the outlines of a subject as complex as a religious civilization in a form as brief as this book. Keys for the understanding of traditional metaphysics and thought have been found in the works of René Guenon.

I am grateful for assistance with the manuscript to: Marguerite N. Howe, Youmna Adal, Kevin Cohalan, Beverly Swabb, Whitall N. Perry, Zaynab Istrabadi, Terry Moore, Lawrence Meehan, Dr. William Stoddart, Alexandra Bonfante-Warren, and to my final editors, Nicholas Drake and the late J. Peter Hobson.

I am especially indebted to Dr. Victor Danner who was generous with his time and advice.

In matters of interpretation I have sought to present views which would not be at variance with those of orthodox Sunnī Islam. If I have strayed, the responsibility is my own.

Cyril Glassé
New York

INTRODUCTION

by Professor Huston Smith

One can wonder whether in all the human sciences there is greater need for a reference work than this one in hand. The question risks hyperbole, but there is reason to take it seriously. The world, especially the Western world towards which this encyclopædia is primarily directed, desperately needs to understand Islam better, and in the face of this need previous reference works are woefully inadequate.

At the height of the US-Iranian crisis in 1979, a journalist called attention to the seriousness of our ignorance in words that are likely to retain their force for some time. "We are heading," Meg Greenfield wrote in *Newsweek*,

> "into an expansion of the American relationship with that complex of religion, culture and geography known as Islam. There are two things to be said about this. One is that no part of the world is more important to our own well-being at the moment – and probably for the foreseeable future. The other is that no part of the world is more hopelessly and systematically and stubbornly misunderstood by us."

Towards alleviating this misunderstanding previous reference works did what they could, but they do not come close to meeting the present need. Hughes' *Dictionary of Islam* dates back to the nineteenth century and has a missionary bias that forces Pakistani editions to white-out objectionable passages on almost every page. The four-volume *Encyclopædia of Islam* which appeared between 1913 and 1938 (and its condensed version, cut down to 600 entries from 10,000, the *Shorter Encyclopædia of Islam*, which appeared in 1961) is more objective; its new edition, which is in progress, will serve specialists well, but only half of the fascicules in which it is being issued have appeared, and the price of the eventual multi-volume set will be beyond the reach of the general public. There is a good work in German, *Lexikon der Islamischen Welt*, but (aside from two volumes by the Ronart husband and wife team that deal exclusively with the Arab world) in English this is the picture.

To return to the Greenfield quote, why is it that Islam is so "hopelessly and systematically and stubbornly" – three exceptionally severe adjectives – misunderstood by the west? One answer is that the west's separation of church and state makes it next to impossible for it to understand people who not only lodge religious belief at the center of their individual conduct, but also at the center of their politics.

This is indeed a major obstacle, but there are two others, the first of which again relates to politics. It is ironic that of the major faiths outside Christendom, Islam stands closest to the Judæo-Christian West both geographically and religiously – geographically, Christianity and Islam have shared common borders for thirteen hundred years, while religiously both are descended from Abraham – yet is the one that is least understood. On reflection, though, while this is indeed ironic, it is not surprising. Common borders provoke border disputes, and these can easily escalate into raids, blood-feuds and full scale wars. During most of their history, Muslims and Christians have been at odds, and rivals are not known for having the most objective views of each other.

Once we think of them, these two causes of misunderstanding are obvious; but the third one is not. Religiously, people tend to fall into two categories. Some find the meaning they seek in religious forms – commandments, observances, and texts straightforwardly, largely literally, interpreted – while others, without bypassing or abandoning these, sense their provisional character and reach out for meanings that the forms contain but which cannot be equated with those forms. If we call the first type of person exoteric, out of his concern for meanings that attach to outward or manifest forms, the second type that is drawn to the meanings that underlie those forms conveniently designated esoteric.

Both types turn up in all the historical religions and very likely in tribal ones as well, but nowhere does the difference surface quite as clearly as in Islam. Exoterically, outwardly, and explicitly – Islam is the *sharī'a*, a revealed, canonic law by which the faithful should live. Concomitantly, though, the Koran and the *Ḥadīth*, or authoritative Traditions that were instituted by Muhammad, abound in references, frequently veiled, to profound, metaphysical truths which the forms of Islam enfold and protect in the way husks protect and conceal their kernels. Esoterics see these references as invitations to serch out those deeper truths and make them the center of their lives. At their best, Sufi orders are associations of such esoterics.

Every reference work on Islam will take note of this esoteric/exoteric distinction somewhere, but in others it turns up only in isolated pockets: a handful of entries such as those on Sufism, Mysticism, *taṣawwuf* – perhaps a dozen items in all. It is a remarkable feature of this new encyclopædia that it takes at its starting point that almost everything in Islam can be viewed in these two perspectives. Beginning with that premise, it proceeds to compile a resource that tries intentionally to do justice to both. A glance at the very first entry on "Aaron" will make this clear.

What is in hand, therefore, is more than just a new reference book on Islam that is up-to-date and has been kept to a manageable compass, i.e. a single volume. By virtue of the "binocular" exoteric/esoteric vision that it trains on its entries throughout, a new dimension of depth comes into view. The result is an encyclopedia that does more than bring reliable information into reach. In the long run it can help its readers to see the phenomenon of Islam in a new light.

It seems almost redundant to say that its able and devoted author, Cyril Glassé, deserves our heartfelt thanks.

Huston Smith

NOTES

1. The principal abbreviations used are as follows:

A.D.	Anno Domini	Lit.	Literally
A.H.	Anno Hegirae	Pers.	Persian
Ar	Arabic	Pl.	Plural
Fr.	French	Sing.	Singular
Gr.	Greek	Turk.	Turkish

2. In most cases, dates are given according to both Hegirian and Gregorian Calendars. The Hegirian date is given first, in italics.

3. The following system of Arabic transliteration has been used:

Transliteration	Arabic Letter	Transliteration	Arabic Letter
’	ء	ṭ	ط
b	ب	ẓ	ظ
t	ت	‘	ع
th	ث	gh	غ
j	ج	f	ف
ḥ	ح	q	ق
kh	خ	k	ك
d	د	l	ل
dh	ذ	m	م
r	ر	n	ن
z	ز	ah/at	ه
s	س	w	و
sh	ش	y	ي
ṣ	ص	t	ة
ḍ	ض		

short vowels (represented by orthographical signs placed above or below Arabic letters)

a	َ (above) eg. ba =	بَ
u	ُ (above) eg. bu =	بُ
i	ِ (below) eg. bi =	بِ

long vowels

ā	آ
ū	وْ
ī	يْ

dipthongs

aw	وَ
ay	يَ
iyy	يِّ
uww	وُّ

4. The numbering of Koranic passages is according to Arberry.

بِسْمِ اللَّهِ الرَّحْمَنِ الرَّحِيمِ

IN THE NAME OF GOD, THE MERCIFUL, THE COMPASSIONATE*

*The *Basmalah*. *See* page 89.

A

Aaron (Ar. *Hārūn*). The brother of Moses. In the Koran, Moses says:

Lord, open my breast....
and do Thou ease for me my task.
Unloose the knot upon my tongue,
that they may understand my words.
Appoint for me of my folk a familiar,
Aaron, my brother; by him confirm
my strength, and associate him with me
in my task. (20:25-35)

The Koran accords Aaron an important place alongside Moses, and he is sometimes deemed a Prophet in his own right; representing the esoteric dimension as Moses represents the exoteric. Moses is identified with exoterism because his revelation consists above all of the Mosaic law. The outwardness of Moses' mission is emphasized in the story of his encounter with al-Khiḍr, the personification of esoteric wisdom. Moses does not see beyond the facts of al-Khiḍr's actions to understand their ultimate nature.

Moses said to him, 'Shall I follow thee
so that thou teachest me, of what
thou hast been taught, right judgment?'
Said he, 'Assuredly thou wilt not
be able to bear with me patiently.
And how shouldst thou bear patiently
that thou has never encompassed
in thy knowledge?' (18:65-69)

Exoterism is the domain of rituals, of moral precepts, of institutions; esoterism claims to be that of transcendent wisdom and mystical union, of realization through direct knowledge of the Divine. While in exceptional cases such knowledge may, through Divine grace, irrupt spontaneously within the soul, it is much more often the fruit of a sustained effort to actualize doctrine or theoretical truth through a method of concentration, that is found in a "Way". As such, it is knowledge that the soul has experienced, and thus confirmed for itself. Ultimately, this process implies a transcendental union between the soul and the truth.

Islam designates the exoteric and esoteric aspects respectively by the terms *sharī'ah* (the religious law) and *ṭarīqah* (the path of mystical realization) or by *aẓ-ẓāhir* ("the outer"), and *al-bāṭin* ("the inner"). Esoterism is also called the "kernel" (*al-lubb*), and the Koran sometimes addresses itself to "those who possess the kernels" (*ulu-l-albāb*)

Another, different, aspect of the relationship between exoterism and esoterism is manifested in the Koranic episode of the golden calf. While Moses is on Mount Sinai, the people make, and pay homage to, an idol. Aaron says to them:

'My people, you have been tempted
by this thing, no more; surely
Your Lord is the All-merciful; therefore
follow me, and obey my commandment!'
'We will not cease,' they said, 'to cleave
to it, until Moses returns to us.' (20:92-93)

When Moses returns he reproaches his brother:

'What prevented thee,
Aaron, when thou sawest them in error,
so that thou didst not follow after me?
Didst thou then disobey my commandment?'
'Son of my mother,' Aaron said,
'take me not by the beard, or the head!
I was fearful that thou wouldst say,
"Thou has divided the Children of Israel,
and thou hast not observed my word."'
(20:94-96)

Because it opens onto the formless, esoterism threatens to shatter dogma, and the *sharī'ah*; nonetheless, its presence inevitably depends upon exoterism's revealed forms. When exoterism is absent, as symbolized in this episode by Moses' absence on the mountain, orthodoxy is lost and disintegration follows: when the formal hold of religious dogmas weakens, fissiparous heresy is given free rein. It can therefore be said that the test of orthodox esoterism is that it does not contradict exoterism. The realization towards which esoterism is directed implies rather the transcending of form through form. The higher the spiritual aspiration, the more important and strict the observance of religious law becomes. Esoterism depends upon exoterism in yet another way: without exoterism, the truth is "invisible". Light in itself is a revelation, but unless it illuminates forms it "shineth in darkness, and the darkness comprehended it not". It is only through form, in the sense of exoterism and also of a defined corpus of revelation, that it is possible to attain to formless truth: "I am the door..." On the other hand, without esoterism the form becomes empty and a dead letter: "They have no wine."

As al-Ḥujwīrī says:

> The exoteric aspect of Truth without the esoteric is hypocrisy, and the esoteric without the exoteric is heresy. So, with regard to the Law, mere formality is defective, while mere spirituality is vain.

While the dichotomy between esoterism and exoterism is thus adumbrated in the Koran by the figures of Aaron and Moses (and developed more explicitly in oral tradition that has spun innumerable didactic tales of Moses), we find in the person of the Prophet the two ways joined in one and harmonized. He was a lawgiver but also the channel for an outpouring of *riḍwān* ("felicitous union"), as took place in the event of the Pact of Ḥudaybiyyah. Among his two hundred names are *Miftāḥ ar-Raḥmah* ("the Key of Mercy"), *Sayyid al-Kawnayn* ("Lord of the Two Worlds"), "the Fount of Grace", "the Master of the Lofty Degree". Many of the Ḥadīth, such as "who has seen me has seen the truth" (*man ra'ānī faqad rā' al-ḥaqq*), completely elude being coherently enclosed in any purely exoteric interpretation. Indeed, Islam, of all religions, is remarkably balanced in this respect.

Theoretically, in Judaism, the esoteric and exoteric were originally one. The "inner", being inseparable from the "outer", manifested itself in God's historic acts towards the nation; and the Torah itself was mysticism and sacrament, as was the tribe's very history. This evidently could not continue indefinitely, since the unmanifest cannot coincide with, or forever be reduced to, the manifest and specific. The tension culminated in the rending of the veil of the Temple, and finally in the destruction of the earthly Temple itself. There remained in Judaism a tendency to transform the esoteric into the exoteric and to make ritual of it. Thus the Qabbalah (the post-Christian mysticism that succeeded the Merkava or Heikhalot school) readily becomes an intensified exoterism or a pietistic fervor; moreover, the Qabbalah sees the sephiroth as the body or substance of Judaism, and of Jews, but considers the rest to be of a "demonic" substance, as if it were not God's creation.

Christianity, by contrast, is so essentially esoteric in nature that it had to adopt the forms of the Roman Empire as its outer, or exoteric shell. It thus exhibited the opposite tendency to that of Judaism, by esoterizing the outer and the horizontal planes of existence. Christian fervor attempted to actualize the descent of the heavenly Jerusalem in its worldly institution. Byzantium sought to accumulate all of the gold in the world, not only out of ordinary human avarice, but because the Bible says that the streets of the New Jerusalem are paved with gold. In Byzantium, the very weights and measures reflected a heavenly perfection, and a baker could be put to death for selling a loaf that deviated from the ideal dimension.

Full-blown esoterism with a minimum of exoterism, is the most subtle of dangers, for it can lead to an "absolutizing" of the relative. The French Revolution, that exalted the merely human and rational, made a shrine in Paris out of a length of metal that it called the "standard"— the absolute— meter bar. The Christian notion that God had become man, in order that man raise his nature to conform with the ideally real, became particularly, after the Renaissance, the idea that man as such, i.e. fallen man, was God. With this came the gradual transformation of the world itself; it led to the invention of "progress"— and the modern world. Man splices genes, and inevitably the idea implants itself that man is God.

The clear presence from the beginning of an esoteric aspect to Islam points to its origin in a form of Gnosis. This is also clear from the very nature of the two testimonies of the Faith, one, an enunciation of a doctrine regarding the nature of reality and the other the recognition of the teacher of the doctrine as the way to and through that doctrine. Islam, however, from the outset has presented a balance between exoterism and esoterism; it is a "rectification" of preceding forms of Gnosis. It affirms that God is a unity and not a duality, and that the teacher of the doctrine is a man and not divine or semi-divine himself. It does not demand spiritual heroism of man; it only asks him to be truly man. Nor does God bind himself to man in an historic covenant with a particular people. His covenant is with man as such, and in it God "returns to his throne" (*istawā 'ala-l-'arsh*, Koran 7:54; 10:3; 13:2; 25:59; 57:4) after creating the world in six days. In Islam God "resumes" (with respect to man's knowledge of God, that hangs upon Revelation) His nature of Absolute, as man resumes his primordial nature, symbolized by "the return to the religion of Abraham" and that of Adam. Islam is both a law to ensure social stability, and a transcendent truth; the latter, its esoterism, is found in the *shahādah* (the testimony of faith), the "seeing" that only God is Reality, that truth is itself the means of salvation. This is one sense of the Ḥadīth: "I [the Prophet] have brought both the good things of this world, and the good things of the next world." *See* al-KHIḌR; MOSES; al-QĀSHĀNĪ; RIḌWĀN; SHAHĀDAH; ṬARĪQAH.

'Abā'. The sleeveless garment, open in the front, that is worn by men in the Arabian peninsula. In Saudi Arabia this male attire is more often called a *busht*, while the generic terms *'abā'* or *'abayah* are commonly used to designate a similar cloak that is worn in black over the head by most women when appearing in public.

al-'Abbās ibn 'Abd al-Muṭṭalib (d. *32*/652). An uncle of the Prophet, noted as a rich and shrewd merchant. Throughout the early struggle of Islam he maintained a cautious balance between the Muslims and the Meccans. He protected the Prophet against the other clans while the latter was in Mecca, but fought on the Meccan side after the Hijrah.

Al-'Abbās entered Islam while held as a captive in Medinah after the Battle of Badr. When he protested that he had no means to ransom himself, the Prophet confronted him with miraculous knowledge of a secret conversation that had taken place in Mecca concerning the disposition of al-'Abbās' fortune if he died in war. That the Prophet knew this proved to al-'Abbās that he must indeed be inspired.

However, al-'Abbās returned to Mecca and only joined the Muslims at the last moment as the Prophet advanced upon Mecca for the final conquest. This flight to the Medinan side at the final hour marked the end of the period of the Hijrah, and the Prophet named al-'Abbās "last of the refugees", (*muhājirūn*). Typical of his good fortune in life, these words entitled al-'Abbās and his descendants to stipends from the spoils of war according to the elevated rank of *muhājirūn* as prescribed by the tables of rank and merit, the *diwān*, established in the Caliphate of 'Umar.

Al-'Abbās had the privilege of supplying Zamzam water to pilgrims. This his descendants kept. His son 'Abd Allāh ibn al-'Abbās became a celebrated interpreter of the Koran, who offered, among his other commentaries, explanations for the meanings of the mysterious isolated letters that are found heading certain Sūrahs. From al-'Abbās sprang the 'Abbāsid dynasty (*132-656*/749-1258), that followed the Umayyads, yet another example of al-'Abbās' enduring good fortune. The 'Abbāsids, as cousins, laid claim to the prestige of being of the Prophet's family, while their rivals the 'Alīds, the direct descendants of the Prophet, were, for most of history, obliged to lie low.

Al-'Abbās was a half-uncle of the Prophet; his mother was not the mother of 'Abd Allāh, the Prophet's father, but both 'Abd Allāh and al-'Abbās had the same father, 'Abd al-Muṭṭalib. Abū Ṭālib and Zubayr, however, were full uncles being both sons of the Prophet's grandfather and his grandmother. This played a certain role regarding how the legitimacy of the 'Abbāsids was presented from the Shī'ite point of view.

His son 'Abd Allāh ibn-l-'Abbās studiously kept out of the way of the political struggles that enveloped early Islam. However, he cultivated a reputation for piety and religious knowledge by collecting Ḥadīth and inventing commentary on the Koran with the help of Jewish converts such as Ka'b al-Aḥbār. Thus he brought, along with Wahb ibn Munabbih, stories about prophets and Biblical events called Isrā'īliyāt, or Jewish folklore, into Koranic studies. He died in Ṭā'if in *68*/687, at the age of 72. A few years before his death, he and his family, and Muḥammad ibn Ḥanifiyyah, along with some seventeen Kūfan notables had been imprisoned in Mecca by 'Abd Allāh ibn az-Zubayr; they were freed by horsemen from Kūfah sent by the revolutionary Mukhtār at the request of Muḥammad ibn al-Ḥanifiyyah. It was thus that the 'Abbāsids learned of the mysterious Shī'ah or partisans supporting the family of 'Alī; and they soon took steps to make these partisans their own allies in what was to become the 'Abbāsid revolution.

'Abbāsids (Ar. *ad-dawlah al-'abbāsiyyah*). The second dynasty of the Islamic Empire that succeeded the Umayyads in *132*/749. The rule of the Umayyads was in many ways a prolongation of the old secular and ethnocentric ways of the Arabs — "the Arab kingdom". Many of the later trappings of the 'Abbāsids, such as the sudden concealment of the ruler behind a curtain during audiences— his exaltation — that prompted an ambassador of the Fāṭimids to ask during a particularly impressive ceremony at the time of the Buyids if he were being shown God, were in the grand style of an Eastern potentate and a heritage of the Sāssānids. But if the Umayyads were like desert kings, with the 'Abbāsids there was a definite consciousness of a supra-national new world order. Under the 'Abbāsids, the genius of the Persians fused with Arab-Islamic civilization to reach a high point. Outstanding accomplishments in the fields of medicine, science, literature, and art date from this epoch. The growing importance of Persia in the Islamic Empire was signaled in *145*/762, in the transfer of the capital eastward, next to the Ctesiphon of the Sāssānids, to Baghdad, that had been newly founded by the second 'Abbāsid Caliph, al-Manṣūr. (*See* BAGHDAD.) The reign of the 'Abbāsids, although for the most part they did not actually control the Empire, lasted over five hundred years until the coming of the Mongols in *656*/1258.

The Umayyads had been notorious for their despotism, and rising discontent with their harsh rule led to their downfall. The descendants of al-'Abbās, uncle of the prophet, had avoided the early struggles for power after the first four Caliphs and planted themselves, around the year 700, in al-Ḥumaymah (Lat. 30 degrees North Long. 35 degrees 20 minutes East) southeast of the Dead Sea, 50 km southwest of Ma'ān, Jordan, halfway to 'Aqabah, on the ancient route between Aylah [Eilat], and Petra, apparently in the middle of nowhere but in reality tapping into the communications line between Medinah and Damascus. The opposition to the Umayyads originally turned to the descendants of the Prophet, the 'Alīds, to find leaders, or rather, figureheads for their movements (as 'Alī had turned to the opposition in 'Irāq for support). These proved incapable of leading a successful rebellion, but thus the so-called Shī'ites were born comprising groups of shadowy affiliation looking for someone who could gather a necessary critical mass of the ruling Arabs for a successful bid for power. After the Kūfans had tried to run Ḥusayn ibn 'Alī up the flag-pole to discover that no-one was prepared to salute, they tentatively chose Muḥammad ibn al-Ḥanifiyyah as their figurehead. His campaign came to nothing. Then they turned instead to the family of 'Abbās who had the virtue of being related to the Prophet, being Arab, and being untainted by prior revolutionary activity and failure. The partners they found turned out to be much more clever than anyone suspected.

The 'Abbāsids demonstrated a remarkable ability to attain power. First they remained in a latent state for almost one hundred years. When they began their political activity they did so behind a mask, and carried their plan through several generations before success was achieved. Beginning around *100*/718 the 'Abbāsids formed a coalition with clandestine groups in Kūfah and Khorāsān who were the organization that had raised the revolt of Mukhtār. These clandestine groups were also those who had tentatively supported the Caliph 'Alī, had tested Ḥusayn's capacity to lead by drawing him fatally to his death, and had later supported a half-brother of Ḥusayn, Muḥammad ibn al-Ḥanifiyyah. Abū Hāshim, son of Muḥammad ibn al-Ḥanifiyyah, grandson of 'Alī but not through Fāṭimah, had inherited this support and these connections from his father. Abū Hāshim, on bad terms with the other cousin 'Alīds (who actually threatened to expose his clandestine activities to the Umayyad authorities), but cared for by his cousin 'Abbāsids, passed these revolutionary connections on to Muḥammad ibn 'Alī the 'Abbāsid, in the form of the *'ilm*, ("knowledge"). This was the information, political and occult, necessary to work with the Kaysāniyyah (also called the Mukhtāriyyah, and subsequently, under Abū Hāshim, also called the Hāshimiyyah) and the ideological requirements for cooperation with this shadowy organization. (For a description of these events, *see* MUḤAMMAD ibn al-ḤANAFIYYAH.) Thus the original anti-Umayyad coalition of 'Alī and the 'Irāqī Lakhmid remnants, remnants who were part of the vast Manichean brotherhood from North Africa to Khorāsān, and Sindh, passed into the hands of the 'Abbāsids. The coalition did not disappear with the coming of the 'Abbāsids to the throne; the downfall of the Barmakids and the end of the miḥnah period were two major milestones on the way to its dissolution. The end was only signaled by the revolt of the Qarmaṭīs and the revolt of the Zanj that the Qarmaṭīs helped to instigate, and of course, the rise of the Fāṭimids (who were not descended from Fāṭimah at all).

But in *103*/721 the coalition was taking its first steps and Muḥammad ibn 'Alī, now the 'Abbāsid

"Imām", sent an emissary to Khorāsān and a supreme council was set up in Merv with twelve leaders called *nuqabā'*. The success of the 'Abbāsid revolution was the result in large part of very well thought out and well executed propaganda, the *da'wah*. This was derived from that used by Mukhtār in his earlier, unsuccessful revolt, the Kaysāniyyah. This program included the messianic nature of the leader, the Imām; the fact that his identity was kept secret and that he was remote from the action, even denying his participation if necessary, and the equalization of the status of the mawālī and slaves to that of the Arabs with whom they fought side by side.

This coalition included the very capable and charismatic Abū Muslim as military leader. The Barmakids, who were political-religious figures from Balkh, became the masterminds. An early leader called Khidāsh revealed the nature of the movement by openly preaching a Mazdakite or Khurramite doctrine of property and women in common, and another group, the Rāwandiyyah, obviously also under the Manichean umbrella, caused the 'Abbāsids embarrasment when they declared that they "knew" that al-Manṣūr, the second 'Abbāsid Caliph, was divine. Both were suppressed as politically incorrect, although Nawbakht called the whole 'Abbāsid movement Rāwandīs.

Of obscure origins, perhaps from Kūfah, Abū Muslim set in motion the propaganda in Khorāsān, of which Naṣr ibn Sayyār al-Laythī of Kināna, leader of the Muḍar of Khorāsān and the Umayyad Governor, described to the Caliph Marwān in these words of poetry:

"I see coals glowing among the embers,
they want but little to burst into blaze.
Fire springs from the rubbing of sticks,
and warfare from the wagging of tongues.
In wonder I say, Oh that I could know,
are they awake the Umayyads all,
or perchance, sunk in slumber deep.
If slumbering they are, of carelessness,
then say: arise, awake!
The time of alertness has arrived.
... the man on the spot sees what the absent
one cannot."

The propaganda called for: *ar-Riḍā min Āl Muḥammad*, "the 'approved', 'elected', or 'anointed' one from the family of Muḥammad" that later became the more cryptic *ar-Riḍā min Ahl al-Bayt* ("from the Family of the House"). In both cases it meant the 'Abbāsids but their identity was not revealed; indeed it was a secret up until the moment when Abū'l-'Abbās as-Saffāḥ rose from the assembly to take the oath of allegiance as Caliph on the minbar of the Mosque of Kūfah. (As-Saffāḥ was a last minute substitute for his brother Ibrāhīm who had just died.) The real meaning of the propaganda phrase was left up to the imagination. But the term "Family of the House", or "People of the House", could mean different things to different people (*see* AHL al-BAYT). The Umayyad observer who said that the followers of the 'Abbāsid *da'wah* in Khorāsān were "worshippers of cats and heads" (i.e. masks and statues that uttered oracles, *see* ḤARRĀN) was probably close to the mark.

When the time came for open insurrection, Abū Muslim unfurled the Black Standard that became associated with the family of al-'Abbās. It was inscribed with the words: "Leave is given to those who fight because they were wronged" (Koran 22:39; which continues: "Surely God is able to help them"). The war cry (*shi'ār*) of Abū Muslim was: "O Muḥammad, O helped of God" (Yā Muḥammad, yā Manṣur). Manṣur ("the Victor") was also the name of a kind of Messiah in Gnostic and mystical circles, a name that continued to reappear among radical Shī'ites and was also the name of the second 'Abbāsid. The use of the black banners apparently came about as a sign of mourning for the 'Alīd leader Zayd ibn 'Alī, who was killed after a period of uprising in *122*/740 in Kūfah, and his son Yaḥyā who was crucified by the Umayyad governor of Khorāsān, Naṣr ibn Ṣayyar in *125*/743. In that year, following the death of these 'Alīds, the Hāshimiyyah (former Mukhtāriyyah) propaganda in Khorāsān came firmly under the control of the 'Abbāsids. But the 'Abbāsids were constrained, after power was in their hands, to murder two of the actual leaders of the revolution, Abū Salamah Ḥafṣ ibn Sulaymān al-Khallāl, the *Wazīr Āl Muḥammad*, and Abū Muslim. Their putatative disloyalty regarding who should be Caliph is unconvincing, but it does indicate that the 'Abbāsids and their revolutionaries had diverging, or ultimately incompatible goals and agendas.

The last ruling Umayyad was the Caliph Marwan II who was defeated at the Battle of the Great Zab river (in the region where Alexander had defeated Darius at the Battle of Gaugamela) and fled by way of Ḥarrān and Damascus to the Egyptian coastal city of Farma. He was finally killed in lower Egypt. However, 'Abd ar-Raḥmān, who was to be called ad-Dākhil ("the Intruder"), an Umayyad who escaped from the subsequent persecution of the deposed clan, went on to found a kingdom in Cordoba. Following the example of the Fāṭimids, the rulers of Cordoba later also took the title of Caliphs and their kingdom became known as the Umayyad Caliphate of Spain.

The 'Abbāsid dynasty was initiated by Abū-l-'Abbās, called as-Saffāḥ, "the Spiller" (of Umayyad blood). The 'Abbāsids were the descendants of al-'Abbās, an uncle of the Prophet. While not directly descended from the Prophet, the family relationship helped to rally nascent Shī'ite sympathies to their side. Eventually, however, as proto-Shī'ism developed into Twelve Imām Shī'ism, and Ismā'īlism, the Shī'ites who actually believed in 'Alī and wished to see a descendant of the Prophet in the progeny of 'Alī and Fāṭimah as ruler, came to look upon the 'Abbāsids as usurpers and persecutors of Shī'ism, while the Ismā'īlīs looked to find a leader among one of their own (who also had, for political correctness, to claim to be descended from 'Alī).

The 'Abbāsid dynasty ruled with the help of the Barmakids, a prominent Persian family from Balkh who, before their conversion, had been priests in the Buddhist monastery of Nawbahar. The skilled administration of several generations of this family as Viziers or ministers fostered the flowering of Arab-Persian Islamic civilization, that reached its imperial peak during the reign of Hārūn ar-Rashīd (*170-194*/786-809), and its cultural peak soon after that. Towards the end of his life Hārūn ar-Rashīd deposed the Barmakids. The reasons for this were deliberately obscured afterwards by sympathizers of the Barmakids, who praised them to the skies, but it is clear that the Barmakids were creating an empire within an empire. Hārūn put to death his former Vizier Ja'far ibn Yaḥyā Barmak in *187*/803. Faḍl, the brother of Ja'far, and his father Yaḥyā, were thrown into prison where they died (*see* BARMAKIDS).

This crucial episode marks the turning point in the 'Abbāsid reign; soon afterwards actual power slipped from their hands. Two of Hārūn ar-Rashīd's sons, al-Amīn and al-Ma'mūn, who inherited respectively the west and the east of the Empire (a third, Qāsim, was governor of Jazīrah), fought a brief but bloody civil war over the succession that brought al-Ma'mūn to the throne. Al-Ma'mūn's reign opens a curious episode in 'Abbāsid history. As prosperity declined from the opulence of Hārūn ar-Rashīd's reign, ever more threats emerged to the Caliph's power; at every turn complex ideologies surged up, along with the ghosts of old religions, to confuse the allegiance of the masses. To secure the sympathies of the Shī'ites, al-Ma'mūn designated the Shī'ite Imām 'Alī-r-Riḍā as his successor and married his daughter to him. The black banners of the 'Abbāsids were changed for 'Alīd green. This did not produce the desired results; the 'Irāqis turned and set up, for a short time, another member of the 'Abbāsid family, Ibrāhīm, as Caliph. Then 'Alī-r-Riḍā died, perhaps indeed poisoned — the Shī'ites insist that each Imām died a tragic martyr's death — and was buried by the tomb of Hārūn ar-Rashīd — al-Ma'mūn's father — in Ṭūs, today's Mashhad in Iran.

A noted intellectual who took an active interest in theological questions and contributed to their development, al-Ma'mūn adopted the Mu'tazilite, or rationalist, philosophy in *212*/827. This opens another turbulent period in the history of Islamic thought marked by the *miḥnah*, or inquisition into the beliefs of religious scholars. The *miḥnah* was instituted in *218*/833, shortly before the death of al-Ma'mūn. The Mu'tazilite period lasted twenty years from *212*/827 until the Caliph al-Mutawakkil restored orthodoxy in *232*/847.

Al-Mu'taṣim, the brother and successor of al-Ma'mūn, installed a Turkish guard around him. Feeling uneasy in Baghdad, he founded a new heavily fortified capital at Samarra', 60 miles north of Baghdad. There the capital remained until the Caliph al-Mu'tamid returned to Baghdad. This defensive move to Samarra' foreshadowed the political decline of the 'Abbāsids for, from then on, Turkish soldiers in the armies beginning with al-Wāthiq, began to exercise their own will over the Caliphs, who increasingly ruled in name only. As the Caliphs withdrew into the military camp-city of Samarra', they became more prisoners than princes. Finally, factions in the Turkish guard supplanted the Caliphs as the real political power. Al-Mutawwakil took the title *ẓill Allāh fī-l-ard* ("Shadow of God on earth") but was murdered by the Turkish guards, as were the four Caliphs who followed in quick succession.

During this period, North Africa slipped from the grasp of the 'Abbāsid Caliphs to the Aghlabids of Kairouan (Qayrawan), descendants of Khorāsāni officers of the 'Abbāsid revolution, who continued a no more than nominal allegiance to 'Abbāsid suzerainty by sending the Caliphs frequent gifts from the booty of conquest, and then to the Fāṭimids. Parts of Persia fell under ṭāhirid rule. Although the 'Abbāsids retained their title for four more centuries, the real power fell into the hands of military leaders of a people called the Daylamites from the Caspian region. Inclined to a political Shī'ism of the Zaydi kind, the Daylamite dynasty, that ruled *de facto* in the name of the Caliphs, was known as the Buyids (or Buwayhids). The Seljūq Turks replaced them as the ruling power in *447*/1055.

Towards the end of the 'Abbāsid dynasty, although some of the later Caliphs such as an-Nāṣir showed initiative and the possibility of resurgence, the Caliphate no longer exercised direct political power but played a different role symbolizing political continuity and the principle of legitimacy. In the incessant power struggles of the eastern Empire, no ruler could ever be certain that control was firmly in his grasp. In these circumstances, formal recognition by the Caliph, in the guise of an investiture, came to be sought as confirmation of claims that had, in any case, to be maintained by constant application of military force. When the Mongols appeared on the scene in the middle of the *7th*/13th century they were much more powerful than any of the rulers they encountered. Not yet converted to Islam, and unimpressed by the Caliphate's residual authority, the Mongols simply swept the Caliphate away. The Shī'ites among the Caliph's subjects increasingly resented 'Abbāsid rule and offered the Mongols no resistance. Indeed many of them helped the Mongol invaders, at least as advisors. Thus the Mongols were not stopped until they came up against the Mamlūks of Egypt, a political and military force that was not fragmented.

Under the 'Abbāsids, Arab-Islamic civilization attained its greatest development in the eastern Empire. Centers of learning flourished, among them, the *Bayt al-Ḥikmah* ("House of Wisdom"), an academy founded by the Caliph al-Ma'mūn for the translation of works of Greek science into Arabic. In part, the endowment of educational institutions was stimulated during the Seljūq suzerainty by the need to counter religious propaganda emanating from Fāṭimid Egypt. Advances were made in medicine and the natural sciences, while the arts, philosophy and literature reached new heights. The location of the capital at Baghdad made it the focal point of influences from as far apart as the Mediterranean and the Far East. Islam also drew upon a rich cultural and intellectual heritage from Byzantium, Persia, India, and even China. The coming of the Mongol Hordes shattered this sophisticated culture and sank its libraries in the Tigris. Yet, as was so often the case with the Mongols, their success against the kingdoms and empires of East and West was really due to the weakness of their enemies.

The 'Abbāsid Caliphs are:

Abū-l-'Abbās 'Abd Allah ibn Muḥammad as-Saffāḥ	*132-136*/749-754
al-Manṣūr	*136-158*/754-775
al-Mahdī	*158-169*/775-785
al-Hādī	*169-170*/785-786
Hārūn ar-Rashīd	*170-193*/786-809
al-Amīn	*193-198*/809-813
al-Ma'mūn	*198-218*/813-833
[rival Ibrāhīm ibn al-Mahdī in Baghdad]	*201-203*/817-819
al-Mu'taṣim	*218-227*/833-842
al-Wāthiq	*227-232*/842-847
al-Mutawakkil	*232-247*/847-861
al-Muntaṣir	*247-248*/861-862
al-Musta'īn	*248-252*/862-866
al-Mu'tazz	*252-255*/866-869
al-Muhtadī	*255-256*/869-870
al-Mu'tamid	*256-279*/870-892
al-Mu'taḍīd	*279-289*/892-902
al-Muktafī	*289-295*/902-908
al-Muqtadir	*295-320*/908-932
al-Qāhir	*320-322*/932-934
ar-Rāḍī	*322-329*/934-940
al-Muttaqī	*329-333*/940-944
al-Mustakfī	*333-334*/944-946
Buyid Suzerainty	*320-447*/932-1055
al-Muṭī'	*334-363*/946-974
at-ṭā'i'	*363-381*/974-991
al-Qādir	*381-422*/991-1031
al-Qā'im	*422-476*/1031-1075
Seljūq Suzerainty from	*447*/1055 to *590*/1194.
al-Muqtadī	*476-487*/1075-1094
al-Mustaẓhir	*487-512*/1094-1118
al-Mustarshid	*512-529*/1118-1135
ar-Rāshid	*529-530*/1135-1136
al-Muqtafī	*530-555*/1136-1160
al-Mustanjid	*555-566*/1160-1170
al-Mustaḍī'	*566-575*/1170-1180
an-Nāṣir	*575-622*/1180-1225
aẓ-Ẓāhir	*622-623*/1225-1226
al-Muṣtanṣir	*623-640*/1226-1242
al-Musta'ṣīm	*640-656*/1242-1258

The Mongols sacked Baghdad in *656*/1258 and put al-Musta'ṣim to death. However, the Mamlūk soldier Baybars, then lieutenant to the Egyptian ruler Qutuz, defeated the Mongols at 'Ayn Jalūt in Syria in *658*/1260, brought an uncle of the last 'Abbāsid ruler to Cairo, and installed him as Caliph. This Caliph, al-Muṣtanṣir, was killed in the following year *659*/1261 leading an army in an unsuccessful attempt to recover Baghdad from the Mongols. The line of figurehead 'Abbāsids in Cairo continued, however, and added prestige to Mamlūk rule until Egypt was conquered by the Ottomans in *923*/1517. Thereafter, no 'Abbāsid laid claim to the title of Caliph and the Ottomans were later to maintain that the last 'Abbāsid in Cairo, al-Mutawakkil III, ceded the rights of the Caliphate to Selim I, the Ottoman Sultan. *See* ABŪ MUSLIM; BAGHDAD; BARMAKIDS; MUḤAMMAD ibn al-ḤANAFIYYAH; CALIPH; RĀWANDIYYAH; KAYSĀNIYYAH; al-MA'MŪN: KHURRAMIYYAH; MONGOLS; OTTOMANS; PATRIARCHAL CALIPHS; RAFI' IBN LEIS UPRISING; SURKH-I 'ALĀM; SINDBĀD REVOLT; BABAK; UMAYYADS; ZANJ.

'Abd (lit. "slave"). One of several terms for "slave" and also that element of many Muslim personal names that is combined with one of the Divine Names. Thus, *'Abd Allāh* means "slave of God", *'Abd ar-Raḥmān* means "slave of the Merciful One", and so forth. "Slave" in this sense refers to a state of complete dependence upon God and conformity to His Will. One of the epithets of the Prophet, along with that of "Messenger of God", is *'abd*, "slave" of God, indeed the "perfect" slave. *See also* SLAVERY.

'Abdāl (lit. "substitutes"; sing. *badal*). In Sufi lore, a set of seventy Saints, of whom a certain number are the *ṣiddīqūn* ("truthful ones", similar to the Jewish *tsadeqs*). One *ṣiddīq* is the *quṭb* ("axis" or "pole"), the center of human sanctity on earth. Another four are called *awtād* ("pegs"). The symbolism is that of tent-pegs without which the tent, that is, the world, would collapse.

These Saints are called *Abdāl* because when one dies his function is carried on by another person. This resembles the doctrine of *tulkus* among the Tibetans, but in transference of spiritual function only, not of personality. (It may be mentioned in passing that it is a widespread popular Sufi belief, of unknown but doubtless extraneous origin, that the number of Saints in Islam at any one moment is constant throughout history up until the last days.)

Although it frequently happens that the disciples of a spiritual Master eulogize him as the *quṭb*, or even *quṭb al-aqṭāb* ("the Pole of Poles"), the identity of the *Abdāl* is considered to be one of God's secrets. Although the *Abdāl* are replaced through history, at the end of time there are less saintly men to fill the role, and when the number lapses below a certain figure, or there are no more at all, it is said that the world will come to an end. This hierarchy resembles, or is the same as, the hierarchy of the Fāṭimid organization and the Manichean hierarchy that would seem to be its origin. *See* QUṬB.

'Abd Allāh ibn Maymūn al-Qaddāḥ (d. *261*/874-5?). 'Abd Allāh, son of Maymūn al-Qaddāḥ, the obscure but pivotal figure who is associated with the ultimate origins of the Fāṭimid dynasty. Ibn Rizām would make him the great-grandfather of 'Ubayd Allāh al-Mahdī. This great-grandfather in modern genealogies is called 'Abd Allāh al-Akbar or the Elder; his sons were Aḥmad and Ibrāhīm; Aḥmad's sons were al-Ḥusayn and Abū 'Alī Muḥammad Abū ash-Shalaghlagh; al-Ḥusayn's sons were Abū Muḥammad and Sa'īd. Sa'īd married the daughter of his uncle Abū ash-Shalaghlagh, was "spiritually adopted" by him, and became 'Ubayd Allāh al-Mahdī, the first Faṭimid Caliph. 'Abd Allāh the Elder's father's name Maymūn would mean the "lucky one" and al-Qaddāḥ is thought to refer either to a profession, or to some characteristic; it may mean an "oculist", from *qadaḥ*, a "bowl", such as would be used for making up a collyrium, that is, "someone whose preparations would lead to clearer sight". Or again, it may be the word *qaddāḥ* ("flint") used attributively. (It has also been suggested that Qaddāḥ means "sharpener of arrows", and "piercer of cataracts".) All of these meanings lend themselves aptly as an allegorical code name for a secret religious leader, one who leads the postulant "to see the light".

Ibn Rizām says that this Maymūn al-Qaddāḥ was a follower of Ibn Daisan, and believed that there were two gods, one of light and one of darkness. (Ibn Daisan, or Bardesane was a Christian heretic theologian of the 2nd century, acknowledged by the medieval Muslims — and modern scholars — as an ideological predecessor of Mani.) Thus, Maymūn al-Qaddāḥ (d. *212*/827) is obviously a secret code name, or revolutionary alias such as the Bolsheviks made up for themselves ("Stalin= man of steel", "Molotov= the hammer", etc.), not a real name, used by the father of 'Abd Allāh the Elder.

A Baghdadi historian named aṣ-Ṣuli (d. *336*/946), in place of the code-name Maymūn al-Qaddaḥ, says that the father of 'Abd Allāh was a certain Salīm son of Sindān. Sindān was a freeman and client of Ziyad the governor of 'Irāq, and also his police chief. Salīm was executed for Manicheism by the Caliph al-Mahdī. 'Abd Allāh the Elder, or, more likely, his father Salīm, under the alias Maymūn al-Qaddāḥ, adapted the pre-Fāṭimid and pre-Qarmaṭī gnostic doctrines of the Dualist groups variously known as Khurramiyyah, that were early Islamo-Manicheism, and made them into the more Islamicized Manicheism of Ismā'īlīsm.

One or the other, as Heinz Halm says (opting for 'Abd Allāh al-Akbar) "was the founder of a gnostic tradition on a par with the well-known creators of earlier Gnostic systems such as Simon Magus, Valentinian, or Mani". Indeed, for this new tradition was these very systems synthesized and repackaged. And yet the genius of it was no more than a change of clothing, as shown in the adoption of the simple Muslim name 'Abd Allāh; the change of thinking, in reality so difficult, is one small step for man, and one great leap for mankind. This was carried out in the framework of a vast and pre-existing organization, an organization that was not created by this family, but this family was one of the administrative functionaries, a position very much like that of a bishop, one of twelve, who brought the new thinking to the fore around the fateful revolutionary year of 899, causing a schism in an already radically shifting situation.

The chief adaptations were dropping the "divinities" of the Seveners (*Qadar, Kūnī, al-Jadd, al-Khayāl, al-Istiftāh*, originally emanations) in the favor of intellectual constructs grounded in Islamic terminology. The fact that Allāh Himself became a demiurgic emanation out of the "Unknowable Abyss" (*al-Ghayb Ta'ala*) did not attract much astonishment and was probably an esoteric teaching not confided to the profane. But even if only half understood the metaphysical consequences for the consciousness involved are immense. This was presented as a decoding of the inner meaning of the Koran, and the Shi'ite Imāms were the legitimizing medium, with whom the Ismā'īlī leaders identified themselves.

Thus the Ismā'īlīs reject the names "Maymūn al-Qaddāḥ", or "Salīm son of Sindān" and those genealogies and instead claim that 'Abd Allāh the Elder (*al-Akbar*) was descended from Muḥammad ibn Ismā'īl and thence from 'Alī and Fāṭimah, and a true Muslim. Everyone agrees that 'Abd Allah came from 'Askar Mukram in Khuzistan and went to Baṣrah.

To confuse the issue, those who do not accept that Maymūn al-Qaddāḥ was a pseudonym for the father of 'Abd Allāh the Elder, claim that there was someone else of that name who is supposed to have been connected with Muḥammad al-Baqīr and Ja'far as-Ṣādiq, the fifth and sixth Imāms. This other Maymūn al-Qaddāḥ is credited with transmitting (as *rāwi*) — or perhaps inventing — certain sayings of Ja'far aṣ-Ṣādiq that are fundamental, in different degrees of interpretation, to the Sevener and Twelve Imām Shī'ite doctrines of the Imām.

The Fāṭimids were accused in violent and caustic terms in the 'Alīd Manifesto of *402*/1011, composed by the leader of the Sharīfs (and Shī'ites) of Baghdad, al-Murtaḍā, his brother ar-Rāḍi, and some 'Abbāsid jurists, of having invented their descent from 'Alī through Fāṭimah. As S. Stern has pointed out, there is too much evidence that Ismā'īlīs themselves held the Maymūn al-Qaddāḥ ancestry to be true for this to be an idea that originated with Ibn Rizām and spread to them from him rather than originating with them and being recorded by him. The 'Alīd Manifesto also alleged, as did Ibn Rizām, that the Fāṭimids were ultimately the descendants of Ibn Daisan (i.e. Bardesane, a Hellenist Gnostic teacher in the Valentinian tradition). Although presented as a genealogy, this is obviously an ideologic pedigree, for the standard medieval Islamic teaching said that Marcion begat Bardesane, and Bardesane begat Mani, not biologically but intellectually, the way that Marx begat Lenin. Ephrem Syrus wrote: "The Babylonian Mani went through the door that Bardesane opened." In other words, all the critical observers affirmed that the Faṭimids were the continuation of some form of Manicheism.

Ibn Rizām (Abū 'Abd Allāh Muḥammad ibn 'Alī aṭ-ṭā'ī al-Kūfī), from Kūfah, the hotbed of these Gnostic movements, was in *329*/940 the head of the Maẓālim court in Baghdad, thus a kind of state prosecutor, who interrogated Qarmaṭīs. Ibn Rizām wrote a memorandum about the Fāṭimids that was quoted by others and in particular by Sharīf Abū-l-Ḥusayn Muḥammad ibn 'Alī, known as Akhū Muḥsin (d. *375*/985) an 'Alīd of Damascus and perhaps even a real descendant of Muḥammad ibn Ismā'īl, but a critic of Ismā'īlī claims. Their writings have been called calumnies, slanders, and "malevolent forgeries" by Ismā'īlīs. However, since they are the main source of information on the subject, they are, nevertheless, scrupulously followed by Ismā'īlīs themselves in every detail except two points: the Ismā'īlīs insist on maintaining the fiction that the Fāṭimids descend from 'Alī, and they deny that the sect was anti-Islamic and/or atheistic and libertine. It is true that the Fāṭimid Ismā'īlīs did not, like the Qarmaṭī Ismā'īlīs, butcher pilgrims in Mecca in 930 while mocking the Koran, nor in 931 (according to Abū Ṭāhir's physician Ibn Ḥamdān), circle naked around a Persian youth called Abū-l-Faḍl proclaimed the true Mahdī shouting [this is] "our God, he is mighty and exalted... the true religion has now appeared! It is the religion of Adam! Moses and Jesus and Muḥammad... are nothing but swindlers and cheats... this is a secret that we and our predecessors kept hidden for sixty years and today we have uncovered it." But, nevertheless, they were constantly calling for an end to Islam and Islamic law, which, taken at its face, would seem somewhat like a rivalry to Islam, one would think.

This particular advent of the Millennium in the year 931 and the return of paradise was very short-lived for obvious reasons. But similar, or identical phenomena, including the naked circling are not uncommon events in the history of religions and have even taken place in the United States in recent times within antinomian sects.

Now the more evolutionary Fāṭimid Ismā'īlīs are precisely the ones, as opposed to the revolutionary Qarmaṭīs, who set about to work within Islam gradually in order to achieve their ends, but these ends also explicitly included the abolition of Islam.

The Fāṭimid Caliph al-Mu'izz li-Dīn Allāh (d. *365*/975) referred cryptically to these allegations regarding his descent from 'Abd Allāh ibn Maymūn al-Qaddāḥ in a *sijill*, or rescript, to the Chief Dā'ī (Fāṭimid propagandist) of Sindh (in what is today Pakistan). In this official document the Caliph in effect admitted the ancestry with a play on words saying that "it was true that he was the son of the 'Divinely blessed with success in his affairs' (Ar. *al-maymūn an-naqībāt*) and the 'striker of sparks of guidance' kindling the light of Divine Wisdom" (*qadiḥ zand al-hidāya*), i.e. Maymūn al-Qaddāḥ, with the symbolic meaning of the name spelled out. Al-Mu'izz also said that 'Abd Allāh ibn Maymūn al-Qaddāḥ was a "nickname" for a son of the supposed Imām, Muḥammad ibn Ismā'il, from whom the Fāṭimids claimed descent, which is exactly what Ibn Rizām said, while denying the actual 'Alīd connection. In the 20th century there arose new motivation and new inducements to restore and maintain the fiction. *See* FĀṬIMIDS; al-JUWAYNĪ, NŪR MUḤAMMADĪ; SEVENERS; 'UBAYD ALLĀH al-MAHDĪ.

'Abd Allāh ibn Sabā', called "after his mother", Ibn as-Sawdā ("Son of the Black One"). A Yemeni Jew from San'ā' who converted to Islam at the time of 'Uthmān's Caliphate. He seems to have propagandized at one time the "return" of the Prophet Muḥammad, and the lieutenancy (*waṣī*) or mediumship of 'Alī (to Muḥammad), whom he is supposed to have regarded with "embarrassing" veneration, causing his "exile" to al-Madā'in, the future Baghdad. This would make him the originator of some of the subsequent Shī'ite doctrines regarding the 'Alīds. It has also been said that the figure is fictitious and only a marker for a certain type: the promoter of a "divine 'Alī". A modern writer, 'Alī al-Wardi says the name is a code for Ammar ibn Yasir, another promoter of 'Alī. *See* SHĪ'ISM.

'Abd Allāh ibn az-Zubayr (d. *73*/692). The son of the Companion az-Zubayr ibn al-'Awwām and Asmā' bint Abī Bakr. 'Abd Allāh led a conservative, non-Shī'ite, revolt of the Meccan aristocracy against the Umayyad tyranny. He declared himself Caliph and seized control of Mecca in *64*/683. He was supported in 'Irāq by his brother. The following year in a siege of Mecca, the Ka'bah was hit by a flaming arrow and burned. 'Abd Allāh rebuilt it on a larger scale to include the *Ḥijr Ismā'īl*. This new Ka'bah was pulled down and rebuilt as before by al-Ḥajjāj ibn Yūsuf. When Mecca was captured, the body of 'Abd Allāh was hung from a gibbet and his head then sent to Damascus. The revolt also involved a split between tribes; the Qays and Muḍar (Tamim and Azd) followed Ibn Zubayr; the Kalb and Rabī'ah supported the Umayyads. The Qays were defeated by Marwān I aided by the Kalb at the battle of Marj Rāhiṭ in *65*/684. *See* ASMĀ'; KA'BAH.

'Abd al-'Azīz, King, *see* IBN SA'ŪD.

'Abd al-Muṭṭalib ibn Hāshim. The grandfather of the Prophet and head of the Banū Hāshim clan of the Quraysh tribe. His real name was Shaybah and his mother was Salma bint 'Amr of the Najjar clan of the Khazraj tribe of the city of Yathrib, later known as Medinah. 'Abd al-Muṭṭalib was born and raised in Medinah. When his uncle, Muṭṭalib, brought him to Mecca after the death of Hāshim, his father, he acquired the name 'Abd al-Muṭṭalib ("the slave of Muṭṭalib") because he arrived sitting on the back of his uncle's camel and was mistaken for his servant. He later became the most respected man of the tribe Quraysh, who had no chief since a division of privileges had been made between their ancestors 'Abd ad-Dār and 'Abd Manāf.

A prophetic dream, seen by 'Abd al-Muṭṭalib while sleeping in the *Ḥijr Ismā'īl* next to the Ka'bah, led him to rediscover the well of Zamzam by digging under the spot where the Quraysh had traditionally conducted their sacrifices. The location of the well had remained unknown after being buried by the Jurhumites who inhabited Mecca before the Quraysh. By rediscovering the well, 'Abd al-Muṭṭalib acquired the rights of supplying water to pilgrims to Mecca. His son al-'Abbās inherited these rights.

At the time he discovered the well of Zamzam, 'Abd al-Muṭṭalib had only one son, Ḥārith. He prayed to the Lord of the Ka'bah to grant him ten sons and promised in return to sacrifice one of them. His prayers were answered and when the time came, the youngest, 'Abd Allāh, was chosen for sacrifice. However, the protests of his family moved 'Abd al-Muṭṭalib to consult a woman soothsayer who lived near the Jewish settlement of Khaybar, in order to ask whether God would accept a substitute for the sworn sacrifice. When the soothsayer's informing spirit confirmed this, 'Abd al-Muṭṭalib cast the divining arrows at Mecca to learn how many camels would be acceptable as a surrogate sacrifice. The answer was "one hundred camels". These being sacrificed, 'Abd Allāh's life was ransomed.

'Abd Allāh was the father of the Prophet Muḥammad, but died before the child was born, so that 'Abd al-Muṭṭalib became guardian. 'Abd al-Muṭṭalib died when Muḥammad was still young, leaving the eight-year-old orphan to the care of one of his sons, Abū Ṭālib, uncle of Muḥammad and later head of the Hāshimite clan.

When Abrahah of the Yemen attacked Mecca with the Army of the Elephant in the year 570, the year in which the Prophet was born, 'Abd al-Muṭṭalib negotiated with the attacker on behalf of the Quraysh and asked for the return of his camels that Abrahah had seized. Abrahah was set upon destroying the Ka'bah. When questioned about the Ka'bah, 'Abd al-Muṭṭalib is said to have answered that, as his camels had a master that cared for them, so did the Ancient House, and its Lord would protect it. Sudden death and destruction came upon the army of Abrahah when birds with pebbles in their beaks and claws attacked it. This Divine portent drove off the invader. *See* ABRAHAH.

'Abd al-Qādir, Emir (*1223-1300*/1808-1883). The leader of the struggle against the French in Algeria from 1832 until his surrender in 1847 He was famous not only as a military leader, whose exploits were epic, but as a scholar, a poet and above all, a man of religion. 'Abd al-Qādir was interned for three years in the Château d'Amboise in France and finally exiled first to Bursa and then to Damascus where he eventually died in 1883. In Damascus in 1860 he was noted for saving a large number of Christians when their lives were threatened by rioters by giving them refuge in his house, and others, several thousands, by extending his protection.

Being himself a *faqīr* (a disciple in a Sufi *ṭarīqah*), 'Abd al-Qādir was entombed next to Ibn 'Arabī in Damascus whom he regarded as his spiritual master; his remains were moved to Algeria in 1968.

During his exile at Bursa 'Abd al-Qādir wrote a book for the Société Asiatique to which he asked admission. This was translated into French by Gustave Dugat and was published in 1858. It is a general overview of philosophy, history and theology, and social questions, in the old Arab tradition, probably the last work of its kind. 'Abd al-Qādir makes an analogy between a game of chess, in which the players are free within the frame of immutable rules, and the exercise of free will. He says that faith is above reason, but both come from God and there need be no incompatibility between them and that reason should be exercised in service of faith; he says that the poor are to be maintained at the charge of the rich; that the law of Moses regards matter, the law of Jesus the spirit, and that of Islam combines them both. He says that the prophets are men with the same father but different mothers.

On 14 June 1830, as the Bourbon dynasty was coming to an end, a French force of 37,000 led by General Louis de Bourmont landed at Sidi Ferruch near Algiers and put to an end the 300 year old Turkish Regency that had ruled the country. In some areas *Rayah* tribes who had paid taxes to *Makhzen* tribes for the benefit of the Turkish rulers revolted and anarchy spread in Algeria. Attempts by the Sultan of Morocco to impose himself in Oran were ended by the threat of French naval pressure on the Moroccan coast. Before the Moroccans left Oran, they appointed Muḥyi ad-Dīn, a marabout, or venerated religious figure and father of Emir 'Abd al-Qādir, as governor of the province.

On 22 November 1832, his father, and other members of his family, and the notables of three tribes, the Hāshim, Gharābah, and Beni Amar made a *bay'ah* or pact of fealty with 'Abd al-Qādir under a tree near Mascara. 'Abd al-Qādir was given the title of *Amir al-Mu'minīn* that was used by the Caliphs. This event was a deliberate re-enactment of the Pact of Ḥudaybiyyah made with the Prophet at a dangerous moment in the history of nascent Islam. Although some Arab historians said the Emir was of Berber ancestry from the Ifferen tribe, the official established belief was that he was a Sharīf, or Ḥasani descendent of the Prophet, and moreover descended from the Idrīsi dynasty of Morocco. His grandfather had been made a representative of a Qādiriyyah Sufi Shaykh whom he had met while on pilgrimage. This led to a position of prestige that granted his village, Guetna Oued al-Ḥammam, immunity from Turkish jurisdiction, and his son Muḥyi ad-Din eventually became head of the Qādiriyyah for all of Algeria.

On a pilgrimage with his father to Mecca in the year 1826 'Abd al-Qādir, who had been eager student, came in contact with centers of Islamic learning in Tunisia, the Zeituna university, and in Damascus. During a visit to Baghdad where 'Abd al-Qādir Jīlānī is buried, both father and son were given *ijāzahs*, or permission to instruct, by the chief of the Qādiriyyah Sufi order there. A hagiographical legend says that during the visit to Baghdad a mysterious old man addressed the pilgrims calling the Emir "Sultan" thereby identifying him with the founder of the Qādiriyyah and also prophesying his future role. Stories of the events in Baghdad circulated in Algeria even before the French incursion. On the return through Egypt, 'Abd al-Qādir studied at the al-Azhar. The return of father and son to Algeria became the occasion for extended festivities that further added to their reputation, which was already that of the most prestigious marabouts in the country.

In the spring of 1832 Muḥyi ad-Dīn, after duly inviting General Boyer to enter Islam, declared holy war on the French in Oran. 'Abd al-Qādir led the attacks and earned a reputation for courage and leadership. He severely punished those who supplied the French by ordering amputation of the right hand, the nose, and ears. (It should be noted that although amputation of the right hand is a threat rarely carried out for theft, even in early times, this kind of mutilation, and mutilation as political punishment, is considered forbidden in Islamic law.) To pay for the fighting, non-combatants in the tribes were assessed special taxes of a certain number of sheep.

'Abd al-Qādir took control of Mascara as seat of government and pronounced a *khuṭbah*, or Friday religious address, in the mosque. He continued to unite the tribes, Berber and Arab, against an outside enemy in the name of religion, constantly invoking a rigorous adherence to Islamic law. His accession to power was accompanied by the propagation of "prophetic" dreams, on the part of other religious figures and the dream visitations of departed Saints affirming 'Abd al-Qādir's mission.

At first reluctant to recognize the Emir for fear of the French, the Sultan of Morocco eventually lent support and allowed sales of arms for what became a policy of guerrilla warfare. Income came first from gifts, fees for military appointments, and finally only from *zakat* and *'ushr*, traditional taxes; circumstances, however, forced the Emir to impose a non-traditional tax that he called *ma'unah*. By harassing the French the Emir led them to conclude a peace treaty in February 1834, a tactic which, like the treaty the Prophet Muḥammad made at ḥudaybiyyah, won him recognition. The peace treaty contained a secret convention in Arabic supplied by 'Abd al-Qādir and signed later by General Desmichels. The General hid the existence of this convention even from the French government; its articles in effect recognized 'Abd al-Qādir as legitimate sovereign over Oran with the exception of the coastal towns; the French had to obtain visas from 'Abd al-Qādir for travel in Oran, while Muslims did not; thereby French jurisdiction was denied, even in occupied areas, in this and also in other particulars. While General Desmichels presented the treaty as an extension of French authority in Oran, 'Abd al-Qādir did the opposite in regard to the Algerian tribes, presenting it as a recognition of his own government. On the other hand, 'Abd al-Qādir exposed himself to criticism of having dropped the *jihād*, causing him to resort to force and to use the *Makhzen* tribes the way the Turks had done to continue collecting taxes.

As an Algerian coalition formed against him, 'Abd al-Qādir actually received military help from the French, which led 'Abd al-Qādir to establish a regular army. With the appointment of General Trézel in Oran in 1835 a new policy emerged causing a realignment of forces that culminated in the Figuier convention with other factions in Algeria, the Zmalah and Dawa'ir who joined the French. A battle with 'Abd al-Qādir on the 26th of June was won by the French; but on the 28th the battle of Macta was one of the worst defeats; although it cost 'Abd al-Qādir 500 casualties, the French losses were 2,000. Thereafter, French efforts grew decisively earnest and Mascara was occupied whereupon 'Abd al-Qādir's allies abandoned him leaving him desolate having robbed from him even his personal effects.

However, unexpectedly in Algerian eyes, the French left Mascara three days after occupying it. This must have created a deep psychological impression that a Divine Edict was at work, and that this Edict was on the side of 'Abd al-Qādir: the Algerians who had abandoned 'Abd al-Qādir returned and begged his forgiveness. In subsequent military operations 'Abd al-Qādir exhibited great shrewdness in using the means at his disposal; he relied heavily on intelligence information obtained clandestinely and by overt means at his disposal, such as reading French newspapers. He got the Moroccans to take part, and in general obtained much help from the Sultan of Morocco who largely succeeded in dissimulating his support for 'Abd al-Qādir by dis-information to French representatives in Morocco. Efforts to involve England and the United States by offering them ports in Algeria failed, but they demonstrated his pragmatism in attempting any avenue that would further his political goals.

The Battle of Sikkak in 1836 was the only pitched, European style battle that 'Abd al-Qādir fought. It was a great defeat, and again he was abandoned by his followers, an example of the liability of having power based upon possessing *barakah*, or divine favor, rather than upon social structures of continuity. Again, failure of the French, this time under General Bugeaud, to follow up and aid from Morocco allowed 'Abd al-Qādir to regain his position. This time he relocated further inland. An incident arose in which he punished the Borjia tribe that had maintained friendly relations with the French. In his actions in this case, and in several similar ones, he again deliberately imitated the Prophet's actions, this time the Prophet's reprisals against the treacherous Jewish tribes of the Bani Qurayẓah, and the Bani Nadir. Extremely pragmatic, as the Prophet himself was when purely practical questions were involved, 'Abd al-Qādir, on the other hand, was sometimes harsh for political and opportunistic goals whereas the Prophet was not, his actions rigorous only when it was a question of religious principles.

In 1837 the Tafna peace treaty was concluded; it also included secret protocols in which arms were supplied to 'Abd al-Qādir from French Army depots, arms whose payment went to improve roads in the département from which General Bugeaud was now an elected deputy, and engagements were undertaken to move tribes not cooperative to the Emir out of Oran. The Emir on the other hand had to make concessions regarding his sovereignty and these he kept hidden from his allies and subjects. The new treaty led to a period of good relations with 'Abd al-Qādir and a moment of quiet while the French consolidated their positions; the Turkish Bey of Constantine was also left in peace.

He received a *fatwā*, or religious decision, from the *'ulamā'* of Fez who supported the actions he had taken. Some 400 European deserters had joined 'Abd al-Qādir, some of them converted to Islam. In the meantime, however, French policy changed through the occupation of Constantine. 'Abd al-Qādir attempted to bring other parts of Algeria under his control through military means and diplomatic maneuvers, preparing material stockpiles for total war, and even building fortresses, all of which, however, were to fall to the French within three years of the renewal of hostilities at the end of 1839, precipitated by the march of a French force led by the Duc d'Orléans and Governor General Valée from Constantine to Algiers. In the meantime, 'Abd al-Qādir caused himself a serious setback by attacking the marabout Muḥammad as-Saghir at-Tijānī in order to seize 'Ain Madhi in the Sahara. He perhaps needed the town as a further fall back position in the future struggle, but the pro-French politics of the Tijānīs must have been a prime consideration. Nevertheless, it was a serious division within the Algerian coalition, one which also cost him dearly in men, materials, and prestige.

While the French had consolidated their holdings in Algeria, 'Abd al-Qādir had built himself a state. Within this state the precepts of Islam were upheld; a hierarchy existed from 'Abd al-Qādir to Khalīfahs to Aghas who administered Khalifaliks and Aghaliks down to Caids. A significant improvement was the existence of salaried Judges; under the Turks the Judges exacted their income from bribes of those judged. He could command perhaps 70,000 troops, but regular adherence could not be depended upon, although there was a regular army of some 6,000. This was an innovation as far as Arabs and Berbers were concerned, although the example could be found in the Turkish Janissary forces that were in fact the model, down to the institution of travelling Army Judges. There were attempts to create factories whose results were rudimentary and ultimately unsuccessful.

The campaign against him that began in 1840 eventually forced him to take refuge in Morocco. Because of harsh oppression by the French in the newly won territories, a widespread resistance came into being in 1845. This gave 'Abd al-Qādir new impetus for a while and led to some military successes. But eventually his situation became untenable; Moroccan support was withdrawn, and in 1847 'Abd al-Qādir, refusing to escape if it meant leaving his family behind instead surrendered to General de Lamoriciäre upon condition of being allowed to go to Alexandria, a commitment violated by the French government. He was imprisoned in the Château d'Amboise in France until 1852 when he was released by Louis-Napoléon and went into exile.

'Abd al-Qādir al-Jīlānī (*470-561*/1077-1166). One of the most celebrated Saints in Islam, 'Abd al-Qādir is the founder of the *Qādiriyyah* order of Sufis. He was born in the region of Jīlān in Persia but lived in Baghdad, where his tomb stands today.

A legend relates that when 'Abd al-Qādir's mother sent him to Baghdad, she enjoined him to be always truthful. She sewed gold pieces into his coat as a provision for his religious studies. When his band of fellow-travelers was stopped by robbers along the way he was asked — his poor appearance offering no promise of gain — if he had any money. To the astonishment of the robbers he told them the truth about the hidden gold. Later 'Abd al-Qādir told the robber chief that he despaired of attaining truth himself if, at the beginning of the search, he had lied. And this brought the robber chief to repent.

Another story, or allegory, tells that a sick man called upon 'Abd al-Qādir to help him to sit upright. When the Saint helped him, the sick man miraculously grew to a great size, and explained that he was Islam itself, who had grown weak with the times but was now restored to health by 'Abd al-Qādir. (The idea that Islam needed Jīlānī rather than the reverse is curious because it places a Messianic emphasis upon a person.)

'Abd al-Qādir did not begin public preaching until after the fiftieth year of his life. He went on to found the *ṭarīqah* ("Sufi order" pl. *ṭuruq*,), that bears his name. Al-Jīlāni was called the *quṭb* ("spiritual axis") of his age, and even the *Ghawīth al-A'ẓam* (the "greatest succor"), no doubt because he promised to come out from the unseen to the spiritual aid of any disciple who called upon him. The most famous words of 'Abd al-Qādir Jīlānī are to the effect: "in distress call upon me, and I will come on a white horse to help you." These are, in fact, words of Mithra in Yasht 10 line 55 of the Zoroastrian Gathas: "if they invoke me by name I will come to help them." Mithra was always mounted on a white horse. His most famous written work is a collection of exhortations called the *Futūḥ al-Ghayb* ("Revelations of the Unseen").

With al-Jīlānī the tradition begins of a group of Sufis holding a particular great man or Saint to be the "founder" of their way. Thus the Qādiriyyah is the first *ṭarīqah* to take on a distinct character, or, simply, the first *ṭarīqah* as such.

In the *Futūḥ al-Ghayb*, 'Abd al-Qādir said:

> Die, then, to creatures, by God's leave, and to your passions, by His command, and you will then be worthy to be the dwelling place of the knowledge of God. The sign of your death to creatures is that you detach yourself from them and do not look for anything from them. The sign that you have died to your passions is that you no longer seek benefit for yourself, or to ward off injury, and that you are not concerned about yourself, for you have committed all things to God. The sign that your will has been merged in the Divine Will is that you seek nothing of yourself or for yourself — God's Will is working

in you. Give yourself up into the hands of God, like the ball of the polo-player, who sends it to and fro with the mallet, or like the dead body in the hands of the one who washes it, or like the child in its mother's bosom.

'Abd ar-Raḥmān ibn 'Awf. A Companion of the Prophet and one of the ten to whom the Prophet explicitly promised paradise. 'Abd ar-Raḥmān led the dawn prayer on the expedition to Tabūk when the Prophet was late in coming to the congregation. When the Prophet arrived, he joined the prayer behind 'Abd ar-Raḥmān; the Prophet also prayed behind Abū Bakr in the last days of his mortal illness.

'Abduh, Muḥammad (*1265-1323*/1849-1905). An Egyptian religious reformer who sought to "modernize" Islam and rectify it through reason. He did not take all of the Koran to be Divinely inspired; what the Koran says of human institutions 'Abduh ascribed to the Prophet's thinking. He also advocated the "precedence of reason over the literal meaning of the Koran in case of conflict between the two". This is, to say the least, completely untraditional; the orthodox view is that all of the Koran is Divinely inspired, from beginning to end; not only Divinely inspired but the uncreated Word of God. But in the climate of Islam's casting about for "renaissance" (*naḥḍah*) in the face of material backwardness in regard to the West, 'Abduh's ideas appealed to those who wished to imitate the West without abandoning their heritage. The movement that embodied this reform was called the *Salafiyyah*, and Muḥammad 'Abduh was its most influential figure.

'Abduh had studied in Paris during a period of political exile. There, he associated briefly with the political agitator Jamāl ad-Dīn al-Afghānī and they founded a political/religious society with a periodical called al-*'Urwah al-Wuthqā* ("The Unbreakable Bond"). In 1885 'Abduh and al-Afghānī parted company, when 'Abduh went to Beirut and taught theology at the Madrasah Sultaniyyah. He returned to Egypt in 1888 and became Grand Mufti of Egypt in 1889. In 1894 'Abduh became a member of the Supreme Council of the al-Azhar University and in 1897 published his book on theology and law entitled *Risālat at-Tawḥīd* ("The Message of Unity"). He collaborated in a periodical called *al-Manār* ("The Minaret") founded by Rashīd Riḍā in Cairo in 1899. *See* SALAFIYYAH.

'Abd al-Wahhāb, Muḥammad, *see* WAHHĀBĪS.

Abenragel, *see* AR-RIJĀL.

'Abjad. A traditional system of calculation based upon the correspondence of each letter of the Arabic alphabet with a number. The letters representing numbers are placed into a diagram of squares that make up a larger square (the figure is related to a "magic square"). The letters are then transposed from one square to another in the diagram according to a certain algorithm or procedure that results in an arithmetical operation of multiplication or division. The square is also used for divination since the letters, while signifying numbers, also produce words. In another approach, the substitution of numbers for letters and then other letters of the same numerical value is a method of mystical exegesis known as the *'Ilm al-Ḥurūf*, similar to the Hebrew Gematria. (*See* 'ILM al-ḤURŪF.)

'Abjad order rather than alphabetical order is used when the letters are used as ordinals. That is, a, b, c, d, as ordinals would in Arabic be *'alif, ba'*, *jim, dal* (instead of *'alif, ba', ta', tha'*, which is Arabic alphabetical order today).

The *'abjad* values are:

1.'alif 2. bā' 3. jīm 4. dāl 5. hā' 6. rā' 7. zāy 8. ḥā' 9. ṭā' 10. yā' 20. kāf 30. lām40. mīm 50. nūn 60. sīn 70.'ain 80. fā' 90. ṣād100. qāf 200. rā' 300. shīn 400. tā' 500. thā'600. khā' 700. dhāl 800. ḍād 900. ẓā' 1000. ghain

The mnemonic formula for the order is: 'abjad hawaza ḥuṭi kalaman s'afaṣ qurishat thakhadh ḍẓagh.

There was also a system of designating numbers with the fingers (*ḥisāb al-'aqd*), something like what stock market brokers use on the trading floors today. This system permitted two negotiators to quote prices to each other, their hands under a cloth, such that bystanders had no idea of what sums were involved.

Ablutions. There are three kinds of ablution that symbolically restore the believer to a state of equilibrium or purity and, for the purposes of ritual, do so effectively.

The first is *ghusl* ("greater ablution"). This involves a ritual washing of the whole body, that removes the impurities (called *junub* or *janābah*)

that are the consequences of: sexual intercourse; intromission; ejaculation with or without coitus; menstruation; childbirth; major bloodletting; and contact with a corpse. The performance of *ghusl* also accompanies conversion to Islam and the putting on of *iḥrām* (consecration for pilgrimage). One must also be in a state of *ghusl* before one can enter a mosque or an area purified for prayer (*see* PURIFICATION), or touch an Arabic Koran.

The second kind of ablution is the *wuḍū'* ("lesser Ablution") that removes the impurities which are called *aḥdāth.* These include impurities in the state of the individual caused by: the bodily functions, breaking wind, touching a dog, minor bleeding (but not as small as insect bites), and by loss of consciousness or an interval of sleep. It is the *wuḍū'*, a brief washing of the hands, face, and feet, which is performed before the canonic prayer (*ṣalāt*), but only if the state conferred by *ghusl* has not been lost.

The third kind of ablution is *tayammum* where — through lack of, or legitimate aversion to, water — a substitute of sand, earth, or unfashioned stone, is used in the place of water in a single, special ritual that replaces either the *wuḍū'*, or *wuḍū'* and *ghusl* together. For descriptions, *see* GHUSL; WUḌŪ'; TAYAMMUM.

Abortion. This is acceptable in Islam, according to most theologians, as long as the foetus is not fully formed; a state that is said to occur 120 days after conception, as described by the fourth Ḥadīth of Nawāwī that summarizes the states of foetal development:

> Verily the creation of each one of you is brought together in his mother's belly for forty days in the form of a seed (*nuṭfah*), then he is a clot of blood (*'alaqah*) for a like period, then a morsel of flesh for a like period (*mudhghah*), then there is sent to him the angel who blows the breath of life into him....

The "breath of life" is the "ensoulment" which was the critical issue for medieval theologians. To call the foetus a human being before this point would have been the same as to equate a "possibility" with an "actuality", or to equate non-existence with existence. It is against this that Aristotle's law of non-contradiction, "the first law of reality" is set. Or as the theologian Sa'd ad-Dīn at-Taftāzānī (d. 791/1389) insisted: "possibility is not a thing." The Ḥanafīs permitted abortion until the fourth month and many Shāfi'īs and Ḥanbalīs did also. The Mālikīs make abortion before the fourth month "discouraged" (*makrūh*) but most did not make it prohibited (*ḥarām*) until after the fourth month.

The doctrine of ensoulment after 120 days was held by the Catholic Church as well, but in the 19th century was de-emphazised as "inopportune" precisely because it was recognized it would be used to justify abortion. The idea is consistent with the traditional view, expressed as early as Aristotle, that the soul attaches itself to the foetus out of the unseen at a precise moment around 120 days after conception, and that only with the soul "attached" has the foetus become a human being. Abortions performed before the term of 120 days are therefore acceptable; others would prolong the term still further. In any case, no objections are raised to abortions performed after this moment if their aim is to safeguard the health or safety of the mother. There is an increase in vociferous anti-abortion polemics in the Islamic world like the Christian because Fundamentalism corresponds to a rebirth of Mu'tazilite-like or dualist tendencies that can be seen in all religions at the present time. Dualisms equate a possibility with the thing itself and believe that this is self-evident.

In the Sunni schools of law the foetus has a right to burial and is given a name. *See* BIRTH CONTROL.

Abrahah The Christian viceroy of the Negus of Abyssinia, who ruled the Yemen in the middle of the 6th century AD He undertook a campaign against the North Arabians and marched against Mecca. Because he brought an elephant with his army, the year of the campaign became known among the Arabs as the "Year of the Elephant, traditionally identified as the year 570, and as the year of the Prophet's birth. Al-Mas'ūdī says that three years after the campaign against Mecca, the Persians invaded the Yemen and Abrahah was killed by a Persian general named Wahriz "in the 45th year of the reign of Anushirwan" (Chosroes I), which corroborates the date within three years. However, some modern scholars believe that the campaign must have taken place a decade or more earlier. In any case, as far as Abrahah's campaign is concerned, the date is likely to be no more than approximate that, as a significant event, became nonetheless a reference point in time. Such reference points were not treated with precision, and many other events were cumulated around the one that stood out in memory.

The invasion by the "Army of the Elephant" is mentioned in Sūrah 105:

Hast thou seen how thy Lord
did with the Men of the Elephant?
Did He not make their guile go astray?
And He loosed upon them birds in flight
Hurling against them stones of baked clay
and He made them like green blades devoured.

(According to a traditional gloss, these stones of baked clay, *sijil*, from the Latin *sigillium*, had the name written on them of the person destined to be killed by them. The stones of baked clay may refer to ancient cuneiform tablets, that the Arabs must have come upon frequently in the desert, and which thus become the poetic trace of a cosmic conflict. (Note: because the Koran says that it is in "pure Arabic" there are those who deny that any words in it are from non-Arab etymologies, even obvious ones such as Rūm, or "Romans", and Firdaws, which is from the Persian "pardes".) Before Abrahah's army was driven off, 'Abd al-Muṭṭalib, the grandfather of the Prophet, came out of Mecca to parley with him. Tradition relates that he asked only for the return of his camels that had been captured, saying: "as for the Holy House (the Ka'bah) it has its Master who will protect it."

Abrahah had built a magnificent church in San'a', the chief city of the Yemen, that was called *al-Qalīs* (from the Greek *ekklesia*, also Arabized as *al-Qulays*). A possible motive for the campaign against Mecca may have been to remove the Ka'bah as a rival to his church. After the unexpected failure of his campaign, the Persians regained control of the Yemen until the advent of Islam.

Columns from this church were used by 'Abd Allāh ibn az-Zubayr in the rebuilding of the Ka'bah in *64*/683. *See* 'ABD al-MUṬṬALIB.

Abraham (Ar. Ibrāhīm). Abraham is the ancient patriarch of Islam, as he is of Judaism. The Old Testament calls his father Terah. In Arabic this is Azar which is from the variant form Athar, from which Terah derives. Abraham is also the ancestor of the Prophet, who is his descendant through Abraham's son Ismā'īl (Ishmael). The Koran names both Abraham and Ismā'īl as Divine Messengers (*rasūl*, pl. *rusūl*), and together they rebuilt the Ka'bah in Mecca (traditionally founded first by Adam). Abraham established the pilgrimage to Mecca calling mankind to the "ancient house" (*al-bayt al-'atīq*).

The Koran says:

And when We appointed the House to be
a place of visitation for the people,
and a sanctuary,
and: 'Take to yourselves Abraham's station
for a place of prayer.' And We made covenant
with Abraham and Ishmael: 'Purify
My House for those that shall go about it
and those that cleave to it, to those who bow
and prostrate themselves.' (2:118-119)

And when Abraham, and Ishmael with him,
raised up the foundations of the House:
'Our Lord, receive this from us; Thou art
the All-hearing , the All-knowing;
and, our Lord, make us submissive to Thee,
and of our seed a nation submissive
to Thee; and show us our holy rites, and
turn towards us; surely Thou turnest, and art
All-compassionate.' (2:122-123)

The Koran (3:67) says that Abraham was neither Jew, nor Christian, but a submitted *ḥanīf* ("adherent to perennial Monotheism"), and he was not of the "idolators". According to this description, Abraham represents primordial man in universal surrender to the Divine Reality before its fragmentation into religions separated from each other by differences in form. This religion of Abraham is a reconsecration, a restoration of the *fiṭrah*, or primordial "norm", a spontaneous and sacred conformity to reality that is not externalized — and thus necessarily reduced — to the level of a law; it is called in the Koran *millat Ibrāhīm* ("the creed of Abraham").

Islam necessarily has a form because it has a codified law, established ritual, creed, dogma, and so forth, but inwardly, in its essence, Islam sees itself as a restoration of the primordial tradition of Abraham. For example, when the believer performs the canonical prayer (*aṣ-ṣalat*), he does so not as an individual but as a patriarch, or rather, in the name of the entire human species. In other words, in ritual the individual acts not as this or another man, but becomes the representative of mankind, or "universal man".

The primordiality of Abraham abolishes idolatry. The Koran says:

When he said to his father and his people,
'What are these statues unto which
you are cleaving?'
They said, 'We found our fathers
serving them.'
He said, 'Then assuredly you
and your fathers have been in
manifest error.'
They said, 'What, hast thou come to us
with the truth, or art thou one of
those that play?'
He said, 'Nay, but your Lord
is the Lord of the heavens and the earth
who originated them, and I
am one of those that bear witness
thereunto.'
So he broke them into fragments. (21:53-58)

The traditional commentary to the story in Koran 21:53-70 is that before a festival to idols Abraham went to his people's temple and cut off the limbs and heads of some of the idols and set the sword he had used by the side of the largest idol. When the destruction was discovered Abraham accused the largest idol of the act and told the people: "But this, their chief has done it, so question them if they can speak." But the people threw Abraham into a fire from which he emerged unharmed because God said: "O fire, be coolness and peace for Abraham" (cf. Genesis 15:17: "And it came to pass, that, when the sun went down, and it was dark, behold a smoking furnace, and a burning lamp that passed between those pieces").

The Arabs, as descendants of Abraham, inherited his monotheism, as did the Jews. They continued to practice this monotheism, unchanged by the revelations of Moses and Jesus until, figuratively speaking, the "water in the goatskin" that Abraham gave to Hagar, the mother of Ishmael, the mother of the Arabs, was spent (Genesis 21:15). But as "God heard" Ishmael (the name means "God hears"), and the spring of Zamzam gushed from the earth saving the mother and child from death by thirst, God also "heard" Muḥammad, when the Abrahamic spirituality had "dried up", and idolatry had overtaken the Arab spirit. At the lament of the descendant of Ishmael, Muḥammad, who was wont to go for month-long retreats on a mountain near Mecca, the spring of revelation gushed forth again, the Koran was revealed and Islam came into the world as the restoration, and extension of Abraham's religion. *See* HAGAR; ḤANIF; ISMĀ'ĪL; PROPHETS; TALBIYYAH.

Abrogation, *see* NASKH.

Abū, *see* KUNYAH; NAMES.

Abū Ayyūb. One of the Companions of the Prophet, Abū Ayyūb was a standard bearer of the Prophet who, tradition recounts, at a very advanced age and long after the Prophet's death, took part in a legendary attack on Constantinople in *49*/669 (the date *59*/678 is also sometimes given), where he was killed. In Turkey, the legend took hold and he is known as Eyüp Sultan. His tomb on the outskirts of Istanbul, is greatly venerated and a meeting place of Sufis.

When, in *857*/1453, the Turks under Mehmet Nasir laid siege to the city, a legend grew up that they were rallied by a light coming from the tomb, that was discovered in a vision by Shaykh ash-Shams ad-Dīn at the outset of the final siege.

The Ottoman Sultans were girded at the tomb with the sword of 'Uthmān or Osman, the founder of the dynasty, who had been himself girded with a sword by his father-in-law Shaykh Edebali, a dervish. The ceremonythe investiture of office was performed by the Imām of the mosque of Ayyūb and the *Büyük Chelebi*, the head of the Mevlevi Dervish order.

Abubacer, *see* IBN TUFAYL.

Abū Bakr. The first Caliph, who held together the Muslim community after the death of the Prophet and consolidated Islam's victories in Arabia. Originally a rich merchant of Mecca he was the second, after Khadījah, to believe in the mission of the Prophet and accompanied him on his escape from Mecca (*see* HIJRAH; in Shī'ite accounts 'Alī is considered to be a convert who preceded Abū Bakr). Celebrated as being the closest personal friend of the Prophet and as having an unswerving loyalty to him and an unshakeable belief in every aspect of the prophetic mission, he was known as *Aṣ-Ṣiddīq* ("the faithful"). He replaced the Prophet as Imām to lead the prayers during the Prophet's last illness. His daughter, 'Ā'ishah was the favorite wife of the Prophet. During the early days of Islam, Abū Bakr used his wealth to help the Muslim community through its difficult times and brought freedom for slaves who were persecuted for their belief in Islam. One such ransomed slave, Bilāl, later became famous as the muezzin of the Prophet.

Long before his conversion Abū Bakr had been well respected among the Quraysh and was known to possess the art of interpreting dreams, for which the Meccans often turned to him. His real name was 'Abd Allāh; Abū Bakr ("father of the maiden") is a *kunyah*, a paternity name, in virtue of its indirectness, a respect name. He is mentioned in the Koran as "the second of the two who lay in the cave", in reference to the cave in Mount Thawr where he and the Prophet hid from the Meccan search party on the Hijrah. Of the Prophet's contemporaries, the Koran makes such direct reference only to the Prophet, Abū Bakr and a blind man who importuned the Prophet.

After Abū Bakr was elected Caliph in *11*/632, 'Umar (who became the second Caliph) saw him going to the market place to sell cloth, which was his commerce as a merchant. 'Umar assured him that in view of his office as the head of the Muslim nation it was no longer necessary for him to pursue his trade, and that the public treasury would provide "a middling pension... a winter garment and one for summer... and a sheep's side a day for provender". Abū Bakr died in the second year of his Caliphate in *13*/634. He is considered to be one of the two who transmitted from the Prophet the esoteric doctrines later know as Taṣawwuf, the other being 'Alī ibn Abī Ṭālib.

Abū Dharr al-Ghifārī (d. *32*/652). Companion of the Prophet. Credited with being one of the early converts to Islam. Little is known about him, but at the present time much is conjectured, making him the proponent of modern polemics. Because he was a highwayman (the calling of his clan), with a Robin Hood bent where Islam was concerned, he is made into a prototype Islamic socialist.

Abū Ḥanīfah al-Nu'mān ibn Thābit ibn Zūṭā (*81-150*/700-767). The founder of the Ḥanafī School of Law, that today has the largest following among the Muslim community. Abū Ḥanīfah, a Persian, was one of the great jurists of Islam and one of the historic Sunnī *Mujtahids*. He was born in Kūfah in 'Irāq, and died in Baghdad. Like Mālik ibn Anas, founder of the Mālikī School of Law, Abū Ḥanīfah studied with Ja'far as-Sādiq in Medinah, as well as with other teachers elsewhere.

Abū Ḥanīfah was the grandson of a slave captured during the conquest of Kabul, and set free as a *mawlā* ("client") by his captor, who was a member of the Taymallah tribe. Abū Ḥanīfah lived by trading silk in Kūfah in 'Irāq, where he taught religious studies. He is also said to have been one of the four chief overseers in the construction of the round city of Baghdad.

Although the school of law that bears his name is known for the breadth of its interpretations, he himself may have been a rather more strict traditionalist. Probably because he had been a supporter of a Zaydi revolt, Abū Ḥanīfah died in prison. His followers later ascribed to him a genealogy that made him a descendant of the ancient Persian Kings; he is pictured as refusing an invitation to serve the Umayyads as religious judge. Under the 'Abbāsids, however, his followers readily entered government service, and gained favor by a willingness to accommodate the needs of the ruling princes in matters of law. Abū Yūsuf, who wrote a treatise on the law of land tax, became the first Supreme Judge (*Qāḍī-l-Quḍāt*) in Islam under the Caliph Hārūn ar-Rashīd, and gained official sanction for what became known as the Ḥanīfi School of Law. *See* FIQH al-AKBAR; SCHOOLS of LAW; SHARĪ'AH.

Abū Ḥātim ar-Rāzī (died in Azerbaijan in *322*/934). The Ismā'īlī dā'ī of Rayy who extended his control to Azerbaijan and Daylam, including Jīlān, ṭabaristān (Mazandarān), and Gurgan, attracting many local rulers including Mahdī ibn Khusraw Firūz. This was a ruler of Daylam who had his seat at Alamūt, the future center of Ḥasan-i Ṣabbāḥ's Nizārī state.

Abū Ḥatim corresponded with Abū Ṭāhir al-Jannābi, the Qarmaṭī leader in Arabia. Abū Ḥatim criticised Nasafī for antinomianism perhaps as a result of the episode of the "Persian Mahdī" in Baḥrayn among the Qarmaṭīs in 931. But Abū Ḥātim belonged to the eastern school of Ismā'īlism that did not recognize the leadership of the Fāṭimids but awaited the return of Muḥammad ibn Ismā'īl as the Mahdī. In the meantime, in the absence of an Imām, the religion was to be headed by twelve "adjutants" (*lahiq*), or Bishops.

Interestingly, and tellingly, Abū Ḥatim is recorded as the first to advance the exegesis that the Docetist doctrine in the Koran that says Jesus did not die on the cross but only appeared to die, should be understood in the light of the Koranic verse (3:169) which says: "Say not of those who have been slain in the way of God that they are dead; say that they are living though ye are not aware of it." *See* BĒMA.

Abū Ḥimār, *see* BŪ ḤAMĀRAH; DHŪ-l-ḤIMĀR.

Abū Hurayrah (lit. "the father of the kitten"). A Companion of the Prophet, very fond of cats, whose real name was 'Abd ar-Raḥmān ad-Dawsi. He is the source of more Ḥadīth than any other individual, and is the link in a number of initiatic chains.

Abū Jahl (lit. "father of ignorance"). A prominent enemy of Islam among the Quraysh. His hostility earned him the appellation of "father of ignorance" from the Muslims, but his real name was 'Amr ibn Hisham. He was killed in the Battle of Badr in *2*/624.

Abū Lahab (lit. "father of flame"). His real name was 'Abd al-'Uzzā. Although he was an uncle of the Prophet, he was, nevertheless, a violent enemy of Islam. Before the Prophet's mission, however, Abū Lahab's sons, 'Utbah and 'Utaybah, had married the Prophet's daughters, Ruqayyah and Umm Kulthūm. With the advent of Islam, these marriages were annulled because neither son accepted the religion.

At the death of Abū Ṭālib, Abū Lahab became the head of the Banu Hāshim clan and withdrew clan protection from the Prophet, thus precipitating the Hijrah, the Prophet's emigration to Medinah. Abū Lahab died shortly after the Battle of Badr.

Abū-l-'Atāhiya (*130-210*/748-825). Arabic poet born in Kūfah, with Manichean convictions. Wrote in a wide variety of poetic genres, including ascetic poems called *zuhdiyyāt.*

Abū 'Īsā al-Warrāq (d. *241*/861). A Manichean and free-thinker, who was at first a Mu'tazilite. He was the teacher of Ibn ar-Rāwandī. Abū 'Īsā wrote on sects, and a book called *al-Maqālāt* ("Sayings"), *al-Gharib al-Mashriqī* ("the Stranger from the East"). What he wrote on Manicheism is lost today but was the basis for an-Nadīm's description in his *Fihrist.*

Abū Madyan, Shu'ayb ibn al-Ḥusayn al-'Ansārī (*520-594*/1126-1198). A famous Sufi Saint born near Seville and buried in the village of al-'Ubbād, also called "Sidi Boumedienne", on the outskirts of Tlemcen, Algeria. He came from a poor family in Spain; when young he was a shepherd; in Morocco, to learn a trade, he became apprenticed to a weaver. It was only much later in life that he fulfilled his wish to learn to read and write.

To search for teachers of esoteric doctrine, he went first to Tangier and later to Fez, where his master was Abū-l-Ḥasan ibn Harzihim. In Fez he supported himself by weaving but lived in such extreme poverty that a story is told of how his fellow disciples made a contribution of money that they hid in his clothes. At night he went, as was his custom, to meditate on the side of the Zalagh mountain outside Fez, a spot called today the *Khalwah* ("retreat") of Abū Madyan. A gazelle would always come to him there. On the night that the money had been sewn into his robe, the gazelle avoided him and the village dogs barked. Thus alerted, he discovered the money and threw it away saying: "it was because of this uncleanness that the gazelle fled." The famous story, if somewhat an exaggeration — money is the means of the living for which he labored — depicts Abū Madyan's independence from things of this world and his identification with the *fiṭrah*, or primordial norm.

Abū Madyan then became the disciple of a master called Abū Ya'zzah Yalannur ibn Maymūn al-Gharbī (d. *572*/1177), a Dukkala Berber, who lived at Fez and at Taghyah. The famous Sufi 'Abd al-Qādir al-Jīlānī whom, it is said, Abū Madyan met in Mecca, is also numbered among Abū Madyan's teachers. Abū Madyan eventually settled in Bijayah (Bougie) in present day Algeria where a circle of disciples gathered around him. He became famous for miraculous knowledge of the Unseen, both in the world at large and within men. He wrote poetry in the style of his native Andalusia.

Abū Madyan is called the *Quṭb al-Ghawth,* which means the (spiritual) "Axis of Succor". The "Pole" or "Axis" is a person who is the expression of a central spiritual presence in the world. Even in the 19th century, the tradition of turning in need to Abū Madyan was exemplified by the instruction of the Shaykh al-Buzīdī (the Darqawi Shaykh of the Shaykh al-'Alawī): "If you cannot find a spiritual master go and pray at the tomb of Abū Madyan." Ibn 'Arabi referred to him as "his master" and "the proclaimer of the spiritual path in the West". Today he can be considered a "patron saint" of Algeria. *See* QUṬB.

Abū Ma'shar (*189-272*/805-885). Known in the West as Albumazar, a pupil of al-Kindī, he was an astronomer of Balkh who had access to the ancient records and tables of the Persians that had been kept in Iṣfahān. He believed that the world began with a conjunction of the seven known planets at the beginning of the constellation of Aries (the yearly date is the Persian new year of the *naw rūz*) and would end in such a conjunction in the last degree of the constellation of Pisces. Abū Ma'shar noted the correlation between tides and the phases of the moon. He lived in Baghdad and in Wāsiṭ and had a great influence upon early European astronomy.

Abū Muslim (d. *134*/755). The leader of the Khorāsān coalition that brought the 'Abbāsids to power by overthrowing the Umayyads. In that revolutionary movement it was important, if not *de rigeur*, to show working class roots; thus Abū Muslim was styled *as-Sarrāj*, "the saddler". He probably was a Persian, originally from Iṣfahān, perhaps born a slave who started his career in Kūfah. Shahrastāni said that Abū Muslim was a Kaysāni, that is, an adherent of an earlier revolutionary movement of the end of the 7th century that centered on Kūfah. The Kaysāni (or Mukhtāriyyah) movement had an alien religious background although it claimed to avenge 'Alī and had a secret figurehead in the person of 'Alī's son, but not by Fāṭimah, Muḥammad ibn Ḥanifiyyah (d. *81*/700) in order to gain legitimacy amongst the Muslims. The leader of this original movement was Mukhtār (d. *67*/687) and he was known to perform a ceremony in front of an empty throne, the clue to his true religion. The 'Abbāsid revolution was an extension of the Kaysāni movement, and the organization which supported them was indeed Mukhtār's organization, in particular its Khorāsāni branch that had not been apparent in Mukhtār's time. When Muḥammad ibn al-Ḥanifiyyah died the organization was renamed the *Hāshimiyyah* as it allied itself with his son, Abū Hāshim. Abū Hāshim at his death (without issue) in *98*/717 let his 'Abbāsid cousins in on the 'Alīd family secret. He told them about the nature of their 'Irāqi contacts in Kūfah; and initiated them in the ideological secrets of the cooperation. This was called the *'ilm*, the "knowledge" and it was given to Muḥammad ibn 'Alī ibn 'Abd Allāh ibn al-'Abbās at the 'Abbāsid homestead in Ḥumaymah. Thus the 'Abbāsid conspiracy was set into motion with the help of a clandestine religion with deep roots in 'Irāq, and as it turned out, in Khorāsān.

But Abū Muslim's story begins in Kūfah where Abū Muslim took Islam (in a way, since his later actions do not argue for the depth of his beliefs) and served, perhaps as a slave, of Abū Salamah. Abū Salamah Ḥafṣ ibn Sulaymān al-Khallāl (meaning the "vinegar seller"), mawlā of the Sabī' tribe from Hamdān, was one of the most important 'Abbāsid propagandists; indeed, he was called "the vizier of the 'Abbāsids" and was the military leader of the 'Abbāsid coalition in 'Irāq. However, eventually he was executed by as-Saffāḥ in 750. The reason given by traditions, that Abū Salamah after the installment of as-Saffāḥ as Caliph, veered to support an 'Alīd instead is hardly convincing; it points to an incompatibility between the realities of the 'Abbāsid situation, and the true goals of the revolution. The success of the 'Abbāsids lay in double-crossing their own conspiracy before it could double-cross them.

Abū Muslim accompanied Abū Salamah to Khorāsān. Later he became the client of Ibrāhīm ibn Muḥammad, the 'Abbāsid leader and original candidate for the Caliphate (in secret) and half brother of Abūl-'Abbās as-Saffāḥ who did become the first 'Abbāsid Caliph. Ibrāhīm, who was captured in 747 by Marwan II and died in prison in 749, had sent Abū Muslim back to Khorāsān as his propagandist (*dā'i*). Because of Abū Muslim, many in Khorāsān took Islam, or appeared to, since he had apparently had another, secret doctrine, that was quite different, for he taught transmigration of souls and had Gnostic ascetic traits. Al-Jāḥiẓ said that Abū Muslim had admonished his army to "have nothing to do with women". Thus, we see a characteristic, anti-cosmic asceticism as an aspect of the movement. Part of the revolution's appeal, as in the time of Mukhtār's revolt, was its claim to "purity"; its claim to defend the weak; the messianic and secret nature of the leader who was remote from the actual carrying out of the revolution; and the large-scale participation of mawālī and slaves side by side with Arab tribesmen. (*See* MUḤAMMAD ibn al-ḤANAFIYYAH.)

After the success of the 'Abbāsid revolution Abū Muslim appears to have declared his own divinity to his followers. He had a follower named Hāshim al-Muqanna' who did the same. Many legends describe Abū Muslim's entry into paradise after death with a ritual of basil and butter, that is related to Zoroastrianism or Persian popular belief.

Abū Muslim unfurled the black flag of the 'Abbāsids in Khorāsān with the motto "the 'anointed' leader from the People of the House". The term "People of the House" had a broad meaning among the Arabs, including, in the Koran (33:33), simply those who venerate the Ka'bah. But it also had different meanings for others. Because the identity of the leaders was kept secret, anyone could be encouraged to believe that his own particular affiliation was in reality behind the revolt. For example, "People of the House" also translated a Manichean Buddhist term, *Buddhagotra*, "family" or "house" of the Buddha, from Sanskrit gotra, house or family; (Balkh in Khorāsān was a center of Buddhism). This term in Manicheism was given to the light, that was for them God Himself, suffering in this world, the "Living Soul" — *viva anima* in Augustine, a designation that can be traced back to 1 Corinthians 15:45 "The first man Adam, became a living soul."

The revolt was declared before the end of Ramaḍan. (The breaking of a fast is symbolically the pronouncing of a secret, as it was later among the Ismā'īlis). The 'Abbāsids became so closely associated with Khorāsān that the litterateur al-Jāḥiẓ and others called the 'Abbāsids "a foreign Khorāsānian dynasty" (*dawlah 'ajami Khorāsāni*).

"On the night of *25 Ramaḍan. 129* (10 June 747), the inhabitants of Safidhanj, a village on the outskirts of Merv, witnessed a remarkable spectacle, part religious convocation and part political demonstration. The Khuza'i shaykh of the village, Sulayman b. Kathir [member of the Azd tribe who were the Arab patrons of the Barmakids], led a group of men dressed completely in black to a place of assemblage near his residence. There they proceeded to raise two large black banners, one that they named 'the shadow' on a pole fourteen cubits long and another, called 'the clouds', on a pole thirteen cubits long. As they did so, a newcomer in the village known as Abū Muslim chanted a verse from the Koran: 'Leave is given to those who fight because they were wronged; surely God is able to help them' (22:39). They then kindled bonfires, and in response, men from surrounding villages, also robed in black, left their homes to join their comrades in Safidhanj."

After the 'Abbāsids came to power, al-Manṣūr invited Abū Muslim to 'Irāq and had him murdered, like Abū Salamah, and for probably similar reasons, namely that the 'Abbāsids had their goals, and the revolutionary tiger on which they rode had its goals, which were different. This political assassination took place in *Sha'aban 137*/February 755 in Rūmiya, one of a group of towns known as al-Madā'in, about 3 miles/5 km from Ctesiphon (and also close to the future Baghdad). (*See* AL-MADĀ'IN.) Abū Muslim had wanted to govern East Khorasan himself, independently. His murder was followed by the anti-Islamic revolt of Sindbād and other revolts in Iran, that the 'Abbāsids survived. These revolts demonstrate the curious popularity of Abū Muslim in Iran as a kind of folk hero of native nationalism rather than the leader of the army of a foreign conqueror.

Favorable legends surrounded him in Iran continuously through the middle ages. His name is also associated with many sects of Dualist nature such as a Mazdakite sect called the Abū Muslimiyyah that existed at the time of Shahrastāni. The Ismā'īlīs saw him as a precursor. But he put down rival Dualist movements, such as that of Bih'āfrīd.

An-Nadīm, in the *Fihrist* says: "Before the period of the sons of [Maymūn] al-Qaddāḥ, there were persons close to the Magians and their [Sāsānian] regime, for the restoration of which they strove. Sometimes [they worked] openly and sometimes secretly with intrigue, causing things to happen that were illegal in Islām. It has been said that Abū Muslim, chief of the 'Abbāsid movement, favored this cause and worked for it, but he was cut off before its attainment. Among those who were dedicated [to the cause], coming out openly and making themselves known, there was Bābak al-Khurrami..." *See* 'ABBĀSIDS; MUḤAMMAD ibn al-ḤANIFIYYAH; KAYSĀNIYYAH; BARMAKIDS; SINDBĀD REVOLT; al-MUQANNA'; BIH'ĀFRĪD; KHURRAMIYYAH; al-MADĀ'IN.

Abū Nu'aym al-Iṣbahānī, *see* ḤILYAT al-AWLIYĀ'.

Abū Nuwās (d. *195*/810). A poet, whose real name was Ḥasan ibn Hānī. He was a Persian who became a protégé of Hārūn ar-Rashīd, the famous 'Abbāsid Caliph. Abū Nuwās was a *bon vivant* who, enjoying drinking and high living, has become famous in folklore as a kind of "court jester" to the Caliph. Various stories, jokes, and irreverent remarks are attributed to his wit, in addition to the poetry he actually composed.

Abū Saʻīd Aḥmad ibn ʻĪsā-l-Kharrāz (d. *286*/899). A famous Sufi of Baghdad who wrote one of the first systematic expositions of Sufism, the *Kitāb as-Ṣidq* ("The Book of Truthfulness"), that takes the form of questions to a master and his answers.

> I said: "Is love according to the number of blessings?" He replied: "The beginning of love is the recollection of blessings: then it proceeds according to the capacity of its recipient, that is, according to his deserts. For the true lover of God loves God both when receiving His blessings, and when His blessings are withheld: in every state he loves Him with a true love, whether He withholds or grants, afflicts or spares him. Love invariably attaches to his heart, according to his compact [with God]: except that it is nearer to superfluity [it is better to love more than to love less]. For if love went according to the number of blessings received, it would diminish when the blessings diminish, in times of hardship and when affliction befalls But he is God's lover whose mind is distraught for his Lord, and who is only concerned to please Him: when he is grateful to God, and when he recollects Him, he is bewildered, as though no blessing ever descended on any man but it descended on him also. His love for God distracts him from all [concern with] creation. The love of God has banished from his heart all pride, rancor, envy, iniquity, and much that concerns his advantage in the affairs of this world — and how much more the recollection of what concerns him not!"

Abū Sayyāf the name of a violent, contemporary Muslim separatist movement in the Philippines.

Abū Sufyān. The prominent and wealthy Meccan merchant who led the opposition to the Prophet and conducted some of the military campaigns against him. His wife Hind was also numbered among the fiercest opponents of Islam, and she and Abū Sufyān were among the last to be converted when Mecca was finally occupied by the Muslims. Ironically, it was the descendants of Abū Sufyān who constituted the first dynasty, the Umayyads, who ruled the Islamic Empire after the death of the four "rightly guided Caliphs" (*al-Khulafāʻ ar-Rāshidūn*).

Abū Salamah, *see* ABŪ MUSLIM; MUḤAMMAD ibn al-ḤANĀFIYYAH.

Abū Ṭāhir Sulaymān al-Jannābī (d. *333*/944). From *311*/923, ruler of the Qarmaṭī state of al-Aḥsāʻ and Baḥrayn that had been founded by his father Abū Saʻīd (murdered in *301*/913-914). He led aggressive campaigns against the 'Abbāsids sacking Baṣrah and Kūfah and attacking pilgrim caravans and almost capturing Baghdad. The Qarmaṭīs had been acting out the scenario that the Ismāʻīlis had set in motion through propaganda more than a half century earlier. They had spread contrived prophecies that when seven conjunctions had taken place between Jupiter and Saturn a new world order would come into being, Islam would be abolished, and the "true religion" appear. The fateful final conjunction would occur in the year *316*/928. Leading up to this moment attempts were intensified to overthrow the 'Abbāsids, unsuccessfully.

In *Dhu-l-Ḥijja 317*/January 930 Abū Ṭahir turned to an easier target, more symbolic, and instead attacked Mecca, massacred the inhabitants and pilgrims, and carried off the Black Stone to al-Aḥsāʻ where it remained until *340*/951 when it was returned by being thrown in a sack into the Mosque of Kūfah, broken into seven pieces and some crumbs.

Shortly after stealing the Black Stone, Abū Ṭāhir added Oman to the Qarmaṭī state. The prophecy regarding the conjunctions of Jupiter and Saturn was coupled with another political prophecy invented earlier and broadcast by the Ismāʻīlīs that said that 1,500 years after Zoroaster, at the end of the year 1242 of the era of Alexander (AD 930), the rule of the Magians would be restored. (The "time of Zoroaster" in this prophecy was an error that had been made much earlier by the Babylonians who had confused Zoroaster with Cyrus, 550 BC, and misled the Sāssānids who had consulted them on this point, also misleading modern scholars until recently. The actual time of Zoroaster, now shown by archaeology and other evidence is at the latest, 1,200 BC or earlier.)

Forced to make good on his sect's predictions, in Ramaḍān *319*/931 Abū Ṭāhir accepted as Mahdī or inspired leader, a certain Zakariyyāʻ, a young Persian from Iṣfahān. The Persian, who belonged to a "Majusi" religion, instituted antinomian and libertine scandals, burning books, cursing the Prophet Muḥammad, repudiating Islamic practices (which the Qarmaṭīs had done in any case), and finally, executing Qarmaṭīs themselves. The latter was the point to which they objected. Abū Ṭahir allowed this to go on for a short time, but finally had the Persian killed drawing the incident, in some ways a foretaste of the Qiyamah of Alamut, to a close. The event caused some shock among the eastern Ismā'īlīs, such as Abū Ḥatim ar-Rāzī. After Abū Ṭāhir, the Qarmaṭīs, like Trotskyites after them, turned from world revolution and fighting the 'Abbāsids to simply struggling with their family rivals, the Fāṭimids. Eventually, the success ringing from the name of the Fāṭimid capital Cairo (literally, the "Victorious City of the Exalter of the Religion of God") worked its magic and Qarmaṭīs and other dissident Ismā'īlīs recognized the Fāṭimid Imāmate and finally dissolved as a separate group towards the end of the 10th century. *See* QARMAṬĪS; 'UBAYD ALLĀH al-MAHDĪ.

Abū Ṭālib. An uncle of the Prophet and father of 'Alī ibn Abī Ṭālib, the fourth Caliph. Abū Ṭālib became the head of the clan of the Banū Hāshim, to which the Prophet belonged, at the time of the Prophet's mission. As clan chief, Abū Ṭālib extended the clan's protection to the Prophet against the enmity of the Quraysh. He had also been the guardian of the Prophet after the death of 'Abd al-Muṭṭalib. Abū Ṭalib (from whom the 'Alīds descend) and Zubayr were full uncles of the Prophet; they had the same father *and* mother as the Prophet's father 'Abd Allāh. 'Abbās (from whom the 'Abbāsids descend) and the other uncles (Hamzah, al-Ḥarith, Abū Lahab, and others) had the same father, the Prophet's grandfather, 'Abd al-Muṭṭalib, but not the same mothers. These genealogical issues were of great importance to the Arabs and were part of dynastic arguments later.

When Abū Ṭālib died in 619, another uncle, Abū Lahab, became the chief of the clan. Abū Lahab, an implacable enemy of the Prophet, withdrew the clan's protection from him, thus exposing the life of the Prophet to danger. This change in his circumstances forced the Prophet to emigrate to Mecca for his safety.

Abū 'Ubaydah ibn al-Jarrāḥ (d. *18*/639). A Companion to the Prophet and one of "the ten well-betided ones" to whom paradise was promised. He was an emigrant to Abyssinia, took part in the battles, and played an important rìle in the events after the Prophet's death, particularly the election of Abū Bakr as successor. The Caliph 'Umar made him commander in Syria and tradition holds that 'Umar would have named Abū 'Ubaydah his successor had he not died before him.

Abyssinia (Ar. *Ḥabashah*). Modern day Ethiopia. The Abyssinians are related to the Semites and their language, Amharic, is ultimately cognate with Arabic. The Abyssinians are an ancient Christian nation whose church is Monophysite, as is the Coptic church of Egypt; the Abyssinian Patriarch formerly resided in Alexandria and now in Addis Abbaba. In the sixth century, when the Jewish Himyaritic King Dhū Nuwās (Yusūf As'ar) destroyed the Christians of Najrān in southern Arabia, the Negus, or King, of Abyssinia Ella Aṣbeḥa assembled an army to punish Dhū Nuwās on behalf of the Byzantine Emperor, whose natural role was protector of all Christians.

The Prophet said of Abyssinia that it was "a land of sincerity in religion". Before the Hijrah, some eighty Muslims, including the Prophet's daughter Ruqayyah and her husband 'Uthmān, emigrated to Abyssinia, where they were received by the Negus and given refuge. The Quraysh sent two emissaries to persuade the Negus to reject the Muslim emigrants as outlaws. To confound the accusations of the Quraysh against them, the leader of the emigrants, Ja'far ibn Abī Ṭālib, recited to the Negus the verses of the Koran which speak of Mary (19:16-24):

And mention in the Book Mary
when she withdrew from her people
to an eastern place,
and she took a veil apart from them;
then We sent unto her Our Spirit
that presented himself to her
a man without fault.
She said, 'I take refuge in
the All-merciful from thee!
If thou fearest God...'
He said, 'I am but a messenger
come from thy Lord, to give thee
a boy most pure.'
She said, 'How shall I have a son
whom no mortal has touched, neither
have I been unchaste?'
He said, 'Even so thy Lord has said:
"Easy is that for Me; and that We
may appoint him a sign unto men
and a mercy from Us; it is

a thing decreed.'"
So she conceived him, and withdrew with him
to a distant place.

This recitation convinced the Abyssinians that the Muslims had received a revelation akin to their own.

The sanctuary the Abyssinians gave the Muslim refugees has been cited as the reason why the Arabs in their conquests to spread Islam did not invade that country. Certainly, there is much historical evidence that great sympathy existed between the Negus and the Prophet. In 625, the Negus performed a ceremony in Abyssinia marrying Ḥafsah, daughter of the Companion 'Umar, to the Prophet by proxy; she then went to Medinah. Later, when news that the Negus had died reached Medinah, the Prophet performed the Muslim funeral prayer for him.

'Ād. A great and ancient people frequently mentioned in the Koran, "who built monuments upon high places". They were the recipients of a Divine Message brought to them by the Prophet Hūd (7:63 and 26:123-135), upon the rejection of which, they were destroyed by God. Their city, or perhaps their tribe was also called "Iram of the pillars" (or perhaps "tent-poles"). Whether 'Ād and "Iram of the pillars" are one and the same depends upon one's interpretation of the Koran 89:6-7; the identification cannot be definitively established.

'Ād is usually placed in the south of Arabia but commentators on the Koran say, doubtless in a symbolical sense, that the Israelites had to fight remnants of the tribe of 'Ād when they entered the Holy Land. 'Ād is considered to be one of the tribes of the original Arabs, the so-called "lost Arabs" (*'Arab al-bā'idah*). *See* ARABS.

Adab (lit. "courtesy", "politeness", "propriety", "morals"; also "literature"). An important subject in traditional literature. Al-Ḥujwīrī wrote as follows:

The Apostle of God said:

"Good breeding is a part of faith."

The beauty and propriety of all affairs, religious as well as temporal, depends on a certain discipline of breeding. Humanly, it consists in noble-mindedness; religiously, in observing the Sunnah; in love, good breeding is reverence. A person who neglects this discipline cannot ever possibly be a saint, for the Prophet said:

"Good breeding is a mark of those God loves."

Towards God, one must keep oneself from disrespect in one's private as well as one's public behavior. We have it from a sound Ḥadīth that once, when God's Apostle was sitting with his legs akimbo, [the Angel] Gabriel appeared and said: "Muḥammad, sit as servants sit before a master."

For forty years Muḥāsibi never sat, but always knelt. "I am ashamed," he replied when questioned, "to sit otherwise than as a servant while I think of God."

Towards oneself, one must avoid what would be improper with a fellow creature or with God. For instance, a man must not lie, representing himself to himself as what he is not... In social intercourse the best rule is to act nobly and observe the Sunnah. Human companionship must be for God's sake, not for the soul's sake nor for interest. He is a bad companion, said Rāzī, to whom you have to say:

"Remember me in your prayers. And he is a bad companion with whom you must flatter or apologize."

In modern times, no less than in the past, great importance is placed in Islam upon proper greetings on meeting and parting. "When you enter houses greet one another" (24:61). The shaking of hands, sitting in such a way as to avoid pointing the soles of one's feet at anyone, not laughing raucously, and a general sobriety of attitude are also insisted upon.

Arabs of the desert — as opposed to sedentary Arabs — normally avoid any physical contact other than handshaking. *Adab* also requires a person to join in the carrying of a bier in a funeral procession, to visit the sick, and to assist those in distress. In general, it is also a part of *adab* that the right side of the body be given precedence over the left in all things. Especially, it is the left hand that is used for unclean things and it is imperative that only the right hand be offered in greetings and used in eating.

Arab rules of hospitality — not specifically Islamic — make it a dishonour to refuse lodging and food to anyone presenting themselves at one's door;

but, by custom, such obligations end after three days. When a guest is received by someone it is unthinkable for the guest to refuse at least one cup of tea or coffee. Later glasses may be subtly declined by putting a finger over the cup and rocking it from side to side. In the Arab West, a third glass of tea may be, according to context, a signal from the host that the visit has reached its end. In Arab societies and some others, one offers an invitation to come, to partake, or to do something, three times at one session and the recipient refuses twice, the first two invitations being considered *pro forma*, and of politeness only, and the third, serious.

As refusal can cause acute embarrassment in many traditional societies, requests of others are often made through go-betweens. This practice allows frank discussions to be held through third parties that otherwise would be difficult face-to-face between persons actually involved. *See* GREETINGS.

Adam (Ar. Ādam). The first man and father of mankind. All Arab genealogies go back to the Prophets and finally to Adam and then say: "and God made him of clay". Adam is also vicegerent of God on earth (*khalifatu'*Llahi fī-l-arḍ; *see* CALIPH). He is the first Prophet and builder of the original Ka'bah.

Created by God in His Image (*'alā ṣūratihi* according to the Ḥadīth related by Ibn Ḥanbal in the *Musnad*), and from earth, Adam was taught the names of all things, that the Angels themselves did not know (2:28-31). As the central being within manifestation, or creation, he actually contained manifestation within himself; this is symbolized by his knowledge of the names; the Angels, not being "central", did not "know" the names.

Adam dwelt at first in the Garden of Eden with his wife Eve (Ar. *Ḥawwā'*), who had been created from a rib taken from his left side. They disobeyed the Divine command and ate the fruit of the forbidden tree. In Islam, however, the responsibility of this sin lies not with man but with *Iblīs*, the Devil, who tempted Adam.

In Christianity, the redemption of the Fall — the sin of wishing to see the world as contingency, in its limitation, rather than in its essence as a prolongation of the Absolute — is effectual through Jesus; the Fall is seen as a fault of the will. By Jesus's sacrifice for man and by man's for Jesus, in denying himself in order to accept Jesus, the Fall is redeemed. In Islam, the Fall is the error of seeing the world and the ego as real instead of God, who alone is Real. Thus the redemption from the Fall lies within the *shahādah*, in realizing the truth that there is no god, or autonomous reality, but Allāh. The affirmation of the *shahādah* in principle corrects virtually the effect of the Fall, and its complete realization within the soul restores man effectively to his original state, that of Adam before the Fall. The Fall clouds the grasp of reality; it introduces reasoning in the place of direct knowledge; the *shahādah* restores the lost direct awareness of the absoluteness of God; it places man back in the Garden of Eden.

We created you, then We shaped you,
then We said to the angels: 'Bow yourselves
to Adam'; so they bowed themselves,
save Iblis — he was not of those
that bowed themselves.
Said He, 'What prevented thee to
bow thyself, when I commanded thee?'
Said he, 'I am better than he; Thou
createdst me of fire, and him Thou
createdst of clay.'
Said He, 'Get thee down out of it;
tis not for thee to wax proud here,
so go thou forth; surely thou art
among the humbled.'
Said he, 'Respite me till the day
they shall be raised.'
Said He, 'Thou art among the ones
that are respited'
Said he, 'Now, for Thy perverting me,
I shall surely sit in ambush for them
on Thy straight path;
then I shall come on them from before them
and from behind them, from their right hands
and their left hands; Thou wilt not find
most of them thankful.'
Said He, 'Go thou forth from it, despised
and banished. Those of them that follow
thee — I shall assuredly fill Gehenna
with all of you.'

'O Adam, inherit thou and thy wife,
the Garden, and eat of where you will,
but come not nigh this tree, lest you be
of the evildoers.'
Then Satan whispered to them, to reveal
to them that which was hidden from them
of their shameful parts. He said, 'Your Lord
has only prohibited you from this tree

lest you become angels or lest you
become immortals.'
And he swore to them, 'Truly, I am for you
a sincere adviser.'
So he led them on by delusion; and when
they tasted the tree, their shameful parts
revealed to them, so they took to stitching
upon themselves leaves of the Garden.
And their Lord called to them, 'Did not I
prohibit you from this tree, and say
to you, "Verily Satan is for you
a manifest foe?"'
They said, 'Lord, we have wronged ourselves,
and if Thou dost not forgive us, and
have mercy upon us, we shall surely be
among the lost.' (7:10-23)

Adat (lit. "normative custom" a Malay word derived from Ar. *'ādah*). In Indonesia, Malaysia, and the Philippines, *adat* denotes those regional customs and practices that are usually unwritten, but which nonetheless have the force of social law alongside Islamic law (*sharī'ah*), and the civil code. Customary laws exist everywhere in the Islamic world, to some degree. The form *'ādah* is common in other parts of the Islamic world for such customary laws. *See* SHARĪ'AH.

Adhān. The call to prayer, which is made one or more times by the muezzin from a minaret, a rooftop, or simply from the door of the place of prayer about a quarter of an hour before the prayer begins. The words of the adhān are:

1. *Allāhu Akbar* ("God is greater")— four times.
2. *Ashhadu an1 lā 'ilāha illā-Llāh* ("I witness that there is no god but Allāh")— twice.
3. *Ashhadu anna Muḥammadān rasūlu-Llāh* ("I witness that Muḥammad is the Messenger of God")— twice.
4. *Ḥayya 'ala-ṣ-ṣalāh* ("Rise up for prayer")— twice.
5. *Ḥayya 'ala-l-falāḥ* ("Rise up for salvation")— twice.
6. *Allāhu Akbar* ("God is greater")— twice.
7. *Lā ilāha illa-Llāh* ("There is no god but God")— once.

The word "Akbar" means "greater than all" and can be translated as "Most great"; there is no specific superlative from the adjective in Arabic.

(The rules of euphony in Arabic, as in Koran chanting, call for the *nun* or n to be assimilated to a following letter having the same point of articulation. Thus the *an lā* in the *shahādah* is pronounced *al-lā* and *Muḥammadan rasūlu-Llah* is pronounced *Muḥammadar-rasūlu-Llāh*.)

For the *ṣubḥ* (early morning) prayer the words: *aṣ-ṣalātu khayrun mina-n-nawm* ("Prayer is better than sleep"— once) are inserted between *Hayya 'ala-l-falāḥ* and *Allāhu Akbar* (that is, between e and f above). Shī'ites, however, omit this because they believe it was added to the *adhān* by the Caliph 'Umar.

On the other hand, the Twelve-Imām and Zaydi Shī'ites add to every *adhān: Ḥayya 'alā khayri-l-'amal*, "rise up for the best of works" (twice) which they believe was originally part of the call to prayer but was suppressed by the Caliph 'Umar. And at the end, Twelve-Imām Shī'ites add: *'Alī walī Allāh*, "'Alī is the Saint of God" (once) and sometimes other formulas as well.

Once the believers have assembled inside the mosque, another call is given within as a signal to rise up and form rows immediately before the prayer begins. This interior call is known as the *iqāmah*, or "raising up". It differs from the *adhān* in that *Allāhu Akbar* (*see* 1. above) is repeated twice, rather than four times, and *Ḥayya 'ala-ṣ-ṣalāh* and *Ḥayya 'ala-l-falāḥ* (4. and 5.) are recited once each rather than twice. After this, and before the final two *Allāhu Akbar* (*between* 5. *and* 6.) the words: *qad qāmati-ṣ-ṣalātu, qad qāmati-ṣ-ṣalāh* ("the prayer is established, the prayer is established") are inserted.

In addition to the call, many mosques will display a white flag as a signal that the prayer is being called; at night, a lamp is lit on the top of the minaret to serve the same purpose.

'Adnān. A descendent of Ismā'īl and traditional ancestor of the North Arabian tribes: the Beduins of the northern and central deserts of the Arabian peninsula who called themselves "the sons of 'Adnān". The ancestor of the South Arabians is Qaḥṭān, the Joktan of the Bible.

Adultery, *see* ZĪNA'.

Aesop, *see* LUQMĀN.

al-Afghānī, Jamāl ad-Dīn (*1254-1314*/1838-1897). A modernist, reformer, and political agitator, and above all, opportunist. He was born in Iran but raised in Afghanistan, where he first attached himself to the royal court and rose to become a minister. After his patron fell, his political career became an Odyssey that led through lands as far apart as India and America, and gravitated towards fashionable society circles and centers of power in European and Oriental capitals. He was received by the heads of state in Cairo and Istanbul several times, where he was awarded government subsidies. An inveterate intriguer, al-Afghānī several times was forced to leave those courts that had shown him favor. His political aims were opportunistic rather than consistent. At one time or another he advocated the union of the Islamic countries under one Caliph; pressed for secular republican governments; sought the largesse of princes; called for their overthrow. He swam with the current, wherever it went. He twice ingratiated himself with then Shah of Iran, Nāṣir ad-Dīn, and twice was expelled, the second time under military escort and in chains.

For a time he collaborated with Muḥammad 'Abduh in Paris in the publication of reformist Islamic periodicals. "Jamal ad-Din al-Afghani published a response to a lecture of Ernest Renan's at the Sorbonne in which Renan characterized Islam as 'the heaviest chain ever borne by humanity.' Afghani's answer in the *Journal des Débats* (May 18, 1883) was the following: 'Muslim society has still not freed itself from the tutelage of religion... I cannot prevent myself from hoping that Muhammadan society will one day succeed in breaking its bonds...' This is in strong contrast to what he would write in the *al-'Urwa al-Wuthqa*, in which he said, 'I wish the monarch of all the Muslims to be the Koran, and the focus of their unity, their faith.' However, 'Abduh eventually broke with him. Right up until the end of his life al-Afghānī continued to exercise a fascination over the powerful. Shortly before his death in 1897 he received a pension and a house from the Ottoman Sultan 'Abd al-Ḥamīd, an autocrat who certainly did not respond favorably to the revolutionary proposals of al-Afghānī.

This political chameleon involved himself in perpetual intrigues, of which he always painted himself as the victim. The fascination he exercised as a politician derived from his skillful admixture and manipulation of religion and anarchy, conservatism and radical liberalism. Although he was accused of involvement in the murder of Shah Nāṣir ad-Dīn and of wishing to subvert the rule of his final patron, the Ottoman Sultan, al-Afghānī avoided human punitive retribution, succumbing to death by natural causes.

Afghanistan. Population estimated to be from 14,448,000 to 25,825,000 of which the overwhelming majority are Sunnī Muslims of the Ḥanafī rite. Twelve-Imām Shī'ites make up perhaps 15% of the population and there is a very small minority of Nizārī Ismā'īlīs, several thousands, mostly in the remote northern province of Badakshan. More Nizārīs live in neighboring Tajikistan where they have recently acquired much more political power through civil war. The Pashtun make up the ethnic majority and comprise around half of the population. They are found in the south, across the center, and in the northeast. All Pashtun share a code of customary law called Pukhtunwali. One group of Pashtun, the Durani (Abdali), who consider themselves to be "authentic" Afghans as opposed to all other groups, including other Pashtun, have created a mythical Koranic identity for themselves by believing that they are descended from the Banū Isrā'īl, that is, from Jews, but Jews who converted voluntarily to Islam at the first instance. Specifically, they claim to be descended from a grandson of King Saul named Afghana, and were deported so far east by Nebuchadnezzar. Such fabled self histories are, of course, ethnic commonplaces.

Although the distinction between *Parsiwan*, or Persian speakers and the Pashtun speakers is a fundamental one in Afghan society, the last King, Ẓāhir Shāh, a Pashtun, did not speak Pashtun himself, but rather the court language which was Persian, the universal Islamic language of culture and civilization east of Baghdad. Persian, in its classical form of Dari, slightly different from the modern Persian of Iran, is the language of the Tajiks, but is also spoken by the other non-Pashtun groups in Afghanistan in addition to their own languages.

Afghanistan dates as a modern state from 1747 when King Aḥmad Shāh was chosen to be ruler by an assembly in Kandahar after the assassination of Nādir Shāh in Iran. He styled his reign the *Dur-i Duran*, "Pearl of the Age" that became the Durrani dynasty and the name of his Pashtun clan, the Abdali. Aḥmad Shāh ruled a territory that included the Punjab and Kashmir, and much of Turkestan with other regions such as Sindh paying tribute; in other words, an area including half of former Soviet Central Asia, Pakistan and parts of India. The present borders of Afghanistan are the result of "the great game" of the 19th century in which Russia maneuvered to gain colonial control of Central Asia and Britain to protect its hold over India. This ended in an agreement to make of Afghanistan a buffer state between the two powers preceded by another series of agreements that defined the borders: the Russian-Afghan boundary commission of 1884-1886 for the northern border, the Pamir Commission of 1895 for the north-eastern border, and the Perso-Baluch Commission of 1904-1905 for the western. The Durand Agreement line of 1893 that separated Afghanistan and British India, is now the border with Pakistan. Because this "agreement" was for the benefit of third parties and thus rather arbitrary as regards the actual population, fourteen million Pashtun live in Pakistan where they are called Pathans (from Pukhtun, the eastern pronunciation of the name Pashtun). Other peoples within the Afghani population are the Baluchis, Tajiks (around 25%), Hazaras (19%), who are Shī'ite, and Turkic peoples (8%) such as the Kirghiz, Turkmen, and Uzbeks. The Hazaras are Turko-Mongols in Afghanistan and Central Asia whose name probably comes from Jenghiz Khan's division of his horde into companies of a thousand (Persian *hazar*). The most numerous Sufi *ṭarīqah* in Afghanistan is the Naqshbandiyyah, although the Qādiriyyah and Chishtiyyah are also widespread.

The so-called Kāfirs (unbelievers) of Afghanistan were actually remnants of an ancient Indo-European paganism, who had been isolated up to the end of the 19th century. Once they were presumed to be converted, by force in 1897, their region was called Nūristān ("the land of light"). Groups belonging to them can still be found in isolated places in Pakistan such as Chitral where they usually claim to be Muslims towards outsiders.

The traditional political structures in the times of the King or Amir were the council, made up of nobles, or Sirdars, and Khans and Mullās. The Khans were elected representatives of the people. This council was divided into two groups, the *Darbār Shāhī* or Royal Assemby and the *Kharwānin Mulkhī* representing the population. A kind of Royal cabinet existed called the *Khilwat*. Tribal assemblies called Jirga were adapted by Amir 'Abd ar-Raḥmān Khan at the end of the 19th century into representative bodies, with some delegates elected, called to take special action. This became part of a constitution proclaimed by King Amanullah in 1923. In 1964 a grand assembly or Loya Jirga was called to ratify a new constitution.

Following a long period of corruption and feudal oppression, King Ẓāhir Shāh was overthrown in 1973 by his cousin and brother-in-law Muḥammad Dawud and went into exile. A Communist government came to power eventually supported by Russian troops airlifted in 1979 after Dawud was killed in a coup. The Russian presence led to continuous war but nevertheless did much to build roads, establish schools, and liberate women, progress which was wiped out by the ṭāliban leaving only the Russian built 2.6 kilometer Salang strategic tunnel through the mountains which connects parts of the country otherwise impassible in winter. (The tunnel, built in 1964, was dynamited in 1997 but has since been repaired.) The Afghan war against the Soviet Union was supported by the United States and the Arab Gulf States; the tide however, only turned after Afghan guerillas were supplied with U.S. Stinger missiles, grounding the Soviet airforce. But U.S. support for Afghan resistence to the Soviets actually backfired into the Mujahidin movement. While the Soviet Union was seriously destabilized by the war, Afghanistan was left a shambles after the Soviet withdrawal in February 1989. Internal fighting opened the way for the ṭāliban and al-Qaedah, and the U.S. intervention in 2001. In June 2002, former King Ẓāhir Shāh returned to Afghanistan, and a Loya Jirgah elected Ḥamid Karzai the new president of a national government while actual control of the country was left in the hands of local warlords.

The physical climate of Afghanistan presents very cold winters with very hot summers. The Moghul Emperor Babur said: "One day's travel from Kabul there is a place where the snow never falls, and two hours travel the snow never melts." The country was formerly divided into five regions ruled by *nā'ibs* or governors: Herat, Badakshan, Kabul, Kandahar, and Turkestan. The latter is the northern area, or *Chahar Vilayat* ("Four Provinces") west of Badakshan, including Mazar-i Sharif and Kunduz. It has historically been bound to the Emirate of Bukhara by ethnic affinity more than to Kabul. Once a part of Achaemenid Iran, Afghanistan was also ruled by the Bactrian Greeks after the conquest of Alexander the Great. In Arabic he is called Iskandar and he founded a city, "Alexandria of the Arachosians", at Kandahar, that is named after him. He also founded a city at Herat. Around AD 115 Afghanistan and the surrounding regions were ruled by Kushan kings beginning with Kanishka I. Balkh and Bamian were centers of Buddhism visited by the Chinese scholar Hsüan Tsang in 632. Balkh was also a center for Zoroastrianism, then Manicheism, and finally, Ismā'īlism. India has also exerted its influence upon the land and people. *See* BARMAKIDS; MAḤMUD of GHAZNAH; MAZAR-I SHARIF; ṬĀLIBAN.

Afshārids. An interim dynasty that ruled in Persia between *1148-1210*/1736-1795. As the previous Ṣafavid power declined and Persia was threatened by invasions from Afghanistan and the Ottomans, a leader appeared from a Turkmen tribe, the *Afshār*, one of the original tribes of the *Qīzīl Bash*. Nādir Shāh (d. *1154*/1741) was at first regent for the last Ṣafavids. A remarkably successful military leader, he preserved the territorial integrity of Persia from possible invaders, the Ottomans and the Afghans. Nādir Shāh captured Bukhārā and Khivā and led campaigns against the Moghuls in India where he seized territory, pillaged mercilessly, and captured the peacock throne that he brought back from Delhi. After driving out the Ottoman Turks from Persia, Nādir Shāh had himself declared Shah by an assembly in *1149*/1736 that he called to nominate a ruler.

As a condition of his rule, Nādir Shāh attempted to make the Persians abandon what he called "the heresy of Ismā'īl" (the first Ṣafavid ruler, who made Twelve-Imām Shi'ism the state religion). Nādir Shāh proposed to the Ottoman Turks that if the Persians eliminated the Imāmī element, becoming thereby Sunnī, the Ottomans should recognize Persian Islam as a fifth school of law (*madhhab*). The legitimacy of this Ja'farī School of Law would be confirmed by being accorded a *maqām*, or symbolic station, around the Ka'bah in Mecca. In addition, the Persians would be allowed to lead a pilgrimage caravan along with the Syrians and the Egyptians. This plan was accepted neither by the grandees in Persia nor by the Ottomans.

Nādir Shāh was from a Shī'ite family, but Turkic by race, and thus not subject to the ancestral attraction that Shī'ism, whose doctrine of the Imāms echoes ancient and indigenous Persian concepts of religious authority and revelation, exercises upon Persians of Indo-European origin. He tried to restore Sunnism perhaps because he saw himself as being potentially a great Asian conqueror, although personal religious conviction cannot be precluded. While the Ṣafavids were able to exploit Shī'ism in order to rally support for their conquest of Persia, it would have been a liability for Nādir Shāh if he attempted to create an empire beyond Persia. Perhaps it was his failure in this respect and the frustration of his imperial designs that led to the instability of the last years of his reign. He blinded his own son who was involved in a plot against him, and was himself assassinated by courtiers. Political instability of one kind or another characterized the reigns of his successors, the brevity and frequency of which soon led to the accession of the Zand dynasty. *See* AKHBARĪS; IRAN; QĪZĪL BASH; ṢAFAVIDS; ZANDS.

Aga Khan. The Imām, or spiritual leader, of the Nizārī branch of Ismā'īlīs. The title *Aga Khan* was bestowed on Abū-l-Ḥasan 'Alī Shāh in 1818 by the then Shah of Persia, Fatḥ 'Alī. In 1841, Aga Khan I fled Persia after an unsuccessful rebellion against the Shah and emigrated first to the city of Kandahar in Afghanistan and thence to Bombay.

The present Aga Khan, Karīm (b. 17 December 1936) is the fourth to bear the title and the 49th Nizārī Ismā'īlī Imām, in the belief of his followers, in unbroken succession of descent. He is the grandson of Muḥammad, the third Aga Khan, who selected Karīm to be his successor, passing over the eldest son 'Alī, father of Karīm, and 'Alī's half-brother Ṣadruddīn. The present Aga Khan was educated at Harvard and resides near Paris. He is noted for carrying on his grandfather'stradition of charitable work both within the Ismā'īlī community and outside it. The Aga Khan is of the Qāsim-Shahī line of Imāms. Another line, the Muḥammad Shahīs, was followed by Syrian Ismā'īlīs, but they lost contact with their fortieth Imām, Amīr Muḥammad al-Baqir in 1796, in India, where these Imāms had been living. *See* ISMĀ'ĪLĪS; SHĪ'ISM.

"Age of Ignorance", *see* JĀHILIYYAH.

Agha (also Aga and Aqa). A title of honour and military distinction among the Turks. As an honourific, it is also the title of any of the eunuchs who supervised the woman's sections of the Grand Mosques of Mecca and Medinah.

Aghlabids. A dynasty that ruled in Ifrīqīyā, the region centered around present day Tunisia, from *184*/800 until *296*/909 when they were overthrown by the Fāṭimids. Founded by Ibrāhīm ibn al-Aghlab from Khorāsān, (of a family of 'Abbāsid revolutionaries) the Aghlabids ostensibly ruled in the name of the 'Abbāsids of Baghdad, but actually were an independent power. Under their dynastic rule, Muslim civilization flourished in Tunisia and Algeria with Kairouan (Qayrawan) as its regional center. Having captured and conquered Sicily from the Byzantines, the Aghlabids incorporated the island into their own empire in *217*/832. Malta was seized and added to their own territories in *255*/868.

Aḥkām. The categories into which all actions fall under Islamic law: forbidden (*ḥarām*), obligatory (*farḍ*), recommended (*mustaḥabb*), discouraged (*makrūh*), permitted (*mubāḥ*). *See* FARḌ; ḤARĀM; MAKRūH; SHARĪ'AH.

Ahl al-Bayt (lit. "people of the house"). The term can simply mean a family of note. In the Koran it may refer to the Quraysh (11:73 and 33:33). The Umayyads referred to themselves as *ahl al-bayt.* However, it became particularly a term for the descendants of the Prophet through his daughter Fāṭimah and his cousin and son-in-law, 'Alī. They had three sons, Ḥasan, Ḥusayn, and Muḥsin (who died in infancy). From Ḥasan and Ḥusayn descend the *sharīfs*, who hold an honoured position in Muslim society. Modern day descendents of the Prophet number many tens of thousands. In some countries, such as Egypt, a register is maintained of the Prophet's descendents.

The Shī'ites believe that 'Alī had an intermediary role between man and God that was inherited by Ḥusayn and particular descendents out of succeeding generations. Thus, for the Shī'ites the notion of the *ahl al-bayt* has a special meaning which it acquired when it was used as a slogan first by Mukhtār and the Kaysāniyyah and then by the 'Abbāsid revolution. At that time it was particularly useful because it could mean whatever its hearers wanted it to mean and could rally disparate partisans to the 'Abbāsid cause. The term may have originally suggested itself because of its resemblance to the Iranian term *vispuhr* ("son of the house") which appears in Manichean literature, and "prince of the house", a title of Manī himself. The Barmakids were also referred to by Maqdisi as *min ahl buyūtāt Balkh*, "from the noble houses of Balkh". *See* SHĪ'ISM.

Ahl al-Ḥadīth (also *Ahl-i Ḥadīth*, lit. "People of the Traditions"). A name given to various conservative traditionalists, especially to those who withheld from theological speculation, during the development of Mu'tazilitism and the Ash'arite reaction. At the present time there are modern groups in India and Pakistan who, not following any *madhhab*, or school of law, call themselves *Ahl-i Ḥadīth.*

One could say that from the beginning of Islam there has been a current that could be called *Ahl ar-Ra'y*, "people of opinion" or speculation, and a current called *Ahl al-Ḥadīth*, those who hold to literal interpretation and who claim to eschew opinion. Of the schools of law, the Ḥanafīs made the most liberal use of opinion, and the Ḥanbalīs the least. The Kharijis and the ẓahiris are *Ahl al-Ḥadīth.* Ibn Ḥazm is the foremost philosopher-theologian of the classical *Ahl al-Ḥadīth.*

Since the early 19th century in India some of the most fundamentalist movements to emerge have been called *Ahl-i Haḍīth* by themselves and by others. These are the movements that say that a man's beard must be longer than what can be grasped in his fist, that if a man's gown is not higher than his ankles it is, if not sin, at least a deviation, and that if the gown is not lower than midcalf it is also a transgression. Generally, *Ahl-i Ḥadīth* do not accept a triple divorce pronounced on one occasion; that "non-compulsion in religion" concerns non-Muslims, but that Muslims can be forced to pray, for example; that rightful government is by an Emir elected by the 'Ulamā', and that Islamic rule over the whole world can be established by Jihād. Since the Afghan war against the Soviets these movements have become very militant and in some cases allied with the al-Qaedah of Usāma Bin Ladin. Regarding the modern *Ahl-i Ḥadith, see* LASHKAR-I-TAYYEBA; FUNDAMENTALISM.

Ahl-i Ḥaqq (lit. "People of the Absolute, the Real, God"). One of several sects called collectively *'Alī Ilāhis* ("The Deifiers of 'Alī"). The Ahl-i Ḥaqq are a minor, heretical, dualist cult found among some Persians, Kurds and Turkmen of 'Irāq and Iran. In Iran, they are concentrated in the west of the country, especially around Tabrīz, but small groups can be found everywhere. They are closely related to the Yazīdis of 'Irāq, and more distantly with the other dualist sects in the Middle East. Their doctrine teaches that there were seven Divine Manifestations beginning with a figure called Khawandagar; they believe that the Prophet's cousin 'Alī ibn Abī Ṭālib was one of these manifestations, and that the series culminated in the direct "founder" of the cult, a figure called Sultan Sohak (Ishāq) who lived in the *9th*/15th century.

The cult practices the sacrifice of cocks, an animal that represents the liminal moment of daybreak. Thus the cock appears as a popular symbol in religions with light/darkness polarizations. The Ahl-i Ḥaqq have a ceremony called *sabz namudar* ("making green") which may hearken back to the beliefs of the Manicheans that the Divine light is hidden in the world in greatest concentrations in plants (which is why the Manicheans were vegetarians). The beliefs of the Ahl-i Ḥaqq, which vary from group to group, incorporate elements typical of the Gnostic or Manichean deviations found on the fringes of Islam, as indeed, around all religions. The Ahl-i Ḥaqq believe in the transmigration of souls, and even in reincarnation; like the Yazidis and the 'Alawis, they seem to be a by-product of the Sevener movement, but without the Islamic clothing. *See* MANICHEANISM; SEVENERS.

Ahl al-Kitāb (lit. "People of the Book"). Those whom the Koran cites as having received revealed scriptures: "Surely they that believe, and those of Jewry, and the Christians, and those Ṣābians, whoso believe in God and the Last Day, and work righteousness — their wage awaits them with their Lord, and no fear shall be on them, neither shall they sorrow" (2:58 and similar to 5:69). In virtue of 22:17, Magians (*al-majūs*) — that is, Zoroastrians, also called Mazdaeans, and, in India, Parsis — are sometimes (but not by all authorities) considered to be "People of the Book" along with Christians, Jews and the Ṣābians.

As for the Ṣābians, their identity has never been definitively established, although the Mandaeans of 'Irāq are the most likely. The fact that one Revelation should name others as authentic is an extraordinary event in the history of religions.

The *Ahl al-Kitāb* could not be forcibly converted, as could pagans or disbelievers. They are entitled to protection within the Islamic state which was granted against payment of a tax called the *dhimmah*.

The Koran also states that revelations have been made to others whom God does not name: "Every nation has its Messenger" (10:47); "We sent Messengers before thee; of some We have related to thee, and some We have not related to thee" (40:78). And:

To every one
of you We have appointed a right way
and open road.
If God had willed, He would have made you
one nation; but that He may try you
in what has come to you. So be you forward
in good works; unto God shall you
return, all together; and He will tell you
of that whereon you were at variance. (5:51)

Such is the Koranic perspective; however, it is almost too much to ask that a man hold another's religion as equal to his own. In the actual beliefs of the overwhelming majority of Muslims, Christianity has "lost its truth" and is simply "tolerated" by heaven. Thus, some Muslims believe as a matter of course that Christians do not attain to heaven, while others concede that Christians achieve salvation. In the latter case, the question arises (but is not addressed): if the efficacy of Christianity has been suspended, in virtue of what are Christians saved? Even more out of the question for the average Muslim is it to identify Buddhism, Hinduism, Confucianism, Shintoism, or the indigenous religions of the Americas, for example, as one of the Revelations of which God says: "and about some have We not told you".

Naturally, there are exceptions to religious "nationalism" within Islam as within other religions. There is the story, by no means unique, of a Sufi, Ibrāhīm ibn Adham, who when starting upon the mystic path, and having failed to find a Muslim master at the outset, unhesitatingly took spiritual instruction from a Christian. In Lebanon in 2006, a Shī'ite woman said on French television that because there was no Imām to perform a prayer over the dead in her village, a Christian priest had to do funeral prayers for them. *See* ṢĀBIANS.

Ahl al-Kisā' (lit. "People of the Cloak"). In the 10th year of the Hijrah a delegation of sixty representatives of the Christian community of Najrān arrived in Medinah. Among them were the Bishop Abū-l-Ḥārith and the vicar 'Abd al-Masīḥ. The Christians sought to make a treaty with the Prophet and agreed to pay tribute to the Islamic state that was by then gaining ascendancy over Arabia. During their stay they were allowed to conduct mass in the Prophet's Mosque in Medinah.

Theological discussions took place concerning the nature of Jesus, who for the Christians is Divine and for the Muslims a Prophet only, which resulted in the revelation of this verse of the Koran:

Truly, the likeness of Jesus, in God's sight
is as Adam's likeness; He created him of dust,
then said He unto him, 'Be', and he was.
The truth is of God; be not of the doubters.
And whoso disputes with thee concerning him,
after the knowledge that has come to thee,
say: 'Come now, let us call
our sons and your sons,
our wives and your wives,
our selves and your selves,
then let us humbly pray and so lay God's curse
upon the ones who lie.' (3:53-54)

The Prophet invited the Christians to meet with him the next day to settle their dispute in this way. When the Christians came, they found that 'Alī was with the Prophet, and Fāṭimah and their two sons. The Prophet was wearing a large cloak that he drew over all of them. It is from this event that the members of the family were called the "People of the Cloak". The Christians declined to go through with the imprecation, but obtained a treaty of protection against the payment of the *jizyah*, or tax.

Aḥmad. One of the names of the Prophet. *See* NAMES OF THE PROPHET.

Aḥmad of Rāe Bareli (Aḥmad Barilwi or Brelvi and also known as Aḥmad ibn Muḥammad 'Irfan) (*1201-1246*/1786-1831). Indian religious reformer, a sharif or descendant of the Prophet, also known as Aḥmad Shahīd, born in Bareilly but educated at Lucknow. He militated against British domination and against Sikhs, thus he was an early figure in the nationalist movement. Having gathered several thousand followers in a Jihād, he died in the Battle of Balākot against Sikhs in what is now the North West Frontier Province of Pakistan. His sayings are contained in a text called the *Sirāt-i Mustaqīm* collected by his nephew. He was the disciple of Shāh 'Abd al-'Aziz, the eldest son of Shāh Walī Allāh. Aḥmad Barilwi was also a reformer with views related to the Wahhabi movement. *See* BARILWĪS.

Aḥmadiyyah. A heterodox sect founded by Mirzā Ghulām Aḥmad (*1251-1326*/1835-1908), a Punjabi. Reacting against the efforts of Christian missionaries, he declared himself a *mujaddid*, a "renewer" (of the faith) in 1882. He identified the Christian West, and particularly the economic, political, and religious colonialism, a dominant characteristic in the 19th century, as the manifestation of the *dajjāl* (the "imposter" i.e. apocalyptic Antichrist). Mirzā Ghulām did not judge the Occident to be anti-traditional, but simply denounced it for its domination of Islamic countries. However, he ruled out holy war (*jihād*) as a course of action against the colonial powers, awaiting instead an "awakening" of the Islamic world.

He went on to enunciate a doctrine that Jesus had escaped death on the cross and had attained the age of 120 before dying and being buried in Srinagar. (In Islam, Jesus' death on the cross was only apparent; according to the Islamic perspective regarding the crucifixion, Jesus did not die and is still in a principial state, that is, in Being, from which he will return to this world to destroy the *dajjāl* and bring the world to its end.) Mirzā Ghulām finally claimed that he was the Mahdī, as well as the Second Coming of Jesus, and moreover, the last *avatāra* of Vishnu.

After Mirzā Ghulām's death, the Aḥmadiyyah split into two subsects, the Qadianis and Lahorites. The Qadianis (after Qadian, birthplace of Mirzā Ghulām) are called the *Jama'at-i Aḥmadiyyah*, maintain his doctrines, more or less as they were propounded, and consider him a *nabī'*, or Prophet. By this, they establish a gulf between those who do not accept Mirzā Ghulām as a Prophet, whom the Qadianis therefore consider to be *Kāfirūn*, or non-believers; the Sunnīs in turn have been obliged to repudiate, by the pronouncements of religious courts, the Qadianis as non-Muslims. The Qadianis make the distinction that Mirzā Ghulām was a Prophet, but not a law-prescribing Prophet (*ghayr tashrī'ī*). To this end they call him a *ẓillī nabī* ("shadow Prophet") or *burūzī nabī* ("a manifesting Prophet").

The Lahorites (*Anjumān-i Insha'at-i Islām*), less heterodox, hold Mirzā Ghulām to be a *mujaddid*, or "renewer" only, and have not wished to lose solidarity with the rest of the Islamic world. They were led by "Maulvi" (or "Mawlānā", a title) Muḥammad 'Alī. Muḥammad 'Alī translated the Koran into English, which was published along with Aḥmadiyyah inspired interpretations and commentaries, and also wrote *The Religion of Islam*.

Both Aḥmadiyyah subsects were noted for energetic proselytizing through missionaries — a technique adopted from Protestants — the establishment of mosques abroad, and publication of propaganda materials, particularly in English, long before such activities were adopted by the Sunnīs. As a result, the Aḥmadiyyah gained footholds in Europe and America, and above all, in West Africa, where they organized schools and hospitals. But while accepting the methods of the Christian missionaries and the ideas of Western civilization, both groups are stridently anti-Christian. Their opposition to Christianity lies in their claim that it has deviated from its original beliefs and can no longer be considered a "Religion of the Book" (a revealed religion), and that it is, moreover, the great force for unbelief throughout the world. Among the first claims of Mirzā Ghulām to eminence, was that "it was a sign of the Mahdī" to recognize the *Dajjāl*, or Antichrist, as Ghulām recognized him collectively, in Christianity.

After the partition of India and Pakistan in 1947, the Qadiani branch moved to Rabwa in Pakistan and is headed by a leader entitled the "Viceroy of the Messiah" (*khalīfatu-l-masīḥ*). The Qadianis are evidently a departure from Islam, but the Lahorites are also considered with extreme reservation by the Sunnī world for their sometimes novel and un-traditional interpretations of Islamic doctrine and practices, which include "conversion rituals" resembling Christian baptism. Nevertheless, there are approximately 500,000 Aḥmadis, mostly in West Africa.

Aḥzāb, ("confederates"). *See* BATTLE of the TRENCH.

'Ā'ishah (613-678). Daughter of Abū Bakr, and the favorite wife of the Prophet. She was betrothed to the Prophet at the age of six or seven, after the death of Khadījah. The marriage was consummated after the Hijrah when she had come of age (that is, reached the age of puberty) according to the custom of the society. 'Ā'ishah was eighteen when the Prophet died.

During the campaign against the Banū Musta'liq, 'Ā'ishah accompanied the Prophet, riding in a litter. At one halt she lost her necklace; she set off alone to find it only to return and discover that the caravan had left without her, the camel drivers thinking she was in her litter. She was later found wandering alone by a young man called Ṣafwān, who brought her back to the caravan. There followed a scandal and 'Ā'ishah's fidelity was questioned.

When asked counsel by the Prophet, 'Alī advised him to divorce her, and contributed to 'Ā 'ishah's subsequent antipathy towards 'Alī later. However, a revelation of the Koran cleared 'Ā'ishah and established the law by which accusations of adultery are not valid unless there are four witnesses of the actual act. If four cannot be produced, the accusers themselves are liable to the same punishment for false accusation.

Because it was evident that the Prophet preferred her above his other wives, there was some jealousy in his household. In regard to this jealousy the Prophet said to Umm Salāmah: "Trouble me not concerning 'Ā'ishah, for verily inspiration does not come to me when I am beneath the coverlet of a wife, except that wife be 'Ā'ishah."

After the death of the Prophet, in the early days of the Caliphate of 'Alī, an insurrection was led against the Caliph by the Companions Ṭalḥah and az-Zubayr; 'Ā'ishah joined them. During the battle between the rebels and the forces of 'Alī she was mounted on a camel. The fighting raged until it came up to her camel and then died down; hence the name: "the Battle of the Camel". The rebels were defeated, and Ṭalḥah and az-Zubayr killed in the fighting. 'Ā'ishah was captured but allowed to retire to Medinah.

Towards the end of her life she was often consulted on matters of ḥadīth and Sunnah. As a wife of the Prophet she had the title *Umm al-Mu'minīn* ("Mother of the Believers"). She is buried in the al-Baqī' Cemetery in Medinah. Some 2,000 Ḥadīth are attributed to he; only 75 are *ṣaḥīḥ*. One of her comments in particular deserves especial attention: she said if someone tells you that there is a secret teaching in Islam, he is a liar. As it is in Bukhārī: "Verily, he who tells you that the Prophet has concealed a part of the Divine Revelation and that he has not delivered it to his people, lies."

On a tradition from Ibn Iṣḥāq (Ibn Hishām: *Sīrat*), which had been disputed because the narrator from the family of Abū Bakr was not named, 'Ā'ishah said that during the mi'rāj "the body of the Messenger of Allāh did not disappear (from his bed at the time) and that he was made to travel heavenwards spiritually only."

'Ā'ishah 'Abd ar-Raḥmān, *see* BINT ash-SHATI.

Aissawa (Aissoua, *'Īsāwiyyah*). A Sufi order in North Africa whose center is the tomb in Meknes of the founder Shaykh Muḥammad ibn 'Īsā (d.

933/1527), called the "Perfect Shaykh" (*ash-Shaykh al-Kāmil*). There, once a year, at the time of the Mouloud, a congregation (*mawsim*) of Aissawa from Morocco and other countries takes place. The scholar of religions, Mircea Eliade, guided by Van Gennep, wrote the observation that the Aissawa are in fact a Maennerbund, that is, a lycanthropic secret society. In other words, were-wolves. During the Ḥaḍrah, or sacred dance, members assume animal states, the most common of which is the jackal (*dib*) or North African wolf. When in this state the adepts can be thrown a small animal which they tear apart with their teeth and eat as if they were really the animal which they imitate in a trance-like state. Some Aissawa are snake charmers. *See* SECRET SOCIETY.

Akbar (*949-1014*/1542-1605). The third Tīmūrid emperor of Hindustan, son of Humāyūn, and grandson of Bābur, the founder of this Moghul (Mongol) dynasty. Akbar, (his imperial name means the "Greatest") achieved distinction as both soldier and administrator. What was extremely unusual about Akbar was the extent of his fascination with other religions. At times he wore a Hindu caste mark on his forehead; he was deeply interested in Zoroastrianism and wore the Kusti and thread under his clothing, stopping short of outright conversion. He called upon the Portuguese Catholics of Goa to present their doctrines at court. He sponsored religious debates in a "house of religion", a special meeting hall at Fatehpur Sikri set aside for this purpose where he sat on a pillar above the protagonists and ajudicated among them. With his minister Abū-l Faẓl 'Allāmī abetting his interests, all kinds of mystics flourished at court.

Based upon his study of other religions including Hinduism and Christianity, as well as Islam, he founded his own syncretistic cult with himself at its head, that was known as Tawhīd-i-Ilāhī "Divine Unity" or *Dīn-i Llahi* "Religion of God"; apparently it did not spread outside his own court, where it had a small number of followers who believed that they drew upon a power coming from the sun.

Despite his intellectual interests, Akbar never learned to read or write; he acquired his ideas through the spoken word. He even had works translated for himself, to be read to him, to satisfy his desire to learn.

Akhbārīs. Among the Shī'ites, Ḥadīth ("Traditions") recording the acts and sayings of the Prophet are referred to as *Akhbār* ("tidings"); the Akhbārīs are the school among the Shī'ite theologians that corresponds to the *ahl al-Ḥadīth* among the Sunnīs, that is, traditionalists who eschew speculation. The division arose at the time of the Buyids and has existed ever since, but the Akhbārīs are outnumbered by the *Uṣūlīs*, who favor theological speculation and extrapolation in the light of religious principles (*uṣūl*).

In the *12th*/18th century the Akhbārīs were driven out of Najaf and Kerbala by the vigorous attacks of an Uṣūlī Mullā named Vahid Bihbahani (d. *1207*/1792) who made a declaration of *takfīr* against them, declaring them unbelievers. This was backed up by the use of force and violence administered by Bihbahani's *mirghadabs*, or religious guards. Thereafter Persia became dominated by the Uṣūlī School which, by permitting speculation, made possible a tremendous growth in the power of the Mullās, or religious authorities. The Akhbārīs still exist, however, in India, in Baḥrayn, and in southern 'Irāq; an Akhbāri leader, Mirzā Muḥammad Akhbārī, resides in Baṣrah; the Akhbārī school also exists in the Khurramshahr region of Iran.

The Akhbārīs restrict the authority and prerogatives of the '*ulamā*', in the belief that, jurisprudence should be limited to the application of existing tradition. Because they are Shī'ites, this body of tradition goes back to Shī'ite Imāms; nevertheless, the Akhbārīs use an approach related to Ash'arite theology and Sunnī principles of jurisprudence. They do admit the existence of *kashf*, rational intuition, in the solution of questions. The great exponent of the School was the Mullā Muḥammad Amīn Astarābādī (d. *1033*/1623) and it reached its high point in Persia during the reign of the Afshārid ruler Nādir Shah (*1160*/1747) who tried to bring Persia back to Sunnī Islam.

The Akhbārīs restrict the sources of religious authority to the Koran and Sunnah, and insist, moreover, that the Koran must be interpreted through the inspired traditions of the Imāms. They do not accept, as do the Uṣūlīs, "consensus" (*ijmā'*), and "intellect" (*'aql*). They consider the Shī'ite "Four Books" of Ḥadīth to be reliable, whereas the Uṣūlīs consider the Four Books to contain unreliable Ḥadīth requiring discriminating interpretation. The Akhbārīs allow traditions from Sunnī sources, recognize only two categories of Ḥadīth, namely "sound" (*sahīh*) and "weak" (*ḍa'īf*); the Uṣūlīs accept as authoritative only the

Four Books, but assign four categories of dependability, namely, "sound" (*ṣaḥiḥ*), "good" (*ḥasan*), "derived" (*mutawātir*, and "weak" (*ḍa'īf*). The Akhbārīs consider that "transmitted" (*naqlī*) sources have precedence over reason; whereas the Uṣūlīs hold that *naqlī* sources, which include the Koran and Sunnah, cannot contradict what can be concluded by reasoning from principles.

The Akhbārīs reject *ijtihād*, or the coming to original and unprecedented conclusions as the result of the investigation of sources, reasoning, and endeavoring to understand, whereas the Uṣūlīs accept both *ijtihād* and even conjecture (*ẓann*), should assured knowledge (*'ilm*) not be available from tradition. The Akhbārīs consider it obligatory to refer to the Imāms, even through intermediary but explicit sources; legal decisions can be made only on the basis of the relevant traditions of the Imāms. The Uṣūlīs accept as *'ilm* only that which was reported by those who were in the presence of the Imāms; after the Occultation of the Hidden Imām, which made direct consultation impossible, the Uṣūlīs hold it necessary to resort to *ijtihād*, even to arbitrate tradition. The Akhbārīs restrict competence to the Imām, and make all men muqallid, that is to say, obliged to follow the established precedent of the Imām; the Uṣūlīs maintain that there are authorities who are *marja' at-taqlīd* ("reference for emulation"), i.e. authorities who are relatively independent of tradition and capable of originating doctrine. Therefore the Uṣūlīs divide their community into the *Mujtahid*, who sets the precedent, and those who follow it, namely, the *muqallidūn*; for them to follow the Mujtahid results in heavenly reward, even if the Mujtahid is wrong.

For the Akhbārīs, to promulgate any decision except upon the basis of tradition is blameworthy. *See* AYATOLLAH; BIHBAHĀNĪ; SHĪ'ISM; UṢŪLĪ.

Akhund. An honourific title given to some religious authorities. It is used in the Indo-Persian world.

Aksakalism. *see* AQSAQALISM.

Alamūt. A fortress in northern Iran, near the Caspian, built around *246*/860 by Wahsūdan ibn Marzubān (d. ca. *251*/865). It became the seat of Ḥasan-i aṣ-Ṣabbāḥ founder of the Nizārī state. *See* ASSASSINS.

Al-'Alawī, Shaykh, *see* AL-'ALAWĪ, ABŪ-L-'ABBĀS AḤMAD IBN MUṢṬAFĀ.

'Alawī (lit. "of 'Alī") 'Alawī is a common family name in the Arab world. 1. The name of the Moroccan royal family who are *sharīfs* descended from Ḥasan ibn 'Alī ibn Abī Ṭālib.

2. A Sufi *ṭarīqah*, the *'Alawīyyah*, named after the Algerian Shaykh Aḥmad al-'Alawī. It is widespread in North Africa and elsewhere in the Arab world, especially in Syria where the members of the 'Alawī *ṭarīqah* prefer to be called *Shādhilis* in order to avoid confusion with the 'Alawīs who adhere to the religion (*see below*) of that name. (*See* al-'ALAWĪ, ABŪ-L-'ABBĀS AḤMAD IBN MUṢṬAFĀ.)

3. A religion, signifying the "followers of 'Alī", professed by an ethnic group of the same name, the 'Alawīs, found mainly in Syria, but also in Lebanon and parts of Turkey, particularly around Antakya where they are called *Alevis*. The Alevis of Turkey may in fact be far greater in number — possibly in the millions — than was previously believed in the times of official Sunnism and later official Laicism. The beliefs of different 'Alawī groups may vary widely.

In Syria they were at one time thought to be different by virtue of being descendants of South Arabian tribal groups who emigrated to the north and mingled with the native population. The total 'Alawī population in Syria is numbered in hundreds of thousands or approximately 6% of the national population. In the past they have usually been called Nuṣayris after one of their most important leaders, Abū Shu'ayb Muḥammad ibn Nuṣayr (d. circa *267*/880). Because of this name they are sometimes confused with the Nasoreans, or Mandaeans, of 'Irāq. It is likely that the 'Alawīs are a relic of the Sevener movement, or simply of pre-Islamic Christian Gnosticism, and that they were closely related to the Syrian branch of the revolutionary Qarmaṭīs (Carmathians) of the *4th*/10th century.

After the withdrawal of the Turks from Syria, and during the French Mandate (*1339-1366*/1920-1946), there has sporadically existed an "'Alawī State" in the region of Latakiah with its center around the Jabal Anṣāriyyah, the principal 'Alawī homeland. The existence of the 'Alawī state has been suppressed several times by the Sunnī majority of Syria. (Over 75% of the population of Syria are Sunnīs; the rest consist of Twelve-Imām

Shī'ites, Christians, 'Alawīs, Druzes, and Ismā'īlīs.) In the course of one of these power struggles in 1946, a leader of an 'Alawī bid for political supremacy, Sulaymān al-Murshid, whose followers believed him to be a Divine manifestation, was hanged in Damascus. As the result of a series of *coups d'état* in the 1960s, however, the 'Alawīs came into control of the country and in 1971 Ḥafez Asad was installed as the head of state and government.

The 'Alawīs are often called Shī'ites but, despite the reference to 'Alī in their preferred name today, their doctrines do not correspond in any way to Shī'ism as such. (They do, however, have a marked affinity and sympathy to Shī'ites.) Their doctrine bears an unmistakable resemblance to Ismā'īlī teachings, with their characteristic Gnostic, or dualist ideas. Their peculiar schema of Muḥammad as *ism*, or "name", 'Alī as *bāb*, or "door", and Salmān al-Farsī as *ma'nā*, or "meaning", with both Muḥammad and 'Alī considered to be emanations of Salmān al-Farsī, point to roots in the earliest stirrings of the Sevener movement, proto-Ismā'īlism, as found in the book called the *Umm al-Kitāb*, which dates from the *2nd*/8th century. The initials *'ayn mim sad*, standing for the "Divine Reality" of Salmān and "its two hypostases Muḥammad and 'Alī", constitute one of the 'Alawī religious symbols. Additional Ismā'īlī influence (which provided a veneer of "Islamic" coloring to the 'Alawīs) was probably absorbed from the Qarmaṭīs and later from the Ismā'īlī Assassin sect when it was active in Syria during the Crusades, as well as from Ibn Nuṣayr. However, despite any influences they may have received from later Ismā'īlism, the 'Alawīs, like the Druzes, stand outside of the Ismā'īlism mainstream. Rather, 'Alawīsm is an offshoot of the Manichean and Iranian substrata from which Shī'ism emerged. Franz Babinger said that the Seljūqs were originally "'Alawīs" when they arrived in Anatolia, and the historian Ibn al-Tiqṭaqa said that Hülāgü the Mongol Khan who destroyed Baghdad was also an enthusiastic 'Alawī. To think of all of these as Ismā'īlīs would be misleading but to recognize in all of them a kinship as derivatives from Manicheism is to see the tie which binds them all together.

The beliefs and practices of the 'Alawīs, as is the case in similar sects, are extremely heteroclite, and vary from group to group. The 'Alawīs have a collection of writings called the *Kitāb al-Majmū'* ("The Book of the Collection") that constitute their "holy book" and this contains, among other things, it is said, scraps of a corrupt version of the Nicomachean Ethics of Aristotle. Another important book, replete with Persian ideas, is the *Kitāb al-Haft ash-sharīf* ("the Book of the Noble Seven") or *Kitāb al-Ashbāḥ wa'l-Aẓilla*, "the book of Phantoms and Shadows" in which God creates in the beginning "a shadow casting light", and light is enclosed within souls. The eclecticism of their doctrines goes far back in time; besides theories of Divine emanations, they include elements of astral religion which are ultimately of Babylonian origin (among these is the use of astral phenomena, such as eclipses, as supports of theurgy; there is a belief that the Milky Way is made up of the deified souls of the true believers). They also have elements of Christianity; the 'Alawīs use certain Christian names and mark, in their own way, certain Christian holidays; it is reported that the religious services of the *khāṣṣah* (the initiate elect) — the rest, being "profane", are called the *'āmmah* — include a mass-like ceremony, the *Quddas*, with a blessing (if not consecration) of the species of communion, in particular the wine, and even includes reference to "body and blood" which are "eternal life". In many ways the ceremony resembles the *agapes* of some early Christian sects, to the eye which expects to see Christian origins. In fact, it would be more accurate to see in this the Bema, or ritual meal of Manicheism. They also practice a religious feast called by a Persian name, *Naw Ruz* ("new year"), and the *Mihrajan* which again clearly points to an Iranian influence. This mixture suggests that, as a small, historically beleaguered ethnic group living in remote mountain regions, with a strong feeling of clan solidarity (the *'asabiyyah* of Ibn Khaldūn), they have absorbed elements from all the religions which have passed by them since Hellenistic times, including the pagan and Christian Gnosticism of Roman antiquity. Whilst maintaining their own beliefs, they have pretended to adhere to the dominant religion of the age in order to escape persecution, in the style of Shī'ite *taqiyyah* (defensive dissimulation).

'Alawī religious practices are carried out in secret, in their own places of congregation, which are not open to outsiders. These practices involve progressive initiations in which the novice ascends by degrees into the inner knowledge of the sect; at the same time he may then be accepted into the ruling oligarchy of the community that is dominated by family clans. The 'Alawīs believe that women do not have souls (which is absolutely contrary to Islamic doctrine). Like the Druzes, the 'Alawis believe that their real number does not change, probably through reincarnation, and that this is 112,000. (A similar belief is found among Sufis in North Africa and perhaps elsewhere, namely that the number of "Saints" is always constant in Islam from the beginning to the present.)

Observers have noted that 'Alawī religious practices do not include any of the rites of Islam although, for public relations purposes, 'Alawi leaders have performed *ṣalāt* (Muslim canonical prayer) in the Grand Umayyad Mosque of Damascus with visiting dignitaries from the Islamic world, and have taken part in the pilgrimage to Mecca. The 'Alawīs requested, and received, a religious proclamation from the late Twelve-Imām Shī'ite leader in Lebanon, Imām Musā aṣ-Ṣadr, to the effect that they are a legitimate branch of Islam. *See* QARMAṬĪS, ISMĀ'ĪLĪS; SEVENERS

al-'Alawī, Abū-l-'Abbās Aḥmad ibn Muṣṭafā (*1286-1353*/1869-1934). He was also known as Ibn 'Aliwah. Al-'Alawī was born and died at Mostaghanem in Algeria. At a young age he entered into the "popular" or "folk Sufi" *ṭarīqah* of the dervishes known as the *'Isayyiwah*, whose practices include the performance of such prodigious feats as stabbing oneself with daggers and the like (*see* AISSAWA). He also learned to charm snakes, but abandoned all these in favor of a spiritual discipline under the direction of the Shaykh al-Buzīdī, a master of the Darqawī *ṭarīqah*. On the death of this master, al-'Alawī became the Shaykh of many of the latter's former disciples in Algeria and founded his own order. He was highly esteemed and hailed by many as the Islamic *mujaddid*, or "renewer", of his age (an identification that derives from a Ḥadīth that "every hundred years God will send a renewer for the community").

As a foremost exponent of Islamic esoterism, or Sufism, he attracted followers to his teachings from many countries and, by the end of his life, the Shaykh al-'Alawī had 200,000 disciples, including a handful of Europeans. His representatives established many *zāwiyahs*, or lodges, outside Algeria, notably in Syria and in the Yemen. The Yemenis, many of whom were seamen, established *zāwiyahs* in foreign ports, including New York, Marseilles, and Cardiff in Wales.

His doctrine stressed the practice of *khalwah*, or systematic spiritual retreats, but above all insisted on *dhikr Allāh*, or invocation of the Divine Name. He was also quick to use new methods of modern media. He founded a newspaper for the propagation of his ideas, and encouraged the use of photographs of himself as objects of veneration. This practice was taken up by his followers. Outwardly modest, in secret his disciples alluded to his divinity, and spread sayings that implied that salvation came from the Shaykh rather than from God.

Coming from a poor family, the Shaykh al-'Alawī learned the trade of cobbler in his youth. Although his formal schooling was limited, he sought out and assimilated the sense of many philosophies and spiritual teachings, including the doctrines of other religions, beyond the orbit of what was immediately at hand in the Muslim milieu. He is the author of a collection of poems, his *Diwān*, several treatises on mystical subjects, and an unfinished commentary on the Koran. He wrote of the *dhikr*:

> "The invocation of God is like a coming and going which realizes a communication ever more and more complete till there is identity between the glimmers of consciousness and the dazzling lightnings of the infinite."

Albania. (Population: 3.3 million; 70% are Muslim; 30% are Eastern Orthodox and Catholic.) Country in Eastern Europe, it was conquered by the Turks in 1415. Many Albanians attained high positions of leadership under the Ottomans. Muṣṭafā Kemal AtatĀrk was of Albanian origin.

Between 1673-1676 Shabbatai Zevi, the Jewish messiah who converted to Islam in 1666 as 'Aziz Mehmed Effendi, was exiled to Dulcingo (Dürres) in Albania where "he died on Yom Kippur", the Jewish Day of Atonement, in 1676. Many of his Dönmeh followers accompanied him there. In 1928 the country also became the seat of Bektashism when mystical organizations were prohibited in Turkey. *See* DÖNMEH.

Albumazar. *See* ABŪ MA'SHAR.

Alchemy. *See* JĀBIR ibn ḤAYYĀN.

'Alevis. *See* 'ALAWĪS.

Alexander the Great (Ar. *Iskandar*). The Koran appears to be referring to him, when, in the Sūrah of the Cave (*Sūrat al-Kahf*), "he of the two horns" (*Dhu-l-Qarnayn*) is mentioned. Alexander had gone to the oasis of Siwa in Egypt to consult the oracle that said he was the son of Ammon, a pagan god with two horns. The widely current coinage of the conqueror, and of the successor states, generally depicted him in the guise of the horned god, Jupiter-Ammon; hence the popular designation customarily used in the age of the Prophet. However, it also has a symbolical interpretation: "He of the two Ages", which reflects the eschatological shadow that Alexander casts from his time, which preceded Islam by many centuries, until the end of the world. The Arabic word *qarn* means both "horn" and "era" or "century".

The Koran accords the Macedonian warrior a remarkable role; in order to protect a people, until the last days, from the depredations of the hosts of Gog and Magog (*Jūj wa Majūj*) — representing symbolically the forces of chaos — Alexander builds them a barrier of iron and copper between two mountains as a "mercy from my Lord" (18:98). This "barrier" is interpreted esoterically as being the Revealed Law, i.e. the *Sharī'ah*, that will apply until the Last Days.

In addition to the above Koranic story and its popular elaborations (rather like the Jewish *midrash* tales of the *Haggadah*), there is a folklore, particularly in Central Asia, that portrays Alexander in a mythic light. For example, legend relates that upon his death his testament decreed that his body be carried through the Empire until the meaning of its open hands should be understood. It was finally a humble cobbler who perceived the meaning, namely that Alexander left everything behind him when he left the world.

The position of Alexander, or *Iskandar*, in Islam may be compared to that of Julius Caesar in Christianity: both fulfilled a destiny as forerunners providentially conquering, and so preparing, or "making straight the way", for the establishment of a world religion, like plowmen preparing the way for the coming of a prophetic sower. It was Alexander who cleared the way for the geographic expansion of Islam, just as Caesar brought the Germanic and Celtic tribes of Europe into the Roman Empire, thus indirectly preparing them to receive Christianity. In recognition of this function Alexander is enshrined both in the Koran and in Muslim memory as a prophet-like figure, if not, as he was to the pagan world, a god-like one. *See* ESCHATOLOGY; GOG AND MAGOG.

"Alexander's Wall". (*Sadd-i Iskandar* or *Qīzīl Yilan*, red snake.) The Sāssānids, especially under Anushirwan the Just (Chosroes, d. 579) built defensive walls in Hyrcania south of the Caspian against the nomads from the northern steppes. The most famous of the Sāssānid defensive walls was at Derbend. The name "Alexander's Wall", however, must have been given to it long after Islam appeared, when its actual origins were forgotten to the Persians. Since it was built less than a century before the revelation of the Koran, it is likely that this wall was also known to the Arabs as a Sāssānid construction. It was of importance for the defense of the Byzantines also and they contributed to its upkeep.

Idrissi's map made for Roger of Sicily shows the land of Gog and Magog to which the Koran refers as being in Mongolia; the Great Wall of China was known to the Roman historian of Greek origin Ammianus Marcellinus (d. c. 391). Thus the wall built by Alexander (Dhu-l-Qarnayn) in the Koran (18:95), an ancient and distant wall, may well be an echo of the Great Wall of China, or a conflation of the Sāssānid Wall with the Chinese one.

There were also trench defenses in 'Irāq against the Beduins (called in Arabic *khandaq sabur*). One was designed to protect Ḥirāh. Yaqut says that Shapur II had the moat dug and a wall built as well as frontier watchtowers, and that he ordered a *khandaq* to be dug from the lower region of the Badiya to "what is before Baṣrah and is joined to the sea". Others say it was Chosroes. Baladhuri adds that the Arabs who lived by the *khandaq* guarded it and had the use of the land as a fief without paying a land tax. With the absorption of the Lakhmid state into the Sāssānid empire about 602, the Sāssānian defences against the Arabs fell apart.

Algebra (from Ar. *ilm al-jabr wa'-l-muqabāla*, "gathering together and transposition" [of the terms of an equation], the name of a treatise by al-Khwarizmi.) A branch of mathematics first elaborated by the Egyptians then by the Greeks, Romans, and Hindus. When the Muslims became the custodians of classical science, algebra was advanced by Thābit ibn Qurrā, al-Khwarizmi, al-Mahani, Abū Ja'far al-Hazin, 'Umar Khayyam, Abū'l Wafā'd. 998), and al-Majariti (in Spain, as his name indicates, "from Madrid", d. 1007).

Algerian Democratic Republic. The population of 22,106,000 in 1986 is composed of Arabs and Berbers. 99% are Muslim, almost all being of the Mālikī School of Law (*madhhab*); a very small minority, less than 100,000, are Ibāḍite Muslims living in the M'zab region. The Shādhilī *ṭuruq* (sing. *ṭarīqah*) are most strongly represented, along with the Qādiriyyah. In the desert villages, it is customary to find that all the adult males belong to a *ṭarīqah*, most often the Wazzaniyyah, whose center is at Ouezzane in Morocco. The name Algeria comes from the Arabic *al-Jaza'ir*, the "islands"; but the word also means religious jurisdictions, or "lodges" of the *Baṭini* or "initiatic-esoteric" religions widespread among the North African Berbers from Roman into Fāṭimid times. *See* 'ABD al-QĀDIR, EMIR; ABŪ MADYAN.

Alhambra (from the Ar. *al-qal'ah al-ḥamrā'*, "the red Palace"). The palace of the Naṣrid princes of Granada, Spain. Largely of *8th*/14th century construction, the Alhambra marks the high point of Islamic architecture in the West. Intricate plaster and tile decorations adorn the walls with elegant calligraphic motifs that repeat the words: "there is no victor except God". These words are attributed to the Spanish Umayyad Prince 'Abd ar-Raḥmān III, who was hailed as victor by his subjects on returning from a battle.

Among the more renowned apartments of the palace are the Court of Lions, with its stylized statues of lions around a fountain, the Hall of Ambassadors, and the Hall of the Two Sisters. Next to the palace are the Generalife Gardens (from the Ar. *jannatu-l-'arīf*, "garden of the knower"). Their fountains are fed with water from the Sierra Nevada mountains, whence Machado's description of Granada as *agua oculta que llora* ("hidden water that weeps").

Alhazen, *see* IBN al-HAYTHAM.

'Alī ibn Abī Ṭālib (*598-40*/598-661). A member of the house of Hāshim, a cousin of the Prophet, who was to become his son-in-law, and eventually the fourth Caliph. One of the first converts to Islam. Early in his mission, after the Koran enjoined him: "And warn thy clan, thy nearest of kin" (26:214), the Prophet called his clan together and preached to them saying: "O sons of 'Abd al-Muṭṭalib, I know of no Arab who has come to his people with a nobler message than mine. I bring you the best of this world and the next. God has commanded me to call you unto Him. Which of you, then, will help me in this, and be my brother, my executor and my successor among you?"

The only one who responded was 'Alī, then thirteen years old, and of whom the Prophet then said: "This is my brother, my executor and my successor among you. Hearken unto him and obey him", whereupon the Hāshimites left, saying in derision to Abū Ṭālib: "He has ordered you to hearken to your son and obey him." Following this meeting, however, several aunts of the Prophet and other women of the Hāshimites entered Islam.

'Alī became renowned as a warrior during Islam's struggle for survival, often leading the army. He married the Prophet's daughter Fāṭimah, and it is from their two sons Ḥasan and Ḥusayn that the *sharīfs*, or progeny of the Prophet, descend. A third son, Muḥsin, died in infancy; they also had a daughter, Zaynab. After Fāṭimah died, 'Alī had another son by a concubine. This son, Muḥammad ibn Ḥanafiyyah, became the figurehead leader of a revolt against the Umayyads. (*See* KAYSĀNIYYAH.)

The Prophet's son-in-law played a minor role during the first three Caliphates. He disagreed with 'Umar's plan that a portion of the income from the enormous spoils of conquest sent back by the victorious armies of Islam should be set aside as a reserve for unforeseen eventualities. This income, less the prudent reserve, was distributed to the Muslims according to the national register, the *diwān*. 'Alī, for his part, said that all this income should be given away to the nation; presumably his point of view was that the Islamic community need make no provisions of its own but should rely only upon God. Whatever disagreements 'Alī may have had with the Caliph, he was not completely ignored, for he was put in charge of Medinah when 'Umar visited Jerusalem after its conquest.

Aṭ-Ṭabarī the historian reports 'Umar as having said to 'Alī that the "Quraysh did not want both Prophethood and the Caliphate combined in the house of Hāshim" (the Prophet's and 'Alī's clan). This assertion shows a reserved attitude on the part of 'Alī's contemporaries towards according him greater leadership in the expanding and increasingly important political affairs of the Quraysh. Their reluctance may have been due to 'Alī's idiosyncratic and independent character which was little given to the arts of social diplomacy and compromise. Also, history makes it clear that he was not a successful, rather even an unpopular, leader. At 'Umar's death the Caliphate was offered to 'Alī on condition that he respect the precedents set by the first two Caliphs. 'Alī either refused this condition, or appeared to refuse it whilst in fact modestly making little of his own abilities; there was, if not outright refusal, at least ambiguity. Thereupon the Caliphate was offered to 'Uthmān who unequivocally agreed to abide by the precedents, and was thus named Caliph.

In *35*/656 'Uthmān was assassinated in a rebellion against his nepotism and the despotism of his clansmen who had been made Governors of the conquered provinces. 'Alī was thus elected Caliph at a time of unrest and mounting difficulties. He immediately had to face a rebellion led by the Companions Ṭalḥāh and az-Zubayr in which 'Ā 'ishah, the widowed favorite wife of the Prophet, also took part. It is made out by 'Alī's partisans that this opposition to him was purely bad will and misled; but it could also be taken as an indication that some responsible members of the community sincerely did not believe in 'Alī's ability or aptitude. Nevertheless, 'Alī defeated the rebels at the Battle of the Camel. Then Mu'āwiyah, Governor of Damascus and relative of 'Uthmān, made a bid for the Caliphate in an insurrection culminating in the prolonged Battle of Ṣiffīn, that was dragged out inconclusively over several months. In the midst of the stalemate or, as some sources contend, when 'Alī was on the point of winning, he accepted the proposal of Mu'āwiyah, actually conceived by 'Amr ibn al-'Āsī, to arbitrate the conflict as a legitimate dispute, because 'Alī allegedly wished to avoid further bloodshed; in any case, 'Alī did not, or could not, conclude the struggle decisively. This agreement to arbitrate led to the secession from 'Alī's army of a bloc of strict traditionalists, some 4,000, a faction thereafter called the Khārijites ("Seceders"), who believed that the question at issue was so vital and indeed sacred, that it could only be decided by the will of God and not by negotiation.

Mu'āwiyah manipulated the negotiations with cunning. 'Alī's negotiator, who may well have wanted to see his own son-in-law (rather than 'Alī) elected Caliph, was deceived by a ruse into going along with Mu'āwiyah's partisans. He deposed 'Alī in a public announcement, on the understanding that an agreement had been made to set aside both contenders. However, Mu'āwiyah's negotiator, instead of then repudiating Mu'āwiyah's claims, declared him Caliph, making this appear to be the agreed outcome of the negotiations. Nevertheless, 'Alī refused to surrender his authority and established himself at Kūfah in 'Irāq. In this conflict, it is important to bear in mind that Mu'āwiyah's power base was Damascus, and an army that included many Arab Christians and new converts. 'Alī had to find another power base, and this was 'Irāq, which meant that 'Alī actually had to rely upon the former rulers, the Lakhmids and their allies. These were largely Manicheans pretending to be new converts who sought to manipulate 'Alī for their own ends. They continued to do so after 'Alī's death, using Ḥusayn and other descendents for their political purposes which created Shī'ism in the process, while Kūfah became a lasting center for subversion against Sunni rule.

After Ṣiffīn, the Khārijites now posed a separate threat, and went on to sack Ctesiphon. At the subsequent Battle of Nahrawān, 'Alī overwhelmingly defeated them, but did not succeed in completely crushing the movement. On *17 Ramaḍān 40*/25 January 661, as 'Alī was preparing to lead the morning prayer at the mosque of Kūfah, he was assassinated by a surviving Khārijite, Ibn Muljam, who carried out the deed at the demand of a woman who had made 'Alī's assassination a condition of marriage.

'Alī's elder son Ḥasan succeeded his father as Caliph for half a year, but was then forced by threat of arms, and a large financial indemnity, to cede the Caliphate to Mu'āwiyah. Ḥasan died a few years later, poisoned, it is said, by his wife who had received a promise of marriage from Yazīd, Mu'āwiyah's son. After the death of Mu'āwiyah and the accession of Yazīd to the Caliphate, Ḥusayn, was invited by the Kūfans to lead an insurrection. He went for the bait (against the advice of 'Umar's son) but could not rally support from anyone else and the Kūfans themselves abandoned him. His tragic death at the hands of the troops of Mu'āwiyah's son was to become, later, the emotional focal point in Twelve-Imām Shī'ism.

'Alī is highly revered by the Sufis as the fountainhead of esoteric doctrine; more generally, he is remembered for his piety, nobility and learning. His image among Sunnis is influenced by the idealization of Shī'ites. Depicted by the Shī'ites as the champion of the Muslims on the field of battle during Islam's struggle for life against the Meccans, he became the model for *futuwwah*, or chivalry. Besides being courageous, he acted towards his enemies with generosity and magnanimity. Before himself becoming Caliph, he had acted as counselor to the Caliphs preceding him.

As a loyal cousin and son-in-law it is certain that 'Alī's personal relationship to the Prophet was special; the Prophet referred to him at least twice as "my brother" and three times (in Shī'ite accounts) as "my heir" (*wāṣi'*). The Sunnī view is expressed in this tradition: "Qays ibn Sa'd ibn 'Ubaydah said: 'I said to 'Alī, may God have mercy on him, had the messenger of Allāh... bequeathed to you anything in this matter?' [the Caliphate]. He answered, 'He did not bequeath to me anything which he did not bequeath to the rest of the people, but the people rebelled against 'Uthmān and killed him and treated him and acted against him in a worse manner than I. I thought, therefore, that I had more right to it than the others and I rushed to take it, but Allāh knows best if I was right or wrong.'" The Prophet blessed the marriage union of 'Alī and Fāṭimah in an extraordinary way by anointing them both on their marriage night (in Shī'ite accounts). As far as is known, the Prophet did this for no-one else, and anointing is not a feature of Islamic ritual.

The position of 'Alī is radically more exalted in Shī'ism from what it is in Sunnī Islam, and this is the ostensible part of the nature of Shī'ism's fundamental doctrinal divergence. In Shī'ism, 'Alī is the first Imām, in the special sense in which they understand this term, that is, an intermediary between man and God in this world, unique in his age, necessary for salvation. In the early 'Irāqi revolt of Mukhtār in 685, which clearly involved Islamo-Manicheans, 'Alī was a code-word and stand-in for Mani. (*See also* MAZĀR-I SHARĪF.) This identity was probably conferred upon 'Alī both deliberately on the part of some, and then inadvertently in the course of history, by a conscious attempt to make out of him an outer shell and support for Mani. This is in keeping with the Gnostic origins of Shī'ism. With time, the rìle thrust upon 'Alī absorbed the historic actor, and even his descendents. As such, according to the Shī'ites, who are the mutation and evolution of Manicheism within the overwhelming confines of Islam, 'Alī had exclusive, Divine, right to the Caliphate which the preceding three Caliphs sinfully usurped from him, and the others from his heirs. In reality, however, the position of 'Alī and his descendents in Shī'ism is an accident of history; the divergence between Shī'ism and Sunnism is actually based on theologically doctrinal grounds, a different view of reality, and the historical elements have been interpreted, and painted, to fit and support the ideological divergence.

In Shī'ism, 'Alī and the Imāms who descend from him are beings of superhuman virtue possessing miraculous gifts and absolute spiritual and temporal authority. They are the indispensable means for salvation in Twelve Imām Shī'ism. 'Alī's tomb in Najaf, 'Irāq, is a place of pilgrimage. The story of 'Alīs burial place however, casts another useful light on how he was regarded in reality, and not in later hagiography. The actual place of burial was immediately forgotten; it was "miraculously" rediscovered when the Caliph Harūn ar-Rashīd was out hunting and he "heard his cousin 'Alī calling to him". Harūn obviously had this mystical experience in order to curry favor with contemporary Shi'ites, but it shows that at the time of 'Alī himself no-one thought of him in the terms which Shī'ites were to ascribe to him later. The meaning of the circumstances of course did not escape the partisans, so the story was invented that the burial place was deliberately obscured; that the dead 'Alī, in keeping with mysterious wishes, was placed on a camel left to wander, and his burial place was thus hidden, and, as it happened, left to be "rediscovered" in a vision by an 'Abbāsid rival! (Interestingly, Harūn's own tomb in Ṭūs is today forgotten, because next to him is buried a Shī'ite Imām; al-Ma'mūn's deliberate purpose in burying the Imām next to Harūn was to enhance the Caliph, but the plan did not work in the end.)

The sayings and sermons of 'Alī, and those utterances attributed to him, are collected, or rather invented, as were the speeched "recorded" by Thucydides, in a book called the *Nahj al-Balāghah* ("The Way of Eloquence") which has long served as a model for the use of Arabic much as the speeches of Cicero once did for Latin (*See* al-MURTAḌĀ). According to tradition, 'Alī was also the one who first laid down the rules of formal Arabic grammar, notably describing language as made up of nouns, verbs and particles. As this was first done, in the same words, by Aristotle, it is clear that a legend was woven around 'Alī by his partisans. Similarly, 'Alī became the spokesman and mirror of other ideas and ideologies thereby assuming the epic role finally created for him. *See* SHĪ'ISM, GHADIR KHUMM, ḤASAN, ḤUSAYN, IMĀM; NAHJ al-BALĀGHAH; NAJAF; MANICHEISM.

'Alī Ilāhīs (lit. "Deifiers of 'Ali"). A spectrum of heterodox sects whose members are found in Iran and 'Irāq and for whom 'Alī is a Divine hypostasis, being seen as a manifestation and human receptacle of the Godhead. These sects are more or less closely related to each other, and are similar to other ethno-sects found in the Levant and Syria, such as the Druzes who substitute the Fāṭimid Caliph al-Ḥākim for 'Alī.

The origins of these sects lie outside of Islam. They are superficial accommodations with Islam as the dominant religion on the part of belief systems that have survived from antiquity, fossils of ancient religions. *See* AHL-I-ḤAQQ; MANICHEISM.

'Alī Shīr Navā'i (also written Navo'i and Nawa'i; *844-906*/1440-1501). Turkic poet of Uighur bakhshā origin (Buddhist monks under the Mongols who became court scribes under the Timurids), he was born and died in Herat, statesman and patron of the arts under Bābur and Ḥusayn Bayqara. He raised Chagatay Turkish to the dignity of a literary language. Friend of the poet Jāmī (who brought him into the Naqshbandi order of Dervishes), patron of the painters Behzad and Shah Muẓaffar, the musicians Qul-Muhammad, Shaykhi Nā'i and Ḥusayn 'ūdī, arts which he practiced himself. He wrote poetry in Turkish and Persian and defended Turkish in his treatise, the *Muḥkamatu-l-Lughatayn* "The Judgement between the two Languages". As a very wealthy statesman he founded, restored, and maintained hundreds of mosques, schools, and public buildings.

'Alīds. The descendants of 'Alī ibn Abī Ṭālib and the Prophet's daughter Fāṭimah. The term 'Alīd is:

1. a generic adjective describing all families of such descent.

2. A particular term for those figures that the Shī'ites supported for the Caliphate. However, the name does not imply Shī'ism; some 'Alīd dynasties, such as the ruling family of Jordan, or that of Morocco, are Sunnī, and enjoy the prestige that descendants of the Prophet have among the Sunnīs — without the overtones inherent to Shī'ism.

Aligarh. A secondary school patterned after European models, founded in India in *1292*/1875 by Sir Sayyid Aḥmad Khan. Aligarh College was later added to the Aligarh High School. In 1920 the college became a university. Because of the ideological outlook behind the school, the name Aligarh became associated with a modernizing movement in India that advocated the adoption of Western ideas, or the reform of Islam in that direction. Among its proponents were 'Amīr 'Alī and Sir Muḥammad Iqbal, the President of the Muslim League.

'Alī ibn Abī Ṭālib, *see after* ALHAMBRA.

Allāh. The Name (*al-ism*) of Majesty (*jalālah*), and the "Supreme Name" (*al-ism al-a'ẓam*). Allāh is the Name of the Essence, or the Absolute. It is possibly a contraction of *al-ilāh* ("the Divinity"); nevertheless, the word Allāh cannot be reduced to theoretical grammatical components. If it is, so to speak, a synthesis of two words, the article *al* and the word *ilāh* ("Divinity") that synthesis, which took place in this world out of the inner logic of the Arabic language, was a revelation hidden in the origin of the Arabic language itself. It re-constituted in language a Reality that surpasses incomparably the dimension of the words it apparently contains. The word Allāh is a proper and true Name of God, through which man calls upon Him *personally*. It is an opening onto the Divine Essence, beyond language and the world itself.

The Name was known and used before the Koran was revealed; for example, the name of the Prophet's father was 'Abd Allāh, or the "servant of God". The Name Allāh is not confined to Islam alone; it is also the Name by which Arabic-speaking Christians of the Oriental churches call upon God. When written, the Name is usually followed by the formula *'azza wa jall* ("Great and Majestic"), or by *jalla jalāluh* ("Great is His Majesty").

The Koran speaks of God in innumerable verses of great beauty and penetration:

God
there is no god but He,
the Living, the Everlasting.
Slumber seizes Him not, neither sleep;
to Him belongs all that is
in the heavens and the earth.
who is there that shall intercede with Him
save by His leave?
He knows what lies before them
and what is after them,
and they comprehend not
anything of His knowledge
save such as He wills.

His Throne comprises the heavens and earth;
the preserving of them oppresses Him not;
He is the All-high, the All-glorious.
(Verse of the Throne 2:256)

He is God;
there is no god but He.
He is the knower of the Unseen and the Visible;
He is the All-merciful, the All-compassionate.
He is God;
there is no god but He.
He is the King, the All-holy, the All-peaceable,
the All-faithful, the All-preserver,
the All-mighty, the All-compeller,
the All-sublime.
Glory be to God, above that they associate!
He is God,
the Creator, the Maker, the Shaper.
To Him belong the Names Most Beautiful.
All that is in the heavens
and the earth magnifies Him;
He is the All-mighty, the All-wise. (59:22-24)

it is God who splits the grain and the date-stone,
brings forth the living from the dead;
He brings forth the dead too from the living.
So that then is God; then how are you perverted?
He splits the sky into dawn,
and has made the night for a repose,
and the sun and moon for a reckoning.
That is the ordaining of the All-mighty,
the All-knowing.
It is He who has appointed for you the stars,
that by them you might be guided
in the shadows of land and sea.
We have distinguished the signs
for a people who know.
It is He who produced you from one living soul,
and then a lodging place, and then a repository.
We have distinguished the signs
for a people who understand. (6:95-98)

To God belongs all
that is in the heavens and earth.
Whether you publish what is in your hearts
or hide it, God shall make reckoning
with you for it.
He will forgive whom He will,
and chastise whom He will; God is powerful
over everything. (2:284)

Say: 'He is God, One,
God, the Everlasting Refuge.
who has not begotten, and has not been begotten,
and equal to Him is not any one.' (112)

With Him are the keys of the Unseen;
none knows them but He.
He knows what is in land and sea;
not a leaf falls, but He knows it.
Not a grain in the earth's shadows,
not a thing, fresh or withered,
but it is in a Book Manifest. (6:59)

His command, when He desires a thing,
is to say to it 'Be', and it is.
So glory be to Him, in whose hand
is the dominion of everything,
and unto whom you shall be returned. (36:82)

We [God] are nearer to him [man] than the
jugular vein. (50:16)

He created the heavens and the earth
with the truth, and He shaped you,
and shaped you well; and unto Him
is the homecoming. (64:3)

All that is in the heavens
and the earth magnifies God;
He is the All-mighty, the All-wise.
To Him belongs the Kingdom of the heavens
and the earth;
He gives life, and He makes to die,
and He is powerful over everything.
He is the First and the Last,
the Outward and the Inward;
He has knowledge of everything. (57:1-3)

God is the Light of the heavens and the earth;
the likeness of His Light is as a niche
wherein is a lamp
the lamp in a glass,
the glass as it were a glittering star
kindled from a Blessed Tree,
an olive that is neither of the East
nor of the West
whose oil wellnigh would shine,
even if no fire touched it;
Light upon Light;
God guides to His Light whom He will.
And God strikes similitudes for men,
and God has knowledge of everything.
(24:35-40)

No affliction befalls,
except it be by the leave of God.
Whosoever believes in God,
He will guide his heart.
And God has knowledge of everything.

And obey God, and obey the Messenger;
but if you turn your backs, it is
only for the Messenger to deliver
the Manifest Message.

God —
there is no god but He.
And in God let the believers
put their trust.
(64:11-13)

Your wealth and your children are
only a trial; and with God is a mighty wage.
So fear God as far as you are able,
and give ear, and obey, and expend
well for yourselves. And whosoever
is guarded against the avarice
of his own soul, those — they are the prosperers.
If you lend to God a good loan, He
will multiply it for you, and will
forgive you. God is All-thankful, All-clement,
Knower He of the Unseen and the Visible,
the All-mighty, the All-wise. (64:15-18)

...God is the All-sufficient;
you are the needy ones. (47:40)

Written, the Name is *'alif, lām, lām* (with shaddah), *hā'*. This is a contraction of its full orthography, which is *'alif, lām, lām, lām, hā'*. Between the final lām and the *ha'* there is a "dagger" *'alif.* This is written suspended between the final *lām* and the *hā'*, or decoratively sometimes above the shaddah, and sometimes horizontally above the Name, especially above the ligature between the final lām and the *hā'*. Often, the "dagger" *'alif* is not shown at all. The first *lām* is not voiced, but, in the words of one commentator, "inserted" (*mudghamah*) into the following *lām*, causing it to carry the shaddah, or doubling. The "daggar" *'alif* in the Name has the unique characteristic that when the Name stands by itself this *'alif* of prolongation is pronounced with velarization making the preceding *lām* sound "heavy" (*takhfīm*). When the Name is preceded by a consonant with a *kasrah*, as in *Lillāh*, that *'alif* is develarized and the *lām* becomes "light" (*tarqīq*). When it is velarized, the pronunciation of the double *lām* is a heavy "l" sound found in no other word in Arabic, although the combination of letters exists in other words as well. According to *'Abjad*, or the mystical science of letters, the visible letters of the Divine Name Allāh add up to the number sixty-six, which, tradition points out, is the sum of the letters in *Ādam wa Hawwā'*, or the words "Adam and Eve". (*See* 'ABJAD.)

The initial *'alif* is a support (*kursī*, "a seat") for the *hamzah*, a letter which is a transition between silence and sound; or, one could also say, between non-manifestation and manifestation. This *hamzah* is a *hamzat al-waṣl*, and is elided with preceding vowels, such that *Yā Allāh* is pronounced *Yallāh.* According to Ibn 'Arabi's Treatise on the Name of Majesty, the voiced *lām*, and the voiced "dagger" *'alif*, represent manifestation in relation to the Absolute.

The last letter, the *hā'*, is ultimately an expiration of breath ending in silence. Symbolically, it is a return to non-manifestation. As such it is also reintegration; a return to Beyond-Being (God as the Absolute) on the part of Being (God as Creator), or, on another level, a return to Being on the part of creation. In the nominative form, *Allāhu*, this final *hā'* also leads to the Name *Huwa. Huwa* is at once simply the third-person pronoun in Arabic, but also at the same time a Divine Name of the Ipseity, or the Divine Essence. Spoken softly, the Name Allāh sounds like a thunderbolt; the first syllable wells suddenly out of silence like an explosion, it peaks its crescendo with the sudden "attack" of the double *ll*, and then fades slowly like thunder rolling on into the distance.

In the words of Muḥammad Bushārah, a representative of a Moroccan Darqawī Shaykh of the beginning of this century:

> The Name is made up of four letters that are read Allāh; if you remove the first letter those that remain are read *Lillāh* ("to God"); if you remove another letter — the first *lam* — what remains is read *Lahu* ("to Him"). Finally, there remains only the letter *Ha'*, which, vocalized, is the Name "He" (*Huwa*: the Name of the Essence). In the same way, when we invoke the Name of God, its form gradually melts into the breath itself. The same happens to the dying man whose soul is resolved into breathing alone and leaves the body with the last breath.

In Islam, God is known also by ninety-nine other Names collectively called "the Most Beautiful Names" (*al-asmā' al-ḥusnā*). These are divided into Names of the Essence (*asmā' adh-dhāt*) and Names of the Qualities (*asmā' aṣ-ṣifāt*). The Names are also divided into Names of Majesty (*jalāl*), or rigor, and Names of Beauty (*jamāl*), or mercy. (*See* DIVINE NAMES.)

The Name *ar-Raḥmān*, "the Merciful One", a Name of the Essence, appears in the Koran almost as a synonym for *Allāh*. Historically, the reaction of the pagan Meccans to this Name (notably their refusal to recognize it when the consecration "In the Name of God [*Allāh*] the Merciful [*ar-Raḥmān*] the Compassionate [*ar-Raḥīm*]" was written in drawing up the Treaty of Ḥudaybiyyah) shows that while *Allāh* was known and used by them, as it was to all speakers of Arabic, *ar-Raḥmān* was not. They saw the Name *ar-Raḥmān* as emblematic of the new revelation, and refused to acknowledge it as long as they were unbelievers.

Among other names mentioned in the Koran are: "The First" (*al-Awwal*), "The Last" (*al-Ākhir*), "The Outwardly Manifest" (*aẓ-Ẓāhir*), "The Inward" (*al-Bāṭin*), "The Holy One" (*al-Quddūs*), "The Integral Peace" (*as-Salām*). Among the Names of God as Creator (*al-Khāliq*) are: "The Producer" (from nothing) (*al-Bāri'*) and "The Shaper" (*al-Musawwir*). And He is also called "The Mighty" (*al-'Azīz*) and "The Ruler" (*al-Hakīm*).

In addition to the descriptions of God found in the Koran, there are those found in pious writings. A litany of the 'Isawiyyah *ṭarīqah* of Morocco says:

> God was alone; around him was the Void. He created the universe to make His power known; He created the world that He might be worshiped. He is the Deity, the excellent Master, the necessary Being. The creature disappears; the excellent Master alone is Eternal; the creature is born perishable, the excellent Master remains. The excellent Master is Immense; Full; the creature is empty; the Master is Glorious, Sublime, Knowing, Perfect; the creature is small, ignorant, incomplete; the excellent Master is Exalted and resembles nothing. The excellent Master is in the heart of those who know...

See ARABIC; BASMALAH; DHIKR; DIVINE NAMES; FIVE DIVINE PRESENCES.

'Allāma Hillī, *see* HILLĪ, 'ALLĀMA.

Almagest. The Latinized form of the Arabic *al-Majisti*, which itself was the Arabization, from the Greek *Megalē Syntaxis*. This is Ptolemy's 2nd century work on astronomy (based on the work of predecessors such as Hipparchus of Rhodes) that explained the apparent motion of the planets through the theory of epicycles and deferents.

In departing from the purely mystical theories of Pythagoras concerning the motion of the planets, the *Megalē Syntaxis* represented an important step towards the empiricism of modern science. Yet its empirical tendency was not a divorce from the perception that the heavens were above all a symbol of a higher reality; the physical world was still contained in an ideal, or spiritual world. Ptolemy, like other Greek philosophers, may have known that the earth went around the sun (it is now known that some peoples of antiquity used both geocentric and heliocentric systems for calculations), but he knew above all that the world came from the Spirit, and his planetary model reflected that knowledge, accommodating the data of observed motion as facts of secondary importance.

Islamic astronomy was based upon the theories of Ptolemy as expounded in the Almagest, and it was through the Arabic translation that the Ptolemaic theory was reintroduced as medieval Europe resumed the study of ancient sciences. The word Almagest also served, in European languages, as a generic term for any of the many and great medieval works on such subjects as astrology, alchemy and science. *See* ASTRONOMY. *Almohads* (*524-667*/1130-1269). Spanish name of a Moorish dynasty and religious movement called in Arabic *al-Muwaḥḥidūn* ("the Unitarians"), who ruled in Morocco and Spain. The Almohads brought renewed piety and fervor to the Arab West through a powerful sense of religion not just as rules (in any case laxly observed towards the end of the Almoravid epoch) but as spiritual interiority. This interiority, or awareness that the world exists in a sacred dimension, gave the Almohads their name which means "The Upholders of (Divine) Unity", for the profound sense that God is One means that this world and this life are plunged in God.

The movement grew out of the teachings of a reformer called Ibn Tūmart (*470-524*/1077-1130), a Berber from the Maṣmūda tribe in the Atlas mountains in Morocco. After making the pilgrimage to Mecca, Ibn Tūmart remained in the East to study in Damascus and Baghdad. He returned to Morocco imbued with both the vigorous theology of al-Ash'arī and the mystical ideas of al-Ghazālī. Wherever Ibn Tūmart went he attempted to reform morals and religious beliefs, sometimes violently. In Fez, he threw the sister of the Almoravid prince from her horse for not wearing a veil. Although such an act could easily earn death, Ibn Tūmart evidently commanded enough respect or even awe for his righteous audacity, that he was not punished.

Ibn Tūmart returned to Aghmat where he converted Atlas Berbers (who, although nominally Muslims, knew next to nothing about their religion). As for those who were believers, he reformed their hitherto superficial faith. In Tinmal he founded a *ribāṭ*, or religious-military community, which was run as a religious dictatorship. From Tinmal he waged holy war upon his neighbors. According to Ibn Khaldūn, Ibn Tūmart, who was called a Mahdī, was descended from the Fāṭimids. This does not necessarily mean by birth but could mean intellectually. But it should be noted that North African Berbers had married into the family of Shī'ite Imāms very early on; the original religion of the Berbers had made common cause with Shī'ism. One North African, Abū Hilāl ad-Dayhūri is known to have become Archegos in Ctesiphon at the time of the Caliph al-Manṣur. In any case, Ibn Khaldūn says: "Al-Mahdī's power did not depend exclusively on his Fāṭimid descent...[which]... had become obscured and knowledge of it disappeared among the people, although it remained alive in him and his family through tradition." After Ibn Tūmart's death (which some say had been kept secret by the leadership for two years to prolong the sway of Ibn Tūmart's charismatic authority), his lieutenant 'Abd al-Mu'min suceeded him as ruler and brought North Africa as far as the Libyan desert under Almohad control by *544*/1149. This expansion took place at the same time as the Almoravid dynasty was collapsing through its own decadence. In *566*/1170 Muslim Spain fell into Almohad hands and for a time Seville became the Almohad capital, although the rulers eventually returned to Morocco to govern from Marrakesh.

The Almohads' resounding victory over the Spanish at the Battle of Alarcos in *592*/1195 marked a peak of political power. However, it was soon followed by the single most important defeat the Muslims ever received in the history of Moorish Spain: the Battle of Las Navas de Tolosa in *609*/1212. A Christian army strengthened by knights from Portugal and from outside the Iberian peninsula, unified by the spirit of the knightly orders created out of the Crusades, devastated the Moorish armies and made the complete reconquest of Muslim Spain by the Christians no more than a question of time.

The Almohad period saw the heights, and the end, of Muslim philosophy in the West in the persons of Ibn Tufayl (d. *585*/1185) and Ibn Rushd (d. *595*/1198). (*See* PHILOSOPHY.) It was also the period of Ibn 'Arabī (d. *638*/1240), the famous metaphysician from Murcia in southern Spain. In craftsmanship and architecture the Almohads introduced a powerful style that marked a new beginning for Moorish art. It is outstanding for its direct expression, in the language of art, of a metaphysical conviction, as is to be seen particularly in the Almohad arch. The Almohads introduced the pointed arch, that became one of the most characteristic elements of Moorish architecture, influencing even Christian architecture in Europe. Magnificent examples of these arches can be seen in the Kutubiyyah mosque in Marrakesh, whose amplitude and sense of spiritual fullness, convey visually the *inshiraḥ* ("expansion"), that is the mystical transformation of the physical body that accompanies surrender to God (the literal meaning of Islām). The Almohad arch is, as it were, the architectural image of that which the Koran speaks of in Sūrah 94:

Did We not expand thy breast for thee
and lift from thee thy burden,
the burden that weighed down thy back?
Did We not exalt thy fame?
so truly with hardship comes ease;
truly with hardship comes ease.
So when thou art empty, labor,
and let thy Lord be thy Quest.

The directness and vigor of the Almohad style influenced Islamic art to some degree everywhere. The monumental legacies of the Almohads are the Giralda, now the vast cathedral of Seville (originally the Grand Mosque), the Kutubiyyah mosque of Marrakesh, the Ḥasan mosque of Rabāṭ (never completed and shattered by the earthquake of 1756 that also destroyed Lisbon), and what remains of the Almohad mosque at Tlemcen.

The Almohad emphasis on acknowledging the Unity of God that, as a call to action in Islamic history, points either to an interiorizing of spiritual life, or to an emphasis on rigor, since the Unity, or Oneness, of God was never in question, and was to some degree a reaction against the tendencies of their predecessors, the Almoravids. As the Almoravids lost their initial zeal, they tended to externalize religion and to reduce it to rules and simplistic conceptions; at the same time, they succumbed to the temptations of hedonism, always present in Moorish Spain. It is true, nonetheless, that the Almohad's integration of all things into the Unity of God reflected, to a greater or lesser degree, the general renewal of spiritual fervor that was then pervading the Islamic East. The Almohads flourished for a short time; by *667*/1269 they were replaced in Morocco by the Merinid dynasty, while in Spain the declining Muslim kingdoms yielded gradually to Christian reconquest. *See* RECONQUISTA.

Almoravids (*448-541*/1056-1147). The Spanish name of a dynasty and its supporting political, military and ethnic organization called in Arabic *al-Murābiṭun*, "those who stand together for the defense of religion" (*see* RIBĀṬ). The Almoravids were an imperial movement arising out of an originally religious impetus that enthused and set in motion the Berber tribes of the Ṣanhāja group in the western Sudan, also called the Lemtuna (from *al-Mutalaththimun*, "the veiled ones", because they covered their faces like the Tuareg, to whom they are related). The tribes rose up from the Sahara and the Niger and Mali region to conquer North Africa and then Spain.

One of the chiefs of the Ṣanhāja, Yaḥyā ibn Ibrāhīm, was returning from the pilgrimage to Mecca at the beginning of the *5th*/11th century when he was introduced by the rulers of Kairouan/Qayrawan to a noted scholar, a missionary called 'Abd Allāh ibn Yāsīn. The mission of 'Abd Allāh was to improve the rudimentary religious knowledge of Yaḥyā's people. Upon arrival in the western Sudan 'Abd Allāh took matters firmly into his hands, ordered the penitential scourging of all new converts and imposed a generally zealous regimen. His preaching sparked a movement that spread from a *ribāṭ* (fortress for the defense of Islam) located on an island in the Senegal river in which religion and conquest joined hands; soon, after the death of 'Abd Allāh ibn Yāsīn, an empire was created and then divided between a leader called Abū Bakr, who held control over the movement from *448*/1056, and his cousin Yūsuf ibn Tāshufīn, who seized Morocco as his portion in *453*/1061. Yūsuf ibn Tāshufīn founded Marrakesh as his capital in *454*/1062.

The Spanish Muslims, divided after the decline of the Caliphate of Cordoba into small princedoms, and beset by the Christians, called on Yūsuf ibn Tāshufīn for help. This he gave by bringing an army of Moroccans and Africans across the straits, and he defeated Alfonso VI at az-Zallaqah (Sagrajas) near Badajoz in *479*/1086. This victory, however, produced the seeds of the ultimate defeat of the Muslims in Spain by changing the nature of the political alignments. Until az-Zallaqah, wars in Spain were internecine struggles between *Spanish* rulers, both Christian and Muslim; however, when the North African reinforcements entered the field, the struggle became one between Christian Europe and Islam. This led to the turning point for the Muslims in the defeat of the Almohads at Las Navas de Tolosa in *609*/1212.

In *483*/1090, four years after he had been invited to fight there, Yūsuf ibn Tāshufīn returned to Muslim Spain and captured the country for himself. He conquered in the name of the restoration of orthodoxy, reforming the lax and enervating luxury of the Andalusian courts. Ibn Tāshufīn accepted the authority of the 'Abbāsid Caliphate, in name at least. However, he adopted the title of *Amīr al-Muslimīn* ("Prince of the Muslims") similar to the Caliph's *Amīr al-Mu'minīn* ("Prince of the Believers"), one of the titles used today by the King of Morocco.

Yūsuf died at the age of one hundred in *500*/1106. His empire extended across southern Iberia and included Valencia, which had been wrested from the widow of al-Cid, and North Africa from the Atlantic to Algiers.

The Almoravid domination lasted a bare century until *541*/1147, and then gave way to another Berber movement, that of the Almohads, with a far higher ideological motivation. The Almoravids are a perfect example of Ibn Khaldūn's theory of Muslim history, according to which periodic nomad invasions from the desert to the settled areas are inevitable; they come to sweep away the decadence of sedentary life, before themselves succumbing to its temptations, once they have escaped the natural discipline of the wastelands. *See* ALMOHADS; IBN KHALDūN.

Alms, *see* BEGGING; SADAQAH; WAQF; ZAKĀH.

Aloes, Fragrant (Greek *alö*, cf. Hebrew *ahalīm*; ultimately from Tamil *akil.*) An incense widely used in the Islamic world for religious and special occasions. In Arabic, the incense is called *al-'ūd al-qumari* or *al-qamari*, which is understood to mean "the wood of the moon". However, this is a corruption, for as al-Mas'ūdī says in the "Meadows of Gold", it is *'ūd al-Qimari*, that is, from the "Kingdom of Qimar" which is the land of the *Khmer* (Cambodia).

The wood of aloes (not to be confused with "bitter aloes", a medicinal shrub called *sabrah* in Arabic) is the precious wood of a tree, *Aquilaria muscaria* and *Aquilaria agallocha*, found in Asia. Some 10% of the trees are infected by a fungus disease; the tree reacts to the fungus by producing a resin. When burned, in very small pieces over charcoal, the resin in the wood of the infected tree produces a remarkable and subtle fragrance. The allegory of its origin reinforces its place in religious usage especially among mystics. The incense is mentioned in the Bible (Ps. 45.8; Prov 7.17; Cant 4.14; John 19:39) and was brought by Nicodemus for Jesus. Aloes is also called Eaglewood (from Portuguese *pao d'Aquila*). In Malay it is called *kayu gahru* (or gaharu). The Portuguese epic poet Luis de Camoes called it the odorous wood; it was once imported into Europe and well known.

Alyasa'. The Biblical Elisha, the disciple of Elijah. He is mentioned in the Koran in Sūrah 6:86.

Amal (lit. "hope"). The condition of expectation of the soul. It is also the name, (an acronym, for *Afwāj al-Muqawamah al-Lubnaniyyah*, "Lebanese Resistance Attachments"), of a political organization founded in Lebanon in 1974 by Mūsā aṣ-Ṣadr. Imām Mūsā aṣ-Ṣadr was an Iranian Mullā who came to Lebanon in 1959 and became the leader of most of Lebanon's Twelve-Imām Shī'ites. The purpose of AMAL was to provide the Shī'ites of the Baqā' Valley and southern Lebanon with a political means of action and self-expression, which, with continuing civil unrest in the country, took on a para-military role in the face of other contending factions, all of which were armed. In 1978 Imām Mūsā aṣ-Ṣadr disappeared while on a visit to Libya. Presumably he was assassinated, a fact that Lebanese Shī'ites have steadfastly refused to admit. *See* LEBANON; METAWILA.

Ameer Ali (Sayyid Amir 'Ali; 1849-1928). Modern Indian authority on Islam, author of the *Spirit of Islam.* Like Sir Muḥammad Iqbal, he was strongly affected by the humanist and secular European outlook of the nineteenth century and took an apologetic and rationalist approach to Islam, treating evil, for example, figuratively, and referring to the "parabolic nature of Koranic expressions".

Amen, *see* ĀMĪN.

Āmīn The Arabic form of Amen, meaning assent, "verily", "truly", and "so be it"). "And all the people shall answer and say, Amen" (Deuteronomy 28:14); and "Blessed be the Lord forevermore, Amen and Amen" (Psalm 89); and "Amen, Amen, I say unto thee, except a man be born again, he cannot see the Kingdom of God" (John 3:3).

In Islam Āmīn is used in the same way as among the Jews and the Christians; it is always uttered at the end of the *fātiḥah*, whether within the ritual prayer (*ṣalāt*), or as *du'ā'*, and as an assent to the prayers uttered by others, the preacher at the Friday prayer, for example. It has been suggested that Āmīn is a Divine Name. *See* FĀTIḤAH.

al-Amīn. A name of the Prophet, given to him by the Quraysh before the revelation of Islam, meaning the "Trustworthy One". The word is used as a title for an organization official in a position of trust, such as the treasurer of a charitable organization, a guild, and so forth. *See* FĀTIḤAH.

Amīnah. Mother of the Prophet. She was the daughter of Wahb ibn 'Abd-Manāf. Most sources put her burial place at al-Abwa.

'Abd ar-Raḥmān son of 'Awf narrates that his mother Shifah declared as follows:

> "I was a midwife to the Prophet's mother Amīnah; and in the night when her labor pains seized her, and Muḥammad Muṣṭafā fell into my hands at his birth, a voice out of the Other World came to my ears, saying: 'Thy Lord show Mercy to thee!' And from the east to west the face of earth became so

illuminated that I could see some of the palaces of Damascus by the light of it."

And it is reported that Amīnah declared:

"In that night a flight of birds turned in to my house, so many that the whole house was filled with them. Their beaks were of emerald, their wings of ruby."

See MUḤAMMAD.

Amīr (or Emir, lit. "commander" pl. *umarā'*, from the root *amara*, "to command".) In the past amīr was usually a military title, now used to mean a prince or as a title for various rulers or chiefs. *Amīr al-Mu'minīn*, or "Prince of the believers", is a title of the Caliph. *Amīr al-Muslimīn*, or "Prince of the Submitted" was used by Yūsuf ibn Tāshufīn of the Almoravids, and has remained a title sometimes used by princes in the Maghreb, or Arab West. The title *Amīr al-Umarā'* ("Prince of Princes") was used by the Buyids who ruled under the nominal control of the 'Abbāsids. *See* CALIPH.

Amir Khusraw Dihlawi (*651-727*/1253-1325). One of the most famous Muslim literary figures of India, he wrote lyrical and epic poetry in Persian. Amir Khusraw used national material in his writings, and described customs and festivals. He was a disciple of Niẓām ad-Dīn Awliyā, the most noted mystic of Delhi.

al-Amr (lit. "the command"). In mystical theology the command given by God: *kun*, "Be!" that creates, translating possibilities from the unmanifest to the manifest. As "the Word of God" it corresponds to an aspect of the idea of the *logos*.

"They will ask thee about the Spirit; say to them: the Spirit proceeds from the Command [*al-amr*] of my Lord..." (17:8). *Al-amr* has thus been one of the terms used for the active pole (in Aristotle *eidos*) of the polarization within Being into act and potency, that is, the Yang and Yin polarization from which creation takes place. The polar opposite of *al-amr* (act, form, power, Yang), is potentiality, the passive pole (Yin), which is also called universal nature (*aṭ-ṭabī'ah*), or primordial substance (in Aristotle, hyle). *See* FIVE DIVINE PRESENCES; al-MUMKINĀT; NAFAS ar-RAḤMĀN.

'Amr ibn al-'Āṣī (d. *42*/663). A Qurayshī who converted to Islam shortly before the conquest of Mecca and went on to become one of the most successful Muslim military leaders. He took part in the campaign in Syria in *14*/635 and conquered Egypt in *20*/641 during the Caliphate of 'Umar.

'Amr's army of 4,000, reinforced by az-Zubayr with 5,000, defeated the Egyptians at 'Ayn ash-Shams (Heliopolis) in *19*/640. Thereafter, months of fighting led to the conquest of the Egyptian fortress of Bābilūn the following year, which forced Alexandria to surrender without further bloodshed.

'Amr became the governor of Egypt and founded a camp city at Fusṭāṭ on the eastern bank of the Nile, near present-day Cairo. There he built a mosque that bears his name and still stands today. 'Amr was removed from office by the Caliph 'Uthmān (the head of the Umayyad clan) but, nevertheless, sensing the victory of the Umayyads in the struggle that ensued after the assassination of 'Uthmān, he joined the army of Mu'āwiyah and fought against 'Alī at the Battle of Ṣiffīn in 37/657. 'Amr is said to have devised the idea of having Mu'āwiyah's troops attach leaves of the Koran to their lances. When Mu'āwiyah's forces were seen to be losing the struggle this act suddenly proved an irresistible call to both sides to turn to God's Word to decide the quarrel. This led to a mediation between 'Alī and Mu'āwiyah that was manipulated in Mu'āwiyah's favor.

When Mu'āwiyah the Umayyad became Caliph he reinstated 'Amr as governor of Egypt. 'Amr died in Egypt holding office at a very advanced age. *See* CAIRO.

Amulets. Magical charms are widely used everywhere in the Islamic world, but especially in North and West Africa, and in the Sahara. Most often the amulets are calligraphed passages of the Koran that are sealed in a leather case, worn around the neck or on the body. In Russia and the Ukraine, many Muslims, particularly Crimean Tartars, wear Koranic amulets stiched into waterproof packets around the neck, the way Christians wear crosses. Sometimes amulets take the form of jewelry, such as the "hand of Fāṭimah", and inscriptions on silver. The wearer hopes in this way to ward off evil by the incantations written on the amulets, and at its best, through the intention of seeking refuge in God, which they express. In Arabic they are called *ḥijāb, ḥamā'il, tamā'īm*, and in West Africa *gri-gri*.

In the Middle East amulets are a domain which preserves obscure beliefs; in amulets and talismans one can find residues of past religions. In Africa it is common for such amulets to incorporate elements of animistic religions. Thus Koranic passages are found side by side with invocations of long strange names that are purported by those who believe in them to be "names of Angels", in Hausa and the like. The art of amulets even has its own classic, a Greek known as Balīnās, or Apollonius of Tyana, to whom a treatise is attributed on talismans. The Imām Shādhilī was noted for creating talismans and composing incantations. *See* HAND of FĀṬIMAH; ḤIZB al-BAḤR; REFUGE.

Analogy, legal, *see* QIYAS.

Anas ibn Mālik. A famous Companion and personal servant of the Prophet. He should not be confused with Mālik ibn Anas, founder of the Mālikī School of Law (*Madhhab*).

Andarūn. The private interior of an Iranian home occupied by the women and off limits to visitors. The term corresponds to the *ḥaramlik* amongst Turks, and the *ḥarīm* amongst Arabs.

Andarz. Persian wisdom literature that includes such genres as the "mirrors for princes" or advice for rulers.

Angels (Ar. sing. *malak* or *mal'ak*, from *la'aka*, "to send on a mission"). The doctrine of Angels within the Semitic religions is related to that of the "guardian spirits" of Babylonia and the *daena* and *fravarti* (*fravarshi*) of the ancient Iranian religions. The elaboration of the concepts of the Archangels in particular, and especially the polarization of Michael and the fallen Archangel, Satan, is influenced by Iranian antecedents. The Angels, who are celestial beings in the supraformal world, called *Jabarūt*, are subordinated in a hierarchy at the head of which stand the four Archangels: Jibrā'īl or Jibrīl (Gabriel, called in Iran by his Zoroastrian name, Sraosh), the Angel of Revelation, Mīkā'īl or Mīkāl (Michael), Isrāfīl, whose blast from the "horn" of primordial sound will shatter forms and creation at the end of time, and 'Izrā'īl, the Angel of Death. These are of the class of Angels called the *Qarībiyyun*, cognate with Hebrew *Kerūbhīm* ("cherubim") and interpreted to mean "those who are near (to God)"; and like the *Mal'ak Yāhwēh* of the Old Testament, they "act" in the place of the Divinity. The Archangels' centrality as expressions of Divine aspects, or as protagonists of God, sets them apart from the other Angels. Except for the Archangels who, as Divine functionaries, partake of a certain ambiguity expressed in Michael's name which is a question in Hebrew: "Who is like God?", the Angels do not possess a central state (a state with objective self-knowledge and capacity to know the Essence), and unlike man, the Angels do not possess freewill. Therefore, although closer to God, they are not superior to man in the perfection of his unfallen primordiality *fiṭrah*), because man can truly know God, whereas Angels cannot. In the story of the *Mi'rāj*, the Prophet's ascent to heaven and the Divine Presence, as told by tradition, the Prophet is carried upwards by Gabriel. There comes a point, however, beyond which Gabriel cannot approach and the Prophet must go on alone.

When Adam was created, God commanded the Angels to bow down to him, and Adam's superiority to them was made evident by the fact that he knew the *names* of the Angels and objects in creation, while the Angels did not. Adam knew the names because human knowledge is possible through an identity in the center of one's being with the Intellect, the center of Being itself. Of this Intellect, that can also be called Spirit, Meister Eckhart said: "there is something in the soul which is uncreated and not creatable; this is the Intellect." The "Intellect" in this metaphysical sense, partakes at the same time of created form within man, and of the uncreated within Being. Its center is not the mind but the heart; in Arabic it is called *'aql* ("intellect"), and also *sirr* ("secret").

Traditionally, the true name of something is itself the object named on a higher plane; the true name contains the object, just as Plato's Ideas contain their "shadows", or the objects of existence. Adam's knowledge of the names showed that he was, in fact, the synthesis of creation, and at the same time its center. Because Adam was defined by physical form, and therefore bounded by limitation, it would seem that this would make him inferior to the station of the Angels, who are formless. But the extreme limitation of the spirit which corporeal existence (as form, not as "matter") represents is itself the means whereby that which lies beyond form — and even Angelic formlessness — may be known.

Because Adam knew directly through the Intellect (one could say that he knew because he contained the object of knowledge within himself as subject), form permitted him to grasp what was beyond form. Our life, which is in the world of forms teaches us to understand death, which is outside the world of forms, it is limitation which brings to our awareness that which is beyond limitation, and it bestows the supreme ability namely, to conceive of the Absolute as Absolute. The Angel's knowledge of the Absolute is necessarily indirect, or "blind", that is, as animals know us, rather than as we know each other.

One of the Angels, Iblīs, refused to recognize, because of pride, the superiority of Adam and was banished, falling from the state of an Angel to that of the *jinn*, a being in the subtle world. This is the symbolical story of the origin of evil. It expresses clearly, however, the inability of evil, or Satan, to "see" in form, anything but form, limitation, and not through or beyond form to the essence. It could be said the Angels could not see it either, but they obeyed God. Ibn Māja the traditionalist (born *209*/824) says of Angels:

> 'It is believed that Angels are of a simple substance (created of light), endowed with life, speech and reason; and that the differences between them, the jinn and shayṭān, is a difference of species. Know that the Angels are sanctified from carnal desire and the disturbance of anger; they never disobey God in what He hath commanded them, but do what they are commanded. Their food is the celebration of his glory; their drink is the proclaiming of His holiness; their conversation, the commemoration of God, whose Name be exalted; their pleasure is his worship; and they are created in different forms and with different powers.'

See also ADAM; FIVE DIVINE PRESENCES; HARUT and MARUT; IBLIS; JINN; MUNKAR and NAKIR.

Anṣār (Ar. "helpers"). The name given by the Prophet to the believers among the people of Medinah as an honourific, and to distinguish them from the *muhājirūn*, or immigrants from Mecca. Descendants of the original Ansār families sometimes still include the title "Anṣārī" in their family name to indicate their origins.

al-Anṣārī, Abū Ismā'īl 'Abd Allāh (*396-481*/1006-1089). Scholar, Sufi, and theologian, at first of the Shafi'ite school and then a Ḥanbalī. In Persia he is known as Pir-i Anṣār. He was born near Herat and spent most of his life there. Anṣarī's teacher in religious studies was Abū 'Abd Allāh Taqī; his master in Sufism Abū-l-Ḥasan Kharaqānī.

Al-Anṣārī is the author of the devotional *Munājāt* ("Intimate Conversations"), the *Ṭabaqāt as-Ṣufiyyah* ("The Chronicles of Sufis"), *Dhamm al-Kalām wa Ahlih* ("Shame of Theology and Theologians"), a Ḥanbalī polemic; a book on Sufi theory called *Manāzil aṣ-Ṣā'irin*, and other works.

In his *Munājāt*, al-Anṣārī says:

> O God, seek me out of Thy Mercy that I may come to Thee; and draw me on with Thy Grace that I may turn to Thee.
> O God, I shall never lose all hope of Thee even though I disobey Thee, and my knowledge of Thy Bounty has brought me to stand before Thee.
> O God, how shall I be disappointed seeing that Thou art my hope; or how shall I be despised seeing that in Thee is my trust?
> O Thou Who art veiled in the shrouds of Thy Glory, so that no eye can perceive Thee! O Thou Who shinest forth in the perfection of Thy splendor, so that the hearts (of the mystics) have realized Thy Majesty! How shalt Thou be hidden, seeing that Thou art ever Manifest; or how shalt Thou be absent, seeing that Thou art ever Present, and watchest over us?

Antichrist, *see* DAJJĀL.

Antinomianism (from Greek *anti*, "against" and nomos "law"). In philosophy an antinomy is the mutual contradiction of two principles or inferences resting on premises of equal validity; in philosophy the matter ends there. When religion enters the picture some mutual contradictions can and must be resolved, in the presence of faith, on a higher plane. Not all contradictions can be resolved in this way, however, and notable among them is theodicy or the existence of evil. When the existence of evil is ascribed to two principles, the resolution of contradictory absolutes into a higher principle, that is necessary by the very idea of reality, becomes literally impossible. The way out is to affirm that ultimate reality as such is unreachable and unfathomable. This appears as a doctrine of the "unknowability of God". This is found, for example, in the Mu'tazilite separation of God from His Attributes, and was attacked by al-Ash'arī (d. *324*/945) and many others until the Mu'tazilite doctrine was pushed out of Sunni Islam.

Those Hellenist pre-Islamic sects that were fatally committed to this course, called such a contradictory God the *Bythos*, or "the Abyss". The Fāṭimids who held this belief translated and transposed the term into Arabic as *al-ghayb ta'la* ("the Great Otherness"). This is what they called God, relegating Allāh as a name for the first emanation out of the unknowable invisible which was called the "First Intellect". This emanation, according to their teaching, was itself created, and limited, thus demiurgic, and lamented its own exile from the Abyss although itself the direct creator of the world. (They said that the Name Allāh derived from a verb — *walaha* — meaning "to lament": which is impossible.)

The orthodox answer to the problem, which is St. Augustine's answer, is to explain the existence of evil as an absence of good, not as another kind of substance resulting from another kind of principle. According to the orthodox theodicy, what actually happens when evil enters the world, is that it is a mistake made by consciousness in taking non-existence to be a different form of existence, a kind of "anti-existence". Since such an "anti-existence" would have to have a principle from which it arose (if it is not already God Himself), evidently the essence of such a hypothetical principle for evil would be "absolute contradiction". The Creed of Sa'd ad-Dīn at-Taftāzānī (d. *791*/1389) found it necessary to affirm that the "non-existent is not a thing".

Antinomianism is specifically religious behavior which is contrary to the law. It is related to philosophical and religious antinomy or dualism because it makes an identity between good and evil and thus between what is permitted and what is forbidden. That which is within the limitation, from which creation results, and that which is beyond limitation, or nothingness, are turned into equal realities, and the sum of the "two realities" becomes principial or divine. Antinomian sects exists in all religious climates; sometimes the antinomianism expresses itself only as a tendency that stops short of actually transgressing religious prohibitions; at other times it consists of deliberately violating religious prescriptions, as for example, the breaking of the fast of Ramaḍan at the declaration of the *Qiyamah* ("resurrection") at the Assassin stronghold of Alamut in 1164.

It also exists as various degrees of libertinism of which Gnostic sects have frequently been accused, rightly or wrongly. The practice of *mut'ah*, or "temporary marriage" for a period as short as a day, prohibited by Sunni Islam, is sometimes at the base of these accusations. Elsewhere there were sects called in Persian the "extinguishers of lamps" which may have been radically libertine. In the West the Cathares, for example, were strictly ascetic until they reached a stage which they considered to be purity or perfection of the individual. Thereafter they believed that they were incapable of sin and that whatever they did was good. They had surmounted the law which still existed for the "profane", or as Moliäre, would say, they discovered that the "purity of their intentions" could rectify the "immorality of their acts".

Antinomian currents in Islam, in addition to the *ghulāt*, or "extremist" sects who divinized their pontiffs (which for Islam is the greatest of sins) are still to be found in Sufism in many forms. They are concentrated in some well-known sayings which are passed on as being Ḥadīth. The most famous is usually attributed to Abū Hurayrah, although sometimes 'Alī is also cited as the source: "I have two bodies of knowledge from the Prophet; one you know; if I were to tell you the other, you would slit my throat." The "other" body of knowledge is never specified; it is left as an obscure spot reserved for the awakening of a spontaneous anti-truth. A variant is that there was something 'Alī could not tell anyone that "he had to whisper in a well".

Another well known pseudo-Ḥadīth of this type says that the Prophet retired during a session into a grove, that 'Alī followed him and when he returned was questioned by 'Umar regarding what the Prophet had said. When 'Umar heard the report he said "this must be kept secret otherwise no-one will strive for salvation." The grove theme figures in a series of other rather obscure accounts that refer to an Antichrist figure appearing in Medinah. These are evidently traces of later attempts to neutralize the original forgery by attaching onto it additional elements or evolving it into a third entity.

Some interesting examples of antinomian ideas are among those sayings known as *Ḥadīth qudsi*, or "God speaking through the Prophet". Many of the so-called *Ḥadīth qudsi* are simply the Koran itself paraphrased. A number of others, however, are antinomian when presented, as they are in practice, in the context of an acroamatic, or secret, oral teaching. One of these is "I [God] was a hidden treasure, I wanted to be known, therefore I created the world." This saying may appear recorded for the first time in the *Mathnawi* of Rūmī; by itself there is nothing necessarily objectionable in it. However, as it is actually transmitted orally, explicitly or by implication, the import is that the world is an emanation of God, and thereby God Himself.

Among Algerian Sufis there is the affirmation that the Prophet frequently asked his disciples "is there a stranger among us" meaning that he was about to teach something that could not be told to everyone, in other words, a secret teaching. The secret teaching is rarely made explicit, the follower being left to reconstruct it for himself, which is the more effective since it takes the form, when it arises, under the effect of the original antinomy, as a sudden realization from within.

The device of a "secret teaching" is at the heart of Mahayana Buddhism, and appears at one point or another in virtually every other religions as well. It is a simple method to introduce an antinomian idea wherever one wishes. In itself this was used early enough for Bukhārī's *Ṣaḥiḥ* to affirm that 'Ā'ishāh, the Prophet's widow said to Masruq: "Verily, he who tells you that the Prophet has concealed a part of Divine Revelation and that he has not delivered it to his people, lies." The secret teaching idea persists and is repeated among otherwise pious and even strict Muslims even though the Koran itself says "O Messenger! Make known that which has been revealed to you from your Lord, for if you do not, you will not have conveyed the message." (5:67).

Behind this stand two doctrines to which the antinomian allusions lead; these are found amongst many Sufis, and among minor sects related to Islam or at its fringes. The first is the divinization of man. A direct example is the case of a well known saying widely accepted today as a Ḥadīth, namely, "Who knows his soul knows his Lord, who has seen me [the Prophet] has seen the Truth." The first part is simply classical Gnosis, and is in any case relative; the second draws an identity between man and God. The central teaching of the Koran is that only God is God, and that nothing created is God; nevertheless the divinization of man (*hulūl*) remains one of the key ideas that appears and reappears in Sufism even after having been extirpated, as happens from time to time, by reformers. The revealing touchstone is how al-Ḥallāj and the other "drunken Sufis" are treated by a particular Sufi group; usually the leading figure of the Sufi order affirms that he could have "corrected" al-Ḥallāj, or that al-Ḥallāj was rightly punished for going "too far" (namely making the "secret" of man's "essential divinity" public), but not that al-Ḥallāj was wrong or that the idea is false. Another touchstone is the emphasis on "past masters" who, by becoming intermediaries, become assimilated to God Himself by function. This takes the form of a ritual invocation of the figures in the *silsilah* or initiatic chain of the order. Antinomianism and divinization of the created are inseparable pairs; the one makes the forbidden, or what lies beyond the limit, licit, and the other makes the limited into an absolute.

The other doctrine is that of the "redemption of Satan" (and along with him the rehabilitation of other villains of the Koran, in particular, Pharaoh.) Al-Ḥallāj writes in the *Tāwāsīn* that Iblīs and Pharaoh were "his teachers". The idea that Satan is the perfect Muslim who would not bow to Adam as commanded because he would only worship God may have begun with Sahl at-Tustarī. It was taken up also by Ibn 'Arabī, 'Attar, 'Abd al-Karīm al-Jilī and by others. Ultimately the "redemption of Satan" was a Trojan Horse brought into Islam, an attempt to elevate an anti-principle or evil to the same status or reality as God.

In the Sunni world this antinomianism lies hidden even today within the folds of Sufism; this is not to say that all Sufis are unorthodox; many condemned it. Abū-l Mawahib ash-Shadhilī said of al-Ḥallāj: "Had he attained the reality of annihilation he would have been saved from the errors incurred through saying 'I am He'." Yet it persists nevertheless. Perhaps antinomianism's reason for existence, like the "fall of man" in the first place, is that by its very contradiction it draws a depth out of consciousness. One could also say that in order to know what we are, we have to know what we are not, and antinomianism teaches this. But it has been condemned by all the religions because by its nature it more often destroys the same consciousness in the process, creating solipsism and an all enclosing subjectivism, not to mention subverting a religion at its base. It was even al-Ḥallāj himself who said: "God threw a man into the sea with his arms tied behind his back, and said to him: Careful! Careful! or you will get wet in the water!" *See* BOUJLOUD; DÖNMEH; "SECRET SOCIETY"; DRUNKEN SUFIS; DUALISM; ḤALLĀJ;

MANICHEISM; "SATANIC VERSES"; SAHL TUSTARĪ; UMM al-KITAB.

Antinomy, *see* Al-KINDĪ.

Anwarī ('Alī Awḥadu'd-Din Anwarī d. *587*/1191?). Persian poet of Khāwarān in Khorāsān, studied science in Ṭūs, died in Balkh, achieved his fame during the reign of Sultan Sanjar. When he was a poor student he saw a man pass by gorgeously attired, on a fine horse, with servants, and upon learning that he was poet resolved to drop science and versify instead at the court of kings. Something which he regretted, because as a court poet he had to be ready on the spur of the moment to congratulate the royal eye upon spotting the "new moon of the month of fasting, or to console for a fall from a restive horse, or a bad throw at backgammon, or even a defeat in battle; even to offer condolence to a friend who had a toothache".

As a court poet he had a *rāwī*, or reciter, someone who had a beautiful voice and skill in declamation. Anwarī wrote a famous poem about the depredations of the Ghuzz in 1155 called the "Tears of Khorāsān".

Anwarī was also skilled in science, and an astrologer. In 1185 or 1186 a conjunction of five or seven planets took place in Libra and Anwarī unfortunately predicted a great wind that would overthrow buildings, trees, and cities. Many were alarmed and dug shelters. But on the fateful night a naked light burned unwavering in minarets, and the year that followed was calm. Naturally Anwarī became the butt of ridicule and another taunted:

> "Said Anwarī, 'fearful gales shall blow
> as houses, nay, e'en hills, shall overthrow.'
> The day proved breathless; Anwarī, I ween you
> And Aeolus must settle it between you."

Apocatastasis (Greek: "full restoration" from the verb *apokathistēmi* "to restore"). The first appearance of this doctrine is with Zoroastrianism where it is the third time of creation, the *wizarishn* when evil is destroyed at *frashokereti* and the world is restored to its state in the beginning before it was attacked by the evil spirit. This inspires the idea of the descent of the "heavenly Jerusalem" and other expectations of a blessed time to come. It also appears in a different form, that of the metaphysical doctrine that there is a "moment" in which there is no creation, no manifestation. In this version of the apocatastasis, beside God the Absolute, there is nothing. Because creation is inherent in the Divine Nature, this interval must be followed by the creation of other worlds anew. However, at this "moment" between creations, or between worlds, both the paradises and the hells of the previous creation disappear and existence is restored to the perfection that it possesses in the Principle.

In the West this doctrine is associated with the Stoic philosophers; it was later inherited by Christianity and was upheld by Clement of Alexandria, Origen, and St. Gregory of Nyssa. It was not understood in the same sense by all; Origen for example, believed that creation was eternal (which is directly contradictory to the principle at the root of the apocatastasis doctrine), and for him, the apocatastasis simply meant universal salvation; it is this "theological" interpretation of the apocatastasis doctrine that kept it from becoming a dogma of the early Christian Church, for fear that no-one would then strive for salvation. In Judaism the apocatastasis appears as the ultimate "return of all things to the One".

In Hinduism the apocatastasis is called the *mahā-pralaya*. The *Srīmad Bhagavatam* refers to it when Brahma says: "My play is ended, my day is done." The doctrine also exists in other traditions, notably in Buddhism in the moment in which there is no *samsāra* and all creatures realize *Nirvāna*, and in Judaism's "Be with Me".

There are allusions to such a doctrine in Islam among metaphysicians who point to this saying (which is so respected as to be often cited as a Ḥadīth): *Kāna-Lāhu wa lā shay'a ma'hu, wa Huwa-l-'ān kamā kān* ("God alone was and with Him nothing was; and He is now as He was"). Allusions to the doctrine appear again in another kind of story, found in different versions and often quoted by the Sufis, in which the Prophet leaves his close Companions; first 'Alī goes to look for him and finds him in meditation in a grove. 'Alī holds speech with him and leaves the grove; he meets 'Umar who asks him what the Prophet said, and when 'Alī discloses the Prophet's words (which are not related), 'Umar says that no one must know of this because then no one would strive for paradise. These words of the Prophet are understood to refer to such a doctrine, that must be kept secret. This is similar to the history of the doctrine of the apocatastasis in the early Eastern church, where it was held that the doctrine could not be made general knowledge for the very reason adduced by 'Umar.

The question of the apocatastasis is also at the root of the classical debate between theologians and Muslim Aristotelian philosophers. The philosophers, such as Avicenna, (Ibn Sīnā) argued that the world was eternal; the theologians argued that it was created in an event *ex nihilo*. The metaphysical perspective of the doctrine of the apocatastasis resolves the issue because in its light creation is "eternal" because, whether manifest or not, it is a permanent and necessary possibility "eternally" within the Absolute. On the other hand, the theological "Absoluteness" of God as Creator is maintained because there is, in a manner of speaking, a "moment", a "time" (an unmeasurable time because there is no reference), when the possibility of creation is *only* inherent and *not* manifest. There is nothing "beside" the Absolute. Then, when creation begins anew, it begins *ex nihilo*, out of nothing.

The import of this doctrine is that the paradises come to an end and that those who dwell in them are restored to a principal state, namely, Non-Being from which all beings issue in the first place (assuming, of course, the existence of an immortal soul). The hells also come to an end, which, for those who have not already been annihilated, is equivalent to a full pardon. Yet, rather than "universal salvation" it is, so to speak, a "reset" of manifestation — which includes the paradises and hells, and an affirmation of the Absoluteness of the Absolute. As a further Ḥadīth says: "By the God in Whose hands is my soul, there will be a time when the gates of hell will be closed and watercress will grow therein." Thus the doctrine appears in paradoxical formulations: if one believes that creation is eternal, the apocatastasis means a restoration of a perfect world before the "fall". If one believes that manifestation is not an essential condition of reality, it is the moment when there is no manifestation. If one believes that manifestation is constant and that creation is always going on, then apocatastasis will be interpreted as something in between. *See* ESCHATOLOGY; FIVE DIVINE PRESENCES; al-KINDĪ; PHILOSOPHY.

Apostasy. Although conversion from other religions to Islam is welcomed, apostasy from Islam is not admitted under Islamic law. However, punishment for apostasy (in any case, extremely rare) was not in practice enforced in later times and was completely abolished by the Turks by a decree of the Ottoman government in *1260*/1844. In Arabic, apostasy is called *irtidād* (or *riddah*) and an apostate is called a *murtadd*. *See* RIDDAH.

Apostasy, Wars of, *see* RIDDAH.

'Aqabah. A hill in Mina just outside Mecca. In June 620, following the Prophet's "year of sadness", six men of the tribe of Khazraj of the town of Yathrib (later to be called Medinah), accepted Islam from the Prophet at the hill of 'Aqabah during the Meccan pilgrimage. The following year, five of the original group returned to perform the pilgrimage in consort with seven others, including two men of the Aws, the other leading tribe of Yathrib. These twelve entered Islam and pledged fealty to the Prophet at night in the very place where the original five had entered Islam the year before.

They swore not to associate anything with God, not to steal, not to commit fornication, nor slay their offspring (*see* MAW'ŪDAH), nor utter slanders. They promised to obey the Prophet in that which is right. This oath became known as the First 'Aqabah. The Prophet accepted their allegiance saying:

> If you fulfill this pledge, then paradise is yours. If you commit one of the sins and then receive punishment for it in this world, that shall serve as expiation. And if you conceal it until the Day of Resurrection, then it is for God to punish or forgive as He wishes.

Mus'ad of the clan 'Abd ad-Dār went with the men to Yathrib and stayed with them eleven months to teach them the Koran and their religion. The following year, again during the pilgrimage, seventy-three men and two women (eleven of the men from the Aws, the rest from the Khazraj) took a similar oath at 'Aqabah. This time the men also pledged to fight and defend the Prophet. This was the oath of the Second 'Aqabah; the women at the Second 'Aqabah took the oath of the year before, without the pledge to fight, and this form of the oath became a model known as the "Oath of Women".

The Prophet's uncle al-'Abbās was present at the oath as a witness, even though he was then still a pagan. A Sūrah revealed before this event speaks of a mounting incline, a steep, which is in Arabic *al-'aqabah*.

No! I swear by this land,
and thou art a lodger in this land;
by the begetter, and that he begot,
indeed, We created man in trouble.
What, does he think none has power over him,
saying, 'I have consumed wealth abundant'
What, does he think none has seen him?

Have We not appointed to him two eyes,
and a tongue, and two lips,
and guided him on the two highways?
Yet he has not assaulted the steep;
and what shall teach thee what is the steep?
The freeing of a slave,
or giving food upon a day of hunger
to an orphan near of kin
or a needy man in misery;
then that he become of those who believe
and counsel each other to be steadfast,
and counsel each other to be merciful.

Those are the Companions of the Right Hand.
And those who disbelieve in Our signs,
they are the Companions of the Left Hand;
over them is a Fire covered down.
(Koran 90; an early Meccan Sūrah).

In September of 622 the Prophet emigrated to Yathrib. *See* HIJRAH; MUḤAMMAD.

'Aqīdah, *see* CREED.

'Aqīqah. A non-obligatory tradition of shaving the hair of a child on the seventh day after birth. Thereupon a sheep is sacrificed and the weight of the hair in silver is distributed to the poor. It is an old Arab practice confirmed by the Sunnah, or example, of the Prophet.

al-'Aql (lit. "intellect"). Sometimes used to mean "reason" or "thinking", but its highest and metaphysical sense, as used in Islamic philosophy, corresponds to the *intellect*, or *nous*, as understood in Platonism and Neoplatonism. It is the faculty which, in the microcosm or in man, is the embodiment of Being or Spirit. It is in this sense that the Rhenish mystic Meister Eckhart said: "There is something in the soul which is not created and not creatable, and this is the Intellect."

It is also what the Koran calls *ar-Rūḥ* (lit. "spirit"). The "Unity of the Intellect", or the essential identity of the Intellect in the metacosm (what is beyond the created world), the microcosm (man), and the macrocosm (the world, which is the manifestation of the possibilities of the metacosm), was expressed as a theory by Ibn Rushd (Averroes, d. *595*/1198), the philosopher and chief interpreter of Aristotle. But it is also implicit in most Islamic metaphysics when the question of *'aql* arises, even where there is little or no apparent connection with philosophy or mysticism.

This "Intellect", in the Eckhartian sense, is veiled behind discursive thought or reason; nevertheless, it is essentially the same — or not other — than its celestial prototype, the Divine Intellect. Through this transcendent Intellect man is capable of the "recognition" of Reality and of knowing the world, because the world is in fact contained within him, as the world is contained in Being. The Intellect makes possible direct knowledge, or *intellection*, that amounts to "revelation" on the plane of the microcosm, where the subject — because of his capacity for perfect objectivity — *comprehends* the object, seizes or "assimilates" it, and realizes an *identity* between the subject (his own mind) and the object. It is thus that Plato, and later St. Augustine, described knowing as remembering.

It is the presence of the Intellect within man that sets him apart from animals who participate in the cosmic Intellect peripherally, but do not contain it, since they do not occupy the "center" as does man. It is thus also that Adam knew the names of the objects of creation, whereas the Angels did not, being also peripheral, that is, not containing the projection of the Divine Intellect within them. The Angels, it is true, were superior to Adam in that they were less limited in their form; yet they bowed to him because he was truly vicegerent of God on earth, *khalīfatu 'Llāhi fī-l arḍ*: "Adam, tell them their names..." 2:33. *See* FIVE DIVINE PRESENCES.

Aq Qoyunlu. The "White Sheep" Turkmen confederation, so called from the emblem on their standards. The Aq Qoyunlu were a branch of the Ghuzz (or Oghuz, a division of the Turkic peoples), a steppe tribe who originally formed a part of the Golden Horde of the Mongol Khans.

The Aq Qoyunlu were rivals to the "Black Sheep" confederation or Qara Qoyunlu. The Aq Qoyunlu dominated a region centered around Diyarbakir in Anatolia. At times their control extended into 'Irāq and Persia. They ruled from

780/1378 until *913*/1507 when their domains were whittled away by the Ottoman Turks on the one side, and the Ṣafavids on the other.

'Aqrabah, Battle of, *see* MUSAYLAMAH.

al-Aqsā (lit. "the farthest" [mosque]). The name the Koran gives to the Temple Mount in Jerusalem and to the Temple of Solomon (also called *al-Bayt al-Muqaddas*, "the Holy House". The sanctuary known as "the Dome of the Rock" (*Qubbat aṣ-Ṣakhrah*, often called the "Mosque of 'Umar") dominates the Temple Mount today. From the rock, that was probably the site of the "Holy of Holies", the Prophet was carried by the Angel Gabriel through the heavens to the presence of God. (*See* NIGHT JOURNEY). At the other end of the Temple Mount stands the mosque called al-Aqsā (*Masjid al-Aqsā*), distinguished by its silver dome from the gold of the Dome of the Rock. The Aqsā mosque, one of the most important in Islam, is famous for its elaborately decorated walls. It was built at the end of the 7th century AD and is the largest mosque in Jerusalem. *See* DOME of the ROCK.

Aqsaqalism (from Turkish, "white beard"). A state sponsored anti-religious modern propaganda term that had been used in Muslim countries of the former Soviet Union to deride traditional respect for elders. This term of opprobrium means "rule by the greybeards".

Arabian Nights, *see* THE THOUSAND AND ONE NIGHTS.

Arabic. The language of the Koran, and the Arabs, today the most important language of the Semitic group, spoken by over 100 million people and understood by many more. The Arabic writing system has an alphabet of 28 consonants. It developed from Canaanite script (from which the later, square Hebrew letters are also derived) through Nabatean. The various Canaanite scripts evolved from a so-called "demotic", i.e. cursive, versions of Egyptian hieroglyphs. The Arabic writing system was introduced into Mecca not long before the revelation of the Koran. It underwent necessary refinements for some time after that, notably the creation of the vowel points. In South Arabia there existed another writing system found in Himyarite inscriptions; this disappeared from use in Arabia although it survives in an attenuated and barely recognizable form in Ethiopic script.

The Arabic of the Koran is similar to the *koine* used by the poets of the age, the *lingua franca* of its time, but cannot be equated with it, as the Koran is in every respect, unique. This *lingua franca* differed somewhat from the various tribal dialects and these gave rise to the different Koranic "readings" (*See* QIRĀ'AH.) Koranic Arabic is today a sacred language used only for reading the holy book and for prayer. So-called "classical" Arabic, as established by the usages found in the Koran and the Ḥadīth, is still used for composing books. It is also retained, with a very restricted and modified vocabulary, for journalism, broadcasting, conferences and so forth. The vernacular has, however, branched out into several principal dialects, mutually comprehensible for the most part as are, say, Spanish and Italian.

Arabic has provided most of the special vocabulary of Islam in use all over the world. In addition to religious vocabulary, vast numbers of Arabic words have been adopted into such African and Asian languages as Swahili, Hausa, Persian, Turkish, Urdu, and Malay. Arabic is also the liturgical language, not only of Islam, but of some Christian churches.

Muslims consider the Koran to be holy scripture only in the original Arabic of its revelation. The Koran, while it may be translated, is only ritually valid in Arabic. This is connected with the notion of Arabic as a "sacred Language". Language itself is sacred, because of its miraculous power to communicate and to externalize thought. In this sense, language is essentially the same as the Divine power of creation. In order to create, God speaks a Word in the Spirit; similarly, man externalizes what is within his mind by formulating words with the breath, by giving breath "form" in sound. The power of words to transmit to another consciousness the knowledge of the speaker lies in the fact that true words *are* themselves what they mean, or were at their origin; they are the object itself in sound. (*See* NAFAS ar-RAḤMĀN.) "Sacred" languages preserve this original power of language to an eminent degree; liturgical languages like Latin, the older forms of Greek, and Church Slavonic, have also preserved this power to a lesser degree.

Modern languages have, for the most part, lost this "sacred" quality; the identity between word, or "name", and the object named has become obscured; it is no longer direct, but indirect, through convention, or sign. This obscuration reflects the passage on the part of man from direct knowledge, or intellection, to reason, or indirect knowledge. The Biblical "mark of Cain", placed upon Cain's forehead, as much to protect him as to punish him, has been interpreted to signify this obscuration that took place at the dawn of time.

Arabic was the language of desert nomads, the most conservative of all peoples; it could be said that the desert protected the primordiality of Arabic over other languages by limiting phonetic decay, and by preventing confusion with other languages, loss of the meaning and the power of words, and syntactic degeneration. When it became the fabric of Islam, Arabic was protected further by the need to preserve the Koran unaltered. Thus classical Arabic has retained an ancient quality into modern times.

The nature of Arabic grammar and syntax, that avoids subordination and architectonic complexity (which are the distinctive qualities of Indo-European languages), assures a directness of style. The fact that Arabic (as some other languages such as Russian) does not need the copulative verb "to be" in definitions of being (*al-wujūd*) means that God can easily be referred to in a supra-ontological sense. The phrase *Allāh Huwa adh-Dhāt al-Mutlaqah* ("God is the Absolute Essence"), not involving the verb "to be" in Arabic, does not imply conceptual confinement to being, even pure Being. The case endings make possible great flexibility in sentence structure; the words of a sentence can be presented in more than one order; the meaning remains the same but points of emphasis can be varied. There is a highly developed system of verbal modes, that, by the introduction of prefixes and infixes, generate additional verbs from a given root with meanings which are for the most part predictable from the form of the verbal mode.

In Arabic, almost every word is derived from a simple "root", usually of three letters, most clearly visible in the verbal noun (*masdar*). The root corresponds to an abstract act. The act may be existential such as that expressed by the triliteral root *b-r-k* ("to settle") whence a deposit of water, such as a well (*birkah*), a blessing or spiritual influence (*barakah*, that is, that which comes down from above), or, again, the kneeling of a camel — all are "settling". Or it may represent a state: *k-b-r* ("to be big") or *r-ḥ-m* ("to be merciful") whence also *raḥim* or *riḥm* ("womb"). The letters or phonemes correspond to *al-a'yān ath-thābitah* ("immutable archetypes") in Being (tradition says the letters were taught to Adam by the Angel Gabriel). But the act of which the verbal root is a mysterious incarnation in sound takes place in consciousness: thus the tree of meaning branches from the verbal act-root — the nouns being derived from verbal forms — and the images that the language brings forth are ultimately to be traced back to awareness itself. The words are understood as concepts but they can also shatter concepts or submerge them and return to a threshold between the world and pure mind, where the vibration of sound faces creation on the side of perception, and the uncreated on the side of cognition. The Arabic grammarian Suyuti in the *Kitab al-Muzhir* compared the triliteral roots to "fixed stars" in the firmament beyond which is the empyrean of Being and said their number was 3,276.

While a given word has a specific meaning determined by convention, it also has a universal sense that is evoked by its "root"; language merges with reality. Thanks to the relationship of words to their roots, as if to a supraformal archetype, a deeper and more universal sense often superimposes itself upon a particular meaning in a phrase in classical Arabic. Simple statements, which are the rule in the Koran, open, under the right conditions of receptivity, into astonishing and vast horizons; the world is reduced to ripples in consciousness. These and other qualities make Arabic an incomparable medium for dialogue between man and God in prayer.

There is a saying that "Persian is the language of Paradise, but Arabic is the language of God." The Koran is recited only in Arabic, and even people who cannot read at all, in any tongue, keep Arabic Korans for the blessing of the Koranic presence. In Arabic, the Koran has a sublime beauty at which translations can only allude. Arabic is also the obligatory language of the canonical prayers (*ṣalāh*).

In the Middle Ages, Arabic was also the intellectual language of the Islamic East and was used by many nationalities and religions for literary and scientific compositions. The Persians in particular were great masters of Arabic. The scientist and scholar Abū Rayḥān al-Bīrūnī, who was born in Central Asia and not an Arab, wrote:

> Our religion and our empire are Arab... subject tribes have often joined together to give

the state a non-Arab character. But they have not been able to achieve their aim, and as long as the call to prayer continues to echo in their ears five times a day, and the Koran in lucid Arabic is recited among the worshipers standing in rows behind the *Imām*, and its refreshing message is preached in the mosques, they will needs submit; the bond of Islam will not be broken nor its fortresses vanquished.

Branches of knowledge from all countries in the world have been translated into the tongue of the Arabs, embellished and made seductive, and the beauties of the language have infused the veins and arteries of the peoples of those countries, despite the fact that each considers its own language beautiful, since it is accustomed to it and employs it in its daily offices. I speak from experience, for I was reared in a language in which it would be strange to see a branch of knowledge enshrined. Thence I passed to Arabic and Persian, and I am a guest in both tongues, having made an effort to acquire them, but I would rather be reproved in Arabic than complemented in Persian.

See also 'ABJAD; ALLĀH; ARABS; 'ILM al-ḤURUF; KORAN; QIRĀ'AH; as-SURYANIYYAH.

Arabs. The Semitic people indigenous to the Arabian peninsula. The name Arab is now applied to all peoples who speak Arabic as a mother tongue, including Muslims and Christians, but not Druzes and Arabic-speaking Jews. However, many Arab speakers have little or no Arab blood; they are instead descendants of the other ethnic families of the Middle East and North Africa.

When the Arabs came out of the Arabian peninsula with the expansion of Islam, their language was adopted by all those peoples who already spoke a cognate, Semitic (or, in some cases, Hamitic) tongue. Arab custom too was adopted far and wide, despite the fact that in many countries the Arabs themselves were a small minority who were absorbed and submerged into local populations. Peoples who are Arabs by blood as well as language are found in the Arabian peninsula from Yemen, and the African coast near Yemen, throughout the Syrian desert and southern 'Irāq. After the expansion of Islam they also emigrated in numbers large enough to maintain a tribal identity, like the Banū Hilāl in North Africa. In Algeria, Morocco and Mauritania Arabs make up less than half the population, while the majority is Berber; in Mauritania there is also a variety of West African peoples with close connections with Senegal. Communities of descendants of Arab emigrants, chiefly from the Hadramaut, are also found in Indonesia and Malaysia.

Geographers of antiquity divided Arabia into Arabia Felix — the Yemen, which receives the rains of the monsoon from the Indian Ocean and is luxuriously fertile, and Arabia Deserta — North Arabia. This also corresponds to the traditional division of the Arabs into two major groups: the South Arabians who believe that they are descended from a patriarch named Qaḥṭān, identified with Joktan of the Bible, and the North Arabians, who claim descent from a patriarch named 'Adnān, and through him, from Ishmael (Ismā'īl), son of Abraham. Both northern and southern groups were also divided further into two social groups: the *ahl al-madar*, or house dwellers, and the *ahl al-wabar* ("the people of goat-hair"), tent-dwellers, or Beduins (from *badiya*, "wilderness").

The name Arab means "nomad". The North Arabs are considered *'Arab al-musta'ribah*, "Arabized Arabs", while the Qaḥṭānis of the south consider themselves *'Arab al-muta'arribah*, or tribes resulting from mixing with the *'Arab al-'aribah*, original, or "true Arabs". From the Qaḥṭānis, through a traditional ancestor called Himyar, descend the Arabs of the ancient South Arabian or "Himyaritic" kingdoms. The completely "true Arabs", descendants of Aram son of Shem son of Noah, (son-in-law of the Arabic-speaking Jurhum who, according to Arab tradition, was with Noah in the Ark) are called the *'Arab al-bā'idah*, "the lost Arabs", who, like the "lost tribes of Israel", are "lost", or rather "remote", because their names, while remembered by posterity, are lost to them: their identity has been submerged in that of other peoples. These are the tribes of 'Abil, 'Ād, 'Imlik, Jadis, Jurhum, Tasm, Thamūd, Umaiyim, and Wabir. The Koranic "Thamūd", who were destroyed by God for turning away from His revelations made through the Prophet Ṣāliḥ, are identified with the Nabateans. Koranic commentators make the people against whom the Jews fought coming out of the Desert after the captivity in Egypt remnants of the tribe of 'Ād (symbolically so, for 'Ād is traditionally located in the south of Arabia, a people the Koran says were destroyed for repudiating the Prophet Hūd).

The distinction between South and North Arabian tribes, and a certain opposition due to different traditions, caused tension in later Arab history, as long as the groups maintained a consciousness of their identities. One example is the differences that erupted in Medinah on the death of the Prophet, between the *Muhājirūn*, North Arabians from Mecca, and the *Anṣār*, native Medinans who were originally of South Arabian origin. After the death of Yazīd I, strife broke out in Syria and 'Irāq between the North Arab tribal group of the Qays, and the South Arab Kalb, a conflict that persisted throughout the Umayyad Caliphate.

Two trees grow in the Yemen that were crucial to the economy of the ancient Arabs and influenced their history. One tree produces frankincense that was burned as a fragrance in large quantities in pagan religious ceremonies. The other, myrrh, was used in cosmetics and the embalming of the dead. In antiquity before Christianity became dominant, these substances were in such demand that they made the Yemen a source of wealth to those who ruled it. Besides the incense trade and agriculture in those areas that could support it, the Beduins lived by the raising of camels and livestock that were traded in the markets of Syria and Egypt.

In ancient times the incense trade of the Yemen attracted settlers from the fertile crescent. On the other hand, population pressures in the Yemen forced some clans into the desert to wander in a pattern that progressed northward often bringing them to settle, finally, after wanderings over the course of centuries, in the north. The Kindah tribe, of which the famous poet Imru'-l-Qays was chief, left the Yemen in the fifth century BC and wandered in the Syrian desert before returning to the Yemen shortly before the revelation of Islam.

The time before Islam was called the *Jāhiliyyah* ("the Age of Ignorance"). Its great events were the feuds and raids between desert Arabs. These were recorded in poetic lays called the *Ayyām al-'Arab*, "the Days of the Arabs", that were handed down orally. The importance of poetry to the Arabs persists to this day. It is the principal art form of the nomad, as pictures are the principal art form of sedentary peoples, because poetry recreates the dimension of time (the "invisible" dimension to the nomad wanderer in space) by the succession of sounds. Poetry thus manifests time, the complement to space, which is the dominant life dimension of the hunter-nomad, who meets his prey in space in the destiny of an instant, or pastures his flocks in the endless wilds. Similarly, the picture manifests simultaneity, or space, the complement to the dominant life dimension of the sedentary-farmer whose existence is based on the cycles of planting and harvesting, and thus upon time.

In the Age of Ignorance great markets existed, such as that at 'Ukaz, in which an important attraction was the declaiming of poetry. The most acclaimed poems were written in gold letters and hung in the Ka'bah at Mecca. The idea of one God, inherent in the very Name Allāh ("the God") was ancient among the Arabs. Christianity and Judaism were practiced throughout the peninsula. Through Byzantine influence, Christian communities arose in such places as Najrān in the south of Arabia, which was important enough to be the seat of a bishop. Christian hermits also lived in the deserts, and there were isolated Christians in the midst of otherwise pagan tribes. Besides tribes of Jewish origin living in Arabia, there were also Jewish converts from among the Arabs. In the Yemen in AD 525 the King Dhu Nuwās, who had been converted to Judaism, tried also to convert the Christians of Najrān to Judaism by force, and when they refused, he had them thrown into a burning pit. The martyrs of Najrān are honoured in the Koran (85:4-8).

Another religious group before Islam were the *hunafā'* (sing. *hanīf*), a word of uncertain origin indicating the generally hermitic adherents of a primordial — or perennial — monotheism that went back to Ismā'īl and Abraham. By the seventh century this Abrahamic monotheistic consciousness among the Arabs had all but disappeared. In its place there was a proliferation of idols. The sanctuary of the Ka'bah, originally dedicated to the one God, was filled with objects made of wood and stone representing deities brought from all the lands with which the Meccans traded. Drinking, boasting and feuding prevailed; worship at the Ka'bah became mere "whistling and clapping of hands" (Koran 8:35). Within twenty years all was to change when the Center irrupted into the history of the Arabs and the world was accorded the last divine message: the revelation of Islam.

The revelation of the Koran began around the year 612; by 636 the whole peninsula was converted. Islam has since been adopted by men and women from every people and nation. Its universality is evident, but at the same time Islam everywhere has been marked by the Arab soul. It incarnates something of the purity of the desert, a liberation from time into space, and from form into act; an awakening from the past and a discovery of the eternal in the present, and the nomad's sense of life as a unique journey. According to Aristotle (and, for that matter, in the doctrine of the Tao), the absence of a quality contains potentially its opposite. The desert is the prototype of existence reduced to its essential, to a kind of void. In its emptiness the desert calls forth plenitude, in its receptivity it calls forth the Absolute. *See* 'ABBĀSIDS; ARABIC; ABRAHAH; 'ĀD; BAGHDAD; DAMASCUS; DHU NUWĀS; HŪD; IBN KHALDŪN; IMRU‘-l-QAYS; ISMĀ‘ĪL; JĀHILIYYAH; MA‘RIB DAM; MECCA; MEDINAH; MUḤAMMAD; NAJRĀN; QURAYSH; SABA‘; ṢĀLIḤ; SHU'AYB; THAMŪD; 'UKAZ; UMAYYADS.

al-A‘rāf Ar. the "heights", or "high ground" (from which a clear view is possible of the sky and the low-lying land) and hence a symbolical place between heaven and earth, a limbo for those who do not merit hell but cannot enter heaven. This otherwordly locus may also be considered a kind of "purgatory" but a beneficent one, with privation but without suffering. This interpretation is based upon several verses in Sūrah al-A‘rāf, notably verses 46 and 47.

And between them is a veil, and on the Ramparts
are men knowing each by their mark,
who shall call to the inhabitants
of Paradise: 'Peace be upon you!
They have not entered it, for all their eagerness.'
And when their eyes are turned
towards the inhabitants of the Fire
they shall say, 'Our Lord, do not Thou
assign us with the people of the evildoers.'

There exists also the concept of a purgatory of suffering, in the sense that many theologians, such as Ibn Ḥazm, have maintained that if a believer went to hell it would be for a limited and not an indefinite duration; he would be released into paradise when the sins that brought him there were exhausted. Non-believers, however, would remain in hell indefinitely, that is, until the awareness of an individual self disappeared. Massignon believed that the Christian concept of an eschatological limbo (*limbus*) may have come from the Muslim interpretation of the *al-Ar'āf* of the Koran. Before the concept of purgatory appeared in either Christianity or Islam, it appeared among the Manicheans. The *elect*, upon death, were led heavenward by a light-maiden sent to guide them. This guide repelled the attacks of the devils, after which the soul rested in the moon, then in the sun, and then entered the light paradise. The *hearers* on the other hand, who were burdened with "lower elements", burned a while in purgatory where these base elements were burned away, and then they proceeded on their heavenly journey. *See* CHILDREN; ESCHATOLOGY.

'Arafāt. A plain 12 miles/19 kilometers southwest of Mecca which lies partly outside the restricted area of the *ḥaram*. One of the culminating stations of the great pilgrimage (*ḥajj*) takes place here. On the 12th *Dhu-l-Ḥijjah*, or *yawm 'Arafāt*, the pilgrims assemble on the plain, continually repeating the talbiyyah formula. Attendance at 'Arafāt, at least for a short time — most pilgrims stay from noon to sunset — is obligatory for the accomplishment of the rites of the pilgrimage.

In the 19th century a Christian disguised as a Muslim, John Fryer Keane (Ḥajj Muḥammad Amīn) visited 'Arafāt. His experience is described thus: "The sides of 'Arafāt were thickly clothed with men, and thence they extended one mile and a half to the south, and half a mile across, 'a rippling sea of black heads and white bodies.' The distant countries from which they came, and the object that brought them, filled him with awe. 'Could all this be of no avail, and all this faith be in vain?' If so, it was enough to make a man lose faith in everything of the kind." (*See* PILGRIMAGE)

The name 'Arafāt, is variously interpreted. It came from the root 'arifa "to know", "to recognize", and is most commonly taken to refer to Adam and Eve, separated from each other by the Fall from Eden, and, according to tradition, reunited here and "recognizing" one another. At one end of 'Arafāt is a prominence called "the Mount of Mercy" (*Jabal ar-Raḥmah*), which is the place of choice to pass the day of the pilgrimage.

The massive gathering of humanity that takes place here in the *ḥajj*, a million or more from all over the world, is unique. It has been interpreted symbolically as a foretaste of the Day of Judgement.

al-Arba'ayn (lit. "the forty"). A family ceremony to commemorate the death of one of the members forty days after the event. The practices vary, but often include inviting religious dignitaries for the reading of the Koran, prayers, and a meal. Another commemoration may be held on the first anniversary of the death. It is common in Arab countries for the women to visit the graves of family members on Fridays. In Arabic the number 40 and the letter *mīm* are the same; *mīm* is written as a circle and represents death, or *mawt* whose first letter is also *mīm*. In religions that have evolved from Semitic beginnings, this meaning of the number is retained. Thus some Christian churches, notably the Orthodox, also commemorate the fortieth day after death, and Jesus spends forty days in the desert (dying to his previous nature after baptism). This is also the etymology of the medical term "quarantine", the time for an illness to die away. *See* FUNERALS.

Archegos (also in Persian *Sardar*, and in Latin, *Princeps Magistrorum*). The Greek name of the head of the Manichean religion and the successor to Mani, the Apostle of the "God of Truth". (In the sect of the Elkhasites it was also the title of Elkhasios.) The Archegos was at the head of a hierarchy below which, there were, in Latin: *magistri* (twelve in number, in Greek *didaskaloi*), *episcopi*, *presbyteri*, and then the *electi* and *auditores* (the "hearers"). Mani died, after 26 days in chains, put to death, as "useless and pernicious", by the King of Iran at the instigation of the Zoroastrian head Priest Kartir, in Jundishapur on February 26, 274. His first two successors were Sissinios (in 281 after an interregnum, martyred under Vahram II in 291 or 286) and Innaios, who was also, according to tradition, and in imitation of the perfect master, martyred. (Innaios, brother of Zabed, had also been sent by Mani, with Mani's father Patticius, to India to consolidate Mani's conversions there, and was probably the Lakhmid King Amar's ambassador to Narses to obtain an end to persecution of Manicheans. The Lakhmid King in Ḥīrah, near present day Kūfah in 'Irāq, was their protector.)

The period of Mani's imprisonment became the Manichean month of fasting (in February or March), and the 30th day ending the fast became the principal religious ceremony, the *Bēma*. (Mani died on the 26th day of the fast and returned to life on the 27th, whence the probable origin of the idea that the Islamic *Laylat-al-Qadr* — the descent of the Koran — took place on the 27th day of Ramaḍan). The *Bēma* was a feast, or *agapé*, held in front of an empty throne celebrating Mani's resurrection, alive and present in the invisible. During the ceremony words are addressed to the throne. (In 687, Mukhtār the 'Irāqi revolutionary, spoke to an empty throne in Aramaic, telling those Arabs who were puzzled, that this was "the throne of 'Alī". Interestingly, to this day, the ruler of Spain addresses Saint James in Compostella, once a year with an account of the year's events.)

This feast in front of the empty throne must be the origin of the Koran's description of martyrs (3:169): "count not those who are slain in the way of God as dead; nay, they are living; with their lord they have food."

According to an-Nadīm, a bookseller of Baghdad, in 985, the leader of the Manicheans, the "Imām", (the Archegos) was obliged by tradition to remain in Ctesiphon (al-Madā'in) the capital of the Sāssānid Persian empire, the way the Pope is expected to remain in Rome. For the Manicheans, the place bore the symbolic title "Babel". Ctesiphon was sacked by the Arabs in March 637 and afterwards declined considerably in importance. With the 'Abbāsids, however, the decision to place the new Muslim capital, Baghdad (thereafter interpreted as meaning "Gift of God"), twenty miles or thirty-three kilometers northwest from Ctesiphon brought the political center of the immediate world back to the residence of the Archegos. It should be noted that an Iranian scholar, Zabih Bihruz has made the claim that al-Manṣūr, who founded Baghdad, was secretly a Manichean, for political reasons. (Coins struck in Ctesiphon/al-Madā'in during the Muslim period called the city *al-Bāb*, "the Gate", similar to the name *Bābā* which the city was called on Sāssānid coins.)

The Manichean religion was repeatedly persecuted everywhere, from Rome to Syria, and later in China. In Iran those who tried to escape these persecutions often fled to the Arab city of al-Ḥīrah (which later was absorbed into Kūfah), where they were given protection by the Lakhmid rulers, and to Yemen, and to Khorāsān. With the Arab conquest, after the oppression of the Sāssānids, the Umayyads in the person of the governor of 'Irāq, al-Ḥajjāj, showed the Manicheans the same tolerant treatment extended to Christians and Jews. A later governor even gave gifts to the Archegos.

In the sixth century or earlier, the Manicheans had split into two groups; those beyond the Oxus (Āmū Daryā) formed a new sect and were called, after the nameof a city, Dinawar, or *dīn* as "pure religion" the *Dēnawārs* or *Dīnāwarīyyah*. (The term meant both this branch as well as "*electī*".) This sect challenged the leadership of the Archegos, and the injunction that the leader must remain in Ctesiphon. They had another leader in Khorāsān: Shād Ōhrmizd. In the seventh century a rich man called Zād Hurmuz joined the sect in Mesopotamia when the Archegos in Ctesiphon was a figure called Mihr, and with the help of the secretary of the Muslim governor of 'Irāq, a reconciliation was brought about between the Archegos (Mesopotamia) and the sectarians, the Dēnāwars (who were in Khorāsān). After Mihr, Zād Hurmuz became Archegos in Ctesiphon and was then succeeded by a new Archegos, who was more orthodox, and stricter, called Miqlāṣ. A new division then became apparent between partisans of the policy of Mihr, which seemed to be compromise and coexistence with the rulers and the changing times, a policy described as "relationship" *wisālat*, and the strict, more orthodox policy of Miqlāṣ which was to not compromise; and this gave a new division, the *Mihriyyah* and the *Miqlāsiyyah*. Mihr, it seems, had received a gift of a mule for riding, a silver seal, and embroidered garments — forbidden luxuries, from the Umayyad governor of 'Irāq, Khālid ibn 'Abd Allāh al-Qasrī (governor 724-738).

This division between hardliners and pragmatists, is hauntingly similar to the division between Trotskyites ("world revolution") and Stalinists ("Communism in one country") in the 20th century, not to mention the obvious parallel between Qarmaṭīs and Fāṭimids that was to occur just a bit later in the 10th century.

This division was for a time mitigated under an Archegos who came from North Africa (Tunisia and Algeria were the greatest center of Manicheism outside the Middle East, a center that produced both Saint Augustine and the unfortunate Faustus. This may account for the name of Algeria which means the "islands" a term for gnostic jurisdictions or bishoprics.) This Archegos, perhaps of Berber origin, as were some of the wives of several Shī'ite Imāms, was Abū Hilāl ad-Dayḥuri who was in office in Ctesiphon when Baghdad was founded by al-Manṣur.

With the advent of the 'Abbāsids, relations between the dominant Muslims and Manicheans were at first *very* good. Reputed Crypto-Manicheans (according to an-Nadīm) like the Barmakids, who had been hereditary chief-priests in an apparently Manichean Buddhist monastery in Balkh took part in the 'Abbāsid revolution and then became viziers. Their leader Khālid ibn Barmak (d. *161*/785) was one of those who chose Baghdad as the new capital. A Manichean-like sect called the Rāwāndiyyah played an important part in the 'Abbāsid revolution, and its chief architects, such as Abū Muslim and his follower al-Muqanna' both had other, highly dualist, religious agendas. The Caliph Mahdī (*158-169*/775-785), however,began persecuting Manicheans, using special judges who were "experts" ('arif) to prosecute in *170*/786 those, as Massignon says, who tended toward "dualism by their contempt for the sexual life on earth and for the eating of meat". (p. 382 *The Passion of al-Ḥallaj*). Innocent though this seems when Massignon describes it, nevertheless, this included a political program that meant overthrowing the Muslims' world order. Ṭabarī says that in *141*/758 the "Master of the Zindiqs" or inquisitor (*ṣāḥib az-zanādiqa*) 'Umar al-Kalwādhi died, and Ḥamdawayh, who was Muḥammad ibn 'Isa of the people of Maysān took his place. The Caliph al-Mahdī discovered that the tutor of his son (this would have been a Barmakid) was a Manichean and understandably became upset and intensified investigations. Al-Mahdī warned his son al-Hādi before his succession about Manicheans; al-Hādi said "if I live I shall certainly exterminate this sect in its entirety"; but he suddenly died two months later, apparently poisoned before his program got rolling.

Hārūn ar-Rashīd who succeeded al-Hādi did not continue the persecution and for seventeen years gave the Barmakids free rein until suddenly in *187*/805 he imprisoned members of the family and had one, his bosom friend Ja'far ibn Yaḥyā ibn Barmak, executed. The successor to Hārūn, al-Ma'mūn (ruled *198-218*/813-833), restored some kind of *entente*, and is counted by an-Nadīm *as a Manichean* "who lied" about his inner convictions. By the end of the *3rd*/9th century a crisis point was reached and around the reign of al-Muqtadir (*295-320*/908-932), the Archegos left Baghdad. As an-Nadīm says:

> But [subsequently] the leader sought out any place where he could be safe. The last time they appeared was during the days of al-Muqtadir, for [after that] they feared for their lives and clung to Khurāsān. Any one of them who remained kept his identity secret as he moved in this region. About five hun-

dred of their men assembled at Samarqand, but when their movement became known, the ruler of Khurāsān wished to kill them. But the king of China [an-Nadīm means the Uighur Khan, the Idiqut, of Chinese Turkestan, a Manichean Kingdom], who I suppose was the lord of the Tughuzghuz, sent to him, saying. "There are more Muslims in my country than there are people of my faith in your land." He also swore to him that if he [the ruler of Khurāsān] should kill one of them [the Manicheans], he [the king of China] would slaughter the whole community [of Muslims] who were with him, and would also destroy the mosques and appoint spies among the Muslims in the country as a whole, so as to slay them. So the ruler of Khurāsān left them alone except for attracting tribute from them. Although they have become few in the Islāmic regions, I used to know about three hundred of them in the City of Peace [Baghdad] during the days of Mu'izz ad-Dawlah [946-967]. But at this time [986] there are not five of them in our midst. The people [the Manicheans], who are called Ajārā are at Rustāq, Samarqand, Ṣughd (Sughd), and especially Tūnkath [Tashkent]. (Bayard Dodge; page 802-803, *Fihrist*)

Louis Massignon said that the Archegos "who was watched closely by the Muslim police from the very beginning of the conquest" left *precisely* in *296*/908, "exiled to Soghdiana". He did not explain how he arrived at this date but the reasoning can be deduced from the following events. The Caliph Muqtadir, the 18th 'Abbāsid Caliph, succeeded his elder brother Muktafī on *13 Qa'dah 295*/August 14, 908 when he was thirteen years old. He was deposed, for a day, on *20-21 Rabī' 296*/December 17-18, 908, by his cousin 'Abū-l'Abbās ibn al-Mu'tazz al-Muntasif bi'Llāh, (and, again towards the end of his reign, for three days, by his brother al-Qahīr bi-Llāh February 28-March 2, 929) and finally killed in *320*/932.

Al-Muqtadir was originally put, and kept, on the throne by Shī'ite bankers and Shī'ite secretaries. The unsuccessful backers of Ibn al-Mu'tazz ("the Caliph for a day") who deposed al-Muqtadir in 908 were Sunnis. Evidently, Massignon saw in this struggle between Sunni and Shī'ite backers, that the Shī'ites were the ones who were more dangerous, and less tolerant, as regards the Archegos and Manicheism in general. The "Hidden Imām" of the Twelve-Imām Shī'ites condemned al-Ḥallāj to death for Crypto-Manicheism five years before al-Muqtadir signed the court's decision for the same crime, and, conversely, al-Ḥallaj had supported the Caliphate of al-Mu'tazz. Also, the Shī'ites, much more than the Sunnis, understood the Manicheans, and recognized them when they were pretending to be Sunnis, because the Shī'ites were themselves related to the Manicheans by Gnostic family ideology, being themselves virtually a by-product of the Manichean attempt to take over nascent Islam. Being related, they knew their rivals and were less tolerant. The Baghdadi Shī'ite leader, ash-Sharīf al-Murtaḍā had the famous blind poet al-Ma'arrī "dragged from his house by the foot", when the latter visited the capital and this is understandable when one knows the theology of the event. Moreover, the so-called "Sunni" secretaries who would have been the supporters of Ibn al-Mu'tazz were precisely a class that had been created by the Barmakids and were, many of them, Crypto-Manicheans to begin with.

Thus Massignon either intuited, or knew by evidence which he did not present, that the defeat of al-Mu'tazz's party, and the victory of the Shī'ites, was a struggle between Manicheans and Shī'ites for the control of the nominally Sunni Caliphate, and it signaled the coming of the final peril for the Archegos which precipitated his departure, which, he says, was for Soghdiana. But there Manicheans were also being persecuted, and were only tolerated by counter-threats from the Uyghur ruler of Qocho (a name for Turfan in Chinese Turkestan, see XINJIANG).

Besides the failed *coup de état* of Ibn al-Mu'tazz, there was a conjunction of Jupiter and Saturn in the constellation of Aries on the 13th of March 908. The Ismā'īlis had been playing on astrological beliefs and using the conjunctions of these two planets, planets relating to royalty and dynasty, as propaganda to create expectations of historical changes of cosmic proportions (another conjunction had taken place in 895 and the last of the prophesied series of conjunctions was to take place in 928). Having created expectations, they then created events to match. Prophecies to this effect had been circulated a century earlier, and the culmination was to take place imminently.

The Archegos left Ctesiphon. When Muḥammad fled Mecca for Medinah, he left in his bed his nephew 'Alī to trick the Meccans into believing that he was still there. When the Assassins agreed to give up a castle to the 'Abbāsids hundreds of years later, they made an agreement; half of the garrison was to leave; if that went well, then the second half of the garrison would leave. The first half left, and warned they must not be harmed because the remainder would not give up if the first half was attacked. The 'Abbāsid army waited for the second half to leave. And waited. And waited.

The Archegos left. But did he leave someone behind to keep the authorities thinking he was still in Ctesiphon in 908 or even later? Did he put out disinformation to mislead people regarding his destination? Did he first send a stalking horse to attract danger to himself, and then follow when the coast was clear? Or did a split occur with the Archegos going in one direction, leading a dwindling number of overt Manicheans adrift into oblivion, while a pretender, say a Bishop, from a party more willing to call themselves Muslims, went in the other direction with more success?

The trial of al-Ḥallāj, executed in *312*/922 in Baghdad for *zandaqah* (crypto-Manicheism) signaled the persecution of thousands of what Massignon called "Ḥallajians" who were vegetarians, just like outward Manicheans (history actually calls Massignon's Ḥallājians Ismā'īlīs). By 985 an-Nadīm writes, the Manicheans who had been numerous in Baghdad, were reduced to five. Classical Manicheism disappeared from the Islamic empire (but persisted in China); at the same time a new sect appeared, divided into two groups, Qarmaṭīs and Fāṭimids. The ones who were willing to make the greatest concessions to Islam, the Fāṭimids, founded a rival empire, and in 962, they also founded a rival capital to Baghdad, called Cairo, whose full name means "The Victorious City of the Exalter of the Religion of God." *See* FĀṬIMIDS; al-MADĀ'IN; BARMAKIDS; al-MA'MŪN; al-ḤALLAJ; MANICHEISM; QUṬB; ABŪ MUSLIM; IBN MU'TAZZ.

'Arīf or 'Ārif (lit. "a knower"). Formerly a term applied to someone who was expert in some field, such as an architect. The gardens of the Generalife in Granada are so called from the Arabic *jannatu-l-'arīf*, the "garden of the architect", or, the "knower". *'Ārif* has the technical meaning in Sufism: "someone possessed of direct knowledge of God". The highest station of Sainthood is an *'Ārif bi'Llah* or "knower by (or through) God", the equivalent of the Sanskrit *jivanmukta* in Vedanta (someone not only saved, or admitted to a superior condition of existence, but liberated, in this case "liberated in life"; that is, liberated from all becoming). *Ma'rifah* describes this state of "knowing" and is generally translated "gnosis".

Ibn 'Aṭā' Allāh says in the *Ḥikam*: "Not all who are most certainly amongst the chosen go on to perfect their liberation."

'Arīf was also the title of the "expert" appointed by the Caliph Mahdī to investigate crypto-Manicheans in the Empire. *See* SAINTS.

Arkān ad-dīn, *see* FIVE PILLARS.

Arqam (d. *55*/674). A Companion and early convert to Islam. Arqam was one of the *muhājirūn* who emigrated to Medinah because of religious persecution in Mecca. He took part in the great battles of Islam's struggle for survival, and lived to an old age.

His house in Mecca stood at the foot of the hill of Ṣafā near the Ka'bah (because he was from one of the important families, one of the "Quraysh of the Hollow"). The house of Arqam was one of the most important early meeting places of the Muslims before the conversion of 'Umar. The site is now incorporated into the present Grand Mosque of Mecca.

Artifice, legal, *see* HILAH.

al-'Arsh (lit. "throne"). The Koran speaks often of the "throne" of God (7:54; 9:129 and others). One interpretation is that the throne symbolizes Being. According to tradition, God's throne is inscribed with the words "My Mercy outstrips My Wrath" (*inna raḥmatī sabaqat ghadabī*). The Koran also refers to *al-kursī*, which is synonymous with *al-'arsh*. In the human microcosm it corresponds to "the heart".

An 'Isawa litany says: "My Master! place me in the shadow of Your throne the Day when there will be no shadow but Thine." *See* al-KURSĪ; FIVE DIVINE PRESENCES.

'Aṣabīyyah (from *'aṣab*, "stalks" that bind together). Tribal or group solidarity in the face of those outside the group. Ibn Khaldūn's observations on society in the *Prolegomena* made the term famous.

Ascetic, *see* ZĀHID.

Aṣḥāb an-Nabī, *see* COMPANIONS.

Aṣḥāb al-Ukhdūd (lit. "people of the ditch"). The Christians of Najrān who were burned alive in AD 525 by Dhu Nuwās, a tyrant from the Yemen who tried to convert them forcibly to Judaism. The people of the ditch are extolled by the Koran as martyrs (85:4). *See* NAJRAN.

Aṣḥāb aṣ-Ṣuffāḥ (lit. "the people of the bench"). Poor Muslims who flocked to Medinah and were to be found sitting on a bench near the Prophet's house, hoping to receive sustenance. At this time the Prophet himself lived in extreme poverty, yet he gave to the "people of the bench" and said "The food of one is enough for four, and the food of four is enough for eight."

Of the early period in Medinah the histories say:

> In those days the Prophet would go to the room of one or the other of his wives and ask: "Is there anything to eat?" And the answer might be "No." "Then I fast today" he would say.
>
> "We used to be as long as forty days on end and never lit a fire, in those times," 'Ā'ishah said.
>
> "Believers," the Prophet said "are content in all circumstances" (*Al-Mu'minūna fī kulli ḥālin bi-khayr*).

The straitened circumstances of the Muslims' lives lasted until the conquest of Khaybar, and improved continually thereafter. When he became Caliph, 'Umar once laughed in disbelief when he was told that half of the year's revenue from Baḥrayn amounted to a million dirhams. But he found out afterwards that it was true. When the people gathered in the mosque for prayer, 'Umar spoke to them: "I have got from Baḥrayn a huge sum of money: will ye take your shares weighed out? Or must I count it over to you coin by coin?"

'Asharah Mubāsharah (lit. "ten well-betided ones"). Ten Companions to whom the Prophet foretold they would enter Paradise. They were: Abū Bakr, 'Umar, 'Uthman, 'Alī, Ṭalḥāh, az-Zubayr, 'Abd ar-Raḥmān, Sa'd ibn Abī Waqqās, Sa'īd ibn Zayd, Abū 'Ubaydah ibn al-Jarrāh.

al-Ash'arī, Abū-l-Ḥasan 'Alī ibn Ismā'īl (*260-324*/873-935). He is considered to be the founder of Sunnī *Kalām*, or theology. Born and raised in Baṣrah, until the age of forty al-Ash'arī was a Mu'tazilite and the student of al-Jubba'ī (d. *303*/915; *see* MU'TAZILITES). At that point he put this famous question (here paraphrased from the many versions recorded of al-Ash'arī's thought-experiment) to his teacher: "Take the case of three brothers, one a believer who did good works, one a sinner, and one who died in infancy. What would happen to them?" His teacher answered that "the believer went to paradise, the sinner to hell, and the infant to limbo." "Well", asked al-Ash'arī, "since according to the Mu'tazilite doctrine of *al-aṣlaḥ*, God always chooses the best for his creatures, why did the infant die?" "Because", the teacher answered, "God knew the infant would go on to be a sinner, and so ended his life at the stage that avoided hell, the most advantageous solution." "Then", asked al-Ash'arī, "why did God let the sinner grow to the age of responsibility and be punished for his sin?" (Regarding salvation of children, *see* CHILDREN.)

To this, Mu'tazilite rationalism had no answer, and with this episode al-Ash'arī abandoned their school, became a Ḥanbalī Sunnī, and made public repentance and repudiation in the mosque of Baṣrah for his errors. (Al-Ash'arī actually stood up in a Mosque and said that he had been in error; public, objective repudiation is a necessary condition to escape from any thought control or cult; conversion to Catholicism requires a statement "renouncing the Devil and all his works".)

Although al-Ash'arī considered himself a Ḥanbalī, the Ḥanbalīs themselves accord little place to theology. Like the Ḥanbalīs, al-Ash'arī asserted that the Koran was completely uncreated, even in its letters and sounds; in the school of theology that bears his name, however, the Koran is uncreated in its essence, but created when it takes on a form in letters and sounds, when, that is, it is written or recited.

Despite his repudiation, however, al-Ash'arī went on to apply the Mu'tazilite use of dialectic and rational methods to the dogmas of orthodox Islam, except that whereas they used logic to bring everything down to a horizontal plane, he accepted the transcendent aspects of divinity but, as it were, set them "off limits" to speculation by the use of the formula *bilā kayfa*, "without asking how". He assumed the acts of God to be inscrutable and beyond accountability. In particular, he exalted God's Will to be so far beyond human comprehension that it became absolute in itself, beyond coherence, and even purely arbitrary. According to al-Ash'arī, God could punish good if He so willed, and send the pious to hell.

This is clearly a reaction to the Mu'tazilite desire to reduce the vertical dimension of Divine transcendence and mystery to that of horizontal, and human, logic. But it was al-Ash'arī who actually legitimized the use of some of the Mu'tazilite methods in many domains because he became one of the most accepted authorities in theology. Thus, in the end, he achieved precisely a reformed rationalism, or even, one could say, a reformed Mu'tazilitism.

Al-Ash'arī, denying the existence of secondary causes, is also known for the doctrine of *kasb* (lit. "acquisition") regarding action. According to him, any act such as the mere raising of the hand, is created by God, but *acquired* by the creature who thus takes responsibility for it. This is a device to ascribe free will for man and therefore responsibility, but to reserve all power of action to God alone. In other words, it is an attempt to resolve the opposition between freedom and determinism without resorting to antinomy or to formulations that are contradictory on one plane and resolved on a higher plane. (Although it could be said that what al-Ash'arī actually produced was a reverse antimony.)

Van den Bergh wrote that the "Ash'arītes... are forced by the weight of evidence to admit a certain irrationality in theological concepts, and their philosophical speculations, largely based on Stoicism, are strongly mixed with Sceptical theories. They hold the middle way between the traditionalists who want to forbid all reasoning on religious matters and those who affirm that reason unaided by revelation is capable of attaining religious truths." Within the Ash'arīte scheme of things it is technically impossible to make a statement about the *present* without saying "if God wills" whereas normally this proviso — *in shā'a-Llāh* — is only applied to the future. The great achievement of Ash'arīsm was to establish an orthodox dogmatic guideline. A mystic such as Ḥasan of Baṣrah could resolve metaphysical problems intuitively, but it required the integration of philosophy into Islamic thought in order to provide the tools and concepts to deal with metaphysical thought precisely and flexibly. In theology, Ash'arism laid down a line of defense against reductive reasoning; inevitably it could also be used against philosophy, and was, by al-Ghazāli. (For the *Creed of al-Ash'arī, see* CREED.)

Through his followers, al-Ash'arī's influence became considerable. Although Ash'arīsm was at first opposed by the Seljūqs, and Ash'arītes were even persecuted, as the ideological struggle with the Fāṭimids became more important, Ash'arīsm revealed itself as a useful weapon, and the Seljūq Vizier Niẓām al-Mulk named Asha'rītes to teaching posts, namely al-Juwaynī, al-Ghazālī, and others. Ash'arīsm also became a cornerstone of the Almohad movement. The Ash'arīte school of theology is widespread in the Islamic West while that of al-Maturidi, which is in practice very similar, is the preferred theology in the East.

Among al-Ash'arī's many works, the most famous are the *al-Ibānah 'an Uṣūl ad-Diyānah* ("The Elucidation of the Foundations of Religion"); *Maqālāt al-Islāmiyyīn* ("The Discourses of the Islamicists") and the *Risālah fī istiḥsān al-khawḍ fī-l-Kalām* ("Treatise on Theology"); *Kitāb ash-Sharḥ wa-t-Tafṣīl* ("The Book of Commentary and Explanation"). Al-Ash'arī played in Islam the role the great councils played in early Christianity, by correcting major doctrinal errors and for this reason, he was credited with "singlehandedly saving Islam". He is remarkably similar to St. Augustine who also was a Manichean to be with, repudiated Manicheism, but brought much Manicheism into Christianity. Al-Ash'ari, a reformed Dualist, removed remainders and intrusions of Manicheism from Islam, but brought its rationalist methods into Islam. Yet al-Ash'ari ended up largely upholding the doctrines of Augustine's arch rival Pelagius. St Augustine was forced by Pelagius to uphold determinism and the apparently arbitrary inscrutability of Grace; al-Ash'ari upheld free will and the apparently arbitrary inscrutability of Divine Judgement. *See* CHILDREN; CREED; KALAM; MU'TAZILITES; QADARIYYAH.

Ashraf. The word means "nobles" in Arabic. In India, it has in addition a technical meaning and refers to what is *de facto* a caste system amongst Muslims. Belonging to the *ashraf*, in descending order, are *Sayyids*, also called by the title *Mir*, who are real and purported descendants of the Prophet; *Shaykhs*, that is, descendants of Companions, as well as holders of the title by virtue of leadership; *Mughals* who are Chagatai Turks, and *Pathans*, often called by the surname Khan. That false claims of ancestry are often made is indicated by this saying; "Last year I was a weaver; this year I am a shaykh, next year I will be a Sayyid."

'Āshūrā'. The tenth of the month of Muḥarram, the first month of the Islamic year. The 'Āshurā', which is derived from Jewish holy days, was observed as an optional fast day by the Prophet. 'Āshūrā' is observed in diametrically opposite ways among Sunnīs and Shī'ites. It is a holy day of happy, *beneficent* character for the Sunnīs. Among the Shī'ites it is the ominous *terrible* anniversary of the murder of Ḥusayn by the troops of the Caliph Yazīd. Shī'ites fast the ninth of Muḥarram; on the tenth, certain Shī'ite groups wander the cities and publicly inflict wounds upon themselves. This mortification is an expression of guilt among the Shī'ites for having abandoned the Imāms in their moment of need. In the days preceding the tenth of Muḥarram the *ta'azīyah* martyrdom plays are performed in Iran.

As a Sunnī holy day the 'Āshurā' has been observed since the time of the Prophet because it is, precisely, Sunnah. As the anniversary of the death of Ḥusayn, the public observance was instituted by the Buyid ruler al-Mu'izz ad-Dawlah, a Shī'ite, in *351*/962.

Asiyah (wife of Pharaoh), *see* PHARAOH.

Asmā' bint Abī Bakr (d. *73*/692). A daughter of Abū Bakr and older sister of 'Ā'ishah, the Prophet's wife. When the Prophet and Abū Bakr hid in a cave in the mountain of Thawr outside Mecca, Asmā' brought them food and water in secret, which she carried suspended from two belts that went over the shoulders. Because of this she was "she of the two belts" (*Dhāt an-Nitaqayn*).

Asmā' became the wife of one of the Prophet's closest Companions, az-Zubayr ibn al-'Awwam, and the mother of 'Abd Allāh ibn az-Zubayr. 'Abd Allāh raised an army of opposition to the Umayyad tyranny, declared himself Caliph, and held Mecca from *64*/683. When Mecca was taken in *73*/692 by al-Ḥajjāj ibn Yūsuf ath-Thaqafī, 'Abd Allāh's body was suspended from a gibbet for several days. Asmā' came to Hajjāj and told him to cut down the body, which he did. She died shortly thereafter. She had been, in fact, a driving force in the old conservative (non-Shī'ite or non-'Alīd) opposition to the Umayyads. Asmā' lived to be around one hundred years old.

'Aṣmah ("sinlessness"). *See* 'IṢMAH.

al-Asmā'u al-Ḥusnā. *See* DIVINE NAMES.

Assassins (often ascribed to the Arabic *ḥashshāshīn*, "consumers of hashish", through Medieval Latin *assassini*). The name was adapted, from local usage, by the Crusaders for members of the Nizārī branch of the Ismā'īlīs at a period when the sect was characterized by extreme militancy. This phase in the history of the Nizārīs extended from *483*/1090 until the fall of Alamūt fortress in *654*/1256. The association with hashish is obscure; there were stories that drugs were used as part of an indoctrination intended to produce perfect obedience to the leaders. Or simply, it may be a disparaging reference to the sect's ideas. Indeed, the first written usage of the term Ḥashishīya was in 1123 in the second anti-Nizārī epistle sent by al-Amir, the rival Ismā'īlī leader in Cairo, who was assassinated by the Nizārīs in 1130. In Syria, where the Assassins occupied a string of fortresses, their chief was known to the Crusaders as *le vieux de la montagne*, "the old man of the mountain" (*shaykh al-jabal*). The most famous of the Syrian leaders was Rashīd ad-Dīn Sinān, but the movement was actually headed by the Masters of the castle of Alamūt in Persia. The first of these was Ḥasan-i Ṣabbāḥ who took over the leadership of the main branch of the Ismā'īlīs when a schism occurred in Fāṭimid Egypt.

Ḥasan-i Ṣabbāḥ was a Persian Ismā'īlī propagandist or *dā'i* descended from an Arab from Kūfah. Around the year *479*/1086 he traveled to Egypt, then the center of Ismā'īlī activity under the Fāṭimid dynasty, and subsequently returned to Persia to carry on propaganda in the name of Nizār, the expected successor to the Fāṭimid throne and the Ismā'īlī Imāmate. However, in *487*/1094 a struggle erupted in which Nizār was imprisoned and supplanted by his younger brother al-Musta'lī, at the instigation of the leader of the armies, al-Afḍal. Ḥasan-i Ṣabbāḥ, who was committed to upholding Nizār, took the occasion to break with the Fāṭimids, and by *483*/1090 had seized the fortress of Alamūt, "the eagle's nest" in the north of Iran near the Caspian Sea. With Alamūt as his center of operations, Ṣabbāḥ succeeded in establishing a power base among the outer tribes in mountainous regions far removed from the centers of political influence.

He built his empire through the propagation of Ismā'īlism, a Gnostic-dualist creed that teaches that out of an unknowable God, because of "an inner conflict" between good and evil within the Divinity Itself, a series of emanations called "intellects" emerged that culminated in the creation of the world. The mythic backdrop from which the doctrines of Ismā'īlism derive declares that the world and the body are evil because in them light and darkness are mixed; however, there is within some men a spark of knowledge, imprisoned and cut off from its source. It is said that at the end of the world, light and darkness, which in themselves are neither evil nor good, are resolved into their separate domains; meanwhile, the chosen ones who possess the spark hear the secret call, awaken to the realization of their true nature of light and, at the end of time, they are saved. The quotation attributed to Ḥasan-i Ṣabbāḥ, a kind of paraphrase of the *shahādah*, "nothing is true, everything is permitted" comes from a book by Hammer-Purgstall who based himself on a line in Maqrīzī's "Topography of Egypt" (*Muhawal Dar al-Ḥikmah*). Rather than a quotation it should be understood as a summary characterization of the philosophy seen from outside. Ṣabbāḥ put both of his sons to death, one for drinking wine. Lest one should think that he was a strict Muslim it should be remembered that the Assassins did not observe Islamic law or practices except as a policy of deception towards the outside world, a measure that they called the "drawn veil" (*satr*); but wine drinking is also forbidden in Manicheism.

The Assassins won disciples by claiming to possess the secret knowledge that is the core of Ismā'īlism, known through the *Imām*, himself a hypostasis of the unknowable God and an intermediary to salvation. The Fāṭimid Caliphs were held by the Ismā'īlis to be the *Imāms*, and thus the spiritual heads of the sect.

Marco Polo passed through the region in *670*/1271, and recorded in the account of his travels what he heard about the Assassins. The castle of Alamūt was conquered by the Mongols in *654*/1256; thus stories told in Morocco that Marco Polo encountered the master of Alamūt are factually impossible (and a blending of recent European influence with what may be authentically indigenous material). But the Moroccan stories are revealing in substance: they say that the leader of the sect set upon Marco Polo's head a helmet made of crystal. He could bear to wear it for only a moment because, when it was struck, the crystal produced the "sound of pure evil itself".

Ḥasan-i Ṣabbāḥ's "Assassins" were known in the Islamic world at the time as the *Ta'līmiyyah*, ("people of the teaching"), the *Bāṭiniyyah* ("the people of the inner truth"), or the *Fidā'iyyah* ("the self-sacrificers"). Marco Polo gave this description of how the Assassins created completely submitted followers: as part of their initiation, novices destined to become self-destructive *fidā'iyyūn* were drugged; they awoke to find themselves in a garden of delights complete with fountains flowing with wine, milk, and honey, and *houris*, the maidens of paradise. (This is most likely based on the story that in Messene Mani converted the Lord Mihrshah by causing him to visit the paradise of light in a trance.) After this heady taste of the "afterlife", the new recruits were drugged again and when they returned to their normal state that were told that they had indeed visited paradise, that would be theirs without fail if they obeyed.

Taken allegorically, and not literally, this could be termed a fair description of the process of intellectual indoctrination into the reality system of, say, a cult or a radical political movement; it is the glimpsing of a different and mysterious way of seeing the world, the unveiling of "hidden truths" that constitute the system's typically subjective explanation of theological, political, or even economic phenomena. This has a psychological impact that, once experienced, changes one's perceptions forever, so that it is usually difficult, if not impossible, to de-program completely. Marco Polo's story (to which there is a parallel in the "Universal History" of Rashīd ad-Dīn aṭ-Ṭabīb) is a traditional model of the process of deliberately modifying someone's perception of reality.

To illustrate the Assassins' complete domination over their adepts, Ibn al-Jawzī reported that the followers of Assassin chiefs had been seen to hurl themselves to their deaths by leaping off precipices at their leader's command. More than likely this was a staged piece of theater intended to frighten their enemies, but it was effective and typical of the Assassin style. In any case, the *fidā'iyyūn* were certainly prepared to sacrifice their lives. Their mission was to sow fear of the sect through terrorism and at the same time to weaken their enemies by the murder of key political figures.

The Assassins infiltrated the ranks of their adversaries, often in the guise of dervishes and religious teachers. When they attained to positions of trust they would kill their selected victims, always through the use of a knife. Apparently by design, they usually perished themselves when they carried out their orders. Among their victims were the famous Seljūqid vizier Niẓām al-Mulk (the first to attempt to put down the Assassins), as well as his brother and his son; the Sultan Mālik Shah; al-Āmir, son of al-Musta'lī, the Fāṭimid who put Nizār to death; two 'Abbāsid Caliphs (al-Mustarshid in 1135 and his son ar-Rāshid in 1138), and hundreds, if not thousands, of others. In Syria, Crusader leaders were among their targets and the Assassins succeeded in murdering Conrad of Montferrat, King of Jerusalem. Saladin himself narrowly escaped Assassin attempts on his life and always had to be on his guard.

Through the profound ideological hold the leaders maintained over their followers, and the political destabilization brought about by their program of murder, the Assassins were able to exist as an invisible kingdom within kingdoms. Their castles in northern Persia and Syria were almost impregnable to siege and attack by reason of their well chosen situations. Ultimately, the opponents of the Assassins preferred compromise to the risk of a fatal dagger stroke at the hands of a trusted servant who turned out to be a member of the dreaded sect.

Al-Ghazālī combatted the teachings of the sect (under the name of *Ta'līmiyyah*) by writing polemics against them. Fakhr ad-Dīn Rāzī denounced them until he was warned at knife-point to desist along with the gift of a bag of gold if he complied. When he ceased to attack them, his students asked why, and he replied, "I do not wish to speak evil of men whose demonstrations are so pointed and whose proofs are so weighty."

The power of the Assassins came to an end when the Mongols under Hūlāgū Khān advanced on Alamūt in *654*/1256 with "an army", writes the historian al-Juwaynī, "of such numbers that Gog and Magog themselves would have been destroyed by waves of its battalions". The last Grand Master, Rukn ad-Dīn, surrendered and was sent to Qaraqorum where he was put to death. The Egyptian Mamlūks conquered the Syrian strongholds soon after. Even earlier, as their power declined, the Syrian Assassins had offered to ally themselves with the Crusaders and to become Christians. This offer was declined by the Christians, who may well have realized that, whatever religion the Assassins professed, it would be no more than an outer garment, and that their "conversion" could not be expected to affect their inner and secret beliefs.

There was more to the Assassins, however, than mere terrorism: true to the serious pursuit of knowledge that marked the first centuries of Ismā'īlism, they amassed libraries and acquired scientific instruments, and did not hesitate, if one is to believe the case of Nāṣir ad-Dīn aṭ-Ṭūsī, to kidnap such scholars as could increase their store of cosmological science. The Nestorians and Shī'ites who accompanied the Mongol horde found books and instruments that showed that Alamūt was not only a center of murder but, strangely, of learning as well. The Assassins' fascination with science can be traced to the nature of Ismā'īlism. The metaphysics of dualism, in Ismā'īlism as in Valentinian Gnosticism and Manicheism, is inseparable from cosmology because the physical universe is considered to be, in a certain sense, itself Divine, a kind of shadow of the metaphysically unknowable "Abyss".

Ḥasan-i aṣ-Ṣabbāḥ, murdered his own sons for disobedience. When he was dying he appointed his lieutenant, Kiya Buzurg Ummīd, the master of the Assassin fortress of Lamasar, to be the new chief of Alamūt and the Ismā'īlīs. Ṣabbāḥ had called his own propaganda the "New Preaching", (*ad-da'wah al-jadīdah*). This was a doctrine of the supremacy of esoteric knowledge or *ta'lim* possessed by the inspired authority and was contained in a document called the Four Chapters (*Fuṣūl-i arba'a*). It marked a break with the Ismā'īlīs of Cairo, the Fāṭimids. The inheritors of Alamūt carried on the tradition of Ṣabbāḥ. Then, Ḥasan, the grandson of Buzurg Ummid, declared himself the Ismā'īlī Imām, making himself the secret descendant through mysterious and improbable means, of Nizār, the deposed Fāṭimid.

While alive, Ḥasan's father Muḥammad repudiated the claims of his son and put 250 of his followers to death, or so it is said. Nevertheless, when Ḥasan assumed control he continued to affirm his claim to the Imāmate. Two years after his accession, during the month of Ramaḍān in *559*/1164, he declared to Nizārī leaders from Khorāsān, 'Irāq, Syria, and the Caspian regions, assembled in the courtyard of Alamūt, and to "*jinn*, Angels and men", that their salvation lay in following his commands and that the religious law of Islam, the *sharī'ah*, was abrogated. Thereupon Ḥasan performed two *raka'āt* or bows of prayer signifying the premature end of the month of fasting, calling the day the *'Īd al-Qiyāmah*, that is, "Festival of Resurrection"— not just of the end of Ramaḍān. Those who were present joined him in eating, drinking, and festivities to mark the formal shattering of the sacred law. A traveler reported that on the door of the library of Alamūt were written the words: "With the aid of God, the ruler of the universe destroyed the fetters of the law; *'alā dhikrihi-s-salām*" ("blessings be upon his memory"). (In Gnostic theosophy the religious law is often consideredto be evil.) This "Resurrection" was the return to the open practice of their original religion before they were forced to pretend to be Muslims.

Not long after, Ḥasan himself was murdered, but his son Muḥammad continued his policies. His grandson Jalāl ad-Dīn, however, made a complete turnabout. He reinstated the practice of the law of Islam, declared himself a Sunnī, publicly cursed his forefathers, and for good measure burned the books of Ḥasan aṣ-Ṣabbāḥ. He allied himself with the 'Abbāsid Caliph and put his own military power at the Caliph's disposal. When he died his son 'Alā'ad-Dīn, a shadowy and corrupt figure, returned temporarily to the principles of his great-grandfather, in which the law of Islam, like the "cosmic illusion" itself was merely "clothing" which could be put on and off at will.

With Ḥasan, and the doctrine of the *Qiyāmah*, the curtain had been drawn back from the Assassin's inner doctrines. With Jalāl ad-Dīn the curtain was closed again, and the period known as the *Satr* ("veiling") resumed, with a brief interruption during the time of 'Alā' ad-Dīn.

The break between the Nizārīs and the Fāṭimids of Cairo was made complete by the establishment of the schism in the line of Imāms. The original sect in Egypt followed Nizār's brother and were called Musta'lī Ismā'īlīs. Nizār himself, his son and perhaps his grandson died in Egypt, but several explanations were devised to explain the sudden reappearance of the Nizārī line at Alamūt. One was that a pregnant concubine of Nizār's, or of Nizār's son, brought the yet unborn Imām there who, when he came into the world, was substituted for a son of the master of the Assassins.

With the death of al-Musta'lī's son al-Amīr, assassinated presumably on orders from Alamūt, the Musta'lī line came to an end. However, some Must'alī Ismā'līs believe that a putative son of al-Amīr called aṭ-Ṭayyib is alive in the unseen world, like the Hidden Imām of the Twelve-Imām Shī'ites, and they await his return as Mahdī at the end of time. Others believe that there exist descendants of aṭ-Ṭayyib who carry on the Musta'lī line in secret. Musta'lī Ismā'īlīs in the Yemen and the Bohoras of India continue this branch of Ismā'īlīsm without manifest Imāms. Instead they are led by a figure called the *Dā'i Muṭlaq* ("Absolute Preacher").

Nor was the "New Preaching" snuffed out in the destruction of Alamūt by the Mongols; its old names faded away but the sect survived, rediscovered its Imāms, and eventually found a new life in Persia, Afghanistan, the Pamir mountains and above all, through the success of its proselytizing (or up-dating an older version of the already established religion), among the Khojas in India. *See* ISMĀ'ĪLĪS; MANICHEISM; SEVENERS; SHĪ'ISM; TA'WĪL.

Astrolabe. The astrolabe was a Greek invention and dates from 200 BC It is a projection of the observed heavens as seen from the earth within a defined region upon a flat surface. The astrolabe was used as a navigation aid. The art of making astrolabes was preserved in the city of Ḥarrān and from there spread throughout the Islamic world where it was refined. The astronomer 'Abd ar-Raḥān aṣ-Ṣufī said that the astrolabe was capable of performing some 350 mathematical functions. There were different styles of astrolabes, in particular the Maghribi from Morocco, and the Persian. Until 1960, a mu'aqqit, or mosque functionary charged with determining prayer times, in Fez still made astrolabes by hand.

Astrology (Ar. *'ilm at-tanjīm*). Astrology as a symbolism attached to heavenly bodies — "the heavens reveal the glory of God"— was accepted in the Middle Ages and was not prohibited. One would be hard put to find any astronomer, East or West, up to modern times who was not also an astrologer, that is, a student of cosmological symbolism. As divination, however, predicting the future, astrology is condemned in Islam, as in most religions, because it is misleading to the soul. The theologian Sa'd ad-Dīn at-Taftāzānī (d. *791*/1389)) made a distinction between astrology as a symbolic science and astrology as divination. In his *Creed* he says, after condemning divination, "the astrologer whenever he pretends to know approaching events is like the diviner."

The danger inherent in astrology, despite what value it may have as a mythological system, is that it may trap the soul in some existential illusion or error; that is to say, divination can throw up some illusion that is actually the projection of a subjective flaw. If what is foreseen by divination then appears to be confirmed by events, the soul is snared in an unreality of its own making. As the Ḥadīth says: "Even when the soothsayers tell the truth, they lie." And: "Let no-one malign fate for God says, 'I am destiny.' (found in the *Muwaṭṭa'*)."

Moreover, Islam commends surrender to fate, and the importance of this attitude precludes from the outset recourse to predictions. In Judaism for example, a practising Jew is considered to have no astrological sign; that is, a sacred identity as a bondsman of God replaces the individual identity; the Talmud says: "Israel has no constellation."

Nevertheless, astrology for the purposes of divination has been widely practiced. In antiquity virtually all mathematicians were astronomers, and all astronomers were astrologers. Such men as Naṣīr ad-Dīn āṭ-Ṭūsī and al-Bīrūnī were famous astrologers. The latter attacked astrologers for poor calculations rather for than their science. Thābit ibn Qurrā said:

> Aristotle said that whoever reads philosophy and geometry and every science and is without experience of astrology, will be hindered and obstructed, because the science of talismans is more precious than geometry and more profound than philosophy.

Astrology was used for political purposes; prophecies around astrological events were spread abroad to destabilize regimes. The Seveners arranged political events timed to coincide with planetary conjunctions and fulfill "prophecies" that had been planted by design. The Astrologer Shādhan al-Balkhi predicted the collapse of the Caliphal empire for 922 at the time of the rise of the Qarmaṭīs; Abū Ma'shar (d. 886) predicted the end of the 'Abbāsids for 1213. A certain Daniali came to the Caliph al-Muqtadir and told him that he had found books of Daniel which predicted that al-Muqtadir would solve his financial problems by using a banker whose description Daniali gave and who was an accomplice. In Baghdad in the unsettled 10th century, there were many anxieties and preoccupations with political events. Oracles and books of apocalyptic interpretations of the future were current. The Seveners and their successors the Qarmaṭīs and Fāṭmids took advantage of this by spreading a prophecy that said that with the seventh conjunction of Saturn and Jupiter (starting from a date that al-Birūnī said was a Zoroastrian cyclic anniversary), there would be a new world order: the advent of "the true religion". These conjunctions took place in the years 809, 829, 848, 868, 888, 908, 928, 948, 967.

For the year 928 a great victory had been predicted for the Ismā'īlīs that did not take place. However, a raid by the Qarmaṭīs of Abū Ṭāhir seized the Black Stone from the Ka'bah in Mecca (*17 Dhu'l-Hijjah 317*/January 21, 930) and took it to al-Ḥasā' (al-Aḥsā'), which is in Arabia's Eastern Province or to Baḥrayn. This dramatic abduction of the stone was probably carried out to create political waves intensified by appearing to be the fulfillment of the prophecy. Perhaps the founding of Cairo (which means the "Victorious") in 969 was also built around these deliberate prophecies. Where the plan also succeeded behind schedule, but remarkably because of great difficulties, was the installation of the Fāṭimid leader in Tunisia and the declaration of the Fāṭimid Caliphate in the year 910.

Arab astrology is derived from the Greco-Egyptian tradition and the *Tetrabiblos* of Claudius Ptolemy. The Arabs added the points on the individual horoscope known as the Arabian Parts. These are derived by taking the arcs that separate planets such as the sun and moon, adding or subtracting other arcs, and mapping the resulting arc on a horoscope starting from the horizon in order to determine sensitive points, such as the "part of fortune", the "point of spirit" etc. This system may indeed have given rise, or at least be related to, a traditional Arab system of fortune-telling, still practiced in the market place, that involves measuring distances on the body of an individual — the arm, the head, leg and so forth — and adding and subtracting the measures to produce a divination. Others methods of divination used sand.

The Arabs assigned to the Moon twenty-eight houses (*manāzil*), one for each day of its cycle. In Arabic the signs are called *burūj*, "towers" or "mansions". Individual stars played a greater role in interpretation than they do in the West, especially, the pairs of *naw'ī* stars, that, at a given moment, are observed on the rising and sinking horizons, corresponding to the ascendant and the descendant. This defined the horizontal axis, or the individual nature. The non-individual, or ontological axis, was the vertical between the *samt ar-ra's* ("the highest point" from which "zenith" is derived; also called the *Media Coeli*) and *samt an-naẓīr* (whence "nadir", *Imum Coeli*).

Naw'ī is derived from *naw'*, "the appearance of the first light", and it refers also to the entrance of the moon into each of its twenty-eight mansions, the *manāzil al-qamar*. The study of the progressions of the moon is called the *'ilm al-anwā'* and constitutes traditional Arab agricultural meteorology. The best known book on this science is the *Kitāb al-Anwā'* of Ibn Qutaybah al-Dinawārī.

Other systems of divination existed among the Arabs, such as the *mandala*, the *'ilm ar-raml* (drawing figures on sand), magic squares (*al-wafq*) combined with interpretations derived from the *'ilm al-ḥurūf* ("science of letters").

In addition to predictions, or perhaps above all, astrology was used as a basis for cosmological theory to understand the secrets of creation in the sense that: "the heavens declare the glory of God." The cycles of events, or of lives, were made intelligible by sacred symbolism in the cycles of the planets. In traditional astrological or astronomical diagrams, the divisions of the zodiac, and even each degree (which represents one revolution of the earth) are assigned to an Angel; the identity of the Angel is the link, or the correspondence, between a celestial mechanics and a higher, supra-individual order of reality. Such diagrams of traditional Arab astrology as are available to us today are not easily comprehensible; some aspects may appear to be arbitrary because they are inadequately conceptualized; nevertheless, they cannot be dismissed, for while they are not systematic, they were intended to be guideposts to an individual contemplation that would yield up an understanding within the scope of a personal experience.

The cycles of the planets were applied to manifestations on the human plane, that is, events and history. These cycles (Ar. *akwār* or *adwār*) range from the precession of the equinoxes, a cycle of slightly less than 25,700 years (a number known to most traditional cosmologies, not from measurements, an impossibility that gives rise to fantastical suppositions, but by induction from ideal proportions in mathematics, or as among the Pythagoreans and al-Farābī, from music) to the cycles of the moon, and the daily turning of the earth.

Among the many stories of fate and astrology that are told in the lands of the *Thousand and One Nights* is the following: legend foretold that Islam would rule in Spain as long as the star Canopus (Arabic, *Suhayl*) was visible. In the 8th century it could be seen as far north as Saragossa. By 1492, due to the precession of the equinoxes, it was barely visible in Europe. Today it is below the horizon as seen from the southernmost point in Spain.

It is also related that when Naṣīr ad-Dīn aṭ-Ṭūsī was with the Assassins at their castles in the north of Persia, the Mongols invaded the land and besieged them. The last master of Alamūt, Rukn ad-Dīn, asked Naṣīr ad-Dīn aṭ-Ṭūsī to cast a horoscope in order to determine the best course of action. Naṣīr ad-Dīn's horoscope advised Rukn ad-Dīn to surrender, which he did. Rukn ad-Dīn was first well received by the Mongols, but after a short time beheaded on the orders of Hülāgū Khan. Aṭ-Ṭūsī, on the other hand, became astrologer and astronomer to Hülāgū Khan, joining the Shī'ites in the Mongol train, being appointed astronomer at the Maragha observatory, and thus contributing to the sparing of Shī'ite holy places by the Mongols. *See* ALMAGEST; ASTRONOMY; 'ILM al-ḤURŪF; MANDALA.

Astronomy (Ar. *'ilm an-nujūm*; also *'ilm al-hay'ah, 'ilm al-falak*). "Surely in the creation of the heavens and the earth, and the alternation of night and day... are signs for a people having understanding" (2:159). In the Middle Ages, the Muslims built a great number of observatories, such as the observatory of the *Bayt al-Ḥikmah* ("House of Wisdom") founded by the Caliph al-Ma'mūn (d. *218*/833). His astronomer was the mathematician Ḥabash al-Ḥāsib, as were also the "Banū Mūsā" (the "sons of Mūsā Shākir"). Other observatories were those of the Fāṭimids in Cairo, the observatory of Maragha founded by Hūlāgu Khān (d. *663*/1265) in *657*/1259 for Naṣīr ad-Dīn aṭ-Ṭūsī, the observatory of Samarkand (c. *823*/1420) founded by Ulug Beg, the observatory of Istanbul established in *983*/1575 by Taqī ad-Dīn, and the observatories of Jai Singh at Delhi, Jaipur and Ujjain founded in the *12th*/18th centuries. Apart from observatories as such, there were many lookout towers to study the motions of the stars; often minarets were used for this purpose.

Muslim astronomers created accurate tables (*zīj*) of planetary motion: the *Zīj aṣ-Ṣābi'* of Abū 'Abd Allāh al-Battānī (called Albategnius in Europe), the *zīj* of al-Khwarizmi, the *zīj al-Ḥākimī* of the Fāṭimids made by the astronomer Ibn Yūnus from his observatory on the Muqattam hills outside

Cairo, the *Zīj IlKhānid* of Maragha, and many others. These often served for the creation of special calendars such as the *Jalālī*, that were noted for their accuracy. Major works on astronomy were written by al-Bīrūnī: *Qānūn al-Mas'ūdī* ("the Masudic Canon"), and the *Kitāb at-Tafhīm* ("Book of Elucidation"); by Quṭb ad-Dīn ash-Shīrāzī: *Nihāyat al-Idrāk* ("the Limit of Comprehension"); by Abū Ma'shar al-Balkhī: *Kitāb al-Ulūf* ("the Book of Thousands"); by al-Farghānī (in Latin Alfraganus): *Kitāb fī-l-Harakāt as-Samāwiyyah wa Jawāmi' 'Ilm an-Nujūm* ("On the Celestial Motions and General Principles of Astronomy"), and so forth.

Islamic astronomy was based upon Greek knowledge and Ptolemaic astronomy (*see* ALMAGEST), the sciences of the Ḥarrānians and of the Nestorians of Jundishāpūr; later, through Persia, it drew upon Indian science, notably the works of Brahmagupta and Aryabhāta, and the Mahāsiddhānta. A Chinese astronomer called Fao-Mun-Ji was associated with the observatory of Maragha in Persia.

The influence of Islamic astronomy upon Europe was very considerable. It made its first impact through the work of Arab astronomers in Spain, such as az-Zarqalī (Azarquiel in Europe) who edited the Toledan Tables, and then showed a direct reflection in the first European books on astronomy such as the *Libros del Saber de Astronomia* of King Alfonso X el Sabio ("the Wise"). Islamic observatories must also have influenced the work of the later European astronomers, Tycho Brahe and Kepler.

The early dominance of Islamic astronomy is indicated by the preponderance of words of Arabic derivation in the technical vocabulary of modern astronomy: the index of the light reflection of a celestial body is called albedo (Arabic *al-baiḍā*, "whiteness"); the zenith (Arabic *samt ar-ra's*, "the direction of the head"); nadir (Arabic *an-naẓīr*, "the opposite"); azimuth (Arabic *as-samt*, "the direction"); the star Vega (Arabic (*an-nasr*) *al-wāqi'*, "the falling eagle"); the star Betelgeuse (Arabic *bayt al-jawzah*, "arm-pit of the centre"); the star Algol (Arabic *al-ghūl*, "the ghoul"); the star Rigel (Arabic *ar-rijl*, "the foot" of Orion); the star Deneb (Arabic *adh-dhanb*, "the tail"); the star Aldebaran (Arabic *ad-dabarān*, "the follower" of the Pleiades) and so forth.

The precise astronomical knowledge of the Muslims also permitted them to make perfected astrolabes that were a vital contribution to the voyages of the age of European exploration. The preeminence of Muslims in astronomy gave them a lead in navigation, and it is for this reason that the school founded by Prince Henry the Navigator in the Algarve in Portugal had Arab astronomers, and it was Arab navigators who guided the Portuguese in many of their voyages: Aḥmad ibn Mājid an-Najdī, who wrote treatises on navigation in verse (to aid memorization) and prose, was pilot in the voyage of Vasco da Gama to India.

As is true of all traditional astronomy, as for example, the jyøtividyā of Hinduism, the science in Islam was inseparable from an interpretation of celestial phenomenon as a symbolic cosmology, or what is now called astrology. *See* ASTROLOGY; al-BĪRūNĪ; al-KHWARIZMĪ; NAṢĪR ad-DĪN aṭ-ṬŪSĪ; MŪSĀ SHĀKIR; 'UMAR KHAYYĀM.

al-Aswad. ("the black one") A false prophet who appeared in South Arabia and the Yemen towards the end of the Prophet's life. He was known as *Dhu-l-Khimār*, "the veiled one". He claimed to have revelations from ar-Raḥmān ("The All-merciful"), a Name of God that was revealed, apparently for the first time, in Islam. For a brief time, al-Aswad seized control of the Yemen, much of which was then under Persian suzerainty, and made Sanā'a' his capital until his assassination in an internal power struggle. *See* MUSAYLAMAH; RIDDAH.

'Atabāt al-muqadassa ("the sacred thresholds"). The Shī'ite Holy Places in 'Irāq: Kerbala (tomb of Ḥusayn), Najaf (tomb of 'Alī), Kaẓimayn and Samarra' (tombs of Imāms).

Atatürk, Muṣṭafā Kemal, *see* KEMAL, MUSTAFA.

Atjeh. A Muslim Sultanate at the north-western tip of the island of Sumatra in what is now Indonesia. When Marco Polo visited it at the end of the *7th*/13th century Islam was already established in Sumatra; by the *12th*/17th century it had attained to a highpoint of culture and politically dominated most of the island. From *1290*/1873 the region resisted Dutch conquest, succumbing only in *1322*/1904.

In Sumatra, Islam was distinctly marked by esoterism of the school of Ibn 'Arabī. A teacher named Hamzah Fansūrī taught the Ṣūfī doctrine of *waḥdat al-wujūd* ("the metaphysical unity of

Being") under the name of the *wujūdiyyah* order; his successor Shams ad-Dīn (d. *1040*/1630) became the spiritual master of the King of Atjeh, Iskandar Muda (d. *1046*/1636), under whose rule Atjeh saw the summit of its cultural development. The great metaphysicians of the Shādhilī ṭarīqah, especially Ibn 'Aṭā'Allāh (d. *709*/1309) were well known and earnestly studied in Atjeh. A later Ṣūfī of Atjeh named 'Abd ar-Ra'ūf of Singkel typified the mystical cast of Sumatran Islam in these words:

> We were lofty sounds [yet] unuttered, held in abeyance on the highest peaks of the mountains. I was in Him and we were you, and you were Heand in Him was He; ask those who have attained.

See INDONESIA; SLAMETAN; SULUK.

Athiest, *see* DAHRI.

'Aṭṭār, Farīd ad-Dīn (d. circa *627*/1229). Persian mystic of Nayshabūr and author of the celebrated *Mantiq aṭ-Ṭā'ir* ("The Language of the Birds"; the name is a Koranic reference to Solomon's powers of communicating with the spiritual world, and David's hymning of the praises of God). This is an allegory of the spiritual path in which the birds, led by the *Hudhud*, or Hoopoe, go off in search of their King, the Simurgh. (The starting point of the allegory is the Koran 38:19: "And the birds assembled; all were turning unto Him.")

> 'I fear death', said the bird
>
> 'Can death exist for one whose heart is joined with God?' replied the Hoopoe. 'My heart is one with Him. Thus time and death no longer exist for me. For death is the suspension of time, and time is born of the attachment to things that perish.'

'Aṭṭār also wrote the *Tadhkirāt al-Awliyā'* ("Recollections of the Saints"), a collection of biographies and anecdotes about famous Sufis.

Attributes. Sunnī theology, among the Divine Names and Attributes mentioned in the Koran, places a particular emphasis upon the "seven Attributes", namely: Life (*Ḥayāh*), Knowledge (*'Ilm*), Power (*Qudrah*), Will (*īrādah*), Hearing (*Sam'*), Sight (*Baṣr*), Speech (*Kalām*).

Avempace, *see* IBN BAJJAH.

Avenzoar, *see* IBN ZUHR.

Averroes, *see* IBN RUSHD.

Avicebron, *see* IBN GABIROL.

Avicenna, *see* IBN SĪNĀ.

Awliya', *see* SAINTS.

Axis, Spiritual, *see* QUṬB.

Āyat al-Kursī (lit. the "Verse of the Throne"). A single verse of the Koran (2:256) of more than average length, it is one of the principal "verses of refuge and protection", that are known as *āyāt al-ḥifẓ*:

Allāh
there is no god but He,
the Living, the Everlasting.
Neither slumber nor sleep overtaketh Him.
To Him belongs whatever is in the heavens and the earth.
And who may intercede with Him
but by His leave?
He knows what is in men's hands
and what lieth behind their backs:
while they cannot comprehend any part of what He knoweth
save by His willing them to comprehend it.
Wide is His throne over the heavens and the earth
Nor is He weary of preserving them.
For He is the Sublime, the Tremendous!

It is recited — in Arabic — as a means of entrusting one's self to God's care and is often written on amulets. The power of the "Verse of the Throne" is praised in Ḥadīth. *See also* REFUGE.

Āyat an-Nūr ("the Verse of Light"). A verse of the Koran (24:35 and 36) highly esteemed by Sufis:

Allāh is the Light of the heavens and the earth.
The likeness of His light is as a niche
wherein is set a lamp.
The lamp within a glass and the glass
like a shining star.
Lit is that light of a blessed tree,

an olive neither of the East nor of the West,
of which the oil would almost utter light
though no fire touched it.
Light upon light!
God leadeth whom He will into his light,
He speaketh in allegories to men,
whilst Himself is the Knower of all things.

This lamp is found in houses
which God hath allowed to be exalted
and that His name shall be remembered therein.
Therein do offer praise to Him
at morn and evening,
men whom neither merchandise nor sale
beguileth from the remembrance of God
and constancy in prayer
and paying the poor their due;
who fear a day when hearts
and eyeballs shall be overturned.

Ayatollah (Ar. *Āyat Allāh* "A Sign of God"). An honorific title for high-ranking Shī'ite religious authorities in Iran. There is also an Ayatollah in 'Irāq, who resides in Najaf. The title came into being only in this century. The handful of Ayatollahs, who are associated with religious centers such as Tabrīz, Qūm, and Mashhad, constitute a kind of theological "college", or synod. Newcomers are admitted to the ranks on the basis of recognition and acceptance by existing Ayatollahs, and by popular acclamation. Like all high-ranking Shī'ite Mullās, the Ayatollahs have personal followings.

This grandiose title came into being in the late 19th century but really is an innovation of the 20th century, becoming widespread only in the 1940's. It arose out of the victory in Persia (but not in southern 'Irāq or Baḥrayn) of the Uṣūlī school of Twelve-Imām Shī'ism over the Akhbārī school in the *12th*/18th century. This cleared the way for a development in the authority of the Mullās. Thereafter, the Uṣūlī religious authorities aggrandized power to themselves, in a way reminiscent of the Priestly class of Mazdeism in the days of the ancient Persian dynasties.

The Uṣūlīs maintain that, despite the absence of the Shī'ite Imām, highly qualified teachers have the capacity to make autonomous religious judgements as *Mujtahids* and that such an authority is a *marja' at-taqlīd*, "a reference of emulation". The Uṣūlī doctrine teaches that a Shī'ite must be the follower of such a Mujtahid; furthermore, the Mujtahid must be living; one is even forbidden to follow a dead Mujtahid. Moreover, the Mujtahids claim the allegiance of lesser Mullās who are not Mujtahids and receive the religious *zakāt* tax, and the special tax perpetuated in Shī'ism known as the *khums*.

In the early 19th century there were only three or four Mujtahids; by the end of the century the numbers had grown considerably, and those who could claim large followings adopted the title *Ḥujjat al-Islam* ("Proof of Islam") to mark their higher status. In this century, with the ranks of the Mujtahids now swollen to several hundred, in addition to a large number of *Ḥujjat al-Islam*, the rank was introduced of the Ayatollah, or "Divine Sign". But then, as the number of Ayatollahs grew apace, there came the need for a further distinguishing title, namely that of the Ayatollah al-'Uẓmā ("the greatest sign of God"). Past Shī'ite history has been reinterpreted to show that such an authority, a *marja' at-taqlīd al-muṭlaq*, an "absolute point of reference", has always existed, and those who represented this authority have been named. The last recognized one was Ḥusayn Bururjirdi (d. 1961). At the start of the Iranian revolution there were thirty Ayatollahs. The number has since declined to under ten. After the revolution of 1979, the Ayatollah Khomeini gave up using the title and adopted the title of "Imām". Since he could not claim to be, in his own person, the Hidden Imām returned, this signaled a new development in Persian Twelve-Imām Shī'ism. At the same time, the Ayatollah Sharī'at Madarī was down-graded to the title of *Ḥujjat al-Islam* for his role in political events, an unprecedented event. There is a woman in Qum, Zohreh Sefeti, who some, but not all, consider to be an Ayatollah. The rank of marja' is explicitly reserved for men only. *See* AKHBĀRĪ; BIHBAHĀNĪ; HIDDEN IMĀM; SHĪ'ISM; UṢŪLĪ.

Ayup Sultan, *see* ABŪ AYYUB.

Ayyūb. The prophet Job. He and the trials he underwent are mentioned in the Koran in 4:163; 21:83; 38:42. *See* PROPHETS.

Ayyūbids (*564-658*/1169-1260; a Sunnī dynasty that lasted in Diyarbakir until *866*/1492), it was founded by Ṣalāḥ ad-Dīn al-Ayyūbī (d. *589*/1193), called Saladin in Europe. Ṣalāḥ ad-Dīn, the great heroic figure of the Crusades, was a Kurd who started his career in the service of Nūr ad-Dīn, the

Emir of Syria. After supplanting the Shī'ite Fāṭimids, Ṣalāḥ ad-Dīn established his family as rulers in Egypt and Syria (he was confirmed as Sultan by the Caliph in *570*/1174 upon the death of Nur ad-Dīn). He consolidated his control of Aleppo and Damascus, and then directed a series of wars against the Crusader kingdoms in Palestine, recovering Jerusalem in *583*/1187 after defeating the Crusaders at the Battle of the Horn of Hattin, when he captured the Christian King and the Grand Masters of the Knightly Orders.

For a time, Egypt, Jerusalem, Damascus, parts of the Yemen, and Diyarbakir, were under Ayyūbid control. The Ayyūbid empire ended in the West at the hands of the Mamlūks; in Syria, the Ayyūbids were overwhelmed by the Mongols. *See* MAMLŪKS; ṢALĀḤ ad-DĪN al-AYYŪBĪ.

Āzād, Abū al-Kalām (1888-1958). Indian journalist writing in Urdu and political figure of the anticolonial movement. He was born in Mecca of an Indian father who was a Sufi, married to the daughter of the Mufti of Medinah. Āzād underwent all the influences of his time, the Khilāfat movement, Sir Sayyid Ahmad Khan the modernist reformer, and imbibed the ideas of other politicians of the Islamic world, but went on to become an opponent of the partition of India and instead the advocate of a multi-cultural Indian state.

He became a journalist at an early age publishing *al-Hilāl* ("the Crescent"), and joined the Congress party becoming one of its influential leaders and a colleague of Mohandas Gandhi. In 1940 he was elected president of the All-India National Congress, a post he held until 1946, and in 1947 became Minister of Education in the government of independent India, a post he held until his death. He wrote a partial translation and commentary on the Koran, his *Tarjumān al-Qur'an.*

Azerbaijan. Republic: population 7,789,886. The capital is Baku. The classical name of this country was Atropatene, the name of a family. It is inhabited by a Turkish people whose culture is strongly influenced by Iran. Indeed, in ancient times Atropatene was the site of a Zoroastrian sacred fire (and into the 20th century there was a sacred fire site frequented by pilgrims and travellers from India on the outskirts of Baku.) The post-Soviet orientation is still largely secular although the religious culture is 90% Islamic with a Shī'ite majority. In addition 3% of the population are Christian and there are some 18,000 indigenous Jews and 3,000 Jews from European Russia. The Muslim religious leader is called with a Turkish title: Shaykh al-Islam. In the neighboring republic of Iran there is a northwest region also called Azerbaijan whose capitals are Tabriz and Rezaiyeh; at least twice as many Azeris more live there.

The division that exists today within this region that begins with the Caucasus mountains and once included Urmia, was created in 1828 by the treaty of Torkamanchai. By this treaty the Russian empire expanded to include Armenia and Azerbaijan to the Aras river at the expense of Iran.

Russian colonization and wealth created by oil in the 19th century made Azerbaijan the most Europeanized of Islamic countries at one time, with the first school for women in the Islamic world, and Western style opera written by Azeris. After the Russian revolution, Azerbaijan was briefly independent and then incorporated into the Soviet Union as the "Republic of Transcaucasia" that included Armenia and Georgia; later these were separated. Along with the breakup of the Soviet Union a war broke out between Azerbaijan and Armenia in which the region of Karabagh, with a majority Armenian population, was seized by Armenia. At the present time Shī'ism in Azerbaijan, in the words of Shaykh al-Islam Shukur Allāh Pashazadeh, is neither Akhbārī nor Uṣūlī. *See* AZERI.

Azeri. A Turkic people a third of whom live in the Republic of Azerbaijan and over two thirds in the neighboring regions of Iran. They appeared on the scene with the Oguz in the 11th century. Their language is Azeri Turkish and they are the only Turkic group that is predominantly Shī'ite. Among them were the legendary tribes of the Shamlu, Rumlu, Ustajlu, Tekelü, Afshar, Qājār, and Zulqadar who were the support of the Ṣafavīd dynasty. The Azeris were much influenced by Iran, to the extent of absorbing many Zoroastrian elements into their culture. *See* FUẒŪLĪ.

al-Azhar (Ar. "the resplendent"). The most famous university of the Islamic world, in Cairo, Egypt. It was founded by the general al-Jawhar shortly after the founding of Cairo itself in *358*/969. Originally it was an institution of the Fāṭimids whose purpose was to train preachers, or *da'ī's*, to propogate Ismā'īlī doctrines. The existence of such a centre for the teaching of a special ideology threatening to 'Abbāsid authority forced the Sunni Seljūqs to create their own schools of orthodox theology as a counterforce. Thus the Vizier Niẓām al-Mūlk (d. *485*/1092) founded several "Niẓamiyyah" Madrasahs in 'Irāq and Persia while Saladin and other Syrian rulers founded schools in Syria and Palestine and provided upkeep for others. In this way the al-Azhar gave an important impetus to the development of higher education in the Islamic world.

The al-Azhar also had an important effect upon the development of educational institutions in Europe. The wearing of black academic gowns, traditions of public disputations, divisions into undergraduate and graduate faculties, derive from the al-Azhar and point to an influence that must have made itself felt in other deeper ways. After the Ayyubids conquered Egypt, the Fāṭimid dynasty came to an end and the al-Azhar became a Sunni university. It acquired a great prestige and reputation for authority in religious domains that it has kept to the present day.

B

Bāb (lit. "door" or "gate"). The Shī'ites often quote this Ḥadīth: "I [the Prophet] am the city of knowledge and 'Alī is the gate (*bāb*)." From this, the term *bāb* lent itself to be used in Shī'ism as the title of a person claiming to vehicle special knowledge. The most famous use of the title *bāb* is that of the spiritual leader of the *Bābīs*, a 19th century branch of the Shaykhis, who were themselves an offshoot of twelve-Imām Shī'ism. In *1260*/1844, Mirzā 'Alī Muḥammad, the leader of a branch of the Shaykhīs, claimed to be the *bāb*, or living door to the Hidden Imām. He later went on to claim to be the Mahdī, and finally, a Divine Messenger. Mirzā 'Alī Muḥammad composed a book called the *Bayān* ("Explanation"). His followers caused revolts in Iran and he was shot by a firing squad in Tabrīz in *1267*/1850. *See* BĀBĪS; HIDDEN IMĀM; SHAYKHIS.

Bābak or Pāpak, (d. *222*/837) called (by Ibn Nadīm) "the Khurrami" (from Khurramiyyah or Khurramdiniyyah, a notorious dualist sect). He could equally be called "the Mazdakite" and Ibn Jawzi said that he was one of the *Baṭiniyyah*. He led one of the most powerful of the early revolts against the 'Abbāsids (among which were those of the Surkhi 'Alām, Sindbād, and al-Muqanna'), a revolt which lasted twenty years. Unlike the others which were mainly in Khorāsān, Babak's revolt was in the western regions, that of Azerbaijan but also in Mesopotamia.

Babak was brought to power by the widow of a chieftain called Jaridan killed in battle with another chieftain, Abū 'Imrān. She married Babak immediately upon the death of her husband, saying to followers of her husband that her husband's spirit had gone into Babak who was to bring to pass for himself and for them "what none had ever brought to pass nor shall ever bring to pass hereafter: for he shall possess the whole earth and slay all tyrants and restore the religion Mazdak brought to men (a communism of wealth and women). By him shall the lowest of you become mighty, and the meanest exalted." Babak told those who followed him that he was God.

The troops of al-Ma'mūn had not been successful against him, but with the accession of al-Mu'tas'im, the Turkic general Afshin subdued Babak by taking the fortress of Badh in *222*/837. Babak himself was tricked by Sahl, a Patrician of the Armenian marches, who received him well, then fettered him and delivered him to Afshin, accusing him of being a cowherd who had sought to depose the feudal nobility. Babak was taken to Samarra', tortured and put to death. About a year later, Afshin, who had been given great gifts, was himself accused, rightly or wrongly, by a Mazyar, or chieftain of Tabaristan, of harboring old Magian ways himself in Ushrushana, in Sughd, and fostering revolt against the Arabs. And so Afshin himself was left to starve to death in prison. *See* KHURRAMIYYAH; MAZDAK; al-MUQANNA'; RAFI' IBN LAYTH UPRISING; SINDBĀD REVOLT; SURKH-I 'ALĀM;.

Bābīs. The followers of a small sect which sprang up in Iran in the middle of the last century, as a schism within the Shaykhis. Its leader, Mirzā 'Alī Muḥammad called himself the *Bāb*, or "door" to the Hidden Imām, but later declared himself the revealer of a new religion. A small number of Bābīs still exist today, but the sect was mainly a springboard to another religion, with a wider appeal, the Bahā'is. *See* BĀB; BAHĀ'IS; HIDDEN IMĀM; SHAYKHIS.

Badā' (lit. "priority"). A doctrine of changes in the Divine Will which was advanced by the Kaysāniyyah to explain why certain expected prophecies did not come true. Traces of the doctrine of *badā'* have a very relative and unimportant place in the theology of Twelve-Imām Shī'ism. *Badā'* is very different from the principle of *naskh*, or abrogation of certain verses of the Koran. (This should not be confused with *bid'ah*, which is "innovation".) Changes in the Divine Will imply the mutability of God, a Manichean concept which St. Augustine attacked in *Contra Secundinum*. *See* KAYSĀNIYYAH; NASKH.

Badr, *see* BATTLE of BADR.

Baghdad. The capital of the 'Abbāsid Caliphate. The unrest arising from the province of Khorāsān directed against the Umayyad tyranny led to frequent revolts which culminated in the defeat of Marwan II at the battle of the greater Zab river in *132*/750 (in the vicinity of Alexander's defeat of the Persians at Gaugamela). The victors established the 'Abbāsid dynasty, and the new capital reflected the shift away from the influence of Byzantium towards that of Persia.

The city was founded by the Caliph al-Manṣūr on the west side of the Tigris river, on the site of an ancient Babylonian town. The date of founding was chosen by astrologers for July 23 762/*145*, under the sign of Leo with Sagittarius rising but work actually started on the *1 Jumadah*/2 August. But most significant is that the site was next to the Sāssānid capital of Ctesiphon-Seleucia (Madā'in).

> Manṣūr rode through 'Irāq seeking the site for a new capital. At the little village of Baghdad on the Tigris (where Euphrates flows near) he was counselled: We think it best to settle here, midway between these four agricultural districts of Buq, Kalwadha, Qutrabbul, and Baduria. Thus you will have palm plantations on every side of you and water near at hand; if harvest fails or is late from one district, you can get relief from another. You can get provisions by the Sarat canal from the Euphrates river traffic; Egyptian and Syrian caravans will come here by the desert roads, and all kinds of China goods upriver from the sea, and Byzantine and Mosul produce down the Tigris And with rivers on both sides, no enemy can approach except by ship or bridge.
>
> "The site is excellent for a military camp." Manṣūr said. And here he built the city of Baghdad, called the Round City by reason of its plan and City of Peace.

Ctesiphon had been reduced to a village around the ruins of the Sāssānid Palace. One resident, and al-Manṣūr knew this very well since both kept a sharp eye on the other, who must have rejoiced at the location of the new capital near the village was the Archegos, the head of the Manichean religion, who was obliged by tradition to remain in the former Persian capital, the way the Pope is tied to the city of Rome. The Arab invasion had devastated Ctesiphon in 637; now, by proximity, it was to come back to life; whatever the pre-Islamic meaning of the name Baghdad, Aramaic or Iranian, it was henceforth interpreted in Persian to mean "Gift of God" or "Founded by God".

The original city built by the 'Abbāsids was called *Dār as-Salām* ("House of Peace"), a circular city in the Parthian-Sāssānid tradition, with three concentric walls, pierced at the four cardinal directions by gates opening towards Baṣrah (SE), Syria (NW), Kūfah (SW), and Khorāsān (NE), and surrounded by a deep moat. Ma'sūdī remarked that the Gate of Khorāsān was in the old days often called the Bab ad-Dawlah, because the dynasty (*dawlah*) or state power of the 'Abbāsids had come to them out of Khorāsān. (Because of this support the 'Abbāsids were also called the "foreign Khorāsāni state".) the circle of the outer wall had a diameter of 1.6 miles/2.6 km. The gigantic Caliphal palace, with an immense throne room modeled after the Sāssānid palace of Ctesiphon, and a grand mosque nearby, formed the city's centre, surrounded by vast gardens 1 mile/1.5 km in diameter. The round city had a green dome which was 48 meters high with a mounted horseman on top. This collapsed in a storm in *329*/941.

The city lay upon the great routes of communication with Persia and India, and was the cultural and political focus of Islam in the eastern empire, as Cordoba was in the west. Its glory is reflected in the splendor of the stories of the *Thousand and One Nights*, whose Arab form crystallized the memory of the legendary height of the'Abbāsid dynasty under Hārūn ar-Rashīd (d. *194*/809). Many kinds of cloth were made in Baghdad, and paper was manufactured there, after the technology had appeared in Samarkand. The population then is estimated to have been one and a half million. A historian wrote that Baghdad was:

> The market to which the wares of the sciences and arts were brought, where wisdom was sought as a man seeks after his stray camels, and whose judgement of values was accepted by the whole world.

The ruin of Baghdad began in *469*/1073; the walls crumbled in *653*/1255; it was destroyed by the Mongol invasion starting with the surrender in *656*/10 February 1258. At least one hundred thousand people were killed. In keeping with the religious law of the Mongols , the Yasa, which prohibited the spilling onto the ground of royal blood (similar laws existed with the early Arabs), the last 'Abbāsid Caliph, al-Musta'ṣim, was executed by being rolled up in carpets and trodden to death by horses. The Mongol Il-Khanid dynasty, which replaced the 'Abbāsids in Persia, made Tabrīz and Maragha their capitals. However, Ḥasan Buzurg, of a rival Mongol group within the Golden Horde, becoming the chief of the Jalāyrid successor state, turned to Baghdad to make it again a royal residence in *741*/1340. This was the prelude to a fresh catastrophe for the city in the form of its sacking by Tīmūr in *795*/1393 and again in *803*/1401. The Mongol invasions and, in addition, the establishment of trade routes by sea in the Age of Explorations made the city's decline inevitable. After passing back and forth between Ottomans and Ṣafavī Persians, the Ottomans took possession under Murād IV in *1048*/1638, and Baghdad again assumed a certain importance but lacked a prosperous economic base.

Today, Kaẓimayn, in a suburb to the north, is a Shī'ite shrine of the first magnitude (whose present architecture dates to the last century). As the tomb of the seventh and ninth Shī'ite Imāms Mūsā ibn Ja'far and Muḥammad ibn 'Alī al-Jawād, it draws many pilgrims. The city also boasts the tomb of 'Abd al-Qādir al-Jīlānī, one of the famous Saints of Islam, the tomb of the famous Sufī Ma'rūf al-Karkhī (originally a Mandaean or a Ṣābian, who was instrumental in establishing religious toleration for his former religion, d. *200*/815), and the tomb of the founder of the Ḥanafī School of Law, Abū Ḥanīfah. Baghdad and its environs also possess a number of Jewish shrines, notably the reputed tomb of Joshua, and those of Ezra and Ezekiel. Until 1451 Baghdad was the seat of the Exilarch, or chief of the Babylonian Jewish community. In different periods, the Exilarch (*Resh Galuta*) was accorded sometimes substantial independent authority by the 'Abbāsids, even to the extent of passing sentence on Muslims involved in disputes with Jews. The Exilarch, who was a descendant of David, has sometimes been called the "Jewish Caliph". Although in 'Abbāsid times his authority was civil, he once also had religious authority before this devolved upon the Rabbis. Although the Jews, who made up 15% of the population in the year 930 and 30% in 1830 have left, there are other ancient ethnic groups who remain, such as the Mandaeans, and Nestorian Christians, all of whom are a living link with the Mesopotamian past.

One of the neighborhoods of Baghdad, at-Tabiah, gave its name to the cloth "tabby", once a kind of richly coloured silk imported into Europe from the city. *See* 'ABBĀSIDS; CALIPHATE; HĀRŪN AR-RASHĪD; 'IRĀQ; MADA'IN; MANDAEANS; NESTORIANS; SHĪ'ISM; THOUSAND and ONE NIGHTS

Bahā'īs. A religion of modern times; an offshoot of the Bābī sect of Persia (itself an offshoot of the Shaykhis, who broke away from twelve-Imām Shī'ism). In the middle of the last century the Bābīs split three ways: original Bābīs, Azalī Bābīs, and Bahā'īs. The Azalīs are now almost extinct. After the death of the *Bāb* Mirzā 'Alī Muḥammad in *1267*/1850, one branch of the Bābī movement followed a young man called by the Bābī name of Ṣubḥ-i Azal ("the Eternal Dawn"). After three Bābī followers attempted to assassinate Shah Nāṣir ad-Dīn in *1269*/1852, the Bābīs were repressed by the government. The talented Bābī poetess Zarrin Tāj, called Qurrat al-'Ayn, or "Coolness of the Eye" was executed, with others, and Ṣubḥ-i Azal left Persia for Baghdad.

Ṣubḥ-i Azal's leadership was successfully challenged by his much older half-brother Bahā' Allāh ("the Splendor of God" *1233-1310*/1817-1892) whose former, pre-Bābī name was Mirzā Ḥusayn 'Alī Nūrī. Bahā' Allāh declared himself "the promised one" of the *Bāb's* prophecies and founded Bahā'ism, taking many of the *Bābī* followers with him.

In *1280*/1863 at the request of the Persian government, the Ottomans imprisoned the Bahā'ī chiefs, first in Edirne (Adrianople), and then sent Ṣubḥ-i Azal to Cyprus, and Bahā' Allāh to Acre (Akko) in Palestine. There was intrigue between the two factions; the Azalīs went into decline. The Bahā'ī branch flourished, despite a heavy 19% levy (*huququ'Llāh*) on the surplus revenue (after exempted basic expenses) of its followers. After the death of Bahā' Allāh in internment at Acre in 1892, there were many schisms, first between his sons. The leadership of 'Abbās Effendi (1844-1921), who took the name 'Abd al-Bahā', ("Slave of Bahā' Allāh") was contested by his younger brother, Muḥammad 'Alī, and was willed to 'Abd al-Bahā's grandson, Shoghi Effendi (d. 1957), but passed effectively to a council of thirty called "Hands of the Cause" who elected nine of their number to head the formerly family-run religion and then to an elected "Universal House of Justice" in 1963. Shoghi Effendi's widow, Ruhiyyih Rabbani, one the nine "Hands" with a great deal of influence, born Mary Sutherland Maxwell in New York in 1910, died in Haifa in 2000.

The shrine of Bahā'ism is in Haifa, Israel. The religion, propounding a mixture of humanism, world peace, and brotherly love, has gained a following of over five million. Nearly two million are converts from Hinduism in India. There are a million and a half Bahā'īs in sub-Saharan Africa and Latin America, and 120,000 in America and 25,000 in Europe. In Iran, the Bahā'īs are now looked upon as heretical and are often persecuted. *See* BĀB.

Baḥīrāh. A Christian monk of the 7th century who lived in Bostra, Syria. His dwelling lay along the route followed by the Meccan caravans. One of the caravans which stopped there was accompanied by the Prophet, then twelve years old, and his uncle Abū Ṭālib. The monk saw portents which led him to recognize in Muḥammad the Prophet-to-come. Al-Mas'ūdī said that the monk's name was Sergius and that he belonged to the tribe of 'Abd al-Qays. There are various versions of the story.

Baḥrayn. (Ar. "the two Seas") Emirate in the Persian Gulf; an archipelago named after the principal island. The population numbers over 409,000 of whom 98% are Muslim. Somewhat less than half are Arabs and Sunnīs, mostly of the Mālikī rite, with some Ḥanbalīs; the other half is an indigenous people called the Baḥarīnī, who are of Indo-European origin and twelve-Imām Shī'ite. The Shī'ites are mostly of the Akhbārī school of Jurisprudence (unlike Iran which is Uṣūlī). There is also a minority of Indians, Pakistanis, and Persians.

Bakhtiār. A semi-nomadic people of south-western Iran related to the Lūrs, who speak a Lūrī dialect. They are Shī'ite and number over half a million. The Bakhtiārī are divided into the Haft-Lang and Chahar-Lang, tribal groupings which were once called the "Great Lūrs" and the "Little Lūrs".

al-Balādhurī, Aḥmad ibn Yaḥyā (d. *279*/892). Historian of Persian origin who wrote the *Kitāb Futūh al-Buldān* describing the early Arab conquests, and *Kitab Ansāb al-Ashrāf*, a book of genealogies and biographies.

Balewa, Sir Abubakar Tafawa (1912-1966). A member of the Fulānī tribe, he was born Maham Abubakar, in a village in northern Nigeria, and later became a schoolteacher. He was one of the founders of the Northern People's Party, which developed into one of the most important political parties in Nigeria during the colonial period. When the Federation of Nigeria became independent, Sir Abubakar was elected the first Prime Minister. Along with Sir Ahmadou Bello, Dr. Naamde Azikiwe and Chief Obatemi Awolowe, Sir Abubakar was one of Nigeria's most outstanding leaders.

Sir Abubakar brought traditional Muslim values to his post and conducted himself with the pious simplicity of a believer. His assassination in a *coup d'état* in 1966 represented the passing of an age.

Balkh. *See* MAZĀR-I SHARĪF.

Baluch. A Sunnī people who number over three million; they are part shepherds and part farmers, who live in Baluchistan in Pakistan, in eastern Iran, and also in Afghanistan. Some Baluch are complete nomads.

Bangladesh. Republic. Estimated population 102,000,000 of whom 80% are Muslim and 15% Hindu. There are also Christian and Buddhist minorities. Of the Muslims 90% are Ḥanafī Sunnīs and 10% Twelve-Imām Shī'ites. The most important Sufi *ṭuruq* are the Qādiriyyah, the Suhrawardiyyah, and the Chishtiyyah.

Banking, Islamic, *see* ISLAMIC BANKING.

Banū Isrā'īl (lit. "the Children of Israel"). The name by which the Koran most commonly calls the Jews whom it calls also *alladhīna hādū* ("those that practice Jewish rites"). In Arabia, before Islam, the Jews lived in oases, and practiced crafts such as silver-smithing and agriculture, through which they traded with the Beduins. There were few Jews at Mecca, but half of the population of Medinah was Jewish, and there had also been Jewish kingdoms in the Yemen.

The influence of Judaism on Islam is very great and well documented. To begin with, the Arabs and the Jews have a common traditional ancestor in Abraham; besides the Abrahamic heritage, Mosaic Judaism was familiar to the Arabs. Many of the laws of Judaism are also found in Islam, and in the first century of the Hijrah, Jews who were converted to Islam brought the Haggadah literature to bear upon Koranic commentary.

What is much less well documented is the influence of Islam upon Judaism. In the light of the Koranic re-affirmation of God as Absolute, and as He was known to Adam, Islamic thought redefined the Aristotelian concept of the First Mover in its assimilation of Hellenist philosophy. This revelation or renewal of the primordial awareness of God probably influenced Jewish mysticism in Moorish Spain to emerge as the *Ain Sof* ("Without Limit") of the Qabbalah. While the framework of the doctrine of the Sephiroth could also have come from Neoplatonism directly, the fact that Islam, a Semitic monotheism, produced a massive synthesis of Hellenist metaphysics, probably inspired parallels within Judaism, derived from the Islamic model. Indeed, most Jews adopted Islamic theology, the Kalām when it emerged. As Joseph Kastein wrote in "The History of the Jews": "the Jews turned the general emancipation which attended the advance of Islam in the East to such good account that their intellectual influence once again began to make itself felt in the world of culture."

Banū Mūsā, *see* MŪSĀ SHĀKIR.

Baqā' (lit. "residue"). A Sufi technical term. According to the Sufis, through the practice of spiritual discrimination, concentration, and virtue, the "unreality" of the worshiper, the mortal and corruptible elements of his soul, fade away (*fanā'*) with the help of Divine grace, and there remains an adamantine and immortal nature, beyond appearances. The origin of the term baqa' is in the Koran (55:26-27):

> All that dwells upon the earth is perishing, yet still abides the Face of thy Lord, majestic, splendid.

Al-Ghazālī wrote:

> Each thing has two faces, a face of its own, and a face of its Lord; in respect of its own face it is nothingness, and in respect of the Face of God it is Being. Thus there is nothing in existence save only God and His Face, for everything perisheth but His Face.

This "remainder" is called *baqā'*. As in the words of al-Junayd: "*tawḥīd* (unification with God) is the removal of the temporal from the eternal."

al-Baqī'. The cemetery in Medinah, located near the *Masjid ash-Sharīf*, where many of the famous figures of Islam, Companions of the Prophet, scholars, Saints, and heroes, from its beginnings to recent times, are buried. The cemetery's full name is *baqī' al-gharqad*, or "roots of the lote-tree". The cemetery was once very colourful, full of tombstones and grave monuments. Since Wahhābīs oppose these, they were removed leaving empty fields, without markers.

al-Baqillānī, Abū Bakr Muḥammad ibn aṭ-Ṭayyib (d. *403*/1013). A Judge and a theologian, born in Baṣrah, 'Irāq. Trained as a Mālikī jurist, he was energetic and effective in spreading and establishing the Ash'arite school of *kalām* (theology). He is the author of the *I'jāz al-Qur'ān* ("the Incomparability of the Koran"). This was connected with another work of his that treated the notion discussed in al-Baqillānī's time, of the "apologetic miracle" that is, miracles substantiating claims to Divine mission. Al-Baqillānī says that an authentic miracle (and not mere trickery) must be a suspension of natural laws. *See* al-ASH'ARI.

Baqqā', Buqqā', *see* "Weeping Sufis".

Barabanshchiki. A name, meaning "drumbeaters" given by Russians to the followers of the Chim Mirza Sufi brotherhood, a branch of the Qadiriyyah ṭarīqah in the Caucasus. An old Sufi order, also called the *Jilālah* in Morocco, it expanded in the Caucuses after 1850 under the leadership of a Daghestani, Kunta Ḥajji Kishiev. *See* QADIRIYYAH.

Barakah. From the root *bā' rā' kāf*, meaning "to settle", whence *birkah*, or "well", and, in a derived meaning of the word, the act of kneeling by a camel. The primary meaning of *barakah*, however, is grace — in the sense of a blessing or a spiritual influence which God sends down. *Barakah* may be found in persons, places, and things. Certain actions and circumstances may also be a vehicle for blessing, as other actions and circumstances can dispel grace. Many religious greetings and expressions include the idea of *barakah*, such as *bāraka 'Llāhu fīk* ("May God bless you"), the most common and traditional way of saying thanks.

Bareilly. City west of Delhi in India, halfway to Lucknow. The theological school, Dar al-Ulūm of Bareilly, is characterized by its tolerance to folk beliefs among Indian Muslims carried over with their conversions from Hinduism in earlier times. The school of Bareilly extends its influence through the political party in Pakistan known as the Jama'at-i 'Ulamā'-i Pakistan. *See* BARILWIS.

Barhebraeus (lit. "the son of the Jew" in Arabic: Ibnu-l-'Ibri, so-called because his father Aaron was a Jew who converted to Christianity.) the epithet of Yuhaannā Abu-l-Faraj (AD 1226-1286) a Jacobite Christian historian, also known as Gregorius, the name he assumed when he was made Bishop of Gubos near Malaṭiyya in 1246. He was born in that town and fled with his father to Antioch in AD 1226 from the terror of the advancing Mongols. In 1252 he was promoted to the See of Aleppo and in 1264 he was elected Mafriyan or Catholicos of the Eastern Jacobites and resided in Mosul and Azerbaijan, where he died, in Maragha.

His history, "Abridgement of the History of Dynasties" was written in Syriac and translated into Arabic at the request of certain Muslims of note. This was published in Latin at Oxford in 1663 and thus made him an oft quoted source for Islamic history in the West.

Barīd (from the Persian *burīdah dum*, "having a docked tail". Hence a "mule" and, finally any post-horse or mounted messenger system or postal system. Or possibly from Latin *veredus* "mule", but doubtfully so). The 'Abbāsids inherited the famous Achaemenid Persian system of postal couriers which Herodotus described in those famous lines paraphrased on the frieze of the New York Central Post Office as "Neither snow nor rain nor heat nor gloom of night stays these couriers from the swift completion of their appointed rounds." the Caliph al-Manṣūr (d. *158*/775) set the precedents for the 'Abbāsid system of government, and like the Umayyads, used the Byzantine and Sāssānid chanceries to carry out the operations of the state. To keep a check on his provincial administration, al-Manṣūr made full use of the institution of the postal directorate and its directors to stay informed. They were thus an intelligence service to the Caliph, supplying information about the conduct and activities of provincial Governors, as well as about agricultural conditions and the state of the crops. Out of the registers of the postal stations came one impetus for the science of geography among the Arabs. It is known that in Sāssānid times this postal system had been penetrated by Manicheans who set up their co-religionists as functionaries and thus Manichean communications also travelled with the Imperial mail! This situation doubtless continued into Islamic times.

Barilwis. 1) Barilwi 'alims, teachers and students of the Madrasah or Dar al-Ulūm of Bareilly in India. 2) A Muslim sect in India, followers of Mawlānā Aḥmad Riḍā Khān (*1272-1340*/1856-1921), who concentrate on experiencing the presence of the Prophet Muḥammad during worship, and believe they find it in ecstasies which sometimes render them insensible. 3. The followers of Sayyid Aḥmad Barilwi (*1201-1246*/1786-1831; also known as Aḥmad of Rā'e Bareli, and as Aḥmad Shahīd), and followers of other leaders with the name Barilwi, Barelwi, and Brelvi. *See* BAREILLY; AḤMAD of RĀE BARELI.

Barmakids (*Āl Barmak* or *al-Barāmika*). A Persian noble family from Balkh who were hereditary Buddhist priests. The family supported the 'Abbāsid rise to power and became powerful government figures but they were suddenly deposed by Hārūn ar-Rashīd in 803.

The name Barmak is a title meaning head priest in Sanskrit (*par mukhi* or *pramukha*, "head of a Buddhist monastery"; in Manicheism the highest priest, *Magister*, after the *Princips* or *Archegos*; the term *mukhi* is still used by Indian Ismā'īlīs). The Barmaki or Barmecides were hereditary priests in a kind of Buddhist monastery in Balkh (today Mazar-i Sharīf in Afghanistan) called in Persian *Nawbahār* (*nava vihara* in Sanskrit or "new monastery"). There they had extensive land holdings and they ran a collective farm of which there were many such on the Silk Road, exploiting the religious initiates. The monastery was destroyed in *42*/663 by the Muslim conquests and the city of Balkh soon after. The city was rebuilt in *107*/725. Barmak, the father of Khālid, set out to investigate the new world order which had come crashing down upon his family. He visited the Umayyad Caliphal court depicting himself as a physician, astrologer, and philosopher from the mysterious East. His sons, Khālid, Sulayman, and al-Ḥasan went to Baṣrah and became clients of the Azd tribe, who had moved from Oman to Baṣrah at the end of Mu'awiyah's Caliphate and were also represented in Khorāsān. Khālid ibn Barmak (d. *165*/781) was an architect of the 'Abbāsid revolution and was on very intimate, family-like terms with as-Saffāḥ and al-Manṣūr, who became the founder of Baghdad. (Khālid helped to lay out the city and choose the site.) to create a strong alliance they had mutually fostered each others' children; the wife of Khālid ibn Barmak nursed the children of Manṣūr, and Manṣūr's wife nursed the children of Khālid. He led military expeditions, was governor, and held state office.

His son Yaḥyā ibn Khālid and his two sons Faḍl and Ja'far became the most famous Barmakids and virtually ran the government during the first seventeen years of Hārūn ar-Rashīd's Caliphate. Yaḥyā had been tutor of Hārūn and became his protector when Hārūn's elder brother al-Hādī became Caliph in *169*/785 and tried to eliminate him. Al-Hādi, who swore to follow his father Mahdī's advice to root out Manicheans had set out to do so when he died *suddenly* (al-Hādi had thrown Yaḥyā into prison for infidelity, and the day Yaḥyā was to be executed, al-Hādi died instead). Hārūn, the new Caliph made Yaḥyā his Vizier while Yaḥyā's son Faḍl was governor of Tabaristan (Mazandaran) and Azerbaijan, although they had to answer to Hārūn's mother Khayzuran. Hārūn called Yaḥyā "Father"; Faḍl ibn Yaḥyā was his foster brother. Ja'far was Hārūn's boon companion and intimate, and the tutor of Hārūn's son Ma'mūn. Faḍl was the tutor of the other son, Āmin. A favorable report — one should say "spin" on the part of many figures in the Islamic world at the time and shortly thereafter, due to some special sympathy towards the Barmakids, made this into a "golden age".

In *187*/803, returning from a pilgrimage to Mecca, Hārūn suddenly arrested Yaḥyā and Faḍl and two other sons of Yaḥyā: Musa and Muḥammad. Ja'far was put to death at the age of 37 and his head was impaled on one bridge over the Tigris river while two parts of his body were placed on either side on two other bridges. Yaḥyā was to die in *190*/805 at the age of 70, and Faḍl in *193*/808 at the age of 45. But a brother of Yaḥyā, Muḥammad ibn Khālid was not harmed. Musa (d. *221*/835) and Muḥammad, sons of Yaḥyā, were released from prison by Āmin when he became Caliph.

The downfall of the Barmakids has been treated as a tragedy and a mystery; it has been speculated that Hārūn had gone insane. However, the Barmakids were not what they appeared to be. Baghdad writers from Jāḥiẓ to Ibn Qutaybah and al-Aṣma'ī noted that "When in an assembly anything irreligious is said, the faces of the Barmakids light up; but when a verse from the Koran is quoted in their presence, they tell stories from the book of Mazdak." Mazdak was a Manichean who tried to institute a form of Communism in Iran in the reign preceding Anushirwan. The *Book of Mazdak* was translated into Arabic by Abān ibn 'Abd al-Ḥomayd ibn Lāḥiq ar-Raqqāshi (d. *200*/815), himself a protégé of the Barmakids, and considered to be Manichean. Many things of the kind were said about them, and about Khālid as well. They were accused of infidelity by al-Hādī. There is a veiled reference to this in Mas'ūdī speaking of the Persian predecessor to the *Thousand and One Nights*, The *Thousand Stories* which were about Sāssānid Kings like Khusraw (Chosroes) II. Mas'ūdī has Khusraw (Chosroes) discover that his vizier Bakhtakān is a Manichean, and has him drowned in the Tigris river. Al-Nadīm, writing a little later, was more explicit in the *Fihrist*: "it is said that all of the members of the Barmak family were *zanādiqah* [crypto-Manicheans] except for Muḥammad ibn Khālid ibn Barmak [the one *not* arrested by Hārūn]. It is also said that al-Faḍl and his brother al-Ḥasan were also [crypto-Manicheans]." This explains why the Barmakids were such successful governors, (Heraclitus says: "a hidden connection is stronger than an apparent one") and also their sudden downfall.

Ibn Khaldūn says that an empire can have only as many provinces as populations with whom it has ethnic ties, and the Barmakids had special religious ties with these far-flung provinces of the 'Abbāsid empire. ["...the group to which a given dynasty belongs and the people who support and establish it, must of necessity be distributed over the provinces and border regions which they take into possession."]

The "Buddhist" monastery in Balkh was a Manichean Buddhist monastery (see the description by the Chinese traveler Hsüan Tsang in MAZAR-I SHĀRIF). Manicheism disguised itself as whatever religion was dominant; today a Manichean Buddhist monastery survives in Fujian, China. For this reason writers such as Ibn Khallikan and Ibn Khaldūn called Nawbāhar a "fire temple" (rather than a Buddhist monastery) because Muslim authors lumped Manicheans together with Zoroastrians since Manicheism rarely appeared in its pure form, and the Muslims were not concerned with the details, calling all Iranian religions "Majus".

The Barmakids were creating an empire within an empire and Hārūn ar-Rashīd realized he was in peril. Manicheans may have brought the 'Abbāsids to power, but thereafter there had been continuous Manichean inspired revolts in Khorāsān from Muqanna', to Babak, to Mazyar. As Ibn Khaldūn said: "The reason for the destruction of the Barmakids was their attempt to gain control over the dynasty and their retention of the tax revenues." They also created a class of state secretaries loyal to themselves, and sympathetic to their philosophy, who were not to be ousted until the Twelve Imām Shī'ites replaced them with their own people at the time of al-Muqtadir. Hārūn, with the ruthless instinct of the 'Abbāsids, double-crossed the Barmakids first before they could double-cross him, the way al-Manṣur had done with Abū Muslim. (It could be added that Hārūn himself came to power probably by having his brother the Caliph Hādi poisoned through his mother's Khayzuran's collusion with the Barmakids themselves.) Now the original alliance with the Manicheans which had brought the 'Abbāsids to power suffered a serious setback leading eventually to the Qarmaṭī rebellions, and the Fāṭimid Empire. Abū-l-Qāsim al-Bustī, a Zaydī Mu'tazilite circa *400*/1000, wrote in his *Min Kashf Asrār al-Bāṭiniyya wa-Ghawār Madhhabihim* ("Revelation of the Esoterist's Secrets and the Destruction of their Doctrine"), that Barmak was the "ancestor" of the Fāṭimids. (This is not to be taken literally, but in the sense of "Father of" when speaking of vast developments.)

The alliance and the power struggle between Sunnis and the non-Islamic elements was also a factor in the succession war between Hārūn's two sons, the half-brothers al-Āmin and al-Ma'mūn. Al-Āmin was supported by conservative Islamic elements. Al-Ma'mūn was supported by Khorāsānis, especially from Balkh. Al-Ma'mūn, although he once led an army against al-Madā'in which was defended by 'Imrān ibn Musa, a grandson of Yaḥyā's, during his war of succession, nevertheless was to reconcile with the Barmakids and restore the precarious alliance which had, of necessity, to be set aside by Hārūn and his son al-Āmin. Al-Ma'mūn was to make Barmakids governors again, in one case, of Sindh, a region with a very ancient Manichean population, later in his reign.

It was after the Mu'tazilite concession instituted by al-Ma'mūn was brought to an end that the Caliphs had to leave Baghdad for the garrison city of Samarra' where, instead of Khorāsāni Persian troops, they were protected by Turkish slaves. They returned to Baghdad in 892 but by this time they were clients of the newly emerging Twelve Imām Shī'ites and Manichean inspired revolts like that of the Zanj and the Qarmaṭīs were raging around them rather than in far off Khorāsān, soon to be overshadowed by the rise of the rival Fāṭimid empire.

The name Barmakid was used by many others who were perhaps clients but not of the family. There was a neighborhood of Baghdad called the Barmakid quarter.There is a story in the *Thousand and One Nights* about "a Barmecide Feast" where the food is imaginary. This is a reference to the Manichean Bēma feast where the chief guest in whose honour the ceremony is held was, for some in any case, also imaginary, since he was invisible; but for others, invisible or not, he was absolutely real. *See* MANICHEISM; MAZAR-I SHĀRIF; 'ABBĀSIDS; BAGHDAD; al-MADĀ'IN; IBN MU'TAZZ.

Barmecides, *see* BARMAKIDS.

Barnabas, Gospel of. An "apocryphal" account of the life of Jesus (not to be confused with the "Epistle of Barnabas") in which Jesus is not crucified, but instead Judas Iscariot miraculously takes his form and is crucified in his place. The disciples steal the dead body of Judas, and Jesus reappears. The crucifixion as appearance is called "docetism", and first appeared with a certain Cerinthus around AD 85. It was associated with the idea that flesh and the physical world are evil and that therefore Jesus could not really take on a physical body. Docetism was the tendency of Gnostics such as Marcion and then became fixed within Manicheism whence it entered Islam.

The "Barnabas" story has became popular as a result of its propagation in the Islamic Middle East in recent times (the first English translation by Lonsdale and Laura Ragg was 1907 followed by a translation into Arabic in 1908) where it is taken to be the "suppressed", "true" gospel which does not conflict with the description of Jesus in the Koran. While the so-called "Gospel of Barnabas" does not actually conflict with the Koran, neither can it be taken in the sense of the Koranic passages in question — for it is clear from the Koran that God willed the people to see what they saw — and is pointless as far as Christianity itself is concerned, making nonsense of God's acts towards man.

Of the crucifixion, the Koran (4:155-158) says:

... and because of their disbelief,
and of their speaking
against Mary a tremendous calumny,
And because of their saying:
'We slew the Messiah,
Jesus son of Mary, Allah's Messenger' —
They slew him not, nor crucified him,
but it appeared so unto them;
and lo! those who disagree
concerning it are in doubt thereof;
they have no knowledge
save pursuit of a conjecture;
they slew him not for certain, —
But Allah took him up unto Himself.
Allah was ever Mighty, Wise.
There is not one of the People of the Scripture
but will believe in him before his death,
and on the of Resurrection
he will be a witness against them —

Jesus is thus considered to be still alive in a principial state from which he will return at the end of time. The Koran does not further explain the nature of the crucifixion, nor the difference between its outward appearance — the death of a man — and its inner truth, which is that Jesus was not killed. The Koran does say that the crucifixion of Jesus is what the people saw, and does not go into the reasons why God let the event take place and let the people see what they saw.

The Koranic passage in question is part of a series of accusations against the Jews, namely, of breaking the covenant, of disbelieving in God's revelations, slaying of the Prophets (which in the Gospels Jesus also says several times), and claiming, as it puts it: "We slew the Messiah Jesus son of Mary." It is the claim that they slew Jesus which the Koran refutes; it then cites sanctions for this and other transgressions.

As regards the "Gospel of Barnabas" itself, there is no question that it is of medieval origin. A complete Italian manuscript exists which appears to be a translation from a Spanish original (which exists in part), apparently written to curry favor with Muslims of the time. The original texts may have been copied or written in Istanbul and thus could be the result of the expulsion of Jews from Spain, whence a great many went to Turkey. It contains numerous anachronisms which can date only from the Middle Ages and not before, has factual errors about geography and history, and shows a garbled comprehension of Islamic doctrines, calling the Prophet "the Messiah", which Islam does not claim for him. Besides its farcical notion of sacred history, stylistically it is a mediocre parody of the Gospels, as the writings of Bahā' Allāh are of the Koran. *See* BIBLE; JESUS.

Barzakh (Ar. "a barrier", "an obstruction" between two things or places; specifically, "an isthmus"). A point of transition where entities similar yet different come together. The word has many applications in metaphysics. The Koran in 25:55 states:

And it is He who let forth the two seas,
this one sweet, grateful to taste, and this
salt, bitter to the tongue,
and He set between them a barrier,
and a ban forbidden.

and in 55:20:

He let forth the two seas that meet together,
between them a barrier they do not overpass.

Thus the isthmus, or *barzakh* between the salt and sweet seas (metaphors for this world and the next) beyond which one cannot cross without permission, is a barrier. There is another barrier (also *barzakh*) at death which prevents return, or reincarnation, to this world (23:100):

Till, when death comes to one of them, he says,
'My Lord, return me;
haply I shall do righteousness in that
I forsook.' Nay, it is but a word
he speaks; and there, behind them,
is a barrier until the day that they
shall be raised up.

A Saint who spans the chasm of human and Divine knowledge may also be called a *barzakh*. Indeed man in general, in view of his conjunction of body and soul, matter and intellect, and above all individual and Divine consciousness, is also a *barzakh*. Because the *barzakh* touches the two worlds it is not only a separation, but also a bridge; thus it is very similar to the concept of man as *pontifex*.

Bashi-Bozūk (Turk.) Vagabonds, or, as *Bashi-Bozūk 'askeri*, undisciplined irregular troops, known for their wildness, with their own leaders, which followed the Turkish armies until they were outlawed after the Russo-Ottoman war of 1877.

Bashhār ibn Burd (*95-168*/714-784). A blind poet, born in Baṣrah of Iranian origin. He was the first major literary figure of the Arabic language who was of non-Arab origin. He was a known Crypto-Manichean and early representative of *Shu'ūbism*, the backlash of nationalist affirmation in literature against the domination of Arabism after the Arab conquest. He believed in transmigration of souls, and according to Jāḥiẓ justified Iblīs' refusal to bow down to Adam, because he, Iblīs, was made of fire, and Adam was made of clay. This was the reason for his violent falling out with Wāṣil ibn 'Aṭā, with whom he had been good friends, who asked rhetorically if there wasn't someone who could kill this blind poet. This early rehabilitation of Iblīs was taken up and further developed by the "drunken Sufis".

Basmachis. ("Bandits"). The revolt of the "Basmachis" or "Bandits" was what the Bolsheviks called the Islamic resistance to Communism in Central Asia in the twenties and thirties. One Tatar who did become a Bolshevik and was extolled by the Revolution was Mir Sultangaliev. In 1921 the Tartar nationalist and Communist Sultangaliev called for the creation of an international organisation of colonial and semi-colonial nations and for its dictatorship over the advanced industrial states.

Uprisings began in Central Asia in 1916 because conscriptions in the Russian army left no-one to till the soil. Oppressions by the Bolsheviks created a resistance army of 20,000. The Bolshevik general Frunze almost put down the rebellion when Enver Pasha, the Turkish leader in WWI who had been groomed by Lenin to sway the Turkic populations to Communism joined the rebels and became their leader. King Amanullah of Afghanistan gave support to what was seen as a pan-Islamic movement. In February of 1922 Enver Pasha and the Basmachis captured Dushanbe but a large force sent from Russia crushed the rebellion by the end of summer, killing Enver Pasha, and leaving isolated guerilla remnants that carried on for a few more years.

Basmalah. The formula *bismi-Llāhi-r-Raḥmāni-r-Raḥīm*: "In the Name of God, the Merciful, the Compassionate." The *basmalah* is spoken by Muslims many times each day as a consecration before undertaking any lawful action. It is never omitted before a meal, where it is the equivalent of "saying grace". The meal is ended with the uttering of the *ḥamdalah*. When beginning ritual action the *basmalah* is preceded by the *ta'awwudh*. When performing ritual slaughter the words *ar-Raḥmāni 'r-Raḥīm* are replaced by *Allāhu akbar*.

The *basmalah* has a clear predecessor in the Pahlavī Zoroastrian formula of the 4th century: *pa nām i yazdan i xvorromand i rāyomand* ("in the name of the blessing and bountiful Divinity"). *See* ḤAMDALAH; PIOUS EXPRESSIONS; TA'AWWUDH.

Basṭ. An expansion or dilation of the soul which is experienced as joy. *Basṭ* is related to the Divine Name *al-Bāsiṭ*, "the Expander" or "He who gives joy". In Sufism, *basṭ* is a technical term for an expanding state of the soul that is inevitably followed, sooner or later, by its opposite which is contraction (*qabḍ*). As it is written in the *Ḥikam* of Ibn 'Aṭā' Allāh:

> Through the existence of joy the soul obtains its portion in expansion, but in contraction there is no portion for the soul.

And al-Ḥujwīrī said:

> John (the Baptist) was in straitness (*qabḍ*), Jesus in joyous expansion (*basṭ*); for John, according to a well-known Ḥadīth, wept from the day he was born, and Jesus from the day he was born smiled. When they met, John used to say: "Jesus hast thou no fear thou wilt be cut off from God?"
>
> "John, hast thou no hope of mercy?" Jesus would reply. "Neither thy tears nor my smiling will change decree."

The concepts are similar to the medieval alchemical notions of *solve* (a spiritual, as well as physical, entering into solution, or a dissolving) and *coagula* (fixation in form). But it is the phase of coagulation (*qabḍ*), paradoxically, which offers the possibility of release through the "narrow gate" of form, while solution (*basṭ*) actually entraps because the essence becomes compounded with the conditional. As Ibn 'Aṭā Allāh says:

> It is more dreadful for gnostics to be expanded than to be contracted, for only a few can stay within the limits of proper conduct in expansion.

There is also this Ḥadīth which demonstrates the benefits of *qabḍ*, or straitening: "Sins fall from a sick man, like leaves from a tree." *See* QABḌ.

Ba'th Political Party. (Ar. *Ba'th* means "resurrection"). The Arab Resurrection Socialist Party founded in Syria by both Muslims and Christians, notably Michel Aflaq and Salah Ad-Din Bitar. It held its first congress in Damascus in 1947. It was based upon principles of Arab nationalism and was not religious. After 1963 it split into Syrian and 'Irāqī branches which are inimical to each other and ruled those two countries. The party is organized in both countries as a revolutionary organisation with a cell structure and strict hierarchy that has brought control of the parties in the hands of narrow elites. In 2003 U.S. forces destroyed the tomb of Michel Aflaq in Baghdad.

Bāṭin (lit. "inward"). One of the Names of God, *al-Bāṭin*, "the Inner" (57:3). *Bāṭin* also means that which is secret and, in particular, denotes esoteric knowledge.

Bāṭini. Any doctrine which is esoteric, secret, or initiatic. It also denotes someone who belongs to a group of such nature. Sometimes, but not always, it is used reproachfully, indicating a doctrine of dubious nature. Ibn Khaldūn said that the Berbers in Tunisia who welcomed the first Fāṭimid amongst themselves had, before he came, a *bāṭini* religion. Bāṭini is also the key word in describing the beliefs of the Seljūq Turks when they appeared on the scene and that of the Turkish princedoms in Anatolia before they were absorbed into the Ottoman empire. *See* ALEVIS; TA'LIMIYYAH.

al-Battānī, Abū 'Abd Allāh Muḥammad. (*244-317*/858-929). Astronomer and mathematician. Al-Battānī was from Ḥarrān (today Altinbasak in Turkey, near Urfa), and belonged to the Hellenist pagan religion of that city, but became a Muslim. He studied in Raqqa in Syria on the Euphrates and died in Samarra'. In medieval and renaissance Europe (where he was known as Albatenius) he was accounted one of the most important authorities on astronomy; indeed his calculations (*az-Zīj aṣ-Ṣābi'*) of planetary motion were remarkably accurate, and he also made original contributions to mathematics, notably in spherical trigonometry.

Battle of 'Aqrabah, *see* MUSAYLAMAH.

Battle of 'Ayn Jalūt ("Battle of Goliath's Spring"; *658*/1260). At this battle near Nablūs in Palestine, the Mamlūks led by Qutuz and his lieutenant Baybars decisively defeated the Mongols (a much smaller force), thus saving Egypt from Mongol expansion. This battle also brought Syria under Mamlūk control.

Battle of Badr (*19th Ramaḍan 2*/Friday 17th March 623). The first major encounter between the Muslims and the Meccans (after the skirmish of Nakhlah). Badr lies 90 miles/125 km to the south of Medinah. The Muslim force numbered 305. Before the battle one Meccan joined the Muslims; there were besides him, seventy-four original emigrants (*muhājirūn*). The rest were Companions (*anṣār*), or Medinans. The force of the Meccans was close to a thousand.

The Muslims had set out to attack a Meccan caravan led by Abū Ṣufyān who, however, learned of the danger from scouts and sent a message to Mecca asking for reinforcements. The caravan itself then hastened around Badr to avoid the attackers completely, but the Meccan army of reinforcement encountered the Muslims.

At the beginning of the battle the Prophet threw a handful of pebbles at the Meccans, saying "abased be those faces". A later revelation of the Koran said that it was not he, but God Who threw (8:17). Angels, led by Gabriel, joined the Muslims; one of two men observing on a hill related that they heard the neighing of stallions that swept past them as if in a moving cloud; the other man died on the spot of sudden fear.

After initial challenges to individual combats, the Muslims fought, under the orders of the Prophet, in a style revolutionary to the Arabs; instead of indulging in sporadic and disorganized hit-and-run skirmishes, the Muslims fought as a disciplined body with an order of battle. To this the Koran attached merit when it says "God loves those who fight in His way in ranks" (61:4). The Muslim casualties were fourteen, those of the Meccans fifty, among them Abū Jahl. Fifty Meccans were captured; of these Umayyah, Nadr, and

'Uqbah, bitter enemies of Islam, were put to death, the rest being held for ransom. After the battle, the Prophet addressed the fallen infidels in their common grave, and when those around him expressed surprise, he explained that the recently dead can still hear the living. (The doctrine in Islam, in respect of the nature of hearing and sound, is that the dead may continue hearing for as long as three days).

The battle amounted to an astonishing victory for the Muslims, and one that gained them political credibility for their cause among other tribes. It became one of the greatest marks of glory for survivors to say that they had fought at Badr. *See* MUḤAMMAD.

Battle of the Camel (*10th Jumada II 36*/4th December 656). The decisive encounter of the army of the Caliph, 'Alī, and the army of dissidents led by the Companions Ṭalḥāh and az-Zubayr, who were joined by 'Ā'ishah. 'Alī won, Ṭalḥāh and az-Zubayr were killed in the battle and 'Ā'ishah was sent back to Medinah without sanctions.'Ā'ishah was in a litter on a camel; the battle raged up to her camel and then stopped; from this the battle got its name. *See* 'ALī.

Battle of Goliath's Spring, *see* BATTLE of 'AYN JALŪT.

Battle of Ḥunayn (*8*/630). After their conquest of Mecca, the Muslims fought a battle against the allied tribes of Hawāzin and Thaqīf at a point between Mecca and Ṭā'if. The Muslim army, although very numerous, at first panicked and fled when the Hawāzin came down upon it in the defile of Ḥunayn. The Prophet drew to one side with his Companions and some of the Anṣār, turned to al-'Abbās who had a strong voice, and had him cry out "Companions of the Tree! Companions of the Acacia!" (of the Pact of *Ḥudaybiyyah*). Thereupon from all sides the Companions responded "*Labbayk*" ("At thy service!"), and rallied to the Prophet. The Prophet stood up in the stirrups and prayed "God! I ask of Thee Thy promise." Then he took some pebbles and flung them in the face of the enemy as he had done at Badr, whereupon the tide of battle turned. Afterwards the revelation came:

God has already helped you on many fields,
and on the day of Hunain,
when your multitude was pleasing to you,
but it availed you naught, and the land
for all its breadth was strait for you,
and you turned about, retreating.
Then God sent down upon his Messenger
His Shechina,
and upon the believers, and He sent down
legions you did not see, and He chastised
the unbelievers; and that is the recompense
of the unbelievers;
then God thereafter turns towards whom He will;
God is All-forgiving, All-compassionate.
(9:25-27)

The routed enemy took refuge in Ṭā'if which was besieged unsuccessfully; but the Muslim victory persuaded the desert tribes to accept Islam and shortly thereafter the rebel tribes and Ṭā'if also surrendered and entered Islam. *See also* RIḌĀ'.

Battle of Nahrawan (*38*/658). (Ar. *waq'at an-nahr* "The Encounter at the River"). Following the Battle of Ṣiffīn (*37*/657) and the arbitration which followed, a group seceded from the army of the Caliph 'Alī and became known as "Khārijites" (from Arabic *Kharaja*: "to secede"). They embarked on a military campaign, taking Ctesiphon (Madā'īn). 'Alī attacked them at Nahrawan and annihilated all but a handful. In revenge he was assassinated by a surviving Khārijite, Ibn Muljam. *See* 'ALĪ; KHĀRIJITES.

Battle of Nihawand (*22*/642). This marked the final defeat of the Persians during the Arab expansion which followed the revelation of Islam. The Persians were led by the General Firozān; the Muslims, at first by Nu'mān ibn Muqarran, who was killed and replaced by Hudhayfah ibn al-Yaman. The battle took place near Hamadhān. Afterwards the last Sāssānid, Yazdagird, fled into Khorāsān, and then to Merv, where he was betrayed by one of his satraps and killed while he hid in the house of a miller. *See* YAZDAGIRD.

Battle of Qādisiyyah (*15*/636). This took place near Kūfah (which became an Arab camp-city, founded after the battle). The Persian army of the emperor Yazdagird, the last Sāssānid, under the general Rustum, was decisively defeated by the Muslims led by Sa'd ibn Abī Waqqās. The legendary Persian war flag, the *Drafsh-i Kavianeh*, made of leather and precious stones, was captured, cut up, and divided among the victors.

Persian resistance continued until their final defeat at the Battle of Nihawand, south of Hamadhān, in *22*/642.

Battle of Ṣiffīn, *see* 'ALĪ ibn ABĪ ṬĀLIB.

Battle of the Trench. (Also known as the Khandaq, lit. "the trench", and the "War of the Confederates"). In *5*/627 the Meccan Quraysh prepared to attack the Muslims in a massed battle with an army, called afterwards the "Confederates" (*al-aḥzāb*). The Quraysh had made an alliance with certain desert tribes, the Banū Ghatafan, and Jews of the Banū Nādir who had emigrated from Medinah to Khaybar. The Prophet, however, forewarned of these plans, perhaps by his cousin al-'Abbās from Mecca, ordered a defensive trench to be dug around Medinah. This stratagem had not been used before by the Arabs but was known to the Sāssānids; they had built a trench against Arab incursions near Ḥirāh which was maintained for them by their clients the Lakhmids. (There had also been a three meter deep ditch around a Sumerian city near present day Samarra'.) By a later tradition it was Salmān al-Fārsī, the apocryphal Persian, who gave the idea to the Prophet. Tradition says the trench took six days of feverish work to dig since the warning came only a week before the attack. This is, however, too short a time to make such a trench; it was probably the result of a longer term strategy following the defeat of the Muslims at the Battle of Uḥud.

The Meccan army was made up of 4,000 from Mecca and 5,000 or more from the allies, with a total of 1,000 cavalry. The Medinans numbered 3,000. The Meccan cavalry was stopped by the trench, and the attackers laid siege for two weeks. The Meccan general Khālid ibn al-Walīd, attempted several times to cross the trench with horsemen at its narrowest point near the Jabal Sal' but succeeded only once. 'Alī fought in single combat with one of the attackers and slew him. Another tried to escape, fell into the trench, and was also killed.

Nu'aym of the Ashjā' was one of the leaders of the Confederates, who before the battle, had been sent to Medinah to sow discord and apprehension; instead, he then began inclining towards Islam. During the battle, he again made his way into Medinah, in secret. He entered Islam and then proceeded to stir up the Banū Qurayẓah This was a Jewish tribe in Medinah who had broken their pact with the Prophet and secretly conspired to give assistance to the Confederates. Nu'aym set the Banū Qurayẓah against the Quraysh by telling them that they would be abandoned by the Meccans and should refuse to help unless they were given hostages from the Quraysh. To the Quraysh, on the other hand, he said that the Banū Qurayẓah would not fulfill their promise to help and would attempt to stall by asking for Qurayshi hostages to share their plight in the case of defeat. Nu'aym's ruse succeeded. Dissension among the Confederates grew and was exacerbated by the tribulation of a violent wind from the sea which blew for three days and nights, unleashing torrents of rain. Discouraged, the Quraysh abandoned the siege. Abū Sufyān, the Meccan leader, left precipitously, almost before all the others.

After the battle, the Medinans executed the Banū Qurayẓah for their treachery. The most notable casualty on the Medinan side was Sa'd ibn Mu'ādh, chief of one of the clans of the tribe of Aws. *See* QURAYẒAH

Battle of Uḥud. Uḥud on the western outskirts of Medinah is a volcanic hill with a plain stretching before it. The Quraysh soundly defeated the Muslims here in the third year of the Hijrah (625). The Meccan army, led by Abū Sufyān, numbered three thousand men,including seven hundred in coats of mail and two hundred horse. On the morning of the battle three hundred Medinans under 'Abd Allāh ibn Ubayy (the leader of the "hypocrite" faction in Medinah), deserted the Prophet as the troops rode out of the city, leaving the Muslims only seven hundred strong.

Nevertheless, the Muslims were close to victory when forty archers whom the Prophet had stationed on the hill to remain there and guard the flank, saw that the Muslims were winning. Afraid to lose their share of the booty, most of them abandoned their post. This left the way open for a counter-attack by a detachment of the Meccan cavalry led by Khālid ibn al-Walīd. The ten Muslim archers who had remained faithful to their orders proved too small a number to hold back the cavalry and were cut down.

Caught by the breakthrough of the Meccan cavalry, the Prophet's army was routed and the Prophet himself was wounded and momentarily knocked unconscious. The rumor of his death caused the Meccans to withdraw thinking the battle won. When the Meccans learned that the Prophet had survived it was too late to launch a counter-attack.

In this battle, Ḥamzah, an uncle of the Prophet and one of Islam's most formidable warriors, was killed, speared by a slave named Waḥshī. Hind, wife of Abū Sufyān, thirsting to revenge her kinsman killed at Badr, had set her slave to this exploit with promises of reward. The Prophet greatly mourned Ḥamzah, foremost of the Martyrs of Uḥud. Another hero is Anās ibn Naḍr who fought so valiantly that he succumbed to eighty wounds. Seventy-two Muslims were killed on the battlefield (and are buried there) and several died afterwards. One man, Usayrim, had not believed in Islam until the morning of the battle. When belief suddenly overtook him he set out alone to join the Medinan army. He is notable for having died a martyr on that day and therefore having entered paradise without ever praying a single ritual prayer.

Two women, Umm Sulaym and Nuṣaybah, followed the army from Medinah to tend the wounded on the battlefield; of these, Nuṣaybah had participated in the Pact of the Second 'Aqabah.

Bay'ah ("a pact"). The installation or recognition of a ruler in his office takes the form of a pact, a *bay'ah*, which is an oath of fealty or allegiance. This is made with the ruler by the subjects, or, on their behalf, by the body of religious scholars, the *'ulamā'*, and political chiefs. Initiation into a Sufi order is also in the form of pact made by the novice with God through the spiritual master. *See* ḤUDAYBIYYAH; RIḌWĀN.

Bay'at ar-Riḍwān, *see* RIḌWĀN.

Baybars I (al-Mālik aẓ-Ẓāhir Rukn ad-Dīn; *632-676*/1233-1277). The greatest of the Mamlūk Sultans of Egypt. He began his career as a Turkish slave who was sold into the bodyguard of the Ayyūbid Sultan of Damascus, al-Mālik aṣ-Ṣāliḥ. Baybars took part in the assassination of the Sultan's son, Turanshah, and fled, entering the service of Qutuz, the Mamlūk Sultan of Egypt.

As Qutuz's lieutenant, Baybars defeated the Mongols at 'Ayn Jalūt in *660*/1260. Then, angry at being denied governorship of Aleppo, he murdered Qutuz, seized the Sultanate for himself, and led the Baḥrī Mamlūks to many victories against the Crusaders, reducing the Crac des Chevaliers castle in Syria (*Qal'at al-ḥiṣn*) and other fortresses. Baybars crushed the last Assassin strongholds in Syria and extended Mamlūk rule to its historic limits.

Baybars installed Abū-l-Qāsim Aḥmad as a figurehead 'Abbāsid in Cairo under the name al-Mustanṣir bi-Llāh. Abū-l-Qāsim, an uncle of the last 'Abbāsid Caliph who was killed by the Mongols when they captured Baghdad, was himself killed in an attempt to recapture Baghdad in *659*/1261; but the dynasty maintained itself in Cairo until the Ottoman conquest in *923*/1517. The presence of a figurehead Caliph in Egypt gave Baybars and his Mamlūk successors a greater prestige and enhanced legitimacy.

Baybars recognized the authority of all four Schools of Law and established the custom of naming *qāḍis* (Judges) for each school in his territories, a practice which the Ottomans continued. Baybars was thus able also to play off the schools against one another when it suited him. He was an energetic if ruthless ruler, noted for his military exploits but also for his public works and patronage of splendid architecture. A power struggle followed his death, as was customary with the Mamlūks, and Baybars' infant son was deposed by another contender, Qala'ūn.

al-Bayḍāwī, 'Abd Allāh ibn 'Umar (d. *691*/1291). A Persian religious scholar, who was *Qāḍī* (Judge) in Shīrāz. He wrote a commentary on the Koran entitled *Anwār at-Tanzīl wa Asrār at-Ta'wīl* ("The Lights of Revelation and the Secrets of Interpretation"). Although he takes many opinions from az-Zamakasharī (d. *538*/1144), a Mu'tazilite, al-Bayḍāwī represents a sifting of all previous commentaries, and is regarded as the soundest and most authoritative commentator. *See* COMMENTARIES on the KORAN.

Bayram. A Turkish name for the festivals of 'Īd al-Aḍḥā (in Turkish: *kurban bayram*) and the 'Īd al-Fiṭr. *See* 'ĪD al-ADḤĀ.

Bayt al-Ḥikmah, *see* HOUSE of WISDOM.

"Beatific Vision" (Ar. *Rūyatu-'Llah*). The Koran speaks of men's "meeting with their Lord" as in the last verse of the Sūrah of the Cave:

So let him, who hopes for
the encounter with his Lord,
work righteousness, and not associate with his
Lord's service anyone. (18:110)

and it speaks of souls "gazing upon their Lord" as in the Sūrah of the Resurrection:

Upon that day faces shall be radiant,
gazing upon their Lord. (75:22-23)

Again, there are references in the Koran, to God's "Face", as in the Surah of the Night:

.... even he who gives his wealth to purify himself
and confers no favor on any man for recompense,
only seeking the Face of his Lord the Most High;
and he shall surely be satisfied. (92:18-20)

The Mu'tazilites, or Rationalists, denied that it could be possible to see God, and said that such passages had to be interpreted symbolically or allegorically. The Twelve-Imām Shī'ites, whose theology is a continuation of Mu'tazilitism, also deny the Beatific Vision, interpreting it symbolically. The traditionalists responded with a Ḥadīth in which the Prophet answers his Companions' questions about "seeing" God in Paradise by saying He will be seen as we "see the full moon against the dark night", that is, indirectly, as the moon reflects the light of the sun.

Al-Asha'rī, himself a former and repented Mu'tazilite and the greatest authority on *kalām*, or theology, went on to say that the seeing of God in paradise was the greatest joy that the Blessed enjoyed there.

The importance of the "Beatific Vision", is not a question of sight, but of awareness or knowledge. Or, to put it another way, "seeing God" is a participation, even indirectly, in the Divine Essence. The Mu'tazilites, in denying the "beatific Vision" deny the possibility of knowing God; an unknowable God does not have even a merciful relation with creation; it is this which constitutes the importance of this Mu'tazilite heresy.

The poet Ḥāfiẓ brought himself into actual danger at the hands of Shī'ites for his verse: "This borrowed life which the Friend hath entrusted to Ḥāfiẓ — One day I shall see His Face and shall yield it up to Him."

Christian theologians, notably St. Thomas Aquinas, also emphasize the importance of the contemplation of God, the intellectual "vision" of God — even though God is "invisible" — in paradise. *See* MU'TAZILITES.

Bedug. A drum used in Indonesia to call the prayer in forested areas where the human voice does not carry well.

Behzad, Ustād Kamāl ad-Dīn (d. *942*/1535). Renowned master of Persian miniatures, who worked mainly in Herāt for Tīmūrid princes but also in Tabrīz for Ṣavafis. His art grew out of the Manichean tradition which had already given birth to the icon in Christianity. Before his time, painting in Islam was considered a form of art below calligraphy; but in the 16th century it flourished beyond its earlier rôle in illustrating text and was brought to India by Humayun in 1555, where, at the time of Akbar (who ruled from 1556-1605) Moghul painting reached its high point.

Begging. A practice frowned upon by Islamic law; on the other hand, the giving of alms (*ṣadaqah*), is a religious duty which purifies the soul. It is not legal to beg as long as one has sustenance for a day and a night. Nevertheless, dervishes sometimes took to begging for a livelihood. As al-Ḥujwīrī said:

> There are three allowable motives for begging, as more than one Shaykh has said: first, for the sake of mental liberty, since no anxiety is so engrossing as worry about getting something to eat; second, for the soul's discipline: Sufis beg because it is so humiliating and helps them to realize how little they are worth in other men's opinion, so that they escape self-esteem; third to beg from men out of reverence for God, regarding all as His agents — a servant who petitions an agent is humbler than one who makes petition to God Himself.
>
> The begging rule is this: if you beg and get nothing, be more cheerful than if you get something; never beg of women or people who hang about the bazaar; as far as possible, beg in a selfless spirit; never using what you get for self-adornment or housekeeping, or buying property with it. You should live in the present; never let a thought of tomorrow enter your mind, or you are lost. A final rule is never to let your piety be seen in the expectation of more liberal alms on that account.
>
> I once saw a venerable old Sufi who had lost his way in the desert come starving into the market place at Kūfah with a sparrow perched on his hand crying: "Give me something, for the sparrow's sake!"

"Why do you say that?" People asked.
"I can't say: for God's sake," he replied;
"one must let an insignificant creature plead
for worldly things.

Being (Ar. *al-wujūd*). In Islamic metaphysics this is *Lāhūt*, the second of the "Five Divine Presences", (*al-ḥaḍarāt al-ilāhiyyah al-khams*). Being is what religions call the "personal God"; the first differentiation of the Absolute, which is Itself Divine but not Absolute. It is Divine in relation to existence because it contains all existence in perfection; it is Divine in relation to the Absolute because it is nothing other than the Absolute, "reflected", but a perfect mirror, nonetheless. The Essence, Beyond-Being, which is the Absolute, *Allāh*, is All-Possibility; which must also embrace the possibility of Its own limitation. This necessary possibility is a perfection of the Absolute, no less than the Omnipotence of the Absolute is a perfection. It is Being which is the first movement in the unfolding of this possibility of self-negation.

What is One, indivisible, All-Possibility in the Absolute, becomes differentiated possibilities in Being. And Being translates the All-Possibility of Beyond-Being into existence and generates the creation of the world. Within Being a polarisation takes place into Act (or Power) and Receptivity (or Substance, which is often used as a synonym for Being). Aristotle, and after him the Scholastics, called this polarisation *eidos* and *hyle*, form and materia. It is what the Koran calls the "pen" (*al-qalam*) and the "guarded tablet" (*al-lawḥ al-mahfūẓ*). This polarisation corresponds to Yang (Power) and Yin (Receptivity) in Taoism. Manifestation or creation takes place "between" this polarisation, as the result of its union. Being is the "locus" of the higher paradises, and the degree of the Divine Names of the Qualities such as *ar-Raḥīm* (but not the Names of the Essence, or the Absolute, such as *ar-Raḥmān*).

Being corresponds to what Neoplatonism calls the logos, or the nous. Seen from different perspectives, Being is also called in Arabic *al-'amr*, *al-'aql al-awwal*, and many more terms as well. *Moksha*, or *mukti*, or "deliverance", is release from all contingency into Being, whereas salvation is conformity with a higher, but still contingent, degree of existence.

The Scholastics of Medieval Europe spoke of existence (from *ex-sistere*, "to stand out") as "accidents" in relation to "substance", or Being. "Accidents", metaphysically, are that which is contingent, or dependent, upon something else. Ibn 'Arabī (d. *638*/1240), and metaphysicians of his school, used exactly the same terminology; that which existed he called accidents (*a'rāḍ*) emerging from substance (*jawhar*). Similarly Jāmī' (d. *898*/1491) and other poets said that beings in this world are "foam" on the waves of the ocean. (Water, which takes any shape, and is virtually a universal solvent, is the immediate symbol of substance; the ocean, in Arabic *al-Muḥīṭ*, "the encircling", an immediate symbol of Being.) The foam, the "accidents" come into existence because of privation, or an absence (*'adam*); the world "exists" because it is something removed from Being, from that which really IS, just as a colour is the result of the removal of the other colours from colourless light, from light as such.

A Chinese Muslim named Ma Fu-Ch'u writing in the 18th century described Being thus in a treatise called *The Three Character Rhymed Classic on the Ka'bah*:

Being's great attribute
is called Consciousness-Potency,
Consciousness foreshadowing the
intelligence of things
and Potency implying forms;
creative change begins
when the archetypes are born;
the Great Command
[Ar. kun, 'Be!'; cf. Koran 16:40]
is given
which is the gate to all marvels;
natures and intelligences are separated out
prefiguring their forms;
the myriad intelligences muster
and the subtle substance forms;
what one calls the Primal Spirit [Ar. *ruḥ*]
is truly all-pervasive
from the limits of the Previous Heaven [the
unmanifest; *al-ghayb*]
to the roots of the Later Heaven
[creation: *ad-dunyā*]
the male and female principles emerge
and the four elements are manifested
and their celestial and chthonic aspects fixed;
when the myriad forms are complete
they make Man.
Now Man
is the Essence of Heaven and earth;
among the ten thousand transformations

his is a special creation;
the quintessence of Heaven
is Man's heart;
the glory of earth
is his body;
the ten thousand intelligent principles
are Man's essential Nature...

See FANA'; FIVE DIVINE PRESENCES; al-INSĀN al-KĀMIL; al-KINDĪ.

Bektashī. A heterodox sect found in Turkey and to a lesser extent in countries formerly part of the Ottoman Empire. The Bektashis are sometimes considered to be a Sufi *ṭarīqah*, since they are organized as such. Rather than an esoterism, however, they represent instead a mixture of beliefs and practices which includes elements from Shī'ism, Christianity, and other sources, including possibly Buddhism.

The sect was widespread among the Janisseries, the military corps composed of boys taken from Christian families in the Balkans and converted to Islam, which accounts for the eclectic syncretism of Bektashi practices, reflecting certain vestiges of Christianity. *See* JANISSERIES.

Beloshaposhniki. A Russian name for the followers of the *Vis* (from the name "Uways") *Haji* brotherhood, a branch of the Caucasus Qadiriyyah ṭarīqah, derived from the Chim Mirza branch ("Barabanshchiki"). The *Vis Haji* were founded in Kazakhstan by Chechen exiles. *See* QADIRIYYAH.

Bēma (from Greek *bēma*, a platform). In ancient Greece, a speaker's platform. In Islam, a similar platform is the pulpit called the *minbar*, also used in Synagogues. In the Greek Orthodox church the area around the altar is called the Bēma. Most importantly, the Bēma is the name of the principal ceremony in Manicheism. Mani was imprisoned in Jundishapur and died on the 26th day of his imprisonment (February 14 or 26, AD 274) He returned to life on the 27th to "live forever". (The word Manicheism comes from Aramaic *Mani Ḥayy* — Mani lives.) This is also called his *parinirvana* and was celebrated yearly by a communal vegetarian meal in front of the Bēma, an empty chair, throne, or platform, the chair of Mani. (According to St. Augustine it was a platform of five steps which would make it very much like the *minbar*.) But the chair was only empty to the un-initiated; to those who knew, Mani was on the empty throne, alive and aware. Words were addressed to Mani in Aramaic, perhaps a report on the world progress of Manicheism, which, once everyone had understood and accepted the "Religion of Truth" would trigger the end of the world (much as Communist party meetings began with a report of the scientific state of progress of the ideology on the local, national, and world level.)

According to St. Augustine, the Bēma ceremony took place before Christian Easter, and the thirty days preceding were the Manichean month of fasting. The Manichean month of fasting must have influenced the institution of Ramaḍan (the month in which the Koran was revealed) as a month of fasting, and in particular the idea that the Night of Destiny, the actual night the Koran was revealed, was the 27th night of Ramaḍan.

Since the Manicheans readily pretended to be members of any religion of convenience, it is not surprising that the Bēma shows up in sects which claimed to be Muslim, and elsewhere. In the brief revolt of the Mukhtāriyyah/Kaysāniyyah (which eventually brought the 'Abbāsids to power), the leader Mukhtār held a ceremony in front of an empty throne, to which he addressed strange words. When asked by Muslims what this was, his ready answer was that it was "the throne of 'Alī". Ṭabarī records that in Kūfah (an Arab centre of Manicheism) there was a certain Hawshab who was "the keeper of the throne of 'Alī". ('Alī had no throne; Arabs of his time sat on the ground.)

The empty throne appears among the Whirling Dervishes, the Mevlevis, who have an empty sheepskin on the floor at their ceremonies where the martyred Shamsi Tabrizī sits, invisible to most. Similarly, many Turkish Sufi sects also have empty sheepskins at their meeting for the founder of their order. In the Thousand and One Night, there is the "Barmecide Feast", which is a feast at which there is no food, at least, the guest does not see it. (The empty chair is here an empty plate, perceptible only to the pure. The Barmecides, were according to al-Nadīm and others, Manicheans.) A very inventive variant is an anecdote about the fourth Fāṭimid Caliph al-Mu'izz li-Dīn-i Llāh ("The Exalter of the Religion of God"). He had a decree scroll (*sijill*) made without writing, sealed, and sent into the city of Cairo with a crier and a trumpeter to be read. (Here the empty chair is an empty scroll). The story of the Emperor's new clothes may well be another echo, since Manicheism spread in Europe in the Middle Ages through travelling weavers, who went into houses to make cloth.

Today, the 'Alāwis (Nuṣayris) of Syria have an agape meal as part of their secret rites. In Judaism, there is an empty chair of Elijah at circumcisions and at seders.

Bench, People of the, *see* AṢHĀB aṣ-ṢUFFĀH.

Berbers. A Mediterranean people found in North Africa from Libya to the Atlantic, and from the Mediterranean to regions just below the Sahara. They include nomads such as the Tuaregs of the Sahara, Mali and Niger, as well as settled farmers in the Atlas mountains of Morocco, in the Souss, the Rīf, the Kabyles of Algeria. They also include the Guanches of the Canary Islands. Berbers speak a number of related languages which belong to the Hamitic group such as Targui, Tamazikht, spoken in the Atlas mountains, Rīfī (Tarifit) spoken in the northern Rif, Tashelhit, spoken in the Souss and Agadir, and others. The Tuaregs possess a script, Tifinagh, which was once widely used by the other Berbers. During the French Protectorate in Morocco there was a college which taught in French, Arabic and Tamazikht (from Imazighen, or "free people" as the Moroccan Berbers call themselves). Berber was discontinued after 1956, but in 2002 a new Royal Institute for the Tamazikht Language and Culture opened. A few private schools had already begun teaching Tamazikht earlier.

The Berbers were partly Islamicized in the course of the first Arab invasions and participated in the conquest of Spain. Some Berber groups were left behind after the retreat of the Arabs from Spain and today survive as Spanish ethnic groups such as the Maragatos of Astorga in Leon.

With the help of Berbers in Tunisia, the Fāṭimids carved out their Kingdom, as did the Idrissids with Berbers in Morocco. The Almoravids, the Almohads and the Merinids were Berber movements that established empires and dynasties. Today the Berbers constitute the majority of the population in Morocco and Algeria, and constitute important minorities elsewhere.

Bey. Formerly, a Turkic title for a chief. Today it is a title of respect in social intercourse. Its alternate form is Beg.

Beylerbey. "Bey of Beys", the Ottoman title for a provincial governor. Today in Arabic the equivalent title is usually *walī*.

Originally, there were two Beylerbeys, one for Anadolu (Anatolia) with headquarters at Ankara (from 1451 at Kütahya), and one for Rumeli (Europe) with headquarters at Sofia. The Anatolian Beylerbey had the higher rank and his standard bore three horse's tail pennants (Turkish: *tugh*) while that of the Rumeli Beylerbey had two. In campaigns in Asia, the Anatolian Beylerbey had precedence, while in campaigns in Europe, the Rumeli. The Beylerbeys were also called Pasha. Towards the end of the Ottoman period the number of Beylerbeys had grown to twenty.

The domain under a Beylerbey's control was a *sanjak* ("banner"). From the original two *sanjaks* there grew to be 290, governed by Beys. These were progressively reorganized to form *pashaliks* and *vilayets*, of which there were more than seventy at the end of the Ottoman period after World War I.

Under Selim I, a Beylerbey of the sea, or Admiral, was appointed with the title of *Kapudanpasha*. Other important Ottoman officials included the *Defterdar*, a kind of Comptroller or accountant, an imperial treasurer, the Shaykh al-Islam, the highest religious authority, and the Viziers, or ministers, who conducted the business of government and held the imperial seal with the *tughra*, or Sultan's monogram. The office of the Grand Vizier was called the *Bāb-i Alī* ("the High Gate"), from a nearby gate, which gave rise to the term "Sublime Porte" for the Ottoman Government. *See* OTTOMANS.

Bhakti marga, *see* MAḤABBAH.

Bible. Three sections of the Bible are cited by the Koran as being Divinely revealed: the Pentateuch, or Books of Moses (*Tawrāt*); the Psalms of David (*Zabūr*); and the Gospels of Jesus (*Injīl*). These provide the basis for the identification, "People of the Book" (*ahl al-kitāb*), meaning those with revealed religions. These are Jews, Christians, Muslims, and others. However, the Gospels and Psalms have found no place in an Islamic canon and their contents are mostly ignored and unknown to Muslims. Moreover, the Gospel poses particular difficulties in Islam. Leaving aside the distinction between direct revelation from God which is the case of the Koran (in Arabic *tanzīl*, which corresponds to *shruti* in Sanskrit), and secondary inspiration (in Arabic *ilhām*, the equivalent of *smriti* in Sanskrit), which is the case of the Gospels, the Christian Gospel clashes with Islamic understanding of doctrine on several points, most importantly regarding the nature of Jesus.

Firstly, although in Islam Jesus has no earthly father and is the Spirit of God breathed into Mary, he is not the *son* of God. (*See* JESUS). Secondly, in the Koran, the death of Jesus on the cross is an *appearance* (4:154); that is, he did not die, but was taken up to God, where he will remain until he returns to earth at the end of time.

A third point of contention is the foretelling in the Gospel of the coming of the Prophet. Taking John 16:7:

> Nevertheless I tell you the truth; it is expedient for you that I go away, for if I go not away the Comforter will not come unto you; but if I depart I will send him unto you.

A slight change in the Greek word *paraclete* of the original text ("Comforter", or "Holy Ghost") turns the word into *paracleitos* ("Praised One") which is the meaning in Arabic of the name Muḥammad and its cognate *Aḥmad*, also used of the Prophet. The Gospel would then echo the words of the Koran:

> And when Jesus son of Mary said,
> 'Children of Israel, I am indeed the
> Messenger of God to you, confirming the Torah
> that is before me, and giving good tidings of
> a Messenger who shall come after me, whose
> name shall be Aḥmad.' (61:6)

Muslims believe that the New Testament as used by Christians is incorrect and has, somehow, been falsified. (Although Muslims today think this means that the Gospel is "falsified" throughout, in fact this claim of "falsification" actually referred to only one concrete instance, that of the word paraclete, mentioned above.) Because the Koran affirms Christianity as a Divinely revealed religion, Muslims expect Christianity to be exactly like the Divine revelation that is Islam. Naturally, Muslims assume that Islam is the essence of true, or universal religion, and as Christianity is also a revealed religion, then the assumption that the two must coincide is inevitable. In practice, however, the religions do not, and cannot, coincide. Because comparison between the two is usually made on the basis of their outward forms, not finding the equivalent of the "Five Pillars", not finding exoteric Islam in Christianity, and finding rather a doctrine of Jesus which contradicts the basis of Islam as salvation through the recognition of God as Absolute, Muslims readily came to the conclusion, now established as dogma, that Christianity has somehow been altered; and this alteration can most easily be ascribed to some corruption (*taḥrīf*) of the original text of the Gospels by later editors. Thus what is a symbolical or virtual "corruption" of the Biblical text (from the Islamic point of view) as regards the Greek reference to the "Comforter"/"Praised One" is extended to cover and explain the metaphysical problem (for Muslims) of the meaning of the crucifixion, and the whole discrepancy between the two religions. *See* BARNABAS, GOSPEL of; JESUS; KORAN; PEOPLE of the BOOK; REVELATION.

Bid'ah ("innovation"). A practice or a belief which was not present in Islam as it was revealed in the Koran, and established by the Sunnah on the basis of the Prophetic traditions; hence something possibly contrary to Islam. For some Muslims *bid'ah* includes any practice, or religious fixture, that was not present at the time of early Islam, such as the construction of minarets on mosques, and which is thus to be rejected. For the majority, the introduction of something new is *bid'ah* only when it contradicts the spirit of Islam.

Since the possibilities of Islam can never be exhausted, anticipated in advance, or made entirely explicit in any one epoch, most exponents of Islamic law allow for the concept of *bid'ah ḥasanah*, or "good innovation", that is, an innovation which does not contradict the essence of the religion. Such an innovation may be, for example, the building of the additional story onto the Grand Mosque of Mecca to permit the larger numbers of pilgrims in the present day to circumambulate the Ka'bah at one time.

Bih'āfrīd ibn Farwardīn (d. *133*/750). An enigmatic Iranian revolutionary and para-Zoroastrian revivalist who claimed to be a prophet capable of incorporating both Islam and Mazdeism into one religion. He appeared around the declaration of the 'Abbāsid revolt near Nishapur after having staged his return to life from being dead. He instituted new rituals in Zoroastrianism (among them turning to the sun to pray) and was opposed as a heretic by the priests of Zoroastrianism who called for his death. He was killed along with his followers by Abū Muslim.

Bihbahānī, Vahid (Aqa Muḥammad Baqir ibn Muḥammad Akmal; *1118-1207*/1706-1792). A descendant of the Shī'ite scholar Shaykh al-Mufīd, born near Iṣfahān. Bihbahānī defined the Uṣūlī system of Shī'ite jurisprudence, which stressed the application of principles to current religious questions in order to arrive at original and unprecedented answers, as opposed to the Akhbārī, or traditionalist school which stressed the application of precedent only.

By taking an extremely militant stance, declaring the Akhbārīs categorically to be *kāfirūn*, or unbelievers, as Muḥammad ibn 'Abd al-Wahhāb had done in Arabia towards his opponents, Bihbahānī drove the Akhbārīs out of Persia. (Akhbārīs still exist in southern 'Irāq, especially in Baṣrah, as well as in Baḥrayn). He also used force to impose his ideas, surrounding himself with *mirghadabs*, or "executors of wrath" (a kind of forerunner of the *pasdarān*, or "revolutionary guards" of modern times), who physically intimidated and punished his opponents, on the spot, if necessary. Thus Bihbahānī, as the ultimately successful proponent, came to be considered the founder of the Uṣūlī school. He made it possible, particularly by his example of how he dealt with his opponents, for the superior Mullās to declare themselves Mujtahids and establish themselves as the absolute arbiters of religious authority in Persia, as the *nā'ibs* or representatives of the Hidden Imām.

Bihbahānī had studied at Kerbala and made Kerbala the centre of Shī'ite scholarship in his time. He wrote the *Risālat al-Ijtihād wa-l-Akhbār*, and *Sharḥ al-Mafātiḥ*. He was also categorical with Sufis, as a competing group; for this he was known as Sufi Kush, or Sufi Terminator. *See* AKHBĀRĪ; AYATOLLAH; SHĪ'ISM; UṢŪLĪ.

Bihzad, *see* BEHZAD.

Bila kayfā ("without [asking] how"). A theological principle of not questioning revelation when it may perplex or defy human understanding. This concept is most closely associated with al-Ash'arī, but has been also used by others, such as Ibn Ḥanbal. Al-Ash'arī invoked the notion of *bilā kayfā wa lā tashbīh* ("without asking how or making comparison") most notably in respect of the Koran's so-called "anthropomorphizing" expressions which speak of God as having human attributes — such as the "Hand of God" or the "Face of God", or God's being "seated" on a throne. Although God could not physically have a hand, according to al-Ash'arī and Ibn Ḥanbal, these expressions have to be accepted literally as they are, "without asking how".

These expressions have also been interpreted not literally, but figuratively, today as in the past. The use of the term "anthropomorphizing" in Western writings on the subject of Islam may be misleading, because the references are isolated and do not actually entail anything beyond the level of certain concepts; they do not in fact imply an "anthropomorphic" idea of God. The device of *bilā kayfā* reflects the need felt by theologians in the past to reconcile the fact that if the Koran has symbolic planes of meaning, it must first of all be accepted as true on the literal plane. Because there was the equal imperative to acknowledge God as completely incomparable, solutions had to be sought of which *bilā kayfā* was the closest at hand.

Resorting to the principle *bilā kayfā* is similar to the recourse to "divine mystery" in Catholicism when dogma and metaphysics cannot be reconciled on the purely theological plane without surpassing theology itself by antimony. *See* ISTAWĀ'.

Bilāl. The first *muezzin* (Ar. *mu'adhadhin*,) or caller to prayer. A black slave from Abyssinia, Bilāl was an early convert to Islam who, because his master severely mistreated him for his religious beliefs, was ransomed and freed by his fellow-convert Abū Bakr. When the call to prayer — rather than a summons by bells — was instituted, Bilāl was chosen for his fine voice and despite his imperfect pronunciation of Arabic. He made the call from the top of the Ka'bah when the Prophet entered Mecca in the pilgrimage of *8*/629 as allowed by the treaty of Ḥudaybiyyah, and again the following year when the Prophet entered the city in triumph. He served the Prophet and was the chamberlain to the first Caliphs. Bilāl accompanied the armies to Syria and some accounts say he is buried there.

Bilali Muhammad. Also known as Ben Ali and Bu Allah, he was a famous Black slave on Sapelo Island in the state of Georgia, U.S.A. at the beginning of the 19th century. It is believed that he was born in West Africa. During the War of 1812 he was armed by his master to resist the British invasion of the Georgia coast, and as overseer led the other slaves in the defense. It is said that he knew French, and Arabic. He had a score of children and many descendants today in the coastal region.

A Muslim by origin, his descendants said that his Koran and his prayer rug were his treasured possessions, and that he always wore a black cap like a fez. He was wise in the ways of nature.

He left a leather bound volume which was called a "diary". When studied this was found to be fragment from an Islamic legal work. It is now in the Georgia State Library at Atlanta.

Bilalians. A name adopted by some members of the "Nation of Islam" in America when Elijah Muḥammad was succeeded by his son Wallace Warith Deen Muḥammad. Bilāl was the first renowned Muslim who was black. (*See* BILĀL; "BLACK MUSLIMS").

Bilqīs. The Queen of Shebā (or Ar. *Sabā'*), a pre-Islamic kingdom in South Arabia. She became a consort of King Solomon and entered his religion. Stories describe how the jinn brought her throne to Solomon in Jerusalem from Sheba. The Koran relates that when Bilqīs visited Solomon, she mistook the polished floor of the throne room for water and raised her skirt to cross it. When she realized her error, and thereby the power of illusion, she accepted the *shahādah*, or testimony of Islam, and surrendered to God.

Bilqīs has come to symbolize the nature of woman as infinitude, in complement to man as centre and Intellect, which Solomon represented. That magical and mysterious feminine nature that Bilqīs represents is expressed by the Arab legend that her father was not human, but a *jinn*, a being from the subtle world.

Bint al-Shati the pen name ("daughter of the shore" — Damietta) of 'Ā'ishah 'Abd ar-Raḥman (1913-1999), an Egyptian woman who was a professor of Arabic literature and famous writer on social issues, fiction and non-fiction, and Koranic exegesis.

Birth. Upon birth it is customary to whisper the *shahādah*, or testimony of the faith, into the ears of the newborn. One can also make the call to prayer, which includes the *shahādah*. Ceremonies which may follow, according to local customs, include the sacrifice of the *'aqīqah*, and celebrations of the giving of a name to the newborn child, after seven days. *See* 'AQĪQAH; NAMES.

Birth control. It has been practiced in the past in Islam, and most methods of contraception are generally admitted upon condition of being acceptable to both parties. In recent times there have been *fatwās* (legal decisions) to this effect, issued by councils of *'ulama'*, reaffirming legal opinions formed centuries ago. *See* ABORTION.

al-Bīrūnī, Abū Rayḥān (*362-442*/973-1048). Born of Persian-speaking parents in what today is Uzbekistan, al-Bīrūnī was a universal genius and polymath who turned his attention to every available field of learning. Called *al-ustādh*, "the teacher", the scope of al-Bīrūnī's inquiries was vast and profound, and he is a great luminary in the history of world science.

When attached to the court of Maḥmūd of Ghaznah, he traveled with the Sultan to India, where he learned Sanskrit and became a bridge between the world of Hindu learning and Arabic-speaking Islamic civilisation. For twelve years he concentrated on studying the wisdom of India and the resulting encyclopedic "Book of India" (*Kitāb al-Hind*) described Hindu systems of philosophy, cosmological theories, and customs. Al-Bīrūnī not only translated the *Patanjāli Yoga* from Sanskrit to Arabic, he also translated Euclid's Elements and his own works into Sanskrit. His knowledge of the sacred books of Hinduism gave al-Bīrūnī an unusually broad framework for his study of history. Hindu notions of cyclic time led him to a remarkable awareness of the vast ages of the geologic past.

In *387*/997 he exchanged letters on Aristotle's Physics with Ibn Sīnā (Avicenna), then living in Bukhārā and no more than seventeen years old. The two later met, when al-Bīrūnī disputed with him some of Aristotle's scientific reasoning, in particular the notion of the "eternity of the world". (*See* PHILOSOPHY.)

Al-Bīrūnī's work on astronomy, the *Mas'ūdic Canon*, is dedicated to the successor of Maḥmūd of Ghaznah. He listed 1029 stars and calculated latitude and longitude using instruments of his own making. His treatise on pharmacology, the *Kitāb aṣ-Ṣaydalah*, lists names of substances in Greek, Persian, Arabic, and Sanskrit. As for botany, al-

Bīrūnī described five times as many plants as Dioscorides. He calculated the specific gravity of various substances, wrote on the properties of gems in the *Kitāb al-Jawāhir*, and on the history of nations in *'Athar al-Baqiyah.*

In *409*/1018, at the fortress of Nandana near present day Islamabad in Pakistan, al-Bīrūnī calculated the radius and circumference of the earth. Using the height of a mountain and its angular relationship to the horizon, he arrived at a figure for the radius of the earth which has been equated to be 6,338 km, only 15 km from the estimate of today. His figures for the circumference of the earth are less than 200 km from today's calculations. One of the proofs he gave for the sphericity of the earth is its round shadow on the moon during lunar eclipses (an observation made more than once even by ancient philosophers).

Al-Bīrūnī's field of study embraced the human world, plants and animals, the physical world, and the abstractions of physics and mathematics. Moreover, he showed a profound interest in the subject of religion and, whilst being fully aware of the differences between his own Islamic faith and others which had resort to radically different forms, he did not conclude that the various creeds were no more than subjective systems, or that one was wrong and the other right. Nor did al-Bīrūnī reduce physical reality to what can be ascertained by empirical observations, lose sight of the Presence of God in what he studied, or put dogma between himself and his researches. He was thus a true scientist in the broadest sense of the term.

al-Bisṭāmī, Abū Yazīd (Bāyazīd) Ṭayfūr (d. *260*/874). A Sufi, sometimes referred to as the first of the "Drunken Sufis", because he went so far as to speak in terms which implied Divinity in himself. Al-Bisṭāmī was born in Bisṭām in northern Persia and is buried there. His father practiced an Iranian religion, and the "deifying" thread in mysticism, (which is even found in exoterism, as some of the early Persian converts to Islam proposed deification of the ruler), probably arose out of the characteristic influences of certain of the indigenous religions of Iran.

> "The vestiges of knowledge," said Bāyazīd, "are effaced; its essence is naughted by the Essence of Another, its track lost in the Track of Another. Thirty years God was my mirror. But now I am my own mirror; that which used to be I, I am no more. To say I am God denies the Unity of God. I say I am my own mirror, but it is God that speaks with my tongue — I have vanished. I glided out of my Bāyazīdhood as a snake glides from a cast skin. And then I looked. And what I saw was this: lover and Beloved and Love are One. Glory to Me!" (Ar. *Subḥānī*, a play on the customary *Subḥān Allāh*, "Glory to God!")

Such notions are not shared by all Sufis, by any means, and al-Junayd of Baghdad, in response to precisely this phenomenon, was the spokesman of rigor and "dryness" (*ṣawḥ*), that is, of "union without deification".

Al-Bisṭāmī left no writings and what is known of his sayings (sometimes referred to as *shataḥāt*, or ecstatic utterances; phrases like "How great is my majesty!") come from later compilations such as the *Kitāb al-Lumā'* ("The Book of Illumination") of as-Sarrāj. Many of these sayings are orthodox, and may represent the attribution of anonymous mystic teachings to a famous Sufi name in order to position their contents; but the question is complicated by the apparent existence of another Sufi of exactly the same name, a transmitter of sayings, called al-Bisṭāmī-l-Asghar, "al-Bisṭāmī the lesser". The obscurity of this "other" Bisṭāmī may be the result of an operation performed by orthodox thinking, namely splitting the historical Bisṭāmī into two persons, a problematic "greater" Bisṭāmī, and a more easily acceptable "lesser".

Of the scandalous, and more instructive, stories regarding Bisṭāmī there is one in the *Masnavi* (and the *Tadhkirat al-Awliya'*) which sums up the problem in a nutshell; that is, that the so-called "Drunken Sufis" ascribed divinity to men and to themselves. It recounts that Bāyazīd was on his way to the Ka'bah when he met a holy man who asked him how much money he had for the journey. Then the holy man advised Bāyazīd to go around himself seven times and give him the money instead because "into this house that is I none but the Living God has gone. In seeing me you have seen God; you have circled about the Ka'bah of Truthfulness. To serve me is to obey and give praise to God... Open well your eyes andlook upon me, that you may see the Light of God in human flesh."

Bisṭāmī also claimed to have ascended into the divine presence; which is little compared with his claims above, but may be the reference to his participation in a certain rite, such as say, the yearly Bēma, since this "nearness" took place seventy times in his life.

It is curious that many Sufis of impeccable repute, such as al-Ḥujwīrī, came and visited the tomb of al-Bisṭāmī, and other marks of respect were accorded him; but this does not mean that they accepted his formulations without reservation. Indeed, some of his sayings are so problematic that he is even reported to have scoffed at believers for their belief. Massignon says that Bisṭāmī was exiled seven times to Jurjan for his dualism. Abū Yazīd Bisṭāmī was also reported to have said, "I used to keep company with Abū 'Alī al-Sindhī and I used to show him how to perform the obligatory duties of Islam, and in exchange he would give me instruction in the divine unity (*tawḥīd*) and in the ultimate truths (*ḥaqā'iq*)." i.e., I gave him the example of how to pass oneself off as a Muslim, while he taught me what we really believed. To say that he learned *tat tvam asi* from Sindhī, is to overlook that very similar doctrines had long been professed by Iranian religions and the saying was known in Arabic as anta takuna dhaka among heterodox groups. *See* al-JUNAYD; ZINDIQ.

"Black Muslims". A sect among blacks in America with its centre in Chicago, the original name of which was "the Nation of Islam". The founder was Elijah Muḥammad; but it was the dynamic leadership of Malcolm X, originally Malcolm Little, (later al-Ḥajj Mālik ash-Shabazz), murdered in 1965, that brought the organisation to international prominence.

The roots of the sect reach back to movements among American blacks in the early years of this century. Marcus Garvey's promotion of solidarity with Africa connected the quest for dignity with the search for links with the old world. Two more immediate influences were a religious sect of Noble (Timothy Drew) 'Alī, the "American Moors" of the Moorish Science Temple in Newark, New Jersey. Another was the Aḥmadiyyah, a heterodox Islamic sect which emerged in India during the 19th century, one of the few groups in Islam that proselytized and established mosques in Europe and America at that period. One of the tenets of the Aḥmadiyyah identifies Christianity with the dajjāl, the "deceiver", that is, with the Antichrist, at the end of time. It is probably the transposition of its doctrine which produced the idea that the white man is the devil; this notion characterized the early phase of Black Muslim ideology. These various influences came together in a man called W. D. Fard who met Elijah Muḥammad (originally Elijah Poole) in Detroit in the 1930s. (The name Fard is symbolic, *see* FARD).

Out of the ideas of Fard (who disappeared in 1953) came the movement of "The Lost-Found Nation of Islam in the Wilderness of North America". These were elaborated by Elijah Muḥammad into a doctrine of black superiority. In its original form, it contended that the white race had been derived from the black at Mecca, and that the criterion of heaven or hell was material prosperity. The Nation of Islam demanded that a separate American state be created and given to the blacks. Meanwhile, the growth of businesses sponsored by the Black Muslims helped to create economic independence for the movement.

When Malcolm X visited Mecca he saw true Islam at first hand and, adopting orthodoxy, broke away from the Nation of Islam. At the same time, other splinters from the Nation of Islam either moved over to orthodox Islam or joined pseudo-Islamic groups centreed around different "Mahdīs", sometimes with apocalyptic and racist appeals.

When Elijah Muḥammad died in 1975, his son Wallace Warith Deen Muḥammad assumed the leadership. He has subsequently persuaded the movement, later known as the American Muslim Mission, to abandon its eccentricities, reconcile itself with the contributions made by Malcolm X, and adopt authentic Islam in its entirety. In its commitment to religious orthodoxy, the American Muslim Mission has sent some of its members to study at such traditional centres of Islamic learning as the al-Azhar in Cairo, and the Islamic University of Medinah. Estimates of followers of the American Muslim Mission range from over one hundred and fifty thousand to almost a million; the number of those sympathetic to it, without being Muslim, is even larger.

A smaller faction under Louis Farrakhan, retained the previous name of "Nation of Islam", and maintained its old policies. The number of followers of this continuation of the Nation of Islam is under fifty thousand. *See also* "ḤANAFĪ MUSLIMS".

Black Sheep, *see* QARA QOYUNLU.

Black Stone (Ar. *al-ḥajar al-aswad*). This is a stone set in the south-east corner of the Ka'bah about one

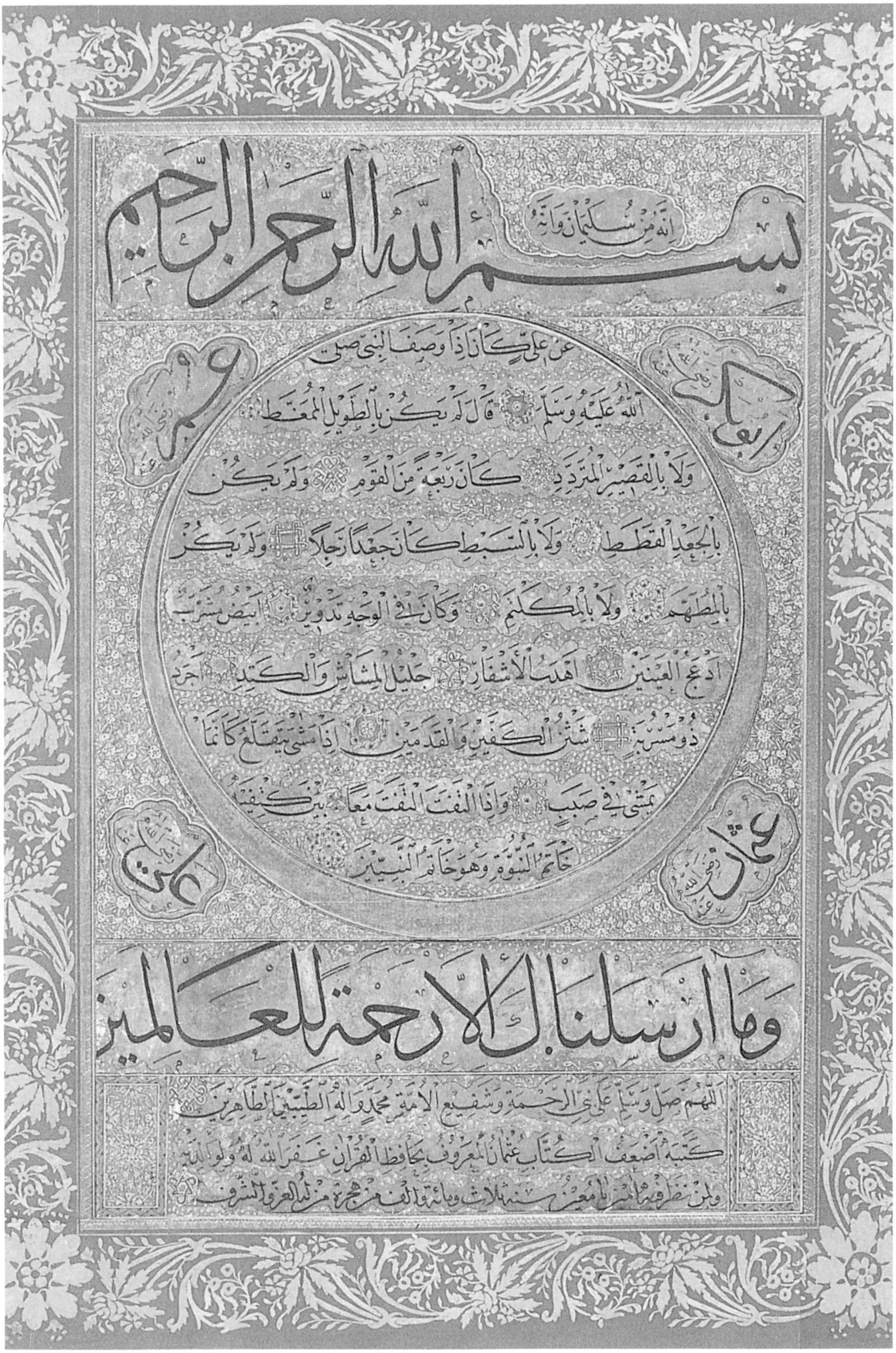
بسم الله الرحمن الرحيم
وما أرسلناك إلا رحمة للعالمين

The *Hilye-i-Sharīf* ("Description of the Prophet") on the *opening page* is by the great 17th-century calligrapher Ḥāfiẓ 'Uthmān.

Opposite page: A set of calligrapher's implements included knives (*bottom right*) for cutting reed-pen nibs (*miqta'*), holders for the reed-pen while it was being cut (*bottom centre*), and burnishing tools (*bottom left*). The pen and ink holder (*beneath table*) and the low scribe's table (*centre*) inlaid with mother of pearl, ivory, ebony and tortoise-shell over goldleaf are of 17th-century Turkish origin. The panel of calligraphy (*top*) reads: "Muḥammad the Guide", and was written in the early 18th century by Sultan Aḥmad II, an accomplished calligrapher. *See* CALLIGRAPHY.

The art of calligraphy assumes a sacred character in Islam, as illustrated by the first line of the Koran to be recorded (*above*): "Read in the Name of Your Lord who Teaches with the Pen." *Bottom*: The *basmalah* ("In the Name of God, the Merciful, the Compassionate") comes from an early 15th-century Persian Koran, and is in *Muḥaqqaq* script. *See* BASMALAH.

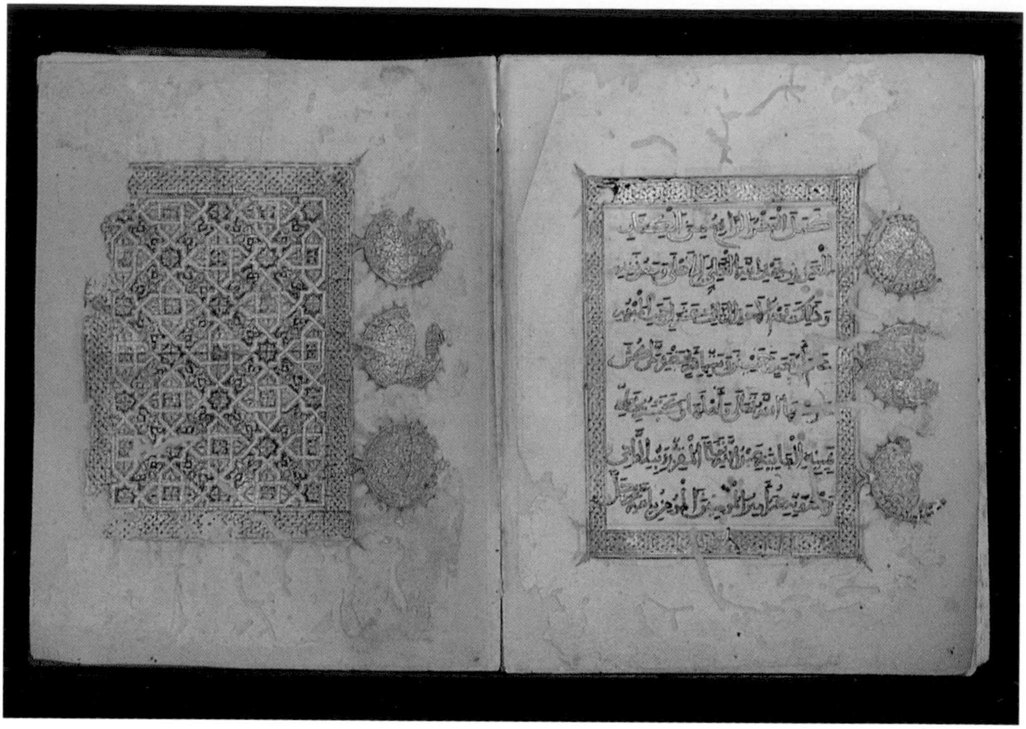

Hand-calligraphed Korans are one of the great art heritages of the Islamic world. That *above* dates from the 12th/13th century, and was executed in a typical North African calligraphy script by the Emir "el Mortada". It is now in the Musée des Oudaias in Morocco. *See* ARABIC; CALLIGRAPHY; KORAN.

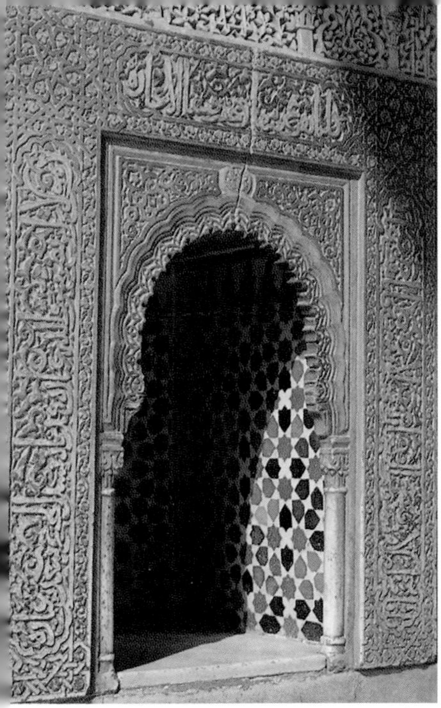

Intricate calligraphic stucco decorations (*top left*) in a tiled niche off the Patio of the Myrtles (*top right*) in the Alhambra in Granada, Spain, the high point of Islamic architecture in the West. The extensive, patterned tile cladding of the mosque in Herat, Afghanistan (*left*) is characteristic of Persian mosque decoration. *See* ALHAMBRA; CALLIGRAPHY; KORAN.

Muslim astronomers built observatories, compiled tables of planetary motion and calendars, and provided much of the vocabulary of modern scientific astronomy. Such precise knowledge, together with highly skilled metalworking, lay behind astrolabes such as that (*above*) now in the Museum of the History of Science, Oxford. Used for measuring the altitude of stars, these precision instruments were a vital contribution to the voyages of the age of European exploration. *See* ASTROLOGY; ASTRONOMY; al-BĪRŪNĪ.

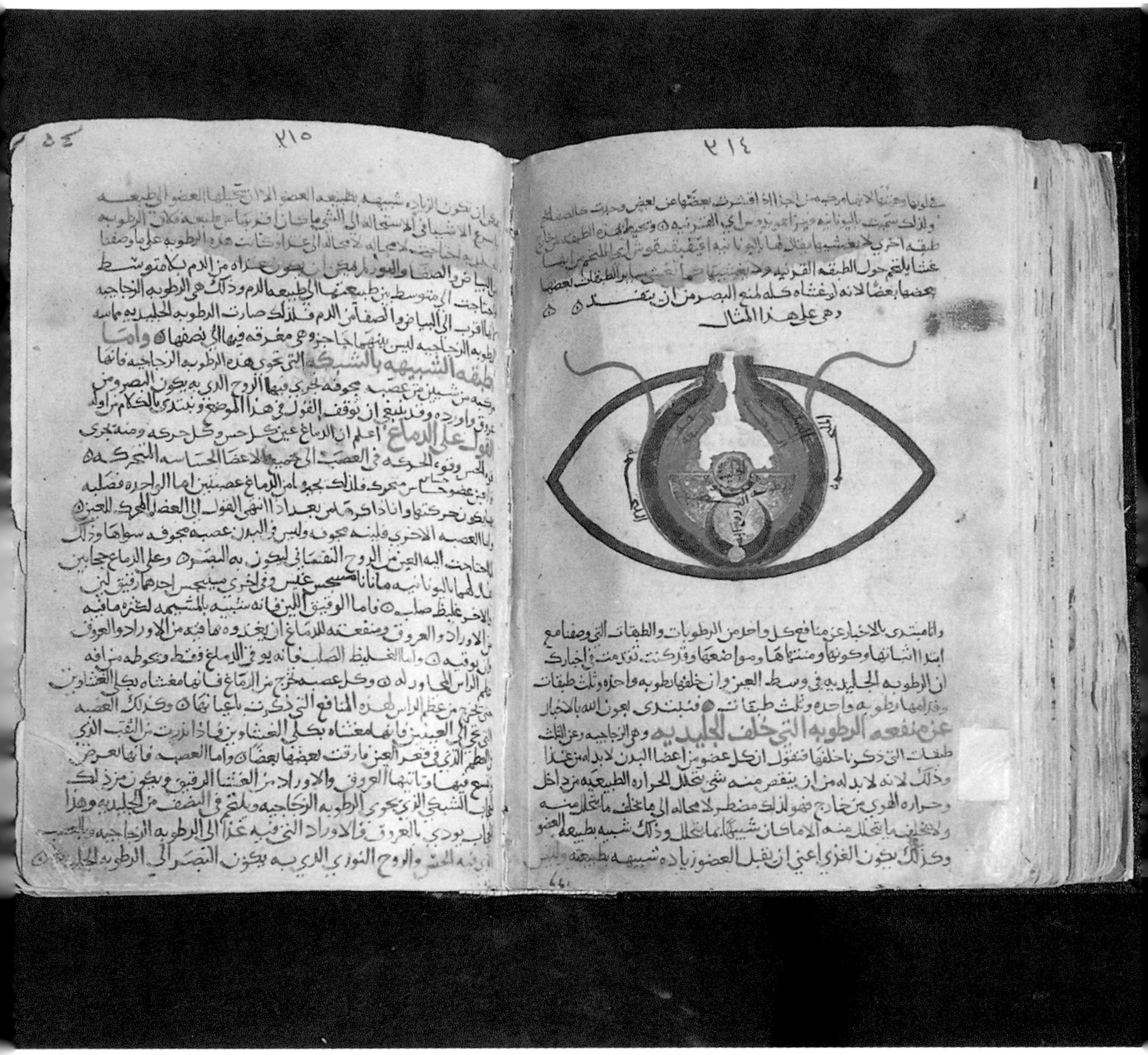

Islamic contributions to medical knowledge included a comprehensive *materia medica* and the establishment of hospitals, first in Baghdad (c. *287*/900) and then in Cairo. Considerable anatomical knowledge is implied by the 13th-century manuscript of the "Anatomy of the Eye", now in the Bibliotèque National, Paris. *See* MEDICINE.

"And thy Lord is Most Generous, who taught by the Pen, taught Man that he knew not" (Koran 96). Islam's sacred text is studied and memorized at Koran schools throughout the Muslim world, as shown here in Afghanistan (*above*), Khartoum (*below*), Mali (*right*) and China (*bottom right*). *See* KORAN; KORANIC SCHOOL.

and one-half yards/meters from the ground. It is black with reddish tones and yellow particles, of ovoid shape about 11 inches/28 cm wide and 15 inches/38 cm high, set in a silver chasing. During the circumambulation of the Ka'bah the worshiper kisses the stone, or makes a gesture in its direction. A Ḥadīth of the Prophet says that it came down from heaven. The Caliph 'Umar once said during *ṭawāf*, or circumambulation: "I know that you are only a stone which does not have the power to do good or evil. If I had not seen the Prophet kissing you, I would not kiss you. Tradition says that Adam placed it in the original Ka'bah. Later it was hidden in the Meccan mountain of Abū Qubays. When Abraham rebuilt the Ka'bah, the Angel Gabriel brought the stone out and gave it to him.

During the siege of Mecca in *64*/683, the Ka'bah caught fire from a flaming arrow and the heat cracked the stone into three large parts and some smaller fragments. In *317*/930 the Qarmaṭīs raided Mecca, captured the stone, and carried it off to al-Ḥasa or Baḥrayn, where it was kept. Ransom was offered for it, which was ignored. Then in *340*/951 it was thrown, the historian Juwayni relates, into the Friday Mosque of Kūfah with a note: "By command we took it, and by command we have brought it back." It was in three pieces before it was stolen; it is in seven pieces today. (*See* QARMAṬIS.)

Because stone is the most durable of substances and the one that comes closest to being eternal, it offers itself readily as a symbol of eternity. The Old Testament of the Bible calls God the "Rock of Ages", and Jesus says to Simon "thou art Peter, and upon this rock I will build my church" (Matthew 16:18). Symbolically, it can also be said that undifferentiated stone hides within itself the essential and refulgent nature of gems, or precious stones (albeit such "latency" is an unorthodox idea; *see* KUMŪN). The Asiatic Mother Goddess Cybele, who was identified with the Cretan goddess Rhea, sister of the Titan Cronus and mother of the Olympian gods, in her earliest sanctuary in Phrygia had a stone fallen from heaven as her effigy.

The Black Stone, because of its colour, the absence of light, lends itself especially to the symbolism of the essential spiritual virtue of poverty for God (*faqr*), that is, a *vacare deo*, an "emptiness for God", or the necessary extinction of the ego that must precede access to the centre which is the heart (*qalb*).

The early Semites used unusual stones to mark places of worship and virtually every culture, ancient and modern, has recognized the inherent symbolism of stones in some hieratic usage or other. Jacob set up a pillar, and on it the stone on which he had rested his head during his dream. He anointed the stone with oil and it became an altar in the sanctuary, already sacred to Abraham, that he founded at Beth-El, near Jerusalem. Ancient British tradition identifies this stone to the "Stone of Scone" which was kept under the royal coronation throne in Westminster Abbey. It was returned to Scotland in 1997. *See also* KA'BAH.

Blessing, *see* BARAKAH; PRAYERS on the PROPHET; RIḌWĀN.

Blue Men (Ar. *ar-rijāl az-zurāq*). Nomad Arab tribes, notably the Reguibat in the western Sahara, that wander over the vast desert between Mauritania and Marrakesh. They are so called because the indigo dye from their turbans and clothes (from a cloth traditionally made in Kano, Nigeria), comes off on their skin. They do not cover their faces by winding their turbans over it as do the Tuaregs, who are Berber, and with whom the Blue Men are often confused.

Bohoras (Vohoras, "traders" from Gujarati *vohorvu*, "to Trade"). An ethnic group in India and Pakistan, originally a Hindu caste, most of whom are today Musta'lī Ismā'īlīs. This is a branch which split with the Nizārīs in *487*/1094 and who do not recognize the Aga Khan as their spiritual leader. Instead they are under the leadership of a *Dā'i Muṭlaq*, or "Absolute Preacher", often called the *Mulla-ji*. They were converted during the early period of Ismā'īlī propagandizing in India before the *5th*/11th century.

Most Bohoras follow that branch of Musta'lī Ismā'īlīsm known as Dā'wūdī; the Dā'wūdī Dā'i Muṭlaq is called the Mulla-Ji and is resident in Bombay. A minority are Sulaymānīs; their leader formerly resided in the Yemen, but in this century transferred his seat to Baroda in India, which was the seat of his Indian *Mansūb* or representative. Their population centres are Bombay and the Gujarat in India and also, through immigration, the commercial centres of East Africa. The 1931 Indian census put their numbers at 212,000. In the *9th*/15th century some Bohoras professed Sunnī Islam rather than Ismā'īlīsm, which gave rise to the Sunnī Bohoras in India and Pakistan. *See* ISMĀ'ĪLĪS.

Bokhārā. City in Uzbekistan. The region around it was called Soghdiana and, by the Arabs *Ma wara'n-nahr*, literally Transoxiana. It was traditionally a seat of learning and again today has a functioning *madrasah*. Destroyed by Jenghiz Khan in 1220 during his invasion of Khwarizm, it became a city of mysticism. It was at the end an Emirate conquered by Russia in 1868. Its muezzins are famous. *See* MAZĀRĪ-SHARĪF; SAMARKAND,

Bosnia and Herzogovina. A republic with a population of over 3,000,000 made up of three ethnic groups: Bosnians, Serbs, and Croats, formerly part of Yugoslavia. The Bosnians are Muslims of the Ḥanafī school of law, the Croats are Catholic and the Serbs are Serbian Orthodox. In 1992 a referendum for independence was passed and war broke out between Muslims, Serbs, and Croats. In 1994 an agreement was made to create a Bosnian-Croat federation. The Dayton accords brought the war to an end but also an uncertain future.

Bosnia had been ruled by Croatian kings in 958 and by Hungary from 1000 to 1200. It then became autonomous and ruled Herzogovina until it disintegrated as a political entity in 1391 after Bosnia, along with the surrounding kingdoms, was invaded by the Ottomans in 1386; in 1463 it became an Ottoman province, an integrated part of the Ottoman empire in 1580, and remained a Turkish province until control passed to Austria-Hungary in 1878. It became a province of Yugoslavia in 1918. In 1946 it became a federated republic in Yugoslavia.

There was a theory once that the Bosnian nobles converted to Islam *en masse* to preserve their land holdings. Now, however, this is no longer believed because the conversion is held to have taken place gradually in the 15th and 16th century, and later, a long time after the conquest. Before the conquest, the "Bosnian Church" of the 13th century was called Bogomil or Patarene and was described by Pope Pius as "Manichee". Besides the economic pressures to convert to Islam in order to avoid certain taxes, did the Bosnians convert because their loosely established Christian church had been in heresy conflict with both surrounding Catholics and Serbian Orthodox in the centuries previously? Was it because of an affinity between their Bogomil beliefs and Islam?

The capital of Bosnia is Sarajevo, which in addition to its historic mosques, the Careva, Alipasa and Gazi Husref Beg Dzamijat, has a 16th-century *madrasah*, the Kurshumli. Besides the myriads of human victims, Islamic monuments throughout Bosnia were destroyed during the war.

Bow, prayer, *see* RAK'AH.

Boujloud (lit. "father of the skins"; in standard Arabic *abū julūd*). A festival in Morocco of pagan origin. It has attached itself to the *'Īd al-Kabīr*, a feast commemorating the sacrifice of Abraham. *Boujloud* is the name of a person who, clothed in the skins of freshly slaughtered sheep, runs through a village or encampment striking the houses or tents with a stick (resembling some rites of the Roman Lupercalia). This is considered to "bless" the households. The psychological meaning is clear, and parallels can be found in most cultures: a person marks himself as impure, in this case by the bloody animal skins, and "draws off impurity"— or its psychological consequences of guilt — onto himself from others, much as in Europe to see a chimney-sweep was thought to bring luck, or as gargoyles were depicted on cathedrals to discharge the tension of an awareness of one's own impurity. The *Boujloud* resembles the practice in Biblical times of sending out a scapegoat into the desert over whose head a priest had confessed the sins of the people.

It has been thought that this scapegoat was dedicated to a desert demon called Azazel; and an important aspect of *Boujloud* is its shadowy nature in that certain practices of the *Boujloud* make mockery of religion. For example, a mock Imām leads a group of people behind him in a ludicrous distortion of the canonic prayer. Taken altogether this is an example of a "carnavalesque" festival, such as can be found in most cultures. Its equivalent is the Roman Saturnalia, its medieval continuations in Europe, in the "Feasts of Fools" with their folk, ecclesiastic, and academic variants, and also the lenten carnival, or sometimes midsummer night ("the eve of Saint John"), the Jewish Purim, and the American (but not European) Hallo'ween. In these events, the laws of religion are ignored for a determined period, while rebellious and shadowy human tendencies come to the surface, spend themselves, and release the tensions caused by daily conformity to social or religious ordinances.

For the sake of social equilibrium religious authorities usually have little choice, given human nature, but to ignore what amounts to a contained rebellion. It has been suggested that Boujloud is an echo of the pagan god Pan, doubtless because of the resemblance to the wearing of the skins of goats during the ancient Greek tragedies, where a similar cathartic function was performed by the enactment of drama. The Boujloud, very little observed today, is peculiar to North Africa but "carnavalesque" festivals are not. One of the principal gates to the walled city of Fez is named Bāb Boujloud. *See* SECRET SOCIETY.

Brelvi *See* BAREILLY.

Brotherhood of Purity (Ar. *Ikhwān aṣ-ṣafā'*). A secret society in Baṣrah, 'Irāq, founded around *340*/951 and probably headed by Zayd ibn Rifā'ah. It served as a forum for discussion and learning, and its members probably included Abū Sulaymān Muḥammad al-Busṭī (al-Muqaddasī), Abū-l-Ḥasan 'Alī az-Zanjānī, Abū Aḥmad al-Maḥrajānī, and al-Awfī. They published fifty-one tracts known as the *Rasā'il ikhwan aṣ-ṣafā'* ("The Treatises of the Brotherhood of Purity"), which constituted an encyclopedia of knowledge in philosophy, theology, metaphysics, cosmology, and the natural sciences, including botany and zoology. The tracts are actually an "infomercial" for the sect behind them. The second Ṭayyibī *Dā'ī al-Muṭlaq*, or supreme leader, Ibrāhim ibn al-Ḥusayn al-Ḥamidi (d. *557*/1162) made the *Rasā'il* part of the Ṭayyibī canon in the Yemen. (He also introduced a mythical "drama in heaven" to the Ṭayyibī Cosmology of ten higher intellects taken from al-Kirmānī, which differed from the Fāṭimid Neoplatonic cosmology.)

The writings of the society reveal a surprising open-minded intellectual curiosity about such civilisations as those of the ancient Greeks, the Persians, and the Indians; their universalism, not surprisingly, went so far as to accept that there is truth in religions other than Islam. Their Neo-Platonic ideas, as well as the method whereby they would raise questions, but not answer them except indirectly and by implication, and their hinting at the existence of a secret authority who could answer all questions, have led them to be identified as an intellectual current flowing from the Ismā'īlīs. Their ethic of brotherhood was linked with self-knowledge and the emancipation of the soul from ignorance leading to a return to God.

Despite this avowed ethic there is a curiously humanistic flavor about the Brotherhood of Purity. The 'Abbāsid al-Mustanjid, who succeeded to the Caliphate in *555*/1160, had their works burned, but the far reaching influence of the *Rasā'il* continued. It may have reached Dante and had repercussions in Europe in the Middle Ages.

The name *Ikhwān aṣ-Ṣafā'* comes from the animal fables of *Kalīlah wa Dimnah* by Ibn al-Muqaffa' (who was himself accused of being a *zindīq*). In the fables the "brothers of purity" are a group of very disparate animals who are caught in a net and have to band together and combine their talents in order to escape. Although the authors of the *Rasā'il* were Ismā'īlīs, and despite later claims of the "official" Ismā'īlī tradition that the "real" author was Aḥmad ibn 'Abd Allāh (c. 827), father of al-Ḥusayn, who was the father of 'Ubayd Allāh, the first Fāṭimid, the Brotherhood did not recognize the Imāmate of the Fāṭimids, nor do they seem to be Qarmaṭīs. Rather, they seem to represent a more neutral current that sought to maintain a common ground among the divergent tendencies that were tearing at that religion. *See* ISMĀ'ĪLĪS.

Brunei. (State of Brunei Daru's-Salam); Sultanate. Population 292,266. Ethnic groups: 64% Malay, Chinese 20%. Religions: Muslim: 63%, Buddhist 14%, Christian 8%. Brunei is located on the north coast of Borneo and is surrounded on the land side by the Malaysian state of Sarawak. The Capital is Bandar Seri Begawan with a population of 52,000. The head of government is Sultan Sir Muda Hassanal Bolkiah Mu'izzadin Waddaulah. The Sultanate of Brunei ruled the island of Borneo in the 16th century and dominated the Sulu Islands of the Philippines. In 1888 it was placed by treaty under the protection of Great Britain. It became sovereign in 1984. Islam of the Shāfi'ī school of law is the official religion.

Bsaṭ (*basā'iṭ*). A plural of *basṭ*, or "expansion". One of its meanings is "humor" as in the "four humors", and also comedy. *Bsaṭ* is the name of an old form of Arab comic folk theatre.

Bū Ḥamārah. "The man with the donkey", a name for a revolutionary in Morocco, who raised a revolt against the Sultan at the turn of the nineteenth century, held northeast Morocco making Taza his provisional capital, and twice threatened Fez with an army of his followers. After long struggles, he was captured in 1909, brought to Fez in a cage, and shot. The theme of "the man with the donkey" is an ancient sign of the Messiah: "Rejoice greatly, O daughter of Zion; shout, O daughter of Jerusalem: behold thy King cometh unto thee: he is just, and having salvation; lowly, and riding upon an ass, and upon a colt the foal of an ass" (Zechariah 9:9). *See* DHU-l-ḤIMĀR.

Bukhārā, *see* BOKHĀRĀ.

Bunyad. (Pers. "foundation"). A type of corporation existing as a "non-profit" institution which has proliferated in Iran since the 1979 revolution.

al-Burāq. The miraculous steed which the Angel Gabriel brought to the Prophet for the Mi'rāj, or Heavenly Ascent, also known as the *Isrā'*, or Night Journey. The root of the word is *bā'-rā'-qāf*, which means "to glitter", especially of lightning. In India the *Burāq* is depicted as having the face of a woman and the tail of a peacock, but there is no basis for this in traditional accounts, in which the *Burāq* is described as a creature for riding, bigger than a donkey and smaller than a horse, of celestial origin. On the other hand, the iconography of the *Burāq* as seen through the Indian imagination, makes of it a fantastical creature, both human and animal, and thus extends its symbolism to that of being the synthesis of all creation which accompanies the Prophet to heaven.

The traditional account of the Night Journey says that the *Burāq* proceeded in flashes of speed; where its glance landed, the next bound brought it, and from this it can be seen that the *Burāq* is an embodiment of the Intellect which, when it perceives an object in Being, or a spiritual reality, can immediately recognize its nature, or "knows" it, without a process of analysis and reason. *See* 'AQL; NIGHT JOURNEY.

Burdah. A mantle, but especially one of the Prophet's mantles, made out of goat's hair. There are two famous poems in Arabic by this name, one by a contemporary of the Prophet named Ka'b ibn Zuhayr, and another by the *7th*/13th century poet al-Buṣīrī.

The Prophet gave away several of his cloaks, a gift which is traditionally a mark of honour; one he threw to the poet Ka'b ibn Zuhayr who had previously been branded as an outlaw for denouncing Islam in his poetry; when the poet repented he recited a eulogy to the Prophet in his presence in Medinah by way of asking for pardon.

> Su'ad is gone, and today my heart is love-sick, in thrall to her, unrequited, bound with chains;
> And Su'ad when she came forth on the morn of departure, was but as a gazelle with bright black downcast eyes...
> Oh, what a rare mistress were she, if only she were true to her promise and would hearken to good advice!
> But hers is a love in whose blood are mingled paining and lying and faithlessness and inconstancy...
> In the evening Su'ad came to a land whither none is brought save by camels that are excellent and noble and fleet...
> One that bedews the bone behind her ear when she sweats, one that sets herself to cross a trackless unknown wilderness...
> I was told that the Messenger of Allāh threatened me with death, but with the Messenger of Allāh I have hope of finding pardon.
> Gently! mayst thou be guided by Him who gave thee the gift of the Koran, wherein are warning and a plain setting out of the matter.
> Do not punish me, when I have sinned, on account of what is said by the informers, even though the false sayings about me should be many.
> Ay, I stand in such a place that if an elephant stood there, seeing what I see and hearing what I hear,
> The sides of his neck would be shaken with terror — if there be no forgiveness from the Messenger of Allāh...
> Truly the Messenger is a light whence illumination is sought — a drawn Indian sword, one of the swords of Allāh,
> Amongst a band of Quraysh, whose spokesman said when they professed Islam in the valley of Mecca, 'Depart ye!'
> They departed, but no weaklings were they or shieldless in battle or without weapons and courage...
> Warriors with noses high and straight, clad for the fray in mail-coats of David's weaving...

Ka'b later treasured this mantle and would not sell it to the Caliph Mu'āwiyah for ten thousand dirhams. It became part of the national treasury after the poet's death.

Although it is sometimes said that this mantle disappeared in flames during the sack of Baghdad by the Mongols in *656*/1258, the Ottomans claimed to possess a cloak of the Prophet (*al-khirqah ash-sharīfah*, in Turkish: *Khirqa-i-sharīf*). Possession of the Prophet's mantle — which already in 'Abbāsid times was considered to be Caliphal regalia and a symbol of the office — was used as an argument in the 19th century by the Ottomans to support their claim to the Caliphate. Today this mantle is kept in the Topkapi Museum in Istanbul. The Ṭaliban in Afghanistan also produced a Prophet's mantle for public display in Kandahar on at least one occasion.

The Burdah is also the name of another famous poem in praise of the Prophet by al-Buṣīrī (*610-695*/1213-1296), a Berber born in Cairo, a Sufi disciple of the Imām ash-Shādhilī and of his successor Abū-l-'Abbās al-Mursī. Al-Buṣīrī was suffering from paralysis when he saw the Prophet in a dream place his own mantle upon him; when he awoke he was cured of his affliction. The poem, which describes the nature of the Prophet, is held in great pious esteem. It is the custom, chiefly in countries that were once part of the Ottoman Empire, to recite this *Burdah*, or "Mantle Poem", of al-Buṣīrī's in mosques during the *Mawlid*, or anniversary of the Prophet's birth. Verse 56 of Busiri's Burdah is especially famous; the Prophet is:

> Like a flower in tenderness, and like the full
> moon in glory,
> And like the ocean in generosity, and like all
> Time brought into one point.

See also KHIRQAH.

Burqa'. In Saudi Arabia it is women's head covering which covers her face, and may go to the ground. In Afghanistan it is the pleated head to foot covering women wear in public with a lattice in front of the eyes to see. In the Gulf States it is a leather face mask worn by women. *See* HIJAB; VEIL.

Buwayhids, *see* BUYIDS.

Butachaqieh. The Persian name for the ancient design that appears on the "peacock throne", which was brought to Persia from Delhi by Nadir Shah. This design was adopted from Indian motifs, in particular from Kashmir, and became known in the west as "Paisley", from the town in Scotland where the design was often woven.

Buyids. A dynasty which controlled 'Irāq and Persia from *320*/932 to *454*/1062. The Buyids (also called Buwayhids) were Daylamis, a people whom Polybius in the second century BC had called "non-Aryan", that is, not Indo-European, who had settled around the Caspian sea. Minorsky called this dynasty an "Iranian intermezzo" but they learned Persian culture only after they came to power although eventually they claimed to be descended from Bahram Gur. By military penetration from within the armies of the Caliphate, and by conquest, they took control of the 'Abbāsid Empire while maintaining the 'Abbāsid Caliphs as figureheads. Under the title of *amīr al-'umarā'* ("Prince of Princes") the Buyid chief ruled as military overlord.

Although the Buyids are known to have been Shī'ites, the exact nature of their Shī'ism cannot be ascertained; it may well have been a kind of Zaydī Shī'ism, and it probably served to rally opposition to the Sunnī political power which they supplanted. In any case, they did not seek to depose the Sunnī Caliph but simply to use him in order to legitimize their own rule, as did later dynasties until the Mongols. In the *3rd*/9th century Ismā'īlī missionaries were active in Daylam and one of the last Buyid leaders, the Marzuban Abū Kalījār (d. *440*/1048) was receptive to the Da'ī al-Mu'ayyad ash-Shirāzī. In *483*/1090 Ḥasan-i Ṣabbāḥ seized Alamut in Daylam and made it his headquarters.

Under the Buyids Shī'ite institutions did grow and develop within the 'Abbāsid empire and Shī'ite holidays were observed. The Buyids were replaced by other dynasties who divided up the areas formerly under their control; the Seljūqs ruled in the west, and eventually the Ghaznavids in the east.

C

Cadi, *see* QĀḌI.

Caesar. Among the Arabs, the term "Caesar" Arabized as *qayṣar*) referred above all to the Byzantine Emperor, and the word *Rūm* (Romans), in the Koran, refers to the Byzantines. In modern times the word *rūmī* has come to mean anything of European, as opposed to native, origin.

Cain and Abel (Ar. *Kābil* and *Hābil*). The sons of Adam. According to tradition, each had a twin sister; Cain married the sister of Abel, and Abel married the sister of Cain. *See* IBN KHALDŪN.

Cairo (Ar. *al-Qāhirah*, "the Victorious", but also "the City of Mars", from *al-Qāhir*, "Mars"). The capital of the Fāṭimids was founded by the general Jawhar, in the name of the Fāṭimid ruler al-Mu'izz, in *358*/969. Cairo then lay between the Nile and the Muqattam hills near the site of the first Muslim capital, al-Fuṣṭāṭ ("the Encampment"). Nearby was the ancient city of Bābilūn, or "Babylon of Egypt", a Greco-Roman fortress, and al-Fuṣṭāṭ, the seat of government of 'Amr ibn al-'Āṣī who conquered Egypt for Islam. Today Cairo encloses that site as well as al-'Askar, the capital of the 'Abbāsids, and al-Iqṭā'āt ("the Fiefs"), the capital under Aḥmad ibn Ṭulūn, and straddles both shores of the river.

The city was founded in accordance with astrological calculation the Fāṭimids being avid students of this pursuit. Legend tells that when the astrologers were poised to pull on bell-ropes in order to raise a pealed signal to the workmen to turn the first clods of earth at the most propitious moment, a raven anticipated them by alighting on the rope and jingling the bells as the planet Mars (*al-Qāhir*) was rising on the horizon; hence, according to this fanciful account, the city's name of *al-Qāhirah*. In fact, Cairo was first called *al-Manṣūriyyah*; it was only when the Fāṭimid ruler entered the country four years later that it became *al-Qāhirah al-Mu'izziyyah* ("The Victorious [city] of [the Caliph] Mu'izz li-Dīn Allāh" [the Exalter of the Religion of God]). The name was intended to send a message to the Qarmaṭīs and other dissident Ismā'īlīs who had not yet accepted Faṭimid leadership.

Although the Fāṭimids (*297-567*/909-1161) were the first rulers of the new city of Cairo, it is the Mamlūks (*648-1250*/922-1517) who left the most evident stamp upon the city's architecture. The great mosques are particularly celebrated: the Mosque of Ibn Ṭulūn, the Madrasah of Sultan Ḥasan, the Mausoleum of Qala'un, the Barqūqiyyah, the al-Azhar, the Ḥusayn Mosque, and many others. Notable too are the *Bāb an-Naṣr* ("The Gate of Victory"), the *Bāb al-Futūḥ* ("the Gate of the Conquests") and the Zuwaylah Gate, built by Armenians who emigrated to Egypt after the Byzantine defeat by the Seljuks at Manzikert in *463*/1071, and such picturesque and lively areas as the market of Khan al-Khalīlī.

However, it is particularly because of the prestige of the al-Azhar theological university, as well as in recognition of its leading role in Islamic history, that Cairo is recognized as one of the great cultural capitals of the Islamic world. *See* 'AMR IBN al-'ĀṢĪ; al-AZHAR; BAYBARS; COPTS; EGYPT; FĀṬIMIDS; MAMLŪKS; MUḤAMMAD 'ALĪ.

Calendar. The Islamic calendar, called today *hijrī* or Hegirian — that is, dating from the Emigration (*Hijr*) of the Prophet to Medinah — has in fact been used by the Arabs since ancient times. Like almost all Semitic calendars, it is based upon the cycles of the moon rather than upon those of the sun, on which are based the Julian and Gregorian calendars. The *actual* beginning of a month, such as the month of Ramaḍān, as opposed to its *predicted* beginning from astronomical calculations, depends upon the physical sighting of the moon. A physical sighting of the new moon, which can take place briefly only at sunset, is generally only possible one day after the astronomical new moon. (Actually, a crescent only forms when ten degrees of separation have elapsed between the conjunction positions of the sun and moon. It is therefore physically impossible to see a crescent moon less than twenty hours after astronomical conjunction.) The insistence upon the actual physical sighting reflects the sense in Islam that it is the immediate surrounding conditions, rather than theoretical ones, that reflect the Divine Will in its relation to men, and that it is these which should determine sacred acts. If the sky is overcast and the new moon is not visible within a territory, the previous month is allowed to run thirty days before the new month can begin. (Judaism had similar rules concerning the beginning of a new month.)

Although in principle a month runs from the sighting of one new moon until the next, in practice, sighting, or adjustments for sighting, are today no longer made, and calendar days run according to astronomical calculations of the moon's motion. Until recently, an exception was still made for the announcement of Ramaḍān and the month of pilgrimage, which, because of their ritual importance should, more than other days, conform to traditional principles. Now, however, with the almost universal abandonment of the traditional point of view, most countries have apparently opted to date Ramaḍān and the religious feasts simply according to astronomical calculation of the new moon without allowing for any corrections dependant upon actual sighting (see astronomical forming of the crescent, above). It is thus not unusual for countries to announce Ramaḍān when physical sighting of the moon would be possible in their territories only one day later, or even before a real sighting could have been made anywhere in the world. Immigrant Muslim communities often celebrate Ramaḍan not according to the country of residence, but their country of origin, which results in different Muslim ethnic groups in France or America often being out of step with each other.

The practice of beginning the months on the basis of an astronomical calculation of the date of the new moon was in fact instituted under the Fāṭimids by the general Jawhar after the founding of Cairo in *359*/969, but was always condemned by the Sunnīs as *bid'ah*, or a false innovation. (Like modern calculations, those of the Fāṭimids were for the astronomical new moon but not for its sighting; the latter would have been far more complex because it would have been necessary to calculate the position of the moon not only on the ecliptic, but also relative to the physical horizon.) The practice of the Ismā'īlis in using astronomical conjunction as the starting point for Ramaḍān was not, however, due to the complexity of calculating physical sighting, since that did not have to be calculated at all, it was enough to see it, but rather to their belief that their doctrines were scientific and above all to their theory that reality derived from physical existence rather than from a metaphysical Being.

The *hijrī* year consists of twelve lunar months, some of twenty-nine, and some of thirty, days; their lengths vary because of the need to round out a year otherwise only 354 days, 8 hours, and 48 minutes long. The annual holidays thus advance about ten days each year so that in thirty-six years, Ramaḍān, the month of fasting, moves around the entire solar year, sometimes taking place in winter, sometimes in summer. The Islamic day, like the Jewish day, runs from sunset to sunset; Thursday evening is therefore part of the Islamic sabbath Friday, which makes it a popular time for religious gatherings.

In pre-Islamic times it had become a custom to intercalate a month from time to time to align the lunar year with the solar. The Council of Mecca, the *Nidwah*, made the decision to intercalate in a given year, which was proclaimed at the fairs of 'Ukāẓ or Minā. This practice of intercalation was prohibited by the Koran in the year of the "farewell pilgrimage". The Koran legislated this change in 9:37: "The month postponed [i.e. a sacred month, *an-nasi'* — meaning here intercalation] is an increase of unbelief whereby the unbelievers go astray..." This was the only change Islam made to traditional Arab custom regarding the calendar. The intercalated days had actually been considered as unpropitious. (Judaism continues the ancient Semitic practice and adds an extra month, Veadar, or Adar Sheni, inserted between Adar and Nisan, approximately every three years or seven times in nineteen years.)

In the year 637, sixteen years after the Hijrah, or "emigration of the Prophet from Mecca to Medinah", the Caliph 'Umar instituted the year of the Hijrah as the first year of the Islamic era, since it had already been the Sunnah of the Prophet to take that event as the reference point in time. Such reference points were commonly used in the past. A previous reference point for the Meccan Arabs had been the Year of the Elephant, AD 570, in which Dhu Nuwās attacked Mecca with an elephant, an event mentioned in the Koran, and also the traditional year for the birth of the Prophet. The cumulation of a number of events around a given year or date reflects a "rounding off" in an age when actual measure of times was of little importance. Modern scholars point out that the attack on Mecca, in fact, probably occurred earlier than 570.

The Hijrah took place in September of 622 (the exact date is not known with certainty); the first day, 1 Muḥarram, of the year in progress coincided with 15/16 July 622, which was thus the first day of the first year of the Hegirian calendar (since the Islamic day begins at sunset the evening of the day before was also 1 Muḥarram).

The names of the months, despite the Semitic preference for a lunar year, and thus for a lunar calendar, in fact reflect an ancient division according to the seasons of the solar year. They are as follows:

1. Muḥarram:	"The sacred month"
2. Ṣafar:	"The month which is void"
3. Rabīʻ al-Awwal:	"The first spring"
4. Rabīʻ ath-Thāni:	"The second spring"
5. Jumādā al-Ūlā:	"The first month of dryness"
6. Jumādā al-Ukhrā:	"The second month of dryness"
7. Rajab:	"The revered month"
8. Shaʻbān:	"The month of division"
9. Ramaḍān:	"The month of great heat"
10. Shawwāl:	"The month of hunting"
11. Dhu l-Qāʻdah:	"The month of rest"
12. Dhu l-Ḥijjah:	"The month of pilgrimage"

Five days of the week are named by the ordinal numbers beginning with the first day, *Yawm al-Aḥad*, which is Sunday. Thereafter, Friday is named "the Day of Congregation" and Saturday is "the seventh day". They are as follows:—

Yawm al-Aḥad: Sunday
Yawm al-Ithnayn: Monday
Yawm ath-Thalāthāʻ: Tuesday
Yawm al-Arbāʻ: Wednesday
Yawm al-Khamīs: Thursday
Yawm al-Jum'ah: Friday
Yawm as-Sabt: Saturday

A solar calendar is indispensable for agricultural purposes, and there are several different calendars in use. Until recently, that most widely used was the Coptic calendar which is based upon the Julian calendar. This calendar is familiar in most Islamic countries but its practical use is now limited to Egypt and the Sudan, countries with Coptic populations. Another is the Turkish fiscal calendar, also a Julian calendar, adopted in the 18th century in the Ottoman empire. In the past, other solar calendars were also created by Muslim astronomers, to an admirable degree of accuracy. One such is the *Jalālī* calendar, made for the Seljūq Caliph Mālik Shah, in the formulation of which 'Umar Khayyam took part. In the Jalālī Calendar New Year's day is the *Naw Ruz*, or March 21st, the Vernal Equinox.

The use of a lunar calendar, and the practice of physical sighting for purposes of dating, has an interesting metaphysical moral. In classical Ptolemaic astronomy the celestial world is understood to be the way it appears to the observer on earth: the universe goes around the earth. This Ptolemaic universe corresponds to the classical theories of metaphysics and is a support for their symbolisms. The observed irregularities were mythologically explained by the perturbation caused by the fall of man. The existence of the seasons, and the variations between day and night, were explained as the result of the shifting of the cosmic axis because of man's expulsion from the garden of Eden or from a state of primordial perfection.

In physical astronomy, the earth and the planets go around the sun. From the mythic point of view, it is as if the celestial consequences of the fall of man and the shifting of the cosmic axis have reached their utmost limit. In this system the ideal reference point, the path back to spiritual universe, seems to be completely lost; there is no metaphysics possible (except perhaps that of two opposing principles). From both points of view, Ptolemaic and modern, mythic and scientific however, the moon does go around the earth; it actually does what it appears to do, unlike the Sun, which appears to go around the earth but in reality does not; the moon remains a source of reflected light (preserving the relationship between Principle and manifestation), and whether it reflects the sun as a support of the Principle or as a source of thermonuclear power, it nevertheless reflects a psychological and metaphysical reality, in keeping with its classical alchemical symbolism as the mind or psyche of man. Thus the moon today is what it was before, or even in the beginning, and the time it measures in the twentieth century is the time it would have measured in the garden of Eden, before the fall.

Another solar calendar was used in the Middle Ages which was dated from events surrounding Alexander of Macedonia. The counting of years began on 1 October, 312 BC, the beginning of the Seleucid era in Syria. It was later used as a universal time reference by the Jews, called the "Dating of Records" (*Minyan Sheṭaroth*). By the Arabs, it was called the age of Alexander (*li-l-Iskandar*). (However, for the Babylonians and, above all, their astronomers, the Seleucid era began on April 3, 311 BC)

In practice, the Western Gregorian calendar, usually referred to in the Islamic world as the *Masīḥī* (the "Messianic" or Christian calendar), is used today as the working calendar everywhere for all purposes except for determining days of religious observance. However, Saudi Arabia, officially at least, uses the Hegirian calendar as the calendar of reference.

THE ISLAMIC HOLIDAYS:

Muḥarram1st — Ra's al-'Ām. (New Year).
The first of Muḥarram, the Islamic New Year, and the first of Ramaḍan, and the first of the month of Ḥajj are calculated to fall upon the following dates in the Gregorian calendar:

Hijrī	*1st Muḥarram*	*1st Ramaḍan*	*1st Dhu-Ḥijjah*
1425	Feb 22, 2004	Oct 15, 2004	Jan 12, 2005
1426	Feb 10, 2005	Oct 4, 2005	Jan 1, 2006
1427	Jan 31, 2006	Sept 24, 2006	Dec 22, 2006
1428	Jan 20, 2007	Sept 13, 2007	Dec 11, 2007
1429	Jan 08, 2008	Sept 2, 2008	Nov 30, 2008
1430	Dec 29, 2008	Aug 22, 2009	Nov 19, 2009
1431	Dec 18, 2009	Aug 11, 2010	Nov 8, 2010
1432	Dec 8, 2010	Aug 1, 2011	Oct 29, 2011
1433	Nov 27, 2011	Jul 20, 2012	Oct 17, 2012
1434	Nov 15, 2012	Jul 9, 2013	Oct 6, 2013
1435	Nov 5, 2013	Jun 29, 2014	Sept 26, 2014
1436	Oct 25, 2014	Jun 18, 2015	Sept 15, 2015
1437	Oct 15, 2015	Jun 7, 2016	Sept 5, 2016
1438	Oct 3, 2016	May 27, 2017	Aug 24, 2017
1439	Sept 22, 2017	May 16, 2018	Aug 13, 2018
1440	Sept 12, 2018	May 6, 2019	Aug 3, 2019
1441	Sept 1, 2019	Apr 24, 2020	Jul 22, 2020
1442	Aug 19, 2020	Apr 13, 2021	Jul 11, 2021
1443	Aug 10, 2021	Apr 3, 2022	Jul 1, 2022
1444	Jul 30, 2022	Mar 23, 2023	Jun 20, 2023
1445	Jul 18, 2023	Mar 11, 2024	Jun 8, 2024
1446	Jul 7, 2024	Mar 1, 2025	May 29, 2025
1447	Jun 27, 2025	Feb 18, 2026	May 18, 2026

10th Muḥarram is *'Āshūrā'*, for Sunnīs a beneficent holy day whose observance is based upon the Sunnah but which is derived almost certainly from the date of the Jewish Day of Atonement, (according to al-Bīrūnī). For the Shī'ites however, because it is coincidentally, or, more likely, by design, the anniversary of the slaying of Imām Ḥusayn, it is the culmination of a period of terrible mourning.

12th Rabī' al-Awwal is *Mawlid* (or *Mīlād*) *an-Nabī* (Prophet's birthday). A festival marked by joyous celebrations, which vary according to local customs.

27th Rajab is *Laylat al-Mi'rāj* (The Night Journey). Joyous celebrations according to local customs.

15th Sha'bān is the *Laylat al-Barā'ah.* This is a non-canonical holiday largely unknown in many parts of the Islamic world; it is observed in Iran and India and among those communities with cultural ties to this part of the world. The origin of this holiday, usually called by its Persian name *Shab-i Barat,* is perhaps the *Farvardin* of ancient Iran for it is connected with the memory of the dead whose souls visit their relatives this day, and with the fates of the living, a kind of "All Souls Day". Hence, the Islamicised legend of the holiday says that the lote-tree of the ultimate limit (*as-sidratu al-muntaha*) is shaken that day and leaves fall with the names of those to die in the year to come.

Ramaḍān is the Month of fasting. The last ten days are particularly holy; the 27th is most often presumed to be the *Laylat al-Qadr,* the night of the descent of the Koran. A very solemn event. Secular festivities are prohibited in this month. (*See* RAMAḌĀN).

1st Shawwal is the *'Īd al-Fiṭr,* ("Feast of fast-breaking"). Three days of festivities marking the end of Ramaḍān.

10th Dhu l-Ḥijjah is the *'Īd al-Aḍḥā,* ("Feast of Sacrifice"). Commemorates the sacrifice of Abraham. It is celebrated throughout the Islamic world. (*See* 'ĪD al-AḌḤĀ). The 8th, 9th, and 10th of this month are the days of pilgrimage to Mecca. (*See* PILGRIMAGE).

The above are holidays observed by Sunnīs and Shī'ites, albeit with other meanings in some cases, particularly that of 'Āshūrā'. The following is a specifically Shī'ite holiday unknown to Sunnīs:18th Dhu al-Ḥijjah is *'Īd al-Ghādir.* A Shī'ite festival instituted by the Buyid Mu'izz ad-Dawlah in *351*/962. It commemorates the event of Ghadīr Khumm, in which Shī'ites believe that the Prophet designated 'Alī as his successor. Not observed by Sunnīs.

In addition to the holidays above, Shī'ites observe many commemorations of events in the lives of the Imāms. In Iran, the celebration of the ancient

Persian solar new year, the *Naw Ruz*, on the spring equinox, 21st March, constitutes an important national holiday. Although secular holidays, usually of a political nature, exist in most Islamic countries, the *'ulamā'* cannot condone the addition of any holidays of a civil nature to those above.

A simple conversion formula to determine in which year New Year's day of a year of the other calendar took place, is the following:

G(regorian year) = H(egirian year) plus+ 622 minus- H/33H(egirian year) = G(regorian year) minus- 622 plus+ (G-622)/32

Another method for determining the Gregorian year is to take the *hijrī* year and multiply it by 970,224. Place a decimal point counting six places from left to right (that is, divide by 1,000,000), and add 621.5774. (It may be more convenient to multiply the *hijrī* year by 0.970224 and not divide by 1,000,000; then add 621.5774). The whole number will be the Gregorian year, and the decimal multiplied by 365 will be the day of the Gregorian year upon which the first of Muḥarram falls.

However, in order to ensure precision in determining dates, it is advisable to consult books containing tables, compiled to give the daily correspondences between the two calendars.

In addition to the Islamic calendar, there is a system of Islamic time which consists in setting the watch to 12 (zero hours) at both sunset and sunrise each day. It is used, rarely, by pious people in addition to the usual time. *See* 'ĀSHŪRĀ'; BAYRAM; 'ĪD al-AḌḤĀ; 'ĪD al-FIṬR; LAYLAT al-BARĀ'AH; LAYLAT al-QADR; MAWLID an-NABĪ; MUḤARRAM; NIGHT JOURNEY; NAW RUZ; RAMAḌĀN. (For prayer-times, *see also* SALĀT).

Caliph (Ar. *khalīfah*, "successor", "substitute", "lieutenant", "viceroy"). The Koran (2:30) refers to Adam as the embodiment of the *fiṭrah*, or primordial norm, and as the Caliph, representative or vicegerent (*khalīfah*), of God on earth. Hence man, in his real nature, and not his fallen one, is cast in the role of viceroy to God. The Prophet, however, was the Caliph of God in the Adamic sense, although his successors could lay claim to the title only insofar as they were his representatives, and carried on his functions as spiritual head and temporal ruler of the Islamic state. The Prophet was at once patriarch, revealer, priest, and prince; and thus the Caliphate has been called his "shadow in history". The successors could not, of course, presume to continue the prophetic function. Nevertheless, the ultimate sense of "Caliph" always clung to the office. As the first four Caliphs, Abū Bakr, 'Umar, 'Uthmān, and 'Alī, had each a spiritual station commensurate with the function they performed, they are called *al-khulafā' ar-rāshidūn*, the "rightly guided" or the "patriarchal Caliphs". Some other Caliphs were also spiritual men, and so, perhaps, also worthy of the name in a true sense, but this term refers only to the first four. The idea of the Caliphate is, however, that of a sacred function and not merely a public office. (*See* PATRIARCHAL CALIPHS).

Originally, after the death of the Prophet the Caliph was elected, except that Abū Bakr himself appointed 'Umar. After the first four Caliphs, the office became hereditary *de facto*. Nevertheless, the procedure of legitimisation was election by the recognized religious leaders or authorities, embodied after the early days of Islam in the corpus of religious scholars known as 'ulamā'. As the supreme military leader, the Caliph, from the time of 'Umar onward, also bore the title of *amīr al-mu'minīn* — "Prince" or "Commander of the Faithful".

The first seat of the Caliphate was Medinah, and then, already under 'Alī, the camp-city of Kūfah. Under the Caliph Mu'āwiyah, the founder of the Umayyad dynasty, the capital moved to Damascus, and under the 'Abbāsids, to Baghdad. For some nine years 'Abd Allāh ibn az-Zubayr (d. *73*/692) claimed the Caliphate for himself in Mecca, which he held in defiance of the Umayyad Caliph 'Abd al-Malik in Damascus. The 'Abbāsid Caliphate came to an end in *656*/1258 when Hülāgū Khan of the Mongol Horde sacked Baghdad and put the Caliph al-Musta'ṣim to death. Thereafter, the title was held by the descendants of the 'Abbāsids in Mamlūk Cairo, but only with a symbolic function. The Ottomans claimed that the last 'Abbāsid ceded the title to Selim I when he conquered Cairo in *923*/1517.

It is possible that the Ottoman claim to the title of Caliph by cession from the last 'Abbāsid is a political fiction invented some time during the last three hundred years. (*See* OTTOMANS.) There are Ḥadīth which can be interpreted to mean that the *khalīfah*, or Caliph, is always to be found in the Arab tribe of the Quraysh; and the Ottomans were certainly not Qurayshīs. Nevertheless, the Ottomans in Istanbul played the role of Caliphs convincingly enough, defending orthodoxy and providing a political centre for Islam. When the Ottoman Caliphate was brought to an end in 1924 through the creation of a secular Turkish state, it was Sharīf Ḥusayn of Mecca who claimed the title. Within the decade his son 'Abd Allāh, King of Transjordan, also claimed to be Caliph. They were, of course, Qurayshīs; but no-one outside their territories acknowledged their claims and no-one has claimed the title since.

Parallel to the 'Abbāsids of Baghdad, there existed rival empires which claimed the Caliphate. These were the Fāṭimid empire in Cairo from *296*/909 to *567*/1171; and the Umayyad Caliphate of Cordoba which presided over a resplendent epoch of Arabo-Islamic civilisation in Spain from *138*/756 to *422*/1031 (using the title Caliph from *317*/929 in imitation of the Fāṭimids; other dynasties followed, without claiming to be Caliphs; Cordoba fell to the Christians in *635*/1236 and Seville in *646*/1248.) The Sultanate of Granada could lay claim to the Cordovan heritage until the fall of Granada itself in *897*/1492 to Ferdinand and Isabella, the "Catholic Kings" of Spain. *See* 'ABBĀSIDS; OTTOMANS; PATRIARCHAL CALIPHS; UMAYYADS.

"Caliph for a Day", *see* IBN MU'TAZZ.

Caliphs, Patriarchal, *see* PATRIARCHAL CALIPHS.

Caliphs, Rightly Guided, *see* PATRIARCHAL CALIPHS.

Call to Prayer, *see* ADHĀN.

Calligraphy. In Islam the art of calligraphy is esteemed as second only to architecture. Because figurative art is forbidden in Islam or, in practice at least, restrained, calligraphy became the foremost among the fine and decorative arts. Moreover, Islam is a civilisation based upon a Book and the Word, both coming from God; thus the arts of writing assume a sacred character. Arabic calligraphy, principally of the Koran, exemplifies its hieratic nature by an extreme regularity or monotony, coupled with an extreme fluidity, or freedom; its ubiquity on architecture serves to render the Revealed Text everywhere visible and pervasive in the traditional ambience.

In the early centuries of Islamic expansion it was considered normal and obligatory that converted peoples should adopt the Arabic alphabet, the letters that give the Koran its physical substance, to write their own languages. Today, the graceful Arabic letters are used by many different languages and cultures. The present form of Arabic writing appeared quite late, shortly before the Koran itself was revealed (other styles of script had existed previously). One of the earliest Islamic styles is the Kufic which has both early and late forms, but which is inherently difficult to read at speed. Very soon, therefore, its use came to be reserved for highly decorative formal use and monumental applications, and the flowing *naskhī* was adopted for writing and communication.

The major styles in Arabic calligraphy are *naskh, ta'līq, thuluth, maghribī*, (which developed in the Arab West and of which an archaic form is preserved in Timbuctu), and the extremely fluid Turkish "chancellery" *diwānī* and Persian *shikaste*. The most common styles used in writing today are a modified *maghribi* used in the Arab West, and the *ruk'ah*, an Ottoman style devised originally for Turkish, which is now used as the customary written script practically everywhere in the Arab world, and which is not considered to have any hieratic character.

Hand-calligraphed Korans constitute one of the great art heritages of the Islamic world. Many rulers, ministers, and other persons of exalted station wrote out the Koran in their own hands, sometimes many times over. *See* ARABIC.

Caravanserai ("Merchants' Inn", from Persian *Kārwān*, "a company of travellers" and *sarāi* "a large inn"). Rulers often built and maintained inns on major communication routes in order to foster the cohesion of their kingdoms. Zubaydah, the wife of Hārūn ar-Rashīd, built inns, wells, and cisterns on the pilgrim route from Baghdad to Mecca, which became known after her as the *Darb Zubaydah* ("road of Zubaydah").

Privately owned inns were to be found in most towns to receive travelers and merchandise, and for this purpose they were also provided with space for storing goods. In the Middle East these inns are usually called *khāns* and, in the Arab West, *funduq* from the Greek *pandokeion* ("guest house"). They usually consisted of courtyards to stable animals, rooms for the travelers, and storage areas for their goods. Inns which have survived to the present day are often excellent historic examples of the civil architecture of their times and today evoke romantic images of a not too distant past. Some are still in use and one, in Iṣfahān, had been turned into a luxury hotel, the former "Shah 'Abbās".

"Carnavelesque Festivals", *see* BOUJLOUD.

Carmathians, *see* QARMAṬĪS.

Castes. In principle, Islam, more than most religions, produces a caste-less society. However, classes did emerge in Islamic society early on. Among the Ottomans there was a division into the military class, the *askeris* and the subjects, the *ra'āyā*, which included peasants and nomads, and town and city dwellers. The *ra'āyā* were prevented by law from riding horses and carrying swords, and wearing certain kinds of dress. After the time of Sulayman the term *ra'āyā* designated the non-Muslim populations.

In Pakistan and India, there exists something like the castes of Hinduism amongst Muslims. There are the *zamindars* or land-owners, the *askeris*, or descendants of warriors, the *lohar-thrukkan* or blacksmith carpenter, the weaver, the cobbler, the entertainer-barber, and the low professions which are the equivalents of "untouchables"; some of whom use different utensils in cafeterias.

Naṣīr ad-Dīn Ṭūsī(*673*/1274) described a view of classes, probably derived from the castes of ancient Iran, which also approximates the caste divisions of India, and for that matter, Medieval Europe:

> "First come the Men of the Pen such as the masters of the sciences and the branches of knowledge, the canon-lawyers, the judges, secretaries, accountants, geometers, astronomers, physicians, and poets, on whose existence depends the order of this world and the next; among the natural elements these correspond to Water. Secondly the Men of the Sword; fighters, warriors, volunteers, skirmishers, frontier-guardians, sentries, valiant men, supporters of the realm and guardians of the state, by whose intermediacy the world's organisation is effected; among the natural elements these correspond to Fire. Thirdly, the Men of Negotiation, merchants who carry goods from one region to another, tradesmen, masters of crafts, and tax-collectors, without whose co-operation the daily life of the species would be impossible; among the natural elements, they are like the Air. Fourthly, the men of Husbandry, such as sowers, farmers, ploughmen, and agriculturalists, who organize the feeding of all the communities, and without whose help the survival of individuals would be out of the question; among the natural elements they have the same rank as Earth."

Casting of stones, *see* RAMY al-JIMĀR.

Cats. The attachment to cats of one of the Companions, Abū Hurayrah ("Father of the Kitten"), is proverbial. Cats, unlike dogs, are considered to be ritually "clean" animals and allowed to roam freely inside mosques, including the Grand Mosque in Mecca. Stories of cats that seek out persons who are praying, and of cats sensitive to the presence of grace, are common.

Chador. In Iran since the Islamic revolution, and some other countries of the Gulf, the black cloak which women wear covering the head and draping to the ground. *See* ḤIJĀB; VEIL.

Chanting of the Koran, *see* KORAN CHANTING.

Charity, *see* FIVE PILLARS; SADAQAH; WAQF; ZAKAH.

Chechnya. Area of the North Caucasus, defined as part of the Russian Federation. Chechens and the neighboring Ingush, to whom they are related, have lived there for millennia. The Chechens converted to Sunni Islam very late, and slowly, from the 17th to the 19th century. The Naqshbendi and Qadiri Sufi sects were responsible for the conversions and wield a strong influence in Chechnya today, as they do throughout the Caucasus. Chechnya became part of the Russian empire in the beginning of the 19th century. The population of the Chechen region was about 1,100,000 before 1989 but 30% were Slavs and Russians were in the majority in the capital, Grozny. Since the Chechen wars much of the Slavic population has left. Several thousands of Chechens live elsewhere in Russia, particularly in Moscow, and other former republics of the Soviet Union. There are also colonies of Chechens in Jordan and 'Irāq dating back before the Russian revolution. *See also* SHAMIL, IMĀM.

Children. There is a Ḥadīth which says that children are born into the world possessing the *fiṭrah*, or a primordial conformity with truth; then their parents turn them into Jews, Christians or Muslims; that is, they acquire a way of being. From this Ḥadīth one can conclude that children who die before the age of reason can be saved by virtue of their innate conformity (*fiṭrah*) with reality.

The Mu'tazilites, or "Rationalists" believed that children who died before the age of discretion went to a limbo; the theologian al-Ash'arī, in refuting the Mu'tazilite beliefs cites this Ḥadīth: "We have heard that the Prophet of God said: A fire will be kindled for all children on the Day that the Dead shall Rise; and they will be commanded: leap into that Fire! And every child who leaps into that Fire will I bring into Paradise. But every child who will not I shall cause to enter Hell."

In other words, according to this doctrine, children who die before they have had the opportunity to be responsible for their own salvation are saved if in their essential nature they are truly innocent. *See* ESCHATOLOGY.

China, *see* HUI HUI; NEW SECT; TĀ SHIH; T'IEN FANG; XINJIANG.

Chinguetti. A town of several thousand inhabitants in the Attar region of Mauritania. The whole country was once known by the town's Arab name *Shinqīt*; it lies on an ancient caravan route along which salt from the the Atlas mountains was transported south to be exchanged for African luxury goods, perfume, exotic wood, and gold.

The town has a small, simple, but lovely mosque that was built in the 13th century, with a sand floor, a roof of palm beams and a stone minaret. Chinguetti had a certain reputation throughout North West Africa as a holy city, not for the usual reason of its containing the tomb of a noted Saint but rather, one imagines, because of its importance as a stopping place for travelers in the ocean of the desert. Like many desert towns, Chinguetti has a private and ancestral library of ancient manuscripts and books which testifies to its past as a spiritual centre.

Chishti, Mu'īn ad-Dīn Muḥammad (*537-633*/1142-1236). A famous Sufi of India, venerated as a great Saint and buried in Ajmir. An important *ṭarīqah* is named after him, the Chishtiyyah Order.

Chivalry, *see* FUTUWWAH.

Christianity. In theory, Islam accepts Christianity as a Divinely revealed religion. Christians in a state under Muslim rule cannot be compelled to become Muslims, their churches are not to be taken away from them, and they are entitled to civil protection. In former times non-Muslims were obliged to pay a special tax (*see* DHIMMI). It is legal for a Muslim man to marry a Christian woman (or a woman of any of the Divinely revealed religions).

The protection of adherents of other religions has been a legal principle in Islam from the beginning, and in most Muslim countries there have been large minorities of Christians and Jews, and lesser ones of other religions such as Hindus, Buddhists, animists, and others depending on the country.

In the Muslim view, the Christian doctrine of the Trinity and the Divine nature of Jesus, and other points of difference from Islam, are deviations from what they believe Jesus's true teachings to have been. Muslims assume that because the Koran says that Jesus was a Divine Messenger like the Prophet, his message could not have been different from the Prophet's; that is to say, that Jesus's message could not have been anything other than Islam as they know it. Despite this perspective, the historic attitude of Islam towards Christianity has been largely sympathetic. Under the Ottomans many churches received privileges which they later lost under secular Christian governments. The Koran says: "and thou wilt surely find the nearest of them in love to the believers are those who say 'We are Christians'; that, because some of them are priests and monks [those devoted entirely to God], and they wax not proud." (5:85) *See* BIBLE; JESUS; COPTS; MARONITES; NESTORIANS.

Chronogram (Ar. *ta'rikh, ramz, ḥisab al-jummal*). A rhetorical device or conceit of enclosing a recorded date in a phrase or epigram. The date, in Hijri years, is obtained by taking the sum of the numerical value of the letters of the phrase according to the rules of *'Abjad* (Each Arabic letter has a numeric value.) The chronogram is sometimes introduced by the word *fī* meaning "in", or written in letters of a different size or colour in a text. Chronograms are found in written works but also engraved on monuments. They are meant to be witty or ingenious, and emblematic. Particularly favored by the Persians, they can be found anywhere in the Islamic world in any language written in Arabic letters.

The year of Jāmī's death is recorded in the chronographs: "And who enters is saved", a quotation from the Koran 3:91 whose Arabic letters equal 898; also "sighs of the heart were taken away from Khorāsān" (this involves subtracting the value of "sighs" or 14 from Khorāsān which is 912 = 898.) The death of a cruel Deccan ruler called Humāyūn was epitomized by a poet as "delight of the world" (*dhawk-i jahan*) = 865.

The Chronograph of Ḥāfiẓ' death is "since he made his home in the earth of Muṣalla (*khak-i Muṣalla*, an oratory near Shiraz which was a favorite resort of the poet), seek his chronogram there". Kh=600; ā= 1; k=20; m=40: ṣ=90 l=30 y (the "a" at the end)=10 the total = Hijri 791 which is AD 1389. As Browne says... "the most ingenious paraphrase in English of a Persian chronogram is by Hermann Bicknell (Hajji 'Abdu-l-Wahīd) the admirer and translator of Ḥāfiẓ...the difficulty in producing a chronogram in English is that only seven letters (C,D,I,L,M,V and X) have numerical values, nevertheless Bicknell overcame this difficulty and thus paraphrased the above chronogram: 'Thrice take thou from MUṢALLĀ'S EARTH (M=L=L=1100) ITS RICHEST GRAIN' (I+I+C+I= 103x3=109: 1100-309=791)."

Browne also cites English chronograms, such as Queen Elizabeth's death: "My Day Is Closed In ImmortalIty" (MDCIII=AD 1603) and for Martin Luther's death : "eCCe nVnc MorItVr IVstVs In paCe ChrIstI eXItV et beatVs", i.e. M.CCCCC.X.VVVVVV.IIIIII = AD 1546.

Other interesting chronograms are *Lodh*= Refuge! for the year H. 736 in which Abū Sa'īd died bringing the dynasty of the Il-Khans to an end and with it anarchy, and the year in which Tamerlane was born. Ulugh Beg was killed by a certain 'Abbās in 853 and the chronogram is *'Abbas kusht*= "'Abbās killed him"; the instigator of this murder was himself killed in 854 by one Bāba Ḥusayn and that date was worked into Bābā Ḥusayn Kusht or "Baba Ḥusayn killed him!"

Circumcision (Ar. *khitān* or *khitānah*). Albeit strongly adhered to, this is a custom rather than a legal obligation. In South East Asia it is called simply *Sunnah*, i.e. "custom". In Muslim countries it may be performed on boys when the child is seven or older. Circumcisions are then occasions for the sacrifice of a sheep or another animal in Africa or the Middle East, and for other festivities elsewhere. However, because of the expense of such celebrations, circumcision is sometimes simply not performed among the poor. Because it is *Sunnah*, but not a requirement of the *sharī'ah*, circumcision is not obligatory upon adult converts.

"Female circumcision", even as a purely symbolic act, a light excision of skin (*khifāḍ*), is not a practice recommended by religion; but it has been apparently tolerated as custom. Such a practice, while serving no purpose except as an imitation of male circumcision, normally did not go so far as to be a mutilation; usually it was harmless. There also exist, however, practices such as clitoridectomy, and/or removal of the labia; these are a grave violence against the person and are strictly forbidden in Islam. Such practices are found in some backward milieus and are due to gross ignorance; they have absolutely no religious basis, and, like all mutilations, are not sanctioned by Islamic law, and legally prohibited in the United States. Attempts have also been made to make it illegal in Egypt and some African countries.

Clothing, *see* 'ABĀ'; IḤRĀM; TURBAN.

Coffin, Suspended, *see* FALLACIES and INACCURACIES about ISLAM.

Commander of the Faithful (Ar. *amīr al-mu'minīn*). A title of the Caliph (since 'Umar, the second Caliph) as military chief. It has also been used by some Kings. *See* CALIPH.

Commentaries on the Koran. Commentaries which are straightforward explanations by way of background information with some degree of interpretation are called *tafsīr*; allegorical and mystical exegesis is more strictly called *ta'wīl*. The latter as allegory (but not necessarily as mysticism) has often, rightly, been considered extremely suspect.

A standard commentary is that of 'Abd Allāh ibn 'Umar al-Bayḍāwī (d. *685*/1282), *Anwār at-Tanzīl wa Isrār at-Ta'wīl* ("The light of Revelation and the Secrets of Interpretation"). It was frequently used in traditional courses of study and includes some of the more dependable opinions taken from earlier commentaries. Another famous commentary, quoted by virtually all later commentators, is the Tafsīr of Abū Ja'far Muḥammad aṭ-Ṭabarī (d. *320*/923), entitled *Jāmi' al-Bayān fī Tafsīr al-Qur'an* ("The Comprehensive Explanation of Koranic Exegesis"). This is a vast compendium of the first three centuries of Koranic exegesis. The *Tafsīr al-Jalālayn*, the commentaries of the "two Jalāls", Jalāl ad-Dīn as-Ṣūyūṭī, the historian (d. *299*/911) and his teacher Jalāl ad-Dīn al-Mahallī (d. *250*/864) is also highly regarded. Also important is the commentary of az-Zamakshari (d. *538*/1144), *al-Kashshaf 'an Haqā'iq at-Tanzīl* ("The Unveiler of the Truths of Revelation"). This commentary is Mu'tazilite and regards the Koran as created.

All of these are based upon oral traditions of the Prophet and the Companions, and in particular upon the interpretations of the nephew of the Prophet, 'Abd Allāh ibn al-'Abbās, called the *Baḥr al-'Ilm* ("Ocean of Knowledge"). Ibn al-'Abbās became somewhat of an "oracle", and it was common to attribute mysterious, speculative, or extravagant interpretations to him as an authority of last resort.

The inimitable quality of the Koran has always been one of the arguments as proof that it is Divinely revealed. Al-Khattabi cites as one of the reasons for the inimitability, along with the internal evidence of *lafẓ* (expression, uttering, vocables), *ma'na* (sense) *nuẓum* (internal coherence), the fact that the Koran launches a challenge to produce its like, which the Quraysh could have tried to answer in order to settle the dispute, but did not.

Many later Muslim scholars wrote commentaries on the Koran, most, if not all of them, incomplete. Some commentaries are specifically Shī'ite and others again, such as those of Ibn 'Arabī and al-Qashānī, are mystical. Fakhr ad-Dīn ar-Rāzī (d. *606*/1209) wrote a commentary called *at-Tafsīr al-Kabīr* ("The Great Commentary") which, on the one hand, is an Ash'arite answer to Mu'tazilite ideas, but which also introduced philosophical thinking into Koranic commentary. The science of Koranic study is part of the *'ilm al-uṣūl*, or "science of the 'roots', or principles, of law".

Much of Islamic Koranic commentary resembles the *midrash* of Judaism in two ways: in content because many commentaries to Biblical stories were supplied by converted Jews and are therefore called *isrā'īliyyāt*; but above all in form, because the method, which is common to all traditional civilisations, is similar. A parable or story is constructed to bring out one or another intention or possibility of the text. Such commentary by parable is usually not to be taken literally, but rather as the expression of an abstract idea. *See* KORAN; TA'WĪL.

Companions (Ar. *ṣāḥib*, pl. *aṣḥāb*, *ṣahābah*). Strictly speaking, those followers of the Prophet who were closest to him in his lifetime, kept frequent company with him, and strove to assimilate his teachings. They memorized and transmitted Ḥadīth and the Koran, before these were written down and compiled.

According to another view, anyone who had seen the Prophet during his life was a Companion, and by this definition the Companions would number tens of thousands. One middle figure which has been been advanced is 12,314 of which 1552 were women. According to this larger view there are categories or "classes" of Companions depending upon the time of their conversion and the key events in which they took part.

According to Ibn Isḥaq, the first person to accept Islam was Khadījah, the Prophet's wife. The next was 'Alī ibn Abī Ṭālib, who was then ten years old and living in the Prophet's household. He had seen the Prophet and Khadījah praying. 'Alī hesitated and thought he should first ask Abū Ṭālib, but the Prophet said "If you do not accept Islam, then conceal the matter" as he was not yet ready for public preaching. The next day 'Alī accepted Islam. The next was Zayd ibn Ḥarīthah, the Prophet's freedman. Then Abū Bakr, of whom the Prophet said: "I have never invited anyone to accept Islam but has shown signs of reluctance, suspicion, and hesitation, except Abū Bakr."

Abū Bakr was open about his religion and invited those whom he trusted to enter it. These were 'Uthmān ibn 'Affan, al-Zubayr ibn al-'Awwam, 'Abd ar-Raḥmān (before conversion 'Abdu 'Amr) ibn 'Awf, Sa'd ibn Abi Waqqās, and Ṭalḥa ibn 'Ubayd Allāh. Abū Bakr brought them to the Prophet and they accepted Islam.

After them came: Abū 'Ubaydah ibn al-Jarrāḥ of the Bani l-Hārith, Abū Salamah, al-Arqam ibn Abi-l-Arqam, 'Uthmān ibn Maẓ'ūn, his two brothers Qudāmah and 'Abdullāh, 'Ubaydah ibn al-Ḥārith, Sa'īd ibn Zayd, and his wife Fāṭimah (the sister of 'Umar ibn al-Khaṭṭāb), Asmā' the daughter of Abū Bakr, and her sister 'Ā'ishah. Another early convert was 'Abdallāh ibn Mas'ūd. it is said the first woman to enter after Khadijah was Umm Fadl, wife of the 'Abbās, famous for his hesitancy, and her sisters Maymūnah, and Salma and Asmā'.

Concealment of Revelation (Ar. *akhfā al-waḥy*). By the device of alleging the existence of "a secret teaching" it is possible to introduce the exact opposite of an intended doctrine into a religion. Mahayana Buddhism, which contradicts much of Buddhism which came before it, claimed that there was a secret teaching for which the world was not ripe before Nagarjuna revealed it. It is also characteristic to sweeten the introduction of an antinomial idea by flattering the recipient as being worthy to receive a teaching which others were not capable of understanding. In the case of Buddhism, the school which does not accept the Boddhisatva idea is furthermore denigrated by being called the "little vehicle" whose followers "are concerned with their own salvation rather than all of humanity".

Thus in Islam, although the single most important idea is that there is no God but Allāh, very early on religious careers were made by claiming divinity for a particular person. This is still done today where one would be hard put to find a Sufi order which does not at least hint that such and such a great teacher of its line was so united with God as to be identical with Him. It is easy to brush off objections of the orthodox by saying that the Prophet was always asking "is there a stranger among us?" meaning that certain things were reserved for the elect, and others could not be expected to understand.

Thus in the *Ṣaḥīḥ* of Bukhāri we find 'Ā'ishah admonishing her pupil Masrūq (d. 62 or 63 A.H.) that the Prophet never kept any part of the revelation concealed: "Verily, he who tells you that the Prophet concealed a part of the divine revelation and that he has not delivered it to his people, lies." The Koran (5:70) also categorically says: "O Apostle! Deliver to the people what has been revealed to you from your Lord. If you do not do so, you will be failing in your duty to deliver His message, to those for whom they are meant."

Confederates, War of the, *see* BATTLE of the TRENCH.

"Constitution of Medinah". A name sometimes given to the *Mīthaq Madīnah*, the agreement made between the Prophet and the Jews of Yathrib, the Arab tribes of Yathrib, and the emigrant Quraysh. Because it calls these "one Ummah" and includes Muslims, Pagans, Jews, and probably Christians among the Arabs tribes as well, this document has been advanced as a model for Muslims in creating a multi-confessional state. It was concluded a few months after the Prophet's emigration to Medinah and was concerned and prompted by questions of mutual defense. In all the "Constitution" comprises eight documents over the space of seven years that regulated inter-tribal relations in Medinah.

Conversion. One enters Islam by surrendering to God. The person who thus actualizes his surrender to God first undergoes the purification of the greater ablution (*ghusl*), and then recites the two testimonies of faith in the presence of two witnesses. Following this recognition of God as the Absolute Reality, and of Muḥammad as the Messenger of God, the new Muslim is committed to keeping the Five Pillars of Islam. Converts from Judaism also bear witness that Jesus is a Messenger of God. *See* SHAHĀDAH; TAWBAH.

Copts. The most important branch of Christianity found mainly in Egypt and the Sudan. The Copts are monophysites who separated from the Christian mainstream after the Council of Chalcedon in 451. Monophysites believe that Jesus had one nature — a Divine nature only — in one person, in contrast to the dominant doctrine, enunciated at the Council of Chalcedon, that in Jesus there are two natures, human and Divine, in one person. The Copts are related to the other monophysite churches such as the Jacobites of Syria, the Ethiopian Church, and, by similarity of doctrine, to the Armenian Church. Their liturgical language is a direct descendant of the ancient tongue of the Egyptians, with the incorporation of an extensive Greek vocabulary of Christian terminology. *See* also CHRISTIANITY; JESUS; MARONITES; NESTORIANS.

Cosmology, *see* FIVE DIVINE PRESENCES.

Courtesy, *see* ADAB.

Creation, *see* KALĀM.

Creed (Ar. *'aqīdah*). Systematic statements of belief became necessary, from early Islam on, initially to refute heresies, and later to distinguish points of view and to present them, as the divergence of schools of theology or opinion increased. The "first" creed is the *Fiqh Akbar* which is ascribed to Abū Ḥanīfah. It is a short answer to the pressing heresies of the time. Later creeds were longer, more elaborate, and complete as being the catechisms of specific schools. Notable creeds are the *Fiqh Akbar II*, representative of al-Ash'arī, the

FiqhAkbar III of ash-Shāfi'ī, and the respective *'aqīdahs* of al-Ghazālī, an-Naṣafī, and al-Faḍālī.

The truly first and most fundamental creed, however, is enunciated in this Ḥadīth:

> A man dressed in white came and sat down so close to the Prophet while he was with his Companions that his knees touched the knees of the Prophet, and said: "O Messenger of God, what is Islam?" The Prophet answered, "To bear witness that there is no god but God and that I am the Messenger of God [*shahādah*]; that one should perform the prayers [*salāt*] and pay the legal alms [*zakāh*] and fast in the month of Ramaḍān [*ṣawm*] and make pilgrimage to the House [*in Mecca, ḥajj*] if that is possible for one."
>
> The visitor said "You have spoken truly. What is faith [*īmān*]?" The Prophet said "That one should believe in God and His angels, and His books, and His messengers, and in the Last Day, the resurrection from the tomb [*ba'ath man fī-l-qubūr*], and the decreeing [*qadar*] of good and evil". The visitor said "You have spoken truly. And what is virtue [*ihṣān*]?" The Prophet answered "That you should worship God as if you saw Him, for if you do not see Him, nevertheless He sees you". The visitor said "You have spoken truly; when shall be the Last Day?" The Prophet answered "The questioned does not know more of that than the questioner." Then the visitor rose and left. The Prophet turned to his Companions and said "That was Gabriel who came to teach you your religion."

The Creed of al-Ash'arī is representative of the fully developed creeds of later Islam:

> The substance of that on which the Followers of the True Way take their stand is the confession of God [Allāh], His Angels, His Script [the Revealed Books], His Apostles [the Messengers sent by God], the Revelation of God and the Tradition [Sunnah] of the trustworthy related on the authority of God's Apostle; not one of these do they reject.
>
> God is One, Single, Eternal. There is no other god.
>
> Muḥammad is His Servant and Apostle.
>
> Paradise is Fact; and Hell is Fact. There is no doubt of the Coming Hour [the Day of Judgment]; and God will raise the Dead from their graves.
>
> God's place is upon His Throne, as He has said. God has two Hands, as He has said — we do not question: in what sense? God has two Eyes, as He has said — we do not question: in what sense? God has a Face, as He has said.
>
> It is not to be said that God's Names or Attributes are anything other than Himself. The Followers of the True Way confess that God has Knowledge as He has said. They assert the existence of His Hearing and His Sight.
>
> They believe that there is no good and no evil on earth except by the Will of God, and that all things are by the Will of God. They confess that there is no creator save God, and that God creates the works of men, and that they are incapable of creating anything.
>
> God gives True Believers Grace to be obedient to Him; He forsakes Unbelievers. He is well able to act for the salvation of Unbelievers; nevertheless He wills not so to act, nor so to grace them that they Believe. He rather wills them to be Unbelievers in accordance with His knowledge, forsaking and misguiding them and sealing up their hearts.
>
> Good and evil depend on the general and particular Decrees of God. The Followers of the True Way believe in His Decrees both general and particular, in His good and His evil, His sweet and His bitter.
>
> They believe that they are not their own masters for weal or for woe, save as God wills, for He has said so. Committing their affairs to God, they declare their dependence on Him in all circumstances, their need of Him at all times.
>
> They believe that the Koran is God's Uncreated Eternal Word.
>
> They believe that God will be seen with sight on the Day of the Raising of the Dead; as the moon is seen on the night of her full shall the Believers see Him; but Unbelievers shall not see Him because they will be veiled from God.
>
> They do not brand any Muslim an Unbeliever for any grave sin he may commit, for fornication or theft or any such grave sin; but

hold that such men are Believers inasmuch as they have Faith, grievous though their sins may be. Islam is the testifying that there is no god but God and that Muḥammad is God's Apostle, in accordance with Tradition; and Islam, they hold, is not the same thing as Faith [*īmān*].

They confess that God changes the hearts of men.

They confess the Intercession of God's Apostle, and believe that it is for the grave sinners of his people and against the Punishment of the Tomb. They confess that the Pool [where the Prophet will meet his Companions in the afterlife] of the Hereafter is fact, and the Bridge [over which the dead will cross] is Fact, that the Rising after death is Fact, that God's Reckoning with men is Fact, and that the Standing in the Presence of God is Fact.

They confess that Faith is both word and deed.

They discountenance argument and disputation concerning Islam. They do not inquire: in what sense? or: Why? because such inquiry is Innovation in Islam.

They believe that God does not command evil, but forbids it; that He commands good, and has no pleasure in evil, though He wills it.

They acknowledge the Elders elect of God to be Companions of His Apostle as Fact; they cherish their virtues and eschew discrimination amongst them, giving priority to Abū Bakr, then 'Umar, then 'Uthmān, then 'Alī, and believing that they are the rightly guided Caliphs, the best of all men after the Prophet.

They approve the Feast and the Friday Congregation and all gatherings for Prayer under the leadership of any Imām, be he pious or be he wicked. They believe in the precept of Holy War against polytheists. They approve Prayer for the welfare of all Imāms of the Muslims and agree that they ought not to rebel against them with the sword, nor fight in any civil commotion.

They believe in the Examining Angels Munkar and Nākir who shall visit the dead with the Punishment of the Tomb, and in the Ascension, and in visions of sleep; and they hold that Prayer for the departed Muslims, and alms in their behalf, after their departing this world, avail for them.

They believe that there is witchcraft in the world, and that the wizard is an Unbeliever, as God says.

They approve Prayer for every Muslim departed, be he pious or be he wicked. They confess that Paradise and Hell are created; and that he who dies, dies at his appointed term; that he who is slain is slain at his appointed term; and that Satan whispers to men and makes them doubt, then spurns them underfoot. They confess that God knows what every man will do, and has written that these things shall be. They approve patience under what God has ordained. For God's Servants they believe in serving Him, the giving of sincere counsel to brother Muslims, and the avoiding of all grave sins; of fornication, of perjury, of party spirit, of self-esteem, of condemning other men.

They approve the avoidance of every person who calls to Innovation; they approve diligence in the Reading of the Koran and the writing of Traditions from the Companions; they approve study of the Law, pursued with humility, restraint, and good manners. They approve the abandonment of all mystification, all evil speaking, and all excessive care after food and drink. Of God alone is our grace, and He is our Sufficiency. How excellent is His Emissary! In God we seek help; in Him we trust. And to Him is our Returning.

See BILĀ KAYFA; FIQH AKBAR; ISTAWĀ'.

Crescent, *see* MOON.

Crown (Ar. *tāj*). A non-Islamic concept; a Ḥadīth puts it thus: "There is no crown in Islam." However, there were, nevertheless, the equivalents of crowns in the turbans and headgears of great Muslim monarchs. The Ḥadīth cited sets itself against rulership for personal aggrandizement and hereditary Kingship which runs counter to the primordial viewpoint of Islam in which distinctions between persons spring first of all from their spiritual state. Also, the Ḥadīth sets itself against the tendency of the age which made monarchs into Divine beings.

Crusades. The expeditionary wars to conquer the Holy Land followed the call of Pope Urban II at the Council of Clermont in 1095. The Crusades were the result of a nascent expansionism in Europe as well as pressures by the Seljūqs upon the Byzantine empire and the destruction of the Church of the Holy Sepulchre by the Fāṭimid Caliph al-Ḥākim in 1009. The enticements were booty, glory, territorial acquisition, and the promised remission of sins and service to God.

The Crusaders captured Jerusalem from the Fāṭimids in 1099 and created a Christian Kingdom with Godfrey of Boulogne as prince. His successor was crowned King Baldwin I. This Crusader Kingdom of Jerusalem (the Duchies of Edessa and Antioch and the others disappeared earlier) lasted until *690*/1291 when Acre fell and all of Palestine passed into the hands of the Mamlūks. Jerusalem had been captured by Saladin in *583*/1187; but from *626*/1229 to *641*/1244 it was restored to the Crusaders by a treaty made between the Muslims and Frederick II.

In Europe, the Crusades stimulated trade, increased the power of the Italian merchant city states, and finally led to the Age of Discoveries. The Knightly Orders of the Templars, the Hospitallers, and the others, which were born out of the Crusades, played a great role in European history. Constantinople, whose protection was one of the original reasons for the Crusades, was sacked by the Christians themselves under the leadership of the Doge Dandolo of Venice during the Fourth Crusade (1204). That ancient Christian Kingdom never completely recovered its strength and could not resist the final Turkish onslaught when it came.

The effects of the Crusades upon the Islamic world, on the other hand, were negligible. In the course of the fighting Saladin consolidated his control and dethroned the Fāṭimids of Egypt, but the Crusades did not unite the Muslims against a common threat. Indeed, some Muslims allied themselves with the Franks. Although in Palestine and Syria the Crusader castles remain as traces of their passage, for Islam the Crusades were ultimately only a transient and localized episode.

Ctesiphon, *see* al-MADĀ'IN.

Custom, *see* ADAT; 'URF.

D

Dahrī (from Ar. *ad-dahr*, "time"). A traditional term for an atheist or materialist. The term originates in the Koran (45:23-24): "Have you seen him who has taken his caprice to be his god?... They say: 'There is nothing but our present life; we die, and we live, and nothing but Time destroys us' (*ad-dahr*)." Hence also the term *ad-dahriyyah*, "atheism". *Ad-Dahr* translates the term *Aeon* (Greek: "the Age"), and *Zurvan* (or *Zervan*) meaning "time". *Zurvan* is the name of a divinity perhaps first found with the Magi of Media, but later identified as Chronos by the Greeks (and Saturn by the Romans). *Aeon* is the Hellenist term for a related Gnostic divinity. Zurvanism was a doctrine which became dominant in Zoroastrianism under the Sāssānids. In Zurvanism Ahura Mazda and Ahriman are made *equal* by being the *twin* sons of Zurvan. In orthodox Zoroastrianism Ahura Mazda does not have a twin brother, and is without an equal; Ahriman, the spirit of Evil, identified by the Greeks as Pluto, appears from nowhere, as if he were the by-product of creation.

Along with Zurvanism a female divinity became prominent, Anahita who began to appear in Sāssānid times on the rock carvings depicting the transmission of kingship to the ruler by Ahuramazda. Before Zurvanism she did not appear in such carvings. In medieval Zoroastrianism, when Zurvanism had declined, a daily prayer remained condemning the *Dahris*, by the Arabic name, perhaps a legacy from a time when one could not attack the Zurvanites directly. The Arabic term *ad-dahr* in the Koran is a reflection of the religious forces that raged among Arabic speakers before the coming of Islam.

Dā'ī (lit. "a caller", "summoner"). In the broadest sense "a missionary" or "a preacher", but specifically it means the propagandists who spread the Ismā'īlī sect. In Fāṭimid Egypt there was a hierarchy of propagandists which culminated in the *dā'ī ad-du'āt* ("the missionary of missionaries"). When the Fāṭimids split into Nizārīs and Musta'līs the leader of the Musta'līs in the Yemen in *526*/1132 assumed the title of *ad-dā'ī al-muṭlaq*, meaning literally "the absolute missionary", or "the supreme propagandist". He is assisted by the ma'dhun. *See* ISMĀ'ĪLĪS.

ad-Dajjāl (lit. "the deceiver" or "the imposter"). A false Prophet; one who misleads people regarding religion. According to Ḥadīth there will be a number of *dajjāls* in history. The last and greatest will be *al-Masīḥ ad-Dajjāl*, the "false Messiah", or Antichrist, who will appear shortly before Jesus returns to earth at the end of time. This *dajjāl* will seek to lead people into disbelief, or to the practice of a false religion. The Ḥadīth states that many unfortunates will follow him with the excuse that they do so "only because he gives them food". In a world overtaken by chaos, the *al-Masīḥ ad-Dajjāl* will be widely believed because he will hold out the false hope of restoring equilibrium. Then Jesus will return, destroy the *Dajjāl* and his forces in a great struggle, and the Day of Judgement will follow.

In a play on words referring to the final *Dajjāl*, the word *masīh* ("Messiah"), has been changed by some traditional commentators to *masīkh*, which means "deformed", thus producing the term *ad-Dajjāl al-Masīkh*, "the deformed deceiver". This play on words is done by the addition of a single dot over the last Arabic letter, *ha'*, changing it to *kha'*, to symbolize how easy it is to deform truth into falsehood. The nature of the *dajjāl* is precisely the deformation of truth into its exact opposite, and a complete inversion, or parody, of spirituality. *See* ESCHATOLOGY.

Dalā'il al-Khayrāt (lit. "guides to good things"). The name of a book of piety which is very popular in the Maghreb, or Arab West. It is a collection of prayers and religious lore with particular emphasis upon the Ninety-Nine Names of God, compiled by Abū 'Abd Allāh Muḥammad al-Jazūlī of Marrakesh (d. *870*/1465).

Dalīl (lit. "a guide"). Professional guides for pilgrims to Medinah. The *dalīls* escort visitors on a circuit of mosques and tombs leading them in the pious recitations of prayers and invocations appropriate to each spot. As guides, the *dalīls* speak the principal languages of the Islamic nations and are familiar with the customs and practices of each of the *madhhabs*, or schools of law.

Their offices are to be found in the vicinity of the Prophet's mosque, and their services can be hired by the day or half-day. Use of a guide is not obligatory, but can be helpful to a visitor unfamiliar with Medinah. Most dalīls can also provide transportation. Because the visit to Medinah is called the *ziyārah*, the Medinan guides are also often called *muzawwirūn*.

Damascus (Ar. *Dimashq*). The capital of Syria at the foot of Mount Qāsiun, Damascus ranks as one of the oldest continuously inhabited settlements in the world. It is mentioned in the cuneiform "Ebla Tablet" which dates from 3,000 BC Indeed, a legend recorded by 'Alī Ḥasan Ibn 'Asākir ("the historian of Damascus", d. *572*/1176) asserts that it was the first city after the Flood to erect a wall and that it was built by the Koranic Prophet Hud. Damascus owes its existence to the Barada river which flows down from mountains to the west of the city, for this river creates a vast oasis garden called al-Ghutah surrounding the city and covers 230 square miles (596 square kilometers), which produces a harvest of apples, pears and peaches and provides a green setting for a number of peaceful villages. In al-Ghutah, at Tell Aswad and Tell ar-Rimād, traces of habitation have been found dating from the Middle and New Stone Age. Although *dimashq* in Arabic means "swiftness", it is the presence of this life-giving water which probably gives the city its name, from the "watered abode" in an early Semitic dialect (in *Arabic ad-Dār al-Masqi*).

But other etymologies, mostly symbolic, also abound. One folk etymology takes the Arabic name and splits it into two words, *dim* and *ashq*, which it interprets to mean "blood flowed", referring to the struggle of Cain and Abel, because tradition places the tomb of Abel (in Arabic, Hābil) on a hill near the city. This spot is particularly favored by Druzes who congregate there on Fridays to picnic and to dance. These legends emphasize that the history of Damascus is woven of the strands of religions ancient and modern. Indeed, one of its traditional gates is even called *Bāb Farādīs* (the "Gate of Paradise").

Within the precinct of today's great Umayyad Mosque, the Aramaean god Hadad was worshiped; under the Seleucids the shrine became the temple of Jupiter before giving way to the Christian Cathedral of St. John the Baptist (according to tradition his head is entombed there today) and in the reign of the Caliph al-Walīd (d. *96*/715, it became a Muslim mosque.

Paul was converted to Christianity in Damascus. Having been struck with blindness on the road to the city where he, a Pharisee Jew, was going in order to seize and persecute Christians, he regained his sight when a Jewish convert to Christianity named Ananias (whose house is today the church of St. Ananias), inspired by the Holy Spirit, put his hands upon him. The trace of the "street which is called Straight" to which Ananias was guided to find Paul (Acts of the Apostles 9:11), exists today; it was one of the two cruciform avenues that were the mark of Roman cities. When Paul's former co-religionists were irate because of his conversion and preaching, he escaped out of the city by being let down the walls in a basket.

As one of the cradles of Christianity, Damascus is the home of ancient Christian communities of many filiations: Catholic, Eastern Orthodox, Uniate, Maronite and Armenian. The Christian centre of the city is *Bāb Toma* (the "Gate of Thomas"). Also, a Jewish community still exists in Damascus which treasures, as part of its heritage, the 2,000 year old Jawbar Synagogue, although the one principally used today is the al-Frange (the "Synagogue of the Frank"), that is "of the European".

When, in *14*/635 Khālid ibn Walīd conquered Damascus from the Byzantines, the Caliph 'Uthmān divided Syrian territory (*ash-Shem*), into the districts of Damascus, Ḥoms (*al-Ḥims*), Jordan (*al-Urdunn*), and Palestine (*al-Filasṭīn*). Mu'āwiyah the Umayyad, the son of Abū Sufyān, on becoming governor of Damascus, was able to use it as a power base in order to compel 'Alī, the fourth Caliph, to abandon Medinah after the death of 'Uthmān and seek a counter-force of his own in the direction of 'Irāq. When the Umayyads came to power in *41*/661, Damascus became, for the next 89 years, the capital of the Islamic Empire, which now stretched from Spain to India. The Umayyads embellished the Grand Mosque in Damascus, and under the Caliph 'Abd al-Mālik (d. *86*/705) built the Dome of the Rock in Jerusalem. Although established in the midst of a sophisticated urban civilisation, the nostalgia of their origins led the Umayyad rulers to build fortified pleasure palaces in the Syrian desert, such as the Qaṣr al-Khayr al-Gharbī, whose ruins remain today.

When the 'Abbāsids defeated the Umayyads at the Battle of the Zab river in *132*/750, the capital of the Empire shifted from Damascus to the newly founded city of Baghdad. From *369*/979 to *567*/1171 Damascus was ruled from Cairo by the Fāṭimids. Under later 'Abbāsid suzerainty, local dynasties ruled it. The Zengīd Atabeg Nūr ad-Dīn (d. *560*/1173) founded the Dar al-Ḥadīth in Damascus as a school for the study of Islamic sciences. Later and larger schools, which afforded a broader approach to the study of the liberal arts, are the *madrasahs* (colleges), called the Jaqmaqiyyah, 'Azīziyyah. 'Ādiliyyah and Ẓāhiriyyah. Under the Ayyūbids (*564-658*/1169-1260), Damascus again became the capital of an Empire which now included Egypt, parts of Arabia, Palestine and northern 'Irāq. The tomb of the Kurdish founder of the Ayyūbids, the great Salāḥ ad-Dīn (*532-589*/1138-1193), better known in the West as Saladin, who successfully opposed the Christian Crusades, is situated by the wall of the Great Umayyad Mosque. When the Mamlūks succeeded the Ayyūbids, Syria was again ruled from Egypt.

In *658*/1260 and *700*/1300 Mongol invasions were repelled, but in *804*/1401 Damascus (and Aleppo) were plundered by Tamerlane. From *923*/1517 to the end of World War I, Syria was under Ottoman rule from Istanbul, except for an interval from *1832*-1840 when Ibrāhīm Pasha, in the name of Muḥammad 'Alī of Egypt, had conquered some parts of the country. After World War I, Syria was under French mandate until April 1946.

The chief of the city's monuments is, of course, the great Umayyad Mosque built under the Caliph Walīd, still magnificent although ravaged many times by invaders and by fire in 1893. But Damascus also boasts a mosque, the Sinaniyyah, built by the great Turkish architect Sinān (*895-996*/1488-1587), and other notable mosques; that of Dervish Pasha and the Tekiyye Sulaymāniyyah, a complex for dervishes built under Sulāyman the Magnificent. Damascus has several excellent examples of medieval caravanserais (*khans* or *fanādiq*), notably that of Assad Pasha.

Buried in Damascus are a number of Companions of the Prophet, near one of the gates of the old city. On the outskirts is the tomb of "Sitt" (Seyyidah) Zaynab, the granddaughter of the Prophet and sister of Ḥasan and Ḥusayn, an important place of pilgrimage for Twelve-Imām Shī'ites. The place in the Great Mosque where the head of Ḥusayn was once kept, is also a pilgrimage spot for Shī'ites. In 1154, the head of Ḥusayn, which by that time was in Ascalan, was moved to Cairo, where it remains today, by the Fāṭimid Vizier Ṭalā'i' ibn Ruzzīk, an Armenian, to keep it out of the hands of the advancing Franks. There is also the tomb of the mystic, Muḥyi-d-Dīn ibn 'Arabī (*560-638*/1165-1240), and that of the Mamlūk Sultan Baybars. The tomb of Emir 'Abd al-Qadir, who, in exile, originally was buried next to Ibn 'Arabī, has been moved to Algeria.

The National Syrian Museum houses a splendid collection of antiquities from Mari, Ugarit (Ras Shamra, where mankind's first alphabet was devised for the Canaanite language), Ebla, Doura Europos and other important archeological sites in Syria.

Dan Fodio, Usumanu, *see* SOKOTO CALIPHATE.

Dara Shikoh, *see* after DAR al-.

Dargāh. A funerary complex with a tomb, often the meeting place for Sufis. Sometimes it is used simply as a name for a Sufi meeting place when no tomb is attached.

Dār al-Ḥadīth (lit. "house of Ḥadīth"). From the beginning of Islam until the present, religious teaching has been given in Mosques. Around the *4th*/10th century the tendency appeared for the creation of special institutions devoted to study. One of the most important of these schools, called the Dār al-Ḥadīth (also a generic name for this kind of institution) was founded in Damascus by the Zengid Atabeg Nūr ad-Dīn Maḥmud (d. *569*/1173). Other such schools existed in Jerusalem, Cairo, Mosul, Nayshabur, and elsewhere.

The further development of more amply endowed and broader based schools came with the Fāṭimids and Seljūqids. The Fāṭimids founded important schools for the preparation of religious propagandists. The Seljūqs countered by creating Sunnī *madrasahs*. *See* al-AZHAR; HOUSE of WISDOM; DĀR al-ḤIKMAH; MADRASAH.

Dār al-Ḥarb (lit. "the abode of war"). Territories where Islam does not prevail. During colonial rule in India, the *'ulamā'* decided that as long as the laws of Islam were not prohibited, or as long as the peculiar institutions of Islam existed, the country could be considered to lie within *dār al-islām* ("abode of Islam"). Symbolically, the *dār al-ḥarb* is the domain, even in an individual's life, where there is struggle against or opposition to, the Will of God.

Dār al-Hijrah (Ar. "house of emigration and refuge"). A place for sometimes clandestine Ismā'īlī propaganda set up at the end of the *3rd century*/9th century. Although the term meant Medinah as Islam's refuge from the pagans before the conquest of Mecca, here it meant the exact opposite: refuge from Islam during the struggle to overthrow it with the "Religion of Truth". The Dār al-Hijrah at Waṣit in 'Irāq (*277*/890) is well known and associated with the Qarmaṭīs, but there were others: in the Maghrib Ikjan (*280*/893) played an important role in the transfer of the Fāṭimid leader 'Ubayd Allāh to North Africa, al-Ḥasa (*282-286*/895-899) in Arabia, Ṭāliqān in Khorāsān and 'Adan Lā'a and al-Janad in the Yemen in *270*/883.

Dār al-Ḥikmah (lit. "the abode of wisdom"). An academy founded at Cairo by the Fāṭimid Caliph al-Ḥakim (d. *411*/1021) in an extension of his palace. The *Dār al-Ḥikmah* was both a seat of learning and a centre for the preparation of *dā'is* (propagandists) to spread the Ismā'īlī sect. An earlier academy called the *Bayt al-Ḥikmah* ("House of Wisdom") was founded near Baghdad by the 'Abbāsid Caliph al-Ma'mūn (d. *218*/833) for the translation of Greek books on sciences and philosophy and for research. Both academies included astronomical observatories. *See* HOUSE of WISDOM.

Dār al-Islām (lit. "the abode of peace"). Territories in which Islam and the Islamic religious Law (the *sharī'ah*) prevail.

Dār Nidwah. The assembly of chiefs of the various branches of the Quraysh Tribe of Mecca founded by their common ancestor Qusayy. Until the Muslim conquest, it was the ruling body of Mecca and had exercised a great influence over the Arabs of the surrounding desert. The site of the original *Dār an-Nidwah*, which was the house of Qusayy, was near the Ka'bah, within the present-day precincts of the Grand Mosque of Mecca, near the King 'Abd al-'Azīz gate. Mu'āwiyah bought the Dār an-Nidwah from the 'Abd ad-Da'r for a million dirhams.

Dār as-Sulḥ (lit. "the abode of treaty"). Also called *Dār al-'Ahd*, a territory not subject to Islamic rule but having treaty relations with an Islamic state. This category is not admitted by all schools of law; the original precedent is the treaty of mutual recognition and protection entered into by the Prophet with the Christian city state of Najrān. *See* NAJRĀN.

Dara Shikoh (d.*1069*/1658). Eldest son of Shāh Jahān, the Moghul Emperor who built the Tāj Mahal. Dara Shikoh became involved in a dynastic struggle with his brothers. His brother Shujā' was a Shī'ite who seized Bengal; Mūrād, also a Shī'ite, took Gujarat.

Himself a Sufi adept, Dara Shikoh was familiar with Vedantic doctrine and Hindu paths of spiritual realisation, but he aroused controversy over his universalist interpretation of the essential agreement between the various revealed religions, and by such statements as: "The science of Vedanta is the science of Sufism." He wrote a book called *Majma' al-Baḥrayn* ("The Meeting of the Two Seas" a term taken from the Koranic Surah of the Cave, 18:60, referring to the *barzakh* [the barrier] which the spritual aspirant must pass beyond to reach the end of the Path) in which he sought to reconcile two spiritual metaphysics.

Both Dara Shikoh and Mūrād were defeated and put to death by their brother Awrangzeb, a Sunnī who applied *sharī'ah* law strictly throughout his empire, and whose devotion was such that he himself sometimes taught the *shahādah* to converts from Hinduism. He took the imperial name of 'Alamgīr ("Seizer of the World"). The brother Shujā' disappeared.

Darar In law, harm, prejudice, constraint, or cruelty. It may be cause for divorce, for example, or it may be a cause for a minor exemption for a legal requirement, such as fasting if it causes harm to health.

Darqāwī, Mulay-l-'Arabī (*1150-1239*/1737-1823). A Ḥadīth states that "Every hundred years God will send a restorer to the community." Mulay-l-'Arabī was considered the nineteenth century *mujaddid* ("renewer", or "restorer" of Islam) in the Maghreb, or Arab West. He brought about a renewal of fervor and a deepening of spiritual penetration whose effects lasted well into this century. He was considered to be the *quṭb*, the "spiritual axis", or "pole", of his age; his personal sanctity and the force of his teaching, stimulated a great outburst of vitality among the Sufi orders in Morocco.

Mulay-l-'Arabī was a Shaykh in a *ṭarīqah* (Sufi order) of the line of the Imām Shādhilī, and it is upon these orders that his influence was strongest. The *ṭuruq* which descend from him are called Darqāwī or Darqāwā after him.

He left only a few writings in the form of letters (*rasā'il*). In one of them he says:

> The soul is an immense thing; it is the whole cosmos, since it is the copy of it. Everything which is in the cosmos is to be found in the soul; equally everything in the soul is in the cosmos. Because of this fact, he who masters his soul most certainly masters the cosmos, just as he who is dominated by his soul is certainly dominated by the whole cosmos...The sickness afflicting your heart, faqīr [Sufi disciple], comes from the passions which pass through you; if you were to abandon them and concern yourself with what God ordains for you, your heart would not suffer as it suffers now. So listen to what I say to you and may God take you by the hand. Each time your soul attacks you, if you were to be quick to do what God orders and were to abandon your will entirely to Him, you would most certainly be saved from psychic and satanic suggestions and from all trials. But if you begin to reflect in these moments when your soul attacks you, to weigh the factors for and against, and sink into inner chatter, then psychic and satanic suggestions will flow back towards you in waves until you are overwhelmed and drowned... it is your business not to forget Him who "grasps you by the forelock" (Koran 11:56).

His immediate spiritual master was the venerated 'Alī ibn 'Abd ar-Raḥmān called al-Jamal ("the Camel") whose tomb is in Fez. Mulay-l-'Arabī, a *sharīf* (descendent of the Prophet) through the Idrīssī dynasty of Morocco, is buried in Bu Berih near Fez, among a tribe called the Banū Zarwal.

Besides famous disciples such as the Shaykh Mulay Muḥammad al-Buzīdī, Shaykh Muḥammad Ḥasan Zāfir al-Madanī, and Shaykh Muḥammad al-Fāsī, through whom the *barakah* ("grace", or spiritual influence) of Mulay-l-'Arabī was carried to Turkey and as far as Ceylon, several descendants of Mulay-l-'Arabī continued his work beyond his life. His son Mulay aṭ-Ṭayyib became a spiritual master as did his grandson, Mulay 'Alī ibn aṭ-Ṭayyib ad-Darqāwī, who was the Shaykh of the Darqāwī branch of the Moroccan Shādhilīs into the thirties in the last century. Mulay 'Alī ibn aṭ-Ṭayyib taught theology at the Qarawiyyīn university of Fez. All over Morocco, his surviving disciples and novices taught by his *muqaddams* (representatives) celebrate his memory in the month of September. *See* QUṬB; SUFISM.

Dassondh. Among Ismā'īlīs, a special tithe, that is, 10% of income paid to the *Imām*. It is paid with extraordinary enthusiasm. This is the name among Khojas. Others call it *ḥaqq-i Imām*. There are also special categories of those who pay much higher percentages with correspondingly higher spiritual benefits.

In some Ismā'īlī texts it is said that the *zakāt* is the "price for the law", which is "all that it is worth", but that the *dassondh* is the price of the esoteric knowledge of the *Imām* and, by implication, that its payment brings with it a kind of absolution. The Aga Khan III was weighed against gold and diamonds at different anniversaries in his life and presented with the equivalent sums of money.

Ismā'īlī groups without Imāms, such as the Bohoras, do not indulge in such lavish occasions, but they too are punctilious about the many payments made in devotion to their leader, the Mulla-Ji.

Dātā Ganj Baksh, *see* al-ḤUJWĪRI.

David (Ar. *Dā'wūd*). The Biblical King and Prophet who received the Divine revelation of the Psalms, called in Arabic *az-Zabūr*. In the Koran, David exemplifies the victory of God's cause against superior odds:

> .... they said, 'We have no
> power this day against Goliath and his hosts.'
> Said those who reckoned they should meet God
> 'How often a little company has overcome
> a numerous company, by God's leave! And God
> is with the patient.'
> So, when they went forth against Goliath
> and his hosts, they said, 'Our Lord, pour out
> upon us patience, and make firm our feet,
> and give us aid against the people of
> the unbelievers!'
> And they routed them, by the leave of God,
> and David slew Goliath; and God gave him

the kingship, and Wisdom, and He taught him
such as He willed. Had God not driven back
the people, some by the means of others,
the earth had surely corrupted;
but God is bounteous
unto all beings. (Koran 2:251-252)

In 4:163 the Koran refers to "Sabbath breakers", living by the sea. Commentaries explain that these were men who set traps to catch fish on the Sabbath and who, by this ruse, were guilty of breaking the law, albeit indirectly. David turned the Sabbath breakers into monkeys for their crime.

In Koran 38:18 two litigants break into David's palace while he is praying:

Has the tiding of the dispute come to thee?
When they scaled the Sanctuary,
when they entered upon David, and he took
fright at them; and they said, 'Fear not;
two disputants we are — one of us has
injured the other; so judge between us
justly, and transgress not, and guide us
to the right path.'
'Behold, this my brother has ninety-nine
ewes, and I have one ewe. So he said,
"Give her into my charge"; and he overcame
me in the argument.'
Said he, 'assuredly he has wronged thee
in asking for thy ewe in addition to
his sheep; and indeed many intermixers
do injury one against the other,
save those who believe, and do deeds of
righteousness — and how few they are!'
And David thought that We had only
tried him; therefore he sought forgiveness
of his Lord, and he fell down, bowing,
and he repented.
Accordingly We forgave him that,
and he has a near place in our presence
and a fair resort.
David, behold, we have appointed thee
a viceroy in the earth; therefore judge
between men justly, and follow not caprice,
lest it lead thee astray from the way of God.
Surely those who go stray from the way
of God — there awaits them a terrible
chastisement, for that they have forgotten
the Day of Reckoning.' (38:20-27).

Commentaries on this passage say that the litigants were two Angels who had come to reproach David for taking Bathsheba and imply, therefore, that his own conscience thus accused him; the story parallels that of Nathan's reproach to David in the Bible (II Samuel:12).

David is credited with discovering chain mail armor (21:78); the hills sing the praises of God with him:

... remember our servant David,
the man of might; he was a penitent.
With him We subjected the mountains
to give glory
at evening and sunrise,
and the birds, duly mustered, every one
to him reverting;
We strengthened his kingdom,
and gave him wisdom
and speech decisive. (38:15-19)

When the Caliph 'Umar visited Jerusalem, the Patriarch Sophronius accompanied him on the Temple Mount while he searched for the *miḥrāb Dawūd* (David's prayer-niche). Later commentaters identified this site with the "Citadel of David".

Da'wah. (from Ar. *da'ā*, "to call", "invoke", "summon", "to invite".) Koranically, the word most commonly means to invoke the deity, and so to place one's faith in that deity. It also means to call to religion, and in this sense Muḥammad is a *dā'ī* or "caller". (Other words for caller are also used to designate a prophet.) It is also the call to the dead to arise from their graves on the Day of Judgement.

In the Middle Ages the term usually referred to the propaganda of such systems as the 'Abbāsid cause, or the Ismā'īlīs. Today it usually means missionary work to bring new believers to Islam, or to reinforce belief.

Dawsah. An annual ceremony performed in Cairo in which the Shaykh of the Sa'dī *ṭarīqah* rode a horse over his disciples who were stretched out on the ground. The disciples would be left unhurt. The ceremony took place on the *mawlid* (the Prophet's birthday). It was prohibited by the civil authorities as anti-modern in 1881.

Dā'wūd, *see* DAVID.

Day of Judgement, *see* YAWM AD-DĪN.

Death. "Die before ye die", the Prophet said, and: "The grave is the first stage of the journey to eternity." And the Koran states:

> ... Say: 'Even if
> you had been in your houses, those for whom
> slaying was appointed would have sallied forth
> unto their last couches'... (3:148)
>
> It is not given to any soul to die, save by the
> leave of God, at an appointed time.
> Whoso desires the reward of this world,
> We will give him of this;
> and whoso desires the reward of the other world,
> we will give him of that;
> and we will recompense
> the thankful. (3:139)
>
> Every soul shall taste of death; you shall surely
> be paid in full your wages on the Day
> of Resurrection. Whosoever is removed
> from the Fire and admitted to Paradise, shall
> win the triumph. The present life is but the
> joy of delusion. (3:182).

"There are those," Ibn al-'Ārif said, "to whom death is as a draught of pure water to the thirsty." As a "last rite", the dying person recites the *shahādah*, just as, at birth, the *shahādah* is recited into the ear of the newborn. In the early days of Islam, when the opponents of the new faith were about to put a Muslim prisoner to death, the condemned man asked to be allowed to make a prayer; this was permitted him, and he prayed two *raka'at* (two bows), rather than the customary four, so it would not appear that he was trying to gain time. Thus, if one is about to be put to death, the tradition is to make a prayer of two prostrations.

Al-Ghazālī wrote:

> When a man becomes familiar with *dhikr* [invocation of the Divine Name], he separates himself (inwardly) from all other things. Now, at death he is separated from all that is not God... What remains is the invocation alone. If this invocation is familiar to him, he finds his pleasure in it and rejoices that the obstacles which kept him from it have been removed, so that he finds himself alone with his Beloved.

'Alī said:

> It is astonishing that anyone, seeing his familiar die, should forget death.

For the prayer for the dead, see FUNERALS.

Defterdar. (from the Greek *dephtar*, "notebook" and ultimately probably from Sumerian *dip-/dup-* "to write", which gave the Sāssānid title of scribe, *dipīr*). Under the Ottomans, an imperial official, a treasurer in charge of accounts and disbursements. Defterdars accompanied the armies on campaigns as well as carrying on civil functions. *See* BEYLERBEY.

Delhi Sultanate (*602-962*/1206-1555). The principal Muslim kingdom in India before the Moghul conquest. Islam was first brought to India by conquering Arab armies during the early years of the Umayyad dynasty. These invaders eventually established the Multān and Manṣūra kingdoms along the Indus, but the major Muslim incursions into India came later under Maḥmūd of Ghaznah (d. *422*/1030). A Turko-Afghan dynasty was established in Delhi by Quṭb ad-Dīn Aybak in *602*/1206, a slave and general of Mu'izz ad-Dīn of the Ghurids, successors to the Ghaznavids. This displaced the previous rulers, the Hindu Rajputs.

Quṭb ad-Dīn's son Iltutmish extended the empire from Sindh to Bengal. In *689*/1290 power passed into the hands of the Khaljis, and in *720*/1320 to the Tughluqids and thereafter to other short-lived dynasties until the Moghul victory by Bābur and the definitive Muslim conquest by Humāyūn. *See* MOGHULS.

Deoband. Islamic university located some 150 kilometers north of Delhi in Uttar Pradesh, India. Popularly called the "Azhar of India", the school, *Dar al-'Ulūm Deoband*, was founded by Qāsim Nanavtavi in *1283*/1866. Its teachers and students were prominent in the movements against British rule. The curriculum is built around traditional religious subjects. At present there are more than three thousand students, and as many as six thousand come to take entrance examinations, including a number of foreigners. The school recently added computers to its curriculum.

The faculty at Deoband takes an ambiguous stand towards mysticism; it accepts mysticism while rejecting some of the more questionable statements of the famous mystics. Thus Ibn 'Arabi is highly esteemed, while many of the things which he said are rejected as not being expressions of ideas which he professed. Indeed the school has created its own mysticism by maintaining that the exoteric teachings of Ḥadīth and law which they pass on are animated by a chain of transmission from teacher to teacher not unlike that of the chain of initiation found in Sufi orders.

The *Dar al-'Ulum Deoband*, by producing religious school teachers throughout the subcontinent, has had an increasingly strong effect on politics and some of the political parties are made up of its graduates, notably the *Jamā'at-i 'Ulamā'i Islam-i* in Pakistan and the *Jamā'at-i 'Ulamā'i* Hind in India.

Determinism, *see* KALĀM; MAKTŪB; QADARIYYAH.

Devil, *see* IBLĪS.

Devshirme. The conscription system used by the Ottomans. It consisted of taking male children from subject Christian populations, chiefly in the Balkans, forcibly converting them to Islam, and raising them to join the ranks of an elite military corps, the Janissaries, or to enter other branches of government service.

The boy-levy (*devshirme*) was carried out largely by force, but to be taken by it held out such promise for a brilliant future, that Ottomans sometimes tried to slip their own children into it. Many of the Viziers came from the higher levels of the pageboy training. At first every fifth boy was drafted in a levy carried out every four or five years, but later every able-bodied boy between the ages of ten and fifteen was liable to be taken in a draft carried out annually. The *devshirme* became obsolete in the seventeenth century. *See* JANISSARIES.

Dhanb, *see* SIN.

Dhāt ("Essence", "quiddity", "ipseity"). This technical term used in Taṣawwuf (Sufism) was devised from the Arabic particle *dhū*, of which it is the feminine form, to correspond to the Greek *ousia* much as the Latin *essentia* was devised for the same purpose. The particle *dhū*, meaning something like "possession of", is used to affix an attribute to a noun. The specialized use of the feminine form *dhāt* in the technical sense of "essence", does not, of course, occur in the Koran. In Islamic philosophy *adh-Dhāt* refers to the nature of something in itself, as opposed to a quality *(ṣifah)* it possesses. The Divine Names are divided by the Sufis into those of the "Essence" and those of the "Qualities" (*ṣifāt*). The Sufic "Paradise of the Essence" *(jannat adh-dhāt)* refers to the Divine Reality itself.

Al-Jīlī wrote:

> The Essence (*adh-dhāt*) denotes Absolute Being stripped of all modes, relations, and aspects. Not that they are outside of Absolute Being; on the contrary, they belong to it, but they are neither as themselves nor as aspects of it; no, they are identical with the being of the Absolute. The Absolute is the simple Essence in which no name or quality or relation is manifested... the Essence, by the law of its nature, comprehends universals, particulars, and relations, not as they are judged to exist, but as they are judged to be naughted under the might of the transcendental oneness of the Essence.

Adh-Dhāt is also called *al-māhiyyah*. *See* FIVE DIVINE PRESENCES.

Dhawq (lit. "taste"). Physical taste; but in mysticism the term means direct experience of truth. In this context, *dhawq* is similar to the word "*sapience*", or wisdom, derived from the Latin sapere, which means primarily to taste and by extension, "to discriminate", "to know". There is a famous Sufi saying: "From the first taste one knows them" [their spiritual nature]. *See* SUFISM.

Dhikr (Ar. "remembrance" either silently or aloud, in which latter case "mention".) *Dhikr Allāh*, or "remembrance of God", "making mention of God" refers to invocation of the Divine Name, or to litanies; metaphysical "anamnesis". The Koran often speaks of *dhikr* as an act of worship: "Remember Me; I [God] will remember you" (*fa'dhkurūnī adhkurkum*) (2:152); "Invoke the Name of your Lord and devote yourself to Him with an utter devotion" (73:8); and: "Remembrance of God is greatest" (*wa-l-dhikru-Llāhi akbar*) (29:45).

For the Sufis, *dhikr* is a spiritual method of concentration, the invocation of a Divine Name or a sacred formula, under the direction of a spiritual master belonging to an authentic chain of transmission (*silsilah*). The spiritual master, or Shaykh, gives the practitioner the necessary "permission" (*idhn*), or mediates the pledge to God (*bay'ah*) that makes the method operative. It is not effectively possible, and can indeed be dangerous, to practice the *dhikr* without an assimilation of the doctrines surrounding the method and above all the revealed doctrine of discrimination between Reality and unreality, the doctrine of the nature of God Himself.

The *idhn* (or *bay'ah*, "pact") is an initiation in which there is a transmission of a blessing (*barakah*) whose origin goes back to the Prophet, and from him to the Angel Gabriel. The *dhikr*, or invocation, should, of course, be accompanied by the observance of all other fitting religious rituals and virtues. It cannot be practiced without adhering to the religion that vehicles and surrounds the method and the doctrine, failing which the method is as dangerous as it is ineffective.

Special forms of *dhikr* exist which include a form of dancing on a fixed spot, introduced by the chanting of religious poetry accompanied by drums, and sometimes by flutes, to create a state of devotional tension. In this dance known as the *dhikr aṣ-ṣadr*, the Divine Name Allāh is chanted; then the Name is reduced to its last syllable *Hu* (of the nominative form *Allāhu*) which corresponds to the shortened form of *Huwa*, "He", a Divine Name of the Essence. Finally, this Name and the act of invocation are reduced simply to breathing, which is, as actualized by the sacred context of the dance, both the Divine Name in its purest form, which is that of breath or of life itself, and, because of the nature of breath, also the cosmological process of creation and its opposite, the re-absorption of creation into God. (*see* ALLĀH) (It should be mentioned that from a medical point of view the rapid breathing of the dance induces hyperventilation.)

This *dhikr aṣ-ṣadr*, or "invocation through the breast", symbolizes a return of essences escaping from the existential illusion of manifestation back to the Creator, a return of creatures out of of the cosmos, even as the Divine Name loses its form and becomes pure breath. The *dhikr aṣ-ṣadr* is also called *'imārah*, and in the Maghreb, or Arab West, haḍrah ("presence").

The word *dhikr* is sometimes used loosely for all the ceremony which may surround a Sufi meeting (*majlis*) in which the *dhikr* proper is only one element, albeit the central one. Such ceremonies may include aspects which are extraneous, that is, outward elements and historical accretions peculiar to a particular tradition. Sometimes these ceremonies have been performed in public, particularly in Egypt in the last century, but their real nature is usually overlooked, obscured, and misunderstood, even in the Islamic world itself. This is all the more true in modern times, in accordance with the Ḥadīth: "Islam was born in exile, and will return to exile."

The power of *dhikr* arises from the identity of the Divine Name with Him who is invoked, the *madhkūr*, God Himself. The act of invocation, *dhikr*, is God's own Act; it is His own Self-knowledge and Self-consciousness. It is God Who invokes Himself through the invoker, the *dhākir*, as He also does through creation. If a man, while asleep and dreaming, calls out the Divine Name or the *shahādah*, he will wake without fail; the *dhikr*, by analogy, does the same for a man caught in the dream called life, for the Prophet said: "When we live, we sleep, and when we die, we wake."

"For everything", the Prophet also said, "there is a polish that takes away rust, and the polish of the heart is remembrance of God." When asked who would be highest in God's esteem on the Day of Resurrection he answered: "The men and women who invoke God much." When asked if they would rank even as those who fought in the way of God, the Prophet said: "Even though a man wielded his sword against unbelievers and idolaters until it was broken... yet would the rememberer of God have a more excellent degree..." *See* ALLĀH; FIVE DIVINE PRESENCES; SUFISM.

Dhimmī. A person belonging to the category of "protected people" (*ahl ad-dhimmah*) in the Islamic state. In classical times, these were the recognized monotheists: Jews, Christians, and "Ṣābians", who were granted autonomy of institutions and protection under Islam. In return they were required to pay a head tax (*jizyah*), and an exemption tax (*kharāj*).

This was usually accompanied by a number of social restrictions which could range from the remarkably oppressive to the remarkably liberal depending upon the place and the epoch. The practice no longer exists as traditional forms of government have been replaced by the modern forms of multi-confessional societies and new forms of taxation. A similar concept exists theoretically among Jews where the non-Jew is called the *Ger Toshaf* ("resident alien") who is considered to be universally subject to the "Noahide Laws"; while receiving some protection in the ideal Jewish state he would also be prohibited (even put to death) from practices which are considered idolatrous. Under these laws Muslims would be considered more in conformity than Christians. *See* AHL al-KITĀB.

Dhirāʻ. A unit of linear measure, the "ell" which is about one foot and a half.

Dhu-l-Fiqār. A famous sword which the Prophet received as booty at the Battle of Badr. It is pictured as having two points and became an attribute of ʼAlī, who used it, although ultimately it was, like the Mantle of the Prophet, the property and emblem of the Caliphs, and as such a copy or simulacrum exists in the Topkapi museum.

Dhu-l-Ḥimār (lit. "the man on the donkey"). In the Near East, the image of the "man on a donkey", that is, someone coming from a far land and arriving in humble circumstances whose real nature is not evident from his appearance, is associated with the advent of an inspired leader. The image is mentioned in Zechariah 9:9:

> Rejoice greatly, O daughter of Zion; shout, O daughter of Jerusalem: behold, thy King cometh unto thee: he is just, and having salvation: lowly, and riding upon an ass, and upon a colt, the foal of an ass.

During the Riddah (the wars of apostasy following the death of the Prophet in 632), a short-lived messianic leader arose in the Yemen called Dhu-l-Ḥimār, who revolted against Islam and claimed revelations for himself. He was also known as al-Aswad ("the Black One") and Dhu-l-Khimār ("the man of the veil").

The "man on the donkey" attribute is also associated with the appearance of Qarmaṭī missionaries at the end of the *3rd*/9th century, also a rebellion in Morocco which ended in 1909, and with other movements.

If it were not already a common emblem, similar to that of "the rider upon a white horse", that is, Mithra, ultimately associated with the apocalyptic appearance of the Angel Michael, the image of "the man on a donkey" became well known through the description of Jesus' entry into Jerusalem in the Gospels. Also, numerous Old Testament images, stories, and interpretations became established as a part of Islamic lore through learned Jews who were converted to Islam. Tales and parables which entered into the corpus of Koranic commentary from the Talmudic haggadah and Jewish legends are called *isrāʼīliyyāt.*

It may well be the Old Testament idea of a future ruler who restores lost righteousness and glory, carried over by converted Jews, which provided the antecedents that led to the acceptance among Sunnis of the concept of the Mahdī. The Sunni idea of the Mahdī is radically different from that of the Shīʻites among whom it originated, beginning with the Kaysāniyyah movement. For the Shīʻites, the figure of the Mahdī has an apocalyptic and Messianic significance; he is endowed with a demiurgic nature and with supernatural powers. The Sunnis later also accepted a certain notion of a kind of Mahdī, at least on a popular level, but in a more earthly sense, that of a "just king". *See* al-ASWAD; BŪ ḤAMARAH; KAYSĀNIYYAH; MAHDĪ; MUSAYLAMAH; RIDDAH.

Dhu-l-Kifl. A Prophet mentioned in Koran 21:85 and 38:49. He is usually identified with Ezekiel. *See* PROPHETS.

Dhu-n-Nūn Miṣrī (*180-245*/796-859). A rather apocryphal Egyptian Sufi, Abu-l-Fayḍ Thawban ibn Ibrāhīm, whose father, a native of Nubia or of Ikhmīm in Upper Egypt, was a slave enfranchised and adopted by the tribe of Quraysh. Dhu-n-Nun had a great knowledge of alchemy and arcane sciences (*ʼilmu-l-bāṭin*), such as magic. He is reputed to have been a link in the transmission of the spiritual sciences of ancient Egypt. He was familiar with Egyptian temples (*barābi*) and it was said that he could read hieroglyphics. He may also have lived in the Hejaz and may have been a student of the Imām Malik ibn Anas, but his master in Sufism was Shuqrān al-ʼAbīd or a Maghribi named Isrāfil. Hehaped the development of Sufism but many in Egypt considered him a *zindiq.*

Among the stories the hagiographer ʼAṭṭār records of him there is the following:

> At nightfall he [Dhu-n-Nūn] entered a ruined building where he found a jar of gold and jewels covered by a board on which was inscribed the Name of God. His friends divided the gold and jewels, but Dhu-n-Nūn said, "Give me this board, my Beloved's Name is upon it": and he did not cease kissing it all day. Through the blessing thereof he attained to such a degree that one night

> he dreamed and heard a voice saying to him, "O Dhu-n-Nūn! the others were pleased with the gold and jewels, but thou wert pleased only with My Name: therefore have I opened unto thee the gate of knowledge and wisdom."

Al-Kalabādhī reported that Dhu-n-Nūn was asked: "'What is the end of the knowers?' He answered: 'When he is as he was where he was before he was.'" He also said, in keeping with the Sufi and Shī'ite tendency to fix honour of God unto men, that a true disciple should be more obedient to his master than to God Himself. *See* DRUNKEN SUFIS.

Dhuwu-l-arḥam (lit. "those of the wombs"; an expression in the Koran). In Islamic law, blood relations through the mother. This relationship establishes claims of rights upon a person and, through inheritance, upon his or her estate.

Dihqān. A member of the rural, land owning gentry in Sāssānid Persia, so called in Arabic, after the Muslim conquest, from the Persian for "head of the village". The *Dihqāns* are credited with preserving orally the stories of ancient Persia which were collected by Firdawsi in the Shah-Nameh ("The Book of Kings").

Dikkah. A raised platform, found mainly in mosques of Turkish influence, from which the Imām can be seen by the congregation during prayers. It is also reserved for the use of the Sultan or dignitaries.

Dīn (possibly related to Ar. *dain*, lit. "debt" but more likely from Avestan *daena* [Pahl. *din*] meaning "vision", "inner consciousness", and especially "religion".). The word employed to mean a religion together with its practices in general. Religion in the abstract is *diyānah* and a specific religion is more often called *millah* ("a way"). *Yawm ad-Dīn*, the "day of the *Dīn*" is universally taken to mean the Day of Judgement.

Divine Names. The Names by which God is known in Islam are divided first into two categories: the Names of the Essence (*adh-dhāt*), such as Allāh and *ar-Raḥmān*, and the Names of the Qualities (*aṣ-ṣifāt*), such as *ar-Raḥīm* and *al-Bāri' ('azza wa jall)*. They can also be divided into the Names of mercy, or beauty (*jamāl*), and the Names of rigor, or majesty (*jalāl*). The Names altogether are called the Most Beautiful Names (*al-asmā'u al-ḥusnā*): "To Him belong the most beautiful Names" (7:179).

The Names consist of those directly revealed in the Koran; others are derived indirectly from certain passages in the Koran, and others are traditional but not derived from the Koran. Not widely accepted are certain Names which are distant grammatical derivations from revealed Names.

The Name Allāh, called the Supreme Name (*al-ism al-a'zam*), stands alone. There is a Ḥadīth which says "To God belong ninety-nine Names..." Therefore, although because of variants the total of any two lists may add up to more than ninety-nine, any one list is limited to this number. The following Names are representative.

1. *al-Awwal*	The First (57:3)
2. *al-Ākhir*	The Last (57:3)
3. *al-Aḥad*	The One (112:1)
4. *al-Badī'*	The Originator (2:117)
5. *al-Bārī*	The Producer (59:24)
6. *al-Barr*	The Beneficent (52:28)
7. *al-Baṣīr*	The Seeing (57:3)
8. *al-Bāsiṭ*	The Expander (13:26) (a derived Name)
9. *al-Bāṭin*	The Inner (57:3)
10. *al-Ba'ith*	The Raiser (16:89)
11. *al-Bāqī*	The Enduring (20:73)
12. *at-Tawwāb*	The Relenting (2:37)
13. *al-Jabbār*	The Irresistible (59:23)
14. *al-Jalīl*	The Majestic (a derived Name)
15. *al-Jāmi'*	The Gatherer (3:9)
16. *al-Ḥasīb*	The Accounter (4:6)
17. *al-Ḥafīẓ*	The Guardian (11:57)
18. *al-Ḥaqq*	The Truth (20:114)
19. *al-Ḥakīm*	The Wise (6:18)
20. *al-Ḥakam*	The Judge (40:48)
21. *al-Ḥalīm*	The Kindly (2:235)
22. *al-Ḥamīd*	The Praiseworthy (2:269)
23. *al-Ḥayy*	The Living (20:111)
24. *al-Khabīr*	The Well-Informed (6:18)
25. *al-Khāfiḍ*	The Abaser (a derived Name)
26. *al-Khāliq*	The Creator (13:16)
27. *Dhu-l-Jalāl wa-l-Ikrām*	Full of Majesty and Generosity (55:27)
28. *ar-Ra'ūf*	The Gentle (2:143)
29. *ar-Raḥmān*	The Merciful (55:1)
30. *ar-Raḥīm*	The Compassionate (2:143)

31. *ar-Razzāq*	The Provider (51:57)
32. *ar-Rashīd*	The Guide (a traditional Name)
33. *ar-Rāfi'*	The Exalter (6:83) (a derived Name)
34. *ar-Raqīb*	The Vigilant (5:117)
35. *as-Salām*	The Peace (59:23)
36. *as-Samī'*	The Hearer (17:1)
37. *ash-Shakūr*	The Grateful (64:17)
38. *ash-Shahīd*	The Witness (5:117)
39. *as-Ṣabūr*	The Forbearing (a traditional Name)
40. *as-Ṣamad*	The Eternal (112:2)
41. *aḍ-Ḍarr*	The Afflicter (48:11) (a derived Name)
42. *aẓ-Ẓāhir*	The Outer (57:3)
43. *al-'Adl*	The Just (6:115)
44. *al-'Azīz*	The Powerful, and also the Precious (59:23)
45. *al-'Aẓīm*	The Great (2:255)
46. *al-'Afuw*	The Pardoner (4:99)
47. *al-'Alīm*	The Knowing (2:29)
48. *al-'Alī*	The High One (2:255)
49. *al-Ghafūr*	The Forgiver (2:235)
50. *al-Ghaffār*	The Forgiving (2:235)
51. *al-Ghānī*	The Rich (2:267)
52. *al-Fattāḥ*	The Opener (34:26)
53. *al-Qabiḍ*	The Seizer (2:245) (a derived Name)
54. *al-Qadīr*	The Capable (17:99)
55. *al-Quddūs*	The Holy (62:1)
56. *al-Qahhār*	The Victorious (13:16)
57. *al-Qawī*	The Strong (22:40)
58. *al-Qayyūm*	The Self-Subsistant (3:2)
59. *al-Kabīr*	The Great (22:62)
60. *al-Karīm*	The Magnanimous, the Generous, the Noble (27:40)
61. *al-Laṭīf*	The Gracious (42:19)
62. *al-Muta'akhkhir*	The Deferrer (14:42)
63. *al-Mu'min*	The Believer (59:23)
64. *al-Muta'alī*	The Self Exalted (13:9)
65. *al-Mutakkabir*	The Superb (59:23)
66. *al-Matīn*	The Firm (51:58)
67. *al-Mubdi'*	The Founder (85:13)
68. *al-Mujīb*	The Responsive (11:61)
69. *al-Majīd*	The Glorious (11:73)
70. *al-Muhṣi*	The Counter (19:94)
71. *al-Muḥyī*	The Giver of Life (30:50)
72. *al-Mudhill*	The Abaser (3:26) (a derived Name)
73. *al-Muzīl*	The Separator (10:28)
74 *al-Musawwir*	The Fashioner (59:24)
75. *al-Mu'īd*	The Restorer (85:13)
76. *al-Mu'izz*	The Honourer (3:26) (a derived Name)
77. *al-Mu'tī*	The Giver (20:50)
78. *al-Mughnī*	The Enricher (9:74)
79. *al-Muqīṭ*	The Maintainer, the Determiner, He Who brings to pass (4:85)
80. *al-Muqtadir*	The Prevailer (54:42)
81. *al-Muqaddim*	The Bringer Forward (50:28)
82. *al-Muqsiṭ*	The Equitable (21:47)
83. *al-Malik*	The King (59:23)
84. *Malik al-Mulk*	Possessor of the Kingdom (3:26)
85. *al-Mumīt*	The Slayer (15:23)
86. *al-Muntaqim*	The Avenger (30:47)
87. *al-Muhaimin*	The Vigilant, the Guardian (59:23)
88. *an-Nāfi'*	The Propitious (48:11) (a derived Name)
89. *an-Nāṣir*	The Helper (4:45)
90. *an-Nūr*	The Light (24:35)
91. *al-Hādi*	The Guide (22:54)
92. *al-Wāḥid*	The Unique (74:11))
93. *al-Wadūd*	The Loving (11:90)
94. *al-Wārith*	The Inheritor (19:40)
95. *al-Wāsi'*	The Vast (2:268)
96. *al-Wakīl*	The Steward (6:102)
97. *al-Walīy*	The Patron (4:45)
98. *al-Wāli*	The Protector (13:11)
99. *al-Wahhāb*	The Bestower (3:8).

See ALLĀH; AMIN.

Divorce (Ar. *ṭalāq*). The Prophet said: "Of all things licit, the most hateful to God is divorce." Marriage in Islam is terminated a) by repudiation by the husband; b) by mutual consent; c) by judicial dissolution by a court upon the request of the wife.

In repudiation, a single statement to this effect, delivered to the wife is sufficient. It must be delivered while the wife is in a state of purity, (*ṭuhr*), that is, not menstruating, and the husband must not have had sexual relations with her during this period of purity; furthermore, the wife must not be pregnant. The repudiation must be followed by a period of waiting for the duration of three menstrual periods, (*'iddah*), to determine if there is a pregnancy (and implicitly to facilitate reconciliation). If the wife is pregnant, the divorce cannot take place until an allotted time after the birth of the child. During the *'iddah*, the husband must supply upkeep, lodging and food. An allowance, *muṭ'āh*, beyond these necessities is morally enjoined, but is not a legal requirement.

The divorce is immediately revocable by the husband at any time during the *'iddah*. Afterwards, remarriage is necessary to restore the marital state. If repudiation, or a statement of divorce, is repeated in each ensuing month or period of purity *ṭuhr*, for a total of three repudiations (*aṭ-ṭalāq bi-th-thalāthah*), reconciliation is not possible until, and unless, the wife is married with another person and subsequently divorced. It is legally possible to pronounce three repudiations at one time but it is morally reprehensible to do so. *'Iddah* must still be observed and if pregnancy is determined, the force of the triple divorce is reduced to the conditions of a single divorce. Such triple divorce at one time is called *ṭalāq badī'*, "innovative" divorce. As such, it is a discouraged form of divorce, reconciliation being the desirable and sought after solution in the view of the law. In Shī'ite law, divorce is seen from a more judicial point of view, and the repudiation must be witnessed.

Divorce by mutual consent has only to be agreed upon by both parties to become effective. Divorce by judicial proceeding upon the request of the wife is obtained on varying grounds in the different schools, but these include the husband's impotence, apostasy, madness, dangerous illness, or some other defect in the marriage.

National laws in recent times have sought, within the framework of *sharī'ah* law, to give more protection to the woman against the husband's easy access to divorce. The *mahr*, or husband's wedding gift to the wife, is normally, and depending upon social status, an endowment of considerable expense; it remains with the wife after any divorce, both as a measure of compensation and also to discourage divorce in the first place. The Syrian Law of Personal Status (1953) makes the payment of maintenance to the wife obligatory for one year, which is thus a legal recourse of the wife against the husband.

The Tunisian Law of Personal Status (1957) makes repudiation by the husband invalid until it has been ratified by a court and provides for further compensation to the wife. Similar laws have been enacted elsewhere, both within an interpretive framework of traditional *sharī'ah* law, and through the operation of civil codes not based upon the *sharī'ah*. Such laws have in some cases made polygamy virtually impossible, or extremely difficult, by reason of a strict interpretation of the *sharī'ah* law which states that all wives must receive equal treatment. *See* also KHUL'; LI'ĀN.

Dīwān. Originally a Persian word meaning a "many leaved book", and hence an account-book, record, collection of poems and, by extension, a government department containing such records. The Italian *dogana* and French *douane* are distant derivations of it. The term was taken into Arabic when Persia first became Muslim, and has since been used to describe a register of financial statistics, a cabinet or almost any kind of government office; it also means, in Arabic as well as Persian, a collection of poetry.

The first Arab *diwān* was copied from the institutions of the Persians, when the Caliph 'Umar established a registry of all members of the Islamic state in order to allot the stipends to which they were entitled from the booty of the conquests. Men, women and children were all graded according to their seniority as converts, and depending upon their being *muhājirūn* (emigrants from Mecca) or *anṣār* (native Medinan converts), their participation in the battles according to merit (Badr was in the first rank), and their family relatedness to those with such merit. According to their standing they received a share in the booty of the conquering Muslim armies.

From this booty and revenue the Caliph 'Umar also set aside a reserve for emergencies. ('Alī disagreed with the principle of such a reserve contending that it should all be distributed, doubtless upon the grounds that reliance should be placed not upon the human resource — such as of a reserve of food — but on God alone.) This actual *diwān* and with it, the original institution, was destroyed in civil unrest during the first century of Islam.

Diyah. The payment of compensation for inflicted injury or death; blood money. This had been part of the customary lex *talionis* of the Arabs before Islam, and came to be covered by the principle in Islamic law of *qisas*, or retaliation. The basis of this law is Koran 5:49. The *diyah* which is best known is the compensation for the taking of a life: one hundred female camels.

This was the ransom for the life of 'Abd Allāh, the father of the Prophet. 'Abd al-Muṭṭalib, who had no sons, had prayed for children. When his prayers were answered, he promised God that in return for sons, he would sacrifice the tenth. However, when the time came for the sacrifice of 'Abd

Allāh, the tenth and youngest son, 'Abd al-Muṭṭalib was grief-stricken, and consulted with a soothsayer whose oracle, after a series of unaccepted offers, confirmed that heaven would accept one hundred camels in expiation of the promise.

In countries where this provision of Islamic law is applied, the traditionally defined *diyah* is today replaced by a sum of money determined by a court of law. In recent years in Saudi Arabia the sums paid in settlement for accidental killings have been as much as sixty thousand dollars. There is a scale of damages for the various grades of bodily injury.

Dogs. These animals are considered to be ritually "unclean", and touching a dog entails a *ḥadath*, or impurity which, in the Mālikī school of law (*madhhab*), is removed by the lesser ablution (*wuḍū'*).

Hunting dogs, however, are not looked upon as unclean, and the Saluki, a kind of Arabian greyhound, is prized by the desert Arabs. It is lawful to eat game caught by a trained hunting dog if the dog is released with the pronunciation of the *basmalah*. For hunting, as for ritual slaughter, the Names of mercy are omitted from the *basmalah*, which becomes *Bismi-Llāh; Allāhu akbar*, "In the name of God; God is greater."

Most schools of law look upon the ordinary dog as unclean in itself; the Mālikī school, in a interesting example of legal reasoning, looks upon all living things as clean in themselves; it reconciles this with the tradition of dogs as unclean by declaring the saliva of dogs to be the polluting agent. The Islamic outlook on dogs clashed harshly with the Iranian: in ancient Iran dogs were highly esteemed and blessed animals. The Zoroastrians had a class of creatures which were considered *khafstra*, or corrupt creatures, but these were snakes, frogs, scorpions and the like.

Dome of the Rock (Ar. *Qubbat aṣ-Ṣakhrah*). A shrine in Jerusalem often (incorrectly) called the "Mosque of 'Umar". It is more a sanctuary than a mosque and it was not built by the Caliph 'Umar but in a much later period, around *72*/691. The Dome stands over the rock on the Temple Mount from which the Prophet ascended to heaven in the Night Journey (*mi'rāj*). The place is revered by the three Semitic religions and may have been the site of the Holy of Holies in the temple of Solomon. (Both Solomon and Jesus are Prophets in Islam). Many stories extoll the spiritual eminence of the Temple Mount which was, in fact, the original prayer direction (*qiblah*) of the early Muslims before the direction of Mecca placed it in the second year of the Hijrah. The Temple Mount is often referred to as the third holy place in Islam (*ḥaram*), after Mecca and Medinah.

The rock itself is oblong and measures 56 feet by 42 feet (18 by 14 meters). Below it is a chamber accessible by a stairway where one can pray in a small area set aside for the purpose (this is a special oratory in addition to the large prayer area on the ground level above). A crack in the rock visible from this grotto is piously explained as having split when the Prophet ascended to heaven; the rock wished to follow. The cave is called the *Bi'r al-arwāḥ*, "the Well of Spirits".

When the Arabs conquered Jerusalem they found the Temple Mount abandoned and filled with refuse. The abandonment of the Temple site was in accordance with Jesus's prophecy that not a stone would be left standing on another. 'Umar ordered it cleaned and performed a prayer there. The sanctuary above the rock, with its golden dome that dominates the skyline of old Jerusalem, was built by the Caliph 'Abd al-Malik ibn Marwan around *72*/691. Its splendid decorative designs are noted for their Byzantine-Syrian motifs. Calligraphic decorations, characteristic of much of Islamic art, majestically dominate the Dome of the Rock. The two hundred and forty yards/meters of inscriptions, famed for their beauty, are in *Kufic* style within, and *ta'līq* on the outside. The inscriptions are all the Koranic verses about Jesus.

The Dome of the Rock's octagonal structure became the model for domed sanctuaries and Saints' tombs from Morocco to China. The octagon is a step in the mathematical series going from square, symbolizing the fixity of earthly manifestation, to circle, the natural symbol for the perfection of heaven. Traditional baptismal fonts are also octagonal in virtue of the same symbolism, baptism being an initiation which opens the door from this world to the next, or to a superior state of being. In Saints' tombs the lower part of the structure is square, or cubic; the octagon is a drum inserted as a transition between the cube of the base and the dome. In traditional Islamic architecture this configuration symbolizes the link between earth, represented by the square, and heaven, symbolized by the dome; in human terms, and according to a similar principle, the Saint is the link between man and God. In Morocco, when the King rides to Friday prayer on horseback, servants hold over him a large parasol, which corresponds to the architectural dome; this is thus a living tableau of the sacred function of man at prayer, for the monarch is also the Imām, or prayer leader, of the nation.

In the case of the Dome of the Rock, the symbolism of its geometric forms echoes the significance of the Temple Mount as the site of the Temple of Solomon. It is the culmination of the revelations of Moses and Jesus in the restoration of the primordial Abrahamic unity which is Islam. The site of the structure is the Temple of Solomon; the calligraphic inscriptions recall the relationship between Jerusalem and Jesus, and the apocalypse to come; and the architecture, above all the octagonal form supporting a dome, is symbolic of the *mi'rāj*, or ascent to heaven, by the Prophet, and thus by man.

Although the Dome of the Rock was built by Syrian craftsmen trained in the Byzantine tradition, it is, nevertheless, the first major example of Islamic architecture, whose more "indigenous" expressions would come later. Situated on the site of the temple of Solomon, it proclaims the ascendancy of Islam. When the sanctuary was built, Mecca was being occupied by a challenger to the Caliphate, 'Abd Allāh Ibn az-Zubayr. 'Abd al-Malik therefore promulgated a decree whereby the Dome of the Rock, rather than the Ka'bah, became the goal of the *ḥajj*, or pilgrimage. This decree was annulled with the reconquest of Mecca, but it demonstrates the sanctity that Islam attaches to the place.

Only the High Priest was allowed to walk in the Holy of Holies, and since the actual position of the Holy of Holies is now unknown, Judaism forbids access to the whole area of Temple Mount; a prohibition which is observed by orthodox Jews. In all likelihood, the Holy of Holies was over the rock which is within the Dome of the Rock. Sacred history and Rabbinical decisions have closed the Temple Mount to the first of the three Semitic religions. In Christianity the veil of the Temple, which separated the Holy of Holies from the rest of the Temple, was rent in twain at the crucifixion of Jesus, to symbolize the going forth of the Shechina into the world. Islam, the third and final Semitic religion which, like Christianity, is universal, makes of the Temple Mount the place where man, as man, is joined once more to God through the restoration of Adam's relationship to God before the Fall, as expressed in the ascent to heaven of the Prophet; thus it is Islam that restores it as a sanctuary.

When the Crusaders controlled Jerusalem, the Knights Templar turned the Dome of the Rock into a church and made it the model for their chapels, or "temples". The only such chapel still extant is in the Templar Castle of Tomar, Portugal, and in the small and ancient church of the True Cross (*la Iglesia de la Vera Cruz*) in Segovia, Spain. The Dome was also the emblem of the seal of the Grand Master of the Order of the Knights Templar. When Saladin recaptured Jerusalem he naturally made the Dome once more into an Islamic shrine. The area around the Dome of the Rock contains a number of minor monuments which were built by the Ottomans. At the other end of the esplanade is the al-Aqsā' Mosque. *See* al-AQSĀ'; JERUSALEM; NIGHT JOURNEY; SOLOMON.

Dönmeh (Turkish: "apostate" from the Turkish root *dön*, "to turn" built on the Arabic model *murtadd.*) A crypto-Jewish sect found in Greece and Turkey with a Muslim outer appearance, and heterodox Jewish beliefs and practices maintained in secret. There arose in Turkey a grand charlatan named Sabbatai Zevi (1626-1676) from Smyrna (Izmir), a descendant of exiles from Spain after 1492. A student of Lurianic Kabbalah, he allowed himself to be proclaimed the Messiah in 1648 after pronouncing publicly the Divine Name in Hebrew which Jews consider to be forbidden. Zevi would enter into striking psychological states in which he acted as a man possessed and advocated the breaking of Jewish religious laws.

With the help of a promoter called Nathan Benjamin Levi of Gaza, Zevi acquired a large following, and his reputation spread over Europe. Samuel Pepys wrote in his diary that Jews in London are speculating on "a certain person now in Smyrna". Tens of thousands of Jews converged on Turkey believing he was the Messiah. Zevi, basing himself upon Christian apocalyptics, proclaimed the year 1666 as the millennium and in that year he attempted to have his followers converge upon Constantinople telling them that they would be able to dethrone the Sultan. The Turkish authorities arrested him; and upon the advice of a Jewish advisor challenged Zevi to an ordeal to prove that he was the Messiah. Thereupon Zevi outwardly converted to Islam, taking the name Mehmet Effendi while preserving his antinomial beliefs inwardly. At that point many Jews abandoned him, and in Italy the Jewish chronicles of the Zevi years were destroyed to wipe out all trace. Some, however, followed him into a kind of Islam and later leaders such as Jacob Josef Pilosof called Querido (b. 1662 in Salonika) carried on the process of further conversions. Zevi himself was exiled to Dulcigno (DurrÍs) in Albania, where he died among his followers.

In Europe a clandestine antinomial Sabbatian movement also arose and produced later variations of which Jacob Frank was a notable example. After various scandals Frank (1726-1791) converted to Catholicism and assumed the title Baron of Offenbach. Frank's antinomianism took the particular form of rampant sexuality which, like Rasputinism and other movements, was a kind of "sanctification through sin". (Zevi, in the pattern of Simon Magus, had been married to Sarah, a prostitute who had been raised in a convent.) David Bakan has traced Frankist Sabbatianism down to Sigmund Freud and sees in him an example of the Sabbatian-Frankist paradigm. He, and others, also *see* Sabbatianism as the origin of Hasidism.

The sect of the Dönmeh were found in Salonika, Edirne, Istanbul, and Izmir before the collapse of the Ottoman Empire when they were estimated as being ten to fifteen thousand. Calling themselves *ma'aminim* the sect was divided into several branches: Izmirlis (who include the Celebis, Karawajo, Cabalieros, and Kara Kashlar), the Yakubis (also called Hamdi-Beyler, a name used by Querido), and the Kuniosos, the latter being followers of Osman Baba. The Izmirlis were also sometimes called the *Tarbishli*, or "those who had taken the turban"; in Edirne they were also called Sazanicos.

While professing to be Muslims and actually honouring Muḥammad, fasting Ramaḍān, going on pilgrimage, they nevertheless believe in Zevi, and others according to the branch, take him to be a Messiah (or simply to be God) and perform rites in respect of this, including a paraphrasing of the *shahādah* and carry on Kabbalistic studies. They believe that the Messiah has been reincarnated some eighteen times since Adam; that Zevi's death was an appearance and that he returned as Querido, and then as Osman Baba. Some groups did not believe in Osman Baba as a reincarnation and these are called *Kapanzylar*, (others did not believe in Querido). Rites are held partly in Ladino (Judaeo-Spanish) and Jewish holidays and rituals are observed, in secret; however, the 9th of Ab, the destruction of the Temple, is not mourned but instead celebrated (antinomially, of course) as the birth of Zvi (the hagiography also makes Yom Kippur his day of death); there was a sacramental meal resembling the Christian *agape*; the followers are said to have maintained two sets of names, a Muslim public name ("for the people") and a secret Jewish name ("for paradise"); to have had houses which were interconnected, and a myriad of sectarian beliefs, practices, and particularities, such as a belief that the lamb contains within itself a secret combination of both male and female natures. To maintain their Jewishness, like the Marranos of Spain, they only intermarried among themselves. Different currents among the Dönmeh would await the return of the Messiah from the north, the south, or by sea, and would go to the seashore for ritual waiting. A number of similarities can be found between them and the 'Alawi sect and Bektashi sects of the Near East.

Many Dönmeh played an important role in the 1908 revolution in Turkey as members of the "Young Turks" and subsequently as laicized statesmen in the Kemalist government. *See* ANTINOMIANISM.

"Drunken Sufis", *see* ANTINOMIANISM; al-BISṬĀMĪ; al-ḤALLĀJ; IBN ABĪ-l-KHAYR; al-JUNAYD; al-KHAMRIYYAH; SAHL TUSTARĪ; TAWḤĪD.

Druzes. A heterodox sect which developed out of Fāṭimid Ismā'īlism and the *5th*/11th century agitation of the Qarmaṭīs. The Druzes, a kind of Ismā'īlī sub-group, call themselves the *Muwwaḥidūn*, the "Unitarians"— which is also the preferred name of the Wahhābīs, and that of the Almohads, a religious movement in Morocco of the *4th*/11th century. However, the Druzes are in no way related to either of these. They are of an altogether different religion, a departure from Islam with which they have no more than an historical link through Fāṭimid Ismā'īlism. There are over 600,000 Druzes who live in Lebanon, Syria, and Israel.

The sixth Fāṭimid Caliph (and Ismā'īlī Imām) *al-Ḥākim*, who died in Cairo in *411*/1021, allowed his followers to announce that he was Divine. Two opportunists who promoted these assertions were Ḥamzah, a Persian, and Anushtegin Darazī ("the cobbler"), a Turk. The latter *dā'i*, or propagandist, left his name to the Druze sect. Darazī's publishing, at al-Ḥākim's behest, of the *bāṭinī* ("inner") doctrine of the Ismā'īlīs concerning the Imām caused an outcry and rioting in Cairo which forced al-Ḥākim to retract. In the recriminations which followed, Ḥamzah and Darazī quarreled; Darazī fled to Palestine or Syria where he continued propaganda concerning al-Ḥākim until his death in *410*/1020; Ḥamzah followed upon the heels of Darazī and had his predecessor duly anathemized, declaring himself instead, in keeping with the practices of the sect, to be the true manifester of the Divine reality of al-Ḥākim. As was the pattern with Ismā'īlī *dā'is*, Ḥamzah hived off what was to become the Druzes from the Fāṭimid Ismā'īlīs, attributing to al-Ḥākim a celestial function, and to himself an earthly one in the role of Imām. After his death, Baha'a-d-Dīn al-Muqtana was the *Tāli'* or successor. The pastoral letters written around that epoch constitute the body of written Druze literature, the *Rasā'il al-Ḥākim*. The doctrine became established among tribes in Lebanon, Palestine and Syria. These tribes in their isolation perpetuated in secret a tradition of Gnostic beliefs going back to antiquity and were the targets of every new wave of Gnostic or Ismā'īlī missionaries, including the Qarmaṭīs. With the propaganda concerningal-Ḥākim, a crystallisation was to take place and fix the form of the dogmas; twenty years after al-Ḥākim died (or according to their beliefs went into a great occultation, the *ghaybah*) entry to the Druze religion was closed. The Druzes believe that their number remains the same since then.

Druze doctrine teaches that al-Ḥākim was a manifestation of the universal intellect, *al-'Aql al-Kullī* and that he is not dead, but mystically and secretly alive in the Unseen and that he will return as the Mahdī. Although this resembles the Twelve-Imām Shī'ite doctrine of the Hidden Imām, which is itself calqued on the Koranic description of Jesus, the two should not be confused. The Druzes believe that emanations of Divine principles are made incarnate, or act through, functionaries in the higher levels of the Druze hierarchy, the "ministers" or representatives of al-Ḥākim. Because of their Ismā'īlī origins, Druze beliefs are characteristically dualist, or Gnostic. The so-called doctrines of reincarnation which are attributed to the Druzes are probably the echoes of the Gnostic teachings of the gathering up of the illuminated souls at the end of time.

The sect is secretive. In practice there are several different degrees of initiation which, along with Druze precepts, are designed to promote obedience, group cohesiveness, and solidarity in the face of pressure from outside. The process of initiation begins at the age of eighteen. The guidance given to the Druzes is represented as being the will of al-Ḥākim expressed through his "ministers". The sectaries are divided into *'uqqāl* (sing *'āqil*; "intelligent") who correspond to the "elect" or the initiates and the *juhhāl* (sing. *jahīl*; "ignorant"). The supreme chief of the Druze is the *Shaykh al-'Aql* with a *ra'īs*, or head, appointed to districts. In Lebanon there is a division into two groups, the Jumblatt and the Yazbakī, each with their own head.

It is sometimes said that the Druzes are descended from the Crusaders, but this is simply a common, catch-all mythology for many groups in the Levant. It has also been alleged that the Druzes have wives in common, but this, similarly, is the most common of slanders in the Near and Middle East, directed at any exotic group by detracting outsiders. Although these various charges are groundless, the Gnostic sects are especially vulnerable to this kind of attack because of their ambiguous attitudes towards religious law; their extreme asceticism on the one hand, and their disregard of the religious law on the other, make for an attitude of independence towards the rest of the world.

Several Druze leaders became prominent in the history of the Levant: the Emīr Fakhr ad-Dīn in the 12th century, Emīr Fakhr ad-Dīn II in the 17th, and the Emīr Bashīr Shihābī in the 19th. The Ottoman Turks found it prudent to allow the Druzes a measure of independence. The Druzes and the Maronite Christians are traditionally hostile to each other; communal warfare between the two irrupted frequently in the last century. Druzes living in Israel are accepted in the Israeli army. *See* FĀṬIMIDS; ISMĀ'ĪLĪS; LEBANON.

Du'ā' (literally a "call" or "plea"). An individual prayer, which may be spontaneous with personal petitions, or a composed individual prayer, such as the *Ṣalāt Mashīshiyyah*, or the *Ḥizb al-Baḥr*, or a special prayer for occasions of distress, the *Yā Laṭif*. The *du'ā'* is different from the ritual, or canonical prayer (*ṣalāh*), which is a non-individual prayer performed five times a day according to a traditionally established form, and which is obligatory. The *ṣalāh* is a kind of liturgy and an act of worship. What Christians usually understand by prayer, is in Islam closer to what is called the *du'ā'*.

The *ṣalāh* is normally followed by a *du'ā'*, prefaced by the recitation of certain expressions of praise and thanks to God thirty-three or more times.

The *du'ā'* itself, which consists of the individual's petitions of God, is voiced inwardly and silently. The *du'ā'*, whether in a group or alone, is performed with the palms of the hands open to heaven; at the end, the words *al-Ḥamdu li-Llāh* ("praise to God") are said and the palms are drawn over the face and down, crossing over the shoulders, as if one were anointing oneself with a Divine blessing. Although there is always a (non-obligatory) *du'ā'* following the *ṣalāh*, a *du'ā'* may be made at any time. *See* FĀTIḤAH; ḤIZB al-BAḤR; IBN MASHĪSH; PRAYER; ṢALĀH; YA LAṬĪF.

Dualism (Ar. *ath-Thunā'iyyah* or *al-Ithnayniyyah*). The doctrine that there are two mutually antagonistic "principles" in the universe, good and evil, also symbolized as light and darkness, or, as in Heraclitus and Hegel, being and non-being, (the latter as an active principal, a determining component of reality, in the sense that something is composed of this much being, and this much non-being; Mullā Ṣadra also made his career with this simple notion). Its empirical starting point is the observation that something like evil exists concretely, although a more philosophical cause lies in the difficulty for the mind to perceive nothingness as truly emptiness, without any shred of materiality. There are numerous variants: in "Christian" Marcionism (d. 160) there is a "good" New Testament God and an "evil" Old Testament God or "Demiurge creator". The doctrine leads to a well-worn circle of reasoning. If the intellectual starting point is that there are two principles or two gods who are at war with each other this assumption inevitably leads to the conclusion that the world is a physical mixture of these two principles. Then the world is not a "creation" but is itself a kind of materialist absolute, or "divine". In other words, the world is God. Or, as in the case of Bardaisan (Ibn Daisan d. 222), and many other Gnostics, an emanation.

If, on the other hand, the starting point is materialism (the doctrines which the Zoroastrians and Muslims called *dahrī*, Koran 45:23) or that I, or someone else, such as 'Alī, the Imām, the sacred teacher, or something in the world, is divine, then the metaphysical conclusion is that two principles are behind the dynamics of such a world. While the mythology that covers the framework is a matter of taste, the crux of the matter is logic: if the ego or matter, is not a "creation" but is itself an absolute, then the limitations which make it individual or discrete are also "absolute" or, "divine". As the Taoists say, it is the absence or empty space which makes a bowl a bowl. But if the bowl is "reality" in itself and not the work of a creator, then the absence that makes the bowl a bowl is also "reality". If nothingness or "Non-Being" is itself "real" and not just a name, or, as in Aristotle, an "accident", that means it has an "essence". The essence of nonexistence (were it to have an essence!), would have to be utter contradiction. This translates as the divinity of evil, as found in, say, Milton, or in Martin Luther.

Such doctrines could be called *radical* dualism and include Manicheism, and such materialist ideologies as Marxism in which the two gods become Thesis and Antithesis. Soviet Communism also saw, quite rightly, Persian Mazdakism as its historical predecessor. (Communism has always been the preferred social system of radical dualism.) Radical dualism also includes philosophical Existentialism, as well as numerous ancient and modern sects and religions. Hans Jonas in *The Gnostic Religion* observed that the keys which unlocked Gnosticism also unlocked Nihilism and Existentialism, that is Heidigger, Nietsche, Sartre, and one could add Romanticism. The philosophical implications of modern science, which emerged from, and abandoned, a non-dualistic Medieval scholastic framework (whose last support, the notion of the "ether", was discarded only at the end of the 19th century and is still being debated), put materialist science also into this family of reality systems. The "Big Bang" theory that makes the origin of the cosmos a "clash" of matter and antimatter, is nothing other than the mythological "war" between two gods. Mani the prophet, Mani the scientist, also said the cosmos began with a "Big Bang" when Darkness attacked the Light.

In recent times it has become fashionable to style as "non-dualism" the idea that God as one sole agent (rather than God and another, such as Satan), is the author of both good and evil). This is of course also dualism because it assumes that evil "exists" on the divine plane or plane of absolute reality; one could say it claims that shadows have their own life. This kind of "non-dualism" is word play but the idea is not new. There were and are those who teach that *tawhid*, "Divine Unity" means only God is God, and there are those who teach that *tawhid*, "Divine Unity" means that everything is God.

Classical Gnostic doctrines which evolved near the watchful eyes of Aristotelianism, in order to mask the illogicality of two realities, had to posit a supra-imaginable level called the *bythos* (Gr. "abyss") or in Islamic gnosis, the *ghayb ta'ala* ("exalted absence") from which even Allāh issued forth. (Some Islamic gnostics spuriously interpreted the Name Allah as coming from the Arabic verb *walaha*, meaning "to lament", referring to an exile from the ineffable).

Sometimes it is one step to move from non-dualism to Dualism. If Yin and Yang are complements it is not Dualism; but if they are incompatible, completely opposed to each other, then it is Dualism. If men and women are by nature friends it is non-dualism, if they are by nature "enemies"...

A second form of dualism could be called *relative* dualism. Here the world is not divine as such, but something in the world — or someone is divine, or "somewhat" divine. "Somewhat divine" could be the "divine spark" which the Gnostics said is found in those whom Paul calls "pneumatics". It could also be the *chintamani* or the "good samsara" of the Western Paradise Sukhavati in certain forms of Buddhism, the "philosopher's stone", the sacred horde or tribe, the particular "guru", the descendant of a sacred family, the holy child, etc. In Islam it is the Shī'ite idea that 'Alī and certain of his descendants possess a divine spark or element of divine light and what is called the *'ilm*, or sacred knowledge. In this form of dualism the element of time, as Ugo Bianchi pointed out, plays an essential role. Whereas in the radical dualisms realisation of final ends can come at any moment between beginning and end, in the relative dualisms there is an inexorable cosmological process which takes a pre-determined duration of time for its accomplishment. The Mahdī is to come at some epiphany in the future and "establish justice in the earth".

The *relative* forms of dualism are more common — at certain times — or more widespread than the "radical" but, in time, the relative dualisms evolve or decay to become in practice indistinguishable from the radical forms, as can be seen from recent developments in Twelve Imām Shī'ism.

Other minor forms of dualism include Monism (Ibn 'Arabi, Christian Science, pantheism, etc.) and a dualism which is termed "Monarchic". In this latter form, the good god, say, Jehovah, is slightly stronger, or has some other advantage over the evil god, Satan, and will defeat him definitively or from time to time in the cosmic drama.

Dualisms are antagonistic to each other; relative dualisms may even be more antagonistic toward a parent or related radical dualisms than to other "relative" competitors, and condemn them as being immoral, or for "going too far". (Al-Ma'arrī was dragged out by his foot — the equivalent expression at that time and place for being "kicked out", when he expected to be welcomed with open arms by Sharīf ar-Raḍīi in Baghdad.) To one extent or another, dualisms are anti-cosmic — they regard the world or the body as evil, or the world as fatally polluted, and require renunciation and asceticism from their followers — purity — unless or until the individual or group is regenerated into a new and perfect entity by the accomplishment of a process or sanctified by the presence of the holy element or person. An inevitable feature is the "external enemy", the political "Great Satan".

There is the phenomenon, of which the ancient sect of "Massalians is the model and technical term, in which the ascetic, having denied himself, becomes a "perfectus" and everything which was forbidden to him or her becomes completely licit. This tendency, of the forbidden becoming permitted, of chastity becoming orgy, can be found at some point or at some time, if not in the beginning then at the "mature" stage of development, in many dualist sects. It may appear as the permission for marriages to be contracted by intention to last for one day (*see* MUT'AH). Thus the heresiarchs accused the Gnostics of orgiastic rituals, "of putting out the candles" at mixed meetings, of regressions to animal states, while their defenders point to the Gnostic's public display of strict and extreme rules of abstinence.

Islam appeared, as many religions do, when dualist doctrines were spreading inexorably throughout the classical world. One story is cited as being the essence of such metaphysical error: The Koran tells how Bilqīs, the Queen of Sheba (the soul) visited Solomon (the intellect), and mistook the reflection on a finely polished floor of his palace (the world) for reality:

> It was said unto her, 'Enter the pavilion.'
> But when she saw it, she supposed it was
> a spreading water, and she bared her legs.
> He [Solomon] said, 'It is a pavilion smoothed of
> crystal.' She said, 'My Lord, indeed I
> have wronged myself, and I surrender with
> Solomon to God, the Lord of all Being.'
> (Koran 27:44-45)

In other words, she mistook a reflection for reality, or "what is not" for a "second" or different kind of Being or anti-Being. To the two gods doctrine Islam replied that there is one God. Islam expunges the errors of dualism by the *shahādah*, the testimony of faith which attests that only God is God. Which is not to say that orthodoxies do not bear the traces of the Dualisms from which they emerged, and back to which they may eventually decay. *See* ISHRĀQ; KHAṬṬĀBIYYAH; KHURRAMIYYAH; MANICHEISM.

Duldul. The mule of the Prophet. The mule was a gift from the Byzantine Viceroy of the Copts of Egypt, the Muqawqīs as the Arabs called him.

Dungan. Or Tungans are a Chinese speaking people of Central Asia and Xinjiang, some of whom are found in eastern Kyrgyztan and Kazakhstan, who are Muslim. Not of Turkic descent, the Dungans are descended from Chinese Merchants who intermarried with Mongols in the 13th and 14th century when China was ruled by a Mongol dynasty, the Yuan.

E

Effendi. Within the territory of the former Ottoman Empire, a traditional title in Ottoman times for a religious or a civil authority. Today, in most cases it is replaced by the honourific Bey, also originally a Turkish term.

Egypt. Republic. Population estimated at 48,500,000 of whom 90% are Sunnī Muslims. The Mālikī school is dominant in upper Egypt and the Shāfi'ī in lower Egypt; some Egyptian Muslims are Ḥanafīs. The non-Muslim 10% are Coptic Christians, Greek Orthodox, Melkites, Jacobites, and members of smaller churches. The prestige of the al-Azhar University has often given the pronouncements of Egyptian religious leaders great weight in the Islamic world; and during the last few centuries Cairo has been the cultural capital of the Arab world. *See* 'AMR IBN al-'ĀṢĪ; al-AZHAR; CAIRO; FĀṬIMIDS; MAMLŪKS; MUḤAMMAD 'AlĪ.

Eid *see* 'ID.

Elijah, *see* ILYĀS.

Elisha, *see* ALYASA'.

Elkhasaios (Also, Elkhasai. Ar. al-Ḥasiḥ). The head of the "baptising" sect (*al-mughtasilah*) or the *Ṣābat al-Baṭa'ih* as an-Nadīm called them, to which Mani had belonged, and from which he emerged with his own religion. Elkhasai's group appears to be a splinter of the Mandaeans. Elkhasai had received a revelation in the form of a "book from heaven". Bell, in *Origin of Islam*, says that a secret watchword of Elkhasai was "I am a witness over you on the day of judgement." This points (along with many other references) to a link between this Mesopotamian sect, through its derivative, Manicheism, and Islam. This phrase is also found in so many words in the Koran (22:78 and elsewhere). Mani (himself the original "Seal of Prophecy") also derived the idea of the cyclical reappearance of the true prophet from the "Book of Elkhasai". Like Elkhasai, Mani also used the word *qerya* for the Gnostic "Call" or as a sign of recognition, along with the clasping of hands.

The handclasp is an important rite among the Mandaeans, and a social imperative among Muslims; the Arabic word *iqra'* (cognate to *qerya*) is a "Call" and the first word of the Koranic revelation in the Surah 96. Among the Gnostics, the "Call" is an important psychological reality (as it still is among some Protestant sects). In Manicheism "the sleep-walking soul of the fallen man comes to life again when he is awakened by the messenger God of the Call". In Manicheism, the first call (*xrustag*) is made by Adam and is answered by the Father of Greatness. Also intriguing in this context, in which stars can be particles of light hidden in creation, is the *najmu ath-thāqiba*, the "piercing or flaming star" of the Koran (86:3), which is followed by the words "over every soul there is a watcher". *See* NAJMU THĀQIBU; MANDAEANS.

Emigration, *see* HIJRAH.

Emīr, *see* AMĪR.

Emre, *see* YUNUS EMRE.

Enoch, *see* IDRĪS.

Eritrea. Since 1993 an independent republic the size of England, formerly a part of Ethiopia. The name is from the Latin for the Red Sea — Mare Erythraeum. The population is three million Ḥanafi Muslims and Christians of the Ethiopian Church. The capital is Asmara with a population of 400,000. The Italian colony of Eritrea was created in 1890 bringing together nine different ethnic groups, including the Christian Tigrinya, the animistic Kunama, the Muslim Afars. In 1952 Eritrea was made an autonomous federated state within Ethiopia by the United Nations. In 1961 a war of independence began which led Haile Selassie to make Eritrea the 14th province of Ethiopia. The war continued under Selassie's successors. *see* ETHIOPIA.

Eschatology. The doctrines of "final ends" which refer to two things: the last days before the end of a cycle of manifestation, and the final, or posthumous, states of souls. The last days, as described in Islam, are marked by the figures of Gog and Magog (Jūj wa Mājūj), the Mahdī, the Antichrist (*Dajjāl*), and Jesus.

The names Gog and Magog are interpreted symbolically by Arab commentators as meaning "flaming fire" and "surging water", that is, violence, destruction, and agitation. According to the Koranic parable recounted in the Sūrah of the Cave (18:93), Gog and Magog, representing the forces of chaos, have been kept at bay, for a time, by the erection of a barrier described as being of iron and molten copper; this was erected by him "of the Two Horns" (*Dhū-l-Qarnayn*), generally taken to refer to Alexander the Great, who was empowered so to do by God. The barrier in the myth may be based distantly on travelers' tales of the Great Wall of China, which existed as trenches in the times of the Warring States and became more formidable in the dynasty of the Chin. Or, closer to the Arabs, a wall built against invaders in Iran by Anushirvan (Chosroes). In the Koran such a wall is also understood to refer to the Divine Law (*Sharī'ah*). At the end of time, chaos will break through the wall of Divinely imposed order, and the world will succumb to "outer darkness".

At the same time, it is believed, there will be a countercurrent, or a brief return to the state of spiritual lucidity and primordial integrity that obtained at the dawn of time. This is the reign of the Mahdī, the "rightly guided one". It is, however, extremely unlikely that the doctrine of the Mahdī goes back to the Prophet himself; probably it is an invention of the early Shī'ite movements of the end of the *1st*/7th century. But a version of the Mahdī idea (different from the Shī'ite one in that it has none of the Imāmī doctrines) has been popularly accepted by some, not all, Sunnī Muslims and is a feature of certain of the Sunnī creeds. It has imposed itself because an eleventh-hour sobriety, like the moment of dispassionate clarity before death, is a well-known experience. Thus, Tradition has the Prophet say: "The Mahdī will be of my stock and he will be broad of forehead and aquiline of nose." This means that he will resemble the Prophet; although the description is physical, it can be taken as a resemblance of character. Under him justice, or a sense of true proportion, and a centre will be restored; law in the place of anomie. The Mahdī's reign of justice will mean the establishment of a spiritual Norm, of what the Far Eastern traditions call the Tao and Hinduism the *dharma*.

The reign of the Mahdī will be followed by that of the Antichrist, *al-Masīḥ ad-Dajjāl* (lit. "imposter messiah"). The word *Masīḥ* ("messiah") by the addition of one dot above the final Arabic letter — the minuscule discrepancy which transforms spiritual truth into falsehood — is changed to *masīkh*, "deformed", and it is by this name that some Sufi masters called the final, great, deceiver.

The deceiver will come at a time when the world is in extreme imbalance, and incapable of distinguishing authentic spirituality from false, if indeed, it does not prefer the false. The deceiver will promise — to use the terminology of Far Eastern traditions — "to stop the cosmic wheel from turning", but will himself be the very incarnation of disorder, pure disbelief, outwardness, and inversion; in short the parody of spirituality.

Better to understand the workings of the Antichrist, it is helpful to distinguish, in the classical religious view, between the psychic and spiritual domains, which, from the viewpoint of the material world, are easily confounded. The psychic or subtle domain resembles the spiritual or supraformal and principial one. An Angel, for example, dwells in the spiritual realm, but to make himself manifest in the physical world, he must take on a subtle form. Magic, or the manipulation of the subtle plane, can be mistaken for miracles, which are transformations wrought in the spiritual or principial plane. This, and the confusion possible between the infra-human and the sublime (arbitrariness appearing to be freedom, lack of conscience to be self-sufficiency, and chaos to be formlessness), are the illusions by which the *Dajjāl* perpetrates his fraud; he substitutes one for the other. However, this is only possible when the ego connives to be deluded. The ego, despite being aware of its own mortality, refuses to yield to the Self which is immortal, and clings to what mirrors it. The reign of the Antichrist is the reign of the ego.

The most significant distinguishing mark foretold of the Antichrist is that he will be one-eyed. To be one-eyed is to be unable to perceive depth or space; that is, to be unable to establish the mutual relationship of objects in a field of vision and to fail to perceive the reality they manifest: to see the fact, but not its significance. Above all, it means to be unable to sense the inward depth of the sacred: the Antichrist reduces the eternal to the momentary. The reduction of consciousness to a point or an instant is not without its attractions, for it implies escape from the majesty and dread of the numinous and the utterly other, as well as from our own responsibility towards the infinite, eternal and transcendental. The Antichrist will "heal" the sick by making their afflictions the norm, or by making sin virtuous. He will win followers by his ability to work marvels or pseudo-miracles.

Concerning the last days the Prophet said: "A body of my people will not cease to fight for the Truth until the coming of the Antichrist" and: "Islam began in exile and will return to exile." This is also cited as prophecy of the sign of the times: "The slave-girl will give birth to her mistress [the inferior will rule and the superior will adopt the inferior as its model]. Suddenly, however, Jesus will appear, and with him the radical correction of the world, the opening of the doors of paradise and the doors of hell, and the discrimination of spirits.

While the last times have the aspect of terrible tribulation, tradition says that when they end a new cycle begins, and with it a new golden age. Also, at the end the spiritual will be easily accessible, although few will want it. The Prophet said: "At the beginning he who omits one-tenth of the law is condemned; but at the end he who accomplishes one-tenth of the law is saved." This echoes the gospel parable of the workers in the garden where those who worked but a short time in the late afternoon were paid as much as those who worked from the early morning. Because of the increase in grace, both garnered a like amount.

With respect to individual eschatology (*al-ma'ad*, the return to God), Islam, like all the monotheist traditions deriving from Zoroastrianism, draws a sharp distinction between the posthumous states of paradise and hell. These are preceded by the end of the world, or individual death, the resurrection (*qiyamah*), in which the bodies are reconstituted and joined again to souls, the gathering (*ḥashr*) and the judgement (*yawm ad-dīn*). The physical end of the world is accompanied by the outward signs of earthquakes, rising of the seas, falling of stars, and melting of mountains. There are two trumpet blasts, the first is the annihilation, and the second the resurrection. In individual death, there is also the "torment in the tombs" (*'adhāb al-qabr*), a punishment inherent in the state of death while awaiting the resurrection and the final judgement.

The Prophet said: "When we live, we dream, and when we die, we wake." Whether we are true to our real selves and to the Real — it is this which determines our state after death. Identification with the Truth leads to paradise, and rejection (disbelief: *kufr*) leads to hell.

These, however, are not the only possible posthumous states. The Sūrah of the Heights (*al-A'rāf*) speaks of those "on the heights" who hear and address the people of paradise, but are not yet in paradise themselves (7:46-47). It is the sanctified who, having fulfilled the requirements of the human state, will enter paradise (*al-jannah*).

'O soul at peace, return unto thy Lord,
well-pleased, well-pleasing!
Enter thou among My servants!
Enter thou My Paradise!' (89:27-30)

Faces on that day jocund,
with their striving well-pleased,
in a sublime Garden,
hearing there no babble;
therein a running fountain,
therein uplifted couches
and goblets set forth
and cushions arrayed
and carpets outspread. (88:8-15)

Those who are not perfected, but are without fundamental fault, may enter into a limbo, or the kind of intermediary state without suffering to which the *al-A'rāf* refers, as they undergo final purification, a state which unfailingly opens onto the state of the blessed. (There are a number of Ḥadīth which Muslim theologians have taken to mean that children who die before the age of reason are saved, or have the posthumous possibility of salvation, because until the age of reason they embody the *fiṭrah* or primordial norm. (*See* CHILDREN.)

Purgatory, or purification with privation or suffering, is not mentioned in the Koran, at least directly, but there are Ḥadīth such as the following: "And God will say: the Angels, the Prophets and the believers have all interceded for them [the sinners] save The Most Merciful of the Merciful (*Arḥam ar-Rāḥimīn*). And He will grasp the fire in his hand and draw out a people who never did any good." This provisional passage through fire corresponds to the idea of purgatory. The provisional passage through Hell is also how Zoroastrianism conceives of Hell: as a punishment in order to correct the soul, a punishment which does not last in eternity. The Andalusian theologian Ibn Ḥazm maintained that if believers went to hell, it was necessarily for a limited time. Al-Ash'arī too admits the possibility, though perhaps less categorically. Ultimately, the Ḥadīth can also refer to an apocatastasis. The Prophet also said: "Those who have merited paradise will enter it; the damned will go to hell. God will then say; Let those leave hell whose hearts contain even the weight of a mustard seed of faith! Then they will be released, although they have already been burned to ashes, and plunged into the river of rainwater, or into the river of life; and immediately they will be revived."

There is, finally, hell itself which lasts in perpetuity — if not in eternity — until the extinction of the personality. A fifth possibility, namely of a transition through a posthumous state, whether happy or fearful to another, necessarily non-human and non-central existence, which may be better or worse that the individual's previous state, depending upon his "Karma", or "what he deserves", is found in some religions but does not enter into the Islamic perspective.

On the other hand, a distinction is drawn in the Koranic Sūrah of the Terror (or "the Event") (*Sūrat al-Wāqi'ah*), between two categories of those not destined to be damned as "Companions of the Left" (*Aṣḥāb al-mash'amah*; 56:9). These are described respectively as the "Companions of the Right" (*Aṣḥāb al-Maymanah*; 56:8) and the "Outstrippers" (or the "Foremost") (*as-Sābiqūn*), the latter being equated with those that are "brought nigh the Throne" (*al-Muqarrabūn*; 56: 10-11). There is clearly a fundamental difference of degree here, which certain of the Sufis have not hesitated to define as that between those who merely achieve salvation and those who attain to Beatitude; salvation is the reward, they say, of the exoteric religion, and Beatitude the aim of the Sufis' esoteric Path.

There is also a cyclical "ratio" of numbers of the "saved" and the "Beatified" respectively: the inevitable decline of humanity as it moves down through time ever further from the pristine norm (*al-fiṭrah*) means that those "brought nigh" will include "a throng of the ancients and how few of the later folk" (56:13-14), whereas the Companions of the Right will consist of "A throng of the ancients and a throng of the later folk". (56: 38-39); as the end of time approaches, salvation remains open to many, but Beatitude to very few; this is not strange, since those "brought nigh" include Jesus and other Prophets and, in fact, the line of Prophets was "sealed" with the death of Muḥammad.

In any event, the Koran speaks of various paradises, each corresponding, no doubt, to different degrees of blessedness: thus there is frequent mention, in general terms, of "gardens beneath which the rivers flow", and specifically of "gardens of Eden" and "gardens of Firdaws" (*Firdaws* being ultimately cognate with the Greek *paradeisos*, "Paradise", both of which are derived from the Persian "Pardes", an "enclosure", recalling the Zoroastrian origin of the idea) whilst the Sūrah ar-Raḥmān says: "But such as fears the Station of his Lord, for them shall be two gardens" (55:46) and "besides these shall be two (more) gardens" (55:62).

The human, or central state is distinguished from all others precisely because it is characterized by the capacity to know the Absolute. To be born human is therefore to arrive at a great crossroads. Islam simplifies the choice of direction into two main paths, because, ultimately, the consequences of being human are either that of becoming sanctified, or that of being reduced to the sub-human, whatever the modes. Damnation is the forfeit, or ultimate loss, of the human state because of revolt, disbelief, or, in the case of the "indifferent" (*ghāfilūn*), of simply abandoning the responsibilities of being God's "viceroy" (*khalīfah*) on earth. Paradise is the realisation of conformity to our true nature; closeness to God because of knowledge of Him; and salvation. *See also* APOCATASTASIS; CHILDREN; HELL; al-JANNAH; TANĀSUKH; YAWM ad-DĪN.

Esop, *see* LUQMĀN.

Esoterism, *see* AARON; SUFISM; ṬARĪQAH; TAṢAWWUF.

Essence, *see* ALLĀH; BEING; DHĀT; DIVINE NAMES; FIVE DIVINE PRESENCES.

Essenes, *see* MANDAEANS.

Ethics. (Ar. *al-amr bi-al-ma'ruf wa-an-nahy 'an al-munkar*, "To enjoin right conduct and prohibit indecency"; also, *ḥisba*.) There are, besides the questions that are legislated, frequent ethical injunctions in the Koran, from:

And whosoever earns a fault or a sin
and then casts it upon the innocent,
thereby has laid upon himself calumny
and manifest sin. (4:112)

to:

Consume not your goods between you
in vanity; neither proffer it
to the judges, that you may sinfully
consume a portion of other men's goods,
and that wittingly. (2:184)and:
Surely those who cast it up on women
in wedlock that are heedless but believing
shall be accursed in the present world
and in the world to come. (24:23)

and:

Woe to the stinters
who, when they measure against the people,
take full measure but, when they measure
for them or weigh for them, do skimp.
Do those not think that they shall be raised up
unto a mighty day a day when mankind
shall stand before the Lord of all Being?
(83:1-6)

These may be summed up by the Koranic formula: "Ye are the best community that hath been raised up for mankind. Ye enjoin right conduct and forbid indecency; and ye believe in Allāh" (3:110). The Ḥadīth express it thus: "*Iḥsān* [virtue] is to worship as if you see Him, for if you do not see Him, nevertheless He sees you"; and "God has prescribed virtue (or excellence, *Iḥsān*) in all things." Other Ḥadīth which deal with ethics are: "No one of you is a Muslim until you wish for your brother what you wish for yourselves." and the *Ṣaḥīḥū Muslim* related on the authority of Abū Sa'īd al-Khudrī: "Whosever of you sees an evil action, let him change it with his hand; and if he is not able to do so, then with his tongue; and if he is not able to do so, then with his heart — and that is the weakest of faith."

In practice, ethics are different in the light of different religions. Christianity makes an ideal world appear to be the reality against which actuality is measured and judges behavior according to ideals. Judaism takes its view of reality from the material world as being real as it is, and instead of the ideal sees a law. Islam's view of reality mixes these two points of view seeing things and situations sometimes from the material and concrete, and sometimes from the ideal. *See* IḤSĀN; SHARI'ĀH.

Ethiopia. Republic. Estimated population: 25,000,000. Before Eritrea became independent some 30% of the population were Muslims of the Ḥanafī School of Law, (with some Mālikīs near the Sudan); the rest are Christians of the Coptic Ethiopian Orthodox Church (which has been Monophysite since the Council of Chalcedon in 451); there remains a very small group of Falashas, or Ethiopian Jews.

By tradition, the first King of Ethiopia was Solomon's son, Menelik, by the Queen of Sheba (in Arabic she is called Bilqīs). In the 13th and 16th centuries there were wars with neighboring Muslim states, which brought increasing numbers of Muslim peoples into Ethiopia. In 1530 there was a considerable influx of Muslim Galla tribesmen from Somalia, which was repulsed by the Ethiopians with the help of the Portuguese. In 1974 the Negus, the Emperor Haile Selassie, was deposed, and a republic declared shortly thereafter. *See* ABYSSINIA; BILQĪS; CHRISTIANITY.

Ethnic Groups, *see* 'ALAWĪS; ARABS; AZERĪ; BAKHTIAR; BALUCH; BERBERS; DRUZES; HUI HUI; KIRGHIZ; KURDS; LURS; MANDAEANS; PUSHTUN; QASHQAI; TUAREG; TURKS; UZBEKS.

"Exaggerators", *see* GHULAT.

Exoterism, *see* AARON; SHARI'AH.

"Extinction", *see* FANĀ'.

"Extremists", (classical theological sects) *see* GHULAT.

Eve, *see* ADAM.

Evil, *see* IBLĪS.

Expressions, Pious, *see* PIOUS EXPRESSIONS.

Eyüp Sultan, *see* ABŪ AYYŪB.

Ezra, *see* 'UZAIR.

F

Fallacies and inaccuracies about Islam. Victor Hugo wrote, in his book *William Shakespeare*, that in the 7th century, a certain Omar [he meant the Caliph 'Umar], "a man who drank only water and no wine", who rode a camel with a bag of dates on one side and a sack of flour on the other, came to Egypt, having laid waste 39,000 towns and villages in his conquests. This Omar, or one under his command, namely Amrou Ibn-Alas ('Amr ibn al-'Asi) destroyed the great library of Alexandria, using it as fuel for the fires of 2,000 bath-houses, which were thus supplied for six months. In actual fact, the libraries of Alexandria had undergone a depredation from the time of the Roman conquest onwards. In 391 they suffered the greatest single blow when the Byzantine Emperor Theodosius I had the pagan temples of Alexandria razed. This particular fallacy concerning the library of Alexandria, born of the mistrust of the stranger and the stranger's religion, is probably no longer current, but others are. Some of the common fallacies in the West are the following:

1. *The Suspended Coffin.* A frequently repeated tale exists that the Prophet's coffin is at Mecca, "suspended between heaven and earth". This is not an Islamic belief. Probably, it is a corruption of the idea, found in Islam, that there is a prototype in heaven of the Ka'bah called *al-bayt al-ma'mūr*, and that Angels circle this celestial centre as men on earth circle the Ka'bah. The tomb of the Prophet is in Medinah, in that part of the main mosque (*al-Masjid ash-Sharīf*), which was once the Prophet's house and where he died. Nearby are the tombs of the first three Caliphs and the sepulchre of Fāṭimah, although she is actually buried in al-Baqī' cemetery nearby.

2. *Muḥammad and the Mountain.* According to this story (proverbial in the West, but unknown in the East) the Prophet Muḥammad called a mountain to come to him and when it did not, he said: "If the mountain won't come to Muḥammad then Muḥammad will go to the mountain." There is no basis in fact for such a story which, moreover, contradicts the spirit of Islam with its emphasis on the non-miraculous and the humble. Viz. Koran 17:39: "And walk not in the earth exultantly; certainly thou wilt never tear the earth open, nor attain the mountains in height." Perhaps the origin of this apocrypha comes from the fact that Ṭabarī recounts that the Prophet was taunted in this way by the idolators:

> Pray to thy Lord, Muhammad, said the men of Mecca, that He move back the mountains that hem us in, and widen the good land for us, and thread it with rivers like the land of Syria and 'Irāq; or that He make our departed fathers rise from the dead, best of all that He send old Qusayy, Qilab's son, who never told a lie, so that we may ask whether what thou tellest us is true or false. If they declare thee true, we will believe in thee.

3. Priests. Many references to "Islamic priests" occur in Western press reports and writing on Islamic countries. This catch-all phrase covers Imāms, Mullās, *faqīhs*, *qāḍis*, and *'ulamā'*. However, the word "priests" is inappropriate, for this implies a consecration to perform a function which cannot be performed by a layman. There is, however, no distinction between priests and laymen in Islam. The dignitaries or functionaries mentioned above are distinguished from ordinary believers only by a higher degree of learning, or doctrinal expertise, but everyone is expected to perform the same religious duties. It is, for example, the ordinary believer who leads prayers, performs sacrifices and officiates; if speaking of priests, it would be more accurate to say that everyone is a priest in Islam.

The function of *Qāḍi* ("Judge") is an appointment on the basis of knowledge, and is clearly not a priestly function; that of Imām, or prayer-leader, is usually performed by someone designated for it because of age or, traditionally, knowledge of the Koran; but it can, in fact, be performed by anyone; the other functions are assumed as the result of qualifications in religious studies. There is no priesthood in Islam, nor anything corresponding to the monastic order: *lā rahbāniyyah fī-l-Islām* ("there is no monasticism in Islam") is a phrase frequently quoted which is based on the Koran's condemnation of "this institution as being invented by men and not prescribed by God" (57:27). Every exoteric function and ritual in Islam can be accomplished by any mentally competent adult Muslim; in the absence of a competent male, a woman can perform any and every ritual on behalf of other women. In other words, every Muslim can perform all "sacerdotal" functions. Among Shī'ites not everyone can be a *mujtahid* or make independent judgements, but this also is a function of aptitude like that of a Judge among lawyers, and results from individual capacities, not consecration.

4. *Epilepsy ascribed to the Prophet.* This formally dates back to a diatribe against Islam written by a Byzantine monk called Theophanes in the 8th century AD Medieval European writers frequently drew upon his writings and Theophanes was the source, or the confirming authority, of other distortions which persist until today. In the 20th century some Western writers about Islam have not hesitated to explain the Koranic revelations as being the result of other kinds of non-specified morbid mental states.

In the 19th century the idea of epilepsy was a popular explanation intended to discredit religious phenomena of many kinds. It appealed to the age because it put them on a solid "scientific" footing. The Prophet's revelations were thus explained, as if the content of the Koran could possibly have been produced by epileptic seizures! St. Paul was also called an epileptic because of his conversion experience and temporary blindness. So was Julius Caesar because he had visions (some of which, as before the crossing of the Rubicon, were shared by the whole legion). There is no basis for these ideas, which are due to rationalist and atheist prejudice.

5. *Pilgrimage to Mecca as the Prophet's birthplace.* It is often said in the Western press that Muslims make pilgrimage to Mecca because it is th birthplace of the Prophet. The birthplace of the Prophet is considered to be of no importance; a library now stands on the spot which is otherwise unmarked and virtually unknown.

The pilgrimage to Mecca is ancient and antedates Islam. According to Islam, the pilgrimage was instituted by Abraham; that is, it is of primordial origin at a sanctuary dedicated to the One God since time immemorial. Thus the pilgrimage is to the sanctuary of Divine Unity and Absoluteness. Like all pilgrimages, it is to the centre of one's own being. It also commemorates the sacrifice of Abraham and pre-figures the Last Judgement. The Prophet is buried in Medinah.

6. *Souls of women.* Women in Islam have souls exactly like men; the Koran is extremely clear on this. The idea that women have no souls is found in some heretical Middle Eastern sects and in Ismā'īlīsm.

7. *Islam comes from Judaism.* In 1833 Rabbi Abraham Geiger wrote a thesis called "Was Hat Mohammed aus dem Judenthume Aufgennomen?" ("What did Muhammad take from Judaism?") This was translated into English as "Judaism and Islam" and followed by "Judaism and the Koran" by Abraham Katsh in 1954 (also author of "Hebraic Foundations of American Democracy"). The ideas set forth in these works generally follow the pattern of *post hoc ergo propter hoc* reasoning. Long before that, Christian polemicists tried to show that the Koran was really written by a Christian monk. These however, were not the origin of this particular fallacy. Rather it is a general illusion created by naive belief in the Bible. In the Middle Ages it was believed, in Europe, that all languages came from Hebrew. And that all other religions were heathenism. It was only around the time of the French Revolution that a true understanding of the development of languages began to emerge (and with it the realisation that Hebrew is rather a dialect of Arabic.)

But the scientific understanding of the development of religions has even greater difficulties to overcome than does a scientific understanding of linguistic development (as can be seen over the struggles in the popular mind regarding the theory of evolution). Since Jews and Arabs are at the origin the same people, the Semitic material upon which the two religions are built is a common heritage, such as the Code of Hammurabi, for example, and various legends. Some of this common material was adapted by the Hebrew Prophets and then bears a Jewish trace when it appears in Islam. However, Islam, like Christianity (or Judaism, for that matter), is decisively influenced by Zoroastrianism. (Monotheism, garden of Eden, Fall of man, baptism/ablution, idea of the individual soul, universal afterlife, heaven and hell, resurrection, Last Judgement, end of the world, all originate in Zoroastrianism.) While it is difficult to quantify, it would be fair to say that 50% of Islam and Christianity come from Zoroastrianism (sometimes literally as translations of Zoroastrian fragment texts). This is the result of the colossal impact of the Persian world view upon the Semitic world view when the Persians conquered Babylon and most of the Semites in the sixth century BC The consequences of that intellectual upheaval continue to manifest themselves to this day in new developments, such as the idea of the "rapture".

Naturally, Islam is not free of its own common fallacies regarding Christianity, for example that Christians worship a piece of wood called the cross. For another, *see* BARNABAS, GOSPEL of.

Fanā' (lit. "extinction"). In Sufism one hopes "to die before one dies", that is, to die to the world and to subsist in God Alone; this latter state is called *baqā'*, "subsisting" or, in fact, "immortality" in the Real. The term *fanā'* thus corresponds exactly to the Buddhist term *Nirvānam*, which also means literally "extinction". While the word *fanā'* exists in the Koran its use by Sufism for this technical concept was probably inspired by Buddhism in Central Asia. The spiritual journey to *fanā'* involves many stages, notably the extinction of the "soul that inclines to evil" (*an-nafs al-ammārah*), and then of the "soul that accuses [itself]" (*an-nafs al-lawwāmah*), which are then replaced by the "soul at peace" (*an-nafs al-muṭma'innah*). This extinction itself is, in a sense, only penultimate; some Sufi masters speak of a *fanā' al-fanā'*, or the "extinction of the extinction". By this they mean the disappearance of *fanā'* itself before the ineffable glory of God, the state of *baqā'* being actually beyond all definition, and involving the loss of all individuality: "extinction in God" (*fanā' fī-Llāh*).

Thus, Ibn 'Aṭa' Allāh wrote in the *Ḥikam*:

> If you were to be united with Him only after the extinction of your vices and the effacement of your pretensions, you would never be united with Him. Instead, when He wants to unite you to Himself, He covers your attribute with His Attribute and hides your quality with His Quality. And thus He unites you to Himself by virtue of what comes from Him to you, not by virtue of what goes from you to Him.

And Niffāri:

> In the hour when I make you spectator of all existences at once in a single Vision, then at that Station I have certain forms, which if you find you know, call on Me by the forms. But if you do not know the forms, then in your agony invoke Me by the pain of that Vision.
>
> The Vision will be thus: you will be given sight of the whole Height and Depth, the whole Length and Breadth, and the All within, and all those modes in which that Totality exists, as a thing manifest, eternal, entirely ordered, and convulsed in endless struggle. You will observe the existence of each thing...its own holy song, each directed towards Me in worship, in its own Praising, staring at Me in a Glorification ...Let no fear alarm you at such a time as will come; and let no companion comfort you in the hour when I shall make you My spectator, and cause Myself to be known to you, though it may be once in your lifetime. For I will tell you in that hour, and you will know, that you are My lover, inasmuch as you will deny all things for the sake of what I have made you see, so that I shall become your Sovereign Disposer; and you will come to where I am on one side and all things on the other side. You will be attached to Me; all things else shall attach to you, and not to Me.
>
> Such is My lover. And know this: you are to be My lover. And all your knowledge then will be knowledge of My Love... no resisting... no describing...

See SUFISM.

Faqīr (lit. "a poor man", pl. *fuqarā'*). A Sufi or initiate in a Sufi order (*ṭarīqah*: plural *ṭuruq*). The term "Sufi" is properly reserved for one who has reached the end of the spiritual path; "the Sufi is not created" (*aṣ-Sūfī lam yukhlaq*) according to the saying. The origin of this use of the word *faqīr* is found in the Koran (47:38): "God is the Rich and you are the poor (*fuqarā'*)."

The word *faqīr* means to aspire to spiritual poverty or detachment (*faqr*, "poverty") which is a *vacare deo*, an emptying of the soul for God. (Cf. Matthew 5:3: "Blessed are the poor in spirit: for theirs is the kingdom of heaven.") In the Near East the Persian word *darwīsh* (dervish), with the same literal meaning, is often used in place of *faqīr*.

Al-Ḥujwīrī said:

> It is not, however, the quantity of money that makes the moneyed man. No one who recognizes poverty as better than money is a moneyed man, though he be a king; and a

man who does not believe in poverty is a moneyed man, however poor he is.

To many in the West the word in its form *fakir* has come to mean a public performer of stunts or magic, which is a deformation of its true meaning. *See* FAQR; MUTABĀRIKUN; SĀLIK; SUFISM.

Faqr (lit. "poverty"). Poverty, both material and spiritual. In the context of religion and especially mysticism, the idea and the word are very important. This is the virtue of spiritual poverty, detachment, and an emptiness making way for God's presence. It is the great spiritual virtue of the Prophet in relation to God. Among the mystics *faqr* is the central virtue, emblematic of all the virtues. On the one hand the Koran states: "and surely Remembrance of God is greatest" (*wa-l-dhikru-Llāhi akbar*); on the other, the Sufis say: "without *faqr* ("spiritual poverty") there is no *dhikr*" ("Remembrance" or "Invocation of God", the central act in the spiritual method of the Sufis).

Jesus says in Matthew 5:3: "Blessed are the poor in spirit: for theirs is the kingdom of heaven." *Faqr* is also the emptiness and removal of obstacles to theophany in the Biblical formulation in Isaiah and Matthew: "The voice of one crying in the wilderness, Prepare ye the way of the Lord, make his paths straight" (Matthew 3:3). A comparison may also be made, in another sense, to the doctrine of *kenosis* (Gr. "emptying", from *kenos*, "empty"); the "emptying" of self by Jesus, or the emptying of one nature in order to take on another (Phil. 2:7). *See* FAQĪR; IBN al-WAQT; IḤSĀN; SUFISM.

Fair, *see* 'UKĀẒ.

al-Fārābī, Abū Naṣr Muḥammad ibn Tarkhān (c. *257-339*/870-950). A philosopher of the Islamic School, which integrates the doctrines of Plato and Aristotle into a single point of view. In Europe he was called al-Farabius (and also Avenasser). Among the Muslims he was called *al-mu'allim ath-thāni*, "the second teacher", after Aristotle, whose works had become available in Arabic thanks to translations made at the Academy of the Caliph al-Ma'mūn in Baghdad.

Al-Fārābī was of Turkish origin and was born in Turkestan; he studied in Baghdad, also traveled in Syria and Egypt, and taught in Aleppo where he carried on his studies thanks to a pension he received from the Sultan. He died in Damascus. Some of his works on Aristotle were translated into Latin in the Middle Ages; a universal thinker, he exerted a great influence on European thought. The philosopher-physician Ibn Sīnā credited al-Fārābī with giving him the first keys that opened the way to his understanding Aristotle.

Al-Fārābī, like al-Kindī, and virtually all Muslim philosophers, also drew upon Neoplatonism for his metaphysics; and he developed al-Kindī's ideas further. Al-Farābī made several distinctions regarding the Intellect (the extension of Being into the centre of man). He divided the Intellect into:

1. The "active Intellect" (*al-'aql al-fā'il*; "intellectus agens"), which is the *nous* of Plotinus and the *logos* of philosophy, or the "world of ideas" of Plato.

2. The "potential Intellect" (*al-'aql al-hayūlānī*; "Intellectus in potentia"), the latent capacity to acquire eternal truths which subsist in the "active Intellect".

3. The "acquired Intellect" (*al-'aql al-mustafād*; "Intellectus acquisitus"), learned knowledge.

Al-Farābī developed the terminology of Arab scholasticism by drawing upon the Koran, a terminology that was to be adapted into Latin and later adapted by St. Thomas Aquinas. Al-Farābī devised terms for necessary and contingent Being, act and potency, substance and accident, essence and existence, matter and form.

Al-Farābī also adapted the theories of Plato's *Republic* in his *Risālah fī Arā' Ahl al-Madīnah al-faḍīlah* and his *al-Siyyāsah al-Madaniyyah* ("Statecraft") but, naturally, as a Muslim, saw the ideal state in the past, and in *al-madīnah al-faḍīlah* ("the virtuous city") he assigned to revelation the same role as Plato did to Poetry, while the perfect rule was that of the Prophet himself. He was himself a musician, a flute-player, and wrote an influential work on Music, *Kitāb al-Musīqa*, in which he drew analogies between music and mathematics. *See* BEING; al-KINDĪ; PHILOSOPHY.

Farā'iḍī Movement (often written *Farā'izī*). A political and religious reformist movement founded in Bengal at the beginning of the 19th century by Sharī'at Allāh (d. 1840), and developed by his son Dūdhū Mīyān. It operated as a secret society of the Muslim peasantry and resisted the oppression of the *zamindars* or landowners and fomented uprisings. Its founder had lived a considerable time in Arabia and seems to have been inspired by Wahhābīsm. Extirpating Hindu influence from Islam in

India was one of its guiding principles and it exhibited the kind of Machiavellian pragmatism and willingness to use coercion that characterized a number of movements then and since that used Islam as the vehicle for acquiring political power. The Farā'iḍī movement declined after the death of the founder's son around 1860.

Faraqlīṭ. Arabic rendering of the word "Paraclete", from John 16:7: "... And I will send you the Paraclete." This is understood by Muslims to mean the Prophet. The word "Paraclete" recalls the Arabic word *faraqa*, "to distinguish" (between truth and unreality); thus a symbolic (not an etymological) meaning of "distinguisher" has been attributed to the word *faraqlīt*. (The practice of assigning or discovering symbolic etymologies is common in all traditional thinking. It assumes that any word has meaning in its very "form" as sound, even if the word comes from a completely foreign language. Traditional thinking looks upon this form or appearance, and its resemblance to known words, not as being arbitrary, but rather as a providential expression of the word's true sense. Thus, traditional etymology does not concern itself with the history of a word, and analysis into its "causal" origins, but takes it as it appears and sees in it something like a "revelation". It seeks to recognize a resonance of thought in the immediate shape of the word. The usefulness of this kind of interpretation depends upon how much intuition and understanding is brought to it by the interpreter. The process mimics the development of language itself. In India, this kind of symbolical, sometimes mystical, "etymological" interpretation is called, in Sanskrit, *nirukta*.

There is an analogy between this sense of *Faraqlīṭ* and a name given to the Koran: the *Furqan*, which means "the Criterion", or "the Distinction" — "between truth and falsehood". *See* BIBLE.

Farāmūsh Khāneh. A secret society founded in Teheran in the middle of the 19th century. Because it sounds like the Persian word for forgetting, this has been called the "house of forgetfulness" but, in fact, it was a Masonic lodge (Freemasonry is *faramāsūniyyah* from the French *Franc-Maçon*; the plural of freemasons is *farāmūsh*). In 1824 James Morier put these words into the mouth of the Mujtahid of Qum: "True Mussulmans always recognize each other in the same manner, as I have heard to be the case among a sect of the Franks, called *Faranooshi* (so the Persians call Freemasons, about whom they are very inquisitive), who by a word, a look, or a touch, will discover one another even among thousands."

The Farāmūsh Khāneh was founded by Mirza Malkom Khān (1833-1908), a Perso-Armenian journalist, adventurer-entrepreneur, and charlatan. This lodge, unlike subsequent ones, may not have had any formal connection with any European lodge and was abolished by royal decree in 1861. The Grand Master was to be the monarch (as is the case of Freemasonry in Sweden) and the direction was to lie in the hands of Qājār princes, but Malkom Khān wanted to use the lodge for modernist reform and for his own purposes.

Masonic lodges exist throughout the Islamic world today. In Israel a Masonic lodge may include Jews, Muslims, and Christians, reminiscent of the way that Templars and Ismā'īlīs met in their day. The Masonic notion of the "Great Architect of the Universe" actually originated in Iran in an apocalyptical doctrine where the *Ban* or "Great Architect" prepared a grave to imprison the powers of darkness after the destruction of the universe in a fire lasting 1,468 years. Secret Societies and Masonic Lodges flourished in Islamic countries at the end of the 19th century as places where the members could promote social progress in emulation of Europe.

Farasu'n-nawba, *see* SENTRY HORSE.

al-Farazdaq (d. *115*/733). A poet who had satirical contests (*naqa'id*) with another poet, Jarir.

Farḍ The obligations God places upon man, such as witnessing to the truth, prayer, fasting, and so on. In most schools of law the term is synonymous with *wājib* ("duty"). However, the Ḥanafīs draw a distinction between *farḍ* and *wājib*. For them *farḍ* is a Divinely instituted obligation whose omission is sin, and *wājib* is an obligation imposed by law, thus indirectly; in this case the omission of what is *wājib* may not necessarily be sin.

A further distinction is made by the *sharī'ah* in general regarding *farḍ* itself: there is *farḍ al-'ayn*, or essential obligation which is incumbent upon all, and *farḍ al-kifāyah*, an obligation which is acquitted in the name of all, as long as it is performed by some. Obligations such as visiting the sick, returning a greeting, fighting holy war, assisting in a funeral procession, are fulfilled in regards of those confronted with the duty as long as a minimum, a specified sufficient number of respondents according to the case, fulfill them. *Farḍ* is one of the categories (*aḥkām*) into which all actions fall. *See* AḤKĀM; ḤARĀM.

Fard (lit. "solitary"; pl. *afrād*). The esoteric possibility exists that a man be illumined spontaneously with a transcendent spiritual truth, without following a path or a spiritual master. Such a "solitary" (*fard*) may not even be affiliated to a particular revealed religion. If the *fard* is outside a tradition, the personal "revelation" is, so to speak, not transmissible, being individual and not destined for a collectivity.

If the *fard* is within a tradition and his illumination is the fulfillment of that tradition's possibilities of inner realisation, it is nonetheless unlikely that it can be taught in its fullness to others, although the person is certainly a witness to the truth. Since the "solitary" has followed no specific way and used no spiritual means to obtain it, his illumination, which is often sudden, remains personal. A *fard* is the recipient of an exceptional destiny, which can only occur in extraordinary circumstances, usually where normal access to revelations and teachings is prevented.

The doctrine of the *fard* is analogous to the Catholic doctrine of spontaneous baptism, or baptism by the Holy Ghost, without human intermediary. *See* al-KHIḌR; SHAYKH.

Fār(i)sī (from Fars, a region of Persia). Persian; the language, and the derived adjective.

Fast (Ar. *Ṣawm*). The Prophet recommended fasting as a spiritual discipline. It was taken up by the early Muslims so enthusiastically that finally the Prophet had to curtail it because excessive fasting by the Companions in Medinah was making them physically weak. In addition to the fasting of the month of Ramaḍān from dawn to sunset, there are many other optional fast days in the Islamic calendar. Some occur regularly every month, and some are scattered through the year. These fast days are Sunnah, or the example set by the Prophet. The Prophet said: "He is not a good Muslim who eats his fill and leaves his neighbor hungry."

Fasting may be undertaken as a penance, for breaking an oath, and the like, and as a substitute for some other obligation. At first, fasting on the day of 'Āshūrā' was obligatory but, with the institution of Ramaḍān, it became only voluntary. *See* RAMAḌĀN.

Fatalism, *see* MAKTUB; QADARIYYAH; KISMET.

Fatawa 'Alamgīriyyah. A collection of *fatāwā* (sing. *fatwā*), or opinions and legal precedents made by jurists in the Moghul empire. It is named after the Emperor 'Alamgīr in whose reign the collection was made in the *12th*/18th century. The *Fatāwā 'Alamgīriyyah* became a fundamental source for Muslim law in India. Also called *al-Fatāwā al-Hindiyyah* ("Indian Jurisprudence").

Fātiḥah (lit. "the opening" chapter and also, by implication, "the victorious" chapter). The *Fātiḥah* is the name of the sūrah which is placed first in the Koran, although the first sūrah to be revealed was Sūrah 96, named *Iqra'* ("recite"). The *Fātiḥah* is the verse of the Koran which is recited in each standing station of the canonical prayer (*ṣalāh*). The *Fātiḥah* — along with a minimum of twelve Koranic verses, including Sūrah 112, named *al-Ikhlāṣ* ("Purity") — is the required minimum that every Muslim must memorize in Arabic. The *Fātiḥah* is often called *as-saba'ah al-mathani* (the "seven oft-repeated verses").

The *Fātiḥah* is the essence of the Koran and sums up man's relation to God.

Bismi 'Llāhi-r-Raḥmāni-r-Raḥīm
In the name of God, the Merciful,
the Compassionate
al-Ḥamdu li-Llāhi Rabbi-l-'Ālamīn
Praise to God Lord of the Worlds
ar-Raḥmāni-r-Raḥīm
he Merciful, the Compassionate
Maliki yawmi-d-dīn
King of the Day of Judgement
Iyyāka na'budu wa iyyāka nasta'īn
You alone we worship, you alone we beseech
Ihdinā-ṣ-ṣirāṭa-l-mustaqīm
Lead us in the straight path
sirāṭa-lladhīna 'an'amta 'alayhim
The path of those upon whom is your grace
Ghayri-l-maghḍūbi 'alayhim
Not of those upon whom is your wrath
wa lā-d-ḍāllīn
nor the astray.
Āmīn.
Amen.

The *Fātiḥah* is remarkably similar to the Paternoster, and its components are also echoed, word for word, in Zoroastrian prayers in Pahlavī which were extant in the 4th century.

Apart from its central place in the canonical, or ritual, prayer, the *Fātiḥah* is frequently recited as part of a *du'ā'*, or individual and spontaneous prayer. It is also recited individually or in a group upon marriage, on visiting a holy place, at a funeral, or in any number of circumstances in which a *du'ā'* prayer is appropriate. The *Fātiḥah* is always concluded by saying *āmīn* ("Amen").

Fāṭimah. One of the three daughters of the Prophet, whose mother was Khadījah, the Prophet's first wife. The Prophet commended Fāṭimah's character, calling her one of the four exemplary women that he extolled in history, and she is usually referred to as *Fāṭimah az-zahrā'* ("Fāṭimah the resplendent").

She married the Prophet's cousin 'Alī ibn Abī Ṭālib, who became the fourth Caliph; and their sons Ḥasan and Ḥusayn are the ancestors of the *sharīfs*, the descendants of the Prophet. For the Shī'ites, certain descendants of 'Alī and Fāṭimah through the line of Ḥusayn are Imāms, in the special Shī'ite sense of the term, which is that of divinely empowered spiritual leaders. A third son of 'Alī and Fāṭimah, Muḥsin, died in infancy.

Fāṭimah died six months after the Prophet's death and is buried in the *al-Baqī'* cemetery in Medinah. (A sepulchre called Fāṭimah's Tomb is located near the tomb of the Prophet in the Prophet's mosque. Some, notably Shī'ites, believe this sepulchre to hold her body, but that is unlikely, despite the name, and it is far more probable that the remains are actually in the nearby *al-Baqī'* cemetery.) She is held in great reverence by the Sunnīs as well as by the Shī'ites. *See* AHL al-KISĀ'I; MUḤAMMAD; SHARĪF.

Fāṭimids (*297-567*/909-1171). The Ismā'īlī dynasty which founded Cairo as its capital in *358*/969, and which ruled an empire extending from Palestine to Tunisia. The Fāṭimid rulers called themselves Caliphs, thus laying claim to supreme political and spiritual authority in Islam in rivalry to the 'Abbāsids of Baghdad. Their name, Fāṭimid, represents a claim to be descended from the Prophet through his daughter Fāṭimah, and her husband 'Alī, the Prophet's cousin; but this claim has been frequently questioned. Contemporaries of the Fāṭimids repudiated it by impugning the authenticity of the Fāṭimid genealogy in a manifesto formulated in Baghdad in *402*/1011 by 'Alīds and jurists; historians, ancient and modern, have largely concurred in this repudiation. The name *al-Fāṭimiyyūn* was first used by a Qarmaṭī tribe, a clan of the Kalb, the Banu-l-Aṣbagh in the Syrian desert when led by Ḥusayn ibn Zikrawayh against the 'Abbāsids around *290*/903, and was later adopted by 'Ubayd Allāh.

The Fāṭimids were Ismā'īlīs, direct descendants of the early Shī'ites; from whom the Twelve-Imām Shī'ites are an offshoot. Other rival Shī'ite groups existed or had existed, including those who rallied around a descendant of 'Alī by another wife known as "al-Ḥanafiyyah", whose son, Muḥammad ibn al-Ḥanafiyyah became the Imām of this sect. The choice of the name "Fāṭimid" may reflect the desire to establish a clear distinction between themselves and other Shī'ites of the Ḥanafiyyah line, or more likely, an attempt to identify Fāṭimah with a female divinity from the pantheon of the Seveners and pre-Islamic Gnostic religions such as the "Mother of the Living".

Propaganda disseminated in North Africa made much of a prophecy contained in the Ḥadīth to the effect that a time would come in which "the Sun would rise in the West". But this "Ḥadīth" and those concerning the Mahdī were clearly invented for this very purpose. Indeed, the claim was rather a challenge to the authority of Islam because the Koran says:

> Bethink thee of him who had an argument
> with Abraham about his Lord,
> because Allah had given him the kingdom;
> how, when Abraham had said:
> My Lord is He Who giveth life
> and causeth death,
> he answered: I give life and cause death.
> Abraham said:
> Lo! Allah causeth the sun to rise in the East
> so do thou cause it to come up from the West.
> Thus was the disbeliever abashed.
> And Allah guideth not wrongdoing folk.

A singularly successful *dā'i*, or propagandist, of the Ismā'īlī organisation, Abū 'Abd Allāh Ḥusayn, also called ash-Shī'ī ("the Shī'ite"), established the dynasty. He was first sent on a mission from Baṣrah in 'Irāq to Yemen and then to North Africa, where he persuaded the Ketama Berbers to accept his chief, 'Ubayd Allāh, as their religious and political leader. The Berbers of North Africa had in many instances been Christian and, and in particular, Manichean before the recent spread of Islam; it is known that Gnostic sects were active among them, as an expression of resistance to the domination of Rome. In the *2nd*/8th century, at least one of the chiefs, the *Archegos*, of the Manichean church at its seat at Madā'in (Ctesiphon-Seleucia) near Baghdad, originally came from North Africa. It is very possible that ash-Shī'ī's remarkable success in converting the Berbers to follow 'Ubayd Allāh (also called 'Abd Allāh and Sa'īd al-Khayr) was due to the fact that he was calling them to a contemporary version of their old beliefs, now clothed in the form of the newly dominant religion. Perhaps the link between the two was even more direct with 'Ubayd Allāh, already the leader of an existing sect in North Africa, simply returning or settling down again among his followers. To this effect, Ibn Khaldūn said in his history, that the Berbers to whom the missionaries addressed themselves had a *baṭini*, or esoteric religion.

Yet, there is an Ismā'īlī tradition among the Druzes, and in the *Ghāyat al-Mawālid* by al-Khaṭṭab ibn Ḥasan al-Hamadānī, a Yemenī *dā'i* (d.*533*/1138), quoted by Bernard Lewis, that 'Ubayd Allāh was not himself the real Imām, but *Imām mustawda'*, a "trustee" or representative of the real Imām; therefore, it could well be that the real leader remained in the East, whence the propogandists had come, and that the real Imām, that is, the *Imām mustaqarr* ("permanent Imām") only settled in North Africa after his representatives had paved the way for him and assured a smooth transition of the seat of power. Thus the second Fāṭimid Sultan, al-Qā'im, as Imām mustaqarr, would be that real leader who took over after 'Ubayd Allāh died in *322*/934, although he may have arrived in North Africa already some time before. There was a Mesopotamian institution: the substitute king, put upon the throne when "omens were exceptionally sombre" as seen in the story of Irra-imitti who put a gardener, Enlil-bāni on his throne to preserve the dynasty. (Only Enlil-bāni did not relinquish the throne as he was supposed to and instead carried on!)

The 'Alīd declaration of *402*/1011 said that the Fāṭimids were descended from Daisan, that is, Bardesanes, a philosopher who had lived near Ḥarrān. This could not mean that they were his physical, but rather his intellectual, descendants. Now Bardesanes was a forerunner of Mani, and was recognized as such by the Arab scholars of the *5th*/11th century, as he is by scholars today. In any event, the Persian historian al-Juwayni (d. *682*/1283) affirmed that the Ismā'īlīs were *Mājūs*, and al-Ḥujwīrī (d. *469*/1077), in the *Kashf al-Maḥjūb*, said this specifically of the Fāṭimids. (For the Muslims, *Mājūs* meant not only Zoroastrianism but also the related Iranian religions and their variants.)

Ash-Shī'ī's propaganda claimed that 'Ubayd Allāh was the *Mahdī*, the Divinely guided leader for the end of time. When, however, 'Ubayd Allāh went to Morocco, by stages, from Salāmiyyah in Syria, he was arrested in *292*/905 by the Aghlabid rulers on behalf of the 'Abbāsid Caliphs of Baghdad and imprisoned in Sijilmassa, in present-day Morocco. By *296*/909 ash-Shī'ī's position had become so strong that he was able to free 'Ubayd Allāh, who then took over the leadership and soon had ash-Shī'ī put to death for his troubles.

'Ubayd Allāh then built himself a capital called al-Mahdīyyah in Ifrīqiyā (Tunisia); in *358*/969 the general Jawhar conquered Egypt in the name of the Fāṭimid ruler al-Mu'izz li-Dīni-Llāh and founded Cairo (*al-Qahirah*), which became the new capital with the cryptic name "*The Victorious* [*city*] *of the Exalter of the Divine Religion*".

From here the Empire grew to include Palestine, while Ismā'īlī propaganda was extended even further through a secret network of agitators. The reign of the Fāṭimid al-Ḥākim (d. *411*/1021) was notable for his erratic, if not actually insane, behavior. (It has been argued that his behavior was rational if understood in the light of metaphysical doctrinal beliefs, the same way Soviet behavior was rational, according to their lights, in the last days when they suddenly revoked all 50, 100, and higher rubles notes to prevent them from being used by a "shadow economy".) He had the church of the Holy Sepulchre in Jerusalem destroyed — one of the events which led to the Crusades — and he had himself publicly declared to be God — a claim he was obliged by the resultant uproar to retract. A similar claim, perhaps less publicly, had been made for al-Mu'izz, the seventh Fāṭimid Imām according to his alleged descent from Muḥammad ibn Ismā'īl, the son of Ja'far aṣ-Ṣādiq. The Fāṭimid Caliphs were the Imāms of the Ismā'īlīs. In their doctrines the Imām is a Divine hypostasis. In the case of al-Ḥākim his supporters had gone too far in making public, to his Sunnī subjects in Egypt, the deepest tenets of the sect. In the Levant, however, successful propagandizing on his behalf among remote Ismā'īlī groups by a Turk called Darazī led to the creation of the Druzes.

In *487*/1094 a coup by the general of the armies, al-Afḍal Shāhinshāh (son of the general Badr al-Jamālī, an Armenian who came to Cairo after the Byzantine defeat at Manzikert, and who built the present walls and gates of Cairo for the Fāṭimids) put the younger heir, al-Musta'lī, on the throne. Badr al-Jamālī had married his daughter to al-Musta'lī in order to consolidate power for himself. Nizār, the eldest son, was put into prison, where he died; his followers attributed to him a son and even a grandson in order that his spiritual succession be kept alive; but as far as the Musta'līs (the followers of al-Musta'lī) are concerned, if there were a son and grandson, these also died in prison.

This disruption of the succession went against the religious expectations of the committed Ismā'īlīs in that the function of Imām was more or less Divine. Thus the succession of al-Musta'lī in *487*/1094, against the superior claims of his elder brother Nizār, confounded many Ismā'īlīs and occasioned a schism. A Persian Ismā'īlī named Ḥasan-i aṣ-Ṣabbāḥ had come to Cairo; upon his return to Persia he spread propaganda in the name of the expected Imām, Nizār. The sudden change of power in Egypt left aṣ-Ṣabbāḥ, already committed to promoting Nizār, little choice but to repudiate al-Musta'lī. It is through Ḥasan-i aṣ-Ṣabbāḥ that a Nizārī branch of Ismā'īlīs survived and flourished. The followers of aṣ-Ṣabbāḥ took over the fortress of Alamūt in northern Persia, probably already in Ismā'īlī hands, as the region had long been a stronghold of sects of ancient Iranian filiation.

This fortress became the Nizārī centre of power. In Medieval Europe these Nizārī Ismā'īlīs were called the Assassins, a name they had been given by the Crusaders. In the East they were known by many different names including *Ta'līmiyyah* ("the people of the teaching"), and by this name the theologian al-Ghazālī (d. *505*/1111) disputed their religious ideas.

This split created the Nizārī and the Musta'lī branches of the Ismā'īlīs. The son of al-Musta'lī, al-Āmir, succeeded his father as ruler in Egypt as an infant, and came first under the tutelage of al-Afḍal. Later, having had al-Afḍal put to death (*515*/1121), al-Āmir was himself assassinated (*525*/1130). This time the followers of al-Āmir claimed that he had a son who would have inherited and perpetuated the spiritual function in that line; this putative son was called aṭ-Ṭayyib, and the Musta'lī faction believe that there exist descendants of aṭ-Ṭayyib living in secret, or that, like the Hidden Imām of the Twelve-Imām Shī'ites, and al-Ḥākim for the Druzes, aṭ-Ṭayyib is alive in a principial state from which he will return. As far as the others were concerned, the putative son, aṭ-Ṭayyib, was assassinated along with his father. The assassination of al-Amīr was carried out by Nizārīs presumably under the orders of Alamūt in Persia.

After the death of al-Āmir, Ismā'īlism in Egypt disintegrated. There it had been the arcane religion of the ruling class and had not been shared by the majority of subjects who were Sunnī. Smaller and smaller groups followed different Imāms in defiance of the Fāṭimid ruler's claims. The army raised a son of the Armenian al-Afḍal ibn Badr al-Jamal to the Vizierate. This son Abū 'Alī Kutayfāt, had survived earlier reprisals as being too sickly; now he deposed the Fāṭimid dynasty, adopted his father's name of al-Afḍal, and made Twelve Imām Shī'ism the state religion, ruling in the name of the Twelfth Imām with himself as *nā'ib* or representative. He also issued coins in the name of the Twelfth Imām. He himself was deposed one year ten days later, in December of 1131. The Fāṭimids returned with a non-linear descendant as Imām-Caliph, named al-Ḥāfiẓ li-Din Allāh. After 1149, there were three more: aẓ-Ẓafir (*544-549*/1149-1154), al-Fā'iz (*549-555*/1154-1160) and al-'Āḍid (*555-567*/1160-1171). By *567*/1171 the Fāṭimids had lost power, and Saladin had the Khutbah read in the name of the reigning 'Abbāsid Caliph al-Mustaḍī'.

Nevertheless, the Fāṭimids had presided over an empire noted for its prosperity and cultural achievements. Jews played an important rôle in their Empire, as they did in Spain. At their high-point the Fāṭimids had posed a serious ideological threat to the 'Abbāsid Empire and called forth the Sunnī reaffirmation embodied in the Seljūqs. The Fāṭimids founded the renowned al-Azhar University, today the most venerable in the Islamic world. Their successors were the Sunnī Ayyūbid dynasty founded by Saladin. Thereupon the Ismā'īlīs virtually disappeared from Egypt, but small groups survived in Syria, Persia, and Central Asia raising havoc out of proportion to their numbers until the coming of the Mongols who destroyed Alamut in 1256; and in obscurity afterwards; the sect later flourished in India. The Fāṭimids, faithful to their origins, brought back the use of Kufic script for monumental writing. The Fāṭimid Caliphs-Imāms are:

297/909	'Ubayd Allāh al-Mahdī
322/934	al-Qā'im
334/946	al-Manṣūr
341/953	al-Mu'izz li Dīn-i Allāh
365/975	al-'Azīz
386/996	al-Ḥākim
411/1021	aẓ-Ẓāhir
427/1036	al-Mustanṣir
487/1094	al-Musta'lī
495/1101	al-Āmir

In *524*/1130 the Caliph al-Āmir was assassinated by Nizārī agents. There followed a Regency, and Abū 'Alī Kutayfāt ibn al-Afḍal ibn Badr Jamal came to power. He ruled in the name of the Twelve Imām Shī'ite Hidden Imām. A year later came the Restoration; the previous Regent, 'Abd al-Majīd al-Ḥāfiẓ became:

525/1131	al-Ḥāfiẓ li-Dīn Allāh
544/1149	aẓ-Ẓāfir
549/1154	al-Fā'iz
555-567/1160-71	al-'Āḍid

The end of Fāṭimid rule in Egypt. *See* ASSASSINS; DRUZES; KŪFAH; ISMĀ'ĪLĪS; MAHDĪ; QARMAṬĪS; SEVENERS; 'UBAYD ALLĀH.

Fatrah (lit. "spiritual lassitude", "a lapse"). 1. The name given to a period of time between two Prophets, for example, the six centuries between Jesus and Muḥammad.

2. A period in the Prophet's life when no revelations descended upon him, causing him despair.

Fatwā. A published opinion or decision regarding religious doctrine or law made by a recognized authority, often called a mufti. Collections of such decisions, such as the *Fatāwā 'Alamgīriyyah*, a collection made in India under the Moghul Empire, form a code of precedents which guide Judges in the exercise of the law. *See* SHARĪ'AH.

Feddayin, *see* FIDYAH.

Festivals, *see* 'ĀSHŪRĀ'; CALENDAR; 'ĪD al-AḌḤĀ; 'ĪD al-FIṬR; 'ĪD al-GHADIR; LAYLAT al-BARA'AH; LAYLAT al-QADR, MAWLID an-NABĪ; MUḤARRAM; NAW ROZ; RAMAḌĀN.

Fez. One of the "imperial cities", or former capitals, of Morocco. The Merinid dynasty (*592-956*/1196-1549) ruled from Fez. The city was founded by Mawlay Idris II in *193*/809, and grew with influxes of emigrants from Cordova (who created the Andalusian quarter), and from Kairouan (creating the Qarawiyyīn quarter). Fez became a centre of culture and learning when the Qarawiyyīn university-mosque was founded, the gift of a wealthy woman. The two quarters, on either banks of the river, were separate rival cities until Yusūf ibn Tashfin, after 1075, had their walls destroyed and replaced by a single rempart which enclosed them both. The Merinid Abū Yusūf in 1276 founded New Fez, or Fez Jdid, a military and administrative city less then a kilometer away from the old medinah.

The old city of Fez, with its walls, gates, palaces, souks, *funduqs*, *madrasahs*, and mosques, is still largely intact, constituting an extraordinary living heritage. The narrow streets and the hilly site make motor traffic impossible in most of the old town. The crafts have not completely disappeared (although in 2006 the formerly large Guild of combmakers was reduced to one man) and Fez is still a singularly remarkable example of a large city which has kept the aspect of a medieval town. Until recently, the countryside began abruptly at the walls of the old city. This was the typical stamp of the ancient city, the distinction, so clear in the traditional mind, of the civilized world as only a small island surrounded by the vast natural world of God's making.

In addition to the Andalusian and Qarawiyyīn mosques (the latter is one of the largest in the world and can accommodate some 10,000 worshipers), there are several Madrasahs or schools of higher learning. These are now monuments, no longer used as schools, although they are still places of prayer. The most famous are the *'Aṭṭārīn*, the "perfumers' madrasah" built by that guild, and the *Abū-l-Ḥasan* built by a Sultan, who when presented with the exorbitant bill for its construction, was taken aback, thought a moment and then paraphrased an old Arabic poem: "What matters the expense as long as it is beautiful; too costly rings not true for what pleases the eye."

Fez has a rich tradition of many Saints and scholars that have walked its streets, and the fragrance of sanctity makes Fez a goal of pilgrimage. At the centre of the city is the tomb of the founder, Mawlay Idris II, a mosque with a roof of green Fez tiles. This is one of the most important sanctuaries in Morocco. Near the city is the *Jabal Zalāgh* where the great Abū Madyan, as an impoverished young man, would go and pray at night. His life, and that of others who gave the city its reputation, is re counted in the collection of the lives of Saints of Fez called the *Ṣalawāt al-Anfus.*

Fidā'ī (lit. "man of sacrifice"). Someone who gives up his life for a cause; origin of the word *fidā'iyūn. See* FIDYAH.

Fidā'iyūn *see* FIDYAH.

Fidyah (lit. "expiation by sacrifice", "redemption"). The expiation of faults, spiritual errors, or other shortcomings by some such means as offering a sacrifice, fasting or feeding the poor (cf. Koran 2:192). Fidyah can also mean to give up one's life for a cause; the word *fidā'iyūn* ("men of sacrifice") has its root in this. *See* FIDA'I.

Fihrist *see* an-NADĪM.

Fiqh. Jurisprudence. The science which deals with the observance of rituals, the principles of the Five Pillars, and social legislation. There are four schools of fiqh, known as the four Sunnī Schools of Law (Ar. *madhhab*, pl. *madhāhib*). In addition, the Shī'ites and the Khārijites have their own schools. Each school has its fundamental written treatises. Someone who is versed in *fiqh* is called a *faqīh. See* SCHOOLS of LAW; SHARĪ'AH.

al-Fiqh al-Akbar (lit. "the greatest or supreme Canon Law"). At one time, the term (*al-Fiqh al-Akbar*) meant theology before the development of theology (*kalām*) as such. *Al-Fiqh al-Akbar* is also the name of several creeds of which the following, by Abū Ḥanīfah (d. *150*/767), is the most famous.

1. We do not consider anyone to be an infidel on account of sin; nor do we deny his faith.
2. We enjoin what is just and prohibit what is evil.
3. What reaches you could not possibly have missed you; and what misses you could not possibly have reached you.
4. We disavow none of the Companions of the Messenger of God; nor do we adhere to any of them exclusively.
5. We leave the question of 'Uthmān and 'Alī to God, who knows the secret and hidden things.
6. Insight in matters of religion is better than insight in matters of knowledge and law.
7. Difference of opinion in the Community is a token of Divine mercy.
8. Who believes all that he is bound to believe except that he says, I do not know whether Moses and Jesus (Peace be upon them) do or do not belong to the Messengers, is an infidel.
9. Who says I do not know whether God is in heaven or on earth is an infidel.
10. Who says I do not know about punishment in the tomb, belongs to the sect of *Jahmites* who go to perdition.

The first article above is a specific refutation of the doctrine of the Khārijites concerning sin, and other articles are responses to the assertions of various sects. The *al-Fiqh al-Akbar* is an important milestone in the development of theology. Statements one to seven succinctly give a wide definition of who is a Muslim; statements eight to ten draw a line and say, in effect, that wide as the definition may be, there is nonetheless a limit beyond which lies error.

This affirmation of a consensus marked the end of a first period of theological turmoil during which different opinions emerged as completely hostile one to another. The Khārijites set an example when they asserted the apostasy of all who did not share their opinion. In the early phase of Islam, each opinion could be taken as excluding the others to such a degree that the holders of another point of view were readily called, if not apostates, then heretics. The *al-Fiqh al-Akbar* of Abū Ḥanīfah marked a new phase in theological polemics by establishing the principle that divergences of belief, within limits, are possible and acceptable. In other words, Islam is here defined as large enough to hold a variety of views, and that rigid homogeneity is not essential to orthodoxy. *See* CREEDS; KALĀM; KHĀRIJITES.

Firāsah. Intuitions about the hidden nature of things, events, and people. The capacity for *firāsah* may be a spontaneous gift in someone, or the result of heightened awareness resulting from spiritual discipline.

Ibn 'Aṭa'Allāh says in his *Ḥikam*:

> Sometimes He reveals to you the invisible domain of His Realm but veils you from knowing the secrets of servants.
>
> Whoever gets to know the secrets of servants without patterning himself on the divine mercifulness (*ar-raḥmah al-ilāhiyyah*), finds his knowledge a tribulation (*fitnah*) and a cause for drawing evil (*al-wabal*) upon himself.

See KARAMĀT.

Fir'awn, *see* PHARAOH.

Firdaws. A Koranic appellation for one of the paradises deriving either from the Greek *paradeisos* or the Middle Persian *paridaiza* meaning originally an "enclosure" and hence an "enclosed garden". The Greek word *paradeisos* and the English *paradise* also derives from the Persian; the idea of paradise comes from Zoroastrianism in both Christianity and in Islam. *See* al-JANNAH.

Firdawsī (*Abū-l-Qāsim Manṣūr*) (*328-411*/940-1020). The poet, born in Ṭūs, who composed the Persian national epic, the "Book of Kings", (*Shahnameh*), recounting the history of the Persian people from mythic times until the Arab conquest. The poem draws upon the records of Persian history compiled in the times of Anushirvan (Chosroe I) and orally preserved by the old landed families known as *dihqāns*. It also incorporates a thousand couplets written by an earlier poet, Daqiqi.

Abū-l-Qāsim was called "Firdawsī" by the Sultan Maḥmūd of Ghaznah, who said the poet's compositions turned the court into an assembly of paradise (*firdaws*). Firdawsī composed the *Shahnameh*, consisting of 60,000 verses, for this ruler, and, according to tradition, spent thirty-five years on it. Disappointed with his pay, Firdawsī satirized the Sultan, and fled into exile where he composed his poem *Yūsuf and Zulaykha*. He later returned, was reconciled with the Sultan, but died before he could receive his reward: legend says a treasure for him as full payment arrived on the backs of camels at one gate of the city of Ṭūs, as his corpse was brought out for burial through another.

Firmān. An Ottoman or Persian royal rescript. The term is also used for religious messages sent by the Aga Khan to his communities.

Fitfir. The name in Arabic of Potiphar, the great man of Egypt into whose household Joseph (Yūsuf) was sold as a slave. When Joseph was freed from prison after interpreting the Pharaoh's dreams, he assumed Fitfir's office. Because of a simple orthographic confusion the name is sometimes said to be Qitfir.

Fitnah (lit. "rebellion, strife"). Any sedition or rebellion against the rightful ruler is *fitnah*. Widespread *fitnah* is one of the traditional signs of the impending Day of Judgement.

Fiṭrah (lit. "primordial nature"). The primordial norm; a harmony between man, creation, and God, such as existed between God and Adam in the Garden. Islam sees itself as the restoration of the religion of Abraham (*millat Ibrāhīm*), which itself is a re-consecration and a prolongation of the religion of Adam as primordial man after his fall, and reconciliation with God. The concept of *fiṭrah*, the primordial norm, is at once the measure of truth in our actions and being, and at the same time the quality of harmony between ourselves and the cosmos. It corresponds exactly to the Hindu notion of universal *dharma*, or to the Chinese *Tao*. *See* CHILDREN.

Five Divine Presences (Ar. *al-ḥaḍarāt al-ilāhiyyah al-khams*). A metaphysical doctrine of the degrees of reality of which there are different versions. The following schema, according to the terminology of Abū Ṭālib al-Makki (d. *386*/996), is the most systematic: in descending order, the five are: *Hāhūt*, Ipseity, the Godhead, the Essence, Absolute Reality; *Lāhūt*, the Reality of Being, namely, the Divinity or Personal God; *jabarūt*, the world of Angels; *malakūt*, the subtle world; and *nāsūt*, the corporeal, or human world.

The Islamic development of the doctrine was evidently influenced by Neoplatonism. It is found in Plotinus and Dionysus the Areopagite (or writing attributed to him, the so-called pseudo-Dionysus). Equivalent teachings are also found in Hinduism, Taoism, and Buddhism, as well as Catholic scholasticism. Thus it was the theory of reality accepted in Europe by both religion and science into the twentieth century up until the existence of the *malakūt*, the subtle world, called the "ether" in science was challenged by the physics experiment of Michelson and Morley. (There is a collection of articles from successive editions of the Encyclopedia Brittanica which feature the entry "Ether" and show a remarkable evolution of how it was conceived from the 1920s to the 50s.) The theory of the Five Presences was first made explicit, however, in Zoroastrianism where it is the cosmology of creation, and it would seem that other religions adopted it from the Iranians. As a universal metaphysical doctrine it reflects the nature of things as seen from human consciousness, but is no more the creation of human thought than the rings of Saturn are the creation of Galileo.

The doctrine of the Five Divine Presences figures prominently among Sufis of the school of Ibn 'Arabī. However, it is to be found, in one form or another, wherever metaphysical considerations arise. Different versions exist, as in the *Ihyā' 'Ulūm ad-Dīn* ("the Revival of the Religious Sciences") of al-Ghazālī, or in the *al-Insān al-Kāmil* ("the Perfect Man") of 'Abd al-Karīm al-Jīlī.

The name of the first Presence, *Hāhūt*, is derived from the word *Huwa*, or "He" (a Divine Name, the Name of the Essence, *adh-Dhāt*), denoting the Ipseity. The Ipseity is That from which nothing can be taken away and nothing added. It cannot be divided; nothing is outside It; "it is not beautiful on one side and ugly on another"— It is beautiful from all sides — there is no privation in It; of which the Voice in the burning bush said: "I am That I am." Of which Sufism says: *lā ana wa lā anta: hua* "not I and not you: He." The Surah of Sincere Religion (112) defines Ipseity thus:

Say: 'He is God, One,
God, the Everlasting Refuge,
who has not begotten, and has not been begotten,
and equal to Him is not any one.'

This is the Absolute, to which the Name *Allāh* properly belongs. *Hāhūt* is often called "Beyond-Being". Plato, in the *Parmenides*, calls It "the One Who is One". In Vedanta It is *Parabrahman*, or *nirguṇa Brahma* ("Brahma beyond Qualities"). It is *All-Possibility*, non-differentiated and non-determined, indivisibly One, or the Divine Name *al-Aḥad* ("The One"). Because *Hāhūt* is Absolute, and All-Possibility, It is also the Possibility, necessarily, of Its own negation or Its own "limitation". This is the invisible root of manifestation or creation, a "negation" of the Absolute. That is, the Absolute "limits" Itself as Its own Absoluteness requires and thus creates the world, which is apparently "other" than God, a "seeming negation" of the Absolute, nonetheless existing in and of the Absolute. A *Ḥadīth qudsī* ("God speaking through the Prophet") puts it thus: "I was a hidden treasure; I willed to be known, therefore I created the world." The ontological bridge between manifestation (the last three presences), and *Hāhūt* is the differentiation and determination of the latter in the second Divine Presence, *Lāhūt*. The first chapter of the Tao Te Ching says: "Nameless is the origin of Heaven and Earth. The Named is the Mother of All Things ('the myriad creatures')."

Lāhūt: from the word *al-ilāh*, or "Divinity". *Lāhūt* is Being and "Personal God"; or as Plato says: "The One Who Is". In Vedanta, *Lāhūt* is *saguṇa Brahma* ("Brahma Qualified"), or *Īshwara*. In relation to the Absoluteness of *Hāhūt*, this Divine Presence has been called the "relatively" Absolute. "Absolute" because seen from "below", from the point of view of existence, it is not different from the Absolute; "Relative" inasmuch as none of its distinct possibilities are absolute in themselves; they are delimited by other possibilities. Nevertheless, *Lāhūt* is Divine because everything in creation is contained within It, and Its differentiations, while not absolute, are nevertheless "perfect".

The Divine Name *ar-Raḥīm*, "the Compassionate", or the "Mercy-Giving" is a Name of the Qualities (*aṣ-ṣifāt*); it is therefore a Name of Being, or *Lāhūt*. It is act; It bestows mercy; It is event and relationship between God and creature. As one Quality among others It excludes other Names or Qualities and is different from *al-Ghafūr* ("The Forgiver"), and *al-Muntaqim* ("The Avenger"), for example. *Ar-Raḥmān* ("The Merciful One"), on the other hand, is a Name of the Essence (*Hāhūt*); It is God "Merciful in Himself". Yet *ar-Raḥmān*, like *al-Quddūs* ("The Holy One") as a Name of the Essence is inherent in all the Names, even in *al-Mumīt* ("The Slayer"). This reflects the difference between God the Absolute and God as Being. The Names of the Qualities, or of *Lāhūt*, may exclude each other but the Names of the Essence may not.

A polarisation takes place within Being into pure act (determining power) and pure receptivity (and infinitude); Aristotle's *eidos* and *hyle*. The latter word has found its way into Arabic as *al-hayūlā*, with the same meaning of "substance" (also called *al-jawhar*, "the jewel"). Pure receptivity ("substance") accepts determining power (act or "bundles of qualities" — "forms" so to speak, in the abstract, the capacity to define distinct entities). From this union of power or essence (essence on a different level from that of *Hāhūt*) and substance, existence springs forth in the succeeding Presences, and possibilities become manifestation. In denoting this complementarity the Scholastics of Medieval Europe called this essence (on the level of Being) "form"; substance, they called "materia". In Vedanta this polarity is called *Purusha* (for the pole of power) and *Prakriti* (for the pole of receptivity). In Taoism, it is Yang (power) and Yin (receptivity-infinitude). The Koranic terms are *al-qalam al-a'lā* (the "supreme pen") for act or power, and al-lawḥ al-maḥfūẓ ("the inviolate tablet") for universal substance or receptivity.

Many terms are used for this polarity, even within the same tradition, because this complementarity within the First Principle may be viewed in many perspectives. Thus the qalam ("power") seen from a different angle is *al-'aql al-awwal* ("first intellect"), also called *ar-ruḥ al-kullī* ("universal spirit"). The *lawḥ* ("substance") is also *aṭ-ṭabī'ah al-kulliyyah* ("universal nature"), or again, *al-unsūr al-azām* ("the supreme element"). Terms multiply as the complementarity is considered in its refractions from Being down to the macrocosm, and finally to the microcosm, or man himself.

In man, the same complementarity reverberates as male and female, and is also reflected within the individual. The active pole of the individual is *al-'aql al-fā'il*, "the active Intellect", while the pole of receptivity is the *nafs*, or his or her soul. (*See* al-'AQL; NAFS.) The pole of receptivity, universal substance, is also reflected in the microcosm by the physical body, and, in particular, by the female body.

The "structure" of man mirrors superior realities. The individual himself, the content of that structure, a personality with its characteristics and its destiny, is a possibility. But while the individual is a differentiated possibility in the *Lāhūt*, it is undifferentiated in the *Hāhūt*, and thus it is possible to say that beyond the personality there is the Self; and that there is only one Self; and that all individual beings, on every plane of existence are refractions of that One Self.

Lāhūt (sometimes also called *'Alam al-'Izzah*, or "World of Glory"), as the domain of the Names of the Qualities, is Creator in regard to the world, and "Personal" God, or God as "Person", God Who hears prayers, Who slays, Who gives life, Who creates, Who accepts repentance. It should be emphasized that what saves in Islam is the recognition of the Absoluteness of God, *Hāhūt*, and His incomparability; but without God as Creator the world is impossible, and without God as Revealer there is no knowledge.

In confronting the Koranic references to "God's Face", "His Hand", and so forth, which are the traces of Being conceptualized, the solution of Ash'arite theology is acceptance without further inquiry, *bilā kayfa*. Metaphysics, however, cannot be satisfied with such a theologic solution, and must enter into the domain of antinomy, whence the need to recognize that certain contradictions are only apparent in analysis but not in their synthesis, which is on a different plane altogether. *Hāhūt* and *Lāhūt* taken together are the Divinity, or in Vedanta, *Ātman*; that which is below, in the succeeding "Presences", is creation, *al-ḥijāb* (the "veil"), or in Sanskrit, *māyā*. Thus it is within *Lāhūt*, or Being, that the created and uncreated meet. There is a Ḥadīth which says:

> The first thing God created was the pen. He created the tablet and said to the pen: "Write!" And the pen answered: "What shall I write?" He said: "Write My knowledge of My creation till the Day of Resurrection."

The third Presence is the *'ālam al-jabarūt* (the "World of Power"; in Vedanta: *vijñānamaya kosha*). It is also the reality which is called the "Throne" (*al-'arsh*). This is the domain of supraformal or Angelic manifestation, which surrounds and contains formal creation, just as it is itself surrounded by Being, and Being by Beyond-Being. This is already part of creation, but is not subject to the same separative conditions as the sensible world. It is the world of Angels; namely "Powers", "Exemplars", "Archetypes", "Thrones". It is also that of the Paradises of the afterlife, with the exception of the Supreme Paradise, the *jannat adh-dhāt*, or "Garden of the Essence".

The *'ālam al-jabarūt* is the level of the created Intellect, or the created Spirit (in Being the Intellect partakes of the uncreated; Meister Eckhart spoke of "something in the soul which is not created and not creatable, and this is the Intellect"). At the "centre" of every Presence is a juncture which joins the Presence above it, and partakes of its nature.

Without this "juncture" (Ar. *barzakh*), the world would be complete unreality and would not exist. These junctures can be thought of as a vertical axis. This vertical axis, which passes through every state and degree of existence, is symbolized, for example, by the sacred "world" trees of primordial religions, such as Yggdrasil of the Norsemen, and the (non-forbidden) "tree of life" at the centre of the Garden of Eden. In the centre of the *'ālam al-jabarūt*, the world of Angels, is a domain within creation which reflects the uncreated. This "reflection" seen, so to speak, from the Divine point of view, is an Angel, himself called *Rūḥ* or "Spirit" (Koran 78:38), who is so great that when the Angels stand arrayed, the *Rūḥ* takes up one row unto himself. The Angel *Rūḥ* corresponds to the Metatron of Jewish mystical metaphysics, and both probably derive from Spenta Mainyu of Zoroastrianism.

The *'ālam al-jabarūt* is thus the created aspect of the *rasūl* ("Messenger of God"), and the created reality of Adam, "true man" or the *al-Insān al-Kāmil*, "the universal", or "perfect man". (The subtle and material worlds correspond to the limitations of ordinary thought and ordinary imagination; the active state of the *al-insān al-Kāmil* is precisely not limited to these, nor, however, is it limited to the *'ālam al-jabarūt*, since in the Koran man is superior to the Angels — whom God instructs to bow to Adam.) (*See* ANGELS.)

The fourth Presence is the *'ālam al-malakūt*, the "World of the Dominion", the subtle, or animic, world. (In Vedanta: *sukshma sharīra*). This is the world of *jinn*, creatures who possess form like man, some of whom incarnate the *'aql* (Intellect) just as man does, and thus possess a "central state". They are therefore capable of Divine knowledge, and upon pain of damnation are compelled to integrate themselves consciously and actively with the superior Presences that confront them upon death, as is man. The revelations that have come into the human world, the *nāsūt*, have also come into the *malakūt*, and are practised there. Islamic dogma specifically holds that there are *jinn* who are Muslim, Christian, and Jewish, and therefore of other religions as well, known to this world and unknown. Man and *jinn* are addressed together in the *Surat ar-Raḥmān* as the "two having weight" (*ath-thaqalān*; Koran 55:31), that is, they possess "form". A band of *jinn*, upon hearing the Prophet recite the Koran in the desert at night on his return journey from Ṭā'if, believed, and came later to Mecca to pledge fealty to the Prophet at the spot which is now called the "Mosque of the Jinn".

> Say: 'It has been revealed to me that a
> company of the jinn gave ear, then they
> said, "We have indeed heard a Koran wonderful,
> guiding to rectitude. We believe in it,
> and we will not associate
> with our Lord anyone.
> He — exalted be our Lord's majesty! —
> has not taken to Himself
> either consort or a son.
> The fool among us spoke
> against God outrage,
> and we had thought that men and jinn
> would never speak against God
> a lie."' (Koran 72:1-5)

The subtle, or animic, world is the place of the lower paradises, and also of the infernal states. The Koranic metaphor for this world is the "Footstool" *al-kursī*, which is "vast... comprising the heavens and the earth" (2:257). The subtle world not only surrounds the sensory world, *nāsūt* (which is its "projection" or "solidification", just as it itself is a "projection" from the Presence "above" it), but also permeates it. Consequently, and because it is the very substance of our minds, the *malakūt* and the phenomena associated with it, psychism, magic, and so forth, are often mistaken and substituted for that which is spiritual, enabling the practice of every kind of idolatry. On the other hand, because it is a part of us — or we are a part of it — the complete denial of it, as a world, and finally as "ether", on the part of scientific and humanistic materialism, distorts and stultifies the way in which we perceive and explain the nature of our own world. (The Michelson-Morley experiment assumed that ether is physical, which it cannot be, otherwise it would be identical with the physical world which is the next, fifth Presence.) (*See* JINN.)

The fifth Presence is our world, the *nāsūt*, "the World of the Human" also called the *'ālam al-mulk*, "the World of the Kingdom". (In Vedanta: *sthūla sharīra*). This is the familiar sensible, or corporeal, world.

Manifestation, or existence, is the last three Presences. It is conditioned, in our experience, by what some metaphysicians reduced to five qualities: time and space — its "containers" — and form, number, and materia, or matter. Plotinus assigned to existence five conditions; Aristotle assigned to existence ten qualities, or categories (Ar. *al-ma'qūlāt*). In Aristotle, substance is itself one of the categories; as a category it is "created"; at the same time, the word was often used to mean "uncreated" Substance which is Being itself. Some writers substitute the concept "life", for substance and include therein some of Aristotle's other categories, such as relation. For those authors, "life" can, in a certain sense, be found in everything in this world, including inanimate objects. Whatever the categories, behind them, behind materia and the ephemeral shadows which exist in creation (*khalq*), is the real, immaterial, substance of Being. Jāmi' and other Sufi poets and writers say that creatures are "foam" from the waves of the ocean, which is Substance, or Being. This is a poetical paraphrase of the explanation that Muslim philosophers, following in the steps of Aristotle, made of existence, saying that the objects of existence are "accidents" (*a'rāḍ*), which emerge from substance (*al-jawhar*).

Some of the Presences are also called by different names. The *'ālam al-malakūt* is often termed the *'ālam al-mithāl* ("World of Symbols"), and this, our world, is called the *ḥaḍrat ash-shahādah al-muṭlaqah* ("Presence of the totally Manifest"). Other nomenclatures combine two Presences together as in *'ālam al-ghayb al-muṭlaq* ("the World of the Absolute Unseen"), which is that of the *Hāhūt* and *Lāhūt* together. Or, *haḍrat al-ghayb al-muḍaf* ("the Presence of the Qualified Unseen") which is the *jabarūt* and *malakūt* together. In the vocabulary of a particular author, a name may be transposed to another Presence (especially *jabarūt* for *malakūt*, and vice-versa) which must be understood from context. Some authors introduce further divisions into the Presences. All the Five Presences taken together have been called *al-ḥaḍrah al-jāmi'ah* ("the Total Presence" or "Synthesis of Presences").

In this connection it might be mentioned that, according to the Koranic vocabulary, man is created of clay (*ṭīn*), the *jinn* of fire (*nār*), and the Angels of light (*nūr*). These terms define three modes of existence and correspond to the three *guṇas* (fundamental qualities) of Vedanta. These are tendencies that characterize everything which exists; ultimately they are modes inherent in the receptivity of substance within Being. The "earth" of man's creation corresponds to the downward tendency towards gross or inferior form which is, in Sanskrit, *tamas* ("gravity", "darkness" "disintegration"); fire corresponds to the expansive tendency, *rajas* ("motion", "rhythm", "multiplicity"); and light to the unitive or upward tendency to surpass form, to rejoin Being, *sattva*, ("cohesion", "light", related to the word *sat*, "being", "perfection", "positivity").

These three tendencies are also the modes of existence referred to in the *fātiḥah* as the path of those upon whom is Thy Mercy (*sattva*), not the path of whose upon whom is Thy Anger (*tamas*), nor the astray (*rajas*).

Tamas is the limitative tendency. It gives separate existence and objectifies; it is the "heaviness" necessary for differentiation. *Tamas* in itself is neutral and necessary. Nevertheless, it is also *tamas*, which, when *it touches consciousness* ("the knowledge of good and evil"), inverts the true, the beautiful, and the good, giving birth to evil. It is the first *guṇa* to emerge in the beginning of all cosmic manifestation, and the last to disappear in the end, "On the day when We shall roll up heaven as a scroll is rolled for the writings" (21:104), and when "To Him the angels and the Spirit mount up in a day whereof the measure is fifty thousand years" (70:4).

The beginning of the Chinese *Three Character Rhymed Classic on the Ka'bah*, by an 18th century Muslim named Ma Fu-ch'u is like an introduction to the study of the Five Presences:

Because there are Heaven and Earth
the ten thousand creatures are born;
because there are sun and moon
Heaven and Earth have light;
because there is the Sage [the Prophet]
enlightening teachings arise.
To hear the teaching of the Sage
is to deepen knowledge and perception,
to know the past,
clearly to understand the future and the present,
to grasp the origin of Heaven and Earth
and the source of the myriad creatures,
to attain to celestial principles
and to see into the hearts of men;
it shows us the road we have come by
and demonstrates the return to Reality:
it makes us aware of our heart and nature
and enables us to penetrate ultimate mysteries;
perpetuated by the wise men of old
it is enshrined in scriptural classics.
The foundation of the Path
is clearly to acknowledge God,
not bounded by space
nor limited by form,

without end or beginning,
not to be apprehended by the senses,
neither near nor far,
and Uniquely Sublime;
not empty nothingness
but Truth and Reality,
mysterious and hard to fathom,
beyond definition,
resembling Goodness and Reason,
yet like empty space,
Reality, Truth and Being,
wondrous and beyond description...

See ALLĀH; ANGELS; 'AQL; al-'ARSH; APOCATASTASIS; BEING; ESCHATOLOGY; DHĀT; al-HAYŪLĀ; NAFS; IBLĪS; AL-INSĀN al-KĀMIL; JINN.

Five Pillars (Ar. *arkān ad-dīn* lit. "supports, or fundaments, of the religion"). The fundamental tenets or requirements of Islam which are accepted as such unequivocally by all branches. The observance of the Five Pillars is required of all Muslims. The non-observance (but not repudiation) of four of the Five Pillars does not constitute departure from Islam, however, and in fact there are many Muslims who do not, at one or another time of their lives, observe the pillars other than the *shahādah*. The *shahādah* is essential, however, and without it no-one can consider himself a Muslim in any sense. Most would agree that the second most important pillar is *ṣalāh*, the ritual prayer, both spiritually, and legally, since there are no grounds for dispensation from the *ṣalāh*, except temporarily for menstruating women, whereas legal grounds exist for prolonged or systematic dispensation of the other three pillars.

The Five Pillars are:

1) the *shahādah* affirming that "there is no god but God (Allāh) and that Muḥammad is the Messenger of God."
2) *Ṣalāh*, the five daily ritual, or canonical, prayers.
3) *Zakāh*, the giving of alms on a stipulated scale. (This is, in a sense, the equivalent of a voluntary religious tax paid directly to the poor.)
4) *Sāwm*, the fasting of the month of Ramaḍān.
5) *Ḥajj*, the performance of the pilgrimage to Mecca once in a lifetime by those physically and financially able to do so without compromising their other responsibilities.

Jihād ("holy war") is sometimes called a "sixth" pillar. It is, however, not universally obligatory. Not all must take part in holy war even if there are valid reasons for it; it is enough that a "sufficient number" take part. Moreover, after the initial struggle for life on the part of the first Muslims in Medinah against the Meccans, *jihād* was rarely declared and could even more rarely be justified.

According to a Ḥadīth related by Ṭalḥāh ibn 'Ubayy, a man came to the Prophet and asked about the religious duties of Islam. The Messenger said:

> "Five prayers by day and night." "Must I perform others?" asked the man. "No," answered the Prophet "unless it is voluntarily." The questions were repeated and answered the same way for the other pillars upon which the man said, "By God I will not add anything to that and I will not take anything away." Whereupon the Prophet exclaimed, "He will be one of the blessed [in paradise] if he is sincere."

A Chinese Muslim, Ma Fu-ch'u, in an 18th-century treatise called *The Three Character Rhymed Classic on the Ka'bah*, describes the Five Pillars thus:

For all lands under Heaven,
the doctrine of the Prophet runs
comprising Rites for human society
and the Heavenly Path.
To confess the Sovereign God
is the first requirement,
and this central ritual
is most wondrous.
The Heavenly Path is cultivated
by the Five Virtuous Acts:
the Virtuous Act of enunciating
the Truth [*shahādah*]
with the heart turned to God;
the Virtuous Act of ritualizing the Truth [*ṣalāh*]
with the body adoring God;
the Virtuous Act of fasting [*ṣawm*]
to master the promptings of desire;
the virtuous Act of heavenly charity [*zakāh*]
to assist the orphans and the needy

the Virtuous Act of pilgrimage [*ḥajj*]
forsaking home and family.

All things, deep and shallow
reside in the heart and breast.
The virtues of the heart
are vehicled by the Path,
which is therefore called
the Vehicle of Reality.

Now the Vehicle of the Rites
is the foundation of all;
the true Vehicle of the Path
is derived from this;
when the Rites are abandoned
the three virtues are obscured.
These five Virtuous Acts
are the five norms.
God commands men
to conquer self
whether they be ignorant or wise,
saints or commoners,
each acting in respectful obedience
as the Rites prescribe...

See CREED; FIQH AKBAR; JIHĀD; PILGRIMAGE; RAMAḌĀN; ṢALĀH; SHAHĀDAH; ZAKĀH.

Fivers, *see* ZAYDIS.

"Flight to Medinah", *see* HIJRAH.

Flood, *see* NOAH.

Folklore, *see* MANDALA; BOUJLOUD; BSAT; FALLACIES; GNAWAH.

Food. Like most religions, Islam makes prescriptions about food. The meat of swine is forbidden (2:167) and that of animals that have not been ritually slaughtered. The consumption of blood is forbidden, but that which remains in meat after draining upon slaughter is acceptable. Wine and inebriating drinks are forbidden (5:92), as are mind-affecting drugs, but drugs used medicinally are not prohibited. Wine mixed with various herbs was used as an anaesthetic by Muslim doctors in the Middle Ages.

In early Islam the eating habits of the Arabs were the criteria for determining what could be eaten and what not, and Ibn Ḥanbal, founder of a School of Law, is said never to have eaten watermelon because he never found a precedent for it in the Sunnah of the Prophet.

In general, scavenger animals are forbidden as food. Shellfish present an exception. Shellfish are scavengers (and thus eaters of carrion, which are prohibited as food themselves, Koran 2:173; 5:3; 6:145; 16:115), and are considered non-kosher in Judaism. The Sunnis, however, eat many kinds of shellfish, nevertheless. (They do, however, consider it *makrūh*, or "a discouraged practice".) Presumably, the acceptance of shellfish as food arises out of the Koranic verse: "the game of the sea and its food is made lawful for you" (Koran 5:96). It could also possibly be an example of *ijmā'* on the part of the Sunnis, that is, usage establishing law. Twelve Imām Shī'ites, however, do prohibit the eating of shellfish, and fish without scales such as shark and eels.

Food that is acceptable is called *ḥalāl*; meat is *ḥalāl* if it consists of the flesh of acceptable animals that have been ritually slaughtered. A Muslim must consecrate the kill by saying the words *Bismi-Llāh Allāhu Akbar*, and cut the throat (both windpipe and jugular vein) with one stroke. Game is *ḥalāl* if the words of consecration are spoken when it is shot, or when a trained dog is released to retrieve it. Fish are *ḥalāl* if caught when alive, but dead fish which have been gathered are not.

If ritually slaughtered meat is not available, it is admissible to consume non-*ḥalāl* meat and "the food of Jews and Christians" provided that prohibited food such as swine's flesh is avoided. When there is no alternative, in cases of necessity, even prohibited food may be eaten. During World War II, Muslim troops fighting in European armies were often obliged to eat canned ham, because other supplies were not available. (In this connection one is reminded — no parallel or conclusion is intended, it is simply a fact — of the Sepoy Mutiny a century ago which was sparked off when Muslim troops serving the British Empire in India were incited to rebel by false rumors that bullets, which they were obliged or wont to bite with their teeth, had been greased with pig fat).

In practice, all authorities would probably approve the eating of prohibited food if there were no alternative for survival, according to the legal principle that "Necessity makes prohibited things permissible." Moreover, there is an injunction in Islam to be reasonable in all things. *See* RITUAL SLAUGHTER.

"Forbidden", *see* ḤARĀM.

Forgiveness, *see* DIVINE NAMES; ISTIGHFĀR.

Forgetting, House of, *see* FARĀMŪSH KHĀNEH.

Formulas of piety, *see* PIOUS EXPRESSIONS.

"Four Books" (*al-kutub al-arba'ah*). The four principal collections of Ḥadīth accepted by Twelve-Imām Shī'ites. These are:

1. *Man la Yaḥḍuruhu-l-Faqīh* ("When no theologian is present") by Muḥammad Ibn Babawayh (d. *381*/991).
2. *Al-Kāfī* ("The Compendium") by Muḥammad ibn Ya'qūb Abū Ja'far al-Kulaynī (d. *329*/940).
3. *Al-Istibṣār* ("the Perspicacious") by Muḥammad aṭ-Ṭūsī (*460*/1067).
4. *Taḥdhib al-Aḥkām* ("The Confirmation of Decisions") also by Muḥammad aṭ-Ṭūsī.

See al-KULAYNĪ; IBN BABAWAYH; ṬŪSĪ, MUḤAMMAD.

"Fourteenth Century". Although quite categorically the Prophet denied any knowledge of the future, there is a popular myth that the Prophet made a comment about each century to come and "wept" when he reached the fourteenth. This myth was created to support a very widespread idea that the world will end in the fourteenth Islamic century, which is the present one. This belief probably arises from the Manichean eschatology which says that once everyone has understood that the world was created in order to rescue the light from the attack of darkness after the Manichean big bang, no more children will be allowed to be born, and the world will come to an end, and will then burn for 1468 years, which is very close to the length of the "Sothic" year (1460).

Free will, *see* MAKTŪB; QADARIYYAH.

Friday Prayer (Ar. *ṣalāt al-jum'ah*). The special Friday midday prayer is performed in a congregational mosque, that is, a large mosque where worshipers come together who may well perform the other daily prayers in a smaller, local mosque. Here an Imām, or prayer leader competent to do so, delivers an exhortation (*khuṭbah*) usually lasting from fifteen minutes to a half hour.

After the *khuṭbah*, the worshipers end the assembly by performing a two-*raka'āt* prayer in place of the normal four-*raka'at Ẓuhr*, or noon prayer. Attendance at Friday prayers is insisted upon as not only meritorious but a duty. Commercial transactions between the moment the prayer is called to the time it is performed are forbidden, although business may be carried on during the rest of the day.

In Saudi Arabia where Sunday is not a holiday, Thursday and Friday are the equivalent of the two-day weekend found in the West. In other countries where European usage prevails, Saturday and Sunday are civil holidays while Friday remains the day of assembly. The observance of the special congregation takes about one hour.

Fundamentalism. The term "Fundamentalism" is Western and misleading because many Muslims are quick to claim that Islam has always been "fundamentalist" and that the contemporary phenomenon by this name is simply a return to Islam as such. It is not, however, an Islam that would have been familiar to al-Ghazālī (d. 1111) or to Abū Ḥanifah (d. 767), or even Ibn Taymiyyah (d. 1328) whom many Fundamentalists regard as their model. The term used, until recently, in Arabic for the phenomenon was not "Fundamentalism", but "extremism" (*mutaṭarifīn*). Now it has been replaced by the more politically correct *Uṣulīyyah*, a literal translation of "fundamentalism". It is characterized by absolutist application of *some* ideas which constitute Islam, and the total rejection of other ideas, which are no less Islam, and no less the Koranic words of revelation. It is marked by the inability to integrate ideas into coherent and stable wholes. Fundamentalism reduces religion to rules and laws and materialism, and ignores transcendence and spirituality.

Following the modern reformer Mawdūdī most Fundamentalists insist in the veiling of all women. The custom arose in some parts of the Islamic world, but not in all; in 'Abbāsid Baghdad it was the reinstatement of a Persian usage. The classical Jurist Ibn Qutaybah (d. *276*/889) a leading Traditionist of the *3rd*/9th century, opposed obligatory veiling saying that veiling was a special Koranic condition for the Prophet's wives only who were a focus of attention and, who unlike other women, were also not allowed to marry any one else after his death. (The "veiling" of the Prophet's wives in the Koran in all likelihood did not mean the wearing of a veil, but that audiences with them should be carried out with a separating curtain.)

Nor are apparently similar schools in the past exactly analogous to modern Fundamentalism. The rise of the Ẓāhirī, or literalist school of law in the *3rd*/10th century, rather than a sclerosis was in some ways actually an escape, an alternative to a rise of legalism in the Islamic world. It was in any case an organic development rather than a reaction to forces from without. Paradoxically, this school was often adopted by extremely liberal thinkers and Sufis seeking greater freedom of thought. Similarly the acceptance by many of predestinarianism in the *2nd*/8th century was a defense against oppression (as well as the logical consequence of certain metaphysical dogmas.) Politics has often disguised itself behind a religious front in the Islamic world as elsewhere. Very often ambitious leaders created their power bases around religious affiliations: the 'Abbāsids and Ṣafavids come to mind, as do the Sanūsiyyah and Tijanīyyah, and the attempt of the Emir 'Abd al-Qādir of Algeria (d. 1883) to build support for his political ambitions through the Sufi movement of the Qādiriyyah. A particular development, however, which led to the modern situation, was to categorically label those who did not belong to one's movement as ungodly, or as unbelievers. This was originally done in order to be able to attack one's neighbors militarily, often not for conquest but simply for plunder, with a clear conscience, for war between Muslims is prohibited. This was the device used by Muḥammad ibn 'Abd al-Wahhāb (d. 1787) the founder of Wahhābism, to justify plundering other tribal groups. Wahhābism became the religious basis of the Saudi state, and also spread abroad in the 19th century, but has now turned against its own original upholders. This characteristic of declaring one's competitors unholy has not only continued down to present times, it has been exploited even more, along with the declaration of "holy war" in circumstances in which not only "holy war" is impossible under the legally prescribed conditions, Islam not being in danger, but any war in the first place from the religious point of view.

Not only do modern fundamentalists equate Western culture with the pagan and barbaric ignorance of the *Jahiliyyah*, or state of the Arab world before Islam, they tend to treat non-Muslims such as Christians who are Koranically held to be believers, as unbelievers. They go further and also treat nominally Muslim leaders of modern governments as unbelievers as well, and finally anyone who doesn't agree with them is called a *Kāfir*, or infidel, no matter what their credentials. In recent years there have been calls for "Islamic Government" in Pakistan even though reasonable religious leaders find the government to be as Islamic as possible, with, for example, constitutional laws prohibiting the adoption of any measures which are contrary to the Koran.

However, these earlier movements had by their nature a very high degree of religious content. The phenomenon of present day "fundamentalism" does not. Islam as religion, Islam as piety, has been replaced by Islam as ideology and as a kind of nationalism. Sometimes this has taken the form of grass roots democracy, but also as the rule by a class claiming religious authority. It has also taken the form of Islam seen as some kind of economic system, not readily definable, and ultimately whatever one wants it to be. It has taken root chiefly among the poor and uneducated as a utopianism without spirituality. One upper class Pakistani woman was quoted calling it "being drunken on bigoted religion". Above all it seems to be a reaction to what are perceived as foreign systems, a reaction which has taken the form of an aggressive, sometimes totalitarian application of religious practices as blind rules. As a rejection of alien influences it can be seen as a defensive mechanism, in which, unfortunately, an awareness of the positive meaning of religion is often obscured.

What is perhaps distinctive about contemporary Islamic Fundamentalism is that it attempts to combine modernism, with its secular and materialist tendencies, with a religious conservatism in a vacuum, cut off from tradition and a matrix of organic process. Some modernist Fundamentalist movements have refused to observe Islamic laws on the grounds that they should not be expected to do so until the whole world does so! As the nature of modern Fundamentalism is contradictory, the precursors do not fall into an orderly group representing similar thinking. They in fact form a composite of the contradictory forces that make up Fundamentalism. Among them are the Indian modernist reformer Sayyid Ahmad Khan (*1232-1316*/1817-1898) who founded the Aligarh College and who saw Great Britain as a model; Jamāl ad-Dīn al-Afghānī (*1254-1314*/1838-1897) who tried to make himself the spokesman of different currents of his time for his own advancement; Muḥammad

'Abduh (*1265-1323*/1849-1905) who attempted to make revisions in Islamic Law to meet modern conditions, such as the *fatwā* which permitted interest on capital; 'Alī 'Abd ar-Razzāq in Egypt who advocated the separation of religion and state as an original historic dogma of Islam; Rashīd Riḍa' who advanced the notion which now is an unquestioned premise of Fundamentalist political theory, the slogan of *shura*, or "consultation" i.e. Islamic democracy; Ḥasan al-Bannā' in Egypt (d. *1368*/1949) the founder of the Muslim Brotherhood is another important figure. The Muslim Brotherhood has tried to overthrow what it considers un-Islamic regimes by force, including terrorism, from within; Muḥammad Iqbal (*1290-1357*/1873-1938) in Pakistan, who combined certain aspects of modern European philosophy, entirely secular and humanistic in its world view, with Islam; Sayyid Abū-l-'Ala Mawdūdī (*1321-1399*/1903-1979), a highly influential Pakistani thinker who advocated authoritarian conservatism with modern dynamism.

Combining the militancy of the Muslim Brotherhood and the legal legitimism of Mawdūdī, Sayyid Quṭb denounced believing Muslims as unbelievers if they did not agree him. Quṭb was executed in *1386*/1966 in Egypt by the Nasser regime. The absolute rejection of those who disagree is in the nature of Fundamentalism, the principle of "consultation" being reserved for adherents of the particular school. Groups derived from Quṭb have been implicated in much violence in Egypt including the assassination of President Sadat in 1981, who himself, along with Nasser when they were "Free Officers", belonged to the Muslim Brotherhood at the beginning of his career. (Sadat, as any politician, looked to various groups for possible support, including Sufis; he belonged to the Shadhilis and even as Head of State he performed pilgrimages to the tomb of Imām Shadhili by the Red Sea.)

In Iran, Dr. 'Alī Shari'atī (d. *1397*/1977) was extremely popular among students for what was a combination of Leftist politics, Western Existentialism, and Iranian Ishraq (the two are fundamentally very similar) served up under the label of Islam. The revolution of Ayatollah Khomeini (d. *1409*/1989) for a time provided a banner for young Muslims in many countries, who, having often been fed a diet of revolutionary rhetoric blaming the West for the under-development of the Third World, rallied around what seemed to be revolution through Islam rather than through some alien ideology. The ultimate failure of the Iranian revolution to provide any real solutions, and the disastrous Iran-'Irāq war blunted enthusiasm, for a time at least, for the promises put forward by "Islamic Government".

The heteroclitic nature of modern Fundamentalism as reaction can be seen from this description of the Muslim Brotherhood by Ḥasan al-Bannā': "A Sunnī ('orthodox') Salafīyyah movement [part of a general reform movement that came into being almost one hundred years ago to restore what was perceived as 'the original Islam' of the 'pious ancestors'], a Sufi truth (i.e. 'a mysticism'), a political organisation, an athletic group, a cultural and educational union, an economic company, and a social idea." From this collection of unconnected and even contradictory appeals it can be seen that the guiding principle of Fundamentalism is the attempt to acquire power, sanctified with the sauce of holy righteousness, on the part of those who do not have power today. It is also the fusion of Islam with technological modernism.

Fundamentalism is a phenomenon which has marked all religions in modern times. Its hallmarks are materialism and literalism, the rejection of tradition, in its place utopianism and millennarianism, appealing to the disenfranchised and oppressed (what Khomeini called the *mustaḍ'afūn*, or the "downtrodden"). It is as if the spiritual power which religions bring into the world at the time of their birth, the power of a beneficent synthesis and a new view of reality, a kind of magic that neutralized what were originally destructive tendencies, evaporates and in its place contrary forces, two gods, burst forth which are at war with each other and with themselves. Forces which had to be confined behind a kind of wall like the Gog and Magog of the Koran now break out anew to wreak the havoc of the ancient times. *See* ḤAMĀS; ḤIZB ALLĀH; KHOMEINI; LASHKAR-I TAYEEBAH; MUSLIM BROTHERHOOD; PAHLAVĪ; WAHHĀBĪS.

Funduq (lit. "an inn", from the Greek *pandokeion*). The word is often used for a modern hotel in the Arab West, but it means first of all a traditional inn, with space for the storage of merchandise, and stables for traveling and pack animals. *See* CARAVANSERAI; KHĀN.

Funerals (Ar. *janāzah* or *jināzah*). Muslims bury the dead as quickly as possible, preferably before sundown on the day of death. Cremation is not practiced in Islam. The corpse is cleaned by persons of the same sex as the deceased and given a ritual ablution, the *ghusl*, an uneven number of times, which may be followed by a *wuḍū'*. The bodily orifices are stopped with cotton wool; the body is shrouded in a winding cloth. Martyrs, however, are buried as they died, in their clothes, unwashed, for their wounds bear testimony to their martyrdom.

A funeral prayer is performed for the recently dead by the mourners and by anyone present in the mosque at the time. Funeral prayers are performed in mosques as a matter of course after the canonic daily prayers. The corpse may or may not be present. An odd number of rows of worshipers is customary for this prayer. The worshipers make an expression of niyyah ("intention") before this as before all ritual acts.

The opening *takbīr* ("*Allāhu Akbar*") is followed by a *du'ā'* which is a personal prayer in one's own words, in this case, pronounced silently in the standing position (*qiyām*). It is customary to use an established *du'ā'*, known as the *qunūt*, which is actually whispered beneath the breath, at this point (*see* QUNŪT). Another *takbīr* precedes a second *du'ā'*, and again, for a total of three such personal prayers. One of these prayers should be a petition for the happiness of the departed soul. After the third *du'ā'*, there is a fourth *takbīr*, and the worshipers say *as-salamu 'alaykum* to the right and to the left. In this prayer there is no *rukū'*, ("bow"), or *sujūd* ("prostration").

As the mourners carry the corpse through the streets to a mosque to be prayed over or to its resting place, the *shahādah* is psalmodied. Piety calls upon those whom the procession passes to rise, join in the chanting, and help carry the bier for a short distance. The body is buried in a grave, lying on the right side with the face towards Mecca. There are no injunctions against the use of coffins, but it more common to bury the body only in its wrappings.

Forty days after death, it is common to recite litanies in remembrance of the deceased. Other customary practices exist, which vary from community to community, and nation to nation. When a deceased person is mentioned, the words *raḥimahu* (*raḥimahā* for a woman) *'Llāh*, "God be merciful to him or her", are spoken.

'Ali said: "Every day an Angel of heaven cries: 'O people there below! produce offspring to die; build to be destroyed; gather ye together to depart!'" (Attributed to 'Ali, this is also found in the poetry of Abū-l-'Atāhiyah, d. *210*/825.) *See* DEATH; MOURNING; PRAYER.

Furqān (lit. "divider", in the sense of criterion or discrimination).1. A name for the Koran because the book is the basis for discrimination between truth and unreality.2. The name of Sūrah 25. *See* FARAQLĪṬ.

Furū' ("branch"). The branches of religious law developed from the principles or *uṣul al-fiqh*. *See* SHARĪ'AH.

al-Futūḥāt al-Makkiyyah (lit. "the Meccan Revelations"). A vast work of esoteric doctrine in 560 chapters by Ibn 'Arabī, the celebrated mystic and metaphysician of the 12th century. *See* IBN 'ARABĪ.

Futuwwah (lit. "Youth", "adolescence" and, by extension, "manliness", "nobleheartedness"). The equivalent of the Western notion of "chivalry". Before Islam social responsibility was determined among the desert Arabs by blood ties alone, with little provision for the outsider apart from the prescribed rules of hospitality for guests. The Prophet in Mecca, before he received his mission, had taken part in a pact of *futuwwah* ("chivalry") to help those without succor.

The pact had come about when a visiting merchant, with no relatives in Mecca to whom he could appeal for aid, was defrauded by a Meccan merchant. The victim, a Yemeni, made a public appeal from the slopes of Abū Qubays, the hill which rises near the Ka'bah. 'Abd Allāh ibn Jud'ān, the chief of the clan of Taym accordingly called for a pact of chivalry among the Meccans. Az-Zubayr, chief of the Hāshim clan, brought the young Muḥammad to take part in the pact. Those who took part poured water over the Black Stone, drank it, and then, with their right hands raised above their heads, made an oath to defend those in need irrespective of clan affiliation. The oath was called the *ḥilf al-fuḍūl*.

The Meccan who had wronged the Yemeni was compelled to make amends. Afterwards, the Prophet said: "I was present in the house of 'Abd Allāh ibn Jud'ān at so excellent a pact that I would not exchange my part in it for a herd of red camels; and if now, in Islam, I were summoned unto it I would gladly respond." Abū Bakr also took part in this pact.

The idea of *futuwwah* in Islam reached its high point during the Crusades when chivalrous acts on both sides were recorded and admired. The nobility of Saladin, who was knighted by Richard the Lion Heart, became legendary in Europe and the Orient.

Under the 'Abbāsids a number of orders of *futuwwah* were created of which the Caliph was occasionally the titular head. These traditions were transferred to Cairo when the 'Abbāsids were installed as figurehead Caliphs by the Mamlūks after the Mongol conquest of Baghdad, and existed later among the Turks and the Persians.

Among the latter a trace of these orders still survive as *zurkhaneh* (Pers. "houses of strength"). Today, these are athletic clubs more than anything else, but they were the embodiment of a traditional Persian practice of the martial arts and they retain a certain sense of ceremony and dedication which recalls their origins. A *zurkhaneh* is the meeting place for a society of athletes who train together and compete as wrestlers. The *zurkhaneh* preserves vestiges of medieval Islamic chivalry, recalled by the ritualistic protocols of the assemblies, and the emphasis on virtue.

Fuẓūlī, Muḥammad ibn Sulayman (d. *963*/1556). One of the first poets to use Turkish as a literary language. He also wrote in Persian and Arabic. As many of his works, among them a "*Layla and Majnūn*", are in a form of Turkish which is close to Azeri, he is reckoned today a national poet in Azerbaijan although he was born in 'Irāq and is buried in Kerbala.

G

Gabriel (Ar. *Jabrā'īl* or *Jibrīl*, "God's Mighty One"). The Angel of Revelation and one of the Archangels. In the Bible, Gabriel is a Divine Messenger sent to Daniel, Mary, and Zacharias. In Islamic tradition Gabriel appears again and again to the Prophets, beginning with Adam, to whom he gave consolation after the Fall, taught the letters of the alphabet, and the skills of working in the world. He brought the revelations of the Koran; in Sūrah 53 (the Sūrah of the Star) he who taught the Prophet is not named, but described; the commentators unanimously accept this to have been Gabriel.

This is naught but a revelation revealed,
taught him by one terrible in power,
very strong; he stood poised
being on the higher horizon,
then drew near and suspended hung,
two bows'-length away, or nearer,
then revealed to his servant that he revealed.
His heart lies not of what he saw;
what, will you dispute with him what he sees?
(53:4-11)

Gabriel also took the Prophet on the Night Journey. Tradition adds that Gabriel interceded on behalf of the Prophet, giving him help on several occasions in a supernatural way.

The Jews of Medinah objected that if Islam had been addressed to them, then Michael would have been the Angel of Revelation. In connection with this the verse 2:92-96 was revealed:

Say: 'Whosoever is an enemy to Gabriel —
he it was that brought it down upon thy heart
by the leave of God,
confirming what was before it,
and for a guidance and good
tidings to the believers.
Whosoever is an enemy to God and His angels
and His Messengers, and Gabriel, and Michael—
surely God is an enemy to the unbelievers.'
And We have sent down unto thee signs,
clear signs,
and none disbelieves in them except the ungodly.
Why, whensoever they have made a covenant,
does a party of them reject it?
Nay, but the most of them are unbelievers.
When there has come to them
a Messenger from God
confirming what was with them, a part of them
that were given the Book reject the Book of God
behind their backs, as though they knew not,
and they follow what the Satans recited
over Solomon's kingdom.

And Gabriel is mentioned again in 66:4:
...but if you support one
another against him, God is his Protector,
and Gabriel, and the righteous among the
believers; and, after that, the angels are
his supporters.

In Iran, Gabriel is usually referred to by his Zoroastrian name, *Sraosh*, and it is perhaps the Zoroastrian connection which explains why, indeed, the Jews of Medinah felt Gabriel was not the Angel whom they would have expected. *See* ANGELS; NIGHT JOURNEY.

Gambling. Games of chance are forbidden in the Koran (2:219 and 5:94). Nevertheless, various indigenous forms of betting, as well as lotteries, do exist, or have existed, in most Islamic countries, due to the colonial influence of European countries.

Garden (Ar. *al-jannah*). The garden is the most frequent Koranic symbol of paradise. *See* al-JANNAH.

"Garden of Death", *see* MUSAYLAMAH.

Gasprinski, Ismā'īl Bey (d. 1914). A Crimean Tatar educated in Russia and abroad, in both traditional and modern institutions who founded an influential Turkic journal in Russia called *Terjuman* ("The Interpreter"). He deplored Islamic backwardness which brought on colonialism. He blamed this backwardness on the short sightedness and rigidity of religious authorities. Gasprinski promoted a movement called *Jadidism*, which sought "renewal" by raising the level of education, awareness, and critical thinking, and the equality of women.

Geber, *see* JĀBIR IBN ḤAYYĀN.

Gematria, *see* 'ABJAD.

Genie, *see* JINN.

Ghadīr al-Khumm (lit. "the pool of Khumm"). An oasis between Mecca and Medinah. Returning from the final, "Farewell Pilgrimage" shortly before his death, the Prophet stopped here with his followers. During the afternoon he called an assembly, took 'Alī's hands, raised them up, and said "Whoever has me as his master (*mawlā*) has 'Alī as his master." Then he prayed: "Be a friend to his friends, O Lord, and be an enemy to his enemies, help those who assist him and frustrate those who oppose him."

The Shī'ites (*see* SHĪ'ISM) assert that this declaration was in reality a designation of 'Alī as successor to the Prophet. The events at Ghadīr al-Khumm are advanced as one of the most important arguments for their thesis concerning 'Alī. The event is celebrated in the Shī'ite world by the *'Īd al-Ghadīr*, or "festival of Ghadīr". The observance of this as a Shī'ite festival dates to *351*/962 when it was instituted by Mu'izz ad-Dawlah, the Buyid ruler who also inaugurated the Shī'ite observance of the 'Āshūrā' as the commemoration of the martyrdom of Ḥusayn. At the time, the Sunnīs of Baghdad countered by making festivals of the 26th Dhū-l-Ḥijjah, the anniversary of Abū Bakr's sojourn with the Prophet in the cave, and the 18th Muḥarram, the death of Mus'ab ibn az-Zubayr who had put down the revolt of a partisan of Ḥusayn; but these observances, being quite artificial, were short-lived.

The Sunnīs deny the existence of a successor in the Shī'ite sense of an Imām in any case, and deny that this event marked the designation of 'Alī as an immediate successor. They cite as evidence the fact that Abū Bakr was unequivocally designated to lead the prayers in place of the Prophet during his final illness; this does not by itself imply that Abū Bakr was intended to succeed the Prophet, but it casts doubt on such a designation regarding 'Alī. Ibn Ḥazm pointed out that if 'Alī had been designated as successor he would not have participated in the *shūra* or council which elected 'Uthmān as Calife.

The Sunnī interpretation of Ghadīr al-Khumm is made in the light of the events immediately preceding it, namely that 'Alī had just been severely criticized by the army he was leading (he had not been present at the "Farewell Pilgrimage" because of a military expedition) for rescinding an order given by his deputy to distribute a ration of new clothing from the spoils of war. The Prophet's statement is seen as intended to still the criticism and justify 'Alī's actions. If the Prophet had intended his statement to be a designation of an heir to the leadership it would be astounding that it was not clearly understood by everyone since the Prophet took pains to make sure that his acts and words were understood clearly by all.

In addition to the Twelve Imām Shī'ite interpretation of Ghadīr Khumm there is an Ismā'īlī one which Henry Corbin explains thus: "the solemn investiture of the Imām by the Prophet at Ghadīr Khumm, a testamentary act by which the Annunciator (*Nāṭiq*) of the religious Law entrusted its secret exegesis (*ta'wīl*) to his spiritual heir and to the Imāms of his lineage". This "secret" interpretation is intended "to transcend the literalism of the Law and of all servitude to texts and men". For the Sunnis there can be no such "secret" interpretation. The easier way "to transcend the Law" would have been not to promulgate it in the first place.

The Fāṭimid Ismā'īlīs also cited Ghadīr Khumm to justify the succession of al-Ḥāfiẓ as Caliph. Until then it was maintained that the succession of the Imām had to go from father to son. (An exception could have been al-Ḥākim who had designated his cousin 'Abd ar-Raḥīm Ilyās as his heir, but rescinded it when his son aẓ-Ẓāhir was born.) Al-Ḥafiẓ was the cousin of the preceding Caliph-Imām al-Āmir who died in 1129, assassinated by the rival Niẓarīs of Alamut, without a son (although it was claimed by some that he did have a son who spiritually disappeared, aṭ-Ṭayyib.) Al-Ḥāfiẓ eventually claimed the Caliphate and Imāmate citing Ghadīr Khumm as the precedent, namely that he had been designated the way 'Alī had been allegedly designated by the Prophet Muḥammad. *See* CALENDAR; SHĪ'ISM.

Ghālib, Mirzā Asad Allāh Khān. (*1212-1286*/1797-1869). Born in Agra, he spent most of his life in Delhi where he was attached to the court of the last Moghul ruler, Bahadūr Shāh Ẓafar. Ghālib wrote poetry in Persian and Urdu, and in a prose work, *Dastanbūy*, described the events of the time of the Sepoy Mutiny which he witnessed. With the wider publication of his works, poetry and correspondence, his fame has grown in the last one hundred years.

Ghāfilūn, *see* GHAFLAH.

Ghaflah (lit. "heedlessness"). Those guilty of *ghaflah*, the *ghāfilūn*, are those who "know only a surface appearance of the life of this world, and are heedless of the hereafter" (30:7). *Ghaflah* is the sin of indifference to the reality of God. It is the "broad way" and the "wide gate". Of the indifferent, or the heedless, it is said: "because thou art lukewarm, and neither cold nor hot, I will spue thee out of my mouth" (Revelations 3:16).

Ghār Ḥīra', *see* ḤĪRA'.

Ghassānīs. A South Arabian tribe, the Banū Ghassān, who migrated to Syria from the Yemen between the 3rd and 4th century AD and settled in the region of Damascus. Many of them became monophysite Christians. Their leaders were accorded a Phylarcate, or status of vassal kingdom, under the Byzantine Emperor Justinian (527-569). The Ghassānīs protected the southern flank of the Byzantine Empire. With the rise of Islam many of the Ghassānīs defected from Byzantine allegiance and assisted the Arabs making possible their invasion of Syria. Those Ghassānīs who did not convert to Islam at the time were accorded a special position as a people not conquered, but rather, allied to the Islamic empire.

In 272 the Roman Emperor Aurelian routed the Palmyrene army at Emesa (Ḥoms). He destroyed Palmyra (Tadmir) a great city in the Syrian desert thus ending the greatest instance, under the Queen Zenobia, of Arab political expansion up to that time. With the loss of this countervailing power against their rivals, the Persians soon thereafter installed the Lakhmids as rulers of a buffer state centreed at Ḥīrah (near the future Kūfah). The Romans followed by sponsoring the Syrian Ghassānīds between Damascus and Petra.

The Jafnid house of the Ghassānīs arose at the beginning of the sixth century when they defeated the Lakhmids. Ḥarith ibn Jabalah was recognized as ruler by the Byzantines and became phylarch. After the Muslim invasion, the Ghassānīd ruler Jabalah ibn al-Āyham accepted Islam after first fighting against it. However, he found it too democratic (he was held equal to a Beduin in an incident while on the pilgrimage), abandoned Islam and returned to Christianity. *See* LAKHMIDS; MARONITES.

Ghaybah (lit. "absence" or "being concealed"). 1. A technical term of Sufism meaning "absence" from the world, that is, withdrawal from all things except the worship and awareness of God.

2. It also refers to the Shī'ite doctrine of the "occultation" or disappearance from human view — or even from the world altogether — of the Twelfth Imām of Twelve-Imām Shī'ism.

The doctrine is a calque after the example of Jesus, who, the Koran says, was not killed on the cross, but rather was raised up to a principial state, a state in Being, from which he will return at the end of the world.

Although the case of the Twelver Hidden Imām is the most prominent example, a similar belief exists among the Druzes who regard the Fāṭimid Caliph al-Ḥākim (d. *411*/1021) as having undergone *ghaybah*. Some Musta'lī Ismā'īlīs believe the same about their Imām Ṭayyib, the alleged son of al-Āmir, who was assassinated in *524*/1129. *See* SHĪ'ISM; HIDDEN IMĀM.

al-Ghazālī, Abū Ḥāmid Muḥammad (*450-505*/1058-1111). Philosopher, theologian, jurist, and mystic; he was known in Europe as "Algazel". He was born and died in Ṭūs, Persia. An extraordinary figure, al-Ghazālī was the architect of the latter development of Islam.

In his youth al-Ghazālī attracted the attention of his teachers because of his capacity and desire for learning. He studied at Nayshābūr with al-Juwaynī, the "Imām of the Ḥaramayn", and was appointed a professor of law at the Niẓāmiyyah in Baghdad by the Vizier Niẓām al-Mulk, the great statesman, patron of learning, and a prolific founder of schools. At Baghdad, al-Ghazālī achieved renown and great success as a lawyer, but after four years experienced a crisis of faith and conscience. A temporary speech impediment, which interfered with his work, made action urgent.

Under guise of going on the pilgrimage, al-Ghazālī turned his post over to his brother (who later became a well known Sufi), and retired to Damascus. After periods of great solitude, he visited the spiritual fountainheads of Jerusalem and Hebron (the site of the tomb of Abraham), as well as Mecca and Medinah. It has been said that during this period of searching he went so far as to question the senses, knowing they could deceive.

He turned his attention to the ways of knowledge one by one: philosophy, theology, and the various schools of the age. In the end he found his satisfaction in mysticism, or Sufism; but of a kind far less extreme than that of the notorious mystics. The Sufism to which he returned was very different than the Sufism from which he issued. His Sufi teacher was called Fārmadhī, a Ḥallājian, and the ideology which Ḥallāj represented was probably also tied up with Ghazāli's family traditions. It is probably this which was at the root of his spiritual crisis, for all these currents were in conflict with orthodoxy. What Ghazāli came to in the end was a synthesis on the side of orthodoxy, and a Sufism very different from that espoused by his radical brother Aḥmad. The resolution of his doubts also led him to write polemics against the Ismā'īlīs.

In the light of this continuity and the certainty which he exhibits even as he describes his searching, it would seem that the crisis of his life was not one of doubt as such, but a turning inward away from the world sparked by discovering that he had been raised in a heretical doctrine; for al-Ghazālī says: "I arrived at Truth, not by systematic reasoning and accumulation of proofs, but by a flash of light which God sent into my soul."

He wrote his great works, the *Ihyā' 'Ulūm ad-Dīn*, ("the Revival of the Religious Sciences"), and *al-Munqidh min aḍ-Ḍ alal*, ("the Savior from Error"), about his search for knowledge. In the *Tahāfut al-Falāsifah* (or "the Destruction of the Philosophers") he refutes the ability of philosophy— on the basis of its own assumptions — to reach truth and certainty, and reduces it to an ancilla of theology. His ethical works are *Kīmiyā' as-Sa'ādah*, ("the Alchemy of Felicity"), and *Yā Ayyuhā-l-Walad*, ("O Young Man"). On mysticism his most famous work is the *Mishkāt al-Anwār*, ("the Niche of Lights"). In all, he wrote about seventy books.

Al-Ghazālī was a Shāfi'ī and as such he used *qiyas* or analogy to arrive at theological decisions. Because the Malikis do not approve of the use of analogy his books were burned in one instance in Seville. He was also an Ash'arite and thus, philosophically a kind of occasionalist. Fire burns cotton, he said, not because fire is an agent, but because it is God's *sunnah*, His "wont" that it should appear to burn cotton and our knowledge of it burning is also this Divine wont; in miracles God changes his *sunnah* and our knowledge changes also. Al-Ghazāli talked about *dhawq*, literally "taste" but meaning "realisation", and like all theologians, the need for "reliable tradition" with which to understand revelation. He says that as an example of mercy in the darkness of the created world there appears God's "gift of knowledge". For him philosophy was irrelevant except for logic which taught one how to think correctly. Aristotle said the soul uses the body as an instrument and through it the soul employs the faculties such as sight and hearing; al-Ghazali, in the "flying man" thought-experiment said a man is aware of his physical existence as he is aware of himself thinking.

Al-Ghazali concluded that the mystics — the Sufis — were the heirs of the Prophet. They alone walked the path of direct knowledge and they were the decisive authorities on doctrine. At the same time, he affirmed the indispensable need for the exoteric framework, i.e. law and theology, to make that knowledge possible. He refuted in particular, after the murder of his patron the Vizier Niẓām al-Mulk, the beguiling teachings of the *Ta'līmiyyah*, or Ismā'īlīs — then active as the Assassin sect — with their enticements of "secret teachings" and "hidden masters".

Towards the end of his life he returned briefly to teach at Nayshābūr and then to Ṭūs, where he lived out his days among Sufi disciples. Al-Ghazālī is a man for all seasons: for the Sufis, al-Ghazālī is a Sufi; for the theologians he is a theologian; for the legalists, he is a jurist.

"To refute" he said, "one must understand". It was clear that he had studied all the schools, had heard their case, taken all their arguments and positions into account, and had understood them. Having established a credible synthesis of philosophy, theology, law, and mysticism in his own person by working back to first principles, al-Ghazālī could put the disciplines themselves in order.

Until his time, Islam had been developing in directions that seemed to exclude each other, and yet each one claimed to be the most authentic view of Islam. With al-Ghazālī an age came to an end and a new age began. The controversies of the Mu'tazilites and Ash'arites had been played out; different sects and points of view had developed and staked their claims to truth and orthodoxy. With al-Ghazālī philosophy crept out of Islam but Islam took a second breath and devotional mysticism took its place. After him the essential doctrines, freed from the entanglements of the groundwork, could develop their fullest expressions. If the prophetic revelation was a concave lens which diffused knowledge from the Divine world into this, al-Ghazālī was a convex lens that took the separating rays of light and refocussed them. He ushered in the second age of Islam. At the end of his *Munqidh min aḍ-dalāl*, as-Ghazālī wrote:

> We pray God Almighty that He will number us among those whom He has chosen and elected, whom He has led to the truth and guided, whom He has inspired to remember Him and not to forget Him, whom He has preserved from evil in themselves so that they not prefer aught to Him, and whom He has made His own so that they serve only Him.

After al-Ghazālī the voices of the different schools were not stilled, but a fresh measure of unity and harmony had been achieved. What had become differentiated in history from the pristine unity of the Prophet's time, became reintegrated anew upon a different plane. With it came a sense of hierarchy and a tighter re-marshalling of society's intellectual faculties to enable it to respond to the needs of a sophisticated civilisation. It was as if the centre had reasserted itself, and as if al-Ghazālī had looked at the pieces of a puzzle, each claiming to be the complete picture of Islam, and put them all in their proper place. There emerged the image of a new organism, a complete body with mysticism or Sufism as the heart, theology as the head, philosophy as its rationality binding the different parts together, and law as the working limbs. Islamic civilisation had come to maturity. *See* PHILOSOPHY.

Ghazwah (lit. "a raid", "an attack"; pl. *ghazawāt*). In particular, the desert raid, and by extension also a battle, war, etc. Related to this is *ghāzī*, "a warrior", or "war leader", which is sometimes used as a title among the Turks. The Italian word *razzia* comes from *ghazwah*. An alternate form of the word is *ghazvat* in Turkey and Persia.

Occasionally *ghazwah* is used to mean *jihād*, or "holy war".

Ghulāt (Persian for Arabic *ghulāh* sing. *ghāli*; lit. "extremists"; "exaggerators"). A polemical name for the Shī'ite sects that endow 'Alī (or others) with Divine qualities, or simply assert that the Divinity resides in someone. Exactly who is and who is not termed *ghulāt* varies according to the school of thought. Generally, those sects that go beyond the Twelve-Imām position are *ghulāt* in almost everyone's eyes. Shahrastānī (d. *548*/1153), the historian of religions, wrote:

> The Shī'ite extremists elevate their Imāms above the rank of created beings and regard them as Divine. These anthropomorphic tendencies are derived from Incarnationists, Transmigrationists, Jews, and Christians. For the Jews liken the Creator to the creature, and the Christians liken the creature to the Creator.
>
> This anthropomorphism is primarily and characteristically Shī'ite; only at a later period was it adopted by certain sects of the Sunnīs, Followers of the True Way.

The Ghulāt were also linked to political discontent on the part of the poor. Tradition recounts that among the early leaders of the ghuluww, there was a weaver, a seller of barley, and a dealer in straw; populists, in other words. *See* SHĪ'ISM.

Ghusl. The "greater ablution", which confers a state of purity necessary to perform ritual acts such as prayer. One must acquire the state of *ghusl* before one can enter a mosque or any area purified for prayer, and before one can touch an Arabic Koran. The impurities which occasion the need for *ghusl* are called *janābāt* (sing. *janābah* or *junub*) and are: intromission; ejaculation; menstruation; childbirth; contact with a corpse (this latter is considered by some to be *Sunnah* only, that is, recommended but not obligatory).

Ghusl is the washing of the entire body beginning with the private parts which cannot be touched again during the performance of *ghusl*. Then the *ta'awwudh* and *basmalah* are pronounced along with the formulation of the *niyyah* (intention). The right hand cups water and is passed over the head, torso and limbs in an order which gives precedence to the upper, the front, and the right side over the lower, the back, and the left. The navel is cleansed eight times. The fingers of one hand clean the interstices of the fingers of the other; the insterstices between the toes are cleaned. The mouth and nostrils are rinsed with water. At the end one pronounces the *ḥamdalah*. This is the most strict procedure, that of the Mālikī school. Other Schools of Law maintain that it is enough to immerse the body in water or simply pour water over the body, that is, to take a shower preceded by the *niyyah* and the sacred formulas above.

When it is impossible to perform ghusl for lack of water or reasons of health, it can be replaced with *tayammum*, or purification with earth or stone, before the performance of a ritual. An additional *tayammum* is performed before entering a mosque and a stone is placed at the doorway for this purpose. A repetition of the *tayammum* is necessary for each prayer (*ṣalāt*).

Ghusl is also performed by a convert before being formally received into Islam, after the washing of the dead, major blood letting, and before putting on *iḥrām* for pilgrimage. By way of custom and "good measure", rather than an obligation, it is performed even if not necessary, the evening before the congregational Friday prayer, and before the festivals of 'Īd al-Aḍḥā and 'Īd al-Fiṭr. *See* ABLUTIONS; BASMALAH; TA'AWWUDH; TAYAMMUM; WUḌŪ'.

Glorification, *see* TAMJĪD.

Gnawah. A loose association of street musicians found in Morocco, with a vaguely religious character. Originally descendants of slaves brought from Guinea, whence their name, the Gnawah practice ecstatic trance dancing, which in various forms is common to the desert and rural areas. The Gnawah are sometimes called upon to play their drums (which are beaten with curved sticks), to beat their iron clapping instruments, somewhat like large castanets, and to dance in relays for days on end in order to draw someone out of a sickness by the invigorating nature of their rhythms and music.

In some Sufi orders the mystical dance (*haḍrah*) has degenerated into trance dancing; the Gnawah are the reverse: trance dancing aspiring to a higher calling by claiming to be a *haḍrah*. To this end some Gnawah have claimed the famous saint 'Abd al-Qādir al-Jīlānī as the authority for their practices. Today the Gnawah are losing their ethnic identity and dying out. They often perform as professional entertainers, and for the purposes of this demand there are today many imitators, who far outnumber the authentic Gnawah.

God, *see* ALLĀH; FIVE DIVINE PRESENCES.

Gnosis, *see* MA'RIFAH.

Gnosticism, *see* MANICHEISM; SEVENERS.

Gökalp, Ziya (*1293-1343*/1876-/1924). A professor of sociology at the University of Istanbul. He promoted Turkish nationalism, or Pan-Turanianism, but his overriding aim was the secularisation of Turkish society. Wishing to turn Islam into a kind of rationalist and "scientific" ethical culture, Gökalp unhesitatingly copied western models even while glorifying Turkishness. He was the precursor of Atatürk, who put Gökalp's ideas into practice with the policy of *laik*, or the laicisation of Turkish life. Until the changes imposed by Atatürk after the First World War, Turkish society was completely immersed in Islam.

Many of the ideas which set modern Turks against Islam can be traced back to Gökalp's propaganda. These blame the Arabic alphabet for the widespread illiteracy which prevailed in Turkey, as it did in all traditional countries. The introduction of the Roman script cut the Turks off from their cultural past, and the subsequent increase in literacy may more logically be ascribed to the introduction of universal and compulsory schooling. The teachings of Gökalp once moved a ministerial committee to recommend putting pews in mosques.

It was until recently the law in Turkey that, except for the minister of religion, one could not wear a brimless hat, the normal headgear of Muslims, in public. (The headgear must be brimless in order to allow the touching of the forehead to the ground in prayer). Such was the extent of Gökalp's influence. Today, Islam is allowed a longer leash in Turkey, and all Imāms are allowed to wear brimless hats.

Gold. The wearing of gold ornaments by men — but not by women — is forbidden by the *sharī'ah*. Nevertheless, gold wedding rings are now commonly worn by men in Islamic countries, as well as gold watches.

The *sharī'ah's* intention behind this prohibition for men is to maintain a state of sobriety, reserve, concentration, and spiritual poverty, that is, the perfections of the centre. Women, who symbolize unfolding, infinitude, manifestation, are not bound by the same constraints.

Gospel of Barnabas, *see* BARNABAS, GOSPEL of.

Grand Mosque of Mecca, *see* KA'BAH.

Greetings. The *sharī'ah* makes the offering and return of greetings obligatory. When one Muslim encounters another, the greeting is *as-salāmu 'alaykum* ("peace be upon you"), and the response is *wa 'alaykumu-s-salām* ("and upon you be peace"). In either case, one may add *wa raḥmatu-Llāhi ta'ālā wa barakātuh* ("and God's mercy and blessings"). The same greeting may be used upon parting company and at any time, day or night, although in the morning the greeting *ṣabāḥ al-khayr* ("good morning"), to which the answer *ṣabāḥ an-nūr* ("morning of light"), is more common. When two groups meet, a "sufficient number" of each group must offer and return greetings.

Because it is used all the time, it is often forgotten that *as-salāmu 'alaykum* is a religious greeting, as *pax tecum* was a greeting of Christians in the Middle Ages. Sometimes Muslims refrain from using this greeting with non-Muslims and substitute some other form of salutation.

It is the practice in letters to write *al-ḥamdu li-Llāhi waḥdah* ("praise to God alone") at the head; the *basmalah* ("In the Name of God") is properly reserved for formal documents.

Gri-Gri. In West Africa, an amulet with Koranic inscriptions sealed inside, for protection from harm. Such an amulet is called a *ḥijāb* in North Africa.

Amulets are widely used everywhere in the Islamic world, but in some regions they are elevated to an extraordinary degree of importance, a practice which receives the disapprobation of strict and informed Muslims. Magic squares are also used as amulets. *See* AMULET; REFUGE.

Groupe Islamique Armé (GIA) An Algerian Islamist clandestine organisation. When the Algerian military annulled democratic elections which would have brought a Fundamentalist party, the Islamic Salvation Front, to power in 1992, the GIA turned on the government and society by killing thousands in an indescriminate terror campaign in the following ten years.

Guarded Tablet, *see* AL-LAWḤ al-MAḤFŪẒ.

Gunbad. Tombs in the form of towers, with two levels inside, used by the Seljuks, and found in the confines of their empire. The style of the gunbad suggests that it is the representation of a Central Asian funeral tent dressed for a great chieftain, rendered in stone.

"Guru", *see* MURSHID.

H

Habous. A common name in Morocco for *waqf*. *See* WAQF.

Ḥaḍana (lit. "care"). The right of children to receive upkeep from the father before and after a divorce. Ḥaḍana also means that the care and custody of a child belongs to the mother, or close female relative, until the child attains a certain maturity, which for boys is considered to be the age of seven, and for girls, the age of puberty. The next stage of custody belongs to the father, or close male relative.

al-Ḥaḍārāt al-ilāhiyyah al-khams, *see* FIVE DIVINE PRESENCES.

Ḥadath. The impurities which are removed by the lesser ablution (*wuḍū'*) before prayer. *See* WUḌŪ'.

Ḥadd (lit. "limit", "borderline", "ordinance", "statute", pl. *ḥudūd*). A legal term for the offenses and punishments which are defined in the Koran.

Hadi of Sabzawar, Mullā (*1212-1295*/1797-1878) One of the foremost Persian philosophers of the 19th century, a continuator of the "School of Iṣfahān", that is, of Mullā Sadra. Mullā Hadi had inherited means but was noted for living abstemiously and giving generously to poor students. He studied at Meshhed and at Iṣfahān but returned to Sabzawar to teach. He died in the course of a lecture, surrounded by students and repeating the words *Hua, Hua* (the Divine Name "He"). Among his works is the *Asraru al-Ḥikam* (Secrets of Philosophy).

Ḥadīth (lit. "speech", "report", "account"). Specifically, Traditions relating to the deeds and utterances of the Prophet as recounted by his companions. "In the time of the Prophet Arabs in the Peninsula would greet each other by asking 'what is your news (*khabar*) of the Prophet?'" (Ṭabarī).

Ḥadīth are divided into two groups: *ḥadīth qudsi* ("sacred Ḥadīth"), in which God Himself is speaking through the Prophet, and *ḥadīth sharīf* ("noble Ḥadīth"), the Prophet's own utterances. Ḥadīth may enunciate doctrine or provide a commentary upon it. They deal with the contents of the Koran, social and religious life, and everyday conduct, down to the tying of sandals. They are the basis, second only to the Koran, for Islamic law (sharī'ah).

The *Muṣannaf* are collections classified by subject: The most respected collection of all is the *Jami' as-Ṣaḥiḥ* of Muḥammad Ibn Ismā'īl al-Bukhārī (d. *256*/870). This has 7,397 Ḥadīth under 3,450 subject headings (*bāb, abwāb*). Next is the *Ṣaḥiḥ* of Abū-l-Ḥusayn Muslim ibn al-Ḥajjāj (d. *261*/875); usually simply called "Muslim"). These two *Ṣaḥiḥs* or *Ṣaḥiḥayn* (the Arabic dual of Ṣaḥiḥ) are the foremost collections. The *Six Muṣannaf*, the principal canonic collections, (i.e. those accepted as authoritative) also known as the "six books" (*al-kutub as-sittah*) are the *Ṣaḥiḥayn*, and: the collection of Abū Dawūd as-Sijistanī (4,500 Ḥadīth, d. *261*/875), Abū 'Isa Muḥammad at-Tirmidhī (d. *279*/892 or *302*/915). The collection of at-Tirmidhī and Abū Dāwūd are *kutūb sunan*, or collections of Ḥadīth specifically relevant to the practices of the Prophet. Finally there are the collections of an-Nasa'i (d. *303*/915), and Ibn Mājā (d. *273*/886), another *kitāb sunan*. These collections include sayings of some of the Companions. Abū Hurayrah is the Companion cited as the primary source of the greatest number of Ḥadīth.

Equally famous is the *Muwattā'* of Mālik ibn Anas, the first collection ever written down. Another kind of collection is the *Musnad*. *Musnads* are collections grouped around the primary source, that is, the transmitter. The most famous (of four well known *Musnads*) is the *Musnad* of Ibn Ḥanbal, founder of a school of law (d. *241*/855). Ibn Ḥanbal's Musnad contains 30,000 Ḥadīth. That of Aṭ-Ṭayālisi (d. *202*/818) is the first *Musnad* with 2,767 Ḥadīth from 600 authorities.

Of later large compilations which drew upon the early collections the best known is the *Maṣabiḥ as-Sunnah* by al-Baghawī (d. *510*/1116) revised as the *Mishkat al-Maṣabiḥ* (over 6,000 Ḥadīth) by Walī ad-Din at-Tabrizī (d. *737*/1337). Many other

Ḥadīth are found in such books as the *Ḥilyat al-Awliyā'* ("Adornment of the Saints") of Abū Nu'aym. There are also small collections of forty significant Ḥadīth (forty as an exemplary number of Ḥadīth that everyone should know). The first is by al-Marwazī (d. *299*/912) and the most famous is the *Forty Ḥadīth of an-Nawāwī* (d. *675*/1277).

At the beginning of Ḥadīth literature there were important "family" collections of Ḥadīth, written down or maintained in memory. These came from Anas ibn Mālik (the Prophet's servant (d. *91*/710); 'Abd Allāh ibn Mas'ūd (d. *32*/653); Zayd ibn Thabit (who like the Caliph 'Umar, did not wish the Ḥadīth to be written down, presumably so as not to rival the Koran); Ibn 'Umar (son of the Caliph d. *73*/692); Ibn 'Abbās (son of the Prophet's uncle, d. *67*/687). Listening to a raconteur of prophetic Ḥadīth was an evening entertainment at the Umayyad court from the time of Mu'awiyah.

'Umar II ('Umar ibn 'Abd al-'Azīz, reigned *99-101*/717-720) the pious Umayyad, desirous of promulgating laws in conformity with Islamic traditions, encouraged systematic gathering of Ḥadīth and commissioned Muḥammad ibn Muslim ibn Shihāb az-Zuhrī (d. *124*/742) to make a collection. Az-Zuhrī died before this was done but he is credited with establishing the standard of attaching to the Ḥadīth a full *isnād*, or chain of transmission. He had students, so Ḥadīth study was becoming a science. It could be said that all the later religious sciences were at this period subsumed under the covering notion of Ḥadīth. Even after the separate development of *fiqh* (law) and *kalam* (theology) schools of theologic study were still called *Dar al-Ḥadīth* ("House of Ḥadīth", a generic name for this kind of institution). The best known Dar al-Ḥadīth was founded in Damascus by the Atabeg Nūr ad-Din (d. *560*/1173). Other such schools existed in Jerusalem, Cairo, Mosul, Nayshabur, and elsewhere.

The *isnād* is the chain of transmission. Distinctions are made according to whether the Ḥadīth was "heard"; "reported"; "disclosed"; "found"; and other categories relating to the circumstances of transmission. The transmission is the *riwayah*; the transmitter is a *rawī*, who, it was admitted, could "edit" the Ḥadīth and improve upon its form and style, whence the same Ḥadīth is found reported in different degrees of amplitude. The *matn*, meaning "letters" (*mutūn*), is the actual text of the Ḥadīth.

The canonical collections grade Ḥadīth according to indices of authenticity. The highest grade is *mutawatir*, that is "recurrent" or reported by many different sources; then *ṣaḥiḥ* "reliable"; *ḥasan* "good"; *da'if* "weak", and *mawdu'a*, or "fabricated". When collections of Ḥadīth began to appear, there were also studies by scholars of what they considered to be fabricated Ḥadīth; there was a saying "that there is no more reprehensible act than the fabricating of Ḥadīth", which shows awareness that many Ḥadīth were not historically authentic.

The collections of Bukhārī and Muslim were scrupulously compiled in the first two and one half centuries of Islam. Their authenticity was assured by the criterion which the people of the time found most valid, that of an authoritative *isnād*, or chain of transmission. The method was based on the assumption that it was unthinkable for God-fearing men to lie about matters which they held sacred; each human link in the chain vouchsafed the others. If in the *isnād* there were persons whose integrity could be doubted for any reason, however small, the authenticity of the Ḥadīth was to that extent weakened. Biographical study also served to establish the plausibility of the transmissions. Naturally, fabricated Ḥadīth also had fabricated *isnād*, but criticism of the *matn* would be equivalent to dogmatic discussions of Islam itself — thus analysis discussions turned around the *isnād*, but often as euphemism for a discussion of the contents. Rather than enter into a debate of verisimilitude, Ibn Khaldūn remarked on the "well known bad memory" of the family of the principle transmitters of Mahdī Ḥadīth as a way of saying that the Mahdī Ḥadīth are false; (they do not appear in the *Ṣaḥiḥayn* and first with Abū Dawūd). But on the other hand, since there were also Ḥadīth which denied the existence of a Mahdī, it was ultimately theological consensus which determined which Ḥadīth would lead to the elaboration of doctrine, and which would not.

The Shī'ites call Ḥadīth by an another word, *khabar* ("news", pl. *akhbār*). For Shī'ites, the authenticity of a Ḥadīth is guaranteed not by an *isnād* which begins with the Companions, but by its transmission through 'Alī and the Imāms of Shī'ism. The Shī'ite collections of Ḥadīth, which were made during the Buyid period from *320-454*/932-1062, are considerably larger than the Sunnī ones, and contain references to the Imāms not found in Sunnī collections. (*See* al-KULAYNī; IBN BABAWAYH; at-ṬŪSĪ, MUḤAMMAD.)

Western scholars have often affirmed that Ḥadīth have been invented in order to justify some legal opinion or school of thought; this is undoubtedly true and even the early compilers rejected large numbers of Ḥadīth as fabricated. However, the sceptical tendency among Western scholars at one time went so far as to reject *ipso facto* any Ḥadīth which appeared to support a particular school or tendency. One orientalist was thus led to maintain that the Sufis had invented the saying: "Remember Me [God] I will remember you", since it so evidently fitted their teachings. In fact, this is not a Ḥadīth at all, but a quotation from the Koran (2:152). Even if, from a historical point of view, a particular Ḥadīth is false, it does not necessarily follow that the opinions, practices, or doctrines linked with it are suspect. A Ḥadīth may be false in the sense that the Prophet never spoke the words, but nevertheless true in that it is wholly consistent with his message.

Islam views the actions of a Divine Messenger as providential and unlimited in their inner nature. Therefore it is with the authority of the Koran, which states: "You have a noble example in God's Messenger" (33:21), that Islam bases its Sunnah upon the Ḥadīth in addition to the Koran. If the Ḥadīth were to play such an important role in the development of an entire civilisation, their scope must be vast. Throughout the centuries, as Islam evolved, it searched out the traditions of the Prophet's life to guide the faithful in situations not touched upon by the Koran. As primordial man, or as the expression of the plenitude of human possibilities, the Prophet in his life may well have manifested all the possibilities of Islam by act, thought, speech or gesture. Yet it is inconceivable that all these possibilities should be discoverable in the received canon of Ḥadīth, for they are as ultimately limitless. Thus, the legitimacy of legal decisions and intellectual developments reposes, ultimately, not upon Ḥadīth but upon their orthodoxy in relation to Islam as such; for Islam is always greater than the sum of its historical parts, and its possibilities could not possibly have been exhaustively treated in the historical Ḥadīth.

The Ḥadīth were accorded the role of basis of law in Islamic jurisprudence by the universally accepted methodology of ash-Shāfi'ī. It then became inevitable that as Islam unfolded in history, the need for the tangible support which Ḥadīth could provide for intellectual and cultural developments called forth the "missing" or "unspoken" Ḥadīth that were now required. If in the first centuries the standard by which Ḥadīth were measured was that of an impeccable *isnād*, the growing needs of an expanding Islam of later times added *de facto* another, one of verisimilitude in the eyes of a developed and sophisticated religious community.

Thus it came about that there grew up a corpus of Ḥadīth which were clearly impossible historically, and yet were repeatedly quoted and rarely questioned. To the modern Western mind this may appear an anomaly which reflects little credit on Islam's intellectual integrity, a confusion which it would be desirable to rectify. To do so would be to call into question, for example, the Sainte Chapelle, because the Crown of Thorns, which it was built to house, could be shown to be a medieval forgery. This relic, which a Byzantine emperor in need of money sold to St. Louis (followed by the baby linen of Jesus, the lance that pierced his side, the sponge and chain of his passion, the reed of Moses, and part of the skull of John the Baptist), called forth one of the most magnificent creations of Western civilisation. The resulting Chapel, rather than being a monument to gullibility, testifies to the authenticity, on the spiritual plane (which is more real than the material one), of its historical cause. Truth transcends historical niceties.

There are so-called "Ḥadīth" and "Sunnah" which are patently, or pointlessly, false, such as the common story that the Prophet went into rages upon seeing a shape resembling a cross, and shattered crosses whenever he found them. This is in such contradiction to the Prophet's nature that it is easy to see it as a zealot fable substituting human pettiness for Prophetic rigor. It is not true, nor does it add any depth or strength to what is in fact true. Then there are the polemical Ḥadīth which were invented as propaganda to support one or another party in dynastic and political struggles. There are also Ḥadīth, which have nothing objectionable in their content, but which the Prophet could not have uttered for historical reasons: "I [God] have a army in the east I call the Turks; I unleash them against any people that kindle my wrath." But there are others again which, although they appear late in history, have an authenticity of spirit about them, and have been accepted as authentic, to the extent that they were frequently repeated by Muslim scholars, and not challenged. This is a consensus of silence which amounts to acceptance. The scholars, and thence the *ummah* ("community"), have found them to be adequate expressions of the spirit of the Prophet's message. Among these are the sayings: "Who has seen me [the Prophet] has seen the Truth," and, "The first thing God created was Intellect."

When the Prophet was leading a prayer in the mosque of Medinah, and had finished the words "God hears him who praises Him", a man called out from the back, "Our Lord, and to Thee praise." The Prophet said that he saw Angels rushing to record those words, which were thereafter included in the canonical prayer.

Tradition records that the ritual, or canonical, prayer was taught to the Prophet by the Angel Gabriel. Yet here, the Prophet unhesitatingly incorporated the isolated words of an ordinary person into the context of a Divine ordinance. This, in effect, is what the Islamic community has done, in accepting as authentic, Ḥadīth which clearly could not be traced back to the Prophet.

These are the expression of a transpersonal genius and the living soul of the religious manifestation, and so, for all purposes, are the utterances of the Prophet. They are *virtually* authentic (just as the accepted Gospels are virtually true) because they are recognized as such by the Muslim community. Just as the Prophet could accept as part of the Divine revelation words spoken by a third party, so Islam has accepted, in effect, that some Ḥadīth are the Prophet speaking outside of time. *See* MUḤAMMAD; SUNNAH.

Ḥaḍrah (lit. "presence").

1. Divine Presence. (*See* FIVE DIVINE PRESENCES.)
2. In later Islam a courtly reference to the Caliph.
3. A title of respect or simply of politeness to any person. In the Near east it is pronounced as ḥazrat.
4. A popular name for the sacred dance of the Sufis. *See* 'IMĀRAH.

Ḥāfiẓ (present participle of the verb *ḥa-fa'-ẓa*, "to protect", "preserve" and, by extension, "to memorize"). One who has memorized the Koran. The goal of Koranic school education is to commit the entire Koran to memory, and many traditional Muslims have done so. As the Koran says of itself, it is easy to memorize; "And we have made the Koran easy for remembrance; are there then men who will be reminded?" (54:17). There are indeed *ḥuffāẓ* (pl. of ḥāfiẓ) who achieve this without understanding the Arabic of the sacred text, particularly in the Indian sub-continent and South-east Asia. In this case, it is the sound or the "form" of the revealed scripture that vehicles a supernatural, saving grace.

Ḥāfiẓ, Shams ad-Dīn Muḥammad (d. *793*/1391). A Persian poet of Shirāz, famous for his *Dīwān*, a collection of Sufic poetry. In Ḥāfiẓ there is a compression of many subjects into one *ghazāl*. The *ghazāl* has hemistichs and the rhyme is aa;ba;ca;da for 9,11,12 or exceptionally 15 lines (the epic is aa;bb;cc;dd). Ḥāfiẓ speaks of love, panegyric, wine songs, all in one, suffused by a mystical spirit producing a multifaceted result. Because of this, in Iran Ḥāfiẓ is often opened for the purpose of oracular divination. Love in Persian poetry is often addressed to an adolescent boy who can represent the divinity (in translations made in the past, such as below by Sir William Jones, the "boy" is made into a "maid"). Translations of Ḥāfiẓ usually are one and one half times longer than the Persian original, and none has ever been able to convey what it is that makes Ḥāfiẓ so famed.

Ḥāfiẓ was much studied by Goethe and influenced the modern school of Russian poetry. He was called the "Tongue of the Hidden".

Sweet maid, if thou would'st charm my sight,
And bid these arms thy neck enfold;
That rosy cheek, that lily hand
Would give thy poet more delight
Than all Bocara's vaunted gold,
Than all the gems of Samarcand.
Boy, let yon liquid ruby flow,
And bid thy pensive heart be glad,
Whate'er the frowning zealots say:
Tell them, their Eden cannot show
A stream so clear as Rocnabad,
A bower so sweet as Mosallay.
O! when these fair perfidious maids,
Whose eyes our secret haunts infest,
Their dear destructive charms display;
each glance my tender breast invades,
And robe my wounded soul of rest,
As Tartars seize their destin'd prey.
In vain with love our bosoms glow:
Can all our tears, can all our sighs,
New lustre to those charms impart?
Can cheeks, where living roses blow,
Where nature spreads her richest dyes,
Require the borrow'd gloss of art?
Speak not of fate: Oh! Change the theme.
And talk of odours, talk of wine,

Talk of the flowers that round us bloom:
'Tis all a cloud, 'tis all a dream:
To love and joy, thy thoughts confine,
Nor hope to pierce the sacred gloom.
Beauty has such resistless power,
That ever the chaste Egyptian dame
Sigh'd for the blooming Hebrew boy!
For her how fatal was the hour,
When to the banks of the Nilus came
A youth so lovely and so coy!
But oh! sweet maid, my counsel hear
(Youth should attend when those advise
Whom long experience renders sage):
While music charms the ravish'd ear:
While sparkling cups delight our eyes,
Be gay: and scorn the frowns of age.
What cruel answer have I heard!
And yet, by heaven, I love thee still;
Can aught be cruel from thy lip?
Yet say, how fell that bitter word
From lips which streams of sweetness fill,
Which naught but drops of honey sip?
Go boldly forth, my simple lay,
Whose accents flow with artless ease,
Like orient pearls at random strung:
Thy notes are sweet, the damsels say;
But O! far sweeter, if they please
The nymphs for whom these notes are sung.

Ḥafṣah. One of the wives of the Prophet, and a daughter of 'Umar. She knew how to read and write and participated in the collecting of the Koran during the Caliphate of 'Uthmān. She was entrusted with the safekeeping of one of the earliest written collections of Koranic verses, a *muṣḥaf* (a copy of the Koran), which had already existed during the Caliphate of Abū Bakr. *See* WIVES of the PROPHET.

Hagar, *see* ISMĀ'ĪL.

"Hagarism". A bizarre theory propounded in 1977 by Patricia Crone and Michael Cook, two Western Islamic scholars according to which Muḥammad never existed and Islam was a fiction which gradually came into existence over time but considerably later than the 7th century. According to this "theory" Islam was invented following Samaritanism as a model and projected back in time in order to dignify something mongrel, indefinable, and nondescript, which they called "Hagarism" from "Hagarenes", a contemptuous, racist, term for Arabs. The book was not purely a hoax or a satire although the idea that the Koran was made up for Hajjāj in order to replace "old Hagarene writings with others composed to his own taste", and that the Koran was based on such sources as the inscriptions on the Dome of the Rock rather than that the inscriptions came from the Koran, would make one think that they were making fun of scholars. As it turned out, the scholars simply could not tell the difference. So what was even more bizarre is that the Academic establishment at the time (or very few) did not summon up any intellectual discrimination to point out the absurdity of the idea, or pounce with characteristic eagerness upon any error, but rather passed over this in silence, or were, in fact, full of admiration over the extensive scholarship! As one Ivy League professor said in his classroom — in 1989 — "they can't be that wrong since they were rewarded with positions at prestigious universities."

It may have helped that the authors in their introduction did say that they did not expect anyone to take it seriously, which, however, explains nothing and does not remedy the fact that some gullible souls have been taken in. (They did say in the introduction that the book was written "by infidels for infidels" and they did not expect any believer to take them seriously; cf: Koran 2:102 Nor did they [Harūt and Marūt] teach it to anyone till they had said: "We are only a temptation, therefore disbelieve not (in the guidance of Allah)." It may be noted that while political correctness dictates what is truth in the Academic world, in private many scholars harbor ideas which they rarely dare whisper to another soul, and this is an example why.

Hagia Sophia (Gr. lit. "Divine wisdom"). The famous basilica of Constantinople, now Istanbul, and today called Aya Sofia, using the modern Greek pronunciation. Under the Ottoman Turks the architect Sinan remodeled the church, by then a mosque, with great skill. Since the time of Atatürk it has been a museum.

When the city of Constantinople fell to the Ottoman Turks under Sultan Meḥmet II on Tuesday 29 May 1453, the conqueror ordered the edifice to be converted to a mosque in time for the congregational prayer on Friday. This consisted of the erection of a wooden minaret, the construction of a *miḥrāb* (a niche to indicate the direction of Mecca), and the addition of a *minbar*, a moveable staircase which served as a pulpit.

Meḥmet was to replace the wooden modifications with brick, and added arch buttresses and retaining walls to the building. The three stone minarets which complete the Aya Sofia's famous outline today were added by the architect Sīnān under Selim II and Murad III. *See* SĪNĀN.

Haidaris, *see* KHAKSĀRS.

Ḥajj, *see* PILGRIMAGE.

al-Ḥajjāj ibn Yūsuf ath-Thaqafī (*41-95*/661-714). The leading general of the early Umayyads. On behalf of the Umayyad rulers Marwān, 'Abd al-Malik, and al-Walīd, al-Ḥajjāj conducted a struggle against enemies of the state. At first he fought 'Abd Allāh ibn az-Zubayr who had raised opposition to the Umayyads, declared himself Caliph, and held Mecca, finally defeating him. Then al-Ḥajjāj was sent to pacify unrest in 'Irāq. He succeeded by unhesitatingly applying cruelty and force, and remained a loyal Umayyad governor of 'Irāq for twenty years until his death.

Al-Ḥajjāj was a competent soldier and strategist, and an able administrator. Under him the Arab armies expanded into India and Central Asia. But his reputation for ruthlessness and brutality completely overshadows any good report of his qualities. It is therefore a great irony that the present building of the Ka'bah dates in large part from his reconstruction of it after the conquest of Mecca from 'Abd Allāh ibn az-Zubayr, and that the introduction of vowel markings into Arabic from Syriac, in order to prevent misreading of the Koran, was initiated under his direction.

Ḥākim. 1. A ruler or governor.
2. The name of a Fāṭimid Caliph who died in *411*/1021. Al-Ḥākim had the Church of the Holy Sepulchre destroyed in Jerusalem, an event which was a contributory cause to the Crusades. The ruler was noted for his erratic behavior and was responsible for events which led to the creation of the Druze sect. He passed a series of laws which have sometimes been considered signs of madness. But these laws have also been explained as attempts to preserve a system, or rather an "anti-system" which was collapsing, by the rules of that anti-system. Thus Ḥākim's law against "women coming out of their houses in the day" was an attempt, according to Vatikiotis, to remove from the system the wealth of his female relatives by not allowing them to participate in the economy, This was rather like measures put forward as the Soviet Union was collapsing, measures such as the sudden, abrupt removal of 50 and 100 ruble notes in one day from circulation which created tremendous upheaval but made sense to the Communist financial authorities. *See* DRUZES.

Ḥākim. 1. Lit. "The Wise", *al-Ḥakīm*, a name of God.
2. In classical times a title for someone learned as a doctor. At that time medicine was part of philosophy and a *ḥakīm* was versed in both fields.

Ḥāl (lit. "a state", "condition"; pl. *aḥwāl*). A technical term in Sufism for a transitory state of illumination, as opposed to a *maqām* ("station") which, once acquired, remains a permanent station of the soul. Ibn 'Aṭā' Allāh says: "When He wants to show his grace to you, He creates states in you and attributes them to you."

The Persian Sufi Abū Naṣr as-Sarrāj (d. *378*/988) lists some typical states in his Kitāb al-Lumā': attentiveness (*murāqabah*); the feeling of nearness to God (*qurb*); love (*maḥabbah*); hope in God (*rajā' fī-Llāh*); longing (*shawq*); familiarity (*uns*); confidence (*iṭmīn*); contemplativeness (*mushāhadah*); and certitude (*yaqīn*).

Ḥalāl (lit. "released" [from prohibition]). That which is lawful, particularly food, and meat from animals that have been ritually slaughtered. The opposite is *ḥarām*. *See* FOOD; RITUAL SLAUGHTER.

Ḥalīmah bint Abī Dhu'ayb. The Beduin foster mother of the Prophet who cared for him as a child. The name Ḥalīmah means the "mild, caring one". Customarily, the town Arabs gave a small boy to the Beduins for several years, against payment, to be brought up speaking the purer Arabic of the desert and to be tempered by the hardships of desert life. Her husband's name was Ḥarīth; they belonged to the Banū Sa'd ibn Bakr, a branch of the Ḥawāzīn. *See* RIḌĀ'

al-Ḥallāj, Ḥusayn ibn Manṣūr (*244-309*/857-922). A Persian mystic born in Baida in southern Iran who was tried for Manicheism or dualist heresy (*az-zandaqa*) by the 'Abbāsid authorities in Baghdad and put to death. Al-Ḥallāj was famed for his poetry which is highly appreciated to this day. He had no small number of disciples in many milieus of 'Abbāsid society, and a degree of popular acclaim.

Miracles were ascribed to him, but so was wizardry. He was a member, or even head of a secret organisation (his father had taken the family to live in Wasiṭ which was a centre for the Qarmaṭīs, and before them, Manicheans), and he was married to a woman from a family, the Karnaba'i, who were Zanj revolutionaries and pro-Zaydi. In his travels to Turkestan he was called by the Manichean title of *muqit*, which means "vegetarian provider". He had apparently many thousands of sympathizers, followers, or co-religionists scattered far and wide who were vegetarians. (Massignon calls them "Hallajians".) In particular, they consumed large amounts of lettuce and endive, which are "light bearing" plants in Manicheism. He may have been involved in stirring up revolt against the civil authorities, or indoctrinating people in some movement, for in the houses of al-Ḥallāj's disciples the 'Abbāsid authorities found

> a great number of documents, written on Chinese paper, some of them in gold ink. Some were mounted on satin or silk, and bound in fine leather. Among other papers were curious files of letters from his provincial missionaries, and his instructions to them as to what they should teach, how they should lead people on from stage to stage, how different classes of people should be approached according to their level of intelligence and degree of receptiveness.

For many years he traveled widely visiting the cells of his co-religionists in 'Irāq, Iran, and Central Asia. He made three pilgrimages to Mecca, went to India (Sindh) twice, and once to Chinese Turkestan, apparently to visit the Idiqut, the Manichean Uighur ruler in Qocho (Turfan) on the Silk Road. From his propagandizing and religious activities he came to be called al-Ḥallāj, short for *ḥallāj al-asrār*, "the Carder (*ḥallāj*) of hearts or consciences" (to card is to disentangle, by combing, the fibers of wool, cotton, etc.). However, in the communistic Qarmaṭī circles in which Ḥallaj evidently travelled many leaders emphasized their "worker" origins because they appealed to discontent of the poorer classes; thus one finds another al-Ḥallaj, this one named Khalaf who was the Ismā'īlī organizer of Rayy, and that Ḥamdān Qarmaṭ was a mule driver.

He remains enigmatic; many consider him a Saint, even a model of esoteric realisation; others considered him to be too ambiguous to be a Saint; that his miracles were theatrical deceptions and staged to impress, involving the collusion of supporters or accomplices, and that his doctrine was un-Islamic. It was reported in testimony against him that al-Ḥallāj himself, and members of his family, had encouraged veneration of him verging on worship. "God is in heaven" he said "but He is also on earth". Even when he was young he had made claims which were startling:

> One day as I was walking with Ḥusayn ibn Manṣūr (said his master al-Makkī) in a narrow street at Mecca, I happened to be reciting from the Koran as we went along. He heard me.
>
> "I could utter such things as that myself", said he.
>
> From that day on, I saw him no more.

When al-Ḥallāj had already achieved a certain notoriety, it was reported of him:

> "At one time" (said Judge Muḥammad ibn 'Ubayd) I sat as a pupil with al-Ḥallāj. He was practicing devotion in the Mosque at Baṣrah in those days as a Koran teacher; it was before he made his absurd claims and got into trouble. One day my uncle was talking to him; I sat by listening. And Ḥallāj said: "I shall leave Baṣrah."
>
> "Why so?" my uncle inquired.
>
> "People here talk about me too much; I am tired of it."
>
> "What are they saying?" my uncle asked.
>
> "They see me do something", said Ḥallāj; "and without staying to make any inquiry, which would have disabused them, they go about proclaiming that Ḥallāj gets answers to prayer, even that he performs evidentiary miracles. Who am I, that such things should be granted me? I will give you an example: a few days ago a man brought me some dirhams and told me to spend them for the poor. There were no poor about at the moment, so I put them under one of the Mosque mats, by a pillar, and marked the pillar. So long as I waited, no one came by; so I went home for the night. Next morning

> I took my place by that pillar and began to pray; and some dervishes, poor Sufis, gathered about me. So I stopped my prayer, lifted up the mat, and gave them the money. And they have set the rumor flying that I had only to touch dust for it to turn to silver!"
>
> He told similar stories, until my uncle rose and said good-bye to him. He never went to see Ḥallāj again. "There's something of the deceiver about the man" he said to me. "We shall hear more of him someday."

An-Nadīm said that:

> There is a difference of opinion about his country and place of upbringing. It is said that he was from Khorāsān, from Naysābur. Then it is said that he was from Marw (Merv), and it is also said that he was from aṭ-Ṭālaqān. Some of his adherents said that he was from ar-Rayy, while others said from al-Jibāl, but nothing is clear about him or his town.

An-Nadīm had read, in the handwriting of Abū al-Ḥusayn 'Ubayd Allāh ibn Aḥmad ibn Abī Tāhir that:

> Al-Ḥusayn ibn Mansur al-Ḥallaj was a crafty man and a conjurer who ventured into the Ṣūfī schools of thought , affecting their ways of speech. He laid claim to every science, but nevertheless [his claims] were futile. He even knew something about the science of alchemy (*al-kīmīyā'*). He was ignorant, bold, obsequious, but courageous in the presence of sultans, attempting great things and ardently desiring a change of governments. Among his adherents he claimed divinity, speaking of divine union. He presented the tenets of the Shī'ah to the kings, but to the common people the doctrine of the Ṣūfīs. In enlarging upon this he claimed that the Divine Power had alighted within him, so that he was He, Almighty God, may He be glorified and sanctified. In connection with this he said "He is my nonexistence, exalted and great."

Al-Ḥallāj began as a disciple in Sufism of Sahl at-Tustarī, whom he left for al-Makkī, whom he also left. Then he attempted to enter the circle of disciples of al-Junayd al-Baghdādī, who refused him, saying: "I do not accept madmen." A well-wisher who followed the young al-Ḥallāj after this meeting tried to calm him: al-Ḥallāj answered: "I only respect [in al-Junayd] his age; the (mystical) degree is a gift and not something acquired." Al-Ḥallāj became well-known, nonetheless. He was often surprised by observers who found him in intimate conversation with God, apparently on exalted terms: "O Thou Whose Closeness girds my very skin." Despite his modest protestations that such utterings went "no further than the novice's first degree", and attempts to restrain those who heard them from proclaiming his apparent spiritual attainments, ample accounts of al-Ḥallāj's piety and nearness to God — indeed, of his Divinity — slipped out.

More than once al-Ḥallāj would cry out in the public marketplace words like these:

> O men! save me from God, for he has ravished me from myself, and does not return me to myself... woe to him who finds himself bereft after such a Presence and abandoned after such a union!

This reduced the people in the market to tears. Another report of a similar public outcry says that when he saw the people begin to weep, he broke out in laughter. (The word *charlatan* comes from the Italian *cerretano*, "one who cries out in the marketplace" and Latin for "seller of indulgences".) His ostentatious miracles often involved money: he pulled back the carpet in his house to reveal a heap of gold coins, and invited the spectators to take as much as they wanted.

In a classical miracle, al-Ḥallāj came to a party on the Tigris river and cast the illustrious guests into confusion by challenging them to solve a mystical word puzzle. The host, in the meantime, implored al-Ḥallāj to heal his sick and dying son. "He's already healed" al-Ḥallāj retorted. The child was sent for, and lo! was brought out in good health, indeed, "looking as if he had never been ill". The host then handed al-Ḥallāj a purse as a reward, containing, *he said*, three thousand dinars. Al-Ḥallāj immediately threw the purse into the Tigris, and left the party, leaving his question unanswered, but saying "You had some questions to ask of me, I think, but what questions could *you* ask of *me*? For I see only too well how right you are, and how wrong I am." The next day, the host recounted the previous events to other guests and expressed regret (in stage magic parlance, "the hook"), saying that had he known al-Ḥallāj would throw the money away, he would not have given it. Presto! a messenger arrived, presenting the purse, dripping wet but full of gold, to the remorseful giver. The publicity stunt is familiar stage magic. It began with the guests being distracted (in magic parlance "misdirected") by being given a word puzzle to solve, the host, in collusion with al-Ḥallāj, never showed the child sick, but only a child "cured". The purse that was thrown in the Tigris was only *said* to contain gold dinars, but was empty. A similar purse, wet from the river but full of gold was presented to the guests who heard the account of the previous evening's events.

Another miracle was: "One day he moved his hand scattering musk over the people. Another day he moved his hand scattering money. Then one of the discerning persons present said to him, 'Now I see well-known money, but I shall believe in you, as will the people with me, if you give me money on which there is your own name and that of your father.' He replied, 'But how? No such thing is made!' Then he [the questioner] said, 'Whoever has caused something nonexistent to appear has produced something which is not made.'" Massignon, who calls Ḥallāj the "martyr of truth" admits as deceitful "miracles" the "case of the inflating clothes", "the disappearing fish", and the "phoney" blind man; to which can be added: the appearance of subsisting without food, producing food out of his sleeve, and restoring a dead parrot to life, after passing the sleeve of his cloak over the dead bird, the *second time* the bird was presented for resuscitation, having had ample time to find a suitable live substitute.

Thus, not everyone, of course, was convinced:

> Ḥallāj converted many people to his system, and some important men among the rest. It was the Reactionaries he most hoped to win over, for he thought their belief as a good preliminary to his own; and he sent an emissary to Ibn Nawbakht, a member of that sect [the intellectual leader of the Shī'ites of Baghdad].
>
> Ibn Nawbakht was a cautious, intelligent man. Your master's miracles, he said to the disciple, may well be conjuring tricks. I am, he went on, what may be called a martyr to love: I enjoy the society of the ladies more than any other thing on earth. Unfortunately, however, I suffer from baldness. I have to let what hair I have grow long, and pull it over my forehead, and hold it there with my turban. And I have to disguise my grizzled beard with dye. Now, if Ḥallāj will give me a head of hair and a black beard, I will believe in whatever system he preaches; I will call him the Prophetic Vicar or the Sovereign if he likes; nay, I'll call him a Prophet, or even the Almighty!

The clue to this account is the description of Ibn Nawbakht as a "cautious intelligent" man; that is, it was not mere incomprehension that led to his rebuffing al-Ḥallāj's advances, but the fact that he saw through him. And it is not without humor that he asked for a cure for baldness.

But al-Ḥallāj had highly placed followers in sensitive government positions, among them the Caliph al-Muqtadir's mother and his chamberlain an-Nāsir; and he preached the existence of Divinity in certain members of the 'Alīd family. (Which did not prevent the Twelver Shī'ite Hidden Imām, by way of his third *wakil* Ibn Rawḥ (Ibn Ruḥ) Nawbakhti, from condemning al-Ḥallāj to death with a *tawqī'* in *308*/920, even before the Caliph Muqtadir issued his own *tawqī'* or sentence.)

In *300*/913 al-Ḥallāj, while in hiding in Sus, was captured by a member of the state intelligence apparatus and placed under arrest. He spent several years in detention for suspicious activities and the propagation of dubious doctrines. After several trials (which created unrest in Baghdad), he was condemned for *zandaqa*, or Manichean heresy, reluctantly, by the civil and religious authorities alike (even including some Sufis). After his execution rebellions broke out in several places including Ṭālaqān.

At the time the Qarmaṭī revolt was underway, the Fāṭimids were rising in North Africa, and the authorities were alarmed by the use of religion for political subversion. Ḥallāj was often accused of being a Qarmaṭī and was once pilloried by the police with an inscription "Qarmaṭī agent" around his neck. Early on he had contacts with the Zanj revolt in which Zaydis and "extreme" Shī'ites were involved. After his execution Hallāj's head was paraded around Khorāsān to prove that he was dead. (All of the splinters of the Dualist movements, Ismā'īlīs, Assassins, and even Druzes were to claim that he had been one of their *dā'īs*, or propagandists. It was Naṣir ad-Dīn Ṭūsi, a crypto-Ismā'īlī, who, as inspector for the Mongols, had Ḥallāj's tomb restored in Karkh.)

With public order at stake, religious orthodoxy, at least as regarded doctrines which cloaked organisations whose scope went far beyond spiritual contemplation, was a critical issue. Also, there was a power struggle in Baghdad over who would control the ostensibly Sunni government: the contest was between Twelve Imām Shī'ites and ghulāt, "extreme" Shī'ites, who also led the revolts in the desert. The Twelve Imām Shī'ites won, in Baghdad. Al-Ḥallāj's execution was followed by that of many of his followers, by Massignon's accounts, as many as ten thousand; and not a few of the followers deliberately sought out execution on purpose to become martyrs in imitation of their religious ideal, that is, Mani, if they were indeed crypto-Manicheans as the authorities alleged. Others sought refuge by leaving Baghdad and going to the regions near Baṣrah (where the Qarmaṭīs were active) and to Khorāsān.

In any case, al-Ḥallāj had publicly proclaimed himself a heretic, saying such things as: "I have renounced faith in God, and this renunciation is obligatory for me, whereas for any Muslim it is execrable."

And: "To claim to know Him is ignorance [in radical Gnosticism Bythos, the Abyss or *al-ghaib* is unknowable]; to persist in serving Him is disrespect; to stop fighting Him is madness" etc. "To think that God can mix himself with the human", al-Ḥallāj said, "is impiety... and *shirk*" ("association"; i.e. he meant that God hidden in some form within the world remained *fully* divine). "I am an orphan (i.e. cut off from outwardly professing my religion, but I have a Father" (the "Father of Greatness" of the Gnostics). Behind this antinomianism was his heretical interpretation of *Tawḥīd* ("Divine Unity"), which was that he, al-Ḥallāj, was God *completely* without any trace of humanity. Once in Iṣfahān, a preacher named 'Alī ibn Sahl was speaking about wisdom; al-Ḥallāj arrived on the scene and said: "Impudent one, you let yourself talk about wisdom while I am still alive!" The preacher was not intimidated and had him chased out of the city as a *zindiq* ("heretic" or Manichean dualist). Al-Ḥallāj finished his career in a public execution on March 26, 922 which drew large and sympathetic crowds; he was scourged, gibbeted, and finally decapitated the next day. Then the remains were burned, as was the accepted procedure with *zindiqs*. An official reported that:

> His disciples asserted that the person who had endured the scourging was not he, but some enemy of his on whom his likeness had been cast. Some of them even claimed to have seen him afterwards, and to have heard something from him to that effect, along with more nonsense not worth the trouble of transcribing.

Al-Ḥallāj is famous for having said: *Ana al-Ḥaqq* ("I am the Truth; the Real", as much as to say "I am God"). *Al-Ḥaqq* was the Gnostics preferred name for God; Mani called himself "the Prophet of the God of Truth" (a Manichean term). Aḥmad ibn Fātik said: "I heard al-Ḥallāj say 'I am the Truth — and the truth belongs to God — clothed with His essence, there is no difference (between us)'." This kind of declaration has earned al-Ḥallāj admiration from some; but arising in the midst of a religion whose beginning and end is the incomparable Absoluteness of God, the revelation of which in the *shahādah* is the cord of salvation, it was bound to raise questions and cause trouble. Al-Ḥallāj said *Ana al-Ḥaqq* in his poetry; according to didactic tradition he also announced it to the Sufi master al-Junayd, the mystic least likely to be impressed by such a proposition. His reply is that of orthodox Sufism: "Not so", said al-Junayd. "It is *through al-Ḥaqq* that you exist."

It is not that al-Junayd, a Sufi, denied knowledge of God without otherness (*tawḥīd*); but he defined it as the removal of obstacles between man and God. At the end of the path man remained man and God remained God, (*al-'abd yabqā-'l-'abd, wa-r-Rabb yabqā-'r-Rabb*), a position which can admit that man's realisation of God is without limit, without contradiction, without reservation, without even the *shirk* ("association of another reality with God") that arises from thought and conceptualisation itself. But al-Ḥallāj, and his school, claimed that there was a *personal* union; the individual was divinized, which naturally led to a cult around an individual in this world.

Ḥallāj spoke mysteriously of the "master of the sparkling light" (reminiscent of the "shimmering light" of the Fāṭimid poet Ibn Hani al-Andalusi); he spoke of "pre-eternities" and "post-eternities" which along with the present, make up three times; he made Satan into a hero, on a level with God; altogether these are the "doctrine of the two principles and the three times" which was the signature of Manicheism. He had all this in common with his teacher, Sahl Tustarī who also spoke of God as particles of light. In Baghdad al-Ḥallāj was called the "dazzled man" (*al-mustalim*). Ḥujwīrī described al-Ḥallāj's compositions and statements, with faint praise, thus:

> Al-Ḥallāj wrote brilliantly, both allegories and theological and juridical formulations. All his mystical utterances are like the first visions of novices, though some are more powerful, some feebler, some more acceptable, some more improper than others. When God grants a man a Vision, and he tries afterward to put into words what he saw in the height of ecstatic power, and helped by Divine Grace, his words are apt to be obscure, and the more so if he expresses himself hastily, and under the influence of self-admiration.

In his own time he was generally held to be a heretic, by Sufis in particular. After his death, however, a propaganda — a "spin"— began in his favor, particularly from the region of Khorāsān and Transoxiana, painting him as a martyr of exoteric incomprehension. Once he was long dead, with his haunting poetry surviving him, there was a partial rehabilitation of his memory. In a certain sense, the historic al-Ḥallāj was split into two persons: Ibn 'Arabī said that he saw in a vision that al-Ḥallāj was a Saint; but Ibn 'Arabī also said that he had a vision in which the Prophet accused al-Ḥallāj because al-Ḥallāj in effect had claimed to be greater than he; and so the Prophet said, it was right that al-Ḥallāj was condemned by the law. (Ibn 'Arabī, better than any one else, knew how to play an audience.) Al-Ḥallāj thus became a kind of conundrum in virtue of which al-Ḥallāj's poetry often turns on apparent paradoxes:

> God threw a man into the sea with his arms tied behind his back, and said to him: Careful! Careful! or you will get wet in the water!

Other poems deal with themes more familiar to mysticism but in a particularly dramatic fashion:

> When in my thirst I stooped my face to wine,
> Dark in the cup I saw a shadow. Thine!

And:

> I am my Love: my Love is I; two ghosts this body occupy. If you see me, He's what you see; When you see Him, you will see — me!

And:

> Prophecy is the Lamp of the world's light; But ecstasy in the same Niche has room The Spirit's is the breath which sighs through me; And mine the thought which blows the Trump of Doom. Vision said it. In my eye
> Moses stood, on Sinai.

On his last day he said: "It is enough for the ecstatic that The One and Only singles him out." But, once deciphered, most revealing of Ḥallāj's secret are the words he spoke on the way to his execution, *laughing*:

"The account of Abū-l-Hasan al-Hulwani who says:

> I was present that day which was the downfall of al-Ḥallāj, when he was brought bound in chains. And he walked happily under the chains, and he laughed, and I said to him: 'Master, whence comes this state?— This is the coquetry of the Beauty, which draws its elect to meet it.' and then he said:
>
> My drinking companion is beyond all suspicion, As to his intention to betray me:
>
> He invites, and greets me, as the host does to his guest; [He, the host, gives me to drink from the cup from which he drank himself]
>
> But as soon the cup will go around, he calls for the mat and headsman...
>
> This is destiny of he who drinks the wine in the month of Tammuz with the dragon."

"Beauty" is a Manichean term for the "Living Soul" or light hidden in the world, or the God of light. (There is a Ḥadīth: "God is Beautiful and loves Beauty.") The "host" is Mani, who martyred, returns in the invisible to preside over a feast, which is the main ceremony of Manicheism, the Bema feast. There are other references in Ḥallāj to the "Night Feast that ends the fast", and also "our naw ruz" meaning the Manichean naw ruz, the commemoration of Mani's revelation (the second visitation of his heavenly twin) which took place shortly after Zoroastrian naw ruz, and was different from it. (The Manicheans are noted for manipulating religious calendars.) Drinking of wine is forbidden for Manicheans as it is in Islam; but disguising one's religion, to the point of denying it altogether, was permitted by Mani, and is found in other Dualisms, as in Shī'ite *taqiyyah*. The Host (Mani) of the drinking party (the Bema) gives the cup from which he drank, that is, martyrdom, to Ḥallāj. (Several sucessors of Mani were martyred and imitation of Mani's life was the ideal, to the point of actually provoking martyrdom for oneself.) Even Ḥāllaj's imprisonment paralleled Mani's and involved healing a court figure, as Mani, in prison, was called upon to answer questions about the whereabouts of the soul of the Shah's dead sister. "Tammuz" the name of a month, is also the name of a pagan god, Tammuz-Adonis, who dies and returns to life, as did Mani, the ever-living, or Mani-Ḥayy (which means "Mani the Living" in Aramaic and Arabic whence the term Manicheism). The "dragon" is Azhi-Dahhaka of the Avesta, or Zohhak, a "fearful serpent" (enchained by Kavi the Blacksmith until he breaks forth again to be finally destroyed by the Saoshyant). The Dragon is a mythic representative of a *foreign* usurper who held the Iranians in bondage for a thousand years after Jamshid. Here, as in the Shah-Namah, the dragon represents the Arab-Islamic conquest of Iran. But not only is Dahhaka depicted as an Arab and chosen instrument of the Devil, he is also someone who was beguiled by the Devil from the primitive and innocent vegetarianism which is supposed to have prevailed before the descent into the eating of animal food and cannibalism. (Ḥāllaj was a vegetarian as were orthodox Manicheans.)

The trial of Ḥallāj was an historic landmark. It was the most important case of a wave of persecution of crypto-Manicheans instigated by the Twelve Imām Shī'ites. Ibn al-Jawzī reports that in the year after Ḥallāj's execution, 923, fourteen sacks of manuscripts confiscated from Manicheans, like those found with Ḥallāj, were burned in Baghdad and that streams of melted gold and silver, characteristic of their illuminations, streamed from the pyre. When Ḥallāj was executed a revolt broke out in Ṭalaqān, near Balkh in Khorāsān. Many other "Ḥallājians" (Massignon preferred this term to "Islamicised Manicheans" which is what he meant but used only reluctantly) were also executed in the year *312*/924 and before and after. Sixteen years after Ḥallāj's death one of his associates, Shalmaghani, was executed in Merv. After this, those overt Manicheans in the empire who had not hidden their true religion now did so, and others, like the Ḥallājians who had already dissimulated in the spirit of *taqiyyah* and had been in disguise already, went further into cloaking their true beliefs and claiming to be the most Sunni of mystics. As an-Nadīm wrote of the Manicheans who had been so numerous in Baghdad at the time of al-Hallāj:

> The last time they appeared was during the days of al-Muqtadir, for [after that] they feared for their lives and clung to Khurāsān. Any one of them who remained kept his identity secret as he moved in this region... I used to know about three hundred of them in the City of Peace [Baghdad] during the days of Mu'izz ad-Dawlah [946-967]. But at this time [986] there are not five of them in our midst. *Fihrist.*

See al-JUNAYD; MANICHEISM; MIRACLES; SAHL at-TUSTARĪ.

Ḥalqah. 1. A circle of listeners sitting in a mosque around a teacher. The term was used for those who attended the audiences of the Prophet. A ḥalqah also means a circle of spectators gathered on a public thoroughfare watching a performer or listening to a story teller.

2. The ruling council of elders of the Ibāḍites is called a ḥalqah.

Haly 'Abbās, *see* al-MĀJŪSĪ.

al-Hamadhānī, Aḥmad ibn al-Ḥusayn called Badi' az-Zamān, "the wonder of the age" (d. *399*/1008). The first writer of the stories called *Maqāmāt.* The narrator or *rāwī* in al-Hamadhanīs stories is a character called Abū-l-Fatḥ al-Iskandarī, and the hero of the action is 'Īsā ibn Hisham. The stories reflect the personalities of recognizable types from society. *See* al-ḤARĪRĪ.

Ḥamā'il, *see* AMULETS.

Ḥamālat al-'Arsh (lit. "bearers of the throne"). The eight Angels whom the Koran mentions as the bearers of the throne of God.

Ḥamās (Ar. "zeal"). Ḥamās is an acronym for "Islamic Resistance Movement" (*Ḥarakat al-Muqāwamah al-Islāmīyah*). It grew out of the *Intifāḍah*, the Palestinian uprising against Israeli occupation in 1987 and the Muslim Brotherhood. Ironically, Ḥamās itself was the result of an Israeli policy originally to support Islamic movements in order to undermine the P.L.O. by causing religious divisions. (The Palestine Liberation Organisation, is a secular Arab or Palestinian organisation.) An Islamist organisation, Ḥamās arose as an Islamic militant resistance organisation, following the lead of Hezbollah, a Shī'ite organisation in Lebanon. Now one of its goals is to destroy the P.L.O. and it is better organized than the P.L.O. has been. Its founder, 'Abd al-'Azīz ar-Rantīsī had Shaykh Aḥmad Yāsīn, a crippled schoolteacher, as his spiritual advisor. Both had been members of the Muslim Brotherhood and had run welfare and educational services in Gaza. Ḥamās came into being when the Muslim Brotherhood was being discredited for not being more active. Its military wing, the Qassām Brigades, is named after Shaykh 'Izz ad-Dīn al-Qassām, a Muslim preacher in Haifa who had led revolts against British rule and Zionist settlers and who was killed in the 1930's dying in battle. He was also the inspiration for the much smaller group Islamic Holy War (Islamic Jihād) dedicated solely to military struggle. Islamic Holy War's leader, Dr. Fatḥī Shiqāqī, was assassinated by Israeli agents in Malta in October 1995.

Yāsīn was arrested in 1989 and jailed in Israel. He was released in 1997 in exchange for two Mossad agents arrested in Amman after a bungled assassination attempt. He had said that Hamas would end its activities against Israel if Israel pulled completely out of the West Bank and Gaza. He had since made statements which are more ambiguous in this regard. In 2004 Yāsīn, along with five others, was killed in a missile attack on him in Gaza. In 1992, 415 Ḥamās activists were deported out of Israel and dumped on a snowy, barren hillside in Lebanon, where they remained for a long time as a reproach to Israeli policy. Under Yāsīn's successor, Muḥammad Musa Abū Marzook, an American educated engineer and native of Gaza, there was a resumption of suicide bombings in protest over the Oslo accords of 1993 for limited Palestinian self-rule. He was arrested in New York in 1995, and released upon condition of deportation, without being tried, in 1997. Then direction passed to 'Imad al-'Alami, an engineer from Gaza who is based in Damascus. Another leader, Maḥmud az-Zahar operated openly as the political leader in Gaza until he was arrested by Palestinians in 1996. The military wing was also run by Yahya Ayyash, known as "the engineer" for his bomb making activity, until he was assassinated by a telephone bomb set by Israeli agents. He was succeeded by Muḥammad Dief.

Ḥamās is a mass movement with the support of at least a fifth of the Palestinians in the West Bank and Gaza. It has an estimated budget of seventy million dollars from the contributions of the Palestinian diaspora, supporters in the Middle east, and some governments. A large percent of the contributions originate in Europe and the United States. Most of the money goes to run charitable institutions such as schools, orphanages and clinics, and the care of families of those arrested by the Israelis, and the families of suicide bombers. Yāsīn was assassinated by an Israeli missile attack. Rantīsī was assassinated in a separate missile attack. In 2006 Ḥamās won democratic elections in the West Bank and Gaza and formed a government. President Bush first welcomed Ḥamās for its using democratic means to come to power, and then cut off financial aid to the Palestinians.

Hamdard Foundation (Urdu: "compassion"). A Pakistani charitable association and pharmaceutical company created in 1953 by Ḥakim Muḥammad Sa'id to provide free medical care for the poor. It has publications and sponsors international scholarly work and lectures. In 1991 it founded Hamdard University.

Ḥammām (lit. "bath"). The custom of Roman baths, with their "cold", "tepid" and "hot" rooms, which fulfill the requirements of the *ghusl*, or greater ablution, were adopted by the Arabs and incorporated into Islamic civilisation. Baths of this type remain an amenity of Muslim towns.

Hammurabi. King of Babylonia in the 18th century BC A famous code of laws is attributed to him. This code of laws is an important forerunner of the laws in the Koran, as it is also a forerunner of Jewish law. After the revelation of the Koran, Roman law and Iranian Sāssānid law played a great role in the shaping of Islamic law as it developed.

Hammurabi was referred to as the "king of justice" and royal decisions were *dinat sharrim*. There are 282 preserved laws in the Code of Hammurabi;

it also resembles the Sharī'ah in that it concerns itself with economic life, morality, ethics, all in one. It is with some exception a lex talionis. The earlier Sumerian code of Ur-Nammu (lived 2112-2095 BC), King of Ur, tended more to punishment of crimes by compensation in payment. The Code of Hammurabi also made provision to protect women and children; and like Islamic law it made distinctions between compensation of damages towards victims having different degrees of social status, that is, free men and slaves.

It provided for a false witness to suffer the punishment that would have gone to the accused: "If a seignior accused another seignior and brought a charge of murder against him but has not proved it, his accuser shall be put to death." "If a seignior wished to divorce his wife who did not bear him children he shall give her money to the full amount of her marriage price and he shall also make good to her the dowry which she brought from her father's house and then he may divorce her." Some women could inherit 1/3 of their father's property or the usufruct thereof. "If a seignior struck another seignior's daughter and caused a miscarriage, he shall pay ten shekels of silver for her fetus." [Similarly in Islamic law when an abortion is caused, the father pays the woman a blood price for the foetus.]

Very similar to the Koran (83:1) are also these Sumero-Akkadian Hymns: "He who handles the scales in falsehood, he who deliberately changes the stone weights and lowers their weight will make himself lie for his profits and then lose his [bag of weights].

Ḥamdalah. The formula *al-ḥamdu li-Llāh*, (also pronounced colloquially *ḥamdillah*), meaning "praise to God". It is uttered at the end of meals, to mark the end of an activity, and as an interjection in appropriate circumstances.

Traditionally, the phrase is a formal beginning to a speech, in which case it is followed by *wa-ṣ-ṣalātu wa-ṣ-salamu 'alā mawlānā rasūli-Llāh*, ("blessings and peace upon our Lord the Messenger of God.") The extended form *al-ḥamdu li-Llāhi waḥdah*, ("praise to God alone") is written at the head of letters. The *ḥamdalah* is used to terminate actions begun by the *basmalah*. The *ḥamdalah* is, in medieval theological and alchemical terms, the *coagula*, and the *basmalah* the *solve*.

Hamzah. One of the letters of the alphabet, an aspiration of breath, or a passage from silence to sound. The first letter of the Arabic alphabet, the *'alif*, is actually a support, or *kursī*, for the *hamzah*. By itself the *hamzah* is without sound, but is the beginning of the sound of following letters, or the interval between sounds. This is highly symbolical and it should be noted that it is the first letter of the Divine Name *Allāh*.

Ḥamzah. An uncle of the Prophet, an early convert to Islam and one of its more ardent champions in the battlefield. He had been a hunter and was a man of prowess. He was killed at the Battle of Uḥud by the lance of a slave called Wahshi who had been promised a rich reward for the life of Ḥamzah by Hind, the wife of Abū Sufyān, leader of the Meccan opposition. The Prophet mourned his death with particular sadness. *See* BATTLE of UḤUD.

Ḥanafī, *see* SCHOOLS of LAW.

"Ḥanafī Muslims". A Black American Muslim group which grew out of the "Nation of Islam". Hamaas Abdul Khaalis left the "Nation of Islam" in 1958 and adopted orthodox Islam of the Ḥanafī School of Law. There were at one time close to one hundred mosques in the U.S. which looked upon Abdul Khaalis as their authority. The number of followers is not known but has considerably diminished today. *See* "BLACK MUSLIMS".

"Hand of Fāṭimah" (Ar. *yadd Fāṭimah*, and *al-kaff*, "the palm"). A stylized image of the palm which is a popular decorative motif for jewelry in the Islamic world. The hand depicted in this way is a magical symbol of power, and is thus used as a talisman, for the hand is the capacity to control nature and bring order out of chaos. The symbol is ancient; it is found in many cultures, notably that of the Indians of North America; in the Middle East, it may be directly linked with the Essenes and the Mandaeans, who traditionally were jewellers and silversmiths, and may have propagated the symbol. Despite its name, it has nothing to do with Fāṭimah, the daughter of the Prophet.

Handasah (supposedly derived from Persian *andāzeh* "quantity", "measure"). The science of land measurement, and then, by extension, the terracing of land and engineering in general. The Arabs built dams for irrigation in very early times. Traces of ancient dams still exist in the region of Mecca. The most famous dam of all, however, was that of Ma'rib in the Yemen, which existed before the Christian era. The collapse of this dam around 580, an event preserved in poetry and legend, sent a signal throughout the tribes as far as the Syrian desert that the epoch of the greatness of the South Arabian kingdoms had passed.

One great early work of Arab engineering was the bringing of water to Mecca from the nearby mountains. The Spanish brought a heritage of Arab engineering to the Americas, even as far north as New Mexico, in the form of irrigation techniques. *See* SĀQIYAH.

Ḥanīf. A word, of doubtful derivation, but perhaps from Syriac *ḥanpa* meaning heathenism. Several religions were called *ḥanputa*, that of Manicheans and the Ṣābians for example. The word *ḥanīf* is used in the Koran to describe one who adheres to pristine monotheism (pl. *ḥunafā'*). A descriptive name in the Koran for Abraham, and for those before Islam who by the purity and uprightness of their nature did not succumb to paganism and polytheism. The *ḥunafā'* between Abraham and the time of the Prophet were thus the faithful representatives of the Abrahamic-Isma'ilite tradition during the period called the *Jāhiliyyah* ("Age of Ignorance") which saw a descent into paganism. One of these, Umayyah ibn Abī-ṣ-Ṣalt, was known as a great poet; another, Quss ibn Sa'īdah, was a famous orator. Others were Waraka ibn Nawfal, 'Ubayd Allāh ibn Jahsh, 'Uthmān ibn Huwayrith, and Zeyd ibn Amr. Waraka and 'Uthmān became finally Christians. 'Ubayd Allāh became a Muslim, migrated to Abyssinia, and there became a Christian. Zeyd could not decide. As he prayed at the Ka'bah he said: "My God, if I knew what form of worship is most pleasing to Thee I would choose it, but I know not." The Prophet said of him: "On the last day Zeyd will rise up, a community in himself."

Ḥaqīqah (lit. "truth" or "reality", cognate with *Ḥaqq*, "Reality", "Absolute"). The esoteric truth which transcends human and theological limitations. In this sense *ḥaqīqah* is the third element of the ternary *sharī'ah* ("law"), that is, exoterism; *ṭarīqah* ("path"), or esoterism, and *ḥaqīqah*, essential truth.

Ḥaqīqah is also called *lubb* ("kernel", "quintessence") related to a Koranic phrase (28:29 and elsewhere): "those who possess the kernels" (Ar. *ūlu-l-albāb*), meaning "those who have insight or grasp the essence". Hence the Sufi adage: "to get at the kernel, you have to break the shell", which means that esoterism "shatters" exoterism, just as essence "shatters" forms in the sense that it cannot be reduced to them.

In India particularly, the concept of *ḥaqīqah* was emphasized to such a degree, especially by the schools claiming *waḥdat al-wujūd* ("unity of being", or monism), that many Sufis dispensed with the practice of the religious law (*sharī'ah*). This prompted strong orthodox reactions on the part of schools which emphasized *waḥdat ash-shuhūd* ("unity of consciousness"), such as the Chishti reaction as in the words of Sayyid Muḥammad Gesūdarāz:

> People keep on saying that *ḥaqīqah* is the Divine Secret; but I Muḥammad Ḥusayni say that *sharī'ah* is the Divine Secret, because I have heard talk of *ḥaqi'qah* from Haidaris, Qalandaris, Mulhids [heretics], Zindiqs [Manicheans]; nay I have even heard it from the mouths of Yogis, of Brahmans, and of Gurus; but talk of *sharī'ah* I have not heard from any one's lips than the people of the true faith and beliefs [i.e. Sunnis]. From this it is evident that *sharī'ah* this the Divine Secret.

See SUFISM.

Ḥaram (lit. "restricted", "forbidden", "sacred" and, by extension, "sacred possession or place"). The sacred areas around Mecca, Medinah, and the Temple Mount of Jerusalem. The first two are often referred to as the *ḥaramayn* (the "two sacred sites"), and in these it is forbidden to take life, except for the extermination of noxious or dangerous animals, along with other restrictions. Non-Muslims are not allowed into these sacred zones which extend around the cities of Mecca and Medinah for a radius of several miles. Jerusalem is sometimes referred to as *thālith al-ḥaramaym* ("the third sacred site").

The Grand Mosque of Mecca is called *al-Masjid al-Ḥarām* ("The Sacred Mosque"), often referred to simply as *al-Ḥaram*.

In Arabic, that part of a house reserved for its women is called by the related word *ḥarīm* (whence "harem"). In modern Arabic, *ḥarīm* may also mean women, sing. *ḥurmah*. *See also* ḤARĀM below.

Ḥarām (lit. "forbidden", for revealed, i.e. sacred, reasons). That which is prohibited. In *fiqh* (jurisprudence) all actions fall into one of five categories (*aḥkām*): prohibited (*ḥarām*), discouraged (*makrūh*), neutral (*mubāḥ*), recommended (*mustaḥabb*), and obligatory (*farḍ*). *See also* AḤKĀM: ḤARAM above; FIQH.

al-Ḥaramayn *See* ḤARAM; MECCA; MEDINAH; JERUSALEM.

Harem, *see* ḤARAM; ḤARĪM.

Ḥarīm (lit. "forbidden [area]"). The women's quarters in a Muslim household, whence the English word "harem". In Turkey it is called the *haramlik*, as opposed to the *salamlik*, the "place of greetings", the salon or men's quarters. *See* ḤARAM.

al-Ḥarīrī, al-Qāsim ibn 'Alī (*446-516*/1054-1122). Famous author of picaresque stories called *maqāmāt*. The genre probably derives from Buddhist *jataka* tales. Al-Ḥarīri was from Baṣrah where he was an official in the bureau of information (*Ṣāhib al-Khabar*), a sort of intelligence service of the Caliphs. His *Maqāmāt* are noted for their literary and linguistic qualities. The dramatic anecdotes centre around an eloquent character called Abū Zayd of Serūj and his narrator companion Ḥārith ibn Hammām. The choice of names, which is as nondescript as possible, is seen from this Ḥadīth "every one of you [Arabs] is a *Ḥārith* [one who acquires gain by trade] and everyone of you is a Hammam [a worrier, one who is subject to cares and anxieties]. The *Maqāmāt* have been translated into English as *The Assemblies of al-Ḥarīrī*. *See* al-HAMADHĀNĪ.

Ḥarrān. An ancient city (the Roman Carrhae) in northern Mesopotamia, in what is now Altinbasak, in southern Turkey, near Urfa (Edessa). Ḥarrān was the ancient Harranu (Biblical Haran) of Sumerian times, perhaps a trading outpost of Ur. It lay, as Ammianus Marcellinus described, on the safer of two roads, avoiding the deserts of the nomadic Amorites, from Ur and Babylon to the Mediterranean. Abraham came to Ḥarrān from Ur of the Chaldees. There Sin (the Semitic name of the Sumerian Nanna) the god of the moon had an important and famous temple (cf. Koran 6:76-88 which describes how Abraham first worshiped the moon, then the sun, then Allāh). Shamash the sun god (Sumerian Utu or Babar, the "resplendent") probably also had a temple. Particularly interesting from the point of view of later developments, Nusku, a god of light, the son of Sin was also venerated in Ḥarrān.

It was in Ḥarrān that Abraham's father Terah (in Arabic Azar) died; it was there that Abraham was commanded to go into Canaan by God in the Old Testament; it was there that Isaac married Rebekah, and Jacob labored for Laban. It was the centre of the Biblical land of Padan-Aram. The land of Padan-Aram was occupied by the Amorites until 1100 BC and thereafter by the Aramaeans until they lost their national identity with their conquest by the Assyrians in 732 BC The adoption by the Aramaeans of the Canaanite alphabet, instead of the cuneiform script, made their language into the *lingua franca* of the Near east.

The philosophical development of Ḥarrān must have been strongly influenced by the proximity of the kingdom of Commagene. In what is now southeast Turkey, in the former Seleucid province of Commagene, made into an independent kingdom in 162 BC by a governor named Ptolemy, Mithridates I, an Iranian prince, established himself and the kingdom became the westernmost Zoroastrian country, which unlike Zoroastrianism elsewhere depicted its divinities in the form of Hellenistic statues. The capital was Samosata. In Commagene wine was used liturgically. The rulers of Commagene were the Orontids who originally ruled in Armenia at the time of Darius. The Kingdom endured until AD 72 when they were wiped out by Vespasian in the course of the Jewish war. Caracalla was assassinated in Ḥarrān. The city was often disputed by Parthians, Romans, Byzantines and Persians.

There was a Manichean church in Ḥarrān (and there had been a community in nearby Edessa where Bardaisan had lived). Archelaus, a bishop of Karkhar (commonly identified with Ḥarrān) in the third century (d. 278?) is depicted as having had a debate with Mani, and in the *Acta Archelai* describes Mani as wearing a blue cloak with yellow trousers, the costume of a Mithraic priest. Cyril of Jerusalem (c. 315-86) was one of the first church leaders to make use of the Acta Archelai in pastoral instruction on the dangers of Manicheism and especially warned against accepting too readily the repentance of those who had turned from Manicheism. The genuineness of their denial had to be ascertained before they could be trusted, and it appears that catechumens who had been Manicheans had to renounce Mani publicly before they could be baptized.

In Islamic times the Ḥarrānians were Hellenistic pagans whom the Christians had not succeeded in converting; nor did the Muslims. According to an-Nadīm, it was the Caliph al-Ma'mūn, who passing through the region learned of the Ḥarrānians being pagans and who informed them that unless they adopted Christianity, Judaism or Islam, they would be put to death as idolators. It was then that they turned to lawyers and hit upon the stratagem of claiming to be Ṣābians, a people mentioned in the Koran as "People of the Book" i.e., those who had received Divinely revealed religions. One of their number, Abū Isḥāq ibn Ḥīkal, a secretary to the Caliphs al-Muṭī' and aṭ-Ṭā'i' obtained a *fatwā* ("legal decision") to this effect. However, it is clear that the Ṣābian status of the Ḥarrānians had been debated earlier, and that in any case, toleration was extended to them from the very moment of conquest by the Muslims who were fully aware of their ancient temples, although later travellers were often taken by surprise.

Shahrastānī (d. *548*/1153), the scholar who carried out a survey of religions, and an-Nadīm (d. *385*/995), called a party of the Ḥarrānians *aṣḥāb ar-ruḥāniyyah* ("spirit worshipers"). Al-Mas'ūdī (d. *345*/956) said that they had temples dedicated to "intellectual substances", and that the Mandaeans were "a dissident sect of Ḥarrānians". He saw written over a temple the slogan "He who knows His being, himself becomes divine" (which became the "Ḥadīth": *man 'arafa nafsahu 'arafa rabbahu*).

The Ḥarrānians played an important role in transmitting the philosophic, scientific, and Hermetic knowledge of the Greeks to the civilisation of Islam. Jābir ibn Ḥayyān (d. *160*/776), the famous alchemist, was of Ḥarrānian origin, as was Thābit ibn Qurrā (d. *288*/901), mathematician, physician, and philosopher, and many other men of learning. Another Ḥarrānian, Theodore Abū Qurra (d. 820), the Melkite Bishop of Ḥarrān, was the first Christian writer of importance to write in Arabic. Shihāb ad-Dīn Suhrawardī founder of the school of Illuminationism (*ishrāq*) acquired some of his notions in Ḥarrān. Its proximity to Commagene doubtless made it a repository of Iranian ideas. Al-Bīrūnī opined that Zoroaster had belonged to the sect of Ḥarrān and had gone there with his father "to meet Elbus the philosopher and acquire knowledge from him". This is not, of course, historically true but it is a significant observation that in Ḥarrān Iranian civilisation and Hellenism embraced each other. It had a Platonic academy. Under the Umayyads a school of medicine from Alexandria established itself in Ḥarrān and it was the capital of the last Umayyad Caliph. The city grew under the Ayyubids and acquired an impressive citadel and a very large Mosque. In 1184 the Spanish Arab traveler Ibn al-Jubayr visited Ḥarrān (the temple of the Moon God had been destroyed in 1081). First conquered peacefully by the Mongols in 1263, the city was partly demolished in 1271, one of several Gnostic centres so destroyed, perhaps at the suggestion of the Mongol's Shī'ite advisers eager to eliminate ideologic competitors. *See* ṢĀBIANS; SHAHRASTĀNĪ; THĀBIT IBN QURRA.

Ḥarrānians. *See* ḤARRĀN,

Harratin. Populations of mixed Arab and Negro blood found in villages on the northern edge of the Sahara in Morocco.

Hārūn. The Arabic name for Aaron, the brother of Moses. (*See* AARON). In Arab folklore, Hārūn is the name of the King of the Jinn and as such is the folk word for an echo, that is, "an answer called back by a Jinn".

Hārūn ar-Rashīd (*147-194*/764-809). The fifth 'Abbāsid Caliph. Baghdad was his capital and the Caliphate reached its apogee during his reign, which declined after the crisis marked by the downfall of the Barmakids, a Persian family that had long provided the 'Abbāsids with able ministers of state. Hārūn ar-Rashīd had diplomatic relations with Charlemagne and with the emperor of China. His sumptuous and celebrated court is associated with the present form of the tales of the Thousand and One Nights. *See* 'ABBĀSIDS; BARMAKIDS.

Hārūt and Mārūt. According to the Koran (2:102), two Angels who taught sorcery to men in Babel (Ar. *Bābīl*; "Babylon" a name for Mesopotamia), and sowed division between husband and wife. However, they never misled anyone without first warning their victims of the consequences of their knowledge. The origin of the names are in Avestan Haurvatat ("wholeness") and Ameretat ("immortality"), in Pahlavī *Hordad* and *Amurdad*, two of the seven Zoroastrian divinities that are the "heptad" of the *Amesha Spentas*. Their presence in the Koran testifies to the upheaval in Semitic religious thought that began when Cyrus conquered Babylon and Mesopotamia and Zoroastrian doctrines revolutionized religious ideas in the Middle east.

When there has come to them a
Messenger from God
confirming what was with them, a party of them
that were given the Book reject the Book of God
behind their backs, as though they knew not,
and they follow what the Satans recited
over Solomon's kingdom.
Solomon disbelieved not,
but the Satans disbelieved, teaching
the people sorcery, and that
which was sent down
upon Babylon's two angels, Harūt and Mārūt;
they taught not any man, without they said,
'We are but a temptation; do not disbelieve'.
From them they learned how they might divide
a man and his wife, yet they did not hurt
any man thereby, save by the leave of God,
and they learned what hurt them, and did not
profit them, knowing well that whoso buys it
shall have no share in the world to come;
evil then was that they sold themselves for,
if they had but known.
Yet had they believed, and been godfearing,
a recompense from God had been better,
if they had but known. (2:95-98)

Ḥasan (*3-50*/625-670). More properly al-Ḥasan, the eldest grandson of the Prophet. He succeeded his father 'Alī to become the fifth Caliph. For most Shī'ites, Ḥasan is also the second Imām. Mu'āwiyah, the Umayyad governor of Damascus, attacked Ḥasan; before a definitive battle could take place, Ḥasan himself offered to give up the Caliphate in return for remuneration and pensions for himself and his brother Ḥusayn. (Ḥasan's offer crossed with a proposal from Mu'āwiyah that the renunciation be temporary for the lifetime of Mu'āwiyah with *carte blanche* regarding the other conditions. Upon receipt of Ḥasan's offer Mu'āwiyah withdrew his own).

According to the historian aṭ-Ṭabarī, among the conditions of the abdication were that Ḥasan would retain five million dirhams then in the treasury of Kūfah, that he would receive the annual revenue from the Persian district of Darabjird, and that 'Alī would not be reviled by the authorities as had been Mu'āwiyah's practice. Others say that the Caliphate was to be restored to Ḥasan upon the death of Mu'āwiyah.

Ḥasan's Caliphate lasted six months in all. He died in Medinah, some eight years after his abdication. Shī'ite accounts say that he was poisoned by his wife upon the instigation of Yazīd, the son of Mu'āwiyah. But this must be taken with caution because according to Shī'ite accounts almost all the Imāms were murdered by the Sunnī rulers.

Ḥasan was famous for his many marriages which numbered more than 130. The rapidity and frequency with which Ḥasan repudiated his wives led him to be called al-Muṭliq ("the Divorcer"). His father 'Alī had to warn men not to give their daughters in marriage to his son, which deterred no-one. Families favored the connection with the Prophet's family and the young women were eager to be, even if only for a short time, the wife of the grandson of the Prophet.

Ḥasan Baṣrī (*21-110*/642-728). A famous Sufi, born in Medinah the son of a freed slave. He settled in Baṣrah ('Irāq), where he became known for his learning. During the reign of the Umayyads, when intellectual activity was at low ebb, Ḥasan of Baṣrah was a lighthouse who attracted a wide circle of students.

In his school were treated all the ideas that were to grow into Islamic law, theology, and Sufism. He is a link in the transmission of many Ḥadīth, having known many Companions in Medinah; most of the Sufi initiatic chains (*silsilahs*), pass through him; the Mu'tazilites started out, according to tradition, by breaking away from his school. Ḥasan, a giant of his age, left no writings, but was quoted widely by others. To judge from his influence, his scope and depth were as great as any of the later major figures whose work was more extensively recorded. Ḥasan is famous for the saying the "world is a bridge upon which you cross but upon which you should not build". (In India this is attributed to Jesus and is an inscription at Fatehpur Sikri). It is reported that he said:

> God made fasting as a training ground for His servants, that they may run to His obedience. Some win that race and get the prize; others fail, and go away disappointed. But by my life! if the lid were off, the well-doer would be too busy about his well-doing, as

the evil-doer in his evil-doing, to get him a new garment or anoint his hair.

The wonder is not how the lost were lost, but how the saved were ever saved.

Fear must be stronger than hope. For where hope is stronger than fear, the heart will rot.

My asceticism is mere lust, and my patience cowardice; and all my asceticism in this world is lust for the Other, the quintessence of lust. But how excellent is a man whose patience is for God's sake, not for the sake of being delivered from Hell; and his asceticism for God's sake, not for the sake of getting into Heaven. One grain of true piety is better than a thousandfold weight of fasting and prayer.

In the *Waṣiyyah* of Maḥmūd ibn 'Īsā can be found these prescriptions of Ḥasan Basrīs to spiritual disciples:

> One must seek to have the ten qualities of a dog: to sleep little during the night, which is a characteristic of a truly fervent soul. Not to complain of the heat or the cold, which is the virtue of patient hearts. Not to leave behind an inheritance, which is the character of true devotion.
>
> Never to be angry or envious, which is the character of the True Believer. To keep away from those who devour, which is the nature of the poor. Not to have a fixed abode, which is the quality of being a pilgrim. To be content with what we are thrown to eat, which is the virtue of moderation. To sleep where we find ourselves, which is the characteristic of a satisfied heart. Never to mistake who is our Master, and if he strikes us, to return to Him, which is the quality of hearts that are aware. To be always hungry, which is the characteristic of men of virtue... to be with the crowd dims the light of the heart...

Ḥasān ibn Thābit, *see* ḤASSĀN ibn THĀBIT.

Ḥasan-i Ṣabbāḥ, *see* ASSASSINS.

Ḥasanah (pl. *ḥasanāt*). A good deed. The *ḥasanāt* are the good actions which will be placed, symbolically, upon the "scales" to determine salvation at the Day of Judgement. Ibn 'Aṭā' Allāh says:

> Do not seek recompense for a deed whose doer [the real active agent being God] was not you. It suffices you as recompense that He accepts it.

Ḥasanī 1. An adjective for the *shurafā'* (sing. *sharīf*), or descendants of the Prophet through Ḥasan; those through Ḥusayn are called Ḥusaynī.

2. The Arab tribes of Mauritania call themselves the "Ḥasanī". They are considered to be "warrior" tribes. The Berbers of Mauritania are often called the "Ḥusaynī" tribes and are considered to be the "religious", or *zāwiyah* tribes, without, in either case, implying a descent from either Ḥasan or Ḥusayn, but rather a function or characteristic. The Arabic dialect of Mauritania is called *al-Ḥasaniyyah.*

Hāshimite. The Meccan clan — the Banū Hāshim — to which the Prophet and 'Alī belonged. The name Hāshimite is sometimes taken as a family name by descendants of the clan, as for example the royal family of Jordan, who are *shurafā'*, or descendants of the Prophet. *See* MECCA; QURAYSH.

Ḥashr (lit. "assembling together"). The term used especially for the gathering together of creatures for the Day of Judgement.

Ḥassān ibn Thābit (d. *50*/665). A poet of Medinah who entered Islam. Ḥassān ibn Thābit composed poetry which extolled the Prophet, the faith, and such deeds of the Muslims as the victory of Badr. He recited his poetry at meetings in which Beduins came to Medinah to hear of Islam. The Prophet gave Sirin — the Coptic slave-girl he had received with her sister Maryah, from the Muqawqīs of Egypt — as a gift to Ibn Thābit. *See* MUQAWQĪS; UMMĪ.

Ḥātim aṭ-Ṭā'ī. A famous figure in Arab folklore. A chieftain's son, Ḥātim aṭ-Ṭā'ī was charged with the care of sheep, or camels, by his father. As a dutiful host he slaughtered several of them in order to feast strangers who arrived at his absent father's tents. The rest of the herd he divided among the guests as a gift.

He became the honoured epitome of Arab hospitality, but was also known as a warrior. His legendary exploits were to find a prominent place in Arab literature but with the spread of Islam were even more extolled in Persia, India and even Malaya.

Tradition recounts that the sister of the son of Ḥātīm aṭ-Ṭā'ī, 'Ādi ibn Ḥatīm aṭ-Ṭā'ī, had been captured by the Muslims, treated well, and released. She told her brother, a recalcitrant pagan, of her impressions of the Prophet. 'Adi came to Medinah to see for himself.

When he arrived he was received with special honour by the Prophet.

> The illustrious man's son, 'Ādī ibn Ḥātim aṭ-Ṭā'ī, announced himself: the Prophet rose to his feet (which he never did for any other unbeliever), took him by the hand, and seated him on a cushion while he himself sat on the ground. The Prophet said: "In this world God has given you all you need; lordship of your people, and a famous name that your father left you. What could you lose if God gave you the other world besides? That world will be yours if you take on the faith I speak of." 'Ādī was silent.
>
> "By the God Who made me!" the Prophet cried, "this faith shall one day prevail from the rising to the setting sun!" 'Ādī entered Islam and his tribe followed him.

Afterwards many from the desert tribes came to Medinah to surrender themselves unto God, and that year, the 9th of the Hijrah, became known as the "Year of Deputations".

Ḥawārī. A term taken from the Ethiopic referring, in the Koran, to the disciples of Jesus. Also, the name of the representatives of the Prophet who were designated after the second *'Aqabah* pact. *See* 'AQABAH.

al-Ḥawqalah. The name for the frequently used expression *lā ḥawla wa lā quwwata illā bi-Llāh*, "there is no power and no strength save in God." It is particularly used in moments of distress to call forth the virtue of submission. The *hawqalah* is also an incantation in the face of evil. *See* PIOUS EXPRESSIONS; REFUGE.

Hawwā'. ("Eve"), *see* ADAM.

Ḥayrah. In mysticism, the terrifying consternation experienced by the first consciousness when it passed from non-existence to existence,

al-Hayūlā (Arabic, derived from the Greek word *hyle*, which originally meant "wood", and later came to be used of material in general and then, as a technical term, "substance", "matter"). *Al-hayūlā* stands for substance in the metaphysical sense of *materia prima*. The Arabs adopted the word from the Greeks as philosophy developed as a branch of Islamic learning.

Another word for *materia prima*, synonymous with *al-hayūlā* but antedating it, is *al-habā'*, literally "dust". Referring to the dissolution of created manifestation, the Sūrah al-Wāqi'ah says: "and the mountains will be shattered and become scattered dust [*habā'an munbatha*]" that is, *materia* disassociated from form (56:5-6). The Caliph 'Alī used the word in this sense when he said that "creation is like dust in the air, only made visible when struck by light." The light in 'Alī's simile corresponds to the *eidos* ("form") of Aristotle, which is the other pole of *hyle*. *Eidos* and *hyle* are the polarisations of Being, and are the equivalents (from the static and philosophic view of Scholasticism) of the Chinese Yang and Yin.

Hyle or *hayūlā* is materia prima (also *natura naturans*) in Being, and materia secunda (also *natura naturata*, in Arabic *al-jawhar al-habā'*) in the world — but *not* matter-quantity, as conceived of by modern science. This latter concept of *materia* as matter, is *materia* seen "from below" and defined only by quantitative distinctions (weight, extension, and what in modern science has become the "quantums"). This special view of materia, divorced from its metaphysical reality, is what the Scholastics called *materia signata quantitate* ("*materia* under the sign of number"). *See* FIVE DIVINE PRESENCES.

Hazāra. A people in Afghanistan of Mongolian descent. Their name probably comes from the Persian *hazar*, or "thousand" which was a military division of the Mongol Horde. The Hazāras are Twelve-Imam Shī'ite.

Heaven (Ar. *as-samā'* pl. *as-samāwāt*). The different heavens mentioned in the Koran represent degrees of spirituality, or domains; sometimes these are symbolically assigned to different Prophets. The origin of the concept is of course the planets visible to the eye. The "seventh heaven" marks the end of supraformal creation, and, in the symbolism of the seven directions of space, is the centre.

The Koran depicts the heavens as being cleft apart at the end of the world (82:1), or being rolled up like a scroll (21:24). The sky, from the point of view of man, is the place where physical reality joins metaphysical reality. The sundering of the sky or the heaven is the irruption of the Divine into the created, which is also the meaning of the apocalyptic trumpet call of primordial sound. Paradise is usually called the *al-jannah* ("garden"), or *firdaws* ("paradise"). *See* FIRDAWS; al-JANNAH; SEVENTH HEAVEN.

"Heights, the", *see* al-A'RĀF.

Hejaz (Ar. *al-Ḥijāz*, lit. "the barrier"). A region, the Red Sea coast of Arabia from the south of Mecca northward beyond Yenbo, and inland as far as Medinah. Its main cities are Mecca, Medinah, Jeddah, Ṭā'if, and Yenbo.

Although the Hejaz was the cradle of Islam, after the founding of the Islamic state the political centre shifted from Medinah to Damascus, then to Baghdad, and the Hejaz became a cultural backwater. The region came under the administration of Sharīfian families who ruled in the name of the Caliphs. In World War I, the sons of the Sharīf of Mecca were prominent in raising the Arab revolt against the Ottoman Turks. When the war ended, Sharīf Ḥusayn of Mecca declared himself King of the Hejaz. In 1924, however, the Hejaz was conquered by King 'Abd al-'Azīz of the House of Sa'ūd from the Nejd. He took the title "King of the Nejd and the Hejaz". As more regions were added by conquest, the new, united Kingdom was called Saudi Arabia. Because of the pilgrimage to Mecca, Jeddah, and with it the Hejaz, has remained the hub of commerce in Arabia.

The Hejaz has its own dialect of Arabic. It also had, until recently, a typical style of architecture. The houses had projecting wooden balconies called *rawshan*, where one could sleep at night, or sit and enjoy the evening breeze. In the north, wind towers on the roofs would catch and circulate breezes through the house. The style is also found on the island of Suakin, in the Red Sea, formerly a colony of the Hejaz. Hejazi architecture is said to be in part the result of influences introduced by Malayan craftsmen, which testifies to the cosmopolitan nature of the region thanks to the presence of the holy cities that have drawn pilgrims and trade throughout the centuries. Today, unfortunately, the examples of this splendid architecture have largely disappeared, to be replaced by modern concrete buildings.

Hell. The place of torment where the damned undergo suffering most often described as fire, "a fire whose fuel is stones and men". Names of hell used in the Koran are *an-nār* ("the fire"), *jahannam* ("Gehenna"), *al-jaḥīm* ("burning"), *aṣ-ṣa'īr* ("raging flame"), *as-saqar* ("scorching fire"), *al-hāwiyah* ("abyss"), *al-ḥuṭāmah* ("crushing pressure"). In Persian it is called *dozakh*).

The physical sufferings of hell are the concretisation of the state of inner contradiction which ensues from the denial of God. Or as the Koran says:

> Nay, but the unbelievers still cry lies,
> and God is behind them,
> encompassing. (85:19-20)

Hell is the manifestation of that denial. The soul undergoing the sufferings is in fact attached to them, that is, enjoys them in a certain way, just as the cruel or self-destructive enjoy the results of their cruelty in this life; those who are or remain in hell do so because they cannot detach themselves from the errors that brought them there in the first place. If they did, they would by that very fact be liberated; but in the place of true joy they put a false one, and the habit of egocentrism that prevented them from surrendering to God in life also prevents them from recognizing the truth of their state in hell.

The consequences of this state of contradiction may be suspended in life, but are inevitable when the protective modalities, time and space, which contain the world, are removed at death. Certain limbos and intermediate states are also possible after life for the soul which is not saved, that is, the soul which is not in conformity with the superior reality beyond manifestation.

Theologians make the distinction that both hell and paradise last for perpetuity (*Khuld*) and not for eternity (*abad*), that is, that they have no limit or end, in the sense that they are indefinite temporally. This distinction is necessary, for eternity is a quality that belongs to God alone. While paradise is not co-extensive with God, it is perpetual in that the blessed finally become one with their metaphysical possibility. The distinction applies all the more so to hell, albeit in another sense, in that hell ends for the individual once the consciousness of personality disappears, which happens sooner or later for all its inhabitants, even those whom Dante placed in the lowest circle.

The Mu'tazilites believed that if one entered hell, one never came out except, so to speak, when no more consciousness of an individual substance, a *persona*, remained; since one entering hell would already possess a somewhat chaotic nature, he could be considered as already on the way to the dissolution of consciousness in this life. However, most other theologians, particularly the school of al-Ash'arī, believe that if the person who entered hell was not an idolater, a *mushrik*, one who associated another reality with God, but a believer, then God could forgive his sins or non-conformities. This could take place immediately, aided perhaps by the intercession of the Divine Messengers whom the believer followed, despite his sins. Or the forgiveness could take place after a sojourn in hell in which the non-conformities had been "burned away".

There is a Ḥadīth which refers to this: "He shall make men come out of hell after they have been burned and reduced to cinders." God can forgive any sin but one: denial of His Reality, which is most easily grasped as His essential Unity; that nothing is absolutely real, except Him.

Existence in the world, the scholastics said, in accordance with the teachings of Aristotle, is "accidents" in relation to Being. In Islamic philosophy, and in its mysticism, which incorporated Aristotle and Plato within the intellectual framework of esotericism, Being is called *al-jawhar* ("the Jewel"), and "accidents", or contingencies which arise out of Being in the form of existence are called *a'rād*. These are due to a privation of reality, since existence is the result of the removal of qualities from plenitude, a privation of what Is. Whatever exists does so because of the removal of something from invisible Being.

Now according to Aristotle, the absence of a quality calls forth its opposite. The same is true of the soul, which at death, when the world's coverings of time, space, and form are removed, is called upon to face the Substance of its reality. All space and all time become one place and event. Adequacy and essential conformity to the Substance at that confrontation, which can readily be likened to the Great Judgement, is what religions call salvation. Identity with that Substance is *moksha*, or deliverance from all contingency; it corresponds to what Islam calls the state of the *'ārif bi-Llāh* ("the knower by God"). The absence of an adequate conformity to that Substance, the absence of the qualities and equilibrium of Being with which one is confronted, the absence, for example, of kindness, uprightness, dignity, (privations of the Divine Qualities of Mercy, Truth, and Majesty) calls forth their opposite. Hell is not the vengeance of a cruel God, but the consequence of the nature of reality.

No! I swear by the Day of Resurrection;
No! I swear by the accusing soul...
What, does man reckon
We shall not gather his bones?
even though he offer his excuses...
(Koran 75: 1-3; 15)

On the day when their tongues, their hands and
their feet shall testify against them touching
that they were doing.
Upon that day God will pay them in full
their just due, and they shall know that God
is the manifest Truth. (Koran 24:24)

When traditional Muslims mention hell in conversation, they set off the idea with invocations of God's protection, for themselves and for the listener, for the magic of words is such that even the thought is frightening, and its appearance in speech may be taken as a dreadful omen. *See* CHILDREN; ESCHATOLOGY.

Heraclius (Ar. *Hīrāql*). The emperor of Byzantium who reigned from 610 to 641. In the sixth year of the Hijrah (628), Heraclius received a legendary written invitation from the Prophet to enter Islam. Traditional stories depict the Christian emperor as wishing to accept conversion, but being deterred by the opposition of his chief nobles; he encounters Abū Sufyān and questions him about the nature of the Prophet, recognizing in him a Divine messenger. The early Muslims also pictured Heraclius as having a prophetic dream of the triumph throughout Syria of the "Kingdom of a circumcised man", or of having seen this by reading the portents of the stars.

The story of Abū Sufyān and Heraclius is reported in the Ṣaḥīḥ of Bukhārī; it is a dialogue of the kind found in Thucydides, somewhat more idealized, and presenting the view of Muslim expectations. But it reports the letter sent from the Prophet to the Byzantine emperor:

'Abd Allāh ibn 'Abbās said that Abū Sufyān ibn Ḥarb informed him: Heraclius sent for him [Abū Sufyān] with a party of the Quraysh, when they had to trade in Syria during the truce which the Messenger of God had arranged with Abū Sufyān and the unbelieving Quraysh. So they came to Heraclius when they were in Jerusalem. Heraclius invited them to his court, and around him were the gathered chiefs of the Romans. Heraclius called them and his interpreter, and said: "Who among you is nearest in relation to this man who claims to be a prophet?" Abū Sufyān said, "I am the nearest to him in relationship." Then Heraclius said, "Bring him nearer to me and keep his companions behind his back. Say to them that I am going to put some questions to this man about the one who claims to be a prophet; if what he tells me is not true, then the others will show it."

Abū Sufyān said that: "By God, if it were not the shame that they would charge me with lying, I would have lied against the Prophet." Then the first question that he put was: "What is his family standing among you?" I said: "He is a man of high birth amongst us." Heraclius said: "Did any one from among you ever advance such a claim before him?" I said: "No." He said: "Was anyone of his forefathers a king?" I said: "No." He said: "Do the men of rank and wealth follow him or the poorer ones?" I said: "Rather the poorer ones." He said: "Are they increasing or decreasing in number?" I said: "Nay, they are increasing." He said: "Does any one of them apostatize out of hatred for his religion after having embraced it?" I said: "No." He said: "Did you ever charge him with telling lies before he said what he now says?" I said: "No." He said: "Is he unfaithful to his agreements?" I said: "No, but we have made a truce with him and we do not know what he will do with it."

Abū Sufyān said: "And I got no opportunity to introduce a disparaging word into this conversation except this remark." Heraclius said: "Have you fought with him?" I said: "Yes." He said: "What was the outcome of your battles with him?" I said: "Fighting between us and him has had different turns — sometimes he causes us loss and at other times we cause him loss." He said: "What is it that he enjoins you?" "He says: 'Serve Allāh alone and do not set up aught with Him, and give up what your forefathers believed.' He enjoins on us prayers and truthfulness and chastity and respect for the ties of relationship."

Then Heraclius said through his interpreter: "I questioned you about his lineage and you said that he was a man of high birth among you. Even thus are messengers raised from amongst the noblest of their people. And I questioned you whether any of you had ever advanced such a claim, and you said: No. I thought that if anyone had advanced such a claim before him, he could be imitating what has gone before. And I questioned you whether there was a king amongst his forefathers and you said: No. Had there been a king among his forefathers then his actions could be a wish to regain the kingdom. And I questioned you whether you had ever charged him with telling lies before he advanced the claim which he now makes, and you said: No. So I knew that it could not be that a man who abstained from telling lies about men should tell lies about God.

"And I questioned you whether men of rank and wealth follow him, or the poor, and you said that it is the poor people that follow him; such are the followers of Messengers. And I questioned you whether they are increasing or decreasing and you said that they are increasing, and such is the case of the true faith until it attains completion. And I questioned you whether any of them becomes an apostate out of hatred for his religion after having embraced it, and you said: No. Such is faith when its joy is infused into hearts. And I questioned you whether he is unfaithful to his agreements and you said: No. Even so, the Messengers are never unfaithful. And I questioned you about what he enjoins upon you, and you said that he called you to serve God and not set up anything beside Him and forbade you the worship of idols; and that he prescribed prayer and truthfulness and chastity."

Heraclius went on: "If what you say is true, he shall soon be master of the place where I stand. I knew that he would appear but I never thought that he would be from among you. If I knew that I could go to him, I would have made an earnest endeavor to meet him, and if I were with him, I would indeed wash his feet."

Then he called for the letter of the Messenger of Allāh, which Dihiyah al-Kalbī had brought to the governor of Baṣrah, and the governor of Baṣrah had sent to Heraclius, and he read it:

In the Name of Allāh, the Merciful, the Compassionate. From Muḥammad, the servant of Allāh and His Messenger, to Heraclius, the emperor of the Romans, Peace be on him who follows guidance. I invite you to the faith of Islam: surrender to God [enter Islam] and you will be in peace. Allāh will give you a twofold reward. But if you turn away, on you will be the sins of your subjects. O People of the Book, come to equitable words between us and you, that we shall not associate anything with Him and that some of us shall not take others for lords besides Allāh. But if they turn away, say, bear witness that we are the surrendered [Muslims].

Abū Sufyān said: "When he had said what he wanted to say and finished the reading of the letter, there was a great uproar in his presence and the voices became loud and we were turned out. I said to my companions, the cause of the son of Abū Kabsha [a disparaging reference to the Prophet] has become great, as the emperor of the Romans is afraid of him; and I was certain then that he [the Prophet] would prevail, until Allāh made me embrace Islam..."

See MUQAWQĪS.

Herāt. City in Afghanistan, then Bactria, founded by Alexander the Great, whom Niẓāmī described as a figure who prepared the way for Islam. The Moghul Padishah Babur described Herāt this way: "The whole habitable world had not such a town as Herāt had become under Sultan Ḥusayn Mirza... Khorāsān, and Herāt above all, was filled with learned and matchless men. Whatever work a man took up, he aimed and aspired to bring it to perfection."

Heresy, *see* ILḤĀD.

Hezbollah, *see* ḤIZB ALLĀH.

Hibah. In Islamic law, a gift of property.

Hidden Imām. Foreign to Sunnī Islam, the doctrine of the Hidden Imām is peculiar to Twelve-Imām Shī'ism (although several Ismā'īlī sects have developed their own variants). Twelve-Imām Shī'ites believe that the twelfth Imām, named Muḥammad and said to be born in Samarra' (*255*/869), disappeared at the age of four in the year *260*/873, upon the death of his father, Ḥasan al-'Askarī, the eleventh Imām. Some say he disappeared into the cellar (*sardib*) of the family house in Samarra', others that he disappeared in Ḥilla near Baghdad. He reputedly made several more or less miraculous reappearances but from that time until today he has been living supernaturally hidden from mankind. He will reveal himself at the end of time as the Mahdī.

From the time of his disappearance until the year *329*/940, when the Imām would have been about seventy years old, his will was made known through four successive representatives, or *wakīls*. The first was 'Uthmān ibn Sa'īd, the secretary of the Hidden Imām's father, Ḥasan al-'Askarī. 'Uthmān had often acted on behalf of the eleventh Imām, and he, along with the women of the household, supplied the accounts of the twelfth Imām, descriptions of his appearance, etc. The other representatives were Abū Ja'far Muḥammad, Abū-l-Qāsim ibn Rūḥ, and Abū-l-Ḥasan 'Alī ibn Muḥammad Samarrī. This period of contact with the Imām is called the "lesser occultation" (*al-ghaybah as-sughrā*). It is also called the *wukalā'*, after the representatives (*wakīls*), or the "period of emissaries" (*as-sifārah*).

On behalf of the Hidden Imām, the *wakīls* collected the *khums*, or special tithe (more literally, "fifth portion") which, among the Shī'ites, is due to the Imāms. In the Medinan community this was the share of the spoils of war, which was the special prerogative of the Prophet to distribute in the interests of religion and the state. Among the Sunnīs this tithe disappeared after the Prophet, but it was maintained by the Shī'ites in favor of the descendants of the Prophet who were Imāms. The last *wakīl*, who died in *329*/940, declined to name a successor to his function of mediating with the Imām, saying "the matter now rests with God." Thus began the period of the "greater occultation" (*al-ghaybah al-kubrā*), which continues to this day.

The Twelve-Imām Shī'ites believe that this twelfth Imām is still alive although invisible — thus there is no successor to him.

It is important to note that the eleventh Imām had no other children. If a descendant (in the event, the Hidden Imām) were not attributed to him, the line of Imāms — whose mediation in Shī'ism between man and God is necessary for salvation — would have come to an end. The theories upon which Shī'ism is based, the Imāmate (the existence of a divinely ordained and inspired intermediary of God on earth) whose principles of succession had become dogmatically and rigidly defined two hundred years previously, would have suffered a serious blow. No less important, there would have been no justification for continuing to collect the tithe of the *khums* — today received by the Mullās from their followers. According to the Shī'ite records known as the *'Aqā'id ash-Shī'ah*, the eleventh Imām, who probably suffered from poor health and died at the age of twenty-eight (his father, the ninth Imām died at the age of forty-one) had no wives; this is a very unusual case because the Sunnah insists upon marriage as "half of the religion" and it was usual to marry at a very young age. (The conditions which make legal marriage impossible also preclude having children). In other words, diabetes may have put an end to the Imāmate. But religious demands required that the Imāmate continue. And so it did, with the flourishes of fable.

As the eleventh Imām had no wives, the twelfth Imām is believed to have been born to a concubine, or female slave of the eleventh Imām. She was called Narjis Khatun, and is said to have been a grand-daughter of the Byzantine emperor, who was captured (not kept for ransom), sold into slavery, and bought providentially by an agent of the tenth Imām for his son for whom she knew she was destined. When Narjis Khatun bore him a son, the eleventh Imām is reported to have said "bring him to me every forty days" (to birds who took the child away for safekeeping), which is to say he was not often seen, the explanation being that the child was always kept in the women's quarters (or by the birds in a secret haven). And then at the age of four he disappeared.

Shī'ites call the Hidden Imām the "Lord of the Age" (*Ṣāḥib az-Zamān*), the rightful ruler of the universe, the spiritual *axis mundi*. He is also called the "Awaited Mahdī" (*al-Mahdī al-Muntaẓar*) who will return at the end of time, manifest his dominion, bring order and justice to the world and — a very characteristic point — "take vengeance on the enemies of God". (The Sunnīs have also adopted the idea of the Mahdī, but of course they do not identify him with any Shī'ite Imām. For the Sunnīs the Mahdī restores spiritual clarity at the end of time, but the aspect "of taking vengeance" is not only absent, but foreign to their conception of the matter.)

Shī'ites believe that the Hidden Imām illumines men and intercedes with God on their behalf. He hears personal prayer, and in particular it is the custom to beseech him by writing sealed letters which are left at the tombs of Imāms, and their close relatives (*Imāmzādeh*), dropped into wells, or thrown into the sea. It has been averred that, at the moment of death, he who is saved has a vision of the Hidden Imām.

It is doctrine in Islam that Jesus — in his reality — did not die upon the cross but exists in a principial state and will return to the world at the end of time. Doubtless, it is this Koranic doctrine concerning a unique prophet with an exceptional function in the world in its last days, that provides the calque, or precedent, for the unusual theory that resolves the Shī'ite predicament regarding the existence of the twelfth Imām. (Also, in Iranian lore, as in European, there are heroes who disappear into enchanted places from which they will reappear centuries later at a historical juncture.) Following this model, other sects, including the Musta'īlī Ismā'īlīs, and also the Druzes, have "hidden" or "occulted" spiritual figures. The dogma of the twelfth Imām, however, is the most highly developed of these doctrines, and has proven to be of tremendous historical consequence for those who believe it.

Ibn Bāṭūṭah travelled through Ḥilla in 1327. He later reported:

> Next morning we went on and alighted at the city of Ḥilla, which is a large town lying along the western bank of the Euphrates, with fine markets where both natural products and manufactured good may be had. At this place there is a great bridge fastened upon a continuous row of boats from bank to bank, the boats being held in place both fore an aft by iron chains attached on either bank to a huge wooden beam made fast ashore. The inhabitants of Ḥilla are all Shī'ites of the "Twelvers" sect, but they are

divided into two factions, known as the "Kurds" and the "Party of the Two Mosques", between whom there is constant factional strife and fighting. Near the principal market in this town there is a mosque, the door of which is covered with a silk curtain. They call this the Sanctuary of the Master if the Age. Every evening before sunset, a hundred of the townsmen, following their custom, go with arms and drawn swords to the governor of the city and receive from him a saddled and bridled horse or mule. With this they go in procession, with drums beating and trumpets and bugles blowing, fifty of them in front and fifty behind, while others walk to right and left, to the Sanctuary of the Master of the Age. They halt at the door and call out "In the Name of God, O Master of the Age, and in the Name of God, come forth! Corruption is abroad and injustice is rife! This is the hour for thy advent, that by thee God may discover the true from the false." They continue to call out thus, sounding their drums and bugles and trumpets, until the hour of sunset prayer, for they hold that Muḥammad, the son of al-Ḥasan al-'Askari entered this mosque and disappeared from sight in it, and that he will emerge from it, for he, in their view, is the "expected Imām".

See GHAYBAH; IMĀM; ISMĀ'ĪLĪS; MAHDĪ; SHĪ'ISM; UṢŪLĪS.

"Highest Initiation, Book of the Policy and the". (*Kitāb as-Siyāsa wa'l-Balāgh al-Akbar)* quoted by 'Abd al-Qāhir ibn Ṭāhir al-Baghdādī in *420*/1029, and Akhū Muḥsin (a nickname, his real name was Muḥammad ibn 'Alī ibn Ḥusayn) of Damascus (himself a descendant of Muḥammad ibn Ismā'īl), at the end of the 4th/10th century, and by others who refuted the Fāṭimid claims of Sharīfian ancestry. The author is not known; the attribution to 'Ubayd Allāh is obviously false but curiously reminiscent of *The Three Imposters*, also falsely attributed to him, which circulated in Europe. Like the "Revelations of the Secrets of the Batinis and the Story of the Qarāmiṭa" by Muḥammad ibn Malik al-Ḥammādī in the 11th century, about which Stern says: "An account of the circumstances which obliged Ja'far ibn Manṣūr al-Yaman to leave his native Yemen and join the Fāṭimid court in North Africa is contained in the invaluable history of the Ismā'īlīs of the Yemen, written by one of their enemies in the middle of the eleventh century..." the "Book of the Highest Revelation", which has been called "a propagandist travesty", was also written by one of their enemies; and it also provides valuable information to understand the operations of the sect. The text may be "fictitious" but may yet correspond to the realities as seen from the outside. Whether the information is flattering or not depends upon your point of view. The works of Ibn Rizām, another "enemy", are used by the Ismā'īlīs themselves to provide information about their own history, although his conclusions about the orthodoxy of Ismā'īlism obviously are rejected as incorrect, and "biased".

It is known that members of the sect went through different stages of initiation (balāgh), seven is the number usually cited, in order to be fully indoctrinated. One of these initiations apparently involved a symbolical pilgrimage to Mecca (referred to by Rūmī, and was one of the irregularities of which al-Ḥallāj was accused). In the Masonic initiation of the first degree, that of the entered apprentice, the postulant arrives at the Temple of Solomon in something like the garb of an Islamic pilgrim to Mecca, which suggests that the Ismā'īlīs had a hand in designing this laymen's outreach program for the Templars.

"The Book of the Highest Initiation" is not actually about an initiation or initiations, but is a very compelling attempt to depict the psychology which results from the indoctrination. That it is reasonably authentic is known from material from China, which says that the mother religion presented itself disguised, as occasion suggested, as any convenient indigenous religion, such as Buddhism, Taoism, and Confucianism. (In fact they went so far as to create a text which presents Lao Tsu as leaving China by the Western Gate, in order to be reborn as Mani, and also, in appearance, Buddhist Sutras which are not Buddhist and teach something different than the Buddha's doctrine.) It is also immediately recognizable as authentic to another type of perennial Manichean-like organisation, the Intelligence agency, for the first precept is: "Make propaganda among the people by approaching each individual according to the manner to which he inclines by making everyone believe that you belong to his sect." This kind of identity concealing adaptation to surrounding conditions is reminiscent of the nature of viruses which are alien but, for a period of time, behave like the surrounding substance and use that substance to replicate themselves. And it follows:

"If you have a Shī'ite to deal with let him understand that you share his convictions. In order to gain his confidence you will dwell upon the injustice with which the Muslim community treated 'Alī and his children, upon the murder of al-Ḥusayn, the serfdom to which they have reduced his womenfolk. You will say that you abjure all loyalty towards Taym and 'Adi, the Umayyads and the 'Abbāsids. You continue in this strain, telling similar tales to please them and to capture their minds. In this way you will have people of this conviction following eagerly your lead; you will get from them whatever you want.

"If you have to deal with a Ṣābian, insinuate yourself into his mind by discourses on the hebdomadal number; you will find his doctrines to be kindred to yours.

"If you have the chance to meet with a Jew, hold his attention by speaking to him about the Messiah; tell him that it is same as the Mahdī; that the knowledge of him procures rest from the duties imposed by religion and of its troublesome obligations, in the same way as his law enjoins him to rest on the Sabbath-day. You will gain his sympathy by speaking disparagingly of the ignorant Christians and Muslims with their assertions concerning Jesus: that he has not been born and that he had no father. Tell him that Joseph the carpenter was his father and Mary his mother; and that Joseph was her husband. By this and similar speech you will soon make him one of your followers.

"Gain the Christians by expatiating on the faults of the Jews and the Muslims; show them that you approve of their making the sign of the cross, but let them know its allegorical explanation. Try to confute their negative views about the Paraclete and prove to them that he is going to come and that you call them to him.

"If you have to deal with a Sunni speak to him with respect of Abū Bakr and 'Umar, mention their excellent character; speak ill of 'Alī and his descendants and do not be sparing of censure of them. Insinuate to him that Abū Bakr and 'Umar were not quite alien to the doctrine you are teaching him. If you gain his confidence by these means, you will be able to lead him on, whenever you like to a higher degree and gain ascendancy over him.

"Be sure to make them enter the most solemn covenant, to make the most severest vows, and the most binding undertakings. These will serve you as a shield and a fortress. Do not be in a hurry to confide to your disciples doctrines that are revolting to their minds; make them advance in the different degrees gradually, step by step.

"In the case of some of them you will have to content yourself with imbuing them with a sympathy towards Shī'ism and with belief in Muḥammad ibn Ismā'īl and that he is alive; do not go farther with these people. Keep up for their benefit, an appearance of unselfishness in matters of money; let your manner towards them be one of great mildness. Order them to keep the seventy prayers, and admonish them to avoid lying, fornication, sodomy and intoxicating drinks. Behave yourself towards them with gentleness, patience and try to win them by clever management. They will prove a great help to you against the vicissitudes of fortune, against enemies you may find, or against those of your followers who, changing their views, might come to oppose you. Do not request such a person to stop the cult of his God, the exercise of his religion and the belief in the Imāmate of 'Alī and his descendants, up to Muḥammad ibn Ismā'īl ibn Ja'far; it will be enough to acquaint him with arguments taken from the hebdomads; break him by an excessive quantity of prayers.

"Others you may advance even to the first notions of the true theology. Make your approach by the doctrines contained in the Book of the Teaching which Heals the Soul (*Kitāb al-Dars ash-shāfī li'l-Nafs*), viz. that there is no God, either as a attribute or a subject. This will help you to teach, when you reach that stage of the initiation, the divinity of that one to whom divinity belongs.

"Those whom you have advanced to this degree you can inform, as we have informed you, of the truth concerning the Imām; you can disclose to them that Ismā'īl and his son

> Muḥammad had been but his Doors (*abwāb*). This will prove a great help for you in destroying the belief in the Imāmate of the descendants of 'Alī ibn Abī Ṭālib when you reach the goal of the initiation and profess openly for the truth for those who are worthy of it.

The book continues mainly in the vein of discrediting established religion and promoting freethinking. The full text is in *Stern's Studies in early Ismā'īlism*. *See* al-ḤALLĀJ.

Ḥijāb (lit. "a veil" or "partition"). A common meaning of *ḥijāb* today, because it does designate the veil, is the adherence to certain standards of modest dress for women. The usual definition of modest dress according to the legal systems does not actually require wearing a veil, but does require covering everything except the face and hands in public; this, at least, is the practice which originated in the Middle east. *See* VEIL.

Aside from its literal sense, in metaphysics *al-ḥijāb* refers to the veil which separates man or the world from God. In particular, it can mean the illusory aspect of creation, about which a Sufi proverb says that it is *khayālun fī khayālin fī khayāl*; "an illusion within an allusion within an illusion".

Ḥijāb has been used as an equivalent for the Indian concept of *māyā*, which is cosmic illusion, existential "magic" or *līlā*, creative play. Ibn 'Aṭā'Allāh says in the *Ḥikam*:

> Were the light of certitude to shine, you would see the Hereafter so near that you could not move towards it, and you would see that the eclipse of extinction had come over the beauties of the world. It is not the existence of any being alongside of Him that veils you from God, for nothing is alongside of Him. Rather, the *illusion* of a being alongside of Him is what veils you from Him. Had it not been for His manifestation in created beings eyesight would not have perceived them. Had His Qualities been manifested, His created beings would have disappeared.

The metaphysical sense of *ḥijāb* is precisely a veil which "refracts" the light of the Divine Intellect, which otherwise would be blinding. Al-Jīlī said: "The Divine Obscurity is the primordial place where the suns of beauty set. It is the Self of God Himself." Ibn 'Aṭā'Allāh also says:

> How can it be conceived that something veils Him, since He is the One who manifests everything?
>
> How can it be conceived that something veils Him, since He is the One who is manifest through everything?
>
> How can it be conceived that something veils Him, since He is the One who is manifest in everything?
>
> How can it be conceived that something veils Him, since He is the Manifest to everything?
>
> How can it be conceived that something veils Him, since He is the Manifest before the existence of anything?
>
> How can it be conceived that something veils Him, since He is more manifest than anything?
>
> How can it be conceived that something veils Him since He is the One alongside of Whom there is nothing?
>
> How can it be conceived that something veils Him, since He is nearer to you than anything else?
>
> How can it be conceived that something veils Him, since, were it not for Him, the existence of everything would not have been manifest?
>
> It is a marvel how Being has been manifested in non-being and how the contingent has been established alongside of Him who possesses the attribute of eternity.

Hijrah (lit. "the migration"; often written "hegira"). The emigration of the Prophet from Mecca to Yathrib (later called *Madīnat an-Nabī*, the "City of the Prophet" or Medinah) at the end of September in 622. In Mecca, persecution of Muslims had grown to the point that the Prophet's life was in danger; but in Yathrib he was offered sanctuary.

Abū Ṭālib, uncle and protector of the Prophet, had died earlier that year, and the leaders of the Quraysh decided to seize the occasion to rid themselves of the man who had caused such great dissension in Mecca. They plotted Muḥammad's murder. It was decided that a member of each of the clans would participate and thus all would share the responsibility. The Angel Gabriel warned the

Prophet, who told Abū Bakr that they would flee Mecca together for Yathrib.

Muḥammad instructed his cousin 'Alī to mislead the conspirators by donning the Prophet's green cloak and sleeping in his bed. Then the Prophet, reciting the words of the Sūrah *Yā Sīn*, "we have enshrouded them so that they see not" (36:9), slipped past the enemies surrounding his house and joined Abū Bakr. The two left Mecca on camel with a flock of sheep driven behind them to cover their tracks. They hid in a cave in Mount Thawr several miles south of the town, while 'Abd Allāh, the son of Abū Bakr returned the camels. At the Prophet's house the conspirators came upon 'Alī and realized they had been tricked.

A search party arrived at the cave but never looked in it because of the sudden, miraculous growth of an acacia tree which blocked the entrance; moreover, the presence of a spider's web over the opening of the cave, and of a dove's nest with an egg in front of the cave, seemed to show that no one had entered.

After several days of hiding, the Prophet and Abū Bakr continued on camels with a Beduin guide and with food brought to them by Asmā', the daughter of Abū Bakr. During the journey of some ten or fourteen days by riding camel to Yathrib, the verse was revealed: "Verily He who has made the Koran a law for you will bring you home again." (28:85).

Some seventy Meccan Muslims emigrated to Yathrib at the same time as the Prophet. These were the original *muhājirūn* (emigrants). More followed over the course of the next few years. "This last *muhājir*—", this was the Prophet's phrase—was an uncle of the Prophet, al-'Abbās, who joined the Muslims just as they were advancing to conquer Mecca. The Hijrah took place in the year 622, at the end of September, probably on the 17th. Sixteen years later, in 637, the Caliph 'Umar formalized the Prophet's custom of dating events from the Hijrah, the moment of the establishment of the first Islamic state. Thus the year of the Hijrah became the first year of the Islamic era. *See* CALENDAR; MUḤAMMAD.

Ḥīlah (lit. "ruse", pl. *ḥiyal*). A legal stratagem to circumvent the intentions of the *sharī'ah* (canon law), without technically breaking it. Such stratagems came into use in the 'Abbāsid Caliphate chiefly among the Ḥanafīs, but were adopted to a lesser degree by the other schools when they offered solutions to otherwise difficult social problems, and were not intended merely to circumvent the law. *See* SCHOOLS of LAW; SHARĪ'AH; "SLEEPING FOETUS".

Ḥilf al-Fuḍūl (lit. "oath of virtue"). The Pact of Chivalry in which the Prophet had participated some twenty years before the revelation of Islam. *See* FUTUWWAH.

Ḥillī, 'Allāma (Manṣūr Ḥasan ibn Yūsuf ibn 'Alī al-Ḥillī; *648-726*/1250-1325). He is also known as Ibn al-Muṭahhar. The leading Shī'ite theologian during the Il-Khanid dynasty. Ḥillī studied for a time with the astronomer and mathematician Naṣīr ad-Dīn aṭ-Ṭūsi, as well as with Sunnī scholars, and was the author of over seventy-five treatises on Shī'ism, such as the *Minhaj al-Karāmah fī Ma'rifat al-Imāmah* ("The Miraculous Way of Knowledge of the Imāmate").

'Allāmah Ḥillī established a Shī'ite methodology and terminology for the critical study of Ḥadīth literature (*dirāya*), modeled upon that of the Sunnīs, and he reorganized Shī'ite jurisprudence. He is buried in Najaf.

al-Ḥilyat al-Awliyā'. A vast compendium in ten volumes of Sufi lore, doctrine, and biography by Abū Nu'aym al-Isbahānī (d. *430*/1038).

al-Himmah (lit. "concentration", or "resolve"). The quality of perseverance or striving towards God. Its opposite is *al-ḥiss* (lit. "noise", "sensation"), distraction or inattention from concentration upon God.

Ḥīrah, *see* LAKHMIDS.

Ḥira'. The cave (*ghār*), or grotto, at the summit of the mountain of that name, now usually called *Jabal an-Nūr*, the Mountain of Light. The grotto is large enough for a man to perform the prayer; inside is a small opening which faces Mecca. The cave is a few miles from Mecca; the ascent to the top takes an hour or two. There the Prophet would retreat to meditate. One of his daughters would bring him food so that he could remain at the grotto the whole month. There, in the last days of Ramaḍān, on the Night of Destiny (*Laylat al-Qadr*), the Koran descended into the soul of the Prophet. *See* LAYLAT al-QADR.

al-Ḥiss (lit. "sensation", "noise"). Physical sensation. Also, a technical term for the distractions which draw the soul away from contemplation of God, and the state of "distractedness". The opposite of *al-ḥiss* in this sense is *al-himmah* (spiritual concentration). Al-Hujwīrī said:

> Beware of distracting your own mind from God by trying to satisfy people whose minds are occupied with vainer things. When you meet a man of nobler mind than your own, then you may safely distract your mind to satisfy his. But otherwise, never distract yourself; "Is God not enough for His servants?" [Koran 39:36].

And Ḥasan of Baṣrah said:

> Beware of this world with all wariness; for it is like to a snake, smooth to the touch, but its venom is deadly. Turn away from whatsoever delights thee in it, for the little companioning thou wilt have of it; put off from thee its cares, for that thou hast seen its sudden chances, and knowest for sure that thou shalt be parted from it: endure firmly its hardships, for the ease that shall presently be thine. The more it please thee, the more do thou be wary of it; for the man of this world, whenever he feels secure in any pleasure thereof, the world drives him over into some unpleasantness, and whenever he attains any part of it and squats him down upon it, the world suddenly turns him upside down. And again, beware of this world, for its hopes are lies, its expectations false; its easefulness all harshness, muddied its limpidity.
>
> And therein, thou art in peril: or bliss transient, or sudden calamity, or painful affliction, or doom decisive. Hard is the life of a man if he be prudent, dangerous if comfortable, being wary ever of catastrophe, certain of his ultimate fate. Even had the Almighty not pronounced upon the world at all, nor coined for it any similitude, nor charged men to abstain from it, yet would the world itself have awakened the slumberer, and roused the heedless; how much the more then, seeing that God has Himself sent us a warning against it, an exhortation regarding it! For this world has not with God so much as a pebble or a single clod of earth; as I am told, God has created nothing more hateful to Him, and from the day He created it He has not looked upon it, so much He hates it.

The Prophet said: "This world is under curse, and everything in it, except for the remembrance of God." The mystical abhorrence of the world, however, is heuristic, intended to lead man out of illusion, for by itself, the world is God's creation, and good as God is good. *See* DHIKR.

History, *see* IBN ĀTHIR; IBN KHALDŪN; al-MAS'ŪDĪ; RASHĪD ad-DĪN at-ṬABĪB; at-ṬABARĪ; al-WAQĪDĪ.

Ḥizb Allāh (lit. "party of God"). A term in the Koran for the Muslims, as opposed to the idolators, during the initial struggle for life.

> Whoso makes God his friend,
> and His Messenger,
> and the believers — the party of God,
> they are the victors. (5:62)

and:

> Thou shalt not find any people who believe in God and the Last Day who are loving to anyone who opposes God and His Messenger, not though they were their fathers, or their sons, or their brothers, or their clan. Those — He has written faith upon their hearts, and He has confirmed them with a Spirit from Himself; and He shall admit them into gardens underneath which rivers flow, therein to dwell forever, God being well-pleased with them, and they well-pleased with Him. Those are God's party; why, surely God's party — they are the prosperers. (58:23)

The term has been appropriated by various movements and groups in the past as a name for their organisation or viewpoint. The 1979 revolution in Iran was marked by the emergence of street vigilantes calling themselves Ḥizb Allāh and organisations called *Komiteh* who enforced the will of revolutionary factions which dispersed counter-demonstrations and closed universities. Ḥizb Allāh went on to become various militias of clerics vying for political power. They were a more irregular grouping than the *Pasdarān* or Revolutionary Guards.

In the Lebanon, in the 1970s as the Twelve-Imām Shī'ites grew more conscious of their group identity under the Iranian Mullā Imām Mūsā's-Ṣadr, the political grouping *Amal* was created in 1974. As civil unrest in Lebanon grew, this was followed, after the Iranian revolution of 1979, by the creation of *Ḥizb Allāh*, a more radical paramilitary group closely linked with Iran. Its leader, Sayyid Muḥammad Ḥusayn Faḍlallāh, a cleric, had come to Lebanon from Najaf, a centre of Shī'ite teaching in 'Irāq. His militant following in Lebanon was reinforced by the arrival of Lebanese Shī'ite theology students expelled from 'Irāq in the seventies. The Iranian revolution and the Israeli invasion of Lebanon gave the impetus for Ḥizb Allāh to emerge as the leading Shī'ite military organisation in Lebanon. Iranian Revolutionary Guards arrived in the Bekaa Valley in Lebanon and the goal of Ḥizb Allāh became the establishment of an Islamic state and the destruction of Israel.

Ḥizb Allāh attacked American, French, and Israeli forces in Lebanon. The killing of 241 U.S. marines in their barracks in Beirut in 1983 led to U.S. and French withdrawal of their peacekeeping forces from Lebanon. Ḥizb Allāh also attacked U.S. and French embassies, carried on bombing attacks in France, hijacked airliners, and took Western hostages in Lebanon, the last of whom was released in 1992. These attacks were carried out to further their policies and in some cases the policies of Iran. The Israelis carried out bombing attacks on Shaykh Faḍlallāh, killing many but not him, and on a Ḥizb Allāh leader Sayyid 'Abbās al-Mūsawi who was killed in 1992. Another leader, Shaykh 'Abd al-Karīm 'Ubayd was abducted in 1988. In 1989 Syria enforced an end to the civil war in Lebanon after the Ṭā'if Accord, and Ḥizb Allāh moved towards parliamentary political participation. Attacks and counterattacks continue between Ḥizb Allāh and Israeli forces in the south of Lebanon. *See* LEBANON; METAWILA.

Ḥizb al-Baḥr. "The Litany of the Sea" composed by the Imām Shādhilī using passages from the Koran (*see* SHĀDHILĪ). Its recitation has been credited with saving Damascus from conquest by an attacker. Its power resides in the ritual recitation of the litany in Arabic. The groups of letters are the mysterious "isolated letters" which stand before 29 Sūrahs. Seven consecutive Sūrahs begin with the letters *hā mīm*, and these, along with other Sūrahs where the letters appear in combination with other letters, are called the *hāwamīm*. In such cases the isolated letters also stand for the whole Sūrah. *Tabārak* and *Yā Sīn* are also the names of Sūrahs.

> O our God, O Most-High, O Tremendous One, O Gentle One, O All-Knowing, You are my Lord and Your knowledge suffices me. The Most excellent Master is my Master and the Most excellent Sufficing is my sufficiency. You help whom you will and You are the Mighty, the Compassionate. We implore security in our movements and our stillness, in words, in willing, in dangers from doubts and suppositions cloaking our hearts from contemplation of the unseen. The believers have been visited by affliction and shaken by a powerful earthquake. And the hypocrites and those with sickness in their hearts say that God and His Messenger have promised us only delusion [Koran 8:49] — Confirm us and aid us and compel for us this sea, as You compelled the sea for Moses, and compelled the fire for Abraham, and compelled the mountains and iron for David, and compelled the wind and demons and *jinn* for Solomon [cf. Koran 38:18,36]; and compel for us every sea that is Yours in the earth and the heaven, in the corporeal world (*al-mulk*) and the subtle (*al-malakūt*) and the sea of this world and the sea of the beyond; and compel for us all things, O You in Whose Hand is dominion of everything. *Kāf hā' yā' 'ayn ṣād; kāf hā yā' 'ayn ṣād; kāf hā' yā' 'ayn ṣād.*
>
> Help us. Lo! You are the Best of Helpers, render us triumphant. Lo! You are the Best of Conquerors, and forgive us. Lo! You are the Best Forgiver, and grant us mercy. Lo! You are the most Compassionate, and provide for us. Lo! You are the Best Provider, and guide us, and rescue us from an erring folk.
>
> Accord us favorable winds — as it is in Your science — and spread them over us from the treasuries of Your mercy. And transport us thereby generously with peace and well-being in the religion (*dīn*) and this lower world (*dunyā*) and the beyond (*ākhirah*), for You have power over all things.

Our Lord, make easy our affairs with repose for our hearts and our bodies; with peace and well-being in matters of religion and matters of the world. And be our Companion in our journeying, and Regent (*khalīfah*) with our folk and quench the faces of our enemies and confound them in their place that they may not go or come to us. "And had We willed, we verily could have fixed them in their place, making them powerless to go forward or go back." [Koran 36:66]. "Yā' Sīn, And the wise Koran, Lo! You are of those sent on a straight path. A revelation of the Mighty the Merciful. That You may warn a folk whose fathers were not warned, so they are heedless. Already the word has come true of most of them for they believe not. Lo! We have put on their necks irons reaching to their chins, so that they are stiff-necked. And We have set a bar before them and a bar behind them, and have covered them so that they see not" [36:1-9]. Confounded be those faces. Confounded be those faces. Confounded be those faces. "And humbled be the faces before the Living, the Self-Subsisting. And already ruined is he who bears wrongdoing" [20:111].

Tā' sīn, hā' mīm 'ayn sīn qāf. "He has loosed the seas, they meet. Between them is an isthmus (barzakh), they do not encroach upon each other" [55:19,20]. *Hā' mīm, hā' mīm, hā' mīm, hā' mīm, hā' mīm, hā' mīm, hā' mīm.* Lo! the Command is come (*humma al-'amru*). And lo! the Aid. Lo! they do not look upon us. *Hā' mīm.* The Book is revealed from God, the Mighty, the Knower, Forgiving sins and accepting repentance, of punishment far-reaching and powerful. There is no God but He. To Him is the journeying.

Bismillāhi is our door; *Tabārak* our walls, *Yā' Sīn* our roof. *Kāf hā' yā' 'ayn sād* is our sufficiency, *hā' mīm 'ayn sīn qāf* our protection. Allāh will be enough for them, Allāh is the Hearer, the Knower. Allāh will be enough for them, Allāh is the Hearer, the Knower. Allāh will be enough for them, Allāh is the Hearer, the Knower. The curtain of the throne is draping over us, and the eye of God is looking at us. With Allāh's strength they do not have power over us and "Allāh, all unseen, surrounds them from behind. It is a glorious Koran on a Guarded Tablet (*lawḥ maḥfūẓ*)" [85:20,21]. "For Allāh is the best of Guardians, and He is The Most Merciful of the Merciful." [12:64]. Lo! my Protector is Allāh who revealed the Book and He befriends the righteous. "If they turn away, say Allāh suffices me, there is no God save Him, in Him I have put my trust, and He is the Lord of the tremendous throne. If they turn away, say Allāh suffices me, there is no God save Him, in Him I have put my trust, and He is the Lord of the tremendous throne. If they turn away, say Allāh suffices me, there is no God save Him, in Him I have put my trust, and He is the Lord of the tremendous throne" [9:129]. In the Name of God, with which nothing in the earth or Heaven can suffer harm. And He is the Hearer, the Knower. And He is the Hearer, the Knower. And He is the Hearer, the Knower. And there is no strength nor power except in Allāh, the exalted, the Mighty.

See ḤURŪF al-MUQAṬṬA'ĀT; REFUGE; SHĀDHILĪ.

Holy Cities, *see* JERUSALEM; MECCA; MEDINAH.

Holy Days, *see* 'ĀSHŪRĀ'; CALENDAR; 'ĪD al-AḌḤĀ; 'ĪD al-FIṬR; 'ĪD al-GHADĪR; LAYLAT al-BARĀ'AH; MAWLID an-NABĪ; MUḤARRAM; NAW RUZ; RAMAḌĀN.

Holy War, *see* JIHĀD.

Hour, the (Ar. *as-sā'ah*). In the Koran, "the Hour" is the end of the world, the Last Judgement, and the events related to it. Only God knows when it will be, but mankind knows that it will be terrible (Koran 53:50), and sudden (12:107). The Prophet said: "The Hour will not surprise the one who saith: Allāh, Allāh."

Also, those who are assembled for the Day of Judgement will believe that the time they spent on earth was but an hour, or less (10:46). *See* YAWM ad-DIN.

Houris (Ar. *ḥawrā'* or *ḥuriyyah* pl. *ḥūr*). The female companions, perpetual virgins, of the saved in Paradise. They are the symbols of spiritual states of rapture. (Koran 44:54; 52:20; 55:72; 56:22; or as companions, 2:23; 3:14; 4:60). There also are in paradise eternal youths (*wildān mukhalladūn*). Western scholars of religion believe that the *houris* of Islam originate with the *Daena* of Zoroastrian eschatology. In Zoroastrianism, if the soul of the departed is saved and destined to enter paradise, it is met by its inner conscience in the form of a beautiful woman, the *Daena*, that leads the soul across the "bridge" into the afterlife. Zoroastrian ideas spread throughout the Near east after the conquest of Babylon by Cyrus in 539 BC and as far as Egypt with its conquest by Cambyses in 525 BC The "bridge" (*sirāt*) of the Zoroastrian eschatology is not mentioned anywhere in the Koran but has nevertheless become a universally accepted feature in Islamic eschatology, apparently simply taken for granted by the early theologians, many of whom, if not the majority, were Persians.

Zoroastrianism, and probably before it ancient Indo-European religion as well, believed (perhaps as a result of observing the decomposition of food set by a grave for the dead) that the soul lingers for three days before beginning a journey into the afterlife. This belief is also preserved in Islam as the idea that the dead can hear for three days. The Prophet addressed words to the bodies of those who had died at Badr, and when asked why, said: "Do you not know that the dead can hear for three days?" The three days also appears in Christianity as the lapse of time between Good Friday and Easter Sunday. The *Daena* is also the figure whom the apostles see on the Sepulchre in the cave whose stone at the mouth has been removed. *See* ZOROASTRIANISM.

"House of Forgetting", *see* FARĀMŪSH KHĀNEH.

House of Wisdom (Ar. *bayt al-ḥikmah*). An academy founded in *215*/830 by the Caliph al-Ma'mūn (d. *218*/833) in Baghdad for the purpose of translating Greek books on philosophy and the sciences into Arabic. The Fāṭimids later founded an academy in Egypt with a similar name, the "Abode of Wisdom" (*Dār al-Ḥikmah*), for the propagation of Ismā'īlī doctrines. These academies had important libraries, that of the Fatṭimids in Egypt being the greatest library of its time. Whether the *bayt al-ḥikmah* actually existed is at present questioned.

"Howling Dervishes". A pejorative colonial name for those Rifā'ī dervishes whose method included calling out loudly *Ya Ḥayyu, Ya Qayyūm*, "O Living One, O Self-Subsisting One." *See* RIFĀ'ĪYYAH.

Hubal. An idol, the God of the Moon. Centuries before Islam, 'Amr ibn Luhayy, a chief of the tribe of Jurhum who dwelt in Mecca before the coming of the Quraysh tribe, brought the idol to the city from Syria. It was set up in the Ka'bah and became the principal idol of the pagan Meccans. The ritual casting of lots and divining arrows was performed in front of it.

Hubal was pulled down and used as a doorstep when the Prophet conquered Mecca and purified the Ka'bah. *See* IDOLS; JĀHILIYYAH.

Hūd. A pre-Islamic Prophet to the Arabs mentioned in the Koran (7:63-70; 11:52-63; 26:123-139). Hūd was sent as a "warner" to the extinct tribe of 'Ād who rejected him. *See* 'ĀD; PROPHETS.

al-Ḥudaybiyyah. A place on the road from Jeddah to Mecca just outside the *Ḥaram* (restricted precinct). Here the Prophet stopped and awaited the outcome of events when prevented from making the pilgrimage by the Meccans. A Koranic revelation (48:27) in the sixth year of the Hijrah declared the Prophet would pray at Mecca. In March of 628 he set out to perform pilgrimage at Mecca with a party of about one thousand men, unarmed and in pilgrim dress (*iḥrām*). The Quraysh stopped the party at Ḥudaybiyyah, about ten miles from Mecca.

'Uthmān, who had powerful relatives among the Quraysh, was sent to negotiate with the Meccans. When he did not return at the expected time, many thought that he had been killed or captured and that all was lost. In this moment of peril, the Prophet's followers individually made a new oath of fealty to the Prophet known as the "Pact of Felicity" (*bay'āt ar-riḍwān*). The Prophet himself represented the absent 'Uthmān by proxy in this oath; one man, Jadd ibn Qays, refrained from taking it, hiding behind a camel.

Then 'Uthmān returned with some Meccans. The Quraysh agreed to a truce, the "Peace of Ḥudaybiyyah". Under the conditions of this treaty the Prophet would be allowed to make the pilgrimage, not then, but in the following year. Mecca would be emptied for three days for the Muslim pilgrims. The peace also stipulated a truce for ten years; that those who were not free but subjects or dependents of the Quraysh and who defected from the pagans to the Muslims would be returned to the Quraysh by the Muslims, whereas those who were subject to the Muslims, and who defected from the Muslims to the Quraysh, would not be returned by the Quraysh.

The Prophet performed the pilgrimage the following year. In doing so, he signalled to the Meccans that one of their main fears regarding Islam, which was that Mecca's position in Arabia as far as pilgrimage and trade was concerned was threatened, was unfounded because his religion maintained the pilgrimage tradition largely intact. The testimony of faith declaring there is no god but Allāh, and that Muḥammad is the Messenger of God rang out in the valley of Mecca. The Quraysh, camped on the hill of Abū Qubays, heard it, a portent of the coming triumph of Islam. Other effects were equally far-reaching. The desert tribes had seen the Meccans dealing with the Prophet as an equal, and as a sovereign, and many turned to the new religion. Shortly thereafter, in the year 630, taking an incident between an allied tribe and the Meccans as a breach of the truce, the Prophet marched upon Mecca and conquered it, meeting almost no resistance. *See* MUḤAMMAD; RIḌWĀN.

Hudhud. A bird, the Hoopoe, a popular image of a kind of celestial messenger in mystical literature. The Hudhud informed Solomon about Queen Bilqīs in Sabā (Sheba), in the south of Arabia, and that her people worshiped the sun instead of God, and about the glory of her throne (Koran 27:22).

Hui Hui. A name for Chinese Muslim peoples of Turkic origin, and loosely, a colloquial and general designation for Muslims in China. It probably originated as a Chinese version of a Turkic tribal name, but was later applied more broadly to include other minorities in Central Asia, and particularly the descendants of Arab and Persian immigrants. *Hei Hui* ("Black Hui") refers to the Uigurs; Hui Chiang ("Hui Territory") means Turkestan.

Hui Hui Chiao ("Hui Hui Doctrine") is a colloquial Chinese designation for Islam, the formal one being *Chen Ch'ing Chiao* ("Doctrine of Truth and Purity"). The number of Hui Hui is estimated to be 7.2 million; the total Muslim population of China has been put at 14.6 million, but the true figure is probably more. *See* TA SHIH..

Ḥujjat al-Islām, *see* AYATOLLAH.

al-Ḥujwīrī, Abū-l-Ḥasan 'Alī (d. *469*/1077). A Persian Sufi, generally known simply as al-Ḥujwīrī, who was born in Ghaznah and died in India at Lahore where he is known as Data Ganj Bakhsh. There is a great shrine-mosque built around his tomb. He is the author of a famous exposition of Sufism called *Kashf al-Mahjūb li-Arbāb al-Qulūb* ("The Unveiling of the Hidden for the Lords of the Heart").

Hülāgu Khān (614-663/1217-1265). Grandson of Jenghiz Khan and brother of Kubilai Khan, Hülāgu led part of the Mongol horde against the 'Abbāsids and sacked their capital, Baghdad, thus ending the Arab Caliphate in 1258. Two years later he captured Damascus, but was finally checked by the Mamlūks at the battle of *'Ayn Jalūt* in 659/1260. Despite the Nestorian Christian influence associated with the Mongol conquests in the Islamic world (the mother and wife of Hülāgu were Nestorians, and Nestorians advised the Mongols in their advance south), the Nestorians lost out. Hülāgu founded the Il-Khanid dynasty in Persia, but the Mongols of the south adopted Islam with the conversions of Maḥmūd Ghazan (d. *703*/1304), and Muḥammad Khudabanda (Uljaytu; d. *717*/1304). The historian Ibn al-Tiqṭaqā said that Hülāgu was an enthusiastic 'Alawī, that is, he belonged to a religion which appears to be a derivative of Manicheism, if not Manicheism itself.

Although the Mongol Golden Horde on the Volga and the Il-Khanids of Persia were nominally under the authority of the Great Khan, they became in practice independent when Kubilai established his capital in China. While the Mongol invasions were disasters, spelling the end of a world amidst wholesale massacres (The historian Ibn al-Athīr called them "the greatest calamity that had befallen mankind") they were also a purge, which, sweeping away the past, ultimately vivified the countries they touched. They could not have taken place if the invaded countries had not already become decadent and stagnant. Like the pruning of trees, although a kind of death, the Mongol invasions led to a renewal on a more homogeneous footing. *See* IL-KHANIDS; JUWAYNĪ, 'AṬA' MALIK;

MAMLŪKS; MONGOLS; RASHĪD ad-DĪN aṭ-ṬABĪB; YASA.

Ḥulūl (Ar. "settling", "alighting", "descent" and, by extension, "incarnation"). In Islamic philosophy it refers to the settling of a superior faculty upon a support. This may be the settling of the soul in the body for example, or, again, the settling of the intellect (*'aql*) in the mind. Most commonly however, *ḥulūl* refers to any doctrine which upholds the idea of Divine incarnation in human form, such as that of the *avatāras* of Hinduism, the solar, Divine, or semi-Divine heroes of Indo-European religion and myth, or the Divinity of Christ in Christianity. In Islam, Jesus is a Prophet, who, although he does not have a human father, being the "Spirit of God" cast into Mary, is nevertheless not considered to be Divine.

Divine incarnation is a notion which Islam is bound to reject, in the sense that this idea, more than any other, compromises Islam's "operative effectiveness". Salvation in Islam depends upon awareness of the Absolute as Absolute and thus Unique. Therefore, it is this critical point of Divine Oneness and incomparability which is defended most strenuously. Naturally, it is also around this notion of incarnation, which challenges God's Absoluteness, that the most serious heresies have arisen. A rural preacher in Morocco once said: "In Jerusalem there is a sanctuary, divided by a wall, with two entrances; on one side the Christians go, and on the other, the Muslims. If a Christian goes in on the Muslim side, the Muslims kill him; and if a Muslim goes in on the Christian side, the Christians kill him."

There is, of course, no such place in Jerusalem, but given the common heritage between the Religions of the Book, one could say there is such a place in the soul. If the *shahādah*, the testimony of the Absoluteness of God were given to a Christian, his Christianity would receive a mortal wound. And if a Muslim were to believe: "This man is God", he would be eating of the fruit of the tree of the knowledge of good and evil, the tree which God forbade to Adam.

Praise belongs to God
who has sent down upon His servant the Book
and has not assigned unto it any
crookedness;
upright, to warn of great violence
from Him, and to give good tidings
unto the believers, who do righteous deeds,
that theirs shall be a goodly wage
therein to abide forever,
and to warn those who say, 'God has taken to
Himself a son';
they have no knowledge of it, they
nor their fathers; a monstrous word
it is, issuing out of their mouths;
they say nothing but a lie. (Koran 18:1-5)

Divine incarnation is not accepted as a doctrine in Islam and thus *ḥulūl*, the word for such incarnation, can be an accusation of doctrinal error.

Ḥurūb ar-Riddah, *see* RIDDAH.

al-Ḥurūf al-Fawātiḥ, *see* al-ḤURUF al-MUQAṬṬĀ'AT.

al-Ḥurūf al-Muqaṭṭā'at. The "isolated letters", also called *al-ḥurūf al-fawātiḥ* ("the opening letters"). These are single letters (*ṣād, qāf, nūn, kāf*) and groups of two to five letters, such as *ḥā' mīm*, or *'alif lām rān* which stand before 29 Sūrahs. Some of the Sūrahs with isolated letters form blocs, such as seven consecutive Sūrahs, which begin with the letters *ḥā' mīm*, and which, along with other Sūrahs where the letters *ḥā' mīm* appear in combination with other letters, are called collectively the *ḥāwamīm* Sūrahs.

One explanation is that the letters are abbreviations standing for the initials of scribes. The Koranic commentator 'Abd Allāh ibn 'Abbās gave interpretations for the letters such as "I, Allāh, am One" for one set of letters. The *ḥā' mīm*, he said, stood for *ar-Raḥmān*, "The Merciful", a Name of God, and *'alif lam mīm* for "I, God, know."

Scholars and mystics throughout history have also attempted to explain or elucidate the meaning of the letters but none have done so conclusively. Whatever the explanation behind them, the letters have taken on mystical significance as magical emblems of the Sūrahs they precede. *See* ḤIZB al-BAḤR; 'ILM al-ḤURŪF; KORAN.

Ḥurūfī. 1. Someone who is versed in the mystical science of letters and words called *'Ilm al-ḥurūf*, its interpretation, and divination through it. *See* 'ILM al-ḤURŪF.

2. An extremely heterodox sect, now extinct, that sprang out of Shī'ism in Iran and Turkey in the *9th*/15th century.

Ḥusayn (*5-61*/624-680) or better: al-Ḥusayn. The second son of 'Alī and Fāṭimah, and grandson of the Prophet. The story of Huṣayn is the central event in Twelve-Imām Shī'ite history.

When Mu'āwiyah died, his son Yazīd became Caliph in Damascus, without the usual election, since Mu'āwiyah had forced some prominent Companions in Mecca to swear fealty to Yazīd some time before. Yazīd had a reputation as a reveler. Dissensions arising from differences as to who was most suited to the dignity of the Caliphate for spiritual, political, and doctrinal reasons, not all of which were merely Shī'ite contentions, led the notables in many cities to refuse to swear allegiance to Yazīd. Among these were 'Abd Allāh ibn az-Zubayr, son of a famous Companion who later declared himself Caliph and held Mecca for a time, and Ḥusayn, the Prophet's grandson, who left Medinah to take refuge in Mecca.

At Mecca, Shī'ite partisans invited Ḥusayn to go to Kūfah (in 'Irāq) and assured him of support there. Ḥusayn sent his cousin Muslim ibn 'Aqīl ahead to prepare the way. The cousin was captured and executed by the Umayyad Governor. Ḥusayn, however, plunged ahead and decided to go to Kūfah with eighteen members of his household and sixty others, of whom thirty were Companions. 'Abd Allāh, the son of the late Caliph 'Umar, advised Ḥusayn against this course of action.

Yazīd then ordered the governor of 'Irāq, 'Ubayd Allāh ibn Ziyād, to intercept Ḥusayn, who had now been reinforced with six hundred men. However, an army of four thousand led by 'Umar Ibn Sa'd (the son of the Companion Sa'd ibn Abī Waqqās) surrounded him at Kerbala, in 'Irāq, near the Euphrates river. Cut off from water for eight days, he parleyed with the Caliph's troops until at length the parties fought, at first in individual combats, as was the custom of the Arabs. Finally, Ḥusayn mounted his horse and went into battle where, weakened by thirst, he was killed. Only two of his children survived the massacre which followed. The martyrdom took place (the date was later fixed by tradition to coincide with a religious day of observance) on the 10th of Muḥarram ('Āshūrā') in the 61st year of the Hijrah (10 October 680 AD). While it had little effect upon the political situation at the time, the martyrdom of Ḥusayn was to become a symbol of capital importance for Shī'ites, first under the Buyids and then even more so after the rise of the Ṣafavid dynasty.

For the Shī'ites, Ḥusayn is an Imām, a figure they understand to be an intermediary between man and God. They believe this function to be hereditary, inherited from 'Alī and passed on to Ḥusayn's descendants. Among the Shī'ites there is an historical and ever-present sense of guilt surrounding the martyrdom at Kerbala. It centres on the misleading invitation made to Ḥusayn and his subsequent betrayal by the early "proto" Shī'ites of Kūfah, who did not come to his aid. This, it is felt, is a repetition of the treatment of 'Alī and the pattern for the "lack of support" shown to the other Shī'ite Imāms after Ḥusayn.

The first Ṣafavids, who succeeded in conquering Persia at the beginning of the *10th*/16th century, exploited and institutionalized this guilt. Like others before them, the Ṣafavids used Shī'ism as a weapon in their struggle to seize and hold power, and as a mechanism of social control, albeit two-edged and perilous. The Ṣafavids made Shī'ism the state religion in Persia, exalting the tragedy of Kerbala to the highest degree and burning it into the national consciousness, where it is maintained by constant remembrance and insistence upon its importance, to the point that, even in taking a drink of water, it is the custom to curse Yazīd and remember how Ḥusayn was forced to thirst before his death.

The death of Ḥusayn is enacted with many gory and pitiful details in a martyrdom play (*Ta'īziyyah*) which is performed in the Shī'ite world in the days preceding the anniversary of Kerbala according to the lunar Islamic calendar.

For the Sunnīs, the event is a deplorable murder of the second closest descendant of the Prophet. But even though it is held as a terrible tragedy, it has not become a personal and national trauma. Apart from the anniversary of Kerbala, the 10th Muḥarram is a religious holiday among the Sunnīs because it was, for other reasons, a religious day of observance in the Prophet's time. It is not a coincidence; the actual date of Ḥusayn's martyrdom at the time was not important enough to record; but by deliberately attaching to an existing day of religious observance it was possible to divert religious energy to another purpose. 'Āshūrā' remains a beneficent holiday for the Sunnīs. For the Shī'ites the 10th Muḥarram is the terrible anniversary of the martyrdom of Ḥusayn and is the most tragic and sorrowful day of the year. At this time some Shī'ite sects work themselves up into a frenzy and beat and wound themselves in the streets. Since Ṣafavid times, Kerbala, the site of the tomb of Ḥusayn, has been the most important Twelve-Imām Shī'ite shrine. *See* IMĀM; KERBALA; RAWDAH-KHANI; SHĪ'ISM: TA'ĪZIYYAH.

Ḥusaynī tribes. In Mauritania, those tribes, chiefly of Berber origin who, having lost military supremacy to the *Ḥasanī* tribes, now maintain a claim to status on the basis of religious devotion. The names Ḥasan and Ḥusayn are emblematic in Mauritania of "warrior" and "sacerdotal" functions rather than any ancestral relations. The *Ḥusaynī* tribes are also called *zāwiyah* tribes.

Ḥuzn (lit. "sadness", "grief"). It means ordinary sadness, grief or melancholy, but for the Sufis it has the special meaning of a "sacred nostalgia", a longing for the Reality, beyond the veil of separation, in regard to which this world is an exile. It is this spiritual longing which motivates the birds in Aṭṭār's allegory *Mantiq aṭ-Ṭā'ir* (the "Language of the Birds") to set off to look for their missing and mysterious king, the *Simurgh.*

Tradition recounts:

> Once in Abū Bakr's time, some folk from the Yemen came to Medinah. When they heard a Reader in the Mosque chanting the Koran, tears fell from their eyes.
>
> We were like that once, the Caliph said; but our hearts have grown harder since.

Hypocrites (Ar. *munāfiqūn*). A party in Medinah which professed sympathy to the Prophet and Islam but whose members were actually supporters of the pagan Quraysh of Mecca. The Koran refers to them as "propped up pieces of wood" and "those in whose heart is a disease".

Their leader was 'Abd Allāh ibn Ubayy, who withdrew his three hundred horseman from the Muslim forces just before the Battle of Uḥud. He was an important figure in Medinah before the Prophet arrived there; almost to the end of his life he was jealous of the Prophet and grudging in his help. It was in respect of him, and his use of some six of his female slaves, that the verse of the Koran (24:33) was revealed:

> ...And constrain not
> your slave girls to prostitution, if they
> desire to live in chastity, that you may
> seek the chance goods of the present life.
> Whosoever constrains them, surely God
> after their being constrained, is All-forgiving,
> All-compassionate.

I

'Ibādah. A technical term in theology meaning acts of worship or ritual, from the verb *'abada* "to serve" and *'abd* "slave", "servitor".

Ibāḍites. Also called *Ibāḍīs*, the only surviving branch of the otherwise defunct Khārijite movement. The Khārijites were a dissident group in Islam (the name means "the Seceders") which established itself around the edges of the Umayyad and 'Abbāsid empires. Although they were usually a minority found only in a few remote places, they did, at one time, pose a military threat to Mecca and Medinah.

The Ibāḍites elect, in secret, a chief of the community called an Imām. Although in practice several different Imāms exist at any given time, the sect admits the possibility of a universal Imām presiding over all Ibāḍite communities, who would in effect be the Ibāḍite Caliph.

They hold that the Koran is created, whereas the mainstream of Islam holds the Koran to be the uncreated word of God. Otherwise, apart from a sectarian spirit due to historical isolation from other communities, there are today only minor differences between the Ibāḍites and the Sunnīs. Although they constitute their own *madhhab*, or school of law, Ibāḍite law resembles the Mālikī school. They are, moreover, often confused with Mālikīs because both pray with their hands at their sides (as do also the Shī'ites) whereas all the other Sunnīs clasp their hands in front of them in prayer. The Ibāḍites today are found in Oman (which is their historical center and where they constitute the majority), and in East Africa, Zanzibar, Libya, the island of Jerba in Tunisia, and the region of the M'zab in Algeria. *See* IMĀM; KHĀRIJITES.

Ibāḥah, (lit. "permissiveness", "licentiousness", "libertinism"). Libertine sects or doctrines are called *ibāḥī*. Dualist sects, particularly the Khurramiyyah and Qarmaṭīs, the Mazdakites before them, and remnants of Gnostic sects in the Middle East today, were persistently accused of libertinism and preaching the holding of women and property in common. In the Middle East such accusations are commonly made against any sect which diverges too far from the dominant norm and is secretive. Such accusations are frequently encountered and are to be interpreted as a sociological phenomenon with one group disassociating itself from another which it does not understand.

The Gnostic sects in particular call these accusations down upon themselves because they propose that evil and good are both present in the Principle and because of their secret (*bāṭinī*) doctrines which they consistently withhold from the scrutiny of outsiders. It is not surprising, therefore, that outsiders should conclude that the sect must involve something lurid. Similar accusations were made against the Gnostic sects in the Roman Empire during their struggle with the authorities representing religious orthodoxy.

The paradox, that both libertinism and asceticism could be ascribed to the same sect, is due to Dualism's conception of religious law as something negative, and even "evil". Believing that the "evil of the law" could be transcended by esoteric and secret knowledge, the Dualist sects did in some respects show contempt towards certain religious laws, but not necessarily towards all laws; they also could seek to transcend the law by extreme discipline and even mortification whereby, again, the disciple made himself independent of the law; hence the reputation for asceticism. When Manicheism spread to Rome, and became prevalent among the upper classes, many well-bred female devotees of the religion of Mani were betrayed by the pallor of their all too zealous fasting. But, some sects prescribed a period of extreme asceticism and thereafter affirmed that the initiate was perfect, and could not sin no matter what he appeared to do. Thus an air of ambiguity has hovered over all "esoteric" sects and somewhere in their makeup an element of libertinism can in fact always be found. This ambiguity is shown by the practice of mut'ah, or temporary marriage among the Shī'ites. *See* KHURRAMIYYAH; MAZDAK.

Iblīs (from Greek *diabolos*, "the slanderer" and hence "the devil"). A personal name of the devil, otherwise called *ash-shayṭān*, (from the Hebrew) and described in the Koran as "the adversary".

Originally, he was one of the Angels, the only one who refused to bow down to Adam when so commanded by God, saying to God, "You made me of fire and him of clay." For this disobedience God cast Iblīs out of heaven, reprieving him however, from annihilation until the Day of Judgement. Iblīs tempted Adam and Eve to eat the fruit of the forbidden tree, which in the Old Testament is the tree of the knowledge of good and evil. In Islamic belief, the guilt for this sin (*ithm*), lies not with mankind as an "original sin" from which man must be redeemed, but with the devil.

Nevertheless, it is mankind that bears the sanctions and consequences of the Fall from Eden. The Fall of mankind is the result of its taking for Reality something other than God: of seeing the world as a separate reality. It is the result of perceiving the relativities of the world as absolute rather than the essences of Being. This is "associating something with God" (*shirk*), which Islam sees as the fundamental sin, the denial of the Divine Unity. It is corrected *virtually* by the *shahādah*, for thereby one becomes aware, at least theoretically, that only the Absolute is real when one testifies that there is no god but Allāh; and it is corrected *effectively* by the complete realization of the *shahādah* with the mind and the heart, whereby the relative vanishes and only the absolute remains, which was the state of Adam before the Fall.

There is a story told of the Sufi al-Junayd:

> "At one period in my life", he said, "I felt a longing to see in vision what Satan was like. And as I stood in the mosque one day, an old man came through the gateway. His face turned towards me; and at the sight of it my heart clenched with horror. He came nearer, and I cried out: 'Who are you? the look of you — the mere thought of you — I cannot bear it!'"
>
> "I am him you wanted to see."
>
> "The Accursed One!" I exclaimed. "Then answer now my question: why would you not bow down to Adam, for which God cursed you?"
>
> "Junayd," said he, "how could you imagine that I should bow down to any except God?"
>
> "This answer startled me. But then a secret voice inside me whispered: Say to him: 'You're lying — if you had been an obedient servant you would not have disobeyed His Command.'
>
> "And as if he heard the whisper in my heart, the old man cried out: 'O God! You've burnt me!'
>
> "And suddenly he vanished."

The devil tempts man and tries to mislead him. The *ta'awwudh* formula of taking "refuge in God from Satan the stoned one" is spoken before reciting the Koran, and before the *basmalah* or consecration through the Divine Name, "In the Name of God", when undertaking ritual action. In Islam, as in all orthodox metaphysics, evil arises within creation when the quality of limitation encounters consciousness. In Sanskrit this limitation is called *tamas*, which in itself is neutral, like many of its consequences such as the property of weight, and which is the source of the differentiation between one object and another, being in fact the separativeness necessary for manifestation to take place at all. However, when the principle of separativeness touches consciousness, reality is inverted and the contingent and relative appear to be Cause and Absolute.

Among the traditional signs of "dark spirits" are the following: first, that they say the opposite of the truth; second, that they deny their own faults and attribute them to others, preferably to someone who is completely innocent; third, that they continually change their position in an argument, the purpose of argument being only to subvert, to turn aside from truth and goodness; fourth, that they exaggerate the evil of what is good, and the good of what is evil, that is, they define good as evil because of a shadow of imperfection, and evil as good because of a reflection of perfection; they glorify a secondary quality in order to deny an essential one, or to disguise a fundamental flaw; in short, they completely falsify true proportions and invert normal relations.

That this must be so is due to the "imperfection" of creation itself. Plato admired creation because it reflected the Absolute Good. But at the same time creation was not, and could not be, the Absolute itself. Jesus says in the Gospels, "Why callest thou me good? Only God alone is Good." The existence of creation arises from the possibility which the Absolute necessarily contains, in virtue of Absoluteness itself, of its own negation. Creation is the "illusorily real" manifestation of this possibility. It is at once nothing other than the Absolute, and at the same time an "otherness" which appears to set itself against God. It is this apparent and inescapable "otherness" in creation that is the introduction of evil, and that is why the Srūah of Daybreak (Sūrah 113) speaks of the "evil of that [the world itself] which He created".

The dualist philosophies take creation as the sign of a flaw within the Absolute. They equate the possibility of self-negation with evil; and they confuse the *necessity* of the possibility of self-negation within the Absolute, the need for God to create, which is a perfection, with weakness, or see it as proof that some power outside God provoked creation. In this way, they claim that evil either exists within God or coexists with Him. Creation then becomes a drama in which God salvages Himself from the consequences of the power of evil that is His equal. It is for this reason that C. G. Jung said that the "trinity should be a quaternity" whose fourth person is the devil; a conclusion drawn from the Gnostic assumption that Satan is really an aspect of God Himself.

In order for there to be a world, there must be limitation, and limitation implies nothingness, which lies beyond the limit. When consciousness looks upon nothingness, the natural tendency is not to see nothingness — that would be enlightenment — but to see "another something". The mind assigns essences to what it sees; the essence of nothing, if it were to have an essence, would be absolute contradiction, or pure evil. (Even Mani says that the nature of "Darkness", or evil which for him is a reality unto itself, is "madness".) But in the mind that has made the error, this anti-essence then arises and makes its abode. Evil is the result of an error which then acts through the consciousness that has made the error. The struggle which results is, as Milton says, "dubious battle upon the plains of heaven", dubious because not real; the outcome is certain. When creation, or manifestation, disappears altogether in that instant between manifestations which is the *apocatastasis*, evil, the apparently "absolute" other reality that *arises only in the world*, disappears also, "shut out by the Angel Michael's sword", before Michael himself disappears and God, the Merciful is alone. *See* REFUGE; SHAHĀDAH; SHIRK; TA'AWWUDH.

Ibn Abī-l-'Awjā, 'Abd ar-Karīm. There are biographical notices about this figure such as: "hanged in Baghdad for making up 10,000 Ḥadīth"; "a man of dangerous heterodoxy, who, on his own admission, invented numerous traditions, falsified the calendar and spread Manichean propaganda by means of insidious questions relating to the problem of suffering and of divine justice, and who was a believer in the eternity of the world and in metempsychosis." In other words, a universal heretic as his name indicates: "son of the father of distortion"; but not a specific real individual even though many Orientalists have been taken in by the joke.

Ibn Abī-l-Khayr, Abū Sa'īd Faḍl Allāh (*357-440*/967-1049). One of the so-called "drunken Sufis" who were wont to claim a union with God in terms of a personal identification. (The Sufis are in fact careful to say, no matter what degree of union is realized, "the slave remains the slave, and the Lord remains the Lord".) Abū Yazīd (Bāyazīd) al-Bisṭāmī (d. *260*/ 874) was the first to be called a "drunken Sufi", and he is remembered for his exclamation, supposedly made in a state of ecstasy, "Glory to me".

To Ibn Abī-l-Khayr is attributed the famous statement, pointing to his clothes: "there is no-one in this robe but God." This does not have the scent of ecstasy about it and seems more calculated; indeed, accounts of his life become increasingly ambiguous towards the end; he lived in an opulent and lavish style glorifying himself. Massignon considers Abī-l-Khayr a follower of al-Ḥallāj. *See* al-JUNAYD.

Ibn Adham, Ibrāhīm, *see* IBRĀHĪM ibn ADHAM.

Ibn Anas, *see* MALIK ibn ANAS.

Ibn 'Arabī, Abū Bakr Muḥammad Muḥyī-d-Dīn (*560-638*/1165-1240). An influential mystic and teacher. In recognition of this pre-eminence he was called "the greatest shaykh" (*ash-shaykh al-akbar*) and the "red sulphur" (*al-kabrit al-aḥmar*), an alchemical reference implying that Ibn 'Arabī could draw knowledge out of ignorance as sulphur "draws" gold out of lead. Ibn Khaldūn called him *ṣahib at-tajāllī*, "a theophanist". Indeed, any number of sects could find support in him for a wide variety of extravagant beliefs. Ismā'īlīs have often claimed him (and also Rūmī) to be one of themselves. Ibn 'Arabī is often called a pantheist and there is justification for this. However, the school which upholds him would vehemently reject pantheism. Thus, curiously, perhaps, many of those who admire him, guided by their own orthodoxy, rectify his ideas in practice and disregard the compromising elements. In other words, the very subtlety of Ibn 'Arabī's formulations has opened him to being integrated into, if not an orthodox mystical perspective, at least not an out and out heresy.

Ibn 'Arabī was born in Murcia in Spain, and studied at Seville and Ceuta. He later visited Mecca and Baghdad, and settled in Damascus. Several women were great sources of mystical inspiration for him. While in Spain he had met two women saints, then already quite old; Shams of Marchena, and Fāṭimah bint ibn al-Muthannā' of Cordova. In his biographical descriptions of Andalusian Sufis, the *Ruḥ al-Quds* ("The Spirit of Sanctity") and ad-Durrāt *al-Fākhirah* ("The Pearls of Glory"), Ibn 'Arabī describes both of them, saying he learned much from their example. In Mecca in the year *599*/1201 he met Niẓām 'Ayn ash-Shams ("the Spring of the Sun"), the young daughter of a friend, Abū Shāja Zāhir ibn Rustam. She was beautiful and young, but learned, and she participated in the intellectual gatherings in her father's home. She inspired Ibn 'Arabī to write the love poems which are contained in the *Tarjumān al-Ashwāq* ("The Interpreter of Longings").

His monumental work on mystical doctrine is the *Futūḥāt al-Makkiyyah*, ("the Meccan Revelations"). Equally famous are the *Fuṣūṣ al-Ḥikam* ("Bezels of Wisdom"). Mystical experiences confirmed for him the unity of religious forms despite their external divergences; he spoke of a *ḥāl*, or a spiritual state, in which he was joined to the nature of Jesus. In a famous passage in the *Tarjumān al-Ashwāq* Ibn 'Arabī said:

> My heart is open to all forms;
> it is a pasturage for gazelles
> and a monastery for Christian monks
> a temple for idols and the
> Ka'bah of the pilgrim
> the tables of the Torah and
> the book of the Koran.
> Mine is the religion of Love
> Wherever His caravans[1]
> turn, the religion of
> Love shall be my religion
> and my faith.

[1][literally "camels", a Koranic symbol for spiritual realities]

Ibn 'Arabī is particularly renowned for audacious metaphysical formulations. *Huwa* ("He"), the third person pronoun, is also a Divine Name of the Essence. Ibn 'Arabī declared that another, "inner" Name for the Divine Essence is *Hiya*, ("She"). The idea that the Divine Essence could contain a polarity is so completely heretical (it is commonly found among the Gnostics) that it lends strong support to the idea that Ibn 'Arabī compiled ideas from many sources but did not himself realize their full import.

Although Ibn 'Arabī is considered to be one of the most intellectual of Sufis, for him *maḥabbah* ("love"), and not *ma'rifah* ("knowledge"), is the summit of mysticism, for it is love which actually makes Divine union (*tawḥīd*) possible. He set down in writing the doctrine of *waḥdāt al-wujūd* (the "unity of being", or Monism), the counterpart within Islam of *advaita vedanta* and of the doctrine of the Tao. The term *waḥdāt al-wujūd* itself was not used by Ibn 'Arabī; it was used by others beginning perhaps with Ibn Sab'īn, and became the technical term for this type of doctrine. Thus Ibn 'Aṭā' Allāh, a great follower of Ibn 'Arabī, one generation removed, but of whose orthodoxy there is less question, says:

> Behold what shows to you His Omnipotence, (may He be exalted): it is that He hides Himself from you by what has no existence apart from Him.

and:

> How can God (*al-Ḥaqq*) be veiled by something, for He is apparent (*ẓāhir*) and has actual being (*mawjūd ḥāḍir*) in that wherewith He is veiled?

Although Ibn 'Arabī is credited with the doctrine, *waḥdat al-wujūd* is more or less the metaphysics of Sufism as such, and Ibn 'Arabī's role was in fact that of expressing more formally, and perhaps more amply, ideas that had up until then been taught only orally. While appearing exotic, *waḥdāt al-wujūd*, or Monism, is much more common than is supposed, forming the philosophical basis, for example, of the modern Church of Christian Science. In addition to formalizing much Sufi doctrine in writing, Ibn 'Arabī was a bridge between the Sufi traditions of Spain and Morocco and the eastern Sufism of Egypt and Syria. It has been said that Ṣadr ad-Dīn al-Qunāwī, whom Ibn 'Arabī may have met in Konya in *607*/1210, was a disciple, and that through him, Ibn 'Arabī influenced Quṭb ad-Dīn ash-Shirāzī and Persian mysticism in general. However, Nasrollah Pourjavadi has pointed out that Persian mysticism already had all the same elements before Ibn 'Arabī came upon the scene. Thus it is probably more accurate to say that all these Sufis manifest a Gnostic brotherhood which already existed from Spain to India even before the advent of Islam. During the great flowering of Islamic intellectuality in Atjeh in Indonesia, the names of Ibn 'Arabī and other proponents of his school of intellectual mysticism, such as Ibn 'Aṭa' Allāh, were bywords.

A famous recent student of Ibn 'Arabī was the Emir 'Abd al-Qādir of Algeria (d. *1300*/1883), a great warrior who fought French colonization in the 19th century. Also a Sufi, the Emir regarded Ibn 'Arabī, who preceded him by almost a millennium, as an important teacher, although the Emir consciously modeled his political and religious career on the Sufi 'Abd al-Qādir al-Jīlānī, of whose *ṭarīqah*, or order, in Algeria, he was the head, succeeding his father in this function. The Emir 'Abd al-Qādir was originally buried next to the Shaykh Ibn 'Arabī in his tomb in Damascus; Now 'Abd al-Qādir has been re-buried in the Cemetery of Martyrs in Algeria. The Mausoleum of Ibn 'Arabī in Damascus, on the slope of Mount Qāsiun, was built by the Turkish Sultan Selim the Grim in *924*/1518 after his conquest of the Mamluks, the first Ottoman structure in Syria. *See* SUFISM.

Ibn 'Aṭā' Allāh, Aḥmad ibn Muḥammad (d. *709*/1309). A mystic of the order founded by the Imām ash-Shādhilī (d. *656*/1258). Ibn 'Atā' Allāh was originally a jurist of the Mālikī School of Law and taught at the al-Azhar school in Cairo, and at the Manṣūriyyah. His father had been a Sufi but Ibn 'Aṭā' Allāh was not only not drawn to mysticism, but was antagonistic towards it, and in particular towards Abū-l-'Abbās al-Mūrsī (d. *686*/1288) who taught Sufi disciples in Alexandria. But in *674*/1276, Ibn 'Aṭā' Allāh met al-Mūrsī, successor to the Shaykh ash-Shādhilī, and became his disciple on the spot.

Ibn 'Aṭā' Allāh wrote a celebrated book of mystical aphorisms, the *Kitāb al-Ḥikam*, which aimed at arousing spiritual awareness in the disciple. He also wrote the *Miftāḥ al-Falāḥ wa Miṣbāḥ al-Arwāḥ* ("The Key of Success and the Lamp of Spirits") on the spiritual method of invocation (*dhikr*), the *Kitāb at-Tanwīr fī Isqāṭ at-Tadbīr* ("Light on the Elimination of Self-Direction") concerning the approach of the Shādhilī school to the practice of virtue, the *Kitāb al-Laṭā'if fī Manāqib Abī-l-'Abbās al-Mūrsī wa Shaykhihi Abī-l-Ḥasan*, about the first Masters of the Shādhiliyyah *ṭarīqah*, and other works. The intellectual mysticism of the Imām ash-Shādhilī, as well as that of Ibn 'Arabī, made a deep impression upon the Muslims of Indonesia, where the works of Ibn 'Aṭā' Allāh are well known, in particular the *Kitāb al-Ḥikam*, which has been translated into Malay.

His aphorisms include the following:

> One of the signs of relying on one's own deeds is the loss of hope when a downfall occurs.
>
> Your striving for what has already been guaranteed to you, and your remissness in what is demanded of you, are signs of the blurring of your intellect.
>
> If He opens a door for you, thereby making Himself known, pay no heed if your deeds do not measure up to this. For, in truth, He has not opened it for you but out of a desire to make Himself known to you. Do you not know that He is the one who presented the knowledge of Himself to you, whereas you are the one who presented Him with deeds? What a difference between what He brings to you and what you bring to Him.
>
> How can the heart be illumined while the forms of creatures are reflected in its mirror? Or how can it journey to God while shackled by its passions? Or how can it desire to enter the Presence of God while it has not yet purified itself of the stain of its forgetfulness? Or how can it understand the subtle points of mysteries while it has not yet repented of its offenses?
>
> How can it be conceived that something veils Him, since He is the one who manifests everything?
>
> Your postponement of deeds till the time when you are free is one of the frivolities of the ego.

He who is illumined at the beginning is illumined at the end.

Your being on the lookout for the vices hidden within you is better than your being on the lookout for the invisible realities veiled from you.

One of the signs of delusion is sadness over the loss of obedience coupled with the absence of resolve to bring it back to life.

The proof that you have not found Him is that you strive for the permanency of what is other than He, and the proof that you are not united to Him is that you feel estranged at the loss of what is other than He.

Travel not from creature to creature, otherwise you will be like a donkey at the mill: roundabout he turns, his goal the same as his departure. Rather go from creatures to the Creator: "And that the final end is unto thy Lord" (53:42). Consider the Prophet's words (God bless him and grant him peace!): "Therefore, he whose flight is for God and His Messenger, then his flight is for God and His Messenger; and he whose flight is for worldly gain or marriage with a woman, then his flight is for that which he flies to." So understand his words (upon him peace!) and ponder this matter, if you can. And peace on you!

Ibn Athir. Famous as literary figures, three Kurdish brothers from northern 'Irāq are known by this name.

1. Majd ad-Dīn (*544-607*/1149-1210) was a lexicographer and assembler of Ḥadīth.
2. Abū-l-Ḥasan 'Izz ad-Dīn Muḥammad (*556-632*/1160-1234) wrote a history called the *Kāmil* ("The Complete").
3. Diyā' ad-Dīn (*559-637*/1163-1239) was a literary critic.

Ibn Babawayh, Muḥammad (c. *306-381*/918-991). Also known by the alternate names Ibn Bābūya, aṣ-Ṣadūq, or al-Qummī. He is one of the principal early Shī'ite theologians, the author of a large number of books of which the most famous is *Man la yaḥḍuruhu-l-faqīh* ("When no theologian is present"). This is one of the foundations of Shī'ite theology and one of the so-called "Four Books" of Shī'ism, *al-kutūb al-arba'ah*, the principal collections of Shī'ite Ḥadīth. The others are *al-Kāfī* ("The Compendium" or "the Sufficient") by Muḥammad ibn Ya'qūb Abū Ja'far al-Kulaynī (d. *329*/940), and the *Istibsar* and *Taḥdhīb al-Aḥkām* by Muḥammad aṭ-Ṭūsī (d. *460*/1067).

The father of Ibn Babawayh is said to have asked the Hidden Imām, through the third *Wakīl* ("representative"), Abū Qāsim Ḥusayn ibn Rūḥ, to pray that a son be granted him. The father received the answer "We have prayed for it", and Ibn Babawayh would say that he was born because of the Hidden Imām's prayers. He also said that he had communicated in a dream at Mecca with the Hidden Imām who commanded him to write his book the *Kamāl ad-Dīn* ("Perfection of Religion"). Ibn Babawayh traveled widely, collected Ḥadīth and was a teacher of another important Shī'ite scholar, the Shaykh al-Mufīd. The father of Ibn Babawayh, 'Alī ibn Ḥusayn, is also called by the same name, and the two together are referred to as the as-Ṣadūqān.

Ibn Babūyā, *see* IBN BABAWAYH.

Ibn Bājjah, Abū Bakr Muḥammad (c. *500-533*/1106-1138). The philosopher known in Europe as Avempace, whose thought greatly influenced Ibn Rushd (Averroes). Ibn Bājjah was born in Saragossa, Spain, and died in Fez, having served as minister to the Emir of Murcia. He wrote a commentary on Aristotle and treatises on the physical sciences.

In one of his works, *Tadbīr al-Mutawaḥḥid*, he speaks of the "solitary", who is in the world as it is, but lives as if he were not in it at all, and adheres rather to the rule of an ideal society. The enlightened individual may attain this "perfect state or republic" inwardly, even if it is not within reach of society as a whole. For him, as for Plato, the Intellect can reach Truth by itself, even without revelation: he believed, in other words, that the capacity for revelation is inherent in the Intellect itself, and revelation is a manifestation of the Intellect. *See* PHILOSOPHY.

Ibn Bāṭūṭah, Abū 'Abd Allāh Muḥammad (*704-780*/1304-1378). An explorer and traveler known as the "Arab Marco Polo". Born in Tangier, he began traveling at the age of twenty-one when he went across North Africa to Cairo, and thence to Mecca to perform the pilgrimage. Thereafter he traveled in Syria, Mesopotamia, Persia, East Africa, Oman, Asia Minor, the Crimea, the regions along the Volga, Samarkand, Bukhara, Afghanistan, India, (where in Delhi he became a Judge), China, the Maldive Islands, Ceylon, Java and Sumatra.

His journeys were wanderings from place to place rather than a purposeful design. He frequently criss-crossed his tracks and returned to the great cultural centers of Islam. During his travels he performed the pilgrimage four times. He returned to Tangier after twenty-four years absence but soon set out again, this time for Spain. He returned and thereafter went across the Sahara to Timbuktu and regions of the Niger.

At the end of his life he dictated a description of his travels (*Tuḥfat an-nuẓẓār fi gharā'ib al-amṣār wa-'ajā'ib al-asfār*). The narrative, known at first in fragments, but then discovered in a complete original manuscript in Algeria, is considered to be a generally accurate account of the countries seen by the most far ranging traveler of the ancient world.

Ibn al-Bayṭār, Abū Muḥammad 'Abd Allāh ibn Aḥmad Ḍiyā' ad-Dīn (d. *646*/1248). A botanist, born in Malaga, Ibn al-Bayṭār traveled widely to study plants. He entered the service of the Sultans in Egypt and died in Damascus. Ibn al-Bayṭār wrote the greatest compilation of medicinal plants made before modern times, the *Kitāb al-jāmi' fī-l-adwiyah al-mufradah.* It contains 1,400 entries including many plants never before recorded, and cites a number of Latin and Greek authors.

Ibn al-Fāriḍ (*578-632*/1182-1235). A famous Arab Sufi teacher and poet who lived in Egypt. His most famous poem is the Khamriyyah (the "Wine Ode"). The Sufis make wine a symbol of invocation of the Divine Name and by drunkenness describe the rapture of the knowledge of God, as in the well-known *Ruba'iyyat of 'Umar Khayyam. See* al-KHAMRIYYAH; SUFISM.

Ibn Gabirol, Solomon ben Judah (*411-463*/1020-1070). A Jewish philosopher, known in the West as Avicebron, born in Malaga. A student of Ibn Sīnā (Avicenna) and Empedocles, his famous philosophical work is *Fons Vitae* ("the Fountain of Life"). In it he explains why circles are often used to demonstrate philosophical theories by saying that they show how effects are contained in their causes. Ibn Gabirol, the first Jewish teacher of Neoplatonism in the West, emerged out of the tradition of Arab philosophy in Moorish Andalusia. He was probably the first to use the term "Qabbalah".

He may have influenced Duns Scotus towards a material conception of the substance of manifestation (which the Scholastics called *materia signata quantitate*, "*materia* under the sign of quantity"). He was better known to the Jews of his time as a poet than as a philosopher and, using Arab meters in Hebrew, he wrote liturgical compositions.

Ibn Ḥanbal, Aḥmad (*164-241*/780-855). The originator of the Ḥanbalī School of Law, which was established by his disciples. He studied in Baghdad and received instruction from the great legal theoretician ash-Shafi'ī. He is the compiler of a large collection of Ḥadīth, the *Musnad.*

When the 'Abbāsid Caliph al-Ma'mūn made the Mu'tazilite doctrine of the created Koran official state dogma, Ibn Ḥanbal staunchly upheld the orthodox dogma that the Koran is uncreated. Although other figures, Judges and theologians, backed down in the face of the threat of physical punishment, Ibn Ḥanbal maintained his beliefs, for which he was at first imprisoned and then scourged. He gained a great reputation for his steadfastness in the face of persecution, and was restored to favor by the Caliph al-Mutawakkil, who put an end to the miḥnah (inquisition into belief), and reinstated the doctrine of the uncreated Koran.

Ibn Hāni', Muḥammad al-Andalusī (d. *362*/973). Maghribi poet, born in Seville. He wrote panegyrics of the Caliph al-Mu'izz li-Din-i Llah stating that the whole world belonged to these Imams. Born of a family of Ismā'īlī missionaries, and intellectually of the line of Ibn Masarrah, he had to flee Spain and became the court poet of the Fāṭimids. He was murdered perhaps while on his way from Ifrīqiyā to Egypt.

Ibn Ḥawshab Abu-l-Qāsim al-Ḥasan ibn Faraj ibn Hawshab al-Kufī called "al-Manṣūr al-Yemen" (d. *302*/914). He was from a prominent Shī'i family from Kūfah. There was a Ḥawshab al-Bursumī who was a keeper of "the Chair or Throne of 'Alī" during the Kaysāniyyah revolt. Ibn Ḥawshab came to the Yemen as an Ismā'īlī da'ī from Kūfah around *268*/881 and founded a *dar al-hijrah* "a house of refuge". By 905 Ismā'īlīs controlled Ṣan'ā'. Ibn Ḥawshab was an architect of the migration of the Ismā'īlī center from Mesopotamia or Ahwaz to North Africa. He instructed 'Abd Allāh as-Shī'i who worked with the Ketama Berbers to prepare the way for the migration of 'Ubayd Allāh. Ibn Ḥawshab also sent his nephew al-Haytham as an Ismā'īlī dā'ī to Sindh. When other Isma'ilis turned against the Fāṭimids, Ibn Ḥawshab remained loyal. Later, his son Ja'far ibn Manṣūr al-Yemen, alone among his brothers, also remained loyal migrating to North Africa and joining the court of al-Qā'im at Mahdīyyah. The son became a leading exponent of *ta'wīl*, "esoteric" or symbolic interpretation or, more accurately, spinning the meaning of religious texts, under al-Mu'izz. *See* 'UBAYD ALLĀH al-MAHDĪ.

Ibn al-Haytham, Abū 'Alī (*354*/965-*430*/1039). Arab scientist born in Baṣrah and died in Egypt. He was known in Europe as Alhazen for his work on optics which was translated into Latin in 1572 by Gerhard of Cremona and which had an important influence on European science. He was also learned in mathematics, medicine and philosophy. He worked at the court of the Ismā'īlī Caliph al-Ḥākim in Cairo and later at the al-Azhar where he proposed that "perception of a form [as distinct from mere seeing], required discernment, inference, recognition, comparison with other signs and judgement".

Ibn Ḥayyan, *see* JĀBIR ibn ḤAYYĀN.

Ibn Ḥazm, 'Alī ibn Aḥmad (*384-456*/994-1064). A theologian of Arab-Persian descent (although he is also regarded as being of native Christian origin) born in Cordova, he was a violent opponent of the Ash'arites (*see* al-ASH'ARĪ). Literalist and singular in his approach, he was a chauvinist in regard to Islam, the Arabs, and Muslim Spain, and a noted poet.

He followed the Ẓāhirī (exoterist) School of Law and so maintained that the only level of meaning in the Koran was the explicit; according to him no hidden meanings were admissible. He wrote many books on a variety of subjects including philosophy, history, and descriptions of different sects and schools of thought. Ibn Ḥazm was a critic of Shī'ism. The Shī'ite doctrine claims that the Imāms possess *'iṣma*, "sinlessness" or "impeccability". As Vatikiotis noted: "Ibn Ḥazm rejects impeccability on purely historical grounds relating to 'Alī. If 'Alī knew the prophetic *naṣṣ* [supposed designation at Ghadīr Khūm] appointing him to the *Caliphate*, why did he participate in the *shūra* (council) for 'Uthmān's selection? If he were famous for his bravery, why did he adopt *taqiyya* or dissimulation? The allegation that he fought against infidels and proselytized more than anyone else is voided by the surpassing activity of 'Umar."

For his highly polemical stands he spent the latter years of his life in a kind of internal exile, and the number of his disciples was restricted by the authorities. He wrote the *Ṭawq al-Ḥamāma*, ("The Neckring of the Dove") about the psychology of love, and the *Kitāb al-Fiṣal wa'n-Niḥal*, a critical discussion of religions and sects.

Ibn Hishām, Abū Muḥammad 'Abd al-Malik (d. *219*/834). Arab Scholar, known for his edition of Ibn Isḥāq's *Sīrat rasūl Allāh* ("Life of the Messenger of God"), the most important traditional biography of the Prophet.

Ibn Isḥāq, Ḥunayn (*194-259*/809-873). A Nestorian Christian, physician to the Caliph al-Mutawakkil, Ibn Isḥāq collected Greek manuscripts, and with his son Isḥāq, his nephew Ḥubaysh, and others, translated these manuscripts into Arabic. These included works by Galen, Hippocrates, Plato, and others. *See* NESTORIANS.

Ibn al-Jawzī (*510-597*/1116-1200). Jamāl ad-Dīn Abu-l-Farāj 'Abd ar-Raḥmān ibn 'Alī, known as Ibn al-Jawzī and called the "Preacher of Baghdad". Ibn Khallikān called him the most learned man of his time and Ibn Jubair gave an enthusiastic account of sermons he heard in Baghdad. He was a prominent follower of the Ḥanbalī school which was vehemently opposed to Shī'ism.

A prolific writer, he composed histories and laudatory biographies. While praising early Sufis for piety, Ibn al-Jawzī was a fierce critic of what he called aberrations of the Sufism of his time, and other Gnostic doctrines. One person's heresy may be another person's truth; Annemarie Schimmel, who was very partial to Sufism, called Ibn al-Jawzī's *Talbīs Iblīs*, the "Delusions of the Devil" a "very poisonous book". (*See* SILSILAH.) Ibn Jawzī quotes Ibn 'Aqil as saying:

"Islam has come to grief between two sects, the Esoterists (*Baṭiniyyah*) and the Literalists. The Esoterists abrogate the literal sense of the code by the interpretation which they claim to give, for which they have no evidence: so much so that there is nothing left in the code to which they do not assign a hidden meaning, causing the obligatory to be non-obligatory, and the forbidden to be non-forbidden. The Literalists, on the other hand, take hold of everything according to the literal expression even where there must necessarily be an explanation that is not the literal sense. The truth is between these two positions, which is that we should accept the literal sense where there is no evidence to divert us from it, and reject every hidden meaning where the code furnishes no evidence for its existence."

He says that the Baṭiniyyah have eight names: Isma'iliyyah, Sab'iyyah, Babakiyyah, Muḥammirah (the "Reds", so-called because they dyed their garments red in the days of Babak and wore such); the Qarmaṭīs; the Khurramiyyah (which he says was a designation of the Mazdakites and that this sect had different premises which nevertheless led to similar consequences), and the Ta'limiyyah.

Ibn Khaldūn, 'Abd ar-Raḥmān ibn Muḥammad (*733-808*/1332-1406). Often called the "Father of Historiography", Ibn Khaldūn was born in Tunisia. His life was extremely turbulent; at one time he served the Merinid Sultan in Fez as a functionary, but was imprisoned because of court intrigue. He regained his freedom and his position, but then other troubles forced him to go to Spain. At first, Ibn Khaldūn was well received at the court of Granada, but political turmoil forced him to flee to North Africa, where he was given a post by the Sultan of Būjiya with whom he had once shared imprisonment. War and vicissitudes forced him to return to Fez, and thence to Tunis where he wrote his *Prolegomena.*

Having set out east to perform the pilgrimage, Ibn Khaldūn entered into the service of the Mamlūk Sultan of Egypt, Barqūq. In Cairo he became the Grand Qāḍi (Chief Judge) of the Mālikī rite. He was dismissed and reinstated as many as five times, this office being notorious for the fact that its holder was bound to come into conflict with the ruler's wishes. On a mission to Damascus Ibn Khaldūn was trapped inside the city by the attacking army of Tīmūr (Tamerlane) and had to escape by letting himself down by a rope from the city walls, in the face of the conquering Tīmūr; the latter allowed him to return to Egypt, where he died.

Ibn Khaldūn was an acute observer of human nature. He noted the tendency to admire and respect power, so that conquered people often adopt the habits and customs of the conquerors, even to the extent of adopting their dress. His observations in this domain were such that he could also be rightly called the "Father of Sociology." In studying human nature, he was led to analyze the significance of sleep and to consider the prophetic character of certain dreams according to traditional psychology. Like the Vedanta, Ibn Khaldūn equates dream sleep with the subtle state, and sleep without dreams to the formless or Angelic state, each with its corresponding possibilities of knowledge. (In Vedanta the four states are: *vaishvānara* [waking], *taijasa* [dream state], *prajn~ā* [profound sleep], and *turiya* [the unconditioned state, which is Being]. *See* FIVE DIVINE PRESENCES.)

However, it is not his speculations on spiritual psychology, or the social sciences that constitute his greatness, but his unique contribution to the understanding of history. Ibn Khaldūn's great work, the *Muqaddimah*, or *Prolegomena*, is the introduction to his *Kitāb al-'Ibar* ("Book of Examples and the Collection of Origins of the History of the Arabs and Berbers").

The Muslim peoples considered by Ibn Khaldūn are those whose habitats alternate between deserts and settled agricultural regions. Ibn Khaldūn's theory explains a recurrent pattern in the history of these peoples: between nomads and sedentaries, who represent a primordial division of human existence in the world, he holds that there is under the best of conditions a natural state of tension. Moreover, town-dwellers inevitably tend to fall into decadence and moral corruption, from which the nomads are preserved by the arduous nature of their daily lives. Among the nomads, Ibn Khaldūn discerns a hierarchy dependant upon the intensity of their involvement with the rigors of the desert: at the summit are the camel herders who penetrate farthest into the desert; after them come the herders of sheep who stay on the fringes of the desert, and last in the hierarchy are the cattle herders, who are obliged to keep to easy pastures.

Periodically, groups of nomads conquer the towns and become the new rulers. According to Ibn

Khaldūn's theory, they at first bring a new vigor, sense of justice, and spiritual acuteness to the royal function, but after three generations, the rigor and the virtue which were needed to establish their sovereignty begin to ebb away from them. The princes of the first generation know what is required of them to become rulers; those of the second generation participated in the conquest, so that they too have first hand knowledge of the requirements of kingship; the princes of the third generation, however, know of this only by hearsay; and those of the fourth believe that power and respect are no more than their due by birthright. Thus the "fourth" generation lives in a distorted, and illusory, memory of the past, and it is only a matter of time before it forfeits the right to rule. Thus, rulers and ruled alike are then laid open once more to a fresh and purifying influx of desert nomads.

Ibn Khaldūn stands apart from mere recorders of observed events; he sees effects in causes, endeavors to find the underlying reasons for historic change and explores a theory whereby future developments may be predicted. What Ibn Khaldūn drew from his observations of the rhythmic movements of history is a model that is not dissimilar to the moral of the story of Cain and Abel in the Bible (although Ibn Khaldūn does not actually use this example; it is from the "Reign of Quantity and the Signs of the Times").

Cain represents the farmer-sedentary who lives in time; Abel the hunter-nomad who lives in space. The farmer plants, and must wait to see the seeds grow and be transformed; he is bound to duration. The hunter stalks a prey, and successfully kills it when an instantaneous identity takes place between the hunter and the prey, as symbolized by the arrow that finds its mark. There is no duration, but a perfect moment. The art of the sedentary is pictures, for pictures represent the other dimension, space. The art of the nomad is words, or poetry, for in poetry there is succession of events, or time, the invisible dimension of the nomad's life. The two art forms are what the Hindus call *yantra*, the sacred picture, and *mantra*, the sacred word.

The murder of Abel by Cain signifies the destruction of space by time. At the beginning, the world was an endless space, and time was eternity, only a rhythm, a return to the same moment. With the Fall, change enters into the world, and thence into society; eventually change begins to dominate it, and time becomes a duration. The Biblical story recapitulates the history of the world as the absorption of space by time as duration, or as Abel's death agony.

In the garden of Eden, Eve was never separated from Adam. But when the wheel becomes the means of transport, when electronic communications impose themselves as the medium, then knowledge that is direct, and recognition that is face to face recede. An inevitable gap opens up, the mirror of identity darkens. It may be only hours between continents by airplane or microseconds by telephone, but in those microseconds the separation is absolute. No matter how swift they are, communications which are born of time are never in the present, but are ghosts out of the dead past. Adam has lost Eve. Cain's sacrifices of time (rather than of himself, as symbolized by Abel's sheep), like his satellites in space, do not win God's blessing. Cain has wandered into "the Land of Nod", the world of history and change, the modern world.

When history begins, as it does with Cain and Abel, there also begins the movement away from unity, which is a movement away from the center. This movement is towards multiplicity, and towards a multitude of illusory "centers". "Perfect" or "absolute" multiplicity is an unattainable limit, but one towards which history tends and which is its ultimate goal. What Ibn Khaldūn observed in the *Prolegomena* was the dynamics of the two poles in human history, still in their traditional phase, a weaving taking place between nomads and sedentaries, before the sedentaries completely engulfed or destroyed the nomads altogether, or before Cain finished killing Abel. *See* RASHĪD ad-DĪN aṭ-ṬABĪB.

Ibn Khallikān, Abū-l-'Abbās Aḥmad (*608-681*/1211-1282) A biographer, he was born in 'Irāq, a descendant of the family of the Barmakids, the able viziers of Hārūn ar-Rashīd. He studied theology in Aleppo, Damascus and Cairo. The Sultan Baybars named Ibn Khallikān the head Judge of Damascus. His book, *Kitāb Wafayāt al-A'yān*, is one of the most important works of reference, along with those of al-Wāqidī, for biographical information on more than 800 of the great men up to his time. Ibn Khallikān said that chess (in Persian satranj) was invented by Zezeh ibn Dāher, an Indian; others attribute its invention to Iran: there is a story in the Shahnameh how chess was invented to show to a Queen how a son died in battle.

Ibn Masarrah (d. *319*/931) Spanish philosopher from the region of Cordova who was associated, in the descriptions of Islamic writers, with the doctrines of the Greek philosopher Empedocles (495 BC-435 BC). Empedocles taught that there were two principles, Harmony and Disorder. According to him matter had a principial nature, that is, it was a self-sufficient reality, not created. He taught something like the divinity of man; he is said to have thrown himself into the crater of Mount Aetna in order that there would be no mortal remains so that it could appear that he was taken up into heaven. Ibn Massarah's ideas were apparently similar; that is, a kind of dualism and its resulting "divine materialism". It is said the he believed the world to be an emanation of God.

Ibn Masarrah could also be described as a Mu'tazilite in that he subscribed to the unknowability of God; but the unknown God is fundamental to most dualist doctrines and was also taught by the Fāṭimids. At one point in his life he traveled to the Middle East establishing links with the schools he encountered on his path.

Ibn Masarrah was a continuator of pre-Islamic religious doctrines that had existed in Spain before the Arab conquest (and which existed in North Africa, the Middle East and Central Asia). Asin Palacios, who studied Ibn Masarrah, concluded that his doctrine was essentially Priscillian Manicheism. Probably, through schools that he established or led in the south of Spain, Ibn Masarrah influenced or initiated the pantheistic and Gnostic outlook of the theosophist Ibn 'Arabi, and Ibn Sab'in, and was a forerunner of the Imām ash-Shādhilī. *See* IBN 'ARABI.

Ibn Mashīsh, 'Abd as-Salām (d. *625*/1228). The spiritual master of Abū-l-Ḥasan ash-Shādhilī, the founder of the Shādhilī order. Ibn Mashīsh, a Berber, was considered the *quṭb* (spiritual axis) of his age. Although he lived as a recluse on a mountain in Morocco, the Jabal 'Ālam, today a place of great pilgrimage, his renown had spread in his lifetime throughout the Islamic world. Nothing tangible remains of him except the *ṣalāt al-Mashīshiyyah* which is recited by all the *ṭuruq* which derive from the Imām ash-Shādhilī. This is a prayer which is a spiritual portrait of the Prophet and thus of the *al-insan al-kamil*, "the Perfect Man".

> O my God, bless him from whom derive the secrets and from whom gush forth the lights, and in whom rise up the realities, and into whom descended the sciences of Adam, so that he hath made powerless all creatures, and so that understandings are diminished in his regard, and no one amongst us, neither predecessor nor successor, can grasp him.
>
> The gardens of the spiritual world (*al-malakūt*) are adorned with the flower of his beauty, and the pools of the world of omnipotence (*al-jabarūt*) overflow with the outpouring of his lights.
>
> There exists nothing that is not linked to him, even as it was said: Were there no mediator, everything that depends on him would disappear! (Bless him, O my God), by a blessing such as returns to him through You from You, according to his due.
>
> O my God, he is Your integral secret, that demonstrates You, and Your supreme veil, raised up before You.
>
> O my God, join me to his posterity and justify me by Your reckoning of him. Let me know him with a knowledge that saves me from the wells of ignorance and quenches my thirst at the wells of virtue. Carry me on his way, surrounded by Your aid, towards Your presence. Strike through me at vanity, so that I may destroy it. Plunge me in the oceans of Oneness (*al-aḥadiyyah*), pull me back from the abysses of Unification (*tawḥīd*) and drown me in the pure source of the ocean of Unity (*al-waḥdah*), so that I neither see nor hear nor am conscious nor feel except through it. And make of the Supreme Veil the life of my spirit, and of his spirit the secret of my reality, and of his reality all my worlds, by the realization of the First Truth.
>
> O First, O Last, O Outward, O Inward, hear my petition, even as You heard the petition of Your servant Zachariah; succor me through You unto You, support me through You unto You, unite me with You, and come in between me and other-than You: Allāh, Allāh, Allāh! "Verily He who imposed on you the Koran for a law, will bring you back to the promised end" (28:85).

"Our Lord, grant us mercy from Your presence, and shape for us right conduct in our plight" (18:9).

"Verily God and His Angels bless the Prophet; O you who believe, bless him and wish him peace" (33:56).

May the graces (*ṣalāwat*) of God, His peace, His salutations, His mercy and His blessings (*barakāt*) be on our Lord Muḥammad, Your servant, Your prophet, and Your Messenger, the un-lettered prophet, and on his family and his companions, graces as numerous as the even the odd and as the perfect and blessed words of our Lord.

"Glorified be your Lord, the Lord of Glory, beyond what they attribute unto Him, and peace be on the Messengers. Praise be to God, the Lord of the worlds" (37:180-182).

Ibn Mas'ūd, 'Abd Allāh (d. *33*/653). A Companion of the Prophet and an early convert, he became an administrator in Kūfah. He is noted for the fact that he possessed and used a version of the Koran different in some respects from that edited under the Caliph 'Uthmān. Some remnants of this variant have survived, but it was condemned by Mālik ibn Anas, who declared that prayer performed by an Imām who recited Ibn Mas'ūd's version of the Koran was invalid.

Ibn al-Muqaffa', Abū Muḥammad (d. *140*/757). A Persian, originally a Zoroastrian of possibly Manichean convictions, who was converted to Islam. He was a secretary in the Caliphal administration and renowned for an elegant style and command of Arabic. Ibn Muqaffa' translated into Arabic the Indian fables of Bidpai (from Pahlevi), which then became the political allegories called *Kalīlah wa Dimnah.* These stories, in which animals act out situations that arise in matters of state, are perennially popular in Arab literature.

Among the subjects of the Lion were two Jackals, named Kalīlah and Dimnah, both cunning and sagacious in the highest degree. And one day Dimnah said to Kalīlah: I wonder why the Lion keeps himself so close retired of late? I think I will solicit an audience; and if I find him in any indecision, I purpose to turn his audience to my own advantage...

You will be playing a dangerous game, Kalīlah said; for there are three things which any man will be wise to avoid, owing to the impossibility of controlling the issues of them; one, incurring the confidence of a Prince; two, trusting a woman with a secret; and three, trying the effect of poison on one's self.

If the chance of failure, Dimnah replied, were sufficient reason for never trying, you would exclude from human endeavor all conduct of human affairs, all commercial enterprise, and all military achievement.

Well, I wish you luck, said Kalīlah; and Dimnah betook himself to the Lion's court...

Ibn Muqaffa' was eventually executed; perhaps in the persecutions, which were beginning around that time, of the practice of clandestine Manicheism; he may have betrayed himself by suggesting that the Caliph should claim Divinity (*Risālah fi as-Ṣaḥābah*). The Caliph in question, al-Manṣūr, may well have been a Manichean in secret for reasons of political opportunism and had already been compromised in this respect by the well meaning devotions of the sect of the Rāwāandiyyah whom he also had slaughtered for embarrassing him in front of the Muslims.

Ibn Muqlah, Abū 'Alī (d. *330*/940). He was vizier to three Caliphs, al-Muqtadir, al-Qāhir, and ar-Rāḍī. With his brother Abū Abd Allāh he learned calligraphy from Aḥwal. He had a turbulent career in unsettled times. He was tortured, had his right hand cut off and his tongue, and was put to death. But his fame lies in establishing a style of cursive writing which was beautifully proportioned. He laid down mathematical rules of calligraphy based on the rhombic dot, the width of the pen, determining the proportion between the elements of a written Arabic letter and its shape. The "standard" 'alif would be seven rhombic dots, and the "standard" circle within which some letters would be inscribed would be the diameter of the standard Alif. Other letters were proportioned also with a fixed number of rhombic dots between their elements. *Ibn al-Mu'tazz, Abū-l 'Abbās 'Abd Allāh* (*861*/247-*908*/296) "The Caliph for a Day", often not counted in dynastic lists, yet his caliphate represented one of the most important turning points in the history of the Caliphate.

After the death of the Caliph al-Muktafi a power struggle which had been building behind the scenes for a long time came to a head. Until then, the powers around the throne were Sunnis and state administration was carried out through Sunni secretaries. In reality however, these so-called Sunni secretaries were from crypto-Manichean families, some assembled from as far away as Balkh. As Brockelmann says "Manicheism, particularly in 'Irāq, still exercised a great influence... and very nearly became the religion of the ['Islamic'] educated classes." In addition, more Crypto-Manicheans were brought into the government by the Barmakids who had helped the 'Abbāsids to power in the first place. The Barmakids themselves were destroyed by Harun ar-Rashid in 805, but their administrative protegés remained, still in control of the mechanism of government because they were in control of the bureaucracy. In 908, a shift was about to take place. The influence of Twelve Imam Shī'ites had grown. At the death of al-Muktafī, Shī'ite bankers and functionaries put the 13 year old Muqtadir on the Caliphal throne as their puppet. Several months later the "Sunni" secretaries struck back and on the 17th of December put Ibn al-Mu'tazz on the throne in Baghdad while the reigning Caliph, al-Muqtadir, was ousted.

Ibn al-Mu'tazz, the grandson of the Caliph al-Mutawakkil, was the son of the Caliph al-Mu'tazz who himself had been put on the throne in 866 until 869 by the Turkish Guards of Samarra' when the Caliph al-Musta'in fled from them to Baghdad. A poet, he wrote "The Epistles", a miniature epic of 450 iambic couplets celebrating the reign of his cousin the Caliph al-Mu'tadid, which Browne called the "nearest approximation to an epic poem to be found in Arabic literature". He also wrote works on poetics influenced by Aristotle's *Rhetoric* which had recently been translated into Arabic. He had led a life away from politics extolling the pure Arabic of the Beduins while occupying himself with literary criticism. But he was opposed to Twelve Imam Shī'ites.

The attempt to restore the *status quo ante* through the palace imposition of Ibn al-Mu'tazz on the throne was short lived. The day after the child Caliph Muqtadir had been deposed, the Shī'ites successfully countered and al-Mu'tazz, "The Caliph for a Day", was executed. Thus the shift of state power into the hands of Shī'ites was decisive and confirmed. The Shī'ites, as direct rivals, were more aggressive against Manicheans than the authentic Sunnis had been, and above all the Shī'ites knew who the Manicheans were when the real Sunnis generally did not have a clue. The Manicheans who until then were usually disguised as Sunnis (but thereafter increasingly as Twelve Imam Shī'ites) were now out of power and under serious threat. (Al-Ḥallāj supported Ibn al-Mu'tazz, for example.) This would have signaled the time for the Archegos, the head of the Manichean religion living in the outskirts of Baghdad, to depart for safer ground. An-Nadīm says this took place in the reign of al-Muqtadir. These events were accompanied by the Qarmaṭī revolt, the founding of the Fāṭimid dynasty and followed by the execution of al-Ḥallāj in 924, an event long time coming, preceded by years of his imprisonment on charges of crypto-Manicheism. After al-Ḥallāj was put to death there followed the executions of thousands throughout the empire of those whom Massignon calls "Ḥallājians" and whom others call Ismā'īlīs. *See* ARCHEGOS; BARMAKIDS; MANICHEISM.

Ibn al-Nafīs, 'Alā' ad-Dīn Abū-l-Ḥasan (*610-687*/1213-1288). Born in Damascus, Ibn al-Nafīs was a physician who worked in Cairo at the Naṣrī and the Manṣūrī hospitals and made remarkable contributions to medicine. (The institution of care for the sick at hospitals was established in the first centuries of Islamic civilization).

Ibn an-Nadīm, *see* an-NADĪM.

Ibn Qutaybah, Abū Muḥammad 'Abd Allāh ibn Muslim (*213-276*/828-889). A philologist born at Baghdad of Persian descent, he wrote about the education necessary for a court secretary, *Adab al-Kātib*; about literature, *Kitāb ash-Shi'r wa-sh-Shu'arā'* ("The Book of Poetry and Poets"); and on moral training; *'Uyūn al-Akhbār*. He said that before Islam appeared, Judaism, Christianity, and *zindiqah* (Manicheism) were practiced in Mecca.

Ibn ar-Rāwandī, Aḥmad Ibn Yaḥyā Abū-l-Ḥusayn. (died either c. *246*/860 or c. *290*/902). Born in Marw ar-Rud, but settled in Baghdad, Ibn ar-Rāwandī was at first a Mu'tazilite, whom he later criticized in the *Kitāb Faḍīḥat al-Mu'tazila*, then a Shī'ite, but became a notorious free-thinker, or zindiq-Manichean under the influence of Abū 'Īsā al-Warrāq (d. 247/861). He wrote the *Kitab az-Zumurrudh* ("The book of the Emerald") which was refuted and quoted in the *Kitāb al-Intiṣār* by al-Khayyāt. (The title refers to a "special quality" of the emerald which was believed had the power to blind snakes.) It listed arguments which supported the existence of prophecy and refuted it, thus attacking the Prophet. In the *Zumurrudh* presumably the arguments against prophecy were presented by the mentor al-Warrāq, under guise of citing criticisms made by the Brahmans of India. Ibn ar-Rāwandī also criticized Islam in general and the Koran, (*Kitāb al-Dāmigh, Kitāb at-Taj*).

He was obliged to flee from Baghdad and hide in Kūfah, at the home "of a Jew" who was "a patron of his". Ibn al-Murtaḍā said that ar-Rāwandī also wrote simply for money, and thus wrote tracts for Jews, Christians, Shī'ites, and Dualists.

Ibn Rizām, Abū 'Abd Allāh Muḥammad. In *329*/940 Ibn Rizām was the head of the *maẓālim* or court of complaints in Baghdad. He wrote an investigation of the Ismā'īlīs which is at variance with Ismā'īlī claims and for this reason he is considered a source of a "black legend". Nevertheless, on many points the Ismā'īlīs themselves have to turn to his account to fill in gaps in their "official" account and thus they credit him with having access to "authentic" sources. Ibn Rizām's account was amplified by Akhū Muḥsin. It is hard to believe that when every subsequent writer confirms Ibn Rizām it can only be because he himself was influenced by Ibn Rizām and had no independent opinion or information.

Ibn Rizām's account says that a non-'Alīd, Maymūn al-Qaddāh was the founder of Ismā'īlism and the progenitor of the Fāṭimids; that he was a follower of Abu-l-Khaṭṭab, the namesake of a Manichean-type sect, as well as the follower of Daysan or Bardaisan, a precursor of Mani. This progression became later considered a genealogy, that is, that the Fāṭimids were considered to be literally descendants of Bardaisan and Marcion. However, the Fāṭimids, Bardaisan, Marcion were not in one family except intellectually.

Ibn Rizām's account is augmented by Ṭabarī whose information came from the interrogation of a captured relative of the Qarmaṭī dā'ī Zikrawayh ibn Mihrawayh. *See* 'ABD ALLĀH IBN MAYMŪN al-QADDĀH.

Ibn Rushd, Abū-l-Walīd Muḥammad ibn Aḥmad ibn Muḥammad (*520-595*/1126-1198). An Arab philosopher who had little influence in the East, coming, as he did, at the end of the development of philosophy in Islam, and perhaps marking its summit. Known, however, as Averroís in Europe, and translated into Latin, he became the great authority on Aristotle's philosophy, and was so celebrated that he could be referred to simply as "the Commentator". For Ibn Rushd, Aristotle was the consummate master of the "Way" of the mind.

In Europe, a school arose around his "Commentaries on Aristotle" which was called "Latin Averroism". Into the 15th century and beyond, he was still a vital force in European philosophy, although his thinking, abstracted from his own Muslim framework and belief, was interpreted as that of a sceptic oriented towards nominalism, or empiricism, rather than of the realist (or nowadays, idealist) that he was.

Ibn Rushd was born in Cordova, the grandson of a Judge. His friend Ibn Ṭufayl, the philosopher, introduced him to the Almohad court and he was appointed *qāḍi* (Judge) in Seville. Because all learning was virtually one continuous science without borders in that age, he was not only a philosopher and a canon lawyer, he also served as physician to Abū Ya'qūb Yūsuf, the Almohad prince.

The Arab West is the most conservative part of all the Arab world, and is devoted to maintaining tradition; this is, in fact, the outstanding characteristic of the Mālikī School of Law. There, broad ideas often came under suspicion, and popular feelings during the rule of al-Manṣūr interpreted philosophy as heresy. For a time Ibn Rushd, who had meanwhile established himself in Morocco, was exiled back to Spain, but he was later allowed to return, and finished his life in North Africa.

In Europe, he is famous for the theory of the "Unity of the Intellect", which, corrupted into the "theory of the common soul", was called "pan-psychism". However, it is really an expression of the Neo-platonic concept that true knowledge consists in the identity of the knower with the known. The faculty of cognition, or "knowing", is the intellect, which is a projection of the metacosmic Intellect— the center of Being — into the individual knower. Creation, which is the object of knowledge, is the differentiation in the cosmos of that Intellect. Awareness of the identity between the two is knowledge; the knower knows because, in a sense, he contains what he knows. The notoriety of the doctrine arose because it was expressed as philosophy; but in Islamic mysticism it is familiar under its esoteric formulations as *waḥdat ash-shuhūd*, ("unity of consciousness"), and the essentially similar *waḥdat al-wujūd* ("unity of being"); the latter was being expounded around the same time by the metaphysician Ibn 'Arabī (d. *630*/1240) but being seen as religion, and not as philosophy, it was not read in Europe.

Ibn Rushd is also associated with what has been called the "two truths" theory; this contends that his doctrine was that there is one truth for philosophers, which is philosophy, and another for the masses, which is religion. But since for Averroís the higher truth lay in revelation and the lower in the formulations of theology, he cannot be guilty of the secret "free thinking" he was accused of in the Middle Ages. Rather, he recognized that there exists truth as such, which must needs resort to ellipses and to apparent contradictions or antinomies in order to express itself in the terms of reason rather than myth; and he recognized too that dogma, for its purposes, either simplifies the truth or expresses it only in part. Theological dogma does this in order to avoid doctrinal contradictions which cannot be resolved by ordinary reason; inevitably, however, at some point, it too is obliged to make up for what is missing from its simplifications by acknowledging certain categories as "mysteries", or by hiving off the inexplicable with the formula *bilā kayfa* ("don't ask why"), as the Ash'arites do. Ibn Rushd actually sought to harmonize the Koran and revelation with philosophy and logic.

Van den Bergh summarizes Ibn Rushd's own summary in the *Incoherence of the Incoherence* [the answer to al-Ghazālīs attack, the *Incoherence of the Philosophers*]) thus: "There are three possible views. A Sceptical view is that religion is opium for the people, held by certain Greek rationalists; the view that religion expresses Absolute Truth; and an intermediate view, held by Averroís, that the religious conceptions are the symbols of a higher philosophical truth, symbols which have to be taken for reality itself by the non-philosophers. For the unphilosophical, however, they are binding since the sanctity of the state depends upon them... Although he does not subscribe to the lofty words of his master [Aristotle] that man because of the power of his intellect is a mortal God he reproaches the theologians for having made God an immortal man. God for him is a dehumanized principle." *See* FIVE DIVINE PRESENCES; PHILOSOPHY.

Ibn Sab'īn, Abū Muḥammad 'Abd al-Ḥaqq (d. *668*/1270). A Sufi of Murcia, Spain, especially known for his Monism (Ibn Khaldūn called him *ṣaḥib al-waḥdah*) and Hermeticism. He may have been the first to use the term *waḥdāt al-wujūd* ("unity of being" that is, Monism). He was asked by the governor of Ceuta, Ibn Khalās, to reply to some philosophical questions put to the Almohad rulers by Frederick II Hohenstaufen, King of Sicily (1194-1250). These four "Sicilian" questions which had also been sent to other parts of the Islamic world, had to do with Aristotelian philosophy. They concerned the eternity of the world, the goal of metaphysics, the immortality of the soul, and the nature of the Aristotelian categories and their number. Ibn Sab'īn's answers (*al-Kalām 'alā al-masā'il al-siqiliyyah*), preserved in the Bodleian Library and translated by M.A.F. Mehren in the July 1879 issue of *Journal Asiatique*, like the questions, are fairly banal, but they showed him to be well versed in Greek philosophy. (The copy of this article in the Columbia University library had only the first three pages, out of around fifteen cut open until 1988!) He was called the "Sufi following the method of the Philosophers" although, using philosophical methods and reasoning, he himself criticized philosophers, as well as Sufis. He said that the world is virtually contained in the Essence of the Divinity, that the goal of Metaphysics is knowledge of God.

The reply to Frederick's questions also show him, or his scribe, insulting the Emperor: "By asking this question you reveal your belonging to the ignorant crowd, lacking in intelligence. You ask how many categories there are after saying yourself that there are ten. This shows how weak your schooling was."

Ibn Sab'īn was known to be haughty and arrogant, having said: "If you are looking for paradise, go to Ibn Mad'in; if you want the Lord of paradise, come to me." Encountering opposition from religious authorities for his radical views, he traveled from place to place until he reached Mecca where some say he committed suicide. As Massignon says, in the fashion of the Stoics, opening his veins "in desire for God... a philosophical, mysterious, death, imitating Socrates, and Empedocles and Cato, the Sati of the Hindu widow, the gymnosophist Brahmachari; even the 'binding of Isaac' by which Rabbis strangled, at the demand of mothers, circumcised Jewish children forcefully baptized by horrid bishops."

Ibn Khaldūn said that he was one of those extravagant Sufis who believed that the world is an emanation of God and that one of his axioms was that "God is the reality of things which exist", which has been repeated in the simplistic proposition that "the world, not being nothing, must be God Himself".

A teacher of Ibn Sab'īn was Abū Isḥāq ibn Dahhāq, and, it was said, a Hermeticist named Ibn Aḥlā of Lorca (d. *645*/1247). Abū-l-Ḥasan ash-Shusterī (*1610-665*/1213-1269) was a noted, and devoted disciple. In a poem, the *qaṣīdah nūniyyah*, Ibn Sab'in mentions Ibn Masarrah (d. *319*/931), into whose tradition he clearly falls. The alien influences show themselves in Ibn Sab'īn's opinion of the Prophet Muḥammad, whom he sees not as the paramount revealer, but one figure out of many, perhaps even inferior to Hermes Trismegistus. He also attacked al-Ghazālī, probably because al-Ghazālī was the defender of orthodox Islam from Gnostic, and thereby the related philosophical, as well as Hermetic doctrines. The name Ibn Sab'īn means literally "Son of Seventy" (or the mystical number seven made "ten-fold"?) and he also used the name Ibn al-Dāra ("Son of the Circle", the circle being also interpreted as a Maghribi symbol for the number "seventy"). The name 'Abd al-Ḥaqq may also be symbolic, because the partisans of certain outlooks preferred to say "Reality" (*al-Ḥaqq*) rather than the theistic "Allāh". He wrote the *Budd al-'ārif* ("the Prerequisite of the Gnostic"), *Duruj* ("the Degrees") and *Fatḥ al-Mushtarak* ("The Shared Revelation"), *Sharḥ kitāb Idrīs* ("the Book of Idris"), *Kitāb al-Iḥāṭa*, ("the Comprehensive work") and many other treatises. *See* IBN MASARRAH; SUFISM.

Ibn Ṣa'd (Abū 'Abd Allāh Muḥammad ibn Ṣa'd ibn Mani' az-Zuhrī, usually called Kātib al-Waqidī, "the secretary of Waqidī" d. *230*/845). Biographer from Baṣrah who lived in Baghdad. He wrote the *Kitāb al-Ṭabaqāt al-Kabīr*, a large biography of Companions, Helpers, and Followers, grouped as "classes" or succeeding generations.

Ibn Sa'ūd, 'Abd al-'Azīz (*1297-1372*/1880-1953). King of Saudi Arabia, known there as King 'Abd al-'Azīz Āl Sa'ūd. He was born in Riyāḍ the son of 'Abd ar-Raḥmān, Sultan of the Najd. His father had been driven out of Riyāḍ in *1309*/1891 by the adversaries of the family, the Banū Rashīd of Hā'il, and had taken refuge in Kuwait. Some ten years later, in *1319*/1901, 'Abd al-'Azīz led a raiding party of forty or so men into the Najd. In the early morning they penetrated into the city of Riyāḍ and attacked the governor on his way from the Musmak palace to perform the dawn prayer.

This daring foray succeeded; the governor was killed and Riyāḍ recaptured. With this the Sa'ud family regained control, 'Abd al-'Azīz became King of the Najd and thereafter his Kingdom grew steadily. In *1344*/1924 he conquered the Hejaz, then the Asir and finally the rest of what is today Saudi Arabia. In *1348*/1929 the King was obliged to fight the Battle of Sibilla against dissident nomad tribe leaders. These were formerly his own supporters, who had continued carrying out raids, now against British-defended 'Irāq, against the King's wishes and despite the program of settlement which he initiated. The battle was fought with the King's troops mounted on Fords and Chevrolets that had been commandeered in Jeddah and driven across the desert.

In 1938 oil was discovered in Dhahran (Ẓaḥrān). The King signed agreements giving Standard Oil of California concessions to exploit the finds; twenty years later oil production led to an era of unprecedented prosperity.

King 'Abd al-'Azīz was by any standards a most remarkable figure. Starting out as a tribal chieftain, he became King of a new and modern nation. He had the ability to make bold political decisions in situations which were completely unfamiliar to him; he also had an immense store of good fortune. But despite his capacity to act independently of past habit and precedent, King 'Abd al-'Azīz, in the middle of the twentieth century, retained the air of a Biblical patriarch. He died in Ṭā'if of ripe old age and went to the grave with forty-two battle wounds received in his youth fighting with lance and sword. He was succeeded as King by his sons in turn, first (Ibn) Sa'ūd, then Fayṣāl, Khālid, Fahd, and 'Abd Allāh.

Ibn Sīnā, Abū 'Alī Ḥusayn ibn 'Abd Allāh (*370-429*/980-1037). Physician and philosopher, and one of the renowned intellectual figures of the Middle Ages, Ibn Sīnā was born near Bukhāra, of a Turkic mother and a Persian father. A precocious student, after learning the Koran by heart at the age of ten, he studied the *Isagoge* of Porphyry and the propositions of Euclid. Logic, philosophy, and medicine were to be his calling in life. He wrote numerous treatises of which the most influential was the *Canon of Medicine*, which remained a basis for teaching medicine in Europe into the seventeenth century, and the *ash-Shifā'* ("Healing"), known in Europe as the *Sanatio*.

Medicine in Islam was a prolongation of the science of the Greeks, and thus Ibn Sīnā's concepts were based on those of the Greek physician Galen. His lofty reputation in Europe earned him the title of "Prince of Physicians". In the East however, where many other physicians wrote similar medical treatises, he was more renowned as an expounder of philosophy, at that time a unified study of Plato, Aristotle, and Neoplatonism. Ibn Sīnā was actually one of the prime targets of al-Ghazālī's attack on the philosophers.

Ibn Sīnā's great accomplishment was to "complete" the philosophy of Aristotle and elaborate an ontology of Being. Ibn Sīnā, probably despite himself, developed for the West as much as for the East, the "philosophy of monotheism". Aristotle had spoken of the First Mover but had not described Him. This became possible only after Islam, and the revelation of the Absolute, the revelation of the "nature" of the "First Mover".

It was Ibn Sīnā who was to describe philosophically the relationship between the Divine Essence and Being. However, he did so "backwards"; Ibn Sīnā said, *because* God exists, therefore He has an Essence, which is Existentialism ("existence precedes essence"). Thus Ibn Sīnā thought of Being as being physical and "existing". (The Ismā'īlīs say that *the soul is a projection of the body*, instead of the other way around.) In orthodox metaphysics, it is the exact opposite which must be true: namely, *because* God has an Essence, therefore "He exists", or rather, has Being in the sense that Being proceeds out of the Divine Essence by way of "creation", and from Being proceeds existence. But to arrive at this, not only was Islam a necessary pre-condition as a Revelation of the Divine Essence, which is why Aristotle himself had gone no further, but it was necessary to arrive at the idea by "backing into it" because the Divine Essence is, in Itself, inconceivable. If nothing else, this certainly demonstrates that error teaches, that limitation brings awareness, or that good can come out of evil, even though, "woe to those through whom evil comes". The fall of man must precede salvation.

Ibn Sīnā wrote that his father was an Ismā'īlī and that Ismā'īlī meetings, which Ibn Sīnā attended as a child, were held in his home. Thus, although Ibn Sīnā claimed to be a Ḥanafī Sunnī, albeit with a very cavalier attitude towards religious laws for he lived the life of a medieval playboy, he came from a background in which the physical world was considered to be "divine", the "body of God", so to speak. He used Ismā'īlī terminology such as *al-Mubdi'* for God. It was this religious formation that allowed him to follow the Koranic doctrine of the Divine Attributes or Names treated as physical, material guideposts back to their necessary center, which, understood in the human mind, would then be the Essence. An Essence that Ibn Sīnā said God "had" because God — or the world — "had" an existence. Similarly to his idea of existence preceding essence, Ibn Sīnā postulated that if a grown man were to be suddenly created in a void, without limbs, without senses, he could nevertheless arrive at self awareness, although how, is not clear unless one assumes that consciousness itself has differentiation, or to put it otherwise, that consciousness is material, that the soul is a thing. In keeping with this possibility, Ibn Sīnā adduced a speculative estimative faculty called which he called *wahmiyyah*, which would be what makes a sheep run away from a wolf even if it has never seen one before.

But once the pathways running between existence-essence-God were established, even in a contrary direction, religious philosophy could forget what led to it; and God's Essence could then be recognized as "existing" independently of the mind of man, and independently of the world; that God was there before the creation of the world, and will there after it is gone.

The objection that the philosophers had to the creation of the world, was that if it were not eternal, then some change had to have taken place within God which was the decision to create; and God cannot have a fluctuation within Himself, a "decision to create" because a change can only take place within that which is relative and mutable, which God as Absolute could not be. (This was also at the root of the problem of God "knowing" particulars and why the philosophers said that, as God, He can only "know" universals.) Thus the philosophers concluded that the world was eternal. But if the world were eternal, the theologians objected, then the world would also be God since it would have a Divine Attribute, eternity.

Although theology says the world is created, and leaves it as a dogma, this problem has never been elucidated philosophically or metaphysically because here doctrine ends; it can only be known as

Although the essential elements of a mosque remain constant, the architectural style may vary greatly. The *Masjid-i-Shaykh Luṭfullāh* in Isfahan (*above*) is perhaps the finest and most important work of the Ṣafavid period (1501-1732). Built on the *Maydān-i-Shāh,* the great polo ground laid out under the direction of Shāh 'Abbās (1587-1628) when the capital of Persia was transferred from Qazvīn to Isfahan in 1598, it has the ornate tiled façade and dome typical of Persian mosques of the period. *See* MOSQUE.

The mosque of Sultan Aḥmad in Istanbul (*below*) completed in 1616, is known as the "Blue Mosque" because of its blue tilework. Both are expansive and ample-domed buildings based on Byzantine models. The Dome of the Rock in Jerusalem (*below right*) was founded by the Caliph 'Abd al-Malik in 687 (completed in 691), from which the *mi 'rāj* ("Night Journey") of the Prophet began. *Opposite bottom left* is the Badshahi Mosque in Lahore, Pakistan; *opposite bottom right* is the resplendent courtyard of the *madrasah* Ben Youssef in Marrakesh, Morocco. The Great Mosque of Cordova is the world's third largest mosque. A Christian church since the 15th century, it was begun in the 8th century, and frequently added to, notably in the 10th century. The hexafoil arches in two tiers (*far right*), whose nineteen aisles form the sanctuary, represent an important departure in Islamic architecture, in the Hispano-Mauresque style. The central dome (*right*) in front of the *miḥrāb* was completed by al-Ḥakam II (961-76) and is supported by a series of intersecting ribs. *See* al-AQṢĀ'; DOME OF THE ROCK; MADRASAH; MIḤRĀB; MOSQUE; NIGHT JOURNEY.

The Djenna mosque in Mali (*left*), made of clay and earth rammed together, is a fine example of the indigenous mosque architecture which developed in countries bordering the Sahara. The spiral minaret of the *Malwiyyah* at Samarra', Iraq (*below*) is thought to have been based upon the form of pre-Islamic ziggurats. The largest ancient mosque still extant, it was begun by al-Mutawakkil in 847/1443. But the largest mosque in the world is now the Shah Alam Mosque in Selangor, Malaysia (*below left*). The *madrasah* school in the Great Mosque complex in Samarkand (*opposite*), where Tamerlane is buried, features the lobed dome and extensive external tiling characteristic of 15th- and 16th-century Persian mosque architecture. The band of ornamental Kufic on the minaret reads "Eternity is for God" (*al-Baqa' li-Llāh*). *See* MADRASAH; MINARET; MOSQUE; TIMURIDS.

The interior of the al-Aqṣā' Mosque in Jerusalem (*opposite*) with the carved wooden *mimbar* and the *miḥrāb* which indicates the *qiblah,* the direction of Mecca. The Ardabil carpet (*left*) was woven for the Ismail Shah Mosque, Tabrīz, in *918*/1512. Almost certainly the largest ever woven in Persia, its fine decoration includes traceries of flowers, Koranic inscriptions and hanging mosque lamps. The 13th-century incense burner (*below*) exemplifies the achievements of Islamic metalwork in a variety of materials, including copper, brass and bronze. *See* al-AQṢĀ'; DOME OF THE ROCK; MIḤRĀB; MINBAR; QIBLAH.

Although some branches of Islam prohibit the veneration of tombs, there is, nevertheless, an important heritage of funerary architecture, the most famous example being the Taj Mahal (*above*) near Agra, built by Shah Jahan (1628-1658) in memory of his wife Mumtaz Mahal, and completed in 1648. The mosque of the shrine of 'Ali, the *Mazār-i-sharīf* (*below*), is in Afghanistan. *See* MAZĀR-i SHARĪF.

the object of a spiritual "realization" of the world and creation as an emptiness or a void. Al-Ghazālī, who attacked the philosophers, had to become a mystic in order to resolve the questions which they had raised but in doing so, al-Ghazālī became a proof that non-dualist Sufism, an orthodox Sufism was possible, despite the abundance of evidence that Sufism has usually hidden within itself precisely the doctrines from which Ibn Sīnā himself derived. Real knowledge, al-Ghazālī said, came from *dhawq* (lit. "taste") or direct intellection of reality.

Ibn Sīnā wrote prolifically, served a number of princes as physician, and had energy left over to enjoy a somewhat hedonistic life-style which would not have earned the approval of more moralistic observers. In seeking patrons, he was often caught in the middle of wars and rivalries and thus his life was not without adventures. At one point he was made a Vizier to the prince of Hamadhān, but mutinying soldiers demanded that he be put to death. Caught in the middle of political strife, Ibn Sīnā had to escape in disguise. He traveled widely and lived in many places in Persia, including Merv, Iṣfahān, Kazwin, and Hamadhān, where he died, his last days spent in pious exercises and repentance, it is said. He is considered the summit of philosophy in the East; after him its cultivation flourished in Muslim Spain and then passed to Europe. *See* PHILOSOPHY.

Ibn Sīrīn, Abū Bakr Muḥammad (*34-110*/654-728). A celebrated transmitter of Ḥadīth born in Baṣrah and a contemporary of Ḥasan of Baṣrah, but above all, the first Islamic interpreter of dreams (ta'bir ar-ru'yā). (Heraclitus said that a dreamer participates in the activity or work of the cosmos.)

Ibn Taymiyyah (*661-728*/1263-1328). Born in Ḥarrān, Ibn Taymiyyah grew up in Damascus, where, following in his father's footsteps, he became a jurist of the Ḥanbalī School of Law. He taught first in Damascus and later in Cairo where he was imprisoned because his so-called "anthropomorphist", or more accurately, literalist interpretations of the Koran outraged scholars, particularly the Shāfi'īs. He took references to "God's Hand", and others like it, literally. He was imprisoned several times in Egypt and Syria for his religious and political opinions. Even while in prison he continued to teach religion, to his fellow inmates, and to write prolifically, so much so that his opponents were driven to deprive him of writing materials, an insult that wounded him perhaps more then prison itself.

He is famous for having said in a Friday sermon that "God comes down from Heaven to Earth [to hear prayers] just as I am now coming down" [the steps of the *minbar*, or pulpit]. His literalist understanding of the Koran led him to attack many authorities in Islam including al-Ghazālī, the Sufis, and, in particular, Ibn 'Arabī. Ibn Taymiyyah stormed against what he saw to be *bid'ah*, or innovation in religious practice. He even inveighed against the competence and authority of the Patriarchal Caliphs, 'Umar and 'Alī.

Treated as an eccentric, sometimes even as a heretic, his zeal and strong opinions nevertheless earned him the respect of many. Ironically, at his death, biographers say, his bier was followed by "twenty thousand mourners", many of them women who believed that he was a Saint. Indeed, his grave became a place of pilgrimage to seek miracles, favors, and cures. This would have earned his fiercest disapproval. Ibn Taymiyyah is one of the principal figures in the fundamentalist strand of Islam, and he is an important forerunner of the Wahhābīs. *See* WAHHĀBĪS.

Ibn Tāshufīn, Yūsuf (d. *500*/1106). The founder of the city of Marrakesh and leader of the Almoravids in their conquest of Morocco and Spain. *See* ALMORAVIDS; RECONQUISTA.

Ibn Ṭufayl, Abū Bakr Muḥammad ibn 'Abd al-Malik (d. *581*/1185). An important Arab philosopher, known in the West as Abūbacer. Born near Granada in Spain, Ibn Ṭufayl was Vizier to the Almohad prince Abū Ya'qūb Yūsuf and introduced Ibn Rushd (Averroïs) to the court. He wrote the famous *Ḥayy ibn Yaqẓān* ("The Living, Son of the Awake"; the "Living" is man, and the "Awake" is God). This philosophical novel describes how a youth growing up isolated on an island, through his own contemplation, arrives at the truths usually considered to be revealed — that is, through the natural faculties of the mind itself — and liberates himself from his lower soul. In his conduct on the island, the youth exemplifies the religious or ethical teachings of a number of different traditions. The relationship of the characters of the novel also implies that philosophy is necessary for the full understanding of religion.

The *Ḥayy ibn Yaqẓān* was translated into Latin by Pococke as *Philosophicus Autodidactus*, and inspired Daniel Defoe to write *Robinson Crusoe.*

Ibn Ṭufayl, along with Ibn Bājjah and Ibn Rushd, formed the avant-garde of Muslim philosophy, which was destined shortly to become virtually extinct, and marked the high point of its development. *See* PHILOSOPHY.

Ibn Tūmart, Abū 'Abd Allāh Muḥammad (*470-524*/1077-1130). The founder of the Almohad dynasty. *See* ALMOHADS.

Ibn al-Waqt (lit. "son of the present"). A term which refers to the state of being entirely present in the immediate moment. As one saying has it: "The Sufi is a man whose thought keeps pace with his foot" (that is, he is entirely *present*, his soul is where his body is, and his body always where his soul is). Although *Ibn al-waqt* is considered to be a mystical term because it is popular with the Sufis, and akin to the precept of Hesychasm, of "keeping oneself inside the heart", or "wakefulness", it is also an interesting expression of the traditional notion of psychology. "Son of the Present" implies that one is perceiving what is really before one, and not something out of one's memory, or anticipations and wishes regarding the future; one is perceiving reality and not interposing the contents of one's psyche between oneself and the world as a filter and a dream.

> Know that the present life is but a
> sport and a diversion, an adornment
> and a cause for boasting among you,
> and a rivalry in wealth and children.
> It is as a rain whose vegetation
> pleases the unbelievers; then it
> withers, and thou seest it turning
> yellow, then it becomes broken orts.
> And in the world to come there is a
> terrible chastisement,
> and forgiveness from God and good pleasure;
> and the present life is but the joy
> of delusion. (Koran 57:19-20)

It is, above all, the reversal of the normal tendency of the psyche to be passive, to receive the impressions of the world and, rather than act, to react to them on the purely horizontal plane and in terms of a subjective, personal, dream projected onto the world. The *Ibn al-Waqt* reverses this natural passivity to the world; he is present and active; if not active in a physical sense — the Prophet said: "My eye sleeps, but my heart wakes"— active in a spiritual sense, in that the physical laws of gravity are reversed in the spirit, and the soul instead of falling, rises, instead of giving in, surpasses itself.

> Have they not regarded the birds among them
> spreading their wings, and closing them?
> Naught holds them but the All-merciful.
> Surely He sees everything. (67:19).

The present that is meant in the term *Ibn al-Waqt* is not an intangible instant, where future is constantly becoming past, rather it is endless; it is always there, an eternal present and also the sense of eternity.

The great Sufi of Baghdad, al-Junayd (d. *297*/910) said:

> The Saint hath no fear, because fear is the expectation either of some future calamity or of the eventual loss of some object of desire, whereas the Saint is the son of his time (*ibn waqtihi*); he has no future that he should fear anything; and as he hath no fear so he hath no hope, since hope is the expectation either of gaining an object of desire or of being relieved from a misfortune, and this belongs to the future; nor does he grieve, because grief arises from the rigor of time, and how should he feel grief who is in the radiance of satisfaction (*riḍā*) and the garden of concord (*muwāfaqāt*)?

See FAQR.

Ibn Zaidūn, Aḥmad ibn 'Abd Allāh (*395*/1003-*463*/1071) The most famous of the Arab poets of Spain, in Cordoba. He was in love with an Umayyad princess, Wallāda, who was also a poet.

Ibn Zuhr, Abū Marwān 'Abd al-Malik (d. *557*/1162). One of the greatest Arab physicians, called Avenzoar in medieval Europe where his work was very influential. He was born in Seville and came from a line of physicians. Ibn Zuhr knew Ibn Rushd (Averroïs) — who may have learned medicine from him — and Ibn Ṭufayl, the philosophic luminaries of the great age of Muslim Andalusia. His works on medicine, which demonstrated a good knowledge of anatomy, were translated first into Hebrew and then into Latin.

Ibrāhīm *See* ABRAHAM.

Ibrāhīm ibn Adḥam (d. *166*/783). A legendary Sufi, born a prince of Balkh. The following is recounted of him by later Sufis:

> Ibrāhīm son of Adham was of a princely family of Balkh. One day, he told: "I was seated on my seat of state, and a mirror was offered for my self-inspection. I looked in it. I saw only a wayfarer toward the tomb, bound for a place where there would be no friend to cheer me. I saw a long journey stretching before me, for which I had made no provision. I saw a Just Judge, and myself unprovided with any proof for my ordeal. My royalty became distasteful in that moment."

And again:

> When he was out hunting one day he followed so hard after an antelope that he left his train far behind him. And God gave the antelope voice. "Wast thou created for this?" it said to him; "who bade thee do such things?"
>
> Ibrāhīm repented of his whole way of life. Abandoning everything he entered the path of asceticism; and after this conversion never ate any food but what he earned by his own labor.

Not finding a Muslim mystic to teach him at the outset, he turned to a Christian. "My first teacher in *ma'rifah*" ("mystical knowledge") he said, "was a monk named Simeon."

> I visited him in his cell, and said to him, "Father Simeon, how long hast thou been in thy cell here?" "For seventy years," he answered. "What is thy food?" I asked. "O Hanifite," he countered, "what has caused thee to ask this?" "I wanted to know," I replied. Then he said, "Every night one chickpea." I said, "What stirs thee in thy heart, so that this pea suffices thee?" He answered, "They come to me one day in every year, and adorn my cell, and process about it, so doing me reverence; and whenever my spirit wearies of worship, I remind it of that hour, and endure the labors of a year for the sake of an hour. Do thou, O Hanifite, endure the labor of an hour, for the glory of eternity." *Ma'rifah* ["knowledge"] then descended into my heart.

Later, he went on to find Sufi masters. Of the path of knowledge Ibrāhīm ibn Adḥam said:

> This is the sign of the knower, that his thoughts are mostly engaged in meditation, and his words are mostly praise and glorification of God, and his deeds are mostly devotion, and his eye is mostly fixed on the subtleties of Divine action and power.

Balkh, the home of Ibrahīm ibn Adḥam, still had remains of Greco-Buddhist civilization when the Muslims arrived; the family of the Barmakids, viziers of Harūn ar-Rashid, had been Buddhist priests, of a kind at any rate, in the Buddhist monastery of Nawbahar (the new *vihara*, "monastery") before converting to Islam and entering the service of 'Abbāsids. (The Sufi term "son of the moment", *ibn al-wuqt*, capable of more than one meaning, was shortly to come into being and may have referred to opportunistic conversion). The occasional Buddhists (called *Sumanis*) even lived in Baghdad under the 'Abbāsids.

The story of Ibrahīm ibn Adḥam is patterned after the story of the Buddha: a young prince sees successive reminders of the transience of the world and turns to the path of enlightenment. Whether it is an edifying story simply adapted to Islam for purposes of instruction or whether an historical Ibrāhīm ibn Adḥam actually existed, one who shed a Buddhist identity in order to adopt an Islamic one, is now perhaps impossible to settle. In any case, the figure of Ibrahīm ibn Adḥam defines a certain spiritual type, what some forms of mysticism called a *pneumatic*; and it is to these schools of mystic thought that Ibrahīm ibn Adḥam belongs.

Another trace in Islam of contact with Buddhism is also found among the Sufis is their use of the term fana', or "extinction". The word is found in the Koran, but its adaptation to the technical concepts of the Sufis is probably a parallel to the Buddhist concept of *Nirvana*. *See* MAZĀR-I SHĀRIF; SUFISM.

'Īd al-Aḍḥā (lit. "the feast of the sacrifice"). Also known as the *'Īd al-Kabīr* ("the great feast") and, in Turkey, as the *kurban bayram*, this is the most important feast in the Islamic calendar. It falls on the 10th Dhū-l-Ḥijjah which is also the culmination of the pilgrimage at Mecca. For those not performing the pilgrimage, the feast is one of communal prayer followed by the sacrifice of an animal; for those who are in Mecca performing the pilgrimage, the sacrifice is the concluding rite.

The feast is a commemoration of Abraham's sacrifice of the ram as a Divine dispensation releasing him from the intended sacrifice of his son. When Abraham had confirmed his obedience to God, the Angel Gabriel brought a ram at the last moment as a substitute for the son. This son is not named in the Koran, but it is usually accepted in Islam that the sacrifice was to be of Ismā'īl (Ishmael). For those commentators who hold that Ismā'īl (Ishmael) was indeed the promised victim, Abraham's willingness to sacrifice his then only son, at an age which left no hope for another, constituted the greatness and depth of his obedience. The second son, Isaac, is precisely understood to be God's reward for Abraham's perfect submission.

In Islam the place of Abraham's sacrifice is held to be Minā, just outside Mecca. The pillars at Minā, which are stoned during the pilgrimage, symbolize the devil's tempting of Abraham, three times, to abandon the sacrifice.

On the morning of the *'Id al-Aḍḥā* the people assemble at the communal place of prayer (*muṣallā*), usually an open field, for the *'Īd* ("feast") prayer is performed in principle, by all members of the community or city together (*see* PRAYER). In keeping with an ancient Semitic tradition, found also in Ezekiel, one returns from the 'Id prayer by a different route than that followed in coming to it. After the prayer, the Imām sacrifices a sheep for the nation, or the community, and then one for his family. The believers return to their homes where each head of a household sacrifices a sheep, a camel, or an ox for his family. The sacrifice is consumed over the course of several days.

The sacrifice is performed by a man, usually, but not necessarily, the head of the household. He faces Mecca, utters the appropriate ritual intention *an-niyyah* (essentially a statement of the clear nature and purpose of the act to be performed), speaks the name of the person or persons on whose account the sacrifice is being made, pronounces the words *bismi-Llāh*; *Allāhu Akbar*, and then cuts the throat of the animal, both wind-pipe and jugular, in one stroke (*see* SACRIFICE). Women who head households ask a man, a relative or the Imām of the local mosque, to perform the sacrifice for them, although a woman could perform the sacrifice herself if no suitable adult male could be found. The celebrations continue for three days and consist chiefly of family visits. The sacrifice renews a sense of consecration towards God and perpetuates a primordial sacerdotal function.

The Prophet instituted the feast in the second year of the Hijrah in Medinah when he and the refugees could not fulfill the pilgrimage to Mecca. *See also* PILGRIMAGE.

'Īd al-Fiṭr (lit. "the feast of breaking fast"). After the *'Īd al-Aḍḥā*, the second most important holiday in the Islamic calendar. It follows the sighting of the new moon that signifies the end of the fast of the month of Ramaḍān. The festival is marked by the special *'Īd* prayer (*see* PRAYER) which is performed by the whole community together in an outdoor prayer ground called the muṣallā. In large cities the *'Īd* prayer is also performed in congregational mosques. A special alms (*zakāh*) called *zakāt al-Fiṭr*, is given at this time. The *zakāt al-fiṭr* consists of a measure of grain for every member of the household (or its equivalent in value). It is given directly to the poor. Celebrations of the *'Īd al-Fiṭr*, also called the lesser feast (*'Īd aṣ-Ṣaghīr*), normally go on for three days. In Turkey it is called the "little" or *kücük bayram*.

'Īd al-Ghadīr (lit. "the festival of the pool"). A purely Twelve-Imām Shī'ite festival observed on the 18th Dhū-l-Ḥijjah, which commemorates the events of Ghadīr al-Khumm, in which the Shī'ites believe that the Prophet designated 'Alī as his successor. The event became a Shī'ite celebration in *351*/962 under the Buyid ruler Mu'izz ad-Dawlah. *See* GHADĪR al-KHUMM.

al-'Īd al-Kabīr, *see* 'ID al-AḌḤĀ.

'Iddah (lit. "number"). The interval of time which a woman must observe after divorce or the death of a husband, before she can remarry. Its purpose is to determine the paternity of possible offspring but also, in the case of divorce which has not been pronounced three times, to provide a space of time in which a reconciliation may take place. The duration of *'iddah* is three months or three menstrual periods in the case of divorce, and four months and ten days in the case of the death of the husband.

In the case of divorce, the husband must provide lodgings and food for the woman for this period and is morally, but not legally, expected to provide upkeep (*muṭāʻ*) beyond the necessities. In one case in classical times when a man had provided only the legal minimum of support for his divorced wife, the Judge had no means to force him to do more; but in a later case this Judge refused to accept that man's testimony as a witness because he was not "morally upright".

'Idgah. A place of communal prayer for festivals, called *musallā* in Arab lands. This is a place where an entire city could perform the 'Id prayer.

Idhn (lit. "permission"). Although *bay'ah* ("pact") is the more common term, *idhn* denotes initiation into the *ṭarīqah*, the path of the Sufis. The initiation is a pact sworn with God to consecrate oneself to Him and fight "in His way" for truth and against illusion with one's life and one's possessions. It involves a ritual handclasp which may have originated with the Mandaens. The pact brings with it the "permission" (*idhn*) to use the means of concentration of the Sufi order, the *dhikr*, usually a litany or an invocation, which, without the initiation and its special blessing (*barakah*), is ineffective. True initiations convey a knowledge which cannot be transmitted in any other fashion; baptism, for example, conveys the ability to see the ideal as Real, and the bay'ah the power to see multiplicity as the silent manifestation of the One. *Idhn* can also mean the Shaykh's permission to a disciple to teach or transmit the *ṭarīqah*. *See* BAY'AH; DHIKR; RIḌWĀN; SUFISM.

Idols (Ar. Sing. *wathan*, pl. *wuthun* and *awthān*; also *ṣanam* pl. *aṣnām*). Many of the idols set up in the Kaʻbah in Mecca during the "Age of Ignorance" (*al-Jāhiliyyah*) had been brought from surrounding countries, in part, no doubt, to encourage trade with those regions. The principal gods at Mecca were Hubal (god of the moon), and the female goddesses al-'Uzza, whose principle shrine was in the valley of Nakhlah, a day's camel ride south of Mecca; al-Lāt, who had a rich temple at Ṭā'if (and at Palmyra); Manāt whose main temple was at Quḍayḍ on the Red Sea; and Wudd, goddess of love. Also known in Mecca were the pair Isaf and Na'ila. In addition, others were Manāf, the sun god; Quzaḥ the rainbow; Nasr, the eagle; Qaʻis, the goddess of fate, and some known as little more than names such as Baʻīm, Jibt, al-Muharriq, Nuḥm, Shay al-Qawm, Ṭāghūt, Yaghūs, Yaʻūq, Zūn, and others. Apart from astral deities representing cosmic principles inherited from the Mesopotamians, many gods were Baʻls like those of the Old Testament, and totems of particular tribes.

The cult of the idols consisted largely of pilgrimages during the months of truce, coinciding with the desert fairs, the great souks, like that of 'Ukāẓ, and Minā. The cult included processions in which a cult object was carried on the back of a camel under a pavilion called a *qubbah*. The ceremonies included singing and dancing, and circumambulations of the cult objects. Sacrifices were a very important part of the rituals.

Of the 360 idols set up in the Kaʻbah, the most important was Hubal, god of the moon. Upon the conquest of Mecca the Prophet cut open some of these idols with a sword and black smoke is said to have issued forth from them, a sign of the psychic influences which had made these idols their dwelling place. The Prophet turned the idol of Hubal into a doorstep.

At the conquest of Mecca, the Prophet sent Khālid ibn Walīd to destroy the sanctuary of al-'Uzzā at Nakhlah. When Khālid returned, the Prophet asked: "Did you see anything?" to which Khālid replied: "Nothing." "Then," said the Prophet "You have not destroyed her." Khālid returned to Nakhlah and out of the ruins he saw a naked woman come, black with long, wild hair. He slew her, saying: "'Uzzā, denial is for you, not worship." When he returned he told the Prophet: "Praise be to God who has saved us from perishing! I was wont to see my father set out for al-'Uzzā with an offering of a hundred camels and sheep. He would sacrifice them to her and stay three days at her shrine, and return unto us rejoicing at what he had accomplished."

The Golden Calf which as-Samīrī brought the Israelites to worship while Moses was on Mount Sīnāi would produce a lowing sound, because as-Samīrī had thrown into it dust which Gabriel, whom he saw passing by on the way to the mountain, had set foot upon. The people themselves, by their frenzied attentions to the idol, contributed to its hold over them; their frenzy, as it were, rendered up to the image some of their own power over themselves. Thus the attraction the idols exerted over their devotees was not arbitrary, but the result of a projected influence; to this in return the worshiper could respond. Abū Sufyān could hope to sway in battle those of the believers whose faith was not firmly established with his war cry: "Al-'Uzzā with us — but not with you!"

In Plato's *Timaeus*, Critias speaks of Neith, a goddess of the Egyptians whom the Egyptians readily identified with Athena. Here is paganism at a stage where its adherents treat their gods as symbols of a reality that the symbol does not encompass but only indicates. The paganism of the Arabs of the *Jāhiliyyah*, however, was the end-point of religious decadence and hardening, not unlike the present hardening of the monotheisms into reductive fundamentalism. The symbols no longer pointed beyond themselves; the unique idol was itself a deity or a power. What may once have been the awareness of a spiritual reality became an enclosure for a reflected mental influence, hellish in its heat and density.

The power of the idols, as of all illusion, depended upon the consent and the cooperation of those who gave themselves up to them. *See* JĀHILIYYAH; al-KALBĪ; KAHIN.

Idrīs. A prophet in the Koran, often identified with Enoch of the Bible who "walked with God" and did not die. He is mentioned in Sūrah 19:57 ("We raised him to a high station") and 21:85. Idrīs for Muslim philosophers and Sufis is synonymous with Hermes Trismegistus, a Hellenist fusion of Hermes with the Egyptian god Thoth. Much of the *Corpus Hermeticum* was translated into Arabic: *Kitab damānūs* (*Poimandres*), *Kitāb asrār*, and many others. "Moses Maimonides... in a letter to Samuel ibn Tibbon, called it (Hermeticism) an 'ancient philosophy' that interferes with Aristotle's more rigorous and intellectually satisfying system of thought."

al-Idrīsī, Abū 'Abd Allāh Muḥammad (*492-576*/1099-1180). A physician born in Ceuta, and educated at Cordova, who established himself at the Arabized court of Roger II of Sicily. He is famous for his books on medicinal plants (*al-Kitāb al-jāmi' li-ṣifāt ashtāt an-nabatāt*), and geography (*Kitāb al-mamālik wa-l-masālik*).

For King Roger he wrote *al-Kitāb ar-Rūjarī* (the "Book of Roger"), a treatise on geography which became the basis of European knowledge of the subject at the time.

al-'Īd aṣ-Ṣaghīr, *see* 'ĪD al-FIṬR.

Ifāḍah (lit. "overflow", "flooding", "unfurling"). Applied to the *ḥajj*, it is a special term for the rush of pilgrims from 'Arafāt to Muzdalifah at the end of the *wuqūf* ("standing") on the Day of 'Arafāt during the pilgrimage. *See* PILGRIMAGE.

Ifrad, *see* IḤRĀM.

Ifrīqīya (from the Roman name: Africa). The Arab name in the Middle Ages for the region which today comprises Tunisia.

'Ifrīt, *see* JINN.

Iḥrām (lit. "consecration"). 1. The state entered into in order to perform the pilgrimage (either *ḥajj* or *'umrah*) and the name of the costume that the pilgrim wears.

2. The consecrated state required for the performance of canonical prayer (*ṣalāh*), is also called *iḥrām*. It is preceded by the purification conferred by the greater ablution (*ghusl*), and by performing the lesser ablution (*wuḍū'*). This *iḥrām* begins with the pronunciation of the words *Allāhu akbar*, that is, the *takbīr* which opens the prayer (*ṣalāh*), and ends with *as-salāmu alaykum*, the salutation that closes the prayer. *See* GHUSL; WUḌŪ'; PRAYER; ṢALĀH; TAKBĪR.

To enter into the *iḥrām* of pilgrimage, the pilgrim performs the greater ablution (*ghusl*), makes the intention (*niyyah*), indicating what kind of pilgrimage he will perform (*ifrād*, *tamattu'*, or *qirān*, *see below*), and pronounces the *ta'awwudh* and the *basmalah*.

Then the pilgrim dons the costume of *iḥrām*. (Only men put on the costume of the *iḥrām*; women enter into the consecration of *iḥrām* but do not wear special clothing; their heads are covered to conceal the hair, and the body is covered to the wrist and to the ankle; veils are not worn, but the headcovering is close to the face). The *iḥrām* garb consists of two large pieces of cloth that must be unstitched and seamless. With the legs apart to ensure that there is enough slack for walking, he wraps the lower cloth (*izār*) around the waist, tucking it in place to hold it firm, or securing it with a belt or some kind of fastening. (The belt and all worn accoutrements must not be sewn; although originally the wearing of metal was forbidden, many modern pilgrims add a safety pin or two to secure the *izār* — an innocuous innovation in an age when most pilgrims wear vinyl money belts for documents, plastic sandals, and a wrist watch).

The pilgrim drapes the upper cloth (*ridā'*), over the left shoulder, and knots it on the right side near the waist. The right shoulder is left bare, but during prayer it should be covered with the *ridā'*, although in practice this last point is often ignored. The person entering into iḥrām performs a two *raka'āt* prayer, and recites the *talbiyyah*: "*Labbayka-Llāhumma labbayk*" ("At Thy service, God! at Thy service"). From this point on the *talbiyyah* becomes the recurring invocation of the state of *iḥrām* (*see* TALBIYYAH). No other clothing is worn, but during cold weather it is permissible to cover oneself with a blanket for warmth.

Women enter into *iḥrām*, but do not put on special clothing nor do they cover their faces. The ritual ability to perform pilgrimage is not affected by menstruation, nor is it prohibited for a menstruating woman to enter the Grand Mosque of Mecca (*al-Masjid al-Harām*).

Once the state of *iḥrām* is assumed one may not make sexual contact, cut the hair, pare the nails, use perfume, cut a green tree or kill an animal, with the exception of noxious insects, rodents or venomous animals such as snakes or scorpions.

Nothing must be worn which is stitched. As special sandals are not made any longer (it is permissible to walk barefoot), most people today resort in practice to plastic sandals; this is unfortunate since the purpose of the *iḥrām* costume is to re-inforce the awareness of a state of primordial simplicity and purity. If clothes may not be sewn then, logically, unnatural materials like plastic should not be used either, for they are antithetical to the timelessness of the rituals. In practice pilgrims wear belts with pouches, fastened with rivets rather than sewn, or carry a shoulder bag (also unsewn) to hold their documents. The state of *iḥrām* is brought to an end by shaving the head, or much more commonly by cutting off a small, symbolic, lock of hair.

Iḥrām must be entered into at the latest before entering the perimeter of the *ḥaram* extending round the city of Mecca. There are places, today generally marked by a mosque, called *mīqāt* (pl. *mawāqīt*) which are situated on access routes to Mecca where it is traditional to enter into *iḥrām*. But *iḥrām* can also be put on at the point of departure from one's home or homeland or again, as is very usual nowadays, at the point of entry to the Kingdom of Saudi Arabia, namely, Jeddah. Everything required can be purchased there without difficulty. One should not enter into *iḥrām* for the *ḥajj* before 1st Shawwal, nor prolong *iḥrām* after the *ḥajj* is finished. In any case, it is not possible to assume *iḥrām* for the *ḥajj* after the dawn of the 10th Dhū-l-Ḥijjah. Once one has entered the consecrated state, whether for the *ḥajj* or the *'umrah*, it is obligatory to fulfill the entire rites unless, for reasons of overriding importance, one is prevented from doing so.

From the time that *iḥrām* is put on, until the end of the *'umrah*, or until the standing on 'Arafāt in the case of the *ḥajj*, the words of the *talbiyyah*, — the response of attentiveness to God's command spoken by Abraham — are constantly on the pilgrim's lips.

The intention of entering into *iḥrām* may be made for the *'umrah* alone. As for the *ḥajj*, which is always performed in combination with the rituals of the *'umrah*, there are three possibilities, one of which should be specified in the niyyah:

A) *Ifrad*. The pilgrim puts on the *iḥrām* with the intention of fulfilling the *ḥajj* alone on, or before, arriving at a *mīqāt*.

With the completion of the *ḥajj*, this form of *iḥrām* comes to an end. The pilgrim then assumes a fresh, second state of *iḥrām* at one of the points situated on the periphery of the Sacred Area (*ḥaram*), resorted to by the residents of Mecca when they need to change into *iḥrām*. These are the mosques of *Tanā'īm*, *'Ā'ishah*, or *Ju'āranah*. Then the pilgrim performs the *'umrah*. The *iḥrām* of this kind of pilgrimage, performed as two separate acts, is called a *mufrid bi-l-ḥajj* while on the *ḥajj*, and *mufrid bi-l-'umrah* while performing the *'umrah*. This is also the technical term for the pilgrim.

B) *Tamattu'*. *Iḥrām* is put on when, or before, one arrives at a *mīqāt* intending to perform the *'umrah*. On completion of the rites, the state of *iḥrām* is foregone until the 8th Dhū-l-Ḥijjah, when the garb of *iḥrām* is donned once more in Mecca — without going to the periphery of the sacred zone — and the *ḥajj* is performed. The pilgrim is called a *mutamatti'*.

C) *Qirān*. The *iḥrām* is worn with the intention of performing the *ḥajj* and the *'umrah* together, and it is not put off until both are accomplished. The pilgrim performs the *'umrah* first, with only one *sa'y* to cover both *'umrah* and *ḥajj*. It is possible to change one's intention to the condition of *tamattu'* provided this is done before the *ṭawāf al-qudūm*, or the first circumambulation around the Ka'bah. The pilgrim is then called a *muqrin*. *See* GHUSL; ḤAJJ; PILGRIMAGE; TALBIYYAH; 'UMRAH.

Iḥsān (lit. "virtue", "excellence", "making beautiful"). The third element in the canonical definition of Islam as: belief (*īmān*), practice (*islām*), and virtue (*iḥsān*). *Iḥsān* is explained by the Ḥadīth: "worship God as if you saw Him, because if you do not see Him, nevertheless He sees you."

Iḥsān also refers to excellence in what we do. The Prophet said: "Allāh has prescribed *iḥsān* for everything; hence if you kill, do it well; and if you slaughter, do it well; and let each one of you sharpen his knife and let his victim die at once." *See* ĪMĀN; ISLĀM.

Ijāzah. A licence or certificate. It refers to any kind of diploma, but an *ijāzat at-tabarruk* is a written testimony from a Shaykh describing what studies a disciple has undertaken and affirming his affiliation with a *ṭarīqah*.

Ijmā' (lit. "assembly"). One of the *uṣūl al-fiqh*, or principles of Islamic law (*sharī'ah*). Its basis is the Ḥadīth: "my community shall never be in agreement in error." *Ijmā'* is a consensus, expressed or tacit, on a question of law. Along with the Koran, Ḥadīth, and Sunnah, it is a basis which legitimizes law.

Ijmā' is above all the consensus of the religious authorities (*'ulamā'*); but popular consensus can well lead the way to this. A perfect *ijmā'* is always possible, but is difficult to achieve because of the divergence of religious views and the lack of an authority recognized by all parties. Thus *ijmā'* does not mean that there are no dissenting views, but that agreement exists among a greater or lesser majority.

Two notable dogmas established by *ijmā'*, neither of which are found in the Koran or the Sunnah, are the veneration of Saints (which is strenuously opposed by the Wahhābīs, who accept only the *ijmā'* of the Medinah community of the Prophet's time) and the "sinlessness of the Prophets", a notion which began among the Shī'ites. *Ijmā'* corresponds to the principle *vox populi, vox dei* ("the voice of the people is the voice of God"). *See* SHARĪ'AH; UṢŪL al-FIQH.

Ijtihād (lit. "effort"). The name comes from a Ḥadīth in which the Prophet asked one of his delegates, Mu'āz, by what criteria he would administer the regions assigned to his control. "The Koran" the man replied:

"And then what?" the Prophet asked.
"The Sunnah" [or example of the Prophet].
"And then what?"
"Then I will make a personal effort [*ijtihād*] and act according to that."
And this the Prophet approved.

Ijtihād is applied to those questions which are not covered by the Koran or Sunnah, that is, by established precedent (*taqlīd*), nor by direct analogy (*qiyās*) from known laws. Those equipped with the authority to make such original judgements are called *Mujtahidūn* and in the Sunnī world the first rank of *Mujtahidūn* (after the four Patriarchal Caliphs) are the founders of the four Schools of Law, or *madhāhib* (sing. *madhhab*). Within diminishing domains of competence there are other ranks of *Mujtahidūn*. Although the possibility of a *Mujtahid* arising today is accepted in theory, the preliminary qualifications expected of him would be tantamount to perfect knowledge of all the laws expounded before him; this would surely be an insurmountable obstacle across his path. Therefore it is said that "the door of *ijtihād* is closed" as of some nine hundred years, and since then the tendency of jurisprudence (*fiqh*) has been to produce only commentaries upon commentaries and marginalia.

Nevertheless, it is also clear that *ijtihād* is always necessary and inevitable because of the need to act in situations which are new or unique, or because information is lacking or competent authorities not present. As long as an individual is responsible for himself until the Day of Judgement, every believer finds himself, at one time or another, in the position of Mu'āz, and has to fall back upon the *ijtihād* of personal decision. Within the Sunnī world, the decisions of Judges in certain domains over the years represent small increments of *ijtihād* at the levels of the Schools of Law.

In the *Uṣūlī* Shī'ite world, but not for the minority *Akhbārī* group, the situation is entirely different. *Ijtihād* is recognized as an ever present necessity and is the prerogative of the higher religious authorities. Ultimately, of course, *ijtihād* is the function of the Imām, but in his absence it is delegated to the senior authorities. Their status derives precisely from the fact that they are *Mujtahidūn*, recognized as competent to make original decisions. Moreover, every Shī'ite Muslim is expected to be under the advice and direction of a *Mujtahid*. It should be borne in mind that what Shī'ites consider *ijtihād* would not always be so considered by Sunnīs. A Shī'ite *Mujtahid* is, in fact, obliged to go through the process of *ijtihād* even when answering a question exactly analogous to one he may have answered in the past. Each act of *ijtihād* is considered unique and related to no more than the question at hand. A major decision in recent times which necessitated *ijtihād* on the part of Shī'ites — but not Sunnīs — was whether or not circumambulation of the Ka'bah was valid on the recently built second level in the Grand Mosque of Mecca. (The Shī'ite *Mujtahidūn* decided that it was.) The *ijtihād* of a particular Shī'ite *Mujtahidūn* is binding only upon his own adherents. *See* AKHBĀRĪS; SHARĪ'AH; UṢŪL al-FIQH; UṢŪLĪS.

Ikhlāṣ (lit. "sincerity", "purity"). That sincerity which is surrender to God, "with all one's heart, and all one's mind, and all one's soul". In Islam this is the affirmation of the Divine Unity. This is accomplished virtually by the first *shahādah*, "seeing" that "there is no god but God".

The degree to which this is understood varies, of course, with human capacity. The realization of the *shahādah* is the purpose of the spiritual life. The first enunciation of the *shahādah* virtually achieves the removal of *shirk* — the sin of "associating unreality with Reality"— in the soul. But as long as the consciousness perceives objects as independent of God, the surrender of the soul is not complete; it has not attained complete "sincerity". "There is no sin compared with the sin of your existence", said the woman saint Rābi'ah al-'Adawiyyah.

Because the eradication of *shirk* within the soul is a life-long work, the most important Sūrah of the Koran, and after the *Fātiḥah*, the most repeated, is the 112th, the *Surat al-Ikhlāṣ*. This, the "Verse of Sincerity" proclaims the unity, or absoluteness, of the Divine Essence, indicated by the word *Hua* ("He"), which is the Name of the Essence. This is amplified and deepened by the further declaration of the metaphysical truth that the Absolute cannot be the result or issue of anything other than Itself, nor, as Essence, act upon something outside of Itself:

Qul Huwa-Llāhu Aḥad;
Allāhu-ṣ-Ṣamad;
lam yalid wa lam yūlad
wa lam yakun lahū kufuwan aḥad.

Say, He, God, is One.
God the Everlasting.
He never begot, nor was begotten,
nor is there an equal to Him.

See ALLĀH; FIVE DIVINE PRESENCES; SHAHĀDAH; SHIRK.

Ikhtilāf al-fiqh (lit. "the divergences of canon law"). The Sunnī world accepts unequivocally the idea that the divergences between schools of canon law and theologians are providential and a "mercy". The concept of *ikhtilāf* is enshrined as the seventh article in *al-Fiqh al-Akbar* of Abū Ḥanīfah. Assuredly, the notion has forestalled greater rigidity, opened the door to some suppleness in interpretation and practice, and prevented conflict, as far as possible.

Ikhwan. The name of the Beduin followers of the Saudi King 'Abd al-'Azīz. *See* WAHHĀBĪS.

al-Ikhwān al-Muslimūn, *see* MUSLIM BROTHERHOOD.

Ikhwān aṣ-Ṣafā', *see* BROTHERHOOD of PURITY.

Ilāhīs. Turkish religious chants used by Sufis. *See* QAWWALI.

Ilḥād (lit. "deviation"). Heresy. Heretics are called *malāḥidah*. The word "religion" has been interpreted as signifying the means of binding oneself to God, which cannot be done if the apprehension of God is false or incorrect. (Thomas Aquinas also said that a "false idea of the universe will lead to a false idea of God"). There is a margin to belief and doctrine which may be broad or narrow, according to whether it touches upon the peripheral or the essential. If the deviation from a true apprehension ("right belief"; Greek: *orthodoxia*) is broad enough, the practice of religion becomes inoperative; it does not perform the goal of binding man to God. Orthodoxy is of two kinds: orthodoxy within a particular religion, and orthodoxy in the relationship of religions to God Himself.

If, to use an extreme example, a religion were based upon the cognition of space through practices built around three-sided objects, the introduction of objects of four sides would then be heretical; the process of realization through three-sided means would be impeded and perhaps even halted entirely thereby. On the other hand, if the object of realization were simply space as such, a four-sided object would not be heretical in relation to space, but only to the three-sided perspective on "religion". The great revealed religions are, in certain respects, mutually incompatible, but each is nonetheless orthodox in respect of God, Who revealed it.

The mixing of religions, that is to say, syncretism (*talfīq*), and even the mixing of such aspects of religion as are separately orthodox before God, actually produces an inoperative system which not only does not lead to God, but which increases the confusion of the adherent.

Revelations are *ipso facto* orthodox; however, because of the power of the "Divine Imagination", each can shatter the pre-conceptions entertained by believers of other faiths. The orthodox elaboration of Divine revelation to meet the specific circumstances of the ensuing religion depends upon a rigorous, and divinely blessed, examination of the contents of revelation (*ijtihād*), confirmed by the affirmation and consensus of the community at large (*ijmā'*). These functions were, in Christianity, carried out by the patriarchs and councils; in Islam they were performed by the founders of the Schools of Law in cooperation with the great theologians and with the grateful recognition of the *ummah* ("community"). These inspired efforts, together with the corpus of confirmed practices, customs, and teachings, constitute Tradition. *See* SUNNAH.

Ilhām. Inspiration or intuition, in principle accessible to all, as opposed to waḥy ("revelation"), and *tanzīl* ("sending down") which is the inspiration of the Word of God into the nature of a prophet. *See* REVELATION.

Il-Khanids. A Mongol dynasty which ruled Persia (*654-754*/1256-1353). It was founded by Hūlāgū Khān, brother of Kubilai, and descendant of Jenghiz Khān. Hūlāgū sacked Baghdad in *656*/1258 putting the 'Abbāsid Caliph al-Musta'sim to death. The Mongols were stopped in their westward advance by the Mamlūks at the Battle of 'Ayn Jalūt ("the Well of Goliath") in Syria in *658*/1260.

The Il-Khanids ruled in Persia in the name of the Great Khān of Mongolia and China, but when Kubilai moved his capital to Khanbalig, and especially after his death in *693*/1294, their rule became, in practice, independent. Maḥmūd Ghazan (d. *703*/1304), who instructed Rashīd ad-Dīn aṭ-Ṭabīb (d. *717*/1317) to write his universal history, and Uljaytu (Muḥammad Khudabanda; d. *717*/1317) were converted to Islam. Shī'ism at this time was making important advances in Persia; the Shī'ites, who had in fact supported the Mongol invasions against the 'Abbāsids, made strenuous efforts to turn the Il-Khanids to Shī'ite Islam.

Under Maḥmūd Ghazan, and the able Vizier Rashīd ad-Dīn, there was agricultural and fiscal reform, the establishment and revision of tax registers, and an energetic program of building which included caravanserais, bridges, and whole towns. The Il-Khanid capital was Tabrīz, which became a center of East-West trade. However, within a hundred years of the Mongol conquest, their domains in Persia disintegrated into small kingdoms, ruled by dynasties such as the Muzaffirids and the Jalayrids; and this state of affairs persisted until the rise of Timūr. *See* HŪLĀGŪ; MONGOLS; RASHĪD ad-DĪN aṭ-ṬABĪB; TIMŪRIDS.

"Illiterate Prophet", *see* UMMĪ.

'Ilm (lit. "science", "knowledge"). There is a Ḥadīth which says: "seek science [*'ilm*], even unto China." In the sense of *'ilm* as "revealed knowledge", the Koran itself had provided the essentials to metaphysical knowledge and to an understanding of the relationship between man and God. A repeated theme of the Koran is that revealed knowledge alone avails man in relation to God, and that speculative thought (*aẓ-ẓann*) is invalid. "They engage only in speculation, and speculation is of no avail with the Real" (53:28). As regards *'ilm* in the meaning of "science", the Arabs at the time of the revelation were not well endowed with it. In the wars of the conquest one desert Arab warrior demanded a ransom of one thousand dinars for a very important hostage. When asked by others why he had demanded so little, the Beduin said "I didn't know there was a number higher than a thousand."

At the height of the 'Abbāsid dynasty in Baghdad, Islamic civilization acquired great sophistication by absorbing some of the intellectual heritage of other peoples, including that of India and China. Because of the dual implication of the word *'ilm* in Arabic, some minds have constantly confused principial, or metaphysical, knowledge with empirical knowledge. Thus it is frequently claimed nowadays that Western scientific knowledge somehow originated in the Islamic revelation, the *'ilm* of modern science being perceived as deriving from the *'ilm* of the Koran. This is to ignore the role of peoples such as the Greeks in the development of modern thought, and to fail to see that words change their meanings.

A special usage of the word *'ilm* in Shī'ism refers to the esoteric knowledge possessed only by the Imām. A very special use of the word *'ilm* was the names of the leaders of the Kaysāniyyah/Mukhtāriyyah Kufite revolutionary group and the political/religious doctrine required to make use of this information. The was the *'ilm* which Abū Hāshim passed on to the 'Abbāsids and which became their key to power. (*See* MUḤAMMAD ibn al-ḤANAFIYYAH.)

The Prophet said: "One of the signs of the Hour is that knowledge [*'ilm*] will be taken away and ignorance reign supreme."

'Ilm al-Ḥurūf (lit. "the science of letters"). A mystical procedure which consists of adding up the numerical *'abjad* values of letters in one word and constructing other words with the same numerical value as part of the mystical interpretation of the Koran. This numerical value is then treated as a kind of archetype which may reflect in another word or words a related aspect of it, yet a different one. When used for divination, usually a magic square is also constructed. Those who use this science are known as *ḥurūfīs*. The science is also known as al-jafr.

This is the Arabic counterpart of the Hebrew *Gematria* of the Kabbalists. A well known example of *'ilm al-ḥurūf* is that *Ādām wa Hawwā'* (Adam and Eve) is contained in the Divine Name Allāh because the numerical value of the letters of the Name and the phrase are both 66. Another is *al-ḥikmah al-ilāhiyyah* ("Divine Wisdom") which is the same sum as *taṣawwuf* ("Sufism").

Ibn 'Arabī, the famous exponent of mystical doctrine, tells of the following example of divination by *ḥurūf*: a "man of God", of the city of Fez told him, in a discussion of the prospects of the Almohad armies which had crossed the straits into Spain, that "God promised his Apostle — peace and blessings of God upon him — a victory this year; He revealed it in His book in the words: 'Indeed We have given you a clear victory.' The glad tidings are contained in the words 'clear victory' (*fatḥan mubīnan*)... consider the sum of the numerical value of the letters."

The numerical value of "*fatḥan mubīnan*" comes to *591* which is the Hijrī year of the victory over the Christians by the Almohad Ya'qūb al-Manṣūr at Alarcos in *591*/1194.

The historian al-Juwaynī describes how the Assassins took the name of their principle fortress, Alamūt (which comes from *aluh*, "eagle"), and by analyzing the name into Aluh Amut, found in it by *'abjad* the year in which they captured it. As letters, the analyzed name is ALH AMWT; which is 1+30+5+1+40+6+400 = 483, a Hijrī year which corresponds to 1090. In the book of *Revelation*, the "number of the beast"— 666 — is the *'abjad* or *gematria* sum for Nero Caesar (NRON QSR in Hebrew) and the alternate, 616, is the same without the second N. *See* 'ABJAD.

Ilyās. The Prophet Elijah, from the Greek form of the name, Elias. He is one of the Prophets mentioned in the Koran:

Elias too was one of the Envoys;
when he said to his people, 'Will you
not be godfearing?
Do you call on Baal, and abandon the
Best of creators?
God, your Lord, and the Lord of your
fathers, the ancients?
But they cried him lies; so they will be
among the arraigned,
except for God's sincere servants;
and We left for him among the later folk
'Peace be upon Elias!'
Even so We recompense the good-doers;
he was among Our believing servants.
(37:123-132)

Ilyās is also mentioned in the Koran 6:85.

Ilyasā', *see* ALYASĀ'.

Images. On the basis of Ḥadīth, the making of images is prohibited in Islam; those who make them will, on the Day of Judgement, be told "to breathe life into what they have created" and, failing to do so, will be punished. The degree to which the religious authorities censure images differs, however, according to whether the images are of a living thing — an important distinction is made between depictions of vegetable and animal life — whether they are on a flat surface, or representations which "have a shadow", that is, statues.

In fact, images of plants have been used as decorative motifs on mosques, in addition to abstract motifs (such as circles, jagged lines and spirals, all legacies of architectural traditions going back as far as Sumeria), at least since the Dome of the Rock was built at the end of the *1st*/7th century by Syrian Byzantine craftsman for Umayyad patrons, and doubtless even before. The use of floral designs interwoven with Koranic calligraphy on manuscript or carved into wood or plaster is very common. One of the most famous works of art in the Alhambra is the fountain with stylized *statues* of lions. Turkish and Persian miniatures represent not only secular scenes but the popular illustrations of the Prophet's ascent to heaven, the *Mi'rāj-nāmeh.* The Prophet's face is customarily veiled in these books. The representation of his face is a line which, for many reasons, is clearly an unbroachable limit. (The Shī'ites, however, display pictures of 'Alī, often with the slogan "there is no warrior like 'Alī and no sword like Dhu'l-fiqār.")

Despite initial resistance to the taking of photographs on the popular level, no modern political figure, regardless of how vehemently religious strictness is proclaimed, has foregone the use of photographs. Today it would be hard to find objections to them voiced anywhere in the Muslim world.

What can be said then, with certainty, is that the setting of an image in a place of prayer, would be reproved for drawing the attention away to a form instead of letting it seek the formless — although nowadays one can find religio-political posters even in mosques. It can also be said that the use of realistic paintings or realistic statues such as one finds in Europe or in Muslim cities which have undergone modern European influence, is alien to the spirit of Islam. By contrast, *stylized* representations which do not seek to create an illusion, or a *pretense of reality*, are acceptable, or are at least tolerated, outside of places of prayer.

The prohibition of images would seem on the one hand to be intended to avoid the concretization or "solidification" of forms in the mind. Such a concretization is an obstacle to the emptying of the mind in order to apprehend the supraformal. A further intention is doubtless to prevent the creation of counterfeits of reality — idols — to which the beholder would "lend life" out of his own soul or substance.

To counter the natural tendency of desert peoples to "condense" ideas and their figurative representations into psychological "hardenings" (the Koran speaks of the "hardening" and the "melting" of hearts), Islamic art has, in addition to not using realistic images, cultivated means which actively produce the opposite effect. That is, Islamic art often seeks to dissolve psychic knots by the rhythmic repetition of design motifs, particularly of geometric designs and arabesques, in order to bring the beholder a taste of infinity, and by abstraction, to restore a sense of space as a means of escape from imprisonment within forms.

Imām (lit. "model", "exemplar"). 1. An Imām is the leader of prayer, for a particular occasion or as a regular function. He leads by standing in front of the rows of worshippers; if only two persons are praying, he stands to the left, and slightly in front, of the other. The basis for the dignity is knowledge, particularly of the Koran, age or social leadership. In groups of equals, the function may simply be performed by each in turn. Every mosque has one or more Imāms who lead prayers, in whose absence any suitable male may be Imām. A woman may lead the prayer for female members of her household.

2. A title, perhaps in addition to other titles, of the head of a community or group. The founders of the schools of law (*madhāhīb*, sing. *madhhab*), in particular, are called Imāms, as are the heads of the Khārijite or Ibāḍite communities. Imām is also an honorific, as in Imām al-Ghazali or Imām ash-Shādhilī.

3. Among the Shī'ites the word has the special significance of an intercessor, unique and predestined to the age, who must be recognized and followed in order to be saved. Imām is the title and spiritual function of 'Alī and his descendants through Fāṭimah (although for one group of Shī'ites, who no longer exist, the function belonged to a descendant of 'Alī by another wife). Most Shī'ite groups believe there can only be one Imām at a time, and disagreement about the identity of the Imām and the nature of his function has caused the Shī'ites to split into sects with divergent dogmas.

In general, the Imām, whose function is called the Imāmate, is credited with supernatural knowledge and authority, and with a station of merit which, as it were, is an extension of, and virtually equal with, that of the Prophet. For the Twelve-

Imām Shī'ites, also called "Imāmīs", the Imām is an intermediary between man and God. In addition to his spiritual authority, the Imām has an absolute right to civil authority, and one who prevents the Imām from exercising temporal power is an usurper. The Imām is the summit of sanctity for Twelve-Imām Shī'ites, who hold to the doctrine of the cycle of sanctity" *(dā'irat al-wilāyah)* which follows the closing of the "cycle of prophecy" by Muḥammad, who is the "Seal of the Prophets" (*khatam al-anbiyā'*) for all Muslims. The sects of Shī'ites known as the *Ghulāt*, or extremists, even consider their Imām to be Divine. *See* SHĪ'ISM.

Immanence, *see* TASHBĪH.

Imām al-Ḥaramayn ("the Imām of the two Sanctuaries"). A title for the theologian al-Juwaynī. *See* al-JUWAYNĪ.

Imām, the Hidden, *see* HIDDEN IMĀM.

Imāmī. An appellation of the Shī'ites (the "Imāmīs"), and an adjective describing their doctrine. It is in particular applied to the Twelve-Imām Shī'ites *(ithna'ashariyyah)*. The Imāmīs are those who believe that there is a figure called an Imām, who, being an intermediary between man and God, has supreme spiritual and temporal authority. *See* SHĪ'ISM.

Imāmzādeh. In Iran, a term for a prominent descendant of one of the Imāms, or the tomb of such a descendant. The most important such tomb is in Qumm, that of Fāṭimah al-Ma'sūmah, the sister of the Imām 'Alī ar-Riḍā'. *See* IMĀM; SHĪ'ISM.

Īmān (lit. "faith"). This is faith in itself and a term designating those articles of belief which are part of Islam. *Īmān* is defined as faith in God, His Angels, His books (revelations), His Prophets, and the Day of Judgement. Islam as religion is divided into a ternary of which *Īmān* is one aspect along with *Islām* (in a second sense, as an aspect of the religion, that is, the rites and the law), and *iḥsān*, or virtue. One could say that in Islam it is faith which saves because God is beyond comprehension by the mind; therefore to know Him one must believe; it is faith which brings knowledge of God. Many Muslims think that it is enough to affirm the testimony of faith to be saved. However, most theologians have been quite explicit that some good acts, an objectification of one's faith, are necessary for salvation in addition to faith.

The Prophet said: "Faith [*īmān*] is a confession with the tongue, a verification with the heart, and an act with the members." *See* IḤSĀN; ISLAM.

'Imārah. The name used in North Africa for the Sufi dance, which is a spiritual means, known also as a *ḥaḍrah*, ("Presence", "Remembrance in the Breast") and technically as the *dhikr aṣ-ṣadr*. *See* DHIKR.

'Imrān. The father of the Prophets Moses and Aaron; in Islam also the name of the father of Mary.

God chose Adam and Noah
and the House of Abraham
and the House of 'Imrān
above all beings, the
seed of one another;
God hears, and knows. (Koran 3:30)

Also:

And Mary, 'Imrān's daughter,
who guarded her virginity,
so We breathed into her
of Our Spirit... (Koran 66:14)

Imru'-l-Qays. One of the most famous poets of the *Jāhiliyyah*, the pagan "Age of Ignorance". He is the author of one of the celebrated poems — "odes written in gold" — which were acclaimed at the yearly fair of 'Ukāz and perhaps hung in honor in the Ka'bah, for which reason they were called *mu'allaqāt* ("hung") and collected under that title.

"Here halt and weep, for one long-remembered love, for an old
Camp at the edge of the sands that stretch from the Brakes to Floodhead,
From Clearward to the Heights. The marks are not gone yet,
For all that's blown and blown back over them, northward, southward.
Look at the white-deer's droppings scattered in the old yards
And penfolds of the place, like black pepperseeds.
The two who ride with me rein closer to my side:

What! take thy death of grieving, man? Bear what's to bear!

I tell ye both, I'll be the better for these tears—
Where is the place among these crumbling walls to weep it out?
The same old tale as ever — the same as with that other
Before her — the same again with her at the Whettingstead.
When women rose and stood, the scent of them was sweet
As the dawn breeze through a clove tree.
I suffered so for love, so fast the tears ran down
Over my breast, the sword-belt there was soaked with weeping.
And yet — the happy days..."

Incarnation, *see* ḤULŪL.

Incense, *see* ALOES.

India. Population 759,000,000 of which 11% are Muslims. Muslim expansion into India began with the first Arab conquests in Sindh under Muḥammad ibn Qāsim in *93*/712. Islam was carried deeper by the Ghaznavid invasions, especially under Maḥmūd of Ghaznah (d. *422*/1030), and firmly established in the Punjab and Kashmir. Under the Delhi Sultanate (*602-962*/1206-1555), and under the Moghuls (*932-1274*/1526-1858), Islamic rule in India reached its height. *See* ALIGARH; CHISHTI; DELHI SULTANATE; DEOBAND; KHAN, SIR SAYYID; MOGHULS; QUṬUB-I MINAR; SHĀH WALĪ ALLĀH.

Indifference, *see* GHAFLAH.

Indonesia. The country with the largest Muslim population in the world. There are 169,442,000 Indonesians of which 80-90% are Muslims of the Shāfi'ī school; the rest of the population are Hindu, Buddhist, Dutch Protestant, and Catholic, with some animist religions. The Islamization of Indonesia is not well documented but it is known that the Sufi *ṭurūq* played a very important role in the process as did expansion through peaceful trade. Unlike Islam in the Middle East and India, no military conquest was involved. Today, the various *ṭurūq* remain influential, and various branches of the Shādhiliyyah, Qādiriyyah, Khālwatiyyah, and other *ṭurūq* are widespread. At the beginning of the *11th*/17th century, the Kingdom of Atjeh in the north of Sumatra marked a golden age of Islam in Indonesia, especially in the reign of the Sultan Iskandar Muda. Indonesian Islam is a remarkable blending of many cultural influences. The Indonesians are noted for the fervor with which they undertake the pilgrimage to Mecca. *See* ADAT; ATJEH; MENANGKABAU; MUḤAMMADIYYAH; SLAMETAN; SULŪK.

Infidel, *see* KUFR.

Inheritance (Ar. *mīrāth*, "inheritance", or *farā'iḍ*, "allotments"). The Koran prescribes the distribution of an estate amongst certain relatives and fixes the proportion of the estate allotted to each (4:11-13). Before Islam, inheritance among the Arabs had always passed to the adult male relatives of the deceased in the interests of consolidating wealth among the powerful in order to strengthen the clan. Thus the Prophet, as a posthumous orphan, received no inheritance from his father and was raised as the poor ward of his grandfather.

The Koran decrees a radical redistribution of inheritance rights entitling nine categories of relative who previously had no share in inheritance. Six of these are women, including the wife, daughter, and sisters of the deceased.

Since not all categories or possibilities are expressly legislated for in the Koran, a complex science of inheritance has arisen as a special branch of law to determine priorities when different relatives compete with one another for an estate.

The amount of a willed legacy (following precedents in Roman law) is limited to no more than one third of the estate after all debts are paid, the remainder to be distributed according to the schedules established by the Koran. If a legacy is made in favor of an inheritor who also inherits according to the Koranic schedules, with the result that his inheritance is greater than the share provided by law, the other inheritors must agree to this, otherwise only the schedule can apply. Shī'ite law provides greater latitude for legacies, possibly as an historical reaction to the verdict that Fāṭimah received at the hands of the Caliph Abū Bakr, who denied her the property of Fadak because of a very strict interpretation of the Prophet's words that a Prophet leaves nothing behind him in this world. Also the oasis of Fadak had been used by the

Prophet as a public or state property for the upkeep of the poor. (The case was reviewed by Caliphs in later history and the property was actually given to the 'Alīds several times and revoked, often because of political revolts. It became one of the historical grievances of Shī'ism.)

The distribution according to the schedules of inheritance may be modified, if complications arise, by means of legal decisions for the resolution of conflicting claims. To avoid the distribution of property according to these schedules, the person may give away or distribute his property during his lifetime, without legal limit, restriction, or constraint.

Koranic law among the Sunnīs is practically always superimposed upon the customary law that has traditionally prevailed locally. Thus, traditional inheritors according to the national custom of the people, continue to inherit, *after* those entitled by the Koran, or even, if there are no surviving relatives as defined by the Koran, to replace them altogether.

Among the Shī'ites, Arab customary inheritance is excluded, and descendants are favored over other relatives. This results, with historical implications in support of the Shī'ite point of view, in greater legitimacy being accorded to the claims of the Prophet's descendents through Fāṭimah, than to claims through the descendants of the Prophet's uncle al-'Abbās, who would be favored by Arab customary law. The Shī'ite law of inheritance would thus have favored the legitimacy of the 'Alīd claims over those of the 'Abbāsids.

Inheritors can be divided into two categories: those who *share* with other inheritors, and residuaries who receive if there are no sharers. A person can be both a sharer and a residuary. The sharers participate in proportions of 1/2, 1/4, 1/8, 2/3, 1/3, and 1/6 according to their priority. The shares may be all reduced proportionately, if there are many inheritors, in order to divide the estate between competing inheritors in a particular category. A fundamental rule is that male relatives receive twice as much as female relatives of the same category. (Islamic law assumes that women have a place in a household headed by a male, and encourages this at every turn.) The nearer degrees exclude the more remote. In practice, the Koranic laws of inheritance have been somewhat modified by statute laws in some countries.

Initiation, *see* BAY'AH; IDHN; RIḌWĀN.

Injīl, *see* BIBLE.

Innovation, *see* BID'AH.

al-Insān al-Kāmil (lit. "perfect, or complete, man"; hence "universal man"). A doctrine of Sufism (found also in other traditions, most notably in the figure of Gayomart in Zoroastrianism) described most fully by 'Abd al-Karīm al-Jīlī (d. *820*/1417) in his treatise *al-Insān al-Kāmil*. The basis for this doctrine in Islam is the Ḥadīth, reported by Ibn Ḥanbal, that "God created Adam in His image [*'alā ṣūratih*]", and certain other "Ḥadīth" of the Prophet advanced by mystics such as: "I have a time when only my Lord is great enough to hold me", and "I am an *'Arab* without the *'ayn*, I am Aḥmad without the *mīm*; he who has seen me has seen the Truth (al-Ḥaqq)." *'Ayn* is the name of a letter of the alphabet, but it is also a word with the meanings of "source", "fountain", "eye"; and abstractly it means "origin" or "differentiation". Without the *'ayn*, and the separation it symbolizes, the word *'Arab* becomes *rabb* ("Lord"). The letter *mīm*, in the symbolism of Arabic letters, stands for death. If the *mīm* of mortality is removed from Aḥmad — a name of the Prophet meaning "the most praised"— it becomes *Aḥad* ("One"), a Name of God.

The doctrine of the "perfect man" (*al-insān al-kamīl*), is akin to the hermetic doctrine of the Emerald Tablet: "As above, so below; the universe [*macrocosm*, in Arabic: *al-kawn al-kabīr*] is a big man, man [*microcosm*, in Arabic: *al-kawn as-saghīr*] is a little universe." This doctrine is first found written in Arabic in a text by Jābir ibn Ḥayyān, the alchemist, in the *2nd*/8th century: "Thus the little world is created according to the prototype of the great world. The little world is man when he has realized his original nature, which was made in the image of God."

The Perfect Man or Universal Man is also to be found in the Qabbalah as "Adam Kadmon" (primordial man), and is related to the medieval theory of the "Great Chain of Being". It asserts that there is a hierarchy of existence which includes all that is in creation, and that man is the synthesis of all creation by his nature. Man contains all the manifested possibilities as potentialities within his own being, or more precisely, within the created and uncreated intellect, or *'aql*, itself the projection into the individual of supra-cosmic, ontological Being, or uncreated Intellect. The center of the supra-cosmic Being is also called *ar-Rūḥ* ("Spirit"), among other names. Al-Ghazālī wrote:

> Before the creation, God loved himself in absolute Unity and through love revealed Himself to Himself alone. Then, desiring to behold that love in aloneness, that love without otherness and duality, as an external object, He brought forth from non-manifestation an image of Himself, endowed with His attributes and His Names. The Divine image is Adam.

Many others voiced similar ideas, Ibn 'Arabī among them. The doorway to the state of the *al-insān al-kāmil* is revelation. The means are the revealed doctrine of discrimination between the Real and the unreal, and concentration upon the Real through the perfection of the virtues both human and supernatural. If it be within his destiny, a man can reach the center of his being, and be man essentially and not "accidentally". Here his every act is in accordance with the Divine Will, with which it is in fact identical; he is in perfect activity but "motionless", because he is identified with the First Cause but not with effects. This is the state of "Ancient Man" (*Adam Kadmon*) or "primordial man" who is in harmony with the *fiṭrah* ("cosmic norm"). This the Chinese Tradition calls "true man" (*chen jen*). If it is the Divine will, man can, by virtue of his theomorphic nature, effectively assimilate all the other states of existence, which are like planes, each being a degree of the vertical axis that passes through the center of each state of existence. One of the most common symbols of that "world axis" is the tree, especially the tree of paradise, the "tree of life" in the center of Eden.

When man has realized all the states of being, he contains the whole universe and has effectively returned to the state of Adam as he was before the Fall: his will and knowledge are in no way contradictory to God's, he is the master of the garden, the perfect "slave" (*'abd*) of God, and thus the "perfect man" (*al-insān al-kāmil*).

Al-Jīlī said:

> As a mirror in which a person sees the form of himself and cannot see it without the mirror, such is the relation of God to the Perfect Man, who cannot possibly see his own form but in the mirror of the Name Allāh; and he is also a mirror to God, for God laid upon Himself the necessity that His Names and attributes should not be seen save in the Perfect Man.

A Chinese treatise called *The Three Character Rhymed Classic on the Ka'bah*, by an 18th-century Muslim named Ma Fu-ch'u speaks of the *al-Insān al-kāmil* thus:

> Now Man
> is the Essence of Heaven and earth:
> among the ten thousand transformations
> his is a special creation;
> the quintessence of Heaven
> is Man's heart;
> the glory of earth
> is his body;
> the ten thousand intelligent principles
> are Man's essential Nature.
> Man's descent into the world
> marked a great transformation;
> when the first ancestor,
> whom we call P'an ku [Cosmic and Primordial
> Man, here meaning
> Adam, and also Abraham],
> first entered manifestation,
> he dwelt in a country of the West,
> the land of the Ka'bah...
>
> ... the servitor
> has no person of his own,
> no desires of his own,
> no heart of his own,
> but fearing the command of God
> he cultivates his person assiduously,
> makes his intentions sincere
> and rectifies his heart.
> The ancient name for this
> is Purity and Truth [a Chinese name for Islam]
> to be able to conquer self
> can be called Purity,
> and to return to the Rites determined by Heaven
> can be called Truth;
> neither to conquer self
> nor to return to the Truth
> can only be called hypocrisy [Ar. *nifā-*].
> A man has a body
> and he has also a heart;
> when the body meets objects
> emotion and desire are joined;
> the heart in relation to human nature

is like the spirit of Heaven [Ar. *rūḥ*];
if the promptings of desire prevail
a man rejoins the birds and beasts;
but if reason masters desire
he becomes a True Man.
[*Chinese Chen-jen*; Ar. *al-insān al-kāmil*]
A man who cultivates goodness
must endeavor to be sincere, [Ar. *mukhliṣ*]
to realize himself in the way of the Prophet
and constantly live the Truth...

See also BEING; FIVE DIVINE PRESENCES.

In shā'a-Llāh (lit. "if God wills"). The Koran 18:24-25 says: "And do not say, regarding anything, 'I am going to do that tomorrow,' but only, 'If God will.'" These words are used to express the conditionality and dependence of human will upon God's will, and are used in all references to futurity and possibility in the future. *See* PIOUS EXPRESSIONS.

Inspiration, *see* ILHĀM; REVELATION.

Intellect, *see* AQL; FIVE DIVINE PRESENCES.

Intention (Ar. *niyyah*). A legally necessary step in the performance of all rituals, prayer, pilgrimage, ablution, sacrifice, recitations of the *Yā Laṭīf* prayer, etc. The believer makes the intention out loud or inwardly to perform the ritual in question.

In Islamic law the basis of judging someone's actions is his intention. The Ḥadīth which defines it is: *innamā 'l-a'māla bi-n-niyyah, wa innamā li-kulli imri'in ma nawā...* "Actions are according to their intentions, and to each man there pertains that which he intended..."

This Ḥadīth opens the canonical collections of Muslim and Bukhārī.

Interest, *see* ISLAMIC BANKING; RIBA.

Intifada (Ar. lit. "shaking off"). The Palestinian Arab uprising which began in December of 1987 after twenty years of Israeli occupation of the West Bank and Gaza. The occupation after the 1967 war led to various forms of oppression of Palestinians: collective punishment, demolition of Arab homes, confiscation of land and the allocation of much of the West Bank to Israeli settlers, imprisonment without trial, torture of prisoners, deportation of Palestinians, etc. The Intifada was characterized by civil unrest, political agitation, and attacks by Palestinian youths and children throwing stones at Israeli soldiers. It led to the growth of increasingly more militant organizations among the Palestinians such as HAMAS and numerous violent incidents. The Intifada came to an end with the Oslo accords and the beginnings of Palestinian autonomy, after several thousand Palestinians and scores of Israelis were killed. The peace process itself broke down in 1997 with the rise of Jewish fundamentalists and hardliners after the assassination of Yitzhak Rabin, and the uprising resumed in the form of suicide bombings inside Israel.

Intoxicants, *see* WINE.

Invocation, *see* DHIKR.

Iqbal, Sir Muḥammad *1290-1357*/1873-1938). Indian philosopher, poet, and politician. Sir Muḥammad studied at Government College, Lahore, at Cambridge University, and the University of Munich. He practiced law and was a president of the Muslim League. He wrote poetry in Urdu which was often Monistic or Gnostic and rather reminiscent of the German "Cherubinischer Wandersmann":

You created light
I made the lamp
You created clay
I made the cup
You created the forest, the mountain, and the desert,
I made the walk, the garden, the orchard.

He is the author of many works on religious reform and self-advancement. He was strongly affected by nineteenth century secular European humanism, writing, for example: "the Qur'anic legend of the Fall has nothing to do with the first appearance of man on this planet."

In his *Reconstruction of Religious Thought In Islam*, Iqbal tried to combine the ideas of modern Western philosophers such as Bergson and Nietzsche with the Koran.

Iqṭa' (lit. "allotment", "parcel"). The granting of fiefs to their Turkish army chiefs by the Buwayhids, Seljūqs, and Ayyubids, Mamluks, and Il-Khans. The revenue from the fiefs provided income for the support of such chiefs, and it was an alternative to direct taxation by the state. In the case of 'Irāq, where agriculture depended upon the maintenance of a complex system of irrigation, the effect of the *iqṭa'* system was harmful in the extreme, for the fief holders sought to extract as much income as they could without returning adequate investment for the maintenance of irrigation. *See* MANṢAB.

Irade (from Ar. *īrādah*, "will"). The term describing a decree issued by the Ottoman Sultan.

Iran. Islamic Republic. Est. population: 43,000,000 of whom 98% are Muslim. Of the Muslims 8% are Sunni and 92% are Twelve-Imām Shī'ites (of the Uṣūlī school; there are some Akhbaris in Khuzistan). Armenian and Assyrian/Chaldean Christians are estimated to be 1% of the population. A small number of Jews remains in Iran. There are also 30,000 Zoroastrians, 50,000 Bahā'īs, and small numbers of 'Alī Ilāhīs, Shaykhis, Bābīs, and Ismā'īlīs. Ethnic Persians are the majority (63%), but 26% of the population speak Turkic languages (Azeris, Baluchis, Qashqai, Turkomans, and others). There are over two million Kurds in Iran, and there is an Arab minority in Khuzistan (called Arabistan by the 'Irāqis). *See* AFSHĀRIDS; AKHBĀRĪS; 'ALĪ ILĀHĪS; AQ QOYUNLU; AYATOLLAH; BĀBĪS; BAHĀ'ĪS; BAKHTĪAR; BIHBAHĀNĪ; DIHQĀNS; ILKHANIDS; IMĀMZĀDEH; 'IRFĀN; ISHRĀQĪ; KHOMEINI; LUR; MAZDAK; MANICHEANS; MULLĀ SADRA; NI'MATU'LLĀH; NURBAKSH; PAHLAVĪ; QĀJĀRS; QANĀTS; QARA QOYUNLU; QĪZĪL BASH; QUMM; RAWDA KHANI; ṢAFFĀRIDS; SAMANIDS; ṢAFAVIDS; SHAYKHIS; SHĪ'-ISM; ṬĀHIRIDS; TAJIKS; UṢŪLĪS.

'Irāq. Republic of Iraq. Population 21,422,292 of whom 95% are Muslim and 4% are Christian. Approximately 55% of the Muslims are Twelve-Imām Shī'ites (and many of these are Persians or Arabs of Persian descent). In southern 'Irāq, where Shī'ites are in the majority, the legal school of the Twelve-Imām Shī'ites is Akhbārī, not Uṣūlī, as in Iran. This Akhbārī branch is centered in Baṣrah. It is important to bear in mind that this school was driven out of Iran by the Uṣūlīs in the 18th century, whereas the northern 'Irāqi Twelve-Imām Shī'ites are largely of the Uṣūlī school, as are the Iranians. 'Irāq is the home of Najaf and Kerbala which are very important Shī'ite shrines, much visited by Iranians. Najaf is the seat of an Ayatollah who commands also disciples in Iran. There are also Shī'ite shrines in Baghdad which are important to Iranians.

The Sunnis, found in eastern and central 'Irāq, are mostly of the Ḥanafī rite. Northern 'Irāq is the home of its Kurdish population. Although the Kurds are often considered Sunni, and may claim to be so towards outsiders, many belong to heteroclite sects of which the Yazīdīs are the most representative. Although Yazīdīs in some estimates comprise only 0.31% of the population, the actual numbers must be considerably higher. There were about 20,000 Mandaeans in the south on the border with Iran, who are not Muslim at all, and are now threatened with extinction because of the war. Many more Mandaeans are found in Iran.

An estimated 77.8% of the population are Arabs; 17.9% are Kurds; 1.2% are Persian (but many of those considered to be Arab are also of Persian descent). 1.2% of the population are Turkmen. Assyrian Christians make up 0.5% of the population; Jacobite Christians make up 0.26%; Chaldeans and Jacobite Uniates (Churches in communion with Rome) are 2.21%. *See* AKHBĀRĪS; 'ABBĀSIDS; BAGHDAD; BIHBAHĀNĪ; MANDAEANS; NESTORIANS; QARMAṬĪS; SHĪ'ISM; YAZĪDĪS; UṢŪLĪS; ZANJ.

'Irfān. Gnosis or esoteric knowledge. The word is used mostly in Shī'ism, and actually corresponds to the general ideas of Sufism removed from the operative context of disciple and master (*ṭarīqah*), and formal transmission through an initiatic chain (*silsilah*).

The Shī'ite authorities have always been rather jealous of Sufism because it tends to displace the role of the Imām. Thus Mullās such as Bihbahānī and Majlisī wrote diatribes against it, seeing in it a dangerous competitor. Hence the schools of *'irfān* and *ishrāq* are a philosophical Sufism, removed from its operative framework and its method, which is the *dhikr*, since they do not engage the individual totally they can all the more easily be accommodated to Shī'ism. Sufi *ṭuruq* do exist in Persia, but they are a relatively small number, and from Ṣafavid times they were forced to subordinate themselves to the exoteric and doctrinal exigencies of Shī'ism. Before he was exiled from Iran in 1963, Ayatollah Khomeini was an exponent of 'irfān in the city of Qumm. *See* NI'MATU'LLĀH.

Irtidād, *see* APOSTASY.

'Īsā, *see* JESUS.

'Īsāwa, *see* AISSAWA.

Iṣfahān. City in Iran, capital under the Ṣafavid dynasty. It is in the center of the country and sits on the river Zayndeh Rūd (formerly Zindeh Rūd) "the life-giving" river. Shah Abbās I (1587-1629) built palaces and mosques, the Hasht Behesht ("eight paradises" palace) and the Masjid-i Shāh (today Masjid-i Emam), a famous mosque on the plaza or maydān, which also fronts the Shaykh Lutf Allāh Mosque. In the time of Shāh Abbās the population of the city was 600,000 and the saying appeared *Iṣfahān nesf-é jahān*, "Iṣhafān is half the world."

A city has been on the site for five thousand years from the time of a legendary king of the Iranians, Jam, whose fortress there was mentioned in Zoroastrian writings. Iṣfahān was also the site of an Achaemenid capital and was called Anshan and Gabae. It is also associated with the legendary blacksmith Kavi, who chained Azhi Dahhaka in Mount Demavend. At the time of the Arab invasion in 640 it was called Jaī. The name Iṣfahān is derived from *Aspadana*, "army camp". The present day city was the result of a consolidation of several towns, Sheheristan and the Jewish town of Yehudieh, which was made by the Buyid ruler Rukn ad-Dīn in the 10th century. Iṣfahān was the capital of the Seljūqs. The city was not destroyed by the Mongols but Timūr made a mountain of skulls there to warn others not to resist him.

Īshān (lit. Persian, "they"). A name for Sufi spiritual masters used in some areas of Central Asia. Elsewhere the term *Pir* is used, and amongst Arabs, Shaykh. In the 1920s a particularly secret order arose out of the Yasaviyyah in southern Kyrgyzstan called the "Hairy Ishans" (Chachtuu Eshander or, in Russian, Volosatye Ishany) who were more markedly opposed to Soviet rule than the other Sufi orders. They were repressed in the 1930s and 1950s but still exist. *See* SHAYKH.

Ishmael, *See* ISMĀ'ĪL.

Ishrāqī (lit. "illuminationist"). A school of philosophy of characteristically Iranian inspiration founded by Shihāb ad-Dīn Suhrawardī (*549-587*/1154-1191), which combined elements of Sufism and Shī'ism with Hellenistic and Orphic philosophy, Hermetics, and Zoroastrian Angelology. The Ishrāqī school, more of a mystical intellectualism than a mysticism, insisted upon an aspect of "wisdom" in philosophy or suprarational realization. It exerted an important influence in Iran up to the 18th century.

Jurjāni in his *T'arifāt* calls the Ishrāqis "philosophers whose master was Plato" while al-Qashanī called them "followers of Seth". As Suhrawardi lived in northern Mesopotamia he must have had contact with the religion of Ḥarrān. He said that in the cosmos were four cardinal points, one of which was "pure light" and the other "pure darkness". At the other two points "darkness was mixed with some light" (as if darkness were itself something positive that exists independently of light!) and where "light was mixed with some darkness". From this, it is evident that Ishrāq is a form of dualism or Manicheism.

The Ishraqi philosophy was refined by Mīr Dāmād and Mullā Ṣadra in Iṣfahān in the *11th*/17th century; it also exerted a strong influence on the Shaykhi sect in Iran. Intellectually it is very similar to Western Existentialism.

The name *'ishraq*, which implies "sudden illumination" is a clue to the hold with which dualist doctrines seize their adherents. When the idea springs up in the mind that there are two forces of light and darkness, good and evil struggling in the world, the balance between conscious and unconscious is so altered that there is a powerful conviction, often inescapable because of its overwhelming subjectivity, that one has realized the fundamental nature of reality, that one has been truly "illuminated" and thereby exalted. For this reason people often remain steadfastly fixed in cults even after their absurdities have become apparent or have been demonstrated to them. The experience of such "illumination" may be found in many sects, Christian, Buddhist, Jehovah's Witnesses etc., and was known as "indoctrination" under the Communists. *See* 'IRFĀN; MULLĀ ṢADRA; SUHRAWARDI.

Islam (lit. "surrender", "reconciliation", from the word *salām*, "peace" or "salvation"). The religion revealed to the Prophet Muḥammad between AD 610 and 632 It is the last of all the Divine revelations before the end of the world. The name of the religion was instituted by the Koran (5:5) during the farewell pilgrimage: "Today I have perfected your religion for you, and I have completed My blessing upon you, and I have approved *Islam* for your religion."

Besides designating the religion, the word has a further technical meaning in the triad *islām, īmān, iḥsān*, the three fundamental aspects of the religion, of which *islām* is here the equivalent of *'ibādah*, that is, acts of worship, the Five Pillars, and the *sharī'ah*. (*See* FIVE PILLARS; ĪMĀN; IḤSĀN.)

Islam is the last of the universal religions and today numbers some 800 million followers. While some countries which are the original home of Islam are almost 100% Muslim, today every country has at least a small Muslim minority. In recent years it has shown itself to be not only the most widespread religion in the world, but also the most dynamic, attracting converts at a faster rate than at any time in the last few centuries.

Islam is the third major Semitic religion and has an intimate relationship with the other two; it accepts all the Prophets of Judaism as Prophets of Islam; moreover it also accepts Jesus, not as the Divine manifestation he is to Christians, but as a Prophet, albeit of an extraordinary kind since in Islam also, he does not have a human father but is rather the "Spirit of God" cast into Mary. Judaism takes God and "nationalizes" Him as the God of a "peculiar" people; Christianity universalizes Him making Him the God of the Gentile as well as of the Jew through the person of the Divine Jesus; Islam, as the third revelation, returns to the unity of the point of departure of the first Semitic revelations before conceptions of tribe and nation had emerged and before the apotheoses of men-gods. Islam restores the primordial relationship between creature and Creator as it existed in the Garden of Eden. In Islam, as in Eden, man in his essence is perfect and unfallen; in his Intellect he is capable of perceiving and recognizing God in the Unseen. God in Islam is known under the aspect of eternity, without commitments in history, neither "repenting" nor sending down "a son", always returning to His Absoluteness, and seen from the abstractness of metaphysics rather than as a participant in a religious drama shared with his creation.

Al-Jīlī said:

> All other revelations are only a reflection of the sky of this supreme revelation, or a drop of its ocean; while being real, they are nonetheless annihilated under the power of this essential revelation, which is exclusively of God by virtue of His knowledge of Himself, whereas the other revelations are of God by virtue of the knowledge of other persons.

See FIVE PILLARS; SHAHĀDAH.

Islamic Banking. The Koran prohibits usury, or interest on loans (*ribā'*). This has been interpreted as meaning that money can be used as a means of exchange, but cannot be treated as a commodity. Since money *qua* commodity is inextricably bound up with modern economics, the general practice in modern times has been to accept the requirements of economic necessity, and disregard the question of interest. Banks in most Muslim countries have long given interest on deposits and taken interest on loans. This is not without legal basis: it is an accepted principle among the schools of law that "Necessity makes prohibited things permissible."

Already in early Islam, the question of interest posed problems because it was implied in certain commonplace economic exchanges. The custom of bartering unripe dates on the tree for ripened dates was a type of such a transaction because it involved the selling of an article today, against expectations of its future price. A pure futures market in the army camp of Kūfah arose out of a speculative buying and selling of army pay tenders that were redeemable for grain, in anticipation of the future cost of the commodity. The reaction of the lawyers to this futures market was that it was usurious, and tenders could not be sold without the owner taking receipt of the grain. In the case of the dates however, Mālik ibn Anas made an exception on the basis of social necessity and established practice.

In the past, various legal devices were used to circumvent the prohibition against interest. In modern times, the prohibition has most often been simply disregarded. Even Ottoman banks, for example, charged and paid interest. However, there have always been those, who, on religious grounds, have refrained from placing their money in banks. For many, the custom of holding the family money in women's jewelry of silver and gold has been the traditional savings system.

A common means of circumventing the whole problem of interest has been to call interest by a different name: commission. Recently, however, renewed attempts have been made to provide banking without interest. These revolve around the classical devices: the *murābaḥah*, whereby a commodity is sold, with a contract to buy the commodity back with a price differential equal to the agreed interest; and *mushārakah*, whereby the depositor is a partner and, setting aside a remuneration for management, shares in the profits, but can also share in the losses; and the *muḍārabah*, "the sleeping partnership", putting up financial backing for operations entrusted to someone else, and profit sharing in the profits of these operations. Several banks promoting these approaches have grown up with various degrees of success and endorsement from religious authorities. *See* MUḌĀRABAH.

Islamic Circle of North America (ICNA). One of the major Islamic organizations in the United States, founded in 1971. It has an annual convention that draws thousands of participants and a monthly magazine called "The Message". The organization has links to the political parties of Asia known as Jamā'at-i Islāmi. *See* JAMĀ'AT-I ISLĀMI

"Islamic Jihād" *see* ḤAMĀS.

Islamic Society of North America. An umbrella organization of Muslim professional groups with a center in Plainfield, Indiana. It grew out of the Muslim Student Association in 1982 and counts 400,000 members. It holds a yearly convention and publishes a monthly magazine.

Ism (lit. "name"; pl. *asmā'*). As well as meaning "name" in the everyday sense, it also designates the Divine Name, Allāh, "the Supreme Name" (*al-ism al-a'ẓam*). The Divine Names taken together are called "The Comely Names" (*al-asmā' al ḥusnā*), and are divided into the Names of majesty or rigor (*jalāl*), such as "the Slayer", "the Mighty", "the Victorious", and the Names of Mercy (*raḥmah*), "the Merciful", "the Restorer", "the Nourisher". The number of Divine Names mentioned in any one list is ninety-nine. *See* ALLĀH; DIVINE NAMES; KUNYAH; LAQAB; NAMES.

'Iṣmah. The doctrine of sinlessness, which originated among the Shī'ites in regard to the Imāms, and then entered Sunnī Islam. The Sunnīs attribute this to Prophets, and the Shī'ites to Prophets and Shī'ite Imāms. This does not render the Prophets free from error; the Koran clearly cites errors on the part of David and Solomon (38:24-26 and 35) as does also the Old Testament, not to mention the Fall of Adam. These errors, however, do not engage their substance; they are "faults" (*dhunūb*, sing. *dhanb*) but not "transgression" (*ithm*). For such faults the Prophets suffer sanctions in this life but not punishments in the afterlife. *See* SIN.

Ismā'īl (Ishmael) 1. The eldest son of Abraham by Hagar, Ismā'īl being the Arabic form of Ishmael; he is the immediate patriarch of the North Arabians just as Isaac (Ar. Isḥāq) is of the Jews.

The Koran does not name the son who was to be sacrificed by Abraham, but it does say that for his obedience Abraham was rewarded, and it is understood by most Muslim commentators that the reward precisely, was a second son: Isaac, born to Abraham and Sarah in their great old age. This, and other arguments, have generally meant that in Islam, Ismā'īl (Ishmael) is considered to be the son Abraham was about to sacrifice, although great commentators who hold the opinion that it was Isaac can also be found.

After the birth of Isaac, Hagar and Ismā'īl were then cast by Abraham into the desert because of the jealousy of Sarah. There are provisions in the code of Hammurabi to protect the sons of the "first wife" against those of the slave girl or concubine and guarantee the children's rights against undeserved disinheritance. Sarah did not have the Code of Hammurabi to call upon, so the fate of Hagar was to be abandoned with Ismā'īl in the desert. When the water in the goatskin given by Abraham was spent, Hagar feared for the life of her son and rushed between two hills in anguish. The Bible says:

> And God heard the voice of the lad [Ishmael means "God hears"]... for I will make of him a great nation. And God opened her eyes and she saw a well of water; and she went, and filled the bottle with water, and gave the lad drink. And God was with the lad; and he grew and dwelt in the wilderness, and became an archer... and his mother took him a wife out of the land of Egypt. (Genesis 21: 17-21)

These events are identified with Mecca. The hills Ṣafā and Marwah are a hundred yards from the Ka'bah; running between the two is a rite of the pilgrimage; between Ṣafā and the Ka'bah is the well of Zamzam which sprang from beneath the foot of Ismā'īl. According to tradition both Hagar and Ismā'īl are buried in the *hijr Ismā'īl* ("Ishmael's enclosure") which is an enclosed area next to the Ka'bah. The place of sacrifice of Ishmael, for whom the angel Gabriel substituted a ram at the last moment, is situated by Islamic tradition at the foot of a hill in Minā, a few kilometers outside Mecca.

Islamic tradition relates that Abraham later visited Ismā'īl and that together they built the Ka'bah, replacing a temple first erected by Adam. Ismā'īl married a woman of the tribe of Jurhum, and his descendants are the North Arabians, including the Prophet himself. Ismā'īl is a Prophet (*rasūl*) with a major revelation, as are Abraham and Muḥammad. *See* ABRAHAM; KA'BAH; PROPHETS.

2. The eldest son of Ja'far aṣ-Ṣādiq, whom the Shī'ites consider the sixth Imām. According to the Shī'ites, Ismā'īl was designated to succeed Ja'far as Imām. However, the designation was revoked and another son, Mūsā-'l-Kāẓim became Imām (after his older brother 'Abd Allāh died without children), at least in the view of Twelve-Imām Shī'ites.

The question of succession arose because Ismā'īl died (*145*/762) before his father. One group, the Seveners, held that the Imāmate passed through Ismā'īl to his son Muḥammad, and either ended there, according to some groups, or continued through his descendants, according to the Ismā'īlīs. Out of this controversy, and more importantly out of the ideological reasons behind it, issued several branches of Shī'ites. *See* ISMĀ'ĪLĪS; SEVENERS; SHĪ'ISM.

Ismā'īlīs. A sect which is usually considered to be a Shī'ite branch of Islam. This classification, however, can be misleading. Ismā'īlism's Shī'ite affinities do not constitute its essential element. Rather, it is the metaphysics of Ismā'īlism which is its singular characteristic. The sect is a manifestation within Islam of ancient Persian religious systems. Islam gives them an outer clothing, a form, and a vocabulary, but the central core of Ismā'īlism is far more ancient. Ismā'īlism is the Islamic parallel to Gnosticism (the alternative Dualist form of Christianity), and is related to Hellenistic pagan Gnosticism, and Manicheism. A further parallel to the appearance of Ismā'īlism in Islam is the emergence of Manicheism among the religions of China as the result of influences transmitted through the Uighur Turks of Central Asia; this produced the *Ming Chiao* ("religions of light"), which are Dualistic forms of Buddhism ("the Buddha of Light") and Taoism.

Around its Dualist core beliefs Ismā'īlism adapts the doctrines and practices of exoteric Islam to the sect's own needs. Sometimes exoteric Islam is practiced fully, sometimes partially, sometimes not at all; in the history of Ismā'īlism all these variants can be found at different times and in different places. However, even when outward Islam is observed, it is modified to accommodate the inner and essential doctrines of Ismā'īlism which are by their nature secret (*bāṭinī*).

The starting point of the Gnostic-Dualist philosophy is to attribute substance, or an essence, to evil. The solution which Gnostic-Dualism offers for the problem of the existence of evil is to say that it must exist within God, the Principle, whereas the theodicy of orthodox theologies sees evil as the absence of good — an "accident" without essence which appears on the plane of existence, but which has no origin in Reality since it disappears when existence is reintegrated back into Being.

If both evil and good were *absolute*, but necessarily in irreducible mutual opposition, then the Principle in which they originate would be inconceivable because of its inherent internal contradiction. It is for this reason that the God of the various Gnosticisms has to be affirmed as being completely unknowable. Classical Ismā'īlism called the Absolute *Ghayb Ta'ālā* ("Supreme Unseen", "Supreme Void" or "This Great Absence", later called *al-Mubdi'*, "originator", "principle"). This corresponds to the "Abyss" (*Bythos*) of Hellenistic Gnosticism. What Ismā'īlism calls Allāh (which, for Sunnīs, is the Name of God both as Being and as Absolute) is for them no more than the first *emanation* or hypostasis (*maẓhar*) of the "unknowable" and nameless God. For this reason Ismā'īlī theologians were able to say that the Name Allāh is derived from the word *walaha* ("to lament"), because this "first intelligence" (*al-'aql al-awwal*) "knows something" of the otherwise unknowable Abyss and "laments" its exile from the Abyss, as in Hellenist Gnosticism Sophia (the "Aeon" or "emanation" of wisdom) laments the same exile. Of course, such an interpretation and etymology are untenable and unacceptable from the point of view of orthodox Islam. (Ibn 'Arabī also professed this etymology which belies the Priscillanist nature of his teachers.)

Although especially associated with Valentinian Gnosticism, it is common to all the Gnostic philosophies to propose that the world is the result of a conflict between the polarization of the two forces of good and evil within the world of emanation, a metacosm called the *pleroma.* As a result of this conflict, they say, the emanation known as the *Demiurge* creates the world. (The Manicheans see creation as a kind of defensive tactic whereby the emanation of the "good" aspect of God takes refuge from attack by the "evil" one. Once hidden in creation in the form of light, they say, God is then "liberated" by the realization and acts of the Gnostics, or "Knowers", who, moreover, expedite the process by the sacramental eating of vegetables which liberates the light particles trapped in them.)

The *pleroma* (Gr. "fullness", "plenitude") is called by some Ismā'īlī writers the "abode of origination" (*dār al-ibda'*); one of the emanations, called the Demiurge, then becomes creator of the world itself. The world is called the *kenoma* ("the emptied sphere", from Gr. *kenos*, "empty"). In the Hellenistic mythological formulation, in this world there are fragments of the emanation known as *Sophia*, the *Aeon* who personifies "Wisdom"; *Sophia* knowing something of the unknowable God from which she emanated, tried to return to this God in a "hopeless leap" whose course was shattered by *Horos*, another Aeon who personifies "limitation". The fragments of wisdom thus shattered reside in men — the Gnostics, the "Knowers"— who hear the *call* that tells them they "are the son of a King" and "gold that has fallen into the world's mud". It calls them to throw off the impure "clothing" of forms, and false, external knowledge, and to realize their "nature of light". It is this metacosmic confrontation, they say, which was a kind of war among the Angels, whence arises the story of Lucifer, the "fallen" Angel, whose revolt caused, or arose out of, the creation of the world and the mixing together of light and darkness. (*See* NOAH.)

The world, however, like the unknowable "God" who contains within himself the two principles in mysterious and unfathomable union, also contains the two principles, but in conflict with each other. Thus, the physical world, also, is "divine" or "absolute" or an "autonomous" reality, in the sense that existentialists say that "existence precedes essence". The Gnostic psychologies often teach that the mind is "a projection of the body" (rather than the other way around, as in orthodox cosmologies). This is a possibility expressed in the arresting literary idea of shadows suddenly declaring their independence of the objects or persons that cast them. In the "realized" consciousness, however, the two principles can coexist, just as they do in the unknown God; and that "realized" consciousness is considered by the Gnostics to be itself an hypostasis of the Divinity; or simply Divine. This does not prevent such a consciousness from manifesting contradiction, as indeed it must; but that very contradiction, inscrutable and inexplicable, is taken as an ipseity to be proof of its unquestionable "Divinity".

The "awakening call" is an essential element in Gnostic mythology; hence the name of "caller" (*dā'ī*) given to Ismā'īlī propagandists. On hearing the call, the Gnostics form communities; their salvation lies in the recognition of the Divinity hidden in the world in the form of the Gnostic teacher; it awaits the end of the world (in the terms of the "New Preaching" of Alamūt in Persia, the *qiyāmat al-qiyāmah*, "the resurrection of the resurrection"). When the world and evil disappear, there remain, along with the Abyss, the principles of light and darkness, which when unmixed are neither good nor evil. The Gnostics reward for waiting is salvation, which is nothing less than Deification.

In Ismā'īlism, the Gnostic doctrine of syzygies (or "alter egos") emerges as the doctrine of dual prophetic functions, or the notion that every Prophet has his counterpart: one Prophet, the *nāṭiq* ("the speaker"), makes manifest what the other Prophet, the *sāmit* ("the silent one") knows secretly. Thus, in most forms of Ismā'īlism, Muḥammad is the "speaking" counterpart to the "ineffable" knowledge of 'Alī. In the early forms of Ismā'īlism (as in the *2nd*/8th century book called the *Umm al-Kitāb*), rather than 'Alī it is Salmān al-Farsī, the apocryphal manumitted Persian who is the hidden manifestation of Divine knowledge. Literal and strange interpretations of scripture, often opposite to their face meaning and those accepted by orthodox authorities, the raising of obscure problems, are characteristic of Gnosis. Regarding this technique of a startling unveiling of "hidden truth", compare Irenaeus' explanation of Ptolemaeus' Gnostic exegesis of Matthew 8:9: when the centurion tells Jesus: "I have soldiers and slaves under my authority, and whatever I command, they do"; according to the Gnostics, the "commanding" Centurion is in reality the Demiurge learning from Jesus that of which he, the creator of the world, was ignorant. According to this view, Muḥammad reveals only a part of the knowledge which 'Alī knows *in toto* as the *asās* ("foundation").

For the purpose of indoctrination, a *dā'i*, or propagandist, could claim that the doctrine in which the Prophet is no more than a spokesman for a higher authority, namely, 'Alī or Salmān al-Farsī, is taken in fact from the Koran. Through the science of allegorical interpretation and the elucidation of secret meanings, a *dā'i* could, for example, throw a light on the following Koran quotation that would reveal an unsuspected meaning such as to startle an ordinary believer:

Say: 'I am only mortal
the like of you; it is revealed to me
that your God is One God.
So let him, who hopes for the encounter
with his Lord, work righteousness,
and not associate
with his Lord's service anyone'.
(Koran 18:110)

Interpreted as a hidden teaching, the word "Lord" could be revealed as actually referring to 'Alī. It is of this Gnostic 'Alī that Naṣīr ad-Dīn aṭ-Ṭūsī wrote in the *Tasawwurāt*:

> 'Abd Allāh ibn 'Abbās says: "No women could give birth to a man like 'Alī Ibn Abī Ṭālib! Verily by God, I saw him in the Battle of the Camel, without armor, riding between the arrayed armies of the warriors, and saying: 'I am the Face of God who has been appointed by Him. I am the side of [pointing towards] God, towards which you have been instructed to turn, whether one is praying for forgiveness, or repenting his sins. I am the lord of the Great Throne [*'arsh-i a'ẓam*], and the mystery of God, I am the face of God, and His hand, and His side, of which God says that you have sinned with regard to it. Who is he who repents? I accept his repentance. Who prays for forgiveness? I may forgive him.'"

An 'Alī so described is no less startling to Sunnī Muslims than the belittling notion of the Prophet given above; Orthodox Islam, needless to say, must reject both definitions.

According to Ismā'īlism, Prophets come in cycles which comprise a "great week" of seven thousand years. Each cycle is presided over by one of the Prophets whom the Koran calls *Ulū 'l-'Azm* ("Possessors of Steadfastness") as its outward Prophet (Adam, Noah, Abraham, Moses, Jesus, Muḥammad), as well as by an "intermediary" (*wāṣi*), (Seth, Shem, Ishmael —Ismā'īl— Aaron, Peter, 'Alī), and a "permanent Imām" (*Imām-Qā'im*), (namely Mālik Shulim, Mālik Yazdaq, Mālik as-Salīm — all different names for Melchizedek — Ma'add, the ancestor of the North Arabians, and, again, 'Alī). The symbolic number seven, the sum of the six directions of space and the center, represents the completion of a cycle of manifestation. Similarly, the counterpoise of light and darkness, and of speaking and silence among the Prophets, is repeated in the relationship between the living Imām and his spokesman, the *Ḥujjah* ("proof"), who discloses part of the knowledge that the Imām possesses. Since it would be invidious for the Imām to declare his own Divinity, it is declared for him by his "alter ego", the *Ḥujjah*. Salvation, in both Ismā'īlism and in Gnosticism, depends upon the secret knowledge which is recognized by the "spark of light" in the gnostic. In those Ismā'īlī systems which possess or emphasize a doctrine of Imāms, this knowledge is embodied in the Imām himself. In Ismā'īlism, the Imām, finally, is one of the hypostases of the Abyss, whence the equation which is frequently drawn between the Ismā'īlī Imām and God. In Gnostic-Dualism any leader of note claimed as much; Valentinus readily affirmed that he was the Logos, as did others. Ḥasan-i aṣ-Ṣabbāḥ, the founder of the "New Preaching" at Alamūt, wrote: "If I assert the *ta'līm* [the Gnostic teaching], and there is none who takes the *ta'līm* position except myself, then the designation of the Imām rests with me."

Thus in Indian Ismā'īlism, the Angels Munkar and Nākir, who interrogate men upon death, ask only: "Did you recognize who was the Imām?" This is, for them, the meaning of the *shahādah*; it is this recognition which saves; not to have recognized the Imām leads the soul back into the world to be reincarnated for an interminable length of painful existence until the opportunity arises again to recognize the Imām of the age. (*See* TANĀSUKH). Abū Muḥammad al-'Irāqī, who scrutinized the Ismā'īlīs after al-Ghazālī, complained that they made the Prophet superfluous since obviously the Imām as conceived by the Ismā'īlīs was superior. Both al-Ghazālī and Shahrastānī took issue with the fact that the Imām had only his own being to present as the saving doctrine.

Historically, Ismā'īlism and Twelve-Imām Shī'ism are branches of a Near Eastern Dualism which sought someone to champion political justice, and its own theology, through successive descendants of 'Alī, whom it turned into Imāms, or intermediaries between man and God. There is a considerable difference between the Twelve-Imām Shī'ite and the Ismā'īlī notions of the Imām, reflecting their divergent theological viewpoints, whereas Sunnīs do not, of course, accept the notion at all; for them, the word refers only to a prayer-leader.

The first dynasty of Islam, the Umayyads, encountered political resistance on the part of those to whom the Umayyad policy of Arab supremacy was intolerable. The resistance often looked to the descendants of 'Alī and Fāṭimah for leadership, precisely because they were of the family of the Prophet. Equally, 'Alī and his descendents looked to a Gnostic power base in 'Irāq, specifically in Kūfah, among the former Lakhmids, in order to counter the Umayyads. This mutual relationship led Ja'far aṣ-Ṣādiq (d. *148*/765), who was widely looked upon as the most suitable leader of a resistance both political and religious in nature. For the Shī'ites, Ja'far was the sixth Imām; and the sixth holder of the spiritual and religious authority inherited from 'Alī. For non-Shī'ites, and probably as far he was concerned, himself, Ja'far, was a scholar who taught notable Sunnis their theology and showed no inclination to lead a movement. His eldest son, Ismā'īl, would have inherited, in the eyes of Shī'ites, Ja'far's authority had he not died in *145*/762, before his father, leaving the group around him (the early Ismā'īlis who had hoped to gain influence with his succession) without a figurehead. At this point the main body of Shī'ites looked first to 'Abd Allāh, the next son of Ja'far, and when he, too, died without a son, to the third oldest son, Mūsā al-Kāzim, as the legitimate successor. The followers of Ismā'īl, whose conception of the Imām was more absolute than that of the other Shī'ites in that for them the Imām was no mere intermediary but Divinity itself, maintained on the contrary that the next Imām should be Ismā'īl's son.

These followers of Ismā'īl came to be called Seveners (by Western scholars) because they declared that Ismā'īl was the seventh Imām, and that, with the number seven, a cycle had now been completed, heralding a new beginning and a fresh doctrine. The identity of the seventh Imām was actually open to argument and interpretation, depending upon the requirements of each doctrine and group; the son, or some other successor, of Ismā'īl could be made the seventh Imām by not counting Ḥasan, usually considered to be the second Imām; Ḥasan could be considered the representative, or *Imām Mustawda'*, of his brother Ḥusayn, usually considered to be the third Imām but now to be seen as the second. The Sevener movement produced many splinters, in keeping with the subtle and fluid nature of its doctrines. The schools were to split and branch out again and again. Some factions maintained a loyalty to certain descendants of Ja'far through Ismā'īl, others to leaders whom they themselves threw up; and others, notably the Qarmaṭīs, dropped the need to believe in a supreme spiritual authority altogether (although it cannot be excluded that Ḥamdān Qarmaṭ and others may have played for them the very role that the Fāṭimid Caliph-Imām played for the Fāṭimids). The various Sevener movements were, in fact, to become a secret insurrection, an underground with branches all over the Muslim empire, seeking to overthrow the 'Abbāsids, the dynasty which followed the Umayyads.

One of these Sevener, or Ismā'īlī, groups succeeded in conquering Egypt, and became the Fāṭimid dynasty. Another, the Qarmaṭīs, succeeded in seizing East Arabia and Baḥrayn, and at one point also seized Mecca. The Qarmaṭīs were to disappear, absorbed into the Fāṭimid Ismā'īlīs, leaving behind such remnant groups as the 'Alawīs of Syria and Turkey and the 'Alī Ilāhīs of 'Irāq and Iran.

In *487*/1094 a coup d'état took place in Fāṭimid Egypt. The leader of the armies, Badr al-Jamālī (an Armenian general who had fought for the Byzantines at the Battle of Manzikert) had married his daughter to al-Musta'lī, the younger son of the Fāṭimid Caliph. When the moment came for succession, Badr al-Jamālī's son al-Afḍal Shāhinshāh deposed the elder son, Nizār, put him in prison, where he died, and made al-Musta'lī Caliph and Imām instead. This caused a schism between the Egyptian Ismā'īlīs, who followed al-Musta'lī, and the eastern Ismā'īlīs, who remained loyal to Nizār. A Persian *dā'i*, or propagandist, named Ḥasan-i aṣ-Ṣabbāḥ, who had captured the fortress of Alamūt in north Persia, became the leader of the Nizārīs, and created his own organization which forged political terror into a deadly weapon. His followers were to be called the Assassins (a European name given them by the Crusaders; the name most commonly used in the Islamic world was the *Ta'līmiyyah*, the "people of the teaching", i.e.

"gnostics"). Alamūt thereafter became the principle center of Ismā'īlism.

In *524*/1130 the Nizārīs assassinated al-Amīr, the son of al-Musta'lī, and the belief developed among his followers that al-Amīr had a son named aṭ-Ṭayyib who had gone into hiding or "concealment" on the death of his father. Thus some of the Musta'lī Ismā'īlīs believe that a descendant of aṭ-Ṭayyib subsists somewhere in secret and fulfils the function of Imām. Others believe that, as with the *ghaybah* of the Hidden Imām for the Twelvers, and al-Ḥakīm for the Druzes, this concealment is supernatural and the function is still held by aṭ-Ṭayyib himself in the invisible world, and that he will show himself again at the end of time. In Egypt, after the assassination of al-Amīr, Ismā'īlī allegiance to the last Fāṭimid Caliphs became ever more fragmented, with sometimes more than one claimant to the function of Imām. Shortly thereafter, in *567*/1171, Ṣalāḥ ad-Dīn al-Ayyūbī (Saladin) conquered Egypt and put an end to the Fāṭimids altogether. Ismā'īlism in Egypt, which was in any case the doctrine of the ruling class rather than of the general population, disappeared from Egypt and took refuge in the Yemen, where the chief of the Ismā'īlīs for a time after the death of al-Amīr was a woman, as-Sayyidah Ḥurra (d. *532*/1138).

Not long before the fall of the Fāṭimids of Egypt the function of Imām reappeared among the Nizārīs at the Assassin stronghold of Alamūt in northern Persia. Ḥasan 'Alā Dhikrihi-s-Salām ("Ḥasan, on whose memory peace"), the grandson of Ḥasan-i aṣ-Ṣabbāḥ's successor, Kiya Buzurg Umud, claimed that he was the Imām. According to other accounts, he claimed to be the *Ḥujjah*, or "witness", to the knowledge of the Imām; there is nothing, however, to stop him from having claimed both at different times. The history of Ismā'īlism is the stripping away of one secret to reveal another known only to the inner circle; nowhere is the labyrinth so complex as when it comes to the multiple and fugitive identities of the Imāms where one person is a mask for another. By various explanations, such as the migration of a pregnant concubine of Nizār's (or his putative son al-Hādī) from Egypt to Alamūt, and the substitution of children at the appropriate time, Ḥasan's followers made him into a descendant of Nizār for those who believed that physical descent was an essential condition of the Ismā'īlī Imāmate.

In *559*/1164, Ḥasan 'Alā Dhikrihi-s-Salām, by a ritual repudiation of Islamic law ceremonially staged as a premature end to the fast of Ramaḍān, proclaimed the *'Id al-Qiyāmah* ("the Feast of the Resurrection"), ushering in a new age in which there was no longer any need to cover the "Religion of Truth" with the appearance of Islam and its religious law, which latter was, moreover, likened to the Flood of Noah. In Ismā'īli *ta'wīl* (allegorical interpretation) the Flood is an allegory of ignorance, which is the *sharī'ah* ("religious law") and its opposite is the *da'wah* (the Gnostic call). "Islands", (*al-Jazā'ir*), a name for the Ismā'īlī dioceses, are the prominences of consciousness which appear as the exoteric flood recedes. Ramaḍān, or fasting is allegorically the keeping of a secret, ended as the truth of the matter was declared and made public.

In the Alamūt *Qiyāmah*, the "veiling of the truth" by the Islamic law was lifted, and the law was superseded by the "inner" and secret "truth" of the Gnostic doctrine. The end of the law expresses the Gnostic doctrine of the falling away of all beliefs "like clothes" when the secret truth is understood and the great awakening comes. However, a successor to Ḥasan, Jalāl ad-Dīn (also called Ḥasan III), drew the outward covering of Islam back over matters again and professed to be a Sunnī Muslim. His conversion was readily accepted by the Caliph an-Nāṣir and other Princes, and Jalāl ad-Dīn was known as the *naw musalman* ("the new Muslim"). This policy of Jalāl ad-Dīn actually bought time for the power of Alamūt; it was accompanied by the building of mosques and bathhouses in Ismā'īlī villages, signifying the acquisition of the status of a civilized state; Sunnī legists were even invited to instruct the villagers in the use of the new mosques. The outward resumption of Islam which followed the *Qiyāmah* was called the *Satr* ("veiling"), and resembled the *Satr* which had preceded it, except that the Divinity of the Imām, in his public aspect of *Qā'im*, having been more or less openly so declared, remained thereafter a more accessible doctrine.

In *654*/1256 the Assassin stronghold of Alamūt fell to the Mongols and shortly thereafter the last Grand Master, Rukn ad-Dīn, was put to death. Ismā'īlism survived in communities scattered through Persia, Central Asia, the Yemen and Syria. Before the Mamlūks stamped out Ismā'īlī power in Syria, the Ismā'īlīs there had offered to ally themselves with the Crusaders and to become Christians. The offer was enthusiastically received by the Christian King of Jerusalem and his court, but nullified by the Knights Templar, who put the Ismā‘īlī envoys to death.

Despite the sharp decline of the fortunes of the Ismaī‘īlīs in Syria and Persia, another great expansion of Ismā‘īlism was yet to come, in India. Ismā‘īlī propagandists had been active and successful in gaining converts in Sindh since the early days of the Seveners, presumably amongst existing followers of pre-Ismā‘īlī Gnostic-Dualisms in India. According to tradition, Ḥasan 'Alā Dhikrihi-s-Salām (himself assassinated in *561*/1166) sent a Nizārī missionary to Sindh named Nūr ad-Dīn, also called Nūr Satagur; others put the date of Nūr ad-Dīn somewhat later, *575-640*/1179-1242; he is also associated with Gujurat and a shrine or tomb at Nawsari near Sūrat (with a tombstone, however, dated 1094). There was a Pir Shams ad-Din also in Sindh with a mausoleum at Multan. A descendant was the most successful of the Nizārī leaders in Sindh called Pir Ṣadr ad-Dīn (*9th*/15th century), also known by Hindu names such as Sahadev. Ṣadr ad-Dīn converted a Hindu caste called the Lohanas to Ismā‘īlism and gave them the name of Khojas, derived from the Persian word *Khwājah* ("Lord"). He is associated with an important Ismā‘īlī book called *Das Avatār* ("the Tenth Incarnation"), and the local name he gave to Ismā‘īlism was the *Satpanth* ("Way of Truth"). It should be noted that there is a Dualist school of metaphysics in Hinduism, as well. All the Ismā‘īlī missionaries in India freely adapted Hinduism to Ismā‘īlism, and vice versa. Indeed, it is in the nature of Gnostic-Dualism to take any religious form as its starting point and then to lead the novice through it to the "hidden and secret knowledge". As part of his approach, Pir Ṣadr ad-Dīn taught that the tenth *avatāra* ("incarnation") of Vishnu was none other than the Caliph 'Alī.

Similarly, Musta‘lī Ismā‘īlīs from Egypt, and later from the Yemen, sent missionaries to India, especially to the Gujarat. Musta‘lī missionaries succeeded in converting another originally Hindu caste, who became known as the Bohoras (or Vohoras, "the traders"). The head of the Musta‘lī community in the Yemen was called *al-Dā‘ī-l-Muṭlaq*, assisted by the *Ma'dhūn* and *mukāsir*. With the growth of the community in India, the *Dā‘ī* moved there from the Yemen in *946*/1539. Not long afterwards, on the death of the 26th *dā‘ī*, a split occurred, with most of the Indians favoring a *dā‘ī* called Dāwūd Burḥān ad-Dīn (d. *1021*/1612) in India, and the Yemenis a *dā‘i* in the Yemen, of Indian origin, called Sulaymān ibn Ḥasan (d. *1005*/1597). The Sulaymanis number about 70,000 in the Yemen, and a few thousand in India. The Da'ūdīs number about 500,000, most of whom live in India, around Bombay. 30,000 also live in Pakistan, mostly in Karachi, another 20,000 in East Africa, and 5,000 in the Yemen. Their leader resides in Sūrat, India and is called the Mulla-Ji as well as *al-Dā‘ī-l-Muṭlaq*.

Splits also occurred among the Nizārīs because any charismatic leader could, and did, claim to be the Imām. Thus the historic lists of Imāms vary considerably, the two major groupings being known as Muḥammad Shāhīs and Qāsim-Shāhīs. But the older factions among the Nizārīs are disappearing, to be replaced by a new self-awareness and assertiveness, as if Ismā‘īlism in this century were awakening after a long period of dormancy. In general, the Bohora Ismā‘īlīs resemble Sunnī Islam considerably more than the Nizārīs do, who more readily treat the ritual principles of orthodox Islam in a symbolic or allegorical fashion. The doctrine in any case is a prerogative of the Imām and can be changed at any time. The Ismā‘īlīs, particularly the Nizārīs, practiced *taqiyyah* (dissimulation of one's real religion to avoid persecution) to a high degree. This was also very much the position of the Manicheans *vis-à-vis* the early Christians, and other religions with which they came in contact. In Persia, the Ismā‘īlīs were often obliged to pass themselves off as Twelve-Imām Shī‘ites, and in this guise a number of Ismā‘īlīs played an important role in the Ni‘matu'llahi Sufi order (*ṭarīqah*).

Today's Ismā‘īlīs are found mainly in India and Pakistan (both Nizārī and Musta‘lī branches), with smaller groups in the Yemen (chiefly Sulaymani-Musta‘lī), Syria (chiefly Nizārī), Central Asia (Nizārī), and Iran (Nizārī). Large numbers of Ismā‘īlīs have emigrated from the Indian sub-continent to various East African countries. Others have emigrated to Europe and America, particularly since the expulsion of Asians from Uganda. The Indian census of 1931 put the number of Musta‘lī Ismā‘īlī Bohoras (of whom the majority are Dāwūdī-Musta‘lī) at 212,000, and the number of Nizārī Ismā‘īlī Khojas at slightly more than that. Nizārī Khojas added to other Indian Nizārī groups such as the Guptis, the Shamsis, the Burusho of Hunza (in Kashmir), and others, were estimated at that time to amount to 250,000 Nizārīs in India. To this can be added a few thousand Ismā‘īlīs in other countries for a total estimate, in the 1930s, of all Ismā'īlīs, both Nizārī and Musta'lī, to be 500,000. Today they probably number several millions. Not all Khojas and Bohoras are Ismā'īlīs; some are Sunnīs and others are Twelve-Imām Shī'ites. The present Imām of the Nizārīs is the Aga Khan IV who resides near Paris.

Among the important books of the Ismā'īlīs is the *Da'ā'im al-Islām* of Qāḍi Nu'mān ibn Muḥammad at-Tamīmī (d. *873*/974), a Fāṭimid work of the *4th*/10th century. It is an expression of Ismā'īlī jurisprudence (*fiqh*), in a period when the outward aspect of Ismā'īlism was at its closest to orthodox Islam. Also, this work, was the lowest level of initiate teachings; it could be taught to all, whereas only a select few could progress on to the next level and thereupon to even more esoteric works whose access was limited to those who showed the necessary adaptation. Thus, in many ways, the book is indistinguishable from ordinary exoterism except for its allusions to the Imāmate. But the view of the Imāmate is radical: "Glorification of the Imams, blessings of God upon them, is a form of glorification of God... we have seen the legates and crown princes kiss the ground as a salute to them, revering them, and knowing their rank." Works of a more doctrinal kind in which the *bāṭin* ("inner doctrines") or *ḥaqā'iq* ("ultimate realities") came far more to the forefront, culminating in the *Qiyāmah* doctrine, were written by the *dā'īs* Abū Ya'qūb Sijistānī (d. *4th*/10th century), Hamīd ad-Dīn al-Kīrmānī (d. *411*/1021), Naṣīr-i Khusraw (d. *452*/1060), who is still highly venerated by the Ismā'īlīs of Central Asia, and Naṣīr ad-Dīn aṭ-Ṭūsi (d. *673*/1274). The book Kalām-i Pīr is ascribed to both Abū Isḥāq and Naṣīr-i Khusraw. The *Umm al-Kitāb*, a book from the *2nd*/8th century, from the very origins of the Seveners, is influential among the Ismā'īlīs of Central Asia and Badakshān in Afghanistan, and is representative of the first, early attempts to integrate the Gnostic doctrine into an Islamic framework. In this sense it is not completely successful; its alien origins are apparent despite the masterly choice of name. (The word *Umm al-Kitāb*, "the mother of the book", is an allusion to the name of the celestial prototype of the Koran among the Sunnīs.) The *Umm al-Kitāb* transposes formulations into Islam which had been developed by Gnosticism in order to infiltrate Christianity; hence a somewhat "trinitarian" approach (perpetuated by the 'Alawīs of Syria) and an echo of the demiurge idea. But in the end, especially after Alamūt, the formulations became so refined that they were transparent to orthodox Islam, and orthodox Islam became transparent to them. Islam became truly married to Gnosticism and its outer garment: the *shahādah* became recognition or knowledge of the Imām; prayer (*ṣalāh*) came to be directed to the Imām; *zakāh* came to be given for the Imām; *fasting* meant keeping his secret; *ḥajj*, visiting the Imām, and so on. The Alamūt period represents the culmination of a perfected Ismā'īlism in which Gnosticism was so closely adapted to Islam (admittedly a Shī'ite Islam), that they fit together like hand and glove.

During the period of their ascendancy, when they ruled Egypt and threatened to topple the 'Abbāsid Empire with the power of the syllogism, the Ismā'īlīs had a profound influence upon the development of Islam. They were the leaven by which intellectual fermentation brought forth a developed mysticism out of inchoate possibilities. Dualism had performed the same function in regard to Judaism from the first contact of the Jews with the Parthians, during the Babylonian Captivity, thereby producing the first school of mysticism in Judaism, in the shape of the *Merkava*. A later Dualist permeation of Judaism, at the time of the Qumrān sect, called forth the response of Christianity. Again, at a still later time, the Ismā'īlī *Rasā'il Ikhwān aṣ-Ṣafā'* (The Epistle of the Brotherhood of Purity) stimulated Jewish rationalists at Baghdad and influenced their interpretation of the 3rd?-6th? century AD *Sefer Yetsira* ("The Book of Creation", which described creation as the result of thirty-two means — ten numbers and the twenty-two Hebrew letters—) and so, perhaps, stimulated the flowering of the Qabbalah. (This, it may be noted, appeared in Provence not far from the irruption of the Christian Gnostic sect of the Cathars, or Albigensians.)

The service that Dualism performed was a challenge to orthodoxy that brought forth a complete development of its possibilities; much as the fragrance of the Eagle Wood tree, aloes (*al-'Ūd al-Qimārī*), much beloved of the Sufis, is a resin which is secreted by those trees to protect themselves from an infection by an alien organism.

Because the metaphysics of Gnostic-Dualism tend to interpret the cosmos as the "shadow" of Reality, the Ismā'īlīs pursued the study of science vigorously. Regarding themselves as heirs to the inward and secret truth of all religions, the Ismā'īlīs demonstrated a great curiosity about other faiths and examined them in greater depth than most

Sunnīs, who were largely content to view other religions from afar, and to interpret them almost entirely from Islamic reference points. The Ismā'īlīs were especially well-informed about Christianity, which, with its doctrine of the incarnation, and of a spiritual truth which goes beyond appearances, provided many parallels to Ismā'īlism — as well as vital differences. The facts account for the great success the Ismā'īlīs and other strands of Gnostic-Dualism enjoyed in penetrating other religions. Certain Ismā'īlī formulations proved useful to Sunnī Islam and were used by many thinkers, some of whom never stopped to wonder where certain ideas, such as the *Nūr Muḥammadī* ("the Muhammadan Light") and Sahl at-Tustarī's *'umūd an-nūr* ("pillars of light") actually originated. By being open to ideas from all sources, as evidenced by the writings of the Brotherhood of Purity (*Ikhwān aṣ-Ṣafā'*), a group founded around *340*/951 in Baṣrah, the Ismā'īlīs facilitated the assimilation and adaptation of Hellenistic thought within Islam. *See also* AGA KHAN; 'ALAWĪS; ASSASSINS; BOHORAS; BROTHERHOOD of PURITY; DRUZES; FĀṬIMIDS; JAM'A'T KHĀNAH; JAZĀ'IR al-ARḌ; KHOJAS; QARMAṬĪS; MŪKHĪ; NŪR MUḤAMMADĪ; SEVENERS; SHĪ'ISM; TA'WĪL; 'UBAYD ALLĀH al-MAHDĪ; UMM al-KITĀB.

Isnād. The chain of transmission supporting a Ḥadīth. The authority, and character, including moral probity, of every member of a chain in the transmission of a given Ḥadīth, and the existence of alternate chains of transmission for a saying, were fundamental criteria for accepting Ḥadīth as authentic. *See* ḤADĪTH.

Isrā', *see* NIGHT JOURNEY.

Israel. Created by United Nations partition of Palestine in 1948. Population 5,916,700 of whom 80.5% are Jewish, 14.6 % are Muslim, 3.2% are Christian, and 1.7% Druze, including Israeli citizens in the West Bank and Gaza strip. Population of Gaza: 924,000; population of the West Bank 1,428,000. Jewish immigration to Palestine began to grow at the end of the 19th century and swelled in the 1930s with refugees from the Nazis. Between 1948 and 1996 2,654,000 Jewish immigrants came. 56% of the immigrant population has come from Europe, 18% from Africa, 15% from Asia, 8% from the Americas and Oceania. *See* PALESTINE.

Istanbul. The capital of the Ottoman Empire was originally called Constantinople, the extension built beginning in AD 328 by the Roman Emperor Constantine to the original city of Byzantium. The name Stamboul at first designated the central quarter of the city. The word presumably meaning "Downtown" comes from the Greek *eis tēn polin* ("into the city"), was already in use before the Turks. The Turks usually called the city Kustantiniyya and did not officially adopt the name Istanbul until 1930.

Istanbul stands at the southern extremity of the Bosphorus, a channel where the waters of the Black Sea, on their way to the Mediterranean, rush into sea of Marmora. The channel, now bridged, narrowly separates Europe and Asia. The city is a promontory with the Sea of Marmora on the south, and a bay of the Bosphorus called the Golden Horn on the north (in Turkish, *Halice*, from Arabic *khalij*, "a bay").

The city of Byzantium was founded by the Greeks under Byzas in 657 BC It had a tumultuous history under the Greeks and Macedonians. When the Roman Empire became dissociated from the city of Rome, its natural center of gravity moved east. The Roman empire had been failing; Valerian had been captured by the Persians (AD 260); the frontiers of the empire could not be defended. Aurelian (AD 270-275) and Diocletian (284-305) had held back decline. Diocletian, who abdicated, travelled incessantly to hold the empire together; he made his capital Nicomedia in Asia Minor; he created the Tetrarchy; when that failed Constantine became the victorious ruler. Constantine, recognizing the strategic advantages of the fine harbor and commanding site defended by natural barriers made Byzantium, which like Rome also has seven hills, his capital. The city of Constantinople was founded on November 8, 324. By tradition, the Emperor was protected by Apollo; Constantine did not immediately stop deification of the Emperor as a result of his conversion, but the founding of the city was the point at which the empire began changing from pagan empire to Christian.

At first thought to be too large, the New Rome grew such that in 413, Theodosius II, not yet emperor, had to enlarge it again leaving his stamp on Christian Constantinople. With extensions to its ancient walls, the city acquired its classical limits in 439.

These walls were a wise investment, for from then on attempts to conquer the city were frequent until Meḥmet Nasir invested the city in 1453 (*See* Meḥmet II). By then the city had been attacked by Huns, Avars, Slavs, Bulgarians, and repeatedly by Arabs, who dreamed of its conquest from the beginning of Islam. But Constantinople was most weakened not by Muslims but by the Fourth Crusade which under the Doge Dandolo sacked the city in 1204 and reduced its population to a quarter of its former size. The city was so depopulated that when the Turks captured the city they sent servants "to all the lands, to say: Whoever wishes, let him come, and let him become owner of houses, vineyards and gardens in Istanbul".

Under the Christians the city was the seat of Eastern Christianity; it was full of churches, the chief of which was the Cathedral of the Hagia Sophia, "the Holy Wisdom" built by Justinian the Great (AD 527-565) who brought to fruition the work begun by Constantine. The city lived out its theology attempting to fulfill the expectations of the heavenly Jerusalem; because the streets of the heavenly Jerusalem were paved with gold, Constantinople collected gold with a religious zeal; because the heavenly Jerusalem was populated with Angels, Constantinople was full of an earthly approximation: eunuchs. Because the heavenly Jerusalem was the fulfillment of Divine Law, heavenly measures with absolute punishments were applied to trade. A loaf of bread had to be baked to a strict weight as if it were the projection of a Platonic ideal into the world. If the ideal weight was off, the punishment was drastic, as if the weights and measures were in the hands of the Angels at the Day of Judgement. The coinage was also, at first, extremely reliable, and assured Constantinople a dominant position in international trade. But the passions of theology were to be surpassed by the passions of chariot racing and the city rivalries of the Blues, the Reds, and other teams. The Hippodrome stands, showing its later importance, in front of the Cathedral, now the mosque of Aya Sofia and next to the Mosque of Sultan Aḥmet.

Ottoman Constantinople continued the cosmopolitan tradition of the city. By the time of Süleyman, the population of Istanbul was at least half a million, and in 1593 an English traveler, John Sanderson, cites the population as 1,231,207. At the end of the 19th century, Muslims were in the minority in the city, surpassed by Greeks, Armenians, and foreigners. There was a quarter where well-off Greeks lived, called Phanari, and many of them, the Phanariot, became families who frequently served the government as diplomats and translators. The reign of Sülayman (1520-66) was the high water mark of the Ottoman empire, and the period of Istanbul's greatest splendor. The architect Sinan built the Sülaymaniyyah Mosque, one of the great examples of world architecture, and embellished the city with other buildings. Much of Constantinople had been rebuilt by the pious Sultan Bayazid II (1481-1512) called the *Veli* "the Saint". At the time of Sülayman the administration was such that it was considered the paragon of the world. The custom of the ruler to sit by the gate of the city to dispense justice and receive petitions associated the word "gate" and government throughout the Middle East. In Istanbul the palace of the Grand Vizier was the effective seat of government and was called the *Bab-i Ali*, "High Gate", whence the Turkish government was called "the Sublime Porte".

In the seventeenth century a poet named Nabi described Istanbul as:

There is no place where knowledge and learning
Find so ready a welcome as Istanbul.
No city has eaten the fruits of the garden of art
So richly as the city of Istanbul.
May God cause Istanbul to flourish
For it is the home of all great affairs.
Birthplace and school of famous men,
The nursery of many nations,
Whatever men of merit there may be
All win their renown in Istanbul.

See MEḤMET II; OTTOMANS; TURKEY; TURKS.

Istibrā'. Washing the private parts after passing water as a preparation for the ablution. *See* ISTINJĀ'; WUḌŪ.

Istawā (from *istawā 'ala-l-'arsh*, lit. "He (God) mounted on the throne", 32:4 and *passim*). One of several Koranic passages which "anthropomorphize" God, or speak of Him as having human attributes. It should be borne in mind that what has often been called "anthropomorphism" in debates around this question is really nothing more than a *conceptual* tendency. References occur to God's Face, His Hands, and His footstool (*al-kursī*). The school of Ibn Ḥanbal insisted that these references be accepted literally, without drawing any conclusions, but without question (*bilā kayfa*). The

Ash'arites did the same, but in addition to the literal aspect, also saw a symbolic allusion to God's assumption of majesty towards His creation. Nevertheless, in modern times these passages are generally understood symbolically. Al-Ash'arī wrote in *al-Ibānah 'an Uṣūl ad-Dīyānah* ("The Elucidation of the Foundations of Religion"):

> Certain Rationalists [Mu'tazilites] have maintained that God's words "the Merciful is seated on the throne" mean merely that He has dominion, reigns, exercises power. God, they say, is everywhere; and this denies that He is on the Throne. They hold that His being seated is merely an expression referring to His Power. If they were right, the distinction between the Throne and the earth would be lost, for the Power of God extends over the earth and all worldly things... so that He would be seated on the Throne, and on earth, and on heaven... and on everything. But since no True Believer regards it as right to say God is seated... it necessarily follows from this consensus of Believers that being "seated" in this passage has a meaning particular to the Throne and does not refer to anything else. Be God exalted above their thought.

See BILĀ KAYFA.

Istidrāj (lit. "a baiting by degrees", "a lure to destruction"). A fall from grace from what may even appear to be an exalted state as a consequence of a hidden chain of harmful causes and effects in a person's being which has not in fact been rooted out or effectively neutralized.

Ibn al-'Ārif says in the *Maḥāsin al-Majālis* ("Beauties of Spiritual Sessions"):

> It was said: "Do not be deceived by good times, because in them lurk the secrets of calamities." In how many springs have the flowers and trees bloomed, and people thought highly of it all, only to be soon inflicted with a heavenly disaster! God says: "Our scourge comes down upon [the crop], by night or in broad day, laying it waste, even though it was in bloom only yesterday" (10:24). How many disciples have shone with the splendor of their will to serve God and felt the intense effects of spiritual joy; they became renowned, were put above everything, and were supposed to be the chosen friends of God. But how often has the serenity of such a man changed into grief, and his spiritual illumination into depravation! So it is that the Sufis recite the following verses:
>
> "You made your thoughts pleasant like the days, Not fearing the disaster which fate was bringing." "The nights soothed you, and you were deceived by them; But when nights are serene, troubles follow."

But as Ibn 'Aṭā' Allāh says:

> Sometimes darknesses come over you in order that He make you aware of the value of His blessings upon you.

Istighfār (lit. "asking for forgiveness"). Seeking the forgiveness of God through the words *astaghfiru-Llāh*, ("and ask for God's forgiveness"). One is in effect asking that the evil incurred in created existence through the breaking of Divine Law should be covered or neutralized by what transcends existence and its evils. When one turns to God for forgiveness in sincere repentance, with the intention of not repeating the offense, God forgives unconditionally, for He is *al-ghafūr*, ("the All-Forgiving", "the One who covers over").

The Prophet recited the *istighfār* one hundred times, or alternately seventy times, each day. There is a famous Ḥadīth: "My heart is clouded until I have asked God's forgiveness seventy times during the day and the night.

'Istiḥsān (lit. "seeking the good", "aiming at the best", "improvement"). A legal principle, akin to the *istislāh* of Mālik ibn Anas, whereby laws are established on the guidelines and injunctions furnished by the Koran and Sunnah. This is the working principle used by Abū Ḥanīfah, founder of the Ḥanafī School of Law. It is, in effect, simply the expression of the idea that it is equity and justice as defined by God that must determine both the formulation and the interpretation of laws. Today the principle of the morality of law seems self-evident, and in most non-totalitarian countries is to be taken for granted. However, the origin of human law cannot be other than Divine law. In this sense, the ideal enshrined in *istihsān* and *istislāh* remains timelessly valid.

Istikhārah (lit. "asking for the best choice", "seeking goodness"). A practice, based upon the Sunnah, of asking God for guidance when faced with important decisions or perplexing situations. *Istikhārah* consists of praying a two *raka'āt* prayer immediately before retiring to sleep along with a *du'ā'* (personal prayer) in which one presents the problem to God and asks for guidance: a response may come in the form of a dream, a sign, or a sudden certitude. Alternatively, one may seek the answer in the Koran, using the same procedure: after a *two raka'āt prayer* and a *du'ā'* to put the problem to God, the Koran is opened and the hand placed upon the page. The verse under the hand, or above or below, may shed light upon the question. Such use of the Koran is frowned upon by many Sunnī authorities, as is — a *fortiori* — the not uncommon use of the Mathnawī of Jalāl ad-Dīn Rūmī in Shī'ite lands in the same way, or the poems of Ḥāfiẓ. *See* MATHNAWĪ.

Istilāḥāt. Technical vocabularies. One of the first signs of the formalization of Sufism was the appearance of detailed technical vocabularies such as those by al-Ḥakīm at-Tirmidhī (*3rd*/9th century), and later by many others, such as al-Ḥujwīrī.

Istinjā'. The practice of washing the orifices to clean the body after calls of nature. If water is not available, sand or earth is used. For some Schools of Law *istinjā'* is obligatory in the preparation for assuming the state of *wuḍū'* for prayers, while other schools only recommend it. As Western style toilets are not equipped, as are toilets in the East, with running water in the cabinets, this practice is not always possible. *See* ISTIBRĀ; WUḌŪ'.

Istiṣlāḥ (lit. "Seeking what is correct, wholesome"). A principle invoked by the jurist Mālik ibn Anas, to the effect that public and individual good must be the criterion for the development of the law. The basis of law is Divine injunctions as found in the Koran and Sunnah. These canonic sources however, make implicit only the framework of Islamic law; the rest being elaborated by such guiding principles as *istiṣlāḥ* or *istiḥsān*. *See* ISTIḤSĀN.

Istisqā'. A two *raka'āt* prayer to ask for rain. It is performed by the entire community, in a *Muṣsallā* (communal prayer ground), in the morning. *See* PRAYER.

Istithnā', *see* PIOUS EXPRESSIONS.

Ithm. One category of sin. *See* SIN.

Ithnā'asharīyyah (lit. "Twelvers" from *ithnā'ashar*, "twelve"). The most important division of the Shī'ites, the Twelve-Imām branch, so-called because they hold that there were twelve Imāms, the last of whom is still mysteriously alive since his occultation in the *3rd*/9th century, and will return as the Mahdī. The Twelvers are the dominant religious group in Iran, constitute the majority in 'Irāq, and are found in Syria, Lebanon, Pakistan, some of the Gulf states, and in several other countries, including the Eastern Province of Saudi Arabia. *See* HIDDEN IMĀM; SHĪ'ISM.

Ithnayniyyah, *see* MANICHEISM; SEVENERS.

Īwān. A feature of Persian architecture which spread to other parts of the Islamic world, notably India, it consists of a semi-circular vault open on one side — which frequently faces onto a courtyard — and closed on the other three. The brick ribbing which supports the vault is concealed, and the outer arch may well be pointed.

Izār (lit. "a wrap", "a cloth sheet"). The lower of the two unsecured cloths which constitute the consecrated pilgrims' garb, or *iḥrām*. It is fastened around the waist and falls below the knees. The upper cloth which is draped over the shoulders is called a *rida'*. *See* IḤRĀM; PILGRIMAGE.

'Izrā'īl. One of the *qarībiyyūn*, or Archangels. 'Izrā'īl is the Angel of death. Although mentioned by name in non-Koranic mythology, in which his description is of a being of cosmic dimensions with innumerable eyes and feet, he is not named in the Koran. The Sūrah as-Sajdah says: "Say thou: the Angel of death that is encharged with you will bring you to your end, and then to your Lord ye will be returned" (32:11). *See* ANGELS.

J

Jabarī or Jabrī (from Ar. *Jabr*, "compulsion"). This designates a member of the Jabariyyah school of early Muslim theoreticians who maintained determinism as opposed to free will. Freedom of the human will was the thesis of the Qadariyyah school. *See* KALĀM; QADARIYYAH; MAKTŪB.

Jābir ibn Ḥayyān (*103-160*/721-776). A celebrated alchemist, not a Muslim, but a Ḥarrānian from the community of the Ḥarrānian "Ṣābians" of North Syria. He may not be a historical figure, but a symbol for a collective process of adaptation into Arabic of Hermetic sciences by Bardesanians of Edessa/Ḥarrān. By tradition Jābir went on to Baghdad. The name became the foremost in medieval science, known and studied in Europe as Geber. The Jābir writings on alchemy and chemistry were still being read in the 16th century.

As an alchemist, Jābir was first of all concerned with the purification of the soul. He is cited in the medieval texts:

> All Metallick Bodies are compounded of Argentvive and Sulphur, pure or impure, by accident, and not innate in their first Nature; therefore, by convenient Preparation, 'tis possible to take away such impurity... It is called by Philosophers, one Stone, although it is extracted from many Bodies or Things.

The importance of the Arab/Islamic contribution to chemistry can be seen in the word "chemistry" itself: it comes ultimately from the Arabic *al-kīmiyā'* ("alchemy") which means "the science of *Khem*", an ancient name for Egypt, which referred to that country's "black earth" together with a symbolic allusion to the color black standing for the metaphysical void, or Beyond-Being, or perhaps to the alchemists' *materia prima.* Likewise, the word "alembic" comes from the Arabic *al-inbīq*, elixir from *al-iksīr*, alkali from *al-qilī* ("potash"), alcohol from *al-kuḥl* ("antimony powder"); athanor from *at-tannūr* (an "oven"), and so on. The Moors brought knowledge of distillation to Spain, whence it spread in Europe and was used to make alcoholic spirits from grains and potatoes, i.e. vodka and whiskey.

Jacob, *see* YA'QŪB.

Jadhb (lit. "attraction"). A term in mysticism for the "Divine attraction" which certain souls experience. It refers especially to states of violent, sudden cognizance of a superior reality, disturbing everyday human equilibrium. One who is subject to such states, the consequence of which may be temporary or permanent, and resemble a benign madness, is called *majdhūb*, "one attracted [to God]" and corresponds to one who would be called in the West "God's fool" or a "holy fool".

Jadidism. (lit. "renewal"). Like similar movements in the Middle East at the time, this movement in Central Asia which began in 1890 sought to bring development of Islamic countries to the level of Europe by imitating its institutions, such as charitable organizations and introducing modern schools, science, and industry. Among its leaders were 'Abd ar-Rauf Fitrat and Maḥmud Khoja Behbudi. Its politics of cultural reform was overtaken by the Russian Revolution.

Ja'farī. An adjective derived from *Ja'far aṣ-Ṣādiq* to qualify the body of religious law of the Twelve-Imām Shī'ites. The expression "Ja'farī Shī'ites", however, refers particularly to the Akhbarī school of Shi'ites found mostly in southern 'Irāq, who do not follow Mujtahids (or Ayatollahs), that is, non-Uṣūlī Shi'ites. *See* JA'FAR AṢ-ṢĀDIQ; SHARĪ'AH; SHĪ'ISM.

Ja'far aṣ-Ṣādiq (*80-148*/699-765). A descendant of the Prophet. A renowned scholar of the religious sciences. Shīite tradition also makes him a master of mysticism and of such cosmological and arcane sciences as alchemy. He had a circle of students in Medinah, and two founders of Sunnī Schools of Law, Mālik ibn Anas and Abū Ḥanīfah, studied with him. The Twelve-Imām Shī'ites consider him to be the founder of their School of Law, which is called *Ja'farī* after him.

Twelve-Imām Shī'ites hold that the Prophet had successors to his function, in the form of intermediaries between man and God. These successor-intermediaries, known as Imāms, were descendants of 'Alī ibn Abī Ṭālib. According to the Shī'ites, Ja'far was the sixth Imām. The doctrine of the Imāmate came to hold that the function was passed on by designation (*naṣṣ*). Thus Ja'far aṣ-Ṣādiq is said to have first named his eldest son Ismā'īl as Imām to succeed him; then, it is said, he revoked this designation in favor of his third son, Mūsā Kāẓim after 'Abd Allāh, the second son, had died without children. Those who chose even so to follow Ismā'īl and his son became the Seven-Imām Shī'ites ("Seveners" or *sab'iyyah*), who survive as present day Ismā'īlīs. Those who followed Mūsā Kāẓim became the Twelve-Imām Shī'ites ("Twelvers" or *ithnā'ashariyyah*).

Ja'far is a pivotal figure in the development of Shī'ism. Before him, the movement had a distinctly political nature with the Imāms acting rather as rallying points for resistance to the Umayyads and as the focus of rival aspirations. After him, it became transformed by the development of new religious currents of which he was held to be the spokesman and authoritative founder. This coincided with the penetration of the, in fact, heterodox doctrines of the Seveners into Islam as what later became known as Ismā'īlism.

In keeping with the tradition that he is a wellspring of esoteric doctrines second only to 'Alī himself, the Shī'ites claim that Ja'far possessed a book of secret knowledge (*Kitāb al-Jafr*, *jafr* meaning "vellum", not the name Ja'far), known only to the family of the Prophet.

Without the least acquiescence in, or acceptance of, the role Ja'far is alleged to have played in Shī'ism, he is nonetheless considered to be a great Sufi by the Sunnī mystics, and appears in the more prominent *silsilahs*, or initiatic chains, of the Sufi orders. *See* 'ABD ALLĀH ibn MAYMŪN al-QADDĀḤ; ISMĀ'ĪLIS; KITĀB al-JAFR; NAṢṢ; NŪR MUḤAMMADĪ; SEVENERS; SHĪ'ISM.

al-Jafr A name for the "science of letters". *See* 'ILM al-ḤURŪF; KITĀB al-JAFR.

al-Jāhiliyyah (from *jāhil*, "ignorant", "untaught"). The "time of ignorance" or period of Arab paganism preceding the revelation of Islam. Since Islam restores the Abrahamic, or primordial, religion the *Jāhiliyyah* is considered to be that epoch which came immediately before the Islamic revelation like darkness before the dawn. During the *Jāhiliyyah*, the pristine monotheism of Abraham declined and gave way to an opaque and oppressive paganism, and general decadence.

Many of the idol cults, and the idols themselves, were brought to Mecca from other parts of the Middle East. Indeed, not all the Arabs were by any means pagan, many tribes being Christian or Jewish. Moreover, there were always certain spiritually gifted individuals called *ḥunafā'*, (singular *ḥanīf*), who remained unattached to these two religions and who continued to hold to the original monotheism of Abraham.

Typical of the period were the great fairs, such as those of Minā and 'Ukāẓ, and the months of truce that made them possible. These great gatherings of pagan times, the *sūq al-'arab*, were replaced under Islam by the *ḥajj* ("pilgrimage") alone. Before Islam, several sites in Arabia with sanctuaries similar to the Ka'bah (the church of Najran was called a Ka'bah) had attempted to rival its attractions as a centre of pilgrimage, but none was as successful as Mecca in either religion or trade. *See* IDOLS; al-KALBI; KAHIN.

al-Jāḥiẓ (*160-254*/777-868) Abū 'Uthmān 'Amr ibn Bahr, called the "goggle-eyed", Arab litterateur. Grandson of a Negro slave, al-Jāḥiẓ wrote theological tracts, a large work on rhetoric (*Kitāb al-Bayān wa-t-Tabyīn*), forty treatises, and a collection of essays called "The Book of Animals" (*Kitāb al-Ḥayawān*), "The Book of Misers" (*Kitāb al-Buḥalā*), "Excellences of the Turks", "The Superiority in Glory of the Blacks over the Whites" and other essays called *rasāil*. He lived in Baṣrah and was favored by Ibn az-Zaiyāt, the vizier of the Caliph Wāthiq and so spent time at the court in Baghdad and in Sāmarrā'. He admired Greek civilization, had wide-ranging and eclectic interests, and was a Mu'tazilite, giving his name to a sect called the Jāḥiẓiyyah. He is considered a master of the Arabic language and is noted for his humor. "Ideas" he said "run about the street. It's how you express them that matters."

It seems that he was also one of the first to write about political theory in the Islamic world. He probably composed the *Risālat al-'Uthmāniyyah* during the reign of al-Ma'mun (d. *218*/833). It was presented to the Caliph by the courtier al-Yazidi (d. *202*/817). The treatise, which long predates al-Mawardi (d. *450*/1058, *al-Aḥkām as-Sultaniyyah*), and Ibn Taymiyyah (d. *730*/1328, *as-Siyasah ash-Shar'aiyyah*) presents the right to rule as belonging to him who is most pious, and is also elected by popular consent, and demonstrates accountability to those who elected him. The ruler must also present qualities (*faḍl*) of superior virtue, knowledge of religious and worldly matters, and moral qualities such as courage, generosity, and truthfulness. But Jāḥiẓ rejects Shī'ite ideas that rulership is by blood and genealogy. This is affirmed in the Koran because when God gives Abraham leadership over the people, Abraham asks "and what of my progeny?" God answers: "Not if they do wrong." (Koran 2:124).

Jahm, *see* JAHMITES.

Jahmites. The followers of Jahm ibn Ṣafwān Abū Muḥriẓ (d. *128*/745), a radical heretic who taught that God had no attributes, i.e. a God beyond any comprehension and apprehension, but who also followed to an extreme the opinions of the determinists, and apparently held that man had no free-will. This implied that salvation was pre-determined and that man, in effect, could not work either for, or against, his salvation. The Jahmites were condemned by Abū Ḥanīfah in his *Fiqh Akbar. See* FIQH AKBAR; MAKTŪB.

Jalāl ad-Dīn ar-Rūmī (*605-672*/1207-1273). One of the most prominent mystics of Islam. There are, nevertheless, salient elements of heterodoxy in his teaching; he believed in metempsychosis, or transmigration of souls, which is a belief that orthodox doctrine must reject or reduce to a metaphor; and his "universalism" went far enough to be "trans-Islamic" and questionable. But above all, his followers, while appearing to seek union with God, actually seek union with Rūmī. For this and other reasons, the Mevlevis do not readily fraternize with other Sufis. However, the effect of tradition has been to disregard these and integrate him into the mainstream.

Rūmī's genealogy is fantastical hagiography and the story of his life is embellished such that its trajectory of apotheosis, as told by Aflaki, is a foregone conclusion; it would have us believe that he is descended from Abū Bakr on his father's side, Khwarizmian royalty on his mother's, and by his father's initiatic lineage from Aḥmad Ghazālī and Najm ad-Dīn Kubrā, that is, from the cream of mystics. It is said that while in Damascus in *618*/1221 Jalāl ad-Dīn had been seen walking behind his father by Ibn 'Arabī, the eminent exponent of Sufi doctrine, who had exclaimed: "Praise be to God, an ocean is following a lake!"

He was of Persian origin from Balkh, but left at an early age with his father Bahā' ad-Dīn Walad, a scholar who had incurred the displeasure of the rulers (who, the story tells, appear in the middle of the night to excuse themselves to Bahā' ad-Dīn). Balkh by this time, as Nāṣir-i Khusraw lamented, was no longer the "seat of the ancient wisdom" but was experiencing the weight of orthodoxy. Indeed, the Ismā'īlīs of Tajikistan have always regarded Rūmī as one of their own, and this would explain the nature of the conflict with the authorities that led to his exile, which Khusraw and others also experienced.

After several years of wandering, making the pilgrimage to Mecca, then sojourns in Aleppo and Damascus, the family was invited by the Seljūq Sultan of Rūm to settle in Iconium, now Konya, Turkey. To show his respect for Bahā' ad-Dīn, the Sultan advanced out of the town to meet the scholar as he approached Konya, dismounted from his horse, and led Bahā' ad-Dīn's mount by the hand into the city, the story says.

Because of the Byzantine past of the region the city retained the name *Rūm* ("Rome") among the Turks; and it is from this that Jalāl ad-Dīn came to be known as ar-Rūmī, "the man of Rome [Byzantium]". In Konya, Rūmī became a religious teacher, and he was already a Sufi when, at the age of thirty-nine, he met Shams ad-Dīn at-Ṭabrīzī(d. *645*/1247), a mysterious, and probably allegorical figure, who was to exert the most powerful effect upon the poet and to vivify, like a veritable sun, the growth of his latent spiritual and literary genius. Rūmī later wrote of him: "Sun of Tabrīz ... the absolute light ... the sun [Ar. *shams*] and the ray of the lights of Divine Truth."

Shams ad-Dīn of Tabrīz, made by tradition to be one of the spiritual poles (*aqṭāb*) of his age, transformed Rūmī, and brought him to taste direct knowledge. The *Mathnawī*, a vast six-volume work of spiritual teaching and Sufi lore in the form of stories and lyric poetry, was one of the outward results of Rūmī's discipleship to Shams ad-Dīn at-Tabrīzī, to whom Rūmī dedicated much of his work. The *Mathnawī* stands as one of the treasures of the Persian-speaking world, known to all speakers of the language and memorized in part by every literate member of Persian society. The inward realization which Shams ad-Dīn called forth gave Jalāl ad-Dīn ar-Rūmī the force which lives in the dervish order of the Mevlevi (Ar. *Mawlawī*) which he founded and whose center is in Konya. It is interesting to note that Shams is depicted as an objectionable, outrageous, "prankster" figure thus coloring him with the attributes of the Demiurge.

After staying with Rūmī for the period of twelve chehals (forty day periods) of retreat, Shams ad Dīn disappeared from Konya and Jalāl ad-Dīn sent men to look for him. Two years later, he was either found or simply reappeared in Konya; after a further sojourn in the home of Jalāl ad-Dīn he was murdered by persons jealous of him. By that time, however, his disappearances and mysterious re-appearances, and his strange nature may well have been blended into an allegory created by ar-Rūmī to symbolize the dawning or unveiling of the spirit, the reflection of Being within the soul. The story of Shams as a revealing martyr, who then reappears as a living presence with the gathering of the brethren has earlier antecedents in Iranian religious mythology.

The Mevlevi order whom Jalāl ad-Dīn ar-Rūmī founded are known as the "Whirling Dervishes" for their dancing and music (*samāʻ*), both of which are supports for their spiritual method. It has even been said, in Prof. Hamid Dabashi's memorable phrase, that it is "intoxicated Theo-Eroticism", and that Rūmī substituted "love for fear, dance for prayer, singing for recitation, poetry for piety". Apart from the dancing and music of the Mevlevi order, Rūmī is associated with music in other ways, for the singing of the Mathnawī has become an art form in itself.

Jalāl ad-Dīn ar-Rūmī came to be a powerful spiritual influence not only in the Persian-speaking world, including Afghanistan and Central Asia, but also among the Turks, and in India. Sage and poet, his tomb in Konya is a place of pilgrimage for the pious and the questing. For eight centuries he has been a living presence for his followers, many of whom experience his *barakah* ("grace") directly as if he were still with them.

Among the many famous quotations from Rūmī is this:

> Every form you see has its archetype in the Divine world, beyond space; if the form perishes what matter, since its heavenly model is indestructible? Every beautiful form you have seen, every meaningful word you have heard — be not sorrowful because all this must be lost; such is not really the case. The Divine Source is immortal and its outflowing gives water without cease; since neither the one nor the other can be stopped, wherefore do you lament?... From the moment that you came into the world a ladder was put before you that you could escape. First you were a mineral; then you became a plant; then you became an animal. Did you not know that? Then you were made man, given consciousness, knowledge and faith. Think on this body made from dust — what perfection it has! When you have transcended the condition of man you will doubtless become an angel. Then you will have finished with the earth: your home will be heaven. Go beyond the angelic state; go into that ocean so that your drop of water will become one with the sea.

And also:

> Appear as you are, be as you appear. You are not this body, but a spiritual eye — what the eye of man contemplates it becomes...

And the famous:

> Tell me Muslims, what should be done? I don't know how to identify myself. I am neither Christian nor Jewish, neither Pagan nor Muslim. I don't hail from the East or from the West, I am neither from land nor sea. I am not a creature of this world...

See KUBRĀ; MAZAR-I SHARĪF; MEVLEVI; QUṬB; SUFISM.

Jamāʻah (Ar. assembly). A mosque used for Friday Prayers. *See* MOSQUE.

Jamāʻat-i Islāmi. Political party founded in 1941 by Sayyid Abū al-Aʻlā Mawdūdī along with several other intellectuals. The party has branches in India and Bangladesh. They call their program *iqamat-i-deen*, the establishment of religion and subordination of all activities to religion and the establishment of an Islamic state, the abolition of bank interest, introduction of *zakat* and Islamic law. They believe in the use of democratic means although they do support guerilla movements in Kashmir.

The party is distinguished by an extremely disciplined organization and stringent selection of cadres, admitting less than 2% of its supporters to full membership. *Jamā'at-i Islāmi* views Islam, however, as an ideology, and virtually as a political activity in this world rather than a spiritual way directed at the posthumous state of the believer. The aim of restoring the conditions of the first Four Rightly Guided Caliphs, which is the goal of all Fundamentalist Islamic groups, can only be called Utopian. It should be noted that the constitution of Pakistan prohibits the passage of laws which contradict Islam, which along with other institutions, has led some scholars to say that Pakistan is in fact as much an Islamic government as is practically possible. Despite its excellent organization, *Jamā'at-i Islāmi* has been relatively unsuccessful in winning political representation in parliament and has recently boycotted elections in Pakistan protesting that the other candidates, contrary to rules, could not be considered as people of "good character". In India, where Muslims are in a minority, the party is dedicated to preserving Islamic values.

The *Jamā'at-i Islāmi* is headed by an emir, or president, who is elected for five years who is assisted by a *Majlis-i Shoora*, an elected consultative council. Since 2001, *Jamā'at-i Islāmi* has been increasingly implicated in armed struggle. *See* MAWDŪDĪ.

Jamā'at Khānah. An Ismā'īlī meeting place.

Jāmī, Nūr ad-Dīn 'Abd ar-Raḥmān (*817-898*/1414-1492). A famous Persian Sufi poet, and a Sunni. He was born in Jām and died in Herat. An Olympian figure, that one can easily see in the company of Virgil, Homer, Dante, Milton, or Goethe, versatile, talented, prolific, "in Jāmī the mystical and pantheistic thought of Persia may be said to find its most complete and vivid expression." He was a wide ranging scholar but his most famous works are poetic: the *Lawā'iḥ*, ("flashes of light"), "Salmān and Absal", "Yūsuf and Zulaykhah", and the *Bahāristān* ("Abode of Spring").

Jāmī wrote:

Being's a sea in constant billows rolled,
'Tis but these billows that we men behold;
Sped from within, they rest upon the sea,
And like a veil its actual form enfold.
Being's the essence of the Lord of all,
All things exist in Him and He in all;
This is the meaning of the Knower's phrase,
"All things are comprehended in the All."

Janābah. A state of impurity which invalidates the performance of ritual acts such as, for example, the canonical prayers. Its causes include intromission, sexual intercourse or emission, giving birth, menstruation, or contact with a corpse. The state of impurity thus occasioned is removed by the greater ablution (*ghusl*). Other, minor, impurities called *ḥadath* are removed by the lesser ablution (*wuḍū'*). *See* ABLUTIONS.

Janāzah. The funeral process, the procession, and the coffin with the corpse. *See* FUNERAL.

Janissary (from Turkish *yeni cheri*, "new troops"). An elite military corps within the Ottoman Empire selected out of the *devshirme*, the boy-levy of Christian children from the Balkans who were compelled to enter Islam and then raised and trained to be soldiers or officials according to their aptitudes. The beginnings of the Janissaries may date back as early as *731*/1330. They and the system of *devshirme* underwent further development under the Sultan Murad II (d. *855*/1451), and both reached the stage of being fully organized in the reign of Selim I (d. *926*/1520). The Janissary corps were put down and disbanded after they rose in rebellion in *1242*/1826 against the Sultan Mehmet II.

The Janissaries were created to meet the need for an infantry corps during the struggle against the Byzantines. The Turks fought normally as mounted horsemen, but warfare against fortresses called for different kinds of military skills, and an infantry had to be formed. To insure their loyalty, the Janissaries were converted to Islam in their youth, and for this reason remained more reliable than other troops created later from adult converts.

The Janissaries rarely numbered over fifteen thousand, until wars with Persia swelled their ranks to several times that number. After they were given permission to marry in *989*/1581, membership of the corps naturally tended to become hereditary, and the subsequent decline in their military effectiveness was perhaps inevitable, since their selection was based less and less upon military ability. As the core of the army, the Janissaries exerted great influence in the sphere of politics, their power being such that they could sometimes dictate a change of Viziers — or even demand his head — and exact enormous bribes before they allowed a new Sultan to accede to the throne.

In *1242*/1826 the Janissaries rose up in opposition to the creation of a new regular corps called the *Muallem Eshkinji* ("drilled guard"). The Sultan reacted vigorously and induced the religious authorities to issue a malediction against the Janissaries, after which their barracks were surrounded by loyal troops, banners proclaiming holy war were unfurled and, in the attack upon them, most of the Janissaries were killed; their flags and traditional headgear were then publicly dragged through the mud to signify their disgrace. The Bektashi religious confraternity which was peculiar to the Janissaries was outlawed. *See* DEVSHIRME.

al-Jannah (lit. "the garden"). The garden is the most frequent Koranic symbol of paradise. The word suggests that which is veiled, covered or surrounded; hence an "enclosed garden" luxuriant with foliage of tall, shadowing trees and sheltered from storm or tempest. A further significance pointed out by the commentators is that the delights prepared therein for the blessed are concealed and hardly imaginable in man's present state of existence; fruits of obedience to God ripen unseen.

...and the Outstrippers:
the Outstrippers [i.e. the Foremost]
those are they brought nigh [the Throne,]
in the Gardens of Delight
(a throng of the ancients
and how few of the later folk)... (56:10-14).

The Companions of the Right
(O Companions of the Right!)
mid thornless lote-trees and serried acacias,
and spreading shade and outpoured waters,
and fruits abounding
unfailing, unforbidden,
and upraised couches...
...for the Companions of the Right.
A throng of the ancients
and a throng of the later folk. (56:27-39).

In the Koran, *al-jannah* also refers to the Garden of Eden where Adam dwelt with Eve before the Fall.

The desert is dead, sterile and odorless. To come out of the desert into an oasis, is to be overwhelmed by the perfumes of plants and flowers, and the sudden proliferation of life; it is also to be blest with coolness, repose after journeying and water after thirst. To a desert people more than to any other, the planted garden with shade and running water is the most powerfully concrete example by which their imagination may grasp the nature of another, supernatural world.

The Koran often speaks of "Gardens [of paradise] underneath which rivers run". Deep in the Arabian peninsula are aquifers which carry water under pressure, drop by drop, through porous rock from the mountains of the Red Sea to the Gulf on the other side. There (and in spots across the deserts, as well as on the sea floor of the Gulf itself) these aquifers well up as springs, sometimes warm springs, which create the vast oasis of al-Ḥāsa. The movement of the life-giving water from one end of the peninsula to the other takes as long as ten thousand years, a mysterious, secret presence hidden in the earth.

This is the similitude of Paradise
which the godfearing have been promised:
therein are rivers of water unstaling,
rivers of milk unchanging in flavour
and rivers of wine — a delight
to the drinkers,
rivers, too, of honey purified;
and therein for them is every fruit,
and forgiveness from their Lord—(Koran 47:15)

Give thou good tidings to those who believe
and do deeds of righteousness, that for them
await gardens underneath which rivers flow;
whensoever they are provided
with fruits therefrom they shall say,
'This is that wherewithal
we were provided before'; that they shall be
given in perfect semblance; and there
for them shall be spouses purified; therein
they shall dwell forever. (Koran 2:23)

We shall strip away all rancour that is
in their breasts;
as brothers they shall be upon couches
set face to face;
no fatigue shall smite them, neither
shall they ever be driven forth from there.
(Koran 15:47-48)

Surely the pious shall drink of a cup
whose mixture is camphor,
a fountain whereat drink the servants of God,
making it to gush forth plenteously.
They fulfil their vows, and fear
a day whose evil is
upon the wing;
they give food, for the love of Him, to the needy,
the orphan, the captive...

... So God has guarded them from the evil of
that day, and has procured them
radiancy and gladness,
and recompensed them for their patience
with a Garden, and silk;
wherein they shall recline upon couches,
therein they shall see neither sun nor
bitter cold;
near them shall be its shades, and its clusters
hung meekly down,
and there shall be passed around them vessels of
silver, and goblets of crystal,
crystal of silver that they have measured
very exactly.
And therein they shall be given to drink a cup
whose mixture is ginger,
therein a fountain whose name is called Salsabil.
Immortal youths shall go about them;
when thou seest them, thou supposest them
scattered pearls,
when thou seest them then thou seest bliss
and a great kingdom.
Upon them shall be green garments of silk
and brocade; they are adorned with
bracelets of silver, and their Lord shall
give them to drink a pure draught.
Behold, this is a recompense for you, and
your striving is thanked. (Koran 76:5-22)

..and wide-eyed houris
as the likeness of hidden pearls,
a recompense for that they laboured. (Koran
56:22-24)

Perfectly We formed them, perfect,
and We made them spotless virgins,
chastely amorous, like of age
for the Companions of the Right.
(Koran 56:35-38)

Gardens of Eden that the All-merciful
promised His servants in the Unseen; His
promise is ever performed. (Koran 19:61)

Therein they shall hear no idle talk,
no cause of sin, only the saying
'Peace, Peace!' (Koran 56:24-25)

See ESCHATOLOGY.

Jarraḥiyyah, *see* KHALWATIYYAH.

Jāpa-yōga, *see* DHIKR.

Jazā'ir al-arḍ. (Lit. the "Islands of the Earth".) The Ismā'īlīs divided the world into dioceses for the penetration of the *da'wa* or the call to spiritual awakening. According to their symbolism the Great Flood was ignorance and was identified in the case of Islam with exoterism or the religious law, the *sharī'ah.* As the flood, or "ignorance" receded, islands of awareness appeared on the surface of the waters, and so the diocese were called "islands". In the *4th*/10 century the world was divided into twelve such diocese or islands. At the time of al-Qaḍi Nu'man, as cited by Daftary, and by Stern, these regions were: al-'Arab (Arabs), ar-Rūm (Byzantines), aṣ-Ṣaqāliba (Slavs), an-Nūb (Nubians), al-Khazar (Khazars), al-Hind (India), as-Sind (Sindh), az-Zanj (Negroes), al-Habash (Abyssinians). aṣ-Ṣīn (China), ad-Daylam (Daylam), al-Barbar (Berbers). But this is a theoretical division; other, operational divisions, each with its bishop or *ḥujjāh* must have existed at that and other times, or on other levels, for there was certainly a *jazīrah* of Khōrāsan, and a *jazīrah* for Syria. The Arabic name of Algeria, which is *al-Jazā'ir* or, "the Islands", is doubtless derived from this usage, and not from some sundry islands off the coast of Algiers, since from Roman times North Africa was a hotbed of Manicheism, subsequently followed by Ismā'īlī activity which led to the establishment of the Fāṭimid empire.

The hierarchy included the *nātiq*, *waṣī* or *asās*, the Imām, his *bāb*, the *ḥujjahs* (or *laḥiq*, or *naqīb*), four of whom were the equivalent of the the *awtād* or "pegs" in the Sufi hierarchy, and then a number of *dā'īs*. At the bottom was the *mu'min*, or initiated believer, and the candidate or neophyte, *al-mustajīb*. Seven ranks separated the *bāb* from the *mukāsir*, or "persuader". *See* ISMĀ'ĪLĪS.

Jazīrat al-'Arab, (lit. "the island of the Arabs"). The Arabian peninsula.

Jeddah. A city on the Red Sea, Jeddah is the main port of Mecca and Saudi Arabia. (In antiquity the port of Mecca was Shu'aybiyyah, now a beach area.) The name "Jeddah" has been variously interpreted as meaning simply "port", or "new city" (cf. *jadīd*, "new"). However, the traditional view is that it means "grandmother", normally spelled *jiddah*, that is, Eve, the grandmother of all mankind whose "sepulchre" of prodigious length once lay in a cemetery which is today covered over in the centre of the city.

Jeddah is one of the largest and busiest cities in Saudi Arabia, the Kingdom's center of commerce and the major port of entry for pilgrims coming by sea and by air. The vast King 'Abd al-'Azīz Airport was opened in 1981. Its centerpiece is the striking open-air mass transit terminal designed as a gigantic tent city to handle the millions of pilgrims who converge on the city at the time of the *ḥajj*. *See* PILGRIMAGE.

Jerusalem (Ar. *al-Quds*, "the Holy", probably originally so called from *al-bayt al-muqaddas*, "the Holy House", that is, the Temple of Solomon). The holiest place in Islam after Mecca and Medinah, Jerusalem is sometimes referred to as "the third *ḥaram*". Its holiness for Muslims derives, in the first place, from its association with the Old Testament Prophets, who are also Prophets in Islam. The association with Jesus is no less important, and Jerusalem figures in popular accounts of apocalyptic events as seen by Islam.

However, the sacred nature of Jerusalem is confirmed for Muslims above all by the Night Journey, in which the Prophet Muḥammed was brought by the angel Gabriel to the Dome of the Rock on the Temple Mount. From here they ascended together into the heavens (Koran 17:1). The Koran refers to Jerusalem as the *al-Masjid al-Aqṣā*, or the "Furthest Mosque" (that is, the Temple of Solomon) "whose precincts We [God] have blessed" (Koran 17:1). The Dome of the Rock sanctuary now stands over the rock, and nearby is the mosque today called al-Masjid al-Aqṣā. The Temple Mount is called *al-Ḥaram ash-Sharīf* (the "Noble Sanctuary").

Other Islamic monuments in Jerusalem include the Ashrafiyyah, Jawliyyah, As'ardiyah, Mālikiyyah, Tankiziyyah, and 'Uthmāniyyah *madrasahs*, the 'Umarī and al-Ḥamrā' mosques, fountains (those of Qa'it Bey, Bāb an-Nadhīr), *khāns* or hospices (of Muḥammad Ibn Zamīn), and gates, palaces, and mausoleums.

Jerusalem's importance is such that when 'Abd Allāh ibn az-Zubayr was elected Caliph in defiance of the Umayyads and seized Mecca in *64*/683, the Umayyads could proclaim that the pilgrimage was to be performed to Jerusalem, which they controlled, instead of Mecca.

The city first came under Muslim rule in *17*/638 when the patriarch Sophronius surrendered it to the troops of Caliph 'Umar. The Caliph visited the city after the conquest and Sophronius accompanied him to the Temple mount to search for the *miḥrāb* (prayer niche) of David, of which 'Umar had heard the Prophet speak. The Temple mount had fallen into great disorder through neglect, and was covered with refuse. The Caliph ordered it cleaned and had a place of prayer built nearby.

The Turkish Caliphs paid a great deal of attention to the city, adding more edifices to its ancient heritage. The present walls were built by Sülayman the Magnificent. *See* al-AQṢĀ; DOME of the ROCK; NIGHT JOURNEY; SOLOMON.

Jesus, Son of Mary (Ar. *'Īsā ibn Maryam*). He holds a singularly exalted place in Islam. The Koran says that Jesus was born of a virgin (3:45-47); that he is a "Spirit from God" (*rūḥun mina' Llāh*), and the "Word of God" (*kalimatu-Llāh*) (4:171). He is usually called "Jesus son of Mary" (*'Īsā ibn Maryam*), and his titles include Messiah (*masīḥ*), Prophet (*nabī*), Messenger of God (*rasūl*) and "one of those brought nigh [to God]". According to the Koran he performed various symbolic miracles; he raised the dead, brought the revealed book of the Gospel (*Injīl*), and called down as a sign from heaven a table laden with sustenance (5:112-114), which symbolizes the communion host of Christianity.

In Islam, on the authority of the Koran, Jesus has a mission as a rasūl, a Prophet of the highest degree who brings a restatement of God's religion (3:46-60). It is said, too, that he did not die upon the cross: "They slew him not but it appeared so to them" (4:157). A crucifixion took place, but Jesus is alive in a principial state, outside the world and time: "But God took him up to Himself. God is ever Mighty, Wise." (4:158).

It is in fact the common belief among Muslims that the crucifixion was an illusion, or that someone else was substituted for Jesus. This idea of the crucifixion as an appearance, called *docetism*, was found among Marcionites and in Manicheism. While popular belief cannot be held to account, the crucifixion as a pointless charade can hardly be meet to God's purpose, and two thousand years have not shown what God could have meant by such sleight of hand. Nor does the Koran warrant such a view. Rather, it is that the crucifixion of Jesus does not play a role in the Islamic perspective any more than does his superhuman origin, for salvation in Islam results from the recognition of the

Absoluteness of God and not from a sacrificial mystery. Since Islam believes that Jesus will return at the end of time, his death was no more than apparent and did not, as in Christian belief, involve a resurrection after the event. In Islam it is the absolute, or higher, reality that takes precedence in the Koran over the appearances of this world, be they of life or of death. It is this verse about the state of martyrs which holds the key to understanding "They slew him not": "Say not of those who are slain in God's way that they are dead; they are living but you perceive not" (2:154). Or: "Think not of those who are slain in the way of God that they are dead. Nay! they are living. With their Lord they have provision" (3:169).

According to various Ḥadīth, Jesus will return before the Day of Judgement, and destroy the Anti-Christ (*ad-dajjāl*) who, towards the end of time, presents an inverted version of spirituality, misleading mankind in a final and fatal delusion. Then Jesus, it is said, will bring the cycle of Adamic manifestation to an end, and inaugurate another, in what is, in effect, the Second Coming.

There are certain Ḥadīth which say that Jesus and Mary did not cry out when they were born; all other children do because, according to the symbolic interpretation, they are touched by the devil in coming into this world. In the words of the Prophet Muḥammed, Jesus and Mary were the only beings in history to be born in such a state of sinlessness.

Although the position of Jesus in Islam is extraordinary in a number of ways, even for a Prophet, that Islam should concede any idea of his divinity or admit that he is "the Son of God" is entirely precluded. This, or any trinitarian idea of God, or any suggestion that Jesus is somehow an hypostasis of God, is rejected by Islam.

Many Muslims think that the Christian trinity includes Mary, and certain Christian sects in ancient Arabia actually held such a belief. However, the trinitarian concept, in any form, is necessarily alien to Islam, because the principle which saves in Islam is precisely the recognition of the Divine *Unity*, the all-embracing Reality of the Absolute.

Because the Koran says that all God's Prophets have brought only the one religion of Islam, it is impossible for most Muslims to conceive that the religion brought by Jesus could, in reality, have been anything other than the Islam of the Muslim believer, the Islam of the "Five Pillars". That there is an Islam beyond form which is the religion of each Divine messenger as he faces God, or that a formless Islam is the essence of each religion, are necessarily esoteric concepts. That Christianity as it exists is based upon the doctrine that Jesus is a Divine incarnation, and that his crucifixion and resurrection have redeemed the sins of mankind and saved those who believe in him, can only be explained in the mind of the Muslim as some extraordinary historical error of interpretation or understanding.

It would perhaps seem therefore that Jesus as he is viewed in Islam, and despite the extraordinary attributes credited to him by the Koran, would actually have a role and a nature that could be interpreted into the Islamic universe only with great difficulty. Such, however, is not the case, because Christianity, like Judaism, is specifically mentioned as a revealed religion and Islamic legislation gives it a protected status. It is the nature of Jesus as a Prophet among the other Prophets of the Old Testament which is decisive for Muslims, and the disturbing elements of Christianity as it actually exists are simply set aside, placed outside of Islam, and in practice pose no great enigma, being seen as a kind of archaic survival which God in the Koran has chosen to tolerate. If this seems puzzling to Christians, they must remember that their rejection of the Prophethood of Muḥammad is an equally incredible act for Muslims. Ultimately, it is perhaps only with the fulfillment of the role that God has assigned in prophecy to Jesus at the end of time, when the world and history are swallowed up by the purely miraculous, that the different cadences of the great religions will resolve themselves into one. *See* BIBLE; DAJJĀL; MARY.

Jihād (from Ar. *jahd*, "effort"). "Holy war", a Divine institution of warfare to extend Islam into the *dar al-ḥarb* (the non-Islamic territories which are described as the "abode of struggle", or of disbelief) or to defend Islam from danger. Adult males must participate if the need arises, but not all of them, provided that "a sufficient number" (*farḍ al-kifāyah*) take it up. The idea of "holy war" seems strange to the modern mind, but every society necessarily justifies its own wars as holy implicitly. Blood is spilled deliberately and the reason for it must therefore be consecrated. In Islam this need arises even before the fact, because of the assumption that war could not exist at all if men were submitted to the will of God; yet war does exist so it must have a religious basis.

An important precondition of *jihād* is a reasonable prospect of success, failing which a *jihād* should not be undertaken. According to the Sunnah, a *jihād* is not lawful unless it involves the summoning of unbelievers to belief, and the *jihād* must end when order is restored, that is, when the unbelievers have accepted either Islam or a protected status within Islam, or when Islam is no longer under threat. It is impossible to undertake a *jihād* against Muslims.

In colonial times, when many Islamic countries were under non-Muslim domination — an anomalous condition from the point of Islamic law — it was concluded that, provided Islam was not prohibited, and indeed as long as certain of the institutions peculiar to it were allowed to continue, holy war could not be justified. Although opportunistic calls to *jihād* have been made sporadically when the interests of particular political leaders could be advanced by such warfare, they have never received general support from the religious authorities (*'ulamā'*).

Those who die in a genuine *jihād* — and the laws determining this are complex — are considered to be martyrs (*shuhadā'*), who, as such, have special merit, and enter paradise directly. The Khārijites made *jihād* a sixth pillar of the religion, and it is still so among their modern descendants, the Ibāḍites. On the other hand, the *jihād* is legally impossible for the Twelve-Imām Shī'ites until the return of the Hidden Imām. A genuine *jihād*, as opposed to merely political warfare, has rarely been invoked since Islam's original struggle for survival against the Meccans.

A *4th*/10th century sermon by a preacher named Ibn Nubata exhorts thus to *jihād*:

> How long, ye men, will ye hear warning and heed not?
> And how long will ye abide the whipping and stir not?
> Your ears shake off the Preacher's words. Or are your hearts too haughty to hear? The Fiend has roused up those others to fight for his lies, and they rise up and follow,
> While the Omnipotent summons you to His Truth, and you ignore His Call.
> Beasts fight for mate and cub; birds will die for their nests; yet Prophet and Revelation have they none. But you, who understand, and have the Law and wisdom, scatter away like startled camels before their foes.
> God claims your faith and steadfastness; God promises His Help and Victory again.
> Do you not really trust Him?
> Do you doubt His Justice or His Goodness?
> Give your soul, man, wholly up to Him unto Whom it doth belong. Put no trust in prudence: your prudence will not put off your appointed term to die.
> War! War! ye men of heart!
> Victory! Sure Victory! ye resolute!
> Paradise! Paradise for you who march on!
> And Hell! Hell for you who fly!
> Victory's reward in this world, and the martyr's in the Next; and of these two how much the sweeter is the last!
> Then stand by God; for "Him who helpeth God, will God most surely help." (22:40)

And the Koran says:

> Leave is given to those who fight because
> they were wronged — surely God is able
> to help them—
> who were expelled from their habitations
> without right, except that they say
> 'Our Lord is God.' Had God not driven back
> the people, some by means of others,
> there had been destroyed cloisters and churches,
> oratories and mosques, wherein God's Name
> is much mentioned. Assuredly God will
> help him who helps Him — surely God is
> All-strong, All-mighty... (22:40-42)

It is said popularly, that *jihād* was once the eradication of polytheism and false belief and the spread of Islam. Then it became defense of Islam; but it is also removing evil with the tongue or by an act, or when that is not possible, by condemning it in the heart.

In the West, *jihād* is often considered a strange institution. However, it should be remembered that no-one who declares a war believes that his war is "unholy". Every country justifies its war by elevating it to a high moral level: "to make the world safe for democracy", to "establish a new world order" etc. Defense of own's country is generally considered a "sacred duty". The notion of *jihād* is no different; in a context of divinely instituted laws it has its place, just as marriage does, or commerce, or the law of contracts. *See* FIVE PILLARS; MARTYRS.

al-Jīlānī, 'Abd al-Qadir, *see* 'ABD al-QĀDIR al-JĪLĀNĪ.

al-Jīlī, 'Abd al-Karīm (*767-820*/1365-1417). A famous mystic, born in Jīl near Baghdad. He was a Sufi of the school of Ibn 'Arabī and wrote the book *al-Insān al-Kāmil* ("the Perfect Man"). This is a treatise on the doctrine of realization of the true self. *See* al-INSĀN al-KĀMIL.

Jinn (from which the English word *genie*). The inhabitants of the subtle and immaterial — or subtly material — world, the *'ālam al-malakūt* into which the material and physical world is plunged, as if into a liquid. If we picture a room in our mind, the "medium" in which that imagined room exists supports form, but is itself subtle; it is the *'ālam al-malakūt*. In traditional cosmology, the physical world is a "crystallization", or projection, out of the subtle world, the "ether"; the "ether" is a projection out of the surrounding formless, or Angelic, world; and the Angelic world is projected out of Being (*see* FIVE DIVINE PRESENCES).

Jinn are the inhabitants of the subtle world, some of whom are "non-central" beings like the non-human creatures of this world, whilst others are "central" beings, like men, *jinn* with free will, endowed with the Intellect and capable of grasping Reality, and thus capable of being saved. The *jinn* who occupy this central state have therefore religions and revelations, and some of their religions correspond to the religions of the world of men.

During the Prophet's journey to Ṭā'if he recited the Koran at night in the desert and a party of the *jinn* came, listened, and believed. Later their chiefs came to the Prophet and made a *bay'ah*, or an allegiance, with him on the spot which is today the "Mosque of the Jinn" in Mecca.

Satan, considered to be a *jinn* who was originally an Angel, forfeited his Angelic nature by disobeying God. Angels, who belong to the formless world, the *'ālam al-jabarūt*, and are formless as are the odors of perfumes, have to take on a subtle nature in order to appear to men. In other words, they take on a substance of the subtle world, which is formal (in that what exists in that world has "form") and then they assume a visible "form". For example, magnetic fields are only "visible" when they work upon a substance that responds to them, and if Angels appear, they must do so in an "ethereal" form.

The Koran says that the *jinn* were created of "smokeless fire" (55:15) whereas man was created of clay, as by a potter; the Angels are created of light. Some *jinn* are friendly to mankind, and others hostile; some are beautiful, and others, the *'ifrīt* and *ghūl* (from which the word *ghoul* derives), are hideous. Solomon is famed for his power to command the *jinn* to his bidding, in building the temple, and in the working of prodigies (38:37-41). Islamic lore says, moreover, that the lives of certain *jinn* are incomparably longer than human lifetimes, and that there are *jinn* alive today in the subtle world who were alive in the time of the Prophet.

Sometimes the Koran addresses men and *jinn* together, as in the Sūrat ar-Raḥmān which is directed throughout to both in the dual person of Arabic. It says: "O ye two having weight" (*thaqalān*), meaning the two species of creation having *form* (55:31): and "O company of *jinn* and men, if ye are able to pass beyond the regions of the heavens and the earth, then pass beyond! Ye shall not pass, except by authority. Which then, of the favors of your Lord, do the two of you deny?" (55:33-34). *See also* ANGELS.

Jinnah, Muḥammad 'Alī (*1293-1367*/1876-1948). The first president of Pakistan. Born in Karachi, he studied law in Britain and entered into politics in India in 1910. From 1913 he played an active role in the Muslim League, whose president he became in 1916. Jinnah was a Nizārī Ismā'īlī and was actually indifferent, if not disdainful to religion and Islam in particular. His first speech after the creation of Pakistan actually called upon its citizens to disregard their religious affiliations in favor of their new national identity.

Nevertheless, he first took part in efforts by the Muslim League and the Congress Party of India to promote Hindu-Muslim cooperation in the political sphere. He withdrew from the Congress in 1930 to pursue a policy which led to the partition of India at independence, and the birth of Pakistan as a nation in August 1947.

Jizyah. A tax formerly levied on such non-Muslim adult males as were able to pay it, provided that they belonged to a religion recognized as Divinely revealed, that is, were "people of the book" (*Ahl al-Kitāb*). Pagans conquered and brought into the Islamic state had, in theory, either to accept Islam or death; however, this provision was rarely, if ever, applied; the Ḥarrānians, who were Hellenist Pagans, eventually obtained the status of people with a revelation and were called "Ṣābians". The infirm and poor were excluded from paying the tax.

The basis of the *jizyah* is the Koran (9:29):

Fight those who believe not
in God and the Last Day
and do not forbid what God and His Messenger
have forbidden — such men as practise not the
religion of truth, being of
those who have been given
the Book — until they pay the tribute out of hand
and have been humbled.

It was normally understood to be a tax for civil protection and the upkeep of the army, but it did in practice sometimes take on the aspect of a tribute. The minimum *jizyah* was one dinar. The word comes from *gēzit*, a personal tax under the Sāssānids. The *kharāj*, another and later tax on non-Muslims, and one not indicated in the Koran, was based on the yield from land. *See* AHL al-KITĀB.

Jñāna Marga, *see* MA'RIFAH.

Job, *see* AYYŪB.

John the Baptist, *see* YAḤYĀ.

Jonah, *see* YŪNUS.

Jordan. Hashemite Kingdom of Jordan. Population 4,212,152. 92% Muslim, 8% Christian. Most of Jordan is desert and the only port is Aqaba, on the Red Sea. In Arabic the country is called Urdunn, and was, in Umayyad times a "military district" called a *jund.* The present Kingdom sprang from the Emirate of Transjordan which was created from the disintegration of the Ottoman Empire. The first ruler was the Emir 'Abd Allāh, later King, son of the Sherif of Mecca, ruler of the Hejaz who had aided the British during the First World War. He took the title of King when the country became independent of the British mandate in 1946. Jordan came into being when East Jerusalem and the West Bank were annexed in 1948 after the creation of Israel and the war which followed. In the Arab Israeli war of 1967 both were lost to Israel, and in 1988 King Hussein renounced them which led to the peace treaty with Israel of 1994. Jordan is a constitutional monarchy since 1952.

Joseph, *see* YŪSUF.

Journey, Night, *see* NIGHT JOURNEY.

Judaism, *see* BANŪ ISRĀ'ĪL; DÖNMEH.

Judge, *see* QĀḌI.

Judgement, Day of, *see* YAWM ad-DĪN.

al-Junayd, Abū-l-Qāsim ibn Muḥammad (d. *297*/910). One of the most famous of the early Sufis, who taught in Baghdad, he was a disciple of the Sufi Sarī aṣ-Ṣaqaṭī. An important figure in the development of Sufi doctrine, like Ḥasan of Baṣrah before him and Imām ash-Shādhilī after him, al-Junayd was widely respected and quoted by other Sufis, to the point of being known as the "Sultan" or "Sayyid" (lord) of the *'ārifīn* ("knowers of God").

He wrote no books, but his teachings are reported in the *Kitāb al-Lumā'* of as-Sarrāj (d. *378*/788), in the letters which he wrote, and in the writings of other Sufis. The doctrine as formulated by him is systematic and sober; he advocated the integration of mysticism into ordinary life, commending that Sufis live as householders and not as wandering mendicants. His approach is characterized by an attitude in which Divine knowledge is stabilized within the soul in this world. This the Sufis call *ṣawḥ* (sobriety), as opposed to *sukr* (inebriation or ecstasy).

In the first centuries of the Hijrah, Islam was exposed to many influences in the course of its expansion. Converts from Iranian religions in particular brought with them a tendency to deify the major exponents of religious realization, whether Saints or charismatic leaders. This gave rise to the emergence of so-called "drunken Sufis", such as Bāyazīd al-Bisṭāmī, al-Ḥallāj and Ibn Abī-l-Khayr, with their intriguing implications of a "personal" union with God. Al-Junayd became the spokesman of rigor and the defender of a Sufism firmly planted in exoteric orthodoxy. A Sufi reported:

> *Intoxication* is a mystic term denoting ecstatic love for God; *Sobriety* proposes the attainment of some end. Bāyazīd and his disciples, who think Intoxication the higher way, maintain that Sobriety stabilizes human attributes which are the greatest of all Veils between God and man. But my own Shaykh, following al-Junayd, used to say that Intoxication is a playground for children, and Sobriety a mortal battleground for men.

Al-Junayd was a merchant and he kept a shop in

Baghdad. He rejected al-Ḥallāj from his circle saying "I do not accept madmen." To al-Ḥallāj's assertion that "I am the Reality" (*Ana al-Ḥaqq*), tradition has al-Junayd respond: "No. It is *through* Reality that you exist."

In his approach to *ma'rifah*, or gnosis, al-Junayd emphasized the aspect of witness and consciousness (*shuhūd*), rather than that of Being (*wujūd*), and the aphorism, "everything that you see is the Act of One" is the very essence of his approach. Of *tawḥīd*, or union with God, al-Junayd said: "It is the removing of the temporal from the eternal." The opposition of the *Shuhūd* ("consciousness") school to *wujūd* ("being") turns precisely on the danger of *wujūd* leading to an identification of the world with God. *See* al-BISṬĀMĪ; al-ḤALLĀJ; SUFISM; TAWḤĪD.

Jundīshāpūr (also called Gandisapora, Gundishahpur, etc.). An academy founded in the third century near Ahvāz, in the region of modern Sānābād in Khuzistān, when Persia was ruled by the Sāssānids. The academy was founded by oriental Christians who became Nestorians after the council of Nicea. It was a center which transmitted the study of Hellenistic learning and philosophy to the Muslims.

Translations were made here from Greek to Syriac, and later to Arabic. In 'Abbāsid times it was also an important school of medicine teaching the methods of Hippocrates and Galen.

A number of famous medical figures were associated with it, notably the Bakhtishishu family and Ḥunayn ibn Isḥāq, all of whom were Nestorians.

Juvaini, 'Alā ad-Dīn 'Aṭā' Mālik, *see* JUWAYNĪ, 'ALĀ ad-DĪN 'ATĀ' MĀLIK.

al-Juwaynī, 'Abd al-Mālik (d. *478*/1085). A Persian Ash'arite theologian who fled persecution under Tughril Beg and took refuge in the Hejaz, teaching at Mecca and Medinah. Because of this he acquired the epithet *Imām al-Ḥaramayn*, "the Imām of the two Sanctuaries".

The initial hostility shown by the Seljūqs towards Ash'arism receded and finally vanished as awareness of the ideological threat represented by the Fāṭimids brought them to realize that Ash'arite doctrine, being clear, vigorous, and unambiguous, provided a defensive weapon. As a result, al-Juwaynī became a protegé of the Vizier Niẓām al-Mulk, who founded the Niẓāmiyyah school at Nayshābūr for him. Al-Juwaynī was one of the teachers of al-Ghazālī and also of al-Anṣārī.

Al-Juwaynī wrote, among a vast number of works, the *Ghiyāth al-Umam* (the "Savior of Nations") which argued that the Caliphate, by tradition a prerogative of the Quraysh, could be held if necessary by whoever could assure just government; it is likely that, in writing it, he had Niẓām al-Mulk in mind.

al-Juwaynī, 'Alā' ad-Dīn 'Aṭā' Malik (*623-682*/1226-1283). A Persian historian, of a distinguished Khorāsān family, his grandfather and father were in the service of the Khwārizm-Shāhīs. When the Mongols drove the Khwārizm-Shāhī Sultan Muḥammad and his son Jalāl ad-Dīn out of the region, Juwaynī's father Baha' ad-Dīn entered the service of the Mongols, administering the conquered territories and frequently visited Qaraqorum.

Al-Juwaynī succeeded his father and accompanied Hūlāgū Khān on his invasions of Persia. He was present at the conquest of Alamūt and inspected the famous library of the Assassins, rescuing what he called "choice books" and burning others which he considered heretical. Al-Juwaynī, a Twelve-Imām Shī'ite, became the governor for the Mongol Il-Khanids of the territories which had been directly ruled by the 'Abbāsids and so took up residence in Baghdad. He acquired great wealth and authority, but several times was accused before the Mongols, by rivals eager to unseat him, of conspiring with the Mamlūks or of embezzling fortunes. These accusations led to swings in his position with the Mongols towards the end of his life. He died of a stroke brought on by grief, and was buried in Ṭabrīz.

In *658*/1260 al-Juwaynī wrote an erudite history of the Mongols in a highly sophisticated Persian style. It is called *Ta'rīkh-i Jahān Kūshā* ("The History of the World Conqueror"), and included a detailed history of the Fāṭimids and the Assassins ("a sect of people...in whose hearts was rooted a fellow-feeling with the Magians"). *See* MONGOLS.

K

Ka'bah (lit. "cube"). The large cubic stone structure, covered with a black cloth, which stands in the center of the Grand Mosque of Mecca. In one corner, the Ka'bah contains the Black Stone. Neither the stone nor the Ka'bah are objects of worship, but they represent a sanctuary consecrated to God since time immemorial, and it is towards the Ka'bah that Muslims orient themselves in prayer; thus the Ka'bah is a spiritual center, a support for the concentration of consciousness upon the Divine Presence. (If one makes the ritual prayer inside the Ka'bah, it can be made in any direction; this is also true at the antipodes of Mecca in the South Pacific Ocean.) The Ka'bah is also called the "holy house" (*al-bayt al-ḥarām*) and "the Ancient house" (*al-bayt al-'atīq*). The Black Stone (*al-ḥajar al-aswad*) is in the southeast corner, set one and one-half meters from the ground. In the opposite corner, set somewhat lower, is another stone of a reddish color called the "stone of felicity" (*ḥajar as-sa'ādah*). It is the center of the Ka'bah which marks the direction of the *qiblah*, the focal point of ritual prayer. Overhanging the roof on one side is the *mith'āb* or rainspout. The foundation at the base of the Ka'bah is called the *shadrawān*. The space between the Black Stone and the door is the *al-multazam*, the "place to hold on to". Around the Ka'bah is a restricted precinct called the *ḥaram* of Mecca; this, in fact, surrounds the city on all sides, in some directions as far as twelve miles or twenty kilometers. In this precinct the taking of any kind of life (except that of noxious or dangerous creatures) is not allowed, and only Muslims are allowed to enter.

The Ka'bah was originally founded, tradition says, by Adam, and after his death rebuilt by his son Seth. When the time came, it was rebuilt by Abraham and his son Ismā'īl (Ishmael). This Ka'bah was built without a roof but with doors at ground level on the east and the west sides. When it was finished, Abraham was commanded by God to go to Mount Thābir nearby and call mankind to pilgrimage to the "ancient house" (*al-bayt al-'atīq*).

Afterwards, the Ka'bah was rebuilt by the clan of the Amālikah, descendents of Noah, and then by the Banū Jurhum, who also descended from Noah through Qaḥṭān, the Joktan of the Bible. Several hundred years before the revelation of the Koran, the Ka'bah was rebuilt again by Qusayy ibn Qilab, who had led the Quraysh tribe to Mecca. At that time, according to the historian Azraqī, the Ka'bah, without a roof, was 4.5 meters high, and there were venerated stones in all four corners.

Eighteen years before the Hijrah it was rebuilt again. A Byzantine ship which had been wrecked in Mecca's port of Shu'aybiyyah provided the wood for the Ka'bah, which was built in alternate layers of teakwood and stone by a Coptic carpenter called Baqūm. When the time came to replace the Black Stone, strife broke out between various persons demanding the honor of putting it back, leading to so serious a dispute that bloodshed was threatened. Muḥammad, then known as the "Trustworthy" (*al-Amīn*), and not yet called to his prophetic mission, appeared on the scene at this crucial moment and was asked to resolve the dispute. He invited the leaders of the clans to carry the stone by holding a cloth onto which it had been placed; he then lifted up the stone himself and set it in the corner of the wall.

After the establishment of Islam, Caliphs 'Umar and 'Uthmān both felt the need to enlarge the Mosque (*al-Masjid al-Ḥarām*) around the Ka'bah. They compensated the owners of the surrounding houses which had to be demolished in order to increase the circumambulation area (*al-maṭāf*), and 'Umar was the first to build an enclosure around the Ka'bah, less than the height of a man, with gates and lamps. 'Uthmān introduced covered porticos for prayers.

When in *64*/684 Mecca, then under occupation by the insurgent 'Abd Allāh ibn az-Zubayr, was besieged by the army of Yazīd, the Umayyad, a flaming arrow from one of the besiegers set fire to the Ka'bah, which was destroyed. The heat cracked the Black Stone into three pieces. On examining the original foundation of the now demolished Ka'bah, Ibn az-Zubayr concluded that the Ka'bah had previously included the enclosure to one side (*al-ḥijr*) containing the graves of Ismā'īl (Ishmael) and Hagar. He therefore rebuilt it on a larger scale, increasing its greatest length to 26 cubits from the previous 18. He also made it higher, raising it from 18 to 27 cubits, and built it of stone, with two doors. The Black Stone was repaired and held together by a silver band around the three pieces. He brought mosaics and columns from a church in the Yemen (originally built by Abrahah who had wished his church to rival the religious attraction of Mecca), using the mosaics for decoration and setting three polychrome marble columns inside. In the tradition of the Caliph Mu'āwiyah, Ibn az-Zubayr covered the Ka'bah with black silk.

'Abd Allāh ibn az-Zubayr, who had declared himself Caliph in opposition to the Umayyads, was slain by the troops of the Caliph 'Abd al-Malik ibn Marwān led by al-Ḥajjāj ibn Yūsuf, in *73*/692. Al-Ḥajjāj, for his part, disliked the changes which had been made and reduced the Ka'bah to its former size, leaving a semicircular wall surrounding the *ḥijr*, and the *ḥijr* itself, outside the Ka'bah. Further building was done by the Caliphs Mahdī, Mu'tamid, and Mu'tadid. Mahdī extended the *maṭāf*, and added three rows of colonnades, himself participating in the work. By *167*/782, the Ka'bah had much the appearance it has today.

In *979*/1571 the famous architect Sīnān, who had already built many resplendent mosques in Istanbul and Turkey, began rebuilding the Mosque around the Ka'bah, the previous mosque having been demolished the year before on the orders of the Ottoman Sultan Selim II. For the sacred mosque, *al-Masjid al-Ḥarām*, Sīnān created a colonnade of 892 columns of marble and stone over which were set 500 arches and cupolas. The interior decoration of gold designs and calligraphy was the work of 'Abd Allāh al-Muftī. The whole was completed by *994*/1586; it had seven minarets and nineteen entrances, and there was prayer space for 12,000 in the covered part of the mosque; another 24,000 could pray in the open courtyard. In *1030*/1620 floods swept away the Station of Abraham (*Maqām Ibrāhīm*), the lamps, and part of the walls of the Ka'bah. Sultan Mūrād ordered extensive repairs which did not, however, involve any restructuring.

However, from *1375*/1955 a massive program of enlargement and rebuilding of the mosque was initiated and carried out in the reign of King Fayṣal of Saudi Arabia. In *1377*/1957 cracks were found in the Ka'bah and repaired — the first work on the structure since *1039*/1629. In this rebuilding the mosque was considerably enlarged. It has since then perhaps held several hundreds of thousands of worshippers at a time. The sa'y course, which until then had been outside the mosque, was roofed over and is now within the precincts of the mosque, which was rebuilt on two levels on both of which the ritual circumambulation (*ṭawāf*) is now performed.

The architects had originally recommended that the mosque of Sīnān be torn down, to be replaced by an entirely new structure. King Fayṣal thereupon called a conference of architects to discuss the question, who proceeded to make the same recommendation. To his very great credit, King Fayṣal insisted that the rebuilding and expansion of the mosque conserve as much as possible of the mosque of Sīnān; this was done, thereby saving this magnificent monument from demolition.

The dimensions of the present day Ka'bah are: the north-east wall 12.63 meters, the eastern wall 11.22 meters, the western wall 13.10 meters, and the northwest wall 11.03 meters (it is not completely regular). Its height is 13 meters. The door on the northern side is 2 meters from the ground and is 1.7 meters wide.

A new *kiswah* (cover or cladding) is made for the Ka'bah each year; it is a black cloth with black calligraphic patterns woven into it, and a band of Koranic calligraphy in gold thread around the top portion. The old *kiswah* is removed and cut up after the annual pilgrimage and the pieces are distributed to pilgrims. The Ka'bah is then covered with a new *kiswah*; while it is being replaced a temporary white covering is placed upon the Ka'bah.

The 12th century Sufi Ibn 'Arabī said that the Ka'bah represents Being. As the Adamic temple, it is the first temple of mankind; and as the temple of the last religion, it is also the final temple of mankind, the once forgotten sanctuary, the keystone. In Christianity, the end of the cycle of Adamic creation is marked by the symbolism of the perfect city, the descent of the new Jerusalem from heaven. The perfect city is a crystalline, geometric symbol from the mineral world, in complementary opposition to the organic symbolism of the beginning of the cycle, which is the garden, vegetation, and, above all, the tree of the knowledge of good and evil at its center. Islam shares the symbol of the garden of the beginning with Judaism and Christianity, but its symbol of the center at the end of time is not that of the city, the abstract, man-made habitat that replaces nature, but of the geometric essence of the city, reduced to its simplest form. This is nothing more than a cube, the abstraction of a crystal, the cube of the Ka'bah. Thus the eschatological paradigm of the symbolic "squaring of the circle" is completed, or transposed; the sphere is made cube, the perfect potentiality of the beginning reduced to the perfect completion and stability of the end. The juxtaposition of the organic and the crystalline is also prominent in the decorative calligraphy that is so striking a feature of Islamic architecture: here, the words of the Koran, the crystallization of Divine speech, intertwine with floral motifs; the Intellect intertwines with existence.

One should add that the Ka'bah represents the ultimate "enclosure" for the Divine Presence that the Old Testament calls the Shekhinah (also "Schechina"). After the covenant with Abraham the Shekhinah "dwelt" in the Ark until, when the Jews ceased to be nomads and Solomon built the Temple, the Shekhinah dwelt in the Holy of Holies. The New Testament says that when Jesus' body was pierced with the lance, the veil of the Temple was rent in twain and the Shekhinah went out of the Holy of Holies into the world. Thus the Ka'bah is both the Ark of the Covenant and the Holy of Holies, not in the sense of enclosing the Divine Presence but, rather, as the center of a Holy of Holies that stretches out in all directions; thus the whole earth becomes the locus of prayer for every Muslim, who each day fulfills the role that the Jewish high priest performed only on the Day of Atonement. Since Islam is the return to the primordiality of Adam, the whole earth is once more symbolically the paradisal garden, from any point of which, man, like Adam, may talk in sacred speech with God. *See also* BLACK STONE; ḤIJR; TAWĀF.

Kābil and Hābil, *see* CAIN and ABEL; IBN KHALDŪN.

al-Kaff, *see* "Hand of Fatimah".

Kāfir (lit. "he who conceals by covering", plur. *kafirūn, kuffār, kafarah, kifār*). The *kāfir* is one who refuses to see the truth; an "infidel" who rejects the evidence of Divine Revelation through the mission of the Prophet Muḥammad or the Divine messengers before him, and who is thus ungrateful to God, and an atheist. One can sometimes hear Muslims refer to Christians as *kafirūn*; but this is loose usage and incorrect according to Islamic law; the People of the Book (and those who believe in God) are not *kafirūn*. Such a misusage once caused a scandal in an Egyptian court of law. *See* KUFR; SHIRK.

Kāhin (a priest, wizard, or soothsayer, akin to the Hebrew *kohen*. Feminine: *kāhinah*). In pre-Islamic Arabia, soothsayers were often the guardians of sanctuaries considered to be holy places, some of which were on heights, and often in groves of trees, that is, places where there was underground water. It was believed that the *kāhins* had supernatural powers; they could confer blessings or cast curses; and remove curses cast by others. They were consulted by those seeking solutions to problems, to find lost animals, and to settle disputes. The *kāhin* would speak with his "familiar spirit" (perhaps his own psychic projection), look into people's souls, and read the future. Sometimes in a consultation the *kāhin* would go into a trance and make pronouncements in rhythmical prose called *saj'*.

The Prophet's grandfather, 'Abd al-Muṭṭalib, consulted such a soothsayer when he sought to find an alternative to fulfilling a vow to sacrifice his youngest son 'Abd Allāh, who became the father of Muḥammad. The Meccans also used special sacred divining arrows (*azlam*) without points, which were kept at the Ka'bah, to make supernatural inquiries about courses of action. This practice was forbidden by the Koran: "...partition by the divining arrows, that is ungodliness..." (5:3) and also: "...idols and divining arrows are an abomination..." (5:90).

After the death of the Prophet, revolts to Islam (*hurub ar-ridda*) arose in Arabia which were often led by soothsayers. One was a woman, called the *Kāhinah*; another was the revolt of Musaylamah, and another that of al-Aswad.

Mukhtār (d. *67*/687), who led the revolt of the Kaysāniyyah which attempted to push Muḥammad ibn Ḥanafiyyah (the son of 'Alī by the Ḥanifite woman) to power, came to 'Irāq, claimed to be inspired by the Angel Gabriel, and preached in a trance-like state in *saj'* prose, in the style of the *kahins*, that Muḥammad ibn Ḥanifiyyah was the Mahdī. *See* 'ABD al-MUṬṬALIB; KAYSĀNIYYAH; MANDALA; MUSAYLAMAH.

Kairouan (*Qayrawān*). A city in Tunisia with a population of over 100,000, famous for its Grand Mosque, the *Zaytūnah* and the Islamic university of the same name. The city was founded by 'Uqba ibn Nafi in *50*/670 and became the capital (*184-*

297/800-909) of the Aghlabids and later, the first capital of the Fāṭimids (*297-309*/909-921).

al-Kalabādhī, Abū Bakr (d. circa *390*/1000) A Sufi, author of a compendium of Sufism entitled *Kitāb al-Ta'arruf li-madhhab ahl at-Taṣawwuf* (translated as "The Doctrine of the Sufis").

Kalām (lit. "speech", or "dialectic"; applied to theology which is the study of "Divine Speech". This use of the word probably follows Greek usage in philosophy as in *logos*, "word" for "logic"). Islamic scholastic theology. Theologians were called *ahl al-kalām* ("the people of *kalām*") or *mutakallimūn*: *dialektikoi*. Simon Van den Bergh wrote that: "Although they [the mutakallimūn] form a rather heterogenous group of thinkers whose theories are syncretistic, that which is taken from different Greek sources is a preponderance of Stoic ideas... and ...they have certain points in common, principally their theory, taken from the Stoics, of the rationality of religion (which is for them identical with Islam), of a *lumen naturale* which burns in the heart of every man, and the optimistic view of a rational God who has created the best of all possible worlds for the greatest good of man who occupies the central place in the universe." Wolfson also noted the preponderance of Stoic influence and wrote that *Kalam* "is a thrice told story... whose plot is: Scripture meets philosophy". The first encounter was Philo (at which time Judaism probably acquired the notion of one God not as a number out of many, or merely one to the exclusion of others — henotheism as Mueller called it, but rather as a philosophic unity, that is, a kind of Monotheism to which Zoroastrianism led the way and which was attributed retroactively to Abraham). Then this prelude led to the Church Fathers who of course had to wrestle with the Trinity. (To this should be added the development of Gnosticism as a Platonic exegesis of the Old Testament.) The third encounter was *Kalam*; it was largely adopted by the Jewish thinkers of the time and also caused ripples within the Christian world.

After the death of the Prophet, the Muslim community tried to carry on applying established precedents in regards to legal decisions and beliefs. The people who preserved the corpus of doctrine, law, and custom, were called *ahl al-ḥadīth*, the traditionalists. As new circumstances arose with the expansion of the empire, there was a need for unprecedented decisions, and guidelines for the future. This gave rise to the Schools of Law, who constituted the Sunnīs, namely, those who follow tradition. At the same time, however, the community was confronted with certain new issues, which, naturally, evoked different responses and opinions. One of them concerned the question of the fitness to rule of a ruler who committed sins. This produced the Khārijites, with their declared opinion that the commission of sin was an absolute disqualification even to be called a Muslim. This in its turn called forth the Murji'ites who maintained that the question of sin should be left to the Divine Mercy, to be determined after death. Thereupon the question of responsibility for sin led to the school of the Qadariyyah, who held man to be absolutely free, the creator of his acts, and completely responsible for them. The reaction to this was the emergence of the Jabariyyah, who held that man's actions were completely predetermined.

These schools came about essentially in response to isolated questions, and none of them attempted a systematic interpretation of revelation. In addition, moreover, to these movements or schools, *ad hoc* responses to problematic situations and cases were made by individuals with greater or lesser influence such as the Companions, mystics such as Ḥasan of Baṣrah, and political leaders.

Theology was originally considered to be part of canon law (*fiqh*), although it was known as the "greater" canon law, *al-fiqh al-akbar.* It was the Mu'tazilites who constituted the first real school of theology, insofar as they sought to apply reason to a broad range of questions and to make use of the methods of argument, reason and dialectic. In fact, they probably representated a faction that existed before Islam and outside of it, and had already prepared a program which they then put into motion within Islam to bring Islam in line with their own ideas. Indeed, an obviously false Ḥadith was circulated which said that the "Mu'tazilites are Majus; do not pray with one as a leader, and do not follow their funeral bier". This invention was intended to unmask their real identity. But they did use the methods of dialectic and with these methods they generated a set of answers which they held to be dogma. Although briefly in vogue, Mu'tazilite solutions were in some ways not orthodox, that is, they did not appear to reflect an adequate understanding of spiritual reality, and this led to vigorous objections on the part of religious thinkers; by the middle of the *4th*/10th century the Mu'tazilites had run their course.

Al-Ash'arī (d. *324*/944) was originally a Mu'tazilite, but abandoned them at the same time as adapting certain of their rational methods into Sunnism. He thus became the real founder of theology along with his follower, al-Baqillāni (d. *403*/1012), the independent al-Māturīdī (d. *333*/944), and aṭ-Ṭahāwī (d. *321*/933). In fact, al-Ash'arī's ideas changed with time, and do not in every case coincide with those of the school which bears his name. At first, Ash'arism, which was not a perfect solution, ran into strong opposition, and Ash'arites such as al-Juwaynī had at one time to flee persecution. But in the *5th*/11th century the Sunnī Islam of the Seljūqs came under attack from the doctrines of the Fāṭimids, and the only viable counter-weapon was the broad response to religious questions which the Ash'arites had built up. They were therefore rehabilitated, to become the foremost defenders of Sunnī theology. They, and the school of al-Māturīdī, who was intuitional and less concerned with rational exposition, but in practice quite similar, have remained the standard theology of Sunnī Islam ever since. (For the Creed of al-Ash'arī, *see* CREED.)

Ash'arite theology in its day presented certain problems, and still does if accepted at its face value. But it was a viable attempt to combine revelation and reason to the minimum requirements of causality. Those whose needs for causality went beyond the minimum, naturally went beyond Ash'arism. Muslim philosophers in many cases provided extremely intelligent answers to intellectual problems, but never succeeded in integrating answers based on logic, Pythagoras, Plato, Aristotle, and Neoplatonism, with a religious expression accessible to ordinary believers. It is for this reason that certain critics — who actually misunderstood them — claimed that they were propagating a double doctrine: intellectual arguments for the elite, and blind belief for the masses. The mystics produced their explanations, which depended even more upon the integration of philosophic intelligence with faith; but these explanations were at the same time highly intuitional, and could be grasped only by those with an aspiration to a spiritual path. Nevertheless, since in later Islam, half — or more than half — of the populations of whole countries belonged to Sufi orders, there is no doubt that the Sufis did produce an exceptionally rich theology which has not been fully assessed or appreciated because much of it was, and still is, restricted to oral teachings. With the rise of Fundamentalism, all of these considerations may end up being steam rollered out of the public consciousness.

It was al-Ghazālī who took large measures of philosophy, theology, and mysticism and put them together in a synthesis broad enough to serve the needs of the community at large, and indeed, the whole civilization. His synthesis remains functional to this day, and in making it he performed for Islam, in his person and his intellect, a function analogous to that which Paul and the Church Councils realized for Christianity. (Interestingly, Shahrastānī, the Persian historian of religions, says that Paul brought philosophy to the "religion of Peter").

Kalām is dominated by the school of al-Ash'arī. Although certain aspects of Ash'arism seem harsh, it must be remembered that Al-Ash'arī was concerned to combat certain Rationalist complacencies and was zealous in insisting on God's transcendence. God deals with man in accordance with his acts; he does not send the pious to hell, but for al-Ash'arī the transcendence of God means that He might do so. Such Ash'arite dogmatisms have in practice been mitigated by attitudes borrowed from the school of al-Māturīdī. The latter prevailed chiefly in Asia and more readily accepted antinomial formulations ("antinomial" here referring to the metaphysical paradigm and having nothing to do with the sects of that name).

For the Ash'arites, the Koran is uncreated in its essence, but created in its sounds and letters; that is, created in its written form and when recited, while inwardly it is the Word of God and Divine. (Al-Ash'arī himself seems to have inclined in the end to the Ḥanbalī belief that the Koran is uncreated even in its written letters and pronounced sounds. Shī'ites, who are Mu'tazilites to this day — Mu'tazilitism came from the same milieu that produced Shī'ism — believe the Koran to be created.) The Ash'arites hold that God's Attributes are eternal and distinct from His Essence; that God is not All-Powerful because He possesses the attribute of being All-Powerful, as the Mu'tazilites would have it, but that the Attribute proceeds from God because He is All-Powerful; and that the Attributes are not the Essence, nor are they different from the Essence.

The Ash'arites uphold that the Koranic references to God's Face, His Hand, His Throne mean that He has a Face, a Hand, and a Throne, but that these cannot be likened to human hands, or a human face; anthropomorphic qualities may not be imputed to God. These Koranic descriptions must be accepted as they are, they say, without asking how. Nevertheless, the Ash'arites, while not admitting that these descriptions are *symbolic*, assert that they must be understood literally *and* spiritually at the same time. Ultimately, therefore, on this question as on many others, the Ash'arites insert several steps into a process that turns out to be an antinomy, whereby a contradiction on one plane is resolved on another. The difference between the Ash'arites and the school of al-Māturīdī is that the Māturīdites admit antinomial formulations more readily.

The Divine Reality is intuited by the human spirit as Real; but It surpasses analysis by the mind. Antinomy is the recognition that this is so. It does not mean that God cannot be known; but it means that God must be known through a means. One can grasp readily what a triangle is by apprehending that it has three sides. The nature of a figure with 943 sides cannot be grasped in the same way as a triangle, but it can be known through a name and some constructs. It is because God cannot be grasped directly, that man is saved through faith (along with a certain minimum of acts, or good deeds, that objectify that faith). And it is because God has a revealed Name, that man can know Him.

The Ash'arites deal with the problems of free-will and causality by their theory of atoms. To explain how the creature, lacking the positive and absolute qualities of God, could exercise will and action, the Ash'arites said that the action itself was created by God and then "acquired" (*kasb, iktisāb*) by the creature. (This is also true in many philosophical systems, that of Descartes, for example.) Their most notable formulation, from the point of view of intellectual history, is their theory that atoms are simultaneously atoms of both space and time — instants in space, but without extension. This is essentially an attempt to explain phenomena — the world being apparently detached from God — by making the physical universe into an infinite collection of mirrors which reflect and refract an invisible Divine Reality into experience. It is a traditional forerunner of the modern and material theories of atoms. The Ash'arite idea precedes Descartes's theory of vortices, and modern science's atomism, which has now become the theory of "super-strings". All of these are also "little mirrors", from which the Divine Reality has been removed; little mirrors which, not reflecting God, create reality out of nothing.

The position of the Ash'arites on free-will is not entirely satisfactory; it holds back from openly admitting that there is great enigma in the question. God knows what will happen from eternity; yet we must still be free in order to be responsible for our acts, whose consequences may result in damnation or salvation. Do we then possess free will? There is one respect in which unquestionably we do: at any moment, we are free to choose or accept God as Reality. We may not be free in respect of our actions towards the world, wherein we undergo a variety of compulsion and a chain of cause and effect. But we are absolutely free and responsible in our rejection or acceptance of Absolute Reality, an act which takes place in consciousness; in that we are as free as God; the rest is cause and effect. (*See* HELL; IBLĪS; MAKTŪB; SHAHĀDAH.)

Apart from the *mutakallimūn*, and without establishing an atomistic theory, many Islamic thinkers say, basing themselves on the Koran, that creation is a continuous process, each instant being a new act of creation. ("Every day He is in act" 55:29). It is thus, for example, that Ibn 'Arabī explains the Koranic story of how the throne of the Queen of Sheba was brought instantly to Solomon by a *jinn*. The *jinn* did not physically bring the throne, but *transposed* on the subtle plane — "redirected", one could say — its *place* of continuous creation. The throne was created in Sheba one moment; the next its continuous creation took place in Jerusalem instead.

Creation thus envisaged is not a process, but an instantaneous act; and the changes which natural and human history imply are the successive revelations of that act in time, which, along with extension, number, and the other conditions of existence, exist for man, but not for God. The links between apparently "successive" creation may appear to be cause and effect on the "horizontal" human plane, giving rise to the theory of evolution, for example; but not *in divinis*. On the earth night becomes day, continents form, mammals appear, empires rise and fall, Alexander conquers as far as the Indus, Napoleon retreats from Moscow. These are events over millennia; for God they are all in the eternal present, along with Adam's fall and the end of the world.

By the *7th*/13th century the development of *kalām* had run its course, although commentaries continued to be written even into modern times. *See* AKHBĀRĪS; al-ASH'ARĪ; BILĀ KAYFA;

CREED; FIQH AKBAR; FIVE DIVINE PRESENCES; al-GHAZĀLĪ; HELL; IBLĪS; IBN 'ARABĪ; ISTAWĀ'; al-MĀTURĪDĪ; MU'TAZILITES; PHILOSOPHY; UṢŪLĪS.

al-Kalbī, Abu-l-Mundhir Hishām ibn Muḥammad (d. *206*/821-822). He was a member of a family of scholars from Kūfah; he addressed himself to the study of Ḥadīth and history. According to an-Nadīm, al-Kalbī wrote 118 works, while Yaqut makes it 121. Among those which have survived is the *Kitāb al-Aṣnām*, "the Book of Idols" which is a source on the idolatry of the *Jāhiliyah*, or "Age of Ignorance". (It was a principle in Medieval Islam that to report on heresy was not itself heresy.)

He relates that the poet king Imru'-l-Qays consulted the divining arrows of the idol Dhu-al-Khalaṣah (a piece of cut quartz crystal) in Tabālah before setting out to attack the Banu Asad. The arrows were called "the enjoiner" (*al-āmir*) "the forbidder" (*al-nāhi*) and "the vigilant" (*al-mutarabbiṣ*). He drew three times the forbidder; Thereupon he broke the arrows and hurled them at the idol exclaiming; "Go bite your father's penis! Had it been thy father who was murdered, thou wouldst not have forbidden me avenging him." He then raided the Banu Asad and defeated them. Thus he was the first to denounce this idol.

Ibn al-Kalbī relates that there was a Ka'bah of Sindād in the region between al-Kūfah and al-Baṣrah; but he says it was not a place of worship but a celebrated edifice. And another, the Ka'bah of Najran, is mentioned by al-A'sha in one of this odes. This too, al-Kalbī says was not claimed as a place of worship but merely a hall. However, in the *Diwān*, al-A'sha says "to visit the Ka'bah of Najrān is an ordinance incumbent upon you".

'Jarīr ibn 'Abd Allāh who entered Islam at the conquest of Mecca or in the last six months of the Prophet's life was sent to destroy Dhu al-Khalaṣah which was located six days south of Mecca in the direction of San'a'. He had to kill "three hundred custodians and others" who defended it. Dhu al-Khalaṣah was a white quartz crystal; it was turned into the doorstep of the mosque of Tabālah which is the site of the idol. Al-Kalbi cites a Ḥadīth which says "This world shall not pass away until the buttocks of the women of Daws wiggle [again] around Dhu-al-Khalaṣah and they worship it as they were wont to do [before Islam]. (Bukhārī: *Fitan*: 24). *See* IDOLS; JAHILIYYAH.

Kalimah (lit. "the word"). A name sometimes used for the testimony of the faith (*shahādah*). In the terminology of Christian Arabs the word *kalimah* means the Logos, or Christ. *See* SHAHĀDAH.

Kalmuck. A Mongolian people found in the Russian Federation, the Oyrat, who are Lamaist Buddhists. They number some 100,000 in Russia. They are related to another larger, Mongol Buddhist group in Russia, the Buryat. One of Lenin's grandfathers was a Kalmuck. The spiritual leader of the Kalmucks and the Buryats is the Khambo Lama whose central lamasery (*daitsan*) is in Ulan Ude.

Kano. A city in northern Nigeria of approximately half a million inhabitants, with a history going back more than a millennium. One of the most important Hausa city-states, with a highly developed economic base and craft industry, Kano had trade links throughout West Africa and even with Europe, where its leather products were known as Moroccan leather. It is still the center for many crafts, including the manufacture of the indigo dyed cloth worn by the Tuaregs and Blue Men of the Sahara.

In the 16th century Islam was adopted in Kano and scholars came from Morocco, the best known being one called al-Maghīlī, to put religion on a firm footing. Kano was ruled by an Emir assisted by several chamberlains, who shared power with a Hausa aristocracy.

Kapudanpasha. Under the Ottomans, the Beylerbey of the sea, or admiral in command of the naval forces. In 1531 Selim appointed the pirate Khayr ad-Dīn Barabarossa as Kapudanpasha in order to prosecute a sea war against the Spanish. *See* BEYLERBEY.

Kara Koyunlu, *see* QARA QOYUNLU.

Karaites (from *qara'im*, *bne' miqra*, "readers", "sons of the scripture"). A Jewish sect founded around AD 800 in Babylonia by 'Anan ben David. The sect does not recognize the Talmud but only the Tanakh, the Old Testament. Until the 11th century the sect was centered in Jerusalem. Now there are around 30,000 members, centered in Beersheba in Israel. Because of their doctrinal differences with Talmudic Jews, Karaites were perceived very differently by outsiders. They were accorded full citizenship in Russia in the 19th century when other Jews were supposed to live outside the pale of settlement (many Karaites lived in the Crimea) and later the Nazis also made a distinction and did not persecute them.

Karāmāt (lit. "acts of generosity"; sing. *karāmah*). Gifts or powers of a spiritual or psychic nature acquired by a Saint, short of miracle working. The term is not used for the psychic powers that could be possessed by a sorcerer, and is equivalent to the Sanskrit *siddhi* in the elevated sense of "spiritual attainment".

Kārīz. One of any immense underground irrigation canals in Iran. These date back to antiquity and a single canal could stretch for as long as 25 miles/40 km. Today they are usually shorter but nevertheless reach a depth of 50 feet/17 meters underground. They are underground to minimize evaporation and have openings to the surface for maintenance. They are also called *qanāt*. Similar, albeit smaller underground irrigation canals also exist in Morocco and Libya.

Karma Marga, *see* MAKHĀFAH.

Kashkul. A vessel carried by some wandering dervishes and beggars in Iran and India. It was made from large nuts called "coco-de-mer" (*Lodoicea maldivica*), 20 to 46 cm long. The black colored, double sided nuts wash up, mysteriously, on the shores of Iran and India. They fall into the Indian Ocean from palm trees on the Seychelle Islands (Praslin in the Vallée de Mai). The cocos can weigh 30-40 kilos; once germinated the seeds take nine months to flower; every seven years the palm lets the nuts drop to the ground.

The nuts were gathered up on beaches, split into two down the central seam, and were hollowed out creating a left hand and a right hand vessel which could be used as a multi-purpose bowl which was carried slung over the shoulder.

After Ṣafavid times the *kashkul*, copying the shape of the original, natural coco-de-mer, was also made by craftsman out of metal, particularly brass, and ornamented (as were natural ones). A folklore developed around the size, and left or right-handedness of the *kashkul*, and mendicant groups could be identified by their bowls. Another emblem of wandering dervishes in Iran, India, and Central Asia, along with the bowl, was an axe, which in addition to being a weapon, was meant to be the equivalent of the sword as a symbol of spiritual discrimination.

Kashmir. Strategic state in the northwest of India next to Pakistan, bordering on China. Many Iranians would migrate back and forth between Iran and Kashmir. The population of Jammu and Kashmir at the time of partition in 1947 was close to 80% Muslim but the Maharajah was Hindu and refused to indicate his decision which country he would join. Events in Kashmir led to an intervention on the part of Pakistan, in the face of which the Maharajah joined India in October 1948. India promised a referendum which has never taken place. The part seized by Pakistan in the course of the war which followed is called Azad ("Free") Kashmir. Although one Muslim faction in Kashmir had favored union with India, there has been a continuous opposition to Indian rule which in 1987 became widespread unrest and resistance leading to Indian military occupation. This has now become guerrilla warfare. The unresolved question of Kashmir has been the stumbling block to the improvement of relations between India and Pakistan.

Kaysānīs, *see* KAYSĀNIYYAH.

Kaysāniyyah. A Shī'ite group, also known as the Mukhtāriyyah, who promoted the rulership of a figurehead Imām, or rightful Messianic leader, after the death of Ḥusayn. This rightful ruler of the Kaysāniyyah was *not* a descendant of Ḥusayn, whom they claimed to avenge, but rather a half brother of Ḥusayn's, one called Muḥammad ibn al-Ḥanafiyyah (d. *81*/700). This was a son (and according to some he was the favorite son) of 'Alī and a wife of the Banu Ḥanifa tribe, who was thus called the Ḥanafite (*al-Ḥanafiyyah*). This early branch of proto-Shī'ism was in fact some form of indigenous Iranian religion seeping into Islam. It lingered on as a distinct sect after the death of the Imām. Although some members of the sect gave allegiance to Abū Hāshim, the son of Muḥammad ibn al-Ḥanafiyyah, others declined, saying that the Imām (Muḥammad ibn al-Ḥanafiyyah) was concealed and would return to the world. Those who supported Abū Hāshim were called the Hāshimiyyah. At his death Abū Hāshim in turn transmitted his *'ilm* ("esoteric knowledge") to Muḥammad ibn 'Alī ibn 'Abd Allāh ibn al-'Abbās. This *'ilm* seems to have been the identity of the Hāshimiyyah leaders in Kūfah, and the terms needed to deal with them. As it turned out, the Kaysāniyyah also had ties in Khorāsān. Thus the Kaysāniyyah carried on as the *da'wah* (propaganda) and the revolution of the 'Abbāsids, and ultimately achieved a shared success when the 'Abbāsids defeated the Umayyads and became the supreme power of the Islamic state.

The term *Kaysāniyyah* may come from a name for the leader of the original sect in Kūfah, or from a name for Mukhtār ibn Abū 'Ubayd ath-Thaqafī, the actual leader who promoted revolt against the Umayyads using Muḥammad ibn Ḥanafiyyah as the figurehead, or from the name of one of his lieutenants. For this reason the Kaysānīs are sometimes called the *Mukhtāriyyah*. Mukhtār, an opportunist, was the nephew of Sa'd Mas'ūd, 'Alī's governor in Madā'in. After the murder of Ḥusayn in *61*/680 there appeared in Kūfah a movement called the *Tawwābūn* ("the Penitents") calling for revenge for the death of Ḥusayn. This movement of persons who were not warriors (they seem instead to have been bent on provoking martyrdom out of religious convictions) came quickly to an end by being annihilated by the Syrian troops of the Umayyads (*65*/January 685). However, they were the real beginnings of Shī'ism and their cry for revenge (*yā latha'arāt al-Ḥusayn* — "rise to avenge Ḥusayn's blood") was taken up by Mukhtār who was much more militarily adept and organized.

After taking part in 'Abd Allāh ibn az-Zubayr's struggle against the Umayyads, Mukhtār appeared in 'Irāq claiming to be inspired by the Angel Gabriel and, in verse imitative of the Koran, preached the appearance of the Mahdī who would eliminate injustice in the earth; Muḥammad ibn al-Ḥanafiyyah, was, in secret, this very Mahdī. (This is the first time the Mahdī idea appeared.)

Raising a force of discontented Aramaic and Persian clients (*mawālī*) of the occupying Arabs, Mukhtār put them under the command of Ibrāhīm ibn al-Malik al-Ashtar, the chief of the Nakh' tribe of Madhḥij, a Shī'ite leader in Kūfah and the son of one of 'Alī's generals. On *Rabī I 66*/October 685 they succeeded in taking Kūfah. The forces of Mukhtār won several victories in 'Irāq and defeated a Syrian army led by 'Ubayd Allāh ibn Ziyād, the Umayyad governor who had sent troops against Ḥusayn at Kerbala. 'Ubayd Allāh ibn Ziyād was killed and Mukhtār celebrated the victory by a ceremony in front of an empty throne, which was represented as being "a chair belonging to 'Alī" (*kursī 'Alī*, whose keeper in Kūfah at one time was a man called Hawshab). (Arabs of 'Alī's generation did not have chairs, much less thrones; they sat on the ground.) This throne, to which Mukhtār spoke, was the seat of the presence of God. In this ceremony, and in his speeches, Mukhtār make extensive use of *saj'* or rhyme, like a *kāhin* or shaman. This throne was the *tabūt* which they carried into battle; when it was first introduced and shown, many of his partisans "who had been influenced by the doctrines of Ibn Saba'" got up and shouted three *takbīrs* by raising their hands.

This ceremony of the empty chair, resembling the "Bema Ceremony", links the Kaysāniyyah to the Manicheans whose center among the Arabs had been Ḥīrah, the Lakhmid capital. The Lakhmids were dispossessed when Islam expanded and their capital dwindled away as the population moved to the nearby newly founded military camp-city of Kūfah. Ḥirah eventually disappeared, or rather took on a new identity, as did the Lakhmids. The Lakhmids had been Manicheans, and the Caliph 'Alī had turned to them for support against the Umayyads who were supported by the Christians, and former Christians of Syria. Indeed, the immediate predecessors of the Kaysāniyyah, the Tawwābūn, also exhibit a Manichean trait in that some four thousand persons without military experience went off in search of apparent martyrdom, as the Rāwandiyyah were to do some seventy years later in the presence of Manṣūr the 'Abāssid. (Mani was martyred, and provoking martyrdom was a fitting and desirable end to the believer's life.)

Mukhtār originated the concept of *bada'*, not accepted by Sunnī Islam. This is the idea that God changes His mind; shown in that, at first God wanted to do *this*, and then decided to do *that* instead. This means that there are possible changes in the Divine Will, and therefore, changes, or contingencies, within God Himself. Before the battle of al-Madhār, as was his usual practice, he told his followers that God had informed him of their coming victory; when in fact they were defeated, Mukhtār explained that "God's will had changed". (The mutability of God is a Manichean idea which St. Augustine attacked in *Contra Secundinum*.)

The Kaysāniyyah pioneered the use of the term *imām* and *imām al-hūdā*. Mukhtār called himself the Wazīr Al Muḥammad ("the Vizier of the Family of Muḥammad".) He transmitted the Mahdīs teachings to the faithful, and received an oath of allegiance, a *bay'ah* on behalf of the Imām. The large-scale participation of mawālī and slaves side by side with Arab tribesmen was innovative and upset some of the conservative Arab leaders in Kūfah and elsewhere. Taqiyyah, or systematic deception regarding one's affiliation (widespread in Shī'ism and other dualist religions) was a fundamental Manichean technique — Mani said his followers could denounce him under duress with equanimity — also makes its appearance within Islam with this movement. Mukhtār himself was killed on *14 Ramaḍan 67*/3 April 687 in a desperate battle against Muṣ'ab ibn Zubayr.

The Kaysāniyyah revolt was a forerunner of the 'Abbāsid *da'wah*. The messianic idea of the leader or Imām who was concealed and remote from the actual revolt, even denying his role if necessary, and the participation of mawālī and slaves side by side with Arab warriors were characteristics which repeated themselves in Khorāsān, during the 'Abbāsid da'wah, this time successfully. *See* MUḤAMMAD ibn al-ḤANFIYYAH; ABŪ MUSLIM; IMĀM; MAHDĪ; SHĪ'ISM; TAWWĀBŪN.

Kazakhstan. Independent in 1991 from the former Soviet Union, population 17,376,615. Over 7,000,000 are Kazakhs, the rest are Russians, Ukrainians, and Germans. The capital is Astana. The Kazakhs are an amalgam of Turko-Mongolian peoples who emerged as a distinct people in the 15th or 16th century. The dominant strain among them are the ancient Qipchaqs. Before the 1917 revolution the Kazakhs were called the Kirghiz, (or Kirghiz-Kazak) while the other people called Kirghiz in the present day were formerly called Kara-Kirghiz. They are Sunni Muslims Islamicised in the 18th century by missionaries from the Tatars. The traditional way of life was sheep herding. Besides the Kazakhs in Kazakhstan, another 800,000 live in the Sinkiang region of China, and some 63,000 in western Mongolia.

Kebatinan. (Indonesian abstract noun formed from the Arabic *bāṭin*, "esoteric"). Esoteric organizations in Indonesia. These include a wide variety of groups from animist and Hindu based movements in Java, to regularly constituted Sufi orders in Atjeh.

Kemal, Muṣṭafā (1881-1938). The first president of Turkey from 1923 until his death in 1938. He was called *Atatürk* ("Father of the Turks") by his supporters known as the "Kemalists". Kemal, who was from Albania, and had gone to school in Thessaloniki, had a marked aversion to the religion of Islam. He made *laik* ("laicization") an important, if not the main, aspect of his political program. The substitution of the Latin alphabet for the Arabic one (the adoption of the Arabic alphabet by any people had historically been part of its adoption of Islam) under the pretended aim of increasing literacy, served to cut the Turks off from their past by making most of them unable to read their literature. The subsequent "Turkification" of Turkish — the attempted removal of as many words as possible of Arabic origin — could only be partly successful, but even so it raised further barriers to communication with other Islamic countries, and even, it has been said, between generations of Turks themselves.

By turning the Aya Sofia Mosque into a museum, and making compulsory the wearing of the European hat, which has a rim and thus impedes the prostration which is intrinsic to Muslim prayer, Mustafa Kemal caused as much controversy in the Islamic world of the time, as he did by the outright ban against wearing turbans in public. His program was imposed with laws which made it a crime to express ideas or even think thoughts that "run counter to... the historical and moral values of Turkishness, or the nationalism, principles, reform and modernization of Atatürk".

Kemal was a model to be emulated by other modernizing leaders of Islamic countries, most notably Reza Shah, founder of the short-lived Pahlavī dynasty of Iran, Enver Hodja of Albania, and others. One of his most famous sayings is: "Happy is he who calls himself a Turk."

Kerbala. The place in 'Irāq where Ḥusayn, grandson of the Prophet Muḥammad, was Martyred in *61*/680. It is now a city. The tomb, *Mashhad Ḥusayn*, is the holiest shrine of the Twelve-Imām Shī'ites. The first edifice was built there in *369*/979 by the Buwayhids (also called Buyids), although an enclosed area (*ḥā'ir*) existed much earlier. The tomb and shrine were destroyed several times by Sunnī rulers to remove this focus of Shī'ite agitation. Today, there is a domed shrine over the (presumed) tomb of Ḥusayn, and the tomb of 'Abbās, his half brother, is nearby.

Clay from Kerbala, "sanctified by the blood of martyrdom", is stamped into little cakes onto which Twelve-Imām Shī'ites rest the forehead during the prostration in the prayer. The clay is also considered to have curative powers. The body of Ḥusayn rests in Kerbala, but the head, which was brought to the Umayyad Caliph Yazīd, reposes in the Ḥusayn Mosque in Cairo. In the Grand

Umayyad Mosque of Damascus, where the head once lay, a sanctuary remains; both places are points of pilgrimage for Shī'ites, and to a certain degree Sunnīs as well. *See* ḤUSAYN; SHĪ'ISM.

Khadījah. First wife of the Prophet, and, during her lifetime, the only one. The Prophet was twenty-five years old at the time of their marriage, and she, a wealthy widow, forty; she died at the age of 65 in the year 619, before the Hijrah.

The Prophet had been master of her caravans before they married. They had two sons, Qāsim and 'Abd Allāh (who both died in infancy), and four daughters, Zaynab, Ruqayyah, Fāṭimah, and Umm Kulthūm. Khadījah is buried in the al-Malā' cemetery in Mecca.

Khaksārs. 1) A Darvishi group in Iran, and 2) A modern political movement in India.

1) Khaksars in Iran (Ṭariqah Aleviyyah Khaksāriyyah Ḥusayniyyah Jalaliyyah). Also called *Ḥaydaris*, these are one of the more numerous of the *darvishi* groups in Iran. *Darvishis* (from *darvish*, Persian for *faqir*, the technical term for a Sufi) are irregular semi-secret organizations common in Iran and among Kurds in Turkey and 'Irāq. They are Sufi-like but the basis of the associations are *not* clearly around a doctrine and method firmly based upon Islam as is the case with more authentic Sufis.

The origins of the *darvishi* associations are obscure and markedly pre-Islamic as can be seen from a characteristic stance found in *darvishi* rituals. This is a stance called *qapi* with the right big toe placed over the left big toe, and with the arms folded over the chest. This is related to a ritual position found in Zoroastrianism (in which the priest's hands are crossed but not folded under the arms; rather the Zoroastrian priest holds his earlobes). Ivanow said the position was also found in Mithraism, and in other ancient Iranian religions. This ritual position is also used by many Turkish Sufi orders such as the Jarrahiyah (Khalwatiyyah) and the Mevlevis.

The most prominent Khaksār meeting place is the Cheheltan in Shirāz. At one point during their meetings the lights are turned out and a dhikr is carried on in darkness often with ritual sobbing. There are many points in common between the Iranian Khaksārs and the Ahl-i Ḥaqq. Since the 19th century the Khaksārs have been divided into two groups: the Ghulam 'Ali-Shahis, and the Ma'sum 'Ali Shahis. The Khaksārs were the last such groups to continue wearing the patched Sufi cloak and their distinctive white girdle and the red cap or *taj*. Crossed axes are their emblems.

Story tellers in Iran are usually Khaksāris.

2. A modern political movement in northern India founded in 1931 by 'Inayat Allāh Khān al-Mashriqī (d. 1963), a mathematician working as a government functionary. He had been educated in Germany. The Khaksārs were modeled on the Nazi S.A. They wore brown uniforms and a badge of brotherhood (*ukhuwwa*) on the upper right arm and carried out community and social services. Their name means "earth" and "head" and they strove to be as "humble as dust" but also drilled in a military fashion carrying spades. They interpreted the Koran "scientifically" and it was their aim to make Islam dominant over the globe. In 1941 the movement had more than a million adherents but became divided during the war, and now has almost disappeared.

Khālid ibn al-Walīd (d. *22*/642). A famous warrior in the war between Mecca and Medinah, and during the early conquests of Islam. A Qurayshī and at first an opponent of Islam, he was converted a year before the conquest of Mecca. The first Caliph, Abū Bakr, made him the leading general of the Muslim armies. He defeated the imposter Musaylimah at the "Garden of Death" during the Wars of Apostasy (*ḥurūb ar-riddah*), and in the campaign to conquer Syria he defeated the Byzantines near Damascus. He was called the "Sword of Islam" (*Sayfu-l-Islām*) by the Prophet. *See* SWORD of ISLAM.

Khalīfah, *see* CALIPH.

Khalil ibn Aḥmad (d. *175*/791). The Grammarian from Oman. He worked out complex metrical theories about Arab poetry (inspired it is said by listening to the rhythms of the coppersmiths beating plates in the market) and compiled the first dictionary (*Kitab al-'Ayn*) using a phonetic scheme according to the origins of sound of use to poets and possibly influenced by Indian ideas. *See* SIBAWAIH.

Khalwatiyyah (from Ar. *khalwah*, "a spiritual retreat"; Turkish: *Halvetiyye*). A widespread Sufi order that was founded by Shaykh 'Umar al-Khalwatī (d. *800*/1397) who is called its first *pīr* ("master"). It is also said that the name originated with Shaykh 'Umar's master, Muḥammad ibn Nūr al-Bālisī who was called al-Khalwatī because of his frequent retreats. The second *pīr* of the order was Shaykh Yaḥyā al-Shirwānī (d. 869/1464), the author of a litany called *Wird as-Sattār*, recitation of which is among the obligations imposed upon the members of most branches.

The foundations of this order are considered to be voluntary hunger, silence, vigil, seclusion, *dhikr* ("invocation"), meditation, maintaining a state of permanent ritual purity, and "binding one's heart to the spiritual master".

The Khalwatiyyah spread in the Caucasus, Anatolia, and Azerbaijan from the late *8th*/14th to the end of the *11th*/17th century. In the *10th*/16th century it spread to Egypt and Muslim Africa. The order is a branch of the Suhrawardiyyah, and has many branches among which are the Jarraḥiyyah, Sha'bāniyyah, Sünbüliyyah, and Sīnāniyyah. The late Shaykh Muẓaffar of the Jarraḥī branch, whose center is Istanbul, established the order in Europe and North America.

Khamra wa ḥalwa (lit. "redness and sweetness"). An Egyptian street vendors' cry to hawk watermelons. Characteristic cries existed for all kinds of wares in the medieval world, including Europe, where now only "cockles and mussels, alive, alive, O" is still remembered. In the Arab world they still exist today. This particular cry also found another colloquial use in describing a pretty girl, and became the title of an Egyptian short story, incorrectly translated as "a donkey and sweets".

al-Khamriyyah. The "wine ode", a mystical poem by Ibn al-Fāriḍ (*577-633*/1181-1235), the most famous of Arab Sufi poets. For the Sufis, wine is a common symbol of Divine knowledge and invocation (*dhikr*). The full moon is the amplitude of the Divine revealer, or the spiritual master; the crescent, the aspirant to Divine knowledge; the army, the warriors engaged in the "greater holy war", against one's own soul...

> We quaffed upon the remembrance of the Beloved a wine
> Wherewith we were drunken, before ever the vine was created.
> The moon at the full its cup was; itself was a sun, that a crescent moon passeth round; how many a star gleams forth, when that wine is mingled!
> And but for its fragrance, never had I been guided unto its tavern; and but for its radiance, never had the mind's imagination pictured it.
> And Time hath not left aught of it save a last gasp; as if its being vanished were a concealment in the breasts of human reasons;
> Though if it be but mentioned among the tribe, the people of the tribe become intoxicated, yet guilty of no disgrace or crime.
> From the very bowels of the vats it has mounted up, and naught remains of it in truth but a name:
> Yet if on a day it cometh into the thought of a man, great joy will dwell in him and all sorrow will depart.
> And had the boon-companions beheld no more than the impress of the seal upon its vessel, that impress would surely have made them drunken, without the wine itself;
> And had they sprinkled therewith the dust of a dead man's tomb, the spirit would surely have returned unto him, and his body been quickened.
> And had they but cast, in the shade of the wall where groweth its vine a sick man, and he nigh to death, his sickness would have departed from him;
> And had they brought nigh to its tavern one paralyzed, he would have walked; yea, and the dumb would have spoken upon the mention of its flavor;
> And had the breaths of its perfume been wafted through the East, and in the West were one whose nostrils were stopped, the sense of smell would have returned to him...
> ...And had an enchanter drawn its name on the forehead of one afflicted with madness, the letters drawn would have cured his sickness;
> And had its name been inscribed above the banner of an army, surely that superscription would have inebriated all beneath the banner...
> ...More ancient than all existing things was the tale of it told in eternity, when neither was shape nor trace to be seen;
> And there did all things subsist through it for a purpose wise, whereby it was veiled from all that had not an understanding mind.
> And my spirit was distraught with love for it, in such a manner that the twain were mingled together in unification, and not as body

is permeated by another:
'Tis a soul and no wine there, when Adam is reckoned my father, but a wine and no soul there, when the vine thereof is reckoned my mother.
Now the subtility of the vessels is really consequential upon the subtility of the inward truths, and the inward truths augment by means of the vessels.
And the division truly has taken place, while yet the whole is one: our spirits being the wine, and our corporeal shapes the vine...
...Then let him weep for himself, whose life is all wasted, and he not in all his days of the Wine taken part or portion.

See DHIKR; IBN al-FĀRIḌ; SUFISM.

Khamsa. A parasol carried over the 'Abbāsid Caliph when he appeared outside in public; the custom probably originated in India. It is still preserved in Morocco where a parasol is carried over the King as he rides to Friday Prayer on horseback.

Khan. 1. An inn and warehouse for traveling merchants (*see* CARAVANSERAI.

2. A Turkic word for chief or prince, used as a title for rulers and incorporated by the Turks as one of the titles of the Caliph.

Khan, Sir Sayyid Ahmad (*1232-1316*/1817-1898). An Indian reformer and modernist who advocated that India adopt Western ideas. Sir Sayyid founded the Muḥammadan Anglo-Indian Oriental Aligarh College in 1875; in 1920 the school became a university. Aligarh gave its name to a modernizing movement in India.

Sir Sayyid served in the East India Company and was a local magistrate at the time of the Sepoy Mutiny; he was noted for his actions in saving Europeans during the disturbances. Although Sir Sayyid was pro-British, he also wished to see an independent India where the religions could exist peacefully side by side.

Khānqāh. The Persian name for a meeting place of dervishes, or Sufis (*see* SUFISM). In the Arabic-speaking world the term used is *zāwiyah* (lit: "corner"). Before many Khāniqahi in Iran were meeting places for Sufis, they had already been meeting places for members of other Persian religions,

Khandaq, *see* BATTLE of the TRENCH.

Kharāj (lit. "produce"). A tax on kind, amounting to a land tax, from non-Muslims within the Islamic state. It was imposed later, and in addition to, the *jizyah*, or poll-tax. In Sāssānid times the state's revenue came largely from the land tax which was a sixth to third of the harvest depending upon the fertility of the land. This was called *kharāg*, and the *kharāj* is modelled on it. The Sāssānid income also came from a personal tax called *gēzīt* which is the model for the *jizyah*. *See* JIZYAH.

Khārijites (Ar. *khawārij*, sing. *khārijī*, lit. "the seceders"). A sect that arose in opposition to both 'Alī and Mu'āwiyah upon the occasion of the arbitration that followed the Battle of Ṣiffīn (*37*/657). The Khārijites had been part of 'Alī's army, but when it was announced that the question of the succession to the Caliphate was to be decided by negotiation, they, some twelve thousand, left; hence the name "seceders". The Khārijites felt that such a matter could not be resolved by compromise; their cry was "Decision is God's alone."

Their starting point was puritanism, a nostalgia for the Islam of the Caliphate of 'Umar; they could be called "old believers" (many of the Khārijites had been *qurrā'*, public reciters of the Koran). Their doctrine of sin, which became the most characteristic aspect (logically so, since they considered the upheavals which befell the Muslim polity a fall from a state of perfection), appeared within a Khārijite sect called the Azraqīs around *74*/693.

The Khārijites were a populist group in revolt against the evident hardening of the Caliphate into an Arab Kingdom. Arab supremacy was expressed in the practice of adopting non-Arab converts into an Arab tribe but at the same time imposing upon each one a "protector"; in order to achieve a status within the community, each convert was made a "client" (*mawlā*, plural *mawālī*) of an Arab, although 'Alī himself was said to be a notable exception to this policy, treating all converts as equals. However, this general relegation of non-Arabs to inferior status naturally provoked resentment and caused new converts to rally around movements that promised redress of wrongs.

'Alī at first ignored the Khārijites, being preoccupied with Mu'awiyah; but he finally turned, and attacked them at the Battle of Nahrawān *38*/658. Most of the Khārijites were killed, but a few escaped and perpetuated the movement. 'Alī himself was later assassinated in the mosque of Kūfah by Ibn Muljam, a Khārijite either seeking revenge for the death of his family, or else, less credibly, induced to it by a woman who demanded the assassination of 'Alī as her bride-price.

For hundreds of years the Khārijites were a source of insurrection against the Caliphate and spread to the far reaches of the Empire including to Morocco. They survive today in one of the more moderate forms of Khārijism, namely the Ibāḍites. Ibāḍī Khārijism is the Islam of Oman, but minority Ibāḍī communities also exist in Tunisia (the island of Jerba), Algeria (the M'zab), Libya, and in Tanzania (Zanzibar was once an Omani colony).

According to the Khārijites, anyone can be the leader of the community if he is morally irreproachable. Their leader is accordingly called an Imām, and is elected, whereas for the Shī'ites their "Imām" must be a descendant of 'Alī and an intermediary between man and God; and for the Sunnīs, the supreme leader of the Islamic state had to be, at the beginning at least, a member of the tribe of Quraysh of Mecca.

The Khārijites hold that there is an obligation to revolt against an Imām that has sinned. Indeed, in their doctrine, major sins forfeit salvation and the condition of believer, making a sinner *de facto* an apostate, without remedy. For them, faith without works does not save, whereas for the Sunnīs there is no despairing of the mercy of God. For the Ash'arites, God in His Mercy may even draw a sinning Muslim out of Hell.

This absolute doctrine of sin may well have been a reaction on the part of the Khārijites against the tendency of the desert Arabs to accept external adhesion to Islam as adequate, without any corresponding inward conversion and commitment. It was also an ideological reinforcement in their struggle against non-Khārijites.

The Khārijites considered the fact of being a Muslim absolute in itself and equivalent to salvation; Islam represented a perfect state of soul and to be a Muslim was already to be saved. Sin was therefore a contradiction which nullified the state of believer, or demonstrated that the sinner had turned against Islam. If a person sinned, he could not possess a perfect state of soul and therefore was not really a Muslim. His sin proved inward apostasy, and for it he could be put to death. Non-Khārijites could also be considered apostates, and they and their families put to death. This doctrine of sin was one of the important points repudiated by the book *al-Fiqh al-Akbar* of Abū Ḥanīfah. Likewise this extreme Khārijite attitude led to the Murji'ite reaction, a pietist philosophy which said that to profess Islam with the tongue made one a Muslim, and that the question of one's inner conversion was deferred to the Day of Judgement. The profound controversy which raged around this question led Abū Ḥanīfah to declare categorically in *al-Fiqh al-Akbar*: "no one is to be considered an infidel on account of sin."

The Khārijites did not accept the authority of the Caliphate after 'Alī's decision to turn to arbitration (nor, did they accept retrospectively the whole of 'Uthmān's Caliphate). They went so far as to consider all but themselves unbelievers and traitors to Islam, and finally believed it impossible even to live among them. The Ibāḍites are a moderating branch in this respect and have survived, whereas the more rigid groups have disappeared. Despite its categorical attitude towards other Muslims, the Khārijites view other religions differently, notably conceding that, provided that the non-Muslim "People of the Book" (*ahl al-kitāb*) acknowledge the Divine mission of the Prophet, they need not automatically abandon their own religion.

A Khārijite sermon of the 2nd century of the Hijrah gives a taste of their point of view:

> Know this, ye men: we did not leave our homes and goods out of a vain restlessness, nor in quest of pleasure, nor to claim old right, nor to win empire. But when we saw the lamps of justice all put out, then indeed "the earth, vast as it is, was straitened" [Koran 9:118]) upon us. We heard as it were a Herald call us to obedience unto the Merciful, and to the Judgement of the Book of God.
>
> We met your warriors. We called them to obey the Merciful and abide by the Judgement of the Book; they called us to obey Satan and abide by the judgement of the children of Marwān. Then they came at us, galloping, clamoring, and riotous, for Satan laughed among them, and their blood seethed with his fires. And the wheel turned; and we went up and they went down, for such a smiting there befell as made the ungodly totter.
>
> When 'Uthman reigned, he walked six years in the ways of Abū Bakr and of 'Umar; and then worked innovation in Islam. And

the bond of unity was loosed; and every man wanted Caliphate for himself. Then reigned 'Alī, who wandered from the path of truth and proved himself no beacon for the guidance of men. Then reigned Mu'āwiyah son of Abū Sufyān, that accursed son of an accursed father, whom God's Prophet himself did curse, who spilt innocent blood as it were water and made God's Servants his own slaves, a man who grasped the moneys of God into his own hands, a traitor to the Faith and a ravisher of women, who did the bidding of his lusts until he died.

And after him came his son Yazīd, Yazīd the drunkard, Yazīd the huntsman, the tender of hawks and leopards and apes, who consulted not the Book but soothsayers, and followed his lusts to his death, God curse and punish him!

Then came Marwān, that excommunicate and accursed son of a father whom God's Prophet cursed, who drowned in the filth of his vices, God curse him and his fathers all! And then sat Marwān's sons upon the throne, children of that accursed House, who have devoured the moneys of God and mocked at his Religion and made His Servants their own slaves. And this wickedness has gone on and on. And O Muḥammad's People, how have ye been unhappy and forsaken!

See AHL al-KITĀB; 'ALĪ; FIQH AKBAR; IBĀḌ ITES; MURJI'AH; SIN.

Khāṭi'ah. A category of sin. *see* SIN.

Khatm al-Anbiya', *see* SEAL of PROPHECY.

Khatm an-Nubuwwah, *see* SEAL of PROPHECY.

Khatm al-Wilāyah, *see* SEAL of SANCTITY.

Khaṭṭābiyyah. A Sevener dualist Manichean sect in 'Irāq in the *2nd*/8th century whose leader, Abū-l-Khaṭṭāb Muḥammad, asserted that Ja'far aṣ-Ṣādiq was Divine, and later that he himself was likewise Divine, a spiritual descendant of Ja'far by "adoption". The Sect was attacked by the 'Abbāsid authorities in 'Irāq and the leader killed. Some of his followers affirmed that his death was only an illusion; there were numerous splinter groups and many eventually joined other Manichean sects. *See* MANICHEANS; QARMAṬĪS; SEVENERS; KHURRAMIYYAH.

al-Khayyām, 'Umar *see* 'UMAR al-KHAYYĀM.

al-Khayzurān. The mother of the Caliphs al-Hadī and Harūn ar-Rashid. She was a Persian (although it is also said that she was a Yemeni slave), and, according to Sir William Muir (he did not cite his source), the daughter of the Iranian Rebel, Ustadh Sīs. She was one of three women who gave birth to two Caliphs along with another Persian, Shah-Parand, the grand-daughter of Yazdigird who was married to al-Walīd the Caliph and bore him Yazīd III and Ibrāhīm.

Al-Khayzurān (the name means the bamboo shaft) had nursed some of the Barmakid children, as Barmakid mothers had nursed 'Abbāsids, a tradition since the time when the two families allied themselves with each other at the origin of 'Abbāsid power. Thus certain Barmakids such as Yaḥyā were particularly attached to her as a "milk-mother". The Caliph al-Hadī continued a persecution of the Manicheans begun by his father, al-Mahdī, and was also not cooperative to his mother who attempted to play a major role in the government. Thus al-Hadī called into opposition to himself two powerful forces, already in close alliance to each other, his mother and the Barmakids, and al-Hadī died suddenly, poisoned some believed, by his own mother in order to put the more amenable Harūn ar-Rashid on the throne.

Al-Khayzuran amassed a large fortune and among her public works she bought the house in Mecca where the Prophet Muḥammad was born and turned it into a mosque.

Khidhlān (Ar. "abandonment"). According to theologians, an "attitude" of God when he leaves someone to his own devices and thus inevitably prey to his weaknesses. It corresponds to the Christian idea of "fall from grace" and is remedied in the same way, by prayer and seeking out blessing.

Ibn 'Aṭā' Allāh said in his *Ḥikam*:

> Sometimes He makes you learn in the night of contraction (*layl al-qabḍ*) what you have not learned in the radiance of the day of expansion (*fī ishrāq nahar al-basṭ*). "You do not know which of them is nearer to you in benefit." (4:11)

See ISTIDRĀJ.

al-Khiḍr (lit. "the green one"; also, and perhaps originally, *al-khaḍir*). A spiritual *persona* identified with the figure in the Koran 18:64: "One of Our servants, unto whom We [God] had given mercy from Us, and had taught him knowledge proceeding from Us." He is not, of course, mentioned by name in the Koran.

When Moses and his servant, as is recounted in the Sūrah of the Cave (Koran 18:61-83), go looking for the union of the two seas, that is, the sea of this world and the sea of the next, or manifestation and Being, Moses is distracted. The fish which they are carrying to eat comes to life and slips away, showing them that they have passed — seeing, but not observing — their goal. In retracing their steps they encounter the figure described above. Moses wishes to follow al-Khiḍr but is told that he will not be able to bear with that mysterious figure. Therefore, Moses promises to ask no questions, but simply to obey. The two, Moses and al-Khiḍr, (the servant of the previous episode is not mentioned further) now encounter three situations in which al-Khiḍr performs apparent outrages, sinking a ship, killing a lad, and repairing a wall for unworthy folk. Moses each time, and despite his promise, expresses dismay at the actions and is finally abandoned by al-Khiḍr, who explains upon parting the hidden reasons behind his acts, which were intended to bring a greater good out of an apparent evil, and which were done at the command of God.

According to the most usual, but not exclusive, Sufi commentary, Moses represents exoterism with its limitations, grasping at the external and apparent, whereas al-Khiḍr represents the inner dimension, esoterism, which transcends form. He appears to men in those moments when their own soul bears witness to an awareness of that dimension. In that rare case when there is a spontaneous realization of spiritual truth on the part of a *fard*, a "solitary" or someone who is by destiny cut off from revelation or from normal channels of spiritual instruction, it is al-Khiḍr who is the teacher as in the saying "when the disciple is ready, the master appears." The Sufis, upon entering an empty room, greet the void, because al-Khiḍr is there, and also say *as-salāmu 'alaykum* whenever he is mentioned, because at his mention his presence is called forth.

Al-Khiḍr is known everywhere throughout the Islamic world. He is a personification of the revealing function of the metaphysical Intellect, "the prophetic soul", the projection into the soul of the center of Being. The Sufi Ibrāhīm ibn Adham said: "In that wilderness I lived for four years. God gave me my eating without any toil of mine. Khiḍr the Green Ancient was my companion during that time — he taught me the Great Name of God." Philologists are no less intrigued by him, and connect him with Elijah or Utnapishtim of the Gilgamesh epic. *See* FIVE DIVINE PRESENCES; SUFISM; UWAYS al-QARANĪ.

Khilāfat Movement. A movement of Muslims in India from 1918 to 1924 to influence British policy towards Turkey after World War I and to preserve the Caliphate as a uniting institution for Islam. The Khilāfat Movement came into full existence with the creation of the All-India Khilāfat committee in 1918. The Turks themselves, however, abolished the Caliphate in 1924. The Movement then split into those who supported an Ottoman Candidate and those who supported a Hashimite. It disappeared not long after that. The Khilāfat Movement had grown out of tendencies gathering at the end of the 19th century. The Khilāfat movement had benefited from Hindu-Muslim nationalist cooperation against British rule that had begun during the war, and was supported by Gandhi after it. Eventually, however, the Islamic nature of the Khilāfat Movement led to an increase in differences in the goals of Hindu and Muslim political groups and led to nationalist aspirations along religious lines.

Khil'ah. An ornately made "robe of honor", often accompanied by other gifts, given by the ruler as a reward or mark of distinction. Such gifts were also made to other rulers. The giving of the robes was a hallmark of the court style of the 'Abbāsids of Baghdad. The Arabic word *khil'ah* has come through Italian into European languages as *gala*.

Khirqa-i-sharīf, *see* BURDAH; KHIRQAH.

Khirqah (lit. "a rag", "a tatter"). A cloak worn by some orders of dervishes. Patched continually as it wears out, the *khirqah* is a sign of poverty and renunciation of the world. In some orders the initiation is transmitted by the Shaykh's laying of a cloak over the disciple. According to the circumstance the act may also represent only a blessing. The patched cloak is also called a *muraqqa'ah*. *See* BURDAH; MURAQQA'AH; SUFISM.

Khiva. City in what is Uzbekistan today, a region once called Khwarizm, whose capital was Urgenj. It is near the Amu Darya, or Oxus, and near lake Aral. Once a satrapy of the Achaemenids, it was ruled by the Khwarizm Shahis until they were destroyed by Jenghiz Khan in 1219. It was a Khanate at the time of the Russian conquest in 1873. It has today a relatively well preserved old city.

Khojas. An ethnic group, in India and Pakistan, formerly a Hindu caste (which still preserves a strong group identity), most of whom today are Nizārī Ismā'īlīs. Most Khoja Ismā'īlīs, but not all, recognize the Aga Khan as their spiritual leader, the Imām.

The *dā'i* (lit. "caller", "propagandizer") Pīr Ṣadr ad-Dīn (also called by the Hindu name Sahadev) converted the Khojas to Ismā'īlism from Hinduism during early Ismā'īlī propagandizing in India in the *9th*/15th century. The sect was also spread in a Hindu form as the *Satpanth* ("true path"). The name Khoja was given to the followers by their missionary leader and means "lord" (*khwajah*) in Persian. Population centers of the Khojas are Bombay and the Gujarat in India and, through emigration, East Africa. Some Khojas have also emigrated to Europe and America, particularly after the expulsion of Asians from Uganda, and the decolonization of Mozambique.

In 1866 some of the Khojas sued the Aga Khan I in the Bombay courts to recover property from his control. The Khojas who are not followers of the present day Aga Khan derive from this split and are mostly Twelve-Imām Shī'ites. Other Khojas are Twelve-Imām Shī'ites going back a much longer time. Until the middle of the last century the Ismā'īlī Khoja self-awareness as a distinctive group was not highly developed; it has since then increased considerably, causing the Ismā'īlī Khojas to distance themselves from Twelve-Imām Khojas. Among Khojas in East Africa, this development did not take place until this century, and caused some social dislocations. Some Khojas are Sunnī Muslims, while others are Hindus. The Indian census of 1931 put their numbers at somewhat over 200,000. Today it would be considerably more, especially taking into account Khojas in Africa.

Khomeini, Ruhollah Musavi (1902-1989). Of a Persian family which had returned to Iran after several generations in Kashmir, Khomeini was born in the village of Khomein. He carried out his higher theological studies with Ayatollah Hā'eri, one of the most noted Mujtahids of his time. 'Abd al-Karīm Hā'eri from Yazd had taught at Najaf and Kerbela; Khomeini studied with him in the Iranian city of Arak and in 1921 accompanied him to Qum. At that time nationalism was on the rise in Iran and Iranians wished to have a center of theological learning to rival those in 'Irāq: this Iranian center was to be Qum.

The Faiziyeh madrasah in Qum had been founded by Fatḥ 'Ali Shah, the second Qājār; Khomeini was to study there and later teach theology and Islamic law. In the early 1960's he had enough followers to be considered one of the rare teachers called Ayatollahs.

In 1962 administrative procedures for local councils were instituted in Iran which allowed counselors to swear when taking office "by the holy book" (rather than the Koran specifically). The Mullās took this to be an open door for non-Muslims and in particular Baha'is to take control of the seats of government. In January of 1963 a land reform law was passed which included lands of religious endowments which the Mullās had wished exempted. The land reform law was popular although the results actually proved counterproductive for agriculture later; it was passed over the opposition of the Mullās. In February the Shah gave women the right to vote, an act which the Mullās opposed. Tensions between the government and the religious teaching establishment led to government raids upon the Faiziyeh in March of 1963 in which a student was killed. Khomeini made a series of inflammatory sermons which climaxed on the sensitive anniversary of Ḥusayn's death at Kerbela. The themes of his sermons decried what he perceived to be insults to men of religion and berated enemies of Islam, which included Israel and oppressive anti-Islamic governments. (The government of the Shah was friendly towards Israel and supplied it with Iranian oil while Israel provided the Shah with support and technical advisors).

On 5 June 1963 Khomeini was imprisoned. Rioting broke out in several cities. After several months in prison he then spent eight months under house arrest. Not long after being liberated, he made a speech in November of 1964 opposing a law being considered by the Iranian parliament which would have given American military forces in Iran diplomatic immunity, making them subject only to American courts and American laws. The embarrassing law passed by a very narrow margin, and was followed by a loan from the American government to Iran. In a characteristic style that absolutized relative points (he once said in a sermon at Qum that in killing Ḥusayn at Kerbela the Umayyad Caliph Yazid wished to exterminate all the descendants of the Prophet), Khomeini called the new law of diplomatic immunity the "enslavement of Iran" which "acknowledged that Iran is a colony; it has given America a document attesting that the nation of Muslims is barbarous... if the Shah should run over an American dog, he would be called to account, but if an American cook should run over the Shah, no one has any claims against him... It is America that considers the Koran and Islam to be harmful to itself and wishes to remove them from its way; it is America that considers Muslim men of religion a thorn in its path."

The sermon was clandestinely printed and distributed on tape cassettes. Several days later Khomeini was exiled to Turkey, but Khomeini's ideas had struck a chord with the mass of Iranians and when he went by invitation in 1965 to Najaf in 'Irāq to teach theology he had become one of the most prominent Shī'ite religious authorities.

In January of 1978 a wave of demonstrations broke out in Iran; Khomeini had to leave 'Irāq and went to Paris. The BBC Persian service carried a speech by Ayatollah Shariatmadari, who until then had been cautious, blaming the government. The demonstrations in Iran led to shootings by the army. Every forty days thereafter, on the occasions of mourning for the dead of the previous demonstrations, new demonstrations and new shootings took place. The bazaars at Qum were closed and remained closed except for forty days until the next year. On August 19 a cinema burned and four hundred people died; the government blamed provocation by religious conservatives; the religious opposition blamed SAVAK. Violence continued until the Shah left Iran on January 16, 1979. On the first of February Khomeini returned.

In 1971 Khomeini had published the *Vilayat-i Faqih*, "The Government of the Jurisprudent" which proposed that in the absence of the Hidden Imām competent Jurists are mandated by the Hidden Imām to govern in his place. In theory, this resolved the tension of Shī'ite political practice which otherwise assumes all government other than that of the Hidden Imām to be illegitimate. In actual fact, the need for legitimate government in the absence of the Imām had already called for its theoretical legitimization. Very early in the development of Shī'ism, serving in the government had become perceived as betraying the Imām; therefore al-Murtaḍā ash-Sharīf 'Alam al-Hudā (d. *436*/1044) formulated the Shī'ite principle that "if the person accepting a government office knew or considered it likely on the basis of clear indications that he would be able, through his tenure of office, to support a right or to reject a false claim or to enjoin the good or forbid evil, and that nothing of this would be accomplished but for his holding office, it was obligatory for him to accept office."

What was new in Khomeini was that the political authority who could govern in the place of the Imām was to be a religious jurisprudent. This development grew out of the movement of the Shī'ite *Uṣūli* school of law, to which a Persian Mullā, Aḥmad Naraqī (*1185-1245*/1771-1829) made the following contribution: In 1829 he collected historical materials and Ḥadīth regarding political authority in a document called the *'Awa'id al-Ayyām*. He quoted what he believed to be an inspired tradition which concluded that while "The kings have authority over the people, the religious scholars have authority over the kings."

In the new government system adopted in Iran following Khomeini's lead, the highest authority must specifically be filled by a jurisprudent. The constitution also provides that there be a *rahbar*, also a jurisprudent, who may impeach the head of government if he deviates from religious principles.

Khomeini was called the *Nā'ib-i Imām* or the "representative of the Imām", a term often shortened to "Imām" implying that he was the returned Hidden Imām, something which Khomeini did not claim to be but a practice which he did not stop.

He had three daughters and two sons. The eldest, Muṣṭafa, had died in 'Irāq in 1977. He wrote stylized *'irfani* ("mystical") poetry, a custom among Shī'ite religious teachers, under the pseudonym 'the Indian.' Many Mullās cultivate characteristics and idiosyncracies which fascinate their publics and focus attention; Khomeini always spoke in an even tone of voice, never raised it, and his students could set their watches by his regular appearance at prayers and the Friday sermon.

Khomeini could set into motion drastic acts in the name of a merciful God without revealing in himself any apparent trace of self-contradiction. He did this with a kind of totality or ipseity. Having thus combined diametric opposites within himself, having become what his particular theology calls a "place between two places", he could exercise a profound fascination over those who came into his presence. This is how an American journalist, Robin Carlsen, described its effect: "A hurricane he was, yet immediately one could see that there was a point of absolute stillness inside that hurricane; while fierce and commanding, he was yet serene and receptive... This was no ordinary human being... none possessed quite the electrifying presence of Khomeini... Imam Khomeini broke into my heart and my brain with a current of emotion that I can only describe as extreme positivity, what I prefer to call 'love'. Yes, despite his call for Islamic executions (and in his very speech that day he called for a pardoning of thousands of prisoners who were amenable to change allegiance) his unwavering sternness of mien, his invulnerability to individual feeling, he was charged with a love that actually seemed to purify my heart, to fill it with a bliss that I had not known before... imagine for a moment the pushing of the body of oneself out of one's mother's womb, or the moment when one might awaken to the fact that one was being created inside a foetal body, or the moment when one was conscious of dying... Khomeini was that powerful, Khomeini was that strong; Khomeini was that ego-less and invincible. In a moment I saw all the impulses of the revolution, the whole history of the overthrow of the Shah, the rhythms of martyrdom... all of this contained in the presence of this man..." (*The Imam and His Islamic Revolution.*)

It is also interesting to note that in 1824 James Morier wrote of the foremost Mujtahid of Persia in Qum: "a man who, if he were to give himself sufficient stir, would make the people believe any doctrine that he might choose to promulgate. Such is his influence, that many believe he could even subvert the authority of the Shah himself, and make his subjects look upon his firmans as worthless, as so much waste paper." (*The Adventures of Hajji Baba of Iṣfahān.*) *See* HIDDEN IMĀM; IRAN; PAHLAVĪ; UṢŪLĪS.

Khul' (lit. "release"). A form of divorce based upon mutual consent in which the wife is obliged to return the bride-price. *See* DIVORCE.

Khums (lit. "a fifth part"). The portion of the spoils of war that the Prophet reserved for himself and for the use of the community. Among the Sunnīs the institution lapsed with the death of the Prophet, but among the Shī'ites it is preserved as a special religious tithe collected by the *Mujtahids* from their followers on behalf of the Hidden Imām.

Khurramiyyah (also called "Khurramdinids"; "the joyful religion"). A grouping of Iranian dualist sects of pre-Islamic origin in the *3rd*/9th century centered around Bādh in north Persia, near Azerbaijan. After the Muslim conquest, many followers of such sects outwardly professed Islam, while secretly keeping their own beliefs. The Khurramiyyah appeared along with the 'Abbāsid propaganda. Its leader was an 'Ammār ibn Dāwūd, a propagandist of the clandestine 'Abbāsid movement. 'Ammār's name was supposedly changed to Khidāsh ibn Yazid by the 'Abbāsid leader Muḥammad ibn 'Alī. Afterwards, the Khurramiyyah had spread and Khidash was put to death by the governor Asad ibn 'Abd Allāh al-Qasrī. The 'Abbāsids were obliged to repudiate Khidash and paint his appointment as a deliberate "test of obedience". A later Khurramiyyah also appeared around Abū Muslim, with one branch claiming him as a future messiah who would return. These events reveal a great deal about the real power basis of the 'Abbāsid revolt.

In the time of the Caliph al-Ma'mūn (d. *218*/833) the Khurramiyyah were led by a figure called Jawīdān and caused civil unrest. After the death of Jawīdān, the Khurramiyyah were led by a successor called Babak, who acquired a great notoriety in the 'Abbāsid Empire.

The Khurramiyyah were held in abhorrence by the Muslims of the age because they were believed to be libertines in the tradition of the Mazdakites, a Manichean sect which arose within Zoroastrianism at the beginning of the 6th century AD who practiced vegetarianism and — or such is the usual accusation — held women and property in common. The Mazdakites sect flourished for a short time under the Shah Kobad (d. AD 531) and was then put down with a massacre. The story of the Mazdakites was cited by the Vizier Niẓām al-Mulk (d. *485*/1092) in his "Book of Government" (*Siyāsat-Nāmeh*) as a warning to the Seljūq princes and the 'Abbāsids regarding the Assassin sect of his age, the inheritors of Mazdakism.

In the reign of the Caliph al-Mu'taṣim (d. *227*/842), at a time of civil unrest caused by famine, the Khurramiyyah rose in revolt; Bābak, however, was captured by Afshīn, a Persian prince and general of the Caliph, and was put to death in

Samarrā' in the year *223*/838. Afshīn was greatly honored and richly rewarded for putting down the revolt. Ibrāhīm ibn Mahdī, an uncle of the Caliph, said in a sermon from the pulpit: "Prince of True Believers, Glory, Glory to God! Thy warfare is accomplished; God is thy Warrior, let God's good slave Afshin take luck for his reward; the blow he struck has fastened a radiance on his face."

After the death of Bābak, the Khurramiyyah persisted under this name for some time thereafter, all the while being progressively Islamicised, at least outwardly.

Afshīn himself, shortly after the execution of Bābak, was accused by Mazyar, another rebel, a chieftain of Tabaristān, of instigating the revolt for which Māzyār was himself captured. According to Mazyar and other captured rebel chiefs from Soghdiana, they were all of them, including Afshin, secretly members of a Magian religion. Afshin, on being tried by the 'Abbāsid authorities, professed himself a dutiful Muslim who had only permitted peoples under his control in Soghdiana (a stronghold of Manicheism) to retain their old religions for the sake of civil tranquility. However, one of his accusers, a Soghdian warlord, said that Afshin received letters addressing him as "God of gods", a title his family had possessed in their old religion as Princes of Surushna. From the revelations against him, and his own admissions, Afshin was found guilty of treason and put to death, as were his accusers and rebelling co-religionists. *See* BABAK.

Khusraw, Nāṣir-i *see* NĀṢIR-I KHUSRAW.

Khuṭbah, *see* SERMON.

Khwārizm Shāhīs (Islamic rulers from the *2nd*/8th century until *628*/1231). Rulers of a Persian kingdom, Khwārizm, situated around the Oxus (Amu Darya) river south of the Aral Sea, and extending in the direction of the Syr Darya (Jaxartes) river. The region had been ruled by Persian dynasties from the 4th century AD on. A slave-vassal of the Seljūqs, Anushtigin, founded the last dynasty around *470*/1077. For a while the Khwārizm Shāhīs filled the power vacuum after the Seljūqs and controlled regions far to the south of Khwārizm until the Mongols arrived on the scene in *617*/1220. Later the region was known as the Khanate of Khiva.

al-Khwārizmī, Muḥammad ibn Mūsā (d. *226*/840). The mathematician, born in Khwārizm, Persia, after whom the *algorithm* is named. The word *algebra* is derived from his use of the word *al-jabr* ("coercion", "restoration"), which first appeared in his book on mathematics *al-Maqālah fī ḥisāb al-jabr wa-l-muqābilah*. It was the Latin translation of this work that introduced the algebraic concept into Europe.

His works on mathematics established the use of the Indian system of counting which became known as Arabic numerals, and the use of the zero. He also made astronomical calculations and did work on geography, sundials, and astrolabes. *See* ALGEBRA.

al-Kindī, Abū Yūsuf Ya'qūb ibn Isḥāq (d. *256*/870). The first important philosopher in Islam, and a student of the sciences and medicine. Born in Kūfah, al-Kindī was known in Europe as the "Philosopher of the Arabs"; some of his works were translated into Latin but many of the three hundred Arabic treatises attributed to him are lost; around seventy survive. Al-Kindī, a calligrapher at the Caliphal court at Baghdad, was the forerunner of the tradition of Islamic philosophy which studied Plato and Aristotle as complements to each other.

Al-Kindī was a polymath; he made contributions in mathematics, astronomy, chemistry and the theory of music. He wrote about Swedish, Norman, Chinese, and Yemen steel. He defined philosophy as the "knowledge of the realities of things according to human capacity" and said there was a universal and supreme Truth (accessible to reason, which in religion and revelation, is taken to be self-evident).

He was one of the first to confront the problem of creation, which according to Aristotelian philosophy is eternal whereas, according to revelation, is an act of God out of nothingness, *ex nihilo*. Al-Kindī's solution was to turn to Pythagoreanism and Neoplatonism, and to propose that creation is an emanation from an ultimate sphere, and that the ultimate sphere is created by God and can be "uncreated" by Him. It can be said that al-Kindī affirmed emanation and creation side by side in a solution resembling the apocatastasis of the Stoic philosophers and the early Church Fathers. Al-Kindī's approach developed in a climate when Mu'tazilite rationalism dominated religious thinking, and when it was important to establish harmony between reason and revelation which he thought should guide philosophy. He accepted the possibility of the resurrection of the body.

Al-Kindī proposed allegorical interpretation of the Koran, or *ta'wīl*, as the solution to a typical problem such as the following: when the Koran affirms that God says to a thing: " 'Be!' and it is" (Koran 2;117; 3:47; 6:73; 16:42; 19:36; 40:70), God addresses something as existing *before* its existence. Allegorical interpretation here resolves the apparent logical contradiction; but what is important is that al-Kindī recognized that antinomy is inherent in metaphysics, antinomy being the recognition that contradictions irreducible on one plan (as opposed to paradoxes, which are a different matter), may be resolved — or cease to exist — on another. If such apparent contradictions exist, they do so because the mind, in order to conceive reality analytically, is forced to reduce its formulations to one or another plane. It is thought itself which creates the kind of problem antinomy resolves. Al-Kindi is notable as one of the few pure Arabs really distinguished in domain of thought or letters. Among his students are Aḥmad ibn aṭ-Ṭayyib al-Sarakhsī (d. *286*/899) and Abū Zayd al-Balkhī (d. *324*/934) *See* APOCATASTASIS; BEING; FIVE DIVINE PRESENCES; KALĀM; MU'TAZILITES; PHILOSOPHY.

Kirām al-Kātibīn (lit. "noble scribes"). The recording Angels are conceived of, in popular Islam, as working in pairs, one to the right and one to the left of each person, inscribing respectively the individual's good and evil deeds (82:11). It is further believed popularly that the salutation of peace to the right and then to the left is directed to these recording Angels.

Kirghiz. A pastoral Muslim people found in the former Soviet Republic of Kyrgyzstan, in China, and Afghanistan. The Kirghiz are *yurt* nomads rather than *tent* nomads. Most of the Afghan Kirghiz have now fled to Pakistan.

The Kirghiz are Turkic-speaking, but of mixed Turkic and Mongol descent who lived in the Minusinsk Steppe on the upper branches of the Yenesei river in southern Siberia. They migrated to the Tien Shan where they merged with Mongols. They belonged to the "White Horde" fraction of the "Golden Horde" of Hūlāgū Khān and separated from the suzerainty of the Uzbeks in the fifteenth century. They came under the control of the Uzbek Khanate of Kokand in the 19th century and were conquered into the Russian empire in 1876. Before the 1917 revolution they were called Kara-Kirghiz whereas the people now called Kazakhs were called the Kirghiz-Kazak. They were Islamicised in the 18th century. There are 2,480,000 Kirghiz in Kyrgyzstan and another 100,000 in Xinjiang (Sinkiang) in China. There were over 25,000 Kirghiz in Afghanistan, most of whom fled to Pakistan during the Afghan war. They have a national epic called the Manas which is 250,000 lines long and is recited from memory by shamans. *See* KYRGYZSTAN; MONGOLS.

Kismet (from Ar. *qismah*, "part", "portion", "lot"). This word for fate made its way into European languages from Arabicized Persian through Turkish.

Kiswah. The black cloth which covers the Ka'bah, it is woven of a mixture of silk and cotton and is embroidered with calligraphic inscriptions from the Koran in gold thread in bands around the top. The whole cloth also has the Divine Name Allāh patterned in black on black throughout.

Tradition (probably to exalt the family of the 'Abbāsids) says that the mother of 'Abbās was the first to drape the Ka'bah with a *kiswah*. Originally the *kiswah* was woven by the Hārīthiya in Najran, a center of weaving; later at the imperial Dār al-Tīraz in Tustar in Iran. In modern times the *kiswah* was woven and embroidered in Cairo from generation to generation by a family called as-Sa'di; now the workshop has been moved to Mecca. The *kiswah* is changed each year; the old *kiswah* is cut up and distributed to pilgrims. During the changing, the Ka'bah is covered for several days with a white kiswah, and is popularly said to be "putting on *iḥrām*" ("consecration") as would a pilgrim. The color black has a sacred meaning (as in the ancient name of Egypt, *Khem*, "the Black Country") because it can symbolize the non-manifestation of Beyond-Being, or the Absolute.

Kitāb al-Jafr (lit. "the Book of Vellum" from *jafr*, a lamb, the book being written on vellum). An alleged book of secret teaching which the Shī'ites believe was compiled by 'Alī for the use of his descendants.

First specific mention of such a book is associated with Ja'far aṣ-Ṣādiq, the sixth Imām. That 'Alī kept a notebook (*ṣaḥīfah*), which may have contained his interpretations of Koranic verses and other thoughts is likely; that it contained anything substantial which he did not transmit to those who came to him for guidance is another matter, and indeed, the Sufis hold that 'Alī was one among others, who transmitted esoteric doctrine; that the notebook contained great secrets is a belief of those who believe there are great secrets. Allusions to such a book have filtered into Sunnī folklore where it is called the "Book of Hidden Things" (*Kitāb al-mughaybāt*), and it has become common to ascribe various predictions, typically of apocalyptic events, to such a book. In modern Arabic the term *'ilm al-jafr* ("the science [of the Book] of Vellum") has come to signify divination and fortune-telling.

The 'Abbāsids had their version of this secret book called the "yellow scroll" (*aṣ-Ṣaḥīfah aṣ-Ṣafra'* or *Ṣaḥifat ad-Dawlah*), which they alleged to have received through Muḥammad ibn al-Ḥanafiyyah which predicted their rise and the coming of the "black banners". This scroll was buried in Ḥumaymah, the 'Abbāsid estate, and then lost.

Koran (Ar. *al-qur'ān*, lit. "the reading", or "the recitation"). The holy book of Islam, the Koran is commonly also called the *muṣḥaf* ("collection of pages", "scripture"), *al-furqān* (lit. "the discrimination"— between truth and unreality), *al-Kitāb* ("the book"), *adh-dhikr* ("the Remembrance") and many other names. In formal speech it is called *al-qur'ān al-karīm* ("the Noble Koran"), or *al-qur'ān al-majīd* ("the Glorious Koran").

The Koran was revealed by God in a form of Arabic closely corresponding to the refined usage of the Meccan aristocracy of the Quraysh, but readily accessible to the speakers of other tribal dialects. However, although the language of the Koran is related to what had already become the poetical *koine* of the Arabs, it cannot be equated with it, for in every respect the Koran is subject to no rule, to no measure, to no standard; it is itself its own law. Its language became the basis of formal or classical Arabic, both literary and spoken, but while unquestionably the standard, its style is nevertheless inimitable (*i'jāz*). The Koran could be called poetry, or poetic prose, though much is of a striking austerity. The earlier, Meccan passages are frequently reminiscent of the pre-Islamic style called *saj'*, which stands between poetry and prose, with assonances, rhymes and near-rhymes, and line-lengths and meters which frequently shift. The following example, the Sūrah 81, gives some idea of this style, necessarily remote in translation:

In the Name of God,
the Merciful, the Compassionate

When the sun is muffled,
And when the stars are darkened,
And when the hills are moved,
And when camels
ten months pregnant are abandoned
And when wild beasts gather abroad
And when the seas surge up
And when souls are assembled
And when the girl-child
that was buried alive is asked
for what crime she was put to death
And when the writ is all displayed
And when the sky is torn away
And when hell-fire is lit
And when the garden is brought near—
Then shall each soul know what it has prepared.

Nay! I call to my witness the planets
that shift and hide
And night as it closeth
And morning as it breathes.
This in truth is the word of an honorable
Messenger,
Strong in the strength he got from
Lord of the throne,
Who must be obeyed, and trusted,
Your comrade is not mad:
He saw him in the clear middle air.
It was no hunger for the unseen,
Nor is this the utterance
of a devil to be stoned.
Whither can ye turn?
This is naught but a reminder to creation,
To whomsoever among you pleaseth to walk
a straight path.
Nor will you so please, unless God please,
Who is creation's Lord,

The revelation of the Koran began about the year 610; the Prophet was engaged, that year as others, in meditation in the cave of Ḥirā' (*ghār Ḥirā*), near the very summit of the mountain Jabal Nūr, during the holy month of Ramaḍān. In one of the last nights of the month (*see* LAYLAT al-QADR) the Angel Gabriel appeared to him with the first revelation, the beginning of Sūrah 96:

Read! [*'iqra*, from which *qur'ān*, "reading"],
in the Name of thy Lord who did create,

create man from a clot.
Read! for thy Lord is the Most Bounteous One,
Who teacheth by the pen,
Teacheth man that which he knew not.

The revelation continued sporadically, reflecting the events attendant on the birth of Islam, and directing the actions and responses of the Prophet as circumstances required. The Koran contains laws for society and warnings of the end of the world, descriptions of judgement, of Heaven and of Hell. There are stories of Biblical figures, but often in a form surprisingly different from that of the Hebrew Scriptures, as if the same events were being witnessed from a different point of view. It also contains stories of figures unknown to the Bible, and passages which are metaphysical and non-descriptive. Sacred history is a secondary preoccupation; the subject of the Koran is above all the Divine Nature and the means of salvation.

Many stories in the Koran resemble those of the Jewish *midrash*, popular and didactic versions of Biblical events which act as commentaries on the Scriptures. Here God is speaking, as it were, in terms of the lore inherited by the Arabs as descendants of Abraham and Ismā'īl (Ishmael), such as the accounts of creation, of Adam, and of Noah, the legends of Moses and Solomon, and events from the Arabs' own history, such as the stories of the Prophets Hūd and Ṣāliḥ. These were well-known to the men of the Prophet's day, and indeed to the Prophet, who incarnated the spiritual heritage of the Arabs.

In order to grasp the phenomenon of the Koran, what needs to be borne in mind is that Divine revelation is destined by God not simply for scholars, historians and those who have knowledge of comparative religion, but for the commonalty of men living at a particular place at a particular time, to whom the revelation is needful in order to encompass the truths of God and immortality. It is addressed, more immediately, to such men of that time and place as God has chosen to lay the foundations of a new society, to establish and consolidate in the world a religion that will endure beyond their time and spread beyond their land. To this end, God addresses men in a language they know, in concepts that are in part familiar (and in part amazingly new), against a background of received common knowledge, hearsay, mythology, and even prejudice. It is not surprising, therefore, that certain of the Koranic narratives or accounts of the creeds of Christianity and Judaism do not correspond to those religions' understanding of their own legends and beliefs.

What is certain, however, is that these Koranic expositions were — and are — appropriate to the knowledge, mentality and emotions of those whom God wished to be Muslims; they necessarily reflected a corpus of "truths" as perceived in the world of that time from which God could lay down a Straight Path leading to His absolute Truth to which, for them, no other faith was possible: "Praise belongs to God, who guided us unto this; had God not guided us, we had surely never been guided" (7:43); to use allegory, analogy, repetition and multiple reflection of the innumerable facets of myth and doctrine is part of the Divine contriving whereby men are saved: "God has sent down the most excellent of records, a book allegorical and many-layered ..." (39:23). "And now We have coined for men, in this Koran, every kind of parable, that perchance they may bethink themselves, a Koran in Arabic, with nothing crooked in it, that perchance they may learn piety" (39:27-28).

The extent to which God has adapted His Message to men's knowledge and questioning — both inevitably relative and inadequate from the perspective of God's absolute and total (and to us unimaginable) knowledge — is indicated by the frequency of such introductory phrases as the following: "They [will] ask: when is the Judgement Day?" (51:12); "They will ask thee: when [will] the Hour fall?" (59:42); "They [will] ask thee about the Spirit" (17:85); "They [will] ask thee about him of the two horns [*dhū-l-qarnayn*, Alexander the Great as mentioned in legend]; say thou: I shall recite to you an account of him" (18:83). Here, as everywhere in the Koran, God is addressing the Prophet; referring to men's questions, God gives the answer to men, through the inspiration vouchsafed to His Prophet.

And because the legends were well known, the Koran's recounting of the myths is frequently so concise, and even elliptical, that an acquaintance with the store of popular oral 'literature' current in the Prophet's day is needed to fill out the details, but not to fill out what the Koran is expounding by them. In practice, these legends remain familiar today; most Muslims know that the name of the Queen of Sheba was Bilqīs, and that the mysterious guide of Moses in the Sūrah of the Cave was al-Khiḍr, although neither name occurs in the text of the Koran.

However, in the concise re-telling of traditional tales and the purveying of understanding about other religions "of the Book", the essential and specifically Islamic doctrines of the Oneness of God, and the duties of men in the face of this re-asserted Oneness, are expounded with an eloquence and profundity that have left Muslims over the centuries in no doubt that the Koran is the direct and saving Word of God. And the miracle of it is that, out of this "material" that was very much of its age and place, there has come forth a Message that is timeless and universal. The Koran was the sole miracle, of any kind, which the Prophet admitted during his entire ministry of prophet-hood.

Western writers who, for reasons of the defence of Christianity and Judaism, or for reasons of their disbelief (*kufr*) in any Divine Revelation, have been wont to disparage the Koran as regards factual, historical accuracy, or have spoken of "Muḥammad's confused knowledge of history" or of his "imperfect or deficient knowledge of Judaism" are, in every respect, wide of the mark. To begin with, such observations presume the Prophet's participation in the composition of the Koran, which is in no way admissible. The accusation is not new; it was made in the Prophet's day and refuted frequently in the Koran itself, as in, for example, the Sūrah of the Star:

By the Pleiades at their setting!
Your comrade erreth not,
He doth not deviate,
Nor speak from any desire of his own.
It is all inspiration. A thing inspired,
Which one of dread power hath taught him—
...And he revealed unto his slave
what he revealed.
What he saw was no lie of his heart;
Will ye dispute with him about what he saw?
(53:1-5, 10-11)

Al-Jurjānī (Ash'arite theologian, d. *816*/1413) asked what it was that made the Koran different from human literature, for the stories could be imitated, and so could the style. The difference, he concluded, was a spiritual presence in the Koran, a force, a blessing, a *barakah*. Although the stories in the Koran have their historical origins, they undergo a transformation which lifts them out of their former context into a retelling which is not that of a human tongue. For example, the story of Dhū-l-Qarnayn and his building of a great wall (18:95), possibly reflects legends the Arabs had heard about the Great Wall of China, or the great wall built at Derbent near the Caspian by the Sāssānid king Chosroes (Anushirvan) against the Huns. Divine revelation then took this "material" and used it for its own purposes; the origins of the story become irrelevant, and it serves instead as a support to mirror heaven's sense, a *mathal*, or similitude. The once Chinese wall becomes the partition of Divine Law erected by God's viceroy between His creation and chaos, which will be breached in the apocalypse. Folklore stripped to its essence becomes pure symbol; "God coins similitudes [*amthāl*] for men, and God has knowledge of everything" (24:36). And: "God is not ashamed to strike a similitude even of a gnat" (2:24).

The Trinity as "seen" in the Koran, is not the trinity of the "Apostles'" Creed, nor the Nicene Creed, but a Trinity empty of all exegesis, a Trinity compared only to the "evidentness" and Absoluteness of the Divine Unity. Similarly, the Docetist doctrines concerning the crucifixion of Jesus as appearance were known among the Arabs. The description of the crucifixion in the Koran as an illusion (4:156), however, is not touched by any Docetist origins and purposes, for these are as alien to Islam as they are to Christianity. Instead, God recasts a cosmic event which, in Christianity, is seen providentially from the human point of view, into God's "vision" of it in Islam. The event seen by God becomes a restatement of the *shahādah: lā ilāha illa-Llāh*: "there is no god but God."

The revelation of the Koran was the ordering of the Prophet's very soul into the form of sacred words according to the Divine Command, to God's disposition of things. This occurred in the "Night of Destiny" or of "Power", the *Laylat al-Qadr*, the night of revelation. This sacred night, according to 'Ā'ishah, the Prophet's favorite wife, was the very "soul" of the Prophet.

Lo! We sent it down on the Night of Power;
And what shall teach thee what is
the Night of Power?
The Night of Power is better than
a thousand months;
in it the angels and the Spirit descend,
by the leave of their Lord, with all commands.
It is peace, until the coming of the dawn. (97)

The words were then brought out of the being of the Prophet into the "day", as Sūrahs, and *āyāt*, called forth in many cases by the immediate circumstances as events unfolded for years to come. The revelations ended with these words:

> This day have I perfected for you your Faith,
> And accomplished unto you my grace, Choosing
> for your religion: Islam! Submission! (5:5).

This was part of the sermon to the multitudes delivered during the "farewell pilgrimage" in March 632 (A.H. *10*), a few months before the Prophet's death on 8 June 632 (A.H. *11*). Abū Bakr wept when he heard these words because he understood then that this was the end of the revelations. The camel upon which the Prophet was mounted during the sermon buckled under the numinous weight which often came over the Prophet when the Spirit settled upon him.

The Koran was written down in part during its revelation, but above all it was committed to memory, as is the custom of traditional and largely preliterate cultures. Until the most recent times the first phase of primary education in the Muslim world was the memorizing of the Koran. In many countries, even today, thousands upon thousands know the entire Koran by memory. According to tradition, a definitive editing of the Koran was carried out in the Caliphate of 'Uthmān in order to avoid complications caused by variant texts. Earlier collections may have been made in the Caliphates of Abū Bakr and 'Umar, but 'Uthmān's definitive text was determined by a commission headed by a secretary of the Prophet, Zayd ibn Thābit, along with 'Abd Allāh ibn az-Zubayr, Sa'īd ibn al-'Ās, and 'Abd ar-Raḥmān ibn al-Ḥārith. The Koran was collected from the chance surfaces on which it had been inscribed: "from pieces of papyrus, flat stones, palm leaves, shoulder blades and ribs of animals, pieces of leather, wooden boards, and the hearts of men".

The Koran is the foundation and primary source of doctrine of Islam. In this, it is followed by the Ḥadīth (traditions of the Prophet) and Sunnah (the Prophet's example). The Koran is recited as a blessing to both reciter and hearer, and studied as the key to the knowledge of God. Islamic law prohibits the touching of the physical Arabic Koran (and formal, but not casual, recitation) unless the person is in a state of purity which corresponds to the greater ablution, or *ghusl* (*lā yamassuhū illa-l-muṭahharūn*). It is a prescription that every Muslim must commit at least twelve verses or lines of the Koran to memory.

The Koran is divided into 114 chapters each of which is called a *Sūrah* ("a row" pl. *sūrāt*). The Sūrahs are composed of verses each of which is called an *āyah* (lit. "a sign" pl. *āyāt*). Today the Koran is arranged in such a way that all the longer Sūrahs precede the shorter; and the whole is divided into thirty approximately equal lengths called *ajzā'* (sing. *juz'*), for the purposes of regular reading. One *juz'* is allotted for each day of reading in a month. Each *juz'* is divided into two *aḥzāb* (sing. *ḥizb*), one to be read in the mosque with the *salāt aṣ-ṣubḥ* ("morning prayer") and another with the *salāt al-'aghrib* ("evening prayer"). This and other divisions are customarily marked in the margins.

The revelations are identified as having been revealed either at Mecca, or at Medinah. The earlier, Meccan revelations have a more poetic and enthusiastic character, throwing forth powerful images of the world's end and existence's reabsorption into the Divine uncreatedness. The Medinan revelations are, on the other hand, like the calm after a storm, and deal mainly with the giving of laws. However, in the canonic recension of the Caliph 'Uthmān, some Meccan chapters contain verses revealed at Medinah and vice versa, so that the text's disjointed and irregular character has tempted Western scholars to try to rearrange it in a more apparent order.

These attempts are ill-advised, however, for the Koran's sudden shifts in meaning, points of view, and depth are in the very nature of the text. The Koran is heaven's sense compressed or refracted into human intelligibility, and it is inevitable that the vicissitudes the Koran has undergone in the world, namely, its first limitation into human language, memory, understanding, and dialect, and then its historic assembly into a written text, reflect the disparity between the human order as it is — not in an ideal world — and the Divine order. Jalāl ad-Dīn ar-Rūmī suggested that it is this very nature, outwardly chaotic, that is a "ruse" of the Koran to approximate the chaotic nature of the human soul, in order then to catch it, as a net catches a fish, and to bring it back to absorption in the Divine from which the soul has wandered. The impression the Koran can make when it is read is like a progression in a labyrinth which suddenly opens out into a secret and transcendent center. Its stories are those of the past, but they are also stories of the present and the future. They multiply themselves into an infinity of reflections, and then without motion bring the subject face to face with the Unity of God.

Fundamental to Islam and self-evident beyond any question to the believer is the fact that the Koran is Divinely revealed, that its author is God Himself. That He sometimes speaks in the first person singular, sometimes in the plural, sometimes in the third person, has never troubled Muslims, and has never been a stumbling block to belief. These shifts confront one with a space or consciousness different from our own, beyond our human limitations, and total, compared to which the human sense of logic is clearly small and fragmentary, incommensurate, and almost irrelevant. Faith is conviction through direct experience, and not the result of a process of reason.

The substance of the Koran is completely wedded to its Arabic form. Because the Koran is what is called in Sanskrit *shruti* ("primary revelation" or God Himself speaking) — unlike much of the New Testament which is *smriti* ("secondary revelation") — and because of the nature of Arabic as a sacred language, a language capable of transmitting *shruti*, it is completely impossible to translate the Koran in its *reality* into another language. Translations are therefore unusable for ritual and liturgical purposes. The sound itself, of inimitable sonority and rhythmic power, is numinous and sacramental.

It is a fundamental doctrine of Islam that the Koran, as the speech of God, is eternal and uncreated in its essence and sense, created in its letters and sounds (*ḥarf wa jarḥ*). It has been asserted that the doctrine of the uncreated Koran was the result of exposure to the Christian dogma of the Logos; that, as the Christians defined Jesus as the Word of God and as having two natures, one human and one Divine in one person, so the Muslims transposed this doctrine by analogy to the Koran as the Word of God made book. The Muslims were indeed aware of the Christian doctrine; the Caliph al-Ma'mūn (d. *218*/833), who supported the Mu'tazilite theory that the Koran *was* created, wrote to one of his governors that belief in the uncreatedness of the Koran resembled "the Christians when they claim that Jesus was not created because he was the Word of God". During the brief Mu'tazilite ascendancy which began in the Caliphate of al-Ma'mūn, belief in the uncreated Koran was temporarily suspended arousing fierce opposition. The Koran was declared to be created, and those opposed to this view were persecuted during an inquisition called the *miḥnah* (*218-232*/833-847) into the beliefs of the religious authorities. Yet lawyers and Judges staunchly upheld the dogma of the uncreated Koran, and nurtured it when necessary in secret. Ibn Ḥanbal went further, and declared that the Koran "was uncreated from cover to cover", that is, also in its letters and its sounds. In this he was certainly not intending to imitate the Monophysites, but he was flogged for his beliefs. When the *miḥnah* came to an end, the doctrine of the uncreatedness was restored, and has not been challenged since, in the Sunnī world. The Khārijites differ from the Sunnīs on this point, and in their dogmas the Koran is entirely created, which is also true for the Shī'ites, both Twelve-Imām and Zaydi, whose theology is actually an extension of that of the Mu'tazilites. *See also* al-ḤURŪF al-MUQATTA'ĀT; LAYLAT al-QADR; MUḤAMMAD; PROPHETS; QIRĀ'ĀT; REVELATION; UMMĪ.

Koran, Chanting. The recital (*tilāwah* or *qirā'ah*) of the Koran is governed by the science of *tajwīd* (lit. "adornment", "making beautiful" or "striving for excellence") which determines the full, smooth and balanced pronunciation, in context, of each letter and syllable. On this basis, which is fundamental as being the necessary and minimum according of respect to the revealed Word of God, there are three "*tempi*" of recitation: slow and measured (*tartīl*); moderate (*tadwīr*); and rapid, as for swift narration (*ḥadr*). One whose mastery of *tajwīd* and psalmody qualifies him for regular chanting in public is known as a "reciter" (*qāri'*, pl. *qurrā*).

Only the canonical Arabic text, as collected and compiled under the Caliph 'Uthmān with the consensus of the Companions (*ijmā' aṣ-ṣahābah*) may be recited, in one of the seven acceptable versions of punctuation and vocalization (*al-qirā'āt as-sab'ah*). These, though fixed only in the fourth century of the Hijrah, are taken to correspond to the seven *ahruf* ("letters", "versions" or, possibly, "dialects") of the Koran which, according to a Ḥadīth, the Prophet referred to as all having divine authority. In practice, only two of the "seven readings" have become customary: in Egypt, for example, the reading of Hafṣ according to the scholar Abū Bakr 'Āṣim; and in the rest of Africa that of Nāfi'.

The punctuation laid down by these *qirā'āt* is important because single verses may well contain more than one sentence, and the punctuation will then indicate the pause that should be made at the end of the sentence, or sentences. Or, on the contrary, a single sentence may run across more than one verse, in which case it would break the sense to pause at the end of a verse. Korans are therefore marked to help the reader to determine where stops and pauses are possible, and where they should not be made. If the meaning of the words is understood, this is usually clear from the text, but many Koran chanters, even those of Arabic mother tongue, do not always fully understand the sense of the words, and there are instances, notably passages which are "embracing" (*mu'āniqah*), where one sense is possible if a stop is made, and another if it is not. In such passages tradition determines how they are to be read. Some Korans have a *mim* and *'ayn* symbol, which stands for *mu'āniqah*, indicating that a line or a word can be understood as referring to either the passage preceding or following; these are then marked with three dots (cf. *fīhi* in Koran 2:2, which can either end the previous phrase, or begin the following; tradition indicates no stop to be made here).

The rules of *tajwīd*, which seem complex considered separately, are essentially the application of phonetic principles inherent in the Arabic language, and can be summarized under three headings:

1. assimilation of certain consonants (cf. Sanskrit *sandhi*)
2. modification of vowels;
3. pausal abbreviations.

1. Consonants with the same point of articulation "blend" in Arabic, cf. the so-called "solar" consonants following the *al* of the definite article: as *al-nūr* is pronounced *an-nūr*, conversely *in-lā* becomes *illā*; the final nasal (*tanwīn*) of, say, *Muḥammadan rasūl* becomes *Muḥammadar-rasūl* (although the nasal remains gently audible); *mīn-ba'd* is pronounced *mim-ba'd*; *an-ya'bud* is pronounced *ay-ya'bud*; *qad tabayyan* is pronounced *qat-tabayyan* etc.

2. The quality of the three fundamental vowels (a i u) is affected by an adjacent, and in particular by a preceding, consonant. For example, the gutturals and palatal hard consonants make for an "open" *a*, in contrast to the tendency for this letter to undergo "umlaut" (*imālah* meaning "leaning" [towards i]) after soft consonants. The open long *ā* in the Divine Name *Allāh* is particularly important and characteristic, for in this word alone in the entire language the consonant l is hard and palatal; however, if the Divine Name is prefixed by the preposition *li*, making the compound *li-Llāh*, then under the influence of the vowel *i*, the double *l* is softened and the following long *ā* is subject to *imālah*.

Long vowels before double consonants or two consonants together are shortened: e.g. *fī 's-samāwāt* is read *fissamāwāt*, the long *i* of *fi* being shortened by the *ss*; and *mā 'ktasabat* is pronounced *maktasabat*. In an apparent exception to this, a long vowel before a double consonant which is historically single is lengthened in compensation, and for the sake of clarity: e.g. *ḍāllīn* from an underlying *ḍālilīn*. Similarly a long vowel followed by the glottal stop called *hamzah* is lengthened by the degree of 3-1 if it occurs within a word, and by the degree of 2-1 if it occurs between two words.

3. In pausal forms, i.e. in words at the end of phrases or sentences, the final element — be it *tanwīn* (nasal), declensional or conjugational vowel (*i'rāb*) or dotted *h* (pronounced *t*) — is dropped: thus, for *waḥdahu*, *waḥdah*; for *khayran*, *khayra*; for *yu'minūna*, *yu'minūn*; for *jannatun*, *jannah* (because two rules, as it were, come conjointly into play).

Other rules of *tajwīd* aimed at clarity and comprehensibility include an emphatic pronunciation of all doubled consonants (*tashdīd*) and particularly of the double *n*, as in *innā*; and, in the not uncommon occurrence of final *m*, the compressing of the lips until after the voicing ceases.

Adherence to these phonetic rules over the centuries has been successful in conserving a smooth, "classical" pronunciation of great beauty, power and sonority; it has also saved the sound of the Koran from being corrupted by the many phonetic reductions that have impinged upon the various Arabic vernaculars.

There are passages in the Koran (cf. 41:37; 96:19 and others) which when read or heard, oblige the hearer, if possible, to make a bow (*rukū'*), or a prostration (*sajdah*). Some such *sajdahs*, in 48:25, are prescribed by some schools, in this case Abū Ḥanīfah and Ibn Mālik, but not by the other schools. If the reader or hearer of a passage calling for a *sajdah* or *rukū'* is seated, he should rise up and perform a *rukū'* if it is called for, but a *sajdah* can be performed directly from a sitting position and the reading then continues. If these occur in the recitation portion of a ritual prayer (*ṣalāt*), a *sajdah* or a *rukū'* is performed at that time and the prayer resumes from the point at which the bow or the prostration occurred. In most Korans these passages are marked with the words *rukū'* or *sajdah* in the margin or between the lines. Not every *sajdah* so marked is obligatory for all schools of law. *See* QIRA'AH.

Koranic School. Traditionally, the first schooling a child receives in Islamic societies. The Koranic school is being replaced by modern systems of education but is still found in many places. Colloquially, these schools are often called *kuttāb* or *m'seyyid*, and here children from four or five years of age learn to read and write, and are sometimes taught arithmetic. The full course of such a school culminates in the complete memorization of the Koran. The voices of a chorus of children reciting the Koran is one of the most characteristic neighborhood sounds of a traditional Islamic town. When the Koran is memorized in its entirety, the student's education is finished unless he goes on to the *madrasah* ("upper school"). As modern systems of education have today replaced the traditional one, the Koranic school has become a largely preschool institution or an educative parallel for young children.

Traditionally, the teacher is paid at intervals as the student learns more of the Koran. The learning of the fifty-fifth chapter, the Sūrah *ar-Raḥmān*, marks an important step; the teacher is paid a bonus, often a certain number of sheep. (The payments are made for portions of the Koran actually memorized. In Arab pre-Islamic and Islamic custom the basis of remuneration is for accomplishment, not for effort or time). In addition, a sheep is sacrificed and a celebration called the *nafas ar-Raḥmān* ("the infusion of the breath of the Merciful One") is held for the child.

In Koranic schools the writing is traditionally done on wooden tablets called *lawḥ* which are painted over with a lime mixture to provide a clean smooth surface and to erase the previous lesson. The ink is a mixture made primarily from burnt wool to which water is added; the pen is a sharpened reed with the point cut at an angle on the left to produce the characteristic thick and thin of Arabic letters. A pupil's tablet may be very beautifully decorated by the calligraphy of the teacher to be brought home to the parents as a sign that some particular stage of Koranic study has been reached.

"Kosher", *see* ḤALĀL.

Kubrā, Najm ad-Dīn ibn 'Umar (Abu-l-Jannāb Aḥmad ibn 'Umar al-Khīwaqī *540-618*/1145-1221). A Khwarazmian Sufi, born in Khiva and buried there, a disciple of Ismā'īl al-Qasrī at Dezful and 'Ammar ibn Yāsir Badlisi of the school of Abū Najib Suhrawardi, but also influenced by and related to the school of *ishraq* of Shihāb ad-Dīn Suhrawardī (d. *587*/1191). He is called *Kubrā* because of his nickname *aṭ-Ṭāmmatu-l-Kubrā* ("the Supreme Calamity") which his admirers say was because of his skill in debate, although his theology and the curses he enthusiastically put on his detractors, which included the Mongol invasion in which he himself died, may be the real reason. He was also called, rather immodestly, *Wali-tirash* ("the Saint Carver") because it was supposed that any one on whom his glance fell in moments of divine ecstasy and exaltation attained to the degree of saintship. (Jāmī said sarcastically this influence was not limited to human beings, but extended to dogs and sparrows.)

Kubrā was the "founder" of the Kubrāwiyyah order which was particularly influential in Central Asia. This Central Asian School of Sufism, related to Rūzbehān Baqlī of Shiraz (d. *606*/1209), evolved a complicated, Gnostic system of symbolism of light and colors as alchemical signs and visions experienced by the adept on his path of transformation. Henry Corbin, who brought this school to the attention of scholars, called this doctrine of colors "photisms".

Najm ad-Dīn Rāzi (*573-654*/1177-1256, (the successor of Kubrā) and Shams ad-Dīn Muḥammad Jīlānī Lāhījī (d. *912*/1506) said that "black light" (in Persian *nūr-e siyāh*) constituted "the highest spiritual stage". (Semnānī said, however, that the "black light" precedes an outburst of perception of green light or the "emerald vision"). "Black light" is a construct for evil divinized. Metaphysically evil is "a lack of good" or an "error" made by a consciousness in treating nothingness as if it were a substance and therefore as if it were derived from a Principle or from God. The Central Asian School is a form of radical Dualism because it treats evil positively and makes it equal to God or makes God into the source of evil. (Lāhījī was a Shaykh of the Nūrbakhshīyyah, closely related to the Kūbrawiyyah, and wrote a commentary of the *Gulshan-i Rāz*, "The Rose Garden of Mystery" of Maḥmūd Shabistarī, d. *720*/1320.) Abu-l-Hasan Busti is said to be the first who used the term "black light" in new Persian, but the idea of "dark light" or "a ray of the divine darkness" is often met with in Dionysus the (Pseudo) Areopagite (c. 500).

This radical Dualism of the Central Asian school parallels the doctrines of *ishraq*, for Shihāb ad-Dīn Suhrawardī also spoke of darkness as having a positive existence and created a cosmology in which there are points at which "light is mixed with darkness", as if darkness exists without light. Both of these schools of thought, and other related ones, are late extensions in Islamic times and within an Islamic framework of heterodox Zoroastrian offshoots and consequently are repositories of Persian legend and metaphysical speculation.

Bahā' ad-Dīn Walad of Balkh (*540-629*/1145-1231), father of Jalāl ad-Dīn ar-Rūmī, is also considered to have been a disciple of Kubrā, although Balkh was itself an ancient home of this type of theosophy, and Bahā' ad-Dīn probably belonged to a collateral branch of the school, as did Rūmī himself. A later well known figure of this school was 'Alā'ad-Dawlah Semnānī (*659-736*/1261-1336), as was Farid ad-Dīn 'Aṭṭār (d. c. 1225). The school had a great influence upon certain branches of Sufism in India through some, but not all, of the Naqshbandiyyah Later branches of the Kubrawiyyah are the Dhahabiyyah (for *silsilah dhahabiyyah*, the school of the "golden initiatic chain") in Shiraz, the Firdawsiyyah (in Bihar, India), the Rukniyyah, Ashrafiyyah (in India), Ya'qubūbiyyah (in India), Ightishāashiyyah, Hamadhāniyyah, Nūrbakhshiyyah, and Lahjāniyyah. Some of these branches are Shī'ite. It is said that Najm ad-Dīn Kubrā kept the number of his disciples to the number twelve; this cannot be taken literally and refers actually to the number of higher representatives or Khalifahs and others, but is interesting in that it observes the hierarchical structures found amongst the Fāṭimids and other related organizations. A Kubrawi, Badr ad-Din Ibrāhīm (d.1322), son of Sa'd ad-Din Ḥamuyi (a Shī'ite Khalifah of Kubrā d. *650*/1252) converted the Ilkhanid Ghazan to Islam in 1295. Another, Saif ad-Dīn al-Bākharzi (d. *658*/1260) converted Berke, Khan of the Golden Horde to Islam. The branch through 'Alī ibn Shihāb ad-Dīn al-Hamadhānī (*714-786*/1314-1385 buried in Khotlan in Tajikistan) was involved in the Islamization of Kashmir. Kubrā is buried in Kunya-Urgench (in Turkmenistan), not far from Khiva (Uzbekistan). Locally, he is called "Shikavrati". *See* ISHRAQI; NAJMU THAQIBU; SUFISM.

Kūfah. Founded as a military camp by Sa'd ibn Abī Waqqās shortly after the conquest of Ctesiphon in 637. According to a millennial political theory of the Caliph 'Umar, the Arab armies were not to settle, not to mingle with local populations, but to continue as a permanent military force until the whole world was conquered for Islam. This was the reason for the founding of several garrison-cities of which Kūfah became the most notable. Later, with the building of mosques, Kūfah became a city in its own right, and acquired the city gates of the conquered Sāssānid capital Ctesiphon along with the pretensions of religious and political Arab supremacy which it absorbed with the population of the nearby city of Ḥirah, which eventually disappeared. This former Lakhmid capital, with its Gnostic traditions, imbued the surrounding Beduin tribes with a religious, philosophical, and political radicalism that has never disappeared. The poet al-Mutannabi was born in Kūfah and nurtured his poetry and politics among its radical desert tribes. The city and the tribes around it transformed their pre-Islamic Gnosticism into what was to become *ghulāt* Shī'ism and later Qarmaṭī insurrection. Kūfah became above all a foyer of millennialist revolt. 'Ali had died in Kūfah at the hands of a Kharijite and his unknown burial place was "discovered" in nearby Najaf a century and half later by the astute Harūn ar-Rashīd in a vision. In 680 the citizens of Kūfah invited Ḥusayn ibn 'Alī to be their leader while in reality watching to see if anyone else followed. When few did, they casually allowed Ḥusayn to be killed by the Umayyads since it turned out he was not enough of a figurehead to suit their aspirations. Centuries later the Ṣafavids would turn this event into a metacosmic paroxysm of guilt. The Muezzins began to cry from the minarets on the day tradition later assigned to the event (originally unrecorded, like the burial place of 'Alī) that "today the body of Ḥusayn lies naked in the desert..."

Since after Ḥusayn no suitable 'Alīd could be found, one of their own, Mukhtār, led the unsuccessful Kaysāni revolt in 685 in the name of a Mahdī whose identity was mostly kept secret but who was Muḥammad ibn al-Ḥanifiyyah. In 739 Kūfah became the scene of a revolt of Zayd ibn 'Alī, and finally, it became an epicentre of the 'Abbāsid's revolution although they themselves never trusted it enough to remain there for long. In between, Kūfah found time to become an early center for philology and Sunni jurisprudence, until the founding of Baghdad eclipsed it forever.

Kufic is the name of a style of Arabic writing

which actually originated in Ḥirah, perhaps, even probably, in order to propagate the books of Mani in Arabic. This style was used to write early Korans after which it went out of fashion, but was restored and favored by the Fāṭimids. *See* LAKHMIDS; MADA'IN; BAGHDAD.

al-Kufr (lit. "covering", "hiding" and, by extension, "disbelief"). Unbelief in God, the state of being an infidel, blasphemy. The word has a more shocking and dreadful associations in the mind even of a Muslim of today than does the word "unbelief" for a Western believer. Unlike the idea of mere unbelief, which implies passivity, *kufr* clearly implies an active striving to block out God's evidentness, a will to oppose Him, a lack of gratitude for life and revelation. It is a denial of God, the *only* sin which God cannot forgive, because it refuses Him and His Mercy. The adjective is *kāfir*, an atheist, and the plural is *kāfirūn*, *kuffār*, *kafarah*, and *kifār*.

Say: "O unbelievers,
I serve not what you serve
and you are not serving what I serve,
nor am I serving what you have served,
neither are you serving what I serve.
To you, your religion,
and to me, my religion!" (109)

See KAFIR; SHIRK.

al-Kulaynī, Muḥammad Ibn Ya'qūb (d. *328*/939). Shī'ite theologian, author of the "Compendium of the Science of Religion" (*al-Kāfī fī 'Ilm ad-Dīn*). The book has two parts, the *Uṣūl al-Kāfī* ("Foundations of the Compendium"), and the *Furū 'al-Kāfī* ("Branches of the Compendium), and contains sixteen thousand Ḥadīth, or traditions, including those particular to Shī'ism. His work is one of the most important to Shī'ites among whom he is called the *Thiqat al-Islām* ("The Trust of Islam"). He died in Baghdad and is buried in Kūfah. *See* SHĪ'ISM.

Kumūn. In Mu'tazilite philosophy the latency or "hiding" (*kāminah*) of an effect within the cause, as in the idea, alluded to in the Koran, that fire is hidden in wood: "Have ye observed the fire which ye strike out; Was it ye who made the tree thereof to grow, or were We the grower?" (Koran 56:71-72). The idea was prominent with Naẓẓām; with this the world could be hidden in matter, only a different balance of qualities (similar to the Indian three *gunas*) allowed one or another aspect to emerge in a particular manifestation at any one time. In this way, matter would be the source of reality as it is in modern physics. *Kumūn* is also an implicit assumption in theories of evolution, which were advanced by all the Gnostic schools who believed that souls transmigrated into higher states of life. Opposed to *kumūn* in Islamic philosophies are the "occasionalists" such as the Ash'arites and the *ashab al-a'rād*, "accidentalists", or Aristotelians. However, because of the similarity of the concept of potentiality, or possibility, in the Aristotelian description of Being, *kumūn* is often wrongly considered to be derived from Aristotle, when in fact the Mu'tazilites received it from the Dualists who said that matter was the mixture of light and darkness. Thus the opponents of the Mu'tazilites underlined the idea that "possibility" is not a "thing", that "possibility" is not a "reality", that it is not hidden within the folds of something else, and, above all, does not have an existence somewhere, waiting to emerge, forseeable by soothsayers.

Kun. The word "Be!" The Divine command which God gives to possibilities to manifest themselves, or be created. "When He decrees a thing, He but says to it: 'Be!' (2:111): and "His command, when He desires a thing, is to say to it 'Be,' and it is." (36:81) *Kun* is better translated as "exist!", for what is involved in this Divine command is a bringing into existence out of Being; God speaks to what already has being but what has not yet undergone the reduction that is manifested existence. It is for this reason that the verbal noun corresponding to *Kun* is *Kawn* which means the manifested "world, cosmos, universe"; and the corresponding causative noun *mukawwin* means "maker", "creator". In the terminology of the Sufis this distinction is made explicit by the use of the word *wujūd* for Being, as in Ibn 'Arabī's *waḥdat al-wujūd* (the "Unity of Being"). *See* al-KINDĪ.

Kunyah. An honorific name of paternity or maternity, as Abū Bakr, "the father of the virgin" or Umm Khulthūm, "mother of Khulthūm". The naming of a parent after the child has itself a name: teknonymy. Often a man will be called by the name Abū, "father of" followed by the name of his firstborn son. A mother may be called Umm, "mother of" followed also by the name of her eldest son.

Such names arise from the idea that calling someone directly by their given name is impolite while a more oblique form of address is more honorable. (In Japan the socially polite word for "I" regularly changes as a particular elliptic form, such as "*boku*" which literally means "your servant" becomes too literally an affirmation of self and becomes itself impolite.)

But such a name can also stand on its own and be given to a child, especially as it is expected that a son will name his own son after the name of his father. Thus a young boy may often be called Abū Muḥammad if his father's name is Muḥammad. In some countries, particularly, Egypt and Morocco, the Abū names are considered rustic. But in 'Irāq the use of Kunyahs has become particularly elaborate. Everyone whose given name is Muḥammad may be called Abū-l-Qasim because this was a kunyah of the Prophet Muḥammad. Everyone whose given name is 'Alī may be called Abū-l-Ḥusayn because 'Alī was the father of Ḥusayn, and thus with other names that are associated with historical figures. The name Abū may also be used to create a name out of an outstanding characteristic. The Companion Abū Hurayrah was known as "father of the kitten" because of his affection for cats; the explorer Richard Burton, when he performed the pilgrimage in disguise, was nicknamed the "father of the mustachios"— Abū Shuwarib — for his appearance. *See* ISM; NAME; LAQAB; NISBAH.

Kurds. An Indo-European people, not Semitic or Turkic, who live mainly in a region referred to as Kurdistan, which includes parts of northern 'Irāq, western Iran, eastern Turkey, and northeastern Syria. Within this region there are about sixteen million Kurds who are nationals of the countries above. There are also some Kurds in Lebanon and the Soviet Union (where they are a recognized nationality).

The Kurds believe that they are descended from the ancient Medes. Although most Kurds are considered Sunni, some in Iran are Twelve-Imām Shī'ites. A large number belong to such minority sects as the Yazīdīs and the Ahl-i Ḥaqq (also called 'Alī Ilahis and 'Alawīs). Amongst those who are considered Sunnis there exist many *darvishī* or folk mystical affiliations which are strongly heterodox. Besides the deeply ingrained folk practices within Kurdish Islam, the established Sufi organizations, the Naqshbandiyyah, and particularly the Qadiriyyah also teach secret beliefs which further augment a climate of sectarianism apparent on the surface and deeply ingrained beneath it. Before Islam the Kurds were Zoroastrians and many traces of Magian religions are preserved among them. Saladin (Salāh ad-Dīn) was a famous Kurd who fought the Crusaders and founded the Ayyubid dynasty.

Kurds have their own Iranian language which is broken into two main dialects and further subdialects. The Kurds were a tribal people; today only about 15% are herders, most are farmers. Under the Ottoman empire the Kurds had a measure of autonomy and were governed by tribal leaders and princes of tribal confederations. The rise of nationalism and the disintegration of the Ottoman empire left the Kurds divided between several countries in each of which they are a minority.

In this century, failing to achieve self-determination at the end of World War I, although the promise was held out by the Treaty of Sèvres, the Kurds have fought lasting rebellions in attempts to gain independence, or at least greater autonomy. Between 1960 and 1975 in particular, because the Shah of Iran gave 'Irāqi Kurds under General Mustafa Barzani support in uprisings against the Baghdad government, the Kurds fought long and hard. Their struggles, however, were without success for the Shah's support was withdrawn once his own goals towards 'Irāq had been achieved.

In 1958 the regime of Colonel Kassim attempted to reach an accord with the Kurds of 'Irāq. General Barzani was allowed to return from exile in the Soviet Union and in 1959 Barzani assisted the government in putting down a revolt. By 1961 when Kurdish expectations had not been met, a revolt broke out. Reactions of the Baghdad government to Kurdish uprisings have been particularly sharp because of the economic importance of oil fields located in or near Kurdish areas. In 1964 talks were opened between the government and the Kurds. Agreements were announced in 1970; Kurdish was to be recognized as a national language along with Arabic; certain political concessions were promised. In 1974 an autonomy law was passed against a background of continuing armed struggle in which Iran and Syria provided staging areas for the Kurds, Israel supplied arms, and the United States economic support while the Soviet Union aided 'Irāq. Throughout the struggles the policy of the Baghdad government was to divide

Kurds among themselves, offering one faction concessions while severely repressing another. There have also been sharp divisions among the Kurds themselves.

Promises were frequently made and broken. Tensions increased between Iran and 'Irāq until an agreement was made in March 1975 in Algiers on borders between the two countries, particularly the status of the Shatt al-Arab waterway. Iranian support for the Kurds was immediately withdrawn. The Iranian revolution led to Kurdish revolts in Iran and the Iran-'Irāq war also involved Kurds on both sides.

Kursī (lit. "stool"). The "footstool" of God's "throne", (*al-'arsh*). It is also held that *kursī* is synonymous with *'arsh* and thus means "throne" as well. There is a famous Koranic verse known as the a*yat al-kursī*, or "verse of the throne".

One of the symbolic interpretations is that *al-'arsh* is Being, and *al-kursī* is non-formal manifestation, or the Angelic world. *See* AYAT al-KURSĪ; FIVE DIVINE PRESENCES.

Kuwait. State on the Arabian coast of the Persian Gulf, bordering on Saudi Arabia and 'Irāq. Population: 1,800,000. The majority are Sunnīs.

Kyrgyzstan. Independent in 1991, formerly part of the Soviet Union. Population 4,769,877, of whom 52% are Kirghiz and the rest are Russians and Uzbeks. Capital Bishkek. *See* KIRGHIZ.

L

Lailat..., *see* LAYLAT...

La'nah (lit. "cursing"). An ancient, but rare ritual of mutual imprecation which can be used to resolve certain disputes. *See* LI'ĀN; AHL al-KISĀ'I.

Lahore. (lit. "iron fort"). First mentioned by Baladhuri (d. *279*/892) as al-Āhvāar, and by the *Hudūd al-Ālam*, it is the most important city in the Punjab in Pakistan. Probably founded around the 2nd century AD, this was a capital of the Ghaznavid empire, and after 1187 that of the Ghurids before being set aside in favor of Delhi. The Mongols sacked it in 1241, but under the Moghuls after its reconquest by Humāyūn in 1555 it became a great city again. It was the residence of Jahāngīr, Shah Jahān, and Awrangzeb. After being fought over by Mahrattas, Persians, Afghans, and Sikhs, it was declared the capital of Ranjīt Singh who was declared Mahārājāh of the Punjab in 1802. In 1849 it came under British control.

Lahore has an excellent museum, the Shālimar gardens, the Bādshāhi mosque, and the tombs of Muḥammad Iqbal, al-Ḥujwīri (Dātā Ganj Bakhsh), Miān Mīr of the Qādiriyyah, and Jahāngīr.

Lakhmids. An Arab dynasty which ruled a pre-Islamic kingdom in the territory of what is present day 'Irāq. Its capital was Ḥīrah. The Lakhmid kingdom extended down the coast of the Persian Gulf to Baḥrayn including what is now the Eastern Province of Saudi Arabia. The Lakhmids depended upon the Sāssānids for their political existence, forming a buffer on the western edge of the Persian empire. The Lakhmids maintained for the Persians a series of strategic trenches used to discourage Arab attacks. When the Arab invasion of Iran came, many of the tribes making up the Lakhmid kingdom, some of whom were Nestorian Christians, joined with the Muslims in the onslaught upon the Persians, helping to bring about the Persian defeat at Qādisiyyah.

After the battle of Qadisiyyah in 636 or 637 the city of Ḥīrah went into decline and was displaced by the newly founded garrison city of Kūfah some fifty kilometers away. Thereafter, those ideas and entities that had been part of Ḥirah re-emerged in Kūfah. Ḥīrah had been founded near Babylon in the 2nd century BC The Lakhmids arose at the end of the 3rd century A.D and lasted until 602. Ṭabarī names twenty of their kings. The Lakhmids had been installed as kings of Ḥīrah by the Persians around 272. (The Romans sponsored the Christians Ghassanis of Syria as an Arab counterweight to the Persian sponsored Lakhmids.)

In 298, after the defeat of the Persians by the Romans in the reign of Diocletian, the Lakhmids under Imru'-l-Qays I went over to the Romans and overran North and Central Arabia even laying siege to Najran, then held by Shammar Yuhar'ish III of Ḥimyar. Soon after, they returned to alliance with the Persians, however, and they reached the height of their rule c. 504-554 with Mundhir III under the Persian suzerainty of Kabad and Chosroes I.

Among their rivals were the tribe of the Kinda to the south who had founded a kingdom in the Yammamah of Arabia with cities whose excavation reveals an hitherto unsuspected degree of Hellenist influence. Around 525, Ḥārith of Kinda, grandfather of the poet Imru'-l-Qays, was killed along with 48 other members of the tribe by Mundhir III the Lahkmid king. In the turmoil following, some members of the Kinda rejoined the Yemen branch of the Kinda tribe. The father of Imru'-l-Qays, the Amīr over the Kinda clan of the Asad, was assassinated. Imru'-l-Qays unsuccessfully tried to avenge his father's death; destiny drove him into exile guarding five coats of mail armor and his family. He was called by the Byzantine Emperor to Constantinople; on his way back he died at Ankara, perhaps poisoned by the Byzantines after having been appointed by them as head of the Arab armies of the Ghassanis under the Ghassanid King Ḥārith ibn Jabalah.

Ḥīrah had played an important role in the expansion of Manicheism (as did Kūfah afterwards). In 293, 'Amr ibn Adi, Lakhmid king of Ḥīrah, became a protector of Manicheism and under him a center of Arab Manicheism developed. 'Amr ibn Adi sent Innaios (the third successor to Mani and, after Mani himself, the second missionary to India along with Mani's father Pattik), as his emissary to the Sāssānid Great King Narses to plead against the persecution of Manicheism. The Manicheans may have had a role in an uprising in Egypt against the Romans, and this may have softened the attitude of Narses who was cited as an enemy of the Manicheans. In order to spread Manicheism clandestinely, Mani had pioneered the use of small books which could easily be concealed even on the body, rather than ponderous scrolls which could not. Since books and writing were critical to the spread of the new Semito-Persian religion which had become established at Ḥīrah (and was persecuted by both Romans and Persians), a system of writing Arabic also developed there. This system of writing Arabic was to shortly benefit the spread of Islam by facilitating the writing of the Koran under the name of Kufic writing.

Ibn Rustah, in the *Kitab al-Al'aq an-Nafisa* reported that Manicheans had come to Mecca from Ḥīrah before Islam. Ḥīrah was also on the route from Mecca to Madā'in, the Persian capital. Thus trading Arabs from Mecca passing through Ḥīrah could have observed the Bēma ceremony, the central rite of Manicheism which commemorates the return of the martyred Mani as an invisible presence seated upon an apparently empty chair before which is spread a feast. A knowledge and image of the Bēma feast reported by travelling Meccans, among whom the Prophet could easily have been one, is perhaps mirrored in this "picture" in the Koran: "Think not of those, who are slain in the way of Allāh, as dead. Nay, they are living. With their Lord they have provision. (*'inda Rabbihim razzaquna*)" (Koran: 2:154 and 3:169). The empty chair later became a mysterious symbol, perhaps the "tabut" that Ṭabari described of the revolt of Mukhtār (685) who carried out a ceremony in front of an empty chair which he called the "throne of 'Alī". Here also, many elements could have found their way into the Prophet's experience of life including the idea of the three groups which are described in the Surat al-Waqi'ah, and the ancient description of the light of the heavens and the earth kindled from the oil of an olive tree "not from the East nor from the West". Above all, this was the atmosphere which would have refracted the light of the "shining star" (*an-najmū thaqibū*).

The universalist and Manichean notion of many religions with one and the same message expressed by messengers sent to different nations may also have come from Ḥīrah to Mecca where revelation transformed it into positive religion; the term "Seal of the Prophets" had originally designated Mani but appears in the Koran as a designation for the Prophet. This along with other Gnostic terminology from Aramaic and Persian would have been adapted to Arabic in that region and put at the disposal of other Arabs and thus found its way into the theological speculation of the desert Arabs.

As Arab speakers acquainted with Persian ideas, the Lakhmids were important transmitters of these ideas to the Arabs further south, a process which had begun with the conquest of Babylon by Cyrus in 539 BC Among those originally Zoroastrian ideas were the conviction that the world will come to an apocalyptic end, a resurrection of the dead, a universal judgement, an afterlife in a paradise or a hell. After Islam appeared on the scene the Lakhmid Arabs were swept up with the new revelation coming out of the desert both in religious and political terms but their heritage continued to manifest itself through the urban center of Kūfah in contributions to theology, scholarship, and art, notably Kufic calligraphy, but also in attempts to re-establish their once leading role through such revolts as the Kaysāniyyah and later through the Qarmaṭīs.

The last king of Ḥīrah, an-Nu'mān ibn al-Mundhir, reigned from 580 to 602. He was the son of a Jewish mother, but adopted Nestorian Christianity after 591. He came to power through the intercession of a famous poet, the Christian 'Adi ibn Zayd, whom he later suspected and put to death. The poet's son acted for the revenge of his father at the Persian court of Ctesiphon, and Nu'mān was eventually put to a royal death by being trampled by an elephant.

During the struggle between Mu'āwiyah and 'Alī, the one relied upon the Ghassanis of Syria for his support, and the other turned to the heirs of the Lakhmids of 'Irāq. This coalition between 'Alīds and Lakhmids brought the descendants of 'Alī into their figurehead role of Shī'ite Imāms. *See* KŪFAH; MADA'IN.

Laqab. Honorific names such as those adopted by Caliphs or Sultans, such as "Exalter of the Religion of God". *See* KUNYAH; ISM; NAMES; NISBAH.

Lashkar-e-Tayyeba. Called the "Army of the Pure", a "mujahid" or paramilitary organization in Pakistan who consider it their duty to bring "death to oppressors". Its parent organization is the

Markaz ad-Da'wah wa-l-Irshad, "The Center for Preaching and Guidance", whose center is in Muridke near Lahore. The *Markaz* runs 130 schools and a university. The founder was a professor at a university in Lahore, Ḥāfiẓ Muḥammad Saeed. The organization was set up in 1986 but grew out of the *Ahl-i Ḥadīth* movement which began in India at the beginning of the 19th century. The Soviet Afghan War gave the impetus to the *Lashkar* followed by the guerilla war in Kashmir, and the U.S. war in Afghanistan. At that time it is believed to have had the support of the Pakistan Inter-Services Intelligence (ISI). In 1999 the *Amir*, or leader, Saeed announced "the breakup of India, if God wills" and their intention not to rest until India is dissolved into Pakistan. They called the U.S. attack on Afghanistan a new crusade (*salibi jang*) by the "Christian" West against the Muslim world. *See* AHL al-ḤADĪTH; FUNDAMENTALISM.

Laṭā'if (the plural of *luṭf*, "subtlety"). Subtle centers in the body mentioned by some, but not all, schools of mysticism. These are similar to the *chakras* of Hindu Tantrism, but their theory is neither so diverse nor so developed.

They vary according to school, but include as most important the forehead as seat of consciousness and the perception of forms; the breast as the focus of breath, or life; and the heart — but not the physical heart — as the junction of the individual with Being, or with what is supra-individual and beyond form. *See* NAQSHBANDIYYAH; SIRR.

Law, *see* SHARĪ'AH.

Lawāmiḥ (lit. "flashes"). Intuitions and understandings of a spiritual order which suddenly settle upon the soul. Also, the title of several books by Sufis.

Ibn 'Aṭā' Allāh says:

> Rarely come the Divine intuitions except on a sudden, lest the slaves should claim them as a result of their preparations.

al-Lawḥ al-Maḥfūẓ, (lit. "the guarded tablet"). The Koran says of itself that it is written on the "guarded tablet" (85:21-22). This has become the term for metaphysical substance (Aristotle's *hyle* or Sanskrit *prakriti*). The corresponding Islamic term for metaphysical form (the Greek *eidos* or the Sanskrit *purusha*) is the "Pen" (*al-qalam*) which writes upon the l*awḥ al-maḥfūẓ*. The tablet is also the repository of destiny (*al-qadr*), giving rise to the expression "it is written" (*maktūb*), for something fated. *See* BEING; FIVE DIVINE PRESENCES.

Laylah... *see* LAYLAT...

Laylat al-Barā'ah. On the night of the 15th Sha'bān religious observances are held in many places in the Islamic world in the belief that destinies for the coming year are fixed that night. (It is the night before the day of the 15th which is the holy night since the Islamic day runs from sunset to sunset.) In Arabic it is called the *Laylat al-Barā'ah* ("night of forgiveness"). In Iran and India it is called *Shab-i Barat*. The origin of this holiday is perhaps the *Farvardin* of ancient Iran for it is connected with the memory of the dead whose souls visit their relatives this day, and with the fates of the living, a kind of "All Souls Day". Hence, the Islamicised legend of the holiday says that the lote-tree of the ultimate limit (*as-sidratu al-muntaha*) is shaken that day and leaves fall with the names of those to die in the year to come. *See* CALENDAR.

Laylat al-Isrā' wa-l-Mi'rāj, *see* NIGHT JOURNEY.

Laylat al-Qadr (lit. "night of power" or "destiny"). The night in the year AD 610 in which the Koran descended, in its entirety, into the soul of the Prophet. It is one of the last ten nights of the month of Ramaḍān. For this reason the last ten days of Ramaḍān are taken to be particularly holy. In that night the Angel Gabriel first spoke to the Prophet, the Koran was revealed, and the Divine mission began.

The Sūrah 97 describes the Night of Power as "better than a thousand months... peace until the rising of the dawn". It is related that 'Ā'ishah, the Prophet's favorite wife, explained that the *Laylat al-Qadr* is "the soul of the Prophet". That is to say, since the Prophet is also all of creation in the form of a man, that night corresponded to his soul. This also implies that the true nature of the human soul is a receptacle for God's revelation. There is a widespread belief that the Night of Power is the 27th of Ramaḍān. It is certain that this common belief originates in Manicheism where the 27th day of the month of fasting is the celebrated anniversary of the death of Mani, for there are no Islamic sources for such an idea. *See* CALENDAR; KORAN.

Lebanon. Population estimated at over 3,575,000. There have been significant demographic changes, or changes in representation in the last twenty years; the population balance has shifted towards the Muslims. It is now estimated that 48% of the population are Muslim; 40% are Christian; 10% are Druze; 2% are 'Alāwīs and Ismā'īlīs. Of the Muslims, it is estimated that 68% may be Twelve-Imām Shī'ite while the Sunnīs are 32% (formerly Sunnīs were in the majority or thought to be in the majority). Of the Christians, 60% are Maronites, and the rest are Greek Orthodox, Melkites, and a number of smaller Christian churches. (There are more than 600,000 Druzes distributed throughout the countries of the Levant including Syria and Israel; since the 1970s, the 'Alāwī sect has been in power in Syria. The various Shī'ites of Lebanon are called *Metawila* inside the country. *See* 'ALĀWĪS; AMAL; DRUZES; ḤIZB ALLĀH; METAWILA; MARONITES; SHĪ'ISM; SUNNĪ.

Leilat..., *see* LAYLAT...

Legacies (Ar. *waṣāyā*; sing. *waṣiyyah*). Bequests made through the will of a testator can amount to only one third of his inheritable property under Islamic law (a condition which is taken from Roman law). As regards the other two-thirds, or indeed the whole estate if no bequest has been made, a complex law of inheritance exists which divides the estate among inheritors according to established schedules. Wills may be oral, but oral or written, they must be attested by two witnesses. A bequest to an inheritor, above the portion due to him by the law of inheritance, must be approved by the other inheritors. The law of a third also limits the property which may be given to endowments for pious works, the Dead Hand (*waqf*). No limit is placed on the portion of one's estate which may be disposed of as gift before one's death. *See* INHERITANCE; WAQF.

Leo Africanus. (1489-1528?) Leo Africanus was al-Ḥasan ibn Muḥammad al-Bassān az-Zayyāti al-Fassī, born in Granada in 1489; he was educated in Marrakesh. A traveler, he was captured by pirates and sold as a slave to the Pope, Leo X Medici. The Pope having found him remarkable, christened him after himself with the name Leo Giovanni in 1520. Leo Africanus taught Arabic at Bologna, wrote several works in Italian, and returned to the Islamic world in Tunis in 1528 where his trace disappeared.

In 1550, a "Description of Africa and the Noteworthy Features found therein" in Italian by Leo Africanus was published in Venice.

"Letters, Isolated", *see* al-ḤURŪF al-MUQATTA'ĀT.

Letters, Science of the *see* 'ILM al-ḤURŪF.

Lex Talionis, *see* QISAS.

Li'ān (lit. "imprecation"). An uncommon form of divorce which is nonetheless possible in Islamic law, based upon the husband's accusing his wife of infidelity. He supports the accusation by taking an oath four times (instead of the requirement, otherwise, for the infidelity to have been seen by four witnesses) and by calling imprecations upon himself in case of falsehood on his part.

The wife then denies the accusation by taking four oaths, and calls imprecations upon herself in case of falsehood on her part. The marriage is thereby dissolved, and the two can never be remarried to each other again. The wife keeps the dowry. *See* DIVORCE.

Libya. (Libyan Arab Republic. Instead of the usual word *jumhūriyyah* for "republic", the word *jamāhīriyyah*, based, no doubt symbolically, on the collective plural, is used). The estimated population in 1986 was 3,654,000. The country is 98% Muslim, of whom some forty thousand are Ibāḍī Khārijites. The Sunnīs are largely of the Mālikī rite. One third of the population is affiliated with the Sanūsī order (which, outside Libya, now only has followers in the Sudan). Libya is the site of spectacular Roman and Greek ruins, notably Leptis Magna, Sabratha, and Cyrene. *See* IBĀḌ ITES; SANŪSĪYYAH.

Limbo, *see* A'RĀF; ESCHATOLOGY.

Lord, *see* RABB; SAYYID.

Lot, *see* LUT.

Loya Jirga. In Afghanistan, the name of a general council made up of elders and leaders of tribes and ethnic groups including elected representatives called to decide matters of state. *See* AFGHANISTAN.

Lucknow. City in India east of Delhi, seat of a theological school called the *Nidwah.*

Luqmān. A figure mentioned in the Koran in Sūrah 31:11, as a man "having wisdom". He was known in Arab legend as a sage, and later tradition attached to his name a corpus of proverbs and moral tales reminiscent of those attributed to Aesop in Western Europe. Luqman was identified by Darmsteter as the homologue of Balaam the son of Beor. The meaning of Beor in Hebrew is to swallow, as Luqman means to swallow in Arabic. Originally the figure was doubtless common to all the Semitic peoples. The tales of Aesop are probably also of Mesopotamian origin.

Lur. A people in Iran, most of whom are of Indo-European origin. They speak a language which is close to ancient Persian or Pahlavī. The Lurs number over 500,000 of whom the majority are Shī'ite. Many are nomadic and graze their flocks in the region of the Zagros Mountains of southwest Iran.

Lūṭ. The Prophet Lot. He is mentioned in the Koran (6:88); (7:78); (11:77); (15:59); (21:71); (22:44); (26:161); (27:55); (29:31); (37:133); (54:33). He is described as a warner to his people, the inhabitants of the "overwhelmed cities" (*al-Mu'tafikah*), of God's impending punishment for their indecency and sodomy, but is rejected. His household are saved except for his wife who "lingered".

Lūṭī. A member of a chivalrous brotherhood. From time to time, and particularly in the 19th century, these turned to brigandage, and the term became synonymous with bandit.

Lycanthropy, *see* SECRET SOCIETY.

M

al-Ma'arrī, Abū-l-'Alā' (*363-449*/973-1057). One of the most famous of Arab poets, al-Ma'arrī was born and died in Ma'arrat al-Nu'mān in Syria. Blind from childhood, he lived to a ripe old age withdrawn from the world but widely celebrated for his powerful verses.

"He achieved originality and urbane elegance while still breathing an air of desert freedom reminiscent of the poets of the pre-Islamic "Age of Ignorance" (*Jāhiliyyah*). Somewhat like the author of Ecclesiastes, al-Ma'arrī described the world from an aloof, aristocratic and slightly scornful point of view."

Paradise, Hell; the sweet, the lurid Light
Both feed on Darkness; so we flit from state
To state like marsh-fire
through the one long Night.

The wailing funeral was not long gone
Before a wedding pomp followed upon.
The Wheel groaned. Both went on into the dark:
The sob, the shouting sounded soon as one.

"There is no God save Allāh!"— that is true,
Nor is there any prophet save the mind
Of man who wanders through the dark to find
The Paradise that is in me and you.

Al-Ma'arrī was a vegetarian and was celibate; besides being steeped in the school of al-Mutannabi, he was well acquainted with the Fāṭimid *dā'ī*, Mu'ayyad fī'l-Dīn Abū Naṣr al-Shīrāzī, possibly a teacher of Ma'arrī, who wrote works called the *Majālis* which are very similar to his. Mu'ayyad, from a Daylami Ismā'īlī family, left Shirāz and went to Cairo where he eventually became the *dā'ī al-du'āt*, but was exiled to Syria for a time. He corresponded with al-Ma'arrī "on the subject of... vegetarianism". This is a code word meaning a proscribed religion with vegetarianism as one of its tenets. Ma'arrī was also visited by Nāṣir-i Khusraw. Ma'arrī had once been "dragged by his foot" (an Arab trope for "expelled") out of the house of al-Murtaḍā, brother of Sharīf ar-Rāḍī of Baghdad. (Ma'arrī probably expected that a Twelve Imām Shī'ite would recognize a kindred spirit in a vegetarian.) While in Baghdad he frequented the Dār al-'Ilm library and aroused the ire of Sunnis as well as the less radical Twelver Shī'ites. Ibn al-Jawzī accused him of being a *zindīq*: "As for Abū-l-'Alā', his poems make no secret of their heresy; he went to all lengths in his hatred of the prophets but floundered about in his attempts to mislead, being afraid of execution, till he died in his destitution. There has been no period without successors to these two parties [Baṭinīs and Kharijites], only thank God, the fuel of the more audacious has been extinguished." Indeed, the title of one of a-Ma'arrīs works, *as-Siqṭ min az-Zand* ("the Spark from the Flint") may have been an audacious flaunting pun on *zand* in Persian and its derived term *zindīq*. Al-Ma'arrī had written:

They all err — Moslem, Christian,
Jew, and Magian;
Two make Humanity's universal sect;
One man intelligent without religion,
And one religious without intellect.

And in *Luzūm mā lā yalzam*:

Now this religion happens to prevail
Until by that religion overthrown —
Because men dare not live with men alone,
But always with another fairy-tale.

In *Siqṭ min az-Zand* he composed panegyrics of Ḥamdānids and Fāṭimid figures. In his *Risālat al-Ghufrān*, al-Ma'arrī describes a visit to the afterworld which may have served as a model for Dante's *Divine Comedy*. This theme is derived from the 4th century Pahlavī book of Ardā Virāz ("Book of the Holy Virāz"); the story is actually older than the 4th century, for Plutarch relates a similar "vision of Aridaeus" who was said to be a man of Soli in Asia Minor. In it, a wise man, chosen by an assembly of wise men, reaches the afterlife in a hashish inspired dream, returns after seven days and relates the punishments and rewards of heaven and hell.

al-Madā'in. (lit. "the cities"). The Arabic name of the twin cities of Seleucia-Ctesiphon This was actually a group of seven towns located 20 miles/33 kilometers southwest of old Baghdad on either side of the Tigris river. The two main towns were the Greek Hellenist city on the west which was founded by Seleucus around 300 BC and opposite, on the east, the Persian city of Ctesiphon (*Ṭaisafun*) which became the capital of the Sāssānids. Since the Tigris changed its course at the end of the Middle Ages much of Seleucia has disappeared. Some distance away from Ctesiphon stood a new town founded by Anushirwan around 550 called by the Arabs Rūmīyah because the inhabitants had been deported there from Syria. Here al-Manṣūr had Abū Muslim killed.

In the south part of Seleucia, and on the West bank of the Tigris, was a town which the Persians called Veh-Ardeshir, the Arabs called Behrasir, and the speakers of Syriac and Aramaic called Kōkhē (the name of the hill upon which the town was built). This was the seat of the Nestorian Katholikos who now has removed to California. Since from here Mani had sent some of his important missions, this was probably also the town which was the seat of the Archegos, head of the Manichean religion, until the Archegos left Ctesiphon and Baghdad at the time of the Caliph al-Muqtadir around the beginning of the 10th century, probably in 908. (Mani's father Pattik joined the sect of the Mughtasila while he resided in Ctesiphon). Seleucia was also the Jewish center of Babylonia and the seat of the Resh Galuta.

In Ctesiphon stood Persian palaces, among them the ancient *Qaṣr al-Abyad* ("white palace") and the *Iwān-i* or, now, *Ṭāq-i Kisrā* palace built in the 3rd century, an arch of which still stands. The Caliph al-Manṣūr wanted to destroy it and tried, but Khālid ibn Barmak argued against it. Nearby is Salmān Pāk, the legendary burial place of the apocryphal Salmān Farsī which is a Turkish built mausoleum from the Middle Ages which contains two tombs.

Ctesiphon was conquered and looted by the Arabs in March 637. From that time it declined in favor of al-Kūfah until Baghdad was founded nearby in 762 which was a kind of spiritual restoration of the center of empire back to Ctesiphon. Al-Madā'in had a large Jewish, Manichean, and Christian population and Arabs, Syrians, and Greeks. *See* BAGHDAD; ARCHEGOS; MANICHEISM.

Madhhab (lit. "a direction"; pl. *madhāhib*). A system of thought, an intellectual approach. Specifically, the term *madhhab* is used to refer to each of the schools of law. *See* SCHOOLS of LAW; SHARĪ'AH.

Madīnah, *see* MEDINAH.

"The Mad Mullah", *see* MUḤAMMAD IBN 'ABD ALLĀH ḤASAN.

Madrasah (lit. "a place of study"; pl. *madāris*). A traditional school of higher study, in the sense that students entering a madrasah were presumed to have already committed the entire Koran to memory. The course of studies corresponded to the *trivium* of the "liberal arts" (grammar, logic and rhetoric) and included law (*fiqh*), traditional systems of mathematics (*'abjad*), literature, history, higher grammar, the calculation of prayer times, Koranic exegesis and chanting, and so forth. Medicine and agronomy were sometimes also taught.

The madrasah was actually more a residence than a place of study, since instruction was given in the mosque itself with students sitting around the teacher (although a small mosque was an indispensable part of the madrasah). Some madrasahs, such as the Abū-l-Ḥasan Madrasah in Fez, were built by princes who then provided a small pension for the students. Others were built by merchant and craft guilds, for example the *'Aṭṭarīn* or perfumer's madrasah in Fez. Many madrasahs that still exist are architectural masterpieces, particularly those in India and Morocco. Usually the madrasah had a central courtyard, a prayer hall, and small rooms where the students lived. It was the custom for the teacher to give the student a certificate (*ijāzah*) at the end of a course of study which could last for several years.

The Fāṭimids spurred the development of schools throughout the Islamic world. On the one hand they founded the al-Azhar university in Cairo as well as schools of the type called *dār al-'ilm* ("house of knowledge") in order to train propagandists for their sect. On the other hand, Sunnīs responded by opening their own schools of theology to meet the threat. Niẓām al-Mulk and the celebrated Saladin, for example, established many madrasahs with the avowed aim of countering the theological subversion of the Fāṭimids. But madrasahs had existed from earlier times; and among the most famous institutions were the *Bayt al-Ḥikmah* founded by the

Caliph al-Ma'mūn in Baghdad in the *3rd*/9th century, the *Niẓāmiyyah* founded by the Vizier Niẓām al-Mulk in the *5th*/11th century, and the *Mustanṣiriyyah* founded by the Caliph al-Mustanṣir in *631*/1234. The madrasahs of Bukhāra were said to hold thousands of students, and some important cities had dozens at one time.

The Muslim madrasahs provided the model for the European university. From the madrasahs came such traditions as the wearing of collegiate black gowns (worn at learned disputations in Fāṭimid Egypt), the division into undergraduate and graduate faculties, and much more besides. In Java, in addition to newer schools of Islamic study called madrasahs, an older form of Islamic school still exists called the *pesantren*. *See* 'ABJAD; DĀR al-ḤADĪTH; FIQH; KORANIC SCHOOL.

Maennerbund. *See* "SECRET SOCIETY".

Mafrūḍ (from *farḍ*, "that which is obligatory"). A religious obligation. *See* FARḌ.

al-Maghrib (lit. "the place of sunset", "the west"). 1. An abbreviation of the term *ṣalāt al-Maghrib*, the evening prayer, which may be performed a few minutes after the sun has set, and until the red glow fades from the western sky. (*See* PRAYER.)

2. *Al-Maghrib al-'Arabī*, The Arab West, the "Maghreb" is the region comprising Morocco, Mauritania, Algeria, Tunisia, and Libya. The classical Arabic name of Morocco is *al-Maghrib al-Aqṣā* (the "farthest west"). The name Morocco is derived from the city of Marrakesh.

Magi *see* MAJUS.

Magic (Ar. *as-siḥr*). Although the distinction is made between *as-siḥr al-abyaḍ* ("white magic") and *as-siḥr al-aswad* ("black magic"), magic as such is condemned in Islam, and its practice forbidden. Nevertheless, it is widely practiced. The term as-siḥr connotes specifically sorcery; *ad-da'wah* means incantation and exorcism; and *kahānah* or *kihānah* is divination. The verses of the Koran known as the *āyāt al-ḥifẓ* ("verses of protection", or "safeguard") are used as talismans against magic as well as for the avoidance of, or escape from, adversity.

According to tradition, the Prophet himself was the victim of a type of sorcery which involved spells cast by breathing on knots. In a vision he saw two Angels who informed him that the spell affecting him was on a rope that had been thrown into a well. The revelation of Sūrahs 113 and 114 dissolved the spell, each of the eleven verses undoing the effect of one of the eleven enchanted knots of the rope. These two verses are called the *al-mu'awwidhatān* ("the two of taking refuge"):

Say: 'I take refuge with the Lord of the Daybreak
from the evil of his creation
from the evil of utter darkness if it comes on,
from the evil of the witches who blow on knots,
from the evil of an envious man in his envy.'
(113)

Say: 'I take refuge in man's Lord.
man's King,
man's God,
from the whispering insinuator's evil
who whispers in man's breast,
from jinn and man.' (114)

A very common form of magic still found today uses the diagram of the *mandala*. *See* MANDALA; REFUGE.

Maḥabbah (lit. "love"). In spiritual psychology the meaning corresponds to the Greek *agape*, the Hindu *bhakti* and the Mahāyānist *Karuṇā*. It is the attitude of soul which implies devotion, "sacrifice of self" (i.e. transcending the *ego*), and "love of God". *Maḥabbah* is also the expansive aspect of the spiritual path, the fulfillment of the primordial norm called the *fiṭrah*, and the imitation of the example of the Divine Messenger, the Sunnah.

Maḥabbah may predominate as an operational attitude, but it is always associated with *makhāfah* ("fear of God", but also purification and "contraction") and with *ma'rifah* (gnosis or "knowledge of God"). Any of the three may constitute the principal spiritual methodology, but all three also are necessary elements of any spiritual development. *Makhāfah*, as purification, precedes *maḥabbah* as expansion. *Ma'rifah*, as union, is the culmination.

In the *Maḥāsin al-Majālis*, Aḥmad Ibn al-'Ārif says that "*maḥabbah* is the beginning of the valleys of extinction (*al-fanā'*) and the hill from which there is a descent towards the stages of self-naughting (*al-māhū*); it is the last of the stages where the advance guard of the mass of believers meets the rear guard of the elect." *See* FIṬRAH; MAKHĀFAH; MA'RIFAH.

al-Mahdī (lit. "the guided one"). A figure many Muslims believe will appear at the end of time to restore righteousness briefly — over the span of a few years — before the end of the world, the Day of Judgement (*yawm ad-dīn*). The doctrine, and the early Ḥadīth literature associated with it, originated with the Kaysāniyyah, who were followers, or rather, promoters, of Muḥammad ibn al-Ḥanafiyyah, a descendant of 'Alī by a woman of the Ḥanafī tribe. Muḥammad ibn al-Ḥanafiyyah tried unsuccessfully to resist Umayyad despotism. His followers maintained after his death that he had disappeared into hiding at Mount Raḍwā in northwest Arabia, in the region of Yenbo and Medinah, and that he would return to bring righteousness into the world. (*See* MUḤAMMAD ibn al-ḤANAFIYYAH.)

If the Mahdī Ḥadīth do in fact date from this movement, as is likely, (although they were recorded much later than other Ḥadīth) the later development of the doctrine of the Mahdī took hold because of the immediate political and religious aspirations of the Twelve-Imām Shī'ites. At the same time, both Shī'ite and Sunnī theologians believed it plausible that a reflection of the "Golden Age" of Islam would take place in history before the end of time, just as, by analogy, the sunset mimes the colors of the dawn. Or perhaps they saw in the rule of the Mahdī a kind of foreshadowing of the Second Coming of Jesus as announced in the Koran. Thus, at the time of the saintly Umayyad Caliph 'Umar ibn 'Abd al-'Azīz (d. *101*/720) the early historians record that: "A man once asked the Traditionist Ṭāūs: 'Is 'Umar the Mahdī?' 'He is a Mahdī,' replied Ṭāūs, 'but not *the* Mahdī.'"

The various Ḥadīth about the Mahdī appear to be inventions to support political causes. There are no Mahdī Ḥadīth in Bukhāri and Muslim; they appear much later in Tirmidhī and Abū Dāwūd. They state that he will be a descendant of the Prophet and have the same name, Muḥammad, possibly in one of its other forms, such as Aḥmad. However, another Ḥadīth, in all appearance an invention to counter pro-Mahdī Ḥadīth, proclaims that "there is no Mahdī but Jesus, son of Mary".

Despite this, some non-Shī'ite Muslims believe that the Mahdī will come in addition to the Second Coming of Jesus, and that the Mahdī is a respite in the darkening of the cosmic cycle. In this anticipation it is held that the reign of the Mahdī will reflect, towards the end of time, the pristine purity of the Prophet's rule and thus unite the schools of law and all the sects; the reign of the Mahdī will be finished before the Antichrist (*al-masīḥ ad-dajjāl*) appears to play his role; and once the Antichrist has led away his followers, Jesus will then come to destroy the Antichrist in the closing moments of the cosmic drama.

Belief in the Mahdī has been rejected by noted Sunni authorities as being a Messianism incompatible with a religion in which salvation does not depend upon intercession, especially intercession at a particular point in time, making all of time dependent upon that event. The Twelve-Imām Shī'ites identify the Mahdī with the Twelfth Imām, called the *muntaẓar* ("the awaited"), who is the "Hidden Imām". Other small Shī'ite groups have their own special interpretations of the Mahdī.

Predictions and lore concerning the Mahdī abound; the places where he will manifest himself are cited many times, and the signs of his coming are enumerated. In Morocco, it is said that the Mahdī and the Antichrist will turn up at the same time on the beach of Oued Massa. While his reign is often understood as being an inward or spiritual one, it has also been interpreted as being outward and temporal, a new universal Caliphate. A number of political leaders have exploited these expectations for their own ends and claimed to be the Mahdī. Ibn Tūmart (*470-525*/1077-1130) of the Almohads, and the Mahdī of the Sudan, Muḥammad Aḥmad ibn 'Abd Allāh (*1259-1303*/1843-1885) are among the historical figures. One of the most remarkable was 'Ubayd Allāh al-Mahdī, founder of the Fāṭimid dynasty. *See* DAJJĀL; HIDDEN IMĀM; JESUS; 'UBAYD ALLĀH al-MAHDĪ.

Mahdī of the Sudan. *See* MUḤAMMAD AḤMAD ibn SAYYID 'ABD ALLĀH.

al-Mahdīyyah. A city in Tunisia, founded by the Fāṭimids as their capital in *300*/912. It was so named because the founder of the dynasty claimed to be the Mahdī. *See* FĀṬIMIDS.

Maḥfouz Naguib. (1911-2005) Egyptian novelist and short story writer who won the 1988 Nobel prize for literature. He wrote about contemporary life and saw religion as an impediment to the advancement of society. For this there was an assassination attempt on his life in 1994 on the part of Islamic militants.

Maḥmal (lit. "litter"). A richly decorated camel litter, of the kind which would normally carry an important personage, it accompanied the yearly pilgrim caravan to Mecca from Cairo, and later from Damascus as well. The *maḥmal* was an emblem of state and rulers. Princes sent it as a token to represent them at the "standing" on the Day of 'Arafāt during the pilgrimage. (*See* PILGRIMAGE.)

The custom began in the times of the Mamlūks or the Ayyūbids, perhaps initiated by the widow of the last Ayyūbid who one year went on the pilgrimage and the next year sent her empty litter. The Egyptian *maḥmal* was often the most lavish, decorated with silk, gold, silver, and precious stones, but empty except for a Koran; the camel which bore it was led and not ridden. The Egyptian caravan also brought the *kiswah*, or covering of the Ka'bah, which is renewed each year. The practice of the *maḥmal* was discontinued when the Wahhābīs conquered Mecca in 1924.

Maḥmūd of Ghaznah (*350-422*/970-1030). Founder of the Ghaznavid dynasty and ruler of Afghanistan and Khorāsān, Maḥmūd was the son of Sabuktagin, a Turkic slave of the governor of Khorāsān, himself a vassal of the Sāmānid rulers of Bukhara. Sabuktagin was a noted successful military leader who bequeathed a kingdom to his son Ismā'īl. When Maḥmūd asked his brother to divide the domains with him, Ismā'īl refused, whereupon Maḥmūd attacked and conquered the whole kingdom. As a vigorous military leader, he made a number of successful expeditions into India, did not retain captured territory for his rule, with the exception of Lahore, but brought back great spoils. No less vigorous was his advancement of Islam, persecuting Shī'ites, especially Ismā'īlīs, and others with whom he did not agree. The 'Abbāsid Caliph al-Qādir invested Maḥmūd with a *khil'ah* ("robe of honor") and titles of sovereignty ending Maḥmūd's titular vassalage to the Sāmānids. Maḥmūd of Ghaznah was one of the first rulers to use the title of Sultan (from Arabic *sulṭān*, "authority").

The court of Ghaznah, on a trade route in Afghanistan between Kabul and Kandahar, was a haven to many scholars, including the great scientist and thinker al-Bīrūnī. The presence of many learned men, riches brought from India, and Maḥmūd's own architectural creations including the great mosque called the "Celestial Bride", made the ancient walled city influential in many ways. Maḥmūd was himself greatly interested in literature and theology, and was an active participant in the intellectual life of his court. He was himself a poet. But he was greedy and it is said was not above accusing someone of heresy merely in order to acquire some or all of his wealth. As Browne says: "he was fanatical, cruel to Muslim heretics as well as to Hindoos (of whom he slew an incalculable number), fickle and uncertain in temper, and more notable as an irresistible conqueror than as a faithful friend or a magnanimous foe." Also, he shortchanged his court poets.

Al-Bīrūnī accompanied Maḥmūd on his campaigns in India and used these as opportunities to learn Sanskrit, to study the intellectual treasures of that nation, and to translate such classics as the Patanjali Yoga into Arabic. *See* al-BĪRŪNĪ.

Maimonides, Moses (1136-1204). A Jewish physician and philosopher. Born in Cordoba, he settled in Egypt and was the court physician to Saladin. He acted, unofficially, as the head of the Egyptian Jewish community and was in correspondence with Jews throughout the Islamic world. At a time when many Jews were converting to Islam, Maimonides wrote the *Guide for the Perplexed*, with the intention of stemming this flight. He took the developments of Islamic philosophy, which was based upon Aristotle, and applied it to Judaism to bring it more in line with the times. Although hailed as a great figure of enlightenment, he was actually controversial in his time for his rationalism and even to this day he is not completely accepted by Orthodox Jews and not at all by Kabbalists. In particular, his condemnation of a belief in the corporeality of God, and magical and superstitious use of amulets like the mezuzah, his exclusion of resurrection in the body, led some Kabbalists to say that he was "reborn as a worm".

Mahr. The bridal gift which the groom pays to the bride, and which remains her property. She keeps all of it in the case of divorce, and half of it if the marriage is dissolved before consummation. The Arabs gave a bride-price before Islam and the Koran authorized the practice (4:4).

For the poor, no dowry is too small — the Prophet said to one poor man an iron ring would do. In modern times the expectation of large dowries, amounting to fortunes, has created social problems.

Majallah. A uniform codification of the laws of contract and obligation, based upon Ḥanafī law, promulgated in Turkey between *1286*/1869 and *1293*/1876 for use in the new secular courts, the *Niẓāmiyyah.* The Majallah was in force throughout the Ottoman Empire. It was replaced in Turkey by the adoption of the Swiss Civil Code in 1927 and elsewhere by other national laws; it is still in use in Jordan.

Majdhūb (lit. "attracted", from *jadhaba*, "to pull", "attract"). One whose sense has been deranged in a benign way, presumably from an overpowering perception of Divine Reality. A *majdhūb* is a "holy fool", one who is in some way mad, or seemingly mad, but possesses an aura of sanctity. The state may be temporary or permanent. One such figure, famous in Morocco for his aphoristic utterances and poetry, was 'Abd ar-Raḥmān Majdhūb, who lived in the *12th*/18th century.

Al-Ḥujwīrī said of such a one:

> It is related that one day when ash-Shiblī (a famous Sufi of Baghdad) came into the bazaar, the people said 'This is a madman.' He replied: 'You think I am mad, and I think you are sensible: may God increase my madness and your sense!'

And 'Abd Allāh ibn As'ad al-Yāfi'ī (d. *770*/1367) said:

> They say: 'Thou art become mad with love for thy beloved.' I reply: 'The savor of life is for madmen.'

And also:

> 'Alī ibn 'Abdān knew a madman who wandered about in the daytime and passed the night in prayer. 'How long,' he asked him, 'hast thou been mad?' 'Ever since I *knew.*'

Majlis (lit. "a sitting", "a session"). A gathering of notables in a Beduin tent, the audience of a Shaykh, an assembly, a ruling council, a parliament. It is also a Sufi gathering for the purpose of reading instructive texts, invocation, and singing — corresponding to what in Hinduism is called *satsang*. In Turkey the word *durgah* is similarly used, and in India, *durbar.*

al-Majlisī, Muḥammad Bāqir ibn Muḥammad at-Tāqī (*1038-1111*/1628-1699). A Shī'ite theologian, author of the *Biḥār al-Anwār* ("Oceans of Light") concerning the Imāms, *al-Ḥaqq al-Yaqīn* ("The Confirmed Truth"), and other books which are classics of Shī'ism, including several written in Persian. The foremost Shī'ite scholar of his time, al-Majlisī was also a popular Shī'ite polemicist and a violent opponent of philosophy. Towards Sufism, in which he saw a rival and competitor to Shī'ism, he was implacably hostile and was able, with the approval of the Shah, to have it banned and ousted from Iṣfahān, where al-Majlisī was born and died. He was a student of the father of Vaḥid Bihbahānī.

Mājūs. Derived from Magi, or Parthian priest, this is a name by which Muslims called Zoroastrians, and other Iranian religions. A more precise name for Zoroastrian is Zardushti, since Mājūs indicated any one of a number of Iranian religions, including Manicheism. The Arabs did not readily distinguish one type of Iranian religion from another, so that when one reads in a European language that such-and-such converted to Islam from "Zoroastrianism", this is usually a mistranslation from "Majūsi" which means he could actually have belonged to any number of sects. For example, during the time of the Fāṭimid al-Mu'izz, Sindh (and also Multan) more or less spontaneously adhered to the Fāṭimids on their own, yet the Sindhīs in question were not outwardly Ismā'īlīs. There was a question then (a question which has posed itself again in modern times) of bringing the practices of these Sindhīs (called "Friends of God") in line with the outer appearance of the co-religionists in Cairo. The Fāṭimid religious leader al-Nu'mān called these Sindhis Majūs, yet they could not have been Zoroastrians, and even less, as Stern has suggested: "probably a vague denomination for Hindus" (!). Evidently they were Manicheans from the early conversions without any Islamic pretensions (but perhaps with Indian or Hindu elements instead.)

The Magi proper were a tribe or a family that formed the priestly class in Zoroastrianism and claimed to be descended from Manuchehar, a mythical figure who was the legislator of grammar. In Sāssānid times the head priest, the head of the Magi or *mōbadān-mōbad*, was appointed by the kings, who themselves were hereditary priests of Anahitā.

The visit of the Magi, or Zoroastrian priests, in the Christian story of Jesus, refers to the accomplishment of the Zoroastrian prophecy. This prophecy in Zoroastrianism says that a virgin will bathe in a lake in which the seed of Zoroaster is preserved and that she will conceive the "world savior (*Saoshyant*)". It is only one of so many Zoroastrian elements in Christianity, that the latter can be considered as a prolongation of Zoroastrianism with a Semitic catalyst. *See* SĀSSĀNIDS; ZOROASTRIANISM.

al-Majūsī, 'Alī ibn al-'Abbās (d. *384*/994). Known in Europe as "Haly Abbās", al-Majūsī, a Persian, was court physician to the Seljūq Sultan, 'Aḍud ad-Dawlah. "The Royal Notebook" (*al-Kunnāsh al-Malikī*), his book on medicine, was translated into Latin and called the *Liber Regius* (later known as "The Complete Art of Medicine").

Makhāfah (lit. "fear"). The state or emotion of fear and reverence towards God. *Makhāfah* implies purification; it is the beginning of awareness as in the Solomonic proverb: *ra'as al-ḥikmati makhāfatu-Llāh* ("the beginning of wisdom is the fear of God"). It is a spiritual attitude towards God that must be sustained permanently being a kind of reflection of, or response to, God's rigor and majesty; it also constitutes a phase, one of the threefold aspects, of the spiritual path. From this point of view it precedes *maḥabbah* ("love") which is sacrifice and expansion into the mold of the *fiṭrah*, or primordial norm. The third and final aspect of the path is realization, *ma'rifah* — gnosis or union. *See* FIṬRAH; MAḤABBAH; MA'RIFAH.

Makkah, *see* MECCA.

Makrūh. (lit. "disliked" from *karaha*, "to dislike"). The category of actions which are discouraged by the Sunnah. The other categories (*aḥkām*) are *farḍ*, or *wājib*, which are the obligatory acts of prayer, fasting, etc.; *mustaḥabb*, or *mandūb*, actions which are recommended, *mubāḥ*, actions which are permitted or neutral, and *ḥarām*, actions and things which are forbidden. *See* AḤKĀM; FARḌ ; ḤARĀM; SHARĪ'AH.

Maktūb (lit. "written", "ordained"). In the sense of "it is written", it is an expression pronounced frequently in resignation to God's Providence. It refers to the Divine decrees written on *al-lawḥ al-maḥfūẓ* (the "guarded tablet"), and to such Koranic statements as: "There befalls not any happening in the earth or in your souls except it is in a book [*Kitāb*] before We [God] manifest it..." (57:22). Ibn 'Aṭā' Allāh says in the *Ḥikam*:

> Antecedent intentions [*sawābiq al-himām*] cannot pierce the walls of predestined Decrees [*aṣwār al-aqdir*].

While Islam views man's life as predestined in the sense that nothing can finally oppose the Will of God, man nonetheless has the gift of free will in that he does make choices and decisions. Resignation to the Will of God is a concomitant to striving in the Path of God. Above all, man is completely free in what is essential, that is, he can accept the Absolute and surrender himself to It, or reject God and pay the price. In this he has absolute free-will. The Talmud also says: "Everything is in the Hands of God, except the Fear of God." *See* LAWḤ al-MAḤFŪẒ; KALAM.

Malāḥida, *see* ILḤĀD.

Malak, *See* ANGELS.

Malā'ikah, *See* ANGELS.

Malakūt, *see* FIVE DIVINE PRESENCES.

Malāmatiyyah (lit. "men of blame"). The *malāmatiyyah* is often referred to as if it were a Sufi order (*ṭarīqah*) since it is characteristic to describe any idea as being a sect, or even a tribe. Indeed, it is said that Ḥamdūn al-Qaṣṣār (d. *271*/884) founded the "sect" in Nishāpūr of those who "proved" their sincerity and devotion to God by cloaking it under an "affected" libertinism. If it were not simply a spin or double-think to take in the gullible, it could be the designation of a tendency, or of a psychological category, of people who attract blame to themselves despite their being innocent. This may be due simply to maladjustment, but it can also be a measure of self-defense in order to hide a spiritual aptitude until a time of ripeness or, as a deliberate self-humiliation, to purify and loosen a positive quality from the grip of the lower soul (*an-nafs*), rather like Edgar, disguised as Tom, in King Lear. This is a very subtle spiritual operation which could well assume a morbid character, but it has, even so, been recognized as a legitimate possibility in Sufi lore. Al-Ḥujwīrī wrote:

> In the Path there is no taint or Veil more difficult to remove then self-esteem. And pop-

ularity does more than any other single thing to deter human nature from seeking to come to God.

The Contemptuary, or votary of Contempt, is careful never to resent whatever is said of him; and for the sake of his own salvation he must commit some act which is legally neither a deadly sin, nor a trivial sin, but which will ensure his being generally disapproved.

I once saw enough of a certain Transoxiana Contemptuary to feel at home with him. 'Brother,' I asked him on one occasion, 'why do you personally do these things?'

'To make other people's opinions unreal to me', he answered.

Others follow the discipline of Contempt from an ascetic motive: they wish to be generally despised for the sake of mortification of the self. To find themselves wretchedly humiliated is their intense joy... I saw... why the elders always suffered fools.

Malaysia. Federation. Population 15,300,000; Islam is the official state religion and the 55% of the population that is of indigenous Malay stock is Muslim of the Shāfi'i School of Law (some elements of the population are Ḥanafīs). The rest consisting of ethnic Chinese, Indian, etc., are Buddhist, Taoist, Christian, Sikh, and animist. Islam came to Malaysia with merchants from the Hadhramaut beginning at the end of the 7th century. Sufi *ṭuruq* include the Qādiriyyah, Shādhiliyyah, and Naqshbandiyyah.

Malik (from the root *mīm-lām-kāf*, "to possess"). A King. In Islam the more usual title for the ruler of a state, after Seljūq times, was Sultan (from the Arabic *sulṭān*, "authority"), for reason of the associations of the word *malik*: as it stands it is a Divine Name (*al-Malik*), which could be construed as impious if used to designate a human office; moreover, when "Kings" are mentioned in the Koran the references are not always flattering, for example: "...as for kings (*mulūkan*), when they enter a city they despoil it..." (27:34).

Mālik ibn Anas, Abū 'Abd Allāh (*94-179*/716-795). Founder of the Mālikī School of Law. He was born and died in Medinah, and received traditions from Sahl ibn Sa'd, one of the last surviving Companions. Mālik ibn Anas studied with Ja'far aṣ-Ṣādiq, the great scholar and descendant of the Prophet. He knew Abū Ḥanīfah, who had also studied in Medinah, then the cultural center of Islam. Mālik's approach to canon law relied heavily on the customary usages (*a'māl*) of Medinah and used *ijmā'* ("consensus") and *ra'y* ("opinion") secondarily.

His book, the *Muwaṭṭa'* ("The Path made Smooth"), is the earliest collection of Ḥadīth, and the first book of law. The Mālikī School of Law which derives from him is dominant in the Arab West and is also found in southern Egypt. *See* SCHOOLS of LAW.

Mamlūks (from the Ar. *mamlūk*, "one owned [by another]", "a bondsman", "a slave"). A military corps made up of slaves originally from beyond the Islamic domains and non-Muslims who were converted as youths. Most came from the steppes and were Circassians, Turkomans, or Mongols. They were raised to be soldiers with loyalty to a single chief.

The Fāṭimid dynasty from the *4th*/10th century on, and the Ayyūbids after them, depended upon them as the back-bone of the army. In *652*/1254 this military corps revolted against the last Ayyūbid and put one of their own number, Aybak, in control by marrying him to the step-mother of the murdered Sultan, thus establishing themselves as the power that ruled until the Turks conquered Cairo in *923*/1517. The Mamlūks remained, however, an influential military and landowning class until Muḥammad 'Alī Pasha crushed them decisively in *1226*/1811.

With few exceptions, Mamlūk Sultans ruled for a very short time, their power being dependent upon the whims of the military class that supported them. One chieftain, Qutuz, defeated the Mongols of Hūlāgū Khān at 'Ayn Jalūt in *659*/1260, thus checking the Mongol advance, but he was soon replaced by his lieutenant Baybars (d. *676*/1277), one of the most celebrated Mamlūk Sultans. It was Baybars who made the descendants of the 'Abbāsids, who had been deposed in Baghdad by the Mongols, into figurehead Caliphs in Cairo in order to legitimize his own Sultanate. He was the first Sultan to maintain all four schools of law on an equal footing in his domains, a practice later scrupulously adhered to by the Turks.

After Baybars, there began a decline in the line of the *Baḥrī* Mamlūks ("Sea Mamlūks"), so-called because their head-quarters were situated on an island in the Nile at Cairo. In their place rose the *Burjī* Mamlūks ("Mamlūks of the citadel"), a line headed by the Sultan al-Manṣūr Sayf ad-Dīn Qalā'ūn (d. *689*/1290), and firmly established with az-Zāhir Sayf ad-Dīn Barqūq (d. *802*/1399).

Struggles against the Crusaders, the Mongols, the Tīmūrīds and the Turks marked the Mamlūk period, as did also the far-reaching diplomatic relations established by them. An enduring stamp of architectural accomplishment rested upon Cairo and the other territories under Mamlūk dominion. The Ottoman Sultan Selim I conquered Cairo in *923*/1517 and incorporated Egypt into the Ottoman Empire, his victory being due in part to the Mamlūks' neglect of cannons and firearms as being beneath them, with the result that they were no match for the Ottomans, whose skill in such weapons was highly developed.

The Mamlūks, transformed into a tax-farming (*iltizām*) landholding aristocracy, were only eliminated as a political factor by Muḥammad 'Alī, the viceroy of Egypt, in *1226*/1811; inviting three hundred leading members of the Mamlūk community to dine in the Citadel, he had them massacred.

al-Ma'mūn, Abū-l-'Abbās 'Abd Allāh (*167-218*/783-833). An 'Abbāsid Caliph, the son of Hārūn ar-Rashīd, he promoted scientific study, and the translation of works of Greek learning into Arabic. He also founded an academy in Baghdad called the *Bayt al-Ḥikmah* ("House of Wisdom"), which included an observatory, for the advancement of science; Greek manuscripts were sought in Constantinople to enrich its library and to be translated into Arabic. A medical school was also founded in his reign.

When his brother al-Amīn was Caliph, Al-Ma'mūn had been governor of Merv, important by reason of its location and its trade links to distant lands. Buddhists, Shamanists, Muslims, Turks, Arabs and Persians rubbed shoulders in its markets; art flourished. It was there that al-Ma'mūn was exposed to the many stimuli which made him one of the great intellectuals among the Caliphs. Because his mother was a Persian, al-Ma'mūn was familiar with Persian civilization, and popular with his Persian subjects.

When his father died, al-Ma'mūn became involved in a power struggle with his elder brother. The orthodox party in Baghdad opposed al-Ma'mūn because he was "under the influence of an astrologer from Balkh" who had been introduced by Yaḥya Barmak and *converted to Islam.* Al-Ma'mūn's troops conquered Baghdad, but various rebellions marked his reign, initiated by members of his own family and also by Shī'ites who supported 'Alīd factions. Towards the end of his life he engaged in military campaigns against the Byzantines.

In a measure obviously seeking to placate Shī'ites, al-Ma'mūn declared the Imām of the Shī'ites, 'Alī ibn Mūsā ar-Riḍā, to be his successor to the Caliphate. The Imām pre-deceased him however, and was buried next to the tomb of al-Ma'mūn's father, Hārūn ar-Rashīd, in Ṭūs on a site now considered holy by Shī'ites and called Mashhad. (The site is holy because of the Imām 'Alī ar-Riḍā; the fact that Hārun ar-Rashīd is also there is ignored.) The Shī'ites maintain improbably thatvirtually everyone of their Imāms was assassinated, but this time they are probably right on the mark.

An interesting conversation is ascribed to al-Ma'mūn and 'Alī ibn Mūsā ar-Riḍā:

> "On what grounds do you [Shī'ites] claim the Caliphate for yourselves?" al-Ma'mūn asked. 'Alī ibn Mūsā replied the nearness in kin of 'Alī to the Prophet, may God save him and give him peace, and by the descent from Fāṭimah, may Allah be pleased with her."
>
> "If it is all nothing but a question of kinship," said the Caliph, "then surely there are amongst the Prophet's relatives — those that survived him — people who are nearer in kin to the Prophet or the same level as he. Whereas, if it is only the descent from Fāṭimah which counts in this matter, then truly the rights of Fātimah belong after her to Ḥasan and Ḥusayn and not to 'Alī. It follows that 'Alī robbed them both in their lifetime while they were in good health, and seized something to which he had absolutely no right."
>
> 'Alī Mūsā had no reply. (Quoted by M. Sharon from Ibn Qutaybah.)

After the Imām's death, the Caliph al-Ma'mūn inclined towards the doctrines of the rationalist Mu'tazilites, to curry the favor of the Shī'ites, and in *212*/827 their dogma of the created Koran was declared official, the obligation to accept this doctrine being enforced in *218*/833 by an inquisition (*miḥnah*), into the beliefs of Judges and religious leaders. (The orthodox doctrine, now everywhere accepted except by Shī'ites, is that the Koran is uncreated in its essence.) Aḥmad Ibn Ḥanbal became famous for being flogged for maintaining that the Koran was not only uncreated in its essence but physically uncreated "from cover to cover". After al-Ma'mūn, the *miḥnah* was abolished and the heyday of the Mu'tazilites came to an end, but for his association with non-orthodox doctrines al-Ma'mūn was nicknamed the "Prince of the Unbelievers" and an-Nadīm in the *Fihrist* even said he was a Manichean, which was the sense of the original charge that he was "under the influence of an astrologer from Balkh". (*See* NADĪM).

Al-Ma'mūn was a pivotal figure in the history of the 'Abbāsid dynasty. It was in his reign that the coalition with the factions of Khorāsān that had brought the 'Abbāsids to power began to unravel (after Harūn ar-Rashīd had the Barmakids put to death). Al-Ma'mūn, more than any other 'Abbāsid, was keenly aware of the theological tiger on which the 'Abbāsids had ridden to power. (Ibn Muqaffa' said that al-Manṣūr, the second 'Abāssid Caliph, was "like the rider of a lion who terrifies those who see him but is himself the most terrified of all".)

In the course of the early political struggles of Islam, the descendants of 'Abbās seemingly retired from the stage to a remote place, Ḥumaymah, southeast of the Dead Sea, 50 km southwest of Ma'ān, Jordan, in the direction of 'Aqabah. However, their retreat lay on the route between Medinah and Damascus and here they could discreetly observe the political scene and tap into the line of communications. The recently conquered Arabs of 'Irāq and the Persians were seeking ways of politically reasserting themselves. The Arabs were in power in the Islamic empire, and a political movement, especially a non-Arab Iranian one, needed to have Arabs as figureheads if it was to succeed. After unsuccessfully attempting to use Ḥusayn, the nephew of the Prophet, and later Muḥammad ibn Ḥanafiyyah, both of them prestigious Arabs, to lead an insurgency against the Umayyads, the leaders of the Kaysāniyyah from the region of Kūfah, and their allied Persian factions from Khorāsān, turned to the 'Abbāsids. In 716, Abū Hāshim, head of the 'Alīds, passed on to the 'Abbāsids the legacy of Muḥammad Ibn Ḥanafiyyah's partisans in 'Irāq, and the *'ilm*, the knowledge of dealing with them.

This gave rise to the coalition of the 'Abbāsids with Abū Muslim and Khorāsān. Propaganda played a very strong role in the revolution and a pseudo-Ḥadīth was launched (the Prophet denied knowing the future) which was even put into the mouth of Mu'āwiyah, the founder of the Umayyads, and said: "When al-Ḥakam's offspring reach the number of thirty males, they will make God's money a source of exploitation amongst themselves, they will turn God's religion into one of deceitfulness, and they will turn God's servants into slaves." Another said "O, Abū Hāshim, our da'wah is Eastern, our helpers are the people of the East and our banners are black; for the messenger of Allāh said: 'When you see the black banners approaching from Khorāsan join them even if you crawl on the snow for it.'"

Many of the Persians in the movement deliberately used Arab names to further make it appear that this was an Arab revolt; nevertheless, al-Birūni and others afterwards referred to the 'Abbāsids as "a foreign Khorasāni dynasty" (*dawlah ajāmiyyah khurasāniyyah*). The 'Abbāsids rallied the Arab elements while the Persians provided a power base, a base which 'Alī was already seeking against Mu'awiyah when he turned towards Kūfah before being assassinated.

The Kaysāniyyah had attempted to use the 'Alīds to come to power; when this had failed they tried to use the 'Abbāsids. The 'Abbāsids, however, turned the tables and used them instead. Once the revolution was successful, they put to death the Khorāsāni architect of the revolt, Abū Muslim who had begun to assume power for himself. Thereafter, however, the 'Abbāsids were a hostage to the hidden forces they had harnessed. If they gave too many concessions to the Persian ideologies left behind by the Sāssānids, and particularly the radical ones of Khorāsān and Kūfah, the Arabs representing conservative Islam would withdraw their support; but so would the Persians if they did not get what they wanted. Early into the 'Abbāsid era a group called the Rāwandiyyah came to the palace of al-Manṣūr and asked him to make known his divinity as they apparently had been promised he would. This was more than an embarrassment to al-Manṣūr; it was dangerous vis-a-vis the essential Arab bloc and he unceremoniously had the Rāwandis, several hundred of them, put to death before further damage was done to his position. (A modern Iranian historian has surmised that al-Manṣūr had actually converted to Manicheism in order to cement the bonds with the Khorāsānis: "Paris vaut une messe.")

Hārūn ar-Rashīd, for his part, catered to the nascent Shī'ism of 'Irāq and Iran (which had been created by the Kaysāniyyah in the first place) by having a vision in which his "cousin" 'Alī revealed to him his grave, which had been forgotten and unknown. In this way Najaf became the shrine of 'Alī. Then, toward the end of his reign, Hārūn ar-Rashīd suddenly turned on the family of his viziers, the Barmakids from Balkh (who represented the new leadership within the Persian bloc), and had them put to death, probably because they were hollowing out a Khorāsāni empire within that of the Arabs. The sudden elimination of the Barmakids by Hārūn ar-Rashīd is reminiscent of Philippe le Bel's elimination of the Knights Templar for similar, indeed almost identical, reasons.

Al-Ma'mūn had been born at Merv, then the economic and intellectual center of Persian Khorāsān (and also a center of Nestorianism); his accession to power was through a civil war with his half-brother who represented the Arab bloc while al-Ma'mūn represented the Persian. Al-Ma'mūn's victory put him even further into the Persian debt. Al-Ma'mūn named the 'Alīd figure, 'Alī ar-Riḍā, the 8th Shī'ite Imām as his successor. In 203/818 'Alī ar-Riḍā suddenly died in Nagaun near Ṭūs, presumably poisoned, and was buried next to Harūn ar-Rashīd, the father of al-Ma'mūn. This double burial place, probably intended to merge loyalties into one symbolic shrine, became Mashhad, after the Ṣafavids come to power. It survives only as a Shī'ite memorial: Hārūn ar-Rashīd is today forgotten and even despised by the Persians; few who visit Mashhad even know that he is also buried there.

The pro-Shī'ite gestures of the 'Abbāsids, such as they were, did not give anything to the non-Shī'ite elements that had actually created Shī'ism and inspired it, and which at the time were the more critical and politically dangerous segment of the Persian religious spectrum. Mu'tazilitism, however, perfectly suited the heterodox indigenous Iranian theologies that had become powerful both religiously and politically — the two being inseparable in Iran — under the Sāssānids. Al-Ma'mūn's imposition of Mu'tazilitism (it was already the house ideology of the 'Abbāsid revolution) as the official state dogma gave the Khorāsānis and these indigenous factions religious *carte blanche* for their beliefs. At the same time, rival ideologies were suppressed; Al-Ma'mūn (perhaps also as a counterbalancing gesture towards Arabs) took measures against the Ḥarrānians. In imposing Mu'tazilitism al-Ma'mūn was paying back the family political debt as the price for the Caliphate; it did not necessarily reflect any belief on his part but was simply *Realpolitik* although the well informed writer an-Nadīm did say that al-Ma'mūn was actually a Manichean.

The founder of Mu'tazilitism, Waṣīl ibn 'Aṭā' (d. *131*/748) was a mysterious figure. A *mawla*, or Iranian "client" convert to Islam, he was apparently the head of a secret organization, for Jāḥiẓ, the famous Arab writer, said of him: "Beyond the Pass of China, on every frontier to far distant Sus and beyond the Berbers, he has preachers. A tyrant's jest, an intriguer's craft does not break their determination. If he says 'Go' in winter, they obey; in summer they fear not the month of burning heat [a cryptic reference to Ramaḍan]" (Jāḥiẓ, *Bayān* I,37). And at this time there arose a saying armored as a Ḥadīth: "The Mu'tazila are the *Majūs* [adherents of Iranian religion]; do not follow one in prayer, nor join in carrying his bier when he is dead." It was these factions, under the leadership of the Persian Abū Muslim, that had provided the 'Abbāsids with the critical support they needed to come to power.

The imposition of Mu'tazilitism by al-Ma'mūn in *212*/827 aroused Arab resistance and had to be accompanied with a religious inquisition beginning in *218*/833. The use of force led to a stony intransigence on the part of the Arabs and the orthodox. Al-Ma'mūn's successor was obliged to lift the *miḥnah* within ten years and to renounce Mu'tazilitism. But he was also obliged to turn to mercenary Turks to protect himself and Turkish slaves replaced the Iranian element in the army; soon he had to leave Baghdad and live in the military garrison city of Samarra'. The Kūfans and Khorāsānis for their part, their aspirations, indeed their plan to acquire power for themselves, ultimately not satisfied by the coalition with the 'Abbāsids, withdrew their support.

Feeling betrayed by those whom they themselves were using, they began to work to subvert and destabilize the regime: first they encouraged the Black slaves to revolt in the Zanj uprising (*257-269*/870-882). Then, in *269*/882, the Governor of Kūfah, Aḥmad ibn Muḥammad aṭ-Ṭā'ī, informed the authorities in Baghdad that a people were grouping in southern 'Irāq *who had a non-Islamic religion*; and they were "prepared to fight the Community of Muḥammad with the sword and impose their own religion"; but no-one listened to him until the Qarmaṭīs began seizing control of whole regions. Further, in the reign of the Caliph al-Muqtadīr (from *295*/908) the head of the Manichean religion, the Archegos, left Baghdad. Rumors had it that he left for Samarkand, where there is no record that he actually appeared, while a man heralded as the Mahdī came to Tunisia, founded a new dynasty and proclaimed himself the true Caliph and rightful ruler of the Islamic world. The 'Abbāsids had become prisoners of forces they could no longer control; by the time they began to reassert themselves history had passed them by, and the Mongols (with Shī'ite advisors) were about to bring this phase of Islamic history to a close.

> "When al-Ma'mūn was dying his brother Mu'tasim bade one of those who stood near to recite the Profession of the Faith in Ma'mūn's ear; and the man did so, raising his voice in the hope that the Caliph might be able to repeat the words after him.
>
> No use shouting, said the physician Ibn Masawayh. At this moment he could not tell the difference between his God and Mani!
>
> Ma'mūn's eyes opened startlingly large, and glittering with an extraordinary light. His hands clutched toward the doctor and he tried to speak. But no words came. His eyes turned towards heaven, and filled with tears."

See 'ABBĀSIDS; MU'TAZILITES.

Man, the Perfect, *see* al-INSĀN al-KĀMIL.

Manāqib (lit. "virtues", "glorious deeds"). Hagiographical literature, such as the *Salwat al-Anfus* ("The Solace of Souls"), or the *Tadhkīrāt al-Awliyā'* ("Memorials of the Saints"), which are lives, records, and anecdotes of the Saints and the pious.

Manāsik al-Ḥajj. The rites of pilgrimage. *See* PILGRIMAGE.

Mandaeans (from Aramaic *Mandā d'Haiyē*, "the Gnosis of Life"). A small sect which probably migrated from Palestine, as a result of persecution from the greater body of Judaism, retracing the steps of Abraham through Ḥarrān, to their present home in the marshlands of 'Irāq. They now number less than 15,000, with some living in Iran, but as a result of the Iraq war they are facing extinction. They have their own quarter in Baghdad, and many are silversmiths. A graphic symbol of their religion has recently appeared which is a banner, the *drafshe*, draped over a cross. This banner and cross (the top above the cross piece is very short) is displayed during all ceremonies. Their religious writings are in a dialect of Eastern Aramaic.

Because of the many resemblances, it is possible that the Mandaeans are descended from the Qumran sect, that is, the Essenes, who had similar beliefs and also practiced sacramental lustrations. The Essenes were also the Jewish sect which had absorbed the greatest influence from Zoroastrianism, whence ablutions formed a central rite. Martin A. Larson wrote:

> "The climactic event in Essene history [in 69 BC]... the Teacher of Righteousness — that is the Essene leader — went boldly into Jerusalem and there, in the very temple itself, he proclaimed and condemned the lawless corruption and aggressions of the priests and authorities who ruled in Israel. He was therefore seized and executed, by what means is not certain, but some scholars believe that he was crucified."
>
> "Shortly thereafter, the persuasion developed among his followers — until it became an actual dogma — that he was the Most High God of the Universe Himself who had appeared for a time as a man among men; that he died a sacrificial death for the redemption of sinners; that he had risen from the grave on the third day; that he had returned to his throne in heaven; and that before the end of the then-existing generation, he would send a representative to the earth. This representative would in due course be invested with unlimited power and would terminate the present dispensation, conduct the last judgement, and establish the communal kingdom of the saints on earth, who would then come into possession of all the property of the wicked, who would, thereafter suffer infinite and eternal agonies in hell."

Besides being originally Essenes, and also related to the Ebionites, some scholars identify the Mandaeans with the *Mughtasilah*, the "washing sect" spoken of by an-Nadīm (d. *385*/995), whom he also calls the *Ṣābat al-Baṭā'ih* ("the Ṣābians of the Lowlands") in the *Fihrist* published in Baghdad in *378*/988. If this is so — and some scholars dispute it — the Mandaeans, or their forerunners, or a branch, would be the "Baptizing" (or, rather, "ritual ablution") sect of the Elkhasites, to which Mani (AD 216-276) belonged with his father Pattik (Ar. *Futtuq*) until the age of 24, when he went off to create his own gnostic religion, Manicheism. The Mandaeans thus would be the crucible in which a series of transformations took place at different times producing Christianity, Manicheism, and finally, Islam.

The principle book of the Mandaeans is the *Ginza* ("the Treasure", also called the "Great Book"), along with the "Book of John", and the "One Thousand and Twelve Questions". They were originally a sect of Judaism, and their beliefs are a mixture of elements from all the Semitic religions, but the essence of their religion is Gnostic-dualism, testimony of the transforming shock which Zoroastrianism produced upon the Semitic world. The "Knowledge of Life", after which they are named, is a celestial "emanation", and represents the Gnostic "call" to recognize one's true nature. Their beliefs include certain elements of Babylonian "astral" religion, evidenced by such things as turning towards the north star for worship, and metaphysical formulations which are heavily influenced by astrology. Manicheans, who probably arose out of the Mandaeans, also turned towards the north star when the sun and moon were not visible, and also used elements of astrology. A ritual handclasp is practiced by Mandaens, whence it spread directly to the Manicheans for whom the handclasp played an important rôle, symbolizing "pulling each other out of the darkness and into the light". Thence it became an insistant social feature in Islam with a ritual aspect in initiations and secret Sufi handshakes. One frequent interpretation of the handclasp in Sufi initiation is "extending a saving hand to a drowning man".

The principal rite of the Mandaeans is repeated sacramental lustrations in fresh running water. They venerate John the Baptist, for which, by a misunderstanding of one of their names, *Nāṣōreans* or the "observers" (of John, *Yōḥāna*), they became known in Europe as "St John's Christians". They no longer call themselves Nāsōreans, but that is still the name of the priestly class (also called *Tarmidē*), their followers being known as *Mandāyē*. This division, typical of all Gnostic sects, resembles the division into *electi* ("the chosen"), and *auditores* ("hearers") of the Manicheans. It may be that there is a filiation (also suspected of the Essenes) with the followers of John the Baptist, and the Ebionites, but the Mandaeans, despite the fact that they were the crucible which produced Christianity in the first place, have no real affinity with Christianity, and are in fact antagonistic towards it, calling Jesus "the prophet of lies". Indeed, they are also hostile towards Judaism (because Gnosticism considers the religious law to be compromised and evil), and call Moses the prophet of the evil spirit *Rūhā*, whilst Adonai they say is a false god. Despite their Gnostic doctrines they were once identified as the *ṣabi'ah*, or "Ṣābians", of the Koran, a people cited as having a revealed religion and thus belonging to the "People of the Book" (*ahl al-kitāb*). Other groups have also been identified as Ṣābians, notably a people of Ḥarrān in Syria. Ma'rūf al-Karkhī (d. *200*/815), a pivotal figure in the history of Sufism, is believed to have been a Mandaean. *See* AHL al-KITĀB; MANICHEANS; SABIANS; ZINDĪQ.

Mandala. A magical operation based on a diagram resembling the Hindu *mandala*, which was once very common and widespread and which may still be encountered in Africa and the East. It involves drawing a design consisting of an inkspot surrounded by several Koranic verses on the palm of the hand of a young boy. One of these verses is always 50:22: "Lo! we have removed your veil and today your sight is piercing." Incantations are then made which are believed to cause him to see visions inside the inkspot in answer to questions put to him concerning things and acts unknown, in the past, or at a distance. In Morocco it is known as "inducing the *ḥarakah*" ("movement"). Although the *mandala* uses Koranic verses, its origin is clearly not Islamic, for Islam does not condone magic. *See* MAGIC.

Mandūb, *see* MUSTAḤABB.

al-Manfaluti, Mustafa Lutfi (d. 1924). Popular Egyptian writer who, in addition to original prose, also produced Arabicized versions of several European works.

Manicheism. A world religion which, from the second century on, spread throughout the Near East and beyond, to Rome, Spain, North Africa, Afghanistan, Central Asia, India, and finally,

China. It was not the first religion of its kind which is Gnostic-Dualism, teaching that there are two opposing gods, light and darkness, which are intertwined in the world and struggling within it, but it achieved a high degree of development and refinement, effective organization and world-wide distribution. In addition to being a specific religion with a particular history, Manicheism is also a type of ideology and religion; it has its secular parallels within philosophies, particularly those of Heraclitus, Empedocles, Hegel, Marx, the Existentialists, and Communism, which was the preferred social system of Manichean polities. Many later dualisms are mutated forms of the original Manicheism, although some doubtless arose spontaneously, as the parable teaches (Matthew 13:24), from seeds that had traveled a great distance in time and space and suddenly sprouted out of nowhere, as if, while men slept, someone came, sowed tares among the wheat and went his way.

Balkh became a center, and in the West, Algeria-Tunisia where Augustine was converted. Indeed, North Africa was so important that in the middle of the *2nd*/8th century, when the 'Abbāsids came to power, the head of the world Manichean Church, the *Arch-Egos*, or Imām, whose seat was twenty miles from Baghdad in the former Persian capital of Ctesiphon, was a North African named Abū Hilāl ad-Dayhūrī. (When the Arabs first conquered the Berbers they called them "Mājūs".) Eventually, along the Silk Road, Manicheism spread to China. There it still survives today as a secret society in the province of Fujian, where a temple of Mani (in Chinese Mo-Mo-Ni from the Aramaic Mar Mani), still exists. (And of course, in Fujianese Chinatowns across the world.)

In the middle ages Manicheism re-appeared in Europe, in mutant strains, spreading from Asia Minor into Bulgaria and Yugoslavia ("the Bosnian Church") and then as "Catharism" the religion of the "pure", to Italy, and Germany, where it created Martin Luther, and France where it was also called the Albigensian heresy. (Often spread by weavers who could talk to the women of the house, it may have given rise to the story of the "Emperor's new clothes".)

The founder, Mani, called "the Apostle of Truth", was born in AD 216 in a region of 'Irāq where the Semitic and the Iranian worlds blend and overlap. Mani was brought up in a sect which practiced repeated sacramental ablutions. Called "baptizing" sects by Christian scholars, these sects, and some major religions, are the result of a collision between Semitic religions and Zoroastrianism, which followed the Persian conquest of Babylon. The particular sect, in some ways similar to that of Qumran and the Essenes, was the Elkhasites, related to the Mandaeans of today, who are probably those whom the Koran calls Ṣābians, one of the "People of the Scripture". Mani's father Patik (Ar. Futtuq) joined the Elkhasite sect after hearing a voice (cf. Koran 74:1-6) while in a temple of idols, perhaps a Buddhist temple, commanding him to purify himself by not eating meat, drinking wine, or procreating (Mani was already on the way). At the age of 13 and again at 26 Mani received revelations and the visitation of his "heavenly twin" (Ar. *Tawm*, Gr. *Syzygy*) and began preaching his own religion.

In 243 Mani had an audience with the Shah of Iran Shāpūr and introduced himself with these fateful words: "I am a healer from the land of Babylon." Mani and his followers often presented themselves as physician philosopher-astrologers, curing people of their illnesses. (Barmak was to introduce himself like this later at the court of the Umayyads in Damascus.) By tradition, Mani was a painter, whose images, considered to be themselves inspired revelation, used gold as a background, which symbolized the Manichean divinity of matter, and were the precursors of Orthodox icons, and Islamic miniatures. His temples were called by the Persians *nagarkhaneh*, "houses of paintings". Indeed, in Iranian tradition Mani is known even today as the consummate painter. Abū Faẓl, Akbar's minister, said of Fatehpur Sikri's decorative embellishments that "even Mani could not have done better".

Mani enjoyed favor under the Persian Kings Shāpūr I (241-272) and his successor Hormīzd-Ardeshīr (272-273). Shāpūr's brothers adopted Manicheism. Mani was permitted to propagate his religion throughout the empire. "His achievement and innovation lay in his ability to address pagans and Christians, Zoroastrians and Buddhists, convincingly in their own terms: in bold mythologizing, in imitating the Church fathers by producing exegetical variations on sacramental mysteries." Tradition says Mani, dressed in a blue frock and yellow-green trousers of a Mithraic priest, a costume which was evidently the "guru suit" of its day, brought the religion to Turkestan and to India, wandering ceaselessly, even though he had a club foot. But as time went on, the authorities looked upon the new religion as a subversive movement with alarm and mistrust, a turn of events which was to happen over and over again in other countries. Towards the end of his life Mani was imprisoned at the instigation of Kartir, the head of the Zoroastrian priesthood. He died in 276, after being imprisoned in heavy chains for twenty six days in the city of Jundishāpūr. The period of Mani's imprisonment during the month of February became a month of fasting for his followers, who said that after his death, which was termed a martyrdom and a crucifixion, he returned to life. (This event was called his *pari-nirvana* in the Buddhist version).

To celebrate his resurrection a feast was held *in his supernatural presence* with the invisible Mani seated on an empty throne. This feast, held at night, on the thirtieth day of the Manichean month of fasting (February, although Augustine cites March), became the principle rite of the religion and is called the *Bēma* from the throne upon which the invisible Mani is supposed to sit. (According to Augustine's description of this throne, it was indistinguishable from what became the pulpit or *minbar* of Islam.) During the ceremony a speech is addressed to Mani. (Mukhtār, the leader of the Kaysāniyyah revolt, also addressed a mysterious speech to an empty throne. When asked, by Muslim Arabs what this was all about, Mukhtār said he was addressing the "throne of 'Ali", which, in a nutshell, is how Shī'ism came about).

The Bēma ceremony, besides the speech to the living, invisible, and present martyr on the throne, was also a meal of the faithful, an *agape*. The Koran (2:154), establishing the doctrine of martyrs, says: "And call not those who are slain in the way of Allah 'dead'. Nay they are living, only you perceive not" [but you cannot see them] and (3:169) adds: "with their lord they have sustenance" (*rizq*, meaning food). Although it also fits the Christian Mass, this probably is a snapshot of first hand experience of the Bēma ceremony which Meccan traders could have seen in 'Irāq in Ḥirah, the Arabic speaking capital of the Lakhmid kingdom, which was a Manichean center that lay on the trading route to Ctesiphon. Several ancient authors also state that Manicheism had appeared in Mecca before Islam.

The term Manicheism itself reflects this existence of Mani in the invisible as it probably derives from the words "Mani lives" (*Mani Ḥayy*) in Aramaic, the primary religious language of the religion. (In an other example of ontogeny recapitulating phylogeny, Communism had several versions of the slogan "Lenin lives" including "Lenin is more alive than any of the living.") Manicheism's own name for itself is "Truth" (cf. the newspaper *Pravda* "Truth") and the "Religion of Truth". One Fāṭimid Caliph took the throne name "Exalter of the religion of God" (*al-Mu'izz li-Dīn-i Llāh*). "Religion of God" was later copied by the 'Abbāsids in their names, but it was originally another code word for what was the Fāṭimids true, but secret religion. But the classical name was the "Religion of the Two Principles and the Three Times" which found its way into the title of a Manichean-Buddhist Sutra in China. The religion is the most radical form of Gnostic dualism; it says that Godhead is two entities which are opposed to each other, and that these entities are *physically* light and darkness, or good and evil.

In the beginning, according to Manichean mythology, the good "god" was in his garden which was "walled on three sides" but open on the fourth. Suddenly and violently, he was attacked by an invisible force, the other pole of his reality. In order to escape, the good god produced emanations from himself in the form of particles of light; light thereafter existed in darkness; progressive emanations led to a Demiurge, creator of the world. Light is hidden in the world, and must be liberated; Gnostics who have heard the "call" proceed to carry out their destiny, namely, to liberate the light which is also their own reality; their salvation is to save the light also hidden within themselves; the return at the end of time of that light to its origin is a kind of deification of which such teachers as Mani were the living manifestation.

Thus Mani invented the "Big Bang" long before modern science drew similar conclusions from materialist assumptions. (Quantum mechanics is the true heir of Gnostic speculations.) Hans Jonas noted in *The Gnostic Religion* that there is a remarkable parallel between Gnosticism and Existentialism, and as it turns out, with other materialisms, including the current scientific one. With Mani, instead of matter and antimatter coming together, or thesis and antithesis as in Communism, the god of darkness attacked the god of light who proceeded to create the world which is a kind of emanation in which these two divinities are *physically* entwined creating matter as we know it. The two opposing principles, the essence of this type of metaphysics, were, nevertheless, accompanied where necessary, by a pantheon of lesser divinities, which included "the Mother of the Living" (who, by being identified with Fāṭimah, created the name of Fāṭimids) and even "an architect of the universe", the great "Ban". These lesser gods from classical Manicheism populate the curious mythologies of the early "Sevener" movement.

But the question of what God really is, beyond and before that supposed split into two antagonistic forces, is consigned to unknowability; Gnosticism becomes agnosticism; the Hellenist systems therefore, called the Absolute that necessarily lies beyond the two absolutes "the unknowable Abyss": *Bythos*; and here consciousness returns to unconsciousness. Thus the Ismā'īlīs spuriously derive the Divine Name Allāh from the verb *walaha*, meaning to "lament" because for them God is only a Demiurge who "laments" his exclusion from the Abyss which they call the *Ghayb T'ala*. Similarly, in the Mu'tazilite theology of Twelve Imām Shī'ism, the names of Divine Attributes are on the level of Being, but not of Essence.

In Manicheism, the god of light, hidden in the world in the form of light particles, is called, among other names: "Beauty" (which must be the origin of the so-called "Ḥadīth" that "God is Beautiful and loves beauty.") These hidden particles were said to be found especially in certain "light bearing" plants such as lettuce, endive, and cucumbers. Those adepts who knew the "truth", or possessed the "secret knowledge" (*gnosis*) about this primordial and perpetual struggle which continues in this world, were thence vegetarians. (Meat was also considered as inspiring passions, clouding reason, and downward tending or "tamasic" by nature.) By this knowledge, and especially through adherence to the spiritual leader, and by observing many life-denying anti-cosmic ascetic rules, they participated in the struggle (cf. *tikkun*) by liberating the light particles in those vegetables they ate. The Manicheans also prohibited drinking wine.

The light was collected out of the believer during prayer, which was made facing towards the sun, the moon, or the polar star. The redeemed light was carried by the waxing crescent moon (symbolized as a kind of "boat" carrying a star) and brought out of the world (cf. Koran 36:39) to be reconstituted as the original divinity (although it was said, some particles would remain, at the end, lost and trapped within the abandoned dead shell of the world). This crescent and star, already an ancient symbol used by Mesopotamians and Persians, was introduced into Islam not by Arabs, but by the Ottoman Turks (*see* MOON). Because it resembles the Arabic letter *nun*, the Sufis attached a mystical meaning to the letter, saying that it was a boat which preserved the kernel of the past by carrying it over to a future cycle of time. (All the letters of the alphabet of course have mystical meanings.)

The Manichean Adept, at his death or at the end of the world, would be escorted, as in Zoroastrianism, by a light-maiden sent as a guide and protector, driving away assailing devils. The soul would rest a while in the moon, then the sun, then would ascend to a light-heaven. Thus the cosmos was seen as a kind of scientific machine in the secret plan to liberate or redeem the God of light from the imprisonment which manifestation had imposed upon Him. Science and theology — a kind of scientology — were one and the same. The Manichean afterlife can also be compared to this description of Ismā'īlī beliefs in India: "salvation lies in recognizing the Imam of the Age... the soul of a disciple... is then drawn at physical death... to a Lower Paradise... they receive the final touch of the 'knowledge of the Imam,' and when the Imam dies he 'combines himself all the pure souls' of his period and carries them to the Tenth Intelligence... The bodies of the faithful are absorbed by the Sun and the Moon and there purified, after which they are absorbed into plants and animals and serve as nourishment for the Imam. The souls of unbelievers, those who have failed to recognize the Imam, 'find no rest and wander to and fro' in darkness. 'They struggle towards subtlety but are set back.' After a long period these darkened souls again assume human form and have a new opportunity to recognize the Imam of the Age. The substance of the bodies of the believers passes through different stages of animal, vegetable and mineral worlds until it too is purified." (Hollister: *The Shi'a of India*, p. 251.)

The Manicheans also were opposed to procreation and believed that once everyone in the world joined them and learned the truth, then procreation, which prolongs the errors of existence as long as they persist in the errors of the mind, would cease and with it the world would come to an end, and then burn for 1,468 years. (Almost the exact duration of the Sothic year, this is obviously the origin of the popular belief in Islam, supported by spurious Ḥadīth — since the Prophet insisted that no-one knows the future — that the world will end in the 14th Islamic century, which is the present one). In the end Evil would be amalgamated in a solid mass. Those who followed the inspired teachers and accepted the esoteric knowledge and became a part of the community, will have been saved in their *individuality*. This amounts to salvation for the ego. Martyrdom, however, was something to aspire to and even seek out, in imitation of Mani. Thus his two successors, Innaios and Sisinnios, are both considered to be martyrs as well, and why al-Ḥallāj was eager to end his life, in old age, with the crowning glory. Manicheans unhesitatingly used hyperbole to extol themselves and to exalt their persecution, and exaggerate their victimhood: thus "crucifixion" was the Manichean term for any kind of suffering or privation on the part of one of them.

Early on, the religion divided into two groups: the Miqlasiyyah and the Mihriyyah. One seemed to advocate the spread of a pure form of Manicheism throughout the world simultaneously, and one advocated a kind of compromise: working with the existing political system to consolidate power, in order, apparently, to acquire sovereignty somewhere or to create a Manichean state as a step towards universal Manicheism. The division suggests that of the Qarmaṭīs and the Fāṭimids, and later that of the Trokskyites and Stalinists. To establish full Manicheism in one country, according to its theory, would be to bring about the end of the world in one country.

Similar revolts and movements reappeared again and again in Iran under the 'Abbāsids who themselves used the Manicheans as the tiger which they rode to power. The vanguard of the 'Abbāsid revolution used names which showed their worker status, such as "saddle maker", "vinegar seller", "wool carder", "tent-maker". The greatest of these revolts, after the 'Abbāsids themselves, was of course, the Qarmaṭī movement but there were many others: among them the revolt of Sindbād (*also* Sonpādh), an anti-authoritarian revolt (*138*/755) in northern and Central Iran sparked by the assassination of Abū Muslim.

In *150*/767 another revolt broke out in Khorasan under the leadership of Ustād Sīs. This was followed by the revolt of the *Surkhi 'Alām 161-164*/778-779 (the "Red Banners") and that of Bābak (d. *222*/837). Marxist historians naturally saw these revolts as prefiguring their own revolution. Manicheism, in fact, is so uncannily similar to so many revolutionary movements, that the Abbé Berrouel attributed all Jacobin movements and the French revolution itself to Mani. The revolts in early Islam dominated Islamic state policy for a time; after the Fāṭimids came to power, the Vizier of the Seljūqs, Nizām al-Mulk, was only one of those who warned of the return of Mazdakism during the height of the Assassin period and who fought the peril by creating schools of orthodox Islamic theology.

The organizational hierarchy of the Manichean church was as follows: the head was called Archegos and lived in Ctesiphon (Madā'in) which was destroyed in the Arab conquest but became, almost miraculously, restored by the 'Abbāsids in the form of Baghdad (which is why Muslim historians interpreted the word to mean "gift of God".). Under him were 12 "Apostles" (*Hamozag*) or magistrates; 72 Bishops (*Espasag*); 360 Priests (*Mahistag*). This hierarchy resembles, not surprisingly, the invisible spiritual hierarchy of Sufism, with the *quṭb* or "pole" at the head, as well as the hierarchy of Fāṭimid da'īs. The community was divided into two groups: the chosen ones, the Elect, (Persian: *Ardavan*, in Arabic *Siddiqun*, or the *Tsadiqs* of Kabbalism, in Latin, the *Electi*) and the "Hearers" (Latin: *Auditores*, Persian: *Niyashagan*, Arabic: *Sammāūn*), rather like the *Salikun* and *Mutabarikun* of Sufism, or the "knowers" and the "ignorant" of many Gnostic groups, such as the Druze. (In the early canonical collections of *Ḥadīth* there are frequent references to the vast numbers of *Siddiqin* to be found living in this or that locality, notably around Damascus.) This doctrine is taken so far in the esoteric interpretations of certain sects, that outsiders are not even thought of as being "real", but as being of illusory or "demonic" substance; this was true of the *Qiyāmah* doctrine of the Assassins of Alamūt, and it is also found in the *Qabbalah*.

This was a justification for a kind of exploitation of the religion's followers, especially in the case of Manichean estates in Central Asia (which included the domains of the Barmakids, originally "Buddhist Priests" in Balkh) and which amounted to a kind of slave labor, not unlike that of the helots in Sparta, or the collective farm workers and masses in the Communist state serving the nomenklatura and the party. *Manicheism divided the twenty four hour day into three eight hour segments for work, rest, and devotion.*

This perception, this "knowledge" of the opposition of the two "realities" produces powerful psychological consequences, first of all as an experience of "illumination" (*see* ISHRĀQĪ). This illumination conditions all further perception of reality as an "insight" into the supposed workings of the universe not known to the profane. The experience of perceiving evil to be a reality creates a powerful psychological conviction that the person has discovered a truth that others around him do not suspect exists; that they are truly blind and ignorant while the postulant has come upon the secret of the universe.

It is mythologized by Gnostic-Dualism into a mystic "call". 'Awake!' it says, and throw off the impure laws which have imprisoned "the noble son, the unknown King"; cast off the deceit which has kept you in bondage and denied you self-knowledge. As a technique of indoctrination, the *absolutely literal interpretation* of established scripture was used to shatter the unity of received perceptions, and thus to begin a train of thought which led to the awareness of a shadow self and a shadow world. To this was joined the raising of doubts by pointing out curious difficulties and subtle questions in theology. When the break with a previous sense of reality was complete, increasingly allegorical interpretations of sacred scripture could then be introduced. At one time, such allegory seems to have taken the form of making the disciple believe he had completed the pilgrimage to Mecca, or if need be the Temple of Jerusalem, through a ceremony within the lodge. The accusations against al-Ḥallāj included testimony to this effect, and Rūmī also alludes to it in his *Mithnāwī*, To this day, many Sufis think they are approaching Mecca when they perform the Ḥadrah, and are physically present in front of the Ka'bah at its culmination.

But the most remarkable feature of Manicheism was not its ability to indoctrinate, although that was prodigious, for all the regions of the world which once contained a critical mass of Manicheism are still spiritually "radioactive" to this day. The most amazing feature is its ability to infiltrate other belief systems, to disguise itself as other religions, and like a virus, to use the structures of other religions to replicate itself. In China, Manicheism readily transformed itself into mutant forms of Buddhism, Taoism, and Confucianism which were called *Ming-Chiao* ("religions of light"). Obviously, Manicheism did the same within other religions, including Christianity, Judaism (Isaac Luria is a striking example among many others), and Hinduism.

Islam seems to have been born out of a rejection of Manicheism. But once Islam was born, Manicheism sought to infiltrate it. The writing known as "The Mother of the Book" (*Umm al-Kitāb*) was one early ideological attempt on the part of a Syrian Manichean center to graft itself onto the new religion. This attempt to subvert Islam around the year 730 was quickly outpaced by Islam's own development although it left its traces by arresting the development of some still existing Manichioid sects. The attempt to impose Mu'tazilitism as a ready made theology for Islam produced a creative fever which was finally brought to an end by Ash'arism. Mu'tazilitism did become the theology of Twelve Imām Shī'ism. Besides the Star Wars of the Qarmaṭī and Fāṭimid periods, which were brought to an end by the Mongol invasions, the most pervasive attempt to turn Islam into Manicheism was through mysticism.

The obvious solution, after several false starts, was to turn the Prophet into the exoteric apostle of Mani, with Mani himself the esoteric revelation of truth. Circumstances and convenience dictated transforming Mani into 'Alī. Sahl at-Tustarī introduced such evidently heretical ideas which remain dear to mystics to this day as the creation of the world through the *emanation* of divine light particles named the "Muhammadan Light" (*Nūr Muḥammadī*). To make this doctrine more respectable, it was attributed to the sixth generation descendant of 'Alī, and supposed Shī'ite Imām, Ja'far aṣ-Ṣadīq. There was also the philosophical exaltation of Iblīs, which elevated the prince of darkness to the level of a second principle. The "three times" of Manicheism appeared as the Tustarī-Ḥallājian idea of "pre-eternity" and "post-eternity" added to the present, but was rather too esoteric to get much play. Sahl at-Tustarī also spoke of "columns of light". Thus Sufism, particularly that of the "drunken Sufis" most of whom are described as converts from "Magianism,, was a major entry point by which Manicheism again penetrated Islam and which persists to this day cohabiting the minds of people who otherwise believe themselves to be orthodox Muslims. These Crypto-Manicheans adapted Manicheism as an inner truth of Islam. Manicheism remains the fountainhead and inspiration of mysticism everywhere, an inside, deeper, esoteric, (*bāṭin, 'ilm*), knowledge of Islam, and indeed of all other religions, and succeeds because Manicheism proposes, not unlike the tempter in the garden of Eden, what everyone really wants, which is the divinity of the ego itself.

Clandestine Manicheism as an intellectual affectation was very widespread in the first three Islamic centuries. It was the religion of the avant-garde cherished by many poets from Bashār ibn Burd to al-Mutanabbī and al-Ma'arrī, and intellectuals from Ibn al-Muqaffa' to Muḥammad ibn Zakariyyā ar-Rāzī. Thus throughout history, Manicheism lived on in subsequent incarnations as a kind of secret twin to Islam.

Manichean writers describe Mani, who billed himself as the "Paraclete" and the "Apostle of Jesus", as being a great hero of religious freedom and a champion of truth, suffering at the hands of incomprehending authorities: his religion, it was said, was better than others; "he was more merciful" than Jesus, whose followers could not deny him without sinning in the process, whereas Mani's could deny him if it were opportune to do so. Mani (like Rūmī later) allowed his followers to repudiate him as much as necessary, if threatened; it was permitted to hide one's beliefs, a practice which became *taqiyyah* in Shī'ism. Thus, the Medieval Muslim litmus test to determine if someone was a Manichean, namely having them spit on a portrait of Mani (and eat a bird, which a vegetarian would find abhorrent), was really of little value. Harūn ar-Rashīd's poet friend Abū Nuwas was hauled in while drunk and exculpated himself (to the authorities, at least) by vomiting on Mani's picture.

When the Islamic state decided (as the Persian, Roman, and Chinese had done or would do) that Manicheism was a subversive threat and began to persecute Manicheans in earnest under the Caliph Mahdī, it was necessary to appoint an expert (*'arif*) to determine if someone really was a Manichean. This was particularly difficult to do since both religions, Islam and Manicheism had "a family resemblance" and many elements in common, such as five prayers (although an-Nadīm says the Manicheans had three prayers; interestingly, the Shiites combine their five prayers such that effectively there are three prayer times). Prohibition of wine, month of fasting, and Docetism are some of many similarities between Manicheism and Islam. (Al-Ghazālī's famous religious crisis probably came about precisely because he did sort out what was what and parted theological ways with his family and in particular with his brother.)

Moreover, few Muslim scholars ever succeeded in sorting out the difference between Zoroastrianism (which itself had been largely infiltrated by Manicheism before Islam arrived on the scene) and Manicheism as such. This can be seen from 'Alī Ṭabarī (not the historian) whose *Book of Religion and Empire* says that Magians worship stars and fire and pretend that God is the creator of good and light and Satan the creator of darkness and evil; that war is never at rest between them and "...that the spirits of their dead come back to them once a year, partake of food and drink put before them and at their withdrawal provision themselves". (This is not present in Zoroastrianism, being a description of the Bēma ceremony which was to appear in many forms within Islam itself.) To this day many Turkish Sufis display an empty sheepskin at their meetings for their deceased founder to sit upon, the most famous of which is the red sheepskin for Shamsi Tabrizī, the "martyred" teacher of Rūmī who is simply a re-made version of Mani. These groups also preserve a ritual position of the feet with one toe over the other. The Mevlevis call it *niyaz* and the other Turkish Sufis *ayak mühülemek* "sealing the feet". This ritual position is found in Zoroastrianism but also in the derivative religions of Persia.

However, once universities were organized by Niẓām al-Mulk to fight the propaganda coming out of the newly established al-Azhar ("the Resplendent") in Cairo, Muslim theologians became somewhat better informed. For example, the philosophical links between Manicheism and its Gnostic predecessors became common knowledge. The medieval Muslim theologians and historians spoke of the historically correct intellectual progression from the theologian Marcion (d. 160), a Christian heretic who taught that the Father of Jesus Christ was a good God, while the creator of the visible world, was the Demiurge, and this Demiurge was the God of the Old Testament, an evil God. They said the next link in the chain was the Hellenist philosopher of Edessa, Bardaisan (154-222), who contributed cosmological notions in which the world is composed of five primal elements. (Edessa is present day Urfa in Turkey, near Ḥarrān.) Thence modern scholars of course put Mani, but typical to the traditional allegorical style of Islamic historians, this line was treated as an actual family tree, skipping Mani by name or rather making him the ancestor-founder of the Fāṭimid dynasty, which was the actual Manicheism, syncretized, evolved, and modified for the times, with which they were concerned at that moment.

Above all, for the Muslims of the Middle Ages, the term *majūs* ("Magians") meant all Iranian religions rolled into one, and when they said that a convert to Islam had been a majūsi, it is quite misleading to translate this as a conversion from Zoroastrianism. To add to the confusion, the Muslims called Manicheans by a Zoroastrian term for them, *zindīq*, which means simply "heretic". (Indeed, for many theologians, including St. Thomas Aquinas, Manicheism, was *the* heresy of heresies.) This was often translated without being completely identified into English, French, and German (cf. "*ketzer*"), vaguely as "rationalist", "freethinker", or "materialist" when in fact it entailed a good deal more. When translated literally as "heresy" this misleads by implying something indeterminate, when in fact it is quite a specific term, generic heresy being *ilḥād*. A less specific term is *bāṭini*, meaning a secret religion, although, when Ibn Khaldūn says that the Berbers of North Africa before the "Mahdī" arrived among them belonged to a *bāṭini* religion, there can be no doubt what it was.

The historian Maqrīzī (*767-846*/1364-1442) and geographer Ibn Rusteh (c. *290*/903 in *A'laq Nafīsa*) said that Manicheism had come to Mecca before Islam. It did so through the Lakhmid capital Ḥīrah, a center of Arab Manicheism which had even developed a script for Arabic in order to propagate the writings of Mani among the Arabs. (This script, Kufic, instead served to propagate the Koran.) Here the traders of Mecca had ample opportunity to come in contact with the religion. The imprint of the subtle religion upon Islam appears in many ways, but notably in the Verse of Light (24:35), in the idea that all the divine messengers come from one source, "the Seal of Prophecy" (which was originally the title of Mani before it became the title of Muḥammad), the division of the saved into three groups in the Sūrat al-Wāqi'ah (56), and the Docetism of the doctrine of Jesus (namely, that the crucifixion was only an "appearance".).

Since we learn what we are when we discover what we are not, above all, Manicheism in Islam appears in the explicit rejection of Manicheism, that is, in the emphasis on divine unity (16:51): "Allāh hath said: Choose not two gods. There is only one God. So of Me, Me only be in awe." Thus, while Islam's starting point, like Gnosticism's, is acquisition of a spiritual knowledge, and the acceptance of the spiritual leader as presented in the two testimonies of faith, in the case of Islam the knowledge, the *gnosis*, is the perception of the reality of the divine unity rather than that of a duality. Islam is not a dualism; rather it is, like orthodox Christianity, a rectified dualism. (The process is reflected in the ambiguous way the Koran describes *Allāh*, as both forgiving and punishing. An Immune reaction has to contain the code of th virus which it is neutralizing.) It is as if Islam were a catalytic reaction to a rising tide of dualism, or the reaction of a spiritual immune system, like Christianity before it, to the cataclysmic dynamics generated by the mixing of Zoroastrianism and Semitic Religion. In Manicheism the idea of God lost a human personality and became a mathematical abstraction of two opposites; in Islam the abstractions became a Unity, an abstract God on a radically transcendent plane. A new revelation of the nature of Reality.

After Islam came out of the desert as a conquering force, the city of Ḥīrah of the Manichean Lakhmids became transformed into the new city of Kūfah but was destined to continue to play a central role. The Umayyads made Damascus their power base and allied themselves with the Christian Ghassanis. This forced 'Alī to turn to Kūfah as his power base and to ally himself with the Lakhmid successors. This marriage of convenience even led to actual marriages; 'Alī's immediate descendants, who became the Imāms of Twelver Shī'ism, frequently had Berber concubines, which was a way of strengthening the alliances, since North Africa had for some time been a stronghold of Manicheism. After 'Alī and his successors were thwarted, and especially after the killing of Ḥusayn in *61*/680, the legend was created of 'Alī's denied and pre-destined right to the Caliphate, and there followed, in Kūfah, the birth of proto-Shī'ism, in the form of the procession of penitents (*tawwabūn*) who sought out martyrdom at the hands of the Umayyads in the year *65*/685. Lakhmid Manicheism turned to an unhistorical image of Mani transformed into an idealized 'Alī for its own support and inspiration.

Thereupon the Kūfan factor re-emerged as the revolt of Mukhtār (*65-67*/685-687). In the course of his rebellion, this Kūfan leader performed a ceremony which mystified the Muslims who were with him: he addressed mysterious words to an empty throne. When asked what this all meant, he explained that he was speaking to the throne of... 'Alī. It is thus that Mani's posthumous Islamic metamorphosis began. Around this time we also find the first appearance of the Ḥadīth concerning the *Mahdī*. From this unsuccessful revolt against the Umayyads came the forces which were to bring the 'Abbāsids to power and establish Baghdad, near Ctesiphon, as the new capital.

A son of 'Alī, Muḥammad ibn al-Ḥanafiyyah was the figurehead around whom the Kaysāniyyah or Mukhtāriyyah revolt raised Muslim support for itself and he was the person for whom the title *Mahdī* was originally created. Although Mukhtār, the leader of the revolt, was killed in *67*/687, Muḥammad ibn al-Ḥanafiyyah escaped sanctions on the part of the Umayyads and even maintained good relations with them because his status with the Mukhtāriyyah (also called Kaysāniyyah) was secret. After the death of the family leader of the 'Abbāsids, 'Abd Allāh ibn 'Abbās in *68*/687, the new family head was Muḥammad ibn al-Ḥanafiyyah, who was also the head of the Alīd family. Thus, for a short time, the leader of both families, the 'Alīds, original allies of the Kūfans, and their cousins the 'Abbāsids, the future allies of the Kūfans and their extension in Khorasan, was one person. He was the last 'Alīd leader to unite the two families, and their *shī'ah*, their partisans, under one authority. When he died in *81*/700, his son Abū Hāshim went to Mecca and then Medinah; the 'Abbāsids for their part had migrated to Ḥumaymah in Palestine under the leadership of 'Alī (d. *118*/736) the youngest son of 'Abd Allāh ibn 'Abbās.

After the death of Muḥammad ibn al-Ḥanifiyyah the titular leadership of the 'Alīd revolutionary organization (the extension of political alliances created by 'Alī himself or created around him by groups seeking to control him) passed to al-Ḥanifiyyah's son Abū Hāshim and the organization whose visible tip was known as the Kaysāniyyah/Mukhtāriyyah became known as the Hāshimiyyah. Towards the end of his life, Abū Hāshim, who had no children, moved from Medinah in *91*/710 to Damascus under arrest because of a dispute with 'Alīd family members, and then, when freed, he moved into the 'Abbāsid family homestead at Ḥumaymah. Before he died in 716, Abū Hāshim initiated Muḥammad ibn 'Alī ibn 'Abd Allāh ibn al-'Abbās into the secrets of the Kaysāniyyah/Mukhtāriyyah organization. This was described as a transmission to Muḥammad the 'Abbāsid of the "*'ilm*", the "esoteric knowledge" of Abū Hāshim and the names of the leaders of the Kūfan secret underground. The Caliph 'Alī's Kūfan connection passed on to the 'Abbāsids. The 'Abbāsids affirmed their leadership of the movement and thus the 'Abbāsids became the new secret leaders of the revolutionary organization which had burst upon the scene as the Kaysāniyyah/Mukhtāriyyah, an organization which was apparently based in Kūfah but which also had an even greater following in Khorāsān (and in North Africa, although this connection did not come into play at this time.) This organization achieved success under the 'Abbāsids, in alliance with the Barmakids, who were crypto-Manicheans from Balkh, and through these allies the 'Abbāsids became Caliphs.

As Brockelmann wrote: "Not pure Zoroastrianism but rather Manicheism, particularly in 'Irāq, still exercised a great influence on those among the new converts not entirely satisfied by the rigid formalism of Islam, and very nearly became the religion of the educated classes." It certainly was the preferred religion of poets.

While Manicheism was at its height within the 'Abbasid empire, outside of it, in the year 762, Manicheism became the religion of the Uyghur Turks, at first in Mongolia near Baikal, and after 840 it became the state religion in Turfan in what is today Chinese Turkestan (Urumchi in Xinjiang). As such it exerted a tremendous influence upon all Turkic groups. When, for example, the Seljūq Turks entered the Islamic world, they were, as Franz Babinger remarked, not as yet Muslims, but "'Alī Ilāhīs", a form of Islamic Manicheism.

After a period of cooperation with the hidden forces behind the 'Abbāsid coalition (with the necessary exceptions of the massacre of the Rawandiyyah who would have embarrassed al-Manṣūr, and the assassination of Abū Muslim who would have overthrown him) the 'Abbāsid Caliph al-Mahdī discovered that his son's tutor was a Manichean. He thereupon began a persecution of Manicheans. When his son Hādī was about to renew this persecution (he promised his father to nail a Manichean to every tree), he suddenly died, probably poisoned by the very Barmakids whom he accused of "infidelity"— rather than by Hārūn's mother Khayzūrān, the usual suspect. Harūn ar-Rashīd did take the throne in *170*/786 and maintained the closest possible relationship, in the family tradition, with the Barmakids. Then in *187*/803 he suddenly turned and executed many of them, since, as Ibn Khaldūn surmised, the Barmakids were moving to create an empire within an empire. In turning on the Barmakids, Hārūn ar-Rashid displayed the remarkable 'Abbāsid survivor instinct of his ancestors, that which had eliminated or double-crossed Abū Muslim, before Abū Muslim could double-cross them.

The persecution of Manicheans abated once again under the reign of al-Ma'mūn, which was not surprising since he was himself named as a Manichean, by an-Nadīm. Al-Ma'mūn was born in Merv and had a Persian mother, and was said to be under the influence of "a philosopher-astrologer from Balkh". He was not the only Caliph who had a close relationship to Manicheism. The contemporary Iranian scholar, Zabih Bihruz thought al-Manṣūr, the first 'Abbāsid Caliph, was also a crypto-Manichean, which is certainly suggested by the incident of the Rāwandiyyah.

But the 'Abbāsid dynasty was founded on a co-existence with Manicheism; what is more surprising is the extent to which Manicheism had also affected the Umayyads: a certain Ja'd ibn Dirham, who was executed by the Caliph Hishām ibn Abd al-Malik, was the teacher of the Caliph Marwan II, and his son, and "brought them to Manicheism" reports an-Nadīm. Similarly, the teacher of Walid II, Abd aṣ-Ṣamad ibn al-'Alā, was held to be a Manichean and it is said that the Caliph kept company with Manicheans, had an richly ornate portrait of Mani, and had the Christian Metropolitan of Jerusalem mutilated for criticizing Manicheans.

But the coalition of the 'Abbāsids and Khorāsānis proved troubled. Al-Ma'mūn tried to continue riding the Manichean Tiger, which was in any case his necessary support in the initial war against his brother, by instituting Mu'tazilitism as the official theology, a policy which proved unpopular.

The occasion when this power shift took place, when Twelve Imām Shī'ites became the power behind the throne, was the accession of the Caliph al-Muqtadir in *295*/908. There was a brief attempt to return to the status quo in the palace revolt of the "Caliph for a day", Ibn al-Mu'tazz, which failed, and the Shī'ites affirmed their control. Shortly thereafter, probably in the same year *296*/908-909, the Archegos, head of the Manichean church, left Baghdad. This had been the seat of the religion for more than half a millennium. The emigration of the Archegos, supposedly in the direction of Samarkand, was preceded by the emigration westward of 'Ubayd Allāh the Mahdī, and followed by the declaration of the Fāṭimid Caliphate in North Africa, and the Mahdī's triumphant entry into Kairouan. Then came the founding of Cairo: the cryptic name is literally "The Victorious City of the Exalter of God's Religion" and with it, the school for Ismā'īlī propaganda, the "Resplendent", *al-Azhar*.

This monumental change had been preceded, as well as accompanied, by the eruption of the Qarmaṭī revolt. The name "Ibn Qarmaṭ" is explained as being from the Aramaic *qarmaṭ*, "a man with red eyes", meaning "a teacher of secret doctrines"; and to walk with short strides; but the name was used before the actual Ibn Qarmaṭ came on the scene, and the Arabic dictionary *al-Munjid* says that *qarmaṭa* also means to write a text in very small letters with a very fine hand, the signature of Manichean writings. The Qarmaṭīs had a "mysterious" ceremony, called the "Night of the Imām", and like the Kaysanis, a "mysterious" tabernacle. Not many details are known but it seems to be the Bēma, again.

In 930, the Qarmaṭīs raided Mecca and stole the Black Stone from the Ka'bah. Public outcry followed the abduction of the Black Stone and unsuccessful attempts were made to ransom it. Muslim historians of the day linked its disappearance with the Fāṭimids, for they said that the earth refused to receive the body of the first Fāṭimid for burial so long as the stone remained stolen.

In 951, the Black Stone was suddenly and mysteriously returned; it was thrown, wrapped in a sack, into the Friday Mosque at Kūfah, with the note: "By Command we took it, by Command we return it." No ransom had ever been asked for nor accepted. We know that in the year 692, when the wooden Ka'bah burned down after being hit by a flaming arrow, the Black Stone was cracked in three pieces; today it is in seven (and crumbs, according to the Report of the Engineer in charge of the rebuilding the Grand Mosque of Mecca in the reign of King Faysal). This fracturing of the stone dates from the abduction. Only a few historians at the time alluded to the stone's fracturing; the 'Abbāsids had every reason to keep this portentous event secret as revolutions swirled around them.

In fracturing the stone the Qarmaṭī's appropriated it as their own; they, in effect, substituted their own stone at the center of Islam. Substitution: an act of magic, an act of dream-thought in broad daylight. As if, say, someone took the Statue of Liberty and put Ishtar in its place. Muslim pilgrims to

Mecca would kiss the stone in reverence as a symbol of Islam, but the Manicheans could say that in reality and in ignorance they were paying homage to their own religion and its eternally living head. The stone, and with it Mecca, in another symbolism, is the key-stone, forgotten and misprized, cast aside in the desert since the times of Adam and Abraham and then brought forth at the end of time to complete the Divine Design. A symbolism which the Manicheans contrived to appropriate to their purpose. Cf. Psalms 118:22 "The stone which the builders refused is become the head stone of the corner. This is the Lord's doing; it is marvelous in our eyes. This is the day which the Lord hath made; we will rejoice and be glad in it."

The advent of Twelve Imām Shī'ites as the dominant force in Baghdad led to the execution of al-Ḥallāj in *309*/922, after a lengthy trial for being a Manichean or *zindīq*. Before the state trial found him guilty, al-Ḥallaj had already been condemned by the Hidden Imām through his representative. In 923, the next year, bushels of Manichean manuscripts were burned in Baghdad; the gold and silver illumination ran in torrents. The execution of al-Ḥallāj signalled a wave of executions of Manicheans in various guises, or as Massignon termed them, "Ḥallājians", while Qarmaṭī-Ismā'īlī revolts broke out into the open across the 'Abbāsid empire from North Africa to India, including that of the Zanj, which Massignon said was inspired by Manicheans. The bookseller an-Nadīm (d. *385*/995) writing afterwards said: "I used to know three hundred of them [Manicheans] in the City of Peace (Baghdad)... but now there are not five of them in our midst."

They had not disappeared into nothing; they disappeared into disguise. They had transformed themselves in the face of increasing opposition; as Ibn Ḥazm (d. *456*/1064) remarked of the Fāṭimids: "I see that Mazdak has become a Shī'ite." And although by the 13th century Islam had developed a certain immunity, it was only the coming of the Mongols which changed the whole face of the Islamic world and meant that a titanic struggle for the soul of Islam was over.

The Persian historian, al-Juwaynī (d. *682*/1283), in the vanguard of the invading Mongols was present at the Mongol destruction of Alamūt. Al-Juwaynī, as a Twelve-Imām Shī'ite (a branch of the Shī'ite movement whose fortunes thereafter continued to rise in Persia), was as passionately opposed to the Assassins as Kartir, the Grand Mobad (High Priest) of the Zoroastrians under the Sāssānids (who were Zurvanites) had been opposed to Mani. Al-Juwayni wrote of the Fāṭimid movement in his *History of the World Conqueror* (Jenghiz Khan): "a sect of people ... in whose hearts was rooted a fellow-feeling with the Magians ..."

See 'ALĪ ILĀHĪS; ARCHEGOS; BARMAKIDS; ELKHASAIOS; al-ḤALLĀJ; IBLĪS; ISHRĀQĪ; KAYSĀNIYYAH; KHAṬṬĀBIYYAH; KHURRAMIYYAH; LAKHMIDS; MANDAEANS; al-MADĀ'IN; MAZAR-I SHARĪF; MAZDAK; NŪR MUḤAMMADĪ; QARMAṬĪS; SEVENERS; 'UBAYD ALLĀH the MAHDĪ; UMM al-KITĀB; XINJIANG.

Manṣab. A military title of the Moghuls, created by the Emperor Akbar (d. *1014*/1605). The title brought with it a fief for the livelihood of its holder, in return for which concession the landholder, the *manṣabdārī*, provided horse soldiers to make up an army for the Emperor upon demand. The numbers could be from 10 to 10,000 horse in accordance with his grant. *See* IQṬĀ'.

Manṣūr. The "Triumphant" "The Victor". A Divine Name, and the name of the second 'Abbāsid Caliph. It was a favorite name among Gnostics such as Manicheans, Isma'ilis, etc. Probably it referred to triumph over death as in the sense of "O Death where is thy victory?" and in the specifically Manichean sense of the resurrection of the martyr.

Manṣūr al-Yaman (d. *302*/914). An honorific title for Ibn Ḥawshab, an Ismāīlī *dā'ī* whose full name was Abū'l-Qāsim al-Ḥasan ibn Faraj ibn Ḥawshab ibn Zadhān an-Najjār ("the cabinet maker") al-Kūfi from Kūfah who was sent to the Yemen to create support for 'Ubayd Allāh by proclaiming the appearance of the Mahdī, a function which 'Ubayd Allāh was to claim in 889. Ibn Ḥawshab may have been, along with Abū 'Abd Allāh ash-Shī'ī, the architect of the transferral of 'Ubayd Allāh to Tunisia. Ṭabarī records that there was a Ḥawshab in Kūfah who was the custodian of "'Alī's throne" during the revolt of the Kaysāniyyah. (Could this be the the Ḥashab who was son of the "Cabinet Maker?") 'Alī, of course had no throne — a desert Arab sat on the ground — but Mukhtār was known to perform a ceremony addressing an empty chair which he called "'Alīs throne" to those who asked what it was. Ibn Ḥawshab attempted to keep the

Yemen faithful to the Fāṭimids and out of the hands of the Qarmaṭīs or other dissidents.

Maqām (lit. "a standpoint", "a station"). A spiritual station such as a virtue or an attitude which becomes the dominant complexion of the soul. A *maqām* may be an aspect of Divine knowledge which is profoundly realized and permanently acquired by the soul, as opposed to a transitory spiritual state (*ḥāl*). A particular *maqām* may be characteristic of a particular Saint or Prophet.

Al-Ḥujwīrī says:

> A station is a man's standing in the Way (*ṭarīqah*). It denotes his perseverance in fulfilling what is at that period of his life obligatory on him. He may not pass on from that *maqām* without accomplishing all he is bound to do there. The first station, for instance, is Penitence, the next Conversion, then Renunciation, then Trust, and so on. A man may not pretend to Conversion without complete Penitence, nor to Trust without complete Renunciation.
>
> A *ḥāl* on the other hand, is something that comes down from God into man's heart quite independently... it is a grace. Junayd says: *ḥāls* are like flashes of lightning... Everyone who longs for God has some particular station, which is his clue at the beginning of his quest. Whatever good he derives from other stations through which he may pass, he will finally rest in one, since one station and its own quest include and call for complex combination and design, not merely conduct and practice.
>
> Adam's *maqām*, for example, was Penitence, Noah's was Renunciation, and Abraham's Resignation. Contrition was Moses' station, and Sorrow David's. The station of Jesus was Hope, that of John the Baptist Fear. Our Prophet's was Praise. Whatever these men drew from other wells by which they dwelt a while, each man returned at last to his original station.

The Persian Sufi al-Qushayrī (d. *465*/1072) lists some typical *maqāmāt*: repentance (*tawbah*; the beginning of the way); withdrawal (*wara'*); renunciation (*zuhd*); silence (*samt*); fear of God (*khawf*); hope (*rajā'*); sadness (*ḥuzn*); poverty (*faqr*); patience (*ṣabr*); trust (*tawakkul*); and contentment (*riḍā*). Lists by Sufis go on to as many as forty five different stations, some of which can, if transitory, also be listed simply as "states" (*hāl*; pl. *aḥwāl*).

The term also has technical meanings in poetry and music. In music, the *maqām* is the opening passage which establishes the mode and style of the piece.

Maqām Ibrāhīm (lit. "the standing place of Abraham"). At a spot a few meters from the Black Stone corner of the Ka'bah, there is a small kiosk which contains a stone with a figurative indentation of a footprint. By tradition this is the footprint of Abraham impressed into rock during the building of the Ka'bah by Abraham and Ismā'īl (Ishmael). In the vicinity of the *Maqām Ibrāhīm* a prayer of two *raka'āt* is performed during the rites of pilgrimage. *See* ABRAHAM.

al-Maqdisī. The name of a famous Jerusalem family (*Bayt al-Maqdis* — "Holy House") which produced a number of scholars and jurists. The most famous of them is Muwaffaq ad-Dīn ibn Qudāmah al-Maqdisī (d. *620*/1223), the author of the *Kitāb al-Mughnī* on Ḥanbalī law.

al-Maqrīzī, Taqī ad-Dīn Aḥmad (*767-846*/1364-1442). An historian and biographer. Born in Cairo, al-Maqrīzī was a *muḥtasib*, or inspector of markets, who later wrote a book on weights and measures. He became a *khaṭīb* ("preacher") in a mosque and a religious teacher. He wrote histories of the Fāṭimid, Ayyūbid, and Mamlūk dynasties.

Maqṣūrah. An area of a mosque set aside for use by important personages, it is usually surrounded by an enclosure of lattice work or some kind of screen. The first *maqṣūrah* may well have been built by the Caliph 'Uthmān in the mosque in Medinah as a protection against attack.

Marabout (a French word derived from the Ar. *marbūṭ*, "attached", in the sense of being bound to God). A term used in North and West Africa for a Saint, or a venerated descendant of a Saint. Although Saints are revered to some extent throughout the Islamic world, in the Arab West and West Africa the respect paid to Saints is a very important dimension of spiritual practice. Only in countries where Wahhābī doctrine prevails have all traces of veneration previously accorded to Saints been expunged.

The Saint is considered to exercise a spiritual influence, grace or blessing (*barakah*), which after his death may remain at his tomb indefinitely and bless those who visit it. The intercession of Saints is often called upon in prayers; indeed, saintly *barakah* may also be recurrent in a family, bursting forth from generation to generation in the descendant of a great Saint as a special piety or sanctity, rather as certain healing powers were attributed to the British royal family, and to the French Kings.

In the Arab West, Saints' tombs with their characteristic domes dot the landscapes and Saints' festivals (*mawsim, moussem* in French), adorn the year, being occasions for gatherings, sometimes of many thousands of visitors, and for fairs, powder-play (the execution of fighting maneuvers on horseback and the firing of matchlock rifles), and other festivities.

"Marabout" is a term used more often in French than in Arabic, and is peculiar to those areas of North and West Africa that were once part of the French colonial empire. In French the word *maraboutism* was invented to describe this veneration of saints.

Ma'rib Dam (Ar. *sadd al-ma'rib*). In South Arabia there were a number of simple earthen dams built for irrigation purposes. Some dated from the 6th century BC and were the pride of the South Arabians, the most famous being that of Ma'rib. When it burst about AD 580 after a long period of neglect, the event had a profound effect upon the Arabs of the south as marking the end of an epoch, and closing the period of their greatness which stretched back into the legendary times of the Queen of Sheba (Saba').

The Koran may refer to the destruction of the Ma'rib Dam in 34:14-17:

For Sheba also there was a sign in
their dwelling-place — two gardens,
one on the right and one on the left:
'Eat of your Lord's provision, and give thanks
to Him; a good land, and a Lord
All-forgiving.'
But they turned away; so We loosed on
them the Flood of Arim, and We gave them,
in exchange for their two gardens,
two gardens bearing bitter produce
and tamarisk-bushes, and here and there
a few lote-trees.
Thus We recompensed them for their unbelief;
and do We ever recompense any but
the unbeliever?

Dams which were built much later, but reminiscent of the style of Ma'rib, can be found today still intact not far from Mecca. *See* SABA'.

Ma'rifah (lit. "knowledge"). Knowledge in general, especially in modern Arabic usage, but in religious literature specifically gnosis, that is, esoteric, or mystical knowledge of God. It corresponds to *jñāna* in Sanskrit. In Sufism, *Ma'rifah* is part of a triad that includes *Makhāfah*, "fear" (of God), and *Maḥabbah*, "love". The three are attitudes any one of which can determine a spiritual way, but they are also phases in every spiritual path. *Makhāfah* is a necessary phase of purification, *maḥabbah* the expansion to fill the "mold" of a Divine messenger, and finally *ma'rifah*, which is wisdom and realization of truth: union. These correspond in some respects to the three "paths" (*margas*) in Hinduism, of deeds (*karma*), devotion (*bhakti*), and gnosis (*jñāna*). *See* MAKHĀFAH; MAḤABBAH; SUFISM.

Maristān. A traditional infirmary, usually for the insane. A *maristān* was often attached to a Saint's tomb where it was hoped that the blessing of the Saint, and the supportive ambiance which prevails in such places, would help recovery. *See* MEDICINE.

Marja' at-Taqlīd (lit. "reference point of emulation"). In the Uṣūlī school of Shī'ism, a Mujtahid is a religious authority of the first rank whose competence is such that he can arrive at original, unprecedented decisions in theology and religious law. A *Marja' at-Taqlīd* is a kind of supreme Mujtahid, present in every age. Everyone who is not himself a *marja' at-taqlīd* is obliged to be a *muqallid*, that is, an emulator, or follower of such a one, as a Shī'ite is obliged to be a follower of a living Mujtahid (it is forbidden to be a follower of a dead Mujtahid). *See* AYATOLLAH; UṢŪLĪS.

Maronites. A Christian Uniate sect in the Lebanon (with some members in Syria, Israel, Cyprus, and Egypt, and through emigration, in the United States and South America), named after an eponymous St. Maron of the 5th century. Since the Crusades, and the year 1182, the Maronites have accepted the supremacy of the Pope and are today in communion with the Catholic church. But the origins of the Maronites lie in the divergence of opinion regarding the nature of Jesus which led to the Council of Nicaea.

Originally the Maronites were probably Monophysites who held that Jesus was entirely Divine, one person with one nature. (The Orthodox belief is that Jesus is one person with two natures, human and Divine.) At the beginning of the Muslim invasions, the Ghassāni Arabs of Syria, who were Monophysite, and at odds with the Orthodox Melkites of Syria, allied themselves with the Muslims and turned against Byzantium. The Byzantines, seeking to win back the support of the Ghassanis, offered the religious compromise of the *Ecthesis* in 638, to bring about greater religious harmony between themselves and the Syrians. This compromise was that of *Monotheletism*, a doctrine that the will of Jesus was one with the Divine Will, a concession to Monophysitism that does not go as far as to posit a continuity between God and creation which is Monophysitism. The Maronites, who were Monotheletists, are apparently the historical result of that compromise between the Byzantines and the Syrian Monophysite Christians.

In 1182, a Maronite Patriarch of Antioch, Amaury, convinced other Maronite Bishops to ally themselves with Rome. Communion with Rome was ratified at the Council of Florence in 1445. Many Maronite practices, however, remained at variance, such as mixed convents of monks and nuns, and in 1736 the Maronite Church received a constitution from Rome which was intended to bring about greater conformity. A married priesthood is still allowed, although not marriage after ordination, and, like the Orthodox, two kinds of clergy exist, married and celibate. French protection of the Maronites began with Louis XIV, permitted by a decree of the Ottoman Sultan. This led to intervention in the 19th century because of massacres of Maronites at the hands of the Druzes. After clashes between the two in 1860, the Sultan established the province or *sanjak* of Lebanon with an Ottoman Christian governor. Representation in the council, or *majlis* of the province was distributed among the religious groups including Orthodox, Druzes, and Shī'ites.

After 1860 a great migration began out of Lebanon while the process of identifying with French institutions continued. After World War I France assumed administration of both Lebanon and Syria, later subdivided into autonomous states. To justify continued outside intervention, a region was created with a Christian majority in the original Ottoman province but now with an added substantial Muslim minority: to Mount Lebanon, the Christian heartland, was added the then predominantly Muslim city of Beirut, Tripoli, Sidon and Shī'ite south Lebanon. Under the terms of the mandate a constitution was adopted in 1926. There began an unwritten tradition that Lebanon's president was a Maronite, the Prime Minister a Sunni, and the President of the Chamber of Deputies a Shī'ite. Defense was usually headed by a Druze. A new constitution was promulgated from Paris in 1934.

A first free election for the Syrian and Lebanese parliaments in 1943 resulted in a defeat for French-supported candidates; the governments demanded control of administration for themselves. The French commander Catroux responded by arresting the President and the cabinet. In Lebanon, the pro-French, Émile Edde was appointed head of state, but he did not succeed in forming an effective cabinet. After the war ended in Europe, fighting broke out in Damascus; with the help of the United Nations, both Lebanon and Syria became independent.

During this period Sunnis favored a union with Syria; the Maronites looked upon Lebanon as a part of Europe, and promulgated a nationalism called "Phoenicianism" that held the Lebanese to be a distinct group from the other nations of the Levant. The Greek Orthodox, however, favored a secular identity as Arabs first (over that of Christians). Reaction to Arab nationalism led to the development of Pierre Jemayel's Maronite dominated (80%) Phalangist movement, with its motto "Lebanon above all".

Three of Lebanon's ethnic-religious groups, Maronites, Shī'ites, and Druzes (in Syria one can also add the 'Alawis) have in common doctrines which absolutize something in creation. In the case of the Christians with a Monophysite and Monotheletist tradition, the physical person of Jesus, in the case of the Shī'ites, the Imām, in the case of the Druzes, al-Ḥākim. Theologically very similar, they are very antithetical on the plane of their outside forms because of the absolute within, the absolute hidden on the material plane. These have co-existed in the past under a hegemony of outside powers, that of the Muslim empires, then the Ottomans, and the French. In this century those hegemonies have disappeared. To the south another absolutism has appeared in the form of the state of Israel which has resulted in the displacement of large numbers of Palestinians into Lebanon; at the same time a demographic shift has taken place in which the Muslims now outnumber the Christians in Lebanon, along with a sharp increase of population within the Shī'ite community, now outnumbering the Sunnis, who have particularly suffered as a result of the Israeli invasion of Lebanon which attempted to oust the refugee Palestinians but succeeded in radicalizing the Shī'ites. A new equilibrium has yet to emerge. *See* GHASSĀNIS.

Marrano. Spanish name for Jewish converts to Christianity who maintain their Judaism in secret often applied to all crypto-Jews but in particular those from the Iberian peninsula. *See* DÖNMEH; MORISCOS; TAQIYYAH.

Marriage (Ar. *an-nikah*). In Islam, marriage is accomplished through a contract which is confirmed by the bride's reception of a dowry (*mahr*) and by the witnessing of the bride's consent to the marriage. If she is silent, her silence is also taken as acceptance; the Mālikīs and Shāfi'īs insist if the bride is a virgin, that she be represented by a male guardian (*walī*), usually a relative, who accepts the terms on her behalf. A woman cannot be forced to marry against her will.

When agreement to the marriage is expressed and witnessed, those present recite the *fātiḥah* (the opening chapter of the Koran). Normally, marriages are not contracted in mosques but in private homes or at the offices of a Judge (*qāḍi*). It is often the national or tribal customs that determine the type of ceremony, if there is one, and the celebrations which accompany it (*'urs*). In some parts of the Islamic world these may include processions in which the bride gift is put on display, receptions where the bride is seen adorned in elaborate costumes and jewelry, and ceremonial installation of the bride in the new house to which she may be carried in a litter. The groom may ride through the streets on a horse followed by his friends and well-wishers, and there is always a feast called the *walīmah*.

In religious law it is legal for a Muslim man to marry a Christian woman, or a woman of any of the Divinely revealed religions. It is not legal however, for a Muslim woman to marry outside her religion. In the past, non-Muslims marrying Muslim women have entered Islam in order to satisfy this aspect of Islamic law where it is in force. It now happens more and more frequently that Muslim women marry non-Muslim men who remain outside Islam. Such marriages, when and where they do not offend against the civil law, meet with varying degrees of social acceptance, depending upon the milieu. *See* WOMEN.

Martyrs (Ar. *shahīd*, pl. *shuhadā'*). Believers who die for the faith, in defense of it, or persecuted for it, are assured of Heaven. They are buried as they died, unwashed and in the same clothes, the bloodstains testifying to their state.

Moreover, the Koran (2:154) says "And call not those who are slain in the way of Allāh 'dead'. Nay they are living, only you perceive not." Koran (3:169) adds the curious detail that they have food: "count not those who are slain in the way of God as dead; nay, they are living; with their lord they have provision." (It was been suggested by the Ismā'īlī Da'i Abū Ḥatīm in the classical age that this elucidates Koran 4:157-158 which states that Jesus was not killed but raised up to God). Assimilated to martyrdom are those whose death has been tragic; their burials, however, follow the normal course of ablution and change of linen, before interment.

Shī'ism historically began with the march of the penitents (*tawwabūn*) out of Kūfah in 65/685 who deliberately sought martyrdom (and found it in battle with Caliphal troops) in repentance for not having come to the aid of al-Ḥusayn *61*/680. Al-Ḥusayn himself is the chief martyr of what became a cult of martyrdom in Shī'ism. The Babī poetess Qurratu-l-Ayn wrote:

> For me the love of that fair-faced Moon who,
> when the call of affliction came to him,
> Went down with exultation and laughter crying, "I am the Martyr at Karbal !"

Starting with colonial times the cult of martyrdom began amongst Sunnis as well.

Ma'rūf al-Karkhī (d. c.*200*/815). A pivotal figure in Sufism. By his father's name Firūz it is known that he was Persian; his original religion is not clear; he is often considered to have been a "Mandaean" and was instrumental in gaining recognition for this religion as being Ṣābians protected under Islamic law. He was from the district of Wāsiṭ and was the mawlā of the Imām 'Alī ibn Mūsā ar-Riḍā and accepted Islam at his hands, which reflects more upon the nature of the 'Alīds' relationships than on Ma'rūf's conversion. Sarī as-Saqaṭī was a disciple of his according to the *isnād* used by virtually all

Sufis, and he related: "I dreamed that I saw Ma'rūf al-Karkhī beneath the throne of God, and God was saying to His angels, "Who is this? They answered, 'Thou knowest best, O Lord' Then God said, 'This is Ma'ruf al-Karkhī, who was intoxicated with love of Me, and will not recover his senses except by meeting Me face to face.'" One day Ma'rūf said to his pupil "When you desire anything of God, swear to Him by me." Although Ma'rūf was not one of the "drunken Sufis" this self-aggrandizement is characteristic of their school. His tomb still exists in Baghdad.

Mary (Ar. *Maryam*). The mother of Jesus. In Islam she is mentioned with her honorific *sayyidatunā* ("our lady"), as the Prophets are titled *sayyidunā* ("our lord"). In the Koran she is the daughter of 'Imrān and Hannah. She was raised by Zakariyya'; it was her custom to retreat in the *miḥrāb*, the "prayer niche" in a holy place, and "whenever Zakariyya' went into the *miḥrāb* where she was, he found that she had food. He said: 'O Mary! Whence cometh this unto thee?' She answered: 'It is from God; God giveth without stint to whom he will'" (3:37). This is almost always the verse which is written on prayer niches when they are decorated with calligraphy.

And mention in the Book Mary
when she withdrew from her people
to an eastern place,
and she took a veil apart from them;
then We sent unto her Our Spirit
that presented himself to her
a man without fault.
She said, 'I take refuge in
the All-merciful from thee!
If thou fearest God...'
He said, 'I am but a messenger
come from thy Lord, to give thee
a boy most pure.'
She said, 'How shall I have a son
whom no mortal has touched, neither
have I been unchaste?'
He said, 'Even so thy Lord has said:
"Easy is that for Me; and that We
may appoint him a sign unto men
and a mercy from Us; it is
a thing decreed."'
So she conceived him, and withdrew with him
to a distant place.
And the birthpangs surprised her by
the trunk of the palm-tree. She said,
'Would I had died ere this, and become
a thing forgotten!'
But the one that was below her
called to her, 'Nay, do not sorrow;
see, thy Lord has set below thee
a rivulet.
Shake also to thee the palm-trunk,
and there shall come tumbling upon thee
dates fresh and ripe.
Eat therefore, and drink, and be
comforted; and if thou shouldst see
any mortal,
say, "I have vowed to the All-merciful
a fast, and today I will not speak
to any man."'
Then she brought the child to her folk
carrying him; and they said,
'Mary, thou hast surely committed
a monstrous thing!
Sister of Aaron, thy father was not
a wicked man, nor was thy mother
a woman unchaste.'
Mary pointed to the child then;
but they said, 'How shall we speak
to one who is still in the cradle,
a little child?'
He said, 'Lo, I am God's servant;
God has given me the Book, and
made me a Prophet.
Blessed He has made me, wherever
I may be; and He has enjoined me
to pray, and to give the alms, so
long as I live,
and likewise to cherish my mother;
He has not made me arrogant,
unprosperous.
Peace be upon me, the day I was born,
and the day I die, and the day I am
raised up alive!'
That is Jesus, son of Mary... (19:16-34)

In Koran 19:28 she is called "Sister of Aaron". This is often understood to mean Aaron, the brother of Moses, on the ground that Mary's relationship to the revelation of Jesus was analogous to that of Aaron in regard to Moses. Like Aaron, she has an inward function rather than an outward one in respect of revelation. On the Prophet's journey to Ṭā'if a Christian slave asked him how he knew of Jonah. The Prophet replied: "He is my brother; he was a Prophet, and I am a Prophet." In other words, brotherhood can be a kinship on a spiritual plane, and the Prophet's point of view specifically included this possibility. Joseph, the husband of Mary in the Gospels, does not appear in the Koranic accounts.

When the Muslims conquered Mecca, the Ka'bah was cleansed of the many stone and wood idols it contained. Inside the Ka'bah, on the walls, were several paintings, among them a picture of Abraham and an icon of the Virgin and Child. The Prophet covered the icon with his hands, instructing that everything else should be painted over. *See also* AARON; JESUS.

Mas'ā. The walkway between the two hills Ṣafā and Marwah, which is today within the precincts of the rebuilt and extended Grand Mosque of Mecca. This space, which is 1,247 feet/394 meters, is walked seven times in the performance of the rite of the *'umrah*. The ritual walking is called the sa'y, and it commemorates the running back and forth of Hagar, when she cast about looking for water for her son Ismā'īl (Ishmael). *See* KA'BAH; PILGRIMAGE.

Maṣallah, *see* MUṢALLĀH.

Masaḥa 'ala-l-Khuffayn (lit. "wiping the inner shoes"). The *khuffayn* are a kind of footwear, a soft shoe worn inside a boot, which modern practice has assimilated to stockings. If they have no holes and are put on while the person is in a state of ablution (*wuḍū'*), then, in renewing the ablution, it is enough to wipe them with moist hands without removing them and wiping the bare feet. This Sunnī practice is not accepted by the Zaydīs. The Mālikī school of law accepts the principle of *masaḥa 'ala khuffayn* but insists that it applies only in the case of actual *khuffayn*, which exist today as a kind of soft leather under-slipper worn in Turkey. Many individual Mālikīs, however, do not make this distinction. However, whereas as many Ḥanafīs only touch the socks with a moist hand, the Mālikīs who assimilate socks to "inner shoes" actually wipe the foot with a moist hand as if it were bare. *See* ZAYDĪS.

Maslamah, *see* MUSAYLAMAH.

Mash'ar. A place where it is traditional to perform a ritual action, as in the two prayer sites in the pilgrimage, *al-mash'ar al-ḥarām*, and *al-mash'ar al-ḥalāl*. *Al-mash'ar al-ḥarām* is in Muzdalifah, within the restricted precinct, the *ḥarām*, and *al-mash'ar al-ḥalāl* is in 'Arafāt, just outside the precinct. *See* PILGRIMAGE.

Mashhad (lit. "the place of martyrdom"). The term used by the Shī'ites for the tombs of their Imāms, such as the *mashhad Ḥusayn* at Kerbala. *Mashhad* without further qualification usually refers to the tomb of the eighth Shī'ite Imām 'Alī ibn Musā 'r-Riḍā (or 'Alī Reẓā) (d. *203*/818) and the town, also sometimes spelled *Meshed*, which has grown up around it, is the capital of Khorāsān province in northeast Iran. Its population today is close to 500,000. The shrine of the Imām is one of the most important in Twelve-Imām Shī'ism, as it is the only tomb of an Imām in Iran itself, and the most important after Kerbala and Najaf (the burial place of 'Alī). The Caliph Hārūn ar-Rashīd is also buried there, having died in the place on a journey ten years before the death of the Imām.

The Shī'ites advance in testimony of the sanctity of Mashhad the following Ḥadīth: "A part of my [the Prophet's] body is to be buried in Khorāsān, and whoever goes there on pilgrimage, God will surely destine to paradise, and his body will be forbidden to the flames of hell; and whoever goes there with sorrow, God will take his sorrow away."

Al-Ma'mūn, the son of Hārūn ar-Rashīd, ordered a tomb to be built there for his father, who died in the place before 'Alī ar-Riḍā. This tomb was successively expanded, particularly by Shah 'Abbās, not because of Hārūn ar-Rashīd, but because of the tomb's other occupant, the Shī'ite Imām. It has since become one of the most lavish shrines in Islam. (As Hārūn ar-Rashīd was not a Shī'ite, and is considered rather as an enemy of Shī'ism, his tomb is not honored and its place in the shrine is coincidental unless, of course, al-Ma'mun had the Imām poisoned, as is claimed, in order to associate the two in the popular imagination of the time.)

In 1911 the city was occupied by rebels, and the Persian government, lacking forces, permitted the Russians, who had military units stationed in Khorāsān, to take action. This they did by bombarding the city; the golden dome of the shrine was damaged, and a wave of opprobrium against the Russians swept through Persia.

Masīḥī (from *al-masiḥ*, "messiah"). The proper name for Christians, pl. *masīḥiyyūn*. This use of the word was first established by Christian missionaries, in preference to the term *Naṣārā* ("Nazarenes").

Masjid, *see* MOSQUE.

al-Masjid al-Ḥarām, *see* KA'BAH.

Masjid an-Nabī ash-Sharīf, *see* MOSQUE of the PROPHET.

Massignon, Louis (1883-1962). Famous for his life long study of al-Ḥallaj, Massignon was one of the great Islamicists of the last century. His first deep contact with the Islamic world, after studying French literature and Sanskrit at the University of Paris and having served as a volunteer in the infantry, was a journey for historic research from Tangier to Fez in 1904. Thereafter he began a study of Arabic and Persian. In 1907-1908 he was on a research mission to Mesopotamia, where he was arrested by the Turkish police for espionage. He escaped and later spoke about an experience in Ctesiphon before the ruins of the palace of Chosroes, where a "visitation of the stranger", kept him from plunging a daggar into himself. The experience led to a religious renewal; he enrolled at the al-Azhar of Cairo where he studied Islamic philosophy.

He kept in touch with Charles de Foucauld (who wanted Massignon to follow himself in his religious and espionage activities) and many other literary and cultural figures. In 1912 he lectured in Arabic at the Egyptian University of Cairo. In the Great War he served in the Ministry of Foreign Affairs and in an infantry regiment. Afterwards he was a diplomatic officer. In 1919 he received his first position at the Coll ge de France and in 1926 became Professor of Sociology and Sociography of Islam. In 1929 he founded the Institut des tudes Islamiques. He also taught at a number of other schools.

He took part in the Jungian Eranos conferences in Ascona, and towards the end of his life was ordained a priest in the Melkite rite. He became a spokesman for certain currents of Catholicism and also took part in political struggles particularly during the Algerian War. Earlier he had founded a small, peculiar religious group which he called the Badaliya in which the members sought to expiate collectively the sins of designated acquaintances.

Throughout his life Massignon was involved with al-Ḥallāj. His research made al-Ḥallāj into one of the most documented figures of medieval Islam. Massignon called al-Ḥallāj "a martyr of truth" and made a hero out of him, making excuses for his fake miracles as "mere leger-de-main to aid belief" and explaining all charges of revolutionary activity as folly "dreamed up" by the authorities . Thus he whitewashed al-Ḥallāj and made him into a "misunderstood" Sunni orthodox saint perpetuating the myth which was originally created by Ḥallāj's gnostic co-religionists.

Rather than admit that Ḥallāj was a Manichean as accused by the Baghdad authorities, something which Massignon actually documented and proved by his research, Massignon made out of him a *tertium quid*, something else. The religion which Ḥallāj followed, became Ḥallājianism and it turned out that it had tens of thousands of followers, many of whom were also executed afterwards, for the same reasons. (In other accounts of history, those Ḥallājians are called Qarmaṭīs and Ismā'īlīs.) It turns out that Ḥallājians ate lettuce, (just as Manicheans did) and to clarify matters Massignon calculated the amount of lettuce required to feed the mythical movement of Baghdadi Ḥallājians, or followers of Ḥallāj. Massignon wrote: "In A.H. 345 the annual consumption of lettuce (*khass*=hindibā, the food eaten by the Hallajians) at one dirham per 20 head of lettuce, brought in 700,000 dirhams (at the new, depreciated rate of 14 dirhams to the dīnār). Two thousand *jarib* of land (=432 hectares) were used for the raising of this lettuce. The fact that lettuce is consumed only during a quarter of the year, and represents in weight only half of the bread consumed in 345, and in money only 5 percent of the cost of bread per person in A.H. 303, confirms, in this instance also, the demographic drop (9/10). Finally, with price of bread, we assign two curves, that of the price of bread in relation to the price of wheat, and that of the silver dirham in relation to the gold dīnār; both are necessary for understanding the revolutionary crisis that occurred in Baghdad at the end of 308 as a result of the monopolizing deals of Vizir Hāmid and his associates in speculation. For bread, let us remember that if 100 kg of wheat yields only 74 kg of flour...." (p. 234, Vol 1; of four).

By such red herrings, thousands in number, he produced the result that the Encyclopedia of Islam, New Edition, says in the article NŪR that while one might think that Ḥallāj was a Manichean, "Massignon clears him of this charge".

Nevertheless, the result is not only of interest to scholars for *La Passion de Husayn ibn Mansūr Hal-*

lāj; martyr mystique de l'Islam, faithfully translated into English as the *Passion of al-Hallāj Mystic and Martyr of Islam* can be read with the enthusiasm one reserves for a mystery novel or a great adventure, in this case, an adventure of the mind.

Massignon had an unusual flair for discovering and unmasking connections, in manuscripts and in ideas. He proposed that the Qarmaṭīs were at the origin of trade guilds in the West but never explained how. Undoubtedly he was correct; the connection must have been through the associations between the Ismā'īlīs and Templars in the Holy Land during the Crusades, both organizations being independent and in some ways opposed to the conventions and principles of their respective civilizations. Having more in common with each other than with their own cultural matrices, the Ismā'īlīs passed the Qarmaṭī social programs on to the Templars who then organized the Masonic Lodges in Europe. When Philip le Bel realized that the Templars were creating a state within a state, he moved against them leaving the Masons without their leadership but with the legend that Jacques de Molay escaped from the conflagration to become a Grand Master of the Scottish Rectified Rite.

Massignon's vast work is a gold mine wherein much treasure remains to be found. His conclusions, often the result of his own philosophy, can now be contested on many points, but his contribution to Islamic scholarship is immense.

al-Mas'ūdī, Abū-l-Ḥasan 'Alī ibn al-Ḥusayn ibn 'Alī (d. *345*/956). An historian, geographer, philosopher and natural scientist, he was a descendant of the Prophet's Companion 'Abd Allāh ibn Mas'ūd. A Shī'ite born in Baghdad of a Kūfan family, al-Mas'ūdī had an excellent education. He knew the great men of Baghdad of his time, and his many teachers included Sīnān ibn Thābit ibn Qurra (d. *331*/943), the Mu'tazilite theologian al-Jubba'ī (who was the teacher of al-Ash'arī), and he knew al-Ash'arī himself (d. *324*/935), the founder of Sunnī *Kalām* ("theology"). He debated with the physician, philosopher, and alchemist Abū Bakr Muḥammad ibn Zakariyya ar-Rāzī (d. *320*/923). Al-Mas'ūdī traveled extensively in the East, including India. He also went to Egypt but, strangely, not to North Africa or Spain. He described the places he visited, and chronicled the events of his times in his book *Murūj adh-Dhahab wa Ma'ādin al-Jawhar* ("the Meadows of Gold and Quarries of Jewels"), and his *Murūj az-Zamān* ("Meadows of Time"). He wrote thirty-four works, most of which are lost.

The "Meadows of Gold" is actually an encyclopedia of medieval Islamic knowledge. It rambles over every imaginable kind of subject: geography, historical notices including the history of the Prophets, the ancient Arabs, the Romans, the Persian Kings, the Islamic dynasties, the French Kings, the peoples of the ancient world together with their customs, religions, curiosities, temples, monuments, commerce, medicine, astronomy, astrology, science, the nature of the soul, psychology, and legends.

Of India, Mas'ūdī says that in the ancient past it was there "that order and wisdom reigned". He makes many interesting observations, among other things, on Indian theories of the cycles of time and history. At the beginning of a cycle, al-Mas'ūdī says, the circumference which contains all the principles to be manifested in it is greater, and there is more freedom to act. At the end of a cycle, it draws tighter and there is compression; the quality of time itself changes: in the beginning of a particular cycle of manifestation time can contain more events, and at the end, less, which gives the impression of rapid succession, speed, and havoc. "Meadows of Gold and Quarries of Jewels" contains an apt and accurate description of this.

Mas'ūdī explains a certain enigma of Iranian history in his *Kitābu't-tanbih wa'l-ishrāf*. Persian and Arab historians habitually reduce the interval between the death of Alexander and the foundation of the Sāssānid dynasty to 266 years when in fact it was five and a half centuries. Mas'ūdī explains this as the result of a prophecy current in Persia that a thousand years after Zoroaster the religion and the Persian empire would fall. According to an erroneous idea (which is still current among many scholars today) Zoroaster lived 300 years before Alexander (actually Zoroaster lived at least 1,000 BC if not much earlier). By this [erroneous] but popularly accepted date of Zoroaster the Sāssānid dynasty founded by Ardashir Babakan in AD 226 had only 150 years to run, thus theoretically ending around AD 380. Ardashir, fearing the effects of a self fulfilling prophecy hoped to cheat destiny by removing 300 years from history in order to attach it to the time which prophecy alloted to his dynasty. It can be said that Ardashir's trick worked because the dynasty lasted 434 years coming to an end with Yazdegird III in AD 651-2, as it would have according to the original thousand year prophecy but instead running according to Ardashir's falsified schedule (and the historically erroneous date of Zoroaster accepted by the Sāssānids based upon consultations with deluded Babylonian chroniclers who confused Zoroaster with Cyrus.) Mas'ūdī called this falsification of history —the removal of three hundred years — an "ecclesiastical and political secret".

Matn. In the analysis of Ḥadīth, the *matn* is the body, or content, of the Ḥadīth; the *isnād* the chain of transmission. In another sense, *matn* may denote the actual text of an author, which may be published with a commentary, the *sharḥ*. Matn means "letters" (*mutūn*) as quoted by Goldziher from a poem by Labid: *wajalā s-sulūlu 'ani 'ṭ-ṭullūli ka'annahā Zubrun tujiddi mutūnahā aqlāmuhā*: "the torrents make the traces of the camps reappear as if they were letters restored by the strokes of a reed pen." *See* ḤADĪTH.

Matter, *see* HAYŪLĀ.

al-Māturīdī, Abū Manṣūr Muḥammad (d. *333*/944). A theologian (*mutakallim*), born near Samarkand. Together with al-Ash'arī and others, he is one of the founders of *Kalām* (Islamic theology). Little is known about the man himself, for his school became established as the result of the writings of his disciples, in particular an-Naṣafi. Traditionally, the doctrinal differences between the school of al-Māturīdī and that of al-Ash'arī are numbered at thirteen, seven of them being only a difference in the way matters are expressed.

The most important difference is that al-Māturīdī accords human free will the logic of its consequences, that is, that the just are saved on that account, whereas with al-Ash'arī God's will is unfathomable: God may send the just to hell. Al-Māturīdī recognizes that God's reward or punishment is in relation to man's actions and this view has largely been tacitly accepted, in practice even by Ash'arites. In general, the school of al-Māturīdī has not hesitated to enunciate dogmatic antinomies, (man has free will, but is predestined; the speech of God is both created and uncreated) which has won more adherents than the Ash'arites have in Central Asia and the Far East. It should be noted, even so, that the school of al-Māturīdī, whilst enunciating these doctrines, has largely avoided explaining them, and left that expansion to the mystics. *See* al-ASH'ARĪ; KALĀM; SUFISM.

al-Ma'ūdah. In the Arab desert society that predated Islam, the *ma'ūdah* was an unwanted female child that was buried alive. The practice was forbidden by Islam. (On the Day of Judgement the victim will be asked "for what sin she was slain" Koran 81:8).

The practice probably originated because of the conditions of perpetual famine in which the desert Arabs lived; infanticide reflected the struggle for survival.

Maudūdi *see* MAWDŪDĪ.

Mauritania. Islamic Republic. Population: 1,850,000 of whom half are Arab and Berber whites, and half are members of various black tribal groups, Sarakollé, Fulānī and Wolof, who are also found in Senegal. Besides Arabic, of the dialect called Ḥasaniyyah, French is the dominant language, especially among the Blacks, for whom, with fourteen native languages, it is the common medium. 99% of Mauritanians are Muslims of the Mālikī School of Law. Mauritania was Islamicised by the Almoravids, whose center was near the city of Aṭṭār, from *442*/1050 on. Many Mauritanians are loosely affiliated with the Qādiriyyah *ṭariqah*, and the Tijāniyyah is influential in the south of the country. The white tribes are divided into *Ḥasanis*, or Arabs, and *Ḥusaynis*, or Berbers. The Berber tribes are also called the *zawiyah* tribes.

There is a caste structure to society: the nomads, Arabs and Berbers, who call themselves the "bones", undisputedly consider themselves the nobles, while the others, who are town dwellers, include musician castes, craft and artisan castes, fisherman castes, and other small groups, each with a distinct place on the social ladder. These are called the "flesh" (*laḥm*). The traditional name of Mauritania is *Bilād al-Bīḍān* ("The country of the Whites"), and in North Africa the country was known as *Shinqīt*, after the holy town of *Shinqīt*, or (in French), Chinguetti. Although there is a republican form of government, in the desert, the chiefs, the Emirs, are the ruling force. *See* CHINGUETTI; ḤASANĪ.

al-Māwardi, 'Alī Muḥammad (d. *450*/1058). A Judge in Baghdad and a figure at court, al-Māwardi wrote one of the important books of political science entitled *Kitāb al-Aḥkam as-Sultaniyyah* ("The Book of Rules of Government"). It is in the genre of a "mirror for princes", (*nasiḥahatu-l-muluk*). Al-Māwardi discusses the *bilad ad-dīn*, a state ruled by religion; *bilad al-quwwah*, rule by power (in respect of the rise in the 10th century of the "sultanate" state based on force), and *bilad ath-thawra*, anarchy. In this al-Māwardi followed Ibn Muqaffa' who said that there were three forms of government, those based on justice and truth, on injustice and political realism, and those of "meddling and squander". Before Ibn Khaldūn addressed the question, al-Māwardi discussed the reasons why rulers lost power.

Al-Māwardi mentions that the Sāssānid state was based upon *maslaḥah*, welfare, and not *sharī'ah*, religious law. The principles of Sāssānid rule, however, in the *Ahd Ardashir* ("The Testament of Ardashir I", the founder of the dynasty), said that "Kingship and religion are twin brothers, no one of which can be maintained without the other. For religion is the foundation of kingship and kingship is the guardian of religion. Kingship cannot subsist without its foundation and religion cannot subsist without its guardian. For that which has no guardian is lost, and that which has no foundation crumbles."

Mawdūdī (or Maudūdi), Sayyid Abū al-A'lā (*1321-1399*/1903-1979). A highly influential Muslim revivalist and politician. Born in Aurangabad, India, he spent much of his life in Hyderabad and later in Lahore, where he is buried after having died in America while on a journey. He came from a family which had been displaced as a result of colonialism and the subsequent loss of political power on the part of the Muslims in India. He was involved in the Khilāfat movement and the early Congress party, but turned towards Muslim nationalism and then Islamic utopianism.

In 1941, along with other intellectuals, Mawdūdī founded a political party, the Jamā'ati Islāmi, which became divided with the partition of India into several branches. This party is an embodiment of his views which treats Islam itself as an ideology and a political activity, setting aside its spiritual aspect. He viewed the Islamic state as a sixth pillar of the religion. In his state social ills can be overcome by the literal meaning of the Koran; a non-Muslim cannot be a member of parliament or hold a high government post. Social evolution, Utopianism, and struggle with non-Islamic forces characterized his outlook.

Much of his life Mawdūdi was a journalist, starting as editor of an Urdu weekly magazine *Madīnah* at the age of sixteen. He was the editor of a daily newspaper *Taj* and later, *Jam'īyat*, which was the newspaper of *Jam'īyat-i 'Ulamā'-i-Hind*, a political party in Delhi. From 1933 to 1979 he was the editor of *Tarjuman al-Qur'an*, a monthly which was the forum for the expression of his ideas. His major works amongst many which he wrote as a journalist are: *Jihad in Islam* (which attracted Muḥammad Iqbal who invited Mawdūdī to come to Lahore); *Towards Understanding Islam*; and his magnum opus, a translation of the Koran and commentary in Urdu, *Tafhīm al-Qur'an*, which is widely read in Pakistan and has appeared in English. As *emir* or leader of his party Mawdūdī was imprisoned several times after the creation of Pakistan.

Mawlā (pl. *mawālī*). During the first century of Arab expansion following the revelation of Islam, converts to Islam outside Arabia were adopted into Arab tribes. This "adoption" was made by the convert becoming a client (*mawlā*) of an Arab who was the protector. This status was a kind of second class citizenship in the Islamic state and was resented, particularly by the Persians. It is said that this system was not practiced by 'Alī, who treated all converts among the conquered people as equals of the Arabs.

The *mawālī* system declined and was abolished by the Umayyad Caliph 'Umar ibn 'Abd al-'Azīz (d. *101*/720), but it had by then contributed to the growth of political Shī'ism which hoped to find greater equity through the overthrow of the Umayyads and the promotion of one of the 'Alids to the Caliphate. The word *mawlā*, in its sense of "master" or "patron", or simply as an expression of respect, has come into modern English as *Mullā* (sometimes Mullah, "religious authority"). *See* UMAYYADS.

Mawlānā Jalāl ad-Dīn ar-Rūmī, *see* JALĀL ad-DĪN ar-RŪMĪ.

Mawlawī, *see* MEVLEVI.

Mawlay (lit. "my master" from *mawla*). A title used in Morocco for *sharīfs*, descendants of the Prophet. It is often encountered in its French form, *Moulay*.

Mawlid an-Nabī. The birthday of the Prophet, the 12th of Rabī' al-Awwal. The observance of the *mawlid* as a public holiday began around the *6th*/12th century. In *690*/1291 the Merinid Sultan Abū Ya'qūb introduced *mawlid* celebrations into Morocco; and in Mamlūk Egypt a century later the fervor of the celebrations reached great heights.

The manner of observing the *mawlid* is a matter of local custom. Most typical is the recitation of various litanies in mosques. In countries that were once part of the Ottoman Empire, it is the custom upon the *mawlid* to recite the *Burdah* ("The Mantle"), a poem by al-Busīrī whose theme is praise of the Prophet.

In some countries there are street processions, such as the procession of wax displays in Salé, Morocco, perhaps inspired by Spanish Saints' processions. *See* BURDAH.

Mawlūd, *see* MAWLID an-NABĪ.

Mawsim, *see* MOUSSEM.

Māyā, *see* ḤIJĀB.

Maymūn al-Qaddaḥ, *see* 'ABD ALLĀH ibn MAYMŪN al-QADDAḤ.

Maẓālim. (Ar. *radd al-maẓālim*, "correction of complaints"). Courts in traditional Islamic society from the middle ages on, which are not under the Qāḍi's jurisdiction, but under the jurisdiction of the ruler. They resolve civil suits, abuses of power, and tax questions. Those questions which are not family law, inheritance, etc. were treated in these courts and now in modern civil and criminal courts. *See* SHARĪ'AH.

Mazār (from Arabic *mazhar*, "appearance", "manifestation"). A term used in Iran and Central Asia for the tomb of a Saint, or a place associated with his life.

Mazār-i Sharīf. A town with a population of less than 50,000 near what was once Balkh in north Afghanistan, near Uzbekistan. It is famed for its splendid shrine which is held to be the tomb of 'Alī. ('Alī was buried in 'Irāq, in an unknown grave which was identified as Najaf by Harūn ar-Rashid in a vision.) Still, piety has insisted that 'Alī's presence graces Mazār-i Sharīf as well. An inscription at Mazār-i Sharīf in Persian declares: "It is said that Murtaḍā 'Alī is in Najaf. Come to Balkh and see how beautiful it is." Sa'dī said that "'Alī is in the land of the two rivers and between the mountains [a description of the situation of both 'Irāq and Balkh]. There is only one sun, but its light shines everywhere."

In the time of Sultan Sanjar, who reigned in the first half of the twelfth century, a report reached Balkh from Sindh (which is in today's Pakistan) that the grave of 'Alī was nearby. A Mullā of the place at first denied it but then 'Alī appeared to him in a dream and confirmed the report. A shrine was erected by Sultan Sanjar which was finished in 1136. It was destroyed by Jenghiz Khan in 1220 when he sacked Balkh. Not long afterwards Marco Polo could still call it "a great and noble city". In 1481 the tomb was replaced by Ḥusayn Bayqara. Thenceforth it became a place of pilgrimage. Mazār-i Sharīf overtook Balkh (which was 23 kilometers from the shrine) as Mashhad had overtaken Ṭūs.

Whoever is actually buried in Mazār-i Sharīf antedates Islam. By identifying him with 'Alī, his partisans thus assured that his tomb became protected and honored by the Islamic establishment. At this point it will be impossible to positively identify the personage so protected, but the circumstances connecting Sindh, 'Alī, and Balkh lead to the guess that it is Mani's traditional Iranian missionary Mar Ammo, or perhaps Mār Shad Ohrmizd who actually founded the eastern Dēnāvāriya school of Manicheism and lived around AD 600. It is not the only tomb of 'Alī in Central Asia; there are other mazār 'Alī, in Shāhī Mardan in Ferghana, for example, so the idea of safeguarding their favorite pre-Islamic heretics through metamorphosis occurred to others as well, and there are also a number of other Saint's tombs in nearby Tajikistan which have been identified as "Majusi" in origin. None of these, however, attained the celebrity, and architectural splendor of Mazārī-Sharīf, thanks to the patronage of the Tīmūrids, at first Shāh Rukh and his wife Jawhar, and then Ḥusayn Bayqara.

According to tradition, Mar Ammo had come to Afghanistan where a goddess named Bagard (Lakhshmi) stopped him. He said that he brought a new religion to which she answered that they had enough religions. Mar Ammo stopped and prayed for two days; the spirit of Mani appeared to him and told him a list of books to read to the goddess whereupon she allowed him to continue.

Balkh was the origin of many astrologers, and center for Ismā'īlīsm, which is still found in Badakshan and the Pamir. Rūmī (who is considered an Ismā'īlī by the Pamiris) and his father were expelled from Balkh and went to Konya when orthodox reaction became too strong. (Similarly, Nāṣir-i Khusraw before them had also been expelled, from Balkh.) Khusraw, railing against the development of orthodox control wrote:

> As for the province of Khorāsān, once the Abode of Learning,
> It has become a cavern of sordid and effeminate demons.
> Balkh! The House of Wisdom! and now fit for the axe, its fortune turned topsy-turvey on its head.
> Khorāsān, once the Kingdom of Solomon —
> How has it become the domain of Satan.

The town of Balkh is ancient; the Iranians said it was founded by Gayomart, the first man, and called it "mother of cities". By legend Zoroaster had lived there, began his mission there and even died there. In Alexander's time it was called Alexandria-Bactra or Zainaspa, and it was the capital of Bactria, which, at times, included Soghdiana, Merv, part of Khorāsān and Ferghana, not including Khwarizm, and saw Greek settlements. Gold from Siberia flowed through it, and later Indian and Chinese trade. After the Seleucids, Bactria was captured by the nomad Yueh-Chi Kushans and became Ṭocharistan. It later was a center of Buddhism, and in Central Asia Buddhism was influenced by Zurvanism and the cult of Amitābha grew.

The Chinese Buddhist pilgrim Hs an Tsang (X anzang) visited Balkh around the year 630 and reported that in addition to about one hundred Hinayana monasteries, with about three thousand devotees, there were, at some distance from them, what he called *Nava Sangharama*, recognizable as *Naw Bahar* or *Nava Vihara*, from Soghdian Buddhist texts. It was from these new, perhaps "Mahayana" monasteries created as a vehicle for Manicheism that the Barmakids, then abbots of a "Buddhist" monastery were drawn to Baghdad to become ministers for the 'Abbāsids. Hs an Tsang said that Buddhism was brought to Central Asia by Trapuṣa and Bhallika (referring to Balkh) two merchants who were the first to offer food to the Buddha after his Enlightenment and who became his first lay followers. Buddhism existed side by side with Islam in Central Asia until around the year 1000 when its decline was observed by al-Bīrūnī. Buddhist monasteries may have influenced the architecture of the *madrasah*. The history of Balkh was colorful and venerable in Islamic times. *See* IBRĀHĪM ibn ADHAM; NAṢIR-I KHUSRAW; KUBRĀ; JALĀL ad-DĪN ar-RŪMI; MANICHEISM.

Mazdak (early 6th century AD). It is said that he was a Magian priest in Persia who became the leader of a cult within Zoroastrian Mazdeism. His Mazdeism could only have been a disguise since his father's name was Bāmdād which was a common name among Manicheans. He preached the holding of women and property in common, and advocated Dualism (Ar. *thanawiyyah*), a system of belief in which evil is equal to good and possesses essence and substance. He preached to the King that "The rich and powerful are the same as the empty handed poor. It is unjust that anyone should have superfluous wealth, the rich are the weft and poor the woof... Women and possessions should be held in common, if you do not wish the Good Religion to be impaired, for from these two things come Envy and Avarice and Want, which secretly unite in Anger and Hatred, and then the devil perverts the body of the sages..."

Communism has always been the social system of choice of Manichean and dualist religions. Along the silk road and in Afghanistan, Manichean communities were organized as collective farms in which the workers were actually exploited by a priviliged priestly class, just as they were in the Soviet Union by the nomenklatura.

The Persian Shah Qobad (Kavadh, 488-531) became a follower of the cult, but was finally convinced of its unorthodoxy or its disadvantage since in 497 he was "deposed by the nobles and shut up in the caste of Gelgard or Andmishn in Susiana... it was known as Anushbard, the castle of oblivion, whose name it was forbidden to mention". But Qobad escaped and with the aid of the King of the Hephtalites regained the throne in 499 which had been occupied by his brother Zhamasp. Eventually Mazdak was put to death, as were thousands of his followers; the succeeding Shāh, Chosroes I (Anushirvan, "Great Soul"), embodied a revival of Zoroastrianism in Persia. After the restoration under Chosroes, many Mazdakites were expelled from Iran to Azerbaijan, to the Yemen, and to the region of Ḥīrah, (later to be Kūfah) where, four centuries later, Mazdakism reappeared as Qarmaṭīsm, and earlier, in the form of numerous peasant revolts in Iran.

Ibn Muqaffa' translated the *Book of Mazdak* into Arabic. The Persian Vizier of the Seljūqs, Niẓām al-Mulk (d. *485*/1092), wrote about Mazdakism in his *Siyaset-Nāmeh* ("Book of Government") as a warning to the rulers of his age, which was also beset by irruptions of Dualist sects. The Mazdak epoch was remembered with anguish in Iran as "the time when children did not know their fathers". The system was, as exactly as possible in a pre-Industrial age, a form of Communism with good and evil playing the role of what in Marxism is thesis and anthesis. Communist theoreticians saw a family resemblance in Mazdakism, as well as other Iranian peasant revolts, and Soviet Orientalists paid special attention to these. Mazdak was cited as a "red hero" in Soviet textbooks. According to Elton Daniel, citing Pigulevskaya, the Mazdakite revolt resulted in destruction of the old slave-owning aristocracy, derogation of the Zoroastrian priestly class, weakening of peasant communities and the victory of the proprietary-military class, the *Shah*, and the central government. According to Bausani, "Mazdakism differs from Manicheism in its insistence on the chance nature of liberation and illumination, which anyone, even a plebeian, could obtain, and perhaps even the ascetic Manichean aristocracy felt this doctrine to be dangerous." Mazdakism as a dominant force came to an end in 524 but continued to exert its influence even into modern times.

Bausani also wrote: "The idea that it was Satan rather than God who created the vile visible world, was regarded as blasphemy. If one thinks of the rock relief of Ardashīr at Naqshi-i Rustam, which shows the king corresponding exactly to Ohrmazd (Ahura Mazda) the Creator God, each trampling under his feet the vanquished, illegitimate rival (the king's enemy is thus equated with Satan) it is quite natural to think that Manicheism's identification of Satan with the Creator might — despite Mani's initial friendship with the highest members of the aristocracy and with the king himself — easily be interpreted by the oppressed masses as the portent and symbol of the overthrow of authority. One should also bear in mind the element of individualism in Mani's teaching. The Manichean myth is one long hymn to the possibility of *personal* salvation from the evil of the world, and it was the individual person that despotic regimes ignored." *See* QARMAṬĪS; MANICHEISM; BABAK; SURKH-I 'ALĀM.

Mecca (*Makkah al-Mukarramah*; lit. "Mecca the Blessed"). From ancient times, Mecca has been a spiritual center. Ptolemy, the second century Greek geographer, mentioned Mecca, calling it "Makoraba". Some have interpreted this to mean "temple" (from *maqribah* in South Arabian) but it may also mean "Mecca of the Arabs". Interestingly, the Dravidian Purāṇas also speak of an ancient holy place there dedicated to the god of wisdom. Originally, Mecca was called "Bakkah" ("narrow"), a description of the site between the mountains that press upon the city and valley of the Holy Places. The Koran says: "The first sanctuary appointed for mankind was that at Bakkah, a blessed place, a guidance for the peoples" (3:96).

Of visible monuments that date back to ancient times there exists today only the Ka'bah, Abraham's temple to God, towards which Muslims throughout the world turn to pray, and which has been rebuilt several times. The landscape surrounding the city is of a striking aridity, as if of immeasurable age. It is nature reduced to its bare foundations, evoking the limitless and the invisible. The Koran calls Mecca the "uncultivated" or "seedless" valley; and, indeed, its inhabitants have always depended upon commerce for their livelihood. The Quraysh of the Kinānah tribe, who descended from an ancestor called Fihr, had inhabited Mecca for several centuries before the revelation of Islam, entered into commercial agreements with surrounding countries and financed caravans to carry trade-goods. The Koran mentions the "Winter and the Summer Caravan" which sometimes numbered thousands of camels; the great incense trade of the Yemen was routed through Mecca.

Two trees grow in the Yemen, one of which produced myrrh and the other frankincense. In the ancient world, these were used in cosmetics, religious ceremonies, and embalming. Since Mecca is at the crossroads of Africa, the Mediterranean, and the East, the location called forth an entrepreneurial spirit. The demand for myrrh and frankincense was high — the state funeral of a Roman Emperor's wife once exhausted a full year's production. The materials were light and precious, their transport profitable, and as a result, many Meccans were always exceedingly rich.

Before Islam, there were as many as six cities in ancient Arabia with temples similar to the Ka'bah. Yet the prestige of Mecca was greater than them all; this, and the wealth that trade brought, made the Quraysh the aristocrats of the Peninsula. After the patriarchal dominance of Qusayy, a council of the chiefs of the important families governed Mecca. The notables (*al-mala'*) met at the general council called the *Dār an-Nidwah* when any important decisions had to be made. The first *Dār an-Nidwah* was built by Qusayy ibn Qilāb himself, the chief of the Quraysh who had established the tribe in Mecca several generations before the Prophet. Qusayy also rebuilt the Ka'bah. This temple, a center of pilgrimage for the Arabs from ancient times, lies in the hollow of the valley. Because it was a matter of pride to live near the Ka'bah, the most important families were called the Quraysh *al-Biṭāḥ*, the "Quraysh of the Hollow". The houses of the Prophet, Abū Bakr, 'Umar, and 'Uthmān, were all located in the area around the present Grand Mosque; the house of Arqam and the building of the *Dār an-Nidwah*, were within what are now the precincts of the Mosque itself.

Because this valley is the lowest part of the city and its environs, it is subject to flooding. When the mountain rains are heavy, as can happen every few years, the water drains quickly and suddenly towards Mecca, unchecked by any vegetation. Flooding then occurs around the Ka'bah to the depth of several meters. On such occasions it has not been unknown for the circumambulation of the Ka'bah (*aṭ-ṭawāf*) to be performed swimming.

The Caliphs 'Umar and 'Uthmān attempted to control these floods by building dikes, but their efforts were no more successful than those of later Caliphs. At the present time there is a storm water project underway to remedy this ancient inconvenience.

During the *Jāhiliyyah*, (the "age of ignorance" before Islam), there were several important yearly fairs (*aswāq*) near Mecca in the truce of the holy months which suspended the perennial fighting and desert feuds. At 'Ukāẓ, desert poets declaimed their compositions, and the most acclaimed was written in gold letters and hung in the Ka'bah, such poems being known as *mu'allaqāt* ("the hung ones"). A number have survived to the present day. Another fair was held at Minā; the *suq al-A'rāb*. Both of these fairs were used as occasions to announce intercalations of extra months every few years in order to bring the lunar calendar into line with the solar, until these intercalations were forbidden by the Koran. Before the Hijrah, the Prophet had preached Islam at Minā and here such opponents as Abū Lahab attacked him with abuse, and hired poets insulted him in verse.

After Islam was established and Medinah became the seat of government, many important Meccan families migrated there. This, and the opening of other trade routes through the expansion of Islam, led to the decline of Mecca as a trading center, although the increase in pilgrimage traffic compensated somewhat for the loss. A number of the descendants of the Companions continued to live there, and it became for a time a place of culture and learning. In general, however, Mecca underwent a period of comparative neglect as political activity shifted to Medinah, Kūfah, Damascus, and finally Baghdad. As a result, there were frequent disorders in Mecca. At one time 'Abd Allāh ibn az-Zubayr seized the town and held it against the Umayyad Caliph, claiming the Caliphate for himself. At another, it was captured by a Khārijite leader, and in *317*/930, the Qarmaṭīs of East Arabia and Baḥrayn raided Mecca and carried off the Black Stone from the Ka'bah, keeping it in al-Ḥāsa, or perhaps Baḥrayn, for a number of years before returning it in *338*/956.

Thereafter, control of Mecca fell to the hands of *Sharīfs* (descendants of the Prophet), who ruled it from *350*/966 down to recent times, under the suzerainty of the Caliphs. In Ottoman times, the Hejaz (the western region of Arabia) was administered by a Sharīfian dynasty in the name of the Sultan in Istanbul, while Turkish troops were garrisoned in its cities.

In World War I, the Sharīf of Mecca, Ḥusayn, encouraged by the British, revolted against the Turks. His sons Fayṣal, 'Alī, and 'Abd Allāh led Arab forces in the fighting. After the war, Ḥusayn declared himself King of the Hejaz; 'Abd 'Allāh went on to become King of Transjordan, and Fayṣal, King of 'Irāq. 'Alī would have succeeded his father Ḥusayn but in *1344*/1924 Mecca, and later the rest of the Hejaz, were conquered by King 'Abd al-'Azīz Al Sa'ūd of the Najd. It was at first administered as a separate Kingdom, and then integrated into the Kingdom of Saudi Arabia.

Mecca today, except for the presence of the Ka'bah, is in outward appearance an ordinary Middle Eastern city. It is unusual only in that the population, in addition to the descendants of the Quraysh and the indigenous Arabs, has communities made up of immigrants from all parts of the Islamic world, as does Medinah. Virtually nothing remains of the characteristic and charming Hejazi style of architecture, with its projecting, latticed *rawshān* windows. Upon the site of Abū Bakr's house, which in his time he had already turned into a Mosque, there stands today a Mosque named after him. Upon the site of the Prophet's house is a library, and on that of 'Alī's, a school. Two Sharīfian palaces survive as administrative buildings. A contemporary mosque called the "Mosque of the *Jinn*" stands upon the site of an oratory where the *Jinn*, or people of the subtle world, were said to have come and pledged fealty to the Prophet. At the top of the hill known as Abū Qubays, which looks down upon the Ka'bah and over the city, stands a mosque called the Masjid Ibrāhīm, popularly known as "the Mosque of Bilāl". In Minā, at the pass of 'Aqabah, where the Medinans made their two oaths of fealty, is a graceful mosque of a simple but authentic Arabian style, which, together with what remains of the Mosque of Sīnān within the Grand Mosque, is the only relic of traditional architecture.

Immediately adjacent to the city lie the pilgrimage places of Minā, Muzdalifah, and 'Arafāt, and also *Jabal Nūr*, the "Mountain of Light" where in a cave at the top (*Ghār Ḥirā'*) the revelation of the Koran began. Also not far away is the *Jabal Thawr*, another cave where the Prophet hid with Abū Bakr on their escape to Medinah.

Mecca has a number of other names of which *Umm al-Qurā*, or "Mother of Cities" is the most frequently used. It is surrounded on all sides by a restricted holy area, called the *ḥarām* of Mecca, where the taking of life, except of harmful or dangerous creatures, is forbidden, and where only Muslims are allowed to enter. *See also* 'AQABAH; 'ARAFĀT; BLACK STONE; KA'BAH; MINĀ; MUZDALIFAH; PILGRIMAGE; QURAYSH; ZAMZAM.

Medicine (Ar. *aṭ-ṭibb*). In classical times the study of medicine was part of philosophy, and all physicians were also philosophers. Medical studies among the Muslims derived from the Nestorian Christians of Jundishāpūr, a city which was located near present day Ahvāz in Iran. Jundishāpūr was a school founded by the Nestorians in the third century under the Persian Sāssānid dynasty. This school, which transmitted both the philosophy of the Greeks and the medical science of Hippocrates and Galen, produced physicians who practiced throughout the Islamic Near East. Among them were such influential figures as the Nestorian Gabriel Bakhtishishu, physician to the Caliph Hārūn ar-Rashīd, and Ḥunayn Ibn Isḥāq, physician to the Caliph al-Mutawakkil. The "Ṣābians" of Ḥarrān (Carrhae) in Northern Syria, now within the borders of Turkey, a pagan religious and ethnic group, also transmitted Greek and Babylonian learning to the Muslims.

Hospitals were founded in Baghdad around the year *287*/900, and later in Cairo and elsewhere. With the spread of such institutions, medicine developed to an advanced state. Al-Muqtadir (Caliph *295-320*/908-932) had physicians in Baghdad licenced so that the incompetent could be weeded out; 860 passed the test. The scientific heritage of the Greeks, Egyptians, Babylonians, Persians, and later of India, was fused into the corpus known as Islamic science. The Muslims established, moreover, a comprehensive *materia medica* based upon the study and classification of medicinal plants by Dioscorides and other Greek scientists.

The most famous figures in the Islamic science of medicine are ar-Rāzī (Rhazes), Ibn Sīnā (Avicenna), Ibn Baytār, al-Bīrūnī, and Ibn Zuhr. *See* MARISTAN.

Medinah. The epithet *al-Munawwarah*, "the radiant", is usually added to the name of this city. Originally it was called Yathrib, a name with pagan connotations, and became known as *madīnat an-nabī*, the "city of the Prophet" after the Hijrah. At the time of the revelation there were two Arab tribes that inhabited Medinah, the Aws and the Khazraj, both of South Arabian origin, and several Jewish tribes, the Banū Naḍīr, the Banū Qaynuqā', and the Banū Qurayẓah.

Medinah was an oasis famed for the dates from its palm groves. It is situated in the midst of volcanic hills around a small plain called the *manakhah* (from *nikh*, the command to make a camel kneel) where caravans to the city would stop and camp.

The two Arab tribes, aided by the Jewish tribes allied with them, had been in an intermittent state of civil war immediately before Islam appeared to call the Medinans to a new way of life. In 620, six men of Medinah of the tribe of Khazraj, on pilgrimage to Mecca, entered Islam by the hand of the Prophet at the pass of 'Aqabah. The first man of Medinah to become a Muslim was named Iyās ibn Mu'ādh. In the following two years, the first Muslims returned to Mecca and brought others with them. In 622 seventy-three men and two women took an oath of fealty to the Prophet which, for the men, also included the duty of protecting him. In September of that year the Prophet emigrated to

Medinah and was joined by seventy emigrant Meccans called the *Muhājirūn*, whilst the native Medinan Muslims were known as the *Anṣār*, "helpers". The creation of an Islamic state led inevitably to war against the Meccans and their Beduin allies which ended in victory for the Prophet and the Muslims in *8*/630. The Prophet remained in Medinah for the rest of his life, and Medinah was the capital of the Islamic empire until the Caliph 'Alī moved his headquarters to the military camp-city of Kūfah. Medinah was a center of intellectual activity for some time, but after *63*/683, when it was sacked by troops of the Umayyads because of unrest and rebellion, the city went into decline and much of the population migrated to Spain.

Almost everyone who makes the pilgrimage to Mecca also visits Medinah to pay homage at the tomb of the Prophet. Next to the Prophet in the Prophet's mosque are also buried the Caliphs Abū Bakr and 'Umar. Not far from the Prophet's mosque is the al-Bāqī' cemetery where the Caliph 'Uthmān and many Companions are buried, as well as other great figures in the history of Islam. Inside the Prophet's mosque is a structure often called the "Sepulchre of Fāṭimah". It stands where the house of 'Alī and Fāṭimah stood, adjacent to the Prophet's house. But Faṭimah was doubtless buried in the al-Bāqī' cemetary. At Qubā', in the suburbs of Medinah, stands the first mosque of Islam, the *Masjid at-Taqwā*. Other famous mosques in the city are the *Ghamāmah* (*Musalla 'n-Nabī*) where the Prophet prayed for rain, the *Sabaq* mosque which was the site of the original festival prayers, the *Jum'ah* mosque, and several small mosques near the *Jabal Salā'*. Just outside the city is the *Jabal Uhud*, where the famous battle took place. *See* 'AQABAH; MOSQUE of the PROPHET; MUḤAMMAD.

Meditation, *see* DHIKR; TAFAKKUR.

Meḥmet II (*833-886*/1429-1481). An Ottoman Sultan, Meḥmet II was known as "the Conqueror" (*an-Nāṣir*) for his conquest of Constantinople in *857*/1453. He also conquered the Balkans, adding vast territories to the empire. Mehmet is credited with the design of the cannons, the largest yet built, needed to bombard Constantinople during its fifty day siege. The Sultan devised much of the strategy and joined in the fighting himself. At one point, overcome with excitement, he drew his sword and rode his horse into the Bosphorus, swimming among the ships and rallying the sailors during a sea battle.

It was his bold decision to carry ships overland, around the chain barriers impeding entrance to the channel of the Golden Horn, which proved to be the decisive maneuver that led to the Turkish victory. Seventy-two light Turkish ships were dragged from the Bosphorus over the isthmus of Pera to the Golden Horn. Thousands of workmen prepared slipways greased with oil, tallow, and fat, working overnight and in secret, for if the Byzantines had realized what was happening, they could have destroyed much of the Turkish fleet. Once inside the Golden Horn, an attempt by the Venetians in Constantinople to sink the intruding Turkish fleet was betrayed by their commercial rivals the Genoese, and failed.

The Turks then built a pontoon bridge of barrels to bring another army over to besiege the city, and attempted tunnelling beneath the walls; they had reached a distance of one-quarter mile inside the city walls before a Byzantine engineer succeeded in heading them off with a counter-tunnel, which connected with the Turkish one, to foil the sappers. The Turks also made a breach in the walls with a siege tower which the Byzantines succeeded, at great sacrifice, in filling. After more tunnels and more siege towers, the Turks offered favorable terms to the Byzantine Emperor but he, even though he had learned that help was not going to come from his Venetian allies, refused, saying "it is not in my power nor in the power of anyone here to surrender this city. We are ready to die and we shall leave this world without regret."

Even so, by 27 May 1453, the Turks were on the point of withdrawal when a military leader named Zagan Pasha, made an impassioned appeal against it; a referundum was put to the army and it was decided to venture another assault. The final attack was amphibious. Two waves of Turks, (the attacking army was over one hundred thousand strong, the defenders only a few thousand) were beaten back. A third was almost repelled. Then confusion developed amongst the defenders, signals were misunderstood, consternation grew, and a Janissary force breached the outer wall and came upon a secret gate, through which the Byzantines were receiving supplies. This gate had not been locked, and suddenly the Turks found an open door through which to enter the city. The Emperor threw off his regalia, joined in the hand to hand fighting and was killed. On 29 May 1453, Constantinople fell.

As a Sultan, Meḥmet II was fairly liberal towards the populations he conquered, extending protection to the Christian churches and monasteries that fell under his sway. In fact, in the end, the Ottomans became virtually the protectors of the Orthodox church. Meḥmet II knew Persian, Arabic and Turkish, as well as some Latin and Greek. He wrote poetry in Persian and was a patron of the arts. *See* HAGIA SOPHIA; OTTOMANS.

Menangkabau. The central region of the island of Sumatra in Indonesia, and its ethnic group, which is matriarchal. This region was one of the first to be Islamicised in Indonesia, starting in the *5th*/11th century, undergoing influences from Atjeh in the north.

Menstruation (Ar. *maḥā'id, ḥā'id*). Considered a state of ritual impurity, it excludes a woman from performing *ṣalāh* (ritual prayers, which do not then have to be made up), from touching the Koran, sexual intercourse; entering a mosque (but not the Grand Mosque of Mecca, which can be entered since *al-Masjid al-Ḥarām* is an exception to many ordinary rules, as are certain other sanctuaries which are open to anyone in any state. Menstruation does not preclude making *du'ā'* (personal prayer).

At the end of a period of menstruation, a woman performs the greater ablution (*ghusl*) to restore ritual purity. The state of menstruation does not affect the performance of pilgrimage, either *ḥajj* or *'umrah*; these can be performed, as well as the circumambulation (*ṭawāf*) of the Ka'bah, but the canonical prayers (*salāh*) are omitted. The *du'ā*, however, are performed. According to legal decisions based on Ḥadīth concerning special circumstances, a menstrual flow which never ceases, or chronic discharge, is disregarded from the point of view of ritual. In such a case, rituals are performed as if the person were in a state of normal ritual purity except that the *wuḍū'*, or *tayyamum*, is performed before every prayer. *See* ABLUTIONS; GHUSL; TAYAMMUM; WUḌŪ'.

Metaphysics, *see* FIVE DIVINE PRESENCES.

Metawila (also romanized as "Metalwi, from Arabic *mutawālin*, pl. *matāwilah*, "successor"). A colloquial designation in Lebanon and Syria for Twelve-Imām Shī'ites, but also applied by extension to the sects of the Ismā'īlīs, 'Alawīs, and Druzes.

The Twelve-Imām Shī'ites of Lebanon have been amongst its poorest and most backward people. In 1959 an Iranian Mullā named Mūsā-ṣ-Ṣadr came to Lebanon, and from that point there began a marked growth in the community's self-awareness. Until that time the community had been dominated by important local Shī'ite families such as the al-As'ad and the Ḥamada. Under Mūsā-ṣ-Ṣadr's leadership, representative organs of political expression were created. In December 1967 the Shī'ite Supreme National Council was set up by act of parliament, and in 1969 Mūsā-ṣ-Ṣadr was elected its president.

In 1974, Mūsā-ṣ-Ṣadr created *Amal* as a political organization to mobilize the Shī'ites in the Baqā' valley and in southern Lebanon. Like other political groupings in Lebanon, *Amal* acquired a militia. Shortly thereafter, other Shī'ite groups of a more expressly military nature came into being, as a result of continued political upheaval in Lebanon, notably *Jihād*, and later *Ḥizb Allāh*, a radical military organization directly linked with revolutionary Iran and associated with a leader called Shaykh Muḥammad Ḥusayn Faḍl Allāh.

Imām Mūsā-ṣ-Ṣadr was mysteriously abducted on a visit to Libya in 1978, and is now presumed dead, a fact which his followers in Lebanon continued to refuse to accept. Before his disappearance he issued, at the request of the 'Alāwīs of Syria, a fatwā to the effect that they are a legitimate branch of Islam. *See* LEBANON; SHĪ'ISM.

Mevlevi (Arabic *Mawlawī*). A Sufi order in Turkey founded by Mevlana (Mawlānā, "our lord") Jalāl ad-Dīn ār-Rūmī (d. *672*/1273). The members of this order are sometimes called "Whirling Dervishes" in the West because part of their method of spiritual realization consists of dancing in which they revolve to the music of flutes, drums, and the chants of *ilahis* (Turkish Sufi songs). The training of a Mevlevi dervish includes exercises for the dance in which the first two toes of the right foot grasp a nail on the floor while the dervish pivots around it. The dervishes' turning requires a great deal of practice to master, but is extremely graceful when performed in a ritual meeting. The presence of the founder, Jalāl ad-Dīn ar-Rūmī, is strongly manifested in the order, and many dervishes experience intense personal relationships with him.

The dancing became a formal part of the Mevlevi method with ar-Rūmī's successor, his son

Sultan Veled. During a Mevlevi dancing session (*samā'*), a red sheepskin is placed upon the floor, symbolizing the presence of Shams-i Ṭabrīz, the mysterious figure who inflamed Jalāl ad-Dīn ar-Rūmī with Divine awareness. The dancing lasts about an hour, in four movements called *salams*; at the end, the *pīr*, or spiritual master, makes his appearance among the dancers. The *ney*, or reed flute, figures prominently in the symbolism of the dervishes. The trembling of the reed as the breath — or spirit — gives it life and its "cry" recalls the nostalgia of its separation from the rushes where it grew, from its origin, as ar-Rūmī's poetry declares. And the reed crying for return to the Principle is the Spiritual Master, or ar-Rūmī himself.

Hearken to this Reed forlorn,
Breathing, ever since 'twas torn
From its rushy bed, a strain
Of impassioned love and pain.

The secret of my song, though near,
None can see and none can hear.
Oh, for a friend to know the sign
And mingle all his soul with mine!

'Tis the flame of Love that fired me,
'Tis the wine of Love inspired me.
Wouldst thou learn how lovers bleed,
Hearken, hearken to the Reed!

The dance is called *muqābalah* ("encounter") and is an expression of the doctrine of the Mevlevis whereby the soul encounters, and awakes to Reality; it is universal in its sentiments, and almost Hindu in spirit. Each dancer sees his own face in that of the others, who are like mirrors to him; but although it is his own face, through the repetition of the reflection in others, his individuality becomes unreal and the other becomes oneself. The dancing moves in a semi-circle. This is creation, the arc of descent proceeding away from God (*qaws-i-nuzūl*). While creation descends, however, creatures within creation ascend. As the dancing progresses, the Shaykh enters and the culmination of the furthest point of the first arc brings the dancers face to face with the Spiritual Master. This is the moment when night changes into dawn (*al-fajr*), the sun rises, and the arc of ascent (*qaws-i-'urūj*) begins which leads to realization. The dancers whirl to the other side, completing in dance one whole cycle of creation and return to the One.

It should be mentioned, at the risk of disturbing what is a compelling metaphor, that this rather powerful imagery of souls passing through different stages of existence in the world is not found in orthodox theology. While it may be useful in evoking a recognition and a desire to return to the source, it also implies a permanence of the substance of the soul, a kind of divinity of created substance. For this reason metempsychosis is not accepted by orthodox Islam or by any monotheism. Islam holds that man is created directly into the human state.

The Mevlevi order was forbidden in Turkey, as were all other Sufi orders, during the initial secularization of the country in 1925, but it has since been allowed to return to the surface of Turkish life. Some Mevlevis have presented performances of their music and dancing in the West.

A contemporary Mevlevi *Pīr*, Shaykh Sulayman Loras has said:

> If we do not strive for inner perfection, we will remain what we are now — talking animals. The world has never been without teachers. Each age has its teachers. Jesus, Buddha, and Muḥammad were some of the great ones, but there are always *aqṭāb* [plural of *quṭb*, someone who fulfills the role of "spiritual axis"], special beings who take care of the world. The perfect man, the complete man, lies within each one of us.

Mevlevis are also found in Syria, Egypt, and other countries which were once part of the Ottoman Empire; however, at the present time only the branches in Konya and in Istanbul are active. Ar-Rūmī said: "Come, come, whoever you are, unbeliever or fire-worshiper, come. Our convent is not of desperation. Even if you have broken your vows a hundred times, Come, come again." *See* JALĀL ad-DĪN ar-RŪMĪ.

Miḥrāb. A niche in the wall of a mosque to indicate the *qiblah*, the direction of Mecca, towards which all Muslims turn in prayer. It also provides a reflecting surface so that the voice of the Imām is clearly heard by those behind him. The *miḥrāb* was introduced around *90*/709; in the Mosque of Qubā', a stone as a direction marker was used in the time of the Prophet. As an architectural device, the miḥrāb-type niche appears in the Hellenist synagogue of Doura Europos. The miḥrāb also has its antecedents in the *cella*, a small room or niche in a temple where a statue of the god or goddess was kept, and to which access was sometimes restricted to priests. When the Koran says that Mary stayed in the *miḥrāb* (3:37), it may be referring to this.

The earliest surviving *miḥrāb* may be that in Jerusalem, in the chamber beneath the rock in the Dome of the Rock (*Qubbat aṣ-Ṣakhrah*). However, the most famous and splendid *miḥrāb* is unquestionably that of the mosque of Cordova. Decorated with multicolored mosaics of melted glass and gold that were a gift from the Byzantine Emperor Nicephoras to the Caliph Ḥākim II, the niche is carved alabaster and marble, and the ceiling is a single piece of marble in the shape of a seashell, creating remarkable acoustics: a mere whisper is reflected audibly a great distance.

The *miḥrāb* embodies the symbolism of the cave, the hidden place, the cavity within a mountain. The cave is a universal token of inwardness, initiation and profound worship amongst all peoples, from the *kivas* of the Hopi to the cave of the thousand Buddhas. In the cave, the sky cannot be seen, and yet it is within it that heavenly reality must be found, just as it is through faith that man is saved. The cave is taken to be the heart, and the mountain which surrounds it is the physical world, or body, which imprisons the spirit. It is within the heart that one encounters the truth.

Or dost thou think the Men of the Cave
and Er-Rakeem were among Our signs a wonder?
When the youths took refuge in the Cave
saying,'Our Lord, give us mercy from Thee,
and furnish us with rectitude in our affair.'
Then We smote their ears
many years in the Cave...
And we strengthened their hearts, when
they stood up and said, 'Our Lord is
the Lord of the heavens and earth;
we will not call upon any god, apart
from Him, or then we had spoken outrage.
These our people have taken to them
other gods, apart from Him. Ah, if only
they would bring some clear authority
regarding them! But who does greater
evil than he who forges against God a lie?
So, when you have gone apart from them
and that they serve, excepting God,
take refuge in the cave, and your Lord
will unfold to you of His Mercy, and will
furnish you with a gentle issue of your affair.'
And thou mightest have seen the sun,
when it rose, inclining from their Cave
towards the right, and, when it set,
passing them by on the left, while they
were in a broad fissure of the Cave.
That was one of God's signs; whomsoever
God guides, he is rightly guided,
and whomsoever He leads astray, thou
wilt not find for him a protector...
(18:9-11, 14-17)

Mīlād, *see* MAWLID an-NABĪ.

Millah. A particular religion, creed, faith, sect or spiritual community, as opposed to *dīn*, which denotes religion in general and Islam specifically. *Millah* is often used in the compound the "religion of Abraham" (*millat Ibrāhīm*). The Turkish form *Millet* was used in Ottoman Turkey as a name for the religions within the Empire; but the word is more usually used in both Turkish and Persian to mean "nation", "people" or "state".

Mimbar, *see* MINBAR.

Minā. Islamic tradition proclaims it the site of Abraham's sacrifice of the ram in place of his son Ismā'īl (Ishmael); the spot is on the eastern side of the rocky valley and is known as the *majār al-kabsh* ("the place of the bleating of the ram"). The small town of Minā, five kilometers/three miles, from Mecca, only comes to life at pilgrimage time.

Not far from the town of Minā is a rise known as the *'Aqabah* ("the incline") where the first groups of Medinans swore fealty to the Prophet; here a mosque called the *Masjid al-Bay'ah* (the "Mosque of the Covenant") stands today, a noble — and rare — example of the traditional Hejazi mosque style remarkably preserved amidst rampant modernization.

The valley is called the *sūq al-'Arāb* ("fair of the Arabs"), for Minā, along with 'Ukāẓ, was one of the great yearly fairs of pre-Islamic Arabia. In the center of this area — now enclosed by gigantic pedestrian ramps so that the thousands of pilgrims can approach on two levels — are the three *jamarāt*, or pillars, which are stoned as one of the rites of pilgrimage. They represent three occasions on the way to the fateful sacrifice when Satan appeared to Ismā'īl (Ishmael) to warn him of Abraham's intention (or to dissuade Abraham), and was three times stoned by Ismā'īl.

The Khayf mosque stands in Minā; here pilgrims pray during the pilgrimage. Throughout the valley are sites now forgotten, where mosques once stood marking the places where Koranic verses were revealed. *See* MECCA; PILGRIMAGE.

Minaret (from Ar. *manārah*, a "lighthouse"). Towers from which the Muezzin (*mu'adhdhin*) makes the call to prayers (*adhān*). The first minarets were built towards the end of the first Hijrah century. *See* MOSQUE.

Minbar (also written and pronounced mimbar). A pulpit in a mosque used by the Imām for preaching the Friday sermon (khuṭbah). It is actually a movable staircase. The first minbar was that used by the Prophet and it had three steps. When Abū Bakr used it as Caliph he only mounted to the second step; 'Umar to the first; but 'Uthmān to the second, and that is what Imāms normally do today, although minbars are usually built with many more steps. A speaker's podium has come into use in some places instead of the minbar. The oldest minbars which have survived today are the minbar of the Kairouan mosque in Tunisia, and the minbar of Andalus mosque in Fez, which are in museums.

The Manicheans had a similar structure which functioned as an altar, also known as the "throne of Mani, called from Greek a bēma, with five steps. Upon the fifth step a picture of Mani was placed and prayers and speech were addressed to it during the Bēma ceremony.

Minorities. When Islamic law was in force (today it has largely been replaced by civil law in most countries), recognized non-Muslim minorities were allowed to retain their own legal systems, at least for their internal affairs. (This recognition would exclude idolators, although in practice non-monotheist religions or other non-conforming religions were assimilated to the status of "People of the Book" [*Ahl al-Kitāb*], sometimes by being considered Ṣābians.) Thus, while wine is forbidden for Muslims, Christians and Jews were not forbidden to make, sell and drink it.

In Morocco, for example, Rabbinic law is still recognized as applicable within the Jewish community. In medieval Baghdad, the ancient head of the Jewish community, the Resh Galuta, was given a wide latitude of authority, which in some periods went so far as to allow him to judge disputes involving Muslims and Jews (and not simply those between Jews). Tribal law, and local customary law (*adat*) exist side by side with Islamic law and civil law in many places. *See* AHL al-KITĀB.

Mīqāt (lit. "appointed time", "date" and by extension, "place and time of meeting"). On the traditional overland approaches to Mecca, and situated in some cases a considerable distance away, are the points each called *mīqāt*, at which pilgrims on their way to perform the greater pilgrimage (*ḥajj*) assume *iḥrām*, that is, consecration and the ritual dress, that marks it. Pilgrims approaching Mecca by way of the Red Sea would, at the latest, put on *iḥrām* when the ship passes the latitude of one of the *mīqāt*. Today pilgrims coming to Jeddah by air often put on *iḥrām* at the point of embarkation.

Some of the *mawāqīt* (pl. of *mīqāt*) are: Dhāt 'Irq, 80 kms to the northeast of Mecca; Dhāt Ḥulayfah 250 kms north of Mecca and 9 kms away from Medinah; Juhfah, to the northwest of Mecca 180 kms distant; *Qarn al-Manāzil* 50 kilometers to the city's east; and Yalamlam, sixty kms to the southeast.

Mīr. A title of respect used in the Indo-Persian world for descendants of the Prophet, it is a contraction of the Arabic amīr, "prince", "commander".

Miracles (Ar. *mu'jizāt*). Some minor traditions attribute a number of miracles to the Prophet but there is nothing conclusive about their nature; they play no role in Islamic theology, nor do they embody any essential element in the life of the Prophet. One event which is thought to be miracle is called the "splitting of the moon". This is deduced from the beginning of Sūrah 54:

> The Hour has drawn nigh; the moon is split.
> Yet if they see a sign they turn away, and they say
> 'A continuous sorcery!'
> They have cried lies, and followed their caprices;
> but every matter is settled.
> And there have come to them such tidings
> as contain a deterrent —
> a Wisdom far-reaching;
> yet warnings do not avail.

The notion that this passage refers to an event called forth by the Prophet in Mecca before the Hijrah appears to be only the result of late Koranic interpretation, and thus conjecture, and is not supported by any contemporary references. It has become a part of Islamic folklore, but the Koranic passage should rather be taken to refer to a coming apocalyptic event, or possibly an allusion to the dissolution of the world at one's own death. The idea that the Prophet split the moon may be a confusion with an illusion said to have been created by al-Muqanna', a revolutionary religious leader and follower of Abū Muslim, who is said to have made the moon appear and disappear by the use of a bowl of quicksilver in a well.

Thus it can be said that while Islam does not deny miracles, neither does it accord them any role of significance. If there is a miracle which is often pointed to, it is the Koran itself. And the Koran says (17:37): "And walk not in the earth exultant. Lo! thou can'st not rend the earth, nor can'st thou stretch to the height of the hills." Then there are writers who have also dismissed miracles:

If thou can'st walk on water
thou art no better than a straw.
If thou can'st fly in the air
Thou art no better than a fly.
Conquer thy heart
That thou mayest become somebody. (Anṣārī)

And, the Persian Bāyazīd al-Biṣṭāmī (d. *261*/875) said:

> Even if you see a man endowed with miraculous powers to the point of rising in the air, do not let yourself be deluded, but investigate whether he observes the Divine precepts and prohibitions, whether he stays within the limits of religion and whether he accomplishes the duties this imposes upon him.

But this is misleading because Biṣṭāmī is really saying that miracles are possible, just not very important. In other words, he is saying do not pay attention to any miraculous powers that I may have (in magic what is termed a "hook" and "load" to created the desired belief). It was in fact the school of the Drunken Sufis, and especially al-Ḥallāj that used stories of miracles systematically to influence the gullible. Al-Ḥallāj's many miracles, which Massignon called "harmless legerdemain", can be explained as stage magic. One famous "miracle" is the following:

> Hallaj wished to convert a certain Ibn Harun, a man who used to hold salons where the better-known Baghdad shaykhs engaged in discussion. When all the guests were seated on one of these occasions, Hallaj opened the conversation with this riddle: "have you no time to recognize me? Then recognize my verity! My first is softer than my fourth, my fifth is longer than my third, My second commonest of all. The thrice three threes. What is the word? Divine; and you shall see me stand upright Where Moses stood, on Sinai, wrapped in light." Everyone was baffled.
>
> It happened that Ibn Harun's little son was sick at that time, and sinking fast. And the host presently said to Hallaj: My boy is sick; I wish you would pray for him.
>
> He is already healed, said Hallaj; don't worry any more. It was only a few minutes later that the child was brought in, looking as if he had never been ill. Everyone present was dumbfounded; Ibn Harun pulled out a sealed purse and offered it to Hallaj.
>
> Shaykh, said he, use this as you will.
>
> Now the salon where they were sitting opened on the Tigris bank. Hallaj, taking the purse, which [supposedly] contained three thousand dinars, threw it into the river.
>
> You had some questions to ask me, I think, he said, addressing the company of shaykhs; but what questions could you ask of me? for I see only too well how right you are, and how wrong I am.
>
> And with these words he went away.
>
> Next day, Ibn Harun paid visits to the various shaykhs who had been present with Hallaj, and showed them the very purse which Hallaj had tossed into the stream. Yesterday, said he, I could not stop thinking about the present I had offered him: and I began to wish he had not thrown it into the river. Scarcely an hour after that thought came into mind, a poor disciple of his came to my gate to say: The shaykh greets you and bids me say to you: Make an end of regret and take this purse; to one who obeys Him God gives power, even over earth and water. And he put my own purse in my hand."

In other versions, the messenger appears with the purse dripping wet while a new company of visitors is present listening as the "miracle" cure of the previous evening is being recounted; the purse is opened in front of the listeners, and the gold is inside. The explanation will be familiar to stage magicians. The riddle is intended to distract the audience's attention ("misdirection"). No one sees the child sick (the "load"), it is only the word of the accomplice, Ibn Harun, and the child is too young to be questioned; a healthy child is brought out; an empty purse is thrown into the river, and a similar purse, wet as if miraculously retrieved from the river is shown to the audience, with the gold.

Explaining al-Ḥallāj's other miracles was a popular pastime in the Middle Ages. *See also* KARĀMĀT.

Mi'rāj, *see* NIGHT JOURNEY.

Mīr Dāmād (d. *1041*/1631). A Persian scholar and philosopher, the teacher of Mullā Sadra. Mir Damad's full name was Muḥammad Baqīr ibn ad-Dāmād. He combined the *Ishraqī* ("illuminationist") philosophy of Suhrawardi with theology and mysticism. This kind of synthesis became characteristic of Shī'ite thinking. His most famous work is *aṣ-Ṣirāṭ al-Mustaqīm* ("The Straight Path").

Mīr Fendereski (d. *1050*/1640). Shī'ite theologian.

Mirzā. An Indo-Persian title of respect.

Miskīn (lit. "poor"). In addition to its meaning of someone who is poor in material terms, it is used to mean, in a very laudatory sense, someone who is meek, or "poor in spirit", and thus worthy of sympathy. As such it is a very frequently heard expression.

Miswāk (from the word *sāka*, "to brush", "to polish"). A toothstick, often mistakenly translated as toothpick. It is a method of cleaning the teeth, highly recommended by tradition, using a suitable twig with the bark cut and the fibers loosened by some preliminary chewing. The end fibers become a convenient brush for scrubbing the teeth after eating. Because it is hallowed by the Sunnah, many pious people use the miswāk in addition to the modern toothbrush.

Miyan. A title of respect in the Indo-Persian world.

Mīzān (lit. "the balance scale"). The Koran's symbol of harmony in creation and of cosmic equilibrium, and also of eschatological justice and retribution for deeds in this life. (The scales are also an important symbol in Zoroastrianism.)

> The sun and the moon are made punctual,
> the stars and trees adore;
> and the sky He hath uplifted:
> and He hath set the balance scale.
> Transgress not in the balance scale,
> but observe the measure strictly,
> nor fall short thereof. (55:5-9)

The scales of this balance weigh one's works of good and evil down to an atom's weight.

> When earth is shaken with a mighty shaking
> and earth brings forth her burdens,
> and Man says, 'What ails her?'
> upon that day she shall tell her tidings
> for that her Lord has inspired her.
> Upon that day men shall issue in scatterings
> to see their works,
> and whoso has done an atom's weight of good
> shall see it,
> and whoso has done an atom's weight of evil
> shall see it. (99)

Some of the early literalist interpreters in Islam took the mīzān, along with God's throne (*'arsh*), footstool (*al-kursī*), the pen (*al-qalam*), the guarded tablet (*al-lawḥ al-maḥfūẓ*), to be actual celestial entities rather than symbols. The term is also used for a "ground design" in architecture, and as a technical term for musical patterns and rhythmic modes. *See* ISTAWĀ.

Modernization, *see* ALIGARH; 'ABDUH; KEMAL, MUṢṬFĀ; SALAFIYYAH; TANẒĪMĀT.

Moghuls. The celebrated Muslim dynasty of India, noted for the cultural refinements of its rule which, by blending elements from Persia and India, created one of the most sophisticated civilizations known to history. Its achievements were outstanding in the spheres of architecture, music, literature, and in all the arts of living, not least cuisine.

The Moghul Empire was founded by Bābur (*888-937*/1483-1530), a descendant of Tīmūr on his father's side, and of Jenghiz Khan on his mother's. The name "Moghul" is simply "Mongol" in a phonetic form adapted to the Persian language and the Arabic script. Bābur became a ruler at the age of eleven in Ferghana in Transoxiana, and conquered Samarkand at the age of fourteen. Then he lost both, and went off to Afghanistan, seized Kabul and then Qandahar. At the Battle of Panipat (*932*/1526) he defeated the Sultan of Delhi and established his own capital there and at Agra. His son Hūmāyūn (*912-963*/1506-1556) warred for years with his brothers over the succession, and only reigned effectively for the last six months of his life. He introduced the art of Persian miniature painting into the court.

Hūmāyūn's son Akbar (*949-1014*/1542-1605), called the Great, ruled over the greatest extension of the Moghul Empire, comprising most of northern India and Afghanistan. He devised a syncretic religion called *din-i-ilāhī* ("religion of God") an amalgam of several religions that Akbar was acquainted with in India, including Christianity. This syncretic mixture, of which he made himself the head, was only practiced at court. In the Moghul Empire of Akbar's time, Hindus played an important role in the government. He created the class of officials called Manṣabdārs (*see* MANṢAB). Akbar built Fatehpur Sikri near Agra to be his capital, but had to abandon it before occupation for lack of water supply.

The next Emperor, Jahangīr (*977-1037*/1569-1627) built palaces at Lahore, as well as the Shalimar gardens. Shāh Jahān (*1001-1077*/1592-1666) built the Tāj Mahal, as well as the Red Fort in Delhi and the Great Mosque. The Red Fort has a famous inscription in Persian: "If there is a paradise on earth, it is here, it is here, it is here" (also ascribed to others). Shāh Jahān's successor Awrangzeb (*1028-1118*/1618-1707), also called 'Alamgīr, was the most zealous Muslim of all the Moghul Emperors. He enforced Islamic rules in a court that was more famed for omitting them, and thereby earned the enmity of his Hindu subjects and officials in a way that had not occurred under his predecessors. It was doubtless this action on Awrangzeb's part that accelerated, if it did not indeed initiate, the decline of Moghul power; disaffection by Hindus and attempts to seize central and local power by Muslim princes and princelings, together with the armies of Afghanistan and Persia, then weakened the dynasty further.

Awrangzeb was the last of the Emperors known as the "Great Moghuls". Although he actually extended Moghul rule into the Deccan, the decline otherwise in Moghul authority was met with renewed vigor on the part of Hindus, and expansion by the British. In *1274*/1858 the last Moghul, who no longer had any real power, was deposed by the British for alleged complicity in the Sepoy Mutiny.

Monasticism. Islam expressly forbids the institution of monks or priests. Christian monks were known in pre-Islamic Arabia and may even have been a familiar phenomenon; but as Islam spreads a net of salvation for every man, in his daily social life, it precludes the setting aside of a class of men in a category different from society as a whole. Nevertheless, numerous men have lived as religious recluses, including such celebrated saints as Ibn Mashīsh. There was even an institution of those called *al-Murābiṭūn* ("the bound ones"), who dedicated some years of their lives to live in isolation in remote outposts called rubuṭ (sing. *ribāṭ*) in order to defend the frontiers of *Dār al-Islām* ("Abode of Islam"). *See also* PRIESTS.

Mongols. The Mongols were a people of the Siberian forests who came from the North into the steppes of Mongolia. Calling themselves the children of "the blue-grey fox and the fallow deer", and mimicking the life of totem animals, they were Shamanists; that is, as in Shintoism and the religion of the Indians of North America, they saw God as a Spirit whose Presence is active in nature. The greatest manifestation of this Great Spirit was "the Eternal Blue Heaven"; but, like the Japanese *Kami*, It also appeared in distinct manifestations called *Tengri*. The Mongols followed as leaders those who, through visions and theurgic power, such as calling forth "a storm of darkness" to confound the enemy, showed that the Spirit moved in them. Even after they became Buddhists, visions and a magical sense of the universe continued to dominate their religious understanding. The Mongol Empire, carved out at the expense of the Ch'in dynasty in North China and the Sung in South China, was founded by Temujin (1162-1227), a great-grandson of Qabul Khan; his family having fallen on hard times, Temujin assumed the power-name of Jenghiz Khān ("Oceanic", or universal ruler, perhaps "Ruler between the Seas"). His former name of Temujin means "Blacksmith" a name also implying powers of sorcery.

The orphaned son of a Khan, whose mother fought like a wolf for the survival of her children, Temujin himself had to regain his stolen bride

Börte, and fight his way back to power, making alliances with his blood brothers, and resorting to mutual oath-taking whereby a follower would abandon his tribal identity to attach himself to Temujin alone. He united the Mongol tribes and was declared paramount Khan of the Mongols by an assembly (*quriltai*) of Mongol chiefs in 1206 at Qaraqorum. Through a Uighur scholar named Tatatonga employed by Jenghiz Khan, the Mongols adopted the Manichean Uighur script which is derived from Aramaic through Soghdian, and in 1240 the first Mongol book was written down: the *Altan Daptīr* ("the Golden Book") of which the Persian historian Rashīd ad-Dīn aṭ-Ṭabīb was given some accounts by the Il-Khanid Maḥmūd Ghazan. He was not shown the book for, in the belief of the Mongols, such a Chronicle represented a fearful magical power that could be turned against them. It was probably this book, or one similar to it, that was taken to China and transcribed into Chinese after the Mongols had lost power, as the *Yuan Ch'ao Pi Shih* ("The Secret History of the Mongols"). The Mongol legends speak of a dream that Temujin saw in a cave, in which a spirit, later identified with a Bodhisattva, commanded him to restore the earth to the primordial condition it had known before civilization hid the face of nature. When Temujin awoke from the prophetic dream, he found on his hand a ring that confirmed his mission. In the subsequent Mongol invasions, it was indeed as if some pent-up force had suddenly exploded with primeval power.

Beginning with campaigns in 1205, 1207 and 1209, Jenghiz Khan led the Mongols and their allied Turkic tribes to destroy the kingdom of the Western Hsia, and drive the Ch'in to the Yellow River. In *615*/1218, after a Khwarazmian governor massacred one hundred Mongol envoys at the Otrar river, calling them — no doubt correctly — spies, the Mongols began invading the Muslim realms. At Jenghiz Khan's death in *624*/1227, the Empire was divided between a grandson and three sons. Batu, son of Juchi, received as his territory the Qipchaq steppe in Russia, in Jenghiz' words: "as far as the Mongol horses had trodden"; Chagatai received territories from Transoxiana to Chinese Turkestan, the former Kara-Khitai empire. Ogedei received outer Mongolia; and Tului, eastern Mongolia and northern China. Ogedei was elected Great Khan; after his death in 1241 (which recalled the Mongol Sabotai from an invasion of Hungary), Ogedei's widow Turakina was regent until Ogedei was succeeded by his son Güyük in 1249. An envoy of Pope Innocent IV, Plano Carpini, was present at the election. But after him the leadership passed to sons of Tului, Möngke and Kubilai.

Mongka (Khan 1251-1259), the son of a Nestorian woman, told the friar William of Rubruk, envoy of Louis IX of France, that religions are like the fingers of one hand; he himself favored Buddhism. He had certain Taoist books burned after public disputation in 1255. His brother Kubilai, who succeded Möngke, followed his example regarding Taoist books in 1258. Kubilai (1214-1294; declared Khan by his armies in 1260) founded the Yuan dynasty in China (1260-1368); Kubilai's brother Hülāgū invaded the 'Abbāsid Empire, sacked Baghdad, took Damascus, and founded the Il-Khanid dynasty.

The military superiority of the Mongols lay in their tribal unity, their extremely strict discipline and ability to endure hardship, and their strategic use of spies, terrorism, and superior siege equipment manned by Chinese engineers. Despite their heavy armaments, the Mongol nomad armies were very mobile, overtaking enemy armies that fled before them. Where they went, accounts of cruelty and barbarism multiplied. The more conservative of the Mongol chiefs, who preserved the *Yasa*, or sacred law of the Mongols, believed that they must not settle among the peoples they conquered, but only collect tribute from them. Others argued for going amongst the vassals and governing. These succumbed to civilization, and lost their power.

After the conquest of China, the Mongol capital became, in 1264, the newly founded Khanbaliq (Peking). The Mongols had been Shamanists, and as such were naively open to other religions, treating their rites as so much magic which could be used in conjunction with each other. Even before their conquest of China, they were influenced by elements of Buddhism, and even by Nestorian Christianity and doctrines current among the Uighur Turks, which they easily blended into their original spirit beliefs. After the conquest of China, the eastern Mongols more formally adopted Buddhism, as they adopted civilization, with Lamaist Buddhism eventually gaining the central and Western Mongol territories. (The title of Dalai Lama means, like Jenghiz, the "Oceanic" Lama, and is Mongol in origin. The Chinese, fearing a new irruption of the Mongols, prohibited successors of great Lamas from being sought among Jenghiz Khan's descendents.)

The Golden Horde of the Volga (in which the Ghuzz/Oghuz Turkic elements soon submerged the Mongols) and the Il-Khanids in Persia became Muslims, followed somewhat later by the Mongols in Transoxiana. Although they were nominally under the authority of the Great Khan, once the center of rule shifted to China they became in practice independent. *See* HŪLĀGŪ KHAN; IL-KHANIDS; JUWAYNI, 'ALĀ-d-DĪN; RASHĪD ad-DĪN aṭ-ṬABĪB; YASA; YURT.

Months, *see* CALENDAR.

Moon (Ar. *al-qamar*). The Arabic term for the crescent moon is *al-hilāl*; the full moon is *al-badr*. Their waxing and waning are a symbol of time's cycles and rhythms, and of existence, which is subject to birth and death, as opposed to being, which is beyond mutability. "And the moon, We have measured it out in stations, until it becomes again like a shrivelled palm leaf" (36:39). The moon measures out not only the months of the year but the passing of the years too, for the Islamic calendar is lunar and the pre-Islamic intercalation to align it with the solar year was abolished by the Koran. When the Prophet saw the new moon he would say: "O crescent of good and of guidance, my faith is in Him who created thee."

The crescent and star feature in the flags of many Islamic countries which were formerly part of the Ottoman Empire. Thus, in the language of conventional symbols, the crescent and star have become the symbols of Islam as much as the cross is the symbol of Christianity. However, this use of the crescent as a symbol for Islam was introduced late and did not originate with the Arabs.

The crescent and star appear on Mesopotamian monuments where the star is the planet Venus or one of the female divinities who represent Venus. In the fifth century the crescent and star appear on a Sāssānid coin. The Manicheans used the crescent and star to symbolize the "moon-boat" which in that religion carried the star representing particles of light dispersed in creation back to its reconstituted origin. In the Islamic world they appear on the Fāṭimid Caliph's robes, and were used by the Ottoman Turks who made the symbols universal ones after they conquered Constantinople in *857*/1453 1452.

A crescent on the cupolas of mosques is used to indicate the *qiblah* (direction of Mecca). Often three golden balls are placed below the crescent; traditionally they stand for the material, subtle, and Angelic worlds (*see* FIVE DIVINE PRESENCES) and the crescent then symbolizes the world of Being.

Sūrah 54 of the Koran speaks of the "splitting of the moon". It is sometimes understood to be a prodigious sign worked by the Prophet. According to this interpretation, the Prophet stood on the hill called Abū Qubays which overlooks the Ka'bah, and made the moon appear to split into two parts which then moved around the Ka'bah. The unbelieving Meccans are supposed to have seen this, but to have replied that the event was only sorcery. The spot where the Prophet supposedly stood, near the later "mosque of Bilāl", (officially known as the Ibrāhīm Mosque) is called popularly *shaqq al-qamar* ("the splitting of the moon"). But while this is the opinion of the commentator al-Bayḍāwī and others, the story appears to be only the result of interpretation of the words of the Koran after the times of the Prophet. There are no contemporary accounts of such an event. It is far more likely that the Koran is speaking allegorically of a sign of the Last Day, rather than of a miracle. *See* MIRACLES.

Moon god, *see* HUBAL.

Moors (from the Latin *maurus*, which is derived from the Greek *mauros*, "dark" [complexioned]). The classical name in Europe of the people of North Africa, who, since the Arab invasions, have been made up of a mixture of Arabs (approx. 40%) and Berbers (approx. 60%). Morocco and Algeria, and, to a lesser degree, Tunisia and Mauritania, correspond to the lands of the Moors. In Spain, Arabs are still called *Moros*, and the Arabs who remained in Spain, outwardly accepting Christianity after the Reconquest, were called *Moriscos*. Starting with the period of European colonial expansion, the term "Moor" came to be synonymous with "Muslim" in many contexts. The Muslims of south India and Sri Lanka are frequently called "Moors", just as the Muslim minorities in the Philippines are known as *Moros*.

Moorish Science Temple. An Islamic based religion founded by Noble Drew 'Ali (born Timothy Drew in North Carolina in 1886). He wrote a book which is usually called the "Circle Seven Koran" to distinguish it from the Muslim Koran. An African-American, he called upon his brethren to call themselves Moors or Asiatics. He started a movement among them which spread through urban centers. He died in 1929, but a number of adherents still exist today.

Moriscos. Muslims who remained in Spain after the fall of Granada in 1492. Many accepted Christianity outwardly in the course of years and because of persecution, but continued to practice Islam in secret. A large number of them were expelled from Spain in 1619.

Some of those who remained in Spain maintained threads of a hidden Islam, sometimes into the 20th century. Before the expulsions, a large number of Moriscos emigrated to North Africa, particularly after the failure of their last attempt to regain Granada in the Alpujarra uprising in 1571. They used a language called *Aljamiado* which was a mixture of Spanish and Arabic, written in Arabic script. *See* MARRANO.

Moro National Liberation Front. Muslim separatist group in the southern Philippines (Mindanao, Sulu, Palawan) which was formed in 1969. "Moro" in popular Spanish means Muslim. It has engaged in a sporadic war with the government seeking independence. There is a splinter group called the Moro Islamic Liberation Front which is smaller but also more aggressive.

Morocco. Kingdom. Population: 23,565,000 (1984 est.). 98% of the population is Muslim of the Mālikī School of Law. There are now less than 150,000 Europeans in Morocco and a small Jewish population. 60% of native Moroccans are Berbers and 40% are Arab. The legal system is mixed. The civil law is based upon French codes, and Mālikī *sharī'ah* law. Jewish Rabbinic law is recognized. Many branches of the Shādhilī *ṭuruq*, such as the Darqawiyyah, Ketaniyyah, 'Isawiyyah, Ouezzaniyyah, are active. Other Sufi orders include the Qādiriyyah (usually known as the Jalālah), and the Tījāniyyah. *See* FEZ.

Moses (Ar. *Mūsā*; to whose name is sometimes added the epithet: "God spoke to him" (*Kallamahu'-Llāh*), i.e. out of the burning bush). In Islam he is a rasūl, a Divine Messenger who brings a new revelation (Judaism and the Mosaic Law), rather than only a *nabī*, who prophecies within the limits of an existing revelation.

The story of Moses in the Koran is told extensively and is very similar in its manifold details to that in the Old Testament. One of the signs associated with him in Islam is the "white hand: during his appearance before Pharaoh, "He drew his hand from his bosom and it was white" (7:108) to signify that his activity in the world had been made sacred. He is also depicted as having a speech impediment which he asks God to remove so that his words may be understood.

Many popular stories of Moses make him representative of the exoteric point of view, the *sharī'ah*, or outer law. This is exemplified in the Koran by the account of his encounter with *al-Khiḍr* (18:61-83), a personification of transcendent knowledge and realization. But Moses could not, as one to whom God spoke, be simply a symbol of the outward; a Sufi interpretation of this same legend makes Moses outwardly the noble and spiritual aspirant, and inwardly the Heart seeking the guidance of the Spirit that "moves where it will".

As a precursor of Muḥammad, the Prophet of Islam, Moses is linked to Abraham, the patriarchal founder of Semitic monotheism; and the Koran describes itself as confirming the teachings revealed to Abraham and Moses as, for example, at the end of Sūrat al-'A'lā: "This indeed was in the first scrolls [revelations], the scrolls of Abraham and Moses" (87:18-19).

Moses' story is told in the following verses: (2:51ff.); (5:20ff.); (7:102ff.); (7:138ff.); (7:150ff.); (9:51); (10:76ff.); (14:5ff.); (17:101ff.); (18:61ff.); (20:9-80, 92ff.); (27:7ff.); (28:3f. 114ff.); (21:48); (40:23 ff.); (42:13); (43:43ff.); (44:17ff.); (51:38); (61:5); (79:15 ff.).

See AARON; al-KHIḌR.

Mosque (from Ar. *masjid*, "a place of prostrations" through French *Mosquée* based on Egyptian dialect *masgid*). In pre-Islamic times the area around the Ka'bah was called the *masjid*. Abū Bakr built a place of prayer next to his house in Mecca before the Hijrah, and a mosque stands on the spot to this day. But the prototype of the first mosque is that of Qubā' in Medinah, which the Prophet built upon his arrival there from Mecca.

The style of mosques varies greatly, but the elements are constant. The fundamental requirement is for a consecrated space, either open or covered or both, upon which the worshipers, ranked in rows behind the prayer-leader (*imām*), perform the actions of canonical prayer, standing, bowing and kneeling. No-one should set foot in this space except in a state of ritual purity. To indicate the direction of Mecca (*qiblah*) which all face in prayer, there is generally a closed arch, of varying degrees of adornment and elaboration, called the *mihrāb*. In very large mosques there may well be more than one *mihrāb*. To the right of the mihrāb in larger mosques stands the pulpit (*minbar*), from which the Friday exhortation, or sermon, (*Khuṭbah*) is delivered.

It is customary for the sacred space to be bright and uncluttered; indirect sunlight may well stream down from openings surrounding a covering dome, as if symbolizing the grace of Heaven descending upon the faithful. Open court-yards supplement the covered space, in which fountains are often placed; it is essential, in any case, that mosques should provide facilities for the ritual ablution preceding all prayers. Another striking feature of the larger mosques in particular, is the illumination, traditionally provided by mosque-lamps that were outstanding examples of the art of the metal-worker and which were able to flood the interior of the mosque with light, particularly during the nighttime ceremonies of Ramaḍān.

The typical Arab mosque is a flat building with arches imitating the original palm trunks which, cut at the top, were the support pillars of the first mosques. At first there were elevated platforms attained by steps to call the prayer. These were to be found in the early mosques in Medinah and in the mosque of 'Amr ibn al-'Āsī in Fuṣṭāṭ (Cairo). These platforms evolved into minarets of which, in later times, the most characteristic were the slender cylindrical minarets of the Turks, which contrast with the expansive and ample-domed mosques built after the style of Byzantine churches. The minarets with elaborate bulbous structures around the muezzin's platform identify a Mamlūk mosque (and similar features are found on some of the Shī'ite mosques of 'Irāq and Iran). The square towers, originally imitations of the square fire towers of the Zoroastrians, identify the minarets of the Arab West. Exceptional styles are the gigantic spiral minaret of the *Malwiyyah* mosque in Samarra', built in imitation of Babylonian ziggurats, and wooden towers found in the Far East. The word minaret itself derives from *manārah*, a "lighthouse".

Almohad art put a characteristic stamp on mosque design, and today some of its features can be found almost everywhere. Mosques in the Sahara are often no more than a half circle of stones. The simple and venerable 13th century mosque of Chinguetti in Mauritania, with a feeling as ancient as the Biblical desert city of Daumat al-Jandal, has fine sand for its floor. The more elaborate mosques of the Saharan cities and sub-Saharan Africa are dried mud buildings that seem to have the ponderous strength of the earth itself, and indeed seem to be part of it. Many of these African mosques, with their tendency towards pure geometry, are exquisite examples of vernacular architecture.

Mosques in Iran and India are famed for the delicacy and profusion of surface decoration, and the most sophisticated of formal styles. In China, mosques are typically built in the styles of Chinese temple architecture, although examples which are strongly Arab in style can be found as far away as Canton, at the end of the sea-route.

In Malay countries traditional mosques are frequently open structures, the walls not fortress-like as in the Middle East. Others, of ancient design, have curved, swallow-tail triple roofs, sometimes surmounted by lotuses, showing the influence of pre-Islamic symbolism, notably the *Triloka*, "Heaven, earth and the underworld", esoterically signifying formlessness, form and desire. Others are characterized by whitewashed courtyards with tall minarets like lighthouses, a style brought by Arabs from East Africa and the Hadhramaut. One of the characteristic architectural traits of all mosques is that in the use of space there is conveyed an absence of "tension between heaven and earth", unlike, for example, a Gothic Christian cathedral which, soaring upwards, seems to call for a spiritual heroism. The architectonics of a mosque express the equilibrium between man and God which is in the nature of Islam. *See also* KA'BAH, MIḤRĀB; MINBAR; MINARET.

Mosque of the Prophet (Ar. *Masjid an-Nabī* also called *al-Masjid ash-Sharīf*, and *al-Masjid an-Nabawī ash-Sharīf*). This mosque in Medinah is the second most venerable mosque in Islam, after the *al-Masjid al-Ḥarām*, or Grand Mosque of Mecca. The first mosque on the site of today's structure was supported by the trunks of standing palm trees that had grown there, and the Prophet himself worked on its construction. It was actually an extension of the Prophet's house. A stone originally indicated the direction of prayer (at first Jerusalem, and later Mecca). In its time, the mosque of Medinah was the principal mosque in Islam, where the Prophet spent much of his time with the Companions.

The mosque was enlarged first by the Prophet, and then by the Caliphs Abū Bakr, 'Umar, 'Uthmān, al-Walīd (the Byzantine Emperor sent gifts on this occasion), and al-Mahdī. The present mosque was built by the Mamlūks, in particular by the Sultans Baybars and Qa'it Bey, and the Ottomans, with additions made in the last century by King 'Abd al-'Azīz Al Sa'ūd and his successors in this. The enormous number of visitors to the mosque at pilgrimage time make further expansion inevitable.

Within the mosque today is the tomb of the Prophet whose house was adjacent. In accordance with the Ḥadīth that "Prophets are buried where they die", the tomb stands on the spot which was 'Ā'ishah's room in the *hujrah*, or women's apartments. Next to the Prophet's tomb are those of Abū Bakr and 'Umar whose burial was admitted in the Prophet's house by 'Ā'ishah. Next to these is a sepulchre which is called that of the Prophet's daughter Fāṭimah, although it is more than likely that she is buried in the *Baqī'* cemetery nearby. (The "sepulchre" stands in the space where the adjacent house of 'Alī and Fāṭimah would have stood.)

Between the Prophet's tomb and a free standing *miḥrāb* a short distance away (this *miḥrāb* is much sought after as a place of prayer of exceptional potency) is a space called the *rawḍah* ("garden"). It is so named because the Prophet said: "Between my house and my pulpit is a garden of the gardens of paradise."

Elaborate ceremonies have grown up surrounding visits to the tomb of the Prophet. The program of a formal visit (*ziyārah*) has specific stations within the mosque which are accompanied by pious recitations. The visitation of the Prophet's mosque is non-canonical, and even frowned upon by fundamentalist circles who insist on a Ḥadīth that advises against the visiting of tombs. Nevertheless, most Muslims aspire to visit the tomb of the Prophet, a visit which is usually combined with the *ḥajj* or the *'umrah*.

Mosque of Qubā'. This Medinan mosque is also known as the "mosque of reverence" (*Masjid at-Taqwā*). Although Abū Bakr turned his house into a mosque while still in Mecca, and prayers were also performed at the house of Arqam, the Mosque of Qubā' is considered to be the first mosque in Islam. A mosque still stands upon the spot today.

Qubā' is about 5km/3 miles from Medinah. Nearby is the *Mabrak an-Nāqah* ("kneeling place of the she-camel"). Upon his arrival in Medinah the Prophet loosed his camel Qaṣwā' to wander and choose where he would stay. Here the camel knelt. The Prophet himself settled nearby, then moved when the larger mosque was built in Medinah.

The name *Masjid at-Taqwā* is a reference to the Koran (9:108): "A place of worship which was founded upon reverence from the first day... wherein are men who love to purify themselves. Allāh loves the purifiers."

Mosque of the Two Qiblahs (Ar. *masjid al-qiblatayn*). A mosque in Medinah where the Prophet suddenly turned towards Mecca during the prayer. Until then he had always prayed facing Jerusalem. The congregation followed suit and a revelation of the Koran later confirmed the establishment of Mecca as the new *qiblah* (prayer direction). *See* QIBLAH.

"Mother of cities", *see* UMM al-QURĀ.

Moulay, *see* MAWLAY.

Mouloud, *see* MAWLID an-NABĪ.

Mourning. Widows are required to observe a period of mourning marked by various abstentions for four months and ten days. *See* FUNERALS.

Moussem (the French form of the Ar. *mawsim*, "term", "season"). A Saint's festival in Morocco, which is the occasion for large fairs. A tent city springs up and, in the case of great festivals such as those of Mawlay 'Abd Allāh near Agadir, or Mawlay Idrīs Zerhun, pilgrims come from distant places. Displays called *tabarrud* ("powderplay") are given, charging on horseback, firing rifles and turning about in the classic Arab cavalry maneuver. At a *moussem*, musicians, story tellers, and street performers congregate, and on some occasions processions take place of which the most famous is that of the *'Isawiyyah* religious fraternity in Meknes.

Some *moussems* may have a different focus. The Imilchil *moussem* is a marriage fair for spouse seekers with no time to waste. Little, or no bride gift is expected, and, apart from a brief stop at the magistrate's booth for registration of the marriage, there is no ceremonial. Other *moussems* are private, albeit large, gatherings of disciples to celebrate an anniversary in the life of a Saint or a spiritual master.

The Arabic word *mawsim* has entered European languages through Portuguese as the season of rains, *monsoon.*

Mozarab (Sp. "*mozarabe*" from Ar. *musta'rib*, one who is "Arabized"). Christians living under Arab rule in Moorish Spain and having adopted Arab life-styles. Today Mozarab denotes the style of their handicrafts and decorative arts, which persisted long after the Arabs had been first subjugated and then in large part expelled from Spain, their style being characteristic of a whole facet of Spanish art.

al-Mu'awwidhatān, *see* MAGIC; REFUGE.

Mu'allaqāt (lit. "the hung ones"). The poems that were acclaimed at the yearly fairs such as Minā and 'Ukāẓ, written in gold letters and said to have been hung in honor in the Ka'bah. A small number of such odes have come down to modern times, the most famous being those of Imru'-l-Qays, 'Antarah, and Labid.

The sequential nature of poetry recreates the dimension of time, and thus is the supreme art of the herding and hunting nomad, whose life unfolds in space. (Similarly, image-making, which recreates space, is the art of the sedentary, who is bound to the agricultural seasons, and lives in time. It is for this reason also that geometry arose among the Greeks, a sedentary people, and algebra, the mathematics of changing relationships, among the Arabs and Persians.) To this day the high point of royal and shaykhly gatherings in Arabia is the recitation of poetry, sometimes in contest. A royal poet may greet guests to a state feast in verse.

The mu'allaqāt are *qasidahs* or odes. The classical ones always have the description of the old beduin camp and the erotic prelude called the *nasib*; the description of a journey on swift-footed camels called the *rakhil*, and the praise of the host or the tribe. The poet is called the *maḍiḥ*. Mu'allim. Any kind of teacher, or master of a trade or craft.

Mu'jizah, *see* MIRACLES.

Mu'ānaqah (lit. "embracing"). Phrases of the Koran which in Arabic can be considered as referring to either the preceding or following word. For example, *fihi* ("therein") in 2:2 which can refer to the word *rayba* ("doubt") before it as: "This book, there is no doubt therein", or to *hudan* ("guidance"), the word after: "therein is guidance for those who strive for piety". As an editorial aid in some Korans the phrase is marked by three dots before and after, and the letters *mim-'ayn* are written in the margin.

Mu'āwiyah (d. *60*/680). One of the sons of Abū Sufyān who led Meccan opposition to the Prophet, Mu'āwiyah became the sixth Caliph and founder of the Umayyad dynasty, having forced Ḥasan, the son of 'Alī, to abdicate. When Caliph, Mu'āwiyah also compelled the leading sons of the Companions to acknowledge his own son Yazīd as successor to the Caliphate, thereby making this originally elective office hereditary *de facto.*

Taking decisive and ruthless action when it was required to achieve his ends, Mu'āwiyah at other times was extremely forbearing. And he understood the style of his people. When a certain Arab said to him:

> 'By God! thou hadst better do right by us,
> Mu'āwiyah, or we'll correct thee, be assured
> of that!'
> the Caliph simply asked:
> 'How will you do that?'
> 'With a stick!' said the man.
> 'Very well', Mu'āwiyah replied, 'I will do
> right'.

"This is the Arab Caesar," the Caliph 'Umar used to say when he saw Mu'āwiyah. Mu'āwiyah was of the family of 'Uthmān, and used revenge for the assassination of 'Uthmān (Mu'āwiyah was at the time governor of Syria) as the pretext virtually to seize the Caliphate out of the hands of 'Alī, who could neither marshal consensus behind him, nor take decisive action to hold onto political power. 'Alī's son Ḥasan, who became Caliph after the death of 'Alī, gave up all authority to Mu'āwiyah without a fight.

> I do not use my sword when my whip will do, was one of his sayings; nor my whip when my tongue will do. Let a single hair still bind me to my people, and I'll not let it snap; when they slack, then I pull; but when they pull, then I slack.
>
> What's approved today was reproved once, he said; even so things now abominated will someday be embraced.
>
> Abū Bakr sought not the world, nor did it

seek him. The world sought 'Umar for all that he sought it not. But ourselves are sunk in it, to our middles.

"I," said he, "am the first King [in Islam]."

See UMAYYADS.

Mubāḥ (lit. "permitted"). The category of actions which are permitted and neutral. The other categories are: *farḍ* or *wājib* for that which is obligatory; *mustaḥabb* or *mandūb* for that which is recommended; *makrūḥ* for that which is discouraged; and *ḥarām* for that which is forbidden. In *fiqh*, or jurisprudence, all actions fall into one of these categories (*aḥkām*). *See* AḤKĀM; FARḌ; ḤARĀM.

Muḍārabah. A business partnership where one partner puts up the capital and the other the labor; a "sleeping partnership". This device, known and used in the past, has now been applied by some Middle East banking enterprises to an arrangement whereby the *muḍārabah* is a deposit of money making the depositor a limited partner in the ventures of the bank, thus earning a return on investment. As interest is forbidden in Islam (but nevertheless often paid by banking institutions either openly or by a different name), the *muḍārabah* is an expedient that has been endorsed by a number of religious authorities as a legal device to authorize earnings on deposited capital. *See* ISLAMIC BANKING.

Mudejar. The Spanish name for Arabs who remained in Spain after the Reconquest. It is also the name of the art style, inspired by Islam, which dominated southern Christian Spain afterwards and remains an influence today. *See* MOZARAB.

al-Mudhākarah (lit. "negotiation", "deliberation", "learning", "memorization"). A spiritual discourse or exposition as might be given during a meeting (*majlis*) of Sufis.

Muezzin (Ar. *Mu'adhdhin*). One who makes the call to prayer (*adhān*) from a minaret or the door of a mosque. During the prayer, the muezzin usually performs the function of respondent to the Imām. Customarily the muezzin chants the Koran from the minarets at night while awaiting the moment to call morning prayer.

al-Mufīd, Shaykh (Abū 'Abd Allāh Muḥammad al-Ḥārithī al-Baghdādī, *338-413*/950-1022). A Shī'ite scholar and author of the *Kitāb al-Irshād* ("Book of Instruction"), a description of the Twelve Imāms.

Shaykh al-Mufīd was called Ibn Mu'allim ("Son of the Teacher", the teacher par excellence being Aristotle). He lived when the Buyids controlled the Caliphate, and the pro-Shī'ite climate promoted an expansion in Shī'ite scholarship. Shaykh al-Mufīd's teachers were Ibn Qulawayh, and Ibn Babawayh. He is a bridge between the "tradition" oriented Shī'ism which preceded him, and the "theologically speculative" kind of Shī'ite scholarship which developed later. Among his own students were ash-Sharīf ar-Raḍī (d. 406/1015) who compiled the *Nahj al-Balāghah* ("the sayings of 'Alī"), and his brother Sayyid al-Murtaḍā (d. *436*/1044). *See* AKHBĀRĪS; BIHBAHĀNĪ.

Mufrad (lit. "singular", "unique"). A particular consecration for the performance of pilgrimage. *See* IḤRĀM.

Muftī. A legal functionary who may be an assistant to a *qāḍi* (Judge) or a *qāḍi* himself, empowered to make decisions of general religious import, called *fatāwā* (sing. *fatwā*). *See* FATWĀ; QĀḌI.

Muhājirūn (from Ar. *hijrah*, the "migration", sing. *muhājir*). That group in Medinah who had fled from persecution in Mecca for being Muslims. Those who were originally of Medinah were called the *Anṣār* (the "helpers").

Muḥammad, the Messenger of God. The name of the Prophet of Islam. It means "the Praised one" or "he who is glorified", and the name Aḥmad, by which the Prophet is also known, is a superlative form meaning "the most laudable:" both from the verb *ḥamada* ("to praise, laud, glorify"). Traditionally, every mention of the Prophet by name or by title is followed by the invocation *salla-Llāhu 'alayhi wa-sallam* ("God bless him and give him peace") or by *'alayhi-ṣ-ṣalātu wa-s-salām* ("upon him be blessings and peace"), a practice also observed following the mention of Jesus, son of Mary, and after the other prophets and the Archangel Gabriel. It is also sufficient to say *'alayhi-s-salām* ("Peace be upon him").

Tradition assigns two hundred names to Muḥammad, including: *Ḥabīb Allāh* ("Beloved of God"), *an-Nabī* ("the Prophet"), *ar-Rasūl* ("the

Messenger"), *Abū-l-Qāsim* ("Father of Qāsim", a son who died in infancy), *Ṭā' Hā'*, *Yā' Sīn* (names of Sūrahs of the Koran), *Dhikru-Llāh* ("Remembrance of God"), *Miftāh ar-Raḥmah* (the "Key of Mercy"), *Miftāh al-Jannah* (the "Key of Paradise"), *Sayyid al-Kawnayn* ("Lord of the Two Worlds"), *Rūḥ al-Ḥaqq* (the "Spirit of Truth"), *Khātim al-anbiyā'* ("Seal of the Prophets"), *Khātim ar-Rusul* ("Seal of the Messengers"), *Sāhib al-Mi'rāj* ("He of the Night Ascent"), *Sa'd Allāh* ("Joy of God"), *Sa'd al-Khalq* ("Joy of Creation"), *'Ayn an-Na'īm* ("Fount of Beneficence"), *Sayf Allāh* ("Sword of God"), *Al-Amīn* ("The Trusty") and so forth. The Bible also gives him a name: Shiloh. In Genesis 49:1-10 it says: "And Jacob called unto his sons and said, Gather yourselves together, that I may tell you that which shall befall you in the last days... The scepter shall not depart from Judah, nor a lawgiver from between his feet, until Shiloh come; and unto him shall the gathering of the people be." Since Jesus (by tradition, at least) is of the house of David, and thus of Judah, the prophecy — and the name — must concern a Prophet coming after him, who is Muḥammad. And Deuteronomy (18:15/18) "I will raise them up a Prophet from among their brethren, like unto thee, and will put my words in his mouth; and he shall speak unto them all that I shall command him."

Muḥammad was born, according to tradition, in, or around, AD 570, the "Year of the Elephant", when Mecca was attacked by the army of Abrahah, an Abyssinian ruler of the Yemen.

The father of Muḥammad was 'Abd Allāh, son of 'Abd al-Muṭṭalib, and grandson of Hāshim, the founder of the Hāshimite clan of the Quraysh. The patriarch of the Quraysh, two generations before Hāshim, was named Fihr of the Kinānah tribe, and it is from his epithet of Quraysh (diminutive of *qirsh*, "shark" or the "biting fish") that his descendants take their name. Since Fihr was able to trace his lineage from Ismā'īl, Muḥammad is a descendant of Ismā'īl and Abraham, and heir to God's promise to Hagar: "Arise, lift up the lad, and hold him in thine hand, for I will make him a great nation" (Genesis 21:18).

Muḥammad was born after the death of his father and, as a minor, unable by pre-Islamic Arab tribal law to inherit from his father, he became the poor ward of his grandfather 'Abd al-Muṭṭalib. In keeping with the custom of the settled Arabs, the infant was entrusted to a Beduin foster mother to be raised in the desert. She was Ḥalīmah of the Banū Sa'd ibn Bakr, a clan of the Hawāzin. While the child was with them, the Beduin family experienced many unaccustomed blessings, but one event frightened them, for, as it was reported by a son of Ḥalīmah: "Two men came dressed in white and opened Muḥammad's breast and stirred their hands inside." In later years the Prophet explained that the visitors were Angels who had washed a dark spot from his heart with snow; he also said that "Satan touches every son of Adam when he is born, except Mary and her son."

Not long afterwards, Muḥammad returned to Mecca. When he was eight 'Abd al-Muṭṭalib died, and an uncle, Abū Ṭālib, became his guardian, his mother having died two years before. As a youth, the Prophet went on caravans and came to take charge of others' trade abroad, being known for his honesty as "al-Amīn" (the "Trustworthy"). It was on one such journey he met a Christian monk in Syria called Bahīrah who recognized in him the signs of his coming prophethood.

At the age of twenty-five, he married Khadījah, a wealthy widow forty years of age, whose caravans Muḥammad had in his charge. Khadījah bore the Prophet two sons who died in infancy, and four daughters. At the age of forty, or around 610, the Prophet, who had already experienced visions which he described as "the breaking of the light of dawn", received the first revelation of the Koran while on retreat near Mecca during the holy month of Ramaḍān. In a mountain-top cave called Ḥirā', the Angel Gabriel came to him with the beginning of the Divine message. (*See* KORAN, REVELATION.)

The Meccans were for the most part idolaters worshiping a miscellany of gods and goddesses, and propitiating them with sacrifices. (*See* IDOLS.) But among the idolatrous Meccans there lived also a certain number of Christians from the oasis of Najrān in the south of Arabia, which was an important Christian center whose bishops came to the great Arab fairs to preach. (*See* NAJRAN; WARAQAH.) Jewish tribes lived in and near Medinah (then called Yathrib); and some Arabs were *ḥunafā'* ("upright ones", sing. *ḥanīf*), still practicing, as individuals, the monotheism which was the legacy of Abraham. Muḥammad had been a *ḥanīf*, and had sought in his retreats to bring himself closer to the one God, the God of Abraham. (*See* ALLĀH.) Now, through the Prophet, began the restoration or renewal of the primordial religion of Abraham, and of Adam, in which man faced God as the Absolute with the same immediacy and simplicity as he did on the first day of creation.

Khadījah was the first to believe that the Prophet had indeed been charged with a Divine mission, followed by 'Alī, his cousin, and Zayd, his servant. The first convert from outside the family circle was Abū Bakr, a respected merchant and Muḥammad's friend. The Prophet began the public preaching of his message by warning his own clan, the Hāshimites, of the danger of punishment for those who did not worship the one God.

However, as followers of the new religion (*al-muslimūn*, "they that surrender to God"), increased, so did the opposition of the pagan Quraysh, who, quite apart from their attachment to their idols, feared for the prosperity of Mecca. The city was a center of pilgrimage because of the Ka'bah, a sanctuary founded by Abraham, sacred indeed to Allāh, but at that time crowded with the idols of neighboring tribes and nations. The Quraysh saw a threat in this new religion which condemned idolatry, fearing that it would deprive them of the respect they enjoyed as guardians of the Ka'bah and diminish the benefits they reaped from the yearly pilgrimage. Although there were several cubic stone sanctuaries like the Ka'bah in Arabia, all of them objects of veneration, it was the Ka'bah of Mecca that was held in the highest esteem. It drew great numbers of desert Arabs who came at the appointed season as pilgrims to worship.

With time, resistance to Islam became virulent. After the Prophet had refused all compromises and even an offer to make him King of the Quraysh, a ban was put upon his clan, the Hāshimites, prohibiting commerce with them. To escape persecution in Mecca, some of the Muslims emigrated to Abyssinia. Eventually the ban was lifted, but soon after, Abū Ṭālib, the Prophet's uncle, died. This uncle, while not a believer in Islam, as head of the clan had protected the Prophet against the animosity of his opponents. Abū Lahab, another uncle, but a fierce enemy of the religion, now became head of the Hāshimites, and let the Quraysh know that Muḥammad no longer enjoyed the clan's protection.

At the same time, some six men of the tribe of Khazraj of Yathrib (Medinah) entered Islam during the pilgrimage to Mecca in the year 620; the next year five of them returned, bringing with them seven others, two of whom were members of the Aws, the other important Yathrib tribe. This time they took an oath pledging fealty to the Prophet. This was the so-called First Pledge of 'Aqabah, named after the 'Aqabah pass, or incline, at Minā, near Mecca, where the event occurred. The next year, seventy-three men and two women took the oath during the pilgrimage, namely, the so-called Second 'Aqabah, whereby the men pledged to protect the Prophet from his enemies.

From this point it became customary for Muslims fleeing persecution at the hands of the Quraysh to emigrate to Yathrib, and shortly afterwards, the Prophet, his life now in danger, left the city with Abū Bakr by stealth and under cover of darkness, evading search parties by hiding in a cave in the Thawr mountain near Mecca. This celebrated journey was the Hijrah ("emigration"). On the 17 September 622 the Prophet entered Yathrib; the year which, according to the Arab and the later Islamic calendar began on 15 July (sometimes said to be the 16th because the Muslim day begins on the previous evening), was afterwards designated by the Caliph 'Umar as the first year of the Islamic era, because the Prophet's arrival in Yathrib marked the beginning of the first Islamic state. Thereafter the city became known as *madīnat an-Nabī*, "the city of the Prophet", Medinah. (*See* HIJRAH.)

The Prophet was soon joined by some seventy fellow emigrants (*Muhājirūn*) from Mecca, and also by his wife Sawdah, a widow he had married after the death of Khādijah. In Medinah, his third wife, 'Ā'ishah, the daughter of Abū Bakr, entered his household; they had been married in Mecca, but the consummation of the marriage was put off until after the emigration because of her tender years. 'Ā'ishah was to be his favorite wife, although the Prophet always retained the highest regard for Khādijah. Thereafter the Prophet was to make other marriages, some of them important as political alliances, others to widows without means, and some for reason of personal affinities. (*See* WIVES of the PROPHET.)

He was of robust health, rarely suffering from anything more than a headache on long campaigns. Of medium height, he had a beautiful face. His long black hair reached his shoulders and he sometimes twisted it in two plaits, sometimes four. Between his shoulders, at the bottom of his back he had a mark, "big as a silver dirham, with hair growing around it". This was the "Seal of Prophecy", the mark of the last Divine Messenger to the world.

> Such force of life was in his walk that a man might think him pulling his feet loose from stone; and yet so light it was that he seemed

> to be stepping ever downhill. And he had such a sweetness in his face that when a man was in his company it was hard to go away.

> People used to ask 'Ā'ishah how the Prophet lived at home. Like an ordinary man, she answered. He would sweep the house, stitch his own clothes, mend his own sandals; water the camels, milk the goats, help the servants at their work, and eat his meals with them; and he would go to fetch a thing we needed from the market.

> He would visit any sick; he would walk as a mourner after any bier he met in the street; and if a slave bade him to dinner, he would go dine with him.

He was a man; it was said "a man, but not like other men, rather like a jewel among stones".

When he laughed, he would throw his head back and one could see his teeth. But he never laughed uproariously, and said that "this world is under curse, and accursed all things in it save the remembrance of God, and such things as help us to remember". And he said: "Be in this world as a stranger or as a passer-by"; but also: "do for this world as if to live forever, and for the next, as if to die on the morrow."

He was fond of milk, honey, and the use of a toothstick (*miswāk*), a kind of brush made of threadwood, with the bark peeled away, still used today in the traditional world, which, when rubbed on the teeth, cleans them. He said that dearest to him were "prayer, perfumes, and women", all that in this world is fragrant of paradise.

A first mosque was built at Qubā', a village near Medinah. Others followed as more and more people of Yathrib joined Islam. Among these were, however, a group the Koran was to call the "Hypocrites" (*al-munāfiqūn*) who in the councils were "like propped-up pieces of wood" (63:4) because their allegiance to Islam was lukewarm and external, and their willingness to do battle for it wavering.

When it became apparent that the Muslims would have to fight for Islam the Koran exempted from their enmity the adherents of the revealed religions, the Christians, the Jews, the Magians (Zoroastrians) and the "Ṣābians". A number of religions which the Muslims of the times deemed to be Divinely inspired, were identified as these Ṣābians. (*See* AHL al-KITĀB.) But idolaters (*mushrikūn*), and unbelievers (*kāfirūn*), who denied the transcendent Divine Reality, could make no claim upon God's indulgence, and had no "right" to peace.

After a skirmish with a Meccan caravan, a small army of three hundred Muslims defeated a force of one thousand Meccans at Badr in March 624. (*See* BATTLE of BADR.) The next year a Meccan force of three thousand defeated about one thousand Muslims at Uḥud, because of the disobedience of a small group of Medinan soldiers. (*See* BATTLE of UḤUD.)

Two years later, in April 627, a massed army of Quraysh, accompanied by the desert tribes of the Ghaṭafān and some Jews from the tribe of the Banū Naḍīr who had been expelled from Medinah, attacked Medinah, where they were unexpectedly confronted by a hastily built defensive trench (*See* BATTLE of the TRENCH.) After a completely unsuccessful siege, known as the "War of the Confederates" (*al-Aḥzāb*), they abandoned their campaign, and thereafter hostilities between Medinah and Mecca all but ceased, although expeditions were sent from Medinah against other tribes.

Tradition relates that during the building of the Trench the Prophet was called to help to remove a large stone. The Prophet split the stone with three blows and three flashes of light emerged, the first of which illuminated for the Prophet the castles of the Yemen, the second the castles of Syria, and the third the palace of Kisrah (Chosroes) at Māda'in (Ctesiphon-Seleucia). This he understood to be a sign that God was opening up the lands to the South, the West, and the East of Arabia to conquest by the armies of Islam. Following this, the Prophet sent out messengers to eight kings, among them Heraclius, Emperor of Byzantium, the Muqawqīs (Coptic ruler of Egypt) Chosroes of Persia and the rulers of the Yemen, bidding them enter Islam before they were conquered and subjugated. The Muqawqīs sent gifts by way of return; the Persian Shah Siroes who had succeeded Chosroes in the meantime tore up the letter. Badhān (*Qā'il* or "ruler") of the Yemen, whose emissaries were in Medinah, seeing that certain prophecies made by the Prophet regarding the death of Chosroe in Persia had already been fulfilled, rebelled against the Persian suzerainty, and entered Islam.

In the following year, a revelation promised the Prophet that he would shortly pray at the sacred mosque of Mecca, at the Ka'bah. In March 628, therefore, he set out with about 1,000 men as pilgrims, not armed for battle, and with seventy camels consecrated for sacrifice. At Ḥudaybiyyah, some twelve miles from Mecca, the Prophet's pilgrimage came to a halt while tense negotiations were conducted with the Quraysh. During a moment of great danger and uncertainty, when the defenseless Muslims could have been annihilated, the Prophet, in a state of rapture like that of his revelations, called everyone to come and take an oath to him; this oath became known as the Pact of Felicity (*bay'at ar-riḍwān*).

God was well pleased with the believers
when they were swearing fealty to thee
under the tree, and He knew what was
in their hearts, so He sent down the
Shechina upon them, and rewarded them with
a nigh victory and many spoils to take;
and God is ever All-mighty, All-wise. (48:18-19)

(*See* ḤUDAYBIYYAH).

The Muslims reached an agreement with the Quraysh by which they stopped short of Mecca that year. The Prophet, however, sacrificed camels at Ḥudaybiyyah and cut his hair as if the pilgrimage had been accomplished. The agreement stipulated that next year the Muslims would be allowed to reach their goal and that Mecca would be evacuated for them for three days. A ten-year treaty of peace was concluded between the Quraysh and the Prophet.

The Koran called this a "clear victory:"

Surely We have given thee
a manifest victory.
that God may forgive thee
thy former and thy latter sins,
and complete His blessing upon thee,
and guide thee
on a straight path,
and that God may help thee
with mighty help.

It is He who sent down the Shechina
into the hearts of the believers, that
they might add faith to their faith —
to God belong the hosts
of the heavens and the earth
God is All-knowing, All-wise... (48:1-5)

The next year the Quraysh, who were watching the proceedings from the hill of Abū Qubays, saw and heard Bilāl, the muezzin of the Prophet, proclaim from the roof of the Ka'bah: "there is no god but Allāh", and "Muḥammad is the Messenger of God." Thereafter, having seen the Quraysh treat with the Prophet and acknowledge him as a sovereign, a rising tide of converts flowed towards Medinah from all quarters of Arabia.

The Quraysh had not anticipated this turn of events: in effect they had given up their struggle without knowing it. The treaty, moreover, freed the Prophet to deal with others, and in the expeditions which followed, the Muslims conquered the redoubtable citadels of the Jews of Khaybar, giving the Jews the choice of entering Islam or paying tribute, thereby bringing riches to Medinah and impressing their neighbors and the Arabs of the peninsula with the growing strength of the Islamic state.

It was on this campaign that the Prophet received by terms of surrender the oasis of Fadak as his personal property; after the Prophet's death his daughter Fāṭimah requested Fadak as her inheritance, but the Caliph Abū Bakr, who, to Fāṭimah's chagrin, refused, retained the oasis for the state, basing this judgement upon a Ḥadīth to the effect that a Prophet leaves no property behind him in this world. It was also on this campaign that the widowed wife of Sallām ibn Mishkam, one of the Jews of Khaybar, attempted to assassinate the Prophet by poisoning a roast lamb. The Prophet took a bite of the shoulder of the lamb but spat it out, warning those with him to stop eating, as the shoulder had told him it was poisoned. However, one of his Companions, Bishr ibn Barā', had also taken a bite which he had already swallowed, so that he soon turned pale and died. The Prophet pardoned the woman who confessed to the deed as revenge for the death of her family; but the Prophet said that a trace of that poison remained with him to the end, making him share in a martyr's death with the others who had been killed outright in the way of God.

But also of the Jews of Khaybar was a woman named Ṣafiyyah, the daughter of one who had counseled the Jews still remaining in Medinah, the Banu Qurayẓah, to break their treaty with the Prophet during the War of the Confederates. This bad counsel and breach led to their demise. Ṣafiyyah had dreamed of a brilliant moon hanging over Medinah, a dream for which she had been rebuked by her family. After the conquest of Khaybar she was among the captives; the Prophet, learning of her dream, offered to set her free to return to her people, but she accepted Islam, and married him on the return to Medinah.

A fight between Beduins, in which the Quraysh took sides against a group allied to the Muslims, was taken by the Prophet as a breach of the ten-year treaty of Ḥudaybiyyah. In January 630, therefore, at the head of an army of 10,000, he invaded Mecca, meeting almost no resistance. The Ka'bah was purified of idols (a painting inside of the Virgin and Child was expressly allowed by the Prophet to remain) and in the course of the following weeks, almost to a man, the Meccans accepted Islam.

The conquest of Mecca was followed by the Battle of Ḥunayn against the Beduin Hawāzin, who were defeated but took refuge with their allies of the city of Ṭā'if, only to surrender later and enter Islam. The Arabs could plainly see that the Prophet's pagan adversaries, if they surrendered to God in Islam, were accepted without rancor, and that Christians and Jews, if they were conquered, could keep all they had by entering Islam, or could accept protection with the new state through payment of tribute. Resistance melted away.

A great expedition of thirty thousand was then sent to Tabūk in the north of Arabia. It returned having encountered no resistance, marking the beginning of Islam's expansion towards Syria and Persia. Upon his return from Tabūk, the Prophet found that some of the lukewarm Muslims of Medinah had founded a separate mosque at Qubā', the "mosque of dissension"; a revelation of the Koran, the Sūrah of Repentance, categorically told the Prophet not to acknowledge it, and the mosque which may have been the hiding place of an opponent of the Prophet, Abū 'Amīr ar-Raḥīb, was pulled down at night:

And those who have taken
a mosque in opposition
and unbelief, and to divide the believers,
and as a place of ambush for those who fought
God and His Messenger aforetime —
they will swear
'We desired nothing but good'; and God testifies
they are truly liars.
Stand there never. A mosque that was founded
upon godfearing from the first day is worthier
for thee to stand in; therein are men who love
to cleanse themselves; and God loves those
who cleanse themselves.
Why, is he better who founded his building upon
the fear of God and His good pleasure, or he
who founded his building upon the brink of a
crumbling bank that has
tumbled with him into the
fire of Gehenna? And God guides not the people
of the evildoers. (9:107-111)

The ninth year of the Hijrah is known as the "Year of Deputations" when delegates came from all over Arabia to accept Islam from the Prophet. The pilgrimage was closed to non-Muslims, and in the following year, in March 632, the Prophet led a pilgrimage caravan from Medinah of thirty thousand men and women. In this, the "farewell pilgrimage", the new law was established: "Verily God has made inviolable for you each other's blood and each other's property, until you meet your Lord, even as he has made inviolable this, your day, in this your land, in this your month." During the sermon of 'Arafāt the last passage of the Koran was revealed:

Today the unbelievers have despaired of
your religion; therefore fear them not,
but fear you Me.
Today I have perfected your religion
for you, and I have completed my Blessing
upon you, and I have approved Islam for
your religion. (5:4-5).

The Prophet looked up and cried: "My Lord! Have I delivered aright the Message I was charged with and fulfilled my calling?" And the multitude answered shouting "Ay, by God you have!"

On 8 June 632, the Prophet died, and was buried, in accordance with his wishes, in his house. As leader of the community he was succeeded by Abū Bakr with the title of *khalīfah* ("he who is left behind", deputy, successor, or Caliph). The expansion of Islam continued. Within a hundred years its realm extended from Spain to India. Today it is found in every corner of the world, and over 800,000,000 people are counted as Muslims, who recite, as the foundation of their faith, the words: "There is no god but God, Muḥammad is the Messenger of God."

God has indeed fulfilled the vision He
vouchsafed to His Messenger truly...
...Thou seest them bowing, prostrating,
seeking bounty from God and good pleasure.

Their mark is on their faces,
the trace of prostration.
That is their likeness in the Torah,
and their likeness in the Gospel:
as a seed that puts forth its shoot,
and strengthens it,
and it grows stout and rises straight
upon its stalk, pleasing the sowers.... (48:27,29)

'Alī and other Companions, questioned concerning the person of the Prophet, said at various times:

> He was a man of medium stature, neither tall nor short. His complexion was rosy white; his eyes black, his hair, thick, brilliant, and beautiful, fell to his shoulders, and he sometimes wore it in plaits. His profuse beard fell to his breast. As to his body his throat was white; and from his breast down to his navel ran a line of black hair, delicate as if it had been drawn with a pen. Other hair low on his body he had none. His head was roundish, and his back stout and sinewy. Between his shoulders he had a growth, big as a silver dirham, with hair growing round it. If I hungered, a single look at the Prophet's face dispelled the hunger. Before him all forgot their griefs and pains.
>
> He was a man of dignity, and seldom laughed; he kept his keen sense of humor under control, knowing its hazards for public men. Of a delicate constitution, he was nervous, impressionable, given to melancholy pensiveness. In moments of excitement or anger his facial veins would swell alarmingly; but he knew when to abate his passion and could readily forgive a disarmed and repentant foe. He put on none of the pomp of power, rejected any mark of reverence, accepted the invitation of a slave to dinner, and asked no service of a slave that he had time and strength to do for himself. Despite the booty and revenue that came to him, he spent little upon his family, less upon himself, much in charity.
>
> He gave considerable time to his appearance — perfumed his body, painted his eyes, dyed his hair. His voice was hypnotically musical. His senses were painfully keen; he could not bear evil odors, jangling bells, or loud talk. "Be modest in thy bearing," he taught, "and subdue thy voice. Lo, the harshest of all voices is that of the ass." He was nervous and restless, subject to occasional melancholy, then suddenly talkative and gay. He had a sly humour. To Abū Hurayrah, who visited him with consuming frequency, he suggested: "O Abū Hurayrah! Let me alone every other day, so that affection may increase." He was an unscrupulous warrior, and a just judge. His acts of mercy were numberless. He stopped many barbarous superstitions, such as blinding part of a herd to propitiate the evil eye, or tying a dead man's camel to his grave. His friends collected his spittle, or his cut hair, or the water in which he washed his hands, expecting from these objects magic cures for their infirmities.

His grandson Ḥusayn, 'Alīs son, said this:

> When I asked my father how the Prophet used to be in his public life, he answered: "He gave people their due always; he never neglected good manners, but would greet his Companions duly and ask after their health. If he came into a company he always sat down in any place he found room. In his council, no one was allowed to shout; if any present was guilty of a fault, he never exposed it, but would always cover it up. Nor did he ever interrupt another man speaking. If he saw anything to disgust him in the person of another, a change might come over his face, but he never remarked on it to the other person.
>
> "He ate kneeling, liking best to eat with a goodly number at table, and used to say: 'The man who eats alone is the worst of men.' Meat was the food he liked best, and he would say: 'Meat is good for the hearing!' But he mostly ate dates. He liked honey, and butter; and he loved milk exceedingly; if anyone gave him a drink of milk he used to say: 'God bless this milk to us and grant us more of the same.'
>
> "On Pilgrimage once, Abu Bakr was angry with one who had let a camel stray, and began to beat the man. The Prophet did not command him to stop, but said, with half a smile, merely: 'See what this Pilgrim is doing!'
>
> "He loved fun. 'Many a jest', said 'Ā'ishah, 'the Prophet made,' and he always said 'God doth not punish a fair jest.'"

The Companion Khawat son of Jabir told the following tale:

Once I was on a journey with the Apostle of God and his people; and we lighted down at a certain halt and pitched our tents. After a while, coming out of my tent, I spied a bevy of women, comely enough, opposite me, sitting talking. So I went in again, and put on my best raiment; then I walked over to the women and sat down in their company.

Suddenly the Apostle of God came out from his tent and saw me. "Abū 'Abd Allāh" said he, "what dost thou there, sitting with the women?"

I was in awe of him, and answered hastily: "Apostle of God, I have a balky drunken camel, and I came to ask these women to twist me a hobble-rope."

He passed a few steps; then turned round on me, and said "Abū 'Aba Allāh, how, more exactly, was that drunken camel acting?" When I replied not, he went on.

After we removed from the halting, whenever the Prophet saw me, he would, after greeting me, ask me that same question: "How was that drunken camel acting?" So when we got back to Medinah, I kept away from the Mosque out of fear that the Prophet would ask me there, to my confusion. I waited my opportunity to catch him alone in the Mosque; and when I saw it I went in and began my prayer. Presently the Prophet came out of his own chamber, and performed a short prayer, two Bows, then sat down near me. I was afraid again, and prolonged my praying, in the hope that he, having finished first, might go indoors again without asking me that question again; but when he saw what I was at, he said: "Abū 'Abd Allāh, pray as long thou wilt; I shall not go away till thou hast finished."

Now! I thought to myself, it behoves to find some excuse to appease the Prophet of God. So I brought my prayer to an end, and greeted him; and having returned my greeting, he asked me once again, "Abū 'Abd Allāh, how was that drunken camel acting?"

"O Apostle of God!" I answered, "by Him Who made thee for a blessing to us, I swear that camel hath given up drinking since I became a True Believer!"

Thereupon the Prophet said solemnly three times: "God had been merciful to thee!" He never asked me that question again.

"Every eye is an adulterer," the Prophet used to say; and again: "Let a man answer to me for what waggeth between his jaws, and what between his legs, and I'll answer to him for Paradise."

"These two are my posterity in the world" the Prophet used to say (meaning his grandsons Ḥasan and Ḥusayn).

One day a certain man met him walking along, carrying his grandson Ḥasan pick-aback, and said: "Tis a great horse thou ridest there, lad!"

"Tis a great horseman too," the Prophet said.

"Of all his family ('Abd Allāh, Zubayr's son, related) the one who resembled him was Ḥasan. Once I saw Ḥasan come when the Prophet was prostrating himself at prayer and climb on his back; the Prophet did not make him get off, till he got off of his own accord.

"His health and energy had borne up well through all the tasks of love and war. But at the age of fifty-nine he began to fail. A year previously, he thought, the people of Khaibar had served him poisonous meat; since then he had been subject to strange fevers and spells; in the dead of night, 'Ā'ishah reported, he would steal from the house, visit a graveyard, ask forgiveness of the dead, pray aloud for them, and congratulate them on being dead. Now in his sixty-third year, these fevers became more exhausting. One night 'Ā'ishah complained of a headache. He complained of one also, and asked playfully would she not prefer to die first, and have the advantage of being buried by the Prophet of Allah — to which she replied, with her customary tartness, that he would doubtless, on returning from her grave, install a fresh bride in her place. For fourteen days thereafter the fever came and went. Three days before his death he rose from his sickbed, walked into the mosque, saw Abu Bakr leading the prayers in his stead, and humbly sat beside him during the ceremony. On June 8, 632, after a long agony, he passed away, his head on 'Ā'ishah's breast."

Will Durant, as a historian, summed him up thus:

If we judge greatness by influence, he was one of the giants of history. He undertook to raise the spiritual and moral level of a people harassed into barbarism by heat and foodless wastes, and he succeeded more completely than any other reformer; seldom has any man so fully realized his dream. He accomplished his purpose through religion not only because he was himself religious, but because no other medium could have moved the Arabs of the times; he appealed to their imagination, their fears and hopes, and spoke in terms they could understand. When he began, Arabia was a desert flotsam of idolatrous tribes; when he died it was a nation. He restrained fanaticism and superstition, but he used them. Upon Judaism, Zoroastrianism, and his native creed he built a religion simple and clear and strong, and a morality of ruthless courage and racial pride; which in a generation marched to a hundred victories, in a century to an empire, and remains to this day a virile force through half the world.

See 'ABD al-MUṬṬALIB; AHL KISA'I; 'Ā'ISHAH; 'AQABAH; BATTLE of BADR; BATTLE of ḤUNAYN; BATTLE of the TRENCH; BATTLE of UḤUD; HERACLIUS; HIJRAH; ḤUDAYBIYYAH; KORAN; MECCA; MEDINAH; MUQAWQĪS; NAMES of the PROPHET; NIGHT JOURNEY; PROPHETS; QURAYSH; RIḌĀ'; UMMĪ; WIVES of the PROPHET.

Muḥammad II, *see* MEḤMET II.

Muḥammad ibn 'Abd Allāh Ḥasan, *see after* MUḤAMMAD 'ALĪ.

Muḥammad Aḥmad ibn Sayyid 'Abd Allāh (*1260-1303*/1844-1885). The "Mahdī of the Sudan". A charismatic religious leader, founder of his own dervish order, in *1298*/1881 he declared himself to be the Mahdī, the Divinely guided leader predicted by Ḥadīth. He declared a holy war, and his followers fought against Anglo-Egyptian control of the Sudan. He succeeded in restoring his own rule in the country but died soon afterwards. In *1316*/1898 the Mahdists were completely defeated by Lord Kitchener, and the Sudan came once more under Anglo-Egyptian control. When the tomb of the Mahdī in Omdurman had become a place of pilgrimage, in order to prevent the site from being used to stir popular unrest, the body was burned and thrown into the Nile.

Muḥammad 'Alī (*1193-1265*/1769-1849). First a pasha, then hereditary viceroy of Egypt, who founded the Khedival dynasty, Muḥammad 'Alī was an Albanian Turk who enlisted as a Bashi-Bazouk, or common irregular soldier, and rose through the ranks to become a commander in the Turkish army. The Napoleonic wars brought him to Egypt. To the end of his life he was illiterate, but when he had wrested control of Egypt from the Turks, he modernized both his army and the government along European lines, and conducted a number of highly successful military campaigns aided by skillful diplomatic maneuvering between the European powers and Turkey.

In *1226*/1811 the massacre of the traditional Egyptian ruling class of the Mamlūks brought Muḥammad 'Alī undisputed control of Egypt. In *1233*/1818 his son Ibrāhīm Pāsha crushed the growing strength of the Wahhābīs in Arabia by besieging and destroying their home town of Dir'iyyah in the Najd. In *1238*/1823 Muḥammad 'Alī conquered the Sudan and laid the foundations of Khartoum.

Muḥammad 'Alī fought for the Ottomans in the Greek campaign which ended in 1827 with the Turkish-Egyptian naval defeat at Navarino. He fought against the Ottomans to secure his independent rule and to acquire Syria, even letting Ibrāhīm Pasha carry the campaign into Anatolia. He was finally forced to back down in the face of European support for the Turks, but made his control of Egypt hereditary; the dynasty of the Khedives lasted until the overthrow of King Faruq in 1952.

"Muḥammadan Light", *see* NŪR MUḤAMMADĪ.

Muḥammad ibn 'Abd Allāh Ḥasan (d. *1339*/1920). A Somalian political and religious leader. After performing the pilgrimage in 1895 he became a disciple of Ibrāhīm ar-Rashīdī, founder of a group called the Ṣāliḥiyyah. Inspired by ar-Rashīdī and the example of the Mahdī of the Sudan, Muḥammad ibn 'Abd Allāh sought to unite around himself his tribe, the Oqaden, and others in Somalia, on the basis of religion and military expansion. In 1899 he declared himself to be the Mahdī.

He fought against British and Italian troops sporadically until he was disowned by his religious preceptor ar-Rashīdī and denounced by the Qādiriyyah *ṭuruq* (religious orders) in Somalia. In 1920 he fled from advancing British troops and died among his tribesmen. In the British press he had meanwhile acquired the sobriquet "the Mad Mullah".

Muḥammad ibn al-Ḥanafiyyah (born *17*/638 or *19*/640 and died *81*/700 or *84*/703 or *86*/705). A son of 'Alī by a wife who was from a tribe called Banu Ḥanif. By some accounts he was the "favorite" son of 'Alī.

After the death of Ḥusayn in *61*/680, 'Abd Allāh ibn Zubayr (killed in *73*/692) began raising a revolt against the Umayyads and eventually seized Mecca. Because 'Abd Allāh ibn 'Abbās, son of the Prophet's uncle 'Abbās and Muḥammad ibn Ḥanafiyyah, son of the Prophet's nephew 'Alī, maintained neutrality in this struggle, they, and seventeen Kūfan nobles who were with Muḥammad ibn Ḥanafiyyah, were thrown into prison by 'Abd Allāh ibn Zubayr. Eventually they were freed by a strong force sent from Kūfah by Mukhtār, the revolutionary. The existence of this partisan support surprised and intrigued the 'Abbāsid side of the family. After this, Muḥammad ibn al-Ḥanafiyyah left Mecca and went to Aylah (Eilat), at the beginning of the year 67 H. (The 'Abbāsids were eventually to establish themselves nearby, at Ḥumaymah.)

After the death of 'Abd Allāh ibn 'Abbās, the head of the 'Abbāsid clan, Muḥammad ibn Ḥanafiyyah was the head of both the 'Abbāsid clan and also the 'Alīd clan. He was the last leader to unite the two families, and their *shī'ah*, or partisans, under one authority.

Muḥammad ibn al-Ḥanafiyyah was the figurehead around whom the Kaysāniyyah/Mukhtāriyyah revolt agitated and was the person for whom the title *Mahdī* was originally created. Although Mukhtār, the actual leader of the revolt, was killed in *67*/687, Muḥammad ibn al-Ḥanafiyyah escaped sanctions on the part of the Umayyads and even maintained good relations with them because his status with the Mukhtāriyyah was secret. When he died in Ṭā'if he was still the focus of the Mukhtāriyyah organization and the legend was created that he was not dead but had gone into supernatural hiding in a place called Raḍwā which could have been either a hill near Medinah or a valley in the Yemen. (The name was perhaps intentionally identifiable with two locations, for the benefit of different groups of partisans.)

After he died, the figurehead leadership of the Mukhtāriyyah (Kaysāniyyah) passed to the son of Muḥammad ibn al-Ḥanafiyyah. The name of this son was Abū Hāshim, and historians therefore called the organization the Hāshimiyyah. But it was an extension in time of the same political alliances originally created by 'Alī himself or created around him by groups seeking to control him. The role of leader had bypassed Ḥusayn, because his misjudgment got him killed, and went instead, in secret, to Muḥammad ibn al-Ḥanifiyyah at the time of Mukhtār's revolt, and thereafter settled on his son Abū Hāshim. The active tip of this movement was centered in Kūfah in 'Irāq (the successor to Lakhmid Ḥīrah). Time would show that it in fact had religious connections which stretched to North Africa and to Khōrāsan, for these were groups bound by the Gnostic tenets of Manicheism.

After the death of his father around 700, Abū Hāshim went to Mecca; the 'Abbāsids had for their part migrated to Syria, under the leadership of the youngest son of 'Abd Allāh ibn 'Abbās, 'Alī (d. *118*/736). The eldest son of 'Abd Allāh ibn 'Abbās and a brother of 'Alī's, 'Abbās ibn 'Abd Allāh, went his own way. He joined Muṣ'ab ibn Zubayr in 'Irāq, and died childless while the other 'Alīds and 'Abbāsids chose to support the Umayyads after the death of the dissenter 'Abd Allāh ibn Zubayr.

Very early on, while 'Alī ibn 'Abd Allāh ibn 'Abbās was still alive, active leadership of the 'Abbāsid family passed to 'Alī's son Muḥammad (who was only fourteen years younger than his father). They bought an estate south of the Dead Sea called Ḥumaymah (lat. 30 degrees North long. 35 degrees 20 minutes East) half-way between 'Aqabah and Ma'ān, Jordan, but spent most of their time in Damascus until the death of Walid I in *96*/715, whereupon Ḥumaymah increasingly became their true center.

Ḥumaymah lay near one of the great caravan routes between Medinah and Damascus; thus, although apparently withdrawn from politics, the 'Abbāsids were strategically placed to collect information. Once they acquired control of Muḥammad ibn al-Ḥanifiyyah's conspiratorial connections and set in motion their own plan to overthrow the Umayyads it was easy for strangers in the 'Abbāsid underground to come discreetly to Ḥumaymah in the guise of merchants; otherwise the 'Abbāsids could meet with their conspirators on the pilgrimage in Mecca.

Towards the end of his life, Abū Hāshim, who had no children, moved from Medinah in *91*/710 to Damascus under arrest because of a dispute with other 'Alīd family members. The dispute was over an inheritance which the 'Alīds believed was due to them because of their descendance from the Prophet through Fāṭimah. (This is a familiar trope.)

In the course of the dispute Abū Hāshim was accused by the senior member of the Ḥasanid branch of the 'Alīds, Zayd ibn Ḥasan, in the presence of the Caliph Walīd I, of having a *shī'ah* or a partisan group, in Kūfah.

The Chief of the Ḥusaynid branch of the 'Alīds, Alī ibn Ḥusayn (known later as Zayn al-'Abidīn and in the course of time considered to be one of the Shī'ite Imāms), came to the help of his cousin and had him released. Estranged from the family of his paternal uncles, Abū Hāshim remained in Damascus but was courted by the cousin 'Abbāsids, to whom he was also related by marriage. Having put up a smokescreen that he was leaving for Medinah, Abū Hashīm in reality went with Muḥammad ibn 'Alī ibn 'Abd Allāh ibn 'Abbās, to the 'Abbāsid headquarters in Ḥumaymah south of the Dead Sea, where he died in *98*/716-717 having spent about a year. Before his death he passed on his function as leader of the conspiracy to Muḥammad ibn 'Alī of the 'Abbāsids. Abū Hāshim was accompanied by six Kūfan partisans. These cadres included: 1. Abū Riyāh Maysarah an-Nabbāl ("the arrow maker"); 2. Abū 'Amr Yaqṭīn al-Bazzār ("the seed and corn chandler") 3. Muḥammad ibn Khunays; 4. Abū Bisṭām Maṣqalah at-Ṭaḥḥan ("the miller"); 5. Ḥayyān al-'Aṭṭar ("the perfumer and spice dealer"); 6. Ibrāhim ibn Salamah. They were not inclined to recognize the transfer and wanted to leave. But Muḥammad ibn 'Alī persuaded them to stay a while until their leader, Salamah ibn Bujayr ibn 'Abd Allāh who had been detained, arrived from Damascus. When Salamah ibn Bujayr arrived he knew already of the arrangement to transfer the Hāshimiyyah to the 'Abbāsids and complied. He gave them the list, the diwan of some members of the conspiracy in Kūfah. It included the name of Abū Salamah Ḥafs ibn Sulaymān al-Khallāl ("the vinegar seller").

The emphasis on trade names proving the craft and populist affiliation was a feature of several revolts including ones in Europe. Having a craft was in fact a requirement to participate in the *Da'wah*, or movement, and Abū Muslim had to learn a trade in order to fulfill his office. His was said to be that of saddler. (This would be like acting Freemasons to actually learn and practice the craft.)

Before he died, Abū Hāshim initiated Muḥammad ibn 'Alī ibn 'Abd Allāh ibn al-'Abbās into the secrets of the Kaysāniyyah/Mukhtāriyyah organization. This was described as a passing on to Muḥammad ibn 'Alī of the *'ilm*, the "esoteric knowledge" of Abū Hāshim and the names of the leaders and their contacts. The *'ilm* was the premisses of the cooperation between a leading Arab faction, one capable of inspiring allegiance in the dominant Arab Muslim hierarchy (initially 'Alī and his descendants, 'Alī himself being forced to turn to 'Irāq for support against the confederates of the Umayyads whose power base was Syria), and an underground religious organization in 'Irāq, centered around Kūfah, but also widespread in Khōrasān. This underground religious organization was the largely clandestine Manichean religion. It had found its interface with the Muslims through its Arab contingent which were the Lakhmid Arabs of Kūfah. The techniques of secret communication between the 'Abbāsids, Kūfah, and Khōrāsan, were elaborate. Muḥammad ibn 'Alī acquired near Ḥumaymah another estate, Kudad, to add another level of security for meetings so secret that not even members of his household could be aware of them.

Thus the 'Abbāsids became the new secret leaders of a vast revolutionary organization. Through them the organization which came into existence at the time of 'Alī finally achieved the goals it was seeking and through the organization the 'Abbāsids became Caliphs. (Al-Jāḥiẓ said that the Khōrāsan gate of Baghdad was important to the 'Abbāsids because the power had come to them from Khōrāsan.)

Abū Salamah the Vinegar Seller, a freed slave, became known as the "Vizier of the 'Abbāsids" for his role in the 'Abbāsid revolution. Towards the end of the 'Abbāsid revolution, however, he changed allegiance from the 'Abbāsids to an 'Alīd who refused to come forward, and thus Abū Salamah was obliged to swear allegiance to Abū-l-'Abbās, but was, nevertheless, murdered in *132*/750, as was Abū Muslim, later. These shifts in allegiance on the part of the revolutionaries on the eve of success suggest that their motivation was not the promotion of the families who were figurehead leaders, but other, clandestine goals, hidden deeper within the revolutionary organization. An uneasy relationship continued between the 'Abbāsids and their clandestine support organization although further conflicts arose. One of these conflicts burst into the open in the destruction of the Barmakids; another followed the death of al-Ma'mūn; and the sign that the coalition fell apart completely was the Qarmaṭī revolt which precipitated the founding of the Fāṭimid empire.

Later 'Abbāsid tradition embellished the account of the acquisition of their revolutionary organization with the invention of the story of the "yellow scroll" (*aṣ-Ṣaḥīfah aṣ-Ṣafrā'*) or the "scroll of the dynasty" (*ad-Dawlah*). In this story Muḥammad ibn Ḥanafiyyah went to his brothers at the death of his father 'Alī the Caliph and asked for his part of his father's inheritance. The brothers said their father had left no property, but Muḥammad insisted that he meant his father's 'ilm whereupon the brothers gave him the scroll which described the future coming of the Black Banners from Khorāsān and the names of the leaders. This legendary scroll was passed to his son Abū Hāshim and then to their cousins the 'Abbāsids who buried it beneath olive trees in Ḥumaymah never to be found again but whose fruit was the dynasty which lasted five hundred years. (The full fascinating story is in *Black Banners from the East* by Moshe Sharon.) *See* 'ABBĀSIDS; KAYSĀNIYYAH; MANICHEISM.

Muḥammadiyyah. An Islamic modernizing and nationalist reform movement founded in Indonesia in 1923 under the impetus of colonization. Like most such movements, it reflected an ambition to imitate the colonizer under the guise of self-expression. It had a separate women's branch, the 'Ā'ishiyyah, and included a Boy Scout organization under the name *Ḥizb al-Waṭan* ("party of the nation"). The Muḥammadiyyah also copied Western missionary techniques and organization, and trained missionary-preachers under the name of *muballigh*. During World War II it was eclipsed by religious organizations sponsored by the Japanese occupation (notably Masjumi), and made only a small comeback afterwards. *See* INDONESIA.

Muḥarram. The first month of the Islamic calendar, the first ten days of which are a period of mourning by the Shī'ites for the death of Ḥusayn. The culmination of this period, the 10th Muḥarram, is the anniversary of his martyrdom. During this time the *ta'ziyyah*, or passion-play representing the martyrdom, is performed, and there are those who wander the streets whipping or wounding themselves in penance. This is part of the Shī'ite syndrome of guilt on the recurrent theme of abandoning and betraying the Imāms in their time of need and peril.

The 10th Muḥarram is completely different in the Sunnī world; the events of Ḥusayn's death are not associated with it. It is instead celebrated according to the Sunnah as a benefic day of blessing corresponding to similar holy days in the Jewish calendar. The first day of Muḥarram is the Muslim new year (*ra's al-'ām*). Traditionally it is noted as a day of piety but without special observances, although presence at the mosque for dawn prayer is highly recommended.

al-Muḥāsibī, Abū 'Abd Allāh Ḥārith ibn Asad (d. *243*/857). A Sufi born in Baṣrah. The sobriquet "al-Muḥāsibī" means "He who has rendered account [of his conscience]". He inclined first towards the Mu'tazilites and their rationalism, but left them, turning instead to Sufism, which he laced with philosophy and theology. Al-Muḥāsibī, a spiritual master of al-Junayd, was an intellectual, and thus a forerunner of the school of the Imām Shādhilī. Al-Muḥāsibī wrote the *Ri'āyah li-Huqūq Allāh*, a practical manual of the spiritual life. *See* SUFISM.

Muḥrim. A person who has put on the clothing and state of *iḥrām* ("consecration") for the performance of pilgrimage to Mecca, whether *ḥajj* or *'umrah*. *See* IḤRĀM.

Muḥtasib. A public functionary whose task, as it has existed since 'Abbāsid times, has been that of supervising the merchants' quality and prices. The *muḥtasib* checks and verifies weights and measures and the use of materials in crafts. He gives expert appraisal of the values of cloth, rugs, woven articles, brass and copper utensils. These estimates are not binding as a price between buyer and seller, but are indicative of the fair market price. The *muḥtasib* is still to be found in some traditional markets.

Mujaddid (lit. "renewer"). A timely "renewer" of the faith. There is a well known Ḥadīth: "At the beginning of every hundred years God will send a renewer for my community." Ash-Shāfi'ī, al-Ghazālī, Abū Madyān, and others have all been considered as the renewers of their age, bringing a drowsing people back to the fountainhead of revelation and faith.

Mujahid (pl. *mujāhidīn*). Someone who takes part in a *jihād* or holy war. The word became known in the West during the PLO struggles with Israel and has now taken on the meaning of an Islamic guerrilla fighter.

Mujtahid (lit. "one who strives"; pl. *mujtahidūn*). An authority who makes original decisions of canon law, rather than applying precedents already established. For Sunnīs, the door of personal effort is now "closed" according to general opinion. The *Mujtahidūn* were the founders of the schools of law and their principal exponents.

For the Shī'ites of the Uṣūlī school the situation is radically different. Not only is *ijtihād* (the making of original decisions) possible, it is also necessary, even when a case is clearly a repetition of a previous decision. Those who make these decisions are the highest religious authorities, originally few, but since the last century, expanding in numbers and very influential because they have vast personal followings, as every Uṣūlī Shī'ite is expected to adhere to one or another *Mujtahid.* They also collect a special tithe called the *khums*, which does not exist among the Sunnīs, and so some *Mujtahidūn* dispose of financial means as well. *See* AKHBĀRĪS; AYATOLLAH; IJTIHĀD; MARJA' at-TAQLID; UṢŪLĪS.

Mukhī. ("priest" from Sanskrit for "face" and Gujurati for "head".) An Ismā'īlī religious dignitary and teacher. He is aided in his functions by an auxiliary called a *Kamadia.* In Western literature the *Mukhī* is sometimes referred to as "the Treasurer", and the Kamadia is called "the Accountant". *Par Mukhī* or "head priest" was a Manichean term for a high priest and is the origin of the name of the family of the Barmaki, or Barmakids, the former heads of a monastery in Balkh who became the allies and viziers of the 'Abbāsids. *See* BARMAKIDS

Mukhtāriyyah, *see* KAYSĀNIYYAH.

Mulay, *see* MAWLAY.

Mullā (also Mullah from Ar. *mawlā*, "master"). In Iran and Central Asia it is a title accorded to religious scholars and dignitaries. It corresponds roughly to the term *faqīh* in the Middle East and North Africa. The use of the term Mullā in Iran and north and east of it for someone learned in religion apparently arose from the fact that the early converts to Islam were adopted into Arab tribes as the clients (*mawlā*, *mawālī*) of a patron (also called *mawlā*). Thus for instruction about Islam one would turn to an established convert, or a *mawlā*; this with time became Mullā in Iran.

Mullā Naṣruddīn. A humorous folk-story character, something like an Islamic Til Eulenspiegel, he appears in folk tales from Morocco to India. He is also known as Jūha and Naṣruddīn Khoja; he is always imposing his comical interpretation of the world on his wife, his neighbors, and the *qāḍi* ("judge"). The character is also linked to Abū Nuwāṣ, a poet and jester-like figure at the court of Hārūn ar-Rashīd in Baghdad.

Mullā Ṣadra (*979-1050*/1571-1640). A Persian scholar and teacher of the school of Iṣfahān. His real name was Muḥammad ibn Ibrāhīm Ṣadr ad-Dīn ash-Shīrāzī; he was a pupil of Mīr Dāmād and one of the most important Shī'ite philosophers. His thought characteristically combined mysticism, philosophy, and theology. Mullah Ṣadra achieved an original intellectual synthesis of Aristotle, Avicenna, Suhrawardī, and Shī'ite Islam. He is the foremost exponent of what has been called "the School of Iṣfahān" and is a remarkable example of a flowering of philosophy long after it had become dormant in the Sunni world. In the last decades in Iran interest in Mullah Sadra has renewed and he is still a motivating force in Shī'ite thinking today. The School of Iṣfahān is essentially *Ishraq*, or "illuminationism" (a form of radical Gnosticism) recast in a more dialectical mode, rather like Existentialism.

One of his most prominent formulations was the idea of the "gradations of Being", namely that Being exists in different degrees in different creatures, strong in some, attenuated in others. In other words, Zayd Fulan is very divine, Qaddur Fulan is a little divine, and Fulan Fulani is not divine at all.

Mulla Ṣadra's theory is similar to the premise of Arianism or Manicheism. In modern times it has led to the assertion in Iran that if two Mujtahids contradict each other, they are both nevertheless right, but to different degrees!

In the *al-Asfār al-Arba'ah* ("The Four Books"), Mulla Ṣadra described the spiritual path as being at first a journey in which a man detaches himself from the physical world and the carnal self, reaching extinction in the Divine. In the second journey he reaches the degree of the Divine Names and Attributes, which is the station of Sainthood, he hears and sees and acts through God. The third journey is the end of extinction (*fanā*), and a transformed remainder of the individual (*baqā'*) subsides in this world. In the fourth journey, the Saint returns to the world (in what the Sufis call *jalwah*) and brings guidance to others, rather like a Bodhissatva.

Mulla Ṣadra's philosophy is extolled by himself as the "sublime wisdom" (*al-ḥikmah al-muta-'aliyyah*), the title of one of his writings, which cannot but recall the title of the Mahāyānist Sutra, "the perfection of wisdom" (Praj~na Pāramitā). Another of his most influential writings is *Shāhid ar-Rubūbiyyah* ("The Witness of Lordship"). *See* 'IRFĀN.

al-Multazam (lit. "that which is held onto"). The space between the Black Stone (*al-ḥajar al-aswad*) and the door of the Ka'bah. Praying before this area (or from any part of the Mosque facing this spot) constitutes one of the stations of the pilgrimage. *See* KA'BAH; PILGRIMAGE.

Mulūk aṭ-Ṭawā'if, *see* TAIFAS, REYES de las.

Mulud an-Nabī, *see* MAWLID an-NABĪ.

al-Mumkināt (lit. "possibilities", fem. pl. of *mumkin*, "possible"). In the metaphysics of Sufism according to ibn 'Arabī, among others, "possibilities" are contained principals in Being in a differentiated state; and in Beyond-Being, that is, in the Absolute, in a non-differentiated state. At some point, and in some world, all possibilities, everything which is possible, must become manifest and existent.

While still in Being the possibilities are said to be in a state of "contraction" (*karb*). When they are "released", or made manifest, they become subject to "dilation" (*tanfīs*), or to "being breathed out" into existence. It is by the Divine command (*al-amr*) that the possibilities become manifest. This Divine command as given in the Koran is the word *Kun*, literally, "Exist!"

Ibn 'Arabi said: "In truth all possibilities resolve principals into non-existence."

There are aspects to this Gnostic theory which many medieval Muslim theologians would have found absurd. Orthodox theologians like Taftāzānī (d. *791*/1389) had to repeatedly hammer home the idea that possibility is a word, a concept, not a reality which exists somewhere, in some state. *See* al-AMR; KUMŪN; NAFAS ar-RAḤMĀN.

Munāfiqūn, *see* HYPOCRITES.

Munkar and Nakīr. Two angels who question the departed in the tomb. They correspond to the Zoroastrian angel Rasht who presides over the eighteenth day of the Zoroastrian month. The Koran describes some "punishment in the tomb" (6:93; 8:52) but the names of the Angels and further elaboration comes from tradition; sometimes in tradition one Angel is named and sometimes two. On the fourth day after death these Angels come and interrogate the deceased regarding their belief. The unbelievers are beaten until the day of Judgement and even the righteous suffer some anguish here. *See* ANGELS.

Muqaddam (lit. "one who is set forward"). A title used for a representative of the civil authorities on the level of a neighborhood, a kind of ward keeper.

While it can mean any kind of representative, it means, in particular, the representative of a Shaykh, or spiritual master, who is authorized to give instruction and initiate disciples in certain Sufi orders.

al-Muqanna' (lit. "he who is veiled or masked"). The sobriquet of Hāshim, a Persian from Merv, who was a follower of the propagandist of the 'Abbāsids, Abū Muslim; after Abū Muslim was put to death, al-Muqanna' raised a revolt in *161*/778 and seized the Persian province of Khorāsān. He claimed to be an incarnation of the Divinity and wore a veil of green silk (or a "mask of gold") to cover his "refulgence" from the eyes of the profane. (Others said it was to hide a hideous deformity.) In *164*/780 after several military defeats, as Ibn al-Athīr relates, he shut himself up in his fortress with his family, gave them poison to drink, and burned it down. He is also known for an illusion of a moon which he caused night after night to rise from a well in Nakhshab for which he is called *Mah-sazanda*, the "moon maker". Al-Qazwini wrote that this illusion was created by a great bowl of quicksilver. His followers were known as the Khurramiyyah, Mubayyiḍah, and Muḥammirah, that is to say, all the usual Mazdakī suspects. *See* ABŪ MUSLIM; BABAK; SURKH-I 'ALĀM; MAZDAK.

Muqarnas. Characteristic decorative devices of Persian origin, used in Arab-Islamic architecture in corners where walls meet ceilings, or as an ornamental articulation of the transition from cubic structures to domes. The *muqarnas* consists of numerous carved pieces of wood wedged together, or of plaster moldings grouped vertically to round out a corner, giving the appearance of a wasp's nest, or, more typically, of stalactites. This beautiful and characteristic geometrical device is found in windows, doors, *miḥrābs*, domes, etc.

Muqawqīs. The title, Arabized, of the Coptic head of Egypt to whom the Prophet addressed a legendary invitation to enter Islam in the sixth year of the Hijrah. A traditional account says that in the building of the trench around Medinah to hold up an attack by the Confederates, the Prophet struck a stone three times which shattered, sending out flashes of light to north, south and east. After this omen, letters were sent to various contemporary rulers, inviting them to submission in Islam. That sent to the Muqawqīs and his reply are preserved in Muslim tradition; he declined politely, but sent gifts and two female slaves, one of whom, Mary the Copt, became a concubine of the Prophet and the mother of his son Ibrāhīm, who died in infancy.

The letter to the Muqawqīs read:

> In the Name of God the Merciful the Compassionate.
>
> From the Apostle of God to thc Muqawqīs, chief of the Copts: Peace be upon him who followeth the guidance.
>
> To proceed: I summon thee with the Call of Islam; make Submission to God as a Muslim and thou shalt live secure; and God shall double thy reward. But if thou wilt not, then on thy head will lie the guilt of all the Copts. O ye people of Scripture, come to a fair covenant between us and you, that we serve God alone, associating no peer with Him, and no more take our fellow men as Lords beside God. But if ye will not, then bear witness: we are the ones who are the Muslims.

The Governor sent reply:

> I am aware that there is a Prophet yet to arise; but I am of the opinion that he is to appear in Syria. For the rest, thy envoy hath been received with due honor; and I send for thine acceptance two virgins such as are highly esteemed among the Copts, and a robe of honor and a riding mule.

See HERACLIUS, MUḤAMMAD.

Muqtaḍi (lit. "one who is appointed or called upon"). He who stands behind the Imām (prayer leader) and calls out the *iqāmah* (the call to prayer made immediately before praying in the mosque), and repeats the *takbīr* (the phrase "*Allāhu Akbar*") in a loud voice so that it is heard in the furthest ranks, and thus initiates the responses within the prayer. In a very large mosque, the *muqtaḍi's* function can be carried out by a number of people. In this way, through a series of men who repeat instructions by calling them out to others who then repeat them in their turn, a congregation of thousands can pray in unison, or a speaker address a vast multitude. The *muqtaḍi's* function is usually performed by the Muezzin, the official caller to prayer. *See* MUEZZIN.

al-Murābiṭūn (lit: "those who are bound, tied, fastened, attached".). Men who, in religious-military organizations, defended the frontiers of the Islamic world (*Dār al-Islām*), often in remote outposts called *rubuṭ* (sing. *ribāṭ*). The institution goes back to the Islamic state under the Caliph 'Umar when, briefly, the Arabs were not allowed to own land in the conquered territories, the intention being to create a permanent mobile class for the expansion of Islam. This code was modified under the successor Caliph 'Uthmān, but the status of *murābiṭūn* reflects this early historical phase. One *murābiṭūn* movement led to an empire in the Arab West, more familiar under the Spanish version of its name, the Almoravids. *See* ALMORAVID.

Murāqabah (lit. "vigilance" "recollectedness"). An aspect of meditation (*tafakkur*), a waiting upon a spiritual presence, a permanent state of awareness. The Prophet said: "My eye sleeps but my heart wakes." It also means an examination of conscience, which in some spiritual methods is performed daily. The methods of Islamic mysticism make meditation a background for invocation (*dhikr*), which is the principal means of spiritual realization, in accordance with the injunction found frequently in the Koran: "And the remembrance of God is greatest" (*wa la dhikru 'Llāhi akbar*).

Al-Ḥjwīrī said:

> When self-will vanishes in this world, contemplation is attained, and when contemplation is firmly established, there is no difference between this world and the next.

See DHIKR.

Muraqqa'ah. A patched garment worn by some Sufi orders in the past as a discipline of poverty. (It is still seen today, albeit extremely rarely.) Some Sufis, who also lived from alms, wore such threadbare frocks that were repeatedly patched rather than replaced, until the whole garment was nothing but patches on patches.

Al-Ḥjwīrī said:

> "A right patch is a patch that is stitched because one is poor, and not for show: if it is stitched for poverty it is stitched right, even if it is stitched badly." And also: "It is not, however, the quantity of money that makes the moneyed man. No one who recognizes poverty as better than money is a moneyed man, though he be a king; and a man who does not believe in poverty is a moneyed man, however poor he is."

It was a characteristic of the Shādhilī order of Sufism *not* to wear such garments. In fact, Imām Shādhilī himself sometimes wore rich garments because he taught that poverty (*faqr*) is above all something inward, that it is not riches which create an obstacle to spirituality, but attachment to them. A cloak in general, as well as the patched cloak, is also called *khirqah*. *See* KHIRQAH.

Mūrīd (lit. "one who is desirous [of spiritual realization]"). A disciple in a Sufi order. A more commonly used name is *faqīr* or *dervish*. *See* FAQĪR.

Muridism. A modern Sufi movement which has become widespread in Senegal. It was founded by Amadou [Aḥmad] Bamba (1852-1927) who has had five successors called *khalifahs* (caliphs), the fourth of whom died in 1990. The present, the fifth, is named Serigne Saliou Mbacké.

Bamba came from a family of religious teachers; he originally led a religious school. Following a familiar pattern, he announced one day to his students that his personal teachings superseded acquired doctrine and that adherence to himself was essential to spiritual progress. Some of the students left him at that point, while those who remained became the core of the new movement. As his influence grew, Amadou Bamba was exiled by the colonial authorities to Gabon in 1895 and later to the Congo. He returned to Senegal in 1902 but was later again exiled to Mauritania for five years in Boutilimit. These events were to give him the aura of a political anti-colonial hero. To his claim for spiritual authority were added accounts of miracles.

The figure of Bamba thus combines the prestige of a champion of the poor and oppressed in a political struggle against a colonizing power (and thereby against the dominance of the West in general) along with miraculous powers and hopes of salvation. This Messianic image has drawn to itself the dispossessed of modern times in West Africa and in particular those Senegalese who have had to face the trials of immigration abroad.

Touba in Senegal is a holy city for the Murids, and in France they have a long established meeting place called a *dahira* in Marseille. There is a sizeable Murid community in New York City, many of whom sell items to tourists on the street and have gone on to found small businesses.

Murji'ah (from Ar. *irjā'*, "postponement", "deferment"). A sect of early Islam that may be termed "quietists". They believed that serious sins are offset by faith, and that punishment for them is not everlasting. Therefore, they withheld judgement and condemnation of sinners in this world. This led to attitudes of political uninvolvement. One of their doctrines, that prayer led by an Imām of doubtful character is, nevertheless, valid, became an accepted principle of Sunnī Islam (but not of Shī'ite Islam).

The Murji'ites appear to have emerged in reaction to the Khārijites, who attribute to sin a quasi-absolute and definitive nature; it is against the Khārijites rather than against the mainstream that the Murji'iah stand out in contrast. Much like St John's "sins unto death", and sins which are "not unto death", the notion of major (*kabā'ir*) and minor (*saghā'ir*) sins is due to the Murji'iah, although the Koran adumbrates it in such passages as:

> "...surely thy Lord knows best who is straying
> from His path, and He knows best who
> it is that is truly guided.
> For to God belong the Heavens and the earth,
> that He may reward them that do evil
> according to what they have done
> and reward them that do well
> according to the best;
> who avoid major sins [*Kabā'ira-l-ithm*]
> and enormities, only falling into minor faults:
> surely thy Lord's forgiveness is broad..."
> (53:30-32).

Some of Abū Ḥanīfah's attitudes derive from the Murji'ite reaction to the extremism of the Khārijites. The Murji'ite doctrine, however, of accepting the outward profession of Islam "with the tongue" as adequate, would inevitably have led to decadence; it was cognizance of this danger that brought about their final extirpation. *See* KHĀRIJITES.

Murshid (lit "guide", "instructor"). An instructor in any field, but in particular a spiritual master, that is, with the ability and a heavenly mandate, in addition to the necessary knowledge, to guide souls. Conversely, no guide (*murshid*) will be accessible to him whom God allows to go astray: "For him whom God sends astray, thou wilt find no guiding pattern [*waliyyan murshida*]" (18:17). A *murshid* is also called a *Shaykh* and, from Turkey to India, a *Pīr*. *See* PĪR; SHAYKH; SUFISM.

al-Murtaḍā, Sayyid (also called ash-Sharīf, and ash-Shaykh Murtaḍa d. *436*/1044). A Shī'ite scholar, student of the Shaykh al-Mufīd, and leader of the Shī'ite community of Baghdad. He was an *Imāmzādeh*, a relative of a Shī'ite Imām, being the great-great-grandson of Mūsā Kāẓīm. He is also known as *'Alam al-Hudā* ("the Banner of Guidance"). Either he, or his brother ar-Raḍī, is the actual author of the *Nahj al-Balāgha*, the speeches attributed to 'Alī.

Murtadd. *see* APOSTASY.

Mūsā Shākir, the Sons of. Three brothers, Aḥmad, Ḥasan, and Muḥammad, who acquired renown as scientists at the court of Baghdad in the *3rd*/9th century. They were mathematicians, astronomers, and engineers who designed the mechanical creations of the time. Known as the *Banū Mūsā*, they participated in the labor of translating Hellenistic writings into Arabic at the *Bayt al-Ḥikmah*, the academy founded by the Caliph al-Ma'mūn (d. *218*/833). A work of theirs on geometry was translated into Latin as the *Liber Trium Fratrum* ("the Book of Three Brothers").

Muṣallāh. A place of prayer, and more specifically the public praying field where, for the festival prayers of the *'Īd al-fitr*, *'Īd al-adhā*, and prayers for rain, the whole population of a city may well meet for communal worship. In Iran the *muṣallā* is called an *'idgah*. The original *muṣallā* was in Medinah, at the site of the present Sabaq mosque (although it is also said that the site is the present al-Ghamamah Mosque).

Musalmān. The Persian and Turkish variant form of the Arabic *muslim* ("one who has surrendered [to God]"), as "Moslem" is the common English form. It is from the Persian that the French acquired *musulmane* for Muslim, usually written "Mussulman" in English.

Musaylamah. The foremost of a number of false prophets who appeared in Arabia towards the end of the life of the Prophet and during the Caliphate of Abū Bakr. Musaylamah claimed to have received divine revelations, and spoke of himself as the "Raḥmān [which is a Name of God] of the Yamāmah" (the east-central region of Arabia). The name Musaylamah, by which the Muslims called him, was a contemptuous diminutive of his real name, Maslamah. He was slain in battle by Waḥshī, the slave who had killed Ḥamzah at Uḥud. The Muslim army was led by Khālid ibn Walīd.

The battle at 'Aqrabah in the Yamāmah between the Muslim forces and those of Musaylamah was the most bloody that Arabia had ever seen. The followers of Musaylamah had already defeated one Muslim force led by 'Ikrimah. At 'Aqrabah, Khālid ibn Walīd divided his army into Beduins, Anṣār (Medinans), and Muhājirūn (Meccan emigrants) to spur competition among them to fight to the utmost. When the Muslims appeared to be losing the struggle, the Anṣār were roused by insults from the rebels and turned the tide. The rebels retreated into a fortified orchard where Musaylamah sat, but then were pursued by the Muslims and there slaughtered. In this battle seven hundred of the Companions were killed, among them some of the oldest, and seven thousand of the followers of Musaylamah. The orchard came to be called "the Garden of Death".

Although more rebellions had yet to be put down in Oman and the Yemen, this battle announced the imminent end of the period of strife which broke out among the desert Arabs after the Prophet's death. During this period, a number of imitators of the Prophet appeared; the *Kahīnah* ("Prophetess") in the north among the Tamīm; Dhu-l-Ḥimār in the Yemen, and others. It is called the *Riddah* (the "period of apostasy").

Mushrabiyyah. (Also *mashrabiyyah* and *mashrabah*). Lattices made of turned dowels, they are typical features of Islamic architecture throughout the Middle East, North Africa, Persia and India. The carved wooden lattice, which forms a pleasing contrast to the often unadorned exteriors of buildings, keep out the hot sun whilst allowing the air to pass.

Mushrikūn (lit. "those who associate"). Idolators. *See* SHIRK.

Muslim (lit. "one who has surrendered to God", from Ar. *aslama*, "to surrender, to seek peace").

1. A Moslem, an adherent of Islam. The word implies complete surrender, submission, and resignation to God's Will. The Muslim is submitted; ideally, therefore, it is not the Muslim who acts, but God, and the actions of the Muslim are an appearance due to his swift and spontaneous obedience to the decrees of fate. This is why the Sufis say that one must be like "a body in the hands of the washers of the dead", moving without resistance to the Divine Will. In this there is peace — *salām*, surrender, wholeness, security. The word "Islam" ("surrender", "submission") is the verbal noun corresponding to the adjective *Muslim* ("surrendered", "submitted"). It is, incidentally, important to pronounce the *s* of *Muslim* sharply as in the English word "slim"; the voiced pronunciation with the s as in "chisel" or "nose", produces a word which means — or sounds somewhat like a word that means — "benighted", "cruel", and which is therefore offensive.

2. Abū-l-Ḥusayn Muslim (*210-261*/816-873), born at Nayshābūr, the great compiler of Ḥadīth. His *Ṣaḥīḥ al-Muslim*, along with the *Ṣaḥīḥ al-Bukhārī* rank as the two most authentic collections.

Muslim Brotherhood (Ar. *al-Ikhwān al-Muslimūn*). A religious organization founded in Egypt in 1929 by Ḥasan al-Bannā', it opposed the tendency towards secular regimes in Muslim countries.

Ḥasan al-Bannā' was assassinated in 1949, and in 1954 the movement was banned in Egypt. It has existed since as a clandestine opposition movement in Egypt, Syria, Sudan, and other countries in the Middle East. Its goal, which is that of the establishment of "Islamic states", is sometimes pursued by assassination and terrorism. In Syria, the first priority of the movement is opposition to domination by the 'Alawīs. The Muslim Brotherhood is held responsible for perhaps more than its share of underground political opposition.

They should not be confused with the *ikhwān* ("brothers"), the desert warriors who helped King 'Abd al-'Azīz in the conquest of Arabia. The name *ikhwān* was also used for Beduin settlement projects in Arabia such as at al-Artawiyyah.

Muslim Council of Britain. A grouping of the major Sunni organizations in Britain founded in 1997 to further Muslim interests and concerns.

Muslim Student Association. In the USA, an active organization founded in 1963 which promotes Muslim awareness.

Muslims, Black, *see* BLACK MUSLIMS.

Musnad. The collection of 30,000 Ḥadīth made by Ibn Ḥanbal (d. *241*/855). *See* ḤADĪTH; IBN ḤANBAL.

Mustaḍ'afūn (lit: "the downtrodden"). A term made current by the Ayatollah Khomeini in the course of the Iranian revolution. Like the "sans culottes" of the French Revolution, or the "descamisados" of Juan Perón, it refers to the disadvantaged whose interests the Iranian revolution claimed to serve. In Iran it is pronounced *mostazafun*. The Pahlavī Foundation was renamed the Mustaḍ'afūn Foundation.

Shī'ism has always been the movement of radical popular causes and has has claimed to be the champion of the oppressed; at the same time the main beneficiaries have been the leadership, the party, the "vanguard". *See* MAZDAK.

Mustaḥabb. The category of actions which, whilst not being obligatory in canon law, are recommended. This is also called *mandūb*. The other categories are *farḍ*, or *wājib*, that is, obligatory; *mubāḥ*, permitted or neutral; *makrūh*, disliked and thus discouraged; and *ḥarām*, forbidden. All actions fall into one of these categories (*aḥkām*), under Islamic law. *See* AḤKĀM; FARḌ ; ḤARĀM.

Mutabārikūn (lit. "those who would participate in blessing"). Those who enter a Sufi *ṭarīqah*, or "fraternity" (lit. "path"), to seek a blessing in addition to the blessings accorded by adherence to the *sharī'ah* ("the outward Divine Law"). The *mutabārikūn* are thus "passive" members of a *ṭarīqah*. The "active" members are those who enter the path because they see in it a way to union with God. The latter are called the *sālikūn*, or "travelers".

The *mutabārikūn* recognize the *ṭarīqah* as a means of grace but do not grasp its possibility as a means of realization. As there are *ṭuruq* ("fraternities") that number hundreds of thousands of adherents, and in the North African desert often include whole communities and towns, it must be assumed that the vast majority are *mutabārikūn*. The division echoes that of the parent tradition which was electi and "hearers".

al-Mu'tafikah (lit. "the overwhelmed ones"). In the Koran, the fated cities of the plain Sodom and Gomorrah, associated with the Prophet Lot (Ar. *Lūt*), which were destroyed.

Mut'ah. Mut'ah (called by the Persians *sigheh*) is allowed by the Twelve-Imām Shī'ites only, and is forbidden by the Sunnīs, thus mut'ah is practiced chiefly in Iran. This is a marriage stipulated to be temporary, sometimes called a "marriage of pleasure". The marriage is automatically terminated at the end of the agreed period. This agreed period can be as short as a day, which has made this a notorious institution, most practiced, ironically enough, in religious milieus. It is associated with Shī'ite places of pilgrimage, where pilgrims would remain for several weeks or months, contracting a temporary marriage for the duration of their stay. It is also associated with religious students who would take up such marriages for the time of their studies. Modernized Iranians typically have abjured this practice.

Mutakallimūn. Arabic for speculative theologians, patterned after the Greek *dialektikoi*, *see* KALĀM

al-Mutanabbī (d. *303-354*/915-965). One of the most famous of Arab poets. The name *Mutanabbī* means the "would-be Prophet", an allusion to the claim, attributed to him, that he was able to write poetry comparable to the language of the Koran. He had, in fact, in his youth been involved in various Shī'ite conspiracies, according to certain of his biographers, and had actually claimed prophethood and the receipt of revelation. His real name was Abū-t-Ṭayyib Aḥmad ibn al-Ḥusayn al-Ju'fī. He was a court panegyrist, one who could easily change his allegiance, and was noted also for his impassioned yet pessimistic view of life. He often extolled Beduin *mores* in his poetry. His quixotic independence, arrogance, boasting and generosity have endeared him to generations of Arabs, who feel an affinity with him; and he was a master of the Arabic language. His most famous line is: "The horseman, night and the desert know me; and the sword and the lance, paper and the pen."

The measure of the resolute is seen
in their resolves
As generous deeds display
the worth of noble souls.
Honor the man of noble soul,
he becomes your slave, but
the mean-souled man when honored
grows insolent.

Naught will suffice for the understanding of men
When the light of day itself
stands in need of proof.
Whoso desires the ocean makes light of streams.
Men bury and are buried and our feet trample the
skulls of those who went before.

Mutaṭāwi'ah (lit. "those who enforce obedience"). A peculiar institution of vigilantes who enforce the performance of prayer and may even inflict beatings for moral laxity. They are found only in some fundamentalist milieus, notably Saudi Arabia. The practice of the public enforcement of morality by such means is not common in Islam as a whole because of the Koran's insistence that "There is no compulsion in religion" (2:258).

Strict public enforcement of morality, not unlike that of the *mutaṭāwi'ah*, was prominent in theocratic republics such as that founded by 'Abd al-Karīm in the Rīf in the 1920s, and in the communities in the Caucasus under Imām Shāmil.

Mutawalli. The administrator of a religious establishment; a term encountered mainly in Iran and India.

Mutawila, *see* METAWILA.

Muṭawwif (from Ar. *ṭāfa*, "to circumambulate", from which comes *ṭawāf*, "circumambulation of the Ka'bah";). One who guides pilgrims in the performance of the rites of pilgrimage, whether *ḥajj* or *'umrah*. The *muṭawwifūn* are residents of Mecca, many of them Qurayshīs. They were a guild in classical times, and the right to be a *muṭawwif* is handed down in the family, but today requires a royal patent.

While it is not necessary to hire a *muṭawwif* in order to perform the *'umrah*, regulations require that pilgrims arriving for *ḥajj* be assigned to a *muṭawwif*, either one of their own choice or one designated by the authorities. The *muṭawwif* works through representatives and handles thousands of pilgrims at *ḥajj* time, providing lodging and transportation, and sometimes food as well. *Muṭawwifs* guide pilgrims according to their respective *madhāhib*, or schools of law. There are published fees covering various aspects of the *ḥajj* services which are fixed by the Saudi government. Arrangements can be made with a muṭawwif in advance of the actual pilgrimage, and it was once the practice for muṭawwifs to travel in Islamic countries in order to prospect for clients.

For the *'umrah*, *muṭawwifs* can be found in the Grand Mosque (*al-Masjid al-Ḥarām*), sometimes at the gates, near the Maqām Ibrāhīm, or near Ṣafā and Marwah. Usually they collect several pilgrims together to perform the rites as a group. *See* ḤAJJ.

Mu'tazilites (from Ar. *a'tazala*, "to take one's distance", "to remove oneself", "to withdraw", perhaps patterned after the Greek *schizmatikoi*). An influential school of theology historically repudiated by Sunnīs but the theological cornerstone of Twelve Imām Shī'ism. This school of thought was born out of, or inserted itself into, the controversies of the civil war between 'Alī ibn Abī Ṭālib and the Companions az-Zubayr and Ṭalḥāh, and the absolute black-and-white condemnatory views of the Khārijites. Faced with a conflict between opposing parties, none of whom could reasonably be considered absolutely reprehensible, the need arose for dogmatic nuances. One response was formulated as: *manzilah bayna-l-manzilatayn* ("a position between the two positions"). This was the answer to a question treated in the circle of Ḥasan al-Baṣrī as to whether a Muslim who had committed a grave sin was a believer or not, in which the Khārijite position was that one who had committed a grave sin was no longer a believer, and therefore could be put to death. Ḥasan al-Baṣrī's answer was that such a one was a believer but a hypocrite; that of Waṣīl ibn 'Atā' (d. *131*/748) was that he was neither a believer nor an infidel, but somewhere between the two, and this marked the beginning of the Mu'tazilite school, those who "had taken their distance" from Ḥasan al-Baṣrī, as the great teacher reportedly had said. This "position between two positions" is what is known in Christianity as the Arian heresy; philosophically it is a violation of Aristotle's law of non-contradiction; which is to say it is a violation of objective reality, and opens to door to total subjectivism, self-contradiction, irrationality, and solipsism. Which is also why the Chalcedonian answer is theologically another version of Aristotle's law and a fundamental statement about the nature of reality. Formulations like the "position between two positions" appear constantly in different disguises and are infinitely tempting for they are the illusory "having it both ways" in the sense of both yes and no at the same time.

The other prominent figures of the new school were 'Amr ibn 'Ubayd (d. *145*/762), and later Abū Ḥudhayl (d. *235*/849) and an-Naẓẓām (d. *225*/840), who was the most important formulator of the Mu'tazilite teachings. The school took stock of the philosophic tools of Hellenistic antiquity, and applied reason to the solution of philosophical problems, leading thereby to the birth of *kalām*, Islamic theology itself. Mu'tazilitism catered to certain ideologies in Persia, and it lent itself easily for a time to being the dominant philosophy of the 'Abbāsids. Its doctrine of free will, moreover, could be used as an arm against the Umayyads, who defended their regime with arguments of Divine predestination propounded by the traditionalists (*ahl al-ḥadīth*).

Although the theology may have been invented in order to move Islam onto dualist tracks, the Mu'tazilites themselves, like antibodies created after vaccination, became opponents of dualism. The Mu'tazilites held, as rationalists (and materialists), that the Koran is created. (The orthodox dogma is that the Koran is uncreated in its essence.) This was proclaimed official doctrine by the Caliph al-Ma'mūn in *212*/827 and enforced by a *mihnah*, a scrutiny of the beliefs held by the various religious authorities, which was a virtual inquisition. Ibn Ḥanbal, founder of one of the schools of law, was scourged for publicly maintaining the uncreatedness of the Koran (in a particularly categorical fashion: he said the Koran is "uncreated from cover to cover"; this could also be taken as an "anti-materialist" stance). But shortly thereafter, when, under the Caliph Mutawakkil, this doctrine was suppressed, the Mu'tazilites went into a sharp decline and fell out of favor, in Sunni Islam. But the doctrine survived in its own milieu, that of Twelve Imām Shī'ism, and is their accepted theology to this day. However, the outlook which results from

Mu'tazilitism is also increasingly evident in modern movements among Sunnis.

Nevertheless, the influence exerted by the school was considerable: it established the widespread use of rational arguments in the subsequent development of theology, and many of its original conclusions were adopted by the mainstream, although the school as a whole was attacked as heretical.

The Mu'tazilites called themselves *ahl al-'adl wa-l-tawḥīd* (the "People of Justice and [Divine] Unity"), and their school was based upon the following five principles:

1. *tawḥīd* ("unity");
2. *'adl* ("justice");
3. *al-wa'd wa-l-wa'īd* ("the promise and the threat");
4. *al-manzilah bayn al-manzilatayn* ("a position between two positions");
5. *al-amr bi-l-ma'rūf wa-n-nahy 'an al-munkar* ("commanding the good and prohibiting evil").

By *tawḥīd* they meant a paradoxical doctrine; Sunnis say that some of the divine attributes ("Names") are of the Essence and some are of Being. By the Mu'tazilite tawḥīd, the essence is unknowable, and none of the attributes are of the Essence; these attributes or Names are reduced to a kind of demiurgic level, to being some kind of created energies.

This unknowability of God led the Mu'tazilites to deny the generally accepted idea that those whom salvation brings into paradise have a "vision" of God, arguing that such "seeing" of God would place Him within space. The Ash'arite and Sunni position is that God is knowable; that some Divine Names are names of the Essence and not some created energy. This controversy became symbolized by the question of "vision" in Paradise. (*See* "BEATIFIC VISION".) The Prophet is credited with saying that the inhabitants of paradise would see God. When asked how, he said "as people see the full moon"; i.e. by "reflection" as the moon reflects the light of the sun.

It is these problems which al-Ash'arī, emerging out of Mu'tazilitism, addressed with his theory of atoms of time and space which are "mirrors" of the One Reality, and his theory of will as "the acquiring of Divine action on the part of the creature" (*iktisāb*).

In the orthodox idea, according to which God is both Absolute and Being (*Hāhūt* and *Lāhūt*), there is a continuity of identity between the Attributes and the Absolute. The Attributes are not the Essence, neither are they anything other than the Essence; an inescapable and necessary antinomy. It is this vertical identity, "with God and One with God", which is true non-duality, in virtue of which the Divine Attributes are not "other Divinities". (*See* BEING; FIVE DIVINE PRESENCES.) The Mu'tazilite *tawḥīd*, like that of some modern philosophers such as Martin Buber, is a unity in name only; the question of how the supposed unity can contain differentiated contraries is simply ignored.

By *'adl* ("justice") they affirmed that man has free will, which is necessary because of Divine justice. (The early Shī'ites believed that God created and determined Men's acts; present day Shī'ites believe in free will). The Mu'tazilites also asserted that God does what is best (*ṣalāḥ* or *aṣlaḥ*) for the world he has created; that God compensates the saved for sufferings they endured in life. What makes this idea of Divine justice scandalous, however, is that it means that what a man does obliges God; it puts God on an equal plane with man; if a man does a good act, God must react accordingly, if a man does an evil act God must react accordingly. What the Mu'tazilite Divine justice means, therefore, is *reciprocity* between man and God. The absurdity of this was not lost on the detractors; but because of the psychology which results from "a position between two positions" neither did it faze the supporters, for whom contradictions are not a problem. It was one thing to make God observe the necessity of his Own Nature, as did Aristotle; it was another to make Him dependent upon something created.

The Ash'arites claimed, not without reason, that Mu'tazilitism "made God into a servant of man", because it made him respond to human acts and made God, as they put it, into "the impregnator of women". The idea of *ṣalāḥ* became the point on which al-Ash'arī revolted against the Mu'tazilites, neatly showing its weakness, (but not, however, disproving the idea that necessity is an aspect of perfection.) (*See* al-ASH'ARĪ; CHILDREN.)

By the third principle they meant heaven and hell. They believed that if someone went to hell, it was forever, he would not leave by reason of Divine Mercy or intercession. (Reciprocity, *see above*, limits God's ability to act; the Ash'arites, on the contrary, believe that sins may be pardoned even in hell, or that a believer may be withdrawn from hell once his sins are expiated.) Present day Shī'ites generally accept that a sinner can be saved from Hell because, ironically, of the power of the Imāms.

The fourth principle, "a position between two positions" was, on the one hand, their philosophical method, but also their political outlook in the historic controversies. This was a middle position between the Sunnīs and the Shī'ites (of the *3rd*/9th century who were more *ghulat* than the Twelvers have been until recently, although this is again changing). The creed of the Mu'tazilites was the chosen theology of the early 'Abbāsids, and the decisive theological influence upon the Shī'ites. It would perhaps be more accurate to say that Mu'tazilitism was the doctrine of those who brought the 'Abbāsids to power, and therefore the 'Abbāsids were obliged to accept it until power shifted. Waṣīl ibn 'Aṭa', the founder of Mu'tazilitism, was apparently the head of some vast clandestine organization for the writer Jāḥiẓ said of him: "Beyond the Pass of China, on every frontier to far distant Sus and beyond the Berbers, he has preachers. A tyrant's jest, an intriguer's craft does not break their determination. If he says 'Go' in winter, they obey; in summer they fear not the month of burning heat" [*Bayān* I 37]. It was precisely this clandestine organization that brought the 'Abbāsids to power.

In present day Shī'ism this idea of the position between two positions, in so far as it relates to the idea of a sinner being between belief and unbelief, has been abandoned. The Shī'ites, apart from the doctrine of the Imāms, developed their theology much later, under the Buyids. By that time Mu'tazilite thinking had already formed the base of Twelve-Imām theology, through the Nawbakhti family of Baghdad, and, being established, was not further modified, while the doctrine of the Imāmate continued to undergo development.

There is in Mu'tazilitism a strong flavor of a metaphysical outlook alien to Islam. This was recognised even before al-Ash'ari, for the following "Ḥadīth" (evidently invented but showing the reaction of an affronted orthodoxy) gained wide circulation: "The Mu'tazilites are the Mājūs [an all-embracing name for the religions of Persia]; do not follow one of them as a prayer leader, and do not attend their funerals."

The fifth principle, the establishment of order in society, was not different from the view of the Sunnīs. *See* al-ASH'ARĪ; "BEATIFIC VISION"; CHILDREN; CREED; ḤASAN BAṢRĪ; ISTAWĀ; KALĀM; KHĀRIJITES; KUMŪN; al-MA'MŪN; MĀTURĪDĪ; MIHNAH; PHILOSOPHY.

al-Muwaḥḥidūn (lit. the "unitarians"). The name by which the Wahhābīs prefer to call themselves, and also the Druzes, and the Arabic name of the Almohad movement. Despite the name, however, there is no connection between the three groups. *See* ALMOHADS; DRUZES; WAHHĀBĪS.

Muwaqqatah (from Ar. *waqt*, "time"). The establishment of the correct times for the daily prayers. Because the prayer times change with the position of the sun, this must be done each day. The need to know exact time encouraged the study of astronomy, and up until this century muezzins often learned to use astrolabes. In 1900 the last man in Fez still skilled in the use of the astrolabe was over 100 years old and had no more disciples.

For a simple means of determining prayer times, *see* ṢALĀH *and also* PRAYER.

Muwatta' (lit. "The Way made Smooth"). This is the name of the first compilation of Ḥadīth. It was made by Mālik ibn Anas (*94-179*/716-795) of Medinah, the founder of the Mālikī School of Law. It is not as systematic as the *ṣaḥīḥān* of Muslim and Bukhari, but it laid the foundation for Ḥadīth studies. *See* MĀLIK IBN ANAS.

Muzawwir (from *ziyārah*, "a visit"). A guide who leads visitors through the steps of a formal visit to the Prophet's mosque in Medinah and the environs. Also called simply a guide, *dalīl*. *See* ZIYARAH.

Muzdalifah. A place between 'Arafāt, 8 km/3.5 miles away, and Minā, 3.5 km/2 miles distant from Mecca. Here pilgrims spend the night after the "standing of the Day of 'Arafat" during the *ḥajj*. They pray at *al-Mash'ar al-Ḥarām* monument and gather pebbles for the ceremony of the stoning of the *jamarāt*, the stone pillars which represent the devil, in Minā. *See* PILGRIMAGE.

Mysticism, *see* SUFISM.

N

Nabī. A Prophet, one who prophesies within an existing revelation, as opposed to a *rasūl* ("Messenger"), who brings a new revelation. *See* PROPHET.

an-Nadīm, Muḥammad ibn Isḥāq (d. *385*/995). Known as *al-Warrāq* ("the manuscriptist") and often called, incorrectly, Ibn an-Nadīm. A book dealer and copiest of Baghdad, he wrote a book called "the Catalog" or "Repertory" (*al-Fihrist*) in 986 which lists books and authors of his times along with notes, commentaries, and observations on religious, spiritual, and metaphysical matters. He was a Shī'ite and the name *nadīm* ("imperial house guest" means he was a companion of the Caliphal court. An-Nadīm was also on close terms with the Vizier 'Alī ibn 'Īsā. He is the most important source of information on Mani which he himself obtained from personal acquaintances (he said he knew 300 Manicheans at one time) and from the now lost writings of Abū 'Isa al-Warrāq. He was an admirer of the ancient philosophers and a major source on the intellectual history of his time. E. G. Browne wrote of him: "...I know of no Arabic book which inspires me at once with so much admiration for the author's enormous erudition, and so much sadness that sources of knowledge at once so numerous and so precious as were available when he wrote should, for the most part, have entirely perished." The *Fihrist* has been translated into English by Bayard Dodge. *See* ARCHEGOS; IBN MU'TAZZ.

Naḍīr Shāh, *see* AFSHĀRIDS.

Nafas ar-Raḥmān (lit. "the breath of the Merciful"). A term in Sufi metaphysics for the manifestation of possibilities, and thus for the creation of the world, based upon the symbolism of the breath. The world is created by God figuratively "breathing out". Creation, and man, receives the breath and with it the means — life — to return to the Creator. The "breathing in" by God is a reabsorption of creation, an extinction of manifested possibilities in Being, and, in the apocatastasis, the disappearance of Being, *Lāhūt*, "the Personal God".

Speech in man, which is vehicled by the breath, is an analogous function. In speaking man makes manifest or objective that which is subjective and hidden within him. The hearer receives the speech and understands it or integrates it into his subjectivity, or consciousness. Breath — *prāṇa* — *spiritus* — which is life itself, is thus the sacred medium in which creation takes place.

The Koran says that God is Creator at every instant (55:29); this eternal creation is sometimes referred to as the "overflowing" (*fayḍ*) of Being, or the "renewing of creation at each instant" or "each breath" (*tajdīd al-khalq bi-l-anfas*). In the *Fuṣūṣ al-Ḥikam*, the chapter on Solomon, Ibn 'Arabi wrote that man does not "spontaneously realize that with each breath he is not, and then again is" (*lam yakun thumma kān*), because the moment of annihilation coincides with the moment of manifestation, and because the act of creation is instantaneous. In history there are progressions of events and change, but metaphysically, the process of creation is continuous and instantaneous, the world being made anew at every instant, differently, reflecting the flux and progression within it.

An incidental meaning of the term *nafas ar-Raḥmān* is a celebration which is held when a pupil in a traditional Koranic school has memorized the Koran from the beginning, the Sūrah *al-Baqarah*, up to the 55th Sūrah called *ar-Raḥmān* ("the Merciful"). *See* ARABIC; KALĀM; SOLOMON.

Nafy (lit. "negation"). The first part of the *shahādah* ("testimony of the faith") is *lā ilāha* ("there is no god"). This is the *nāfy*, the negation of unreality, which precedes the *ithbāt* ("affirmation") *illā' Llāh* ("except Allāh"). *See* SHAHĀDAH.

Nāfilah (pl. *nawāfil*). The voluntary prayers consisting of one, two, or four *raka'āts* which the pious add before and after canonical prayers (*ṣalāh*). Nawāfil are not performed, however, after the performance of the dawn prayer (*ṣubḥ*) until the sun has risen, and after the mid-afternoon prayer (*'aṣr*) has been performed until the evening prayer (*maghrib*)

The *nawāfil* provide a means for the increased exercise of zeal and devotion on the exoteric plane.

In addition to the *nawāfil* which accompany the canonical prayers, there are additional prayers which can be performed at certain times: for example, the *ishrāq*, a supplementary prayer in the morning after sunrise; the *ḍuḥā*, performed before noon; and the *tahajjud*, at night. There are also special prayers such as the *istikhārah*, or "asking for help in choosing the good". Religious teachers recommend that, if one does perform the supplementary prayers, they should occasionally be omitted to underline their optional character.

Nafs. The soul. The Arabic *nafs* corresponds to the Latin *anima* and the Greek *psyche*. It is the individual substance, and corresponds to the receptive pole of Being. It exists alongside *rūḥ* ("spirit"), corresponding to Latin spiritus and Greek *pneuma*, which is non-individual and represents the active pole of Being in man, also called the *'aql* ("Intellect"). (*See* 'AQL.)

Often the term *nafs* is used in a pejorative sense, because in its fallen, unregenerate state, admixed with passion and ignorance, it is *an-nafs al-ammārah bi-s-sū'* ("the soul which incites to evil", 12:53). Passing through the stage of *an-nafs al-lawwāmah* ("the reproachful soul", 75:2), which corresponds in a way to conscience advocating conversion, it can become purified and reconciled to the source of its reality as *an-nafs al-muṭma'innah* ("soul at peace") assured of paradise:

'O soul at peace, return unto thy Lord,
well-pleased, well-pleasing!
Enter thou among My servants!
Enter thou My paradise!' (89:27).

See FIVE DIVINE PRESENCES; RŪḤ.

Nahj al-Balāghah (lit. "the way of eloquence"). A collection of sermons, sayings, and speeches attributed to 'Alī ibn Abī Ṭālib. It was compiled by ash-Sharīf ar-Raḍī (d. *406*/1015), a Shī'ite scholar, the brother of Sayyid al-Murtaḍā (himself a possible author of the book, d. *436*/1044), and a disciple of the Shaykh al-Mufīd (d. *413*/1022). In response to a remark by one Shī'ite scholar that 'Alī could not possibly have written the book, the 'Allama Taba'taba'ī was heard to say: "our 'Alī is not the same as the historical 'Alī."

The book is a model for classical Arabic style, as Cicero is for Latin.

Nahr. The sacrificial slaughter of a camel. *See* SACRIFICE.

Nā'ib. A deputy of a civil authority; also, in certain Sufi orders, the representative of a Sufi Shaykh, superior to a *muqaddam* ("representative").

Najaf. The site in 'Irāq of the tomb of 'Alī ibn Abī Ṭālib, the fourth Caliph. The actual place of burial is not known, or rather, it was simply forgotten, for Shī'ism did not yet exist. 'Alī was assassinated at Kūfah and some say that he was buried there in the courtyard of the Mosque. The present tomb is elsewhere; the Shī'ites explain the discrepancy by saying that the dead body, according to 'Alī's wish, was placed upon a camel and the place where it knelt became the burial place, Najaf being four miles from Kūfah. But this place was not "found" for more than a hundred years. It was "discovered" in a politically inspired vision by Caliph Harūn ar-Rashīd while hunting; he heard "his cousin" 'Alī call to him, and that is how the burial place was found. Then the story of the camel followed, to make the original oversight into an act of Providence and mystery.

The Caliph built a shrine there. Doubtless, this was a political exercise on his part (other such gestures were to follow by successive 'Abbāsids) to curry favor with Shī'ites. From *366*/977 an important tomb built by the Buyid chief Adūd ad-Dawlah stood at Najaf; it was destroyed and rebuilt a number of times.

The shrine of 'Alī is known among Shī'ites as the *Mashhad Gharwah* ("the wondrous place of martyrdom"). Because of the tomb of 'Alī, Najaf is the place of preference for a Shī'ite to be buried and over the centuries the city became surrounded by what is perhaps the largest graveyard in the world known as "the Valley of Peace". Mazār-i Sharīf in Afghanistan also claims to be the tomb of 'Alī. This is, of course, impossible. *See* MAZĀR-I SHARĪF.

Najd (lit. "the highlands"). The central plain of Arabia where Riyāḍ, the capital of Saudi Arabia, is located.

Najm ad-Dīn Kubrā, *see* KUBRĀ, Najm ad-DĪN.

Najmu thāqibu. (Ar. "blazing star"). Koran 86:3, "the star of piercing brightness". One of the names of the Prophet. Some have said that Saturn is the "piercing star", and some Sirius. If *najmu thāqibu* refers to a planet or star, and not to an idea, it is far more likely to be Venus. In Hebrew Venus as the morning star was called Heylel ben Shachar as in Isaiah 14:2 and was applied by Isaiah to Tiglath Pileser III, a King of Babylonia: "How are you fallen from Heaven, Day Star, Son of the Dawn! How you are cut down to the ground, you who laid the nations low!" In the Septuagint Heylel was translated as Phosphorus and in the Vulgate as Lucifer, the Roman name of the Morning Star. (Hesperus was the name of the Evening Star.) The name Lucifer was associated with Satan by St. Jerome. But aside from being a planet and used as an epithet for princes, prophets, and demons, the star in Manicheism symbolizes the particle of divinity hidden within the world, and the blazing star, the exceptionally shining particle of light, may be the divine messenger. The shining star or glittering star also appears in the Surat of Light (24:36) as the *kawkabun durriun*. The distant and strange is often closer than one thinks: the blazing star also appears in the form of the star of Texaco Oil which is of Masonic inspiration (as, doubtless, is also the "lone star" itself). *See* ĀYAT an-NŪR.

Najrān. A city and region in southern Arabia near the Yemen, before Islam, it was an oasis, with a Christian population and the seat of a bishopric. A Himyarite king called Dhū Nuwās ("he of the curls", his actual name was Yusūf As'ar), a convert to Judaism, called upon the people of Najrān to abandon Christianity for his own Jewish religion. When they refused, he had them slaughtered and thrown into burning ditches. When the Emperor of Byzantium, Justin I heard of the massacre, as protector of Christianity he called upon the Negus of Abyssinia, Ella Aṣbeḥa, another Christian king, to punish Dhū Nuwās. The Negus sent an army in AD 525 and Dhū Nuwās was killed. The martyrs of Najrān are remembered in the Christian calendars and are mentioned in the Koran 85:4-8:

> ...slain were the Men of the Pit,
> the fire abounding in fuel,
> when they were seated over it
> and were themselves witnesses
> of what they did with the believers.
> They took revenge on them only because they believed in God
> the All-mighty, the All-laudable...

The traces of the original Najrān can still be seen in the desert. The bishops of Najrān, who were probably Nestorians, came to the great fairs of Minā and 'Ukāẓ, and preached Christianity, each seated on a camel as in a pulpit.

In the tenth year of the Hijrah a delegation of sixty Christians from Najrān came to Medinah to make a treaty with the Prophet, and were permitted by him to pray in his mosque. Najran was a center of cloth making and originally the *kiswah* or covering of the Ka'bah was made there. The church of Najran was called the Ka'bah Najran. (Several other shrines in Arabia were also called Ka'bah). Since around *1088*/1677 up until recently Najran was the seat of the *dā'ī al-muṭlaq*, spiritual leader of the Sulaymānī Ismā'īlīs, a community of about 70,000 in the Yemen and a few thousand in India. The function has been in the Makrami family. *See* AHL al-KISĀ'Ī; CHRISTIANITY; NESTORIANS.

Nāmāz (Pers. "prayer"). This Persian word replaces the Arabic word *ṣalāh* as the name for the canonic prayer from Turkey to India.

Name (Ar. *al-ism*). Muslim names are made up of a proper name followed by a *nasab*, a name referring to an ancestor in the form of *ibn* ("son") or *bint* ("daughter") and the name of the father, then the grandfather, and so on for as many generations as one has patience. A person could also be called by a *kunyah*, an indirect honorific name whose form was that of "father of" (*Abū*), or "mother of" (*Umm*). *Kunyahs* could become proper names in themselves, without the person actually being the "father of 'Abbās" (Abū-l-'Abbās), and be combined with an *ism* ("name"), a *naṣab*, and so forth. To the name by usage could also be added a *nisbah* (an "association"), which could be the place of birth, such as ar-Rūmī, ("from Rum", that is, Byzantine Konya) or ar-Rāzī ("from the town of Rayy"), or the name of a profession such as al-Khayyām ("tentmaker") or al-Ḥāsib ("accountant" or "mathematician"), or a clan or tribal name such as al-Hāshimī ("of the Hashimites"), or a distinction, such as al-Anṣārī, one descended from the original Muslim converts of Medinah. The Qarmaṭīs favored "worker" names, those or trades, such as *Sarrāj*, "saddlemaker".

Then one could have an honorific formal name, which replaced the given name in ceremonial usage, a laqab. Such names were adopted by the later 'Abbāsids when they became Caliph, such as al-Manṣūr ("the Victor") and were given out, in very ostentatious forms, to the Buyid princes such as *'Imād ad-Dawlah* ("Pillar of the State").

When the Prophet accepted converts to Islam, many of them had distinctly pagan names, such as "Slave of the goddess 'Uzzā". These he changed for Muslim names; when a person already had an acceptable name, the Prophet sometimes left it as it was, adding a Muslim name to it. Since then, when one enters Islam, he is given or chooses a Muslim name. As a name has a great and mysterious resonance upon the soul, giving it a sacred identity and a dignity towards which it must grow, or, if a profane name, a weight of triviality or profanity which drags the soul down, the choice of a name which transmits a presence of nobility and piety is a matter of gravity. Therefore, it is common to consult the Koran when the choice of a name comes up, and nothing otherwise directly suggests itself.

Names define the object or person named; thus the more important, sacred, or profound an object or a person is, the more names there are to describe it. For example, there are many names for the Koran, and for the cities of Mecca and Medinah. The Names of God are limited by those which have been revealed, but the Prophet is identified by two hundred names (of which, however, only a handful would be commonly recognized). *See* DIVINE NAMES; ISM; KUNYAH; LAQAB; NASAB; NISBAH.

Name, Divine *see* ALLĀH; DIVINE NAMES; ISM;

Names of the Prophet. The *Dala'īl al-Khayrat* ("Guides to Good Works") of al-Jazūlī lists two hundred names of the Prophet; others list even more. This is a selection of the traditional names:

'Abd Allāh	The Servant of God
Abū-l-Qāsim	Father of Qāsim
Abū Ibrāhīm	Father of Ibrāhīm
Aḥmad	The Most-Praised
Ajmal Khalq Allāh	The Most Beautiful of God's Creation
'Alam al-Hudā	The Banner of Guidance
al-Amīn	The Fount of Blessings
Bāligh	The Proclaimer
al-Bashīr	The Bringer of Good Tidings
al-Burhān	The Proof
Dalīl al-Khayrat	The Guide to Good Deeds
Dār al-Ḥikmah	The Abode of Wisdom
Dhikr Allāh	The Remembrance of God
al-Fātiḥ	The Opener
al-Ghawth	The Redeemer
Habīb Allāh	The Beloved of God
al-Ḥāshir	The Gatherer on the Day of Judgement
al-'Ilm al-Yaqīn	The Knowledge that is Certitude
Imām al-Muttaqīn	The Model Leader of the God-Fearing
al-Kāmil	The Perfect
Kāshif al-Karb	The Effacer of Grief
Khalīl ar-Raḥmān	The Friend of the All-Compassionate
Khātim al-Anbiyā'	The Seal of the Prophets
Khātim ar-Rūsūl	The Seal of the Messengers
Madīnat al-'Ilm	The City of Knowledge
al-Mahdī	The Rightly-Guided
al-Ma'sūm	The Infallible
Miftāḥ al-Jannah	The Key of Paradise
Miftāḥ ar-Raḥmah	The Key of Mercifulness
al-Miṣbāḥ	The Niche of Lights
Muḥammad	The Praised
al-Muḥyī	The Reviver
al-Munīr	The Illuminator
al-Muṣṭāfā	The Chosen
an-Nabī	The Prophet
an-Nadhīr	The Warner
an-Najm ath-Thāqib	The Piercing Star
an-Nūr	The Light
al-Qamar	The Moon
Rāfi' ar-Ruṭab	The Exalter of Ranks
Raḥmah li'l-'Ālamīn	A Mercy to the Universe
Rahmaṭ Allāh	The Mercifulness of God
ar-Rasūl	The Messenger
Rūḥ al-Ḥaqq	The Spirit of Truth
Ruḥ al-Quddūs	The Holy Spirit
aṣ-Ṣādiq	The Truthful
Ṣāḥib al-Bayyān	Master of the Clarification
Ṣāḥib ad-Darajah ar-Rafī	Lord of the Exalted Degree
Ṣāḥib al-Mi'rāj	The Possessor of the Ascension
as-Sayyid	The Liege Lord
Sayyid al-Kawnayn	Liege Lord of the Two Worlds
Sayyid al-Mursalīn	Liege Lord of the Messengers
Shāfi' al-Mudhnibīn	The Intercessor for Sinners
ash-Shāhid	The Witness
ash-Shams	The Sun
ash-Shāri'	The Legislator
aṣ-Ṣirāṭ al-Mustaqīm	The Straight Path
Tā' Hā'	Ta' Ha' (Sūrah of the Koran)
aṭ-Ṭāhir	The Pure

The Ḥajj is the great annual pilgrimage which now brings together as many as 2 million worshipers. The Rites of Pilgrimage are performed in the Grand Mosque of Mecca (*left*) and in the desert environs of the city. The Ka'bah (*above*), the stone structure at the centre of the Grand Mosque, contains the Black Stone, and is the sanctuary towards which Muslims turn in prayer. *See* BLACK STONE; HAJJ; KA'BAH; MECCA; PILGRIMAGE.

'Bilāl's Mosque", or the *Masjid Ibrāhīm* (*above*), overlooks the Grand Mosque from Abū Qubays hill. Pilgrims in the costume of *iḥrām* (*left*) pray before the Ka'bah; (*opposite*), they circle the Ka'bah, shown with its door to the right, with its covering of black cloth, the *kiswah,* inscribed with gold thread (*below*). *See* IḤRĀM.

The *sa'y* of "walking" between the hills of Ṣafā and Marwah, is performed (*above*) immediately after the circumambulation of the Ka'bah. In the plain of 'Arafāt, 12 miles/20 km southwest of Mecca, the pilgrims assemble around the Mount of Mercy (*opposite top*) for the "standing" (*wuqūf*), said to be an occasion which foreshadows the Day of Judgement. The pilgrims proceed *en masse* along gigantic pedestrian ramps to Minā (*opposite bottom*), where they stone the three *jamarāt,* or pillars (*below*). *See* 'ARAFĀT; MINĀ; ṢAFĀ AND MARWAH; SA'Y; WUQŪF.

Ṣalāh, the canonical prayer, is performed five times each day; here it is being led by an Imām in the Nin Jie Mosque, Peking (*opposite top*) and (*opposite bottom right*), during Ramaḍān, in the Regent's Park Mosque, London. Worshipers celebrate the end of Ramaḍān (*opposite bottom left*) with dawn prayers in Yogyakarta, Java, Indonesia. A Touareg in a desert *muṣallā* (prayer-ground) in Algeria (*above*) faces Mecca to perform the *ṣalāh*. *See* IMĀM; MUṢALLĀ; RAMAḌĀN; ṢALĀH; TUAREG.

A *Rak'ah* is a cycle of ritual actions and sacred phrases, with minor variations between different Schools of Law, performed in Arabic, the sacred liturgical language of Islam. A prescribed number of these make up each *ṣalāh*. The worshiper must be in a state of ritual purity to perform the five basic actions which are: (1) the raising of the hands to proclaim *Allāhu akbar* (*top left*); (2) the standing position for the pronouncing of the *fātiḥah* (*top right*); (3) the bow (*rukū'*)) in which the phrase "Glory be to God the Mighty" is repeated three times (*centre left*); (4) the prostration (*sujūd*), also accompanied by the formula "Glory to My Lord the Most High" (*centre right*); (5) the seated position (*jalsah*). *See* FĀTIḤAH; RAK'AH; RUKŪ'; SCHOOLS OF LAW; SUJŪD.

aṭ-Ṭayyib	The Good
Walī Allāh	The Friend of God (The Saint)
al-Wakīl	The Advocate
al-Wāṣil	The Joiner
Yā Sīn	Ya Sin (Sūrah of the Koran)

See MUḤAMMAD.

Nāmūs (from Greek *nomos*, "law"). An archaic term, borrowed from the Christians, for Being, or the personal God. It was personified as an Angel who imparted knowledge or brought revelations. This was the Angel, one could say, of *intellection*, or knowledge obtained through the universal contents of the mind being brought to consciousness in the lightning flash of recognition, a "natural" revelation. "As often as it [lightning] flasheth forth for them they walk therein and when it darkeneth against them they stand still." (2:20).

Waraqah Ibn Nawfal, a cousin of Khadījah, the Prophet's wife, identified the Angel bringing revelations to the Prophet as the *Nāmūs*. *See* WARAQAH IBN NAWFAL.

Naqshbandiyyah. A prominent Sufi order founded by Muḥammad ibn Muḥammad Bahā' ad-Dīn Naqshband (*717-791*/1317-1389) of Bukhārā. Silence as a method of recollectedness and concentration is characteristic of the order, which is particularly widespread in the Caucasus and Central Asia. (Imām Shāmil was a Naqshbandī.) One of the special Naqshbandī prayers is called the *khatm al-Khawājagān* ("the seal of the masters") and is recited after some of the canonic prayers. (Most Sufi orders have something similar, which is invocation of its initiatic chain, in effect a belief that the past masters can help the disciple.) The principal spiritual method of the Naqhshbandīs is silent *dhikr* ("invocation") with the heart. The Divine Name is invoked not with the tongue, but with the consciousness centered on the spiritual heart, the subtle symbolical center of the person, which may or may not coincide with the awareness of the physical heart. It is this spiritual center which calls upon the Name in an existential rather than mental invocation. The method bears some resemblance to the Hesychast prayer of the heart, but is not identical with it. Because of the "silent *dhikr*" the Naqshbandīs were called in Russian Sheptuni in the Soviet Union, "the Whisperers". But in fact, silent *dhikr* is widespread throughout Sufism. The Naqshbandīs also practice concealment in society, which they call *khalwat dar anjoman* or "retreat in the world", and *safar sar vatan*, "journeying towards God in the midst of society". *See* KUBRA: LAṬĀ'IF.

Nasab. (lit. "lineage", "descent", "derivation"). Generally used of a name which refers to a parent, as Ibn Sa'ūd, "the Son of Sa'ud", or Bint Jaḥsh, "the daughter of Jaḥsh". The *nasab* may be employed serially to indicate a line of descent from grandfather, great-grandfather and so on. The *nasab* may be used in addition to other given names indicating profession, ancestral home, etc. *See* NAME.

an-Nasafī, Muḥammad ibn Aḥmad (also called an-Nakshabī, executed by the Sāmānids in Bukhara *332*/943). Ismā'īlī dā'ī of Khorāsān and Transoxiana who introduced Neoplatonic philosophy into Ismā'īlī thought in the *Kitāb al-maḥsūl*. He represented a current of thought which was ideologically allied with the Qarmaṭīs rather than the Fāṭimids and expected the reappearance of an earlier Imām, Muḥammad ibn Ismā'il as the Mahdī. Nasafī's antinomian views were criticized by the dā'ī Abū Hātim in a book called *al-Iṣlāḥ. When as-Sijistānī* recognized the Fāṭimid al-Mu'izz as Imām, probably after the conquest of Egypt, the Neoplatonic philosophy of an-Nasafī was incorporated into Fāṭimid cosmology. The original Ismā'īlī pentad of the pleroma was revised by the Caliph al-Mu'izz lī-Dīn-ī Llāh to include *al-'aql, an-nafs, al-jadd, al-fatḥ*, and *al-khayal*.

Naṣārā (lit. "Nazarene", sing. *naṣrānī*). An Arabic name for Christians. Today the formal name is *Masīḥī*, from *Masīḥ* ("Messiah"), a usage established by Christian missionaries.

Naskh (Lit. "deletion", "abrogation" or "copying", "transcription"). The principle by which certain verses of the Koran abrogate (or modify) others, which are then called *mansūkh* ("revoked"). What is generally at issue is the modification of a universal meaning by a more specific one, a modification caused by an historic change of circumstance. It is also a question of the "style" natural to a Divine revelation, which cannot speak with clauses, exceptions and qualifications in the manner of a legal document, but must be direct and absolute. One set of such direct and absolute statements may condition another set of direct and absolute statements which are thereby rendered *mansūkh*, or conditional; the original statement is not untrue, but is subordinated to another which is more immediately relevant. In this way, by *naskh*, or self-limitation, the "absoluteness" of the Koran accommodates itself to the relativities of the human situation. The Koran itself speaks of the principle in 2:106 and 16:101.

Naskhī. One of the most common styles of Arabic writing. *See* CALLIGRAPHY.

Naṣir-ī Khusraw, (*394-452*/1003-1060). A Persian poet, born in Qubadian near Merv. He says he visited the court of Maḥmud of Ghaznah. Khusraw was a financial secretary in Merv and perhaps a court poet who eulogized kings but later destroyed these poems when he underwent a mystical experience at the age of 41. In the experience someone appeared to him and rebuked him for drinking wine; this led him to go on pilgrimage to Mecca. Mecca may have been incidental to Fāṭimid Cairo as his real destination, for he went there first, stayed for six years and became invested as an Ismā'īlī *dā'i* ("propagandist") of high rank, the Ḥujjat of the Jazirah of Khorāsān by the Fāṭmid Caliph al-Mustanṣir. He also met Abū-l-'Alā' al-Ma'arrī, the "freethinking" and "vegetarian" poet.

From Mecca he visited the Qarmaṭīs in al-Aḥsa, probably on a Fāṭimid diplomatic mission. On his return to Persia, he carried on Ismā'īlī agitation in Balkh until the Seljūq authorities forced him to flee. His opponents incited a mob to attack his house and his life was threatened. He fled to Mazandārān, and eventually to the valley of Yamgan ruled by the Emir of Badakshān in Afghanistan, where there was a Gnostic community dating back to pre-Islamic times. There he called himself the "prisoner of Yamgan" and there he is buried, venerated as the founder of a mystic order.

Khusraw expressed his religious ideas and philosophy in poetry, and his main works are the *Dīwān*, the *Safar-Nāmeh* ("The Book of Travels"), and the *Rawshanāī Nāmeh* ("Book of Light" probably written in *444*/1053. This is about Ismā'īlī concepts of Divine Unity, Logos, Universal Soul, the Human Soul and its Becoming, the necessity for a Spiritual Guide, and reward and punishment in the hereafter. It is 582 lines and is known as the *Shish Faṣl* ("The Six Chapters"). Also, he wrote the *Wajh-i Din* ("The Face of Religion"), *Gushāyish va Rahāyish* ("Release and Deliverance"), *Khwān al-Ikhwān* ("Feast of the Brethren" perhaps referring to the Bēma; here the author draws on many Ismā'īlī works which are no longer extant), the *Zād al-Musāfirīn* ("Provision for the Road") and the *Jāmi' al-Ḥikmatayn* {"Harmonization of the Two Wisdoms"), his attempt to harmonize Greek philosophy with the tenets of Islam and particularly Ismā'īlism, written at the request of the Emir of Badakshan. Sholomo Pines pointed out that not all of these works which are attributed to Naṣir-ī Khusraw could have been written by him, since they express divergent opinions on some subjects. *See* MAZĀR-I SHARĪF; ISMĀ'ĪLĪS.

Nasoreans, *see* MANDAEANS.

Naṣṣ (lit. "designation", "appointment", "stipulation"). The designation of a successor. The Shī'ites contend that the succession to the Prophet, that is to say, the Caliphate, could not possibly be a matter for election, although, in the event, election is what happened, following the customs of the desert Arabs regarding their chiefs. For the Sunnīs the succession was largely, although not entirely, the temporal matter of selecting a leader from several possible candidates to oversee the worldly continuation of the Islamic community. For the Shī'ites the succession concerned the eminent and indispensable, spiritual functions of the Imāmate, which could only be filled first by 'Alī, and then by his descendants. For them, the statements the Prophet made at Ghadīr Khumm amounted to the designation or appointment (*naṣṣ*) of 'Alī, although the Shī'ites would say that the matter was determined in heaven at the time of creation itself. An early appellation for the Shī'ites was *Ahl an-Naṣṣ wa-t-Ta'yīn* ("People of Designation and Appointment").

The question of who was the true successor arose again later, and reached a head with the sons of Ja'far aṣ-Ṣādiq, the sixth Shī'ite Imām. The eldest son, Ismā'īl, who would normally have inherited the office, died before his father, thereby throwing the various partisans into confusion. *Naṣṣ* is Twelve-Imām Shī'ism's answer to the problem of this succession and the discrepancies of fate. The Twelvers explain that Ja'far withdrew the *naṣṣ* from Ismā'īl and gave it to the next oldest brother, Mūsā Kāẓim. For good measure, and as a reason for the revocation, the partisans of Mūsā revile Ismā'īl as a "drunkard"; this accusation is also a symbolic rejection of the Sevener's theology and their attitude towards Islamic law. The Seveners, however, countered by maintaining that *naṣṣ* exists, but once given is irrevocable, and hence that Ismā'īl, pre-deceasing his father, had inherited the Imāmate even so, and passed it on to his son.

The development of the doctrine of *naṣṣ* affected the adherents of another branch of Shī'ism, the Zaydīs, causing them eventually to take a stand on the issue when it arose. For the Twelve-Imām Shī'ites the line of Imāms passed through Muḥammad al-Bāqir upon the death of 'Alī Zayn al-'Ābidīn, Shī'ism's fourth Imām. For them, it is thus Muḥammad al-Bāqir who received the *naṣṣ*. Yet it was Zayd, the brother of Muḥammad al-Bāqir, who actually headed resistance to the Umayyad Caliphate. The descendants of Zayd were politically successful in the Yemen, and thus Zaydism, or "Five Imām Shī'ism" came into being. The refutation of the doctrine of *naṣṣ* is therefore as fundamental to Zaydī Shī'ism as is its affirmation to the Twelvers. *See* GHADĪR KHUMM; IMĀM; SHĪ'ISM; ZAYDĪS.

Nāsūt. A technical term of Sufism describing the sphere of what is human and mortal, as contrasted with *lāhūt*, the sphere of the Divine nature. The Sufis make a pun on the word *nās* ("men", "mankind"), purporting to derive it from the verb *nasiya* ("to forget"), thus equating human nature with forgetfulness of God.

The root of *al-insān* ("man") with its collective plural *nās* is actually *anisa* ("to experience", "to perceive", "to be sociable or intimate"). From it is derived the noun *uns* ("Intimacy"), another technical term of Sufism related to love for God. *See* FIVE DIVINE PRESENCES.

"Nation of Islam". The former name of the sect popularly known as the "Black Muslims" of America. The original Nation of Islam, at first known as "The Lost-Found Nation of Islam in the Wilderness of North America" underwent great changes after the death of its founder Elijah Muhammad in 1975 the majority being led by stages to orthodox Islam by Elijah Muhammad's son Wallace, now named Warith Deen Muhammad. This orthodox branch, centered in Chicago, took the name "American Muslim Mission". A dissident faction, led by "Brother" Louis Farrakhan, retains the name "Nation of Islam" as well as the sect's original anti-white and separatist doctrines.

An off shoot of the Nation of Islam is the "Five Percenters" among young people with roots in "Hip-Hop" culture. This group explicitly believes that Blacks are God; addresses its members as "G". The number seven is a prominent symbol of power (G, meaning God, is the seventh letter of the alphabet). They use the phrase "word is bond" and interpret Allāh to mean "arm leg leg arm head". *See* "BLACK MUSLIMS".

Navā'i, *see* 'ALĪ SHĪR NAVĀ'I

Naw ruz (Pers. originally meaning "new light" [*ruz* being cognate with Latin *lux*], later coming to mean "new day"). It is the name of the festival of the new year, according to the Persian solar calendar, after the spring equinox on 21 March. It is of ancient origin but is a most important holiday celebrated in Iran, and cultures influenced by Iran. As are so many Islamic holidays, it is observed by family visiting. In ancient Iran there also existed the *Mihrajan* ("feast of Mithra") a harvest festival celebrated in the autumn, on the 16th day of the month bearing his name. *Sadak*, in modern Persian *Sade*, was a festival commemorating the discovery of fire by a mythical king of ancient times.

The Manicheans in most host religions re-arranged familiar holidays, "scientifically correcting" their dates, as they corrected calendars. Thus there is a quotation recorded of al-Ḥallaj: "Aḥmad ibn Fātik said: 'We were with al-Ḥallaj in Nihāwand on the New Year (*Naw ruz*) when we heard the trumpet sound.' Al-Ḥallaj said: 'what is happening?' I told him 'today is *Naw ruz*.' He then sighed and said: 'Ah, when will our *Naw ruz* come?' And I said, 'What do you mean by *when*?' He said 'the day when I will be strung up on the gibbet.'

"Now when the day came [not his final execution but another brush with the authorities] — thirteen years later — he looked at me from the pillory and exclaimed: 'Aḥmad, now is our *Naw Ruz* come!' And I answered : 'O Master have you received the gifts of the feast?' — He said to me : 'Indeed. I have received them. Revelation and certitude, so much so that I am ashamed! But it is too early for me to enjoy them.'"

Among the numerous double and multiple meanings here is that the Manichean *Naw Ruz* was different and came later than the orthodox holiday. Al-Ḥallaj also meant by "when will our *Naw Ruz* come", when would they be able to practice openly without disguise, and when would martyrdom, the desired imitation of the master's destiny and fulfillment of all symbolism, come. Certitude (*al-*

yaqin) early on became an interchangeable symbol for death.

Naw'ī. A pair of planets or stars, one of which is rising on the east horizon while the other is sinking on the west horizon at any moment, but particularly at sunrise and sunset. These pairs of planets play an important role in Arab astrology, more so than the descendant and ascendant in European astrology. *See* ASTROLOGY.

Neighbors (Ar. *jār, jirān*). In Islamic law, a person whose land is adjacent to a plot of land being sold has priority rights to buy that land over anyone else, except, possibly, close relatives. If the neighbor is absent, the seller must await his return to allow him his option before selling to anyone else.

Kindness to neighbors is also a social responsibility. There is a *Ḥadīth* which says: "He is not a good Muslim who eats his full and leaves his neighbor hungry." For other purposes, the general notion of neighbor has other legal definitions which vary according to school, such as someone living within a radius of forty houses or forty cubits, or someone who worships at the same mosque.

Neoplatonism, *see* PHILOSOPHY.

Nestorians. A branch of Christianity which separated from the mother church after the stormy Council of Ephesus, called in 431 to decide the controversy raised by the opposition of St. Cyril, Patriarch of Alexandria (supported by Pope Celestine I and representing the views of the majority of Christendom) to the views of Nestorius of Constantinople. Nestorius (d. 451), who had been named Patriarch of Constantinople in 428 by the Emperor Theodosius II, taught that Jesus possessed two natures, one human and one Divine. In that, he was in agreement with the general view, but he differed from it insofar as he taught that in Jesus there were also *two persons* (in the majority opinion there is one person), and that Jesus was at one time the Divine person and at others the human one.

The Council of Ephesus, after great struggles between the opposing factions, affirmed that in accordance with the Nicene Creed, Mary could be called "Mother of God" and that the Divine and human natures in Jesus were so coherent that they could not be separated into two persons; this was confirmed by the Council of Chalcedon of 451. Nestorius was then deposed by the Council and sent into exile at Antioch, where many of his sympathizers were to be found. From there he went to Arabia and finally to Egypt. Nestorius' doctrine has been called *dyophysite*.

The sect which followed his teachings flourished, and Edessa (modern-day Urfa in Turkey) became its center. It adopted Syriac as its liturgical language in place of Greek. The Sāssānid Persians welcomed the Nestorians as a Christian group inimical to the Byzantines, and thus it is that the Nestorians maintained a school of philosophy and medicine founded in the 3rd century AD at Jundishāpūr, near Ahvāz, modern Sānābād, in Khuzistan. Together with Syriac-speaking Christian schools in Syria, the school of Jundishāpūr played an important role in transmitting Hellenistic learning to Islamic civilization. The Nestorian Bishopric of Urmia, in Western Persia, was, and still is, one of the ancient seats of this branch of Christianity. Nestorianism also spread throughout the Yemen and was probably the form of Christianity practiced in Najrān, in southern Arabia. Co-operation between the Nestorians and the Persians helped to lead to the Sāssānid conquest of the Yemen at the end of the 6th century AD Nestorian Churches used to keep a copy of the agreement concluded between the Prophet and the Christians of Najrān, giving them the protection of the Islamic state (*see* NAJRĀN.)

Nestorian influence was at its height from the 7th century to the 12th, during the whole of which period the sect was very active, with scholar missionaries establishing churches in Persia, Central Asia, India, China, and among the Mongols. In AD 735 a group of Nestorian missionaries, whose leader was called in Chinese transcription A-lo-pen, received permission from the T'ang Emperor T'ai Tsung to found a church in Ch'ang An, then the capital of China. The Nestorians in China carved an intricate stone tablet which retold Old and New Testament versions of world history in Chinese and Syriac, and described their mission. At the beginning of the 9th century the tablet was buried as a result of persecutions of the Nestorians in China, and remained hidden until 1625 when it was unearthed in the course of excavations for buildings. It is today one of the great relics of religious history.

The Nestorians developed close relations with the 'Abbāsid dynasty and supplied the Muslims with many teachers, advisors, scholars, and physicians. The physician of Hārūn ar-Rashīd was

Jibrā'īl Bakhtishishu, from a Nestorian family of seven generations of physicians.

The Nestorians, however, were also closely linked to the Mongols of Hūlāgū Khān whose horde destroyed Baghdad in 1258, for both the mother and the wife of Hūlāgū were Nestorian Christians, and perhaps the Nestorians had hoped to convert the as yet shamanist Mongols to Christianity, and to succeed where they had failed with the Muslims. They were, therefore, together with the Shī'ites, prominent advisors to the Mongols during their invasions of the Near East. In the end, however, it was Sunnī Islam that gained the conversion of the Mongols.

The Nestorians accord a great veneration to the Cross (which may account for the ancient and erroneous notion held by many Muslims that Christians worship the cross); they believe that their special altar bread is a "holy leaven" derived from the leaven of the bread at the Last Supper.

In 'Irāq the Nestorians and their Kurdish allies fought unsuccessfully against the Turks at the turn of the last century and again during World War I. During the mandate in 'Irāq, many Nestorians served in the British forces keeping order in the country. When the British left, the Nestorians found themselves again vulnerable, so that after harsh persecutions in the 19th and 20th centuries, many emigrated to America. Among the emigrants was the head of the church, the Catholikos, also called the "Patriarch of the East". The Catholikos now resides in California. The function of Catholikos is hereditary from uncle to nephew, as is that of Bishop.

The Nestorians are now frequently known as "Assyrian Christians", and groups are found in Syria, 'Irāq, Iran and the Malabar coast of India. Beginning centuries ago, a large group of the Assyrians have entered into communion with Rome and are called "Chaldean Catholics". *See* AHL al-KISĀ'Ī; CHRISTIANITY; JESUS; NAJRĀN.

"New Sect". A militant movement among Chinese Muslims directed against the Manchus. It was inspired by a Naqshbandi leader called Ma (Muḥammad) Ming-hsin (d. *1195*/1781). The "New Sect" was opposed to the acquiescence in the rule of non-Muslims that had become customary among Chinese Muslims, an attitude which was thereafter called the "Old Sect". The emergence of the New Sect led to rebellions, and for a short time in the 19th century, to an independent Muslim state.

New Year, *see* CALENDAR; NAW RUZ; MUḤARRAM.

an-Niffarī, Muḥammad ibn 'Abd al-Jabbār ibn al-Ḥasan (d. *354*/965). A Sufi, probably born in 'Irāq. Very little is known about his life, but his mystical writings, the *Kitāb al-Mawāqif* ("Book of Spiritual Stations") and the *Mukhāṭabāt* ("Discourses") are famous for their compelling vigor and enigma. *See* FANA'.

Nigeria. Federal Republic. Population: 103,912,489 of whom 50% are Muslim of the Mālikī School of Law with a large number of Aḥmadiyyah. 35% are Christian, and the others are animists. The Islamization of Nigeria began in the *8th*/14th century and received great impetus during the Hausa-Fulbe struggles at the beginning of the 19th century which led to the Sokoto Caliphate. The Tijāniyyah, Qādiriyyah, and Shādhilī *ṭuruq* are important Sufi orders in Nigeria. Recent years have seen the rise of small heretical groups such as the 'Yan Tatsine, which are the result of social dislocation. *See* BALEWA, Sir ABUBAKAR TAFAWA; DAN FODIO; KANO; SOKOTO CALIPHATE; 'YAN TATSINE.

Night Journey (Ar. *isrā'* and *mi'rāj*). Some time before the Hijrah, the Prophet experienced that which came later to be called the Night Journey (*al-Isrā'*), or the Ascent (*al-Mi'rāj*). The original account of the event is extremely terse; it is tradition which has supplied the details. One night he was sleeping in the sanctuary (*ḥijr*) next to the Ka'bah, when the Angel Gabriel woke him and led him to a beast called the *Burāq*, "smaller than a mule but larger than an ass", according to Bukhārī, and winged.

Mounted on *Burāq* with Gabriel alongside, the Prophet was borne through the sky to Jerusalem where, with the Prophets, Abraham, Moses, Jesus, and others, he prayed at the site of the Temple of Solomon. This Temple had once been the meeting place between Man and God, but in the 7th century it lay in ruins after its destruction by the Romans, for it had been left as it was, in keeping with Jesus' prophecy that not a stone would be left standing.

Two vessels were there offered to the Prophet to drink, one of wine and one of milk. The Prophet chose milk, whereupon Gabriel said that he had chosen the primordial path for himself and his people. Carried by Gabriel, the Prophet rose to heaven from the rock of the temple mount, doubtless the site of the Holy of Holies of the Temple, which the Koran calls the "Farthest Mosque" (*al-masjid al-aqṣā'*). The Dome of the Rock sanctuary stands there today, and close by is the *al-Aqsā'* mosque which is named after the Koranic name for the whole Temple Mount.

The Prophet ascended to the Divine Presence through the "seven heavens", which symbolize the degrees separating non-manifestation from manifestation. As he did so, the Archangel assumed his celestial and spiritual form, as did the Prophets with whom he had prayed but whom he now encountered on the ascension as spiritual realities, each in his heavenly sphere. (Of himself the Prophet had said: "I was a Prophet while Adam was yet between water and clay.")

At the summation of the ascent was the "Lote Tree of the Uttermost Limit" (*sidrat al-muntahā*), the limit of Being before the Absolute. The Koran says: "When there enshrouded the Lote Tree that which enshrouds, the eye wavered not, nor did it rebel. Indeed he beheld of the signs of his Lord, the greatest" (53:16-18).

There the Prophet received the command from God that men should perform the prayer fifty times each day; when the Prophet descended, Moses advised him to return in order to ask that the number be reduced to one more within men's capabilities; it was finally reduced to five.

As he was returning from Jerusalem to Mecca the Prophet saw caravans making their way across the desert. In the morning he made it known that he had visited Jerusalem during the night; the Quraysh mocked him and told Abū Bakr of this, who retorted: "if he says so, then it is true", which earned him the title *aṣ-Ṣiddīq* ("the truth-witnessing"). To the Quraysh the Prophet said nothing of his ascent to heaven, speaking of it only to his Companions. Later the caravans which he had described seeing during his return journey arrived in Mecca, confirming his statement.

The journey from Mecca to Jerusalem is called the *isrā'*, and the ascent from Jerusalem to heaven, the *mi'rāj*. Together they are known as the Night Journey, which has often been pictured in books of Persian miniatures called the *Mi'rāj-Nameh*. Although the date of the *mi'rāj* is not known, the event called the "night of the journey and the ascension" (*laylat al-isrā' wa-l-mi'rāj*) is often celebrated as the 27th Rajab. The event is referred to at the beginning of the *Sūrat Banī Isrā'īl*:

Glory be to Him, who carried
His servant by night
from the Holy Mosque to the Further Mosque
the precincts of which We have blessed,
that We might show him some of Our signs.
He is the All-hearing, the All-seeing. (17:1-2)

See BURĀQ; DOME of the ROCK; HEAVEN; SEVENTH HEAVEN.

Night of Power, *see* LAYLAT al-QADR.

Ni'mat Allāh, Shāh Walī (d. *834*/1431). The founder of the Ni'matu'llāhī Sufi order, he settled at the court of Tīmūr in Herāt and died near Kirmān. Some of his successors moved to Hyderabad in India, whilst those who remained in Persia became Shī'ites under the Ṣafavids. With its branches, the Kawthar 'Alī Shāhī, Gunābādī, Dhū-r-Riyasatāni, Ṣāfi 'Alī Shāhi, and the Shams 'Urafa', the Ni'matu'llāhī is the most important and widespread Shī'ite Sufi order, and is itself a branch, along with the Dhahabī, of the Kubrawiyyah. Shī'ite Sufi orders refer to their Shaykh as the Nā'ib ("representative") of the Hidden Imām.

Nisbah. That part of a name which indicates a profession either of the holder or his forebears, such as Khayyām ("tent-maker"), or place of origin, such as ar-Rūmī ("the Roman", Byzantine). Such a name may be used in addition to other given names. The Qarmaṭīs favored nisbahs with a "worker" connotation, such as Khayyām, Sarrāj (saddler), etc. *See* KUNYAH; LAQAB; NAME; NASAB.

Niyyah, *see* INTENTION.

Niẓām ad-Dīn Awliyā (*636-725*/1238-1324). Sufi saint buried in Delhi in a complex where he is surrounded by tombs of his disciples, including the poet Amīr Khusraw. Niẓām ad-Dīn was a member of the Chishti line. He was born in Badaun in India the only son of Aḥmad Bukhari and Zulaykha. His parents had fled Bukhara from the Mongols. His father died when Niẓām ad-Dīn was five years old. When he grew up, Niẓām ad-Dīn came first to Delhi and then became the disciple of Baba Farid at Ajodhan. After he had succeeded his teacher, he founded his own khanaqah in the village of Ghiyaspur on the banks of the Jumna river. This is now the Durgah or tomb within Delhi which is the focus of Muslim spiritual life in the capital.

Niẓām al-Mulk (d. *485*/1092). An intriguing figure in the history of the Caliphate, when the Seljūq Turks established their Sultanate in the name of the Caliphs of Baghdad, Niẓām al-Mulk was their Vizier or first minister, serving first the Sultan Alp Arslan, son of Toghrul Beg, the founder of the dynasty, and later his son Mālik Shāh.

The reins of empire were held firmly in the hands of Niẓām al-Mulk; the Sultan himself exercised little authority and the Caliph in Baghdad even less. It was Turks who held military control, but it was Niẓām al-Mulk, a Persian, who directed policy; as the Vizier he established schools, built roads, diminished taxes and presided over a period of prosperity.

Niẓām al-Mulk was a patron of the arts and sciences who had himself studied Islamic law at Nayshābūr under Hibat Allāh al-Muwaffaq. In his time the Fāṭimids of Egypt and allied Ismā'īlī sects throughout the 'Abbāsid Empire posed a political and ideological threat. This danger led Niẓām al-Mulk to turn to the Ash'arites, a Sunnī school of speculative theology previously held in opprobrium by the Seljūqs, for a line of doctrinal defense. To uphold religious orthodoxy against the propaganda of the Shī'ite sects, particularly the Ismā'īlīs, he founded the *Niẓāmiyyah* university in Baghdad. Students lived and studied at the expense of the Sultan, and the *madrasah* set the model for all other schools of higher education. Niẓām al-Mulk also founded a less renowned *Niẓāmiyyah* at Nayshābūr, and others elsewhere.

He appointed the Ash'arite theologian al-Juwaynī, known as "the Imām of the Ḥaramayn" and a teacher of al-Ghazālī, to teach at Nayshābūr. Al-Juwaynī wrote his *Ghiyath al-Umam* ("The Savior of Nations") with Niẓām al-Mulk in mind, in order to promote the notion that political rule, or the Caliphate, belonged to the leader who could best advance the interests and stability of the Islamic polity, irrespective of dynasty and the traditional criteria of legitimacy to the Caliphate. Later Niẓām al-Mulk appointed al-Ghazālī to teach in the *Niẓāmiyyah* of Baghdad. Al-Ghazālī also taught in Nayshābūr at the end of his life.

An intriguing, but apocryphal, story is recorded in a work called the *Waṣāyā* (spuriously attributed to Niẓām al-Mulk.) This story is also found in the biography of Ḥasan-i Ṣabbāḥ, the *Sargudhasht-i Sayyidna* and it is also told by the Persian historian Rashīd ad-Dīn aṭ-Ṭabīb, to the effect that Niẓām al-Mulk, 'Umar Khayyām, and Ḥasan aṣ-Ṣabbāḥ studied together at Nayshābūr, and vowed that he who succeeded in life would help the others. When Niẓām al-Mulk became Vizier, Ḥasan-i aṣ-Ṣabbāḥ came to him and was given a post. However, he embroiled himself in intrigue, and was obliged to leave, going first to Fāṭimid Egypt and then back to Persia, where he organized his followers into the Assassin sect. 'Umar Khayyām was given a post as astronomer and scholar, and took part in the creation of the Jalālī calendar for the Sultan Mālik Shāh. A romantic story of fate; what is true is that 'Umar Khayyām made his calculations to reform the solar calendar during the Vizierate of Niẓām al-Mulk in *467*/1074, and that Niẓām al-Mulk fell victim to an Ismā'īlī assassin despatched from Alamūt. The Ismā'īlīs feared him not only because he opposed them on religious grounds, but also because his strong rule was a threat to their political designs of terrorism and fragmentation.

Niẓām al-Mulk wrote a treatise on politics called the *Siyāsat-Nāmeh* ("The Book of Government", also called *Siyaru-l-Mulūk*, or "Biographies of Kings").

Niẓāmī (Abū Yūsuf Muḥammad Ilyās ibn Yūsuf Niẓām ad-Dīn) (*535-598*/1141-1202). A Persian poet and mystic, he was born and spent his life in Ganja, called in Tsarist times Elizavetpol and in Soviet times Kirovābād, in Azerbaijan. His most famous works are a rendition of a tragic Arab love story, "Laylah and Majnūn", and the "Seven Princesses", about the wives of the Sāssānid King Bahram, but more an allegory about illusion and paradise. One of these stories, that of the Russian princess, was used by the eighteenth century Italian dramatist Carlo Gozzi in his *Turandot*, which became the opera. These, together with other writings, make up a collection called the *Khamsah* ("the Five").

Noah (Ar. *Nūḥ*). In Islam, Noah is considered to be a *rasūl* ("Messenger") although he does not have a revealed book. The story of how he built the Ark and filled it with two of every species to save the righteous from the Deluge (*ṭūfān*) is very popular and has received much embellishment in tradition. The origin of the holy day of the '*āshūrā'* is made by tradition the commemoration of the day the Ark came to rest on Mount Jūdī. The Deluge is the great traditional divider between the primordial cycles of time and those at the dawn of history, that is, between pre-history and history.

Al-Mas'ūdī says that the Angel Gabriel brought Noah a sarcophagus containing the bones of Adam, to put into the Ark; that on the Ark were forty men and forty women; and that when, after five months, the ark came to rest on land, they founded a city called *Thamānīn* ("The Eighty") at the foot of Mount Jūdī. Forty is the letter *mīm*, a circle, which represents death; hence the symbol of the forty days in the desert, etc.

The flood is a myth reflecting universal human experience. Before it, there prevailed the Adamic consciousness of the Divine Unity, first as the Sole Reality in the Garden, and then as a fading memory for mankind. In the individual experience this is the state of childhood; Islam says that every child is born innately a Muslim, that is, aware of Divine Transcendence. The flood symbolizes the submerging of the awareness of God as God by the overpowering experience of the *world* as God. In the progress of mankind, the stone age and before, consciousness of the Divine Reality is submerged (the Flood) by an awareness of a Divine Multiplicity in which God and the world are merged; the lightening flash is perceived as Divine, the seasons are perceived as divine, the heat, the cold, the moist, the dry, the subtle, the hard, the fluid, the transforming, are perceived as divine. In other words, existence and experience dominate the sense of Reality. Consciousness is mixed with creation. When the "Flood was over"— the dawn of history — and the waters gone down, awareness of the Divine Unity — preserved in the Ark, the "conscience", the "inner observer"— re-emerged.

In the Flood, God and the world merged. As the "waters" (this confusion of self and the world around us which is, for the individual, the experience of adolescence, the emergence of the sexual power of creation into the mind) receded, they left behind in the mind, gods and goddesses, of which the divinized heavenly bodies, as the most abstract, were the last to lose their power.

The Ark came to rest on solid ground; the adolescence of mankind was over. In Abraham the separation of consciousness from creation was complete; Abraham renounced the stars, moon, and sun, as God (which his forefathers had taken to worshiping) and recognized the God of Adam again as God, Who is unlike anything in Creation, and Master of it. Monotheism returned, and in Abraham a reconsecration took place of the primordial religion.

The universal symbol of the Flood is the projected metaphor for this experience of adolescence on the part of the individual and on the part of mankind as a whole. In the individual it is the transition from the innocence of childhood to the knowledge of adulthood which brings in its wake knowledge of the world. For mankind it is the passage from an age of pre-history to history, and brings with it knowledge of cosmology and the sciences, crafts, and arts.

The Canaanite myth of "God's struggle with the sea monster" (*Chaoskampf*) is not really God struggling with the world, but the world struggling with the idea of Divinity in the mind of man, attempting to retain its hold over man at the moment when it is being superseded by the new awareness of God from the point of view of man's maturity and the cycle of prophetic revelation.

The story of Noah is told in the Koran in the following verses: 3:33; 4:163; 6:85; 7:59; 10:72; 11:25; 14:9; 17:3; 21:76; 22:42; 23:23; 26:106; 29:14; 33:7; 37:75; 42:13.

The Ismā'īlīs interpreted the flood as ignorance or unconsciousness. They called the missionary jurisdictional regions "islands" *jaza'ir*, in the center of which the *dā'ī* or missionary caller stood, with his followers, on an island of awareness emerging out of the flood of unconsciousness.

Nūr Muḥammadī (Persian, lit. "Muḥammadan light" or "light of Muḥammad"; a reduction of the Arabic form *an-Nūr al-Muḥammadiyyah*). The essence of the Prophet, also called *al-ḥaqīqah al-Muḥammadiyyah* ("Muḥammadan Reality" or "the Reality that is Muḥammad"), was created before the creation of the world, when "God took a handful of light and commanded it to be Muḥammad." From it the world itself was created. Much emphasis is placed upon this idea by the Shī'ites, who find this light eminently manifest in their Imāms, but the term is also encountered, mainly in the context of mysticism, among the Sunnīs, as a doctrine not unlike that of the *logos.*

Its origin is a corpus of sayings attributed to Ja'far aṣ-Ṣādiq, and repeated among Shī'ite theologians. In one form it is reported by Mas'ūdī in his *Murūj adh-Dhahab* ("Meadows of Gold"), in which the following words are attributed to 'Alī ibn Abī Ṭālib:

> When God wished to establish creation, the atoms of creatures, and the beginning of all created things, he first made what he created in the form of small particles. This was before He stretched out the earth or raised the heavens... He cast forth a ray of light, a flame from his splendor, and it was radiant. He scattered this light in the midst of invisible atoms, which he then united in the form of our Prophet. God the Most High then declared to him: "You are the first of those who shall speak, the one with the power of choice and the one chosen. To you I have trusted my light and the treasure of my guidance... For your sake I will appoint the people of your household for guidance. I will bestow upon them the secrets of my knowledge: no truth will be hidden from them and no mystery concealed. I will designate them as my proof to mankind, as those who shall admonish men of my Power and remind them of my Unity..." He had chosen Muḥammad and his family...

Ja'far aṣ-Ṣādiq is also reported to have said:

> The light descended upon our most noble men, and shone through our Imāms, so that we are the lights of heaven and earth. To us is heaven committed and from us are the secrets of science derived, for we are the destination that all strive to reach... the Mahdī will be the final Proof, the seal of the Imāms... we are the most noble of mankind, the most exalted of all creatures, the Proofs of the Lord of the Worlds, and those who cling to our friendship will be favored in this life and in death they will have our support...

This concept of the "man of light" is a component of Shī'ism as one more item of perfection in their Imāms, and an important constituent of their doctrine of the Imāmate. But it brought in its wake the overtones of emanationism ("a flame from His splendor"), illuminationism, and arcane knowledge.

It appealed to Sunnīs in a different way, as underpinning the concept that the *rasūl* ("the Divine Messenger") is the manifestation of Being; this is the Intellect in the Platonic sense.

However, the real origin of this doctrine, as put into the mouth of Ja'far aṣ-Ṣādiq, is the Manichean myth of creation, according to which the Creator, under assault from the principle of evil (which Dualism assumes to be as absolute as God Himself), created the world and made Himself into particles of light which he cast into creation, in order to "take refuge" from evil, the "other side" of the Absolute. In Manicheism, this light is God Himself who is liberated and restored through the Elect, the Gnostics, who free the light imprisoned in nature and in themselves against a final universal salvation of the "knowers" at the end of time. It is for the Dualists that the concept of this light has the widest and deepest and, indeed, the original meaning; it came into Islam when Dualism assumed its Islamic form as the Sevener movement. *See* 'ABD ALLĀH ibn MAYMŪN al-QADDĀH; JA'FAR aṣ-ṢĀDIQ; MANICHEANS; SEVENERS; SHĪ'ISM.

Nūḥ, *see* NOAH.

Nūn. Letter of the Arabic alphabet in the shape of a semicircle with a dot in the center. It looks like a boat and Sufis teach that it is a boat carrying the elements of the past which are to be preserved towards a new cycle of time. This doubtless comes from the Manichean doctrine that the liberated particles of light are carried from exile in the created world back to their origin in the Sun, Moon or Polar star in a cosmic boat, and is also part of the symbolism of the crescent and star.

Nūrbaksh, Muḥammad. (Muḥammad ibn 'Abd Allāh; *795-869*/1393-1465). A Sufi, a descendant of the Prophet, born in Persia of a family from eastern Arabia. A charismatic figure, he was given the name Nūrbaksh ("gift of light") by his spiritual master, Isḥāq al-Khutlānī, a Shaykh in the spiritual line (*silsilah*) of the Sufi 'Alī al-Ḥamadhānī. Nūrbaksh declared himself to be the Mahdī and, taking the title of Caliph, tried several times unsuccessfully to lead popular revolts and seize power in Persia. He was captured and pardoned. A Sufi *ṭarīqah*, the Nūrbakshiyyah, descends from him; this order became Shī'ite in Ṣafavid times. One of his followers, Shams ad-Dīn 'Irāqī from Jīlān also propagated the order in Srinagar in India.

Nuṣayrīs, *see* 'ALAWĪS.

O

Occulted Imām, *see* HIDDEN IMĀM.

Occultation, *see* GHAYBAH.

Oman. Sultanate. Population: 2,186,548. The great majority are Ibāḍite Muslims, 25% are Sunnīs, and a smaller minority are Twelve-Imām Shī'ites. Ibāḍite *sharī'ah* law is largely in force.

Omar, *see* 'UMAR.

Omar Khayyām, *see* 'UMAR al-KHAYYĀM.

Omar, Mosque of *see* DOME of the ROCK.

Orthodoxy, *see* FIVE PILLARS; ILḤAD; SUNNAH.

Osman, *see* 'UTHMĀN.

Osmanlis, *see* OTTOMANS.

Ossetians. An Iranian people of the North Caucusus. According to the census of 1979 they numbered 542,000, of whom 365,000 live in Ossetia, the south part of which was the South Ossetian Autonomous Oblast of the Georgian republic, and the north was the North Ossetian ASSR. Since the break up of the Soviet Union they are divided between the Russian Federation and the republic of Georgia. The language of the Ossetians is an Iranian language; the majority are Russian Orthodox although some are Sunni Muslims.

Othman, *see* 'UTHMĀN.

Ottomans (*7th*/13th century-*1342*/1924). Also called Osmanlis, they were a clan of the Ghuzz (Oghuz) branch of Turks, descended from a chieftain of the *7th*/13th century called Ertoghrul, whose son 'Uthmān (alternate spellings are Othman, Osman, and Usman) founded a principality in Asia Minor. The clan controlled Western Anatolia, and in *758*/1357 began a series of conquests which brought Macedonia, Serbia, and Bulgaria under their control; regions which the Turks called "Rumelia", from *Rūm*, the Byzantine ("Roman") Empire. Bāyazīd I, called *Yildirim* ("the lightning bolt") acquired the title of "Sultan" from the 'Abbāsid Caliph in Cairo. The ascent of the Ottomans was temporarily checked when the same Bāyazīd was captured in Battle by Tīmūr (Tamerlane) in *804*/1402.

Constantinople had been the great prize since the Prophet's time, and Muslim armies had made many unsuccessful attempts to conquer it. Ironically, the blow from which it never recovered was delivered by Christians, when in 1204, Doge Dandolo of Venice led the Fourth Crusade against Constantinople, which was taken and sacked. The Turks, and others before them, had been nibbling at the Byzantine Empire, so that by the mid-*9th*/15th century, only a small remnant of territory surrounding the city remained in Christian hands. In *857*/1453 the Ottoman Turks led by Meḥmet II Nāṣir ("the Victor") conquered it and renamed it Istanbul.

The city was besieged for fifty-four days by a Turkish force of 150,000, whilst defense depended upon an army of only 8,000 led by some 400 Venetian mercenaries. The Turks attacked not only by land, and by tunneling, but by sea as well. Because entry into the Bosphorus was impeded by a chain, the Turks were compelled to carry their ships overland by way of Pera, a narrow isthmus, in order to bring their small navy to bear upon the city. At one point the Sultan Meḥmet, a man of fiery temperament, rode his horse into the Bosphorus and swam among the ships, shouting orders to the brandishing of his sword. He was not only daring, but also ingenious; he designed some of the special high trajectory cannons which bombarded the city.

With the conquest of Constantinople the great age of the Ottomans began. In *923*/1517 Selim I *Yavüz* ("the Grim") conquered Egypt, thus marking the end of the 'Abbāsids who had lived in Cairo under the Mamlūks as figurehead Caliphs since the conquest of Baghdad by the Mongols in *656*/1258. The Ottomans later claimed that the last 'Abbāsid in Cairo, al-Mutawakkil III, had relinquished the Caliphate to them; certainly no 'Abbāsid after him claimed the title. According to modern scholars, however, Selim I had neither the political foresight nor the desire for titles that would have suggested the obvious step of acquiring a useful and not inglorious claim to legitimacy by adding the name of Caliph to those of Sultan and Khan.

Instead, it now seems to be accepted among European scholars that the title to the Caliphate "disappeared"; its transference to the Ottomans was a fiction invented in the 18th century when the idea of a Turkish Caliphate became a useful stratagem to bolster waning military power. According to this view, the Turkish claim to the Caliphate was inspired by the treaty of Kuchuk Kaynarja of 1774, when the Russian Tsar acquired the right to protect the Orthodox Christian Church in the Turkish Empire, and the Russians were induced in turn to acknowledge the Turkish ruler's religious authority over Muslims in the Russian Empire. In virtue of this, the Ottomans did not demand travel documents of Muslims coming from outside their empire because they wished to demonstrate that they were all spiritually subject to the Ottoman Caliph. This was essentially to imitate those European policies of "protection" that frequently foreshadowed open colonization. The Treaty of Kuchuk Kaynarja, and such political "fictions" as it embodied, were a mirror held up to European designs.

As time passed, the Turks certainly exploited the idea of the Caliphate further to support their imperial claims; their holding the regalia of the Caliphate, the mantle of the Prophet, in Istanbul, was made much of in token of their legitimacy; even if their claims were invented, they were taken seriously by the Europeans; the British in particular saw the Turkish Caliphate as a threat to the stability of the Muslim areas within the British Empire. They therefore attacked the notion of the Ottoman Caliphate on religious grounds, declaring that the 'Abbāsids had "no right" to relinquish the title, or alternately, that the 'Abbāsids would have been within their rights to do so, were it not for the technical irregularity raised by the Ḥadīth which said that rule belongs to Arab Quraysh so long as there are two Qurayshis left, one to rule and one to be subject.

Given that it had not occurred to most Muslims to contest the validity of a Turkish Caliphate, this disparagement of Turkish claims was somewhat as if the Mufti of Cairo had advised the British Monarchy that, on technical grounds, they could not be "defenders of the faith".

In the end, the Ottomans fulfilled *de facto* the role of Caliphate; in the absence of ruling Qurayshis, they provided Islam with a clear political center, if not in the persons of the Caliphs themselves (who, as individuals, after Sulaymān the Magnificent sank so abysmally low that it has been suggested they could not have been genuine descendants of their predecessors), then certainly in the institution of the Caliphate. It defended Islamic orthodoxy, and in so doing reflected the religious fervor of the Turkish people, who thought of themselves as Muslims first and Turks second. In any case, Ottoman rulers had used the title of Caliph before the conquest of Egypt, as early as Mūrād I (d. *761*/1360). Indeed, they had used the title even before Bāyazīd acquired the title of Sultan from the 'Abbāsids. Ultimately, the authenticity of their claim depended upon its credibility, and this was accepted by the Islamic world. (*See* CALIPH.)

Being Ottoman, Itzkowitz wrote, was "not merely dynastic, but also cultural. The Ottomans were a small minority in the *askeri* [military] class, for to be an Ottoman one had to satisfy three conditions: serve the state; serve the religion; and know 'the Ottoman Way'. Serving the state meant working for the government in a position that gave the privileged status associated with askeri class. Serving the religion meant being a Muslim. 'Knowing the Ottoman Way' involved being completely conversant with the High Islamic cultural tradition, including being at home in the Turkish language (for which a knowledge of Arabic and Persian was also necessary) and conforming in public to the conventional manners and customs for which that speech was the vehicle."

Although the Ottoman Turks are characterized as staunch Sunnis and defenders of Orthodoxy, which they were *politically* by virtue of their opposition to the Shī'ite Persians, Anatolian Islam internally was, and is, far from being completely orthodox itself. The Turkish Sufī orders permeated the society and were replete with practices derived from the same sources as those of the Shī'ites. The Mevlevis and Bektashis are so heterodox they could be considered as separate religions, and the official fa₇ade of Sunnism masked the enormous clandestine presence in Anatolia of the religion of the 'Alawīs whose numbers today are constantly being revised upwards. When one adds to this the sects which are widespread among the Kurds, the nature of Anatolian Islam becomes extremely multifaceted.

In early times, various branches of the Turks adopted Christianity, Manicheism, and Buddhism, in addition to their own Shamanism. When they arrived in Anatolia their religion, according to Franz Babinger, was not Islam, but 'Alawi, and their culture was largely Iranian and remained so to the end of the Ottoman empire. Also, he said that "folk traditions rather than formal Islam" and a Sufism tantamount to Shī'ism informed these folk traditions. Beneath the surface of Islam in Turkey all of these elements persist.

The Ottoman Empire reached its height under Sulaymān the Magnificent (d. *974*/1566), known as *al-Qānūnī* ("the lawgiver"). He controlled Asia Minor, Syria, 'Irāq, Egypt, North Africa, the coastal regions of Arabia, Azerbaijan, the Balkans, Hungary, and vassal states in the Volga region and the southern steppes of Russia. Apart from military prowess, this period also saw great Turkish achievements in administration, social institutions, architecture and public works. Istanbul became, again, one of the great cities of the world.

In *943*/1536 Turkish military power was everywhere unmatched but, by *979*/1571, in the sea battle at Lepanto, the Turks lost control of the Western Mediterranean, although the European powers did not then exploit their victory fully. The Portuguese had meanwhile already wrested supremacy from the Turks in the Indian Ocean, and the Russians had begun making inroads against the Turks. The Tartars were vassals from the time of Ivan the Terrible and the Russians continued to pursue their dream of conquering Constantinople into the 20th century. Although the Ottomans besieged Vienna for a second time in *1094*/1683, where they were narrowly routed by Jan Sobiesky, King of Poland, they were by this time in rapid decline.

Before decline turned to stagnation, however, there ensued the 19th-century reforms (*tanẓīmāt*) whereby Turkey began the process of Westernization. This led to the stirrings of Turkish nationalism which finally displaced the Turks' first and foremost identity as Muslims, culminating in the creation of a completely secular Turkish state under Muṣṭāfā Kemal Atat rk, once the empire had been completely lost in World War I. The Ottoman Sultanate was abolished in 1922 with the establishment of a republic, and the Caliphate was abolished in *1342*/1924. *See* BEYLERBEY; DEFTERDAR; DEVSHIRME; JANISSERIES; ISTANBUL; KAPUDANPASHA; MEḤMET II; QADI 'ASKER; SHAYKH al-ISLĀM; SĪNĀN; SUBLIME PORTE; SULAYMĀN the MAGNIFICENT; TANẒĪMĀT; TURKEY; TURKS.

"Ovliad" (from *awlad*, Arabic "children"). A tribe in Turkmenistan claiming apocryphal descent from the first four Caliphs. Such claims are more correctly understand as implying an Arab origin or strong Arab influx within the group at some point in the past, rather than literal descent from a particular figure. For example, some Pushtun clans in Afghanistan claim to be descended from Biblical Jews, a claim which is purely mythological, and in Mauritania, the Arabs and Berbers claim to be entirely descendants of Ḥasan and Ḥusayn. (*See* AFGHANISTAN.)

P

Padishāh. A Persian title for the ruler, also used among the Turks.

Padri Movement. An Indonesian reform and colonial resistance movement in the beginning of the 19th century. It gave impetus to the rise of Islamically orthodox religious authorities.

Pahlavī. A dynasty in Persia from *1343-1399*/1924-1979. The first Shah of this dynasty was Reza Pahlavī, originally the leader of an Army Cossack Brigade. (Cossack brigades in Iran were Russian trained military units.) Like Atat rk in Turkey, Reza I sought to modernize Persia, and took a hostile stand towards the representatives of religion, the Mullās. He set the tone for a nationalistic policy laying claim to territories which were at that time outside Persian control.

In *1351*/1934 the name of Persia was changed to Iran. At the beginning of World War II, Iranian territory was occupied by Allied troops, and the Shah, obliged to abdicate, went into exile. His son Muḥammad Reza replaced him on the throne (although his coronation did not take place until over thirty years later).

The first ten years of Muḥammad Reza's reign were marked by political turbulence of every kind, made much worse by the foundation of the *Tudeh* Communist party in *1361*/1943. The question of oil revenues and the Anglo-Iranian Oil Company, the subsequent attempt at nationalization and the assumption of dictatorial powers by the Prime Minister Dr. Mossadegh, together with the outbreak of popular disaffection, led the Shah to leave the country on 16 August 1953. Following brief hostilities in Teheran and its seizure by General Zahedī, there was a turnabout of public opinion (often attributed to the activities of a few US CIA agents) and the Shah returned on the 21st to the acclaim of the populace.

The period before and after the first departure of the Shah was marked by the volatile influence of *Bāzārī* elements (that is, the merchants of the Bazaars) in the traditional economic sector, agitation by the Communist Party, and initiatives on the part of religious leaders, the Mullās. A member of the *Majlis* ("parliament"), Ayatollah Qashānī, spoke publicly about the will of the Hidden Imām and was implicated, through the confession of a Persian Fedayyin assassin, in the direction of political terrorism.

Nevertheless, the oil revenues of the sixties and seventies, brought a climate of growing prosperity, offset only by unexpectedly severe failures in agriculture as a result of inept agricultural innovations. The 1970s saw an ever more insistent exacerbation of the profound tensions inherent in Shī'ite political theory. The victory in the *12th*/18th century of the Uṣūlī school over the Akhbārī had cleared the way for a startling growth in the influence and power of the Mullās, comparable to the resurgence of priestly power under Mazdeism in ancient Persia. The Mullās moreover controlled vast sums of money acquired through the religious taxes of *zakāt* and *khums* (the latter does not exist among the Sunnīs) and were closely linked by family with the conservative and rich *Bāzārī* merchant class.

The Shah's regime was becoming ever more irksome to the religious authorities who, ever since Shī'ism became the state religion at the beginning of the *10th*/16th century, and during the last two hundred years in particular, had been formulating doctrine which accorded greater power and competence to themselves. Although the Shah attempted by such means as his lavish coronation held in Persepolis to assert himself as the legitimate heir to ancient Persian sovereignty, it was the Mullās who incarnated a more telling claim, and one which had been alive in Persia ever since the Arabs first invaded and introduced Islam.

The Shah stood for modernism; even if he had stood for religion, by the very definition of political legitimacy as deriving from the Hidden Imām, he could not have claimed that legitimacy; but the Mullās could. Therefore the rule of the Shah became synonymous with foreign influence and centuries of foreign domination; in the revolutionary code words, his government was referred to as "the Umayyads", and himself as Yazīd, the Arab persecutor of Ḥusayn. Combined with the social dislocations of modernism, the continuing affirmation of the ethos of ancient Iran brought about a revolution which overthrew the Shah in 1978. The Ṣafavid Ismāʿīl I had come to power by exploiting a desire for revenge in the name of the Imāms who had been denied their right, as they saw it, to rule; the force he had unleashed now turned against his successors. *See* AYATOLLAH; HIDDEN IMĀM; ṢAFAVIDS; SHĪʿISM; UṢŪLĪS.

Paighambar (Persian: "prophet"; in Turkish: *peygamber*). A Persian word which generally replaces both *nabī* and *rasūl* in the Indo-Persian world.

Pakistan. Islamic Republic. Population: 129,275,660 (estimates run as high as 144.6 million) of whom 97% are Muslim, 1.2% Christian. There are small minorities of Hindus, Parsis, and others. 20% of the Muslims are Twelve-Imām Shīʿites and perhaps a million are Ismāʿīlīs; the rest are Sunnīs of the Ḥanafī school of law. The Suhrawardi, Chishti, and Qādiriyyah *ṭuruq* are the most important Sufi orders. Urdu is the national language but 58% also speak Punjabi, 12% Sindhī, and 8% or more speak Pashtu. *See* IQBAL; JINNAH.

Palestine (Ar. *Filasṭīn*). "Land of the Philistines", inhabited from 3,000 BC by Canaanites and Egyptians and later by Hyksos, Hittites, and Philistines, conquered by the Jews around 1020 BC, and ruled by them until 587 BC and then again, partially, from 164 BC until Roman rule in 63 BC It was also conquered and ruled by the Assyrians and Persians, the Byzantines, and from AD 635 by the Muslims who called it a *jund*, a military administrative district, like that of Jordan. Under the Crusaders it was a Frankish kingdom. Under the Ottomans it was divided into several administrative areas. In 1923, the region corresponding to the Roman province of Palestine became a British Mandate. In 1947 the United Nations divided Palestine making part of it the Jewish State of Israel. A war ensued after which Jordan annexed the Arab part of Palestine and held it until it was conquered by Israel in the 1967 war. Since the 1993 Washington accords parts of the West Bank had become autonomous, for a time, starting with Jericho.

The population of Palestine at the turn of the century was extremely heteroclite and included many groups such as Armenians, Greeks, Bosnians, Circassians, groups of Persian descent, Kurds, as well as descendents of ancient populations, such as Canaanites, Arabs, Jews and Samaritans. After the Jewish diaspora, a small Jewish population remained in Palestine throughout the Middle Ages. From 1870, with the growth of Zionism, this Jewish population grew by immigration from Europe, and in 1939 totaled 400,000.

In 1910 it was estimated that the population of Palestine was 650,000, of whom two-thirds were Muslims and the rest Christians of many sects, and about 60,000 Jews, or about 11% of the total. In 2000 the population of Israel was 6,600,000 of whom 80.5% were Jewish, 14.6% Muslim, 3.2% Christian, and 1.7% Druze, including Israeli citizens in the West Bank and Gaza strip. Before the Israeli pullout of 2005 the Population of Gaza was: 1,100,000 Arabs and 7,000 Jews who control 25% of the territory (and most of the seacoast), which is 26 miles long and mostly 4 miles wide. The Arab population of the West Bank and Jerusalem is 2,200,000 and there are 383,000 Jewish settlers. In 2002 the BBC reported that 40% of the West Bank was in the hands of Israeli settlers. There were also 3,926,787 registered refugees who left Palestine in two waves in 1947 and in 1967; 1,864,601 live in camps, most of them in surrounding countries.

Pan-Turanianism. Pan-Turkish nationalism. The word *Tūrān*, designating the nomadic homeland of peoples speaking cognate non-Indo-European languages, was employed by the Persian poet Firdawsi who, in his *Shāhnāmeh* ("Book of Kings", circa AD 1000) wrote: "The whole part of the earth which is comprised between the Jihūn and the frontiers of Rūm [Byzantium] and which extends from there in a continuous line to China and Khotan became... the empire of the people of Tūrān." The term is an ancient one, which occurs repeatedly in the Zoroastrian *Avesta*, and appears to designate the Altai mountains and the dry, steppe region in Central Asia including the Amu Darya and the Syr Darya rivers, and the Kara Kum and Kizl Kum deserts, all occupied by Turkic peoples. The Pan-Turanian movement began in Turkey in the 19th century as Muslim awareness began to yield to that of ethnic identity under the impact of Western ideas. Its aim was to unite the peoples of Turkic origin in the Middle East, Russia, Persia, Afghanistan and Central Asia into a potent political bloc, most of whom were Muslims. Its broader aim was to embrace all the related Finno-Ugric and Magyar nations; in this it failed.

However, Pan-Turanianism still exists as a latent force between the Turkic peoples of, for example, the Crimea, Azerbaijan, Central Asia and so forth.

Paradise, *see* al-JANNAH.

Pasha. A Turkish military and civil title of high rank. It is still used in Arab countries to designate a civil authority such as a regional ruler or mayor.

Pathans, *see* PUSHTUN.

Patriarchal Caliphs (Ar. *al-khulafā' ar-rāshidūn*). The so-called "rightly guided Caliphs" were the first four Caliphs, Abū Bakr, 'Umar, 'Uthmān, and 'Alī, whose spiritual stations are considered, by Sunnis, to be commensurate with the dignity of being successors to the Prophet; all having been his close Companions during his prophethood. In the hands of later Caliphs, although there were some men of true sanctity, the office became one of political authority alone, although it carried the prestige of its religious connotations.

The Shī'ites, however, recognize as legitimate only the Caliphate of 'Alī and the brief Caliphate of his son Ḥasan who succeeded him. They consider the first three Caliphs to be usurpers. The Khārijites (today's Ibāḍites) do not recognize all of 'Uthmān's Caliphate as being legitimate, nor 'Alī's after the Battle of Ṣiffīn.

The Sunnīs, on the other hand, who comprise at least 90% of the Islamic world, greatly respect and venerate the first four Caliphs.

The reigns of the Patriarchal Caliphs are:

Abū Bakr	*11-13*/632-634
'Umar ibn al-Khattāb	*13-23*/634-644
'Uthmān ibn 'Affān	*23-35*/644-656
'Alī ibn Abī Ṭālib	*35-40*/656-661

This was followed by the short-lived Caliphate of Ḥasan, the son of 'Alī, in *40*/661. Thereafter followed the dynasty of the Umayyads, a family which had been the main opponents of the Prophet during his lifetime. *See* 'ABBĀSIDS; CALIPH; ḤASAN; UMAYYADS.

"The Pen is in the Hand of the Enemy". The simple formula by which Shī'ite divines dismiss any facts which contradict their theses.

People of the Bench, *see* AṢḤĀB aṣ-ṢUFFĀH.

People of the Book, *see* AHL al-KITĀB.

People of the Cloak, *see* AHL al-KISĀ'Ī.

People of the House, *see* AHL al-BAYT.

People of the Scripture, *see* AHL al-KITĀB.

Perfect man, *see* al-INSĀN al-KĀMIL.

"Permitted", *see* MUBĀḤ.

Persia, *see* IRĀN.

Pharaoh (Ar. *fir'awn*). The title of the rulers of Egypt in ancient times. The Pharaoh with whom Aaron and Moses would have dealt is depicted in Islam as the epitome of evil; the Koranic account sees him overwhelmed in the Red Sea, in pursuit of the Children of Israel, but saved alive by his repentance:

And We brought the Children of Israel
over the sea; and Pharaoh and his hosts
followed them insolently and impetuously
till, when the drowning overtook him, he said
'I believe that there is no god but He in whom
the Children of Israel believe;
I am of those that surrender.'
'Now? And before thou didst rebel, being of
those that did corruption.
So today We shall deliver thee with thy body,
that thou mayest be a sign to those after thee.'
(10:90-92)

The sin of Pharaoh is seen as, above all, pride; he rejected guidance and a Divine Message and, by asserting his own "Lordship", as it were challenged God:

... So he showed him the great
sign, but he cried lies, and rebelled,
then he turned away hastily, then he
mustered and proclaimed, and he said,
'I am your Lord, the Most High!'... (79:20-25)

The Koranic accounts are, as is usual, amplified in their detail and trends by contemporary tradition which declares, in illustration of the Pharaoh's pride, that he built a tower which darkened the sun and from its summit shot an arrow into the sky at the God of Moses which, by God's contriving, returned bloodied; Pharaoh's pride was thereby heightened and his doom made more certain; a tradition which echoes a legend of the Jews about the Tower of Babel. Where the Koran differs from the popular traditions is in the significant theme of Pharaoh's repentance and forgiveness. It is frequently forgotten that each Sūrah of the Koran but one begins with a reference to God's mercy. Perhaps not unrelated to this theme is the fact that the wife of the Pharaoh who pitted himself against Moses is, in the Koran, described as a believer, and is considered in tradition also to have been of an exalted spiritual station. Her name, according to Islamic tradition, was Asiyah:

> God has struck a similitude
> for the believers — the wife of
> Pharaoh, when she said, 'My
> Lord, build for me a house in
> Paradise, in Thy presence, and
> deliver me from Pharaoh
> and his work, and do Thou
> deliver me from the people
> of the evildoers.' (66:11)

Philosophy (Ar. *falsafah*). Islam came into the world without philosophy; it was God reaching down to man rather than man, through his own efforts, discovering the ways of God.

For its first century, Islam had no philosophy as such. There was, of course, its great philosophic breakthrough, the essence of the revelation, which was the doctrine of one abstract Divinity. Freed from human form, this was a new vision of Reality, the result of the new religion's repudiation of the Manichean dualism which had been spreading throughout the classical world from its birthplace in 'Irāq for already three hundred years. In Manicheism there were two divinities which had been defined by their mutual opposition to each other. With Islam there is one abstract God, and this created a wave of spiritual liberation into a new dimension. But although it is possible to speak of Islamic epistemology or ethics even at this early period, there was no conscious method or system. However, Islam was soon to become a consumer of classical philosophy, in particular Stoicism, and Aristotelianism, as well as Epicureanism and Pythagoreanism. Above all, Islam studied Aristotle. Then Islam passed him on to Europe thereby awakening the Renaissance. (Early Christianity had abandoned and stifled philosophy bringing on the Dark Ages; as Tertullian said: "What does Jerusalem have to do with Athens?" Irenaeus put it thus: "It is better if a man knows nothing and does not perceive a single cause of things created but abides in faith in God and love, rather than that, puffed up by such knowledge [*scientia*], he falls away from the love that makes man alive... and rather than that he falls into godlessness through the subtleties of his questioning and through hairsplitting [*per quaestionum subtilitates*].)

But first, as Islam expanded in the direction of Persia, it was exposed to the philosophies of antiquity. Where Islam spread, Alexander the Great had gone before, leaving behind the legacy of Hellenistic learning which the Eastern churches put to use. Thus the Nestorians had maintained a school of philosophy in Jundishāpūr (or Gandisapora) near Ahvāz in Persia from the 3rd century AD on.

The Mu'tazilites, or rationalists, were the first to embody the influence of Hellenistic philosophy within Islam. In the long run their efforts were perceived by the orthodox as an intrusion, alien in spirit and dangerous to the faith, for too often doctrine was diminished to fit the measures of reason.

After *212*/827 the Mu'tazilites succeeded in exerting the dominant influence on official doctrine during the Caliphate of al-Ma'mūn (*198-218*/813-833). The movement then declined and was so severely denounced by the theologian al-Ash'arī (d. *324*/935), himself a former Mu'tazilite, as to lose all hope of regaining its former prominence. In later days its name merely served to disguise the freethinker or the agnostic. But al-Ash'arī himself, it should be noted, was a thinker in the Greek philosophical tradition, particularly that of the Stoics, and incorporated the dialectical methods of the Mu'tazilites into Islamic theology.

In the early Christian world, and beyond its confines even as far as India, Neoplatonism had flourished. Greek wisdom had permeated the soil that Islam conquered, and Hellenistic thought did not fail to find adherents among the thinkers in Islam, as well as in the various heterodox sects, of whom the Seveners are the most remarkable example; in the event it was the Dualist Seveners who became the channel whereby the arcane and Gnostic teachings of late classicism entered Islam. The most important flowering of this hidden tradition (which also produced writings that alarmed theologians and rulers alike) was the Brotherhood of Purity

(*Ikhwān aṣ-Ṣafā'*) around *350*/961, who elaborated an encyclopedia of universal knowledge.

When Baghdad (founded in *145*/762) became the 'Abbāsid capital, the intellectual dominance of Islam by Persians was in the ascendent. The second 'Abbāsid Caliph, al-Manṣūr (d. *136*/754), had encouraged Greek learning, but Aristotle was not translated into Arabic until the reign of al-Ma'mūn (d. *218*/833). Then there began the momentous study of the Greek philosopher which came to an abrupt end in the Islamic world some centuries later, first in the East and then in Arab Spain, but not before being transmitted thence to Christian Europe. In Europe this took the form of Latin "Averroism", named after Ibn Rushd, or "Averroes" as he was called, an Aristotelian school of thought which lasted well up into the 17th century.

The Muslims have been accused of combining Plato and Aristotle into one philosophy. This had already been done to some extent by the Neoplatonists and the Syriac and Nestorian Christians. The synthesis was carried further in the works of al-Kindī (*2nd*/9th century) and al-Fārābī (c. *257-339*/870-950). (*See* al-KINDĪ; al-FĀRĀBĪ.) In one sense, however, the Muslim philosophers did not create a synthesis; rather, they simply found no conflict between the two great philosophers and looked upon Aristotle as the primary commentator on Plato. That said, the famous quotation attributed to Aristotle: "I love Plato, I love truth, but I love truth more" was originally found in Arabic (and translated into Latin as: "Amicus Plato, sed magis amica veritas."

Questions of authorship, authenticity, or historical sequence concerned them little. Even less were they inclined to separate out the Neoplatonism that colored their perceptions of Greek thought. Whether Aristotle was truly the author of all the works attributed to him was of little importance; the ideas were what counted.

In Plato they found the analogical view which absorbed all discontinuities, the vertical dimension which united all levels of reality; in Aristotle, the study of the horizontal and apparently separate levels. Between the two they found a complementarity, and moreover, a system of thought that was compatible with the Islamic revelation. Or at least they made it so; Aristotle's concept of the Prime Mover evidently had to yield to the Islamic revelation of the Absoluteness of God and His nature in the Koran, and continuing existence must permanently depend upon Him.

Above all, the Muslim philosophers were Realists, never Nominalists. They believed in one, higher reality, a realm of essences, more real than the realm of things; and that the world is the manifestation of that reality. They believed that universals exist before things (*ante res*). This line of thought is more evident in Plato and his world of ideas than in Aristotle, but the Muslim philosophers did not find Aristotle opposed to it.

Nominalism is the tendency to assert that universals are mere "names" which exist after things (*post res*) or that reality is a function of physical existence and that universals exist "only in the mind". Today, this tendency has gone so far in certain quarters as to declare that behavior is a function of biology, that atoms alone constitute reality. A kind of Nominalism may have been voiced as early as Porphyry (d. 304) but was not taken seriously until after William of Ockham (d. 1349).

The attribution of Nominalism to Aristotle is the result of interpretation or emphasis; above all, the idea that Aristotle is a Nominalist is the result of the banishment of God from philosophical thought, which probably never happened among the Muslim philosophers; it finds its justification in the idea that Aristotle allowed universals a place in things (*in rebus*), that is, within existence itself. Aristotle attributed a substance to individuals; in Plato's formulation, the world is pure illusion; Aristotle, in enunciating the principle of non-contradiction, namely that something cannot be and not be at the same time, found it logical to say that while the world is not real in the same sense as its Principle, it is nevertheless real on its own plane. This he expressed by attributing a substance to individuals. But he was not a Nominalist in that substance is not merely a name or an appearance; the individual substance, or the world, is real; but its reality and existence derives from the removal of the qualities of absoluteness from Reality itself. Its reality is like that of a particular color (manifestation), which is the result of the removal of the other colors from "white" light (the Principle in regard to light and colors), which itself is colorless but contains all the colors. According to Plato, the world can be reduced to God if its illusion is removed; according to Aristotle there is no illusion; but the world is always less than God. He perfectly well recognized the absolutely transcendent nature of the First Mover, beyond the "sublunary sphere" of change, and it is therefore no surprise that the Muslim philosophers found in him the means by which the mind extends its field of knowledge, without denying the supremacy of the Ideal, or supra-Real.

Unlike doubt-ridden modern philosophy, the classical philosophy of the Muslims was based upon the certainty of God and revelation. For Plato and Aristotle, revelation was a function of the intellect itself. Not a few Muslim philosophers came to this conclusion themselves, notably Ibn Ṭufayl (d. *581*/1185). This view never led them to deny Koranic revelation, but, nevertheless, horrified the theologians. Al-Ghazālī (d. *505*/111) was harsh towards those who held that the world was eternal, that God's knowledge being universal did not extend to particular events, and that there was a resurrection of the soul but not of the body. Like al-Ash'arī, he upheld transcendence and revelation against reason. Al-Ghazālī was obliged, in the name of religious orthodoxy, to denounce the philosophers by writing his *Tahāfut al-Falāsafah* ("Refutation of the Philosophers") in order to forestall a neo-pagan renaissance within Islam. In Europe a similar suspicion arose concerning some of the philosophers; the great commentator of Aristotle, Ibn Rushd or "Averroes", was strongly associated with humanism in the European reading of him, but religious scepticism was certainly not the view of the *qāḍi* of Seville himself; it is sometimes forgotten that Ibn Rushd was, after all, a judge (*qāḍi*) according to the religious law of Islam. It was the Western philosophers, and not the Muslims, who took the further step beyond the edge and looked at the world purely empirically.

The Muslim philosophers, then, were realists in their understanding of Aristotle and, necessarily, of Plato. They were predominantly Aristotelian insofar as he is the dialectical means of understanding the Ideal, or the Real. For the Muslim philosophers, Aristotle, the student of Plato, was also his greatest commentator, building an intellectual infrastructure out of the Ideal world up to the edge of the manifested world, or world of things. Al-Fārābī and others fashioned a vocabulary for Aristotelian philosophy in Arabic, drawing upon the Koran. Being or substance they called *jawhar* ("jewel"); "accidents" (or contingencies within Being which are existence) they called *'araḍ* (pl. *a'rāḍ*), which arise out of the "privation" of Being (*'adam*), the categories they called *ma'qūlāt.*

In the classical mold, the Muslim thinkers were never exclusively philosophers in the modern sense, but natural scientists, physicians, and often poets too. Thus Ibn Sīnā, or "Avicenna" (d. *429*/1037), was still published in Europe as a physician into the 17th century, long after his influence as a philosopher and a logician — the most famous of philosophers in Europe and the Orient — had waned. Ibn Bājjah, or "Avempace" (d. *533*/1138) was famous as a philosopher, and the precursor of Ibn Rushd's theory of the "One Intellect", but he also influenced Galileo (through Averroes) by equating the speed of a moving object to the force which set it into motion, minus the factor of friction, and by affirming an identity between the force which moves physical objects on the earth and that which moves the planets. For him, however, this force was not merely a physical phenomenon but had its origin in the spiritual sphere and in the Divine.

The most Aristotelian of all the Muslim philosophers was Ibn Rushd, or "Averroes" (d. *595*/1198). Yet he was responsible for the most Platonic of notions, that of the "One Intellect". (*See* FIVE DIVINE PRESENCES.) The idea is a variant on the fundamental metaphysical notion that the principle of knowledge and cognition, the intellect (*al-'aql al-fā'il*) at man's center, is the same as the principle of creation at the center of Being (*al-'aql al-awwal*, or what Christians would call the *logos*, and Hindus *buddhi*), and that the objective world is Being differentiated, "woven" into existence. Hinduism expresses the same idea in its concept of Brahma and Ātmā. Sufism already had an aphorism to this effect: "Everything that you see is the Act of One." The mystic Ibn 'Arabī (d. *638*/1240) was to develop this further in a more complete and esoteric form in the theory of *waḥdat al-wujūd* ("the unity of Being") in the time immediately following Ibn Rushd. The idea had also been taken up by Ibn Tufayl (d. *581*/1185) in his *Ḥayy ibn Yaqẓān*, an allegory in which natural philosophy and thought lead to insights which parallel those of revelation and mysticism. Through Averroism in Europe, the idea of the "One Intellect" spread quickly, but in the absence of a developed philosophic framework became corrupted into a "theory of one soul" common to all mankind, called "panpsychism".

It was this capacity of philosophy to intoxicate its votaries and ultimately to become independent of religion that led al-Ghazālī to write his "Refutation of the Philosophers", which accomplished just that. He attacked them, with Ibn Sīnā in mind, for, among other things, maintaining the "eternity of the world" and for ascribing knowledge to means other than revelation. Al-Ghazālī specifically denounced twenty theses; three he said were *kufr*, or disbelief: the eternity of the world; the idea that God does not know particulars; the denial of bodily resurrection. The other points he called *bid'ah*, or "objectionable innovation". He only argued with philosophers who were *ilahiyyun*, or those who professed to believe in God, and did not bother with the atheist materialists nor the naturalists (by whom he meant Galen). What he sought was to establish the limits of philosophy: to have it be "the handmaiden of theology" and no more; and if not that, then nothing. Philosophy had created various means of studying and analyzing the world and thought itself, but for al-Ghazālī a dangerous frontier had been reached. The development of philosophy was leading away from the light of revelation and ideas *into* the darkness of Plato's cave, by virtue of a purely empirical view of a material world. Beyond it lay the abyss into which Christian Europe was to fall: Renaissance humanism, which led fatally to a de-humanizing materialism. It was the fall into this abyss that al-Ghazālī wished to avert: providentially so, for he had no means of foreseeing its full consequence, which is the modern world.

To the philosopher's quest to know reality with the mind or thought alone, al-Ghazālī opposed Divine transcendence. Theologically he was an Ash'arite and played towards the philosophers the role that al-Ash'arī had played towards the Mu'tazilites. But remarkably, he was also a mystic who strove to redirect the energies of the thinkers towards the mystic path. His success indicates that the pruning of the philosophical tree made it grow higher and attain to a different world altogether, for after al-Ghazālī there was a tremendous flowering of mysticism.

Philosophy in Baghdad had seen its day. But in Spain the books of al-Ghazālī were burned by the Almoravids in disagreement with certain of the views expressed in the *Iḥyā' 'Ulūm ad-Dīn* ("The Revitalization of the Religious Sciences"), specifically the use of qiyas or "analogy" in law which was a hallmark of the Shāfi'īs of whom al-Ghazālī was one. In the brief reprieve thus afforded, Ibn Rushd and other Spanish thinkers completed their work. Ibn Rushd answered al-Ghazālī by writing his work *Tahāfut at-Tahāfut* ("Refuting of the Refutation"). Indeed, he could easily argue that the "eternity of the world" was implied in the immutability of God, that as God is always Creator, and He never undergoes change, therefore creation is permanent; hence the philosophers conclude that the world is eternal. At the same time theologians see this as a threat to the notion of the Absolute itself; Plato himself calls creation a "second god". The resolution of the apparent contradiction between these two views (of, on the one hand, theology denying the eternity of creation, and on the other, philosophy affirming it), lies in the metaphysical idea of the apocatastasis, or the Hindu *mahāpralaya*, the "moment between creations" when the Absolute is without the *ḥijāb*, the "veil" of manifestation.

At the apocatastasis all manifestation comes to an end; there is God Alone: "My play is ended", says the Srimad Bhagavatam. Then, because God is the Absolute, and the perfection of the Absolute includes the possibility of the negation of the Absolute, God creates anew. This metaphysical idea receives little attention in religion because it undermines all notions of striving for salvation, reducing them to a "joy of return", since the damned are released from hell, and the saved from paradise; it also resolves, however, the question of the "eternity of the world"; the world is "eternal" as a permanent possibility of the Absolute, an "inner dimension".

Similarly, the Philosophers also raised another problem, that of the omniscience of God, concluding that God's knowledge embraced all universals, but did not extend to particulars. The Theologians, naturally, maintained that God's omniscience had no limit.

Philosophy was eclipsed as an active force in Islamic thought after Ibn Rushd, who represents the summit and terminus of Aristotelian thought in Islam. For Europe too, he was a figure of such importance that Dante called him the author of the "great commentary", and placed him, along with Avicenna (that is, Ibn Sīnā) in the first circle of his *Inferno*, with the other great philosophers who await the harrowing for their salvation; upon the single figure of Averroes a whole school of European philosophy was founded.

The great period in which the works of Muslim philosophers were translated into Latin began with the conquest of Toledo by the Christians (*478*/1085). Archbishop Raimundo patronized this task until his death in 1151, and others, including Frederick II of Germany, carried on after him. To emulate the intellectual sparkle of Arab courts, Spanish kings too commissioned translators, often converted Spanish Jews, to put Arab books into Latin. It was by way of this that the Greek classics came again to the attention of Europe.

Islamic thought did not disappear after Ibn Rushd. Rather, it was swallowed up in a tremendous flood of mysticism which broke out from Moorish Andalusia in the *7th*/13th century and spread to the East. This effusion of mysticism attracted and nourished, from then on, the greatest minds in Islam and affected all levels of intellectual activity. Even in its decline, this trend marked many Islamic countries right up to the colonial period and the advent of modernism. Nor was the contribution of philosophy lost; it provided the groundwork for the great metaphysical formulations which followed. That philosophy was indeed integrated into esoterism can be seen from the fact that the celebrated exponent of metaphysical Sufism, or mysticism, Ibn 'Arabī, could be called *Ibn Aflaṭūn*, or "the son of Plato". *See* ALEXANDER; APOCATASTASIS; al-ASH'ARĪ; BEING; BROTHERHOOD of PURITY; al-FARĀBĪ; FIVE DIVINE PRESENCES; al-GHAZĀLĪ; KALĀM; al-KINDĪ; KUMŪN; IBN 'ARABĪ; IBN BAJJAH; IBN RUSHD; IBN SĪNĀ; IBN ṬUFAYL; MU'TAZILITES; RŪḤ; SEVENERS; SUFISM.

Pictures, *see* IMAGES.

Pietists, *see* MURJI'AH.

Pilgrimage. The idea of pilgrimage is expressed by three ideas and words, namely, *al-Ḥajj*, *al-'Umrah* and *az-Ziyarāh*.

Al-Ḥajj ("the greater pilgrimage"), the canonical pilgrimage, one of the "five pillars" of Islam (*see* FIVE PILLARS), is an elaborate series of rites, requiring several days for their accomplishment, performed at the Grand Mosque of Mecca and in the immediate environs of the city, at a particular moment of the Islamic year, which, because of the lunar calendar, advances some ten days each year.

The *Ḥajj* is obligatory upon those who can "make their way" (Koran 3:97) to Mecca. That is to say that the requirement is not absolute, but incumbent upon those whose health and means permit it, and who, in doing so, do not compromise their responsibilities towards their families. Those who have made the pilgrimage are entitled to prefix their names with the appellation "Pilgrim" (*al-Ḥajj*).

In the last century the number of people performing the *ḥajj* in one year could be as few as 10,000, before World War II, and may well exceed a million today. Air transport has in one way made the *ḥajj* easier, but now that over a million pilgrims participate together, it has become far more arduous because at certain moments all the pilgrims are performing the same rites in the same place. Thus, by force of numbers, the circumambulation of the Ka'bah, for example, can overflow outside the Grand Mosque, and be very difficult to perform.

Al-'Umrah ("the lesser pilgrimage", or "visitation"), an abbreviated version of the *ḥajj* — and also one of its constituent elements — can be performed at any time. Its rites can be accomplished in one and one-half hours, and they now take place entirely within the reconstructed and extended Grand Mosque in Mecca. The *'umrah*, which consists essentially of seven circumambulations of the Ka'bah and seven courses, partly walked and partly run, between Ṣafā and Marwah, may be performed at any time of the year except during the "greater pilgrimage" (when it is combined with the *ḥajj*), and at any time of day or night. It is possible to perform the *'umrah* for another by proxy, making an intention to that effect. *'Umrah* does not fulfill the requirement of *ḥajj*, but those who perform the *'umrah* are called, loosely, *ḥajjī* while accomplishing it. (The proper term for one performing *'umrah* is *mu'tamir.*)

Az-Ziyārah ("visit"), a non-canonical custom — not a religious rite (it even contradicts a Ḥadīth expressly forbidding it), of visiting the tomb of the Prophet in Medinah. By extension, the word *az-ziyārah* is sometimes applied to the visiting of any holy place. Such visits are often carried out according to a traditional program, but do not in fact have ritual elements, although the *Fātiḥah*, the fundamental prayer (*see* FĀTIḤAH), is always recited in connection with a visit of this kind, and canonical prayers may be performed.

Pilgrimage to the Ka'bah antedates Islam. The Koran says that the pilgrimage of the Arabs of pagan times had become so degenerate that "their worship at the House is nothing but a whistling and a handclapping" (8:35). Taking elements of the pilgrimage as it then existed, the Prophet gave a new model based upon his two pilgrimages after the founding of the Islamic community; the pilgrimage of the year 7 of the Hijrah (March 629), after the treaty of Ḥudaybiyyah, and the "farewell" pilgrimage of the year 10 (March 632). The latter was the more important from the point of view of exemplary situations.

However, the Koran says that the founder of the rite of pilgrimage is Abraham:

And when We settled for Abraham the place
of the House: Thou shall not associate
with Me anything. And do thou purify
My House for those that shall go about it
and those that stand, for those that bow
and prostrate themselves;
and proclaim among men the Pilgrimage,
and they shall come unto thee on foot
and upon every lean beast, they shall come from
every deep ravine
that they may witness things profitable to them
and mention God's Name on days well-known
over such beasts of the flocks as He has
provided them: So eat thereof, and feed
the wretched poor.
Let them then finish with their self-neglect
and let them fulfil their vows, and go about
the Ancient House'. (22:26-30)

The *ḥajj* is performed at the Grand Mosque (*al-masjid al-ḥarām*), and in Minā, Muzdalifah, and 'Arafāt, which are places directly adjacent to Mecca and contiguous one to the other. 'Arafāt is the farthest from Mecca, being an extensive plain, part of which lies beyond the sacred environs (*ḥaram*) of Mecca; on one side of it rises a small hill called the Mount of Mercy (*jabal raḥmah*). The whole plain is suitable for the rite of the "standing" (*wuqūf*) at 'Arafāt. Minā, which is closest to Mecca, is hemmed in by mountains, and here the pillars are located which are stoned during the *ḥajj*. Muzdalifah lies between Minā and 'Arafāt.

The *ḥajj* and/or the *'umrah* begin, as do all rites, with the stating of intent (*an-niyyah*), and this is bound up with the putting on of *iḥrām* (*see* IḤRĀM), the state of consecration, and the primordial costume which goes with it of two seamless — unsewn — pieces of cloth.

The *'umrah* consists of the following: before setting foot in the sacred area around Mecca, the pilgrim intending to perform the *'umrah* dons the *iḥrām*. Those who are already in Mecca go to certain mosques on the boundary of the sacred area, such as the Ju'ranah mosque, in order to do this. Most visitors from abroad put it on in Jeddah, although it is possible to assume it even in one's country of departure.

1) Upon arriving at the Ka'bah the pilgrim performs seven circumambulations of the Ka'bah.

2) This is followed by a personal prayer (*du'ā'*) whilst pressing oneself to the wall of the Ka'bah at the spot called *al-multazam* between the Black Stone and the door. Since it is difficult because of the number of pilgrims at any time actually to perform this at that precise point, in practice, the pilgrim usually recites his prayer facing the Ka'bah at a point some distance away, near the Station of Abraham (*maqām Ibrāhīm*).

3) The pilgrim then performs a *two-raka'āt* prayer at the Station of Abraham, a small kiosk which contains an imprint, said to be of Abraham's foot, in stone.

4) The pilgrim drinks of the water of Zamzam which is found at the watering place, reached by a flight of steps, where the spring in the courtyard of the Great Mosque has been channeled, or from the drinking fountains set up throughout the Mosque.

5) He then proceeds to the ritual walking (*sa'y*) between the two hills Ṣafā and Marwah, seven times. (Ṣafā to Marwah is one course, Marwah to Ṣafā another.) This is begun at Ṣafā and ends at Marwah, at the far end of the Mosque, where a lock of hair is cut from the pilgrim's head signifying the end of the rite and of the state of *iḥrām*.

Commonly, a new pilgrim hires a professional guide, called a *muṭawwif*, to lead him in the rites of *'umrah*. There are recitations traditionally associated with each step of the rites, but these have no binding character and may be replaced by simple spoken prayer.

The *ḥajj* is a more extensive ritual lasting several days. Iḥrām is assumed at a greater distance from Mecca than that of *'umrah*, at one of the "boundaries", each known as *al-miqāt* (*see* MIQĀT). Many pilgrims put on *iḥrām* as they leave their own countries, particularly those arriving by air.

The intention (*niyyah*) formulated for the *ḥajj* varies according to how the *'umrah* is combined with it. There are three possibilities:

1. *Ifrād*; the *ḥajj* alone; a second intention for the *'umrah* is then formulated at Mecca as the starting point. The second iḥrām is put on at the boundary for the Meccan *ḥaram*.

2. *Tamattu'*; an interrupted pilgrimage; iḥrām is put on for the 'umrah which is performed sometime before the pilgrimage; the state of iḥrām is then terminated, to be resumed when the moment comes for the greater pilgrimage.

3. *Qirān*, the combining of *'umrah* and *ḥajj* without interruption of the consecrated state of *iḥrām*. (*See* IḤRĀM.)

The daily stages of the greater pilgrimage are as follows:

The First Day: 8th *Dhū-l-Ḥijjah*

The name of this day is the *yawm at-tarwiyah* ("the day of deliberation" or "reflection"). The pilgrim must have entered into iḥrām outside Mecca at one of the *mawāqīt* (sing. *mīqāt*) before arriving in Mecca. If he is performing an interrupted pilgrimage according to *tamattu'* (*see* IḤRĀM) and has put off his *iḥrām*, he should resume it early in the morning after cutting his hair and nails, performing the ritual ablution, and pronouncing the *talbiyah* invocation: *labbayka-Llāhumma labbayk* ("At Thy service, My God, at Thy service!").

1. If the pilgrim has not yet performed the *ṭawāf al-qudūm* (the "circumambulation of arrival") he must now do so; one walks seven times around the Ka'bah. (*See* ṬAWĀF). The circumambulation at this point in the pilgrimage is optional, but the Mālikī School of Law considers it obligatory (*farḍ*). Because of the number of people, it is difficult to approach the Black Stone to kiss it; therefore a gesture towards the Stone as one walks past, without actually touching it, suffices.

2. After the seventh round is completed, the pilgrim makes a personal prayer, at the area between the Black Stone and the door of the Ka'bah, or at a spot facing this area.

3. The pilgrim then goes to the Station of Abraham (*maqām Ibrāhīm*), or any place near it, and performs a prayer of two *raka'āt*.

4. The pilgrim drinks the water of Zamzam. Thus far, the rites have been exactly the same as those of the *'umrah*, which is a component of the *ḥajj*; but from this point they can diverge. If one is performing pilgrimage in conjunction with the *'umrah* (*qirān*) (*see* IḤRĀM) (the pilgrim is then called a *muqrin*) one should now perform the "running" (*sa'y*) which will count for both *'umrah* and *ḥajj*; alternatively it may also be postponed until the second ambulation (*ṭawāf al-ifāḍah*). Those performing the *ḥajj* alone (*ifrād*) or separate from the *'umrah* (*tamattu'*) will perform the *sa'y* after the *ṭawāf al-ifāḍah* (also called the *ṭawāf az-ziyārah*). After the rites performed in the Grand Mosque, the pilgrims leave for Minā to spend the night until the dawn prayer. For Ḥanafīs and Mālikīs this stay at Minā is obligatory, whereas for others it is recommended. Therefore some pilgrims stay at Minā while others go directly to 'Arafāt from Mecca.

The Second Day: 9th *Dhū-l-Ḥijjah*

This day is called the *yawm al-wuqūf* ("the day of standing"), and also *yawm 'Arafāt* ("the Day of 'Arafāt"). Those who are not already at 'Arafāt go there after the dawn prayer at Minā. At 'Arafāt the afternoon and late afternoon prayers are combined, under the leadership of the Imām, and also shortened. One *adhan* (general call to prayer) is performed with two *iqāmahs* (call to the assembled worshipers immediately before the prayer).

The *wuqūf* ("standing"; it is not necessary actually to stand) is an essential element (*rukn*) of the *ḥajj*. Usually the pilgrims stay at 'Arafāt from noon until after sunset, that is, some part of the day and some part of the night. This is the opinion of the Mālikī, Ḥanafī and Shāfi'ī schools. Ḥanbalīs stay there all day from morning. Some insist on staying at 'Arafāt until sunrise on the 10th, but it is sometimes pointed out that in accordance with one Ḥadīth, *any time* spent at 'Arafāt fulfills the requirement of presence or "standing", as long as this is accomplished *before* the sunrise of the 10th. After sunrise the time for this requirement has definitely lapsed, and without the standing at 'Arafāt there is no *ḥajj*.

During the "Day of 'Arafāt", the pilgrim should recite the *talbiyah* frequently. (*See* TALBIYAH.) This is indeed the central invocatory prayer of the pilgrimage. The symbolism of this day which is one of solemnity, invocation of God, and the examination of conscience, has been interpreted as a foretaste of the Day of Judgement.

It is not necessary to climb the hill of the Mount of Mercy (*jabal raḥmah*) at 'Arafāt, and indeed because of the number of people, it is safer not to do so. Any spot at 'Arafāt is suitable for the performance of the rite. One must not wear anything on the head, but one may carry a parasol, which is, in fact, advisable. After sunset most pilgrims leave for Muzdalifah in what is called the *ifāḍah* ("overflowing") or the *nafrah* ("rush"). The invocation of the *talbiyah* comes to an end. At Muzdalifah the pilgrims perform the sunset and night prayers combined together and pray these at the time of the night prayer (*'ishā'*). The pilgrims pass the night at Muzdalifah.

The Third Day: 10th *Dhū-l-Ḥijjah*

This day is called the *yawm an-nahr* ("the day of sacrifice"). The dawn prayer is performed at Muzdalifah and the monument called *al-mash'ar al-ḥarām*, an open area, is visited. The pilgrim gathers 49 pebbles if he is going to stay at Minā for two days, and 70 if he will stay three. These pebbles should be approximately the size of a chickpea and they will be used to stone the symbolic pillars (*al-jamarāt*) during the following days.

On the way to Minā the pilgrim passes though a depression called *Wādi Muḥaṣṣar* (also called *Wādi Nār*). This is the place where the Army of the Elephant was turned away and, as it is "a tormented place", the pilgrim hurries through without lingering.

Upon reaching Minā, the pilgrim casts seven stones at the *jamarat al-'aqabah*, the largest pillar, which represents the temptations of Satan. The casting of stones on this day is obligatory.

After casting the seven stones, the pilgrim may perform the sacrifice at any time until the end of the 13th. (There is a rush for sacrifice on the 10th; the well advised pilgrim puts off the sacrifice until a following day.) The sacrifice may be a camel, an ox, or a ram. Actual blood sacrifice may be replaced by fasting three days during the pilgrimage and seven days at a later time for a total of ten days. For followers of the Shāfi'ī school the blood sacrifice is irreplaceable.

At this point the hair of the pilgrim is clipped. Woman cut only a symbolical lock of hair, but many men have the head completely shaved. Cutting a lock, however, is acceptable for men as well. The state of *iḥrām* is terminated, that one may resume normal dress. However, the conditions of abstinence associated with *iḥrām* continue until the pilgrim has definitively left Minā.

Now the pilgrim goes to Mecca and performs the *ṭawāf al-ifāḍah* (also called *ṭawāf az-ziyārah*). However, this, and the "running" (*sa'y*), if not performed earlier, may be performed until sunset on the 13th.

The Final Days: 11th, 12th and 13th *Dhū-l-Ḥijjah*

During these days, called the *ayyām at-tashrīq* ("days of drying meat"), the pilgrim stays at Minā and each day throws seven stones (*ramī-l-jimār*) at each of the three *jamarāt*, first pelting the small *jamarah* closest to 'Arafāt, then the middle *jamarah*, and ending with the large *jamarah*. These pillars stand in a row in the valley of Minā, now accessible by ramps on two levels. Stoning may not be carried out between sunset and sunrise, and it is Sunnah to do it before noon on the first day, and after noon on the other days. It is permissible to end the pilgrimage by leaving on the 12th, as long as one departs before sunset, or has effectively made preparations for departure by sunset. If not, one must remain for the third day. If one needs more pebbles for stoning, they may be gathered in Minā. Upon leaving Mecca one usually performs the *ṭawāf al-wadā'* ("circumambulation of farewell"), which is not obligatory, but commended.

It has been said: "the pilgrimage is a journey to the heart". The yearly flood of pilgrims from the remotest places of Islam has been a remarkable means of spiritual renewal for distant communities which are thus brought closer to the manifest center of Islam.

Historically, the pilgrimage has been a means of knitting together the many races and nations that make up the Muslim community, and there is no other event on earth that can compare with it. Besides its contribution to social cohesiveness, it has, in the past, been a journey for learning and for the interchange of ideas. For many scholars the journey to Mecca has been the turning point of their intellectual careers because of the encounters it provided with other minds. The Almoravid movement was set, it is said, into motion as a result of the pilgrimage of one man, and other events no less momentous can be traced to the sacred journey.

In the days when travel was done by land or sea, people unable to hire transport could well go on foot to Mecca from, say, West Africa. There are many alive today for whom the pilgrimage was such a journey, when, typically, it took two years in one direction and two years back, because pilgrims would sojourn along the way. Many remained in the Middle East, and in Mecca and Medinah especially, where there are communities of Indians, Malays, Indonesians, and Africans, erstwhile pilgrims who settled there. Similarly, Cairo, Damascus, and Baghdad were great stages of the journey, catering to the yearly flood of pilgrims who today travel by air instead.

The caravans which assembled in these cities for the last stage of the journey to Mecca disappeared only towards the middle of this century. In a way, these caravan routes are still viable; pilgrims now come by automobile from neighboring countries. The economic importance of the pilgrimage has increased with the number of pilgrims, and dominates the economic life of Mecca and Medinah, and to some extent, Jeddah. But the pilgrimage is no less important to the economies of Pakistan, Turkey, Nigeria, and Indonesia, whose nationals continue to take part in the pilgrimage in very large numbers to this day. *See* 'ARAFĀT; FĀTIḤAH; FIVE PILLARS; ḤARĀM; IḤRĀM; KA'BAH; MAQĀM IBRĀHĪM; MĪQĀT; MINĀ; MULTAZAM; MUZDALIFAH; RAMY al-JIMĀR; ṢAFĀ and MARWAH; ṢALĀH; SA'Y; TALBIYAH; ṬAWĀF.

Pious Expressions. Koranic formulas are used in every day expressions. The most important is the *basmalah*, or *Bismi 'Llāhi 'r-Raḥmāni-r-Raḥīm* ("In the Name of God the Merciful, the Compassionate") which can begin any lawful, positive activity and must be spoken at the beginning of all rituals.

The *ḥamdalah* or *al-ḥamdu li-Llāh* ("praise to God") marks an end to an action expressing thanks and acceptance, wonder and reverence, as do likewise *subḥān Allāh* ("God be praised!") and *Allāhu Akbar* ("God is Greater" or "Greatest"), or *Lā hawla wa lā quwwata illā bi-Llāh* ("there is no power nor strength save in God"). The istithnā', or In shā'a-Llāh ("if God wills") is used in reference to any action or state in the future. *Innā li-Llāhi wa innā ilayhi rāji'ūn* ("we belong to God and to Him we return") is said when in distress or upon hearing of a death. *Ṣabrun jamīlun wa-Llāhu karīm* ("Patience is an adornment and God is gracious") is another expression in moments of trial. *Al-mu'minūna fī kulli ḥālin bi-khayr* ("believers are blest in all circumstances"). *Tawakkal 'ala-Llāhi wa huwa ni'ma-l-wakīl* ("trust in God, for what a Guardian is He!"). *Ma sh'a-Llāh* ("May God's will be done.") These expressions echo daily in a Muslim's life and, at their most heart-felt, are the support of an unflinching reliance upon God; one may, in the nature of things, fall, but with faith one will "fall upward", and be held by *ar-Raḥmān* ("the Merciful") as he supports the dove in flight. Similar expressions, such as *in nomine Deo, Deo gratia, laus Deo*, were used in the same way in Christian Europe in the Middle Ages. *See* BASMALAH; ḤAMDALAH; al-ḤAWQALAH; REFUGE; TAḤLĪL; TALBIYYAH; TAMJĪD; TA'AWWUDH.

Pīr. A spiritual master, a teacher (*murshid*). From Turkey to India this title is used in preference to the Arabic word *shaykh*.

Pish-Namāz. In Iran, the term for the leader of the prayer, to avoid confusion with the Shī'ite meaning of Imām, which is the term among Sunnis. *See* IMĀM.

Plotinus (AD 205-270) Greek philosopher, known to the Arabs as the *Shaykh al-Yūnānī*. His philosophy, called Neoplatonism, was developed by his disciple Porphyry (d. AD 300) and Porphyry's disciple Iamblichus (d. AD 330). Porphyry published the *Enneads*, or writings of Plotinus. The philosophy was further systematized by the philosopher Proclus (d. AD 485) According to Plotinus reality consists of emanations from the *One*. The first emanation is the *Nous* (mind or intelligence) and the second is the *Psyche* (soul).

In the *3rd*/9th century Neoplatonism began to bear upon philosophy in Islam and especially upon Sufis and eastern Ismā'īlīs. Arabic translations of works claiming to be Aristotelian, the *Theology* of Aristotle which, rather than Aristotle, contained excerpts from Plotinus' *Enneads* and the *Liber de causis* (*Kītab al-īḍāḥ fi-l-khayr al-maḥd*) based upon Proclus' *Elements of Theology* became the most influential sources of Neoplatonism.

In later Plotinian philosophy the ideas became gods; an opposite movement can be seen in Ismā'īlīsm in which what appear to be gods in the 8th century, such as Kūni and Qadar become abstract ideas in the 9th and the 10th. The Plotinian (and Gnostic) idea of the unknowable God in particular was useful to the Ismā'īlis and Shī'ites, both of whom, unlike Sunnis, maintain that God as Beyond-Being is unknowable, like the "Gnostic Abyss". (The Fāṭimids said that the name "Allāh" was derived from *walaha*, meaning to "lament" because this is metaphysical Being "exiled" from the true Absolute, which they called *al-ghayb ta'ala*, "the Great Void", all of which is the pinnacle of heresy in orthodox theology of any religion. The Twelve Imām Shī'ites do not go this far but place the names of the Essence and the Qualities on different levels.)

The dā'ī of Khorasan, Muḥammad ibn Aḥmad an-Nasafī from Central Asia, executed by the Samanids in Bukhara in *332*/934, (along with Abū Ḥātim Aḥmad ibn Ḥamdan ar-Rāzī) is credited with having introduced Neoplatonism into

Ismā'īlism. It also appears in the *Ikhwān aṣ-Ṣafā'* (Brotherhood of Purity), all Ismā'īlis who did not recognize the Imāmate of the Fāṭimids. The Neoplatonic developments within Ismā'īlism were admitted into Fāṭimid cosmology by the Imām and Caliph al-Mu'izz.

Neoplatonism also found its place in the philosophy of the Christian philosophers, as it did among Islamic philosophers up to Ibn Rushd and continues to feed modern mystical currents.

Pole, spiritual, *see* QUṬB.

Polo. (probably from Tibetan *pulu*, "ball"). The game is said to have originated in the steppes of Central Asia with peasant horsemen pelting balls with willow branches at makeshift goals. It became a royal sport and was played by King Darius. Khusraw Parviz played it with his wife Shireen and their courtiers and ladies in waiting as described by Niẓāmī. It was also played by Jenghiz Khan and the Moghul Emperors, almost disappearing with their empire. It was known as a Persian game to the 'Abbāsids who called it *Ṣuljan*. It survived in remote Gilgit and Manipur where the British rediscovered the game and in 1859 Lt. Joseph Shearer of the Bengal Army founded the first Polo club. Calcutta became a center of the British version of the sport from whence it was reintroduced to Indian royalty with new rules evolved by the Hurlingham Polo Club.

Polygamy. *See* POLYGYNY; WOMEN.

Polygyny. ("The state of having two or more wives"). Islamic law, like Jewish law, both deriving from common Semitic tradition, allows up to four wives. Polygamous marriage accounts for less than 3% of marriages in the Islamic world. (It is estimated that there are 35,000 practicing polygamists in America, the majority of them Mormons.) Given the fact that adultery is practically non-existent in most of the Islamic world, and there is no bigamy as in the West, single partner relationships are by far more the norm in the Islamic world than in Western society. Thus while polygyny is still sometimes brought up in the West as a reproach to Islam, Muslims are much more shocked by sexual mores in the West, and with good reason.

In some countries with a majority Muslim population such as Syria, polygyny is forbidden by civil law. Under Islamic law polygyny requires equal treatment of the wives which means in practice a separate house for each wife, making it financially unthinkable for most people. On the other hand, the facility with which divorce is obtained in traditional law, does mean that numerous consecutive marriages are frequently found among the poor. Also, polygyny is unfashionable at the present time in Westernized milieus, and often marriage contracts specifically preclude the husband from taking a second wife. It is ironic that in Central Asia, where polygyny was also forbidden by Soviet civil law (which also prohibited more than five consecutive marriages), it was clandestinely practiced, albeit very rarely, as a sign of wealth among members of the Communist Party, much as in France or Japan a man takes on a mistress as a sign of his social status. *See* WOMEN; MARRIAGE.

Polytheism, *see* SHIRK; IDOLS; JĀHILIYYAH.

The Pool (Ar. *al-ḥawḍ*). This is part of the symbolical "topology" of the afterlife. The pool is a lake fed by the spring of *Kawthar* at the entrance to paradise, attained by crossing over the "Bridge" of death and Judgement. The believers who enter paradise will drink from the spring of *Kawthar*; it was by the Pool that the Prophet promised to meet his Companions. The spring of *Kawthar* is interpreted as being the inexhaustible plenitude of God; the word contains the root *kathara*, indicating abundance amplified by the letter *waw* (w or o) which stands, according to Sufi interpretations, for *al-Wāhid* (the "Single", the "One"; a name of God). The price demanded by God for this plenitude is prayer and sacrifice:

> Surely We have given
> thee abundance (*al-kawthar*);
> so pray unto thy Lord and sacrifice.
> Surely he that hates thee
> he is the one cut off. (106)

It should be noted that the "Bridge" in Paradise, taken for granted by so many, if not all Muslims, is not actually mentioned in the Koran; it is, as the concept of Paradise itself (as indicated by its Persian name, Firdaws) a purely Zoroastrian idea, one which did not make the transition to Christianity as another Zoroastrian concept, the Last Judgement did, but because of the inclusion of Iran within the Islamic world, the Zoroastrian Bridge of the afterlife has found unquestioning and universal acceptance in Islam.

Postal System, *see* BARID.

Pōstakī. In the meetings of Turkish Sufis the sheepskin upon which the founder of the order sits (in the invisible) or the presiding Shaykh.

Power, Night of, *see* LAYLAT al-QADR.

Prayer. This English word serves to translate three different concepts in Islam, namely *du'ā'*, *ṣalāh* and *dhikr*.

Du'ā' (lit. "calling") is an "individual" or spontaneous prayer in which the worshiper expresses his personal sentiments and petitions God. A special form of *du'ā'* is the *Yā Laṭīf* prayer which is used in moments of distress, or in cases of grave illness.

Ṣalāh (lit. "worship", from an Aramaic word whose root meaning is "to hallow") is the "canonical" or "ritual" prayer which must be performed at five appointed times each day. The basic unit is the *rak'ah* (a round of ritual actions and sacred phrases), so that each canonical prayer consists of a prescribed number of *raka'āt* (pl. of *rak'ah*). Superogatory *raka'āt* are permitted and, indeed, encouraged. Conversely, if for any valid reason it is not possible to pray the canonical prayers at the appointed time, they are to be made up afterwards. The form and contents of the *ṣalāh* are fixed by the Sunnah, the Prophet's example, and by the traditions of the schools of law. *Ṣalāh* is an act of worship, a religious service, special forms of which are prescribed for the occasions of death, religious festivals, and solar eclipses, or to ask for guidance in particular circumstances (*istikhārah*), or to pray God for rain (*istisqā'*).

The third category of prayer is the inward prayer of "remembrance" of God, invocation, *dhikr*. For further descriptions *see* DHIKR; DU'Ā'; FUNERALS; ṢALĀH; YĀ LAṬĪF.

Prayer for the Dead, *see* FUNERALS.

Prayer of Ibn Mashīsh, *see* IBN MASHĪSH.

Prayer Niche, *see* MIḤRĀB.

Prayers on the Prophet (Ar. *aṣ-ṣalāh 'ala-n-Nabī*. The word *ṣalāh*, which denotes the ritual prayer of Islam, and its verb *sallā* "to praise", "to bless", often translated as "to pray upon", appears to originate from Aramaic, the root meaning being "to hallow"). The Koran says: "Verily, God and his Angels send blessings upon the Prophet. You who believe, call blessings upon him and peace." (33:56). Muslims use a number of such invocatory prayers in various rituals and ceremonies. The *du'ā'* (petitioning prayer), which follows the *ṣalāh* (ritual, or canonic prayer), is always introduced with a prayer on the Prophet. This is one version used in North Africa:

> *Aṣ-ṣalātu wa-s-salāmu 'alayka yā Nabiyya'Llāh, aṣ-ṣalātu wa-s-salāmu 'alayka yā Ḥabība-Llāh, aṣ-ṣalātu wa-s-salāmu 'alayka yā Rasūla-Llāh; alfu ṣalātin wa'lfu salāmin 'alayka wa 'alā ālik wa-r-riḍā'u 'an aṣḥābika, yā khayra man-i'khtāra'Llāh.*
>
> Blessing and peace be upon you, O Prophet of God; Blessing and peace be upon you O intimate of God; Blessing and peace be upon upon you O Messenger of God. Thousandfold blessing and thousandfold peace upon you and upon your people, and God's felicity upon your Companions, O best of the chosen of God.

Or:

> *Allāhumma ṣalli 'alā Sayyidinā Muḥammadin 'adada khalqika wa riḍa'i nafsika wa madadi kalimatika. Subḥāna-Llāhi 'ammā yaṣifūn, wa salāmun 'alā-l-mursalīn, wa-l-ḥamduli-Llāhi Rabbi-l-'ālamīn.*
>
> Our Lord, bless our master Muḥammad as much as the number of your creations, the felicity of your essence, and the ink necessary to write your words. Magnified be God above what is attributed to Him, and peace upon the Messengers, and Praise to God, the Lord of the worlds.

When a believer mentions the Prophet — and he is rarely mentioned by name, but rather by the title Prophet (Nabi), or Messenger of God (*Rasūlu-Llāh*) — it is customary to add: ṣalla-Llāhu 'alayhi wa sallam ("May God bless him and give him peace"). The "blessings" (*ṣalāh*) refer to "vertical" graces descending into the soul, and "peace" (*salām*) to a "horizontal" grace of inward dilation which receives and stabilizes those blessings. *See also* QUNUT.

Presences, Five Divine, *see* FIVE DIVINE PRESENCES.

Priests (In Arabic, *rāhib*, pl. *ruhbān*, referring only to Christian anchorites or monks). "There are no priests in Islam" is a Ḥadīth which states the position simply enough. Therefore, the term "Islamic Priests" sometimes used in the Western press to mean a functionary such as an Imām, a faqīh, or a *Mullā*, is misleading and alien to Muslim understanding.

Whereas the Christian sacerdotal function implies a special consecration of the person and the power to carry out rituals which a layman cannot perform, there is no ritual in Islam which cannot be performed by any believer of sound mind, either a man, or a woman if no man is present. Some functions, such as that of prayer leader (Imām), may fall to a particular person because of knowledge (particularly of the Koran), respectable repute or age, but could be performed by anyone. Most public functions such as Imām, *qāḍi* ("Judge"), *'ālim* (a doctor of religious science) are based upon knowledge and scholarship (one might say skill), but do not require a consecration that sets the performer of the function apart from other believers. This is consistent with Islam's claim to restore the religion of Abraham, or the "primordial religion"; it could be said that Islam needs no priests because every Muslim is a priest. *See also* MONASTICISM.

Primordial Norm, *see* FIṬRAH.

Prophets (Ar. sing. *nabī*, pl. *anbiyā'*). The Prophets are divided into two classes according to their missions:

1. *Rasūl* (lit. "Messenger", "Envoy", pl. *rūsūl*; the Koran, moreover, frequently refers to *al-mursalūn*, "those who are sent"). A Prophet who brings a new religion or a major new revelation. This category include Adam, Seth, Noah, Abraham, Ismā'īl (Ishmael), Moses, Lot, Ṣāliḥ, Hūd, Shu'ayb, Jesus, Muḥammad. The Koran calls some of the *mursalūn* the "possessors of constancy" (Ar. *ūlū-l-'azm*; 46:35); the Koran does not name them, but commentators have proposed their candidates.

2. *Nabī* (lit. "Prophet"). A Prophet whose mission lies within the framework of an existing religion. A Prophet is also called *bashīr* ("he who brings glad tidings") and *nadhīr* ("a warner") according to the nature of the message they bear; but most are both bringers of glad tidings as well as warners, since the Mercy and the Rigor of God, which these categories respectively reflect, are complementary, as are Beauty and Majesty.

The Koran says that there is no people to whom a Prophet has not been sent (10:48) and Ḥadīth literature puts the number, symbolically, at one hundred and twenty-four thousand, that is, a number so large that humanity cannot claim it was not adequately warned of the universal Judgement. (The Prophets in their inner nature are one: "We make no distinction between any of His Messengers" (2:135-140 and 2:285) and: "And those who believe in God and His Messengers and make no division between any of them, those We shall surely give them their wages" (4:152).)

The Koran mentions four Arab Prophets, or Prophets sent specifically to the Arabs: Ṣāliḥ, Hūd, Shu'ayb, and Muḥammad. In addition, Abraham is equally the patriarch of both Arabs and Jews.

In the *Nihāyat al-Iqdām fī-'Ilm al-Kalām* ("Limits to Prowess in Theology") Shahrāstāni says: "By my life, the Prophet's soul and temperament must possess all natural perfections, excellent character, truthfulness and honesty in speech and deed before his appointment to the office, because it is by virtue of these that he has deserved Prophetic mission and has come into contact with Angels, and received revelation."

The following are the Prophets mentioned by name in the Koran: Adam, Alyasa' (Elisha), Ayyūb (Job), Dā'ūd (David); Dhū-l-Kifl (Ezekiel), Hūd, Ibrāhīm (Abraham), Idrīs (Enoch), Ilyās (Elijah, Elias), 'Īsā (Jesus), Isḥāq (Isaac), Ismā'īl (Ishmael), Luqmān (Aesop?), Lūṭ (Lot), Muḥammad, Mūsā (Moses), Nūḥ (Noah), Ṣāliḥ, Shu'ayb (Jethro), Sulaymān (Solomon), Yūnus (Jonah), 'Uzair (Ezra), Yaḥyā (John the Baptist), Ya'qūb (Jacob), Yūsuf (Joseph). There are also possible references to others, such as Isaiah. Also mentioned by name are Azar (father of Abraham, Terah in the Old Testament, a transformation through the common form Athar), Dhu-l-Qarnayn (Alexander the Great), Hārūn (Aaron), Maryam (Mary), Zakariyyā (Zacharias, father of John the Baptist), and others. *See* ABRAHAM; ADAM; HŪD; ILYĀS; ALYASA'; JESUS; LUQMĀN; MARY; MOSES, MUḤAMMAD; NOAH; REVELATION; ṢĀLIḤ; SHU'AYB; YAḤYĀ; YŪNUS.

Psalms, *see* ZABUR.

Purdah. In Afghanistan and India, the covering of the face and body by women in public, and their general seclusion. *Ḥijāb* ("veil") is becoming the modern term for such observance in Western Islam.

Purgatory, *see* 'ARAF; ESCHATOLOGY.

Purification. A ritual which consecrates a place for prayer, it does not normally precede prayer in the open air, but is used for interiors such as a mosque, a room in a house, or office, or simply a carpet.

The believer cleans the space or carpet to be purified, often with a brush, and then sprinkles water over it after having pronounced the *ta'awwudh* and the *basmalah*. It is recorded that when the Prophet held babies in his arms which were incontinent, he would remove the impurity from his clothes by sprinkling water and pronouncing the *basmalah*.

A mosque or place of prayer is normally purified by cleaning with water and pronouncing the *basmalah*; if a person in the state of major impurity, which requires the greater ablution (*ghusl*) should enter, the purification of the place is deemed to have been lost, and it is necessary to re-purify it. For this reason non-Muslims are not, strictly speaking, allowed into mosques which are actually used for prayer. In some countries this condition is observed; in others, special slippers are provided for non-Muslims to wear when they enter mosques, or else the ground is covered to provide walking areas. In others again, the condition is simply ignored. *See* ABLUTIONS.

Purity, Sūrah of, *see* IKHLĀṢ.

Pushtun. (better *Pashtūn*, pl. of *Pashtāna*). The Pashto-speaking tribesman who live in Afghanistan, where they are one of the main ethnic groups, and in Pakistan, where they are generally called by the variant term Pathan (Hindi and Urdu). The majority are nomads and live in black goat's hair tents. They are Sunnī Muslims and number over fourteen million.

Q

Qabḍ (lit. "contraction", "spasm"). A term in Sufism meaning a contraction, or straitness of soul. The rhythms of life and particularly of the spiritual life, inevitably call forth periods in which the soul experiences its limitations as distress. The opposite is "expansion" (*basṭ*). Spiritually, however, it is contraction which is beneficial, for it is by trials that one is purified; al-Ḥujwīrī says:

> *qabḍ*... is the contraction of the heart in the state of being veiled... *basṭ* the heart's expansion in the illumined state... both are the result of the same spiritual effusion from God upon man, which either stimulates the heart and depresses the soul, causing basṭ, or enlargement, or depresses the heart and stimulates the soul, in *qabḍ*, or straitness.

Ibn 'Aṭā' Allāh says in the Ḥikam:

> He expanded you so as not to keep you in contraction and contracted so as not to keep you in expansion, and He took you out of both so that you not belong to anything apart from Him.
>
> Whoever worships Him for something he hopes from Him, or in order to stave off the arrival of chastisement, has not concerned himself with the real nature of His Attributes.
>
> When He gives, He shows you His kindness; when He deprives, He shows you His power. And in all that, He is making Himself known to you and coming to you with His gentleness.

See BASṬ.

al-Qadam ash-Sharīf (lit. "the noble footprint"). The footprint is often used in Islam as the symbol of the immaterial "trace" of the Divine Messenger. The stylized "footprint" of Abraham is enshrined in a kiosk near the Ka'bah.

The image of a footprint in which are written the praises of the Prophet is a popular decorative motif. The poet Jalāl ad-Dīn ar-Rūmī said: "If you do not know the way, seek where his footprints are."

Qadaris, *see* QADARIYYAH.

Qadariyyah (from Ar. *qadar*, "power", "will"). Those who upheld the notion of free will against the advocates of predestination (the *Jabarīs* or *Jabariyyah*) in Islam's early theological debates. A solution to the problem of free will and determinism was sketched out by the Ash'arites in their theory of man's acquisition of acts which originate with God. Later, the mystics proposed an antinomial solution to the problem which suggested that the individual does indeed possess free will, and is thus responsible for his decisions, but that these decisions — which are seen in time — nevertheless ultimately fulfill a destiny determined "outside time". In other words, they contended that although Divine Will has determined all things, the freedom of human will lies in its capacity to choose, or to deny, the Absolute. In any case, the word *qadar* means "capacity" and implies limitation, and thus destiny; that is, the word for will and destiny is in fact one and the same. For this reason, at other times *Qadari* has had an opposite meaning, that of determinist.

Ibn 'Aṭā' Allāh said:

> To soften for you the suffering of affliction, He has taught you that He is the One who causes trials to come upon you. For the one who confronts you with His decrees of Fate is the same Who has accustomed you to His good choice.

And Jalāl ad-Dīn ar-Rūmī said:

> If we let fly an arrow, that action is not from us: we are only the bow, and the shooter of the arrow is God.

See KALĀM; MAKTŪB.

al-Qaddāḥ, *see* 'ABD ALLĀH ibn MAYMŪN al-QADDĀḤ; IBN RIZĀM.

Qāḍī (pl. *quḍāh*). A judge, appointed by a ruler or a government on the basis of his superior knowledge of Islamic law. This Arabic word is sometimes rendered as "cadi" in English, and produced the Spanish *alcalde* for "mayor". The *Qāḍī's* decisions are binding and final. In the Sunnī world, the "door of *ijtihād*", or decisions made on one's personal assessment, has been "closed", and judges are thus expected to apply only the precedents of the past in making their decisions. In practice, however, judges have applied new solutions (*ijtihād nisbī*, "relative *ijtihād*") to legal problems, at least by small increments, finally producing a new corpus of legal decisions; this could be called *ijtihād* by degrees. In the Shī'ite world, on the contrary, a decision is made only by a mujtahid, a high religious authority, and is a new "unique" decision, even if an identical precedent exists, or if the mujtahid has just answered the same question for another client.

The *qāḍī* must be free of business interests which could compromise his impartiality. Because *qāḍīs* are subject to great pressures from political authorities, the office has sometimes been turned down by men of repute to avoid the stigma of complicity with the political power.

Although a *qāḍī* is a necessary functionary for a community, many disputes are decided by civil authorities such as Shaykhs and Governors, since legal power and political authority are inseparable in traditional Islam. In West Africa the term *qāḍī* has a broader meaning, being sometimes used to designate any man who is well-informed on religious matters but has no official position; such a one would be called a faqīh in North Africa. *See* SHARĪ'AH.

Qāḍi 'Asker ("Army Judge"). An important office among the Ottomans. The Army judges followed the armies on their campaigns.

Qaḍīb. A staff which had become a sign of the Caliph's authority in Umayyad times. Eventually it was believed to have belonged to the Prophet, and was also used by other Caliphates.

Qādiriyyah. A famous Sufi order founded by 'Abd al-Qādir al-Jīlānī (d. *561*/1166) in Baghdad. He is one of the great Saints of Islam, and veneration of his memory is a hallmark of the Qādiriyyah. The Qādiriyyah was the first *ṭarīqah* as such to emerge in Sufism; until then the path had been relatively undifferentiated, although groupings had formed around particular spiritual masters called *ṭawā'if* (sing. *tāifah*) groups, bands or factions. With 'Abd al-Qādir the tradition begins in Sufism of looking back to a particular teacher and considering him as a watershed in method and doctrine; until then Sufis had looked directly to the Prophet as the founder, and considered their own spiritual masters as his representatives; they still do so, in principle, but with an awareness that has, in the individual case, to be actualized.

'Abd al-Qādir's tomb is in Baghdad. He is credited with saying that if someone in spiritual distress calls upon him, "he will come riding on a charger" to bring him help. (This is in fact, an attribute of Mithra.)

The Qādiriyyah is widespread from India to Morocco. In the Arab West the order is called the *Jilālah* and its practices are marked by an intrusion of "folk" Sufism, resulting in the degeneration of the *ḥaḍrah* (sacred dance) into trance dancing, and an emphasis on unusual states of mind and prodigious feats to the detriment of a coherent doctrine of spiritual development. Like the *Ḥamidsha* and *'Isawiyyah*, their ecstatic dancing to an accompaniment of characteristic flute and drum music is often performed in public. *See* 'ABD al-QĀDIR al-JĪLĀNĪ.

Al Qaeda (Ar. *al-qa'idah*, "the command headquarters"). A global terrorist organization that grew out of the Soviet invasion of Afghanistan and American support to drive out the Soviets but was mainly inspired by the Israeli takeover of Palestine. A loosely knit entity once led by Osama bin Ladin and at first financed by the contributions of rich Saudis, it has created spin-offs and has links to other militant Islamic groups such as *Jemā'ah Islamiyah* in South East Asia, *Abū Sayyaf* in the Philippines, *Kumpulan Mujahideen Malaysia*, and *Laskar Jihād* in Pakistan.

al-Qāhīrah, *see* CAIRO.

Qājārs. A dynasty in Persia from *1209-1343*/1794-1924, they were the leaders of a Turkmen tribe, one of the original tribes of the *Qīzīl Bash*. The first Qājār, Aga Muḥammad, fought his way to power. It was under the Qājārs that Teheran, a small town, became the capital of Persia and the country became more involved in world affairs. In *1343*/1924 the Qājārs were deposed by Riḍā Pahlavī, who founded a new dynasty. *See* PAHLAVĪS; QĪZĪL BASH.

Qalam (Ar. "reed", "pen" from Greek *kalamos* of the same meaning). The Koran says several times that God teaches men by the pen, that is, by the revelation of scripture. The *qalam* is also symbolically the instrument of creation, inscribing existence onto the cosmic tablet (*lawḥ*). The *qalam* corresponds to Aristotle's *eidos* ("form"), the Sanskrit *purusha*, while the tablet corresponds to hyle ("substance"), or *prakriti*.

The *qalam* also symbolizes the "writing" of individual destinies onto the "tablet of fate". The concrete nature of this and similar images in the Koran was a stumbling block to some early theologians. Ibn Ḥanbal and al-Ash'arī insisted that these images be taken literally without further elaboration and without questioning, *bila kayfa* ("without asking how").

Qalandar. A name used in the East, chiefly Iran and India, for wandering "dervishes" who lived on alms, the word became popular because of its frequent occurrence in the *Thousand and One Nights*. Obscurity surrounding Qalandar beliefs, and stories that their founder was expelled by the Bektashis (themselves a heretical syncretism) suggest that rather than an order of mystics whose rule required perpetual wandering and poverty, it was really a catch-all term for beggars whose ornate bowl was a mere pretension of spirituality.

In this context a supposed distinction is made between so-called Sufi orders which are *ba-shar'*, or formal ("within the *sharī'ah* or law"), and those which are *be-shar'* ("without the *sharī'ah* or law"); this is no more than a fiction or euphemism, for the so-called *be-shar'* are in reality a class of social outcasts, pariahs, who would more accurately be called unbelievers (*kāfirūn*), and the mentally incompetent. *See* GNAWAH; KASHKUL.

Qalansuwa. A high pointed conical cap worn by noble families of the Sāssānid empire and adopted by the Umayyads, sometimes with a turban wound around it. This also became a distinctive headgear of the 'Abbāsids.

Qanāt. Water irrigation channels in Iran (in Persian *kārīz*), which run underground in order to minimize loss from evaporation, with openings to the surface at regular intervals to give access for maintenance. They are sometimes as long as twelve miles (although in the past they were sometimes 25 miles/40 km). The word can also mean any kind of channel. Less elaborate, but similar, systems of water channeling also exist in Morocco and in Spain, the Alhambra being an example, and in Libya (*foggara*). *See* SĀQIYAH.

Qānūn (from the Greek, *canon*, "a rod", "a carpenter's rule"). A civil law (as opposed to *sharī'ah*, or religious law). A related term is a *ẓāhir*, or decree made by a ruler. A Divine decree however, is *qaḍā'*. *See* SHARĪ'AH.

Qarāmiṭah, *see* QARMAṬĪS

Qara Qoyunlu. The "Black Sheep", a Turkmen horde of the Steppes which arose as a political confederation in Anatolia, 'Irāq, and West Persia, whose name came from the black sheep on their standards. They were a branch of the Ghuzz/Oghuz, once part of the Golden Horde. Qara Yusuf, who conquered Tabrīz in *791*/1389, founded the dynasty. They were driven out by the Tīmūrids but reconquered Tabriz in 1406. The dominion of the Qara Qoyunlu, who were indoctrinated with Shī'ite beliefs, some of them in extreme forms, was supplanted by that of their Sunnī rivals, the Aq Qoyunlu, the "White Sheep", after *873*/1468.

Qāri' (lit. "a reader", pl. *qurrā'*). 1. A reciter in public of the Koran by reason of his skill in *tajwīd*.

2. In the early days of Islam when few people could read, so that those who could were of great importance in spreading the faith, sometimes it would happen that a tribe newly entered into Islam had to rely even upon a child to lead their prayers, if he was the only one who could read. To be a "reader" was, therefore, the equivalent of being an authority in religion, and these "readers" formed a political block, representing the first "conservatives" within the religion. For a time they were the main supporters of 'Alī ibn Abī Ṭalīb in his struggle with Mu'āwiyah. Later, many of them left him, dismayed by his willingness to negotiate the question of succession to the Caliphate which the readers believed was a matter Divinely ordained. These seceders became the Khārijites.

3. *Qāri'* also denotes the authorities whose reading of the Koran originally set the model for vo-

calization, punctuation and so forth. They are known as the "seven readers" (*al-Qurrā' as-Sab'ah*). *See* QIRĀ'AH.

Qarmaṭa fī-l-khatt. A term in calligraphy meaning to write in a small, fine hand, with the ligatures close together. Particularly a style of Eastern Kufic.

Qarmaṭīs (Ar. *al-Qarāmiṭah*, also called Carmathians). An early offshoot of the Seveners, the resurgent Gnosticism which emerged in Islamic guise after the death of Ismā'īl, the son of Ja'far aṣ-Ṣādiq, in *145*/762, after whom they were also called Ismā'īlīs. The Qarmaṭīs became prominent around *277*/890 and it was once thought that they were named after Ḥamdān Qarmaṭ, a peasant who was one of their leading propagandists (*Dā'ī*). However, it now seems that Qarmaṭ, who was himself inducted as propagandist in 874, was named after the movement because the movement was already called Qarmaṭa as attested by earlier documents. The name *Qarmaṭ* means, in Aramaic, "he of the two red eyes", which Ibn Jawzi, in the *Talbīs Iblīs*, said meant "piercing vision" in Nabatean (Aramaic), probably signifying "a teacher of secret doctrines". However, most significantly, according to the Arabic dictionary the *Munjid*, the verb *qarmaṭa* means "to write in extremely fine letters" (arising from its other meaning of "short legged"), a noted characteristic of Manichean books of antiquity. Thus, before they became active militant revolutionaries, they were simply the "sect which wrote in small letters". Many of the Qarmaṭīs, like the classical Manicheans, were vegetarians, and so were also known as the *Baqliyyah* ("the greengrocers"). The more orthodox among them reproached their fellow travelers for laxity in this respect. (The Syrian poet al-Ma'arrī, another crypto-Manichean, was a vegetarian, and corresponded with the Fāṭimid *dā'ī*, Mu'ayyad fi-l-Dīn Abū Naṣr al-Shīrāzi, from a Daylami Ismā'īlī family, "on the subject of... vegetarianism".)

In the beginning, the chiefs of the ascetic Qarmaṭīs were called, among other titles, "Lords of Purity" (reminiscent of the *cathares* of Europe, "the pure ones"). The Qarmaṭīs combined secret religious doctrines with revolution and a program of "social justice" and redistribution of wealth, and property in common (*ulfah*). Ḥamdān's brother-in-law 'Abdān wrote a treatise on what was originally seven degrees of initiation.

The Qarmaṭīs emerged from the region of Wāsiṭ, in 'Irāq, which had been a Manichean center in pre-Islamic times, as described by Theodore Bar Konai, a Bishop of Kashkar (Wasiṭ) in the 8th century. Historians of the time put the Qarmaṭīs at 100,000 concentrated in the Sawad (the "Black Earth" agricultural region) of Kūfah, and the Yemen, and Yamamah (in Arabia). They were a conspiratorial insurrection against the Caliphate referring to their base as *dār al-hijrah* ("the House of refuge"). This is a very Islamic allusion to the Prophet's flight (*hijrah*) from Mecca to Medinah; however, for the Qarmaṭīs this meant "refuge *from* Islam" since their explicit goal was to bring an end to Islam and its rule and law. The Qarmaṭī leader, Ḥamdan Qarmaṭ established his center in southern 'Irāq at a village called Mahtamabad in the district of al-Fūrat in the Sawād of Kūfah, around 890. According to the *Fihrist*, "Qarmaṭ had read in the stars that the Iranians were about to regain control of the Arab empire".

This was propaganda planted a century earlier using the fact that Iranians reckoned conjunctions of Saturn and Jupiter as indicative of the change of dynasties. But already in 882 the Governor of Kūfah, Aḥmad ibn Muḥammad aṭ-Ṭā'ī, informed the authorities in Baghdad that there were people grouping in southern 'Irāq who have a *non-Islamic* religion; these were prepared to fight the Community of Muḥammad with the sword and impose their own religion; but no-one listened to him (Ṭabarī III 2127). In 897 the Governor of Kūfah first undertook a raid against Ismā'īlī villages of the Sawād and sent a series of Qarmaṭīs in chains to Baghdad, where it emerged that a state secretary (*kātib*) had been in correspondence with them. The secretary was arrested, but the connection between the Qarmaṭīs (or Manicheans) and the 'Abbāsid state apparatus had very deep roots and actually went back to the Barmakids.

The Qarmaṭīs, at least in that part of the empire, had originally been under the control of a "Bishop" in Salamiyyah in Syria. This was one of twelve such called a *Ḥujjah*, and elsewhere a *Lāḥiq*. The supreme head would have been the Archegos residing in Baghdad; but as the Qarmaṭī uprisings grew along with 'Abbāsid reactions, he disappeared, probably in *296*/908, in the direction of Samarkand, according to an-Nadīm. At the death of the current Bishop in 899 a conflict arose between the new leader in Salamiyyah and the *Dā'ī* Ḥamdan Qarmaṭ: "Qarmaṭ used to correspond with the man in Salamiyyah... Now when that one died who had been there during his time, and his son succeeded him, he [the son] wrote to Ḥamdan Qarmaṭ. But when Ḥamdan received the letter, he wanted nothing to do with what it contained, for it seemed to him that certain expressions to which he was accustomed had now been changed; to him this was suspicious." The Qarmaṭī Dā'ī 'Abdān (Ḥamdān's brother-in-law) went to Salamiyyah to find that the Ismā'īlī Bishop Abū-l-Shalaghlagh was dead, that 'Ubayd Allāh, his nephew and adopted son, was the new leader, and there was a new doctrine, regarding the leadership. 'Ubayd Allāh claimed not to represent the inspired secret leader, as previous Bishops had done, but to be himself the leader. His fateful and adroit efforts were to lead to the founding of the Fāṭimid dynasty. But aside from those already close to him, no one followed, except perhaps, for the *Dā'ī* Zikrawayh ibn Mihrawayh, yet even that is doubtful, although he did have the dissident 'Abdān killed. Following this development, Ḥamdān Qarmaṭ went to a village named Kalwādhā (near Baghdad) whence he was never heard from again.

In 899 Baghdad chroniclers also recorded the appearance of Abū Sa'īd Ḥasan ibn Bahrām al-Jannābī at the head of a force of Beduin warriors, the tribe of the 'Abd al-Qays. Abū Sa'īd al-Jannābī (who would be killed by a slave in *301*/913-914), was also originally an Ismā'īlī missionary or *Dā'ī*. He occupied the city of al-Qaṭīf in Arabia on the Persian Gulf and founded another *dār al-hijrah* as well as an independent Qarmaṭī state centered at the vast oasis of al-Aḥṣā (or al-Ḥāṣa). His followers named their capital *al-Mu'miniyyah* (from *Mu'min*, "believer"), present day Hofūf in the Eastern Province of Saudi Arabia. This survived to *470*/1077-1078, whereupon rapprochement took place with the Fāṭimids. After Abū Sa'īd, his son Abu-l-Qāsim Sa'īd ruled (*301-311*/913-923) and then another son, rather better known, Abū Ṭāhir Sulaymān (d. *332*/943-944). The Qarmaṭīs of al-Ḥasa and Baḥrayn had a ruling council called al-'Iqdāniyyah. The Qarmaṭīs had branches in Syria among the Banū 'Ulays (under Zikrawayh ibn Mihrawayh al-Dindānī, d. *293*/906), in 'Irāq, and Khorāsān. (For an account of the Syrian Qarmaṭīs *see* 'UBAYD ALLĀH al-MAHDĪ).

The Qarmaṭīs were an uprising by the peasantry and the dispossessed, a social revolution, carried along by a highly ideological leadership like the French or Russian Revolutions. The "worker class" who passionately hurled their heretical religion back at the orthodox establishment and attempted to seize its considerable wealth by conspiracy, rebellion, and terrorism. A movement of peasants and laborers, they bear a remarkable resemblance to modern "liberation armies". Casting far and wide for every dissenting thought they could find to fashion their own system, they brought about a ferment of ideas by using Greek, Persian, and Indian sources without reservation to build complicated and speculative doctrines of cosmology and metaphysics.

The most puzzling sects in the Islamic world, such as the 'Alī Ilāhīs and the 'Alawīs, may well be remnants of Qarmaṭī propagandizing. The Qarmaṭī social philosophy was a kind of communistic egalitarianism, including property in common. The existence of a ritual "love-feast" (*agape*,) with the consumption of the "bread of paradise" is attributed to the Qarmaṭa. This is, of course, the *bema* ceremony around the empty throne, which Mukhtār called the "throne of 'Alī" two hundred years earlier. In al-Ḥāsa this secret ceremony was called the "the Night of the Imām". Although the Qarmaṭa were nominally a vague kind of "Shī'ite" in the view of outsiders, this Imām of theirs, was explicitly *not* 'Alī, even in the tenuous, non-historical sense accepted by other Shī'ites. One historian recorded this account by a Sunni captive held in al-Ḥasa: one evening the Qarmaṭī captor asked the captive what he thought of the first four Caliphs. The captive gave guarded answers, and the captor gave surprising responses. The Qarmaṭī captor who was "drunk" (that is, candid) revealed what he thought about the first four Caliphs. He declared that Abū Bakr was a nobody, that 'Umar had been a brute, and had an equally low opinion of 'Uthmān. This far, normal Shī'ite views. But when he came to 'Alī there was no exaltation as would be expected from a Shī'ite. The Qarmaṭī unexpectedly declared with contempt that 'Alī was "an old woman". The Prophet, however, he respected as someone who was forceful and knew how to command men and rule a state. This account was meant to inform the reader that the leaders of the Shī'ite movement only used the figure of 'Alī and his descendants to move the masses, but did not believe their own propaganda, and that these "Shī'ites" were the ones who knew the real doctrine and dispensed it rather than received it.

It may be that the trade guilds which took on an importance in medieval Islamic society as well as in Europe, (and still exist today, in Fez, for example), were a restoration by the Qarmaṭīs of ancient initiatic orders based on crafts who used these for indoctrination. The ideology of the Qarmaṭīs, like that of the Ismā'īlīs, of whom they were a branch, was a Gnostic Dualism, which sees evil as having a reality and substance of its own, that is, a divinity like unto the substance and divinity of the good. The vital point on which they differed from the Fāṭimid Ismā'īlīs, with whom they otherwise had great sympathies, is that they rejected allegiance to the Fāṭimid Imām. They nevertheless maintained close ties. Naṣir-i Khusraw, a propagandist from Balkh in Khorāsān (Afghanistan), was given an official function by the Fāṭimids in Cairo, and stopped off in al-Ḥāsa on his way back home, obviously on a mission. The Ismā'īlīs in Iran and elsewhere, did not follow the Fāṭimids until the success of the Fāṭimids was convincing enough to over-ride ideological differences. There came a point when all Qarmaṭī old believers were obliged to join them.

The ideological differences had a long history and early precedents. Manicheism divided into two branches early on, already in the fourth century AD There had been a Manichean sect beyond the Oxus called "The pure ones" or Denawars, in Arabic Dīnāwarīyyah. Later this division appeared as the Mihriyyah, who collaborated with outside rulers [Mihr, an Archegos, had received the gift of a mule from the Governor of 'Irāq] and the Miqlasiyyah, who were more opposed to compromises with the ruling power or with circumstances. This could be compared with the division that the Communists experienced in the twentieth century: the Trotskyites who proposed that the eschatological goals could only be achieved by simultaneous world transformation through world revolution, and the other branch, the Stalinists who believed that Communism could exist by first being established in one state. (This led to the anti-Soviet joke in Russia that the Orthodox Church's Prelate wrote his doctoral dissertation in 1928 on the question: "Can the end of the world take place in only one country?)

To precipitate the millennium according to a timetable which they had set forth in ingenious propaganda a half-century earlier in the form of prophecies concerning conjunctions of Saturn and Jupiter, in *317*/930 the Qarmaṭīs raided Mecca, slaughtered pilgrims and carried away the Black Stone. (An earlier conjunction was the declaration of the Fāṭimid Caliphate.) They kept the Black Stone in al-Ḥāsa, or perhaps Baḥrayn, before returning it in *340*/951. According to the historian al-Juwaynī, the stone was thrown into the Friday Mosque at Kūfah with a declaration saying: "By command we took it, and by command we returned it." The Qarmaṭīs had not accepted offers of ransom; (at least not openly). They preferred to reap the propaganda effect.

When the Qarmaṭīs stole the Black Stone it was in three pieces and smaller fragments; when they returned it, it was seven (and smaller fragments) as it is today. Evidently, they deliberately broke it to bring the number of pieces in line with the new age marked by the seven Imāms (or perhaps seven jurisdictions — out of a theoretical total of twelve — dioceses, which they called *jazā'ir* — islands — arising out of the primordial flood which they interpreted as the ignorance of mankind and in particular the Islamic law, the *sharī'ah*). They also alluded to the fact that only they knew if it was indeed the original stone; thus they had effected a tremendous sleight of hand, substituting *their* stone for Islam's stone, as they had already substituted their own 'Alī for the historic 'Alī. Dream thought, as psychologists know, proceeds by substitution, and the Qarmaṭīs were working the magic of thought control like the hidden master of the show.

Opinion of the times linked the Fāṭimids to the Qarmaṭīs; it was said that the Fāṭimids prevailed upon them to return the Black Stone. Indeed, both the Fāṭimids and Qarmaṭīs were the same philosophy under different guises. The story was told that the earth refused to accept the burial of the Fāṭimid ruler 'Ubayd Allāh until the Stone was returned, and that this was done at the order, or urging, of the third Fāṭimid Caliph, al-Manṣūr.

In 969 the Fāṭimid general Jawhar aṣ-Ṣiqillī ("the Sicilian") conquered Egypt and founded Cairo, which in full means "the Victorious City of the Exalter of the Religion of God". (The name of the city was a message to all and especially to the Qarmaṭīs.) Al-Jawzi reports that Jawhar's soldiers on expedition to Syria destroyed the "tabernacle", used in rituals by the Qarmaṭīs. This "tabernacle" was perhaps the "empty chair" that Mukhtār the Kaysāni leader also used in ceremonies, calling it "the throne of 'Alī". (In Kūfah, Ṭabarī reported, there had been a certain Hawshab who was "a keeper of the throne" two centuries earlier.) Yet in 977 there was a high point of Qarmaṭī influence at Kūfah; when the news of the death of Abū Yūsuf Ya'qūb, a Qarmaṭī chief, arrived in Kūfah, shops were closed for three days in sign of mourning. Even in 984 a Qarmaṭī army advanced near Baghdad and was appeased by concessions. But in the next year, after several victories near Kūfah, they were so completely defeated that they went clearly into decline. Also the evident success of the Fāṭimids was convincing. The Qarmaṭīs were absorbed by the Fāṭimids and when the Fāṭimids themselves collapsed, they eventually became Nizārī Ismā'īlīs under the leadership of Alamūt. While they existed their revolutionary presence was dreaded within the 'Abbāsid Empire, and the influence they exerted on a number of heterodox sects which survive was considerable. Travellers to this day report that Qarmaṭī villages still exist in Oman and in Yemen. And the Ba'ath parties of Syria and 'Irāq are their modern heirs. For details of the Qarmaṭī revolt *see* 'UBAYD ALLĀH al-MAHDĪ. Also: *see* ABŪ ṬĀHIR SULAYMĀN al-JANNĀBĪ; FĀṬIMIDS; ISMĀ'ĪLĪS; ARCHEGOS; al-MA'MUN; MANICHEISM; MAZDAK; al-MUQANNA'; RAFI' IBN LAYTH UPRISING; SEVENERS; SINDBĀD REVOLT; SURKH-I 'ALĀM.

al-Qāshānī, 'Abd ar-Razzāq Kamāl ad-Dīn. (d. *730*/1329). Commentator on the *Fusūs al-Ḥikam* of Ibn 'Arabī. Al-Qāshānī also wrote a treatise on Sufi vocabulary, but he is especially known for his Esoteric Commentary on the Koran (*Ta'wīlāt al-Qur'ān*). The latter is very reminiscent of Jakob Boehme's commentary on the book of Genesis, where the operative principle is poetic substitution. Words having one meaning are purported to really mean something else. For example, if the Koran says that glass beakers are passed among the blessed in Paradise, al-Qāshānī says this means "certain kinds of deeds" which they performed in life, when it says they sit on "cushions" this means other deeds and so on. This kind of "explanation" of a sacred text or revealing its "true meaning" by substitution dates back long before Islam. It could also be used to completely subvert a text. 'Ubayd Allāh the Fāṭimid Mahdī claimed that his miracle was just such an explanation, or "decoding" of the Koran.

Qashqai. A Turkic people, pastoral nomads of the Zagros Mountains of southwest Iran, numbering over 400,000, the Qashqai are divided into many tribes. They profess Twelve-Imām Shī'ism, with some latitude. The average man may be fervent, but as is the case with many nomads, his grasp of formal dogma is loose. The simplicity of Islam is precisely one of its great advantages: its fundamentals fit easily into a nomad's packs.

Qaṣwā'. The Prophet's camel, which he rode into Medinah when he left Mecca. Upon arrival in the outskirts of the city, the camel was set loose to find the place where the Prophet would stay. The spot where the camel stopped is called the *mabrak an-nāqah* ("the kneeling of the she-camel"). The Prophet's riding mule was called Duldul, a gift from the Byzantine viceroy of Egypt. The Prophet's horse was called Sakb.

Qaṭar. A Shaykhdom on the Arabian coast of the Persian Gulf. The population is 547,761 and most are Wahhābīs, with a minority of Twelve-Imām Shī'ites.

Qawwali. A form of Sufi singing in Urdu, but also in Persian, found in India, Pakistan, and Afghanistan, and neighboring regions. It resembles the Sufi liturgical singing heard in other parts of the Islamic world, such as the *ilāhīs* in Turkey, and the mystical *qasīdahs* in Arabic, but can be distinguished by its particularly ardent and effusive style. A *qawwal* begins with praises on the Prophet, proceeds to poetry of love directed at God or the Prophet, passes through a phase exemplifying extinction in God called *fanā'*, then through subsistence in God (*baqā'*), and finishes by a return to sobriety (*sawh*). *See* FANĀ'; MAJLIS; SUFISM.

Qayrawān, *see* KAIROUAN.

Qayṣariyyah. A market for fine goods such as cloth, jewelry, perfumes, and gold. In dialects this is often rendered as *qīṣariyyah*. The word comes from *qayṣar* ("Caesar") in Arabic because usually such markets were established upon the sites of forums — the place of Caesar — in cities formerly Roman.

Qiblah. The direction the Muslims face when performing the *ṣalāh* ("ritual prayer") toward the Ka'bah in Mecca. The *qiblah* was originally orientated on the Temple in Jerusalem, but was changed to the direction of Mecca in the 2nd year of the Hijrah. One day, when the Prophet was leading the mid-day prayer in the mosque of the Banū Salīmah in Medinah, after the first two *raka'āt* ("prayer rounds"), he was suddenly inspired to turn towards Mecca to complete the following two *raka'āt*. The congregation naturally followed his example. Henceforth the mosque was called *Masjid al-Qiblatayn* ("the Mosque of the two *qiblahs*").

The *qiblah* is usually marked in mosques by the *miḥrāb* ("prayer niche"). Originally, it was often indicated simply by a stone. To help orient those praying outside the mosque, the *qiblah* may be indicated by a decorative device which can be seen from a distance, for example, the figure of a crescent moon on the top of a minaret spire; the center of the circle forming the crescent indicates the direction of Mecca.

On May 28 and on July 16 the sun at noon in Mecca is directly over the Ka'bah; if the sun is visible at this time locally, it gives the direction of the *qiblah* in great circle terms along the surface of the earth as a sphere, sometimes in contradiction to what one would conclude from looking at a map. In this sense, the *qiblah* in North America is towards the northeast, and not the southwest as one would conclude from looking at a flat conventional Mercator map.

It was established in certain mosques by mean of accurate measurement long after they were built that the building's orientation was imperfect; in some cases it is the custom to make the necessary correction towards the true *qiblah* by having each worshiper in the prayer line turn slightly to the side, while the row faces in the original orientation of the building. This is the practice in the Qarāwiyyīn Mosque in Fez. But in other mosques in the same situation, with a less exalted reputation to maintain, it has not been considered necessary to insist upon the precise, mathematical, accuracy of the *qiblah*, the general opinion being that the *approximate* direction of Mecca is adequate. When it is impossible or impractical to determine the qiblah, the prayer is performed in any direction, all ultimately being valid. ("To God belong the East and West and wheresoever ye turn, there is the face of God," 2:115).

Qipchaq. A Turkic steppe people, who progressively invaded the Islamic world before the coming of the Mongols, they were related to the Seljūqs. The Russians called them Polovsti and Cumans. They were shamanists before being converted to Islam. They dominated the regions north and south of the Caspian and the lower Volga. The Mongols, after their invasions, were for the most part absorbed into the Qipchaq peoples, and the fusion of the two produced many kingdoms, among them the Khanate of the Qipchaq Steppe.

Qirā'ah (lit. "reading", pl. *qirā'āt*). A Ḥadīth declares that the Koran was revealed (*unzila*, "sent down") in seven scripts (*aḥruf*, "letters", plural of *ḥarf*), each of which is valid. The meaning of the word *aḥruf* has occasioned debate, and has been taken by some to refer to the seven principle dialects spoken by the tribes of Arabia. However, the Arabic of the Koran is, of all Arabic, the most elegant, copious and pure, by the common consent of Muslims and Arabs alike, and corresponds in its forms — with minor exceptions — to the morphology and best usages of the dialect of the Quraysh, the aristocrats of Mecca; there is no question of its being, in any literal sense, a blend of differing dialects. The Sufis take *aḥruf* to mean rather "modes" or "levels"; that is to say, they accept that there are seven levels of meaning from the most outward and concrete to the most inward and hidden, corresponding to the seven layers of the Heavens and presenting, therefore, ascending degrees of understanding and approach to the Truth, the Real.

Historically speaking, after the definitive recension of the Koran made at the command of the Caliph 'Uthmān, certain variant readings existed and, indeed, persisted and increased as the Companions who had memorized the text died, and because the inchoate Arabic script, lacking vowel signs and even the necessary diacriticals to distinguish between certain consonants, was inadequate; in practice, the authority of oral transmissions and reciters was an essential complement to the recorded, written text. As Islam became diffused among peoples whose Arabic fell far short of the Quraysh standard, or for whom Arabic was not even a mother tongue, it became a matter of urgency to remedy the deficiencies of the script, formalize grammar and preserve the integrity of the revealed text and of Arabic, the sacred language. The rapid vulgarization of Arabic that ensued in the first centuries of Islam when the language, no longer protected by its isolation, became the *lingua franca* of a vast realm, was a phenomenon noted and deplored by the scholars of the age.

In the 4th Islamic century, it was decided to have recourse to "readings" (*qirā'āt*) handed down from seven authoritative "readers" (*qurrā'*); in order, moreover, to ensure accuracy of transmission, two "transmitters" (*rāwī*, pl. *ruwāh*) were accorded to each. There resulted from this the seven basic texts (*al-qirā'āt as-sab'*, "the Seven readings"), each having two transmitted versions (*riwāyatān*) with only minor variations in phrasing, but all containing meticulous vowel-points and other necessary diacritical marks. These "Seven Readings" have, in the course of time, come to be associated with the seven *aḥruf* of the Ḥadīth.

The authoritative "readers" are: Nāfi' (from Medinah; d. *169*/785); Ibn Kathīr (from Mecca; d. *119*/737); Abū 'Amr al-'Alā' (from Damascus; d. *153*/770); Ibn 'Āmir (from Baṣrah; d. *118*/736); Ḥamzah (from Kūfah; d. *156*/772); al-Qisā'ī (from Kūfah; d. *189*/804); and Abū Bakr 'Āṣim (from Kūfah; d. *158*/778).

The predominant reading today, spread by Egyptian Koran readers, is that of 'Āsim in the transmission (riwāyah) of Ḥafs (d. *190*/805). In Morocco, however, the reading is that of Nāfi' in the riwāyah of Warsh (d. *197*/812) and Maghrebin Korans are written accordingly.

Qirān. One of the forms and intentions of consecration for the pilgrimage, whereby the ḥajj and the 'umrah are performed in conjunction. *See* IḤRAM.

Qiṣāṣ. The principle, introduced by the Koran, of retaliation for harm inflicted. Where a life is lost and the victim and perpetrator are of equal status, the death of the perpetrator is an expiation for the death of the victim. In harm short of the taking of life, a similar harm to the perpetrator is an expiation. Along with the establishment of these principles, which are those of the *lex talionis* of the Mosaic Law, Islam explicitly recommends the substitution of compensation on another plane, i.e., pardon for the guilty person (an act which expiates sins for the pardoner), or material compensation for the harm suffered (5:45).

In actual practice, the Prophet inclined to the milder punishments or to the minimum prescribed penalty for the crimes brought before him. Nevertheless, he judged according to the intrinsic nature of the case, once ordering the execution of a man who had murdered a woman. In the circumstances of that case he put the nature of the crime (murder) before the question of the relative status of the two parties.

In the case of manslaughter, or accidental killing, retaliation cannot be exacted; only compensation may be claimed. The compensation for death is called a *diyah*, and was once fixed by law at one hundred camels, and today by statutory sums.

The principle of *qiṣāṣ* effected a profound modification in the Arab sense of justice. Previously, Arab tribal law had called for revenge for harm suffered; in the case of personal injury this was *tha'r*, or blood revenge, and it could be taken upon any member of the clan of the perpetrator. *Qiṣāṣ* made the actual perpetrator alone guilty, and alone liable to punishment; moreover, the punishment must be the exact equivalent of the crime. This, the reestablishment of social, or indeed, cosmic, equilibrium after it has been disturbed by an infraction, could also be transposed onto a different plane by a material or spiritual compensation. Thus, *qiṣāṣ* is the very essence of justice, the recognition that consequences are contained in acts, or that effect is contained in the cause. In Islam, as in Judaism, *qiṣāṣ* objectified was made the principle of law. This replaced the older, subjective, and thus non-differentiated, tribal sense of revenge.

Qitfir, *see* FITFIR.

Qiṭmīr. The name, according to tradition, of the dog of the Seven Sleepers of Ephesus. The dog slept at mouth of the cave. The name is used in mysticism or magic to invoke a protection for one's interests or some object. *See* SEVEN SLEEPERS.

Qiyās (lit. "measure", "scale" or "exemplar" and hence "analogy"). The principle by which the laws of the Koran and Sunnah are applied to situations not explicitly covered by these two sources of religious legislation. Ash-Shāfi'ī (d. *204*/820) was one of the foremost developers of the use of *qiyās*. *See* SHARĪ'AH.

Qīzīl Bash (Turkish, lit. "red heads"). The name of seven Turkic nomad tribes in Azerbaijan who supported Ismā'īl, the first Ṣafavid, in his struggle for power. These tribes were the Shamlu, Rumlu, Ustajlu, Tekel , Afshar, Qajār, and Zulqadar, and several others. The Qīzīl Bash wore red caps with twelve black tassels, standing for the twelve Shī'ite Imāms, and shaved their beards but let their mustachios grow long (seen in portraits of Shah 'Abbās the great), and shaved their heads except for a tuft. Their relationship to the Ṣafavids was loyalty with a religious flavor, since Ismā'īl was seen as a descendant of the seventh Shī'ite Imām, Mūsā-l-Kāẓim. Later, two of these tribes in turn, the Afshārids and the Qājārs, became the power bases of short-lived dynasties.

A Shī'ite may still be called Qīzīl Bash in Afghanistan. The Qīzīl Bash are also a sect of *ghulāt*, or Shī'ites who divinized their leaders, akin to the Ahl-Ḥaqq and the Alevis of Turkey, and the Alawīs of Syria. *See* ṢAFAVIDS.

Qubā'. A village immediately outside Medinah where the Prophet first arrived after his emigration (*al-hijrah*), from Mecca, and where he built the first mosque, later known as *Masjid at-Taqwā* (the "Mosque of Reverence"). *See* MOSQUE of QUBĀ'.

Qubbat aṣ-Ṣakhrah, *see* DOME of the ROCK.

al-Quds (lit. "The Sanctuary"). The usual Arabic name for Jerusalem, referring to *al-bayt al-muqaddas* ("the holy house"), the Temple of Solomon. By extension, the name is sometimes applied to the whole of Palestine. *See* JERUSALEM.

Queen of Sheba, *see* BILQĪS.

Quietism, *see* MURJI'AH

Qumm. A small city in central Iran which contains an important shrine of the Twelve-Imām Shī'ites. It is the tomb of the sister of the eighth Imām 'Alī ar-Riḍā, called Fāṭimah al-Ma'ṣūmah, or Fāṭimah "the sinless". As it is one of the few tombs of the immediate relatives of the Imāms within Iran, it is much revered.

Qumm is a desert city lying on the crossroads between Iṣfahān and Rayy. It had undergone cultural influences coming from the city of Kūfah, home of political and religious radicalism under the Umayyads. Refugees from Kūfah, the Yemeni dynasty of Āl Sa'd ibn Mālik of the tribe of Ash'ar, as *marzbāns*, or rulers, gave asylum to a number of heretics and Shī'ite jurists between *125*/742 to *278*/891. Afterwards Qumm was ruled by a *wālī*, or governor, appointed by Baghdad, but by then Qumm was already a Shī'ite center.

Qumm, however, did not have an important madrasah until Fatḥ 'Alī Shah, the second Qājār, founded the Faiziyeh madrasah to rival centers of Shī'ite learning in 'Irāq. Since the last century Qumm has become the main center of Shī'ite religious studies in Iran.

Qunawī, Ṣadr ad-Dīn (d. *729*/1329). A Persian Sufi in the Khorasāni tradition.

Qunūt. A prayer, or supplication (*du'ā'*) occasionally inserted in the canonical prayer (*ṣalāh*), a practice based upon the Sunnah. The Prophet would sometimes utter requests of God at some point in the *ṣalāh*. Different supplications are called *qunūt*, although what is most commonly meant is a calling of blessings upon the Prophet. This is recited in the "sitting" position (*julūs*), after the "greetings" (*taḥiyyāt*) and before the ending of the prayer.

A frequently used qunūt is:

Allāhumma ṣalli 'alā sayyidina Muḥammadin wa 'alā āli sayyidinā Muḥammadin kamā ṣalayta 'ala sayyidinā Ibrāhīma wa 'alā āli sayyidinā Ibrāhīma, wa bārik 'alā sayyidinā Muḥammadin wa 'alā āli sayyidinā Muḥammadin kamā bārakta 'alā sayyidinā Ibrāhīma wa 'alā āli sayyidinā Ibrāhīma, innaka anta-l-ḥamīdu-l-majīd.

Our God, bless our Lord Muḥammad and the people of our Lord Muḥammad, as you blessed our Lord Abraham and the people of our Lord Abraham, and prosper our Lord Muḥammad and the people of our Lord Muḥammad, as you prospered our Lord Abraham and the people of our Lord Abraham for you are the Praised, the Magnified.

See PRAYER.

Qur'ān, *see* KORAN.

Quraysh. The tribe of Mecca. The name comes from the root to "bite" (*qarasha*), whence also the word for the shark, "the biting fish" (*qirsh*), sometimes thought to be the "totem" of the tribe. Possibly *Quraysh*, which is a diminutive form, "little shark", was the nick-name of Fihr, the ancestor of the tribe, whose other name was *an-Naḍr*. The tribe was settled in Mecca by an ancestor of renown called Qusayy who displaced the previous inhabitants, the Khuzā'ah. The clans who lived in the immediate vicinity of the Ka'bah, in the lowest part (*al-Baṭhā'*) of Mecca, were known as *Abṭaḥī* or *Biṭahī*, or as *Quraysh al-Biṭāḥ* (the "Quraysh of the Hollow"). Less illustrious families, who lived further out, were known as *Quraysh aẓ-Ẓawāhir* (the "Quraysh of the Outskirts").

The location of Mecca on important caravan routes across the peninsula, and the prestige of the Ka'bah in the Age of Ignorance (*jāhiliyyah*), gave it a considerable advantage as a trading city, with the result that the Quraysh became one of the richest and most powerful tribes. This, together with their descent from the Kinānah and Ismā'īl, gave them claims to an aristocratic pre-eminence.

The Prophet Muḥammad was of the Banū Hāshim clan of the Quraysh: and all of the Arab Caliphs were of the Quraysh (except the Fāṭimids whose claims were repudiated.) Indeed there is even a Ḥadīth which has been taken to mean that rulership and the Caliphate is a prerogative of this tribe alone. (*See* MECCA; MUḤAMMAD).

The Quraysh are mentioned by name in the Koran:

For the taming of Quraysh,
for their taming are sent the winter and
summer caravans!
So let them serve the Lord of this House
who has fed them against hunger,
and secured them from fear. (106)

According to a Sufi interpretation, this refers also to the soul's vicissitudes and to the protection afforded by God to the noblest elements in the soul in its spiritual economy.

Qurayẓah. A Jewish tribe of Medinah that betrayed the Muslims during the Battle of the Trench (*see* BATTLE of the TRENCH). When the Quraysh abandoned the siege of the city, Gabriel commanded the Prophet not to lay down arms until the Qurayẓah were subdued. Their hands freed by the departure of the Quraysh and their confederates, the Muslims turned upon the Banū Qurayẓah and besieged their defensive towers for twenty-five days.

When the Banū Qurayẓah surrendered, they were judged, *as a concession*, by Sa'd ibn Mu'ādh, a chief of their former allies, the Aws; lying on his deathbed, in pain from a wound inflicted during the fighting with the Quraysh, he passed a rigorous judgement: the adult men should be put to death and the women and children sold into slavery.

And He brought down those of the People of the
Book who supported them from their fortresses
and cast terror in their hearts; some you slew,
some you made captive. (33: 25-27)

In books written in the West, this episode has been the occasion for criticism as an example of extreme cruelty. For readers of the King James Bible it should not have seemed an unusual event; in Numbers 25 Moses destroys the Midianites, who received him as a refugee and whose leader's daughter he married. In that case he is instructed to destroy even the male children. In the 137th psalm: it says: "O daughter of Babylon, who art to be destroyed; happy shall he be, that rewardeth thee as thou hast served us. Happy shall he be who taketh and dasheth thy little ones against the stones." Outside the Biblical context similar punishment was meted out elsewhere, as in the destruction of the Albigensians in France, for example, and for much the same reason. It can be seen as a case of the final judgement overtaking a people while still in this world.

Here, the punishment had a special sense: Jewish law itself prescribes such treatment for non-Jews in the conquest of a city as a matter of course, even when betrayal is not in question: "When the Lord thy God hath delivered it unto thy hands, thou shalt smite every male therein with the edge of the sword: but the women, and the little ones, and the cattle, and all that is in the city, even all the spoil thereof, shalt thou take unto thyself" (Deuteronomy 20:12). This is why Sa'd ibn Mu'ādh, who was familiar with the traditions of the Jews in his midst, gave the Qurayẓah this sentence; that their own law should be used on them. *See* BATTLE of the TRENCH.

Qurb (lit. "nearness"). The grace of the nearness of God. Those most exalted in paradise are those who are "brought nigh" (*al-muqarrabun*).

Qurbān (from *qarraba*, "to bring near"). Any practice that brings one closer to God. In particular, it means sacrifice, and especially the animals sacrificed in the *'Īd al-Aḍḥā* ("Feast of Sacrifice"), which in Turkey is called *Bayram Kurban*. Among Arab Christians, the word *qurbān* refers to the Eucharist.

Qurrā', *see* QĀRI'; QIRĀ'AH.

al-Qushayrī, Abū-l-Qāsim (d.*465*/1072). A Persian Sufi, author of a highly respected treatise on the doctrine of Sufism called the *Risālah*. He also wrote a mystical commentary on the Koran.

Qusṭā ibn Lūqā (d. *311*/923). A Christian philosopher and scientist born in Baalbek. He wrote treatises, and translated Aristotle and other Greek works into Arabic.

Quṭb (lit. "axis", "pole"). The "center" which contains the periphery, or is present in it, is a primordial spiritual symbol. The idea of the *quṭb* is the recognition that the function of "spiritual center" can reside in a human being, or be associated with a human being. The *quṭb* is at the same time a celestial reality, and when actualized as the delegation of authority upon earth, it implies a sanctity of the highest order.

Quṭb has been given as an honorific title to great Saints, but it is rather considered to be a *function* which manifests itself, not in a continuous manner but from time to time, through a person, or indeed through some other support in the world. A story is told of the famous Moroccan Shaykh Aḥmad ad-Darqāwī of the 19th century, who, when he was walking in the Resīf market of Fez, crossed shoulder to shoulder with an otherworldly figure dressed in white. As they crossed, the person — an Angel, it is understood — said: "*al-Quṭb*", without indicating whether he meant himself, ad-Darqāwī, something else, or even the moment itself. The nature of the *quṭb* or the spiritual axis, which can work through a person, is thus an elusive reality.

The first four Caliphs, because their personal station was commensurate with the function they fulfilled, are thought of as being each the *quṭb* of his age, by Sunni Sufis. They were not so at all times, but only in those moments when they transcended their individual limitations while acting on those around them as heaven's true vicegerents. The spiritual center then manifested itself through them. The function of *quṭb*, or celestial axis, can also manifest itself through more than one person at a time. Ibn Khaldūn, the historian, says that the Sufis got the idea of the *quṭb* from the extreme Shī'ites. *See* ARCHEGOS; SUFISM.

Quṭb, Sayyid (1906-1966). Egyptian of Indian origin, member of the Muslim Brotherhood, he was executed by the government of Egypt on charges of sedition and terrorism. When he travelled to Europe and North America, he was repelled by contact with an alien view of reality, and became an opponent of the West. Between 1948 and 1950 he stayed in the United States. He described a church dance in Greely, Colorado: "Every young man took the hand of a young woman. And these were the young men and women who had just been been singing their hymns! Red and blue lights with only a few white lamps illuminated the dance floor. The room became a confusion of feet and legs: arms twisted around hips; lips met lips; chests pressed together."

He became a propagandist for an absolutist view of Islam, although he found the basis for Islamic democracy in the Koran and in the idea of *shūrā* or council. Quṭb declared the leaders of modernist Islamic governments no longer Muslims thereby legally justifying their overthrow as infidels. His ideological influence was vast, especially during the Iranian revolution.

Quṭub-i Minar (lit. "the axis minaret"). A minaret in New Delhi, India, famous for its height (240 ft/73 m), built by the Sultan Shams ad-Dīn Iltutmish (d. *633*/1236) around *627*/1230. His tomb is next to the Quwwat al-Islām mosque, which was begun by Quṭb ad-Dīn Aybak (d. *607*/1210).

Originally a victory column, the minaret is almost 50ft/14m around its base and 9ft/3m around the top. It is decorated with calligraphic inscriptions in stone. The minaret was restored in *770*/1368, and again in *1245*/1829 after being damaged in an earthquake in *1218*/1803.

R

Ra'āyā (plural from Ar. *ra'iyyah*, "flock", "sheep", "common folk"). A name given to the non-Muslim populations, subject to poll-tax (the Muslims paid only poor-tax, *zakāh*), in the domains of Muslim rulers. This was a metaphor used in this sense in Mesopotamia from ancient times.

ar-Rabb (lit. "the Lord"; "He who, like a parent, watches, guides and sustains the growth of what is in His care"; "the Sustainer"). A Divine Name of the qualities (*ṣifāt*) but not of the essence (*dhāt*). The most common forms of this Name are the phrases: *Rabb al-'Alamīn* ("the Lord of the Worlds") and *Rabb al-'Izzah* ("the Lord of Might"). In other combinations, however, it may simply mean "owner" without being a name calling upon God. *See* DIVINE NAMES.

Rābi'ah al-'Adawiyyah (*95-185*/713-801). One of the most famous Saints in Islam, she extolled the way of *maḥabbah* ("Divine love") and *uns* ("Intimacy with God"). Her mystical sayings are noted for their pith and clarity; some have become proverbs throughout the Islamic world.

In reply to one who claimed not to have sinned for a long time she declared: "Your existence is a sin to which no other sin can be compared." That is, the affirmation that we exist is itself a sin (*dhanb*) because in reality only God Is. To remove the idea that we are an independent reality is to remove the origin and possibility of sin.

Rābi'ah also said: "I am going to light a fire in paradise and pour water in hell so that both veils may completely disappear from the pilgrims and their purpose may be sure. Thus the servants of God may see Him, without any object of hope or motive of fear."

She was born, lived and died in Baṣrah. Originally from a poor family, she was stolen as a child and sold into slavery. Freed, by reason of her evident sanctity, she gathered a circle of disciples around her and lived a life of extreme asceticism. The Sufis who came after her acknowledge their doctrinal debt to her, and she is mentioned in most biographies of the saints.

ar-Rābiṭah al-Islāmiyyah. The Islamic Association, often referred to as the rābiṭah, an organization for the promotion of Islam sponsored by the Saudi government. Its headquarters are in Mecca.

Rafi' Ibn Layth Uprising (*806-810*/190-195). This was a revolt by peasants, some landowners, and Turkic nomads against the 'Abbāsids caused by the taxation policies of the 'Abbāsid minister 'Alī ibn 'Isa. The leader, Ibn Layth, also had a personal grudge against the minister. Ibn Layth seized Samarkand and Khwarizm and held it. Harūn ar-Rashīd's son al-Ma'mūn put down the revolt in 810/195.

Rāfiḍīs (lit. "repudiators"; in Arabic generally *ar-Rāfiḍah* or *al-Rawāfiḍ*). A general name, abusive in tone, given by the Sunnīs to the Shī'ites because they repudiate the validity of the Caliphs who preceded 'Alī. These Caliphs, Abū Bakr, 'Umar, and 'Uthmān, along with 'Alī, are considered to be "the rightly guided" Caliphs by the Sunnīs. Shī'ites believe that only 'Alī and his descendants had the right to the Caliphate, and so consider the first three to be usurpers.

Rafīq. Literally "comrade" in Arabic; plural: *rafīqān*. At the time of Niẓam al-Mulk (d. *485*/1092) the title by which the Persian Ismāīlīs, those with full membership who were ready to sacrifice themselves for the cause, called one another. The term appears from time to time in Sufism also, where there is a saying: "When setting on the road ('path' or 'mission') take a comrade with you." Also used by Communist parties in modern times.

ar-Raḥīm (from the root *rā', ḥā', mīm*, "to show mercy", "be merciful", which is also the root for "womb"). This Divine Name, which is often translated as the "Compassionate", refers to God's Mercy under the aspect of action reaching into the world, and leading beyond the world back to God. The Divine Name *ar-Raḥmān* means "Merciful by His very Nature", and is a Name of the Essence (*dhāt*). *Ar-Raḥīm* is one of the Names that describe the Divine Qualities (*ṣifāt*). It is most habitually used in the combination *ar-Raḥmān, ar-Raḥīm* ("the Merciful, the Mercy-Giving"). Another combination, characteristic of Arabic rhetorical construction, is *Arḥam ar-Rāḥimīn* ("the Most Merciful of Those Who give Mercy"). *See* DIVINE NAMES; ar-RAḤMĀN.

Raḥmah (lit. "mercy" from the root *rā', ḥā', mīm*, "to be merciful", "to show mercy"). This is an attribute of God which the Koran emphasizes over and over again, in keeping with its nature as the last revelation. At the end of time, man's weakness and confusion is greater than ever, but God's mercy is also nearer.

Al-Ghazālī said: "The Divine Mercy is perfect, in the sense that it answers every need. It is universal, in the sense that it spreads alike over those who merit it and those who do not merit it."

ar-Raḥmān (lit. "the Merciful One"). A Divine Name of the Essence, (*ism min asmā' adh-dhāt*). After the Name Allāh, *ar-Raḥmān* is the most frequently cited Name of God, and is used very often in the Koran almost as the equivalent of Allāh. "Say: call upon Allāh or call upon ar-Raḥmān; whatever ye call Him, His are the Most Beautiful Names" (17:110). This Name is most often used in the combination *ar-Raḥmān ar-Raḥīm* ("the Merciful in Himself, the Mercy-Giving"). The Quraysh refused to recognize this Name in the treaty that was made with the Prophet at Ḥudaybiyyah. From this (and other evidence) it appears that this Divine Name was revealed along with Islam, and was unknown to the Arabs, unlike the Name Allāh. Nevertheless, it should be noted that among the Zoroastrians of the 4th century there existed the formula *pa name yazdan xvorromand rayomand. See* ALLĀH; DIVINE NAMES; NAFAS ar-RAḤMĀN; ar-RAḤĪM.

Rainbow (Ar. *qaws* Allāh, "the bow of God", doubtless so called after the sign God gave Noah, but also known by many popular names). A symbol associated with Noah and the flood, signifying the end of one cycle and the beginning of another.

Rajā'. "Hope".

Raj'ah (lit. "return", "restitution"). The dogma found in several Shī'ite and related sects regarding the return to the world of their spiritual leader, the Imām. In particular, the return of the Twelfth Imām in Twelve-Imām Shī'ism. *See* SHĪ'ISM, HIDDEN IMĀM.

Rajm. Lapidation, or stoning to death. The term *ar-rajīm* ("the stoned one") is applied to Satan. *See also* RAMĪ-l-JIMĀR.

Rak'ah (lit. "a bowing", from the verb *raka'a*, "to bow"). One complete cycle of sacred words and gestures during the ritual prayer (*ṣalāh*). It includes standing, bowing, prostration, and sitting. Each prayer is made up of several such cycles, or *raka'āt. See* ṢALĀH.

Ramaḍān. The ninth month of the Arab and Islamic calendar. The word *Ramaḍān* meant originally "great heat", a description which originates in the pre-Islamic solar calendar. This month was holy in Arab tradition before Islam and was one of the months of truce. Fasting during the month is one of the Five Pillars of Islam (*ṣawm Ramaḍān*).

> ...the month of Ramaḍān, wherein the Koran
> was sent down to be a guidance
> to the people, and as clear signs
> of the Guidance and the Salvation.
> So let those of you, who are present
> at the month, fast it; and if any of you
> be sick, or if he be on a journey,
> then a number of other days; God desires
> ease for you, and desires not hardship
> for you; and that you fulfil the number, and
> magnify God that He has guided you, and haply
> you will be thankful. (2:182)

The month of fasting begins with the physical sighting of the new moon. This is different than astronomical calculation of Sun and Moon conjunction. (A new moon cannot be seen with the naked eye until it has waxed for at least twenty hours after the astronomic new moon, or conjunction of moon and sun.) If the new moon is not sighted on the twenty-eighth day of the previous month, the current month may be lengthened to twenty-nine or thirty days before Ramaḍān is considered to have begun conclusively. Non-sightings of the moon were deemed to be possible because of overcast sky. In practice this theoretical provision has probably never been invoked, because claims of sighting the new moon were always made at the time when astronomic conjunction was expected and such claims were routinely accepted. Aside from questions of overcast sky preventing sighting, there was an official practice in Egypt of accepting claims of sighting even within five minutes of calculated astronomic new moon or conjunction when such sightings were physically and scientifically impossible. In recent times Ramaḍān has been declared in the Middle East when such astronomic new moons have taken place when the sun and moon were over the Pacific Ocean hours after the sun has set and night begun in Arabia! (Sightings of the new moon are made moments after sunset; the new moon sets minutes after the sun.) It is yet to be seen whether new, more scientific thinking which is actually more in line with Islamic law will replace the traditional way of determining Ramaḍan or whether the fiction of a new moon being sighted when such sighting is impossible will persist.

There is also a new problem in determining the beginning of Ramaḍan in that immigrant communities begin Ramaḍan when it is official in their country of origin, rather than in their country of residence, which means that different groups in one country, such as France, may begin Ramaḍan on different days according to the beginning of Ramaḍān in their parent country.

Following Turkish custom, many countries signal the beginning of the month of Ramaḍān, meaning the authorities have registered what they consider to be credible sightings of the moon, to the population by the repeated firing of cannon on the eve of the first day. (In the Islamic calendar a day runs from sunset to sunset.) Cannon are also used to signal the beginning and end of each fast day.

During Ramaḍān a Muslim does not eat or drink from daybreak, when a thread of light may be seen on the horizon, until the sun has set. After the evening prayer (*maghrib*), a breakfast is eaten. Somewhat later in the night a larger meal is taken. It is common to take a meal, sometimes called *suhūr*, in the early morning before the fast begins. Musicians and criers walk through towns at night to wake the people to take this meal; the criers often do this as a pious act.

The daily fast is begun by formulating the intention to perform the fast as a rite. Children begin fasting gradually, first half a day, then several days, until they grow old enough to fast without injuring their health. No one is required to fast if his health is not up to it, and if a fast threatens health it should be stopped. Pregnant and nursing women are exempted from fasting. Menstruating women are also exempted but must make up the lost fast days afterwards during the course of the year.

Travelers are exempted from fasting (but not forbidden to fast), if the distance traveled is great, or if they are on a journey which continues for more than three days. Fast days which are lost for reasons of health or travel must be made up during the year. Exemption from the entire period of fasting is theoretically allowed if one feeds thirty poor people *each* day of the fast, as is partial exemption on the same terms, but it is, in fact, frowned upon and never resorted to by people of means. It is clear from experience that there is a great blessing in ritual fasting; Ramaḍān itself is a blessed month, a moment in the year when God's graces seem closer and more easily accessible.

During the daytime fast, not only must the believer not eat or drink, but he must also abstain from sexual enjoyment, listening to music, and as far as possible from all pleasures of the senses. During the night, pleasures of the senses are again licit, although extraordinary events of enjoyment, such as celebrations, should not be held during Ramaḍān.

The principle of fasting is related to that of limitation. Without limitation, knowledge is impossible, for it is when we come to the end or limit of a thing that its true nature becomes evident. (For example, we know ourselves when we know what we are *not.*) Ramaḍān's marking the end to indulgence, or imposing a clear limit to it day after day for a month, offers an unmistakable spiritual lesson. It also constitutes a purification and a kind of sacrifice, which, like the pruning of trees, leads to renewal and fresh strength. On the moral plane it also brings a direct understanding of the suffering of the hungry. Ramaḍān, which moves through the year because of the lunar calendar, sometimes takes place in the winter months, when it is easier, and sometimes in the summer months, when the sacrifice is greater. Despite its solemn nature, it has a joyous atmosphere about it, even one of festival, although festivities during the month are forbidden.

The Koran was revealed in one of the last ten nights of Ramaḍān, the *Laylat al-Qadr*, the holiest night in the Islamic calendar. During the month of Ramaḍān supplementary prayers called *tarāwīḥ*, numbering twenty or thirty-two *raka'āt* each, are performed during the small hours before the dawn prayer (*ṣubḥ*), and also before the night prayer (*īshā'*). The month is the occasion for intensive reading of the Koran. *See* FAST; FIVE PILLARS; LAYLAT al-QADR.

Ramī-l-Jimār. One of the rites of the pilgrimage, the throwing of stones at three columns in Mina on the 10th, 11th, and 12th day of Dhū-l-Ḥijjah. The pebbles, called *jimār*, are gathered at Muzdalifah the night before, where the pilgrims stop on the way from 'Arafāt.

As are the other rites of pilgrimage, the throwing of the stones is linked to Abraham. As Abraham proceeded to Minā to carry out God's command to sacrifice his son Ismā'īl (Ishmael), the devil appeared three times to tempt his son, who was lagging behind his father, to run away. On each occasion Ismā'īl pelted Satan with stones at the spot marked by the three columns or pillars (*al-jamarāt*) representing the apparitions of Satan.

The three pillars, aligned in a row in the flat valley of Minā, are today accessible from ground level and from above by way of an overhead ramp constructed to accommodate the millions that now come to perform the pilgrimage. The first pillar from Muzdalifah is called *al-jamrah as-sughrā*, or *al-jamrah al-ūlā* ("the small", or "first pillar"); the second is *al-jamrah al-wuṣṭā* ("the middle pillar"); and the third is the *al-jamrah al-kubrā*, or *jamrat al-'aqabah*, ("the large pillar" or "the 'Aqabah pillar").

On the 10th of Dhū-l-Ḥijjah the pilgrims throw seven pebbles, one after the other, at the large pillar, repeating the words *Allāhu Akbar, lā ilāha illā Llāh* ("God is Greatest, there is no god but God"). On the 11th, the actions are repeated at the first, middle and large pillars, and again on the 12th. This completes the usual lapidation of the pillars, for which 49 pebbles are gathered at Muzdalifah. If one stays for another day, the 13th, then 70 pebbles are gathered. A pilgrim remaining past this time will continue stoning the pillars on following days, and he will have gathered more stones at Muzdalifah accordingly. This rite is a means, in a palpable, easily understandable way, of purification, or of taking a distance between oneself and evil in all its forms, not just temptation.

Failure to perform this rite during the pilgrimage may be expiated by fasting or sacrifice. The repetition of the essential *talbiyah* invocation comes to an end with the final stoning of the pillars, although some say the *talbiyah* ends just before the lapidation begins. *See* PILGRIMAGE; TALBIYAH.

ar-Rāqid, *see* SLEEPING FOETUS.

ar-Rasā'il Ikhwān aṣ-Ṣafā' *see* BROTHERHOOD of PURITY.

Rāshid ad-Dīn Sinān (d. *589*/1193). The leader of the Syrian Ismā'īlīs who was known to the Crusaders as the "old man of the mountain" (*shaykh al-jabal*). He was born in Baṣrah and educated in Persia, at Alamut; presumably he was appointed to his place as the chief of the castle of Masyāf by the head of the sect at Alamūt, Ḥasan II called *'ala dhikrihi's-salam*. Rāshid ad-Dīn fought both the Crusaders, and then Salāḥ ad-Dīn al-Ayyūbī (Saladin). After Rāshid ad-Dīn, the Nizārī Ismā'īlī power in Syria declined and was brought to an end when the Mamlūks captured their castles. A community of Ismā'īlīs exists near Masyāf to this day.

William of Tyre relates that in 1171 Rāshid ad-Dīn sent an emissary to the Crusader King Amalric I proposing that the Ismā'īlīs become Christians. The King accepted but the Grand Master of the Templars, Odo of St Amand had the Ismā'īlī envoy killed by a knght named Walter of Mesnil. The Templars had very close relations with the Ismā'īlīs and probably suspected this conversion was only tactical to infiltrate the Crusaders. On the other hand, the Templars had the occasion to learn a great deal from the Ismā'īlīs, including military architecture and methods of social organization and indoctrination, from which Freemasonry doubtless springs.

Rashīd ad-Dīn aṭ-Ṭabīb, Faḍl Allāh *645-717*/1247-1318). A Persian, son of an apothecary, Rashīd ad-Dīn was converted to Islam from Judaism at the age of thirty. He was born in Hamadhān, belonged to the Shāfi'ī school of law, and was a physician. He became Vizier, or minister, of the Mongol Khan Abaqa of the Il-Khanid dynasty. As Vizier, Rashīd ad-Dīn was a noted builder of mosques, *madrasahs*, and public works in the various cities which the Mongols used as their capitals in Persia. He built complete neighborhoods in Tabriz and Sulṭāniyyah.

At the bidding of the Mongol Khān Ghāzān, Rashīd ad-Dīn wrote a monumental history of the world in Persian, *Kitāb Jāmi' at-Tawārīkh* ("The Universal History" also known as the *Ta'rīkh-i Mubārak-i Ghāzān-ī*). It encompasses Adam and the Patriarchs, the Prophets, the history of the Persian Kings and the Muslim dynasties, and gives accounts, together with genealogies of the ruling houses of the Jews, Arabs, Persians, Turks, Mongols, Chinese, Indians, and Buddhists, and it even includes material on the Franks, about whom Rashīd ad-Dīn was remarkably well-informed, describing the Popes and Emperors. One of its most valuable sections was that describing the history of the Mongols, for Rashīd ad-Dīn learned this from Ghazan himself, and from Balad Ching-Sang, the Mongol representative in Persia of the Great Khans.

Perhaps knowing that the history of the Mongols, preserved only in the memory of the people he met and in a secret book which he was not allowed to see, was likely to be lost forever now that they had abandoned their nomadic life on the steppes for a sedentary existence, Rashīd ad-Dīn made great efforts to see that many copies of his history were made and widely distributed.

Rashīd ad-Dīn also wrote other works in Arabic: *Kitāb al-Aḥyā wa-l-Āthār* ("The Book of Animals and Monuments", on botany, agriculture, and architecture) which has not survived, and a collection of smaller works, *al-Majmū'āt ar-Rashīdiyyah*, on metaphysics and mysticism, religious disputations, and correspondence on political and financial matters. He also wrote a commentary on the Koran called *Miftāḥ al-Tafsīr* ("The Key to Commentary").

After the death of the Khan Uljaytu in *717*/1317, who had entered Islam as Muḥammad Khudabanda, Rashīd ad-Dīn was pursued, as he had been before, by political enemies who accused him of poisoning the Khan. This time they succeeded and Rashīd ad-Dīn was executed. *See* al-JUWAYNĪ; MONGOLS.

Rashīd Riḍā, Muḥammad (1865-1935). *See* RIḌĀ, MUḤAMMAD RASHĪD.

Rasūl, *see* PROPHETS.

Rationalists, *see* MU'TAZILITES.

Rāwandiyyah. A radical Gnostic sect (*Baṭinis*) named after 'Abd Allāh ar-Rāwāndī and centered in Khorāsān but related to the Kaysāniyyah of Kūfah. It was a component of the Hāshimiyyah which became the political base of the 'Abbāsids that brought them to power. Theirs was an extremist *ghulāt* Shī'ite doctrine which held that the Imāmate had passed from 'Alī to Muḥammad al-Ḥanafiyyah, to his son Abū Hāshim (d. *98*/716) and, was "legated" to Muḥammad ibn 'Alī ibn 'Abd Allāh ibn al-'Abbās, father of Ibrāhīm. A leader of the Rāwandiyyah, a leper called al-Ablaq, also said that the spirit of Jesus had passed from 'Alī into Ibrāhīm ibn Muḥammad, the 'Abbāsid leader. They believed in the divinity of certain 'Abbāasids and the Prophethood, at least, of Abū Muslim.

After the 'Abbāsid revolution succeeded, in the year *137*/754 (although Ṭabarī says it could have been 138 or 141) a group of six hundred Rāwandīs (from Ṭaliqān in Khorāsān?) came to the Caliph al-Manṣūr in his pre-Baghdad capital called Hāshimiyyah, and declared that they knew he was God, and said "thou art that" (*anta takuna dhaka*, similar to the Indian formula *tat tvam asi*) and asked "for food and drink". This, like the "Chair or throne of 'Alī" of the Mukhtāriyyah (also called the Kaysāniyyah), is most likely a reference to the Bēma ceremony, which included a ritual meal. Members of the sect leaped to their death from the dome of a building in the belief that they would be resurrected in a better state. (In the Bēma ceremony Mani was believed to sit, spiritually alive but invisible, on an empty throne in front of a feast, as he did, triumphant over death, three days after his martyrdom. Martyrdom was thus a desirable end, an end which could be provoked.) Al-Manṣur at first met them in a friendly fashion but had to escape from them and then had several hundred of them put to death.

Zabih Behzade, a Persian scholar, has theorized that al-Manṣūr, if not also others of the early 'Abbāsids, had become a Manichean in secret in order to cement his family's alliance with the Manichean groups that had brought them to power. This is very plausible, given his name al-Manṣūr which had a Gnostic and Messianic significance, that of a "victory over death", and his ostentatious show of asceticism on certain critical occasions. But the "Day of the Rāwandiyyah" was too much, and compromised the 'Abbāsid Sunni credentials with the Muslim majority which were essential for their staying in power. Thus the Caliph swept this embarrassing constituency under the rug by having them massacred despite their evident loyalty and desire to honor him. It was such groups that an Umayyad adversary had in mind when he called the supporters of the 'Abbāsid revolution "worshippers of cats and heads" (talking oracular masks or statues of heads in temples, *see* ḤARRĀN.) The

Rāwandiyyah gradually disappeared as such and merged into the Khurramiyyah. *See* 'ABBĀSIDS; BARMAKIDS.

Rawdah Khānī. (also: *rawzah khāneh*). In Iran, the ritual recitation of the sufferings of the Shī'ite Imāms, in particular of Ḥusayn ibn 'Alī. These are frequently carried out in homes and mosques by preachers who specialize in playing upon the emotivity of the occasion by recalling the sufferings of the Shī'ite martyrs and moving their listeners to expressions of grief. On the 10th day of the month of Muḥarram, the anniversary of the death of Ḥusayn (which for different reasons going back to early Islam is also a Sunnī holiday) these *rawda khānī* lead to public frenzies in which some devout Shī'ites cut themselves with swords and knives, and beat themselves with chains in paroxysms of guilt towards the Imāms, and in joyous expiatory self-punishment.

Martyr plays are also put on in Iran for the same reason, perpetuating deep complexes of guilt, resentment, and desire for vengeance which, for centuries, the religious, and sometimes the political, authorities have not hesitated to cultivate, control, and exploit.

The Rawdah khānī is so called from a book, the *Garden* (rawdah) *of the Martyrs*, an account of the sufferings of the Imāms. There is an imitation called the *Deluge of Weeping* and the *Mysteries of Martyrdom*. The Rawdah khanī reciters are given access to private quarter of homes, the *andaruns* which no other group in society has. *See* SHĪ'ISM; TA'ZIYAH.

ar-Rawḍah (lit. "the garden"). The area in the Mosque of the Prophet (*al-Masjid ash-Sharīf*) in Medinah, between a free-standing prayer niche (*miḥrāb*), and the tomb of the Prophet. It is thus called because of the Ḥadīth: "Between my house and my pulpit is a garden [*rawḍah*] of the gardens of paradise." The Prophet's tomb is on the spot where he died, in what was his house, which was adjacent to the mosque.

Ra'y (lit. "opinion"). A legal principle, that of the personal opinion of the jurist, which is the last resort after the Koran, Sunnah, and precedents have been exhausted in resolving a legal issue.

Ray'ah, *see* RA'ĀYĀ.

ar-Rāzī, Abū Bakr Muḥammed ibn Zakariyyā (*236-313*/850-925). Better known in the West under his Latinized name of Rhazes, he was a Persian physician. His Arabic works which were current in Europe were later translated into Latin and Greek, and finally into modern European languages. Throughout the Middle Ages in Europe he exercised a strong influence upon medicine. His most famous books are the *Liber Pestilentia* (in which he distinguished measles from smallpox), the compendium *Almansor* (*al-Kitāb al-Manṣūrī*), and the Encyclopedic *Liber Continens* (*al-Ḥāwi*). This first became available as a manuscript translated by a Jewish physician in Sicily and was later one of the first books to be printed. Ar-Rāzī recognized the role that psychosomatic medicine or autosuggestion plays in healing and wrote a treatise explaining why untrained practitioners, quacks, laymen, and "old-wives' remedies" often have greater success in healing patients than trained doctors.

In the great tradition of the Middle Ages ar-Rāzī was a universal thinker and pursued all the sciences including theology, astronomy, and music. It was, however, as an alchemist that his other great contribution to European science was made, and his descriptions of the alchemical processes were put into practice by European alchemists such as Nicholas Flamel and Paracelsus.

Ḥujwīrī called Rāzī "a disciple of Ḥallāj" which is to say, of the same ideology; he was known for his freethinking, deliberately avoided Islamic formulas in his writings, and thus may have been a practicing Manichean. He expounded a very Gnostic Pentad of five realities: God-Creator, World-Soul, Original Matter, Absolute space, and Absolute time.

ar-Rāzī, Abū Ḥātim, *see* ABŪ ḤĀTIM ar-RĀZĪ

ar-Rāzī, Fakhr ad-Dīn (*544-606*/1149-1209). Philosopher, historian (he wrote the "History of the Dynasties"), and theologian, he belonged to the Shāfi'ī school of law and was a defender of orthodox views in his book, *Kitāb al-Muḥaṣṣal*. His commentary on the Koran is called the *Mafātīḥ al-Ghayb* ("The Keys of the Unseen"), itself a quotation from the Koran (6:59: "With Him are the Keys of the Unseen"). He was born south of Teheran and he died in Herat.

Readings of the Koran, *see* QIRĀ'AH.

Red Banners Revolt, *see* SURKH-I 'ALĀM.

Reconquista ("reconquest"). The reconquest of the Iberian peninsula by the Christians. The first serious setback to the Moorish invasion of Spain which began in *93*/711 was their defeat at the battle of Covadonga around *102*/720 at the hands of the Asturian chief Pelayo. This was followed by their being decisively checked and defeated at the battle of Tours (*114*/732) by Charles Martel.

Visigoths driven out by the Arab-Berber invasion flocked to Pelayo the Asturian, naming him their King, and the province of Asturias maintained its sovereignty throughout the whole Muslim domination of Spain. From that area and, on the east, from the Spanish March (*Marca Hispanica*), that is to say, border, created by the Franks, began the resistance to the Moorish rulers which eventually developed into the reconquest.

Spreading out from the Asturias there grew a line of fortification which expanded, eventually centering upon Burgos. The area enclosed by the fortification was called "Castilla", the land of castles. A rallying point of the reconquest was the legend of Santiago Matamor, St. James the Apostle, "Killer of Moors", who had appeared to the Christian defenders at the battle of Tours. His tomb had been "discovered" in Galicia at the end of the 8th century, and he was believed to help the Christians in their battles.

The development of the Christian kingdoms in the *4th*/11th century corresponded to a weakening of the Caliphate of Cordova. This took place after the reigns of 'Abd ar-Raḥmān III and al-Manṣūr Bi-Llāh, and the Caliphate then disintegrated into the small principalities called *ṭawā'if* (sing. *ṭā'ifah*). The rivalry between the *ṭawā'if*, their willingness to ally themselves with the Christians against their co-religionists, as well as their inability to create stable institutions and thus ensure continuity from ruler to ruler, led to their downfall. The reconquest, until then a series of back and forth skirmishes over the same territory, now entered a new and more important phase. In *428*/1037 Ferdinand I of Castile, claiming to represent "the Spains", captured Leon and led an increasingly united offensive against the Moors.

The fall of Toledo in *478*/1085, long protected by its strategic position and spared by Alfonso of Castile for reasons of friendship with the Emir, made the rulers of the other *ṭawā'if* realize that their situation was perilous and look to North Africa for help. It was a dangerous step because it meant calling in powers foreign to Spain. But as al-Mu'tamid the 'Abbāsid prince of Seville said: "I do not want to be held responsible for handing Andalusia over to the Christians... I do not want to be vilified from the pulpits of Islam. If I had to choose, I would rather tend camels for the Almoravids, than pasture swine under the Christians."

Help for the Muslim princes of Spain came from the Almoravid ruler of North Africa, Yusūf ibn Tashfīn, and the now reinforced and combined Muslim forces delivered a setback to the Christian armies at az-Zallaqah (Sagrajas near Badajoz) in *479*/1086. This was followed, however, shortly afterwards, by the formation of the knightly orders of Calatrava, Santiago, and Alcantara, and the added impetus of the Crusades. In Portugal, the first King, Alfonso Enriquez, completed the reconquest of his country by *543*/1148 with the assistance of English, French, and German Crusaders who had actually been driven onto his coasts by a providential storm. In Spain, during a period of pronounced French influence, the adoption by the Church of the Roman rite in place of the Visigothic, signified that the country was now a salient of Europe, and no longer an "island" on its own.

Against the Almohads, who succeeded the Almoravids, the Spanish kingdoms rallied a united force from Castile, Aragon, and Navarre, reinforced with Portuguese knights. They defeated the Almohads at the battle of Las Navas de Tolosa in *609*/1212, the single most important battle of the reconquest, which led, eventually, to the fall of Cordova in *634*/1236 and of Seville in *646*/1248; the remaining kingdoms of Granada, its dependency Malaga, and Cadiz, were reduced to the status of tributary states. The battle standard of the Muslims, captured at the battle of Las Navas, now hangs in the convent of Las Huelgas Reales in Burgos.

With the union of Spain under the "Catholic Kings", Ferdinand and Isabella, the moment had arrived for the balance to swing completely to one side. It came then as a great surprise when a massed assault by a vast Christian army against Granada was successfully repulsed. At the siege camp of Santa Fe, Isabella swore she would not remove her shirt until Granada fell, an oath she surely came to regret because Granada held out for two more years and then collapsed only because of internal dissension. In 1492, Granada, the last sovereign Moorish kingdom in Spain surrendered. The morning after, the prince "Boabdil" or Abū 'Abd

Allāh, halted for a moment in a pass of the Sierra Nevada on his way to exile in Morocco, looked back on the Alhambra resplendent in the dawn sun, and wept. The spot is now called *el ultimo sospiro del moro*, ("the last sigh of the Moor").

Nevertheless, there remained a large Moorish population in Spain for some time thereafter. In the middle of the 16th century the Spanish Moors rebelled in a final, unsuccessful, attempt to retake Granada. In 1619, the *Moriscos*, or Moors superficially converted to Christianity, were expelled. Some remained, practicing Islam in secret, perhaps up to recent times. Today, ethnic groups such as the Maragatos of Astorga in Leon, are the descendants of Moorish groups left behind in the reconquest of Spain. *See* ALMOHAD; ALMORAVID.

Reforms, *see* ALIGARH; 'ABDUH, MUḤAMMAD; MUḤAMMADIYYAH; ṢALAFIYYAH; TANẒĪMĀT.

Refuge. Many passages in the Koran are incantations in which the believer can take refuge from evil. The foremost is the so-called "taking of refuge" (*ta'awwudh*): *a'ūdhu bi-Llāhi min ash-shayṭāni-r-rajīm* ("I take refuge in God from Satan the stoned one"). Then the last two Sūrahs (113 and 114) of the Koran are called the "two Sūrahs of refuge" (*al-mu'awwadhatān*) about which it is related that a spell was cast upon the Prophet by an Arabian form of magic which consisted of tying knots in a rope and blowing upon them while making incantations, to which verse 114:4 refers. Angels informed the Prophet of what had been done and the location of the well where the rope had been thrown. The revelation of the two Sūrahs undid the spell, each verse dissolving one of the enchanted knots. For the Sufis the "knots" are also psychic knots or entanglements and the "women that blow on knots" are uncontrolled emotivity, anger, rancor, resentment, jealousy, desire, lust and so forth. (*See* MAGIC.)

Say: I take refuge in the Lord of the Daybreak
From the evil of His creation,
From the evil of utter darkness when it comes on
From the evil of witches who blow on knots,
From the evil of the envious man in his envy.
(113)

Say: I take refuge in man's lord
Man's King,
Man's God,
From the whispering insinuator's evil
Who whispers in man's breast
From (the evil) of Jinn and men. (114)

Some other verses of refuge (*āyāt al-ḥifẓ*) are: 12:64 ("God is the best protector, and He is the Most Merciful of those who show mercy"); 13:11 ("Nor have they a defender beside Him"); 15:17 ("And we have guarded it from every outcast devil"); 37:7 ("With security from every froward devil"); and (4:81); (33:3); 33:48 ("Put your trust in God; God suffices as a guardian"); 39:62 ("He is Guardian over all things"); and the most famous, "the verse of the throne", *āyat al-kursī*, 2:256 (*see* ĀYAT al-KURSĪ) and the *āyat al-'arsh* (also meaning "verse of the throne"), 9:130 ("Now, if they turn away (O Muḥammad) say: Allāh suffices me. There is no God save Him. In Him have I put my trust, and He is Lord of the Tremendous Throne"). The efficacy of these verses resides in their invocation in Arabic.

In many countries, Saints' tombs and places of worship have been places of political refuge where the ruler's agents would not seize anyone fleeing from his authority. In Islam, mosques everywhere have been used as sanctuaries inviolable to pursuit. In the Mawlay Idrīs Mosque in Fez there is a room accessible from a narrow passageway which has been used as a haven by fugitives.

In Persian, the taking of refuge and the place of refuge is called *bast*. Great Shī'ite asylums are the 'Abd al-'Azīm mosque a few kilometers outside of Teheran at Rayy, where Jamāl ad-Dīn Afghānī took refuge from the Shah. Mosques within the city of Qumm, but also the royal stables of the Shah and foreign legations were used as places of refuge. When the telegraph was built between India and Europe across Iran and inaugurated in 1865, the popular belief arose in Iran that the telegraph wires ended at the foot of the Persian throne. Telegraph offices became places where one could claim refuge from the authorities. In 1893, 2,000 people, following bread riots, marched on the telegraph office in Shiraz insisting that a message be sent to the Shah. The crowd swelled to 10,000 and held the staff prisoner until an answer was received from Teheran. *See* AMULETS; ĀYAT al-KURSĪ; ḤIZB al-BAḤR; MAGIC; RUQYAH; TA'AWWUDH.

Reincarnation, *see* TANASUKH.

Resignation (Ar. Islām, "peace through surrender", or *ṣabr*, "patience", or "endurance"; also *idh'ān* and *ruḍūkh*, "humble compliance"). This is one of the chief virtues and fundamental attitudes in Islam. The joyful is accepted with the words *al-ḥamdu li-Llāh* ("praise be to God"), and the sorrowful with equanimity, and therefore with the same words "praise be to God", perhaps amplified with *'alā kulli shay'* ("in all things"). An oft-uttered saying in this context is: *mā shā'a-Llāh* ("whatever God has willed"); likewise, as regards the outcome of events in the future one qualifies every hope or purpose with the words in *shā'a-Llāh* ("if God wills"). *Innā li-Llāhi wa innā ilayhi rāji'ūn* ("we belong to God and to God we return") expresses a resignation that goes beyond the vicissitudes of this life. There is a famous Ḥadīth which says that "half of Islam is enduring (*ṣabr*)".

Resurrection (Ar. *ba'th, nushūr*). The doctrine of the resurrection of the bodies from the graves, and their reuniting with souls to face the great Judgement is a fundamental dogma of Islam. It is much insisted upon in the Koran, and is present in numerous creeds. The Koran says:

They say, 'What, when we are bones
and broken bits, shall we really
be raised up again in a
new creation?'
Say: 'Let you be stones, or iron,
or some creation yet more monstrous
in your minds!' Then they will say,
'Who will bring us back?' say: 'He
who originated you the first time.'
They will shake their heads at thee,
and they will say, 'When will it be?'
Say: 'It is possible
that it may be nigh,
on the day when He will call you, and
you will answer praising Him, and
you will think you have but tarried
a little.' (17:51-54)

What, does man reckon
We shall not assemble his bones?
Yes indeed; We are able
to put his fingers back together. (75:3-4)

Again, the Koran compares the resurrection to the revivification of the parched earth by rain:

God is He that looses the winds,
that stir up cloud,
then We drive it to a dead land
and therewith revive the earth, after it is dead.
Even so is the Uprising. (35:10)

The Rabbinic explanation of the apocalyptic reconstruction of the bodies of the dead from the "indestructible" bone at the bottom of the spine (*luzz*) was known to Muslim thinkers in the Middle Ages. (Islamic doctrine does not specify how the body is resurrected.)

When Indian doctrines were encountered through the Persians, the *luzz* was easily identified with the *piṇḍa* of Indian yoga and cosmology. This is the microcosmic reflection, within the person, of the macrocosmic *hiraṇyagarbha* ("world egg"), designated in Persian *majmā-i anāsīr hasti* ("the totality of elements of existence"), or what the Koran (97:4) calls the *kulli amr* ("all decrees").

The Christian doctrine of the resurrection of Jesus does not exist in Islam. It is understood that the crucifixion was an appearance only; that Jesus did not die on the cross but instead passed into a principial state; that he is in this state alive in the invisible and will return from it again in the Second Coming which will mark the end of the cycle, or the end of the world. *See* JESUS.

Retaliation, *see* QIṢĀṢ.

Revelation. In Arabic this is denoted by two words: *waḥy* and *tanzīl*. *Waḥy*, from a root meaning "to inspire", implies a Divine source that is beyond the world and beyond the recipient; *tanzīl* ("sending down") is used particularly for the revelation of the Koran or other *direct* revelation as the descent of a form from heaven. *Waḥy* and *tanzīl* are thus complementary, and may be called "direct revelation" from God, corresponding to what is called *shruti* ("what has been heard") in Sanskrit. *Ilhām* ("inspiration" or "intuition") is the source of a secondary or indirect revelation, arising within the individual, or reflected within him. This corresponds to the Sanskrit smriti ("what has been recommended, or held in the mind"), "secondary revelation". The difference between the two is shown by the Apostle Paul's distinction between that which came "from the Spirit" and that which came from himself.

The Ḥadīth which are called *ḥadīth qudsī* ("holy Ḥadīth"), are the utterances of God through the

Prophet, and come thus from *waḥy*, whereas the *ḥadīth sharīf* ("noble Ḥadīth") may be inspired utterances of the Prophet himself and, if so, come through *ilhām*.

The Koran speaks of Jesus as having received *tanzīl* from God. The Gospels, without pretence to the contrary, are for the most part, except for the words of Jesus, secondary inspiration, being a description of events by his disciples, and not *tanzīl*. Muslim commentators were surprised to find doctrinal divergences between the Gospels and the Koran, and this has given rise to the historic accusations on the part of Muslim theologians that the Gospels have been changed (*takhrīf*). Rarely has it been suggested that the *tanzīl* of Christianity is in the person of Jesus himself as the Messenger of God and His Word (*Kalimatuh*) (4:17).

The theory of the revelation of the Koran is particularly complex. The Koran was revealed, or descended, in its entirety in one night, the "Night of Destiny" (*Laylat al-Qadr*), into the soul of the Prophet, *which itself is that night*. Thereupon it became manifest through him, in segments, sometimes entire Sūrahs, as particular circumstances and requirements in the world and the Prophet's life called them forth. The Prophet said that this manifestation of the Koran came in two ways: "Sometimes Gabriel reveals to me as one man to another, and that is easy; but at other times it is like the ringing of a bell penetrating my very heart, rending me, and that way is the most painful." *See also* BIBLE; FARAQLĪT; KORAN; MUḤAMMAD.

Rhazes, *see* RĀZĪ, ABŪ BAKR.

Ribā (from the root *rabā*: "to grow, increase, exceed"). Usury or profit — interest — from the loan of money or goods, which is prohibited in any degree. Today the prohibition is hardly observed in any Islamic country. Either it is simply disregarded — the Egyptian Mufti Muḥammad Abduh once declared "moderate interest" lawful — or else it is referred to by some such euphemism as "commission". To stay within the letter of the religious law and soothe consciences, some banks offer the solution of *muḍārabah* (sleeping partnership): this defines the placing of capital as a co-investment, which naturally brings a return to both parties. *See* ISLAMIC BANKING.

Ribāṭ (pl. *ribāṭāt* and *rubuṭ* from the verb *rabaṭa*, "to bind"; "a post", "a hospice", "a fort"). A fort on the frontier of Islam, the origin of the word is perhaps associated with "tethering a horse in enemy territory". The performance of garrison duty at the frontiers of *dār al-Islām* ("the abode of faith") was viewed as a pious duty from the time of 'Umar, when it was accepted that the Arab armies would advance without laying down their arms until Islam was established on the edges of the world.

Those who performed this duty of vigilance and defence in later Islam were called *al-murābiṭun* (the "ones bound [to religious duty]"). This became the name of the movement of the Almoravid (the Spanish name of the dynasty derived from the term *al-Murābiṭ*). The most famous of their forts was the *Ribāṭ al-Fatḥ* ("the camp of victory") from which the Almoravids set out on the conquest of southern Spain and North Africa. The *Ribāṭ al-Fatḥ* has given Morocco the name of its present capital, Rabāṭ. The institution of the *ribāṭ* mingled military service with religious observance and some ribāṭat became with time the meeting places of Sufis, that is, *khānaqahs* or *zāwiyahs*. *See* ALMORAVIDS.

Ridā'. The cloth which constitutes the covering of the upper body over the shoulders in the consecrated pilgrim's garb, the *iḥrām*. *See* IḤRĀM.

Riḍā'. The act of suckling a baby which establishes a foster-kinship, which, in certain degrees and under certain conditions, is an impediment to marriage.

After the conquest of Mecca the clans of the Beduin tribe of Hawāzin gathered to attack the army of the Prophet. The battle took place in a defile called Ḥunayn; eventually the Hawāzin were routed. To increase the valor of the Hawāzin men, their families had accompanied them, and so it came about that the women and children of the Hawāzin were captured. When one of these captives, an old women of seventy years, claimed to be the sister of the Prophet, she was brought before him. Asked for proof of her claim, she showed him the scar of a bite he had inflicted on her when she carried him as a child, for she was the daughter of Ḥalīmah and Ḥārith, two Beduin of a Hawāzin clan, to whom for a time the Prophet had been entrusted as a child, in order to be raised and strengthened in the desert, according to the custom of the Arab city dwellers. The Prophet recognized that the old woman, Shaymā', was indeed his foster sister; he offered to bring her back to Medinah with him, but she preferred to remain with her desert clan of the Banū Sa'd ibn Bakr. She was therefore set free with gifts. Thereupon the Hawāzin all claimed to be related to the Prophet as cousins, a claim which he, however, did not countenance.

Riḍā, Muḥammad Rashīd (1865-1935). Muslim reformer, born in Syria (in what is today Lebanon), associated with Muḥammad 'Abduh, published with him a magazine called *al-Manār* ("the Lighthouse") in Cairo. He was concerned with the decline of the Islamic world, looked upon the Arabs as its champions, believed in the existence of a Caliphate for the sake of unity and promoted democratic consultation, which he called *shūrā*, on the part of the government. He equated Western culture with the *Jāhiliyyah* or the age of barbaric ignorance which existed before Islam but believed that Islam could be combined with modernism.

His legacy is a coherent body of thought and especially an idea of democracy based upon Islamic precedents, namely that of the *shūrā* or consultative assembly.

Riddah. Apostasy from Islam. An apostate is called murtadd. The word is also applied to the period of insurgency and the rise of false prophets among the desert tribes which followed the death of the Prophet. *See* APOSTASY; al-ASWAD; DHŪ-l-ḤIMĀR; MUSAYLAMAH.

Riḍwān (lit. "felicity"). The word is used to mean "God's good pleasure" as in Mark 1:11, and has the same meaning as the Greek eudokia. The verb from which it is derived is used to call blessings upon the Companions of the Prophet: *raḍiya-Llāhu 'anhu* ("may God be well-pleased with him"). This formula is said when the name of a Companion or acknowledged saint is mentioned. The pact which the Prophet made at Ḥudaybiyyah with his followers, which is the model for the ritual of initiation in Sufism, is called the "pact of felicity", or *bay'at ar-riḍwān* ("God was well pleased with the Believers..." 48:18).

In Sūrah 9:74, *riḍwān* means something higher again, the removal of the veil of separation from God which exists even in paradise:

> God has promised the believers,
> men and women,
> gardens underneath which rivers flow, forever
> therein to dwell, and goodly dwelling-places in
> the Gardens of Eden; and greater,
> God's good pleasure [*riḍwān*];
> that is the mighty triumph.

Or again as this Ḥadīth clarifies:

> God will say to the people of Paradise: 'Are you well pleased?' and they will say: 'How should we not be well pleased, O Lord, inasmuch as You have given us that which You have not given to any of your creatures else?' Then will He say: 'Shall I not give you better than that?' and they will say: 'What thing, O Lord, is better?' and He will say: 'I will let down upon you My *riḍwān*'.

In other words, *riḍwān* in its ultimate sense is the final and absolute acceptance of a soul by God:

> 'O soul at peace, return unto thy Lord,
> well-pleased, well-pleasing!
> Enter thou among My servants!
> Enter thou My Paradise!' (89:27-30)

See also ḤUDAYBIYYAH.

Rifā'īyyah. A Sufi order founded by Abū-l-'Abbās Aḥmad ar-Rifā'ī (*500-578*/1106-1182) which became widespread in Syria and Egypt. Ibn Bāṭūṭah visited the tomb of Rifā'ī in Wāsiṭ, 'Irāq in 1327 and in the account of his travels he said:

> Three days march through this district brought us to the town of Wāsiṭ. Its inhabitants are among the best people of Iraq — indeed, the very best of them without qualification. All the Iraqis who wish to learn how to recite the Koran come here, and our caravan contained a number of students who had come for that purpose. As the caravan stayed here three days, I had an opportunity of visiting the grave of ar-Rifa'i, which is at a village called Umm 'Ubayda, one days's journey from there. I reached the establishment at noon the next day and found it to be an enormous monastery, containing thousands of darwishes. After the mid-afternoon prayer drums and kettledrums were beaten and the darwishes began to dance. After this they prayed the sunset prayer and brought in the meal, consisting of rice-bread, fish, milk and dates. After the

night prayer they began to recite their litany. A number of loads of wood had been brought in and kindled into flame, and they went into the fire dancing: some of them rolled in it and others ate it in their mouths until they had extinguished it entirely. This is the peculiar custom of the Ahmadi darwishes. Some of them take large snakes and bite their heads with their teeth until they bite them clean through. After visiting ar-Rifa'i's tomb I returned to Wāsiṭ, and found that the caravan had already started, but overtook them on the way, and accompanied them to Baṣra.

"Howling Dervishes" is a pejorative colonial name for those Rifā'ī dervishes whose method includes calling out loudly *Ya Ḥayyu, Ya Qayyūm*, "O Living One, O Self-Subsisting One." *See* SUFISM.

Rightly guided Caliphs, *see* PATRIARCHAL CALIPHS.

ar-Rijāl, Abū-l-Ḥasan 'Alī (d. *432*/1040). Spanish mathematician, astronomer and astrologer known in the West as Abenragel.

Risālah (from *arsala*, "to send", "a missive", "message" or "epistle"; pl. *rasā'il*). 1. The mission or "ministry" of a Divine Messenger (*rasūl*).

2. *Risālah* also means a treatise, such as the *Risālah* of al-Qayrawānī on Mālikī law, the *Risālat al-Aḥadiyyah* ("Treatise on Unity") by Ibn 'Arabī, or *Rasā'il*, a collection of "belles lettres", etc. *See* PROPHETS.

Rizq (lit. "sustenance"). The "Sustainer" is a Divine Name: *ar-Razzāq*. The Shaykh al-'Arabī ad-Darqāwī wrote in his *Rasā'il* ("collected letters"):

> Nothing makes us so vulnerable to psychic and satanic attacks as concern for our sustenance. And yet our Lord (be He exalted) vowed to us by Himself: "Your sustenance and all ye have been promised is in Heaven; by the Lord of Heaven and earth, this is as true as it is true that ye have speech" (51:21-22). And He also said: "Prescribe prayer for thy people and be constant therein. We ask thee not to provide sustenance; We will provide for thee and it is piety that will gain the issue" (20:132). The same meaning is to be found in many other passages from the Koran as also in the many sayings of the Prophet (may God bless him and give him peace). There is also the saying of the Saint Abū Yazīd al-Bisṭāmī (may God be well pleased with him): "My part is to worship Him, as He commanded me, and His part is to feed me as He promised me," and so forth. I mention all this only because I am afraid you may lapse into the misfortune that afflicts most men. For I see them busy with many activities, religious as well as worldly, and fearing nothing so much as poverty. If they knew what riches are to be had from being occupied with God, they would forsake their worldly activities entirely and busy themselves with Him alone, that is, with His commandments. But in their ignorance they keep on increasing their worldly and religious activities while remaining uneasy from fear of poverty or from fear of creatures, which is serious forgetfulness and a deplorable state; and this is the state in which the majority of people — almost all — exist; may God preserve us from it! Therefore be on guard, my brother, and devote yourself entirely to God; then you will see marvels.

God's sustenance is given to men both here and in the hereafter, and is essentially the same in all states of existence; the Blessed who are given the fruits of paradise as sustenance recognize that they were given the like on earth.

> Give thou good tidings to those who believe
> and do deeds of righteousness, that for them
> await gardens underneath which rivers flow;
> whensoever they are
> provided with fruits therefrom
> they shall say, 'This is that wherewithal
> we were provided before'; that they shall be
> given in perfect semblance... (2:23)

Rites (Ar. *mansik*, pl. *manāsik*, also *nusuk*). The rites of Islam are few: the pronunciation of the *shahādah* into the ears of a newborn child, the sacrifice of the *'Īd al-Kabīr*, the prayers for special purposes, and the recitation of the Koran, are virtually all the rites which exist in addition to the Five Pillars. The most intricate of all the rites are those of the *ḥajj* ("the greater pilgrimage"). *See* FIVE PILLARS.

Ritual Slaughter. Animals, with the exception of game, must be ritually slaughtered to be legally acceptable (*ḥalāl*) as food. After formulating the intention (*niyyah*) of performing ritual slaughter, the Divine Name is pronounced over the animal, which consecrates its death, the formula for this being *bismi-Llāh; Allāhu akbar* ("In the Name of God; God is Most Great"). Before such an act as slaughter, the Names of Mercy (*ar-Raḥmān ar-Raḥīm*) are not pronounced. The throat of the animal is cut, severing both the windpipe and the jugular vein in one stroke. The slaughter must be performed by a Muslim. If the animal is sacrificed for a purpose such as the *'Īd al-Aḍḥā*, the sacrificial feast of "the greater pilgrimage", this fact and the names of those for whom the sacrifice is being made are mentioned as part of the formulation of intention. Game can be used for food. If hunting is carried out, it must be done with the intention of consecrating the kill; for example, while loosing a hunting dog or firing a shot, the formula of consecration used in slaughter should be recited either aloud or mentally.

The blood of the slaughtered animal must be drained as completely as possible. Blood is forbidden as food in Islam, as in Judaism, because it is considered to be the substance which joins the physical body and the psyche in the individual, and can therefore transmit psychic elements from one creature to another.

When *ḥalāl* meat from ritually slaughtered animals is not available, it is permissible for Muslims to resort to meat slaughtered by Christians or Jews in accordance with the Koranic principle that "necessity creates exceptions". *See* FOOD.

Riwāyah. Oral transmission or tradition; in particular the traditions of the ways of reciting the Koran. *See* QIRĀ'AH.

Rock, Dome of, *see* DOME of the ROCK.

Rosary (*Subḥah*, pl. *subuḥāt*; or *misbaḥah*, pl. *masābiḥ*). The rosary in Islam is made up of 99 beads, the number of the Names of God. The Name Allāh is represented by the alif, or the piece in which the two threads of the rosary are joined together. The most common subdivision is into three sections, each of 33 beads, but other subdivisions exist depending upon the litanies (*awrād*, sing. *wird*) which are to be recited. Such litanies are used particularly in Sufi orders, although some are in general use. Various formulas including the *shahādah* ("There is no God but God"), the *ḥamdallāh* ("Praise be to God"), the *tasbīḥ* (*subḥāna' Llāh*; "God be Glorified"), or phrases from the Koran, form the recitation of the rosary which is essentially a means of concentration. The systematic repetition of the same words fixes them, or their idea, in a moment outside the flow of time, reinforcing concentration.

Because the Prophet himself used his fingers to keep count of recitations, moving the thumb across the finger-joints of one or both hands, typically to count out formulas recited 33 times after the end of the prayer (*ṣalāt*), the Wahhābīs opposed the use of the rosary as an innovation, even though it had been used for a long time in Islam. Its use is so deeply established, however, that opposition is rarely heard today.

The members of some Sufi orders wear a large rosary around their necks as a sign of their commitment. The widespread habit of the Turks, and some other Islamic peoples, of carrying a rosary in the hand at all times, ostensibly as a mnemonic device to encourage constant remembrance of God, was taken up in the Balkans as a profane custom of busying the fingers to pass the time which led to the unfortunate expression "worry beads". *See* WIRD.

Rozah. The Persian term for the Arabic sawm, or fast. *See* FAST; RAMAḌĀN.

Rubā'iyyāt, the (from sing. *rubā'iyyah*, or *quatrain*). Any poem written in quatrains, but above all a collection of verses in Persian attributed to the mathematician and astronomer 'Umar Khayyām (d. *517*/1123).

The free translation by Edward Fitzgerald (1809-1883) became justly world famous and is perhaps more remarkable, both as poetry and substance, than the original, which it brought to everyone's attention. Fitzgerald's poem is made up of variations on themes found in Khayyām's poems, and is a distillation of Platonism in Sufi guise. Few of Fitzgerald's verses exist as such in the Persian; yet all, or almost all of them, echo something from the Persian originals. What Khayyām himself wrote cannot be known with certainty, for his Rubā'iyyat exist only in manuscripts which date centuries after his death; more than 1,500 quatrains are attributed to him, and many of these are also attributed to other poets. It may be that the name Khayyam simply was a peg upon which were hung intellectual, free-thinking, or gnostic verses from all sources. Moreover, the popularity of Fitzgerald's work inspired the creation of a number of forged manuscripts in this century which added more corridors to the Khayyām labyrinth; in many ways, Khayyām in Persian has become the reflection of Khayyām in Fitzgerald's English.

The Fitzgerald translation is an extremely intelligent compilation of Sufi (and anti-Sufi) ideas so successfully disguised as hedonism that it is often, perhaps even usually, thought to be praise of the pursuit of pleasure. Which it is, but in its antinomianism it is sometimes also the exact opposite: the tavern is the *khānaqah*, or meeting place of dervishes, wine the remembrance of God, and the Beloved, God Himself. Being two opposite tendencies at the same time, it draws the mind into itself all the better. Fitzgerald himself professed to take its disguise at face value; yet as the real creator of the "Rubaiyat of Omar Khayyam", he crammed it as full of Sufi lore as only a 19th-century Victorian orientalist could. But he was not the only one to do so: in 1853, Captain Sir Richard Burton (1821-1890) wrote the "Kasīdah of Hājī Abdū el-Yezdi (translated and annotated by His friend and Pupil F.B.)" The F.B. (Francis Baker, his middle and his mother's name) is Richard Burton himself. This rubā'iyyat becomes philosophical in the same way as Fitzgerald, quotes Ḥāfiẓ and Khayyām and deals with the same themes, almost as successfully as Fitzgerald, who published his in 1861. *See* 'UMAR KHAYYĀM.

Rūdakī, Farid ad-Din. (d. *343*/954). The first great modern Persian poet (although there was a predecessor called Ḥandhala of Badghis under the Ṭahirids.). He was born in Transoxiana and was the court poet of the Sāmanīd ruler al-Amīr as-Sa'īd Naṣr II ibn Aḥmad (d. *331*/943). He wrote this panegyric for this ruler:

The Ju-yi Muliyan we call to mind,
We long for those dear friends we left behind.
The sand of Oxus, toilsome though they be,
Beneath my feet were soft as silk to me.
Glad at the friend's return, the Oxus deep
Up to our girths in laughing waves shall leap.
Long live Bukhara! Be thou of good cheer!
Joyous towards thee hasteth our Amir!
The Moon's the Prince, Bukhara is the sky:
O sky the Moon shall light thee by and by!
Bukhara is the mead, the Cypress he:
Receive at last O mead, the Cypress tree!

The Ju-yi-Muliyan is a stream near Bukhara. The poem went on "Surely are renown and praise a lasting gain, even though the royal coffers loss sustain." The hint was well taken and he received a great reward. Also legend said that the Amir set out immediately for Bukhara without waiting to put on his boots.

Only a small number of the vast opus attributed to him has survived, but he had a decisive influence on every genre of Persian literature. Hedonist and unconventional. Legend has it that his eyes were put out at the orders of his royal patron for being an Ismā'īlī or Qarmaṭī, (i.e. a Manichean). More likely he went blind naturally rather than for his beliefs since such metaphysics were not unusual in Central Asia at the time; it is later commentators who probably felt it necessary to assure posterity for the sake of morality that Rūdakī's freethinking, or indeed, outright Manicheism, had not gone unpunished.

Rudaki the harp will play,
'Gin ye the wine, as he the lay.
Molten ruby or ruby wine,
None who sees it may divine,
Since Nature of one stuff did shape
The solid gem, the liquid grape.
Untouched it stains the fingers red:
Untasted, flies into the head.

Rūḥ (lit. "spirit"). The word is used in all the possible meanings of "spirit", but in particular means the non-individual aspect of the soul, the intellect or *nous*, in Arabic *al-'aql al-fa'āl* (or *fā'il*) ("active intellect"), as opposed to the lower individual soul, the psyche, in Arabic an-nafs.

The spirit (*ar-rūḥ*) in the individual is continuous with Being itself, *al-wujūd*, or *al-'aql al-awwal* ("first intellect"), and is the dignity which exalts man above animals, and even above Angels. This is signified by the ability of Adam in the garden to name the objects of existence, which the Angels could not do and by which they recognized Adam's superiority over them, except of course Iblīs, the devil, who saw in Adam only clay — and not spirit — and so revolted against God.

Within the individual, *ar-rūḥ* is also referred to as *al-ḥaqīqah* ("reality") or *as-sirr* ("the secret"). The center of Being, which is the point of transition to creation, is symbolized by an Angel (also called *ar-Rūḥ*), who is so great that, whereas the other Angels can form rows, *ar-Rūḥ* occupies a whole row by himself. This Angel corresponds to the *Metatron* in Hebrew or to *buddhi* in certain contexts in Sanskrit. The origin of the Ruh is doubtless the *Spenta Mainyu*, or 'Holy Spirit of God' in Zoroastrianism.

Rūḥ Allāh (the "spirit of God"), is a special name of Jesus (4:169) in the Koran (and also of Adam, but it is not used as his epithet: 15:29). *See* FIVE DIVINE PRESENCES.

Rukhkh. The Arabic name of the phoenix, but *rukhkh* has also been used for other mythical and gigantic birds such as the Hindu *Garuḍa*. The name is presumably derived originally from the Hebrew *ruakh* ("spirit"), corresponding to the Arabic *rūḥ*. The phoenix is, in fact, the spirit; more exactly, it symbolizes the vertical intervention of the spirit in the processes of transformation, "rebirth" from ashes, new life emerging out of the corruption of death, and the transmission of the seeds from one cycle of manifestation to the other. It is an important symbol in alchemy and in cosmology, and mirrors both the immortality of the soul in its victory over death, and also the transcendence of the Intellect in relation to the soul. The Arabic *rukhkh* comes into English as "rook", the alternative word for the "castle" in chess, *rukhkh* alone being used in the game as played in Persia and the Middle East.

ar-Rukn al-yamanī (lit. "the southern" or "Yemeni corner"). The corner of the Ka'bah which contains the Black Stone. *See* BLACK STONE; KA'BAH.

Rukū' (Ar. "a bow"). The name of the bow in the canonical prayer (*ṣalāh*). There are certain passages in the Koran where it is clear from the sense of the words, and also from there being some symbol or the word *rukū'* in the margin, that the reader and his listeners should bow, at that moment, which is done in the direction of Mecca. This is done even if the passage occurs during the recitations within the prayer (*ṣalāh*); after the bow the prayer continues normally. There are also passages in the Koran where a prostration or sujud is similarly performed.

A *rukū'* is also the name of a section of a Sūrah of the Koran often marked in texts by a ḥamzah or an *'ayn* in the margin. *See* RAK'AH; ṢALĀH.

ar-Rūm (lit. "the Romans"). The name the Koran and the Arabs gave to both the Byzantines and the Romans of the western empire as well. To this day in dialectical Arabic, the adjective *rūmī* refers to that which is western or non-indigenous.

Rumelia. Lands of the Ottoman Empire in Europe. The word is derived from Rūm ("Rome"), a term used by Muslims to designate Byzantium, and the whole of Christian Asia Minor before its conquest by Islam.

ar-Rūmī, Jalāl ad-Dīn, *see* JALĀL ad-DĪN ar-RŪMĪ.

Ruqayyah. One of the daughters of the Prophet and his first wife Khadījah. She emigrated to Abyssinia with her husband 'Uthmān ibn 'Affān. After the Hijrah they both went to Medinah. She died in Medinah while the Battle of Badr was taking place.

Ruqyah (lit. "incantation"; pl. *ruqā*). These are incantations, sometimes in unrecognizable sounds, which are used to ward off evil or harm. Many have existed since pre-Islamic times. The Arabs presented the incantations they knew to the Prophet who, one by one, accepted some as lawful and rejected others. Some were ascribed to anterior Prophets. Most surviving incantations today are based on the Koran. *See* AMULETS; ĀYAT al-KURSĪ; ḤIZB al-BAḤR; REFUGE.

Russia. Russian Federation; population 149,909,089; Ethnic Russians are 82%; Peoples of Muslim origin (not all of whom are believers) are around 30,000,000. Besides Christians and Muslims there are two peoples, Kalmuck and Buryat who are nominally Tibetan Buddhist; others belong to other schools of Buddhism and, in addition, many peoples are Shamanist. The largest single ethnic group of Muslim origin are the Tatars who are 4%, followed by Kazakhs and Bashkirs; the majority of the others are also, like Tatars, of Turkic origin, with the exception of the Tajiks and the Ossetians who are Iranians. Most of those Muslim ethnic groups found in the Caucasus and the Daghestanis are not Turkic, except for the Balkars. Ethnic groups who are of Muslim origin are: Abkhazi, Adygei, Aguls, Azeris, Balkars, Bashkirs, Chechens, Cherkess, Crimean Tatars, Dargins,

Dungan, Gypsies (Central Asian Gypsies are Muslim; in other regions they are mostly Russian Orthodox); Ingush, Iranians, Kabardians, Karachai, Karakalpaks, Kazakhs, Kirghiz, Kumyks, Kurds, Laks, Lezgins, Nogai, Ossetians, Rutuls, Tabasarans, Tajiks, Talysh; Tatars, Tats, Tsakhurs, Turkmen, Turks, Uighurs, and Uzbeks. Many individuals of Muslim origin have a very tenuous understanding of Islam. Some ethnic groups have their own republics within the Russian Federation and outside of it. The Tatars are centered around the Volga and Kazan, and are scattered throughout European Russia (and are found in Poland, as well); in the Crimea (now part of the Ukraine) there are large Muslim populations, and the Caucasus are almost entirely peoples of Muslim affiliation. A great deal of inter-marriage between Christians and Muslims has taken place within the former Soviet Union. Most Russian Muslims belong to the Ḥanafī school; a few are Shāfi'ī. The dominant Sufi orders are the Naqshbandī, the Qādirī (in the North Caucasus a more radical branch called the Vis ("Uways") Haji appeared in the 1950s), the Yasavī (with two offshoots: the Laachi, who were pro-Soviet in the beginning of the Bolshevik revolution, and the "Hairy Ishans" who were actively anti-Soviet starting in the 1920s), and the Kubrawī, all of whom are from Central Asia, closely related to each other, and are among the most explicity radically dualist of mystic groups.

Ru'yā (lit. "vision"). The word is often used metaphysically for intellectual understanding or, again, psychic visions or intuitions. It may refer to a prophetic dream, as when the prophet dreamed before the treaty of Ḥudaybiyyah, that he and his people had entered the Sacred Mosque at Mecca without hindrance, in order to perform the rites: "God has already fulfilled in truth the dream [vision, *ar-ru'yā*] for His Prophet..." (48:27).

Rūzbihān Baqlī (d. *606*/1209). Persian Sufi of Shirāz, nicknamed *Shaṭṭah al-Fars*, "the Braggart of Fars" perhaps on account of such verses as:

That which the eyes of Time have never seen,
And which no tongue to earthly ears hath told,
Its tint hath now displayed in this our day:
Arise, and in our day this thing behold!

'From Farthest East to Threshold of the West
I in this age am guide to God's Straight Road.
How can the Gnostic pilgrims me behold?
Beyond the Far Beyond's my soul's abode!"

He travelled widely, preached in Shirāz, wrote the *Laṭā'ifu-l-Bayān* ("Subtleties of Enunciation"), *Mashrabu-l-Arwāh* ("Fount of Inspiration of Souls"), *Mantiqu'l-Asrār* ("Language of Mysteries") and was part of the current to which Ibn 'Arabi belonged, and Najm ad-Dīn Kubra.

S

Sabā'. One of the kingdoms of ancient South Arabia, the capital of which was Ma'rib, near a famous dam that collapsed around AD 580, an event which sent a wave of lamentation through the desert tribes. For the Arabs this was one of the few markers in an otherwise timeless world; an age had passed.

In the Bible this kingdom is called Sheba, and it reached the heights of its development in the 6th century BC, having colonized Abyssinia four centuries previously. The Queen of Sabā', known in Islam as Bilqīs, is accorded a prominent place in Islamic lore as the consort of King Solomon. *See* BILQĪS; MA'RIB DAM.

As-sab' al-Mathānī (lit. "the seven repeated [lines]"). A popular name for the Fātiḥah, or opening Sūrah of the Koran. The Fātiḥah is recited several times in every ritual prayer (*ṣalāh*), and on numerous occasions as a universal prayer.

Ṣābians (Ar. *Ṣābi'*, pl. *Ṣābi'ūn* or, collectively, *aṣ-Ṣābi'ah*). A people named in the Koran (2:59; 22:17), along with Christians, Jews, and Magians (the Zoroastrians), as having a religion revealed by God. Many religious groups, including various Christian branches, and various groups in India, have at one time or another been identified as Ṣābians.

An ethnic group in Ḥarrān in northern Mesopotamia (today Altinbasak in Southern Turkey near Urfa), who were more or less Hellenistic Hermeticist pagans with roots in ancient Babylonian religions, once claimed to be the Ṣābians as a means of escaping persecution for their non-Islamic beliefs. A number of famous scholars, particularly mathematicians, originated among these people, including the astrologer and scientist Thābit ibn Qurrā and the alchemist Jābir ibn Ḥayyān. However, it is the Mandaeans or Nasoreans of 'Irāq, or their predecessors, who are the people most likely to be the Ṣābians of the Koran.

Al-Bīrūni thought the Ṣābians were a synthesis of Judaism and the religion of the Magians. A very profound observation: all the Gnostic groups were not by any means all Jewish but in fact extensions of Semitic Babylonian and Syrian cults mixed with religious influences of Iranian origin to which Neo-Platonism was added later. Christian scholars, who saw many religions as Christian "heresies" still persist in calling Gnosticism the result of Christianity. But Christianity itself, with its obvious Zoroastrian antecedents, along with the more purely Gnostic sects, are indeed the result of the vast philosophical-religious reaction that took place when Zoroastrianism mingled with Semitic religions after the conquest of Babylon by Cyrus in 550 BC The Indo-European tendency is to create metaphors, or abstractions out of things material; the Semites had a tendency to take the abstract, to take ideas and concretize them, almost literally in fact, by making divinities into stones. The reaction between the diametrically opposed tendencies, like the reaction between acid and alkali was dynamic, and new religions resulted, the Gnostic sects and currents on the Semitic side along with Christianity and Islam, and, and Zurvanism, Mithraism, and Manicheism on the Iranian side.

The very fact that many different groups were assimilated to the name and that it is difficult to fix the Koranic term definitively to any one of them, made the concept of the Ṣābians into an open door for toleration to any religion which upon examination appeared to be an authentic way of worshiping God. Nevertheless, the word "Ṣābians" derives from the Aramaic *ṣb'*, a meaning of which is "to baptize". (Baptizing, however, need not be taken literally, for it may refer to ritual ablutions of the kind learned from the Zoroastrians, which are at the origin of Christian baptism and Muslim ablutions). This, along with numerous indications in the Koran, points to the identification of the Ṣābians with the ancient "baptizing" sects of 'Irāq, forerunners of the Mandaeans of today, and with the Elkhasites in particular, out of whom came Mani. Indeed, some have maintained that the term actually means the Manicheans themselves. (In the *Encyclopedia of Islam* 2nd Edition, the article Ṣābi' maintains that they are not Elkhasites but Manicheans; the article *Ṣābi'a* inclines to Elkhasites.) In any case, Elkhasites, Mandaeans, and Ebionites are so similar, that it hard to believe that they could be anything but different branches of the same stock. Wellhausen recorded the fact that the followers of Muḥammad were originally called Ṣābians by the Meccans. *See* ELKHASAIOS; ḤARRĀNIANS; MANICHEISM; MANDAEANS.

Sabīl Allāh (lit. "way of God"). The general name, used in the Koran, for all those acts which are pleasing to God.

Sacrifice. The Arabic words *aḍḥā*, *dhabaḥa* and *naḥara* all mean primarily "to slaughter an animal", "to immolate"; the noun "*qurbān*" implies a sacrifice with or without slaughter, and is derived from the verb *qaruba* ("to draw near"), related to the Hebrew *qorbān*, of the same significance. *Al-'Īd al-Kabīr*, or the *'Id al-Aḍḥā*, which commemorates Abraham's sacrifice of the ram in the place of his son, is the most prominent sacrificial rite, and takes place on the 10th of Dhu-l-Ḥijjah. The 10th, 11th, and 12th are possible days for the sacrifice which may be any of the acceptable animals: a sheep, a camel, a cow, or a goat. The sacrifice is performed according to the rules of ritual slaughter with the words *Bismi-Llāh*; *Allāhu akbar* (instead of *Bismi-Llāhi-r-Raḥmāni-r-Raḥīm*), the blood is drained and the meat used for food. It is not lawful to sell the animal for gain after sacrifice.

Sacrifice may be performed at any time with the intention of coming closer to God. It is the custom to perform the sacrifice called *al-'aqīqah* when a child is born. *See* RITUAL SLAUGHTER.

de Sacy, Baron Silvestre (1758-1838). The most distinguished Orientalist of his time and the founder of the modern school of Arabic scholarship in Europe. The son of a notary, de Sacy was born in Paris. Educated for the civil service, he studied jurisprudence and in 1781 obtained a government post which he held until 1791.

An indefatigable worker, he had little need of rest; in the course of his work and studies he learned the principle Semitic languages and published studies on the Bible. He began the decipherment of Sāssānid Pahlavī inscriptions. During the French revolution he retired from the civil service and lived in seclusion until 1795 when he was called to be professor of Arabic in the newly founded École Spéciale des Langues Orientales Vivantes.

This was the occasion of furthering his already vast knowledge of Oriental languages. He wrote *La Grammaire Arabe* and *La Chrestomatie Arabe*. He was deeply familiar with Arabic literature. Among his works are a translation of the *Maqāmāt* of Ḥarīrī; he prepared an edition of *Kalilah wa Dimnah*, and the *Alfiyyah* of Ibn Malik. Many subsequent Arabists were his students: Freytag, Fluegel, Fleischer, Ahlwardt, Tornberg, Rosegarten, De Slane, Quatrem re and Reinaud. Several chairs of Oriental studies were created in French universities upon his recommendation, as also in Prussia and Russia. He was a founder of the Societé Asiatique in whose publication his own work reached the public; he was peer of the realm of France, a grand officer of the Legion of Honor, and the holder of many foreign titles.

Sa'd ibn Abī Waqqāṣ (d. *55*/674). One of the most famous Companions and earliest converts to Islam, also a veteran of all the Battles. He is one of the "Ten well-betided ones" who were told by the Prophet that they were assured a place in paradise.

Under the Caliph 'Umar, Sa'd ibn Abī Waqqāṣ led the armies in the battle of Qādisiyyah against the Persians in *16*/637 and was the first governor of Kūfah, which he founded. He was one of the electors of the third Caliph, 'Uthmān. *See* COMPANIONS.

Sa'd ibn Mu'ādh (d. *5*/626). The chief of the tribe of 'Aws and one of the early converts from Medinah. Upon his deathbed, after being wounded in the Battle of the Trench, Sa'd passed the judgement which sealed the fate of the Jews of the Banū Qurayẓah. *See* QURAYẒAH.

Ṣadaqah (lit. "righteousness", from the root *ṣadaqa*, "to speak truth", "to be true"). The voluntary giving of alms (as opposed to *zakāh* which is obligatory) to the needy. In the Koran the word is used very frequently in the plural *ṣadaqāt* ("deeds of kindness and generosity"). "God will efface usurious increase [*ar-ribā*] but will increase [profit] from deeds for charity [*aṣ-aṣadaqāt*] and God has no love for any disbeliever or sinner." (2:276) A particular form of *ṣadaqah* is the distribution to the poor of a quantity of grain at least equal to about two quarts, or its monetary equivalent, for every member of the household upon the *'Īd al-Fiṭr* at the end of Ramaḍān.

Sa'dī, Muṣlaḥ ad-Dīn (*580-692*/1184-1292). A famous poet of Shirāz in Persia, and a didactic moralist. His major works are the *Bustān*, ("The Fruit Garden"), the *Gūlistān* ("The Rose Garden"), and his *Dīwān*. He studied at the Niẓāmiyyah of Baghdad and took the name Sa'dī from his protector Sa'd ibn Zengī, the Atabeg of Fars.

Sa'dī was a Sufi, having been the disciple of Shihāb ad-Dīn Suhrawardī. Much of Sa'dī's life was spent in travel. He visited the Gujarat and Delhi (where he learned Indian languages), the Yemen, and North Africa.

Near Jerusalem he was captured by the Franks and worked at hard labor until ransomed. In Syria he was appointed prayer-leader (*Imām*) and preacher (*khatīb*) at a Friday congregational mosque. He died in Shirāz where he returned after the age of 70.

Ṣadr ad-Dīn Shirāzī, *see* MULLĀ ṢADRĀ.

Ṣadr-i a'zam. In Ottoman Turkey and Iran, the chief minister, or what in Arab lands was called the Wazir.

aṣ-Ṣādūq, *see* IBN BABAWAYH.

Ṣafā and Marwah. Two small hills, one now partly removed to make a roadway, near the Ka'bah in Mecca. What remains of both hills is enclosed within the Grand Mosque (*al-Masjid al-Ḥarām*). The two hills are separated by a distance of 394m/1247ft. Between them is a course which is called the *mas'ā*. This distance (293m/927ft) is walked, and in part run, seven times by those performing the *ḥajj* or *'umrah*. This ritual going back and forth between the two hills is called the *sa'y* (the "run", "course" or "endeavor"). The names of both hills are different words for rock or stone, and the origin of the rite of the *sa'y* is the casting to and fro of Hagar looking for water for her son. *See* HAGAR; ISMĀ'ĪL; PILGRIMAGE; SA'Y.

Ṣafavids. A dynasty which ruled Persia from *907-1145*/1501-1732. The first Ṣafavid, Ismā'īl, used Shī'ism as a power base to rally support and to deny the legitimacy of those he was supplanting. The Ṣafavids made Twelve-Imām Shī'ism the state religion of Iran, thereby establishing the basis for internal unity, but tending also to isolate Iran from its Sunnī neighbors, as well as laying it open to the tensions inherent in Shī'ism.

The actual Shī'ism of the Ṣafavid and the *Qīzīl Bash* who were their support, at least since Junayd the father of Haydar and grandfather of Ismā'īl, was a good deal more extreme than Twelver Shī'ism because Ismā'īl left an important collection of poems in Turkish in which he clearly refers to himself as "God", as did Shaykh Junayd who ruled over the military religious brotherhood from 1447 to 1456. The Ṣafavids appear to have been of Kurdish stock with followers in Anatolia who became feudal lords of Ardabil; but they spoke a Turkish dialect of Azerbaijan.

Ismā'īl claimed to represent the Twelfth, or "Hidden" Imām, and, in order to intensify political passions he introduced the cursing of the first three Caliphs. In the long run, however, his emphasizing the claims of the Hidden Imām made all rulers theoretically illegitimate substitutes, thus introducing the seeds of political instability (*See* HIDDEN IMĀM.) Moreover, since the efficacy of the religion also depended upon the Hidden Imām, the door was open to others who could claim to represent him; in the 19th century this led to the birth of dissident sects, one after the other: the Shaykhīs, the Bābīs, the Bahā'īs.

The Ṣafavid dynasty originates from Shaykh Isḥāq Ṣafī ad-Dīn (d. *735*/1334) who lived in Ardabil in Azerbaijan. He was the head of a Sufi order called, after the Shaykh, the Ṣafavī Order; this name was adopted to designate the dynasty. (In Europe it became confused with Sufism, so that the Shah was sometimes called the "Grand Sophi".) The order was associated with Shī'ism and its adherents were seven Turkic tribes called the *Qīzīl Bash*, or "red caps", after the caps they wore, which had tassels standing for each of the twelve Imāms. Legend said that some of the followers were descended from captives freed by Tīmūr to honor Shaykh Ṣafī ad-Dīn, who was given control of the region. The Ṣafavids later claimed that Shaykh Ṣafī ad-Dīn was descended from the seventh Shī'ite Imām, Mūsā-l-Kāẓim, and thus, improbably, from 'Alī.

A descendant of this Shaykh, Junayd, married the sister of Uzun Ḥasan, one of the last Aq Qoyunlu rulers. The son of this union, Haydar, was married by Uzun Ḥasan to his daughter. The son of Haydar, Ismā'īl, turned against the Aq Qoyunlu ruler, however, and with the *Qīzīl Bash*, using Shī'ism as a political and ideological base, began expanding his power. He took the title of Shah and became the first Ṣafavid king.

At first the Ottomans were the greatest threat to Ṣafavid rule but, when they became increasingly preoccupied with expansion into Europe, Shah 'Abbās I ("the Great") took the opportunity to make peace with them, and was thus able to turn his attention to repressing the Uzbek tribes that perennially raided into Persia. Shah 'Abbās moved his capital from Qazvīn to Iṣfahān. His reign marked the peak of the Ṣafavid dynasty's achievements in art, diplomacy, and commerce. It was probably around this time that the court, which originally spoke a Turkic language, began to use Persian.

Following the example of the Ṣafavids, and with military help and propaganda from Persia, other Twelve-Imām Shī'ite regimes were established in various parts of India: Yūsuf 'Ādil Shāh in *908*/1503 made Shī'ism the state religion of Bījāpūr in the the Bahmānī kingdom; Sultan Qūlī founded a Shī'ite dynasty, the Quṭb Shāhī, in Golconda in Hyderabad. Shams ad-Dīn 'Irāqī from Gīlān, a follower of Muḥammad Nurbaksh, propagated Sufism of a Shī'ite inspiration in Srinagar, and Bābūr the Great, the Moghul Emperor, was helped by Ismā'īl I, and his troops wore the *Qīzīl Bash* cap for a time.

In Persia, the Ṣafavid dynasty was followed by that of the Afshārids. *See* AFSHĀRIDS.

Ṣaffārids (*253-900*/867-1495). A dynasty in Sistān, in eastern Persia. The founder, Ya'qūb ibn Layḥ, whose dynastic name came from the profession of coppersmith (*ṣaffār*), raised an army about him at a time of unrest and instability in which the Khārijites who had fled from the west played a role. Although the Ṣaffārids were laid low first by the Sāmānids of Transoxiana, and later by the Ghaznavids, they frequently returned to power as local rulers or governors.

Ṣaḥābat an-Nabī, *see* COMPANIONS.

Ṣāḥib az-Zamān (lit. "the Lord of the Age"). A title given by the Shī'ites to the Twelfth Imām whom they believe to be the Mahdī. *See* HIDDEN IMĀM.

Ṣaḥīfah (lit. "a portion of writing", pl. *ṣuḥuf*). 1. Any of the books revealed to the Divine Messengers who came before the Prophet.

2. The name of a notebook that may have been kept by 'Alī ibn Abī Ṭālib, which gave rise to the legend of a book of secret prophecies, supposedly known only to the descendants of the Prophet and called the *Kitāb al-Jafr*; Shī'ites maintain that this was retained in the hands of those descendants of 'Alī who were considered to be Imāms. *See* KITĀB al-JAFR.

aṣ-Ṣaḥīḥ (lit. "the sure", "the authentic"). The name of two different collections of Ḥadīth, one by Muslim, and the other by Bukhari. Both are highly authoritative. Together, the collections are called *aṣ-Ṣaḥīḥān*. *See* ḤADĪTH.

Sahl at-Tustarī (*203-283*/818-896). An early mystic who was born in Tustar, Persia and died in Baṣrah, he is credited with many fundamental Sufi intellectual formulations of doctrine and an analysis of the steps in the movement of *metanoia*, repentance or turning to God (*tawbah*), and devotion.

Highly unorthodox, he was one of the teachers of al-Ḥallāj. Sahl at-Tustarī explained the famous Sufi saying ascribed to the Prophet: "I am He and He is I, save that I am I, and He is He" (*ana huwa, wa huwa ana, ghayra an ana ana, wa huwa huwa*) as "a mystery of union or realization" at the center of the Saint's personality, called the *sirr* ("the secret"), or the heart, where existence joins Being. Sahl at-Tustarī said: "God is [only] known by the union of contraries attributed to Him."

He said that he was the disciple of "ancient masters" (thus, presumably pre-Islamic ones) and spoke of the essence of Muḥammad as "a column of light" *'amud an-nur* which had *emanated* from God Himself and "which had bowed down before Him a million years before the Adamic Covenant, and which has been disseminated in particles of uncreated certitude (*yaqin*) in a certain number of hearts, those of the intimate elect... In his pristine perfection man exists in the form of a particle of light as an atom (*darr*)." "Tustarī claimed to have met 'One thousand five hundred righteous ones (*siddiqin*, among them forty substitutes (*budala'*) and seven pegs (*awtad*),' and said: 'Their path (*ṭarīqah*) and their way (*madhab*) is the same as mine.'" This formulation was also used by Shibli in referring to Hallāj, and may have been a formula of recognition, like a secret handshake. Tustarī addressed people as *dost* meaning friend in Persian, perhaps a forerunner of the title *rafiq* (Arabic "comrade") later used by the Assassins, or an address of sects which called themselves "Friends of God" (which is as much as to say that they called themselves "saints"). That this detail was preserved by history shows that someone deemed it to be a clue to Tustarī's ideology.

At-Tustarī compiled, along with a group that he led, a commentary on the Koran, called simply *Tafsīr al-Qur'ān*. He said that the Koran contained several levels of meaning. These could be reduced to the outer (*ẓāhir*), accessible to the common man (*'āmm*), and the inner (*bātin*), accessible only to the elect (*ḥāṣṣ*). (In addition there were, he said, a "limit", ḥadd, and a *maṭlā*, "point of transcendence"). By this device of splitting doctrine into "inner" and "outer", at-Tustarī
and his colleagues adapted such philosophy of Persian inspiration into the "inner meaning" as would have normally been rejected by Islamic doctrine had it been taken at its face value. Tustarī treated time as three moments: "Man's existence in this world is suspended between the Day of Covenant and the Day of Resurrection. On his course from pre-existential infinity (*ibtida'*) to post-existential infinity (*intiha'*) man passes through his phenomenal existence, marked by the moment of his creation and the instant of his death." He created a construct of individual "pre-existence" in the form of a "Day of Covenant" (*yawm al-mithāq*), in which, he said, individuals had already existed in the form of light particles. Something like this can be found in the Koran as the eternal acknowledgment by Adam's *descendants* that God is the Absolute. In the Koran, however, there is no question of "light particles", and without the meaning which the event takes on in at-Tustarīs overall schema.

Then he took the "Day of Resurrection" (*yawm al-Qiyamah*), which of course also exists in the Koran, but in a different sense, as a "post-existence" leading to reintegration of the individual into the Principle after the drama of manifestation; in other words, a kind of divinization. These two, pre-existence and post-existence, together with the present time (which becomes a kind of duration without qualitative evolution), are recognizably the Zurvanite, and above all, Manichean, "doctrine of the three moments" which in this way was Islamicised, (as, by a similar process, it was also introduced into some forms of Chinese Buddhism through the *Sutra of the Two Principles and Three Moments*). With this doctrine, creation is no longer *ex nihilo*, but is instead a transformation or exile of a divine Substance into matter which will ultimately return "to itself" as principle or God. An equation is thus drawn between matter and God. In fact, the whole idea of creation is turned upside down; rather than the world being created out of nothing, it is instead created out of God, and God for Tustarī was a form of light.

At-Tustarī was one of the early "drunken Sufis" who ascribed divinity to himself and made *shatahāt*, or so-called "ecstatic utterances" to this effect. He also used the idea of the *nūr Muḥammadi*, or "Muhammadan Light" which has since become common to many Sufis. Much more strikingly, from the point of view of Iranian comparative religion, he tried to introduce into Islam the idea of "columns of light" (*'umūd an-nūr*); this latter did not find much acceptance outside of some Central Asian and Iranian Sufi groups.

What did leave a big trace was the notion, apparently first introduced by at-Tustarī, that Satan was really the strictest believer, the most perfect monotheist, and the most faithful and unwavering servant of God. This rehabilitation of Satan amounts to the introduction into Islam of a second Absolute in the form of evil or as the "other side" of God. This extremely heretical idea was taken up by some other Sufis (although, of course, not all), notably by al-Ḥallāj (the most prominent pupil of at-Tustarīs school), and by Ibn 'Arabī, 'Aṭṭār, and 'Abd al-Karīm Jilī. An important consequence of this makes God the creator of evil as well as of good, which, though less dramatic than Satan being actually turned into God, is no less far-reaching. An examination of these doctrines which are: God as Light; Satan on a level with God; the three times, and various other motifs, make it clear that Tustarī was a Crypto-Manichean, or *zindiq*. But radical as at-Tustarī was, he was only exiled from his home town; his formulations were so innocuous on the surface that he escaped serious censure during his own lifetime. However, many of his disciples, such as al-Ḥallāj (d. *309*/922), and his later followers such as 'Ayn al-Quḍāt Hamadhānī (d. *525*/1131,) (a disciple of Abū Ḥamīd Muḥammad al-Ghazalīs black sheep brother Aḥmad), Shihāb ad-Dīn Yaḥyā Suhrawardī (d. *587*/1191), and Muḥammad Nūrbakhsh (d. *864*/1465) who enthusiastically presented the same ideas to the public rather than to private circles, aroused the authorities sufficiently to be all put to death. ('Ayn al-Quḍat al-Hamadhāni should not be confused with other equally radical Sufis such as Yūsuf al-Hamadhāni, who died in Merv, today Bayram 'Alī Turkmenistan in *535*/1140, and Sayyid 'Alī ibn Shihāb ad-Dīn ibn Muḥammad al-Hamadhāni, a propagator of the Kubrawiyyah in Kashmir, died *786*/1385 in Pakhli, Kashmir, believed buried in Khotlan, Tajikistan.) *See* ANTINOMIANISM; al-ḤALLĀJ.

Sahm-i Imām ("the share of the Imām"). Monies sent to the Shī'ite holy places for their upkeep, the support of the *'ulamā'*, and for distribution at their discretion.

Saḥūr (or suḥūr). A light meal taken before the dawn and the beginning of the day's fasting in the month of Ramaḍān. In cities and towns many people make rounds in the street at night, calling out or beating drums and playing flutes, as a pious duty to wake the dwellers to partake of the meal.

Sa'i. *See* SA'Y.

Saints (Ar. *awliyā'*, sing. *walī*, from *walī Allāh*, "friend of God"). The term *walī Allāh* ("saint") comes from the Koran (10:63): "Lo, the friends of God, there is no fear upon them, neither do they grieve." There is a widespread cult of Saints throughout the Islamic world, and there are various degrees of sanctity; below the degree of *walī* there is that of *ṭāhir*, or one who is "purified", which could well correspond to the Catholic degree of one who is "blessed".

According to popular belief, above the *walī* there is an invisible hierarchy of Saints who are necessary to cosmological equilibrium. These are the four *awtād* ("the pegs"), the forty *siddīqūn* ("the truthful ones", whence the Jewish idea of *tsadeqs*), and so on.

The doctrine of sanctification is defined by a famous Ḥadīth:

> My servant does not cease to approach Me (God) with acts of personal devotion, until I love him; and when I love him I become the Hearing with which he hears, the Sight with which he sees, the Hand with which he grasps, the Foot with which he walks.

Another Ḥadīth says:

> The Heavens and earth cannot contain me (God) but the heart of my believing servant can contain me.

The highest degree of sanctity in this life is the *'ārif bi-Llāh*, ("the knower through God"), which is the supreme state of realization. This state is the equivalent of *mukti* ("liberation", "realization"), the *'ārif bi-Llāh* corresponding in Sanskrit exactly to the Hindu *jīvan mukta* ("the liberated in life").

Saints' tombs dot the countryside in the Islamic world. Commonly the tomb has a dome (whose sphere symbolizes heaven) which rests upon an octagonal drum (the number eight here represents transformation from one state to another. Eight is the first number in a mathematical progression from four — the stable, material world — to the sphere, heavenly perfection). The octagonal drum rests in turn upon a cubic structure which symbolizes the earth. Thus, symbolically, the tomb resumes the Saint's role as a bridge between heaven and earth.

Many countries have a Saint who is virtually the national patron, or one of several national patrons, for example Mulay Idrīs I in Morocco, and Abū Madyān in Algeria. The French created the name "Maraboutism" from the Arabic marbūṭ (one "who is bound [to God]") for the cult of Saints in North and West Africa.

The Wahhābis categorically deny the idea of Saints on the grounds that it infringes *tawḥīd*. This word means "acknowledging or asserting the Oneness or Uniqueness of God", but the Wahhābis take it to mean the exclusion of the Divine or sacred from anything in creation. Paradoxically, *tawḥīd* is used by others for the idea of "union with God", it is the verbal noun of the verb *waḥḥada* ("to make one", "to unite" "to consider, or admit, as one").

Ibn 'Aṭa' Allāh said in his *Ḥikam*:

> Glory be to Him who has not made any sign leading to His saints save as a sign leading to Himself, and who has joined no one to them except him whom God wants to join to Himself.

See QUṬB.

Sajdah (lit. "a prostration"). The touching of the forehead to the ground during the prayer (*ṣalāh*). There are, moreover, many places in the Koran where the sense of the words advises the performance of a prostration. When one of these passages is read (for example 84:21 or 19:60) readers and listeners perform a brief prostration, either directly from the sitting position, if one is sitting, or from the standing position if, for example, the passage is uttered during the prayer; the prayer is then resumed in the normal order and fashion.

The sense of a Koranic text calling for a prostration is sometimes amplified by printing a line above the determinative words, and the word *sajdah* is then inscribed in the margin. In some cases a *sajdah* during a particular passage of the Koran is a custom of one school of law, but not of the others, and this may also be indicated in the margin of the Koran.

A small prayer rug is called a *sajjādah*, and the word also is the root for *masjid*, a mosque, a place of prostration. *See* PRAYER; ṢALĀH.

Sakb. The Prophet's stallion, which he rode to the Battle of Uḥud. One of the Prophet's camels was called Qaṣwā', and his mule, Duldul.

aṣ-Ṣakhrah, Qubbat, *see* DOME of the ROCK.

Sakīnah (lit. "tranquility", "peace", "calm", from the root *sakana*, "to be quiet", "to abate", "to be still", "to dwell"). In Islam the word designates a special peace, the "Peace of God" which settles upon the heart. "He it is Who sent down the *Sakīnah* into the hearts of the believers, that they might add fresh faith to their faith..." (48:4). Although the word is clearly related to the Hebrew *Shekhinah*, and is used in the Koran to refer to the Ark of the Covenant (2:248), it does not go so far as to mean the indwelling of the Divine Presence. (9:26; 9:40; 48:4; 48:18; 48:26).

Saladin, *see* ṢALĀḤ ad-DĪN al-AYYŪBĪ.

Salaf (lit. "predecessors", "ancestors"). The first generations of Muslims, considered by later generations to be the most authoritative source for Islamic practice and guidance. The comments of these first Muslims are used to elucidate questions whose solutions are not explicit in the Koran and in the Sunnah. The *salaf* cover three generations: that of the Companions of the Prophet, that of the *Tābi'ūn* ("the successors") who knew the Companions, and that of the *Taba' at-Tābi'īn* ("the successors of the successors"). Each successive generation's testimony is less authoritative.

The Wahhābīs do not accord a special validity to the opinions and practices of any authority after the Tābi'ūn, and regard all practices introduced after that generation to be unwarranted innovation, at least in theory; in practice this original severity of view has now been much softened. *See* TĀBI'ŪN.

Salafiyyah. A movement, begun at the turn of the century, whose name derives from the phrase *salaf aṣ-ṣāliḥīn* ("the pious ancestors"), it was founded by Jamāl ad-Dīn al-Afghānī and Muḥammad 'Abduh while they were in exile in Paris. Its influence was centered in Egypt, and increased when 'Abduh became Mufti. Through Egypt, it had a profound influence on the other Arab countries, and similar movements sprang up in other parts of the Islamic world, such as the Aligarh in India and the Muḥammadiyah in Indonesia.

Contrary to the implication of its name and to its claim to be a restoration of the original Islam, it was rather a movement of modernization. Although it denounced lukewarm devotion, its exhortation to piety clothed a call to humanism and "progress". The *Salafiyyah* sought to accommodate Islam to the ideas of secular materialism, and did not hesitate to declare that, where there was conflict between classic Islam and modern needs, Islamic law could be changed. As Mufti, Muḥammad 'Abduh declared that "moderate" interest on deposited capital was legal; he called for the dissolution of the four schools of law, which he saw as an archaism, and for the establishment of a unified law which, in the reshuffling, would incorporate modifications to comply with the demands of modern times. The movement emulated Christian missionary endeavor, and sponsored the training of Islamic propagandists to spread a religion presented as *rational* ("the fast of Ramaḍān is healthy and good for the stomach"), *progressive*, and *better* than Christianity or Judaism. The *Salafiyyah* encompassed the first feminist movements in Islam. By declaring itself disposed to accept the theory of evolution, the movement took modern science as a higher authority than the Koran. The publication *al-Manār* in Egypt was for many years the principal mouthpiece of the *Salafiyyah*.

The movement has now run its course, but its influence has been considerable. Many Muslims with a modern education tend to feel that their beliefs are more surely supported by scientific evidence and rational arguments, than by appeals to the authority of revelation. They find, somehow, that the atomic bomb is mentioned in the Koran and this is, apparently, a solid argument for faith. On the other hand, the curious notion that the totality of modern knowledge is due to Islam alone can also be traced to the *Salafiyyah*. If the idea of making Islam submit to the dictates of the modern world has not found general acceptance, the principles of the *Salafiyyah* have, nonetheless, succeeded to the extent that, in the face of any embarrassing or inconvenient contradiction, Islam has often been simply ignored in favor of the imperatives of the times. In recent times the original ideology of the *Salafiyyah* has been overshadowed by a fundamentalist reaction and has become a term for fundamentalism of the type of the Ahl-i Ḥadīth. The term today is applied not to thinking which seeks accommodation with rationalism, but to groups which are literalist and categorical appliers of Islamic law rather than adaptors as was 'Abduh.

Ṣalāḥ ad-Dīn al-Ayyūbī (*532-589*/1138-1193). The son of Ayyūb, a Kurdish general in the army of the Sultan of Mosul, Saladin, as the Crusaders called him, began his career as a lieutenant to his uncle who led the Sultan's armies against the Fāṭimids of Egypt. The Christians of the Latin kingdom of Jerusalem intervened because the Fāṭimids were not an active and outright enemy and, in fact, sometimes allied themselves with the Crusaders. Saladin's uncle was killed in the campaign; Saladin replaced him as commander, and went on to become Vizier, or minister. In *566*/1171 Saladin supplanted the Fāṭimids in the name of Nūr ad-Dīn, Sultan of Mosul.

From Egypt, Saladin began the conquest of Syria and attacked the Christians. By *571*/1175 he had taken Damascus and declared himself an independent sovereign, recognized by the 'Abbāsid Caliphs. Thereafter he consolidated his empire which extended into Konya in Anatolia, and pressed hard upon the Crusader states by creating a unified kingdom around them. In *583*/1187 he defeated the Crusaders at the Horn of Hattin above Tiberias and conquered Jerusalem, but did not succeed in taking the last Christian stronghold of Tyre.

From Tyre the Crusaders received reinforcements, and in *589*/1191 Richard the Lionheart arrived and took Acre. Thereupon began the period of Crusader warfare which made Saladin a famous figure in the West, the match of Richard in knighthood and the epitome of chivalry. He was acknowledged as a warrior remarkable for his sense of justice and goodwill towards the weak and defenseless.

Saladin died in Damascus, leaving the control of Syria, Palestine, and Egypt divided among his descendants, having founded the Ayyubid dynasty.

Salamlik. 1. In traditional Turkish homes the *salamlik* is the reception area for visitors and, in a general sense, is the part of the house open to men, as opposed to the *haramlik*, the area for women.

2. It was also the name of the ceremonial visits made by the Ottoman Sultan to the royal mosques in Istanbul to take part in Friday prayers.

Ṣalāh (lit. "prayer", "worship", pl. *ṣalawāt.* The verb from which it derives is *ṣallā* ("to hallow"); as an act of God it is translated as "to bless"; as an act of men it is translated as "to pray". It is possible, since the word is used only in its so-called second mode, that it is not originally an Arabic word, but one derived from Aramaic.) *Ṣalāh* is the canonical, or ritual, prayer, as opposed to the spontaneous petitioning of God which is called *du'ā'*. It consists of a series of movements and recitations, and is thus a ritual, more of a liturgy, or an act of worship, than the supplication usually associated with the word "prayer" in the West. As an act of worship, the *ṣalāh* is a yoga which models the body, mind, and soul — the latter in the form of speech — to the invisible prototype of awakened consciousness, or of the individual aware of God. The performance of the *ṣalāh* five prescribed times daily is obligatory (*farḍ*), beginning at the age of reason, which is deemed to be seven years. The performance of additional *ṣalāh* prayers is possible but not obligatory. These voluntary prayers are called nawāfil (sing. *nāfilah*). The obligatory *ṣalāh* is, however, one of the Five Pillars, and is clearly the most important after the *shahādah.*

The *ṣalāh* is composed of a series of movements repeated several times. Each series, or cycle of sacred speech and movement, is called a *rak'ah* (pl. *raka'āt*), a "bowing". Some prayers are "silent" in whole or in part; that is to say, the *fātiḥah* and the chosen passage of the Koran are then not pronounced out loud. Others prayers are spoken aloud throughout, and others again are mixed, two cycles being voiced and the rest silent. Prayers which are performed aloud at their correct time are performed in silence when they are made later.

The obligatory prayers, and a simple method of determining their time (*mīqāt*), are the following:

1. *Ṣalāt aṣ-Ṣubḥ*, or morning prayer; two raka'āt, out loud. Its time is between the moment of dawning when "a thread" of light appears on the horizon, until the actual rising of the sun (*ash-shurūq*). This period of time is called *al-fajr*; this is also the name for a voluntary, silent prayer of two *raka'āt* which can be performed at this time. The same word, *al-fajr*, is loosely sometimes applied to

the canonical morning prayer itself. The *ṣalāt aṣ-ṣubḥ* is commonly performed as a "missed" prayer, that is to say, it is performed upon waking, and in silence.

2. *Ṣalāt aẓ-Ẓuhr*, the noonday prayer; four *raka'āt*, silent. It is performed after the moment when the shadow of a stick set vertically in the ground has reached its shortest length at noon and has begun to lengthen as the sun passes its zenith, until the time of *al-'aṣr.*

3. *Ṣalāt al-'Aṣr*, the late afternoon prayer; four *raka'āt*, silent. It is performed from the moment when the shadow of a vertical stick is equal to the length of the stick *and* the minimum shadow of the stick at noon, at the sun's zenith (from about 3:30 pm), until the setting of the sun. According to Ḥadīth, once the *'asr* prayer is performed, no other prayer can be performed until after the sunset prayer is completed.

4. *Ṣalāt al-Maghrib*, or sunset prayer; three *raka'āt*, the first two *raka'āt* are out loud, the third silent. The prayer may be performed any time during the period of approximately twenty minutes starting four minutes after the sinking of the sun below the horizon until the last red glow (*shifāq*) in the sky.

5. *Ṣalāt al-'Ishā'*, or night prayer; four *raka'āt*, the first two out loud, the last two silent. It is performed after the onset of night until the dawn, but is preferably accomplished before midnight. In congregational prayer it is accomplished within one and one-half hours after the sunset prayer.

In polar regions, where special conditions prevail, the prayer times must be determined by some agreed convention such as, for example, choosing the intervals that would occur at Mecca. Such has been the decision of councils which have considered such special situations.

The *farḍ* prayer may be performed alone, or in groups led by an Imām. A call, the *adhān*, is made at the beginning of the prayer period to summon people to the mosque for prayer. Sometimes this call is repeated twice. It is preferable (*mustaḥabb*) in each case to perform the prayer early in its allotted time period, with the exception of the *ẓuhr*, which may be delayed to avoid the hottest part of the day. For the convenience of the congregants, the *ẓuhr* and the *'aṣr* may be performed together, one after the other, at either the time of the *ẓuhr* or the time of the *'aṣr*. The call for the second prayer in combination is reduced to the *iqāmah*, the secondary call for assembly and rising, which is made inside the mosque immediately before the prayer. The *maghrib* and *'ishā'* prayers may be similarly combined when it is difficult or impossible for the congregation to assemble many times during the day; it is also admissible when praying alone, at the individual's discretion.

There are moments when *ṣalāh* is forbidden: at the rising of the sun; when the sun is overhead at the zenith; and at the actual moment when the sun is setting. A prayer should not be begun at these moments, but may be continued through these if begun before. On Fridays the *ẓuhr* prayer is replaced by the congregational prayer (*ṣalāt al-jum'ah*) for those present in the congregational mosque; it consists of two *raka'āt* prayed silently under the leadership of an Imām. On a journey (in the days of camelback travel the minimum distance of such a journey was the equivalent of forty-five to sixty miles, or seventy-five to one hundred kilometers) in which the traveler spends the night away from home, or spends less than three nights in one place, prayers of four *raka'āt* may be prayed in the shortened form (*bi-t-taqsīr*) of two *raka'āt*. From the fourth night spent in one place the normal prayer length is resumed.

To perform the prayer, the person must be in the state of ritual purity conferred by the greater ablution (*ghusl*) and the lesser ablution (*wuḍū'*). The prayer must be performed in a clean place (not, therefore in a bath house, cemetery, slaughterhouse, and so forth) facing the *qiblah* (direction of Mecca), if this can be determined. If it cannot be determined, prayer can be performed in any direction (as it is done when one is *inside* the Ka'bah).

A man's body must be covered from the navel to the knees; a woman's from the neck to below the elbow and to the ankles. The shoes are removed in a place of prayer. (Some Imāms wear slippers or sandals which they wear only inside a mosque.) If there is coming and going, the space in front should be symbolically delimited by some object placed in front of the worshiper (*sutrah*). For this reason, those praying a solitary prayer choose for preference to stand before the wall or a pillar. The worshiper must formulate the intention of the prayer to be performed by naming it (*niyyah*).

The motions of the prayer are as follows:

1. Standing with the feet only slightly apart, the worshiper raises his arms to the level of his ears, palms open forward, and declares out loud the *takbīr al-iḥrām* ("the consecratory magnificat"): *Allāhu akbar.* (This raising of the hands to the level

of the head occurs only at this first *takbīr*. Some schools, and in practice, some individuals of all schools, raise the hands partway up at every pronunciation of a *takbīr*.) This opens the prayer. Then the hands are placed at the sides in the Māliki rite (as also among the Khārijites), or clasped right over left at the waist above the navel in the Ḥanafī rite, (which was the traditional position of a worshipper in the presence of divinity in ancient Babylonia) or clasped at the center of the chest in the Ḥanbalī rite, or above the heart in the Shāfi'ī rite. (All of these have precedents in the Sunnah of the Prophet; each rite has opted for one possibility without excluding the others, and all are acceptable.) In this standing position, which is called the *qiyām*, the worshiper pronounces the *fātiḥah* (which may or may not be preceded by the *Basmalah*). At the end of the *fātiḥah*, the worshiper says: "*āmīn*". If there is an Imām, and the *fātiḥah* has been said out loud, this āmīn is pronounced as a response by the congregation. In the first two *raka'āt* of the prayer (but not in subsequent *raka'āt*), after the *fātiḥah*, some verses from the Koran are recited, as for example, the *sūrat al-Ikhlāṣ* (112). This recitation is called the *qirā'ah*. Among the Sunnīs, the verses recited at this point are the choice of the person praying or leading the prayer. Among the Shī'ites, the verse is almost always the *sūrat al-Ikhlāṣ*. This ended, the worshiper says: *Allāhu akbar* (the *takbīr* are always said aloud), and bows, placing his hands upon the knees.

2. In this position, which is called the bow (*rukū'*), he says silently: *subḥāna-Llāhi-l-'Aẓīm* ("Glory to God the Mighty") three times, or a similar formula.

3. Rising now to the standing position called *wuqūf*, the worshiper says out loud *sami'a-Llāhu liman ḥamidah* ("God listens to him who praises Him"). Then he, or the congregation following an Imām, says as response: *Rabbanā wa laka-l-ḥamd* ("Our Lord, and to Thee belongs praise").

4. Saying: *Allāhu akbar* out loud while still standing upright, the worshiper then prostrates himself, touching the forehead to the ground and with both palms on the ground. In this position, which is called the *sujūd* or the sajdah, he says silently: *subhāna Rabbiya-l-A'lā* ("Glory to my Lord the Most High"), or a similar formula, three times.

5. He raises himself to a seated position and says: *Allāhu akbar*. In this seated position, called *jalsah* or *julūs*, the Mālikīs say nothing, but the Ḥanafīs add a formula such as: *Rabbī-ghfir-lī*, ("Lord, cover my transgressions"). The correct posture for this seated position involves placing the outside of the left foot underneath oneself with the right foot crouched and the big toe of the right foot hooked on the ground. As hooking the toe on the ground is very difficult, and even painful if not practiced from childhood, no insistence is placed upon this precise position, and all sitting positions with the knees upon the ground can be seen.

6. After having marked a momentary halt seated thus, the worshiper pronounces again: *Allāhu akbar*, and makes a second prostration (*sajdah*) exactly as the first. This completes one cycle (*rak'ah*). If this is the first *rak'ah* of any prayer (except the single *rak'ah* of the voluntary night prayer, the *witr*), the worshiper stands up, pronounces: *Allāhu akbar*, and repeats the cycle again as the second *rak'ah*. At the end of the second and fourth (and final) *rak'ah* of all prayers, and the third (final) *rak'ah* of the sunset prayer, before rising from the sitting position (*jalsah*), or before ending the prayer, while in this sitting position, the worshiper utters a formula known as *at-taḥiyyāt*, or the *at-tashahhud*:

> *At-taḥiyyātu li-Llāhi wa-s-ṣalawātu wa-ṭ-ṭayyibātu; as-salāmu 'alayka ayyuha-n-nabiyyu wa rahmatu-Llāhi wa barakātuh, wa-s-salāmu 'alaynā wa 'alā 'ibādi-Llāhi-ṣ-ṣālihin. Ashhadu an la ilāha illā-Llāh, wa ashhadu anna Muḥammadan 'abduhū wa rasūluh.*

> Salutations, prayers, and good works are all for God. Peace on thee, O Prophet, and God's Mercy, and His blessings. Peace be on us and on all God's righteous servants. I testify that there is no god but God; and I testify that Muḥammad is His servant and His Messenger.

There are in practice minor variations to this formula, as to all others used during the prayer. While reciting these words, the Mālikīs, and sometimes the other schools, move the forefinger of the right hand in a counterclockwise circle, while the hand rests on the knee. During the saying of the *shahādah*, it is the custom to stop the circling movement and to point the finger upwards. If this is the end of the prayer (the second *rak'āt* of the *ṣubḥ*, the third of the *maghrib*, or the fourth of all other prayers), it is the non-obligatory custom to recite at this point a formula called the *qunūt* (*see* QUNŪT). Thereupon the worshiper seals the prayer by turning his head to the right and saying: *as-salāmu 'alaykum*, and then repeating these words to the left. The salutation of closing is called the *taslīm*. Alternately, it can be said once with the head turned right for the beginning of the greeting, and left for the end.

In the Shāfi'ī rite, when the *fātiḥah* is said out loud, the Imām utters the *fātiḥah* first and then pauses to allow those following him to recite the *fātiḥah* silently themselves. At each uttering of the *Allāhu Akbar* (and not only for the opening *takbīr*), the Shāfi'īs raise their hands upwards, as all the schools do for the opening *takbīr*. (For these subsequent *takbīrs*, the Shāfi'īs do not raise their hands upwards as high as for the first.)

It is usual, after the public prayer, to remain seated in order to recite one or more formulas repeated thirty-three times, counting on the fingers. This is an introduction to a *du'ā'*, an individual supplication, which is made with the hands upraised slightly, the palms open upwards. At the end, marked by the words: *al-ḥamdu li-Llāh* ("praise be to God"), the open hands are drawn across the face as if a blessing had fallen into them. Then the worshipers rise and greet those next to them with the words: *as-salāmu 'alaykum* Some then perform individual, voluntary prayers, except after the *'aṣr*. These are usually of two *raka'āt*.

In addition to these voluntary, or Sunnah prayers performed before or after the main prayers, there are additional voluntary and optional prayers at specific times: *ishrāq* after sunrise, *ḍuḥā* before noon, and *tahajjud* at late night along with the witr. The Prophet certainly performed all of these at one time or another, but not necessary all of them all the time. Piety makes numerousness of prayers the preferred expression of zeal. This said, it should perhaps be repeated that the number of obligatory prayers is *five* daily. Multiplicity being the easiest way to express quality or profundity, it was related of the great teacher al-Junayd of Baghdad that he performed three hundred *raka'āt* each day at his shop in the market and four hundred at his house each night, in addition to reciting certain formula thirty thousand times each day. The eloquence of the Arabs has failed here to find a better way than big numbers of saying that al-Junayd was not forgetful of God!

The Friday congregational (*jum'ah*) prayer of two *raka'āt*, replaces the normal noonday prayer and is preceded by a sermon (*khuṭbah*). The Friday prayer is performed in a large congregational mosque which can accommodate a greater number of worshipers than can a neighborhood mosque. It also has a preacher in addition to an Imām, or a preaching Imām; to preach requires in principle greater knowledge than does leading the prayers, which is the minimum that everyone must know. The Friday prayer brings together a larger number of people from different neighborhoods, thus increasing a sense of community. Other exceptional prayers are those of the festivals. On the morning of the festivals of the 'Īd *al-Aḍḥā* and the *'Īd al-Fiṭr*, there is a special prayer of two *raka'āt* for which, in principle, the whole community, or even the whole city, gathers together in a special prayer ground called the *muṣallā* (also called *'idgah*). The peculiarity of the *'Īd* prayer is that it is opened with eight *takbīr*, pronounced slowly one after the other, before the first *fātiḥah*. Six *takbīr* are pronounced before the second *fātiḥah*.

A *ṣalāh* is considered to have been interrupted, and to need repeating from the beginning, by the following actions: talking to others, yawning, laughing (but not suppressing a smile or a yawn), and breaking wind. Chronic conditions such as incontinence and bodily discharge, however, are disregarded as far as effect upon the prayer is concerned; the prayer is performed as if these conditions did not exist.

It is best not to interrupt a prayer except for reasons of *force majeur*, but a prayer which is interrupted is simply said again. Different procedures exist for "repairing" an error made in a prayer, such as losing count of the number of *raka'āt*; the lower number of *raka'āt* is assumed, and the worshiper continues until the end of the prayer. After the closing salutation, he immediately performs two prostrations (*sujūd*) from the sitting position, called the prostrations of *ṣahw* ("attentiveness"). They are finished by the greetings (*taḥiyyāt*) and *as-salāmu 'alaykum* just as if it were the final two *sujūd* of a prayer. If there are other defects, for example of errors added to a prayer, it is customary to add two extra prostrations (*sujūd*) before the closing of the prayer, and then the two *sujūd* described above.

Prayers which are missed at the correct time should be made up afterwards. These are called *qaḍā'* and are prayed silently. Menstruating women do not pray and do not make up missed prayers.

With this exception, despite popular opinion to the contrary, the obligation of *ṣalāh* for women is no less than for men.

If one is prevented by illness or infirmity from praying, it is possible to reduce the motions of the prayer to gestures, or even to intentions of gestures, as it is also possible to pray with gestures on camelback, or horseback, and therefore on any means of conveyance when so obliged.

Special prayers, with some modifications, are also recited upon solar and lunar eclipses, to ask for rain (*istisqā'*), to ask for guidance (*istikhārah*), and for funerals (*janāzah*).

Three people in prayer, one leading and two following, constitute a congregation. If two persons pray together, they pray in one row, and the one who acts as Imām stands on the left and slightly forward. If there are three persons, the two following form a row to the back of the leader, and to one side. Three followers form a row behind the Imām. If a row is complete and can hold no more, a new arrival draws a person from the end of a row — not the middle since this would leave an empty space — to join him to form a new row, and he can do this even if the prayer has begun, during the standing for the *fātiḥah* and *qirā'ah*, even though normally one cannot move oneself once the prayer has begun. Joining others for prayer is recommended rather than praying alone, when possible.

If one comes late to a prayer which has already begun, one joins immediately by saying the *takbīr* of consecration, while the congregation is in the standing position (*qiyām*) or in the bow (*rukū'*). Once they have risen from the *rukū'* and the words: *sami'a-Llāhu*... have been spoken, joining in that cycle of prayer is not possible, and one must wait for another *qiyām*. Having joined, one continues individually after the congregation has stopped, to complete on one's own the total number of *raka'āt* which make up the prayer at hand. If prayer is joined during the *rukū'*, the worshiper pronounces two takbīr, one for entering the prayer and one for moving to the bow.

The form of the *ṣalāh* is a creation of the Sunnah. The inspired nature of the *ṣalāh* is indicated by the tradition that Gabriel came and performed it five times at the right moments of the day and night; the Prophet joined in prayer with the Angel, having learned it from him.

In the *ṣalāh* it is not the individual who prays, but rather it is man as such, a representative of the species or all mankind recognizing his relationship to the Absolute. Or again it is creation, with the voice of man as a universal patriarch, praying to the Creator. The *takbīr*, or *Allāhu akbar* — "God is greater (than anything)" — which opens it, is the door into the Divine Presence, and the subsequent *takbīr* are the acknowledgment that all activity, that all power, is God's alone.

The prayer must be performed in Arabic, which is at once a sacred and a liturgical language, that is, a language which has preserved in its forms and sounds a close correspondence — an analogy — to the metaphysical prototype of the reality it designates, and not merely a convention which subsists after a process of phonetic and linguistic decay. In all prayer, and in the *ṣalāh* in particular, it is *reintegration* into the uncreated which is at issue. The *ṣalāh* vehicles this by its nature, and by its symbolism: the individual is diminished in the bow (*rukū'*), and is extinguished in the protestation (*sujūd*), which takes the shape of the letter *mīm*, the letter of death. The first *sajdah* is the *fanā'*, or the extinction of what is created, leaving, in the symbolism of the sitting, the *baqā'* or "that which persists", which is the immortal soul. In the second prostration, the *fanā' al-fanā'* ("the extinction of the extinction"), all remnants of the contradiction or disequilibrium that creation illusorily poses in the face of the Divine Reality symbolically disappear. The Arabic words, which are sacred words in a sacred language, are an essential aspect of the efficacy of the rite.

Ibn 'Aṭā' Allāh says in his *Ḥikam*:

> Ritual prayer is the place of intimate discourses and a mine of reciprocal acts of purity wherein the domains of the innermost being are expanded and the rising gleams of light ray out. He knew of the existence of weakness in you, so He made the number of ritual prayers small; and he knew of your need of His grace, so he multiplied their fruitful results.

And:

> Ritual prayer is a purification for hearts and an opening up of the door of the invisible domains.

See ABLUTIONS; ADHĀN; ARABIC: DHIKR; 'ĪD al-AḌ ḤĀ; 'ĪD al-FIṬR; ISTISQĀ'; ISTIKHĀRAH; KHUṬBAH; PRAYER.

Ṣalāt *see* ṢALĀH.

Ṣalāt al-Ḥājjah (lit. "prayer of necessity"). A prayer of four to twelve *raka'āt* recited at night to seek Divine remedy from distress.

Ṣalāt al-Jum'ah. The congregational Friday prayer of two *raka'āt* performed in place of the normal noon prayer (*ẓuhr*). It can only be performed in a group and normally follows the *khuṭbah* (sermon).

Ṣalāt al-Khawf (lit. "The Prayer of Fear"). A special form of the canonical prayer used, theoretically, by soldiers in times of imminent danger. The prayer is performed in four *raka'āt*; part of the group prays the first two *raka'āt* and ends its prayer while the Imām stands paused; the other part of the group then prays the next two *raka'āt* behind the Imām while the first resumes guard. It could not have been very practical as a method of worship but could certainly unnerve an unbelieving enemy if performed in the middle of a battle, as it was by Khālid ibn al-Walīd.

Aṣ-Ṣalāh al-Mashīshiyyah, *see* IBN MASHĪSH.

Ṣalāt at-Tarāwīḥ (lit. "prayer of rest"). A voluntary prayer consisting of twenty, thirty-two, or forty *raka'āt* recited at the end of the night before the canonical morning prayer (*ṣubḥ*), and in the evening after the evening prayer (*'ishā'*), only during the month of Ramaḍān. Contrary to the practice of normal prayers, the Imām chooses long Koranic passages for recitation aloud. A pause is made every four *raka'āt* for personal prayer (*du'ā'*).

Because of the long recitations, those behind the Imām who are tired are permitted to remain sitting after the previous *rak'ah* for most of the Imām's standing recitation of the Koran, and to rise just before the first bow (*rukū'*) of the *rak'ah*. The name of the prayer, *Tarāwīḥ* ("rest"), is a euphemism for one of the most strenuous exercises designed to tap religious fervor, when Imāms often have to pray in relays, one taking over for another as his voice or energies fail. *Tarāwīḥ* prayers are not admitted by Shī'ites who regard them as an innovation.

Ṣāliḥ. A Prophet with the rank of Divine Messenger (*rasūl*) mentioned in the Koran as having been sent to the tribe of Thamūd. The symbol of the essence of his message, or *ḥaqīqah*, was a she-camel which his people ham-strung, rather than giving the camel water, as they had been asked. The camel lends itself readily as a symbol of humble endurance and submission to God and of a gift from God to be cherished. Indeed, the Koran makes many references to the camel and to caravans, the support of life. Ibn 'Arabi spoke in a poem of the essences of different religions as camels.

God's punishment came down upon the people of Thamūd in the form of an earthquake (7:73-79). Because the people of Thamūd hewed their homes from rock (7:74), the city has been identified as the Nabatean ruins of Madā'īn Ṣāliḥ (lit. "the cities of Salih") in North Arabia.

Sālik (lit. "a traveler"; pl. *sālikūn*). A member of a Sufi order whose intention is actively to seek the realization of God. This distinction is made because in fact most members of Sufi orders are *mutabārikūn* (sing. *mutabārik*), "those seeking to share in blessings", that is, members whose understanding of spiritual possibilities is limited and whose vocation is above all to seek an increase in blessing for themselves. The *mutabārikūn*, seek more of the viaticum as provided by the exoteric religion, rather than seeking to broach the different dimension to which esoterism is the door.

At one time, the *sālikūn* were travelers not only in a spiritual sense, but also in the sense of going from place to place seeking teachings from different masters. The Prophet said: "Be in the world like a traveler, or like a passer by, and reckon yourself as of the dead." The two categories clearly echo those of electi and auditores.

Salmān the Persian (Salmān al-Fārisī). A Companion who was so close to the Prophet as to be called by him a member of the family (*ahl al-bayt*). Salmān was a Persian who, after becoming a Christian, followed various teachers to Syria. Learning from one of them of the imminent advent of a Prophet in Arabia, he went there. After being betrayed, he was sold into slavery and brought to Yathrib, the town destined to become *Madīnat an-Nabī* ("the city of the Prophet"). When the Prophet arrived, Salmān recognized him as the one foretold.

Among the signs of which Salmān had heard was that this Prophet would have a large lump at the bottom of his back, a symbol of the Seal of Prophecy. One day when Salmān was close to the Prophet and filled with thoughts about this sign, the Prophet, who was facing the other way, nonetheless sensed what was preoccupying Salmān, and he let his cloak drop from his shoulders. When Salmān saw the sign he leaped forward and kissed it.

With the Prophet's help he bought his freedom from slavery and went on to become one of the most important figures of early Islam, ending his life as a governor in the newly conquered regions of 'Irāq during the Caliphate of 'Umar or 'Uthmān. Salmān is a link in many initiatic chains (*salāsil*, sing. *silsilah*), of the Sufis. He is credited with the idea of defending Medinah from the attack of the clans allied with the Quraysh, or the *Aḥzāb*, by building a trench around the city. Referred to by its Persian name *khandaq*, this stratagem was supposedly "unknown" to the Arabs, and it confounded the attacking army. (In fact, there were trenches maintained by the Lakhmids before Islam on territory which was a buffer to the Sāssānid Empire.) After the death of the Prophet and the events of the Saqifa of Medinah in which Abū Bakr was elected Caliph, the Shī'ite traditions say that Salmān said the cryptic words in Persian: *kardīd o nakardīd*: "you have done and you have not done." (That is, according to the Shī'ites, 'Alī should have been elected.)

Because he is pictured as one who offered the Prophet crucial, and one might even say, arcane advice, certain Dualist sects on the fringe of Islam have attributed some curious identities to Salmān al-Fārisī. Some have said that he was the Angel Gabriel in disguise; the 'Alawīs make of him one, and perhaps the highest, of three aspects of Divine theophany along with the Prophet and 'Alī ibn Abī Ṭālib; others have seen in him a secret "Divine emanation". As a foreigner in Medinah, Salman has been assigned the role of *Allogenes* ("he who is born elsewhere") by those sects who are inspired by Hermetic tradition.

The significance of Salmān's being providentially very close to the Prophet in his lifetime has been interpreted as more convincingly foreshadowing the great role that the Persian genius was to play in Islam. Salmān represented the very spirit of the nation that provided so many of the great thinkers, theologians, doctors, philosophers, and scientists who brought the power of their synthesizing imagination and inspiration to shape the historical development of Islam. He is, in all likelihood, not a historical figure, but an allegory. Massignon saw in him a literary projection of the Iranian primordial man, Khormuzta, into events that were to affect the Iranian world so profoundly from the outside. As an allegory he plays no historical role after the death of the Prophet as do actual Companions and his burial place is symbolically the Taq, the ruined Sāssānid palace of Ctesiphon, outside of Baghdad.

Samā' (lit. "listening"). The use of music by most Sufis as a means of inspiration or as an aid to contemplation. Music is forbidden in Islam, because it can bear the soul away, but is, nevertheless, practiced everywhere. It is now tolerated even by the Wahhābīs who, when taking Mecca in 1924, were aroused to religious fury by the sound of military trumpets sounding reveille.

Despite the legal prohibition on music, it was, even from early times, and still is today, a common practice among many Sufi *ṭuruq* to use music together with religious poetry to call forth a contemplative attitude in the soul. In particular, music is used to create the appropriate state of mind for the performance of the *ḥaḍrah*, or sacred dance. It is because of this esoteric aspect of music that it was admitted by the Sufis even while being prohibited by exoterism.

Al-Ḥujwīrī says:

> Theologians agree that listening to instrumental music is permissible so long as it is not merely for amusement, and does not induce sinful thought. But the merely permissible is proper for a beast alone. A man ought to seek spiritual good in everything he does. Right listening consists in hearing everything as it is. Men are seduced, and their passions stimulated, by instrumental music because they hear unreally. Music is a presentment of Reality, which rouses the heart to long for God; those who listen with what is real in themselves participate in Reality; those who listen in selfish soulfulness participate in Hell. And ash-Shibli describes music as an outward temptation and an inward premonition: if you know the password you will safely hear the premonition, but if you do not, by inviting temptation you are courting disaster. Another Shaykh puts it thus: Music makes the heart aware of what keeps it in exile, so that its effect is the heart's turning to God.

Sāmānids (*204-395*/819-1005). A Muslim Persian dynasty founded by Sāmān-Khudā, who originated from the region of Balkh, a member of the old Persian aristocracy, the Dihqans. The Sāmānids ruled in Khorāsān and Transoxiana as vassals of the 'Abbāsids. Until the conversion to Islam of the Turkic peoples of the steppes, the Sāmānid domains amounted to a buffer state. But when the Turks became Muslims, Sāmānid rule, in part eroded by internal instability, declined in the face of Turkish penetration into the 'Abbāsid Empire. The Sāmānids were replaced by the Turkic dynasties of the Ghaznavids and Qarakhanids.

As one of the first purely Persian dynasties (following the Ṭāhirids) to return to power after the Arab conquest, the courts of the Sāmānids in Samarkand and Bukhara were the focal points of continuity of old Persian culture and the staging place for the renewal of Persian literature.

Samarkand. Today a city in Uzbekistan, a country which was called in the Middle Ages Soghdiana. It was once the capital of Tamerlane who brought artisans from the four corners to beautify it. His tomb called the Gur-Amir stands there today. The center of Samarkand boasts one of the greatest architectural monuments in the world, the Registan. This square is bounded by the *madrasahs* of Ulug Beg, Shir-Dar, and Tilla-Kari. Nearby is the madrasah of Bibikhanum erected in 1388 by a Chinese wife of Tamerlane. The summer palace of Tamerlane, called the Hazrat Shah Zindeh, is near the tomb of Qasim ibn 'Abbās, which is a shrine.

Outside the city lie the ruins of the original town of Maracanda, whose citadel was perhaps built by Cyrus. The town was also called Afrasiab after an Iranian hero. Near the ruins is the observatory of Uleg Beg. The city of Maracanda was destroyed by Alexander the Great in 329 BC The Arabs under Qutaiba ibn Muslim conquered it in 711 and called it Samarkand. It was the capital of the Samanids (*204-395*/819-1005). It was destroyed again by Jenghiz Khan in 1221. In 1389 it was rebuilt as the Tīmūrid capital. It was made part of the Russian empire in 1868. In the middle ages it was a trading and manufacturing city and particularly known for its paper factory using Chinese technology.

A poet described it and its sister city thus:

Samarkand saikal-i rowi zamin hast
Bukhara quwwat-i Islami din hast

Samarkand is resplendent
upon the face of the earth,
Bukhara is the strength of Islam.

Samarkand, and especially the region to the south, including Balkh (today Mazār-i Sharīf), was a center of Manicheism. Some time after the Archegos left Baghdad in the year 908 there was a conclave in Samarkand attended by five hundred Manicheans, according to an-Nadīm. Maqdisi speaks of the existence in the villages of Transoxiana "of the people in white raiment whose rites resemble those of the Zindiqs". The white clothes were also the distinctive sign of the party of Abū Muslim, the *sāpid-jāmagān* ("the wearers of white raiment", in Arabic *al-Mubayyiḍa*. (White was the prescribed color of garment for the performance of Manichean rites.) Into the middle ages many of the mystics in the region were still vegetarians.

as-Sāmirī. The name which the Koran gives to the tempter who beguiled the Jews to the worship of the golden calf while Moses was on the mountain (20:85). As-Sāmirī gave the calf the power to make a lowing sound by casting into it dust from the footprints of Gabriel who had brought revelations to Moses. As-Sāmirī's punishment was to warn men not to touch him, a reference to the implied connection between him and the Samaritans, a people held by the Jews to be impure.

Sanā'i, Abū-l-Majd (d. *526*/1121). Prolific poet at the court of Ghaznī, who went on to become a Sufi in Marv.

Sanūsīyyah (the "Sanūsis"). A political-religious organization, with at one time a somewhat military outlook, found in Libya, where a third of the population is affiliated to it, and to some degree also in the Sudan. The Sanūsīs were founded by an Algerian named Sayyid Muḥammad 'Alī as-Sanūsī (*1206-1276*/1791-1859), who studied first in Fez and later went to Mecca, where he became imbued with Wahhābī ideas. It was in Mecca that he founded the first lodge of his organization, the Sanusīyyah. Calling himself the "Great Sanūsī", the ideals he propagated were a curious mixture of Wahhābī puritanical fundamentalism with a dash of Sufi teachings eclectically adapted from several different orders. The legal basis of his organization was Mālikī *fiqh*, but his claims to *ijtihād* were soundly denounced by the religious authorities of

Cairo. Essentially, the Sanusīyyah preached a return to exoteric puritanical religion and, much in the style of the Wahhābī movement, and even more like the Tijāniyyah, used this preaching to establish a power-base.

From Arabia, as-Sanūsī moved to Jabal Akhḍar in Cyrenaica, Libya. After his death, the work of expanding the organization was carried on by his sons, and the chief among them, Sayyid Muḥammad al-Mahdī (d. *1320*/1902), established hundreds of lodges, or *zāwiyahs*. His son became King Muḥammad Idrīs of Libya, first under Italian tutelage, and later as the monarch of an independent kingdom in *1370*/1951. In *1389*/1969 the King was overthrown in a coup led by Colonel Mu'ammar al-Qaḍḍāfī.

Saqīfah. The name of the assembly of the Medinans. After the death of the Prophet the *Anṣār* met at the *Saqīfah* to decide the critical question of leadership. The Medinans proposed choosing one leader from the *Anṣār* (natives of Medinah), and another from the *Muhājirūn* (Meccans who had emigrated). To head off a split, 'Umar proposed that Abū Bakr should be the sole leader. The "affair (*amr*) of the Saqīfah" figures retrospectively as an important event in the history of Shī'ism because 'Alī ibn Abī Ṭālib was absent from the meeting attending to the funeral preparations. Still young at the time, being in his thirties, he was not, in fact, a prominent candidate for political leadership in a society which favored age. Nonetheless, the Shī'ites allege, in the light of their theory that a Divine function subsists within the family of 'Alī, that the election of Abū Bakr to succeed the Prophet was in effect a conspiracy to deprive 'Alī of his right as the only legitimate and providential successor.

Sharon makes the following observation: "Following the Prophet's death, the prompt action of Abū Bakr, 'Umar and Abū 'Ubaydah quashed the demand of the Anṣār of Madīnah for a share of the leadership. This action proved to be of great historical significance, because it decided the future political nature of Islam. The Meccan disciples were those who seized the government. What developed consequently was an Islam influenced by the Meccan breadth of outlook which had its roots in Mecca's international commerce; the Madīnans could have easily reduced Islam to a local oasis-found religion." *See* SHĪ'ISM.

Sāqiyah (or *siqāyah*; "irrigation", "water-supply"). The Arabs inherited the science of irrigation from the civilizations of Mesopotamia. The very name of 'Irāq, which derives from a verbal root describing the spread of water, appears to refer to these ancient irrigation systems. The Arabs themselves devised sophisticated irrigation systems for crops. Some of these in the Sahara involved placing sea shells along a water channel so that the wind would blow away deposited sand and thus keep the channel from silting.

Water wheels, sometimes of the giant size that are still in use in Syria, were a common feature of such irrigation systems. In Persia and elsewhere, irrigating channels called qanāt were sometimes run underground for great distances to cool water and keep it from evaporating. *Qanāt* had openings at the surface to provide access for maintenance.

In Marrakesh a system of underground channels called *khettara* exists to make possible the gardens of the palmeraie. According to al-Idrisi it was introduced by 'Alī ibn Yūsuf.

The Spanish word *acequia* ("watering ditch") is derived from the Arabic *sāqiyah*. The *Acequia Madre* irrigation systems used by the Spanish in South America and the American southwest are ultimately contributions of Arab science to the New World. *See* HANDASAH; QANĀT.

Sardar. A Persian title meaning a prince with a military command. The title was adopted by the Turks, and by the Indians into Urdu.

Sarts. A group in Central Asia, especially in the cities of Uzbekistan, who are a mixture of Turks and Tajiks, predominantly with Tajik culture.

Sāssānids. Persian dynasty founded in AD 226 and destroyed by the Arabs in 637. It was founded by Ardāshir (Artaxerxes) I when he conquered Babylon and made triumphant entry into Ctesiphon, having deposed the Parthian Arsacid King Artabanus. With this dynasty the divinity Anāhita came to the fore. Ardashīr claimed a legendary ancestor called Sāsān (son of Bahman — or Vohu Manu — the son of Zoroaster's patron Gushtasp), making the Sāssānids the descendants of the mythical Kayānīs. Both the father, of Ardāshir, also called Sāsān, and his grandfather had been priests at Istakhr in the temple of Anahitā, the goddess of the waters, who was a fertility goddess of Mesopotamian origin, derived from Ishtar. Henceforth Anahitā appeared on royal rock carvings which showed Ahura Mazda passing the *khvarenah*, or blessing, upon the king in her presence.

The Sāssānid capital was established in the Parthian capital, Ctesiphon-Seleucia while Istakhr (an hour away from Persepolis which had been ruined by Alexander the Great) replaced Persepolis as spiritual center. The dynasty represented a restoration of an earlier period of Iranian history after the Hellenist break caused by Alexander the Great.

The Sāssānīds learned — erroneously — from the Babylonians that Zoroaster had lived three hundred years before Alexander the Great (in reality Zoroaster lived considerably before 1,000 BC; the Babylonians had confused Zoroaster with Cyrus). Now there was prophecy current among the people, that one thousand years after Zoroaster the religion and the Persian empire would fall. Thus, according to prophecy (and the defective Babylonian chronology), the Sāssānīd dynasty could hope to continue only for some 150 years. To cheat prophecy and extend the duration of the dynasty, Ardāshir created the official fiction that only 266 years separated the Sāssānīds from Alexander, whereas in fact there were some 550 years. Arab and Persian historians, hampered by the Sāssānīds' control of archives and information, maintained the fictitious interval between Alexander and the Sāssānīds as 266 years. This falsification was explained by Mas'ūdī in the *Kitabu'-t-Tanbih wa-l-Ishraf* as a "political and theological secret". The Sāssānid dynasty lasted for 434 years, and Yazdigerd III was murdered in 651-2; thus Ardeshir in effect did add the time by removing the years he did from history, and the prophecy ran according to his new timetable! (If the prophecy was created after the fact according to the, on the one hand incorrect date of Zoroaster, and on the other hand falsified and shortened interval separating them from Alexander, the mystery would remain why the Sāssānids would have made the excision of time; it is hard to believe it was simply a mistake which they had not noticed rather than a deliberate contrivance as explained by Mas'ūdī.)

The Sāssānīd state was highly centralized. In its time there appeared a state religion which was a new form of Zoroastrianism, Zurvanism, which was a result of the "alchemical" reactions which began when Iranian civilization mixed with Semitic. This took place when Cyrus conquered Babylon. (Zurvanism was a result on the Zoroastrian side along with Mithraism; on the Semitic side the reaction resulted in the development of Jewish Apocalyptic Mysticism, Gnosticism, Christianity, Islam, and other developments which are still continue to appear. In between the Iranian and Semitic worlds, or on both sides, the fusion produced Manicheism.)

In original Zoroastrianism, Ahura Mazda was the supreme divinity, without a beginning, and Ahriman, the personification of evil, appeared into the Cosmos, *out of nowhere*, several thousand years after its creation. In Zurvanism, the relationship between the two is radically changed: Ahura Mazda and Ahriman *were represented as twins* whose father was Endless Time, or Zurvan (Chronos.) This was a very significant change metaphysically and psychologically.

Sāssānīd society was divided into four professional classes, priests (*asravān*), warriors (*arteshtārān*), the administrators (*dipīrān*), and the common people, *vastryoshan*, farmers, and *hutūkshan*, artisans. Except for the administrator-scribes, who were of Mesopotamian origin, this is very close to the social division in medieval Europe. In addition, there were four social classes: princes (*shāhrdārān*), heads of great families (*vaspuhran*), the grandees (*vuzurgān*), and the nobles (*āzādān*) who included the village heads (*dehkānān*). The Latin historian Ammianus Marcellinus said that the official title of the King was: "King of Kings, Companion of the Stars, Brother of the Sun and Moon". In other Sāssānid inscriptions it was: "Worshipper of Mazdā, the Divine, King of Kings of Iran and non-Iran, descendant of the gods". *See* ZOROASTRIANISM.

Satan, *see* IBLĪS.

"Satanic Verses". Within the first three centuries of Islam an assertion was made, recorded by Ṭabarī, that during the revelation of the surat 53, "The Star", the devil succeeded in inserting some words after line 20, where the Koran says: "Have ye thought upon al-Lat and al-'Uzza and Manat, the third, the other?" These were pagan female divinities. The assertion is that the Devil inserted the words: *tilka-l-Gharāniq al-'ulā minhā shafā'a turtajā* into the revelation: "These are sublime swans whose intercession may be sought."

The assertion was cemented by an appeal to plausibility that the Prophet was seeking to win support of the Meccans and was disposed to compromise. The assertion said the verses were allowed to stand a little while before being repudiated. The story of the "Satanic Verses" was denied by al-Bayḍāwī and by others. Indeed, there is no contemporary record of such a perturbation in the revelation taking place and the nature of the event, the import of the verses, is in complete contradiction to the nature of the Prophet. It is this very contradiction which is a clue to the origin of the story of the "Satanic Verses".

In 895 a missionary in North Africa preparing the way for 'Ubayd Allāh the first Fāṭimid spread a fabricated Ḥadīth which said that "in the third century of the Hijrah, the sun will rise in the West". This is a retort, as exactly opposite as possible, to the Koran 2:258: "Bethink thee of him who had an argument with Abraham about his Lord, because Allāh had given him the kingdom; how, when Abraham said: 'My Lord is He who giveth life, and causeth death,' he answered: 'I give life and cause death.' Abraham answered: 'Lo! Allāh causeth the sun to rise in the East, so do thou cause it to come up from the West.' Thus was the disbeliever abashed. And Allāh guideth not wrong-doing folk."

The central mechanism of the "Ḥadīth" about the "sun rising in the West" is the strategic establishment of an antinomial idea, here an equality of a second "Principle", proposed in such a direct "head on" way that denial seems even more improbable than the original assertion. The Koran affirmed that God made the sun rise in the East, and challenged an opponent to make it rise in the West. In saying the sun would rise in the West a rival was being raised to God Himself. In a Muslim climate such a defiance is so unthinkable that even denial of such a saying is thereby curtailed. (In a similar free-thinking vein, also ascribed to 'Ubayd Allāh, is the epistle of *The Three Imposters.*)

The "Satanic Verses" follow a similar pattern. Line three of the surah in question says "By the Star when it setteth, Your comrade erreth not, nor is deceived; nor doth he speak of his own desire. It is naught save an inspiration that is inspired, which one of mighty powers taught him" (50:1-5). Thus in the midst of the Koran's own affirmation that something could not be inserted into the Koran, the most unlikely place to attempt to insert a contradiction, in fact such an attempt was made, as if to affirm the power, again, of a rival to God. The audacity of the imposture of the "Satanic Verses" at that particular point in the Koran made them almost plausible by their very improbability. For example, the story of "the Satanic Verses" has often been defended as "a story so unlikely it could not be invented". Yet this is what an inventor seeks, that human psychology itself work in favor of his invention.

A similar case is the creation of a book around *100*/750 with doctrines completely antithetical to Islam deliberately entitled *Umm al-Kitāb* (lit. "Mother of the Book"). The Koran says "He it is Who hath revealed unto thee the Scripture wherein are clear revelations —they are the Essence of the Book [*Umm al-Kitāb,*] —and others are allegorical" (5:7). In these cases the words of the Koran are used as points of departure for doing precisely that which the Koran says cannot or should not be done; this is the signature of antinomial movements which arise in all religions and mirror backwards the tenets of that religion. (For similar reasons the Sufi Bisṭāmī was accused of practising a "backwards prayer" (*salat maqlubah*). There were several religious currents within Islam that introduced female divinities such as "Kuni" as intermediaries between God and the world. The "Satanic Verses" story probably reflects an attempt to introduce a support for these new female divinities as a kind of "lost" or "secret" revelation. What probably followed was the subsequent neutralization of this intervention on the part of defenders of orthodoxy as being verses the devil had once produced and which the Prophet had already repudiated in his time.

With the perspective of time, however, it is clear that the idea expressed in the "Satanic Verses" is so completely against the spirit of the Islamic message that it is impossible to believe that the Prophet could have actually entertained them as authentic even for a moment. After the point at which the verses were supposed to have arisen the Koran goes on: "They are but names which ye have named, ye and your fathers, for which Allāh hath revealed no warrant." (53:23). The pseudo Ḥadīth about the sun rising in the West still circulates as an "esoteric" teaching. *See* ANTINOMIANISM; DUALISM; UMM al-KITĀB.

Saudi Arabia. Kingdom. Estimated population: 22,800,000. Except for foreign nationals employed in Saudi Arabia, the population is 100% Muslim. There is a small Twelve-Imām Shī'ite minority in the Eastern Province.

Many Yemenis are permanent residents in Saudi Arabia, and many of these are Zaydī; there are also many Zaydīs in the southern province of 'Asīr. The populations of Mecca and Medinah include peoples from virtually all Muslim countries, and thus every form of Islam is represented. The cradle of Wahhābism is the Najd and there it is strongest, although it is also the dominant school of thought throughout Saudi Arabia. *See* IBN SA'ŪD; MECCA; MEDINAH; WAHHĀBISM.

Sawdā' bint Zam'ah. After the death of Khadijah, the second wife of the Prophet. She was the widow of one of the emigrants to Abyssinia and had returned to Arabia upon the death of her first husband. *See* WIVES of the PROPHET.

Ṣawm, *see* FAST.

Sa'y. The walking back and forth seven times between the hills Ṣafā and Marwah in Mecca. This is one of the rites of pilgrimage, both *'umrah* and *ḥajj*, and is performed immediately after the circumambulation of the Ka'bah is completed by the prayer at the Station of Abraham (*Maqām Ibrāhīm*) and the drinking of Zamzam water. At each hill there are recitations which are made standing, and which begin with the words: "Ṣafā and Marwah are among the signs of God..."

The *sa'y* is performed walking except for a portion in the middle, today marked by green lights, where the pace is quickened. The fast pace, for a distance of some twenty meters/yards, is described by the verb *harwala* ("to hurry, make haste"). The covered course of the *sa'y* is called the *mas'ā* and is today paved and enclosed within the precincts of the Grand Mosque; its length is 293m/927ft. Before the present mosque was built in the 1950s, the sa'y took place, as it always had, in the area adjacent to the market, the *Sūq al-Layl*, where the human traffic of the town mingled with the pilgrims walking back and forth between the hills.

The completion of the *sa'y* marks the completion of the rites of the *'umrah* and at the Marwah gate the pilgrim's hair is clipped, or even shaved completely, to signify the end of the state of consecration (*iḥrām*). Near Ṣafā it is possible to hire wheelchairs and litter bearers to assist the infirm in the performance of the *sa'y*.

The origin of the rite goes back to Hagar who, despairing for the life of Isma'il (Ishmael) when the water in the goatskin that Abraham had given them was spent, ran back and forth between the two hills. Then suddenly the water gushed forth from the well of Zamzam. The *sa'y* may therefore represent the casting to and fro in this world from illusion to illusion until true guidance and true life come. *See* HAGAR; PILGRIMAGE; ZAMZAM.

Sayyid (lit. "liege lord"). A title of respect used for the descendants of the Prophet through his daughter Fāṭimah and 'Alī ibn Abī Ṭālib. These are the *shurafā'* (sing. *sharīf*). In the Arab West they are more often referred to as *mawlay* (*mulay*, and in French-speaking countries written *moulay*), since *sayyid* (or *seyyid*) is also a general title of address like sir, monsieur, or mister. It can also be a proper name.

Sayyid Ahmad Khan, Sir, *see* KHAN, Sir SAYYID.

Sayyid al-Murtaḍā, *see* al-MURTAḌĀ.

Schechina, *see* SAKINAH.

Schools of Law (Ar. *madhhab*, pl. *madhāhib*; lit. "movement", "orientation", "trend", " direction"). There are four schools of law among the Sunnīs: the Ḥanafī; Ḥanbalī; Mālikī and Shāfi'ī. These schools are sometimes, in the context of religious practices, referred to as "rites". Each school, or "rite" is a legal system developed out of the so-called "foundations of sacred law" (*uṣūl al-fiqh*). The founders of the schools are Mālik ibn Anas (d. *179*/795); Abū Ḥanīfah (d. *150*/767) Muḥammad ibn Idrīs ash-Shāfi'ī (d. *205*/820); and Aḥmad Ḥanbal (d. *241*/855). The Mālikī school is dominant in the Arab West and West Africa; the Ḥanafī school is dominant in most countries that were formerly part of the Turkish Empire and in India. The Ḥanbalī school is only observed in Saudi Arabia and in Qatar. Technically, the Wahhābīs consider themselves to be "non-imitators" or "not attached to tradition" (*ghayr muqallidūn*), and therefore answerable to no school of law at all, observing instead what they would call the practice of early Islam. However, to do so does correspond to the ideal aimed at by Ibn Ḥanbal, and thus they can be said to be of his "school". The Shāfi'ī school is dominant in Indonesia, Malaya and the Philippines; it is also important in Egypt, where the Ḥanafī and Mālikī schools are also represented, and in some parts of Central Asia and the Caucasus.

In addition, there are also several Shī'ite schools. The most prominent is the Ja'farī school of the Twelve-Imām Shī'ites and the school of the Zaydīs. The Khārijites (Ibāḍites), have their own school.

Among the Sunnīs, each school (today) regards the others as orthodox, but a Muslim is expected to adhere to one school. The mixing of precedents and applications between schools is called *talfīq*, and is frowned upon. *See* SHARĪ'AH.

Science, *see* ASTRONOMY; al-BĪRŪNĪ; BROTHERHOOD of PURITY; DĀR al-ḤIKMAH; HANDASAH; JĀBIR IBN ḤAYYĀN; HOUSE of WISDOM; al-KHWĀRIZMĪ; MEDICINE; at-ṬŪSI, NĀṢIR ad-DĪN.

"Science of the letters", *see* 'ABJAD; 'ILM al-ḤURŪF.

Seal of Prophecy (Ar. *khatm an-nubuwwah*, and also *khatm al-anbiyā'*). 1. A title of the Prophet because he is the last Prophet, and the last Divine Messenger (*rasūl*) before the end of time and the Day of Judgement. That there will be no new revealed religion between his message and the end of the world is an important point of Islamic doctrine.

2. It is also the name given to a large lump of flesh "the size of a pigeon's egg" in the small of the back of the Prophet, which was taken as a physical sign of the "Seal of Prophecy". Analogously, Jesus is sometimes referred to as being the "Seal of Sanctity" (*khatm al-wilāyah*), in virtue of being the Prophet who externalized his inner sanctity to the highest degree.

Seal of Sanctity (Ar. *khatm al-wilāyah*). A title given to Jesus, as the prophet whose sanctity manifested itself outwardly to the highest degree. The Prophet Muḥammad is called the "Seal of Prophecy", as the final Messenger to mankind.

Seceders, *see* KHĀRIJITES.

"Secret society". The technical term, in the science of religions, is *Maennerbund.* A Maennerbund is a secret society whose members undergo an initiation in which they take on, at certain times, as far as possible, the personality of different animals. The origin of the Maennerbuende lies with the dawn of time; stone age man, in order to hunt successfully, imitated one or more of the salient hunting animals around him as a model. It was a form of sympathetic magic in which the instincts of hunter animal as well as those of the prey were learned or acquired by man by identifying with the animal. This began with an initiation in a cave under the direction of a shaman, probably as a puberty rite, and probably with the aid of mind affecting plants such as the *amanita muscaria* mushroom, still used in Siberia, and other plants, *ephedra* sometimes thought to be the *haoma* of the Iranians, for example. These plants varied according to what could be found locally in different regions. It was a method of teaching what society had learned as techniques of survival. These simulations were part of religious rites. Usually the hunter model was the wolf, which was especially suitable for man since wolves hunt in packs, and humans could act in concert. Also, primitive men sometimes followed wolf packs in order to scavenge from them.

The members of such initiatic groups in traditional settings are usually either men or women (the "Amazons" of antiquity and the *Maenads* of Euripides), mixed groups being exceptional. Initiation is practiced in three steps: 1. Seclusion from everyday life (*rites de séparation*); 2. Living at the margin of society (*rites de marge*); 3. Initiation proper (*rites d'agrégation*) (A. van Gennep).

During the ice age, when men often had to share caves with bears, the bear, and in particular the now extinct cave bear (Ursus Spelaeus) was also an animal of imitation and hunt. Cave bear worship cults in the Alps have given us one of the oldest altars of sacrifice found thus far, and traces of primitive man's relationship with bears exist abundantly in language and myth. One of the best known Maennerbuende was that of the Viking "berserkers", literally "bear-skin-men". Most words for bear are euphemisms for the real word (bear in English means "brown one"; *medved* in Russian means the "honey lover") in order to avoid calling up the actual presence of the feared animal through the magic of names. In other areas of the world animals such as jaguars and tigers provided the instinctual training model. ("Judah is a lion's whelp... Benjamin is raven as a wolf" (Genesis:49). The werewolf (Ar. *al-quṭrub* from the Greek *lycanthropos*) is now a strange, seemingly distant phenomenon, but even the foundation of the city of Rome is tied up with it as seen from the myth of Romulus and Remus being suckled and raised by a wolf. Secret societies have continued to play the role of nation founders into the twentieth century (the Free

Masons in America, the Society of the Gray Wolf in Turkey).

The Maennerbuende were superseded by other forms of religious expression but persisted in some areas of the world into classical and even modern times. Maennerbuende were particularly influential in the region around the south Caspian which was called Hyrcania (the Greek form of Iranian *Varkana* "land of the wolf"). It was noted for the presence of "two-legged wolves" (*varka bisagra*) among the early Iranians, and Firdawsi said in the *Shahnameh* that Mazandaran was a region of "demons". Around the southern Caspian the antinomialism of the Maennerbuende tradition later fueled the radical Shīʻism of the Assassins, the *Qīzīl Bash* ("the Red Hats") supporters of Shah Ismaʻil, and the Shaykhis. The "red hat", probably the forerunner of the Fez, had a tassel, probably representing the tail of an animal, although the interpretation later was that the strands stood for the twelve Imāms. Hats symbolizing animals were very common; the "dog ear" cap of Nigeria even gives the wearer the look of a wolf.

In ancient Greek mystery rites the wolf was the usual animal of transformation for men, and the mare for women. It is thought that the wearing of goatskins by the acolytes of rites in which cathartic dramas were performed is at the origin of the word tragedy (from *tragos* for goat). The school known as the Lyceum was the grove near Athens where Aristotle taught and was so called because of the temple of Apollon Lykeios, or Apollo the Wolf-god. Many classical statues exist of "satyrs" — a man with a wolf skin folded up next to him. Even in modern times there are records of Maennerbund activity in Europe such as a werewolf trial in Latvia in 1691 recorded in the *Geheimbuender der Germanen*, published in 1928. Today traces still appear, in the Tongs of China, the lodges of the American Indians, or as folklore, for example in the men's societies of the Alpine countries in which men emerge at the dawn of Mardi Gras costumed as animals and take mild liberties with any women who are found on the street, reminiscent of the Roman Lupercalia. These practices, hidden throughout the year, are permitted to show themselves at the moment when everyone wears a mask, echoes of what were once ancient rites that culminated in the fertility festivals of Easter and May.

Similar practices were found in Russia at the eve of Saint John, or Midsummer's eve, which commemorates Maennerbund religious holidays. In some places in Iran, a practice which has now disappeared since the turn of the century, the populace would work themselves into in a frenzy during the 'Id al-Ghadir and tear with the teeth into honey filled cakes representing the first three Caliphs (who in later Shīʻism became despised).

The transformation into an animal is a widespread taboo. The Bible and other religious legislation forbids the eating of blood because the psychic nature of the animal was believed to be in the blood. It is probably because red is the color of blood, and blood is the medium that joins body and consciousness, that it was associated with the Qarmaṭīs, and esoterism in general. A similar, perhaps related, secret organization called the Red Scarf existed in pre-Ming China (which was at the origin of the dynasty, the dynasty of "Light"). Also red are the Azerī Qīzīl Bash, "the Red Hats", and other Gnostic societies. The sheepskin reserved for Shemsi Tabrizi among the Mevlevis, "his empty throne", is red. The leader of the Qarmaṭīs was described as mounted on a camel and wrapped in a red cloak. The red robe is also associated with Jesus. In the case of Jesus it is his own blood which becomes a viaticum, at once forbidden and sacred, in a rite of multiple transformations, wine into blood, blood into a sacrament.

The positive contributions of the Maennerbunde to religions are two central and important ideas. One is initiation into an unknown reality, which in Christianity has become baptism, and in Islam a pact made with God. While transformation into an animal today has only negative and regressive connotations, it still has something liberating about it (cf. the *Hell's Angels* experience), being a surpassing of one's state. Thus the transformation into something entirely alien, initially into an animal, also introduced the idea of self-transcendance, a possibility in an "upward" rather than a "downward" direction. In the mind of the primitive hunter, when animals escape they do so into lairs which were perceived as "holes in the universe", three such "escape holes" to which the animal bolts took on special and almost universal cosmological symbolism in all cultures. The first is the *cave*. This readily takes on the symbol of the "heart" or center of the being and here secret and initiatic rites were often held. Another is the "bottom of the sea". Here Gilgamesh looked for the plant of immortal life, a story which appears in the Koran as the search for immortality at the invisible "meeting of the seas" as described in Surat 18 (which is called *The Cave*). And the third "hole" is the sun, the supreme spiritual escape out of the cosmos through the center of creation. What Spanish city does not have its *Puerta del Sol*, the principal gate? In Hinduism it is the way which the soul goes to attain *moksha* or "deliverance".

But the Maennerbund's essential characteristic lies in making licit in secret that which society forbids outwardly. Secrecy and antinomialism, or the practice of what is forbidden under guise of transcendence or "esoterism", are bound up in the Maennerbund phenomenon, not always with positive results. Historically these are found in Gnostic movements which often legitimize what is usually forbidden, as for example, "temporary" marriage in Shī'ism.

Mircea Eliade correctly identified the Aissawa in Morocco as being a Maennerbund disguised as a Sufi order; the founder of the Aissawa was supposed to have given his followers permission to eat scorpions and snakes, and other animals, alive — as animals do — "while they were obliged to cross a desert". This is, however, an innocuous explanation for the fact that the Aissawa take on animal states in which they eat small animals as if they themselves were wolves. Lycanthropy is still very common in Africa today, as reported by Albert Schweitzer, and by others. In Senegal it is simply called "loup". Besides the Aissawa, a number of other North African pseudo-Sufi orders such as the Ḥamidsha are in reality Maennerbuende and the folklore phenomenon known as the *Boujloud*, the "father of the skins", during which the antinomialism emerges as a deliberate breaking of religious laws, is also of Maennerbund origin.

As well as pseudo-Sufi orders which are entirely Maennerbuende, other Sufi orders have undergone strong Maennerbund influence, in particular, the Qādiriyyah. Others, especially in Turkey, have preserved a particularly shamanistic role for the Shaykh. Even those Sufi orders which are close to religious orthodoxy nevertheless have some Maennerbund characteristics. Almost all have hidden somewhere what is most radically antinomial for Islam: the notion that men are or can become God. This is rarely explicit and is sometimes submerged for generations, but because of the nature of secret beliefs, the idea reforms itself and surfaces even after having been denounced and its proponents subjected to persecution.

A common Sufi story in Iran and Turkey tells of a disciple who, at the wave of the master's hand, or because he disobeyed him in some small instance, sees the other disciples, or even people on the street, take on the appearance of animals. Francis of Assisi also talks to animals and in particular to the Wolf of Giubbio. Maennerbund manifestations can emerge spontaneously when certain conditions are present; secrecy, authorization to perform what society forbids, secret knowledge. These then call forth a primordial identification with animals. The *oprichnina* or secret police of Ivan the Terrible carried a wolf's head, the Nazi SS imitated Roman legions in carrying animal skins and had a special affinity for leather, as did the Commissars of post-revolutionary Russia. Other examples, innocent and sinister abound in all societies.

In summary, the Maennerbund has, sociologically, a strong hierarchic order; entails separation from everyday life; promotes measures which prevent weakening the links of the member with the group and prevent his re-solidarization with society at large; a tendency to absolutize the group's aims and put them beyond all other moral considerations. In other word's the group beliefs, or practices, or goals are "morally exempt"; in fact, the use of what others would call evil can be justified to achieve the group's wishes. Psychologically this exalts the individual and makes him feel part of an elite, if not in this world then in the next and makes the old personality fall apart because of the segregation from one's past life and from society. Reason is deemed to be inadequate to understand the teaching. Will is similarly broken down and replaced by obedience and passivity. Myths of a "sacred horde" play a useful role in this process, with the death of the individual and his rebirth into the "new life" of the sacred group. Predestinarian ideas are also useful in creating the state of mind propitious to the process of indoctrination. These tendencies can easily be seen in many modern political groupings especially radical and terrorist groups and in such sociological manifestations as "Wilding" in the big cities of America or cults everywhere. *See* ANTINOMIANISM; BOUJLOUD; QĪZĪL BASH.

Seeking Guidance, *see* ISTIKHĀRAH.

Seljūqs. A Turkic people from the Steppes, a branch of the Ghuzz/Oghuz, who entered military service within the 'Abbāsid Empire and succeeded in seizing control for themselves under their leader

Toghril Beg. Toghril Beg assumed the title of Sultan, which had never been used before, and this was stamped on his coinage. The dynasty which he founded began in *429*/1038 and lasted until *582*/1194. An offshoot, the Seljūqs of Rūm in Anatolia, existed as a power until shortly before *707*/1307.

Without abolishing either the Caliphate or the 'Abbāsids, the Sunnī Seljūqs in *447*/1055 entered Baghdad and displaced the Shī'ite Buyids who had preceded them as the effective masters of most of the eastern part of the 'Abbāsid Empire. Seljūq expansion to the west, encroaching upon the Byzantine Empire, was one of the causes of the Crusades. The second and third Seljūq Sultans, Alp Arslan and Jalāl ad-Dawlah Mālik Shāh, benefited from the services of their Persian Vizier Niẓām al-Mulk, who achieved fame as one of the most able political figures in Islamic history.

After Mālik Shāh, the Seljūq Empire underwent progressive fragmentation, giving way to other dynasties such as the Khwarizm-Shāhīs, originally governors for the Seljūqs, and finally to the invading Mongols. The period of the Great Seljūq Sultanate did, however, provide a stability and political unity to a degree rarely achieved afterwards. It marked a broad Sunnī restoration in the Empire after the expansion of Shī'ism under the Buyids. Although at first the Seljūqs were opposed to Ash'arite theology, and theologians like al-Juwaynī were obliged to go into exile, when their great Vizier Niẓām al-Mulk saw the need to counter the religious propaganda of the Fāṭimids, the Ash'arites were rehabilitated and made the theological spokesmen of the dynasty. The Seljūq invasions changed the demographic configuration of the Middle East; Iṣfahān was their capital. According to Franz Babinger, when the Seljūqs arrived on the scene they were not Muslims but 'Alawis. *See* al-ASH'ARĪ; NIẒĀM al-MULK.

Senegal. Population 9,092,749 (1986 est.). The Islamization of Senegal began with the Almoravid movement, around *442*/1050. Islam experienced a second period of substantial growth this century, with the result that 86% of the population is now Muslim and adheres to the Mālikī school of law. Some 4% are animists and the rest consist of various Christian groups of which the Catholics are the most numerous. Although the importance of Islam is overwhelming, Senegal is not a theocratic state, and civil law is based upon French models, with certain allowances made in the direction of religion. Religious tolerance is the rule. The Tijāniyyah Sufi order (*ṭarīqah*) is very widespread, with the Qādiriyyah represented as well. A recent development out of the Tijāniyyah is the movement known as Muridism. *See* MURIDISM.

"Sentry Horse" (Ar. *farasu'n-nawba* and Pers. *asp-i-nawbati*). The 'Abbāsids came to power by allying themselves with more or less clandestine sectarians in 'Irāq and Khorāsan; in so doing they identified themselves with these sectarians probably to the extent of making show that they were actually practising members of the sect. In *141*/758 a group of these sectarians, 600 or so, came from the city of Rāwānd (possibly near Iṣfahān or in 'Irāq) to Hāshimiyyah in 'Irāq, one of several cities of this name established as temporary capitals by the 'Abbāsids before the building of Baghdad. There the Rāwāndiyyah, called sometimes "ultra Shī'ites" paid their homage to al-Manṣur the 'Abbāsid; but they did so proclaiming that they knew that he was God, by throwing themselves to their death from cupolas (in the expectation of holy martyrdom in al-Manṣur's presence assuring them of eternal life) and by asking al-Manṣur to give them "food and drink", a reference to the agape meal of the Bēma ceremony, in virtue of which they also carried an empty throne. This had been the basis of their secret special relationship with the 'Abbāsids, who could not now afford to let the secret be known to their orthodox Muslim and Arab supporters, a secret which most likely would have caused widespread disaffection if not revolt. Al-Manṣur had the Rāwāndis killed, but until enough troops arrived he was in peril for a short time for lack of a good horse with which to escape.

Thus began the institution of the "sentry horse", saddled, bridled and equipped, which was henceforth always in readiness at the Caliph's palace to permit the Caliph to escape if necessary, a practice also copied by the Persian courts, notably the Sāmānids. It was perhaps the echo of this which led to the wide spread rumor in Iran at the time of the revolution that the Shah had a vertical-take-off-and-landing jet at the ready at the palace for evacuation at a moment's notice.

The 'Abbāsid's secret "special relationship" with this "other religion" continued until the Qarmaṭī revolt which coincided with advent of Twelve Imām Shīites as power brokers behind the throne beginning with the reign of the Caliph al-

Muqtadir (reigned 908-932). *See* IBN al-MU'TAZZ; BARMAKIDS.

Sepahi (A Turkish word meaning a mounted soldier). The name of several new clandestine organizations in Pakistan made up of vigilante militants. The *Sepahi Ṣaḥāba* are Sunni vigilantes who attack and assassinate Shī'ites. The *Sepahi Muḥammad* are Shī'ites who attack and assassinate Sunnis. The *Sepahi Masiḥ* is a Christian militant defense organization. An attempt to bring the Muslim vigilantes to discussion is the Mille Yakjahti or National Solidarity Council in Karachi organized by Shah Aḥmad Nawrani.

Sermon (Ar. *khuṭbah*). The exhortation made on a Friday in a congregational mosque before the special prayer (*ṣalāt al-jum'ah*) is called a *khuṭbah*. The custom goes back to the practice of the Prophet in Medinah, who first delivered his sermons standing, and then later, sitting, on a small series of steps, the *minbar*, which was built as a pulpit. It is from such a pulpit, or in some countries a speaker's podium, that the sermon is delivered.

The schools of law prescribe that a khuṭbah must contain certain elements: it must open with the ḥamdalah ("Praise be to God"); then blessings are called down upon the Prophet, the two witnessings of faith (*ash-shahadatān*) are uttered and the unity of God is proclaimed. These are followed by an exhortation or spiritual message, at the close of which blessings are called upon the believers and supplication is made for those in distress. By custom, blessings are also called upon the ruler of the country and divine aid invoked for him. The *khuṭbah* thus became the occasion for a declaration of sovereignty. In addition, the name mentioned in the *khuṭbah* was an indication, in areas of doubt, of the political allegiance of the region. The calling of blessings upon the ruler is still practiced where there are traditional rulers today, and it is reported that the practice in some places in East Africa is to call down the blessings on the last Turkish Caliph, like the persistence of a habit whose causes have long been forgotten. (The Turkish Caliphate disappeared in 1924.)

Once during the sermon the Prophet's grandson Ḥasan came up to him with a toy. The Prophet interrupted the sermon to attend to the child, an example of how the Sunnah is multifaceted. In this case the Prophet taught by concrete example that no matter how busy an adult is, he must not ignore a child's needs. *See* ḤAMDALAH; PRAYERS upon the PROPHET.

Seveners (Ar. *sab'iyyah*, referring to the followers of the seventh Imām; however, the term originated in the West and is used only there). The Seveners are Ismā'īlis in their pre-Fāṭimid and pre-Qarmaṭī period. They are the transition from the Manichean Proto-Shī'ites, the *tawwabūn* who marched out of Kūfah to martyrdom at the hands of Caliphal troops in *65*/685 and the subsequent Mukhtāriyyah (Kaysāniyyah) movement to the Neo-Manicheans, a sophisticated alternative religion emulating Islam as a outward shell while maintaining an inward Gnostic Dualism expressly dedicated to abolishing Islam itself. In the course of this development, which paralleled the development of Islam itself, they produced what became Twelve Imām Shī'ism as a byproduct of their own evolution. At this stage of their development they still had curious divinities such as *kūnī* and *qadar*, *al-jadd*, *al-istiftāh*, and *al-khayāl*, and others, who were various *emanations* of God. (Creation by emanation is a characteristic of Dualism.) These were remnants of the original Manichean pantheon of lesser divinities who played a demiurgic role beneath the level of the two "principals". (*Kūnī* and *qadar* could still be found among the Qarmaṭīs and later Ismā'īlīs.) The emergence of the Seveners marks the point at which early Shī'ism, or Islamo-Manicheism, splits into two streams: movements adhering to their original Dualist nature seeking to return to the outward practice of their religion (until the Mongol invasion) while maintaining a disguise but promoting their own leadership, and a Gnostic form of Islam finding its leaders in the historic descendants of 'Alī which is Twelve Imām Shī'ism.

Ismā'īl, who was claimed as a leader by an early Shī'ite group, died in *145*/762 before his father Ja'far aṣ-Ṣādiq, the sixth Shī'ite Imām. This led to a radical realignment among the various Shī'ite factions, for the death of Ismā'īl, their heir apparent, left the succession in doubt, and the opportunities thus created were eagerly seized upon by the contending parties, each leader seeking in the climate of confusion to advance his own cause. One would declare that the line of 'Alīd Imāms had come to an end in accordance with imputed principles of cyclic manifestation; another that he himself was the successor, through "spiritual filiation", if need be, of Ismā'īl; whilst others committed themselves to follow, or perhaps control, the fortunes of Ismā'īl's infant son. The mainstream of Shī'ites — in all, a very small number at that time — recognized the next eldest son of Ja'far, 'Abd Allāh, as Imām. He, however, died without an heir, and so the leadership devolved to yet another son, Mūsā al-Kāẓim, whose followers were to become the Twelve-Imām Shī'ites. That others pinned their hopes on other, younger sons, suggests that the doctrine of *naṣṣ*, or "designation" of the succeeding Imām by his predecessor, became established precisely as the aftermath of this situation, and in response to the problems it raised.

One explanation advanced by these sects to account for the anomaly in the succession, and its results, was the theory that the number seven, always symbolic because it is the sum of the directions of space (right, left, forward, backward, above, below, and the center which resumes the others), signified the completion of a cycle. Those who took this opportunity to divest themselves of the idea of Imāms altogether or, at any rate, of 'Alīd Imāms, arranged the count so that their last Imām, called *at-tamm* ("the final") was the seventh, who closed the cycle, terminated the conditions which ruled it, and perhaps opened another. A Fāṭimid ruler, Mu'izz lī-Dīni 'Llāh, wrote an esoteric prayer which referred to the son of Ismā'īl, Muḥammad, as the "Seventh *nāṭiq*" ("speaking messenger") and the "founder of a new *sharī'ah*" ("religious law"). Mu'izz was himself, according to Fāṭimid claims, the Imām seven times removed from Muḥammad ibn Ismā'īl, and thus the culmination and beginning of another cycle. By calling Muḥammad ibn Ismā'īl the *nāṭiq*, Mu'izz left open for himself the far higher role of the *sāmit*, or "silent" manifestation, of which the "speaker" is merely the mouthpiece.

In the power struggle after the death of Ja'far, those who did not follow Mūsā al-Kāẓim chose the number seven as symbolic of their new point of departure, the beginning of a new cycle. A number of Sevener groups came into existence in this way, but their adherents were certainly very few, at least in the beginning.

Two of these groups became prominent: the Fāṭimids, whose rulers were the Imāms of the sect, and, under Ḥamdān Qarmaṭ, the ("relatively") Imām-less Qarmaṭīs. (It is not clear whether Ḥamdān Qarmaṭ, or one of the other leaders, was their Imām, whether they considered the Fāṭimid rulers their Imāms, or whether the Qarmaṭīs were a school of "everyman his own Imām".) The Qarmaṭīs followed a populist ideology of collectivism (*ulfah*) and pursued a program of political insurrection, while yet maintaining a certain sympathy with the Fāṭimids. These, and many other groups, constituted the Seveners. They were called *bāṭinīs* (the "inner" or "secret ones") because they professed to have secret teachings. Indeed, they had not only secret teachings, but an altogether secret religion, differing from orthodox Islam radically on several vital points. Not only an alternate religion, the Seveners were also an alternate political allegiance which threatened the 'Abbāsid Empire for centuries, all of which made them into an inevitably clandestine movement.

Their teachings were imparted through indoctrination which sought to break down the certainties of the ordinary believer and to replace them with submission to the authority of a chief or master, more often than not a hidden figure. Perhaps the nominal chief was sometimes imaginary, as a mythical leader can be more awe-inspiring than one of flesh and blood. The abandonment of outward religious practice was encouraged, for it represents a compelling step towards the acceptance of some other authority. The step could be justified by claiming that the presence of a divinely guided leader (or, rather, in Gnostic terms, of a leader who was himself divine), made the religious law (*sharī'ah*) superfluous. Since the presence of the Prophet had not made the *sharī'ah* superfluous in his time, this naturally suggested that here before one's eyes or yonder in the shadows there was an even higher authority; this objection was strenuously voiced by al-Ghazālī, Shahrastānī (although it is very likely that he was himself, in secret, an Ismā'īlī) and others. This tendency took its most explicit form in the abolition of the *sharī'ah* by the doctrine of the *qiyāmah* ("resurrection") declared by Ḥasan, called "'Alā Dhikrihī-s-Salām", the fourth master of Alamūt. (*See* ASSASSINS.)

The intimation of alternate or allegorical meanings to accepted religious truths was another Sevener technique. The postulant was led by degrees to a "realization" of the "hidden" meaning of the Koran as, for example, when it says: "Serve thy Lord until the irrefutable [*al-yaqīn*, "the certain"] comes to you" (15:99). The "irrefutable" in the Koran means "death", but was used by the Seveners to open onto another, unsuspected, world, and in allusion to the acquisition of a superior knowledge supplied by the sect. The Koran 43:84: "And He Who is God in heaven and God on earth" could be used to spring the idea that there were *two* (or more) "Gods" or, again, that someone on earth is God. (Al-Ḥallāj was specifically accused of using this verse in this way.) This higher knowledge could suggest that God had two natures, or that He Himself had his own "God", or that He was not completely all-powerful and had to cede in some respects to another principle, etc. In other words, it was the fateful knowledge of Dualism. (*See* DUALISM.)

It is understandable, then, that Sevener doctrines are only rarely to be discovered in any full or explicit form; mystery had value both as a defense and as an allurement. A cryptic hint would serve to start a potential recruit on the path into a parallel system of belief, virtually into a different world from that of orthodox Islam.

Historically, the Seveners played a fascinating role. In the nascent moments of their entry into Islam, they exercised a definitive influence upon Shī'ism. They infused into Shī'ism the ideas which made possible, as if by catalysis, the subsequent development of Shī'ite speculative theology and the doctrine of the supernatural nature of the Imāms, a development of which Ja'far aṣ-Ṣādiq is portrayed as the watershed. Although it happened that orthodox theology sometimes stumbled into the Sevener labyrinths and came out intoxicated, it is through them that much Hellenistic learning flowed into Islam. The Seveners were aware of the buried treasure of pre-Islamic thought beneath their feet and they provided a channel for tapping the intellectual power of Neoplatonism, Hermetic sciences, and Hellenist philosophy to stimulate intellectual development within orthodox Islam. For their own purposes, the Seveners found great use for these neglected wisdoms before the mainstream of Islamic thought did.

It could be said that the Seveners came upon the syllogism and discovered in it a force to destabilize the 'Abbāsid Empire. In effect, they precipitated a struggle which wrested control of whole kingdoms from Baghdad's grasp. The movement manifested itself as a flurry of small sects but also as major uprisings: the Khaṭṭābiyyah, the Khurrāmiyyah, the Qarmaṭīs, and others, some of which have been called "'Alīd revolts".

Saladin was obliged to take measures to protect himself from them, when as the sect of Assassins, they used political assassination as a means for furthering their power. Not only did Saladin have to defend his life from them, he had to compete with them politically and militarily to preserve his own power and his Sunnī dynasty, the Ayyūbids. Even when the Fāṭimids in Egypt had fallen, Saladin felt compelled to found *madrasahs*, or schools of theology, to counteract Fāṭimid propaganda. Similarly, the Seljūqs had found themselves obliged to turn to the Ash'arites in order to create a doctrinal bulwark and founded many schools to offset the *da'wah* ("preaching") coming out of Fāṭimid Egypt. Al-Ghazālī saw in them, under the name of *Ta'līmiyyah* ("the people of teaching"), a most serious threat to orthodox religion which he fought polemically. Numerous sects that exist today, the Druzes, the 'Alawīs, the 'Alī Ilāhīs (the Ahl-i Haqq), are the remnant of the heyday of the Seveners, preserving fragments of their ideology and perpetuating their methods of obedience.

The accusations of libertinism which have often been made against Sevener sects — for the most part a simple expression of abhorrence at their utilitarian view of exoterism — may at first appear to contradict the pronounced asceticism of the Manicheans in the time of Augustine. But both attitudes are different sides of the same coin; they reflect the conviction of the gnostic's independence of revealed laws, which they look upon as being "evil", and the conviction of the superiority of the knowledge they believe to possess through Dualism. The fragmentary and unstable nature of the Seveners and their offshoots bears witness to the normalizing function of the *sharī'ah*, the sacred law; when it is present a coherence is maintained even in the face of powerfully subtle doctrines, and when it is absent, the providential discrimination of form disappears, and with it, intellectual order. Al-Ḥujwīrī (d. *469*/1077) remarked in the *Kashf al-Maḥjūb*: "At the present day the Shī'ites of Egypt, who are a remnant of these Magians, make the same assertions...that everything stated by the Moslems has an esoteric interpretation, which destroys its external sense." *See also* ASSASSINS; DUALISM; FĀṬIMIDS; ISMĀ'ĪLĪS; KHAṬṬĀBIYYAH; KHURRĀMIYYAH; MANDAEANS; MANICHEISM; NŪR MUḤAMMADĪ; QARMAṬĪS; TA'WĪL.

Seven salams. Seven instances in the Koran where the word *salam* ("peace") is used in the sense of blessing either upon the person being blessed or upon the Prophet: 36:57; 37:79; 37:109; 37:120; 37:130; 37:181; 97:5. (There are also many instances of its use in different senses.) These verses are recited in times of distress or upon auspicious occasions. Other series of phrases or references in the Koran are also deemed to have special power; those Sūrahs recited together which have the opening letters *hā' mim*, for example.

Seven Sleepers of Ephesus. Story in the Koran (18:9-22)) of some young men who were persecuted for believing in one God, in a time before Islam. They took refuge in a cave, and slept there for many years, in an act of grace from God. The pious legend story was known in Arabia before Islam. The Quraysh went to Jewish Rabbis of Yathrib and consulted with them on how to determine if the Prophet was really sent by God. The Rabbis advised the Quraysh to put three questions to the Prophet, one of which was how long the sleepers had slept.

The question was put to the Prophet, in order to trap him, and test his Prophetic knowledge. The Prophet said that he would give the answer on the morrow, but a number of days went by. When the answer did come, it was in the form of the Surah of the Cave (18). Having recounted the legend the Koran says that the time they slept was known only to God, and laid down the rule: do not say that you will do something on the morrow, without saying "If God Wills". The incident shows the Prophet's sincerity in believing that God was sending him revelations. (The Koran's words "three hundred years or three hundred and nine" are understood to refer to human speculation, but not God's word on the matter.) There is a Church in Turkey, near Ephesus, dedicated to the Seven Sleepers.

Seven Speeches (or "Seven Scripts", Ar. *sab'at aḥruf*). A Ḥadīth says that the Koran is revealed in "seven speeches", "readings", "scripts" or "versions"; the meaning of *aḥruf*, which is a plural of *ḥarf* ("a letter", "a written character"), is problematical, and the best interpretation is almost certainly that of seven levels of meaning. There have, on the contrary, also been schools of thought which declare anything but the literal meaning to be heresy; for example, Ibn Ḥazm said that there could be no "inner" meanings (*bāṭin*). The interpretation which refers the "seven readings" to the dialects of seven Arab tribes: the Quraysh, Tayyi', Hawāzin, Yamānī, Thaqīf, Ḥuzayl, and Tamīm, is dubious. *See also* QIRĀ'AH.

Seventh Heaven. The degrees of Being which separate creation from the Absolute are spoken of in the Koran symbolically as the seven spheres, "skies", or heavens, the seventh being furthest from the material world and nearest to Beyond-Being. The final gulf between the two is marked by "the lote tree of the uttermost limit" (*sidrat al-muntahā*, 53:14), the limit of Being itself, which in some traditional accounts, together with the throne, the shade of paradise and the words of revelation, will not disappear when all of manifestation is withdrawn, when, as the Koran says, "the sun will be folded up". This is as much to say that these are not created. (The question of defining the relationship between created and uncreated was one of the great problems debated between philosophy and theology. The Koran and the Divine command *Kun!* ("Be!") were focuses of the debate; *see* al-KINDĪ.)

The notion of seven heavens appear prominently in early Jewish pre-Qabbalah mysticism, the Merkava ("chariot"; i.e. the chariots of Ezekiel) or Heikhalōt ("the Divine Palaces") school. In the Heikhalōt, the mystic in his search for God in the Divine "palace" ascends to the seventh heaven. At each heaven he is opposed and must struggle to gain entry with the use of Divine Names and secret signs, that is, with the knowledge of God. The origin of the idea of seven heavens appears to be Babylonian, or perhaps Persian, the seven heavens being the spheres of the planets visible to the eye, beyond which lies the sphere of fixed stars, which in symbolic astronomy corresponds to Being. *See* HEAVEN; NIGHT JOURNEY.

Sex. In Islam, sexual relations are not considered to be only a step in procreation, tolerated because of the need to continue the species. The pleasure of sexual relations does not have a negative connotation; rather it is considered to be a Divine Mercy — even sacramental — and thus completely legitimate within social rules.

Mankind, fear your Lord, who created you
of a single soul, and from it created
its mate, and from the pair of them scattered
abroad many men and women; and fear God
by whom you demand one of another,
and the wombs; surely God ever
watches over you. (4:1)

Men and women complete each other; a Ḥadīth says: "the world is a possession and the best possession is a virtuous woman." There is no obstacle in Islam towards admitting a tantric perspective and the Prophet himself, as well as many Sufis, gave evidence of drawing spiritual inspiration from earthly love. Literary sources affirm that when the Prophet saw Zaynab, with whom he fell in love, he said: *Yā Muqallib al-qulūb, thabbitnī qalbī* ("O Overturner of Hearts, make mine steadfast").

As can be seen from the literature of Islam, sexual union readily prefigures the felicity of paradise, and eroticism within marriage is condoned. One author could say: "When a man looks at his wife and she looks at him, God looks upon them both with mercy. When the husband takes his wife's hand and she takes his hand, their sins vanish between their fingers... Pleasure and desire have the beauty of mountains. When the wife is with child, her reward is that of fasting, prayer, *jihād.*

"Mundhir III the Lakhmid (a pre-Islamic dynasty), had captured a daughter of Ḥarith ibn Jabala the Ghassani. He decided to present her to Khusraw I Anushirwan. He sent him this description which was quoted in Ṭabarī:

> She is of middle height, has a clear complexion, beautiful teeth, a shimmering white skin, well-drawn brows, big clear jet-black eyes, a long slightly arched nose, long lashes, and a well-shaped profile. She has a lovely figure, thick hair, a fine neck, with a good height between ear ring and shoulder, an ample chest with high-drawn breasts, solid shoulders and arms, shapely wrists, slender hands and fingers. She is flat-bellied, slim-waisted, neat at the hips, generously wide in the flanks, and has well-set well-rounded quarters, full thighs, strong knees, firm legs so that her ankle rings sit tight, and slender ankles and feet.
>
> She is unhurried, used to leisure and keeps her skin smooth even where it is exposed. Always ready for her master, she is neither slavish nor brazen, but patient, aware of her station and background, and has an affectionate, quiet and self-assured way. Her high birth is evident from her father's name even before her clan's and from her clan even before her ancestry. Fine manners are second nature to her. She is high-minded, yet practical and skilled with her hands. She checks her tongue and speaks in a soft modulated voice. She is an ornament to her people, and a model to her enemies. When you want her, she is a woman; when you leave her, she is content. Rouse her, and her eyes grow passionate, her cheeks blush and her lips quiver in anticipation of your embrace.

Khosro II Parvez heard that one of Nu'man the Lakhmid's daughters fitted this description and asked for her which led to a falling out between the two, and the end of the Lakhmid dynasty when Nu'man first refused, then went back and asked for pardon and was executed by trampling by an elephant.

Celibacy or continence in marriage was not encouraged by the Prophet; against excess of asceticism al-Bukhārī records this Ḥadīth: "I fast, and I break the fast, I pray, I sleep, I go in unto women; beware! Whosever deviates from my *sunnah* is not among my followers." Nevertheless, some infrequent example of celibacy as part of a spiritual renunciation of the world can be found among the stories of the Sufis.

Al-Ḥujwīrī says:

> God said: "Women are a garment for ye, and ye for them" [Koran 2:187].
>
> Marriage is permissible to all, both men and women. It is obligatory on all who otherwise cannot abstain from sin. And Satan, who is with the solitary, adorns lust and presents it beautified to the mind.
>
> No human Companionship compares with marriage in quality of reverence and saving power where husband and wife are well suited. But no pain or care is a worse evil than an uncongenial wife. Therefore the dervish must consider well what he is about, weighing in his imagination the evils of marriage against the evils of celibacy, so that he may choose that state whose evils he personally can more easily master. Neither marriage nor celibacy are disastrous in themselves: the mischief lies in self-assertion, and in surrender to desires. The root of the matter is the difference between Retirement and Companionship as modes of life. Those who choose Companionship are right to marry; but to those who would retire from human affairs celibacy is an ornament.

But if there are some grounds for celibacy in the world, from the description of paradise in the Koran, it is hard to imagine celibacy there. Legally a marriage must be consummated and forty days are allowed for this, failing which the marriage contract is void.

A Ḥadīth says: "Marriage is half of the faith; the other half is patience." Its esoteric meaning is clearly tantric; not only is pleasure of union sanctioned, but marriage is a means of reintegration of man and woman into their metaphysical prototypes within Being; a return to the Principle. The female becomes infinitude in face of the Absolute, the male is absorbed and disappears into the infinitude of the female, each becoming one's real Self.

Islam tolerates polygamy but does not encourage it. The number of wives is fixed at four. The existence of polygamy in Islam is a recognition of the universal social conditions of the times and corresponds to a view of man in which the male reflects the unity of the metaphysical principle, and the female its infinity, and thus the multiplicity of the *ḥijāb*, or Divine power of manifestation.

Fornication and adultery are condemned. Intercourse during menstruation is prohibited, as is anal intercourse, and also violence and force against a partner's will. But these are the only restrictions; the Koran says "Your women are your fields; go to your fields as you wish" (2:224). From very early times various methods of birth control have been practiced in Islam and legal opinion generally admits the use of contraceptive devices if the partners agree. *Qāḍis* ("Judges") are known to admonish husbands whose wives complain that they have not carried out their duties towards them, and *vice versa*.

Ibn 'Arabī said: "The most intense and perfect contemplation of God is through women, and the most intense union [in the world] is the conjugal act." And Jalāl ad-Dīn ar-Rūmī said: "I do not wear a shirt when I sleep with the Adored One."

Shab-i-Barat, *see* LAYLAT al-BARA'AH.

ash-Shādhilī, Abū-l-Ḥasan 'Alī ibn 'Abd Allāh (*593-656*/1196-1258). Usually called "Imām ash-Shādhilī", he is the founder of the *Shadhiliyyah*, one of the most important Sufi brotherhoods; it is named after him, and includes the *Darqawiyyah*, the *'Alawiyyah*, and many other orders.

Born in Ghumara, Tunisia, his first master was Muḥammad Abū 'Abd Allāh ibn Ḥarazin (d. *633*/1236), himself a spiritual descendant of the famous Abū Madyān. He also followed for a time a Shaykh called Abū-l-Fatḥ al-Wāsiṭī, but desired to find the *quṭb* ("spiritual axis") of his age, and upon the advice of Abū-l-Fatḥ went to seek him in Morocco.

There he found 'Abd as-Salām ibn Mashīsh of Fez, who lived in retreat in the Rif on the Jabal 'Ālam. This was to be ash-Shādhilī's definitive teacher who, at their first meeting told him to perform the *ghusl*, or greater ablution. When ash-Shādhilī did so, Ibn Mashīsh told him to perform the *ghusl* again. The third time ash-Shādhilī understood, and said: "I wash myself of all previous knowledge and learning," removing from himself the obstacle of provisional knowledge before accepting the spiritual illumination of the Saint.

After he left Ibn Mashīsh, ash-Shādhilī made Egypt the center of his activity and teaching, and was well received there. His teaching insisted upon the inward nature of the spiritual path, thus his disciples did not wear the patched cloak (*khirqah*) that was frequently worn as an outward badge of asceticism by many Sufis, nor did they abandon their livelihood to undertake mendicant wandering, or renounce property and material comfort, or even hesitate to wear fine clothes. For ash-Shādhilī, detachment from worldly things did not mean a need to mortify the flesh or to despise beauty. Above all, the emphasis of the Shādhilī perspective is upon *ma'rifah*, discernment and the intellectual penetration of reality. This is no mere intellectualism, but corresponds to the initiatic process of finding the center through the maze of existence, as exemplified in the myth of Theseus and the labyrinth, or of Aeneas' arrival at the city of Dido where he traverses, mentally, a maze drawn on the city walls. Symbolizing the intellectual process and the spiritual journey, there is a maze drawn in stone on the floor, between the entrance and the altar, of the Cathedral of Chartres. A postulant who traverses this maze seeking its center will find himself approaching it and receding from it, from time to time lost, and obliged to retrace his steps, before he can attain to it. It is a game of hide and seek, of losing and finding, played with God.

Imām ash-Shādhilī had a vision in which he saw the names of his disciples written in the "inviolate tablet" where God's decrees are inscribed (*al-lawḥ al-maḥfūẓ*), and understood this to be a promise from heaven that those of his spiritual descendants who held to his precepts and the precepts of his successors would be spared the fire of Hell. A provisional or temporary entering into the fire for those who will ultimately achieve a paradisal state corresponds to the notion of "purgatory"; to achieve paradise directly is, however, considered to be an exceptional possibility, and ash-Shādhilī's vision is understood to be a dispensation in which, if further purification after death were necessary, the soul would undergo it as a temporary deferring of paradise, in a state which is neither hell nor yet paradise, whereby the soul would be purified in a beneficent way rather than through expiatory suffering.

Imām Shādhilī is buried in Humaithra, a village near the Red Sea, where he died while returning from the pilgrimage.

He left no writings except for a half-dozen litanies such as the *Ḥizb al-Barr* ("the litany of the earth"), and the *Ḥizb an-Naṣr* ("the Litany of Help"), all of which he claimed were inspired. The most famous is the powerful litany known as the *Ḥizb al-Baḥr* ("the Litany of the Sea"). The essence of his teaching is masterfully contained in the writings of Ibn 'Aṭā' Allāh al-Iskandarī (d. *709*/1309), the *Kitāb al-Ḥikam* ("Book of Aphorisms") which has been frequently translated and commented upon. Ibn 'Aṭā' Allāh was himself a disciple of Abū-l-'Abbās Aḥmad al-Mursī (*616-686*/1219-1287), an Andalusian from the circle of ash-Shādhilī in Alexandria who played an important role in perpetuating and establishing ash-Shādhilī's teachings. It was said of ash-Shādhilī that it was enough that a disciple spend a few days with him for an opening (*fatḥ*) to be made in the soul that would begin to dissolve the existential illusion and start him on the way to realization. *See* DARQĀWĪ; ḤIZB al-BAḤR; IBN 'AṬĀ' ALLĀH; SILSILAH; SUFISM.

ash-Shāfi'ī, Muḥammad ibn Idrīs (*150-205*/767-820). The architect of systematic Islamic law, he was born in Palestine and raised in Mecca. He was a Qurayshi who had lived in contact with Beduin tribes, thereby deepening his knowledge of Arabic and poetry. He studied law in Medinah with Mālik ibn Anas, and also pursued studies in Baghdad, to which he returned several times, thus becoming intimately acquainted with Ḥanafī law.

As against the customary usages (Sunnah), of the Medinah community upon which Mālik ibn Anas drew to amplify the law, and against the deductions and speculations of the Ḥanafī school, ash-Shāfi'ī promoted the Ḥadīth and Sunnah of the Prophet as being the primary authority for the interpretation of Koranic injunctions. These, he said, were more important than *qiyās* ("analogy"), and were followed in degree of importance by *ijmā'* ("consensus") as the legitimizing basis of law. Koran, Ḥadīth and Sunnah, *qiyas* and *ijma'* thus became jointly *uṣūl al-fiqh* (the "roots of jurisprudence"), that is, the systematic basis of law.

Ash-Shāfi'ī did not himself found a school of law; this was done by his disciples. His methodology was universally adopted by the other schools. Ash-Shāfi'ī is buried in Cairo. *See* SHARĪ'AH.

Shah of Iran, *see* PAHLAVĪ.

Shah Walī Allāh (*1115-1175*/1703-1762). A religious leader who promoted a reformed, active, and more militant Islam in India. His writings drew upon all fields of Islamic study — jurisprudence, theology, and mysticism — synthesized in accordance with his own original approach and intuitions.

Shahādah (from the verb *shahida*, "to observe", "to witness", "to testify"; "a perceiving", "a testification"). The affirmation and creed that is fundamental to Islam; the first and most important of the "Five Pillars of Islam". The Prophet said: "I have brought nothing more important than the *shahādah.*" When it is accepted sincerely — or "seen" — the consequence is surrender (*islām*) to God, Allāh, and becoming muslim.

It is made up of two statements, the "two testifications" (*ash-shahādatayn*); the dual of *shahādah.* In this context it should be noted that the word *shahida* (and hence the noun *shahādah*) has double significance typical of the genius of the Arabic language: it embraces the acts of seeing or perceiving and then of declaring that one has seen or perceived. The key to this is the link between act and speech which, in the Arabic soul, is so swift and spontaneous that many words bear a double significance reflecting it. For example, *dhikr* ("memory") is also "mention", that is, the verbalization of memory. It is for this reason that the first meaning of "observe", "see", "perceive" passes on to the complementary meanings of "bear witness", "testify", "live out the truth that has been perceived" and, even, "die for that truth": the word shahīd means "martyr".

The Arabic *shahādatayn* are:

Ashhadu an lā1ilāha illā-Llāh, wa ashhadu anna Muḥammadan[1] *rasūlu-Llāh*

I perceive (and bear witness) that there is no god except Allāh and I perceive (and bear witness) that Muḥammad is the Messenger of God.

([1]The rules of euphony in Arabic elide the *nun* into the following *lam* and *ra'*; thus this is correctly pronounced *Ashhadu al-lā ilāha illā-Llāh and Muḥammadar-rasūlu-Llāh.*)

It is the Arabic alone that carries the ritually effective and sacramental force of the words. Ultimately, the one condition of salvation is the complete acceptance of the *shahādah.* The *shahādah* expunges the error of Adam — symbolized by the eating of the forbidden fruit — of seeing objects as reality, in place of God. The sense of the *shahādah* is that one sees that only the Absolute, only Allāh, is Reality. The second *shahādah,* in defining the Prophet Muḥammad, also defines through him the relationship of manifestation or creation as a message or revelation from God.

It is sometimes held that a single uttering of the *shahādah* is sufficient in order to be saved. But while the encounter of the *shahādah* is a unique event out of time, man lives in time and multiplicity; the depth of his affirmation and the extent to which he is transformed by it cannot be conclusively demonstrated from one utterance. Therefore the *shahādah* must be repeated and lived until the implicit realization has penetrated to the center of his being, until through concentration upon the truth, and virtue, the individual substance is transformed and made itself adequate to the truth. Also, most Muslim theologians upheld the idea that faith must be accompanied by good works to save the soul.

> The Bedouins say, 'We believe.'
> Say: 'You do not believe; rather
> say, "We surrender"; for belief
> has not yet entered your hearts...
> The believers are those who believe
> in God and His Messenger, then have
> not doubted, and have struggled
> with their possessions and their selves
> in the way of God; those — they are
> the truthful ones. (49:14-15)

The primary *shahādah* is made up of two elements: the first is the *nafy* ("negation"): *lā ilāha,* (there is no god"). The second is called the *ithbāt* ("affirmation"): Allāh. Between them is a bridge, *illā,* which is a word made up of a conditional (in, "if") and a negation (*lā,* "not"). The conditional "side" of the bridge *illā* faces the negating nafy, and the negation "side" of the *illā* faces the affirming of the *ithbāt.* Thus it says that "there is no reality if it is not the Absolute Reality, God"; its juxtaposition of "if" and two negatives is a kind of magical or miraculous pathway out of the world towards that which can never be negated, *Allāh.*

The first *shahādah* casts man into an endless ocean, that of the Eternal, the Tremendous. The second, *Muḥammadun rasūlu-Llāh,* in which Muḥammad is at once Prophet, revelation and creation, is a vessel coming from the unique Reality, and thereby existing through It, which saves man from drowning in the infinite depths of the Absolute. It is interesting to note that the book of the *Kephalaia* says that man must not believe unless he sees what is to be believed with his own eyes. *See* FIVE DIVINE PRESENCES; FIVE PILLARS.

Shahīd (lit. "witness", pl. *shuhadā'*). A martyr, first of all he who dies fighting, bearing witness to the faith. Such are assured a place in paradise and are buried in the clothes they wore in battle. At the resurrection their bloodstains will testify to their merit. Assimilated to martyrdom are those whose death has been tragic or arousing compassion. *See* MARTYRS; SHAHĀDAH.

Shahrastānī, Abū-l-Fatḥ Muḥammad ibn 'Abd al-Karīm (*469-548*/1076-1153). Historian and student of religions, he was a Persian born in Shahrastān, in Khorāsān. Shahrastānī was nominally a Sunnī, even an Ash'arite, yet he had strong attachments to the Ta'līmiyyah or Ismā'īlīs. Naṣīr ad-Dīn aṭ-Ṭūsī asserted that not only was he an Ismā'īlī but a *da'ī ad-du'at,* or upper echelon propagandist. (Shahrastānī was the teacher of Ṭūsi's father's maternal uncle.) Shahrastānī studied jurisprudence with Abū-l-Muẓaffar Aḥmad al-Khawāfī and Abū Naṣr ibn al-Qushayrī, and theology in Nayshābūr with al-Anṣarī, a student of al-Juwaynī. Shahrastānī wrote a book on theology called *Nihāyat al-Aqdām fi'ilm al-Kalām* ("The Limits of Prowess in Theology"), and a circumscription of philosophic competence in *Muṣana'āt al-Falāsifah* ("The Productions of the Philosophers").

It is because of the remarkable survey of the religions of his time, *Kitāb al-Milal wa-l-Niḥal* ("The Book of Religions and Systems of Thought") that he is highly regarded, for he was an observer who saw to the heart of the matter in regard to religious doctrines and beliefs.

Placing Islam at the center, Shahrastānī studied other religions and graded them according to their proximity to Islam. It is interesting to note that, although this appears at first sight to be a purely ethnocentric approach, it is a classification that would make little sense around any other religion, for example Buddhism; but it is in fact a natural way to proceed in the case of Islam, since it is the religion of the Absolute revealed as such. Shahrastānī showed his sense of objectivity by freely admitting that some of the practices of Islam were against reason (though not false for all that).

Shahrastānī analyzed the divergences among Shī'ite sects, treated of Christianity and Judaism, the Philosophers, Hellenists, the Gnostic sects such as the late Valentinians, or Bardesanians, and the Buddhists. In the Hindus, Shahrastānī recognized in their esoterism the same theories as in Pythagoras, who, as an Indo-European, was indeed kindred to the Hindus, Greek Paganism being in certain ways an attenuated form of Hinduism. Of the link between Pythagoreans and Hindus, Shahrastānī said that a student of Pythagoras named Qalanus went to India and taught a disciple called Brahmanan who became ruler of the country; which can perhaps be thought of as a very condensed account of the Aryan invasions of India. Shahrastānī provided precious information on Zurvanism, a heretical form of Zoroastrianism, and on other long vanished religions.

Shahrastānī classified religions according to four categories:

1. Those who possess a revealed book: Muslims, Jews, Christians.
2. Those who possess something like a revealed book: Magians and Manicheans.
3. Those who subscribe to laws and binding judgements without benefit of a revealed book: Ṣābians (Hellenist Pagans).
4. Those who have neither a book nor fixed laws: worshipers of stars and idols.

He was very sympathetic towards the Ṣābians, by which he meant the Hellenist Pagans of Ḥarran, calling a group of them *aṣḥāb ruḥāniyyah* ("people of the Spirit", or non-Muslim peoples with an apprehension of revelation). He recognized their origins as coming from a primordial Prophetic tradition which he called that of the *Adhimun*. In particular, Shahrastānī thought that their Prophet was Hermes (who is often identified with the Prophet Idrīs, or Enoch, in Islam).

Shahrastānī presented the beliefs of the Ṣābians in the form of a discussion between them and the *ḥunafā'*, the pre-Islamic Abrahamic Monotheists. Of Christianity, he recognized "that Paul had introduced philosophy into the religion of Peter". In reporting strange mythologies, he spoke of the legend of the Phoenix, *al-'anqā' al-khurāfiyyah* ("the legendary griffon") a bird consumed by fire within itself, and then reborn, which the Muslims held to be one of the mythological marvels of India. *See* AHL al-KITĀB; GHULAT; ḤARRĀN; RUKHKH; ṢĀBIANS; TA'LĪMIYYAH.

Shah Walī Allāh, *see* before SHAHĀDAH.

Shām. The old Arab name for Syria and also Damascus.

Shāmil, Imām (*1212-1288*/1797-1871). The courageous and tenacious leader of the Muslim tribes of Daghestan in the Caucasus, who led his people in the war against Russian conquest from 1834 until his capture in 1859. Himself an Avar, he lead a coalition of Avars and Lezghians while Daghestan was organized as a theocracy, run strictly according to the *sharī'ah.*

The discipline imposed by Shāmil, who was of the Naqshbandī order of Sufis, inspired a desperate resistance against increasing odds. When he was captured and Daghestan annexed to the Russian Empire, Shāmil was received with honor by the Tsar, and albeit in exile, lived on a pension with his family in St. Petersburg. He was allowed to go on the pilgrimage, in the course of which he died. He is buried in the *Baqī'* cemetery in Medinah.

ash-Sha'rānī, 'Abd al-Wahhāb (*898-973*/1493-1565). Egyptian Sufi author.

Sharī'ah (from the root *shara'a*, "to introduce", "enact", "prescribe", "revealed religious law"; also *shar'* and *shir'ah*). The canonical law of Islam as put forth in the Koran and the Sunnah and elaborated by the analytical principles of the four orthodox schools (*madhhab*, pl. *madhāhib*), the Shāfi'ī, Ḥanbalī, Ḥanafī, and Mālikī, together with that of the Shī'ites, the Ja'farī. The Zaydī Shī'ites also have their own school of law as do the Ibāḍīs, or Khārijites.

The *uṣūl al-fiqh* (lit. "roots of jurisprudence") are the basis of Islamic law among the Sunnīs: Koran, Ḥadīth and Sunnah (acts and statements of the Prophet), qiyās ("analogy"), and *ijmā'* (popular consensus of the community, or *ummah*). Another principle, *ijtihād* ("effort"), is the extrapolation from these principles to specific cases. In the Sunnī world, and among *Akhbarī* Shī'ites, the age of *ijtihād* is considered to be passed in the sense of having been the prerogative of the period in which the systems of law themselves were established. At least this is the official, or doctrinal, position, for, in fact, a certain degree of *ijtihād* is always inevitable and has always gone on. Among the *Uṣūlī* Twelve-Imām Shī'ites in Iran, the situation is the opposite; ijtihād has not only continued officially, but since the victory of the *Uṣūlī* school in Persia over the *Akhbarīs* two hundred years ago, it has been continuously intensified, and modern developments are carrying the Shī'ites into completely uncharted territory.

The Wahhābīs and Ḥanbalīs limit *ijmā'* to the generation of the Companions and their immediate followers, the *tābi'ūn*; Khārijites limit *ijmā'* to their own community; Twelve-Imām Shī'ites add the teachings of their Imāms to the Sunnah, and *Uṣūlīs* admit the *ijtihād* of qualified contemporary Shī'ite religious authorities.

According to Islamic law, every act fits into one of the following categories called *ahkām*: *farḍ*, obligatory under law, such as the performance of prayer; (to this is added *wājib*, obligatory through legal extrapolation but not expressly mentioned in the primary sources of law so that its omission is no sin); *mustaḥabb* or *mandūb*, not obligatory but recommended; *mubāḥ*, neutral or permitted; *makrūh*, not forbidden but discouraged; and *ḥarām*, forbidden.

The principle of retaliation for an offense, which corresponds to the Mosaic law, is called *qiṣāṣ*. In place of the revenge embodied in the tribal custom which preceded it, *qiṣāṣ* introduces the principle that the consequences of an act are contained in the act itself. Intention (*niyyah*) is the critical factor in determining the nature of every act, in accordance with the Ḥadīth: "Actions are according to their intention..."

Islam makes no distinction between religion and life, nothing being excluded from religion, or outside it and "secular". Islamic law covers not only ritual but every aspect of life. It is often said that in practice today Islamic law is limited in many Muslim countries to questions of family and religious practice, whereas civil administration and commerce are covered by separate legal systems. In fact, a similar situation prevailed from early times; the parallel system of law was the civil law of the prince, which, being also of indigenous origin, did not raise the kinds of objections which are being raised today by traditionalists against the modern legal systems which represent modern times and are therefore borrowed from European models. Because Islamic law is extremely idealistic in its approach, assuming a natural desire to conform to the truth, and the existence of a "holy" society disposed to religious conformity, there has always existed a parallel system of justice administered by the state.

It is not possible to incriminate someone in *sharī'ah* law upon circumstantial evidence; there must be witnesses, or the confession of the accused. This makes the prosecution of criminal cases difficult, if not impossible, in practice. Thus the justice carried out by the political authorities was always a necessary complement to the *sharī'ah*; and the ruling prince could administer punishment and hand down rulings which superseded those of the religious courts. This exercise of judicial authority by the civil authorities, the prince and his delegates down to the local level, was called *siyāsah shar'iyyah* and accounted for as much administration of justice as did the religious courts. This is also called *radd al-maẓālim* ("the correction of wrongdoing") and was carried on by the ruler or in *maẓālim* courts which were not under the jurisdiction of the Qāḍi. The Prince also promulgated *qānūn*, or civil law (from the Greek, *kanōn*, "canon"), and published edicts (*aẓ-ẓahīr*), prerogatives which are taken over by modern governments and legislatures.

In addition, *sharī'ah* law is in practice traditionally limited by the customary laws of people who adopted Islam. Among the Arabs this has meant that the customary rules of Medinah and Kūfah were integrated into sharī'ah as such, but for peoples who came upon the scene later, such as the Berbers or the Qashqai, for example, this meant that as long as the community maintained its tribal or group identity, the traditional customs of the tribe were interpreted into the community's legal usages. In many cases these tribal customs (*'ādāt*) supersede *sharī'ah* law. This situation is particularly marked in the Malay countries, and above all in Indonesia where the customary law, called adat, plays a very prominent role.

Nowhere today, with the exception of Saudi Arabia and some Gulf states, is *sharī'ah* law the dominant legal system. In some countries it has been replaced entirely by legal systems copied from European countries; in others it has been relegated to deciding cases of family law; and in others it exists side by side with European legal systems adopted in the 19th century and first applied to commercial transactions. The Code Napoleon was established in Egypt by Muḥammad 'Alī; in Turkey during the *Tanẓīmāt*, the period of reforms in the last century, a synthesis was made from European legal systems; Jordan still uses the 19th century Ottoman legal system, while Turkey itself, since the abolition of the Sultanate, has adopted codes drawn up even more closely upon European models. Countries that underwent European colonialism adopted in large part the legal codes of the colonial power, and the creation of modern constitutions has led to further adoption of European law.

The desire to return to a more religious society, or to rediscover expressions of political life though indigenous forms rather than borrowed ones, and the rise of modern fundamentalism and new nationalisms as a way of "protest" and revolution, have obliged many governments to make gestures of "a return to Islamic law". These have taken the form of superficial, symbolic, and sporadic applications of the more rigorous aspects of such punishments as public flogging in order to play up to popular sentiments. However, like Catholic Church Canon law, *sharī'ah* law never existed alone in the past, it was always supplemented by legal decisions made by princes and rulers and other courts established precisely because of social needs not covered by *sharī'ah*. Thus the call for a "return to Islamic government" in a country where *sharī'ah* law is applied even in part is rhetorical rather than practical or realistic. Such a call is often heard in Pakistan despite the fact that *sharī'ah* law is largely in effect. Indeed, in Pakistan, there is actually an article of the constitution which says that no law can be promulgated which conflicts with *sharī'ah*, and in the opinion of many Pakistani Islamic thinkers the government is as Islamic as possible; which means that the call of "return to Islamic government" is a call for Utopian perfection which never existed.

Nor is there an imperative need for such a return if one accept the following Ḥadīth attributed to the Prophet: "In the beginning, if one omits a tenth of the law, one will be punished, but at the end of time, if one accomplishes a tenth of the law, one will be saved." *See also* ABŪ ḤANĪFAH; AḤKĀM; AKHBARĪS; CREED; DIVORCE; FARḌ ; FATWĀ; FIQH; al-FIQH al-AKBAR: FIVE PILLARS; ḤADĪTH; ḤARĀM; IBN ḤANBAL; IJTIHĀD; IKHTILĀF; INHERITANCE; INTENTION; ISTIḤSĀN; ISTIṢLĀḤ; KORAN; LEGACIES; MADHHAB; MĀLIK IBN ANAS; MAẒĀLIM; MUWAṬṬA'; QĀḌI; QIṢĀṢ; SCHOOLS of LAW; ash-SHĀFI'Ī; SUNNAH; TALFĪQ; TANẒĪMĀT; THEFT; UṢŪLĪS; WĀJIB; WAQF; ẒĀHIRĪ.

Sharī'atī, 'Alī (1933-1977). Modernist Iranian political thinker and activist. Although he was Iranian, he died in Damascus and is buried there. He was noted for his eclectic ideas and his opposition to the West and to capitalism, to which he thought the answer lay in his understanding of Islam, an understanding which appears to have been fashioned by a kind of Existentialism drawn paradoxically from Western sources, rather than from Iranian ones. He was popular with university students.

Sharīf (lit. "noble", pl. *Shurafā'*). The descendants of the Prophet through his daughter Fāṭimah and 'Alī ibn Abī Ṭālib. The Prophet had other daughters, but upon the marriage of Fāṭimah the Prophet called a special blessing (according to possibly Shī'ite sources). Each *Sharīf* draws his line of descent from one of the two grandsons of the Prophet, Ḥasan and Ḥusayn.

Today there are many thousands of *Shurafā'* in Islamic communities. They are treated with respect and addressed in traditional societies by a particular title: Sidi, Sayyid, Mawlay etc. In some countries special registers exist to inscribe those who are entitled to be called *Shurafā'*. Two ruling families today are Sharīfian, those of Morocco and Jordan.

Shaykh (lit. "old man", "elder"). The title of the head of a village, or of a whole tribe, usually elected. It is also the title of one who has authority, whether spiritual or political, and in particular of a savant or a learned, or otherwise venerable, person.

A special meaning of the word is that of a spiritual master, a *guru*, the head of a Sufi order, which in Arabic is also *murshid* ("guide"). In this sense, its equivalent in Iran and India is *Pīr*, which is used in place of "Shaykh".

Distinctions are made regarding the function: a *Shaykh al-barakah* (or *Shaykh at-tabarruk*) is one who gives initiation into a Sufi order. One who gives, in addition, doctrinal or spiritual teaching is a *Shaykh as-sālikīn*; one who has achieved a knowledge not through an application of doctrine and method, but through ecstatic exaltation, is a *Shaykh al-jadhb*. Such a one, who may possess something of a spiritual state because of his experience, has little means of conveying a useful teaching for the edification of others.

The Shādhilīs make the following three distinctions: a *Shaykh at-ta'līm*, one who knows doctrine, what the Hindus would call a *paṇḍit*; a *Shaykh at-tarbiyah*, or master who can give effective instruction in the spiritual path; and a *Shaykh at-taraqqī*, a "Master of ascension" who possesses a degree of spiritual realization of the truth, and can bring others to his degree of direct knowledge. *See* SUFISM.

Shaykh al-Islām (lit. "the Elder of Islam"). A title which came into use at the time of the Buyids, a period in which very extravagant names and titles were popular, it was applied occasionally as an honorific to religious leaders of high standing.

The title acquired an increasingly specific function during the Ottoman Caliphate, and finally became the office of Mufti of Istanbul. The Shaykh al-Islām was appointed by the Caliph. Towards the end of the Caliphate, the office had become a sizable institution with a secretariat to carry on its duties, but was abolished in 1924 along with the Caliphate itself.

Shaykhis. A Persian Shī'ite sect founded by Aḥmad ibn Zayn ad-Dīn al-Aḥṣā'ī (*1166-1241*/1753-1826). After the disappearance of the Twelfth, or "Hidden Imām" in *260*/873, four successive persons claimed to represent him until *329*/940, when there began the "greater occultation" (*al-ghaybah al-kubrā*). During this period, which continues today, contact with the Hidden Imām, except for several legendary occasions, has been broken off.

Eight hundred years later, Aḥmad al-Aḥṣā'ī, calling each of the four original *wakīls*, or representatives of the Hidden Imām, the *bāb* ("door"), believed himself to be under a special guidance from the Imām and gathered followers. He evolved a neo-Sevener doctrine which was branded as heretical by the Shī'ite authorities. Its speculative theory that earthly bodies are a mixture of material and subtle natures, and that there exists an intermediate spiritual world, which he called the *hurqalya* (something very like the *pleroma* of Gnosticism), posed no threat to Shī'ite essentials and was common enough; but the new doctrine exalted the Imāms and their role in creation beyond the claims of ordinary Shī'ism to the point of polytheism.

The successor to al-Aḥṣā'ī was Sayyid Karīm Reshti (d. *1259*/1843), who claimed to be guided by the Hidden Imām in dreams. By this time the sect was already regarded with great suspicion by the authorities, and grounds for their concern were to grow when, after Sayyid Karim died, some of the Shaykhis found a new leader in the person of Mirzā 'Alī Muḥammad ash-Shirāzī. The year *1260*/1844 was believed to be the year in which the Twelfth Imām would return to the world; Mirza went so far as to claim publicly to be the *Bāb* ("door") — a more direct link than before — to the Hidden Imām. He was brought before the courts — such a claim having serious religious *and* political implications in Persia — and spent much of his career imprisoned. In 1848 he claimed to be the Twelfth Imām. He was shot by a firing squad at the age of thirty in Tabriz in *1267*/1850, after his followers had caused riots.

In addition to claiming to be the spokesman, the *Bāb* ("door"), to the Hidden Imām, and the Imām himself, Mirzā 'Alī had in his brief career gone on to found a new religion. This incorporated modernist elements such as the equality of women and abrogation of the Koran, advocated the removal of the Ka'bah and the tomb of the Prophet, and proposed a bizarre set of pseudo-mystical practices centering on the numbers 19 (the lunar metonic cycle) and 28 (another lunar cycle). The number 19 is also the numeric value of the Divine Name *al-Waḥad* ("The One"). The claims of the *Bāb* expanded into prophethood and beyond. He also predicted a "promised one" who would fulfil his teachings.

The proselytizing of his followers led to civil disturbances, insurrection, and his own demise. The writings of the *Bāb* are the *Bayān*, or "Explanation", and his followers, called *Bābīs*, exist to this day in Iran in small numbers.

The question of his succession, in the characteristically unstable fashion of such doctrines, led to further developments. Some followed the *Bāb's* original teachings, but a new group arose which was shortly to split into two new sects. The new group was led first by a figure called by the cult name of Ṣubḥī Azal ("Eternal Dawn"); and a schism occurred with the emergence of another leader called Bahāʼ Allāh ("the Radiance of God"), thus creating two sects, the *Azalīs* and the *Bahā'īs*.

Not all the original Shaykhīs had adhered to the Bāb, and those who had not now proceeded, under the leadership of one Muḥammad Karīm, a descendant of the imperial Qājārs, to form the "new" Shaykhīs, of whom thousands still exist in Iran today, along with the "Old Shaykhis", survivors of the *Bābīs*, and the Bahā'īs.

Al-Aḥṣā'ī had changed the Twelve-Imām Shīʻite doctrine of "Five Supports" (Divine Unity, Prophecy, Resurrection of the Body, Imāmate, and Justice) to four, combining some supports and eliminating others; the fourth he made the principle of the "perfect Shīʻite" (*shīʻa kamil*) who is in communication with the Hidden Imām and acts as a channel of grace. At the present time, although the Shaykhīs possess two of their own schools of theology, many, if not most of them, have beliefs and a conception of Shīʻism indistinguishable from that of the Twelve-Iman Shīʻites of Iran.

Nevertheless, this series of fissioning sects is clearly a reaction to the tension created in Twelve-Imām Shīʻism by the doctrine of the Hidden Imām. The absolute importance of the Imām in the perspective of Shīʻism on the one hand, and the absence of anyone for a thousand years to fulfill the role — were it possible to do so — has caused innumerable convulsions of this kind in Persian history, and continues to do so today. *See* BĀBĪS; BAHĀ'ĪS; HIDDEN IMĀM; SHĪʻISM.

Shīʻah (lit. the "factions", "party", from *shīʻat 'Alī*, "the party of 'Alī"). Any faction or supporters, but specifically those who supported the claim to the Caliphate of 'Alī ibn Abī Ṭālib are called the *shīʻah*. They did so because they alleged that 'Alī had a Divine right to the Caliphate, or successorship, and that he had received a special mandate from the Prophet; and because of their presuming a unique, spiritual authority in 'Alī, which was passed on to certain of his descendants. It should be noted that such supporters with such an ideology appeared only twenty years or so after 'Alī's death, and the ideology itself took more than a hundred years to develop. *See* SHĪʻISM.

Shīʻism. A branch of Islam comprising 10% or less of the total of all Muslims, with doctrines significantly different from those of the orthodox Sunnī majority. The nature of these doctrines implies the existence of superhuman or divine qualities among some selected leaders, the Imāms, and special authority among others, the clergy. Thus Shīʻism is a form of Islam distinguished by gnosticism of all kinds inherited from many sources in antiquity. Shīʻites themselves are divided into three principal groups:

The largest division by far, Twelve-Imām Shīʻism, also called "Twelvers" (*ithnā ʻashariyyah*), has been the official religion of Iran since the Ṣafavid dynasty came to power in *907*/1501. Twelve-Imām Shīʻites make up 60% of the population in 'Irāq and Lebanon, and Twelve-Imām Shīʻite minorities are also present in Afghanistan, Pakistan, India, and Syria, as well as in the Eastern Province of Saudi Arabia and some Gulf States.

The Zaydīs, also called "Five-Imām Shīʻites" or "Fivers" (a Western term, like "Seveners"), are found in the Yemen, where they make up about 40% of the population. The third largest group, today several million, are the Ismāʻīlīs, who have also been called "Seven-Imām Shīʻites" (they broke off from the mainstream at the seventh Imām; but the term is of Western origin which became Arabized). Their two main divisions are Bohoras and Nizārīs. They are concentrated in the Indian subcontinent, and scattered across Central Asia, Iran, Syria, Yemen and East Africa. Many have also emigrated to Europe and the Americas.

These groups each contain further subdivisions, and in some case have given rise to offshoots, such as the Shaykhīs, whilst certain sects on the fringes of Islam have been influenced by ideas of a dominantly Shīʻite — and often Ismāʻīlī — stamp.

It is commonly said that Shīʻism is a theory that 'Alī should have been the immediate successor to the Prophet Muḥammad. However, the first stirrings of this idea appeared long after 'Alīs death, and the real rudiments of this theory first came into existence more than a hundred years year. It is still a continuously evolving mythology which spins itself backwards from the present, revising the past, and those historical figures who were its main actors would have been amazed to see the rôles which have been posthumously created for them.

The name Shīʻite or *Shīʻah* means "partisan". Shīʻites purport that there was a *shīʻat 'Alī* (the "party of 'Alī"), which, if it actually existed, would have been a small circle, fewer than a dozen men, who advocated, or rather, could have advocated that 'Alī ibn Abī Ṭālib succeed the Prophet; a succession which eventually became the Caliphate. At the time of the death of the Prophet there is absolutely no sign that such a group existed, although when 'Alī actually did become Caliph, twenty four years later, he obviously had some support, and a great deal of opposition. 'Alī was a cousin of the Prophet as well as his son-in-law, having married the Prophet's daughter Fāṭimah. He was, moreover, one of the first converts to Islam and later gained fame, or had fame created for him, as a warrior.

Shī'ism came into existence as a front for alternative political and religious tendencies. In the course of time it created the idea that evil exists in the world because of a monumental historical flaw, a mistake on a cosmic scale. History is interpreted by Shī'ism as a prop or a mythology, still being embellished today, for this underlying idea. The mistake is that 'Alī was not given his rightful place, at the right time. This mistake was disastrous for mankind because Shī'ites attribute to 'Alī and certain of his descendants a Messianic nature. They say that God intended that 'Alī and his descendants, the Imāms, should rule Islam, and thereby the whole earth, and that individual salvation is obtained through them. Some went so far as to say that the Angel Gabriel made the first mistake by bringing the Message (the Koran) to Muḥammad instead of 'Alī for whom it was intended! They contend that it is because of the evil acts of God's enemies that these Imāms and God's plan was thwarted. That when 'Alī (and his son Ḥasan) actually did become Caliph their true Messianic nature was not recognized; that this terrible error was repeated when his son Ḥusayn (who was also so anointed by destiny) was not helped by the people of Kūfah, and worse, killed by the troops of the Umayyads, and that no subsequent albeit legitimate successor to the divine function was recognized and made head of state. The injustice was so great that the Twelfth successor (who in all appearance was never born, the eleventh Imām probably having no issue) went into a magical state and has been hidden from the world for almost twelve hundred years, and is still alive today.

Rather than lament the Fall of Man as the cause of evil in the world, Shī'ites lament the death of Ḥusayn. But they await the glorious reappearance of the Twelfth Imām who will make the world whole again by "filling the world with justice", rather like the restoration of holiness in creation by the descent of the heavenly Jerusalem for some Christians, or the Second Coming. "Filling the world with justice" in no small way implies punishing the "guilty".

Immediately following the Prophet's death, Abū Bakr was elected as Caliph (*khalīfah*, "lieutenant" or "successor" to the Prophet) at the popular assembly (*saqīfah*) in Medinah. The election was carried out in haste as the worsening rivalry between the *Anṣār* (native Medinans) and the *Muhājirūn* (Meccan immigrants) threatened to split the Islamic community. M. Sharon makes the very interesting observation "that the prompt action of Abū Bakr, 'Umar and Abū 'Ubaydah quashed the demand of the Anṣar of Madīnah for a share in the leadership. This action proved to be of great historical significance, because it decided the future political nature of Islam. The Meccan disciples were those who seized the government. What developed consequently was an Islam influenced by the Meccan breadth of outlook which had its roots in Mecca's international commerce; the Medinans could easily have reduced Islam to a local oasis-found religion."

'Alī was not present at this crucial event, since he had stayed at the Prophet's deathbed. He was then just thirty years old; Arab respect for age naturally favored claimants of riper years, although historical exceptions to such a rule did exist. Shī'ites contend that at that moment 'Alī' had been unjustly cheated of the leadership, and more the pity, because he concerned himself with the Prophet's burial while the usurpers concerned themselves with politics. There is, however, no evidence that 'Alī had even a remote possibility of being chosen as leader, or that he thought of himself as a natural successor. If he was a leader, by his absence at the turning point of the events of the *Saqīfah*, he simply disqualified himself, and his supernatural qualities seemed to escape everyone's notice.

'Umar, designated by Abū Bakr as his successor, became the next lieutenant or Caliph. When, upon 'Umar's death, 'Alī, now twelve years older, was offered the Caliphate on condition that he abide by the precedents set by Abū Bakr and 'Umar (a condition which shows that the community had doubts about 'Alī's leadership), he refused to be bound, or expressed himself inconclusively, and the function was instead awarded by an arbiter to 'Uthmān. When 'Uthmān was assassinated during an insurrection in Medinah, in a climate of growing dissension within the Empire because of the despotism or opportunism of the Umayyad clan, 'Alī was elected as the fourth Caliph in *35*/656. He immediately had to face an insurrection on the part of two Companions, Ṭalḥāḥ and Zubayr, who were joined by 'Ā'ishah, a widow of the Prophet. The three were defeated by 'Alī at the Battle of the Camel. But 'Alī also encountered opposition from Mu'āwiyah, a relative of 'Uthmān and governor of Syria, which led to the prolonged and inconclusive Battle of Ṣiffīn in *36*/657, and to the secession of the Khārijites, or "Separatists", from 'Alī's army. While Mu'āwiyah depended upon the Syrian army (largely Christian or newly converted) for his power base, 'Alī turned for help from 'Irāq and thus to the power structures of the former Lakhmid state whose remnants subsisted in Ḥīrah and in the new city of Kūfah. These became his allies. The Lakhmids had been supporters of Manicheism since the King 'Amr ibn Adi made the second Archegos or successor of Mani his emissary to the Persians in 293. From this point 'Alī and, above all, his descendents became instruments of Manichean policy towards Islam. Ḥadīth literature about this period is full of curious references to the large numbers of those called "siddiqin" (i.e. "the Manichean elect") in various places who could be expected to give their support to 'Alī. However, in *40*/661, 'Alī was assassinated by the Khārijite Ibn Muljam. His son Ḥasan was elected Caliph, but under threat of attack from Mu'āwiyah ceded the Caliphate to him in exchange for a sum of money. Having sold the Caliphate, and his supposed holy birthright, the story actually makes the picture even more ironic by saying that the price Ḥasan had asked was less than what Mu'āwiyah was prepared to offer, Ḥasan's demand having crossed with Mu'āwiyah's offer, for, it is said, Mu'āwiyah was actually prepared to give Ḥasan a share in the rulership.

After the death of Ḥasan (according to Shī'ite accounts, poisoned by the Umayyads) his brother Ḥusayn, the only other son of 'Alī and Fāṭimah (there were other half-brothers), was led to show hostility to the Umayyad Caliph Yazid ibn Mu'āwiyah, by reacting to the offer of revolutionary support promised to him by "the people" of Kūfah. When Ḥusayn left Medinah for Kūfah, and was attacked by Umayyad forces, this support did not materialize. It would seem the offer was actually an attempt on the part of Kūfan strategists to test Ḥusayn's political usefulness to their interests rather than a serious offer to risk themselves for him. As it happened, Ḥusayn drew forth no popular backing from other Arabs and the Kūfans did not show their hand, which led to Ḥusayn's tragic death by Mu'āwiyah's forces at Kerbala in *61*/680.

The idea that Shī'ism arose because of a difference of opinion as to who should be Caliph because 'Alī had a divinely ordained function recognized by supporters is belied by the fact that no one took note of 'Alī's burial place after his death; it had to be discovered in a politically inspired vision by the Caliph Hārūn ar-Rashīd more than a hundred years later. Nor was Ḥusayn's death an important event at the time; its date was not noted; it had to be associated with the holiday of the 'Ashura' afterwards to give it importance. Ḥusayn's death was followed by the relatively more successful revolt of 'Abd Allāh ibn az-Zubayr. This was a "Sunni" conservative revolt and did not involve the indigenous elements of 'Irāq. 'Abd Allāh ibn az-Zubayr was an alternative Caliph (sometimes called "Anti-Caliph") who managed to hold Mecca for a time and was supported by the Meccan aristocracy in opposition to the principle of dynastic authority demonstrated by the Umayyads. This also led to divisions among the tribes; Qays and Mudar supporting 'Abd Allāh ibn az-Zubayr and the Kalb and Rabī'ah the Umayyads. But the death of Ḥusayn was later to take on a mythic quality.

The actual historical emergence of Shī'ism in its original radical form begins, not with the succession of Abū Bakr, but with a procession of penitents (*tawwabūn*) who had walked out of the city of Kūfah chanting *yā latha'arāt al-Ḥusayn* — "rise to avenge Ḥusayn!" It was a suicidal desire to seek martyrdom. They were slaughtered by Umayyad troops during a three day confrontation that started on the 4th of January 685 (22 Jumāda I, 65H) at 'Ayn al-Wardah (Ra's al-'Ayn). Before they met their doom they stopped at the grave of al-Ḥusayn and spent a night lamenting his death. Out of 16,000 who had enrolled in the dīwān of Sulaymān ibn Ṣurad al-Khuzā'ī, 4,000 had mustered in the city. But only 1,000 or so old men, not seriously capable of fighting, bent on martyrdom, left Kūfah in a procession. The circumstances suggest that in actuality the Tawwābūn were Islamicised Manicheans. Manicheism extolled martyrdom in imitation of their religious founder Mani, a martyrdom which promised resurrection into eternal life. This was the actual birth of Shī'ism. With this event the gnostic underground of 'Irāq became the Shī'ah and adopted the cause of the 'Alīds (but the fuller ramifications were to follow much later). The procession of the Penitents was observed by Mukhtār ibn Abū 'Ubayd ath-Thaqafī. Mukhtār realized its political potential, was not seeking simply ritual martyrdom as a crown to an ending life, but had a program of political and ideological resurgence to oppose the new religion of Islam. The Gnostic strategists were now following the popular Gnostic groundswell. Ḥusayn had posthumously developed a following. Before Ḥusayn, his father 'Alī had turned to the pre-Islamic religious establishment of 'Irāq (and by extension Khorasan) for support, and now that establishment turned to the 'Alīds for legitimacy within the growing new world order.

In October of that year 685 Mukhtār raised a real revolt and seized the city of Kūfah. Mukhtār did it in the name of 'Alī, enrolled former allies of 'Alī from Kūfah, and held a ceremony in front of an empty throne, to which he addressed strange mysterious speech. He called this the "throne of 'Alī". It is this empty throne which is the key to the underground religion which inspired and shaped Shī'ism. Once a year, at the end of the Manichean month of fasting, the Manicheans hold an agape meal and ceremony in front of a Bema, a chair upon which the invisible founder and foremost martyr, Mani sits in front of the congregation. Like the Emperor's New Clothes, only the pure can see him and words are spoken to him in Aramaic, presumably on the progress of the Religion of Truth. Mukhtār also had a political program which intended to put a living 'Alīd, not a descendant of Fāṭimah and not a descendant of Ḥusayn, but rather Muḥammad ibn al-Ḥanafiyyah, as the head of the movement's political aspirations. The revolt failed, and the movement later allied itself with the 'Abbāsids, and brought them to power instead, until the clandestine movement and the 'Abbāsids had their own falling out. But it was this, an obscure religious underground coinciding with the political resistance of the time, which produced a hybrid that became Twelve-Imām Shī'ism. Somewhat later, Ja'far aṣ-Ṣādiq, head of the 'Alīd clan, eminent scholar and religious authority, at least posthumously, was made to be the spokesman of the doctrine of the Imāmate, by successors and continuators to the *tawwabūn* and the Mukhtāriyyah (also called Kaysāniyyah). After Ja'far aṣ-Ṣadiq, at the split creating the so-called Seveners, the movement divided into those conscious of the original and underlying nature of the religious development, who knew the empty chair was the throne of Mani, and those who believed the propaganda, namely, in Mukhtār's own words, that the empty chair was the throne of 'Alī. (*See* SEVENERS.)

From this march to martyrdom of the penitent *Tawwābūn*, the death of Ḥusayn and perpetual penitence became the central theme of later Persian inspired Twelve-Imām Shī'ism, comparable to Christ's crucifixion in the powerful emotions it evokes. It became the focus of profound themes of guilt for betrayal, of the expectation of vengeance and justification, and, with messianic overtones quite alien to Sunnī Islam, of the chosen one's death as a sacrifice in expiation for the sins of others. The anniversary of the event, (whose actual date was not recorded) has been symbolically identified as the 10th of Muḥarram, which coincides with an auspicious holiday observed in the Sunnī calendar since the Prophet's time. This date for Twelve-Imām Shī'ites is the culmination of a turbulent ten day period of mourning. At this time some Shī'ites scourge themselves publicly in atonement for their ancestors' abandonment of Ḥusayn to Caliph Yazīd's army, and for the perceived betrayal, or for not having supported strongly enough, subsequent Imāms or descendants of 'Alī who inherited his spiritual mandate. According to Shī'ite accounts, the Imāms, almost to a man and even in harmless old age, were poisoned by the Caliphs, perpetuating a theme of persecution of monumental proportions closely bound up with the Shī'ite ethos. (Dualist doctrines often require that there be an external enemy who is held to threaten a mortal danger.)

The fate of 'Alī and his sons, then, is of the highest import in the Shī'ite scheme of history. There was also a sister, Zaynab, a daughter of Fāṭimah and 'Alī, who has a revered position in Twelve-Imām Shī'ism. Her tomb in Damascus is a Shī'ite pilgrimage site, as is also the place in the Great Umayyad mosque where the head of Ḥusayn temporarily reposed, and the mosque in Cairo where it rests today. The sons of 'Alī by other wives, who, not being born of Fāṭimah, were not descendants of the Prophet. They do not play a role in Twelve Imām Shī'ism but do in other Shī'ite branches, and also, ironically, in the first Shi'ite revolt, that of the Mukhtāriyyah or Kaysāniyyah, which used one of these sons, not by Fāṭimah, as its figurehead.

The Sunnīs, also assign 'Alī a high place since, for them, he is the great champion of Islam in its early fight to survive, and the venerable fourth Caliph, one of *al-khulafā' ar-rāshidūn*, the "rightly guided" or Patriarchal Caliphs. It is clear however, that the image of 'Alī in Sunnīsm, is also influenced by his exaltation in Shī'ism. For the Sufis, the other heirs of Near Eastern gnostic traditions, who dominated much of Sunnī theology from the *7th*/12th century on, 'Alī is the fountainhead of esoteric knowledge and, along with Abū Bakr, figures in most of the initiatory chains, or *silsilahs*. The Shī'ites credit 'Alī with laying down the first rules of Arabic grammar. (The terms by which he is supposed to have done so show that it is actually Aristotle's statements about grammar which are being credited to 'Alī.) Thus, 'Alī became the repository of all knowledge, and 'Alī, who barely knew how to write, became the author of whole libraries which have disappeared without a trace. The descendants through Fāṭimah are also descendants of the Prophet, beginning with Ḥasan and Ḥusayn. (Interestingly, Sunnis who respect the descendants of the Prophet through Fāṭimah, calling them Sharīfs, or "noble" have disregarded the descendants of the Prophet through his other daughters, as have the Shī'ites.)

The Shī'ites (and not the Sunnis) hold that 'Alī had a special spiritual function alongside that of the Prophet which, according to them, gave him pre-eminent sanctity that entailed the absolute right to spiritual leadership, known as the Imāmate. This function was passed on by designation to his descendants, who, together with 'Alī, are the Imāms. This meaning of the word is peculiar to Shī'ism: for the Sunnīs an Imām is simply a prayer leader; the first significance, from which the others devolve, is "exemplar" or "model". For the Shī'ites, however, the Imām in his person is something superhuman.

The differences among the various Shī'ite groups hinge in part upon the identity of the Imāms, that is, which of 'Alī's descendants inherited his authority and spiritual power, and also upon the question of the extent and nature of this authority. At one end of the spectrum are the *ghūlāt* (from *ghuluw*, "exaggeration"), the most extreme of whom, make 'Alī into nothing less than Divine. They are sometimes called "ultra-Shī'ites", but sects like the 'Alī Ilāhīs ("'Alī-Divines") are really "*trans*-Shī'ites", beyond Shī'ism and Islam altogether. At the other end of the spectrum is a sect like the Zaydīs who see in the Imāmate a function which may or may not be exercised at a particular time by a descendant of the Prophet, and which does not necessarily include a claim to sanctity. Midway between these points of view, the Twelve-Imām Shī'ites assert that the Imām holds a spiritual and political pre-eminence and possesses special graces, miraculous powers, secret knowledge (*'ilm*) and favor which God has bestowed on no-one else. The Imāms channel a Divine light (the *Nūr Muḥammadi*) and are also considered to be "sinless". The Imām is necessary both for creation to be sustained, and for the believer to win salvation. A saying is attributed to Ja'far aṣ-Ṣādiq, the sixth Imām: "Who dies without knowing the Imām of his time dies an unbeliever." At a stroke this sends the vast majority of Muslims, including the Companions of the Prophet, to oblivion. And, in other words, Twelve-Imām Shī'ites make the Imām into an intermediary between man and God; a necessary and irreplacable intermediary.

This clearly resembles the idea of the *Logos*; the Imāms are envisaged as half-human and half-Divine means of salvation, and this is an idea which the rest of Islam precisely avoids in favor of salvation by direct surrender to God without intermediaries. Moreover, such a conception of 'Alī and the Imāms necessarily implies a profound ambiguity regarding the Prophet himself. No such claims are made for the Prophet in Shī'ism and this inevitably gives the Prophet a lesser role, in fact if not in name, as compared to 'Alī. It is this which creates the real divergence with orthodox Sunnī Islam. H.A.R. Gibb made the observation that all the Gnostic doctrines of the Middle East had flowed into Shī'ism. This in itself created a tension with orthodox Islam which was a reaction to such tendencies in the first place and in Shī'ism the ideological resistance joined hands with political resistance.

The *Shī'ite* doctrine of the Imāms can be summarized by certain details which are found in Twelve-Imām versions of the *mi'rāj* (the Prophet's ascent to heaven): the ancient Prophets whom the Prophet Muḥammad encounters affirm that their missions were in part intended to prepare the way for him *and for the Imāmate of 'Alī*; God instructs the Prophet to look out from heaven into the empyrean, and he sees the twelve Imāms performing the prayer in seas of light; God says of them: "These are my proofs, vice-regents, and friends, and the last of them will take vengeance on my enemies." (Vengeance is a major theme in Shī'ism.)

Whereas no reference at all to 'Alī and his descendants is made in the Sunnī account of the *mi'rāj*, Shī'ite understanding makes the Prophet *share* his spiritual station and function with 'Alī and eleven descendants, emphasizes the miraculous and outwardly avataric nature of their role, and, in the case of the last Imām, prescribes revenge and vindication for itself. This capital variation in the Islamic doctrine was the source of great upheaval for the Shī'ites.

According to Twelve-Imām Shī'ism the Imāms are:1.*'Alī ibn Abī Ṭālib* (d. *41*/661) presumed buried in Najaf, 'Irāq, one of the most important shrines.2. *Ḥasan ibn 'Alī* (d. *49*/669) buried in Medinah. (Some Ismā'īlīs considered Ḥasan a "viceroy" of Ḥusayn, and not an Imām in his own right.)3. *Ḥusayn ibn 'Alī* (d. *61*/680) buried in Kerbala, 'Irāq, perhaps the most important Shī'ite shrine of all.4.*'Alī Zayn al-'Ābidīn* (d. *94*/712) buried in Medinah. *Shī'ites believe that his mother was a daughter of the last Persian King of the Sāssānid dynasty*. Thus his descendents, the subsequent Imāms, would perpetuate the royal blood of the Persian pre-Islamic dynasties. (This is, however, in all likelihood a legend. This putative daughter of Yazdagird, "Shahrbanu", has been identified by Mary Boyce as a cultic name for Anahid, or Anahita, a Zoroastrian divinity of particular importance under the Sāssānids who represents an incorporation into Zoroastrianism of the Babylonian goddess Ishtar. Such legendary and mythological genealogies were common among the Persian royal houses as virtually obligatory supports for claims to legitimacy. Also, early on, the mothers of some Imāms are supposedly Berbers from North Africa; this is indicative of the real links which existed between the Manicheans of 'Irāq and their co-religionists in North Africa, a link which emerges to the fore with the Fāṭimids and with the identity of one of the known Archegos.)5. *Muḥammad al-Bāqir* (d. *113*/731) buried in Medinah. A faction recognized his more active brother Zayd as Imām, giving rise to another branch of Shī'ites, the Zaydīs, known as "Fivers".6. *Ja'far aṣ-Ṣādiq* (d. *148*/765) buried in Medinah. Famous as a scholar, teacher of religion, and fountainhead of hermetic sciences, he is credited with originating the Shī'ite school of law, and many sayings which shape Shī'ite doctrine are attributed to him. Some Shī'ites believe that he designated his eldest son Ismā'īl to succeed him as Imām, then revoked the designation in favor of Mūsā-l-Kāẓim, another son. The adherents of Ismā'īl (who predeceased his father) asserted that the Imāmate rested with Ismā'īl's son Muḥammad. From this schism derive, (in name, but not in substance) the Ismā'īlīs, another Shī'ite sect who are one of a number of groups comprising the historical "Seveners", and who gave rise to the Fāṭimids and the Assassins. This divergence went deeper than the question of the identity of the Imāms, however; its roots lie in the radically different religious doctrine at the center of Ismā'īlīsm.7. *Mūsā-l-Kāẓim* (d. *183*/799) buried at the great shrine of the Kāẓimayn in Baghdad with his grandson Muḥammad al-Jawād. In his time some Shī'ite groups claimed two of his brothers as Imām in his place; he was imprisoned and executed by Harūn ar-Rashīd.8. *'Alī ar-Riḍā* (also called *'Alī Reza*; d. *203*/818). The 'Abbāsid Caliph al-Ma'mūn named him as his successor to the Caliphate, but the Imām died, while traveling, in the village of Nagaun near Ṭūs in Iran, and was buried, deliberately, near the tomb of the famous Caliph Hārūn ar-Rashīd, father of al-Ma'mūn. The town is now called "Mashhad" (which means "place of martyrdom" and is technically the name of all the shrines of the Imāms, all being considered "martyrs", or indeed a kind of sacrificial victim who purifies the people). This, the only tomb of an Imām within the borders of modern Iran, is perhaps second only to Kerbala and Najaf as a Shī'ite holy place. The Shī'ites more or less believe that all the Imāms were murdered by their political opponents, who are considered usurpers of the Imām's authority. The 'Abbāsids came to power with the help of the Manicheans of 'Irāq and Khorasan, but al-Ma'mūn was the last to successfully ride the Tiger, and since the split into Seveners and what was to become Twelvers, Islamo-Manicheism and Shīism began to go their separate ways, with separate leaderships. 'Alī ar-Riḍā, as the front man for the Shī'ites may have actually been assassinated by al-Ma'mūn, as the Shī'ites say, by eating poisoned grapes. With the Caliphate of al-Muqtadir, beginning in *295*/908 the Twelve-Imām Shī'ites became the power behind the throne.9. *Muḥammad at-Taqī* ("the Pious") *al-Jawād* (d. *220*/835) buried at the *Kāẓimayn* in Baghdad. 10. *'Alī an-Naqī* ("the Pure"; d. *254*/868 at the age of forty-one), buried in Samarra', 'Irāq, a garrison city where he was kept under surveillance by the Caliphs. *'Askarī* ("of the army") is one of his epithets.11. *Ḥasan al-'Askarī* (d. *260*/873 at the age of twenty-eight, apparently of ill health) also buried in Samarra', where, like his father, he was kept under surveillance. According to the *'Aqā'id ash-Shī'ah*, he had *no legal wife* but, according to Shī'ite tradition, he had a son by a concubine named Narjis Khatun, whom Shī'ite tradition calls granddaughter of a Byzantine Emperor. She was supposedly captured while on a journey, sold into slavery, and destined for the household of the Imām.12. *Muḥammad*, called *al-Mahdī-l-Muntaẓar* ("the awaited Mahdī"), and *al-Qā'im* (the permanent Imām until the end of time) said to be born, according to Shaykh al-Mufīd, on the 15th of Sha'bān, a festival known as the "night of forgiveness" (which exists independently of this event) in *255*/869. He is said to have disappeared from the world in what is called the "lesser occultation" (*al-ghaybah as-sughrā*), upon his father's death in *260*/873. During the "lesser occultation" the wishes of this Imām were represented in the world by four representatives. In *329*/940, at the death of the fourth representative, who did not name a successor, the "greater occultation" (*al-ghaybah al-kubrā*) began, during which no one has been in communion with the Imām. He is considered to be alive in the unseen, the "Hidden Imām" who is expected to return as the Mahdī.

This Twelfth Imām is called the "Master of the Age" (*ṣāḥib az-zamān*). Shī'ites believe that at the age of four, when his father died (*260*/873), he disappeared into the cellar (*sardib*) of the family house in Samarra'.

The four consecutive intermediaries who represented the Hidden Imām in the world until *329*/940 were called *wakīls*. The first was 'Uthmān ibn Sa'īd, the secretary of the father, Ḥasan al-'Askari, who had often taken charge of the affairs of the eleventh Imām (who was probably in poor health, possibly impotent, and died at the age of twenty-eight). Together with the women of the household, this representative supplied information about the Twelfth Imām, describing his appearance, etc. The fourth and last *wakīl* declined to name a successor, but said on his deathbed: "The matter now rests with God."

Adherents, however, continued to believe in the existence of a successor to the eleventh Imām, and thus the period of the "lesser occultation" (when the Hidden Twelfth Imām had a representative, the wakīl) ushered in the period of "greater occultation" (without an intermediary) which continues today. The Twelfth Imām is considered to be alive today, and will return (the *raj'ah*) as the *Mahdī*, and so is called the "awaited *Mahdī*" (*al-Mahdī-l-muntaẓār*). (The appearance of a leader called the *Mahdī*, or "Guided One", before the end of the world is mentioned in Ḥadīth, but not in the canonical collections, and historically the idea is of Shī'ite origin, appearing some fifty years after the death of the Prophet. Nevertheless, many Sunnī Muslims today share this idea; it is the identification of the *Mahdī* as the Twelfth Imām which is specifically Shī'ite.) Shī'ites believe that the Twelfth, or "Hidden Imām", hears prayers and intercedes in the affairs of this world. (*See* HIDDEN IMĀM; MAHDĪ.)

Originally, Shī'ism was largely a political movement. The Umayyad dynasty imposed a system of Arab dominance in which conquered peoples, in accepting Islam, were adopted into Arab tribes as inferior clients (*mawlā*, plural *mawālī*) dependent upon an Arab protector. This was put to an end by the Umayyad Caliph 'Umar ibn 'Abd al-'Azīz (d. *101*/720), who also ended the execration of 'Alī from the pulpits which had been common since the time of Mu'āwiyah. But this, and Umayyad oppression, had sparked continuous insurrection. Revolts among the Christian populations of Syria were rare, but frequent among converted populations in 'Irāq and Persia. Rebellions seeking redress against Umayyad oppression made descendants of 'Alī, among them also Muḥammad ibn Ḥanafiyyah, a son of 'Alī by another wife, popular rallying points. Although all political movements, in this climate of expectation of imminent reform and millennial fulfillment, had something religious about them, early Shī'ism amounted broadly to political resistance, as is shown by the Shī'ism of the Buyids (Buwayhids), and that of other Daylamis and some Azeri Turks, and by the surviving Shī'ism of the Zaydīs. It was the influence of the Gnostic movements who emerged as the Seveners in the middle of the second *Hijri* century — a contemporary variant of ancient dualism that had penetrated Islam in order to escape persecution and to gain ascendancy — that introduced the notion of "Divine leaders" into the body of Islam.

After Ja'far aṣ-Ṣādiq, these aspirations and expectations took an increasingly supernatural turn. Personal salvation became a matter of "knowing the Imām of the age" and the Imāms became quasi-messianic redeemers, destined by God to be His indispensable instruments in the world. This phase coincides with the rise of the Sevener movement.

Thereafter, there are the "pre-Sevener" Zaydīs, sometimes called "Fivers" who stuck to their conception of the Imām as being, above all, a political leader; the Seveners, or Ismā'īlīs, for whom the Imām is absolutized as a Divine hypostasis; and the "post-Sevener" Twelve-Imām Shī'ites, who lie somewhere between the two.

The next phase in Twelve-Imām Shī'ism was the development of speculative theology during the rule of the Buyids from *320*/932-*454*/1062 which codified the doctrine of the Imāmate. These pro-Shī'ite Daylamīs controlled the 'Abbāsid Caliphs and the Empire and permitted the open expression of Shī'ite thought and literature, which proliferated. It was also under the Buyid Mu'izz ad-Dawlah in *351*/962 that the Shī'ite celebration of the 'Īd al-Ghadīr and the formal public mourning for the death of Ḥusayn on the 10th of Muḥarram were instituted. Imāmate doctrine was thus complete.

The Ṣafavid dynasty, claiming to be related to the Imāms, came to power in Persia at the beginning of the *10th*/16th century. They exploited the Shī'ite complex of persecution, of being surrounded by "enemies", that is to say, by Sunnīs, on all sides, and they turned the anger generated by the displacement of the rightful ruler, the Imām, to the furthering of their dynastic interests. After gaining political control, they promoted Shī'ism from a minority sect to being the state religion in Persia.

The doctrines of Shī'ism are not the same for all Shī'ite groups, and not even within the groups themselves. Twelve-Imām Shī'ism, having been the state religion in Persia for five hundred years, has developed the greatest homogeneity and the largest corpus of established dogma. Nevertheless, a wide variety of beliefs and interpretations of the accepted doctrine exists among the various social and intellectual levels of Shī'ism. Even between *Mujtahids*, or religious leaders within Twelve-Imām Shī'ism, there are considerable divergences. Moreover, all the doctrines have been greatly modified over the years, although an appearance of uniformity has been contrived through the retroactive realignment and adjustment of Shī'ite theory. In the last two hundred years, with the victory in Iran of the Uṣūlī school, which not only allows the leading authorities to exercise original judgements in theology and law, but makes it necessary that someone should do so, a process of accelerated change in Shī'ite doctrine has been set in motion. This process is still active, and recent changes that have overtaken Iranian Shī'ism, are today widening the gap with Sunnī Islam; in the early part of the last century, this gap had seemed to be disappearing. (*See* AKHBARĪS; UṢŪLĪS.)

Twelver Shī'ite theology is, in fact, Mu'tazilitism. It now includes a doctrine known as the five supports: these are Divine Unity (*tawḥīd*), prophecy (*nubuwwah*), resurrection of the soul and body at the Judgment (*ma'ād*), the Imāmate (*imāmah*), and justice (*'adl*). The first three are found in Sunnī Islam, albeit with some differences of emphasis and meaning; the Imāmate, however, is the essence of Shī'ism, and the last, justice, is an inheritance from the Mu'tazilites, or rationalists, whose system is in many ways perpetuated in Shī'ite theology, its brittle and reductive aspects being compensated for by the mystical doctrine of the Imām. By the term justice, what is meant is a *reciprocity* between man and God; God is *obliged* to react in certain ways to man's acts. What it means, in effect, is that man's actions are also absolute or, in effect, divine. This caused the greatest objection on the part of the Sunnis, who said in response that God does what he wants, that God is not obliged to react to man's acts, and does not carry out the bidding of man; God does not depend upon man, as many Gnostics hold.

As regards rituals, the differences between Zaydīs, Twelve-Imām Shī'ites, and Sunnīs are slight in practice when it comes to such matters as the prayers. All Shī'ite sects naturally have their own schools of law; the Twelve-Imām school is called the Ja'farī after Ja'far aṣ-Ṣādiq. (It is interesting to note that both Mālik Ibn Anas and Abū Ḥanīfah studied with Ja'far aṣ-Ṣādiq, but came away without any trace of Shī'ite doctrine: both went on to found two of the four Sunnī schools of law.)

Twelve-Imām Shī'ite practice differs from the Sunnī in such small points as adding a few lines to the call to prayer (*adhān*), notably *'Aliyyu waliyyu-Llāh* ("'Alī is the friend [that is, Saint] of God") added under the Ṣafavids. They also add extra utterances of *Allāhu Akba'r* to the funeral prayer. During the pilgrimage they use only open-roofed buses especially made for them, whereas Sunnīs use vehicles which can be either open or closed. Shī'ites *systematically* combine the two afternoon prayers together and two evening prayers together, something which the Sunnīs do only occasionally. They do not accept, as do the Ḥanafī

Sunnīs, that it suffices to wipe over the covering of the feet (*masaḥ 'alā khuffayn*) during the ablution. They permit the consumption of meat not slaughtered by Muslims, which Sunnīs admit only under reserve of necessity. Shī'ites prohibit eating shellfish which Sunnīs tolerate. More important differences are that the Shī'ites, unlike the Sunnīs, accept temporary marriage (*mut'ah*), and the doctrine that God changes his decisions (*badā'*); the latter was introduced by Mukhtār, and survives in an attenuated and transposed form in Twelve-Imām Shī'ism. Shī'ites deny the efficacy of prayers led by a morally unworthy prayer leader, whereas Sunnīs make a distinction between the function and the person, and accept a prayer as valid regardless of the character of the prayer leader, provided that the prayer is technically in order. Shī'ites also entertain the doctrine of a "cycle of sanctity", a series of saints which begins with 'Alī and runs to the Day of Judgement; the Sunnīs too have Saints (except for such groups as Wahhābīs), but no such doctrine. For both Sunnīs and Shī'ites the "cycle of prophecy" has been closed by the Prophet, who is the "Seal of Prophets". Because Shī'ite theology is a prolongation of Mu'tazilite rationalism, the Shī'ites deny both the uncreatedness of the Koran and the "beatific vision". They also make a distinction between the Divine Qualities and the Divine Essence, but do not quite go so far as the Ismā'īlīs who make the Essence the Gnostic Bythos or *ghayb ta'la*. (*See* "BEATIFIC VISION".)

The greatest single difference, however, between the two resides in the emotional, messianic climate of Shī'ism. Sunnīs find Shī'ism's vilification of the greatly venerated first three Caliphs repellant; and, indeed, the political theories resulting from the conception of the Imāmate as the source of all temporal and spiritual authority, and of the Imām as a kind of "priest-king", have not found sympathy in the Muslim world at large. However, many Sunnis have very little knowledge of what Shī'ites believe, and vice-versa.

For centuries, Umayyad and 'Abbāsid rulers were hostile to the Shī'ite minority, who posed a permanent political threat. It was to protect themselves from this hostility that Shī'ites resorted to the deliberate dissimulation called *taqiyyah*, and pretended to be Sunnī, which, by force of practice, many became. However, similar concepts of *taqiyyah*, or deception, are found in all Gnostic and Dualist sects. Mani not only permitted his followers to deny him under duress, but, Manicheism consciously disguised itself as other religions and claimed to be Buddhism, Taoism, and Confucianism in China. It is easy then to see how they could claim to be Islam, the real Islam, in the Caliphate.

From the Sunnī point of view, Shī'ites are Muslims because their doctrines coincide for the most part with orthodox Islam; the Shī'ite belief in the mystic role of the Imāms, while deplorable to Sunnīs, does not necessarily put them beyond the pale. (In some times and places, of course, Sunnīs do and have regarded Shī'ites as absolute heretics.) For most of the 20th century, differences between Sunnī and Shī'ite tended towards being overlooked, and, perhaps even, forgotten; but this tendency has now been reversed with the growth of Islamic militancy.

For centuries the absence of the Imām caused tension in Shī'ism, since he is indispensable in all domains; for example, some held that the Friday prayers must be suspended until his return. This tension ultimately produced such movements as the Shaykhīs and the Babīs, who claimed to represent the Hidden Imām. The absence of the Imām continues to perturb Iranian society even now, for it is understood — and from Ṣafavid times this has been official, and even written into recent constitutions — that the only legitimate ruler is the Twelfth Imām, whose return is awaited. It was for this reason that the Shah paid a symbolic rent for his palaces, which he was considered to be holding in trust until the return of the Imām. Anyone who rules in the climate of Shī'ism is necessarily held to be a usurper. In the Sunnī world the religious authorities have often been controlled by the political authorities; but in Iran the Mullās have usually maintained a sharply independent, not to say occasionally hostile, attitude towards the throne.

In the 1920s the Shah Reza Pahlevi tried to put down the power of the religious leaders, thus ending the centuries-old policy of previous dynasties which had sought warily to maintain a cordial relationship with them. In the past, this had been done as if the religious authorities were a sovereign entity, so that marriages had even been arranged to cement or create bonds between the royal and religious spheres.

Unlike the Sunnī world, where no allegiance to a religious authority is required other than accepting the procedures of a school of law, Shī'ites must in principle adhere personally to a superior authority called a *Mujtahid.* The *Mujtahids*, the most important of whom are called *Ayatollahs*, not only decide religious matters for their followers, but also control considerable sums of money, because they collect a special tax called the *khums* (a "fifth"), which was, during the Prophet's life, his share of the spoils of war, held by him in effect for the public treasury. The *Mujtahids* collect this tax from their followers on behalf of the "Hidden Imām". By their unique authority to make religious decisions, their control of sometimes vast sums of money, and their influence on the *bāzārī* sector of the economy, the traditional, small, shopkeepers, the *Mujtahids* or eminent Mullās wield a power that the Sunnī *'ulamā'* normally never have. (*See* AYATOLLAH.)

The idea that there was a mistake at the beginning of Islam — the denial of 'Alī and the installation of the wrong authority in the world — a mistake which perpetuated evil in the world, contributed to the overthrow of the Shah. This led to a new development in Twelve Imām Shī'ism which is the doctrine of *Vilayat al-Faqih*, a doctrine which says that the Shī'ite clerics are the rightful political rulers of the state in the absence of the Twelfth Imām. Indeed, it almost replaces the return of the Twelfth Imām altogether, at least as long as clerics remain in power.

The custom of the Arabs of the North Arabian desert to simply elect a leader, and in the event a successor to the Prophet, was unthinkable to some peoples; perhaps even to Arabs of South Arabian origin; but it was, above all, unthinkable to the Persians, with their traditions of priest-kings. Such a matter could not be left to human choice but had to be determined by a Divine decision; moreover, the Divinely designated leader could not be other than Divinely empowered. To this the martyrdom of Ḥusayn added the aspect of a "passion". This drama of suffering and injustice appealed irresistibly to the Persians, a proud people with an ancient culture vastly superior to that of the Arabs, yet humiliated by defeat at their hands. Not only were they conquered and compelled to undergo centuries of foreign domination, but their national religion was replaced, by conquest as much as by conversion, and by a revelation from outside their traditional past. It was also a nostalgia for the Gnostic religions, centered upon God in human form and upon the principle of sacrifice, that led them to exalt the person of 'Alī, whom they called the *haydar* (the "lion") and *shāh-i wilāyat* (the "King of Sanctity"). In 'Alī and his descendants, through the doctrine of the Imāms, they recreated the Divine, redeeming, solar heroes that the austere religion of the desert denied them. *See also*: AFSHĀRIDS; AKHBARĪS; AHL al-BAYT; 'ALĪ IBN ABĪ ṬĀLIB; 'ĀSHŪRĀ'; AYATOLLAH; BĀB; BIHBAHĀNĪ; GHADĪR KHUMM; ḤASAN; ḤILLĪ, 'ALLAMĀ; ḤUSAYN; HIDDEN IMĀM; IBN BABAWAYH; 'ĪD al-GHADĪR; IMĀM; IMĀMZĀDAH; IRAN; ISMĀ'ĪLĪS; KAYSĀNIYYAH; KHOMEINI; al-KULAYNĪ; MAHDĪ; MAJLISĪ; MASHHAD; METAWILA; MĪR DĀMĀD; MĪR FENDERESKĪ; al-MUFĪD; MULLĀ; MULLĀ ṢADRĀ; MUJTAHID; MARJĀ' at-TAQLĪD; MUT'ĀH; NAṢṢ; NAW RUZ; NŪR MUḤAMMADĪ; PAHLAVĪ; PAIGHAMBAR; QUMM; RAWḌA KHĀNĪ; SAQĪFAH; SEVENERS; SHAYKHĪS; TAQIYYAH; TAWWĀBŪN; at-ṬŪSĪ, MUḤAMMAD; UṢŪLĪS; ZAYNAB bint 'ALĪ; ZAYDĪS.

Shirk (lit. "association"). This is what Islam considers to be the fundamental error at the root of all sin or transgression. It is the "association" of something with God, other than God Himself. God is the Absolute. This means that He is Complete, He is Totality, He is Reality. Nothing can be added to Him, and nothing can be taken away. He is One and Indivisible.

To set anything alongside God as Reality is to commit the sin — the error that engages our consciousness and our being — of "association", which is the *only* sin that God cannot forgive, because it denies Himself, and prevents forgiveness:

> God forgives not that aught should be with Him
> associated; less than that He forgives
> to whomsoever he will. Whoso associates
> with God anything, has gone astray
> into far error. (4:116)

The sin of *shirk* ("association") is a name for paganism; pagans are called "the associators" (*mushrikūn*). But *shirk* is the fundamental state of being in revolt against God, irrespective of any professed belief in other gods. It is also atheism, or the putting of nothingness in the place of God. *Shirk* is the opposite of surrender to God, which is acceptance and recognition of His Reality: knowledge, or Islam. Because Islam is knowledge, it is initiated by the act of recognition: the *shahādah*. The *shahā-*

dah is perceiving and declaring that "there is no god but God". *See* KUFR; SHAHĀDAH.

Shu'ayb. One of the Prophets mentioned in the Koran whose mission took place in the interval between Abraham and the Prophet. He was sent to the people of Midyan, and he has sometimes been thought to be Jethro, the father-in-law of Moses. (7:83-91). *See* PROPHETS.

Shu'ūbiyyah. (Nationalism, ethnocentricity). From the early Islamic Empire onward, converted peoples, resenting the policy of Arab supremacy, have tended to engage in forms of national and separative self-expression, politically and in the arts, especially literature. In no case, however, has *Shu'ūbiyyah* involved apostasy from Islam.

Shuhūd (verbal noun of the verb *shahida*, "to witness", "be witness", "observe", "experience"). This can mean simply "consciousness" or refer to the transpersonal Self that is ultimately the only Doer and the only Witness. This corresponds exactly to the Hindu notion of God as *kartr* ("doer") and *bhoktr* ("witnesser" or "enjoyer"). It is particularly in this sense that the word was developed by the Sufi al-Junayd (d. *298*/910) in his theory of the one actor: "everything that you see is the Act of One". The Koran says: "And God sufficeth as Witness" (48:28). *Shuhūd* is thus a complement to *wujūd* ("being").

Shūrā "consultation". The Koran (3:158/159) says: "So pardon them and ask for forgiveness for them and consult with them upon the conduct of affairs. And when thou art resolved, then put thy trust in Allāh." A consultative assembly (*shura*) elected the third Caliph 'Uthmān. The term now refers to representative democratic institutions rooted in Islamic tradition, and in particular to parliamentary democracy. The concept that traditional *shura* should be understood in these terms was much promoted by Muhammad Rashīd Riḍā (d. 1935).

Sībawaih, 'Amr ibn 'Uthman (d. *177*/793). A Persian philologist, called "the little apple" a student of Khalīl ibn Aḥmad, one of the earliest authorities. He is the author of "The Book" (*al-Kitāb*) which determined the principles of Arabic grammar and remains the most authoritative book on the language. Sībawaih died young, perhaps at 33.

Ṣifah (from the verb *waṣafa*, "to describe", "an attribute" pl. *ṣifāt*). An attribute of objects in the philosophic sense, but also an Attribute of God as distinct from His Essence. In Islamic theology, seven particular Attributes of God are posited thus: Knowledge, Life, Power, Will, Hearing, Seeing, and Speech. Other Divine Attributes are often expressed as a Divine Name, such as the "Magnanimous" (*al-Karīm*); the "Compassionate" (*ar-Raḥīm*); and so forth. Some of the Names are not attributes, but Names of the Essence (*adh-dhāt*). *See* DIVINE NAMES.

Sigheh, *see* MUT'AH.

Sihr, *see* MAGIC.

as-Sijistānī, Abū Ya'qūb Isḥaq ibn Aḥmad. (executed ca. *386*/996 by the Ṣaffārid Khalaf ibn Aḥmad). Also known as as-Sijzī and nicknamed "Cottonseed" he succeeded an-Nasafī (executed by the Sāmānids in *322*/934 along with Abū Ḥatīm ar-Rāzī, as the Ismā'īlī dā'ī of Khorāsān. He was one of the first eastern Ismā'īlīs to stop denying the Fāṭimid Imāmate and recognize al-Mu'izz li-Dīn-i Llāh, probably after the conquest of Egypt. With this recognition the intellectual developments of the eastern Ismā'īlīs, notably the Neoplatonism of an-Nasafī, were officially adopted into Fāṭimid ideology. The Original Ismā'īlī pentad of the pleroma was revised to include *al-'aql, an-nafs, al-jadd, al-fath*, and *al-khayal*.

As-Sijistānīwrote the *Kitāb al-iftikhar* and *Kitāb an-nusra*.

Silsilah (from *salsala*, "to concatenate", "interlink"; a "chain", "series"). In Sufism, the initiatic chain of transmission of a Divine *barakah* ("blessing") is called a *silsilah*, *barakah* being a grace or a Divine influence which comes from God alone. A *barakah* was transmitted by the Angel Gabriel to the Prophet, and from him to his Companions. *Silsilahs* consist, therefore, of persons who have subsequently received that pristine *barakah* and who been passed it on. Most recorded *silsilahs* come back to the Prophet through Abū Bakr, 'Umar, and 'Alī jointly, bringing together many collateral strands, particularly in the early stages of each *silsilah*. These chains originate in pacts of allegiance made with the Prophet on three occasions: the pacts of the first and second 'Aqabah and in particular, "the Pact of Felicity" (*Bay'at ar-Riḍwān*) which was made in a moment of extreme danger at

Ḥudaybiyyah just outside Mecca.

Completeness and authenticity of the initiatic chain is indispensable to the legitimacy of anyone claiming to be a Sufi Shaykh. Ibn Jawzī (d. *597*/1200), the theologian, preacher, and universal scholar who wrote Talbīs Iblīs or the *Devil's Delusions*, denounced many deviant practices and notions. Among them he easily demonstrated that several Sufi *silsilahs* were historically impossible; that the persons who were supposed to have passed on the chains could never have met. In answer to this common defect some Sufis claimed that the historically impossible connections were *Uwaysian* links, that is, transmissions across time and space when physical reality interposed itself. (*See* UWAYS al-QARĀNĪ). A more serious deviation than the occasional corruption to which religious organizations are prone, is the fairly common practice which had arisen from early times among many Sufis which was that of systematically reciting *silsilah* prayers. Even when they are presented as merely a pious remembrance of the past masters, these become a regular, weekly ritual invocation of the human beings themselves, something which the Koran categorically prohibits, saying call upon none other than God: "Say: Can ye see yourselves, if the punishment of Allāh come upon you or the Hour comes upon you, (calling upon other than Allāh?) Do ye then call (for help) to any other than Allāh? (Answer that) if ye are truthful." (6:40 and 6:71; 7:37; 10:66; 10:106; 13:14; 17:67; 31:30; 43:86; 72:18). On the other hand, what is often called canonic prayer among the Ismā'īlīs is actually a recitation of the names of the Imāms, or a case of a silsilah prayer carried to its limit.

There are two singular *silsilahs* in Sufism, namely that of the Tijāniyyah Order, whose founder, Sidi Aḥmad at-Tijānī, in the last century claimed to have received his initiation directly from the Prophet in a vision, and that of the Khāḍiriyyah order which claims to have its transmission, not from the Prophet, but independently from al-Khiḍr, a figure who represents the incarnation of the universal Intellect. Such a prodigy is hard to justify historically because of the ubiquitous presence of normal chains in the Islamic world; nevertheless, Sufis themselves refrain from dismissing these out of hand. Religions recognize such possibilities as valid, and Catholic canon law, for example, admits the efficacy of baptisms received in visions or dreams.

An example of a typical *silsilah* is the following:

Gabriel
Muḥammad
'Alī ibn Abī Ṭālib
al-Ḥasan
Abū Muḥammad Jābir
Sa'īd al-Ghazāwī
Fatḥ as-Su'ūd
Sa'd
Abū Muḥammad Sa'īd
Aḥmad al-Marwānī
Ibrāhīm Baṣrī
Zayn ad-Dīn al-Qazwīnī
Muḥammad Shams ad-Dīn
Muḥammad Tāj ad-Dīn
Nūr ad-Dīn Abū-l-Ḥasan 'Alī
Fakhr ad-Dīn
Tuqay ad-Dīn al-Fuqayyir
'Abd ar-Raḥmān al-'Attār az-Zayyāt
'Abd as-Salām ibn Mashīsh
Abū-l-Ḥasan ash-Shādhilī
Abū-l-'Abbās al-Mursī
Aḥmad ibn 'Aṭā'illāh
Dāwūd al-Bakhīlī
Muḥammad Wafā'
'Alī ibn Wafā'
Yaḥyā al-Qādirī
Aḥmad ibn 'Uqbā-l-Haḍramī
Aḥmad Zarrūq
Ibrāhīm Afahham
'Alī as-Sanhājī ad-Dawwār
'Abd ar-Raḥmān al-Fāsī
Muḥammad ibn 'Abd Allāh
Qāsim al-Khaṣṣāṣī
Aḥmad ibn 'Abd Allāh
al-'Arabī ibn Aḥmad ibn 'Abd Allāh
'Alī al-Jamāl
al-'Arabī ibn Aḥmad ad-Darqāwī
Muḥammad ibn 'Abd al-Qādir
Muḥammad ibn Qaddūr al-Wakīlī
Muḥammad ibn Habīb al-Buzīdī
Aḥmad ibn Muṣṭafā-l-'Alawī
(*1286-1353*/1869-1934)

See ḤUDAYBIYYAH; al-KHIḌR; RIḌWĀN; SUFISM.

Sīma. A dark spot on the forehead which develops from touching the head against the ground in prayer. The Koran mentions it: "Their mark is on their faces, the trace of prostration." (48:29). There are many dialectical names for this mark.

Sin (Ar. *dhanb*, pl. *dhunūb*; or *khaṭi'ah*, pl. *khaṭāyā*; or *ithm*, pl. *āthmām*). In Islam sin is divided into two categories. The first is that of *dhanb*, which is a fault or shortcoming, a limitation, an inadvertence, the consequence of which is a sanction rather than a punishment. Sin as *dhanb* is distinguished from wilful transgression (*ithm*), which is more serious and clearly incurs punishment rather than sanction. Moreover, since *ithm* engages will and intention to the highest degree, it necessarily contains the aspect of *dhanb* as well, whereas *dhanb* by itself can exclude *ithm*. The term *khaṭi'ah* is used in practice indiscriminately for both concepts of sin.

The concept of original sin does not exist in Islam. There is a Fall, the expulsion from Paradise of Adam, but not an inherent guilt which entails punishment or requires redemption. Indeed, the responsibility for the Fall is not Adam's; rather, it is Satan's. Adam's part in it is *dhanb* ("fault"), and its consequence is the earthly exile of Adam and his descendants, but not an infirmity which condemns them to a state of "original sin". The restoration of the damage of the Fall is anticipated by the acceptance of the *shahādah*, and accomplished by its complete realization.

The Islamic doctrine of the "sinlessness (*'iṣmah*) of the Prophets" excludes the possibility that sin as *ithm* should have existed in the acts of Adam, although *dhanb* was possible, and occurred. It follows that, in Islam, sin as transgression did not enter the world until Cain killed Abel. The Shī'ites have a similar doctrine which they apply to their Imāms.

The remedy for *dhanb* is to remove it, and for *ithm* to repent and seek God's forgiveness. The interpretation of the meaning of sin in early Islam was the principal doctrinal point which occasioned the schism of the Khārijites; and it was reactions within Islam to this schism, in particular that of the "Pietists" (Murji'ites), which gave impetus to the development of orthodox theology. The problem led to the enunciation of *al-Fiqh al-Akbar* by Abū Ḥanīfah, which says: "We do not consider anyone to be an infidel on account of sin; nor do we deny his faith." The Murji'ites developed the concept of "small" (*saghā'ir*) and "great" (*kabā'ir*) sins which found its place in theology. This is similar to the Christian division into "sins unto death" and sins "not unto death".

The creed of al-Ash'arī says:

> They [Muslims] do not brand any Muslim an Unbeliever for any grave sin he may commit, for fornication or theft or any such grave sin; but hold that such men are Believers inasmuch as they have Faith, grievous though their sins may be. Islam is testifying that there is no god but God and that Muḥammad is God's Apostle, in accordance with Tradition [Sunnah]; and Islam, they hold, is not the same thing as Faith.
>
> They confess that God changes the hearts of men.
>
> They confess the intercession of God's Apostle, and believe that it is for the grave sinners of his people and against the Punishment of the Tomb.

Sinful thoughts do not constitute sin if they are not put into action, and God can forgive any sin except *kufr* (disbelief and ingratitude), for which there is nevertheless the remedy of *tawbah* (turning to the Truth of God). It says in the *Ḥikam* of Ibn 'Aṭa' Allāh:

> Sometimes He opens the door of obedience for you but not the door of acceptance; or sometimes He condemns you to sin, and it turns out to be a cause of arriving at Him. There is no minor sin when His justice confronts you; there is no major sin when His grace confronts you.

And the Prophet said of God (in a Ḥadīth Qudsī):

> So long as you call upon Me and hope in Me, I forgive you all that originates from you: and I will not heed, O son of man, should your sins reach the horizon of the heavens, and then you asked My pardon and I would pardon you.

Sīnān (*895-996*/1488-1587). The renowned Turkish architect who built some of the most famous mosques in Istanbul and Turkey. Among these, one of the most successful is the Selimiye Mosque of Edirne which, like other Turkish mosques, takes the Hagiah Sofia as its model, with a central dome and surrounding smaller ones. Sīnān, however, makes of the model a more perfectly geometric form, less redolent of religious mystery, but more reposed. In addition to mosques in Istanbul, he also rebuilt the Grand Mosque of Mecca. (This mosque was again rebuilt in the 1960s when, most fortunately, King Fayṣal ordered that Sīnān's structure be preserved and the new mosque built around it.)

Sīnān was of Christian origin, one of the *devshirme* (Balkan "boy-levy") who had been converted to Islam and inducted into the Janissary corps. As a soldier he took part in the campaigns of Belgrade, Rhodes, and Mohacs, and in the seige of Vienna he was chief of the Corps of Engineers. He then went to Baghdad, and when he returned to Istanbul, he entered the service of the palace as chief architect.

His output was enormous: seventy-five large and forty-nine small mosques, forty-nine madrasahs, seven Koranic schools, seventeen public kitchens, three hospitals, seven viaducts, seven bridges, twenty-seven palaces, eighteen caravanserais, five treasure houses, thirty-one baths, and eighteen burial chapels. After building the Suleymaniyye Mosque, Sinan said ("according to tradition") to the Sultan: "I have built for thee, O Emperor, a mosque which will remain on the face of the earth till the day of judgement: and when Ḥallāj Manṣūr comes, and rends Mount Demavend from its foundation, he will play at tennis with it and with the cupola of this mosque..."

Sincerity, *see* IKHLĀṢ.

Sindbād Revolt (*also* Sonpādh, Sunfādh, Sunpādh). An anti-Sunni revolt (755/*138*) in northern and Central Iran sparked by the assassination of Abū Muslim. It involved Khurramite, Majūsi, Mazdakite, and Shī'ite elements and was put down around Hamadhān; the leader, Sindbād, was killed. Sindbād claimed that Abū Muslim was dead only in appearance and that he was in fact in the company of the Mahdī in a mysterious castle, along with Mazdak and that all three would appear in triumph. (The preservation of the hero in a suspended state in a magic castle is a theme of Iranian folklore.) In 767 another revolt broke out in Khorāsān under the leadership of Ustād Sīs, and in *161*/778, a similar revolt, that of al-Muqanna', another follower of Abū Muslim. *See* ABŪ MUSLIM; KHURRAMIYYAH; SURKH-I 'ALĀM REVOLT.

Sinf. A tradesman's guild.

Sinlessness, *see* 'IṢMAH.

Sinkiang, *see* XINJIANG.

al-Sirhindī, Aḥmad al-Farūqī (d. *1034*/1625). Indian religious scholar, known as *Mujaddid al-Alf ath-Thānī* ("The Renewer of the Second Millennium"). Sirhindī was very critical of the mystical school known as *waḥdāt al-wujūd.* He said "the mental condition of these so-called Sufis of the last type... is artificially produced (*maj'ul ast*), they cannot be regarded as possessed of a spiritual state (*ḥal*); they do not even know what 'the station of the heart' (*maqam-i-qalb*) is...nor do they possess reasoned knowledge (*'ilm*). It is these who misinterpret the genuine experiences of the real Sufis (*tawḥid-i shuhūd*) into a popular form of the unity of Being (*tawhid-i wujūdi*) and lead people away from the Sharī'ah that is, the moral law into licentious perfidy (*ilḥad-i zandaqah*)."

> Since the great Shaykh Muḥyi al-Din has overlooked the real evil, badness and corruption of the Essences of the contingents, he has regarded them as Ideas of the Mind of God the Exalted. These ideas for him, have cast a reflection in the mirror of the Being of God — besides Whom, according to the Shaykh, nothing exists externally — and have acquired an external shadow being (*namūd*). And (since) he does not consider these Ideas to be anything except the Names and Attributes of the Necessary Being, he inevitably declares the doctrine of the Unity of Being, and affirms the identity of the contingent with the Necessary Being. Holding that evil and badness are relative, and denying that there is an absolute evil or pure badness and says that there is nothing evil in itself.

See IBN 'ARABĪ.

as-Sirr (lit. "secret"). The spiritual center of one's being, the *'aql* ("intellect"), whose symbolic location is the heart. It is in this center that the mystics speak of there being a "union" (*ittiḥād*) with God.

Slametan (from Ar. *salāmah*, "well-being", "security", "integrity"). A religious ceremony of Islam as practiced in Indonesia. It represents an adaptation of Islam to the national religious ethos.

A feast is prepared to greet the ancestors; the word *salāmah* becomes in the Indonesian languages *selamat* ("greetings!"). The *shahādah* is recited in the course of the ceremony, as is the *Fātiḥah* Afterwards, the meal is eaten by those present. The ceremony is carried out at home at regular intervals, as often as once a week. This practice is Indonesian in origin and central to religious practice in that country. The *slametan* is observed even by those Muslims who do not regularly attend prayers in a mosque.

How different traditional Islam in Indonesia is, or was, from Islam elsewhere, before modern fundamentalist influences began to infiltrate the country, can be seen from the fact that in Javanese puppet theater there is an outstanding clown called Semar who is known to be Brahman, and thereby also recognized as Allāh, in secret. Such juxtaposition, God as a comic figure, would be unimaginable in Arab countries.

Slavery. This is an institution which, as elsewhere in the ancient world, Islam took for granted both at the time of the Koran's revelation and subsequently. However, Islam mitigated slavery by recommending kindness and the freeing of slaves as acts of great merit, and declaring that their mistreatment would cause damnation, at the same time as insisting that pagan slaves be taught Islam, and stipulating that free Muslims or protected populations could not be pressed into slavery.

Legally, slaves could only be obtained as captives of war or as the progeny of existing slaves.

In the early years of the Prophet's mission in Mecca, Abū Bakr spent his wealth in ransoming slaves who had accepted Islam and were persecuted for it by their masters. The acceptance of Islam by a slave does not, however, entitle him to freedom. Freedom can be bought through agreement with the master. The child born of a slave and a master is free (and the slave mother is free after the death of the master). Many rulers in the Islamic world were sons of such unions.

The corps of slave bodyguards such as the Mamlūks and Janissaries often used their position to seize power. The slaves who were not a military force were usually treated as members of the household and sometimes given a measure of autonomy. It even happened that slaves were given a position at court, and slaves in notable households frequently had more status than they might have had as free men. Sometimes rulers of one country, or generals, or ministers, were the slave vassals of another.

At the present time slavery has been prohibited in most countries. In Saudi Arabia, where the maintenance of *sharī'ah* law in its totality militates against the prohibition of an institution recognized in the Koran as legal, the statute of slavery was eliminated by King Fayṣal, who purchased and freed the existing slaves and prohibited the importation of new ones.

"Sleeping Foetus" (Ar. *ar-rāqid*). The idea that the period of human gestation may extend for a maximum of two years in the Ḥanafī school of law, and five, or even seven, years in the Mālikī. The "sleeping foetus" is a legal fiction designed to avoid the application of punishments which the illegitimacy of a child would entail. In some countries this has become a folk belief taken as literally true.

Similarly, if a case is brought to court of an unwed mother who has never been married, and thus cannot plead the "sleeping foetus", the legal stratagem which has become the acceptable solution is to determine that the woman had visited a public bath around the time of conception. As public baths normally alternate between women's days and men's days, upon learning that the woman visited the bath right after the men's hours, the Judge concludes that accidentally she came in contact with the sperm of conception by sitting on a bench where a man had sat only a short time before. This stratagem was accepted from Indonesia to Africa before the rise of Fundamentalism and the new literalism *See* ḤĪLAH.

Sokoto Caliphate. A kingdom founded in northern Nigeria around *1225*/1809 by Usumanu dan Fodio. In *1217*/1802, Usumanu dan Fodio (Fodio means *faqīh*, "religious teacher") went on pilgrimage to Mecca. He returned inspired by Wahhābī ideas and began preaching among his people, the Fulanis (also called Fulbe and Peulh). He declared holy war on the pagan Hausa, and succeeded in conquering a growing territory reaching to Niger and Chad. Upon his death in *1232*/1816 he was succeeded as ruler by his sons Muḥammadu Bello and 'Abd Allāh. The Sokoto state grew weaker with time, diminished by opposition to its unpopular stringent moral reforms regarding music and dancing, and suffered attrition at the hands of diverse groups including the Saharan Tuareg. In *1322*/1904 the British occupied Sokoto.

Solomon (Ar. *Sulaymān*). A Prophet held in Islam, and its sister religions, to be the paragon of wisdom, the author of the saying: "the beginning of wisdom is the fear of God" (*ra's al-ḥikmah makhāfat Allāh*). His wisdom is also knowledge of the unseen, and the traditional sciences of cosmology. He could speak the "language of the birds" (*manṭiq aṭ-ṭā'ir*), and had powers over the subtle world. He is traditionally associated with stories of the marvelous.

Solomon is also the epitome of the mystical love of women, as in the Old Testament's "Song of Songs". In Islam, this mystical love is expressed in the story of Bilqīs, Queen of Sabā' (Sheba) who was converted from paganism through being brought to see the difference between illusion and the One Reality, as in the *shahādah*: "there is no God but God", and thus became his consort. When she entered the palace she had taken the polished floor to be water, and lifted her skirt; then realizing her error, and opting, as it were, for reality, she "surrendered to God". In traditional accounts, her father is a *jinn* ("genie"), which is a way of indicating that she incarnated a supernatural nature and was, so to speak, an expression of cosmic infinitude which complemented Solomon, as Wisdom or Self, in the same way that Māyā complements Ātmā.

The chronicles of Solomon tell of prodigies: he could command the *jinn* who, when he set them to build the Temple for him, went on toiling even after his death, tricked because they saw his petrified body, or a statue, standing in the courtyard and seemingly alive. Then the staff on which the body was propped up collapsed because a worm had eaten through it, giving away Solomon's last ruse. At the command of Solomon the throne of Bilqīs was brought miraculously and instantly from the Yemen and placed in his palace in Jerusalem. Ibn 'Arabī explains this in the *Fuṣūṣ al-Ḥikam* by reference to the traditional theory of creation as an instantaneous and continuous act, not a process. At one moment the throne was being created in Bilqīs' palace in Sabā', and the next its creation was continued in Solomon's; the Jinn who brought the throne had done no more than move the site of its creation, but not the object itself.

For a month Solomon lost the graces of heaven, his kingdom and his powers — signified in the loss of his signet ring — because of idolatry in his palace: one of his wives had returned to the worship of her old idols. As a sanction, a "mere body" (one of Solomon's servants) was set upon his throne, while Solomon himself was forced to wander unknown in Jerusalem and to beg for his bread. In the Koranic account, the fault of his wife was "unknown" to him, that is, the fault did not incur his substance and responsibility, but he had committed a *dhanb* ("fault", *see* SIN), for which he underwent a sanction. When Solomon realized what had happened, he sought forgiveness; his signet ring was miraculously restored to him and with it his sovereignty and his dominion over the spirit world (38:35-36). The story of Solomon being replaced by a double probably derives from a Babylonian practice of substituting someone for the ruler in times of danger or when omens were sombre. When the danger was passed the substitute king would be put to death. In one case, however, a gardener doubling for the ruler ended up remaining in power. A Babylonian Chronicle described such an event:
ex:

> That the dynasty might not end, King Irra-imitti made the gardener Enlil-bāni take his place upon the throne and put the royal crown upon his head. Irra-imitti died in his palace because he had swallowed boiling broth. Enlil-bāni who was upon the throne did not relinquish it and was installed as king.

For twenty-four years he ruled the kingdom of Isin. The "Seal of Solomon", the six pointed star, has been a frequent motif used on coins in the Islamic world, and as decoration.

Somalia. Republic. Population: 9,639,151. The country is almost completely Muslim. Some of the Muslims are Zaydī Shī'ites, mostly Arabs from the Yemen. Otherwise the Somalis are Sunnīs of the Shāfi'ī school of law. Islam was established in Somalia from the first century of the Hijrah through trade contacts. Almost all Somalis belong to a Sufi brotherhood (*ṭariqah*). The major *ṭuruq* are the Qādiriyyah, Ṣāliḥiyyah, and Rifā'iyyah. Somalia is noted for possessing an oral literary tradition, memorized and not recorded, of great richness.

After independence from Britain and Italy in 1960 Somalia was ruled by Siad Barre, a Marxist dictator closely allied with the Soviet Union. Driven from power in 1991, Somalia has since been ruled by clans: Isaaq, Darod, Hawiye, Digil, Dir and Rahanwin.

"Son of the Moment", *see* IBN al-WAQT.

"Son of the Widow". Manicheism divides Jesus Christ into several different aspects among them the True Christ, and an apparition from the world of light clad in a phantasmal body. According to Manicheism this is not the person who is crucified on the cross; Jesus' counterpart and *antagonist*, the "Son of the Widow" is instead the person crucified in place of Jesus. Such a doctrine is called Docetism from the Greek word for appearance, often erroneously attributed to "early Christian sects" (which could have been Manichean branches in Christianity). Docetism also appears in an abbreviated form as the Islamic doctrine of crucifixion, namely that Jesus did not die on the cross, but it so "appeared to them". The "Widow's Son" is also a name for Hiram the architect in Freemasonry.

Soul, *see* NAFS; RŪḤ.

Spiritual axis, *see* QUṬB.

Station, *see* MAQĀM.

Subḥah, *see* ROSARY.

Sublime Porte (a French rendering of the name *Bāb-i 'Alī*, "the high gate"). The designation of the Grand Vizierate of the Ottoman Turkish Government and hence of the Turkish government as a whole.

Subud. A sect founded originally in Java by an Indonesian named Muḥammad (called *Bapak*, or "father") Subuh, but fostered in the West by followers of Gurdjieff in Britain and America where the sect has adherents. The name Subud is said to be a composite word from three Sanskrit terms: *Sulisa* ("right living"), *Bodhi* ("enlightenment"), and *Dharma* ("the cosmic norm"). Its central "ritual" is a psychic experience called *latihan* (Malay for "an exercise" or "training") which manifests itself outwardly as moans, crying, laughter, dancing and various involuntary body movements. The *latihan* is experienced in groups at regular meetings.

Subud has nothing to do with Islam although it is often associated with it because of its origin in a Muslim country where it has some practitioners, the fact that adherents in the west sometimes took Muslim names, and that some Muslims were attracted to it, thinking it was an offshoot of Sufism.

In fact, the founder claimed to have attained to a spiritual realization without following any master, Sufi or otherwise, and affirmed that various masters had told him so, naming in particular a Naqshbandi Shaykh 'Abd ar-Raḥman. Subuh was born in 1901; in 1925 he had the experience of a ball of light descending upon him; by 1933 he was proselytizing in Java. In 1956 he was invited to the Gurdjieffian center at Coombe Springs in England, which had been founded by J.G. Bennett, in the hope and expectation on the part of certain Gurdjieffians that he represented the fulfillment of a prediction by Gurdjieff concerning the future of his school.

In the course of his visit, over four hundred people in one month underwent the experience of *latihan*, (or, in Subud terms were "opened"), one of them being so affected by it that he died on the spot. Many who leave the sect find themselves afflicted by various mental and psychological ailments.

Sudan. Population 31,065,229. 70% of the population are Muslims of the Mālikī rite, although the legal system is very much influenced by Ḥanafī law; the rest are largely Christians of various denominations. There is a Muslim theological university at Ummdurman. Important Sufi *ṭuruq* are the Qādiriyyah, the Anṣār (who are "Mahdists", or the continuation of the Mahdī movement in the Sudan), and a number of Shādhilī *ṭuruq*. The Sanusiyyah Order of Libya also has a following in the Sudan.

aṣ-Ṣuffah, Aṣḥāb, *see* AṢḤAB aṣ-ṢUFFAH.

Sufi, *see* FAQĪR; SUFISM.

Sufism (Ar. *at-taṣawwuf*). The mysticism or esoterism of Islam. The word is commonly thought to come from the Arabic word *ṣūf* ("wool"): rough woolen clothing characterized the early ascetics, who preferred its symbolic simplicity to richer and more sophisticated materials. Indeed, there is a Persian equivalent *pashmina-push* "wool wearer". But it could also come from the Greek *sophistēs*, or "sophist", with the association with wool thrown in.

Sufism's doctrines and methods are derived from the Koran and Islamic revelation but their development was influenced by other, ubiquitous mystical teachings. Like exoteric Islam, Sufism freely makes use of paradigms and concepts from

Greek, Buddhist, and even from Hindu sources, and it is not at all strange that the most recent of the great revealed religions should take account of the intellectual developments which preceded it. It is true that philosophies of antiquity, in particular certain Persian schools of thought, played the role of catalyst or "leaven", forcing Muslims to develop the potentials of Islam, and here and there a trace of these "foreign" influences remain, like the blows of a hammer upon a sword. That it resembles other esoteric doctrines is certainly not accidental, for God is One and man universally aspires to knowledge of God. Sufism is found everywhere in the Islamic world; it is the inner dimension of Islam, from which the efficacy and force of Islam as a religion flow.

The character of Sufism remained the same in the later period, when Sufis spoke the intellectual language of Plato and Aristotle, as it was in the age of its inception, before philosophy was integrated into Islam. As the Koran 2:20 says: "The lightning [revelation, or intellection] well nigh snatches away their sight; whensoever it gives them light, they walk in it, and when the darkness is over them, they halt." The spiritual development of a Ḥasan of Baṣrah (d. *110*/728), at a time when the conceptual structures of Islamic thought were still rudimentary, could be likened to a series of flashes of intuition and realization. Yet if he had somehow encountered a philosophically adept Sufi of later times, such as Ibn 'Arabī (d. *638*/1240), whose dialectic made use of many intellectual bridges, Ḥasan of Baṣrah would have had no difficulty in recognizing in him the very doctrines that had already been enunciated in monolithic and religiously didactic terms.

In the early days, Sufism was not recognized as an "inner dimension of Islam", but was often identified with Islam as such. Indeed, to disparage the weakening of human aspiration after Islam's first efflorescence, Sufis have said: "In the beginning Sufism was a reality without a name, today it is a name without a reality." For the Sufis the great Master, the true Master, is none other than the Prophet himself, who taught the essential doctrines of esoteric Islam to his Companions, who in turn passed them on to succeeding generations. It is from this source that the Sufis trace their inspiration and their teachings. The Companions also transmitted the grace, blessing, or spiritual influence (*barakah*) which the Prophet received from God at the beginning of his mission and which he thereafter conveyed to his disciples through the *bay'at ar-riḍwān* (the "Pact of Felicity"), made at Ḥudaybiyyah (Koran 48:10). The chain of transmission whereby the original pact made with the Prophet is passed on from Shaykh to Shaykh is called a *silsilah*, an initiatic chain. All authentic Sufi orders are linked into one of these chains.

Historically, the Sufis have been grouped into organizations called *ṭawā'if* (sing. *ṭā'ifah*), or *ṭuruq* (sing. *ṭarīqah*, "path"), the latter word being used more commonly in the later period, from the time of the Qādiriyyah order. *Ṭarīqah* is now also a technical term for esoterism itself. *Ṭuruq* are congregations formed around a master, meeting for spiritual sessions (*majālis*), in *zāwiyahs*, *khānaqahs*, or *tekke*, as the meeting places are called in different countries. These spiritual meetings are described in the words attributed to the Prophet: "Whenever men gather together to invoke Allāh, they are surrounded by Angels, the Divine Favor envelopes them, Peace (*as-sakīnah*) descends upon them, and Allāh remembers them in His assembly."

In the beginning of Islamic history all the *silsilahs* that go back to either Abū Bakr or 'Alī are actually intertwined; many of the early Sufis (not yet, of course, so named) made pacts with several of the original Companions, including Anas ibn Mālik, Salmān al-Fārisī and others. In the 2nd century of the Hijrah these chains diverged outwards with the geographic expansion of Islam, and later, the names that succeeded one another, such as Ibn Mashish in Morocco and Imām ash-Shādhilī in Egypt, reflect journeys undertaken across the earth in search of masters whose reputation bespoke their spiritual realization.

'Alī is the great early link in these chains; independently of his role in Shī'ism, he is held by Sufis everywhere to be the fountainhead of esoteric knowledge. Another is Ḥasan of Baṣrah who, lacking the philosophical tools available to later generations, left no corpus of written teaching, although he was widely quoted by others; the universal respect he was accorded and the wide circle of his disciples testify to his having possessed wisdom of a very profound order.

Certain Sufis of the later period such as al-Junayd (d. *297*/910), 'Abd al-Qādir al-Jīlānī (d. *561*/1166), Abū Madyān (d. *594*/1198), and Imām ash-Shādhilī (d. *656*/1258) were all famed throughout the Islamic world during their lifetimes. Imām Shādhilī is noted for an approach to Sufism which is especially intellectual. Some of these Sufis left writings as well as oral teachings, and Sufi doctrines have been described in great depth and detail in the works of Ibn 'Arabī, Jalāl ad-Dīn ar-Rūmī, al-Jīlī, al-Ghazālī, Ibn 'Aṭā' Allāh and many others. A number of Sufis likewise wrote allegories; of which an outstanding example is the *Language of the Birds* (*Mantiq at-Ṭā'ir*) by Farīd ad-Dīn 'Attār, in which the birds (souls) set out on a journey to find their king (God). Above all, it has been characteristic of Sufis to express their spiritual insight in great poetry; Ibn al-Fārid's "Ode to Wine", which likens the imbibing of Divine knowledge to drunken ecstasy, is one example of this. Sufism is an "inward" path of union, which complements the *sharī'ah*, or "outward" law, namely, exoterism, the formal "clothing" of religion. Sufism is esoterism, the perception of the supraformal essence which is "seen" by "the eye of the heart" (*'ayn al-qalb*). All true belief has the "taste" of Sufism in it, for without it belief would be theoretical knowledge which committed one to nothing and engaged one in nothing. Sufism takes Islam, and the testimony of faith (*shahādah*), and removes limitations from the understanding of its meaning until the dividing line between "world" (manifestation), and Reality (God), has been "pushed back" to the very limit and nothing but God remains. The Koran calls those who know the essence of things "the possessors of the kernels" (*ūlū-l-albāb*); in turn, the Sufis liken esoteric knowledge to a "kernel" (*lubb*), hidden within a shell. This kernel is the "essence" or "intrinsic truth" (*ḥaqīqah*), which resides at the center of the circle of knowledge and, at the same time, contains the circle itself. Leading to this center from the circumference, which is exoterism, is the radius, the Sufic spiritual path (*ṭarīqah*).

The Persian Sufi Bāyazīd al-Biṣṭāmī said: "This thing we tell of can never be found by seeking, yet only seekers find it." Contrary to notions sometimes encountered in the West, to embark upon the path of Sufism it is absolutely necessary to be a Muslim, for Sufism's methods are inoperative without this religious affiliation, and may even prove destructive to the individual who lacks the protective and normative consecration of the religion of Islam, which is its vehicle. While exoterism is incumbent upon all, for all are called to salvation and to conformity with Divine law, esoterism is a matter of individual vocation. Initiation (*al-bay'ah* or *al-idhn*) is the necessary point of entry from the exoteric, for this transmits a spiritual influence (*barakah*), a grace conveyed by the Angel Gabriel to the Prophet at the time of revelation; initiation plants a seed in the soul; like baptism, it is the beginning of a new life, for the initiation bestowed by a spiritual master (*shaykh*) has a lineage that goes back, through the entire series of spiritual masters, to the Prophet. The master, who is always an orthodox Muslim, must incarnate the truth of the doctrine of which he is the living example; only he who has achieved a realization — in some degree at least — of the Divine Truth can "put in motion the wheel of the doctrine" for an individual seeker. Ultimately, as al-Kalabādhī said: "The Sufis are agreed that the only guide to God is God Himself."

Sufism takes many forms, but it always contains two poles: doctrine and method. Doctrine can be summarized as intellectual discrimination between the Real and the unreal, the basis for this being found essentially in the *shahādah*: "there is no god but God" or "there is no reality but the Reality". Method can be summarized as concentration upon the Real by the "remembrance of God" (*dhikr Allāh*), the invocation of the Divine Name (*dhikr* means "remembrance", "mention", "invocation"). Both doctrine and method must, however, be complemented by perfect surrender to God and the maintenance of an equilibrium through the spiritual regime, which is Islam. Invocation, called in Sanskrit *japa-yoga*, and exemplified in Christianity by the "Jesus Prayer", is the quintessential means of actualizing the Divine Presence and passing from intellectual theory to experience and realization. In Scholastic terms this is a movement from potency to act — in effect to "union" with God (*ittiḥād*) or the realization of the Oneness of God (*tawḥīd*), which is the goal of Sufism. The Koran often underlines the importance of invocation in words such as these: "Remember God standing and sitting" (3:191); "...Those who believe and do good works, and remember God much..." (26:227); and "Surely the Remembrance of God is greatest" (*wadh-dhikru-Llāhi akbar*) (29:45). The principle of reciprocity between God and man is expressed by God's revealed words: "Therefore remember Me; I will remember you" (*fādhkurūnī adhkurkum*) (2:152).

All spiritual method also necessarily involves the practice of the virtues, summarized in the concept of *iḥsān*, the surpassing of self, which a Sacred Ḥadīth defines thus: "Worship God as if you saw Him, for if you do not see Him, nevertheless, He sees you." To this, the Sufis add: "And if there were no *you*, you would see," and make the summation of mystical virtue the quality of "spiritual poverty" (*faqr*). By faqr they mean emptying the soul of the ego's false "reality" in order to make way for what God wills for the soul. They seek to transform the soul's natural passivity into re-collected wakefulness in the present, mysteriously active as symbolized by the transformation of Moses' hand (*see* IBN al-WAQT). Humility and love of one's neighbor cut at the root of the illusion of the ego and remove those faults within the soul that are obstacles to the Divine Presence. "You will not enter paradise," the Prophet said, "until you love one another." The disciple should live in surroundings and in an ambience that are aesthetically and morally compatible with spiritual intermediation, in the sense that "The Kingdom of God is within you". The need of such supports for the spiritual life can be summed up in the Ḥadīth: "God is beautiful and He loves beauty." Ibn 'Aṭā' Allāh wrote:

> Amongst the attributes of your human nature, draw away from every one that is incompatible with your servanthood, so that you may be responsive to the call of God and near His Presence.

As he also points out, the path is the surpassing of self:

> The source of every disobedience, indifference, and passion is self-satisfaction. The source of every obedience, vigilance, and virtue is dissatisfaction with one's self. It is better for you to keep company with an ignorant man dissatisfied with himself than to keep company with a learned man satisfied with himself. For what knowledge is there in a self-satisfied scholar? And what ignorance is there in an unlearned man dissatisfied with himself?

Sufis divide the path into three movements: *makhāfah* ("the way of fear", or "purification"); *maḥabbah* ("the way of love", or "sacrifice and conformity"); and *ma'rifah* ("the way of knowledge"). Here knowledge is not mere mental knowledge, but identity between the knower and the object of knowing. This is why the Sufi in the highest or final degree is called the "Knower by God" (*'Ārif bi-Llāh*). This supreme degree is beyond temporary spiritual states of soul (sing. *ḥāl*, pl. *aḥwāl*), and even beyond permanent stages of realization (sing. *maqām*, pl. *maqāmāt*). He has reached the end of the path, and is "perfected", or completely divested of ignorance; this corresponds exactly to the Vedantine notion of the jīvan-mukta, or one who is "delivered in life", from all duality, alteration, and becoming.

Ma'rifah ("knowledge") is also frequently translated by the word "gnosis" (not to be confused with the Dualist heresy known as "Gnosticism"), which is cognate with Sanskrit *jnāna*. An aspect of *ma'rifah* is self-knowledge in the sense of the Ḥadīth: "He who knows his soul, knows his Lord." Besides direct metaphysical knowledge, *ma'rifah* can also encompass spiritual psychology (knowledge of the microcosm), and cosmology (knowledge of the macrocosm); this does not mean empirical science, but the intuitive, traditional science which discerns clearly the supernatural Cause in all effects, and the trace of the Absolute everywhere.

Alchemy, for example, combines an awareness of ultimate causes with a study of effects. The purification of souls and their union with their center is viewed as a cosmological process carried out by analogy on metals. Speaking of this, Jābir ibn Ḥayyān (known in the West as "Geber" (d. *160*/776) said: "It is called by Philosophers, one Stone, although it is extracted from many Bodies or Things." And: "These imperfect Bodies are not reducible to Sanity [purified from chaos] and Perfection, unless the contrary be operated in them; that is, the Manifest be made Occult, and the Occult be made Manifest." These statements echo the Sufi saying: "Our bodies have become our Spirits, and our Spirits have become our bodies," or that, in reality, according to another saying: "trees have their roots in the sky".

In a similar vein, Abū-l-Qāsim al-'Irāqī, an alchemist of the 7th/13th century, wrote:

> At the beginning of the operation it [the metal to be transformed, or, analogously, the soul] is a mixture of various things. Then it is placed in coction in a light fire and putrifies; and changes; and goes from state to state until it becomes finally *one nature*.

This is a symbolical view of physical processes, and its purpose, like that of mysticism, is to lead to becoming one *nature*, that is, to union. Thus alchemy, unlike a purely empirical science such as chemistry, was a symbolical science and in reality constituted a spiritual way, parallel to Sufism and sometimes blended with it.

To a greater or lesser degree, all traditional sciences, whatever the civilization, look upon natural phenomena as not merely material, but above all symbolical. Thus the traditional four elements, air, earth, fire, water, are not the physical elements, but *modalities* of existence, modified by the *qualities* of cold, warm, dry, and moist, and themselves contained in the quintessence. When it is understood that traditional science views physical reality as of secondary importance and as being dependent upon a higher and principial reality, it cannot be considered "primitive", for it stands in a category which makes great use of symbolism and is altogether different from modern and material science.

The threefold division of the path into *makhāfah, maḥabbah,* and *ma'rifah,* is the equivalent of the Vedantine ternary *karma* ("action"), *bhakti* ("devotion"), and *jnāna* ("knowledge"). And while these are "different ways", they are also each phases of the Path present in differing degrees in each of the ways. Moreover, the three ways offer us an insight into the character of the three Semitic religions: Judaism is the way of fear or obedience, Christianity the way of love and sacrifice, and Islam is the way of knowledge, predominantly, although each necessarily contains the other elements.

The Sufi doctrine has been likened to Neoplatonism, to Vedanta, to the mystical theology of Eastern Christianity, and even to Taoism, all of which it clearly resembles. Jahāngīr, the Moghul Emperor, took instruction from a Hindu teacher called Jadrup and said: "His Vedanta is the same as our *taṣawwuf* ("Sufism"). The famous Sufi Ibrāhīm Ibn Adhām said: "My Master in Spiritual Knowledge was a [Christian] monk called Father Simeon."

The most celebrated expression of Sufi doctrine is "the unity of being" (*waḥdat al-wujūd*), which asserts that everything which exists can only exist because it is an aspect of Divine Reality, hence an aspect of the Divine Unity Itself. This doctrine can be called Monism although it is a literal extension of the Koran's declaration that "Everywhere you turn, there is the Face of God" (2:115). *Waḥdat al-wujūd* does see God everywhere, but does *not* reduce God to everything. God remains supremely transcendent; even though everything which arises out of substance, everything which exists resembles Him (*tashbīh*), He resembles nothing but Himself (*tanzīh*).

In recent times more than ever, especially as Islamic modernists make Sufism the scapegoat for the technological and industrial backwardness of the Muslim nations, Sufism has been accused of "unorthodoxy"; Sufis, however, are often the most fervent of Muslims. This does not mean that there are not, or never have been, deviant manifestations, for that is inevitable; but in itself, Sufism can be orthodox because if it exists within and depends upon the framework of exoterism, although it ultimately surpasses it; as such, it is not always understood by purely theological thinkers. But the charges of unorthodoxy were in fact laid to rest by al-Ghazālī (d. *505*/1111), who was at once jurist, theologian, and Sufi. In his person and his writings he bridged the gap between the outer and the inner, for those for whom such a gap had appeared to exist. As Duncan Black MacDonald has written, al-Ghazālī saw that "the light in which they [the Sufis] walk is essentially the same as the light of prophecy". Of his own turning to Sufism al-Ghazālī speaks in *al-Munqidh min aḍ-Ḍalāl*:

> Then I turned my attention to the Way of the Sufis. I knew that it could not be traversed to the end without both doctrine and practice, and that the gist of the doctrine lies in overcoming the appetites of the flesh and getting rid of its evil dispositions and vile qualities, so that the heart may be cleared of all but God; and the means of clearing it is dhikr Allāh and concentration of every thought upon Him. Now, the doctrine was easier to me than the practice, so I began by learning their doctrine from the books and sayings of their Shaykhs, until I acquired as much of their Way as it is possible to acquire by learningand hearing, and saw plainly that what is most peculiar to them cannot be learned, but can only be reached by immediate experience and ecstasy and inward transformation.
>
> I became convinced that I had now acquired all the knowledge of Sufism that could possibly be obtained by means of study; as for the rest, there was no way of coming to it except by leading the mystical life. I looked at myself as then I was. Worldly interests encompassed me on every side. Even my work as a teacher — the best

thing I was engaged in — seemed unimportant and useless in view of the life hereafter. When I considered the intention of my teaching, I perceived that instead of doing it for God's sake alone I had no motive but the desire for glory and reputation. I realized that I stood on the edge of a precipice and would fall into Hellfire unless I set about to mend my ways... Conscious of my helplessness and having surrendered my will entirely, I took refuge with God as a man in sore trouble who has no resource left. God answered my prayer and made it easy for me to turn my back on reputation and wealth and wife and children and friends.

In any case, after al-Ghazālī, most of the religious authorities in Islam at all levels have been at least nominal Sufis; even Muḥammad ibn 'Abd al-Wahhāb (d. *1201*/1787), the founder of Wahhābism, could not in his time avoid being affiliated at one point with Sufi *ṭuruq*.

Nevertheless, any esoterism, including Sufism, will always be "suspect" in the eyes of exoterism, just as Christianity could not be other than "suspect" in the eyes of Judaism. The *raison d'être* of esoterism is precisely the knowledge of Reality as such. This is a realization which exoterism can only point towards but cannot attain, since it means shattering forms, and with them, exoterism's necessarily dogmatic formulations. Ibn 'Aṭā' Allāh said, quoting the Koran 27:34 (the Queen of Sheba alluding to King Solomon): "Surely, when Kings enter a town, they destroy it," just as the oak tree destroys the acorn from which it grew. The Sufis say: "To get the kernel, one has to break the shell."

"Metaphysical" Sufism, as taught by the great spiritual masters, is different from "folk" Sufism. In some countries hundreds of thousands of disciples have at times been attached to a single master, more than could possibly have had a true vocation for an integral spiritual path. A kind of Sufism has evolved which reflects a popular idea of spirituality. As happens in every civilization, this popular spirituality confuses piety (augmented by great zeal and a multiplication of ritual practices) with pure spiritual intuition and lustral, transcendent knowledge. Needless to say, folklore hawked as the "wisdom of idiots" may be exactly that, but it has nothing to do with Sufism of *any* kind, nor is it a "self-development" divorced from its religious framework.

An offshoot of popular devotional Sufism seeks reassurance above all in psychic phenomena, communication with spirits, or *jinn*, trance dancing, magic, prodigies such as eating glass, piercing the body with knives, and so forth. In psychic powers and extraordinary mental states it finds proofs of spiritual attainment. It has given rise to the European use of the word *fakir* (which comes from the word for an authentic Sufi disciple, a dervish, or *faqīr*, literally a "poor one") to mean a marketplace magician or performer, and has attained notoriety not only among Western observers, but also in Islamic societies.

Metaphysical, or true, Sufism is a spiritual way at the heart of Islam. Its starting point is discrimination between the Real and the unreal, its method is concentration upon the Real, and its goal is the Real. In the words of a Sacred Ḥadīth: "My servant does not cease to approach Me with acts of devotion, until I become the foot with which he walks, the hand with which he grasps, and the eye with which he sees." Bāyazīd al-Bisṭāmī said: "For thirty years I went in search of God, and when I opened my eyes at the end of this time, I discovered that it was really He who sought me." *See also*: AARON; 'ABD al-QĀDIR al-JĪLĀNĪ; al-'ALAWĪ, ABŪ-L-'ABBĀS AḤMAD ibn MUṢṬAFĀ; ABŪ SA'ĪD AḤMAD ibn 'ISĀ al-KHARRĀZ; 'ĀRIF; BASṬ; BARAKAH; BEGGING; al-BISṬĀMĪ; CHISHTĪ; DARQĀWĪ; DHIKR; FANĀ'; FAQĪR; FAQR; FIVE DIVINE PRESENCES; al-GHAZĀLĪ; ḤĀL; al-ḤALLĀJ; ḤAQĪQAH; ḤASAN BASRĪ; ḤIJĀB; al-ḤISS; ḤIZB al-BAḤR; ḤUDAYBIYYAH; IBN ABĪ-L-KHAYR; IBN 'ARABĪ; IBN 'AṬĀ' ALLĀH; IBN MASHĪSH; IBN al-WAQT; IBRĀHĪM ibn ADHĀM; al-INSĀN al-KAMĪL; ISTIDRĀJ; JALĀL ad-DĪN ar-RŪMĪ; al-JUNAYD; KHALWATIYYAH; al-KHAMRIYYAH; al-KHIḌR; KASHKUL; MAQĀM; MALĀMATIYYAH; MEVLEVI; MURIDISM; MUTABĀRIKŪN; NAQSHBANDI; PĪR; QABḌ ; QĀDIRIYYAH; QUṬB; SAINTS; SĀLIK; SANŪSĪYYAH; SHĀDHILĪ; SHAHĀDAH; SHAYKH; SHIRK; SILSILAH; SULŪK; ṬARĪQAH; TAWḤĪD; WAḤDAT al-WUJŪD; ZĀWIYAH; ZUHD.

Suhayb. Companion of the Prophet; the first Byzantine Greek to be converted to Islam.

Suhrawardī, Shihāb ad-Dīn Yaḥyā (*549-587*/1154-1191). The founder of the *ishrāqī* ("illuminationist") school of philosophy which exerted a powerful influence on thought in Iran. Suhrawardī's most influential work was the *Kitāb Ḥikmat al-Ishrāq* ("the Book of Illuminationist Wisdom"). Suhrawardī was born in Persia, but later established himself in Aleppo; there he was imprisoned by the authorities of Saladin under suspicion of seditious heresy, and put to death. Thus he is often called *al-Shaykh al-Maqtūl* ("the murdered master"), or "Suhrawardī maqtūl" to distinguish him from other famous members of his family: 'Abd al-Qāhir ibn 'Abd Allāh Suhrawardī (*491-564*/1097-1168), a Sufi and a scholar; and Abū Hafs 'Umar Suhrawardī (*540-632*/1145-1234), also a Sufi and a statesman. *See* ISHRĀQĪ.

Sujūd (lit. "prostration"). The phase of the prayer (*ṣalāh*) which consists of the act of touching the ground with the forehead. *See* ṢALĀH.

Sulaymān the Magnificent (*900-974*/1494-1566). The Ottoman Caliph under whose reign the Empire reached its high point, Sulaymān conducted successful military campaigns in Europe, besieging Vienna and annexing Hungary, advancing through Persia, and along the Arabian coast, and gaining control of the Hejaz. He was an able administrator and lawmaker (in the Islamic East he is called *al-qānūnī*, "the lawgiver").

In *937*/1530 he handed down the *Kānūnnāmeh*, a corpus of laws which sought, among other things, to remedy abuses in the administration of the military fiefs. He withdrew from the Beylerbeys ("governors") the right to bestow fiefs, requiring them to submit a request called the *tezkere* to the Bāb-i 'Alī, the office of the grand Vizier. Sulaymān was also a patron of the arts, and great builder of public works, including many important constructions in Jerusalem, among them the present city walls. The famous architect Sīnān worked for Sulaymān.

Sulaymān was very attached to one of his concubines, Roxelana, a Russian slave whom he preferred to the mother of the heir, and raised to a unique position of power as legal wife from which she intrigued to have one of her favorites, Rustem, made Grand Vizier, and eventually contrived to have her son Selim, a dissolute drunkard, succeed to the throne. The elder son Muṣṭafā (by another mother), who was popular with the army and had the qualities of a leader, found death at his father's command, and Bāyezīd, a younger but more capable brother of Selim, was eliminated through an unsuccessful bid for power. From then on the harem had an increasing hold over the rulers in Ottoman Turkey, and the Sultans who followed exhibited few qualities as either statesmen or warriors. *See* SĪNĀN.

Sulūk (lit. "journeying"— to God). The Sufis' state of soul or activity seen as "journeying" to God. The term also denotes a quasi-magical and spiritualist ceremony, of local inspiration, performed in Indonesia, known as the *suluk ceremony*. In this ceremony the aspirant seeks to obtain psychic or magical powers by withstanding terrifying assaults from the spirit world during a night in which he symbolically dies. *See* SĀLIKŪN.

Sumayyah bint Khubbāṭ A woman whose name is highly honored as the very first martyr in Islam, killed by the Meccan Abū Jahl for her belief. She was the mother of the Companion 'Ammār ibn Yasar.

Sunbādh Revolt *see* SINDBĀD REVOLT.

Sunnah (lit. "custom", "wont", "usage", pl. *sunan*). A general term that can be applied to the usages and customs of nations, the predominant meaning of Sunnah is that of the spoken and acted example of the Prophet. It includes what he approved, allowed, or condoned when under prevailing circumstances, he might well have taken issue with others' actions, decisions or practices; and what he himself refrained from and disapproved of.

The Sunnah is the crucial complement to the Koran; so much so, that there are isolated instances where, in fact, the Sunnah appears to prevail over the Koran as, for example, when the Koran refers to three daily prayers (24:58 and 11:116), but the Sunnah sets five. On the other hand, there are cases from the earliest days of Islam of universal practices which appear to contradict express Sunnah.

Moreover, the Koran does not make explicit all of its commands; not even all those which are fundamental. Thus it enjoins prayer, but not how it is to be performed: the form of canonical prayer (*ṣalāh*) is based entirely on Sunnah.

The importance of the Sunnah arises from the function of the Prophet as the founder of the religion, and hence the inspired and provident nature of his acts, and the Koran's injunction to pattern oneself after him: "You have a good example in

God's Messenger" (33:21). The Prophet himself was aware of his acts as establishing custom and precedent, although he may not have known that such details as the way he tied his sandals would be a matter of record.

The Sunnah falls into several categories: *as-sunnah al-mu'akkadah*, that which is "confirmed", by being demonstrably repeated in the Prophet's lifetime, so that it has assumed an almost obligatory character, sometimes legally binding when it concurs with clearly essential aspects of ritual and law; and the *as-sunnah al-zā'idah*, the supplementary or elective Sunnah in matters less essential. Whilst emulation of the Sunnah is clearly commendable, there are some aspects that can apply only to the Prophet himself, but are not "legal" for all believers, such as the number of the Prophet's wives, for example.

The applicable aspects of the Sunnah form an element of the *uṣūl al-fiqh* ("basis of law"), after the Koran, and along with *qiyās* ("analogy"), and *ijmā'* ("consensus"), which determine the religious law of Islam. A remarkable example of how strictly some Muslims have sought to emulate the Sunnah, and the literal way in which it has been interpreted, is the case of Ibn Ḥanbal: in his life he never ate a watermelon because he could not find an example of the Prophet's having done so. *See* MUḤAMMAD.

Sunnī (the adjective from Ar. *sunnah*, "custom [of the Prophet]"). The largest group of Muslims are the Sunnīs, often known as "the orthodox", who recognize the first four Caliphs, attribute no special religious or political function to the descendants of the Prophet's son-in-law 'Alī, and adhere to one of the four Sunnī schools of law.

Those who are not Sunnī include the Shī'ites (*see* SHĪ'ISM), the minority sects of the Khārijites, or Ibāḍites (*see* KHĀRIJITES), and other small groups such as the Aḥmadiyyah (*see* AḤMADIYYAH). These non-Sunnīs make up less than 15% of Muslims. The full name of the Sunnīs is *ahl as-sunnah wa-l-ijmā'*, "the People of the Sunnah [the custom of the Prophet] and the Consensus." *See* CREED; SCHOOLS of LAW.

Sūq al-'Arab *see* 'UKĀẒ.

Sūrah (lit. "a row", pl. *sūrāt*). A chapter of the Koran of which there are 114. The names of the *sūrāt* frequently derive from some notable word mentioned in them, such as "the Cow", "the Heights", "the Emissaries", etc. Others are named after the mysterious Arabic letters that appear at the head of certain *sūrahs*, such as *Yā' Sīn* and *Tā' Hā'*. *See* KORAN.

Sūrat al-Ikhlāṣ, *see* IKHLĀṢ.

Surkh-i 'Alām Revolt. (lit. "Red Banners" Revolt). A peasant tax revolt in the Gurgan region of Iran in *161-164*/778-779. It was inspired by Khurramite religious doctrines and had communal ownership of land as its goal. It was one of many Mazdak-like revolts in 'Abbāsid times.

At the same time the revolt of al-Muqanna' took place. His followers wore white and the two revolts are sometimes distinguished by being called those of the "white ones" and "red ones" (*Mubayyida* and *Muḥammira*).

Surkh-i 'Alām means "Red Banners" and this is considered by Marxists as the earliest use of the color red for popular uprisings. The use of a red flag by the Paris Commune in modern times, which before then had been a warning to workers to disperse or be fired upon in France, made this the color symbolizing popular revolts. Red was also used by the Red Scarf society in China that brought the first Ming ruler to power in China, and was the color of the Qarmaṭī leader who wore a red cloak. But the idea that red is an "esoteric" color is doubtless very old since it is the color of blood which is the medium, mysterious by its nature, that joins the body, mind and soul together. Jesus' cloak is traditionally also pictured as being red. *See* MAZDAK; BABAK; KHURRAMIYYAH; al-MUQANNA'; RAFI' IBN LAYTH UPRISING; SINDBĀD REVOLT.

as-Sūryāniyyah, al-Lughah (lit. "The Syriatic language"). The name given to the universal language supposedly spoken by mankind before the Flood (*ṭūfān*), a language common to mankind before the "Tower of Babel", the dispensation of races and the evolution of different tongues. It would have been the language spoken by Adam in paradise although some writers say, illogically, that Adam spoke Arabic in paradise, and *Sūryāniyyah* after the Fall).

It is said that there are traces of *Sūryāniyyah* in Arabic, in the words implied by the isolated letters before certain Koranic Sūrahs, in mysterious utterances and exclamations of Prophets and Saints, and in the speech of children before they learn conventional language.

Sutrah (lit. "covering"). A symbolic barrier established by an object, often a rosary, placed in front of one when the canonical prayers are being performed (*salāh*) in order to demarcate the space needed, particularly that which is touched by the forehead in the prostration. If this area is encroached or trodden on by another person during the prayer, the prayer is considered — by some authorities, but not all — "interrupted" and must be repeated. Without the *sutrah*, an indefinite area in front of the person praying could be considered as the precinct of the prayer and thus violable.

For this reason, a solitary worshiper in a mosque usually chooses to pray, when possible, immediately in front of a wall or pillar. In practice, and in the absence of a *sutrah*, a prayer is only considered interrupted if someone walks upon the space where the head would touch during the performance of the prayer. A different opinion also exists, to the effect that the prayer is not in fact interrupted, but that he who violates the space incurs blame. In sum, the establishment of a *sutrah* in such situations is desirable *adāb* ("courtesy"), but not an absolute requirement.

Sword of God. (Ar. *sayf Allāh*). A name by which the Prophet once addressed his general Khālid Ibn al-Walīd, which then became his honorary title.

In the seventh year of the Hijrah, the Prophet had sent messages to various rulers, calling upon them to enter Islam. The second messenger to the governor of Bostrah in Syria had been put to death by the Ghassanids, Christian Arab allies of the Byzantines, and a party of fifteen delegates sent to Arab tribes in Syria had also been attacked, and fourteen of them killed. To avenge these deaths, an army of three thousand was sent from Medinah under the leadership of Zayd, the adopted son of the Prophet. They learned on route that a far superior force of Ghassanids and Byzantines was gathering to confront them, but in a council of war the Muslims decided to continue. At Mu'tah the two forces met.

In a vision, the Prophet saw Zayd fall wounded and, as he lay dying, pass the white standard to Ja'far, his second in command; thence it was handed to 'Abd Allāh ibn Rawāḥah, and then to Thābit ibn Arqam, who finally handed it to Khālid ibn Walīd, the famous warrior who, not long before, had abandoned the cause of the Meccans and entered Islam. Khālid collected the forces and led them in a retreat to safety. Of his vision the Prophet said to his Companions: "... One of God's swords took the standard, and God opened up the way for them"; thus Khālid came to be called the "Sword of God". *See* HERACLIUS.

Sword of Islam (Ar. *sayf al-Islām*). A stylized wooden sword held or presented by the Imām during the Friday sermon (*khuṭbah*). The sword was symbolic of the Prophet's words after a battle: "we have returned from the lesser holy war (*al-jihād as-aṣghar*), to the greater holy war (*al-jihād al-akbar*)", by which he meant that the greatest holy war is to overcome the weakness of one's own soul and to rescue it from vice, ignorance, and disbelief. The use of this ceremonial sword disappeared during the last century.

Syria. (Syrian Arab Republic). Population 10,075,000, of whom 11% are Christians, 6% are 'Alawīs, 1.2% are Druzes, and some 30,000 are Ismā'īlīs. The rest are Muslims with a small minority of Twelve-Imām Shī'ites. 88% of the population is considered Arab; 6% are Kurds and there are also ethnic Turks, Armenians, and other groups. *See* 'ALAWĪ; DRUZES; ISMĀ'ĪLĪS.

T

Ta'awwudh. The expression: *a'ūdhu bi-Llāhi mina-sh-shayṭāni-r-rajīm* ("I take refuge in God from Satan the stoned one"), often shortened to *a'ūdhu bi-Llāh* ("I take refuge in God"). It precedes the *basmalah* before ritual actions and the recitation of the Koran.

If a provocation
from Satan should provoke thee,
seek refuge in God;
He is All-hearing, All-seeing.
The godfearing,
when a visitation of Satan
troubles them,
remember, and then see clearly. (7:199-200)

See also ĀYAT al-KURSĪ; REFUGE.

aṭ-Ṭabarī, Abū Ja'far Muḥammad ibn Jarīr *(225-310*/839-923). A scholar born in Tabaristan in northern Iran, aṭ-Ṭabarī was a prolific writer on the subjects of theology, literature, and history. Two of his works became definitive reference-works in their fields: the commentary on the Koran called the *Jāmi' al-Bayān fī Tafsīr al-Qur'ān* ("The Full Exposition of Koranic Commentary"), and the universal history of the world from creation until his own times, the *Tarīkh ar-Rusul wa-l-Mulūk* ("History of Prophets and Kings"). Because of his polemics against the so-called "anthropomorphist" interpretations of the Ḥanbalīs he attracted the hatred of popular elements and was forced to live his last years unable to leave his house in Baghdad.

aṭ-Ṭabī'ah (lit. "nature"). As used in *ṭabi'at al-kull* it means "universal nature", that is, substance, from which the world is created. *See* FIVE DIVINE PRESENCES.

Tābi'ūn (from *tabaa*, "to follow", "followers", "successors"; sing. *tābi*). The generation which followed that of the Companions of the Prophet, and thus received his teachings at second hand. Those who succeeded them are the *tābi'ū-t-Tābi'īn* (the "followers of the followers"). Together they constitute the *salaf* (the "first generations"), whose authority in religious opinions is superior to that of succeeding generations, proximity to Prophetic times being taken as an index of orthodoxy. The Wahhābīs regard the *tābi'ūn* as the limit of authority, and exclude the*tābi'ū-t-tābi'īn* from the qualification of exemplary orthodoxy.

This is in accordance with a Ḥadīth: "The best of my people are those of my generation; then those who follow them; then those who follow them." This is the opposite of the idea of progress, and is instead the point of view of tradition, that the height of inward perfection is that which is closest to the moment of revelation, the beginning. From the beginning, from the moment of revelation which is origin and center, the immutable law of manifestation is that of decay, even though there may be outward signs of development as seminal possibilities which are inward become externalized.

But in this externalisation, as when the Temple replaced the Ark of the Covenant, there is nevertheless a loss. Appearances may argue a new richness, but it is a wealth due to a "devaluation", so to speak, caused by slipping from a higher to a lower state of equilibrium. Despite this, there are necessarily moments of restoration as a cycle unfolds, and its final moments, when the traditional norm is forgotten altogether, presages a sudden, cataclysmic reversal, when the Center once again irrupts into the world.

Speaking to his people of the inevitable law of decadence, the Prophet said: "You will follow in the ways of those who came before you [the Jews and the Christians], and even if they were to descend into a snake's lair, you will follow them."

Tablīghī Jamā'at. The Society for Teaching and Propagation founded by Mawlānā Muḥammad Ilyās (1885-1944) in India for the propagation of Islam. It is now an international revivalist movement directed by a *shura* council and holds an annual convention in Raiwand, Pakistan, and in North America.

The conference in Raiwand, which is some thirty kilometers from Lahore, is attended for three days by almost one million people. Tablīghī Jamā'at sends missionaries to hundreds of countries in groups of eight to twelve persons under the leadership of one member who is called the *amir*. They pay their own way and subsist on a bare minimum. They do not seek to convert non-Muslims but to strengthen the religious resolve of believers. They scrupulously avoid all politics and controversy. The missionaries spend four months at Raiwand discussing their methods and witnessing to each other much like evangelicals do in America. They critique their successes and failures. At any one time up to seven thousand people are undergoing seminars at Raiwand.

The Tablīghī have a six point program which is made up of 1) the testimony of faith; 2) performance of prayer with concentration and devotion; 3) *'ilm* and *dhikr*, knowledge and invocation; 4) nobility of character which includes wishing well of unbelievers; 5) sincerity and the examination of conscience so that their intentions are only to serve God; 6) going out on mission in the path of Allāh. The ambience of the Tablīghī is suffused with mysticism without actually practicing any form of mysticism. Muḥammad Zakariyya Kandhalavi (b. 1898), an Indian Ḥadīth scholar, wrote seven essays explaining Islam which are required reading for missionaries.

The *amir*, or president, of the Tablīghī Jamā'at in 1989, Maulana Inamu-l-Ḥasan, said to a conference: "Go and take the eternal message of Islam to the four corners of the globe. Remind your brethren of their religious duties; remind them of the day of Judgement; and call them to the remembrance of Almighty Allāh, to submission to His Will, and obedience to Prophet Muḥammad, peace be upon him."

Tābūt. The elevated sepulchre, or tomb, usually draped with cloth, in which persons of rank, Saints, and Prophets, are buried. A special meaning of the word is the Ark of the Covenant (*tābūt al-'ahd*). The word *ḍarīḥ* refers to a mausoleum as a whole. Ṭabarī says that the Kaysāniyyah revolt of 685-687 carried a *tābūt* with them, even into battle.

Tadjiks, *see* TAJIKS.

Tafakkur (a verbal noun from *tafakkara*, "to ponder", "contemplate", "meditate"). A word often used to describe contemplation or meditation, it should not be confused with *dhikr*, which is invocation or "remembrance". *See* DHIKR.

Tafsīr (a verbal noun from *fassara*; "to explain", "elucidate"). Any kind of explanation, but especially a commentary on the Koran, *tafsīr* designates opinions, elucidation, background information and commentary on the Koran. *Ta'wīl* is another kind of commentary, an exegesis of the inner meaning of the Koran or other text, most often of a mystical nature. The first commentator on the Koran was 'Abd Allāh ibn al-'Abbās, son of the Prophet's uncle, al-'Abbās, who drew heavily on the *Haggadah* for inspiration, of which he learned from Jewish converts to Islam. *See* COMMENTARIES; TA'WĪL.

Ṭāhā Husayn (d. 1971). Egyptian writer, critic, and reformer. Although he became blind at a young age, he was educated at the al-Azhar University in Cairo and in France. He became Minister for Education in Egypt and was the prolific author of short stories, novels, and articles. One of the major figures in Arab literature in the 20th century, his most famous work is his autobiographical *al-Ayyām* ("Days").

Tahajjud. The practice of keeping vigils at night. It was widely observed by the Companions in Medinah during the first years of the Hijrah, but to such a drastic degree that their strength began to suffer, so that it had to be curtailed.

Night vigils are still commonly practiced today, particularly during the early morning when the Koran says figuratively that "God descends close to the earth to hear prayers".

The voluntary prayers performed after the *'ishā'* are often also called *tahajjud.*

Taḥannuth (lit. "pious practice"). Seeking after God by shunning the world and distraction in the soul. The Koran says: "Say Allāh, then leave them to their pointless disputation" (6:91). The word "disputation" (*khawḍ*) implies involvement in things, argument, and haste; "pointless" (*yal'abūn*), lit. "they play", means that the worldly are not committed to any serious purpose; hence it is clear that the Koran is contrasting the single-minded purposiveness of the *dhikr*, "say Allāh", in order, among other purposes, to counter distraction and dissipation either in the world or in the soul.

Tahārah (lit. "purification"). The act of purification, spiritual and physical. Its implications can be extended to cover all forms of ablution and is often applied to circumcision as well.

aṭ-Ṭaḥāwi, Abū Ja'far Aḥmad ibn Muḥammad (*229-321*/843-933). Theologian, born in Ṭaḥā and died in Egypt. He first studied Shāfi'i law with his maternal uncle Abū Ibrāhīm al-Muzanī, a celebrated student of Imām Shāfi'ī and then changed to study Ḥanafī law with Abū Ja'far Aḥmad ibn Abū 'Imrān, who was to become the chief Qāḍī of Egypt. Among his many written works is the *Bayān as-Sunnah wa aj-Jamā'ah* known as the *'Aqīdah aṭ-Ṭahawīyyah* ("The Ṭahawi Creed"). His theology is a continuation of Imām Shāfi'ī and Abū Ḥanifah (*A'ṣḥāb ar-ā'i wa al-qiyās*).

Ṭāhir (lit. "the purified one"; feminine: *ṭāhirah*). A degree of sainthood, below that of *walī* ("Saint"), comparable to the station of "Venerable", or "Blessed" in Catholicism. *See* SAINTS.

Ṭāhirids (*205-259*/821-873). A Persian dynasty in Khorāsān founded by Ṭāhir ibn al-Ḥusayn, from a family of clients (*mawālī*) of the conquering Arabs. First serving the Caliph al-Ma'mūn, Ṭāhir soon made himself virtually independent, but he and his descendants, beginning with his son Ṭalḥāḥ, continued to send tribute to the 'Abbāsids. The court at Nayshābūr became the first focal point of the renascent Persian cultural consciousness after the Arab conquest. The Ṭāhirids were replaced by the Sāmānids and Ṣaffārids.

Tahlīl (lit. "making lawful"). The uttering of the *shahādah*: *lā ilāha illā-Llāh* ("there is no god but God").

Taḥmīd. The uttering of the *ḥamdalah*: *al-hamdu li-Llāh* ("praise be to God").

Taḥrīf (lit. "corruption"). The charge made by Muslim theologians against the Christians, of having modified, and falsified, the Gospel (*al-injīl*) to suppress predictions of the Prophet. In the *Radd al-Jamil al-Ghazālī* expresses the opinion that it is not the text of the Bible what has been altered, but rather the interpretation. *See* BIBLE.

Ṭā'if. A city near Mecca, built on a high plateau, it is considerably cooler than Mecca or Jeddah in the summertime. It was famous for its grapes, and many notables of Mecca owned vines there. The Prophet went to Ṭā'if to preach during his Meccan years, before the migration to Medinah, but was driven out. On the return journey from Ṭā'if he recited the Koran in the night and the Jinn gathered around to listen to him in the desert.

After the conquest of Mecca the Prophet besieged the town unsuccessfully. Shortly thereafter, seeing the mild treatment accorded to those who accepted Islam, the town and its allies surrendered.

Taifas, Reyes de (Sp. "Kings of the factions", Ar. *mulūk al-ṭawā'if*). The epoch of four centuries of Muslim rule in Spain which followed the disintegration of the Caliphate of Cordoba after *422*/1031. The epoch of factions lasted, in effect, until the defeat of the Naṣrids of Granada in *897*/1492.

During this time the Muslim Empire of Spain was ruled by local princes, including the early Zīrids of Granada, the Banū Ḥammūd of Malaga and Algeciras, the Banū 'Abbūd of Seville, the Banū Ḥūd of Saragossa, and others.

Tajalli (lit. a "coming forth into the light", "an effulgence", a "revealing"). A term in mysticism meaning an epiphany, a manifestation of the numinous, an emanation of inward light, an unveiling of Divine secrets, and enlightening of the heart of the devotee. The related word *jalwah* has been devised by the Sufis to echo the word *khalwah* ("withdrawal", "emptiness") and to describe the complement of "emptiness" for God, namely, "being filled" by God's revealing peace.

Tajikistan. Population 5,916,373. Former republic of the Soviet Union, with Uzbek, Russian and other minorities. The language of the majority is a Persian dialect; Russian is also spoken. 80% of the population is Sunni Muslim, but strongly influenced by the kind of Sufi sentiment which is a close kin of Sh'ism; 5% is Ismā'īlī. Capital: Dushanbe. *See* TAJIKS.

Tājīks. (In Russian the word is Tadjik). An agricultural people who are Sunni Muslims of Persian stock and language. There are three million in Tajikistan, which borders Afghanistan, including the groups which exist in all the bordering ex-Soviet republics and especially in such cities as Samarkand and Bukhara. Another four to ten million live in Afghanistan speaking Dari-Tājīk. The "mountain" Tājīks of the Pamir are Ismā'īlīs, as are those of Badakshan in Afghanistan, and for this reason are sometimes considered as a completely alien people by other Tājīks. Among the Pamir peoples the Shchugnantsi and Rumantsi have preserved early Indian and Iranian beliefs and customs.

An early mention of Tājīks is in the *Ta'rīkh-i Mas'ūdī* by Abu'l-Faḍl-Bayhaqī in 1041; they had their own language, West Iranian which is close to contemporary Farsi and to the Dari of Afghanistan. Originally they had come from West Iran to Central Asia where they had been forced by Soghdian Bactrians and Khwarezmians. Sundermann, the great Manichean scholar, notes that the name also appears in a Turfan text. Barthold explained that the Islamic armies which from the end of the seventh century on raided and occupied Soghdian territory were no longer purely Arabs but largely mixed with Persians and spoke New Persian and these were called Tajiki by the Soghdians and later by the Central Asian Turks.

Early Tājīk took on East Iranian words especially from Soghdian in the 10th century by which time they already had a literature whose outstanding figure is Farid ad-Din Rūdakī, the "Sultan" of Persian poets. This literature could be called Tājīko-Persian and besides Rūdakī, includes Firdawsī. The first dynasty which restored Persians to rule after the Islamic invasions, the Sāmānids, were Tājīks. Bukhara was their center but their domain was greater than Central Asia for it also included Afghanistan. The Tājīks are Europoid, they are Brachycephalic (Iranians are Dolocephalic.) Other Iranian peoples in the former Soviet Union are the Ossetians, Novo-Sogdians in the hills of Zarafshan who have now moved to the plains; these are East Iranians.

Tajwīd, *see* KORAN CHANTING.

Takbīr (the verbal noun from the verb *kabbara*, "to declare greatness", "to magnify"). The expression *Allāhu akbar* ("God is greatest") is described by the word *takbīr* ("magnificat", "declaring (God's) greatness"). In Arabic the same form is used for the comparative and the superlative forms of the adjective. *Akbar* thus means "greater" than anything else or than anything conceivable, and hence also "greatest". The *takbīr* punctuates the canonical prayer (*salāh*) and is used constantly in daily life as a pious exclamation. In recent times the takbīr has become a kind of cheer at Islamic rallies and meetings.

Takfir (from *kufr*, "disbelief"). A practice in Shī'ite Islam, but relatively unknown amongst the Sunnis, of declaring someone an unbeliever. (A rare example among Sunnis was Ibn 'Arabī who was declared an unbeliever). It reached its height in the 19th century in Iran, when a mujtahid, or several mujtahids, would declare someone an unbeliever for one or another of his tenets. This was done to Shaykh Aḥṣa'i, the founder of the Shaykhis (for denying the resurrection of the body), to the Bab, to Jamal ad-Din al-Afghani, and to any of a number of religious or political enemies. The device has now appeared amongst Sunni Fundamentalists. There was also a precedent for this among Kharijites.

Takiyyah. A place of religious retreat, a sanctuary, a meeting place of dervishes, or a pilgrim inn. In Turkey the Turkish form of the word is used: *tekke*, together with another word, *durgah*. As a meeting place for dervishes, two other terms are common: in Persia, *khānaqah*, and in the Arab West, *zāwiyah*. *See also* TAQIYYAH.

Talbiyah. The words which the Koran attributes to Abraham when he called mankind to the pilgrimage to Mecca:

Labbayka-Llāhumma labbayk
labbayka-Llāhumma labbayk
lā sharīka laka, labbayk
inna-l-ḥamda wa-n-ni'mata laka wa-l-mulk
la sharīka laka, labbayka-Llāhumma labbayk

Here am I, God! here am I!
Here am I, God! here am I!
and associate none with Thee; here am I!
Surely Praise and Blessing are Thine,
and dominion!
and associate none with Thee, here am I, God!
Here am I!

This is the central, ritual recitation of the greater pilgrimage (*ḥajj*) to Mecca, recited from the moment of taking the consecration and donning the pilgrim's garb (*iḥrām*), until the end of the Day of Arafāt. It is also repeated during the lesser pilgrimage (*'umrah*). It expresses the state of awareness of God's presence by a "readiness" and "watchfulness" of the heart and mind. The *talbiyah* recalls Isaiah 6:8:

Also I heard the voice of the Lord, saying,
Whom shall I send, and who will go for us?

Then said I, Here am I; send me.

See PILGRIMAGE.

Talfīq (lit. "invention", "concoction", "patching together"). The mixing of elements of the four schools of law. In some respects, the rituals differ according to each school (*madhhab*), and legal methods and conclusions differ also. The mixing of the approaches or practices of the different schools is frowned upon; a practitioner and a lawyer are expected to remain within the guidelines of one school. In modern times, however, precedents have increasingly been set for using decisions made in the other schools.

Ṭalḥāḥ ibn 'Ubayd Allāh (d. *64*/683). A Companion, one of the "Ten Well-betided Ones" who were assured of paradise by the Prophet. He took part in the insurrection against 'Alī ibn 'Abī Ṭālib, the fourth Caliph, and was killed in the Battle of the Camel.

Ṭālib (lit. "an asker", "a seeker"). A student, formerly only a student of Divinity. In some countries *ṭālib* is also used to mean a disciple of a spiritual master.

Ṭaliban. (Lit. "students"). The political movement which arose among the children who grew up in refugee camps during the Soviet invasion of Afghanistan. Many of the Ṭaliban came from camps which were in the region of Quetta in Pakistan and many of them had been war orphans. They were raised and taught by religious teachers who had graduated from the Dar al-'Ulum Deoband, a large religious school in India. With only rudimentary education, spurred on by fundamentalist teachers who provided meager religious instruction and much jihād theology, they became an army which captured Kabul and imposed a harsh and primitive form of religious dictatorship in that part of Afghanistan which they controlled. The breakdown of traditional society through war and the loss of traditional Islamic values played a major role in creating the Ṭaliban. In Afghanistan this loss of traditional values has been through war but in other Islamic societies it has also taken place because of drastic population growth.

Their financial support came from the Jamāat-i 'Ulamā'-I-Islam-i, a political party in Pakistan made up of graduates of the Deoband school in India and also from sources in Saudi Arabia and the Gulf states, many claim with the encouragement of the United States.

The rise of the Ṭaliban began in 1994 when the Ṭaliban captured a munitions depot in Afghanistan at Spinbaldak near the Pakistan border which brought the Ṭaliban 800 truckloads of arms and ammunition that had been stored in caves since the Soviet occupation, making them the best supplied group in the country. Units of the army and other guerilla units came over to their side. The Ṭaliban also gained the support of Naṣir Allāh Babar, Pakistan's Interior Minister at the time and subsequently the Pakistani Intelligence Service, ISI. After they took control of Kandahar he saw them as the means to an economic alliance with the states of Central Asia who need a way to the sea. The project of building a gas pipeline from Turkmenistan to Karachi, over Afghanistan instead of Iran, has played an economic role in the strategic reasoning. The potential of the Ṭaliban in destabilizing the Northwest Frontier Province and Baluchistan was to give Pakistan second thoughts, however.

In September 1996 the Ṭaliban captured Kabul. The government of Burhannudin Rabbani and his troops fled northward. The Ṭaliban hanged Muḥammad Najibullah who had headed the Soviet backed government during the Afghan war and his brother Shahpur Aḥmadzai and later two more such leaders, Turkhi and Jafzar. When they came to Kabul they encountered a society which to them was shocking. Kabul was a relatively cosmopolitan city and as a result of Communist rule, the status of women was fairly emancipated. The Ṭaliban program then fell upon women most heavily. Women were prohibited from going about without the head to ground covering, the *burqa'*, from working, from being "provocative" which could simply mean walking with their shoes making a tapping sound. In the name of Islamic Fundamentalism the Ṭaliban prohibited women physicians from practicing medicine and girls from going to school. They made children caught foraging for food stand in the street with their faces smeared with ordure as a punishment for theft short of amputation because they were minors. The Ṭaliban also prohibited showing all pictures of living things, flying kites, television, confiscated cassette tapes, and ordered that men grow beards of a certain length. By their literalist interpretation of religious rules they showed a similarity and a sympathy with the ideology of strict Wahhabis and such groups known as Ahl-i Ḥadīth, which are on the rise in Pakistan.

A Backlash ensued against the Ṭaliban. Anti-Ṭaliban forces, such as those led by General Aḥmad Shah Massoud, an ethnic Tajik, were supported by Iran and Russia. Uzbekistan supported General Dostum, an Uzbek, against the Ṭaliban. General Massoud's troops made the Pathan Ṭaliban retreat from positions north of Kabul. They subsequently recovered much lost ground pushing Massoud's Northern Alliance, who are mostly Tajiks, into a small corner of Afghanistan bordering on Tajikistan.

Since the Ṭaliban are themselves Pathan (Pashtun), Kandahar, a Pathan area, became their center from which they expanded their control over Afghanistan. Their leader was a one-eyed village cleric called Mullā Muḥammad 'Umar. At least one Afghan doctor said he suffered from seizures or outright episodes of insanity.

The program of the Ṭaliban was the "promotion of virtue and the prohibition of vice". This did not stop them from using traffic in narcotics for their revenue as other guerilla groups have done before them. However, towards the end of 1997 they made promises to cooperate with a U.N. program to eliminate the drug trade, which, by all reports, they actually stopped for a time in 2000 by prohibiting the growing of poppy. This prohibition showed results in 2001, but poppy growing was resumed after the U.S. attack on Afghanistan.

The Ṭaliban were very centralized and hierarchical as concerns decision making. They had a *shūra* or consultative council in Kabul. However, in carrying out their program in the streets they were extremely idiosyncratic, individually making up the rules as they went along. From the beginning the Ṭaliban were joined by radical Pakistanis, Chechens, and especially Arabs, many of them Saudis. Above all, there was a close cooperation with al-Qaeda, the terrorist network of Usama Bin Ladin.

In 2001, despite world outcry, the Ṭaliban destroyed two colossal statues of the Buddha in Bamiyan under pretext of destroying "idols". One statue was 53 meters high and the other 36. These statues dated from the Gandharan period and had survived previous attacks by Genghiz Khan and Aurangzeb. The Ṭaliban also destroyed other works of art. The Minister of Culture Mawlawi Qudratullah Jamal termed it "not a big issue" and observed that "it is easier to destroy than to build".

Two days before the attack on the World Trade Center on September 11, 2001 Aḥmad Shah Massoud was mortally wounded in an assassination attempt carried out by al-Qaedah agents posing as reporters. Osama Bin Ladin and his terrorist network were also held responsible for the attack on New York. After the Ṭaliban refused to hand over Osama bin Ladin, the United States attacked Afghanistan in October of 2001.

Ta'līmites, *see* TA'LĪMIYYAH.

Ta'līmiyyah (lit. "people of the teaching"). A name for the Ismā'īlīs, around the *6th*/12th century, because their propaganda promised secret, gnostic, teachings. It is under this name, and that of "Bāṭiniyyah", that al-Ghazālī attacked the Assassins in his writings, particularly in the Fadā'ih al-Bāṭiniyyah. Al-Ghazālī concentrated on the problems he knew were raised by the exoteric and outer aspects of their doctrine. As cited by Ibn Jawzi, al-Ghazālī said that:

> Among the principles of the Bāṭiniyyah is the belief in two gods, both without beginning in time, yet one is the reason for the other's existence. The *Sābiq* (the former or one that precedes) is not described in terms of existence or non-existence, because it neither exists nor does not exist, it is neither known nor unknown, neither describable nor indescribable. In addition, the former emanated the latter, who is the first creator and then in another emanation, the universal soul came into being. According to them, the Prophet is one on whom the former (the *Sābiq*) by way of the latter emanates a holy and pure force. Jibrail, on the other hand is considered merely the intelligence which was emanated on the Prophet and not an individual per se... they deny the next life claiming it merely represents the return of things to their origin. As for religious obligations, they are known for their unrestricted licentiousness: however, when confronted with this position, they deny it and instead confirm the necessity of obligations and restrictions.

Abū Muūḥammad al-'Irāqī, who scrutinized the Ismā'īlīs after al-Ghazālī, complained that they made the Prophet superfluous since obviously the

Imām as conceived by the Ismā'īlīs was superior. Both al-Ghazālī and Shahrastānī (himself probably an Ismā'īlī) took issue with the fact that the Imām had only his own being to teach as the saving doctrine. *See* ASSASSINS; al-GHAZĀLĪ; GHŪLĀT; ISMĀ'ĪLĪS; SHAHRASTĀNĪ.

Talqīn (verbal noun of *laqqana*, "to instruct", "inspire", "insinuate").

1. Spiritual teaching or instruction.
2. The suborning of witnesses (a term used in Islamic Law, *sharī'ah*).

Tamattu'. The combining of the greater and the lesser pilgrimages (*ḥajj* and *'umrah*) by taking a single consecration (*iḥrām*) to cover both. *See* PILGRIMAGE.

Tamjīd (verbal noun of *majjada*, "to glorify"). The frequently used expression *subḥāna-Llāh* ("may God be glorified"). Some authors also use the word *tamjīd* to refer to the so-called *ḥawqalah*, the expression: "There is no power and no strength save in God." *See* ḤAWQALAH; PIOUS EXPRESSIONS; REFUGE.

Tanāsukh (from *nasakha*, "to abrogate", "to copy"). This single word is used to mean, according to context, any of the following: transmigration (the passing of a soul from one state of existence to another, starting from the lower degrees to the higher until the arrival in the human state); metempsychosis (the transmission after death of psychic *elements*, such as memories or aspects of personality, from one person to another as in the Tibetan doctrine of spiritual teachers known as *tulkus* who succeed each other from generation to generation); and, finally, reincarnation (rebirth in a human state of the integral soul of one who has existed already in the human state). Although they are important to the Druzes and other heretical sects such as the 'Alī Ilāhīs, who say: "Men! Do not fear death! The death of men is like the dive the duck makes," such doctrines play virtually no role in Islam. The metaphysical objection to them is that they imply that what transmigrates is real; that it has a substance or a sufficient cause unto itself. This would be as if it were a "piece of God"; which is unthinkable. Transmigration played a role in the doctrines of "Brothers of Purity" and the idea is the prototype of Darwinian evolution and appears as such in Rūmi when he says "I was a plant, I became an animal..." etc.

Islam emphatically denies "reincarnation" after human life, defining human life as the point of ultimate decision, of definitive meeting with the Absolute. From the Islamic point of view, because God is Absolute, and because the human state exists precisely in order that the creature may know God and through that knowledge proceed to a posthumous state in paradise, a human birth carries with it a responsibility which is unique to that lifetime and not repeatable. Otherwise, it would not truly be a human life. However, because humans are capable of rejecting God and thus of leading lives below their nature, it is not only paradise that is a possible consequence of human life, but hell too.

In one lifetime, only a few of the possibilities of the individual in regard to the world can be manifested; the number of combinations of the relative with the relative may be innumerable; but it is not the labyrinthine encounter of the individual with the world which constitutes the reason for creation and thus for life, but the encounter with God. In this regard, one lifetime is unbounded. A Ḥadīth says:

> I [God] was Hidden Treasure; I desired to be known; therefore I created the world.

Because of the nature of the confrontation of the limited individual with God the Unlimited, even a single, unique, lifetime is enough to determine one's destiny for eternity. Indeed, life is precisely that unfolding of the contents of the soul. Once unfolded and spread out there is hardly any reason to pack it up to repeat the process in a different order.

When heaven is split open,
when the stars are scattered,
when the seas swarm over,
when the tombs are overthrown,
then a soul shall know its works,
the former and the latter.

O Man! What deceived thee as to thy generous Lord
who created thee and shaped thee
and wrought thee in symmetry
and composed thee after what form He would?

No indeed; but you cry lies to the Doom;
yet there are over you watchers
noble, writers
who know whatever you do.

Surely the pious shall be in bliss,
and the libertines shall be in the fiery furnace
roasting therein on the Day of Doom,
nor shall they ever be absent from it.

And what shall teach thee what is the Day of Doom?
Again, what shall teach thee
what is the Day of Doom?
A day when no soul shall possess
aught to succour another soul;
that day Command shall belong unto God. (82:1-16)

In this encounter there is one decisive element, the recognition and acceptance of the Divine Reality on the part of the "central" creature whose awareness is capable of knowing God. We are that central creature in this world, for our subjective sense, our awareness of ourselves, is not different from God's own "subjectivity" save that as "fallen" man we are born with the desire to see a "fallen" world, the world of limitation and contingency that replaced the Garden of Eden. Divine revelation makes it possible to "see", through the means of salvation which God offers, what Adam saw before he fell, or, to repair the defective will which chooses the "fallen" state as normal, or simply to obey a sacred law which brings with it that state of conformity of one's individual substance to supra-individual substance, which is essential in order to enter into a beatific state after death. In any case, revelation and providence provide a sufficient glimpse of the Truth to give birth to a faith in the soul that will save it, and then nourish that faith. In Islam this recognition is the *shahādah*, the testification that one sees that only God is Real. The moment that it takes for faith to enter the soul, the moment that it takes to formulate the *shahādah* with the tongue and heart constitutes all, finally, what matters in life. By its nature, this encounter with God, which is human life, cannot be made into a "rehearsal" whose consequences are merely provisional.

Till, when death comes to one of them, he says,
'My Lord, return me;
haply I shall do righteousness in that
I forsook.' Nay, it is but a word
he speaks; and there, behind them,
is a barrier until the day that they
shall be raised up. (23:101-104)

From the human state, because of man's capacity to understand the Absolute, and his free will in respect of either choosing the Absolute — surrender to God (Islām), or rejecting the Absolute — disbelief (*kufr*, or also *kidhb*, "refusal" or "lying"), the path divides at the judgement after death to lead either to heaven or to hell but not back into the world. Limbo, or some other solution is evidently a possibility in the case of infants who have died, and souls that otherwise have not reached maturity or responsibility, but those capable of desiring heaven are thereby also competent to take the one step of faith which leads to it, or suffer the consequences.

Gardens of Eden they shall enter; therein
they shall be adorned with bracelets of gold
and with pearls, and their apparel there
shall be of silk.
And they shall say, 'Praise belongs to God
who has put away all sorrow from us. Surely
our Lord is All-forgiving, All-thankful...
...As for the unbelievers, theirs shall be the fire of Gehenna;
they shall neither be done with and die,
nor shall its chastisement be lightened for them.
Even so We recompense every ungrateful one.
Therein they shall shout,
'Our Lord, bring us forth,
and we will do righteousness,
other than what we have done.
'What, did We not give you long life,
enough to remember in for him who would remember?
To you the warner came; so taste you now!
The evildoer shall have no helper.' (35:30-34)

In one passage through life the soul plays out its drama on many planes, given that intentions also amount to acts, and that what is done also implies what is not done in any given situation. On more than one plane a full range of choices is also presented to a soul which acts or reacts accordingly; one life is thus, in fact, already "many lives". A reincarnation would be a mere repetition in different modes. This redundancy, like that of a game, would take away the importance and significance of human life, whose superiority over that of animals, its majesty, lies precisely in its definitive aspect, its absoluteness.

The pre-existence of souls (which is denied by Avicenna on Aristotelian grounds) is another matter. The Koran pictures all the descendants of Adam being called forth at the beginning of the world to testify that there is no God but Allāh. Thus they come into this world knowing the truth of the nature of things, a knowledge to which religion only recalls man. In al-Ghazāī's *Mishkāt al-Anwār* ("The Niche of Lights"), 'Ā'ishah relates that the Prophet said: "Souls before they became united with bodies were like assembled armies, and afterwards they were dispersed and sent into bodies of mankind." *See* ESCHATOLOGY.

Tanzīh (the "elimination [of blemishes or of anthropomorphic traits]"; and hence, the "assertion of [God's] incomparability"). This is a technical term which describes the viewing of God in the light of those aspects which are transcendent and incomparable. The Koran constantly affirms that God has no equal and that nothing is like God. The complement of this (or the opposite) is *tashbīh* ("immanence"), or what is analogous. *See* TASHBĪH.

Tanzīl (a "sending down [from Heaven]"). A major revelation, such as that of the Koran, having an uncreated, celestial source. *See* INSPIRATION; KORAN; REVELATION.

Tanzimat. The period of government reforms in Turkey which began in *1255*/1839 with the reign of Abdalmecid I, the first reform being the edict known as the *Hatt-i Sharīf* of G lhane; this latter word was the name of a particular pavilion in the palace which lies on the sea of Marmara outside Istanbul, to which dignitaries of the Sublime Porte, foreign ambassadors, and representatives of the Ottoman and subject populations were summoned for the edict's proclamation. It promised all subjects in the Empire, regardless of nationality and religion, security of life, honour, and property; regular military service for Muslims; the lifting of oppressive monopolies; the abolition of confiscations; the end to the leasing of the right to taxation of the provinces to the highest bidder. It made the death penalty dependent upon judicial verdicts following systematic investigation. A series of other laws followed.

The period came to an end when the *Qanun-i Asasi*, proposed by the Vizier Midhat Pasha in *1293*/1876, which would have created a constitution and parliament, was rejected by 'Abd al-Ḥamīd II in *1298*/1880, marking a return to absolutist rule. This came as a reaction to Turkish military defeats at the hands of European powers.

This constitution was finally put into effect in *1326*/1908. By that time the upheavals of the Second World War were imminent; in its aftermath the Sultanate was abolished in *1339*/1920 and in *1342*/1923 the Turkish republic declared. In March of *1342*/1924, the office of the Caliphate, filled by 'Abd al-Majīd II, brother of the last Sultan ('Abd al-Majīd had succeeded to the Caliphate but not the Sultanate), was abolished. *See* OTTOMANS.

Taqiyyah (from the root *waqā*, "to safeguard"; "self-protection" and hence "dissimulation" [in order to protect oneself]). The principle of dissimulation of one's religious beliefs in order to avoid persecution or imminent harm, where no useful purpose would be served by publicly affirming them. It is contained in the Koran 16:106:

> Whoso disbelieves in God, after
> he has believed — excepting him
> who has been compelled, and his heart
> is still at rest in his belief —
> but whosoever's breast is expanded
> in unbelief, upon them shall rest
> anger from God, and there awaits them
> a mighty chastisement...

A Prophet, however, cannot dissimulate the truth. Otherwise, recourse to this refuge is universally accepted in Islam. It is, however, associated most closely with the Shī'ites who practiced *taqiyyah* systematically and widely during periods of Sunnī domination to hide their beliefs from Sunnī Muslims. The Ismā'īlīs have also practiced it in regard to Twelve-Imām Shī'ites and Sunnis. It is the same, or not unlike, the case of Marrano Jews who pretended, sometimes for generations, to be Christians. Although one usually thinks of Spain and Portugal in this connection, there were numerous Jews in England of Shakespeare's time who carried on the pretense of being Christians. Lorenzo da Ponte, Mozart's librettist of Don Giovanni, who later became a professor of Italian literature at Columbia University in New York, while in Italy carried the pretense to the point of becoming a Catholic priest.

Permission to delude was also given by Mani to his followers; they were explicitly permitted to deny him, for which Mani claimed to be "more merciful" than Jesus. Rūmī likewise welcomed those who repudiated him.

Taqlīd (lit. "to hang around the neck"). Originally it meant a practice, now extinct, of designating an animal destined for sacrifice by hanging a marker around its neck so that it would not be used for any purpose that could render it ritually unsuitable. A related meaning was to appoint persons to a public duty by hanging a badge or chain of office around their necks; from this there evolved the now more general meaning of "public acceptance", "tradition", or the received way of doing things in human affairs, from crafts to religion. In religious matters it is the opposite of *ijtihād*, the pursuit of original solutions to questions; in law it is the reliance upon the decisions and precedents set in the past. In many modernizing Islamic societies today, the word has become pejorative, implying what is old-fashioned and retrogressive.

Taqwā. The piety which comes from the awe of God.

Tarāwīḥ *see* ṢALĀT at-TARĀWĪḤ

Tarḍiyah. The expression *raḍiya Llāhu 'anhū* or *'anhā* ("May God be pleased with him" or "her"), a formula inserted into speech or writing immediately following the name of a deceased figure of note, such as a Companion of the Prophet or a Saint. For the recently deceased the formula is *raḥimahū* or *raḥimahā Llāh* ("May God have mercy on him" or "her").

Ṭarīqah (lit. "path", *pl. ṭuruq*). A generic term referring to the doctrines and methods of mystic union, and rightly synonymous, therefore, with the terms esoterism and mysticism (*taṣawwuf*, or Sufism); it refers also to a "school" or "brotherhood" of mystics, of which there are very many, all ultimately linked to a single source.

The names of the *ṭuruq* are rather loosely applied, and if a teacher becomes renowned, his branch may be called after him from that moment on. Thus the apparent number of *ṭuruq* has grown to hundreds. They are, however, ramifications which may be brought back to several main "lineages" descending from the great masters.

All *ṭuruq* trace their authority through a "chain of transmission" (*silsilah*) back to the Prophet himself through his Companions. The time of the Prophet witnessed mysticism, or esoterism, as the pure, inner dimension of Islam in which all the Companions shared. Later Sufi masters, in response to different circumstances or to clarify certain nuances, chose different formulations for making explicit what had been implicit only. At the same time Islam became partitioned to a growing extent between the exoteric (the *sharī'ah*, "the wide road") and the esoteric (the *ṭarīqah*, "the path"), just as the souls of men became a dark forest following the progressive spiritual darkening of the age. This accounts for the development and diversity one finds in Sufism today.

The first *ṭarīqah* to emerge was the *Qādiriyyah*. One *ṭarīqah*, the *Tijāniyyah* claims that its origin is from the Prophet, in a vision made directly to its founder in the last century, without an historical chain, and another, the *Khāḍiriyyah*, claims to have originated in a direct initiation of its founder by al-Khiḍr. *See* AARON; 'ABD al-QĀDIR al-JĪLĀNĪ; BEKTĀSHĪ; FAQĪR; KHALWATIYYAH; al-KHIḌR; QĀDIRIYYAH; MEVLEVIS; NAQSHBANDĪ; QALANDĀR; SĀLIK; SILSILAH; SUFISM; ZĀWIYAH.

Tartīl, *see* KORAN CHANTING.

Tarwiyah (lit. "watering"). The name, coming from pre-Islamic times, which is given to the eighth day of *Dhū-l-Ḥijjah*, one of the days of the greater pilgrimage. On this day the pilgrims set out from Mecca to be present at 'Arafāt on the ninth. The Ḥanafīs make a night stopover at Minā obligatory at this time. However, other schools of law regard this stopover as recommended but not obligatory, so that many go straight on to 'Arafāt. *See* PILGRIMAGE.

Taṣawwuf. Esoterism, Islamic mysticism, or Sufism. The word apparently originates from *ṣūf* ("wool"), the preferred fabric, because of its simplicity, for the garments of the early ascetics. It is often noted that through *'abjad* (the science of the relationship between the numeric values of letters and their meaning) *taṣawwuf* corresponds to the value of the words *al-ḥikmah al-ilāhiyyah* ("Divine Wisdom"). *See* SUFISM; ṬARĪQAH.

Tasbīḥ. The expression *subḥāna-Llāh* ("glory to God"). This is often used in everyday speech to express marvel.

Tashahhud (lit. "testifying"). A station within the *ṣalāh* (ritual prayer), in which the *shahādah* (testimony of faith) is pronounced.

Tashbīh (lit. "the making of comparisons or likenesses"). That there is in the nature of God, an aspect — or aspects — to which analogy can be made is the metaphysical point of view expressed by this term. That which admits, or stresses, God's incomparability is *tanzīh*, for the Koran says that "God is not like anything." There is also the well-known Ḥadīth, reported by Ibn Ḥanbal, that "Adam was created in God's image" (*'alā ṣūratih*). Thus controversy has raged in history as to what is comparable and what is not, and is complicated by the numerous "anthropomorphic" references in the Koran to God as sitting on a throne, speaking, seeing, hearing, having a hand, and so forth. Beyond the historical controversies, however, it can be said that
tashbīh finally refers to immanence, while *tanzīh* refers to transcendence.

The comparability arises out of the fact that the world reflects the Divine Names which are its archetypes; the mystic Ibn 'Aṭā' Allāh described that matter as follows:

> By the existence of His created things (*āthār*), He points to the existence of His Names (*asmā'*), and by the existence of His Names, He points to the immutability of His Qualities (*awṣāf*), and by the existence of His Qualities, He points to the reality of His Essence (*dhāt*), since it is impossible for a quality to be self-subsistent. He reveals the perfection of His Essence to the possessors of attraction (*arbabu-l-jadhb*); then He turns them back to the contemplation of His Qualities; then He turns them back to dependence (*at-ta'alluq*) on His Names; and then He turns them back to the contemplation of His created things. The contrary is the case for those who are progressing (*as-sālikūn*): the end for those progressing (*nihāyatu 's-sālikīn*) is the beginning for the ecstatics (*bidāyatu-l-majdhūbīn*), and the beginning for those progressing is the end for the ecstatics. But this is not to be taken literally, since both might meet in the Path (*aṭ-ṭarīq*), one in his descending (*fī tadallīh*), the other in his ascending (*fī taraqqīh*).

The durability of stone reflects the Divine Name *al-Bāqī* ("The Enduring") and the fire's power of reducing forms to nothing reflects the Divine Name *al-Jalīl* ("The Majestic"). Thus creation resembles God. But God resembles nothing. *See* ISTAWĀ; TANZĪH.

Ta Shih. An ancient Chinese name for the land of the Arabs. Accounts which reached the Chinese from the lands of the various Western barbarians were necessarily garbled and the realities somewhat entangled with fantasy. Arabs were frequently confused with Persians, then as now.

> A T'ang dynasty writer described Ta Shih as follows; *Ta Shih* comprises a territory which formerly belonged to Persia. The men have large noses and black beards. They carry a silver knife on a silver girdle. They drink no wine and know no music. The women are white and veil the face when they leave the house. There are great temples. Every seventh day the king addresses his subjects from a lofty throne in the temple in the following words: "Those who have died by the hand of the enemy will rise again to heaven; those who have defeated the enemy will be happy." They pray five times a day to the Heavenly Spirit...
>
> At the time of the Sui dynasty, a man from Persia [Arabia] was feeding his cattle on the western mountains of Motina [Medinah]. A lion said to him: "On the western side of the mountains are many holes. In one of these is a sword, and close to it a black stone with the inscription in white, "Whoever possesses me becomes ruler." The man proclaimed himself king on the western frontier and overcame all who withstood him.

See HUI HUI.

Tashrīq (lit. "drying of meat"). The name of the 11th, 12th, and 13th days of *Dhū-l-Ḥijjah* (the "days of drying meat") *ayyām at-tashrīq*, so called because the pilgrim will then have made the animal sacrifice bringing the pilgrimage to a close.

Taslīm. The saying of *as-salāmu ʻalaykum* ("Peace be upon you") as a greeting, and in particular at the close to the ritual prayer (*ṣalāh*).

Tatars, *see* RUSSIA,

Ṭawāf. The ritual circumambulation of the Kaʻbah. This is done counterclockwise with the Kaʻbah on the left hand side, seven times. Because there are large numbers of worshipers constantly performing the *ṭawāf* day and night, with the exception of actual prayer times, it is difficult to reach the Black Stone (*al-ḥajar al-aswad*) to kiss or touch it on each round as the Sunnah prescribes. It suffices, therefore, to make a gesture reaching out towards the stone when one passes by it.

The lesser pilgrimage (*ʻumrah*) begins with the circumambulation (*ṭawāf*) as does the greater pilgrimage (*ḥajj*), during which it is performed several times. The opening circumambulation of the ḥajj is called *ḥawāf al-qudum* ("the circumambulation of arrival"). The first three turns are done with the quickened step known as the *harwalah*, as was done by the Prophet on his pilgrimage in the year 8/629 to indicate to the Meccans that he and his Companions were not tired after the journey. The last four turns are walked at a leisurely pace called *taʻammul*. Each turn is called a "round" (*ṭawfah*, pl. *ṭawaf*), or a "course" (*shawṭ*, pl. *ashwāṭ*). One complete cycle of seven turns is an *usbūʻ* (a "sept"). In performing the circumambulation, men who are wearing the consecrated garb of two seamless cloths (*iḥrām*) — for it is only in the *ʻumrah* and certain circumambulations of the *ḥajj* that it has necessarily to be worn — leave the right shoulder uncovered during the first three rounds but cover it for the remainder to avoid sunburn.

Apart from the circumambulation of the Kaʻbah carried out at certain prescribed moments of the pilgrimage, it is also possible to perform them at any time, when they are referred to *asṭawāf sunnah* ("customary circumambulations") and the state of purity conferred by the greater ablution (*ghusl*) is not obligatory for them.

Traditionally, certain recitations are made during the ritual which are inscribed in manuals of pilgrimage, but these are not obligatory apart from the opening *basmalah* and the closing *ḥamdalah*. It is permissible to go round the Kaʻbah ritually mounted on a camel, pushed in a wheelchair, or carried in a litter.

Circumambulation is an ancient rite which appears in all the Semitic religions. It (Hebrew *hakkafot*) is found in the Jewish marriage ceremony, Sukkot, Hoshana Rabba, Simchat Torah, processions around the Bimah, and in archaic magical ceremonies preserved amongst Sephardic Jews. Its origin lies in Mesopotamian astral religions for it imitates the apparent motion due to the rotation of the earth of the stars and planets around the polar star. The symbolism and meaning of the rite is to establish an identity between the circumambulator and what is circumambulated. In the pilgrimage, the pilgrim is of course not identifying with the Kaʻbah but with the center of his being, and through the symbol of the number of completion, the totality of directions of space which is seven, and does this in terms of his final ends or destiny. *See* PILGRIMAGE.

Tawakkul. The virtue of trust, or reliance on God, expressed in numerous Koranic sayings such as: "Whosoever puts his trust in God, He shall suffice him" (65:3); "And therefore upon God let them that trust put all their trust" (14:13). Trust must also be joined to adequate human action and precaution where possible, for the Prophet said: "Trust in God but tie your camel."

Tawbah (lit. "turning"). Conversion to the truth, *metanoia*, change of heart, and also repentance. As the Old Testament speaks of God "repenting", that is, relenting or manifesting a different attitude, the Koran also uses the word *tawbah* as a figure of speech, for God's willingness to "turn" towards those who "turn" towards Him.

Tawḥīd (the verbal noun of *waḥḥada*, "to make one" or "to declare or acknowledge oneness"). The acknowledging of the Unity of God, the indivisible, Absolute, and the sole Real. This doctrine is central to Islam and, indeed, it is the basis of salvation, but is understood within Islam in two diametrically opposed ways, as it were, that of exclusivity and that of inclusivity.

One, a comparatively modern view represented most clearly today by the Wahhābīs, intends by *tawḥīd* the utter exclusion of any analogy, similarity, or quality in creation that reflects or transmits God. This admirably strict and upright definition also removes the possibility of all holiness or sacredness from the world. An exception is the Koran, which doctrinally is conceded to be uncreated, and, according to the Ḥanbalīs, uncreated not only in its essence, on which all Sunnīs agree, but even in its letters and sounds.

This Wahhābī idea of *tawḥīd* is not carried so far as to say the world does not exist, however, and makes a *de facto* assumption of the world's materiality in a sense very much like that of modern science (that is, in complete separation from a transcendent principle) without drawing any conclusions as regards the consequence, which is namely, to leave unanswered the question: whence does the apparent reality of the world derive? This view of *tawḥīd* is based upon the negation (*nafy*), within the *shahādah*, the testimony of faith ("There *is no god* except Allāh").

The other understanding of *tawḥīd* is all-inclusive, that nothing is outside God. It is based upon the affirmation (*ithbāt*), within the *shahādah* ("There is no god *except Allāh*"). It is perhaps this latter view of *tawḥīd* which predominates outside of fundamentalist milieus today, and which certainly dominated Islam in the past.

For the Sufis, the realisation of *tawḥīd* is union with God; by this they mean the removal of the consciousness of all that is not God, in the sense that "what is it that could possibly veil the reality of God?" The fundamentalist understanding of *tawḥīd* considers the Sufi view as unthinkable. It is important to bear in mind that as regards *tawḥīd* as "unification" with God, the Sufis were very careful to emphasize that: "The Lord remains the Lord, and the servant remains the servant" (*ar-Rabb yabqa' ar-Rabb, wa-l-'abd yabqa' al-'abd*). Al-Hujwīrī declared:

> Unification disproves what human knowledge affirms about things. Ignorance merely contradicts knowledge; and ignorance is not Unification, which can only be attained by realizing the falsity of that appropriation of ideas to oneself in which both knowledge and ignorance alike consist. Unification is this, says Junayd again: that one should merely be a *persona* wielded by God, over which His decrees pass, dead to both the appeal of mankind and one's answer to it, lost to sense and action alike by God's fulfilling in onself what He has willed, namely that one's last state shall become one's first state, and that man shall be what he was before he existed.

The most celebrated expressions of the metaphysical understanding of *tawḥīd* are found in Ibn 'Arabī's *Risālat al-Aḥadiyyah* ("Treatise on Oneness") and in the doctrine of "The Unity of Being" (*Waḥdat al-Wujūd*), which pervades his writings and those of his followers. The fundamentalist point of view is best preserved in Muḥammad Ibn 'Abd al-Wahhāb's treatise, *Tawhīd*. *See* SHAHĀDAH; WAḤDAT al-WUJŪD; WAHHĀBĪS.

Ta'wīl (lit. "reducing to its beginning"; hence: "interpretation"). Allegorical or symbolic interpretation of the Koran, especially with a view to elucidating its most profound, inward doctrine. This is a complement to, and part of, *tafsīr*, which is also commentary, but which can be of a more outward and circumstantial nature. Some schools in Islam insist upon a literal interpretation of the Koran only; others, theologians, philosophers, and mystics, turn to symbolic interpretations when circumstances demand it. (*See* al-KINDĪ.)

Ta'wīl especially means allegorical interpretation. The Ismā'īlīs took this to its utmost possibilities and applied this to the Koran extensively and in a special, and abusive fashion, for the purposes of their doctrine.

The Ismā'īlīs also extend, when circumstances allow, allegorical interpretation of aspects of the *sharī'ah*. For them, the *shahādah* (the testimony of faith) can become the formal recognition of the Imām, the *Fast* becomes keeping his secret, and so on.

That this transgresses the orthodox bounds of *ta'wīl* is made clear in the statement of al-Hujwīrī above: an allegorical interpretation may never contradict the apparent and exoteric sense, and may not replace it; for this, obviously, is the prerogative of God, and His revelation. This has always been understood by authentic Sufis. *See* ISMĀ'ĪLĪS; KORAN; SEVENERS.

Tawwābun (Ar. "the Penitents"). After the murder of Ḥusayn ibn 'Alī in Kerbala (*Muḥarram 61*/October 680) there arose in Kūfah the first serious manifestation of proto-Shī'ites. These called for vengeance for the death of Ḥusayn with the slogan "*ya lathar'arāt al-Ḥusayn*" "Rise to avenge Ḥusayn's blood".

Sixteen thousand men had been enrolled in the *dīwān* or conscription of Sūlayman ibn Ṣurad al-Khuzā'ī, the leader who sought to involve people not only from Kūfah but Baṣrah and Mada'in as well. Four thousand appeared in *65*/end 684 to fight against the Umayyads in what was apparent to others as a suicidal attempt. One thousand old men, hardly fit for a military undertaking left the city to be destroyed in a battle with Syrian troops at 'Ayn al-Wardah in the Jazīrah in *22-24 Jumādā 65*/4-6 January 685. Before the three day battle they spent the night at Kerbala at the grave of al-Ḥusayn lamenting his death. They were apparently seeking martyrdom as a religious sacrament; which raises the question: what was their religion? The city which they left was Kūfah, the prolongation of Ḥirah, the former capital of the Lakhmids, and center of Arab Manicheism, a religion which actually had been born in 'Iraq. The movement did not seek out a political leader from among the 'Alīds nor did they have a political program. Their motto of revenge was shortly thereafter appropriated by the revolt of Mukhtār. *See* LAKHMIDS; SHĪ'ISM; KAYSĀNIYYAH.

al-Tawrāt. The Torah or Books of Moses, which are accepted as Divine revelations by Islam. *See* BIBLE.

Tayammum. The purification by sand or stone, instead of water, replacing the customary ritual ablution (*wuḍū'*), or, if necessary, the greater ablution (*ghusl*) as well. The substitution is made if water is not available or if, for health reasons, one cannot use water.

The *tayammum* is performed by formulating the intention of purification, pronouncing the *ta'awwudh* and the *basmalah* together, as is done before all ritual actions, rubbing the hands over a natural stone, uncut and not worked by man (not, therefore, over concrete blocks, or the walls of houses as is thought allowable in some popular belief), then rubbing the hands together, touching the stone again and rubbing the face and neck. The stone or sand is touched again and the left hand is passed over the right hand and arm up to the elbow, then the right hand is passed over the left hand and arm up to the elbow both arms being bared to the elbow. This completes the *tayammum*.

It is performed immediately before the prayer, after the "call" (*iqāmah*) which directly precedes the act of praying has been made. If earth or sand is used in place of a stone, it is only touched with the palms and then shaken off. The hands are passed over the face and arms but the earth is not rubbed in; the purpose is contact and not a "cleaning" by spreading earth on the skin. It is necessary to perform a separate *tayammum* for each prayer, even if the prayers are performed one after the other.

The principle which is invoked here resides in the primordial nature of earth and stone, and its capacity — given the mysterious efficacy of rituals consecrated by revelation — to symbolize purity and convey purification, as water obviously does. The rites *wuḍū'* and *tayammum* give water and earth the power to purify and renew, in the way that metaphysical substance can re-absorb its own creations and renew them, removing psychic pollution and imbalance. It is because of this that worked stone or manufactured materials, even if made from earth and stone, are unacceptable for tayammum; only that which God has fashioned, and not man, opens us to this power of nature.

Because one cannot enter a mosque in the state of sexual impurity (*janābah*) which necessitates the greater ablution (*ghusl*), a stone is often placed at the door of the mosque so that *tayammum* to replace *ghusl* may be performed there by those not able for any valid reason, to use water. This is a special use of *tayammum* which is often ignored, or unknown.

It is admissible to use the *tayammum* when the time needed to perform *wuḍū'* with water would cause the person to miss an irreplaceable prayer such as that of a festival, *'īd*, or a funeral prayer; but this dispensation does not apply to ordinary prayers which can be made up individually.

Pronouncements made in the 19th century by religious leaders in Nigeria have resulted in the *tayammum's* being frequently accepted there as a normal substitute for *wuḍū'* even when water is available; but this practice has not been sanctioned by the consensus (*ijma'*) of the Islamic community.

Ta'ziyah (lit. "solace" "condolence"). 1. A representation of the tomb of Ḥusayn carried by Shī'ites at mourning ceremonies at the anniversary of his martyrdom at Kerbala, the 10th of Muḥarram.

2. It is also the name of a "passion play" performed in Iran at that time which recreates the martyrdom with details designed to arouse frenzied pity for Ḥusayn on the part of observers. These rites may have their origin in the rites for the Persian hero Siyavosh.

Ta'zīr. Punishments or sanctions for offenses at the discretion of the Judge (*qāḍi*), ranging from admonishment to public shaming or whipping. Limits are imposed on the extent of such punishments. As opposed to *ta'zīr*, certain offences incur a punishment defined by the Koran, and are not subject, therefore, to the Judge's discretion.

Tazkiyah (lit. "purification"). 1. A technical term of Islamic law (*sharī'ah*) referring to the testification of the integrity of a witnesses.

2. Purification in general or in a moral sense, through the virtues of giving and generosity. *See also* ZAKĀH.

Testimony of the Faith, *see* SHAHĀDAH.

Tenth Day of Muḥarram, *see* 'ĀSHŪRĀH.

"Ten well-betided ones", *see* 'ASHARAH MUBĀSHARAH.

Thābit ibn Qurrā (*221-288*/836-288). Mathematician, astronomer and physician. Through Muḥammad ibn Mūsā ibn Shākir, one of the "Three Brothers" known as the "Banū Mūsā" who were noted scientists, he was associated to the scientific academy founded in Baghdad by the Caliph al-Ma'mūn. Thabit ibn Qurra was not a Muslim, but a member of the Hellenist sect of Ḥarrān, where he originated. (Ḥarrān is today called Altinbasak, and is in Turkey, near Urfa.) He was instrumental in gaining his co-religionists the status of *Ṣābians* which, by making them "People of the Book" (*Ahl al-Kitāb*), or a people with a divinely revealed religion, protected them from the bout of religious scrutiny begun under the Caliph al-Ma'mun and exempted them from forced conversion to Islam. The scrutiny of al-Ma'mūn was probably feigned for show, because he himself was known as the *Amiru-l-Kāfirin*, "the Commander of the Unfaithful".

Of Thābit ibn Qurra the poet Sarī ar-Raffā said: "Philosophy was dead, and he revived it amongst us; the traces of medicine were effaced and he restored them to light."

Thamūd. A people mentioned in ancient records as well as in the Koran, according to which a Divine revelation was sent to them through the Prophet Ṣāliḥ. His message was symbolized by a camel which the people killed; for the rejection of the revelation they were destroyed by an earthquake and a thunderbolt. They have usually been identified as the Nabateans, whose capital was Petra in Jordan, and who had a colony in Arabia. The ruins of this Nabatean city, northeast of Medinah near al-'Ulā, are called *Madā'in Ṣāliḥ*, or the "cities of Salih" by the Arabs, and their civilisation has, for this reason been called "Thamūdic". *See* ṢĀLIḤ.

Theft (Ar. *sariqah*). The conditions of theft are minutely detailed by Islamic law and precedent. For theft to be established, the stolen goods must have been in custody, namely, in a location belonging to someone, such as a home or a shop, or under watch. The punishment for theft prescribed in the Koran (5:42) is the cutting off of the right hand, and this sanction can be applied for the theft of articles of an established minimum value, for example ten dirhams, but not to articles of insignificant value.

In practice, as in the case of other harsh punishments found in Islamic law, this punishment is rarely applied, but plays the role of a deterrent. There must be either confession by the thief or the testimony of two witnesses; and in that event, the Judge would normally seek mitigating evidence or testimony to throw doubt upon the act and reduce its seriousness. Moreover, punishment can be avoided if the thief provides restitution and is forgiven by the injured party, which, in the eyes of the law, is the desirable outcome which the Judge would encourage.

> But whoso repents, after his evildoing,
> and makes amends, God will turn towards him;
> God is All-forgiving, All-compassionate. (5:43)

Actually, since early times, the punishment for theft has in practice been imprisonment. The sporadic application of amputation for theft in the modern world is not normative; it goes against the current of legal precedent and is, more than anything else, a byproduct of cultural and political upheaval. *See* SHARĪ'AH.

Theodicy, *see* IBLĪS.

Theology, *see* KALĀM.

Theory of Reality, *see* FIVE DIVINE PRESENCES.

Thousand and One Nights, (Ar. *alf laylah wa laylah*). A collection of oriental stories, many of them erotic, some simply entertaining, and others with a profound symbolic and spiritual meaning. The framework is the story of King Shahryār, who, betrayed by women, marries one after the other and puts each to death before she can cuckold him. Then he marries Shahrazād, the daughter of his Vizier, who entrances him with story after story, for a thousand and one nights, in the process giving him three children. In the end he is cured of his wickedness and anguish, and Shahrazād (meaning "of noble blood", "Royal born"), the image of *māyā*, creating reality out of the void, puts an end to this mistreatment of womankind.

Most of the stories originated in India, either in the *Jātaka* tales of the Buddhists or in the collection of Hindu moral tales called the *Hitopadesha*. They passed into Persian where they were known as the *Thousand Tales*, and spoke of Khusrow and Shirin. Mas'ūdī (d. *345*/956) said they were translated into Arabic around the *3rd*/9th century at the height of the 'Abbāsid Caliphate in Baghdad, the city with which they became associated, as they had once been associated with Ctesiphon. They were also popular, later, in Mamlūk Egypt where they took on their final Arabic and Islamic form. The *Thousand and One Nights* first became known in Europe in the French translation of Antoine Galland in the beginning of the 18th century and were immediately popular. Anonymous translations published in "Grub Street" in London appeared shortly after the French edition, and other languages followed. Some of the stories such as that of Aladdin did not appear in the original Arabic Text, now in the Bibliotheque Nationale, which was the basis of the French translation, but translated out of European sources then entered later Arabic texts. Some of the stories, such as that of Sindbad are from other sources, the story of the King Sannabara — Sonpadh in Persian. In addition to his written sources, Arabic and Turkish, Galland also heard stories from a Christian Maronite woman, Hannah Diab who visited France. These also became part of his translation. Charles Perrault, who wrote the Mother Goose tales in France, was an admirer of the *Thousand and One Nights* and many Western writers were influenced by them. Well into the 20th century they usually appeared in European editions which were often expurgated; the parts considered obscene were either omitted or put into Latin, for the benefit of deserving men of reasonable education.

Many stories describe the journey of the soul through life; the treasures which are sought are realisations of reality, and the magicians who are vanquished are the different kinds of illusions which the ego throws up to keep its hold over the immortal self which must be freed from the imprisonment of the earthly condition. Along with these sometimes profound and mysterious elements, the *Thousand and One Nights* were the Hollywood of their age, perfected by storytellers and still alive right up until the moment when television wiped away the traditional spoken arts.

"Three Imposters". A free-thinking pamphlet in French which was published in Holland in 1719 along with some works by Boulainvillers on Spinoza, and in 1721, and frequently thereafter. It was believed to be a translation of a treatise, *De Tribus Impostoribus* in Latin, written by Frederick II Hohenstaufen, King of Sicily (1194-1250) around 1230 and addressed to his friend Othon. This was an attack on positive religion which said that the three imposters were "Moses the Magician", "Jesus", called "the Shepherd" by those who cite the pamphlet, and "Muhammad", called the "Camelherder" although, except for "the Magician" these epithets don't actually appear in the pamphlet itself. Voltaire believed that it was written by Henri Comte de Boulainvilliers (1658-1722).

However, such a treatise was mentioned earlier in 1659 in *Theophrastus Redivivus*. Also, Boulainvillers, who did have a free-thinking circle, nevertheless wrote a life of Muḥammad in which he expressed a significantly higher opinion of the Prophet than the author of the pamphlet in question.

Frederick himself, as a very pro-Islamic monarch in whose court Arabic was spoken and Islamic customs observed, also would have had a higher opinion. He is named as the author because he was the "bad boy" of ecclesiastic history, having got himself excommunicated twice. 'Ubayd Allāh was also associated with the authorship of the pamphlet, because the ideas were common in Qarmaṭī milieus. (In 931, according to Abū Ṭāhir's physician Ibn Ḥamdān, the Qarmaṭīs of Bahrain and the East of Arabia circled naked around a Persian youth called Abū-l-Faūḍl proclaimed to be the true Mahdī, shouting [this is] "our God, he is mighty and exalted... the true religion has now appeared! It is the religion of Adam! Moses and Jesus and Muḥammad... are nothing but swindlers and cheats... this is a secret which we and our predecessors kept hidden for sixty years and today we have uncovered it.")

Probably the pamphlet had an anonymous author in the 13th century and circulated in manuscript form until the day dawned when it could be printed without the parties concerned being burned at the stake. It popped up several times in the 17th century and once a Dr. Morinus even wrote a satire addressed to himself under the pseudonym "Panurge" naming three contemporaries as the imposters. At some point the authorship of the pamphlet was also ascribed to the Fāṭimid 'Ubayd Allāh, and thus "the Three Imposters" appear from time to time in books of Islamic history. *See* HIGHEST INITIATION, BOOK of the.

"Throne verse", *see* ĀYAT al-KURSĪ.

T'ien Fang, (Chinese: "cube of heaven"). The Chinese Muslim name for the Ka'bah. *See* HUI HUI.

Tijāniyyah. A *ṭarīqah*, or religious brotherhood, widespread in Morocco, Algeria, and sub-Saharan Africa. It was founded by Abū-l-'Abbās Aḥmad at-Tijānī (*1150-1231*/1737-1815) who is buried in Fez. He studied the religious sciences in Tlemcen, Cairo, Mecca, and Fez, and joined several other *ṭuruq* before founding his own. He claimed to have received the command to found a *ṭarīqah*, and an initiation directly from the Prophet in a vision. To emphasize the objectivity of this vision, the Tijānis insist that it took place in daylight.

Thus, despite the founder's previous affiliation with at least three other religious fraternities (*ṭuruq*), the Tijānīs claim that the line of descent (*silsilah*) of their blessing (*barakah*) runs directly from the Prophet to Aḥmad at-Tijānī rather than through the links from generation to generation as with other *ṭuruq*. They also claim that only at-Tijānī is to be honoured and obeyed and only his *ṭarīqah* recognized as authentic. This is alien to the spirit of most, if not all, the other ṭuruq who generally accept that the esoteric viewpoint has at any one time different representatives; acknowledge each other; and respect the sanctity of great spiritual masters even of other lines. This customary universality is replaced in the Tijāniyyah by an adherence to at-Tijānī to the exclusion of all other spiritual teachers before or since. To further loyalty to himself, at-Tijānī made the claim to a special privilege that no other Saint possessed, that is, to admit to paradise a follower who had committed major sins. At-Tijānī also claimed to be the "Seal of Sanctity" (*khatm al-wilāyah*) and the "Pole of Poles" (*quṭb al-aqṭāb*).

The general tone of the Tijāniyyah is exoteric, that of adding a greater degree of zeal to one's religious life. Two special du'a' prayers are used by the Tijānīs: the "Prayer of Victory" (*Ṣalāt al-fatḥ*) and the "Jewels of Perfection" (*Jawharat al-kamāl*). The Tijānīs believe that the Prophet taught the latter to the founder. After an initial period of unsuccessful struggle with civil adversaries for political and military supremacy, the Tijāniyyah adopted a policy of accommodation with rulers, particularly with the French in North Africa. This policy was successful and the sect became widespread in French West Africa, through the efforts of traveling merchants. In this region it is one of the most prominent religious organisations today, particularly among the poor. In many ways it bears a certain resemblance to the Sanusiyyah, another politically inspired religious organisation, as well as to the Wahhābīs. The tomb of Aḥmad at-Tijānī is in the heart of Fez, near the Qarāwiyyīn Mosque. The artistic style of this sanctuary, the most important Tijānī mosque, bears the marks of European influence.

Tilāwah. Recitation of the Koran. *See* KORAN CHANTING.

Tīmūrids. A dynasty (*771-906*/1370-1500) founded by Tīmūr, also called Tīmūr-i-Leng, or Tamerlane (*737-807*/1336-1405), a Turkoman prince of Samarkand in Transoxiana. His tomb bears his claim to be a descendant of Jenghiz Khan (which he was not). Tamerlane's armies ranged over the northern steppes down to Persia and India, his name becoming a synonym for terror, and recalling the image of heaps of skulls piled up outside the cities he conquered. He was not notably religious himself, but became the patron of the tomb of Aūḥmad Yasavi north of Tashkent built c. 1397 and was noted for forcibly bringing vast numbers of craftsmen and artists into his empire to build great monuments. He himself took part in constructing some of his projects.

His descendants were not so bloodthirsty. Shāh Rukh (*780-850*/1378-1447) "desired not so much to extend but to repair the ravages caused by his father". His wife Jawhar is credited with the building of her mosque at Mashhad and the mausoleum complex at Herat, including an educational institution (*madrasah*). A grandson of Tīmūr, Ulug Beg, built an observatory, now destroyed, outside the walls of Samarkand, made astronomical calculations himself, and helped to recalculate the calendar. There was a Tīmūrid Renaissance in the fifteenth century. After the destructions of the Mongols, the Tīmūrids led the way to a new consolidation of faith; the Turks lost contact with Chinese materialism and now, after having already accepted Islam as a religion, made it the basis of their social institutions.

Afterwards, however, the Tīmūrids fell to fighting amongst themselves and so lost their sovereignty; but from them is descended the dynasty of the Moghuls. *See* MOGHULS.

at-Tīrmidhī, Abū 'Īsā Muḥammad (*209-279*/824-892). The author of one of the six canonical collections of Ḥadīth, called *as-Ṣaḥīḥ* ("the Authentic"), or *al-Jāmi'* ("the Collected"). *See* ḤADĪTH.

Tombs. The use of funerary monuments was forbidden by the Prophet in keeping with the primordial nature of Islam and its view of life as a temporary exile. Nevertheless, Islam as a civilisation could not avoid marking its history, and it became the custom to erect tombs for Saints and rulers. Thus, despite the prohibition, a very rich funerary architecture flourished whose high point is, of course, the Taj Mahal.

An exception to it today are the Wahhābīs who prohibit the custom of visiting family graves on Fridays, and keep their own graves as inconspicuous as possible. The site of the grave of King 'Abd al-'Azīz, for example, is unknown outside the family, despite the fact that he is the founder of modern Saudi Arabia. When the Wahhābīs conquered Mecca and Medinah they removed the multitudes of grave markers and mausoleums from the major cemeteries, including the most renowned resting place in Islam, the *Baqī'* cemetery in Medinah. They were even going to raze the domed mausoleum over the Prophet's tomb when international outcry prevailed upon the King, and this tomb was spared.

Trench, Battle of, *see* BATTLE of TRENCH.

Transcendence, *see* TANZĪH.

Translation of the Koran. It is sometimes said that the Koran "cannot" be translated, in the sense that translation is prohibited by religious law. The Koran has in fact been "translated" from the very beginning when there were variant readings because of variations in Arabic dialects. Partial translations always existed for the use of non-Arabic speakers, and complete translations were made, for example, by Sa'di Shirāzī and Shaykh Walī Allāh into Persian, and by the sons of Walī Allāh into Urdu. Printed Arabic Korans with interlinear Persian and Urdu translations have existed for some time. However, a translation of the Koran cannot be used ritually, for prayer, for invocation, or for serious study; for these only the Arabic Koran can be used. (In Asia, exceptionally, there are some Muslims who use the Koran in translation for certain ritual applications.)

It is inevitable that translations of the Koran imply some point of view. For example, the very popular translation into English by A. Yūsuf 'Alī is translated from the Bohora Ismā'īli point of view and contains their doctrinal notions. That of Mawlana Muḥammad 'Alī is a translation which incorporates the view of the Aḥmadiyyah. For Sunnis, one of the translations into English with the least number of objections is the Muḥammad Marmaduke Pickthall rendering, *The Meaning of the Glorious Koran*. *See* KORAN.

Tuareg (spelled "Touareg" in French). A Berber people of the Sahara, their language, Targui, is written in its own script. Formerly they were herding nomads and famed as fierce warriors whose resistance to the French continued into the 1920s, when the use of motor vehicles in the desert made the nomads too vulnerable.

Their society is matriarchal and they are noted because the men, for an unknown reason, cover their faces at all times with the cloth of their enormous blue turbans. These are often more than ten yards/meters long.

The Tuareg are often confused with the "Blue Men", certain tribes of the western Sahara who are Arabs, notably the Riguebat tribe. The Blue Men do not cover their faces, but both wear a costume called a *durrā'ah* or, in West Africa, a *bubu*. This is of blue cloth formerly made with indigo dye from Kano, Nigeria. The dye comes off on the skin, giving them the name of "Blue Men".

Tubba'. The title of the ruler of some of the South Arabian, or Himyaritic, kingdoms in pre-Islamic times. *See* ARABS.

Ṭūfān, *see* NOAH.

Tughrah. Elaborate calligraphic seals used by the Ottoman Sultans for official documents.

aṭ-Ṭūl (lit. "length" or "height"). A mystical term for spiritual exaltation, or a state of spiritual development, the highest degree of which is of course that of the Prophet. It has a complement in the concept of *'umq* ("depth", in a spiritual sense).

Tunisia. Republic. Population 9,019,687. 99% are Muslims of the Mālikī School of Law. A small minority, under 50,000, are Ibāḍites who lived on the island of Jerba. This community has become somewhat dispersed in recent years. Although the constitution requires that the president be a Muslim, there is considerable secularisation of Tunisian institutions, and the fast of Ramaḍān has been formally discouraged. The principle *ṭuruq*, the Shādhilī branches, the Qādiriyyah, and the Tijāniyyah, have also lost their influence under the onslaught of modernism.

Tunku, 'Abd ar-Raḥmān (1903-1973). The son of the Sultan of Kedah, Malaya, he was the first Prime Minister of Malaya from 1957 until his retirement in 1970. He studied law at Cambridge and held posts in the civil service. During World War II he was active in clandestine resistance to the Japanese. In 1961 he put forth a plan for the Federation of Malaysia which was approved in 1963.

Turan, *see* PAN-TURANIANISM.

Turbah. A cake of baked clay-like earth, the size of a bar of soap, from Kerbala, the place where Ḥusayn was killed and is buried. It is placed by the Shī'ites on the ground before them in the prayer so that the forehead touches it during the prostration.

Also called *muhr*, these earth cakes are sold in the Shī'ite holy places in 'Irāq and also in Iran.

Turban (Ar. *'imāmah*, pl. *'amā'im*). The characteristic headdress, elegant in its simplicity, used by Muslims and some other peoples in Asia, as well as oriental Christians and Jews. The experienced observer can distinguish nationalities and tribes simply from the style of wrapping the turban which can vary in length from only one meter, to more than ten meters. In some societies the elaboration and size of the turban became a badge of social standing, and the excesses to which notables in Turkey carried the practice of wearing giant, impractical turbans, led to the adoption of the Fez (*tarbush*) as official head covering by the government in the 19th century.

Since then, other variants on headgear have been introduced in attempts to appear modern. The use of the western hat in Turkey, whose rim is an obstacle to the prostration (*sujūd*) in the prayer, as opposed to the traditional headgear which is naturally compatible with praying, was viewed both in Turkey and abroad as distinctly anti-Islamic. Its inclusion as a point in the Kemalist program of laicisation raised great controversy at the time.

The importance of the turban lies in the fact that the head is the seat of the sovereign function of consciousness — that in man which recognizes and most directly mirrors God. To cover the head during prayers is part of traditional custom (Sunnah), and to cover the head, even inside the house or on the street, has been regarded as befitting the theomorphic dignity of man. The skull cap, which is worn by itself or under the turban, is called a *taqiyyah* ("piety") because of the traditional rule that the head should be covered. Up until recent times it would have been completely unthinkable to show oneself in public with the head uncovered, and this is still the case in Beduin societies. Other forms of Islamic headgear include the headwindings called *kavuk* in Turkey, the high crowned caps worn by dervishes in Turkey and Persia, the *kulah*, the *qalansuwa* and, in Central Asia, the cap called the *kalpak*.

Türbe. The Turkish word for a funerary monument, referring both to the enclosing structure (Ar. *ḍarīḥ*), and to the sepulchre (Ar. *tābūt*). It is also the name given to the characteristic Turkish headstone of a grave, with a turban carved in stone at the top; a familiar sight in the cemeteries of the lands of the former Ottoman Empire.

Turfan *see* XINJIANG.

Turkey. Population 62,484,478. Recent estimates of the population run as high as 63 million. Two million (some say ten million) of the population are Kurds and there are some ethnic Arabs in the south, as well as Christian minorities, notably the Armenians. It is usual to think that 98% of the population are Sunnī Muslims, although, as a result of the policy of laicisation carried out this century, many are consciously non-practicing; in addition it is now believed that many who were considered Sunnis belong to sects like the Alevis. This heterodox group, related to the 'Alawis of Syria, and another called Yezīdīs, is found mainly among the Kurds. It is actually a crime in Turkey for a political party to suggest that "minorities exist in the Turkish republic based on national, religious, confessional, racial or language differences". Thus the estimates of such groups in the past was very low; since the development of a more liberal attitude towards religion in Turkey in recent years, the estimations of the number of Alevis has risen into the millions. In 2001, Turkish Alevis in Germany, by asking for Government allocated funds for religious education in schools, have asked for de facto state recognition as a religion separate from Islam.

Since the time of Atatürk there has been an ongoing state program to "Turkify" the language by removing Arabic words (which were very common in Ottoman Turkish) and replacing them with new Turkish based ones. Since Muslims could not be expected to object to the Arabic words which are the carriers of Islam, and which therefore exist in all Muslim languages, the impetus for such a program must lie with a non-Islamic group. *See* BEYLERBEY; DEFTERDAR; DEVSHIRME; DÖNMEH; GÖKALP, ZIYA; ISTANBUL; JANISSERIES, KAPUDANPASHA; KEMAL, MUṢṬAFĀ; MEHMET II; OTTOMANS; PANTURANIANISM; QĀḌI 'ASKER; SELJŪQS; SUBLIME PORTE; SHAYKH al-ISLĀM; SĪNĀN; SULAYMĀN the MAGNIFICENT; TANẒĪMĀT; TURKS.

Turkmenistan Former republic of the Soviet Union, independent in 1991. Population: 4,075,316, of whom 73% are Turkmen, and the rest Russian and Uzbek. The capital is Ashkhabad. The Karakum desert covers 80% of the country. The Turkmen or Turkoman are Sunnis with small divergent religious groups like the Qīzīl Bash. The extinct city of Marv (or Merv), once a major city of Iranian civilisation, today Bahram 'Alī, as well as the Parthian capital of Nish, are located in Turkmenistan.

Turkomans. A nomadic people related to the Turks, found in Central Asia and Sinkiang. *See* TURKMENISTAN.

Turks. A people whose original homeland appears to have been in the Altai mountains of the Tien Shan range in China from which they had migrated to many areas of Central Asia, and at one time controlled the steppes and regions far north into Russia. Others came West with the horde of Jenghiz Khan. Before their conversion to Islam they were shamanists.

Many dynasties ruling in the name of the 'Abbāsids were of Turkic origin; the Ghaznavids, the Seljūqs. Most of the kingdoms to the north of the 'Abbāsid Empire were Turkic, such as the Qipchaq Khanate. So were a number of Persian dynasties including the Ṣafavids, Afshārids, and Qājārs. The greatest of the Turkish empires was of course that of the Ottomans, so named after their original tribal leader Osman (or 'Uthmān). Such was the importance of the Turkic peoples that a Sacred Ḥadīth (*ḥadīth qudsi*) is attributed to the Prophet, in which God says: "I have an army in the East which I call the Turks; I unleash them against any people that kindle my wrath."

Peoples related to the Turks inhabit the regions from Turkey to Sinkiang and include Tartars, Turkomans, Uzbeks, Kirghiz, and others. Most are Sunnī Muslims. *See* AZERBAIJAN; AZERI; KIRGHIZ; TURKEY; TURKOMAN; UZBEKS.

Ṭuruq, *see* ṬARĪQAH.

aṭ-Ṭūsi, Muḥammad ibn Ḥasan (*385-460*/995-1067). Shī'ite theologian, author of one of the so-called "four books", the principal Shī'ite collections of Ḥadīth, the *Istibṣār* ("Examination"). He also wrote the *Fihrist* ("Index") of Shī'ite works, and the *Tahdhīb al-Aḥkām* ("Correcting of Judgements"), as well as many other works. Aṭ-Ṭūsī was also known as the Shaykh at-Ṭā'ifah; he was a student of the Shaykh al-Mufīd and Sayyid Murtaḍā.

aṭ-Ṭūsi, Naṣīr ad-Dīn (*598-673*/1201-1274). An astronomer, mathematician, and astrologer born in Ṭūs, Persia, died in Baghdad. For some time he stayed at the Assassin stronghold of Alamūt, and at Maimundiz, and wrote Ismā'īlī treatises. After the destruction of Alamūt by the Mongols under Hūlāgū Khān, he claimed to have been held by the Ismā'īlīs against his will, having been kidnapped by the Ismā'īlī governor of Quhistan. On the other hand, he did induce the last Chief of Alamut, Ruknu'd-Din Khurshid to surrender himself into the hands of the Mongols whence he was first catered to and then put to death. But he also facilitated the demise of the ʻAbbāsid Caliph by assuring Hūlāgū that there would be no heavenly retribution on him if he put the Caliph to death. Nevertheless, he is the author of a well known and quoted work on ethics. He was, therefore, an opportunist, and joined the Mongols in the capacity of astrologer, professing to be a Twelve-Imām Shīʻite. As he was teacher to the important Twelve-Imām Shīʻite theologian ʻAllamā al-Ḥillī, and the mystic Quṭb ad-Din Shirazi, the Twelvers have also supported the claim that he was not an Ismāʻīlī despite the overwhelming evidence to the contrary.

Accompanying the Mongols he profited from the plunder of many libraries to enrich his own, (as did ʻAlā ad-Dīn al-Juwayni, the Mongol's *Ṣāḥib ad-Diwān.*) Nevertheless, Ṭūsi did save the life of the latter and others on one occasion by playing on the superstitions of Hūlāgū the Mongol. According to Ibn Shakir, Ṭūsi's library counted 400,000 volumes.

As an astronomer at the observatory of Maragha in Azerbaijan he compiled the astronomical tables known as the *Zīj Il-Khānī* for the Mongol Khans. He proposed a model for the study of planetary motion, the "Ṭūsi couple", which has been named after him. A prolific writer he produced numerous treatises on theosophical and theological subjects including the *Tajrīd al-Iʻtiqādāt* ("Definition of the Articles of Faith") and *al-Akhlaq an-Nāṣiriyyah* ("The Nasirean Ethics"), and the *Rawdat at-Taslīm* ("Garden of Submission"). Shahrazurī says of him however, that his scientific reputation was less due to his scientific accomplishments than to his violent temper which brooked no contradiction and led him to impose himself over others.

Tustari *see* SAHL at-TUSTARI.

Ṭuwā. The sacred valley where Moses saw a fire, approached it and was addressed: "Surely I, even I, am thy Lord; therefore take off thy shoes for this is the sacred valley of Ṭuwā; and I have chosen thee. Hearken, therefore, to what shall be inspired (in thee)" (20:12-13). This is also the name of a well and its surrounding district in the city of Mecca, where the Prophet halted during his triumphal entry.

Twelve-Imām Shīʻites, *see* ITHNĀʻASHARIYYAH; SHĪʻISM.

Twelvers. *See* ITHNĀʻASHARIYYAH; SHĪʻISM.

U

'Ubayd Allāh al-Mahdī (*Hijri: born 12 Shawwal 260-died 15 Rabī' I 323* / AD: born July 31 874-died 4 March 934). Founder of the Fāṭimid dynasty; also called 'Abd Allāh and several other names. The name 'Ubayd Allāh is a *diminutive* of 'Abd Allāh, used contemptuously by those of his co-religionists who did not accept his claims and mocked his assumption of this very Islamic name; he was originally called Sa'īd Ibn Ḥusayn and perhaps also 'Alī. His son (born *280*/893) was originally called 'Abd ar-Raḥman and later acquired the titular name of Abū-l-Qāsim Muḥammad al-Qā'im. (His father's assumption of the name 'Abd Allāh thus conferred upon the son the same full name, with patronymic, as the Prophet Muḥammad himself whose father was also 'Abd Allāh, a name literally by which to conjure.)

'Ubayd Allāh al-Mahdī is said to have been born in 'Askar Mukram in Khūzistān (northeast of Baṣrah in today's Iran); he came to Salamiyyah in Syria in *269*/882, where his family had already moved much earlier. (This account may be only an example of literary ontogeny recapitulating phylogeny, that is, each individual biography repeating the family history; he may himself have been born in Salamiyyah, and it was only his great grandfather, 'Abd Allāh the Elder, who was born in 'Askar Mukram.) His father Ḥusayn ibn Aḥmad ibn 'Abd Allāh died when 'Ubayd Allāh was eight years old and he was raised by his uncle, his father's brother, Abu-l-Shalaghlagh (also known as: Abū Shala'la', and: [Abū 'Alī] Muḥammad ibn Aḥmad, and, also: Sa'īd al-Khayr). Abu-l-Shalaghlagh was a *Ḥujjah* (also called a *Lāḥiq*) or Bishop of the Ismā'īlīs in Salamiyyah. (They divided the world into twelve diocese, or "islands", in Arabic, *jazāir*, from which the name Algeria — *al-Jazāir*, probably comes. Some of these diocese may have been only theoretical, but the North African ones were real and active from Roman times.) His grandfather 'Abd Allāh the Elder (*al-Akbar*) is the one who is said originally to have come from al-Ahwāz east of Baghdad and then moved north to 'Askar Mukram, both in Khūzistān. After conflicts with Shī'ites, Mu'tazilites and others, the family fled to Baṣrah.

In Baṣrah 'Abd Allāh the Elder claimed to be descended from 'Aqil ibn Abī Ṭālib, an uncle of the Prophet. Later 'Ubayd Allāh would claim to be descended from another uncle, 'Aqil's brother Abū Ṭālib, and his son 'Alī, through Ja'far aṣ-Ṣādiq, although through which descendant of aṣ-Ṣādiq was a matter that was modified several times. (*See* 'ABD ALLĀH ibn MAYMŪN al-QADDĀḤ.) Conflicts followed the family and 'Abd Allāh the Elder went to Salamiyyah near Ḥamāh in Syria where they stayed, settling first, interestingly, in a so-called "Christian" monastery, *Dayr al-'Uṣfūrayn* ("Monastery of the two Sparrows"). He was not, as some have thought Ibn Rizām to mean, a Christian, but what he really was, was a follower of a religion that disguised itself, or had a branch, within every religion worth the investment of subversion, including, as in the case of the Barmakids, Buddhism. Salamiyyah was a Christian center and seat of a Byzantine autocephalic Archbishop and still had at the time many monasteries. In other words, it was an established religious center which attracted representatives from all religions. Under the 'Abbāsids a new area of Salamiyyah had grown with colonists from as far away as Balkh, in today's Afghanistan. (*See* BARMAKIDS.) 'Abd Allāh the Elder (d. *261*/874) carried on his own religious propaganda and was supported by other missionaries; his activity took him as far away as Daylam on the Caspian Sea near Azerbaijan, where he married and where his son Aḥmad was born (whom the Ismā'īlī tradition credits, interestingly, but improbably, with writing the *Rasā'il Ikhwān aṣ-Ṣafā'*, "The Encyclopedia of the Brotherhood of Purity"). This Aḥmad was the grandfather of 'Ubayd Allāh, and outlived his son Ḥusayn, 'Ubayd Allāh's father, who died in 880.

A certain Ḥusayn al-Ahwāzi who fled with 'Abd Allāh the Elder to Salamiyyah worked as a missionary in the Sawad of Kūfah and recruited Ḥamdān ibn al-Ash'at, called Qarmaṭ (*see* QARMAṬĪS). At the same time, 'Abd Allāh the Elder sent Khalaf al-Ḥallāj to Rayy in Iran.

According to the *Fihrist*, "Qarmaṭ had read in the stars that the Iranians were about to regain control of the Arab empire." (The Iranians reckoned conjunctions of Saturn and Jupiter as indicative of the change of dynasties; the prophecy was planted a century earlier deliberately.) The Qarmaṭīs, another name for the Ismā'īlīs at that time and place, had an evolved social program of equality and property in common (*ulfah*), and very strict commercial laws. (A common factor in many previous Mazdakite-type religious revolts.)

In 881 one Ismā'īlī *Dā'ī* named Ibn Ḥawshab, also known later as Manṣur al-Yemen, went to Yemen from Kūfah disguised as a cotton merchant (a favorite front of the sect when travelling, cf. al-Ḥallāj, or the Cathares in Europe). There he proceeded to build several fortresses, one of which, at Bayt Rayb, he called the *dār al-hijrah*; "the place of refuge". Centers known by such a name were also established by others in 'Irāq (at Wasṣṭ, another ancient place that had known centuries earlier both Christian and Manichean monasteries, under the name Kashkar), at Tāzrūt in North Africa, and in al-Aḥsā' in Arabia. The words *dār al-hijrah* have a very Islamic ring to them as an echo of the Prophet's flight from Mecca to Medinah. This Islamic ring is misleading, deliberately so, since the actual program for which these places existed called for an end to Islam and its institutions. These "*houses of refuge*" were for refuge from Islam and their establishment was the prelude to the revolt which followed. At the same time envoys went to Sindh in India.

In 882 Ḥamdan Qarmaṭ sent Abū Sa'īd al-Jannābi to Bahrayn to organize affairs there. The Governor of Kūfah, Aḥmad ibn Muḥammad aṭ-Ṭā'ī, informed the authorities in Baghdad that there were people grouping in southern 'Irāq "who have a non-Islamic religion; that these were prepared to fight the Community of Muḥammad with the sword and impose their own religion"; but no one listened to him (Ṭabari III 2127). In that year 'Ubayd Allāh is supposed to have come to Salamiyyah from Aḥwaz (Khūzistān) retracing in his great-grandfather's footsteps.

The Baghdad Chronicler aṣ-Ṣūlī (d. *336*/946), an expert in Shī'ite matters, said that the family had in reality descended from 'Abd Allāh ibn Sālim ibn Sindān who was from an Arab tribe called Bahila and that Sindān had been a freedman and client of the 'Irāqi ruler Ziyad, while Sālim, the father of 'Abd Allāh, had been condemned as a Manichean (*zindiq*) in the time of the 'Abbāsid Caliph al-Mahdī (775-785). Ibn Rizām from Kūfah said that 'Abd Allāh was the son of an "oculist" called Maymūn al-Qaddāḥ and that both were followers of Bardaisan (or Bardesane) the Christian Gnostic from Edessa, whose belief Ibn Rizām characterized as a dualism of two gods, one of darkness and one of light. Moreover, Ibn Rizām also makes al-Qaddāḥ a follower of the Khattabiyyah, an early "Islamic" Dualist group. This 'Abd Allāh ibn Sālim (a.k.a. under the code name Maymūn al-Qaddāḥ) would have died in *261*/874-5 and would be the great-grandfather of 'Ubayd Allāh. Often the histories of revolutionaries are murky since they have to conceal their activities, and the use of code names or aliases is common. Ibn Rizām is considered to be an anti-Ismā'īlī polemicist; and, as the Shī'ites say about facts which they do not want to accept, "the pen is in the hands of the enemy". Out of necessity however, everyone, including Ismā'īlīs, are forced to draw on the "enemy's pen" for certain information; however, they choose to accept what they want and reject what they don't. Thus it is recognized by everyone that Ibn Rizām did have access to some early "authentic" sources. The Qaddāḥ ancestry is today officially repudiated since the Fāṭimids claimed to be descended from 'Alīds, and they allege discrepancies about chronology. On the other hand, no objective authority has ever seriously accepted Fāṭimid claims. And discrepancies about chronology, in any case, are the least concern; the number of other discrepancies makes anything possible. One can add that there were a number of Qarmaṭī leaders who did not follow the Fāṭimids but who themselves chose to claim descent from Qaddāḥ, and several times the Fāṭimid Caliph al-Mu'izz accepted descent from Qaddāḥ figuratively, and literally, ("yes we are descended from the 'happy one' — *al-maymūn* — 'the striker of the spark of right guidance' — *al-qādiḥ zand al-hidāya*"). Certainly, the figurative sense is what counted for many Muslim historians for whom the symbolic or philosophical sense mattered more than the material facts. Al-Mu'izz (from S. Stern) also said that 'Abd Allāh Maymūn al-Qaddaḥ was a nickname for the Imām, "the son of Muḥammad ibn Ismā'īl", i.e. 'Abd Allāh the Elder. But the Baghdad 'Alīds refuted Fāṭimid claims of descent from 'Alī, and Ja'far as-Sādiq, and his son Ismā'īl, and his supposed son Muḥammad; they said the Fāṭimids were descended from Bardaisan, the dualist philosopher, because for them Bardaisan-Marcion-Mani were one package, and this philosophical pedigree was the true identity of the Fāṭimids.

It is most interesting that Ibn Rizām also said that the second Fāṭimid Caliph, al-Qā'im, was not the son of 'Ubayd Allāh, but a "foundling"; an idea which also appears among the Druze and some other Ismā'īlī groups creating the idea of "Trustee Imāms". According to this discrepancy, 'Ubayd Allāh would have been acting on some else's behalf, and not his own. Other traditions claim the second Fāṭimid to be the grandson of Abu-l' Shalaghlagh (paternally presumably, since in the official descent he would have been in any case since his mother was supposedly the daughter of Shalaghlagh). Was this paternal blood connection the crucial one in some people's eyes? Or was the second Fāṭimid someone altogether different for whom 'Ubayd Allāh was a stalking horse, designed to draw away attention and danger upon himself?

In any case, the religion which came to be called Ismā'īlī was originally called *din al-ḥaqq*, "Religion of Truth" or simply "the Truth" whose followers were the *ahl al-ḥaqq*, "the People of Truth". Other religions were merely a shell for this Gnostic inner (*bāṭini*) esoteric truth. Its propagation was called *da'wat al-ḥaqq* the "Call to the Truth" or *ad-da'wah*. It came to identify itself with Islam (originally only one of the shells) while constantly calling for an end to Islam and the reinstatement of the "true religion". Since at least the time of 'Abd Allāh the Elder the propaganda had centered on promoting a certain Muḥammad ibn Ismā'īl, a putative descendent of the Caliph 'Alī through Ḥusayn ibn 'Alī and Ja'far aṣ-Ṣādiq, as the Mahdī or promised leader.

In addition to the general revolt, another plan was being executed, of which Ibn Ḥawshab of Kūfah, called the Manṣur al-Yemen, may have been a chief architect. In 893 he sent an Ismā'īlī missionary named Abū 'Abd Allāh ash-Shī'ī, like himself also originally from Kūfah, from Sana'a in the Yemen to Ifrīqiyā, or North Africa. Having made contact with pilgrims to Mecca from Tunisia the year before, Abū 'Abd Allāh ash-Shī'ī called the Berbers of Tunisia to accept among them as leader a Mahdī who would come to them from the East. The Mahdī, a "divinely guided leader", was a familiar feature of Shī'ite political movements since the Muktāriyyah (Kaysāniyyah). Abū 'Abd Allāh ash-Shī'ī's mission among the Berbers was to prove spectacularly successful; but its secret lay in the fact that he was preaching to the converted: Ibn Khaldūn later wrote that the Berbers *already* belonged to a certain *baṭini* or (Gnostic) sect. Indeed, the "Religion of Truth" had been well established among the Berbers in Roman times, centuries before Islam. St. Augustine had belonged to it before his conversion to Christianity, and around the year 750 the Archegos in Baghdad was a Berber from North Africa named Abū Ḥilal ad-Dayhuri. It is interesting to note that many Shī'ite Imāms had Berber wives; this was doubtless to strengthen alliances with ideological kindred.

Abū 'Abd Allāh spread a fabricated Ḥadith which says that "in the third century of the Hijrah, the sun will rise in the West". This was inspired (or one could say "decoded") from the Koran 2:258:

> Bethink thee of him who had an argument with Abraham about his Lord, because Allāh had given him the kingdom; how, when Abraham said: My Lord is He who giveth life, and causeth death, he answered: I give life and cause death. Abraham answered : 'Lo! Allāh causeth the sun to rise in the East, so do thou cause it to come up from the West.' Thus was the disbeliever abashed. And Allāh guideth not wrong-doing folk.

In other words, the disbelievers were now taking up the challenge to make the sun rise in the West the way Allāh made it rise in the East. Cloaked in Islamic allusions, the purpose of the establishment of the reign of the Mahdī was to bring to an end the era of Islam, and thereafter bring about the *qiyamah*, or "resurrection", of something which had itself been engulfed by Islam; the original "Religion of Truth" which was the basis of the revolt.

March or April 893 (Muḥarram *280*) is also given as the birth of 'Abd ar-Raḥmān, the Qā'im, son of 'Ubayd Allāh (who at this point was 19 years old himself) and Abū-l-Shalaghlagh's daughter. Soon the following event took place: according to the *Sirat Ja'far*, the *Dā'ī* Abū-l-'Abbās, brother of Abū 'Abd Allāh as-Shī'ī asked Fayrūz, *Dā'ī-l-du'āt* (the "Caller of Callers") and also the *Bāb al-Abwāb* ("the Door of Doors") who controlled access to the powers in Salamiyyah, that he be allowed to make his Ismā'īlī vow of allegiance to the "head" of the organisation in Salamiyyah. This was done with a curtain between the parties; after the oath, the curtain was drawn away revealing the "Imām" or leader (Abū-l-Shalaghlagh) the Mahdī-to-be ('Ubayd Allāh, supposedly Shalaghlagh's nephew) and the Qā'im-to-be, (presumably

'Ubayd Allāh's son, and, ostensibly, Shalaghlagh's grandson). Up until then Abū-l-Shalaghlagh was considered to be a *Ḥujjah*, or Bishop, probably one of twelve, representing either the official leader of the religion, the Archegos, or, another shadow leader seeking to impose himself. This shadow leader's personal identity was secret, and in a sense, imaginary since he was supposed to be an actually non-existent descendant of the Shī'ite Imām Ja'far aṣ-Ṣādiq named Muḥammad ibn Ismā'īl. This drawing of the curtain was a change in the party line; Abū-l Shalaghlagh previously only claimed to *represent* the leader, now he claimed to be the leader, at least as regards one *Da'i*. A secret leader of one or another name may well have existed (as far as some level of the organisation was concerned), or may have been fictitious, but this substitution or sleight of hand was an attempt to take over the leadership from him, or, in any case, from the other Bishops, and the Archegos himself. It would also unleash a flood of pretenders claiming to be Muḥammad ibn Ismā'īl.

Shortly thereafter, in *286*/899 Abū-l-Shalaghlagh ('Ubayd Allāh's uncle), died, apparently without direct living male descendants, having designated, it is claimed, his nephew (also to be known as his "spiritual son") as his successor to whatever old and new roles which he had played. (Obviously some people were privy to one reality and some to another.) The role of Mahdī usually presumed succession by descent; this, later, 'Ubayd Allāh would call an act of "spiritual adoption" in his *Letter to the Yemeni Community*. According to Ibn Rizām, whose account on this point is accepted by those who otherwise see him as a polemicist not worthy of belief, says that a conflict broke out between the leader in Salamiyyah and the *Dā'ī* Ḥamdan Qarmaṭ: "Qarmaṭ used to correspond with the man in Salamiyyah... Now when that one died who had been there during his time, and his son [sic] succeeded him, he [the son] wrote to Ḥamdan Qarmaṭ. But when Ḥamdan received the letter, he wanted nothing to do with what it contained, for it seemed to him that certain expressions to which he was accustomed had now been changed; to him this was suspicious." The Qarmaṭī leader 'Abdān went to Salamiyyah to find that the Ismā'īlī leader was dead, that 'Ubayd Allāh was the new leader, and that there was a new doctrine. He was confronted with Sa'īd, that is, 'Ubayd Allāh, presenting himself to be the Messiah, the Mahdī for whom revolution was being made. Soon he would also designate his young son 'Abd ar-Raḥman, later to be known as Muḥammad, as his successor, and endow him with further Messianic titles which were al-Qā'im (the "Enduring"), al-Imām al-Muntaẓar ("the awaited leader"), and Ṣāḥib az-Zamān ("Lord of the Age"). This caused consternation among followers and affiliates.

After 899, most of the *Dā'īs* refused to follow the former Bishopric of Salamiyyah, which now claimed to be the supreme center. Some even went so far as to attack the Mahdī with the intention of destroying him. Ḥamdān Qarmaṭ went to Kalwādhā (a suburb of Baghdad) whence he was never heard from again. (However, some Ismā'īlīs believe, more than highly improbably, that he reappeared later under a different name as a loyal Fāṭimid *Dā'ī* in Egypt!) Then, in 'Irāq, a mysterious messenger appeared from Ṭalīqan (in Daylam rather than Ṭalīqan in Khorāsān) looking for Qarmaṭ; not finding Qarmaṭ he went to the *Dā'ī* 'Abdan to recall him to 'Ubayd Allāh. Ibn Rizām: "'Abdan let him [the messenger] know that they had discontinued the *da'wah* or propaganda because *his father* [Abū-l-Shalaghlagh? The "spiritual" father of 'Ubayd Allāh? Ḥusayn the father of 'Ubayd Allāh and his brother Abū Muḥammad? Aḥmad the grandfather of 'Ubayd Allāh and father of Shalaghlagh? Or "'Abd Allāh ibn Maymun al-Qaddaḥ", the great grandfather of them all?] had deceived them. [This has led some to believe that the messenger was 'Ubayd Allāh's brother, Abū Muḥammad.] He had claimed a false pedigree for himself, and had made propaganda for the Mahdī Muḥammad ibn Ismā'il, and we did likewise. But when it became clear to us that none of this meant anything... and it was only your father behind the affair, we turned in repentance to God. It is enough for us that your father made us into unbelievers, do you now wish to make us into unbelievers once again? Vanish, and go back to whence you came." However, the mysterious messenger did manage to bring one 'Irāqi *Dā'ī* to the Mahdī's side, if that is the right conclusion (since the Fāṭimids were subsequently to disavow him and his two sons): Zikrawayh ibn Mihrawayh (also called Zakarōye ibn Mihrōye) *Dā'ī* of western 'Irāq (whose father had beenrecruited by 'Abdan). Next, 'Abdan was murdered at the instigation of Zikrawayh ibn Mihrawayh. However, Abū Sa'īd al-Jannābi, another *Dā'ī*, had the *Dā'ī* Abū Zakariyyā' ad-Ḍammāmi, who sided with 'Ubayd Allāh, killed. Zikrawayh went into hiding.

In Western Persia and Rayy the Ismā'īlīs did not join with 'Ubayd Allāh and remained "dissident" until after 934, or perhaps until the time of the fourth Fāṭimid Caliph al-Mu'izz (953-975). The Musāfirids of Azerbaijan also sided against the Fāṭimids. In Khorāsān some *Dā'īs* may have sided with the Fāṭimids. Yemen first sided with the Fāṭimids, then in *291*/903 one *Dā'ī*, Ibn al-Faḍl edged towards independence and in *299*/911, after reoccupying Ṣan'ā', himself claimed to be the Mahdī. The other *Dā'ī* in the Yemen, Ibn Ḥawshab (Manṣur al-Yemen), an architect of the Ifrīqiyā policy of preparing the Berbers for an emigration of the leadership to North Africa, sided loyally with 'Ubayd Allāh the Fāṭimid.

In the meantime the Qarmaṭī revolt had broken out in earnest. In 897 The Governor of Kūfah undertook a raid against Ismā'īlī villages of the Sawād and sent a series of Qarmaṭīs in chains to Baghdad, where it emerged that a state secretary (*kātib*) had been in correspondence with them. The secretary was arrested, but this shows how widely agents of the secret religion had infiltrated the structures of Islam. (They had been put there by the Barmakids.) In 899 Baghdad chroniclers recorded the appearance of Abū Sa'īd al-Ḥasan al-Jannābī at the head of a force of Beduin warriors. Historians of the time put the Qarmaṭīs at 100,000 concentrated in the Sawad (the "Black Earth" agricultural region) of Kūfah, and the Yemen, and Yamamah in Arabia. Abū Sa'īd al-Jannābī (who would be killed by a slave in *301*/913-914), occupied the city of al-Qaṭīf in Arabia and he founded another *dār al-hijrah* and an independent Qarmaṭī state centered at al-Aḥsā on the Persian Gulf. In the year 900 Qarmaṭīs raided in the neighborhood of Baṣrah; Abū Sa'īd al-Jannābi besieged Hajar, the fortified capital of the Baḥrayn oases, two miles from Ḥofuf in al-Aḥsā'; and for the first time the Caliph al-Mu'taḍid sent 2,000 troops against the Qarmaṭīs, who defeated the Caliph's forces.

In 901 Zikrawayh ibn Mihrawayh sent his son Ḥusayn to the tribe of the Kalb in Palmyrene Syria "to pose as a descendant of Muḥammad ibn Ismā'īl ibn Ja'far and to proselytize among them for the Imām from among his progeny..." Ḥusayn succeeded in recruiting many of the Kalb; the messenger depicted as "son of the *Ḥujjah*" who is presumed to be the brother of 'Ubayd Allāh the Mahdī appeared again, sought out Zikrawayh who in turn sent him to Ḥusayn. Ḥusayn presented this man to the tribes as the true chief (*ṣaḥib al-amr*) of their movement. In the meantime Zikrawayh ibn Mihrawayh organized Qarmaṭī revolts between 902-908 in 'Irāq and Syria. One of the Qarmaṭī tribes, the Banu-l-Aṣbagh, a clan of the Kalb, adopted the name *al-Fāṭimiyyūn*, or Fāṭimids, a name later adopted by 'Ubayd Allāh himself.

'Ubayd Allāh left Salamiyyah because he was warned by carrier pigeons from Baghdad that the 'Abbāsid authorities had learned his identity and had taken measures to arrest him. Women of the family were left behind, including 'Ubayd Allāh's mother and the ten-year-old Qā'im's "childwife". 'Ubayd Allāh went to ar-Ramla in Palestine where it is recorded he watched a meteor shower with the Governor on the roof of the Governor's house (the Governor was a secret co-religionist). He said the meteor shower (which took place 28 October 902) was a miraculous sign of his identity. He hid in Ramla and then he went to Egypt in *291*/903.

In North Africa Abū 'Abd Allāh's followers (who called themselves the "Friends of God" *awlia Allāh*, which means "the saints", or *perfecti*) occupied Mila — the Roman Mileve — which alerted the Emir of Kairouan to the danger growing in the West. Pilgrims carried messages between the Mahdī and Abū 'Abd Allāh; but the army (*jund*) of Kairouan beat back Abū 'Abd Allāh who was obliged to abandon Tāzrūt and re-establish the *dār al-hijrah* in Ikjan.

In the same year Abū-l-Qāsim Yaḥyā ibn Zikrawayh, son of Zikrawayh ibn Mihrawayh, having successfully gathered Beduins from the Syrian desert, threatened Damascus from December 902 to July 903 but died in the siege perhaps incinerated by a naphta projectile. Abū-l-Qāsim Yaḥyā was known as the "Master of the Camel" (*Ṣāḥib an-Nāqa*); Ivanow cites a pseudo-Ḥadith apparently preserved orally in India that "the Prophet once saw God [sic] wearing a red cloak riding on a camel at 'Arafat" (the root of 'Arafat means to "recognize" or "to know"). Abū-l-Qāsim Yaḥyā may also have let himself be taken to be the Mahdī. Abū-l-Qāsim Yaḥyā's brother Ḥusayn took over leadership. Ḥusayn, known as *Ṣaḥib ash-Shāma* ("the man with the birthmark") and *Ṣaḥib al-Khāl* captured Salamiyyah. Just before, Abū Muḥammad (the mysterious messenger from Talīqan of Daylam?), the brother of 'Ubayd Allāh died in Salamiyyah. Ḥusayn also captured Ḥamah and Baalbak, and forced Damascus to come to terms. He seemed to have set up a state expecting a Mahdī, presumably 'Ubayd Allāh, to come and take control; but in a battle near Ma'arrat al-Nu'man with an 'Abbāsid Baghdad army under Muḥammad ibn Sulayman, the Fāṭimid army was catastrophically defeated. Thereupon Ḥusayn in Salamiyyah ordered a massacre of the inhabitants of Salamiyyah, the destruction of the residence of 'Ubayd Allāh and the members of the Mahdī's household who had been left behind (this did not include the women who had been removed earlier). Was he disappointed with 'Ubayd Allāh or was he all along seeking his own interest? This, as so many details in this story, is not clear. The coalition supporting Ḥusayn broke up. Ḥusayn was captured near Salihiyye (Doura Europos), and brought to Raqqa' before the Caliph al-Muqtafi, whence the captives were brought to Baghdad. In Northern Syria remaining Ismā'īlīs were neutralized. Several *Dā'ī's* presented themselves to the authorities asking for pardon. Ḥusayn was executed early in *291*/904 in Baghdad along with hundreds of others, after receiving two hundred lashes. His body was exposed for a year. Another son of Zikrawayh, Abū-l-Faḍl tried to lead Qarmaṭī revolts in Syria. In this connection (Ṭabari, III 2226 — Goeje 51) tells the story of a woman whose son had joined the Qarmaṭīs; she went looking for him. When she found him, he said to her: "What is your religion?" She was surprised at this question; her son went on to say "Everything that we knew before was folly; the *true religion* is what we practice now." Ṭabari's account of the Qarmaṭīs is based upon the interrogation by an 'Abbāsid, Muḥammad ibn Dawud al-Jarraḥ, of an Ismā'īlī captive related to Zikrawayh ibn Mihrawayh

With these mounting reversals to the Ismā'īlī cause, 'Ubayd Allāh went to Egypt. Internal struggles among the Aghlabids allowed Abū 'Abd Allāh ash-Shī'ī in North Africa to reconquer Mila and take Saṭif as well while 'Ubayd Allāh spent a year in Egypt, until November 904, under the protection of one of his initiates in al-Fusṭāṭ. In 905 Egypt, which had been under the independent Ṭūlūnids, was taken under direct 'Abbāsid rule by the 'Abbāsid War Minister Muḥammad ibn Sulaymān (who had destroyed Ḥusayn the son of Zikrawayh.) 'Ubayd Allāh was now abandoned by the *Dā'ī* named Fayrūz, who went to Yemen and joined opponents. Thereupon 'Ubayd Allāh did not himself go to Yemen from Egypt as was planned but instead went first to Tripoli in North Africa. Halfway between Alexandria and Cyrenaica his caravan was attacked by Berber robbers, and his books were lost; this library was much lamented; one of the books was a compilation of prophecies of the future, an echo of the legendary "Kitāb al-Ja'fr", or mythical book of the 'Alīds. Years later these books were regained by 'Ubayd Allāh's son, the Qā'im.

Before 'Ubayd Allāh left Egypt he sent Ja'far his Chamberlain back to Salamiyyah to recover hidden money left in the ruined family house; earlier he had sent a servant back to Salimiyyah to incite the people to curse himself — 'Ubayd Allāh — and encourage the people to destroy what was left of the house in such a way as to preserve hidden treasure in the house which had earlier been collected as part of the religious tithe from 'Irāq and Syria. Ja'far was to use the recuperated money to buy several camel-loads of cotton to disguise his activities. Upon 'Ubayd Allāh's departure from Egypt, the *Dā'ī* Abū 'Alī (in whom some see — believe it or not — Ḥamdan Qarmaṭ resurfaced under a new name) remained in Egypt as the contact for the only Ismā'īlī community which was still on 'Ubayd Allāh's side, that of the *Dā'ī* Ibn Ḥawshab in the Yemen (where, nevertheless, another former *Dā'ī* had turned against 'Ubayd Allāh and headed a rival community.)

From Tripoli 'Ubayd Allāh went to Sijilmassa in south Morocco. There, after several years in hiding, 'Ubayd Allāh was arrested and imprisoned by the Midrarid *Amir*, a Kharijite wholly independent of Baghdad, but who was presumably acting on the advice of the 'Abbāsids or the Aghlabids, or in any case, in their interest.

But in 906, mutineers against the Aghlabids freed Abū-l-'Abbās (brother of Abū 'Abd Allāh ash-Shī'ī) from prison in Kairouan. Abū 'Abd Allāh ash-Shī'ī captured the city of Tubna with Roman war methods. There he applied Islamic principles of taxation, but strictly and orthodoxly (which was not to be expected, since he was actually spreading another religion, albeit one related to Islam.)

In Syria, Zikrawayh who had been in hiding near Qadisiyyah, met his forces in October 906: "Beduins, Non-Arab Muslims (*mawālī*), Aramaean peasants (*nabaṭī*)." Removed from the view of his forces, concealed, he was addressed as "Lord" (*sayyid*). On 10 January 907 a government army sent from Baghdad battled Zikrawayh in the Wadi Dhu Qār, "near the ruins of Iram" for two days. Zikrawayh was wounded, captured by the 'Abbāsids, and died two days later having failed to create a Qarmaṭī state in 'Irāq and Syria. His corpse was preserved and exposed to view in Baghdad. Another *Dā'ī*, "The Smith" (*al-ḥaddād*), and others, surrendered in Baghdad. Remnants of his followers, joined by Persians, continued limited activities under the name of the *Baqliyyah*, or "Vegetarians" under the leadership of Abū Ḥātim az-Zuṭṭī (and others) until they were absorbed into the Qarmaṭīs of Bahrayn around 932.

In North Africa the Ismā'īlīs were much more successful. On March 25, 909 (1 Rajab *296*) Abū 'Abd Allāh ash-Shī'ī entered Raqqāda, the royal suburb of Kairouan in Tunisia. On 26 August, 909 (*6 Dhu-l-Hijjah 296*) 'Ubayd Allāh and his son the Qā'im were freed from detention in Sijilmassa, Morocco, by Abū 'Abd Allāh and formally presented (for the first time) to the Kutama Berber army and *Dā'īs*; the Fāṭimids take this to be his enthronement as Caliph. 'Ubayd Allāh, who had lived in Sijilmassa from 905 to 909, was at the end, before the arrival of the Ketama Berber troops, placed under house arrest by the ruler, while his servants were tortured to determine their true identities and purposes. After his liberation, on the way to Tunis, 'Ubayd Allāh, now al-Mahdī saw for the first and last time the *dar al-hijrah* from which his propaganda had been initiated in Ikjan. Al-Mahdī ordered that all the treasure which had heretofore been collected should be turned over to him.

On Rabī' II *297*/Friday 5 January 910, 'Ubayd Allāh al-Mahdī made his triumphant entry into Raqqāda, where he was publicly proclaimed Caliph and his name read in the Friday sermon. This was the founding of the Fāṭimid dynasty, which would claim authority over the leadership of the whole Islamic world. 'Ubayd Allāh took the throne name al-Mahdī Bi'Llāh. A new genealogy was put forth claiming descent from Ismā'īl the son of Ja'far as-Ṣādiq; originally descent had been claimed from another son, 'Abd Allāh al-Aftaḥ; who was known himself to have no sons (and thus no contestants to object); this alternative was now definitively abandoned. Ibn Ḥazm, the famous theologian and literati in Spain remarks of all this: "I see that Mazdak has become a Shī'ite." [Mazdak was a Manichean or Manichioid revolutionary who had established a Communist-type state in Iran in the early 6th century; the name became a synonym for Manicheans, especially those with revolutionary social programs.] Later, the Fāṭimid Caliph al-Mu'izz in Cairo is depicted by objective observers as (allegorically) answering questions in Egypt about his ancestry thus: "he drew his sword from its sheath and replied: 'This is my pedigree!' and, throwing gold pieces to the assembly, he added, 'And here is my noble ancestry'..."

With the installation of al-Mahdī "the period of concealment (*dawr al-satr*) of the hidden Imāms in the history of early Ismā'īlīsm, had come to an end, being followed by a period of unveiling or manifestation (*dawr al-kashf*), when the Ismā'īlī Imām appeared publicly at the head of his community" (Daftary).

Al-Mahdī was reunited with his mother, his daughters, his nieces, and his son's wife who had been brought from Tripoli by the slave Ṣu'lūk who years earlier had been sent to Salimiyyah to recover them. The expectations about his role, which were of course unrealizable, were transferred to his son (or adopted son) who acquired the title al-Qā'im and the full name of the Prophet, Abū-l-Qasim Muḥammad ibn 'Abd Allāh.

In any case, doubts soon arose among the Berbers and even Abū 'Abd Allāh ash-Shī'ī regarding the Mahdī's authenticity. From circles opposed to him reports say there was dismay over his appearance and demeanor: "They found [around him] silk and brocade clothing, gold and silver vessels, Greek eunuchs, and indications of the use of alchohol. In their Berber simplicity [or rather, since their religion technically prescribed asceticism, celibacy, renunciation of the world, and prohibited wine] they disapproved of all this..." The spokesman of the Ketama confronted the Mahdī before his throne and told him to his face: "We have doubts as to your affair! Perform a miracle for us if you really are the Mahdī, as you have maintained." Al-Mahdī reacted with the inevitable indignation and recalled that the miracle of Muḥammad the Prophet was the Koran; but as the Ismā'īlīs claimed that the Koran has another, "true" albeit very different meaning from what is obvious if taken at face value, the decoding (ta'wil) of this alternate meaning was the miracle of Muḥammad's spiritual successors, who were al-Mahdī's ancestors. This actually brilliantly sums up how Islam was turned into a receptacle for the "Religion of Truth" — it was "decoded".

The tensions were eased in February 911 when the first Fāṭimid Caliph had Abū Abd Allāh ash-Shī'ī, who had prepared his arrival among the Ketama Berbers, and his brother Abū-l-'Abbās, murdered. Deservedly, in the eyes of the true believer. Al-Mahdī had already created a secret police (*diwan al-kashf*). There was also a purge of leaders of the Ketama Berbers who, nevertheless, retained primacy in the new alliances. However, having laid the claim to ruling the Islamic world (and ruling in practice a population most of whom were orthodox Muslims and not of their sect), forced the Fāṭimid Ismā'īlīs to adopt a new attitude towards the institution, the Caliphate, which they had previously tried to destroy, and towards Islam which they claimed to nullify and replace. Instead of the expected New Age, a different kind of new age would take place in which there would be ever repeated cycles of seven Imāms succeding each other until the last *nāṭiq* (speaker-prophet) appeared.

Towards the end of the year, *The Letter to the Yemenite Community* openly detailed the supposed family tree which al-Mahdī thought would unite Yemen and his North African armies in Egypt. In Yemen however, the *Dā'ī* 'Alī ibn al-Faḍl expressed his disaccord with al-Mahdī and declared war on Ibn Ḥawshab (*Manṣur al-Yemen*) besieging him for eight months. Then al-Faḍl himself declared the Millennium by way of abolition of the Islamic religious law, the *sharī'ah*.

On 18 August 912 the new Islamic century began: the year 300 of the Hijrah. With the new century, the Fāṭimids adopted what had been an imperial privilege exercised by Baghdad and Byzantium: they coined a gold Fāṭimid dīnār. The Umayyads of Spain followed their example in *324*/935 in striking coinage. (The Fāṭimid coins eventually had concentric inscriptions and a raised dot in the center, reminiscent of the original Round City of Baghdad. The concentric circles had a mystic sense, that the Bāṭin, or Ismā'īlī esoteric enclosed the Sunni exoteric, and the coin's gold content, higher than that of their competitors insured the acceptance of the coin outside their borders. The Crusaders struck counterfeit Fāṭimid coins, with lower gold content, in order to debase their acceptance). In 921 The Fāṭimid Mahdī and his court entered into al-Mahdīyyah, the new capital whose construction began in 916. The son (or adopted son) of al-Mahdī returned from his second unsuccessful Egyptian campaign to this new capital.

Ivanow reports this tradition from the *Sharḥu-l-akhbār*: "I (i.e. Qadi Nu'man) heard the Imām al-Mu'izz narrate a story about al-Mahdī. He said: once a certain important man asked him: art thou (really) the expected Mahdī, under whose authority God shall gather His slaves, making him the king of the whole earth, and shall the religion of the world become one under thee? He (al-Mahdī) replied to him: the mission of the Mahdī is enormous. I have a considerable share in it, and those who are coming after me shall also share it. (And al-Mu'izz added): if it should be the lot of one person only, how could anything from it come to me? Then al-Mu'izz continued: al-Mahdī was the key which opened the lock of the Divine bounty, mercy, blessing, and happiness. By him God has opened all these to his slaves. And this shall continue after him in his successors, until the promise of God which He made to them in His bounty, might and power, will be fulfilled."

In 934 al-Mahdī died having accomplished a historical feat in every sense including the most literal, that of manufacturing history itself, along with a colossal magic show. The framework for this accomplishment lay in the fact that a sometime secret world religion, the "Religion of Truth" or Manicheism, already established by many others from Spain to India centuries before, arose out of the shadows to stand in the light, at once both disguised and revealed. Where numerous other contenders had failed, al-Mahdī brought that religion from backstage to center stage, and to the open control of an empire, an event to be commemorated in the name of the city of Cairo, founded by the Fāṭimids in 969, which literally in full, means the "Victorious City of the Exalter of the Religion of God". All in all, a truly stunning achievement. *See* 'ABD ALLĀH ibn MAYMUN al-QADDAḤ; ISMĀ'ĪLĪS; MANICHEISM; QARMAṬĪS; SEVENERS; ASSASSINS.

'Ubūdiyyah (from *'abada*: "to serve" (as a slave) or "to worship"). Literally meaning both "slavehood" and "adoration" or "worship", the term defines the Islamic normative relationship of man to God, who is the Perfect Master. It implies complete obedience and resignation, but also expresses elliptically, and transposed into human terms of a human relationship, the nature of Being to Beyond Being, that is, of *wujūd* to Allāh (or in technical terms *Lāhūt* to *Hāhūt*; *see* FIVE DIVINE PRESENCES).

The highest example of the relationship of man to God is the Prophet's service and ministry, for he represents the prototype of *'Abd Allāh* ("Slave of God"). *'Abd* is one of his titles, along with "Messenger" (*rasūl*), "Prophet" (*nabī*), and "Intimate of God" (*ḥabīb*).

'Ūd al-Qimārī, *see* ALOES, FRAGRANT.

Udu, *see* WUDU'.

Uḥud, *see* BATTLE of UḤUD.

Uighurs, *see* XINJIANG.

'Ukāẓ (also transcribed as *Okadh* and *'Ukadh*). A site in the Hejaz southeast of Mecca in the region of Ṭā'if at which, once a year in the "Age of Ignorance" (*Jāhiliyyah*) before Islam, a fair was held beginning on the first day of the month Dhu-l-Qa'dah. It was here that the desert poets recited their odes (*qasīdahs*), describing the great deeds of times past, the so-called "Days of the Arabs" (*ayyām al-'Arab*). It is probable that the most acclaimed of the poems recited at 'Ukāz were written in gold letters and hung in the Kābah. Thence they were known as "the hung ones" (*al-mu'allaqāt*), of which of some ten have survived, the most famous being that of Imru'-l-Qays.

The fair lasted for weeks and was one of the great occasions when the scattered inhabitants of the Arabian peninsula came together. Not only poets came, but also religious preachers, among them the Bishops of Najrān, which was then a flourishing Christian oasis in the south. But as the fair was predominantly a pagan institution, it was abolished by the Prophet. *See* IMRU'-l-QAYS.

'Ulamā' (pl. of *'alīm*, "learned", "savant"). Those who are recognized as scholars or authorities of the religious sciences, namely the Imāms of important mosques, Judges, teachers in the religious faculties of universities and, in general, the body of learned persons competent to decide upon religious matters. Normally, even in hereditary monarchies, the sovereign is officially "elected" by the *'ulamā'*, who thus confirm his authority to rule. The *'ulamā'* have always represented legitimacy in state and religion, and been a confirmatory thread from regime to regime which survived the fall of sultans and dynastys. Among the Twelve-Imām Shī'ites the *'ulamā'* are the superior *Mullās*, the *Mujtahids* whose leading members are called *Ḥojjatalislam* (*Ḥujjat al-Islām*), and *Ayatollah* (*Āyat Allāh*).

Because in the Shī'ite world these leaders have a personal following, and from them an independent income, and have the prerogative of making legal decisions (*ijtihād*), they are a more direct and independent political force than the *'ulamā'* of the Sunnī world. *See* AYATOLLAH.

'Umar ibn al-Khaṭṭāb (d. *23*/644). The second Caliph and the second of the Four Patriarchal Caliphs, one of the most notable figures in Islam, he was famed for his strong will and direct, impetuous, and unambiguous character. Before he became Caliph, 'Umar was known to be uncompromising and even violent. When the responsibility of the Caliphate was given him he became more even-tempered, but still forceful. Under his rule the Islamic Empire expanded with almost miraculous speed, and it is fair to say that it was 'Umar who, after the Prophet, was most influential in molding the Islamic state, and in determining its nature.

He had, at first, been a fierce enemy of Islam, the circumstances of whose conversion four years before the Hijrah are famous: he had set out to kill the Prophet, when he learned that his sister Fāṭimah and her husband Sa'īd ibn Zayd were converts to the new religion; coming to admonish them, he let them recite verses of the Koran to him and was converted on the spot. Once converted, he became the most steadfast of the Companions, and on his deathbed said: "It would have gone badly with me, if I had not been a Muslim."

In the indecision which followed upon the death of the Prophet, 'Umar thrust the leadership onto Abū Bakr, and was the first to swear fealty to him in order to forestall a split in the community between Meccan immigrants, the *Muhājirūn*, and the Medinans, the *Anṣār*. 'Umar himself being later designated Caliph by Abū Bakr on his deathbed, he was the first to assume the title *Amīr al-Muminīn*, generally translated as the "Commander of the Faithful". It was he who determined that the year of the Hijrah should be the first year of the Islamic era, and organized the administration of the newly conquered territories. He instituted scourging as punishment for certain crimes. In his reign Syria and Jerusalem were conquered; also Egypt, Libya and 'Irāq; the Persians were defeated at Qādisiyyah. The wealth which poured in was distributed among the Arab Muslims according to a register called the *dīwān*, which included a proportionate stipend for all, according to merit and station, down to slaves and children.

> Am I a king now? Or a Caliph? 'Umar once asked Salmān the Persian.

If thou tax the land of Believers in money, either little or much, and put the money to any use the Law doth not allow, then thou art a king, and no Caliph of God's Apostle.

By God! said 'Umar, I know not whether I am a Caliph or a king. And If I am a king, it is a fearful thing.

I went to a festival outside Medinah once, said a Believer from Iraq, and I saw Omar: tall and bald and grey; he walked barefoot, drawing a red-broidered cloth about his body with both hands; and he towered above the people as though he were on horseback.

During 'Umar's Caliphate, the Arabs were prohibited from owning land in order to be, instead, a permanent fighting force carrying Islam to the ends of the earth. His era, marked by his powerfully simple and puritan character, came to be looked upon as a golden age, particularly by the Khārijites, who recoiled from the increasingly complex political and theological questions that arose afterwards. All later movements that attempted the restoration of a "pure Islamic state" looked back to the Caliphate of 'Umar as the ideal model, with the exception of Twelve-Imām Shī'ites, for whom all rulers not of the family of 'Alī are usurpers, especially the first three Caliphs.

'Umar was assassinated in *23*/644 by a certain Abū Lu'lu'ah Firōz, a Persian slave of the governor of Baṣrah, Mughīrah ibn Shu'bah. The slave had made complaints to the Caliph about his duties, but had been dismissed, in revenge for which he stabbed 'Umar as he was marshalling worshipers in the mosque for the daybreak prayer. On his deathbed 'Umar appointed a council, the *Shūrā*, to elect a new Caliph, consisting of 'Alī, 'Uthmān, 'Abd ar-Raḥmān ibn 'Awf, Zubayr, and Sa'd ibn Abī Waqqāṣ. Talḥāḥ would also have been a member had he not been absent from Medinah.

'Umar al-Khayyām (*439-525*/1048-1131). A mathematician and astronomer, who is most famous as a poet. The name "Khayyām" means "tent maker" and is reminiscent of the predilection for trade names found among the radical Kufan revolutionaries. His collection of poetry in four-line stanzas called *rubā'iyyāt* ("quatrains"), has been translated into many languages. Khayyām's fame in the West is due to a powerful 19th-century English translation by Edward Fitzgerald. It is curious that his fame in the East, even in Persian, is also largely due to this translation, without which Khayyām would not have reached the level of acclaim he enjoys today.

More than one thousand quatrains are attributed to him, many of which are also attributed to others; as the extant manuscripts of Khayyām's poems date from two centuries after his death, it is difficult to say which he actually wrote, if, indeed, any. It is his reputation as a clear thinker that has resulted in the attribution to him of the most sapiential and perceptive of the quatrains. In recent years, manuscripts in Arabic and Persian attributed to Khayyām, which are straightforward treatises on metaphysics and Sufism, as well as works on mathematics, have been discovered and published in Iran.

The historian Rashīd ad-Dīn aṭ-Ṭabīb recounts in a legendary story known as the *Sar-Guzasht-i-Sayyidnā* ("The tale of the Three Schoolfellows"), that 'Umar Khayyām, Niẓām al-Mulk, and Ḥasan-i aṣ-Ṣabbāḥ were schoolfellows together in Nayshābūr. The three swore that if one succeeded in life he would help the others. Niūẓām al-Mulk became Minister to the Seljūqs; Ḥasan aṣ-Ṣabbāḥ came to him and acquired an important post. Then, because of intrigue, aṣ-Ṣabbāḥ was forced to flee, went to Fāṭimid Egypt, and returned as the chief of the Assassin sect in the fortress of Alamūt in northern Persia. Niẓām al-Mulk fell as a victim of an assassin sent from Alamūt.

What is certain about the rather enigmatic 'Umar Khayyām is that under the Vizier Niẓām al-Mulk, Khayyām worked with a group of mathematicians to reform the Persian solar calendar. The result was the *Jalālī* calendar of *467*/1079, named after the Seljūq Sultan Jalāl ad-Dawlah Malik Shāh. This calendar was not put into use, but its astronomical basis is more accurate than the Gregorian calendar with a discrepancy, it is said, of only one day in 3,770 years. To this end Khayyām compiled astronomical tables called the *Zīj Malik Shāh.* Khayyām was the first to solve cubic equations, of which he distinguished thirteen kinds, providing both algebraical and geometric solutions. *See* RUBĀ'IYYĀT.

'Umar, Mosque of, *see* DOME of the ROCK.

Umayyad (Ar. *ad-dawlah al-umawiyyah*). The first dynasty of Islam which began with the reign of

Mu'āwiyah in *41*/661 and ended with that of Marwān II in *132*/750. The Umayyad capital was established in Damascus by the son of Abū Sufyān, Mu'āwiyah, who had been governor of Syria under the Caliph 'Uthmān, his relative. The family name is that of a clan descended from Umayyah of the Quraysh.

The dynasty became notorious for running the Empire for its own benefit as though it were its personal fief, and it was the worldly and tyrannical nature of the Umayyads, more characteristic of the pagan age than of Islam, which led to their downfall. Typical of their tyranny is their association with al-Ḥajjāj ibn Yūsuf, a figure notorious for his cruelty, who crushed dissent in 'Irāq and the revolt of 'Abd Allāh ibn az-Zubayr in Mecca. An exception, however, to the run of the Umayyads was the saintly and abstemious Caliph 'Umar ibn 'Abd al-'Azīz. It was noted that Abū Bakr, 'Umar, and 'Alī had been bald, and so was 'Umar ibn 'Abd al-'Azīz; but after him, there were no more bald Caliphs.

In Arabia, the practice had always been to regard individuals as no more important than their tribe or clan. Despite Islam, this attitude was carried beyond Arabia by the Umayyads; the people of newly conquered territories, who had no tribal affiliation to protect them, were regarded as lacking status entirely unless, as was necessary, they each acquired an Arab protector. This ubiquitous client dependency in the Empire naturally caused great resentment and was emblematic of the oppressiveness of Umayyad rule, occasioning unrest, rebellion and finally the overthrow of the dynasty. The system was brought to an end by 'Umar ibn 'Abd al-'Azīz but it had by then already done its damage. It played no small role in the development of Shī'ism, the 'Alīds representing, in the eyes of the oppressed minorities, the hope of a more just government. The 'Abbāsids, who were also related to the Prophet, used these Shī'ite aspirations to rally popular support to themselves.

Revolution broke out in Khorāsān, incited by an 'Abbāsid agitator named Abū Muslim. After the defeat of the Umayyads at the battle of the Zab river in *132*/750, the 'Abbāsid forces hunted down all the Umayyads they could find, but one of them, 'Abd ar-Raḥmān ibn Mu'āwiyah, called later *ad-Dākhil* (the "Intruder"), escaped the destruction of his house at the hands of Abū-l-'Abbās ("the Spiller"), the first 'Abbāsid ruler. In *138*/756 'Abd ar-Raḥmān founded an Umayyad kingdom in Spain at Cordoba and, when the Fāṭimids of Egypt declared themselves to be a Caliphate, the Umayyad 'Abd ar-Raḥmān III an-Nāṣir of Cordoba did the same.

The Umayyads in Spain, however, turned out to be vastly different from the tyrants in Damascus. They ruled from *138*/756 until *422*/1031, when Moorish Spain disintegrated into the small kingdoms called "factions" (*aṭ-ṭawā'if*). At the height of Umayyad rule, the Islamic realm in Spain attained to unprecedented prosperity and cultivation. The arts and sciences flourished, particularly philosophy. Under 'Abd ar-Raḥmān III (d. *300*/912) the court and the capital of Cordoba were the most brilliant in Europe.

al-Manṣūr, the second 'Abbāsid ruler, said once to his courtiers: "Who deserves to be called the Falcon of the Quraysh?" "Yourself, surely" the courtiers answered. "No, the Falcon of the Quraysh is 'Abd ar-Raḥmān [the founder of the Umayyad kingdom of Spain], who wandered alone through the deserts of Asia and Africa, and had the great heart to seek his destiny, with no troop at his back, over the sea in an unknown land."

Between the Patriarchal Caliphates and the Umayyads, there was the short-lived Caliphate of Ḥasan, the son of 'Alī ibn Abī Ṭālib, in the year *41*/661. Then followed the Umayyad dynasty.

The Umayyad Caliphs are:

Mu'āwiyah ibn Abī Sufyān	*41-60*/661-680
Yazīd I ibn Mu'āwiyah	*60-64*/680-683
Mu'āwiyah II	*64*/683
Marwān ibn al-Ḥakam (I)	*64-65*/684-685
'Abd al-Malik	*65-86*/685-705
al-Walīd I ibn 'Abd al-Malik	*86-96*/705-715
Sulaymān	*96-99*/715-717
'Umar ibn 'Abd al-'Azīz	*99-101*/717-720
Hishām	*105-125*/724-743
al-Walīd II	*125-126*/743-744
Yazīd II	*126*/744
Ibrāhīm	*126*/744
Marwān II al-Ḥimār	*127-132*/744-750

(Marwān II nickname, "*al-Ḥimār*", or "the Wild Ass of Mesopotamia" was meant in admiration, the wild ass, or onager, being an animal of the hunt. He received it because his reign was spent in constant warfare in defense of his kingdom.)

Thereafter the Caliphate continued under the 'Abbāsids in Baghdad. A separate branch of Umayyads was established in Cordoba and became the "Western Caliphate". The Western Umayyads adopted the title Caliph after the Faṭimids. The Western Umayyads of Cordoba are:

'Abd ar-Raḥmān I ad-Dākhil	*138-172*/756-788
Hishām I	*172-180*/788-796
al-Ḥakam I	*180-206*/796-822
'Abd ar-Raḥman II	*206-238*/822-852
Muḥammad I	*238-273*/852-886
al-Mundhir	*273-275*/886-888
'Abd Allāh	*275-300*/888-912
'Abd ar-Raḥman III an-Nāṣir	*300-350*/912-961
al-Ḥakam II al-Mustanṣir	*350-366*/961-976
Hishām II al-Mu'ayyad (1st r)	*366-399*/976-1009
Muḥammad II al-Mahdī (1st r)	*399-400*/1009-1009
Sulaymān al-Musta'īn (1st r)	*400-400*/1009-1010
Muḥammad II	*400-400*/1010-1010
Hishām II (2nd r)	*400-403*/1010-1013
Sulaymān (2nd r)	*403-407*/1013-1016
'Alī an-Nāsir (Ḥammūdid)	*407-408*/1016-1018
'Abd ar-Raḥman IV al-Murtaḍā	*408-408*/1018-1018
al-Qāsim al-Ma'mūn (Ḥammūdid 1st r)	*408-412*/1018-1021
Yaḥyā al-Mu'talī (Ḥammūdid 1st r)	*412-413*/1021-1022
al-Qāsim (Ḥammūdid 2nd r)	*413-414*/1022-1023
'Abd ar-Raḥman V al-Mustaẓhir	*414-414*/1023-1024
Muḥammad III al-Mustakfī	*414-416*/1024-1025
Yaḥyā (Ḥammūdid 2nd r)	*416-418*/1025-1027
Hishām III al-Mu'tadd	*418-422*/1027-1031

Towards the end of the Spanish Umayyad dynasty of Cordoba, real power passed to the Chief Minister or Chamberlain, called the *Ḥājib*, and into the hands of the Ḥammūdid dynasty of Malaga. The most famous Chamberlain ruler was Ibn Abū 'Āmir, known as *al-Manṣūr* (*Almanzor*). After 1031 the Cordovan kingdom fell apart and rulership passed to the hands of petty kingdoms, the "Kings of the Factions" or *Mulūk aṭ-Ṭawā'if*. *See* 'ABBĀSIDS; CALIPH; PATRIARCHAL CALIPHS.

Ummah. A people, a community; or a nation, in particular the "nation" of Islam which transcends ethnic or political definition, at least traditionally and before the days of modern, Western-style nationalism. Among the Sunnīs the consensus (*ijmā'*) of the *ummah* is a legitimizing principle in the interpretation and application of the *sharī'ah* (Islamic law).

Umm al-, *see* after UMMĪ.

Ummī (lit. "unlettered"). An epithet of the Prophet. Although *ummī* is understood by Muslims to refer to the fact that the Prophet was unlettered, the etymology of the word is disputed by some Western scholars who have claimed that it means "gentile", by connecting *ummī* with *ummah* ("nation") because, they say, the Prophet preached an Abrahamic revelation to the gentiles or non-Jews. However, *ummah* does not mean a "nation" in the sense of the Hebrew goy, and Islam is not a religion coming out of Judaism, as is Christianity; St. Paul's distinction of: "first to the Jew, then to the Gentile" is not meaningful to Islam. Nor is the Muslim understanding of the word *ummī*, as yet other Orientalists have also maintained, a polemical support to argue the miraculous quality of the Koran. The Koran is miraculous, were the Prophet literate or not. But it is the Koran itself which says that the Prophet was illiterate (29:47) "Not before this (Koran) didst thou recite any writing, or inscribe it with the right hand."

The Medinan poet Ḥasan ibn Thābit, a contemporary, devoted himself after his conversion to composing verses praising the Prophet. He once characterized the Prophet's mission in these words: "revelation written on a smooth page". The "smooth page" is the soul of the Prophet, which is unlettered because God's writing could not be inscribed where human writing had gone before. That the Prophet should be considered symbolically, or, in fact, unlettered is linked with the mystery whereby Revelation made him the inviolate instrument of the Koran, for *no other writing* had touched him. The first meaning of *ummī* is "maternal", from *umm*, "mother". The uncreated prototype in Heaven of the Koran is called the "Mother of the Book" (*Umm al-Kitāb*). It is, therefore, in evocation of the mystery and glory of revelation that the Prophet is referred to as *an-Nabī al-Ummī* (the "unlettered prophet"). *See* MUḤAMMAD.

Umm al-Kitāb (lit. "the Mother of the Book"). 1. The Koran is said to have a prototype in heaven. This prototypal Koran is inscribed symbolically on the "guarded tablet" (*al-lawḥ al-maḥfūẓ*), the pole of substance within Being. Also, *Umm al-Kitāb* means the "Essence of the Book" (the Koran) as in 3:7; 13:39; and 43:4: "And Lo! We have appointed it a recitation (*qur'ān*) in Arabic that haply ye may understand, and lo! in the Mother of the Book which We possess, it is indeed sublime, decisive." (*See* BEING; FIVE DIVINE PRESENCES.)

2. *Umm al-Kitāb* is also the name of a book of proto-Ismā'īlī teachings in which the Dualist doctrine of this sect is most openly expounded. As M.S. Hodgson permitted himself to remark: it (the book called *Umm al-Kitāb*) "smacks of Manicheism" (*The Order of Assassins*). It dates from the *2nd*/8th century. As the premises of this book are alien to Islam, and its use of Islamic concepts crude and wide of the mark, it is clearly an early attempt to enter into Islamic terminology and structure, rather than a case of Islam's acknowledging Ismā'īlī tenets. As the penetration of Islam by the various Dualist sects of antiquity continued, their propaganda became more sophisticated and more difficult to distinguish from orthodox doctrine.

Umm Kulthūm. The youngest daughter of the Prophet and his first wife Khadījah. Umm Kulthūm was married to a son of Abū Lahab, the uncle of the Prophet who became an implacable and vicious enemy of Islam. This marriage was dissolved and later she became the wife of 'Uthmān, the third Caliph.

Umm al-Mu'minīn (lit. "Mother of the Believers"). A title given to each of the wives of the Prophet, but used in particular of 'Ā'ishah. *See* WIVES of the PROPHET.

Umm al-Qurā (lit. "Mother of Cities"). A name for Mecca (42:7) which, because of the sanctuary of the Ka'bah, is symbolically the center of the world.

Umm Salmah. One of the wives of the Prophet, the widow of Abū Salmah who was killed at the battle of Uḥud. *See* WIVES of the PROPHET.

Umm al-Walad (lit. "mother of the child"). As concubinage is allowed between a female slave and her master, the status of "mother of the child" is conferred upon a slave who gives birth to a child of the master. The child thus born is free and legitimate. The mother cannot be sold, and automatically becomes free upon the death of the master, if she is not freed before. In the case of royal children who became heir to the throne, the status of the mother increased accordingly. In Turkish she is called the *valide*.

'Umrah. The "lesser pilgrimage", or visit to Mecca, which can be performed at any time; its ceremonies take place entirely within the precincts of the Grand Mosque of Mecca and require a little over an hour to accomplish.

The *'umrah* is also a part of the "greater pilgrimage" (*al-ḥajj*) a rite that requires several days to accomplish and can only be performed at a fixed date of the Islamic year.

The *'umrah* is composed of the seven circumambulations of the Ka'bah (*ṭawāf*), followed by a prayer of two *raka'āt* facing the space between the Black Stone and the door of the Ka'bah known as *al-multazam*, the drinking of the water of Zamzam, and finally the ritual walking between the hills of Ṣafā and Marwah, seven times (*as-sa'y*).

The consecrated garb for the *'umrah*, consisting of two pieces of unseamed white cloth (*iḥrām*), is usually put on in Jeddah or at one of the mosques around the perimeter of the Ḥarām of Mecca. The state of consecration is ended at the seventh passage between Ṣafā and Marwah by the cutting of a lock of hair or even by shaving the head. The *'umrah* may be performed by proxy on behalf of one who is absent simply by formulating the intention of performing the *'umrah* on behalf of another, the rest of the rites then being performed normally. For a more detailed description, *see* PILGRIMAGE. *Also see* IḤRĀM; SA'Y; ṬAWĀF.

Unbeliever, *see* KĀFIR.

Union des Organisations Islamiques de France. Since 1983 a federation of French Muslim associations. In 1991 it created the first seminary for the training of Imāms in France.

United Arab Emirates. A federation of small states on the Arabian coast of the Persian Gulf. The states are: Abū Dhābī, Ajmān, Dubai, Fujairah, Rā's al-Khaimah, Sharjah (Shariqah), Umm al-Qaywayn. The total population of the UAE is over 200,000. Most of the population is Sunnī with small Shī'ite minorities. The schools of law practiced are Ḥanafī, Ḥanbalī, and Mālikī. Formerly the states were known as the Trucial States.

Unity, Divine, *see* ALLĀH; FIVE DIVINE PRESENCES; IKHLĀṢ; TAWḤĪD.

'Unṣurī, Abū-l-Qāsim Ḥasan ibn Aḥmad, (d. AD 1040 or 1050). A Court poet of Maḥmūd of Ghaznah, called *maliku ash-shu'arā* "king of poets". 'Arūḍī of Samarkand said of him: "How many a palace did great Maḥmūd raise, At whose tall towers the Moon did stand to gaze, Whereof one brick remaineth not in place, Though still re-echo 'Unṣuri's sweet lays."

'Urf. Local customs or laws which may exist alongside Islamic laws. *See* ADAT.

'Ushr (lit. "a tenth part"). Sometimes confused with the *zakāh*, the *'ushr* is a tithe on property owned by Muslims, as opposed to *kharāj*, a tax on property owned by non-Muslims. Since the tax on property (*kharāj* or *'ushr*) persisted even if the property changed hands from non-Muslim to Muslim, the distinction between them became blurred, particularly when, as a concession, the Caliph 'Umar permitted the Christian Arab Ghassanids, who had voluntarily allied themselves with the Muslims to the West of Syria from the Byzantines, to pay their tax under the name of *'ushr*, that is, as an unconquered people with the same status as Muslims.

Ustād Sīs, a direct successor to Bihāfrīd, a neo-Zoroastrian sectary who was put to death in Nishāpūr around *130*/747-8 by an officer of Qaḥṭab ibn Shabib, on the orders of Abū Muslim. *See* BIHĀFRĪD.

Uṣūl al-Fiqh (lit. "roots of jurisprudence"). The bases of Islamic law. Among the Sunnīs these are: the Koran, the Sunnah (acts and statements of the Prophet), *qiyās* ("analogy"), and *ijmā'* (popular consensus or agreement). *Ijtihād* ("effort") is the extrapolation from these principles to specific cases.

The Wahhābīs and Ḥanbalīs limit *ijmā'* to the generation of the Companions, that is, to the generation of the Prophet, and their immediate followers, the *tābi'ūn*. The Khārijites limit *ijm'ā'* to their own community. The Twelve-Imām Shī'ites add the teachings of their Imāms to the Sunnah and admit the *ijtihād* or decisions of qualified contemporary religious authorities. *See* SHARĪ'AH.

Uṣūlīs. The dominant school of Shī'ite theology consisting of those who favor speculation and extrapolation on the basis of principles (*uṣūl*). They exist in distinction to the *Akhbārīs*, or traditionalists, now in the minority and found only in India, Baḥrayn, and southern 'Irāq. The victory over the Akhbārīs by the Uṣūlī Mullā Vahid Bihbahānī (d. *1207*/1792) led to a very great expansion in the power of the Shī'ite religious authorities.

The Uṣūlīs maintain that competence to arrive at original decisions and interpretations of the religious law resides in living authorities entitled the *marja' at-taqlīd* ("exemplars for emulation"), or Mujtahids. Every Uṣūlī Shī'ite who is not himself a *marja' at-taqlīd* is an "emulator" (*muqallid*), who must adhere to a Mujtahid — it is considered obligatory — to whom he pays *zakāh* (religious tax), and the *khums*, a special revenue originally due to the Prophet from the spoils of war which has lapsed in Sunnī Islam but still exists in Shī'ism. To follow a Mujtahid brings a heavenly reward, even if the Mujtahid's views are in fact erroneous. It is forbidden to follow a dead Mujtahid.

The "exemplar for emulation" (*marja' at-taqlīd*) is considered to be a general representative (*nā'ib 'amm*), of the Hidden Imām. There is no one Mujtahid who is a unique representative (*nā'ib khaṣṣ*) of the Hidden Imām, not, at least as yet, for the development of the Uṣūlī tendency has not run to the limit; attempts to establish one unique representative of the Hidden Imām and thereby, by implication, of God, were made notably by the Shaykhīs and the Bābīs in the last century. The decisions of the Mujtahid are taken to have the agreement of the Hidden Imām; if two Mujtahids differ, and the Hidden Imām does not manifest his approval or disapproval by what would be an act of God, then it is considered that the Imām is in agreement with both, at least to some degree. (*For the doctrine of the presence of Being in relative degrees, see* MULLĀ SADRĀ.)

Since every Uṣūlī Shī'ite is obliged to be a follower of a Mujtahid, the numbers of Mujtahids have grown from modest numbers at the beginning of the last century to hundreds now. The leading Mujtahids have moreover adopted titles of ever increasing grandeur, calling themselves first *Ḥojjatul-islam* (*Ḥujjat al-Islām*, "Proof of Islam"), and, in the beginning of the 20th century, *Ayatollah* (*Āyat-Allāhi*, "Sign of God"). The distinction between the *marja' at-taqlīd* and the ordinary believer, has led to the establishment of a priestly class, or more precisely, of a caste with the unique prerogative of interpreting God's Will. This is a further step towards the affirmation of the principles including caste, pervading the ancient and indigenous religions of Iran before Islam. At the same time, it affirms Iranian nationalism, repudiates foreign domination, of which the persecution of the Imāms is made a mythic theme, and aims at the re-establishment of Persian influence as it was before the rise of the Islamic Empire. (*For the differences between Akhbārīs and Uṣūlīs, see* AKHBĀRĪS.) *See also* AYATOLLAH; HIDDEN IMĀM; PAHLAVĪ; SHĪ'ISM.

Usury, *see* RIBĀ.

'Uthmān ibn 'Affān (d. *35*/656). The third of the Four Patriarchal Caliphs (*al-khulafā' ar-rāshidūn*), 'Uthmān was elected by a council called the *shūrā*, which had been appointed by 'Umar as he was dying of the wounds inflicted by a disaffected slave. 'Uthmān's reign was marred by nepotism in favor of his clan, the Umayyads. Dissatisfaction with the tyranny of Umayyad governors and the Umayyad conspiracy (in which 'Uthmān was probably not involved) against the son of Abū Bakr, who had impugned Umayyad usurpation of power, led the latter to stage a revolt against the Caliph and murder him after twelve years of rule.

The first half of 'Uthmān's Caliphate had been peaceful; the troubles began, legend says, when 'Uthmān lost the seal-ring of the Prophet which he dropped accidently into a well on the outskirts of Medinah; assiduous search failed to recover it. Afterwards, revolts began in 'Irāq and Egypt, civil wars arose between the Companions and, with the hostility that ensued between Mu'awiyah and the 'Alīds, the unity of the Prophet's time was shattered.

It was 'Uthmān who ordered the compilation of the Koran from the memories of the Companions and such written records as existed, after which it was then edited and a definitive recension which bears his name, was copied and sent to the four corners of the Islamic Empire.

'Uthmān was called *Dhū-l-Nūrayn* ("he of the two lights") because he had, at different times, married two daughters of the Prophet, Umm Kulthūm, and Ruqayyah.

One of the earliest converts to Islam, one night in the desert when he was returning from Syria with a caravan, 'Uthmān had been awakened by a voice crying: "Sleepers, awake! for Aḥmad hath come forth in Mecca" (Aḥmad is a form of the name Muḥammad); he then consulted Abū Bakr (who was known to the Quraysh as an interpreter of signs), who brought him to the Prophet to declare his testimony of the faith (*shahādah*).

Despite the troubles of his Caliphate, 'Uthmān is held innocent of them, and the Creed of al-Ash'arī says: "his murderers killed him out of wickedness and enmity".

Uways al-Qarānī. A legendary figure, described as a contemporary of the Prophet and already a mystic before the coming of Islam, it is said of him that he lived in the Yemen and, although he had not met the Prophet, knew of him, as the Prophet knew of Uways, and that Uways communicated with the Prophet in dreams and visions. Uways is the prototype of the *fard*, the exceptional person in whom spiritual realisation is spontaneous. The legend goes on to say that Uways came to Medinah after the death of the Prophet and received a mantle that the Prophet had left for him. The term "Uwaysian transmission" means to lay claim to a link with some spiritual figure with whom contact would have been clearly impossible. A form of pious or impious deceit, according to the case, some Sufis have asserted an "Uwaysian" transmission of authority, that is, across space and time without the two persons actually meeting. *See* FARD; al-KHIḌR.

Uyghurs *see* XINJIANG.

'Uzair. This name is often identified as being that of the Biblical Ezra, especially in Muslim folklore. It is mentioned once in the Koran 9:30: "And the Jews say: Ezra is the son of Allāh, and the Christians say: the Messiah is the son of Allāh." The reference to Ezra as "son of God" is obscure, and cannot be explained by anything in the Bible or from other sources. Rather than Ezra, the Hebrew scribe, prophet and religious reformer of the 5th century BC the name in the Koran may actually be that of a fallen Angel in some Gnostic sect which has disappeared. Or, it may reflect some secret Jewish sectarian belief of the time.

Uzbekistan. Population: 23,089,261 (estimates run to over 25 million) of whom 71% are Uzbek. Independent in 1991, formerly part of the Soviet Union. 80% of the population is Uzbek with Russian, Tajik, and other minorities; however, the majority of the population considered to be Uzbek is actually Sart, a mixture of Uzbek and Tajik. The capital is Tashkent. Uzbekistan contains the cities of Bukhara and Samarkand which were once major centers of Islamic civilisation. The majority are Sunnis and the Naqshbandi ṭarīqah is very widespread. *See* UZBEKS.

Uzbeks. A Turkic speaking people of Central Asia living today in Uzbekistan with minorities in other Soviet republics such as Kazakhstan, Tajikistan, as well as in Afghanistan and China. They number over sixteen million, which made them the largest single non-European ethnic group in the USSR.

The Uzbeks, who are a remnant of the Turkic Ghuzz/Oghuz tribes of the Golden Horde of the Mongols, take their name from their leader Uzbeg Khan (d. *741*/1340). In the *9th*/15th century they settled between the Syr and Amu Darya rivers. At the height of their power, they ruled an empire that extended into Persia, Afghanistan and China. They have been much influenced by Persian culture, and some Uzbek dialects have been much affected by Persian, but they are nevertheless Sunnīs of the Ḥanafī School of Law. Today Uzbek is more often written in the Cyrillic script than in the Arabic, which is customary for Muslim peoples.

The Naqshbandī *ṭarīqah* is the most widespread Sufi order among the Uzbeks, and in Central Asia in general. The most important cities of the Uzbeks are Samarkand, Bukhara, and Tashkent. Their national costume is a sleeved gown called the *chapan*, worn with a black and white cap whose rim is squared off. *See* MONGOLS.

al-'Uzzā. One of the more important idols of the pagan Arabs, closely associated with al-Lat and al-Manāt. All three were considered to be females. It is known that human sacrifice had been made to them on occasion. The other principal idol of the Meccans was Hubal, god of the Moon. *See* IDOLS.

V

Valide, *see* UMM al-WALAD.

Veil (Ar. *ḥijāb*, "cover, drape, partition"; *khimār*, "veil covering the head and face"; *lithām*, "veil covering lower face up to the eyes"). The covering of the face by women is usually referred to by the general term *ḥijab* in the present day; it is called *purdah* in the Indo-Persian countries, and Iran has furnished the use of the word *chador* for the tent-like black cloak and veil worn by many women in the Middle East. The Koran advises the Prophet's wives to go veiled (33:59).

Koran 24:31 speaks of covering women's "adornments" from strangers outside the family. In traditional Arab societies, even up into the present day, women at home dressed in surprising contrast to their covered appearance in the street. This latter verse of the Koran is the institution of a new public modesty rather than veiling the face; when the pre-Islamic Arabs went to battle, Arab women seeing the men off to war would bare their breasts to encourage them to fight; or they would do so at the battle itself, as in the case of the Meccan women led by Hind at the Battle of Uḥud.

This changed with Islam, but the general use of the veil to cover the face did not appear until 'Abbāsid times. Nor was it entirely unknown in Europe, for the veil permitted women the freedom of anonymity. None of the legal systems actually prescribe that women must wear a veil, although they do prescribe covering the body in public. The prescription that a woman's body must be covered in public to the neck, the ankles, and below the elbow is not in the Koran, which, for its part, enjoins modesty. Covering to the neck, wrist, etc. is simply the interpretation of one particular society in the Middle Ages as to what modesty is. In many Muslim societies, for example in traditional South East Asia, or in Beduin lands a face veil for women is either rare or non-existent; paradoxically, modern fundamentalism is introducing it. In others, the veil may be used at one time and European dress another. While modesty is a religious prescription, the wearing of a veil is not a religious requirement of Islam, but a matter of cultural milieu.

In India the introduction of the use of the veil among Muslims, which happened comparatively recently, amounted to a great liberation. *Purdah*, the separation of women from men, meant that women of the classes that could afford to practice *purdah* could not leave their homes. The introduction of the veil amounted to a "portable" purdah and allowed women a mobility they had not previously enjoyed. This aspect of mobility granted by the use of the veil, a freedom to come and go, is an unsuspected advantage in those societies; there are some Muslim societies where women go sometimes veiled and sometimes unveiled according to their desire to be seen or unnoticed, as the case may be. *See* ḤIJĀB; WOMEN.

"Verse of the throne", *see* ĀYAT al-KURSĪ.

"Verse of light", *see* ĀYAT an-NŪR.

Vilayat-i al-Faqih, *see* WILĀYAT al-FAQĪH.

Vizier, *see* WAZĪR.

W

Waḥdat al-Wujūd (lit. "unity of being"). The doctrine of the unity of being, associated with Ibn 'Arabī and his school, is a form of Monism. It closely corresponds to the Hindu doctrine of nonduality known as Advaita Vedanta and states that there is only one Self which is refracted by manifestation into the multiplicity of beings, persons, creatures, and objects in existence; and that this Divine Self, *Allāh*, God, the Real, the Absolute, is the hidden identity of all that is; "the more He reveals Himself (by the limitless variety of His creatures) the more He conceals Himself" is a well-known saying of the Sufis. Individual natures are two-fold; on the one hand they are masks that partly reveal the one Self, and on the other, they are illusions caused by ignorance, which hide it. The ego is at once a reflection of the Self which thus conveys an idea of what the Self is, but it is also its own impediment to union with the Self when, through delusion and pride, it refuses to admit its own provisional nature and give up its claims to self-sufficiency (*istighnā'*).

According to this doctrine the creature in existence appears to be separate from the Principle, or the Self, although God tells man that He is closer to him than his jugular vein, and indeed it is through revelation, and only through revelation, that creatures are re-united to God, because only a way opened up by God Himself could lead back to Him. Reintegration requires purification, conformity to the Divine norm (*fiṭrah*), and recognition of the Principle within manifestation. What is involved is the dispelling of the illusion of separateness and of a multiplicity apart from God, and this is made possible by two inseparable and indispensable means: doctrine and method. Doctrine renders Reality intelligible and teaches discrimination between the Real and the unreal; method, concentration upon the Real, leads to union with the Real.

The Persian Sufi Bāyazīd al-Biṣṭāmī said:

> Dost thou hear how there comes a voice from the brooks of running water? But when they reach the sea, they are quiet, and the sea is neither augmented by their in-coming nor diminished by their out-going.

And al-Jīlī said:

> Unity has in all the cosmos no place of manifestation more perfect than thyself, when thou plungest thyself into thy own essence in forgetting all relationship, and when thou seizest thyself with thyself, stripped of thy appearances, so that thou art thyself in thyself and none of the Divine Qualities or created attributes (which normally pertain to thee) any longer refer to thee. It is this state of man which is the most perfect place of manifestation for Unity in all existence.

Although the doctrine of the unity of being (*waḥdat al-wujūd*) is ascribed to Ibn 'Arabī, it is in fact the fundamental and central doctrine of all Sufism. Ibn 'Arabī did not himself use the term. What he did was to respond to the needs of his age by making more explicit that which before him had been taught orally and in synthesis with a method which enables a whole style of life. However, "Unity of Being", which is a form of Monism, could also be interpreted as meaning a continuity or identity of substance between the world and God, that the world is God in disguise or a "dismembered serpent" which has to be reconstituted. Against this ever present danger or abuse which rages more fiercely in one age than another, there arose the school of "Unity of Consciousness" (*waḥdat ash-shuhūd*) which put awareness in the place of existence. The Sufi Junayd of Baghdad (d. *297*/910), often held up as a model of "restrained" Sufism, as contrasted with al-Ḥallāj, is described as one of its exponents. However, the actual term appears with Semnanī in the 14th century, and, in the end, may be only cosmetically different. *See* FIVE DIVINE PRESENCES; IBN 'ARABĪ; SUFISM.

Wahhābīs. A sect dominant in Saudi Arabia and Qaṭār, at the beginning of the 19th century it gained footholds in India, Africa, and elsewhere. Adherents of this sect named after its founder Muḥammad ibn 'Abd al-Wahhāb (*1115-1201*/1703-1787), prefer to call themselves

Muwaḥḥidūn ("Unitarians"). However, this name is not often used, and is associated with other completely different sects extant and defunct.

Wahhābism is a steadfastly fundamentalist interpretation of Islam in the tradition of Ibn Ḥanbal, founder of the Ḥanbalī School of Law, and the theologian Ibn Taymiyyah. The Wahhābīs are often said to "belong to the Ḥanbalī School of Law (*madhhab*), but strictly speaking, like the *Ahl al-Ḥadīth* ("the People of Tradition") they are *ghayr muqallidūn* ("non-adherents"), and do not see themselves as belonging to any school, any more than the first Muslim generations did. Wahhābism is noted for its policy of compelling its own followers and other Muslims strictly to observe the religious duties of Islam, such as the five prayers, under pain of flogging at one time, and for the enforcement of public morals to a degree not found elsewhere.

The founder, Ibn 'Abd al-Wahhāb, was born in 'Uyaynah in Arabia, into the Tamim branch of the Banū Sīnān tribe. After studying in Medinah he traveled in 'Irāq and Iran. On his return to Arabia he first preached his austere doctrines in his native town but encountered resistance there. He cast about until he came to the village of Dir'iyyah in the Najd desert, near present day Riyāḍ, where his dogmas were well received by the Emir, Muḥammad ibn Sa'ūd.

Ibn 'Abd al-Wahhāb branded all who disagreed with him as heretics and apostates, thereby justifying the use of force in imposing his doctrine, and political suzerainty with it, on neighboring tribes. It allowed him to declare "holy war" (*jihād*), otherwise legally impossible, against other Muslims. To this end, Ibn 'Abd al-Wahhāb also taught the use of firearms in place of the sword and the lance, the traditional weapons of the desert.

The alliance of Ibn 'Abd al-Wahhāb, as religious or ideological head, with Muḥammad Ibn Sa'ūd, as political and military chief, was sealed by the marriage of the daughter of Muḥammad ibn Sa'ūd to the preacher; this marked the beginning of a military expansion, which proceeded rapidly under the leadership of 'Abd al-'Azīz, son of Muḥammad ibn Sa'ūd, eventually encroaching upon the Ottoman Empire. In 1802 the Wahhābīs captured Kerbala, the site of Ḥusayn's tomb in 'Irāq, and in 1803 they seized Mecca, putting a red *kiswah* ("covering"), on the Ka'bah.

By now the Turks were becoming alarmed. Muḥammad 'Alī of Egypt and his son Ibrāhīm Pasha suppressed the first Wahhābī state on behalf of the Ottomans by the reconquest of the Hejaz in 1813. But the Wahhābīs were not crushed; only in 1818 did Ibrāhīm Pasha finally devastate Dir'iyyah after a very long siege and bombardment with canon brought laboriously across the desert.

However, the Sa'ūd clan succeeded in recouping its control over the Najd under the leader Turkī, making nearby Riyāḍ the new capital. Then a fresh challenge to the Sa'ūd dynasty came from a cousin who seized control of the Jabal Shammār in the north, established a dynasty of his own clan, the Rashīd of Ḥā'il who did not espouse the Wahhābī cause and, moreover, drove the Sa'ūds out of Riyāḍ in *1309*/1891.

In *1319*/1901 the young 'Abd al-'Azīz Āl Sa'ūd (*see* IBN SA'ŪD) dramatically recaptured Riyāḍ with a handful of companions in a daring raid, and from there his new kingdom grew with astonishing success: in *1332*/1913 he captured al-Ḥasā from the Turks, in *1343*/1924 the Hejaz, and thereafter the 'Asīr.

After the conquest of the Hejaz, an attempt was made to settle the Wahhābī Beduin raiders, called *Ikhwān* ("brothers"), in agricultural communities, the first of which was named Irtawiyyah. The policy of settlement at first failed, and certain tribal groups attempted to continue the Wahhābī holy war (*jihād*), with raids into 'Irāq. The firearms introduced earlier led to the use of machine guns in the 20th century, thus threatening wholesale extermination of the Beduins in the course of the traditional desert raids, which had been far less destructive when fought with swords and individual combat. The new weapons were one more reason to turn warriors into settled farmers.

The Beduin revolt was, however, doomed from the outset, for the *Ikhwān*, attacking across the border, would have been no match for the airplanes of the R.A.F. which defended 'Irāq. Moreover, King 'Abd al-'Azīz reacted decisively to this threat to his authority by immediately raising a force which set out from Jeddah and defeated the insurgents at the Battle of Sibilla in 1929. This was fought in the desert; the fighters on the King's side were mounted on camelback and also in automobiles, Mercedes, Chevrolets, and Fords, which had been driven across the desert from Jeddah to bring warriors loyal to the King to put down the revolting Beduins.

This internal struggle with the Beduins was the only serious obstacle to the growth of the Kingdom of Saudi Arabia after the reconquest of Riyāḍ. Wahhābī doctrines and practices were imposed by the conquests although in a progressively gentler form as more urban areas passed into Sa'ūdi control. This was particularly true of the Hejaz, with its more cosmopolitan traditions and the traffic of pilgrims which the new rulers could not afford to alienate. Thus, although the sound of a trumpet calling reveille in Mecca when it was newly conquered was enough to cause a riot among the Wahhābī soldiers — music was forbidden — such that only energetic intervention on the part of the young Prince Fayṣal, later King, prevented a massacre, today music flows freely over the radio and television.

The creed of Wahhābism centered upon the principle called *tawḥīd* (*see* TAWḤĪD), the assertion of Divine Oneness. Ibn 'Abd al-Wahhāb had written a book by this name upon his return to Arabia from his theological studies and travel abroad. But what he actually understood by *tawḥīd* was the exclusiveness of the Divine Reality, and not the Oneness that encompasses everything, which is the usual meaning of the term in Islamic metaphysics. Moreover, Wahhābīs do not take into doctrinal consideration any opinions other than those expressed by the generation of the Prophet and his Companions and those of the generation immediately following. Therefore Wahhābism precludes the principle of *ijmā'* ("consensus") as a basis of *sharī'ah* ("Islamic law"). The legal approach of Wahhābism is in many respects unique, but it coincides most closely with the school of Ibn Ḥanbal, and may be considered a kind of Ḥanbalism, although the Wahhābīs would deny this, or any other, affiliation. The sign of changing times in Saudi Arabia is that the exigencies of the modern world and pragmatism have opened the door to accepting the legal precedents of the other schools.

The Wahhābīs consider, or previously considered, many of the practices of the generations which succeeded the Companions as *bid'ah* ("objectionable innovation"); these included the building of minarets (today accepted) and the use of funeral markers. The cemeteries of Mecca and, above all, Medinah, were once filled with colourful sepulchral markers which were all removed at the Wahhābī conquest, leaving bare fields. Even the tomb of the Prophet was almost destroyed by Wahhābī zealots; it was left untouched through the forbearance of King 'Abd al-'Azīz, protests by the diplomatic representatives of various Islamic countries, and the bad aim of Beduin gunners. When Medinah was conquered, the — perhaps groundless — rumor spread rapidly to the effect that the desert tribesmen had turned Turkish cannons captured in Medinah on the Prophet's tomb, its presence being a scandal in their eyes because of the Prophet's saying: "Do not make of my grave a place of pilgrimage as the Christians make of theirs."

Wahhābism vigorously denies all esoterism or mysticism, and rejects the idea of Saints, including the visiting of Saint's tombs or any tomb or grave, exception being made only to the pressure of universal custom as regards visiting the tomb of the Prophet.

To call upon Saints for aid or protection, and even to entertain the notion of *barakah* ("blessing") rouses indignation in Wahhābī breasts as being nothing less than polytheism (*shirk*). They also reject all notions of the holiness or sacredness of objects or places as detracting from the exclusive holiness of God and as infringing Divine Unity. This attitude would actually be more comprehensible if it were defending God's *Absoluteness*, which fundamentalists feel is threatened when secondary causes are admitted. Compared to traditional Islam, the Wahhābī view is extremely "dry" and tends to reduce religion to a set of rules.

Typical of Wahhābī Islam are the *muṭawwi'ūn* ("enforcers of obedience"), who are, in effect, religious police. While in some countries for a Muslim to eat in public during Ramaḍān is legally public scandal or disorderly conduct, among the Wahābbīs *private* nonobservance too can be a matter for sanction. In Saudi Arabia the *muṭawwi'ūn* patrol the streets to punish those who do not perform the prayer or to enforce prompt closing of shops at prayer time. They keep a close eye on what elsewhere would be matters of private conscience and not public morality. In old Riyāḍ, if the enforcers of public morality smelled tobacco, they did not hesitate to enter a private house to beat the offender; today the *shisha* cafe, where water pipes are smoked, is found almost everywhere.

Wahhābī Islam has now become much milder than it was on the day that it sprang out of the Najd desert. Attitudes prevalent in other Muslim countries have crept in, so that the stringent denunciations made by the founder, Ibn 'Abd al-Wahhāb, are now explained as having been a reaction to an improbable lapse into idolatry on the part of some tribes in Arabia two centuries ago. Ibn 'Abd al-Wahhāb's descendants are today known as the ash-Shaykh family. Their fortunes naturally followed those of the Sa'ūd half of the original "alliance" made in Dir'iyyah at the end of the 18th century between Ibn 'Abd al-Wahhāb and Muḥammad ibn Sa'ūd. *See* TAWḤĪD.

al-Wahm. Illusion, fantasies arising out of the mind which are substituted for reality, as distinguished from the cosmic illusion, shared by everyone, due to the "veil" (*ḥijāb*) drawn across Being. The term is used in mystical as well as ordinary psychology.

al-Waḥy. Inspiration from God, and also revelation. *See* REVELATION.

Wajd (lit. "ecstasy"). A mystical term referring to states of ecstasy produced by the Divine Presence.

'Abd al-Qādir al-Jīlānī said:

> Rapture [*wajd*] is the blessed plenitude of spirit provoked by the exercise of invocation, and the blessed plenitude of soul, in communion with the spirit. Allāh then gratifies His friend with a cup filled with wine that has no equal, and which intoxicates him with a spiritual drunkenness. His heart then seems endowed with wings, which raise him to the gardens of sanctity. At this moment the enraptured one, submerged by this indescribable magnificence, swoons away losing all consciousness.

Al-Junayd said: "When Truth cometh, ecstasy itself is dispossessed." *See* BASṬ.

Wājib. That which is "obligatory", specifically religious duties. All actions fall into one of the following categories (*aḥkām*) according to the religious law (*sharī'ah*): *wājib*, obligatory; *ḥarām*, prohibited; *mubāḥ*, permitted; *mustaḥabb* or *mandūb*, recommended; and *makrūh*, discouraged. *Farḍ*, which also means obligatory, is that which has been made obligatory by Divine institution. *See* SHARĪ'AH.

Walī (pl. *awliya'*). Saint; more properly Walī-Allāh ("friend of God"). *See next and* SAINTS.

Wāli A governor. A province is a *wilāyah*. *Wāli al-'ahd* is the heir apparent to a ruler. *See also above.*

Walīmah. A feast accompanying a wedding. *See* MARRIAGE.

Waqf (lit. "standing, stopping", hence a "perpetuity"; pl. *awqāf*). The giving of property by will or by gift in perpetuity to the Islamic state for pious works or for the public good. It is then managed by a ministry, or *Awqāf*; in North Africa the term *ḥabs*, *ḥubus*, pl. *aḥbās* is more usual. The proceeds pay for the upkeep of mosques and charities. Property given over to the waqf cannot normally be regained by the original owners, its distinguishing feature being precisely that it is given in perpetuity.

In the time of the 'Abbāsids when the government simply confiscated the wealth of the rich in order to make up its deficits, *waqf* trusts were set up to be proof against government expropriation; the donor continued to manage the trust and the right was inherited by the eldest son. The Caliph al-Qāhir (d. *332*/934), when in need of money had a number of such trusts pried away from the mother of his half-brother al-Muqtadir, by a court order which declared them void.

In modern times the accumulation of *waqf* property administered by the state has amounted to a considerable proportion of the land of the whole nation, and this has posed economic problems. Legal devices have sometimes been found to return such properties to private ownership so that land may be used more efficiently. *See* INHERITANCE.

al-Wāqidī, Abū Muḥammad ibn 'Umar (*130-207*/747-822). One of the most important early historians, born in Medinah and attached to the court of Hārūn ar-Rashīd in Baghdad. Author of the *Kitāb al-Maghāzī* ("Book of Campaigns"), sources for the early history of Islam and biography of the Prophet. *See* IBN SA'D.

Waraqah ibn Nawfal ibn Asad. A cousin of Khadījah, the first wife of the Prophet. He is considered to have been a "*ḥanīf*", one who practiced the Abrahamic monotheism inherited by the Arabs which, however, had in general lapsed, except for a few individuals, during the period preceding Islam. Khadījah told him of the Prophet's revelation and Waraqah said that the revealing Angel was the *Nāmūs* (Greek, *nomos*), the Angel who had spoken to Moses: Waraqah thus declared that he recognized the mission of the Prophet. He knew the Christian scriptures and told the Prophet that Jesus had prophesied his coming. *See* NĀMŪS.

Waṣi (lit. "inheritor"). A title which Shī'ites give to 'Alī ibn Abī Ṭālib, who, they claim, was the designated inheritor of the Prophet's functions as spiritual and political head of the Islamic nation. *See* SHĪ'ISM.

Waṣīl ibn 'Aṭa', (d. *131*/748). The founder of Mu'tazilitism. He was a convert to Islam, a *mawla* who lived in Baṣrah and at one time frequented the circle of Ḥasan al-Baṣrī whom he quit when he, Waṣil ibn 'Aṭa', put forth the doctrine of Mu'tazilitism. He was said to have an "amazing ingenuity" for although he could not pronounce the letter "r" (which may not have been literally true but would mean he could not pronounce the second half of the Shahāda which says that Muḥammad is the Messenger of God, or part of the *basmalah*, for example) he could say anything he wished in "beautiful Arabic" by finding circumlocutions.

Waṣīl ibn 'Aṭa' was apparently the head of some vast clandestine organisation for the writer Jāḥiẓ said of him: "Beyond the Pass of China, on every frontier to far distant Sus and beyond the Berbers, he has preachers. A tyrant's jest, an intriguer's craft does not break their determination. If he says 'Go' in winter, they obey; in summer they fear not the month of burning heat" (*Bayān* I 37).

Waṣīl ibn 'Aṭa' was a friend of Bashshar ibn Burd, a Iranian poet known as a zindiq, or Dualist, and the first major poet in Arabic of non-Arab origin, and he wasrelated by marriage to 'Amr ibn 'Ubayd Abū 'Uthmān, the number two Mu'tazilite.

Wasm (Ar. "mark"). A totemic mark or symbol by which a tribe or person marked property, including cattle. It is also the symbol on carpets identifying the tribal designs or the weaver.

Wazīr (from *wazara*, "to carry a burden"). A Vizier, or minister of government or, in Caliphal times, close advisors to the Caliph; under the Ṣafavids and Ottomans, *Wazīr* was a name for governor. The most famous *wazīrs* are the Barmakids, a family that served the 'Abbāsids until Hārūn ar-Rashīd wiped them out to a man, for apparently striving to create an empire within an empire under his nose.

The most celebrated *wazīr* of all, however, was Niẓām al-Mulk, the minister who completely ran the government under the early Seljūqs. Among the Druzes the term is used for certain important religious figures who are considered to be the "ministers", or representatives, of the Fāṭimid Caliph al-Ḥakīm, who for them, exists in the unseen world.

"Weeping Sufis", Sufis who sought, by constant weeping, to draw closer to God (as Thomas · Kempis advised the spiritual postulant "to seek the gift of tears"). The Prophet wept sometimes during the ritual prayer (*ṣalāh*). The Koran 17:107-109 says:

> Say: 'Believe in it, or believe not;
> those who were given the knowledge before it
> when it is recited to them, fall down
> upon their faces prostrating, and say,
> Glory be to our Lord!
> Our Lord's promise is performed."
> And they fall down upon their faces
> weeping; and it increases them in humility.
> (17:107-109)

Apart from those who sought occasion to weep intensely and "methodically", most Sufis have passed through phases of weeping as a sign of the "melting of the heart" or the melting of existential knots.

> In Abū Bakr's time, some folk from Yaman came to Medinah. When they heard a Reader in the Mosque chanting the Koran, tears fell from their eyes.
> We were like that once, the Caliph said; but our hearts have grown harder since.

Werewolves. *See* BOUJLOUD; SECRET SOCIETY; AISSAWA.

Whistling. This is forbidden in Islam, doubtless because of its association with sorcery and the casting of spells in pre-Islamic times, for which reason it is still considered popularly to be "communication with the Jinn". It also has connotations of mindlessness or vulgarity.

Whirling Dervishes, *see* MEVLEVI.

White Sheep, *see* AQ QOYUNLU.

Widows. A widow must observe a period of waiting called *'iddah*, of four months and ten days before remarrying. If the widow finds herself with child from the deceased husband she must refrain from marriage until the pregnancy is brought to term.

Wilāyat al-Faqīh. (lit: "guardianship or government of the Jurisprudent"; in Iran: *Vilayat-i Faqih.*) The Shī'ite theologian al-Muḥaqqiq al-Ḥillī (d. *728*/1326) asserted that religious leaders, the *'ulamā'*, had a function in exercising "guardianship" (*wala' al-imāmah*) over the Imāmate of the Hidden Imām. In 1829, following the establishment of the Uṣūlī school of Shī'ism in Iran, an Iranian Mullā, Aḥmad Naraqī (*1185-1245*/1771-1829), collected historical materials and Ḥadīth regarding political authority in a document called the *'Awa'id al-Ayyam.* He quoted what he believed to be an inspired tradition which concluded that while "The kings have authority over the people, the religious scholars have authority over the kings."

In 1971 Khomeini published *The Government of the Jurisprudent* which proposed, in an argument similar to that once used by Ḥasan-i Ṣabbāḥ to assume authority, that in the absence of the Hidden Imām competent Jurists are mandated by the Hidden Imām to govern in his place. In theory, this resolved the tension of Shī'ite political practice which otherwise assumes all government other than that of the Hidden Imām to be illegitimate. In actual fact, the need for legitimate government in the absence of the Imām had already called for its theoretical legitimisation. Very early in the development of Shī'ism, serving in the government had become perceived as betraying the Imām; therefore Murtaḍā 'Alam al-Hudā (d. *436*/1044) formulated the Shī'ite principle that "if the person accepting a government office knew or considered it likely on the basis of clear indications that he would be able, through his tenure of office, to support a right or to reject a false claim or to enjoin the good or forbid evil, and that nothing of this would be accomplished but for his holding office, it was obligatory for him to accept office."

What was new in Khomeini was that the political authority who could govern in the place of the Imām was to be necessarily a Jurisprudent (*faqīh*) instead of an emir or a prince, or other secular figure who was not a religious scholar.

In the new government system adopted in Iran following Khomeini's lead, the highest authority must specifically be filled by a Jurisprudent, or Mullā. The constitution also provides that there be a *rahbar*, also a Jurisprudent, who may impeach the head of government if he deviates from religious principles. Practical problems in implementation and even theory emerged from the start and are still in flux. *See* HIDDEN IMĀM; KHOMEINI; IRAN; SHĪ'ISM; UṢŪLĪS.

Wine (Ar. *al-khamr*). This is forbidden in Islam, as are all intoxicating drinks and drugs which affect consciousness (2:219; 5:92). Wine, however, is not a substance without spiritually redeeming qualities; thus the Koran says that in paradise there are rivers of wine (47:16); it is on earth that the negative effects of wine are felt, and these outweigh its benefits.

Nevertheless, in many Islamic countries, there are now, as there generally have been in the past, those who consume alcohol (and drugs) despite social disapprobation which may be mild or severe according to the milieu. In some otherwise Islamic countries, the use of alcohol is officially admitted by civil laws which regulate and license its sale.

Clearly, the use of psychotropic drugs for medical purposes, such as anaesthesia, is legal from every point of view. Medieval Muslim physicians used wine mixed with herbs as an anaesthetic. It might be mentioned that wine is forbidden because in a sense it is too elevated for man to enjoy without a loss of equilibrium; there is wine in paradise, where it is licit and does not cloud the understanding, and which flows in celestial fountains along with pure water and milk.

Among the Sufis, or Mystics, wine is a popular symbol of mystical knowledge. Wine is also prohibited in Manicheism. *See* al-KHAMRIYYAH.

"Wiping of the inner boots", *see* MASḤ 'ALĀ KHUFFAYN.

Wird (pl. *awrād*). A series of Koranic formulas, each recited usually a hundred or more times, which constitute a daily religious exercise of concentration, at morning and evening. These are used by the Sufi congregations (*ṭuruq*), and by others as well. The style and formulae of the *awrād* vary greatly but often include an asking for forgiveness (*istighfār*), a prayer on the Prophet, and the *shahādah.* Sometimes other Koranic excerpts are used such as *a-lā bi-dhikri-'Llāhi taṭma'innu-l-qulūb* ("Is it not in the remembrance of God that hearts find rest?" 13:28).

There is a famous Ḥadīth: "My heart is clouded until I have asked God's forgiveness seventy times during the day and the night."

Ibn 'Aṭā' Allāh wrote:

> Only the ignorant man scorns the recitation of litany (*al-wird*). Inspiration (*al-wārid*) is to be found in the Hereafter, while the litany vanishes with the vanishing of this world. But it is more fitting to be occupied with something for which there is no substitute. The litany is what He seeks from you, the inspiration is what you seek from Him. But what comparison is there between what He seeks from you and what you seek from Him?

Witr (lit. "odd number"). A prayer of an odd number of prayer-rounds (*raka'āt*) performed after the night-prayer (*'isha'*), and before the dawn prayer (*subḥ*). It is a voluntary prayer except in the Ḥanafī School where it is a duty (*wājib*), but not one that is imposed by Divine institution (*farḍ*).

Wives of the Prophet. Like the great figures of the Bible, including David and Solomon, the Prophet had more than one wife. Few of his marriages were contracted because of personal affinity; some of his wives were widows who had no-one to turn to, and other marriages were political, for the purposes of creating allies. Polygamy was normal to those times; Islam codified the practice by requiring that each wife be treated equally. In the early part of his life the Prophet had one wife only, Khadījah, who was forty years old and twice a widow when, at the age of twenty-five, he married her around the year 595. She was the first to believe in his mission, and he always revered her memory. She was, moreover, the only wife to bear him children; two, some say three, sons, (who all died in infancy) and four daughters, Umm Kulthūm, Ruqayyah, Zaynab, and Fāṭimah. All the daughters married, but died before the Prophet, except for Zaynab and Fāṭimah. Khadījah died in the year 619, before the Hijrah.

Thereupon the Prophet married Sawdah, aged thirty-five, the widow of a Companion named Sakran. Soon afterwards, he also married the daughter of Abū Bakr, 'Ā'ishah, who was six years old when they were married in Mecca; the marriage was not consummated until she came of age, after the Hijrah. The marriage to 'Ā'ishah has been a pretext on the part of Western writers looking for material with which to attack Islam, in this case with aspersions on the moral character of the Prophet because of the early age of 'Ā'ishah. These attacks have clearly been in bad faith, since the marriage was only completed when 'Ā'ishah reached the age of puberty which is an unmistakable biological signal, and has been for all peoples; those looking to cast blame may as well attack the nature of things and all societies which considered maturity as beginning earlier than the age deemed correct in the 19th century in certain milieus in Europe. 'Ā'ishah was to be the Prophet's favorite wife, and a presence that kindled his intuition and sense of spiritual immanence.

In February of 625 in Medinah, after the Battle of Badr, the Prophet married Ḥafṣah, the eighteen-year-old daughter of 'Umar. She was the widow of Khunays, and had returned from the first emigration to Abyssinia. One year after Badr, the Prophet married Zaynab bint Khuzaymah, a widow of 'Ubaydah, who had died at Badr. She was known as the *Umm al-Masākīn* ("the mother of the poor") for her generosity. She died not long after the marriage.

Umm Salāmah, the widow of Abū Salāmah who died at Uḥud, became another wife. The Prophet married Zaynab bint Jaḥsh, the divorced wife of his adopted son Zayd. She became a fifth wife at the time. A revelation of the Koran authorized more than four wives for the Prophet (Islam limits marriage to four wives at one time). Revelation also authorized marriage to a wife formerly married to a son by adoption, adoption having had for the Arabs the same quality as blood relationship until that time. This was the occasion by which the Koran denied the validity of such a view of adoption. Zaynab was forty years old then, and the Prophet was sixty. Unlike some of the marriages which were political alliances, the marriage to Zaynab was one of personal affinity.

After the Battle of the Trench and a campaign against the Banū Mustalīq, the Prophet married Juwayriyyah bint Ḥārith, daughter of the chief of the Banū Mustalīq, who thus became allied to the Prophet. Umm Ḥabībah, the daughter of Abū Sufyān, the leader of the Meccans fighting Islam, and widow of 'Ubayd (who had been converted to Christianity in Abyssinia, where he died) became the next wife. She was married to the Prophet by proxy by the Negus of Abyssinia while still in Abyssinia. Thus Abū Sufyān became the father-in-law of the Prophet.

Ṣafiyyah, the eighth wife and the tenth marriage, was the seventeen-year-old widow of Kinanah, chief of the Jews of Khaybar who had been conquered. She became a Muslim and married the Prophet on the return journey to Medinah. Maymunah, the eleventh and last marriage — after the pilgrimage to Mecca — was the sister of 'Abbās, and a widow.

In addition, the Prophet had at least two concubines, Rayhanah, captured from the Banu Qurayẓah, who was originally Jewish, and Maryah, a Christian slave who was a gift from the Muqawqīs, the Byzantine viceroy ruling the Copts in Egypt. She bore the Prophet a son, Ibrāhīm, who died before his second year.

Women. In discussing the status of women in Islamic societies it is important to bear in mind that Islam cannot be equated to the norms or the style of a particular society. In some Muslim societies, that of the Berbers, for example, women are very free; in others they are not; these differences are due to cultural factors rather than to Islam. In ancient Arab society, the coming of Islam brought women rights where they had none, or few, before. "You have rights over your women," says a Ḥadīth, "and your women have rights over you." These rights were conferred as an integral part of Divine legislation without being demanded; that is to say, there is no evidence that they were the result of any struggle on the part of Arab women. A spirit of freedom which women had under early Islam may in fact have been curtailed later, under the 'Abbāsids. In the last hundred years, modern societies, Arab as well as European, have given women greater freedom as the natural outcome of new forces at play in the modern world. Such freedoms are not necessarily incompatible with Islam.

It is essential that the traditional Islamic viewpoint concerning the respective roles of man and woman be understood in its own terms, setting aside modern polemics. The traditional perspective cannot be fully grasped without taking into account its metaphysical dimension. Islam views man as a soul encountering God in this life in order to know, love, and obey Him, thereby gaining entrance to paradise and immortality; consequently, Islam views men and women as equal before God. Indeed it views them as identical in this respect, and the Koran says that man and woman were "created of a single soul" (4:1; 39:6 and elsewhere).

Biologically and psychologically, however, men and women are different, male and female corresponding to different prototypes in the metacosm or in Being. Consequently, Islam views it as entirely in the nature of things that man and women should play different roles in society.

From the point of view of salvation men and women are according to Islam identical, and are so treated. However, the concept of equality, implying some sort of quantifiable measure to ascertain it, is alien to Islam, which does not view man as a material entity, either as a "social animal", or as a unit of production.

That men and women are not held to be socially equal by Islam (which does not mean one is inferior to the other) may appear unjust; yet it arises from their inherent differences and is in the nature of things. "Male and female created He them:" this corresponds to the polarity within Being of *eidos* and *hyle*, potency and receptivity (in Sanskrit *Purusha* and *Prakriti*; *see* FIVE DIVINE PRESENCES). It is the pure receptivity of substance in the principial state that foreshadows the qualified receptivity of the feminine pole in the world. *By its receptive perfection*, it yields precedence to the qualified power of the masculine pole, the reflection of pure act in Being. One may object that this is no more than an abstraction and an ideal, but for traditional societies the ideal is real, and the norm around which it seeks its equilibrium. In the world, it is normal for men and women each to contain both male and female poles. But in each person a different pole predominates and is expressed through different modalities, particularly as regards the psychic and the physical natures.

In pure Being, the relationship is perfectly harmonious, as symbolized by the Far Eastern depiction of Yin and Yang. In the world, the perfect harmony of Being encounters the margin of imperfection inherent in manifestation. Human relationships exist in the shadow of this imperfection; doctrinaire egalitarianism, while professing to correct injustice, makes the margin of imperfection the criterion. On the plane of the world, Islam must make prescriptions which translate the difference between masculine and feminine from the traditional point of view into the complexities of social legislation. This plane can never be ideal; it is, at best, a balance between the greater good and the lesser evil. Certain social inequalities are inevitable; the testimony of women in court is less than that of men, because their life of the home does not force them to objectify themselves as the world forces men to do; women are not socially independent in Islam, but legally need a man to act on their behalf; their share of inherited property is less, and so on. However, women have rights that men do not, such as the right to be supported and to a certain inviolability which is respected even by the most rude and warlike Beduins.

On the other hand, the identity between man and woman is affirmed by the capacity of woman to perform all rites; the sacerdotal function in Islam is as much woman's as it is man's (with precedence given to men as concerns the communal performance of rites, leading the public prayer, performing the sacrifice and similar functions).

How the Koranic framework is carried out in practice is largely determined by cultural factors and differs from society to society. While the spirit of Islam is clearly patriarchal, some Islamic cultures, notably those in the Sahara, certain parts of Africa, and regions of South-East Asia are matriarchal. Among Berbers, or the Kirghiz, women have a great deal of social liberty, while in neighboring, or even surrounding, Muslim cultures they may be crushingly restricted. It would be incorrect to attribute abuses that undoubtedly exist within the Islamic world to Islam itself rather than to human nature.

As the spirit of Islam is vast enough to embrace peoples of such diverse human types as Africans and Chinese, the range of social relationships possible within it must be equally vast. The Middle Eastern norm for relationships between the sexes is by no means the only one possible for Islamic societies everywhere, nor is it appropriate for all cultures. It does not exhaust the possibilities allowed within the framework of the Koran and Sunnah, and is neither feasible nor desirable as a model for Europe or North America. European societies possess perfectly adequate models for marriage, the family, and relations between the sexes which are by no means out of harmony with the Koran and the Sunnah. This is borne out by the fact that within certain broad limits Islamic societies themselves differ enormously in this respect.

The existence of polygamy within Islam reflects the cultural norms of ancient Semitic society. It was perpetuated on the one hand because it corresponds to metaphysical possibility, wherein the man represents the oneness of the Principle, and woman the multiplicity of Divine Infinitude, and on the other because desert societies always had a surplus of women, the men being killed off in continual warfare:

> Marry the spouseless among you, and your
> slaves and handmaidens that are righteous;
> if they are poor, God will enrich them
> of His bounty; God is All-embracing,
> All-knowing. (24:32)

Polygamy thus fulfilled a social need, giving women security when independent life was virtually impossible outside marriage, the household and the family. As it says in Isaiah 4:1: "And in that day seven women shall take hold of one man saying, We will eat our own bread, and wear our own apparel: only let us called by thy name, to take away our reproach." The limitation of four wives comes from Judaism where it is a Talmudic injunction.

Because the legal statute of polygamy requires fair treatment and equal support of all the wives, it is in practice becoming rare today for economic reasons, as well as for reasons of the social stigma of being looked upon as un-modern. Using the Koranic requirement of equitable treatment as a justification, and the injunction that the "door to abuses should be closed", some countries like Syria have actually prohibited polygamy. In most of the Islamic world where it is still practiced, only 1 to 3% of marriages are polygamous.

> Men and women who have surrendered,
> believing men and believing women,
> obedient men and obedient women,
> truthful men and truthful women,
> enduring men and enduring women,
> humble men and humble women,
> men and women who give in charity,
> men who fast and women who fast,
> men and women who guard their private parts,
> men and women who remember God oft—
> for them God has prepared forgiveness
> and a mighty wage. (33:35)*See* VEIL.

Wuḍū'. The "lesser ablution", commonly called in Persian *abdast.* This is performed, when the conditions of the "greater ablution" (*ghusl*) have been fulfilled, in order to be in the correct state to perform the canonical prayer, the *ṣalāh.* Once the purification of *wuḍū'* is acquired it is valid until lost by the following impurities termed *aḥdāth*: calls of nature, breaking wind, loss of consciousness, deep sleep, light bleeding (but not a "flow" of blood from insect bites or the like), for a man, touching his private parts, or any of the circumstances which necessitate *ghusl.* A chronic condition such as incontinence of urine is disregarded for the purposes of ablution, and the person performs a *wuḍū'* before each prayer. In effect, the conditions of the state of purity are of a subtle nature and the legal definitions are indicative rather than absolute.

The *wuḍū'* consists of the following actions:

1. Formulating the intention.
2. Pronouncing the *basmalah.*
3. Running water over the right hand and then the left and washing the hands by rubbing one over the other three times. (Rubbing between the fingers, which is a part of *ghusl*, is sometimes added also to *wuḍū'* and considered a requirement, as well as moving a finger-ring, if possible, to allow water to penetrate around it.)
4. Cupping water in the right hand and rinsing the mouth three times (*maḍmaḍa*).
5. Raising water in the cupped right hand to the nostrils (*istinshaq*) and squeezing it out with the left (*istinsar*), three times.
6. Washing the face three times with both hands.
7. Washing the right arm up to the elbow three times with the left hand, and then the left arm up to the elbow three times with the right.
8. Passing the wetted right hand over the head, first back and then forward using the left hand to raise the turban or headgear, once. If both hands are free for this operation, then both wetted hands are passed over the head. It is not necessary in the *wuḍū'* to use much water. The head is only lightly wiped. At this point the *shahādah* is recited.
9. Putting the wetted forefingers in the ears, and with the thumbs behind the lobes, moving both fingers upwards following the conformation of the outer ear, and then from the top of the ear down along the outer ridge, thus wiping the entrance to the ear, and the outer ear.
10. Washing the right foot with the left hand by wiping the outside of the foot with the fingers, palm against the sole, starting at the heel and moving to the toes; from the toes back with the palm against the inside of the foot, fingers along the sole, and then up to the ankle. Similarly the left foot is wiped by the right hand, palm against the inside, fingers against the sole starting from the toe down to the heel, then upwards palm against the sole, the fingers around the foot wiping the outside, and then up to the ankle. (Wiping between the toes is a condition of *ghusl*, but popularly is believed to be a requirement of *wuḍū'*.)

The ablution is completed with the pronunciation of the *ḥamdalah.* It is Sunnah to perform each gesture of the *wuḍū'* three times, but legally once is sufficient. Under certain conditions *wuḍū'* with water may be replaced by a variant, shorter purification with sand, earth, or stone, called the *tayammum.* There are some small differences in how Shī'ites perform the *wuḍū'*.

It is an assumption of the *wuḍū'* that water or earth has been used to cleanse the bodily orifices after calls of nature (*istibrā'* and *istinjā'*). In Islamic countries, privies are provided with a tap of running water for this purpose. As toilet-paper generally replaces water in the West, this practice of washing becomes difficult if not impossible, but not all schools insist upon the *istibrā'* and the *instinjā'* as indispensable for *wuḍū'*.

Normally, water for *wuḍū'* must be running water, or water poured from a container from a source which can be considered clean. If it is necessary to use water which is not running, but nevertheless clean and thus suitable for ablution, a special problem is posed if there is no utensil with which to pour it. It is usually believed that dipping a hand into still water before that hand has itself been washed, ritually, compromises the water for ablution. If there is no way to raise the water to pour, the popular expedient is to scoop water from the surface with a rapid motion of the left hand until the right hand is wetted and can then be dipped in to continue the ablution. Although there are certainly situations more trying, this is perhaps a small example of the firmly established principle: "Necessity makes prohibited things permissible."

Usually, mosques have fountains in the entrance courtyard or other sources where water for ablution can be obtained. If an area of skin is covered with bandages, such that water does not reach it, it does not affect the validity of the ablution.

It was the Sunnah to use a very small amount of water for w*uḍū'*, showing that its primary nature is not a physical cleaning, since that is already presumed, but a purification — the re-establishment of an existential equilibrium, through the symbolism of water as primordial substance, made possible by the ritual. It is because it is a ritual, a series of acts established by heaven, or consecrated by Divine "approval", that the symbolic nature of water can effect a spiritual purpose. *See* ABLUTIONS; GHUSL; ISTIBRĀ'; ISTINJĀ'; TAYAMMUM.

Wuqūf ("standing"). One of the rites of the greater pilgrimage (*ḥajj*) is that of the "standing" (it is not physically necessary to stand) on the plain of 'Arafāt on the 9th day of *Dhū-l-Ḥijjah.* While some schools of law prescribe the presence of the pilgrim for the whole day, and others from noon onwards at least, it is admitted on the basis of Ḥadīth that even a momentary presence there before sundown fulfills the requirement of *wuqūf.* Failing that, however, the pilgrimage is incomplete.

An Imām delivers the sermon (*khuṭbah*) at 'Arafāt at the time of the noon prayer. The "standing" is the time when the invocation of the *talbiyah* is at its height. Altogether, the rite, which today brings millions of worshipers from around the world to one sacred place, is a foretaste of the Day of Judgement. At sundown the pilgrims proceed in a ritual "hastening" (*ifāḍah*) to nearby Muzdalifah which lies in the direction of Mecca. *See* PILGRIMAGE.

X

Xinjiang. (Sinkiang: Chinese: "New Frontier" or "New Territory"). Formerly called Chinese Turkestan (*Hui Chiang*: Uighur territory), this western province comprises many cities of the "Silk Road"; Kashgar, Urumchi (in Chinese also called "Tihwa" or "Return to Civilisation"), Yarkand, Khotan and the sites of Turfan (Qocho) and Dun Huang ("Blazing Beacon"). It is also home to the Chinese nuclear test center of Lop Nor. It contains the Taklamakan desert and the Tarim river basin. The northwestern province of China, Xinjiang borders on Afghanistan, Pakistan, and Kashmir and the Central Asian republics of Kazakhstan, Kyrgyztan, and Tajikistan. Xinjiang is inhabited largely by Uighurs (in Chinese *Hei Hui*, "Black Hui"), a Turkic people from the Altai who are Muslim.

Xinjiang covers one-sixth of China and the Uighurs and other Muslim groups living there have been involved in centuries' long struggle with the Chinese. Official Chinese figures put the Uighur and other Muslim nationalities population in China at 17.6 million. This includes the Uighurs and the Hui, and others. The Hui, although the word is derived from the word "Uighur" denotes a people who are more Han than Turkic and most of whom do not live in Xinjiang. In Xinjiang the percentage of the population who are Muslims is 8 million Uighurs and 1.2 million Kazakhs and other groups, or 48%, while Han Chinese make up 6 million, or 38%. Uighur groups outside China put the total figure of Uighurs in China higher, at 25 million, and say that almost all the Han Chinese settled in Xinjiang since 1950, raising the percentage to its present figure from an original proportion of 4%. There are also Uighurs in neighboring Kazakhstan and Kyrgyzstan and Uzbekistan as well.

In 762 a Uighur army liberated the T'ang Chinese eastern capital of Lo-yang, on the Yellow river, south of Peking. Among those who greeted the victors were Soghdian Manichean priests (Manicheism had been prohibited in 732 but this edict had not been enforced), and the Uighur leader, the Khagan Mo-yu (Bögü Qan) was converted to Manicheism in an event which is recorded in a tri-lingual inscription in Karabalghasun on the river Orkhon in Mongolia. The Uighur ruler became a protector of Manicheism in Central Asia, including that area which was under Muslim control, because he threatened to slaughter the Muslims in his territory if Manicheans were harmed in Khorāsān. In 840 the Uighur kingdom collapsed in the face of an attack by the Kirghiz, a related people, and Manicheism which had been allowed temples in the Yang-Tse basin in China was again proscribed by the Chinese rulers from 843 onward while Manichean priests were even massacred and dressed to look like Buddhists in death to remove traces of the religion (as well as to humiliate the Manicheans). This came at a time of weakness of the T'ang dynasty and when Taoism gained over Buddhism while foreign ideas in art, science and religion penetrated China.

With the fall of the first Uighur Empire, the Uighurs moved south to Turfan from their former power base near lake Baikal. The second Uighur Empire flourished also as a Manichean kingdom, at least as far as the ruling elite was concerned. It was centered at Qocho (Kao-chang also known as Idiqut Shahr) which is 40 kilometers east of modern Turfan.

Before the Uighurs, Turfan in the 7th century was a Buddhist Indo-European culture, whose language, Tokharian, is closely related to Italo-Celtic. The German scholar-explorer von Le Coq called this culture one of "belated antiquities" and Grousset as "lost in space". It was a mixture of Persian, Indian, and Hellenist with Buddhism as its religion, and the most easterly occurrence of Hellenic figures of Gandharan Buddhas. Indo-European in a Turco-Mongol ocean, Tokharian art demonstrates a longing and nostalgia for its cultural kindred. Because of its Persian connection, Turfan was irrigated with 1,000 miles of underground canals in the Iranian fashion, some of them 25 miles long, making Turfan an agricultural region. Turfan had been visited by the Chinese Buddhist scholar and traveller Hsüan Tsang.

The Uighur ruler of Qocho, the Idiqut, was visited by the Sufi al-Ḥallāj in the early 10th century. In the mid-13th century the Tarim basin was conquered by the Mongols under whom, later, Islam was to replace Buddhism and Manicheism in the region ever since.

After seventy years of struggles with the Dzungar Mongols, in 1759 Eastern Turkestan was conquered by the Qing dynasty but the local populations continued to resist the conquerors on and off. Under the Manchus there were a number of Muslim revolts in China and wars against them in 1820-28 (Lanchu), 1830 (Che Kanio), 1847 (Xinjiang), 1857 (Yunan), 1861 (Shansi). Led by Yaqub Beg, Turkestan became independent from 1867 to 1877. In 1884 the region was renamed Xinjiang and declared China's 19th province. After the republic of Sun Yat Sen in 1912, Turkestan rose in the Qumul rebellion which led to an independent Turkestan republic in 1933, and from 1944 to 1949.

In the last few years there have been many incidents in the province indicating resistance to the policy of imposing Chinese language and cultural dominance. These include Baren in 1990, Khoten in 1995 and Ghulje (Yining) in 1997. They include alleged arrests of over 57,000 ethnic Uighurs, massacres, and summary executions of hundreds because of anti-Han Chinese demonstrations or activities. *See* HUI HUI.

Y

Yaḥyā. John the Baptist, an important figure in Islam as a prophet mentioned in the Koran. The prayer of his father Zakariyyā (21:89) for a child in his old age is often cited as a model of a petition answered by God. He is also mentioned in the Koran 6:85; and 19:14-15:

'O John, take the Book forcefully';
and We gave him judgement, yet a
little child,
and a tenderness from Us,
and purity; and he was
godfearing, and cherishing
his parents, not arrogant,
rebellious.
'Peace be upon him, the day
he was born, and the day he
dies, and the day he is raised
up alive!'

Yalamlam. One of the stations on the approaches to Mecca known as *mawāqīt* (sing. *mīqāt*) where pilgrims must put on consecrated garb (*iḥrām*) if they have not already done so. Yalamlam is the *mīqāt* for pilgrims from the Yemen.

Yā Laṭīf. A supplementary prayer (*du'ā'*) invoking the Divine Name al-Laṭīf ("the Subtle", "the Gracious"), which can be recited in situations of distress, particularly serious illness, when Divine remedy is sought. It is very often performed by several persons on behalf of one who is afflicted and probably absent. Its form and order are as follows:
1. Formulation of the intention (*niyyah*) of the Yā Laṭīf prayer.
2. The *ta'awwudh* ("I take refuge in God from Satan the stoned one") is pronounced.
3. The *basmalah* ("In the name of God the Merciful, the Compassionate") and the *Sūrat al-Ikhlāṣ* (the Chapter of "Sincerity", Koran 92) is recited three times.
4. Then the following Koranic verse (42:19) is said: *Allāhu laṭīfun bi'ibādihī yarzuqu man yashā'u wa huwa-l-Qawiyyu-l-'Azīz* ("God is gracious to His servants; He succors whom He will and He is the Strong, the Mighty").
5. A personal petition is silently made.
6. A prayer on the Prophet (*ṣalāh 'ala-n-nabī*) is said. For example:

aṣ-ṣalātu wa-s-salāmu 'alayka yā sayyidī yā
ḥabība-Llāh; aṣ-ṣalātu wa-s-salāmu 'alayka yā
sayyidī yā nabiyya-Llāh; aṣ-ṣala^tu wa-s-salāmu
'alayka yā sayyidī yā rasula-Llāh; alfu ṣalātin
wa alfu salāmin 'alayk;
wa ṣalla-Llāhu 'alayka wa
'alā ālika wa raḍiya 'an aṣḥābika, yā khayra
man ikhtāra-Llāh.

Blessings and peace be upon you
O Intimate of God;
blessings and peace be upon you
O Prophet of God;
blessings and peace be upon you
O Messenger of God.
Thousandfold blessing and
thousandfold peace, God
bless You and Your people,
and may His Grace be upon
Your Companions,
O best of them that God has chosen!

7. The petitioner says *Yā Laṭīfu* turning the head to the right, and *Yā Laṭīf* turning to the left, for a total of 129, or 300, or 500 or 1,000 times.
8. Then the petitioner repeats (6) the *ṣalāh 'alā n-nabī*.
9. A personal petition is made.
10. The prayer is closed by saying *al-ḥamdu li-Llāh* ("Praise to God").

See BASMALAH; al-IKHLĀṢ, SŪRAH; TA'AWWUDH.

'Yan Tatsine. A heretical movement centered around Kano, Nigeria. Its members rose in rebellion against the civil authorities in December 1980 and were put down by the Nigerian Army in bloody fighting at the end of that month. The leader of the movement, Mallam Muḥammadu Marwa, of Cameroonian origin, was dubbed Mallam Maitatsine for his habit of calling God's curse (*tatsine*) on "anyone who doesn't agree with me."

Although the movement claimed to teach the Koran, it regarded the Prophet with derision, while the Mallam took the prophetic function to himself. The movement appealed to the dispossessed young who had lost their roots in social upheavals of recent years. The Mallam was killed on December 29, 1980, and police inquiries put the total number of dead at over 4,000. Since then, similar movements have arisen in Nigeria among the poor, as a result of social and economic dislocations, although not on such a scale.

Ya'qūb. The Jacob of the Bible; he is mentioned several times in Sūrah 12 of the Koran and also in 2:132-140.

Yasa. The tribal and religious law of the Mongols, who were shamanists. On several points the *Yasa* distinctly clashed with the prescriptions of the *sharī'ah*. The *Yasa* prescribed the slaughter of animals by a blow to the head; the Muslims slaughter animals ritually by cutting the throat and draining the blood. The *Yasa* looked upon water as a magical substance not to be used for washing (a Mongol was only washed after birth, and after death; in life he was only washed by the rain). The Mongols feared that the Muslim ablutions would bring down catastrophe through lightning and that the ablutions were in reality a magical ceremony. An additional point of antipathy as far as Muslims were concerned was that the Mongols were heavy drinkers, even the women regularly drinking themselves into a stupor.

The Mongol overlords inflicted punishment on their Muslim subjects because of the tensions between the *Yasa* and the *sharī'ah* until they were themselves converted to Islam. This was particularly true in Transoxiana, the *ulus*, or territory, of Chagatai (d. *639*/1241), a son of Jenghiz Khan. Eventually, the southern Mongols were converted to Islam. The law of Jenghiz Khan says:

> When there is no war raging against the enemy, there shall be hunting; the young shall be taught how to kill wild animals so that they become accustomed to fighting and acquire strength and endurance and will subsequently fight without sparing themselves against an enemy as though against wild animals.

In 1222, returning from the first Mongol incursion into the Muslim world, Jenghiz Khan stopped in Bukhara and expressed an interest in Islam, which was explained to him. He approved its principles and said that Allāh was not other than the Supreme Deity of the Mongols, the "Eternal Blue Sky" (*Tengri*). But he thought the pilgrimage was unnecessary since the *Tengri* is everywhere. *See* HŪLĀGŪ KHĀN; IL-KHANIDS; MONGOLS; RASHĪD ad-DĪN at-ṬABĪB.

Ya' Sin. The name of the thirty-sixth Sūrah ("chapter") of the Koran, so called after two letters of the Arabic alphabet with which the Sūrah begins. There is no unanimity about their interpretation; according to Ibn 'Arabī they stand for two Divine Names: *al-Wāqi* ("the Protector") and *aṣ-Ṣalām* ("Peace"). This Sūrah was called by the Prophet *qalb al-qur'ān* (the "heart of the Koran"). Dealing with the mysteries of revelation; immortality; life, death, Judgement, Heaven and Hell; the great cycles of time and the movements of the heavenly bodies; the mystery of the "pairs" (the dualities in manifestation); resurrection; creation, and so forth in passages of surpassing power and beauty, it is believed to contain all the essentials of the revelation. It is particularly recited for the dead (and recalls Matthew 25:21), and also to aid the recovery of the sick.

> And a sign for them is the night;
> We strip it of the
> day and lo, they are in darkness.
> And the sun — it runs to a fixed resting-place;
> that is the ordaining of the All-mighty,
> the All-knowing. And the moon — We have determined it by stations,
> till it returns like an aged palm-bough.
> It behooves not the sun
> to overtake the moon, neither
> does the night outstrip the day,
> each swimming in a sky. And a sign for them is
> that We carried their seed
> in the laden ship,
> and We have created for them the like of it
> whereon they ride;
> and if We will, We drown them,
> then none have they to cry to,
> neither are they delivered,
> save as a mercy from Us, and enjoyment
> for a while. (36:36-44)

It contains a famous parable introduced by the words: "And coin a parable for them, of the people of the city when the Messengers came to it" (36:13). This has been interpreted, as is possible with parables, in many ways; but within the context of this Sūrah's message about the Islamic revelation and the role of the Prophet as one of those that have been sent by God: "Yā' Sīn, by the Generous Koran, verily Thou art one of them that have been sent, upon a straight path, in a sending down [revelation] by the Almighty, the Compassionate." (36:1-5), the parable appears to refer to the Semitic monotheisms; the first two messengers are Abraham and Moses, the third Jesus and the fourth and last, the Prophet Muḥammad.

In virtue of this, *Yā' Sin* is one of the two hundred names of the Prophet.

Strike for them a similitude —
the inhabitants of the city,
when the Envoys came to it;
when We sent unto them two men,
but they cried them lies,
so We sent a third as reinforcement.
They said, 'We are assuredly Envoys unto you.'
They said, 'You are naught but mortals like us;
the All-merciful has not sent down anything.
You are speaking only lies.'
They said, "Our Lord knows we are Envoys unto you;
and it is only for us
to deliver the Manifest Message.'
They said, 'We augur ill of you.
If you give not over, we will stone you
and there shall visit you
from us a painful chastisement.'
They said, 'Your augury is with you:
if you are reminded?
But you are a prodigal people.'
Then came a man from the furthest parts
of the city, running; he said,
'My people, follow the Envoys!
Follow such as ask no wage of you,
that are right-guided.
And why should I not serve Him
who originated me, and unto whom
you shall be returned?
What, shall I take, apart from Him,
gods whose intercession,
if the All-merciful desires affliction
for me, shall not
avail me anything, and who will now deliver me?
Surely in that case I should be in manifest error.
Behold, I believe in your Lord; therefore hear me!'
It was said, 'Enter Paradise!'
He said, 'Ah, would that my people had knowledge
that my Lord has forgiven me and that
He has placed me among the honoured.
And We sent not down upon his people,
after him, any host out of heaven;
neither would We send any down.
It was only one Cry and lo,
they were silent and still.
Ah, woe for those servants!
Never comes unto them a Messenger,
but they mock at him.
What, have they not seen how many generations
We have destroyed before them,
and that it is not unto them that they return?
They shall every one of them
be arraigned before Us. (36:14-33)

In the *Kitāb Jawāhīr al-Qur'an* al-Ghazali explains that the surah Yā' Sīn is the heart of the Koran because it speaks of the entry of the saved one into paradise, and this is an awakening of the individual himself; the opening of one's own eyes is superior to the knowledge through the eyes of others.

Yathrib. The original name of Medinah. The latter name of the city comes from *madīnat an-nabī* ("city of the Prophet"). *See* MEDINAH.

Yawm ad-Dīn (lit. "the day of the religion" or "of the Judgement"), also called the "day of resurrection" (*yawm al-qiyāmah*), and the "hour" (*as-sā'ah*), and many other names. On that day the world is rolled up like a scroll, and the dead issue from their graves and are reunited with their bodies; the limbs testify to reveal the owner's good or evil deeds. On the scales of God's judgement nothing is overlooked: an atom's weight of good is manifest, and an atom's weight of evil. According to their deeds, and their belief, men are judged and their real nature revealed. Those who clove to the truth enter Paradise, and those who did not, enter Hell. The Koran as the last revelation looks forward to the end; many passages speak of the final day, when the trumpet is blown and the world struck down. The trumpet is blown again and the dead rise up. The blowing of the trumpet symbolizes the destruction of forms by pure sound or transcendence, or again, the separation of forms and their contents. The Koran speaks thus of that day:

... 'When shall be the Day of Resurrection?'
But when the sight is dazed
and the moon is eclipsed,
and the sun and the moon are brought together,
upon that day man shall say,'Whither to flee?'
No indeed; not a refuge! (75:6-12)

Upon that day faces shall be radiant,
gazing upon their Lord;
and upon that day faces shall be scowling,
thou mightest think the Calamity
has been wreaked on them.

No indeed; when it reaches the clavicles
and it is said, 'Who is an enchanter?'
and he thinks that it is the parting
and leg is intertwined with leg,
upon that day unto thy Lord
shall be the driving. (75:22-30)

When earth is shaken with a mighty shaking
and earth brings forth her burdens,
and Man says, 'What ails her?'
upon that day she shall tell her tidings
for that her Lord has inspired her.

Upon that day men shall issue
in scatterings to see their works,
and whoso has done
an atom's weight of good shall see it,
and whoso has done
an atom's weight of evil shall see it. (99)

...upon the day when the earth
and the mountains shall quake
and the mountains become
a slipping heap of sand. (73:14)

If therefore you disbelieve, how will you
guard yourselves against a day that shall make
the children grey-headed?
Whereby heaven shall be split, and its promise
shall be performed. (73:17-18)

So be thou patient with a sweet patience;
behold, they see it as if far off, but We
see it is nigh.

Upon the day when heaven
shall be as molten copper
and the mountains shall be as plucked wool-tufts,
no loyal friend shall question loyal friend, as
they are given sight of them.
The sinner will wish that he
might ransom himself from the
chastisement of that day even
by his sons, his companion wife, his brother,
his kin who
sheltered him, and whosoever is in the earth,
ll together, so that then it might deliver him.

Nay, verily it is a furnace
snatching away the scalp,
calling him who drew back and turned away,
who amassed and hoarded.

Surely man was created fretful,
when evil visits him, impatient,
when good visits him, grudging,
save those that pray
and continue at their prayers,
those in whose wealth is a right known
for the beggar and the outcast,
who confirm the Day of Doom
and go in fear of the chastisement of their Lord
(from their Lord's chastisement
none feels secure)
and guard their private parts
save from their wives
and what their right hands own,
then not being blameworthy
but whoso seeks after more than that,
they are the transgressors),
and who preserve their trusts
and their covenant,
and perform their witnessings,
and who observe their prayers.
Those shall be in Gardens, high-honoured.
What ails the unbelievers, running with
outstretched necks towards thee
on the right hand and on the left hand in knots?
What, is every man of them eager
to be admitted to a Garden of Bliss?
Not so; for We have created them
of what they know.

No! I swear by the Lord of the Easts and the
Wests, surely We are able
to substitute a better than they; We shall
not be outstripped.

Then leave them alone to plunge and play
until they encounter that day of theirs
which they are promised,
the day they shall come forth from the
tombs hastily, as if they were hurrying
into a waymark,
humbled their eyes, overspreading
them abasement. That is the day
which they were promised. (70:5-44)

God is He that looses the winds,
that stir up cloud,
then We drive it to a dead land and therewith revive the earth, after it is dead.
Even so is the Resurrection. (35:10)

And what shall teach thee what is the Day of Doom?
Again, what shall teach thee
what is the Day of Doom?
A day when no soul shall possess
aught to succour another soul; that day
the Command shall belong unto God. (82:17-19)

See ESCHATOLOGY; al-JANNAH.

Yasawiyyah. A ṭarīqah found in Central Asia named after Aḥmad ibn Ibrāhīm Ibn 'Alī of Yasi from Turkestan (d. *562*/1166). Yasavi belonged to the tradition of Yusuf Hamadhāni; originally his ṭarīqah was one of wanderers. It is not as large today in Central Asia as the Naqshbandiyyah, but it is related to it very closely as Yasawi was a spiritual predecessor of Baha'u ad-Dīn Naqshband. The Yasawis are also closely related to the Kubrawiyyah, all three being really branches of one original group. *See* SUFISM; KUBRAWIYYAH.

Yazdagird (d. *31*/651). The last Sāssānid ruler of Persia whose armies, led by the general Rustum, were defeated at the battle of Qādisiyyah in 'Irāq in *14*/635. After the definitive Persian defeat at the Battle of Nihawand in *22*/642, Yazdagird fled into Khorāsān to seek help from his satraps, but found none; one by one his followers abandoned him. Finally, near Merv, he took refuge with a peasant, a miller, who, in a traditional account, asked him: "Who art thou?"

A Persian and a fugitive, said the King.

If thou canst content thee with barley bread, and the poor cresses that grow by the banks of the brook, I offer it to thee freely, said the miller, for that is all I have.

Content, said he, but get me some holy barsom twigs for my ritual besides.

So the poor miller went out to borrow barsom. But those he met with took him before the traitor Mahwi, the King's enemy; and Mahwi said to the wretched drudge; For whom does the like of thee seek barsom? The miller told his tale; and Mahwi knew it must be Yazdagird. Go back, said he; and cut off his head straightway; if not, thine own shall fall.

The poor man heard the word; but little he knew the reach of the deed. It was night when he got home, and came into the presence of the King. Shame and fear in his heart, dry at the lips, he drew softly near, as he would whisper in his ear; then struck a dagger in his breast. And death was in the stroke. One sob the King gave; then his diademed head tumbled on the ground beside a barley loaf he had before him.

The world's soul is a mindless void; and witless is the turning Heaven. A mystery is its hatred or its grace. 'Tis wisest not to care — to watch changes without anger, and without love.

Then came in two cruel-hearted serving men, and dragged out the King's body bleeding. They heaved it into the whirling eddies of the Zark; and there the corpse of Yazdagird drifted, face up for a while, and then face under.

There is a Shī'ite legend that one of the daughters of Yazdagird was married by 'Alī to his son Ḥusayn, thereby bringing the blood of the Sāssānid dynasty into the 'Alīd line, which Twelve-Imām Shī'ites were to venerate. This is unlikely, and the name of the putative daughter, Shahrbanu ("Lady of the Land"), appears to be a particular cult name for the goddess Anahid (or Anahita), a Zoroastrian adoption of the Babylonian goddess Ishtar. Anahid was particularly important to the Sāssānids who promoted a Zurvanite and heretical form of Zoroastrianism. Every Persian dynasty has claimed relation to the dynasties of the past.

Yazīdīs. An obscure dualist sect found among some Kurds in northern 'Irāq and also in Syria, Turkey and Iran. They may number a hundred thousand or more. Much religious practice is centered on the tomb of a certain Shaykh 'Ādī ibn Musāfir in Lalish in the district of Mosul, who was probably an Ismā'īlī preacher. Nestorian Christians considered the tomb, notable for its depiction of a serpent at the entrance, to be that of a Christian. Various dates are given for his death: *557*/1162, *695*/1296, and also *133*/750. He is considered to be the author of a book called the *Kitab al-Jalwah* ("The Book of the Emergence"). Another canonic book is the *Mishaf Resh* or "Black Book" by Shaykh Ḥasan ibn 'Ādī.

The Yazīdīs' own name for themselves is *Dawasin* or *Dasnayye*. (Yazidi, implying for some a connection with the Umayyad Caliph Yazid at whose orders Ḥusayn was killed, probably originated as a name of abuse given them by Twelve-Imām Shī'ites; or perhaps, and more likely, the word comes from Persian *yazata* or *yazdan* meaning "divinities").

They are often called scornfully "devil worshipers". The "Peacock Angel" (*Malak Ṭā'ūs*) is their euphemism for evil, or the devil, which they fear and seek to appease, and do not call by the customary term in Arabic, *Shaytan*. They believe that evil is part of the Divinity, along with good. The Yazidis make representations of this Peacock Angel which they carry in festivals. The Yazidis believe that evil is to be found in lettuce, or as their traditions put it "the devil once hid in a lettuce patch". This belief is ridiculed by their neighbors; it probably goes back, as an inversion, to the Manichean practice of vegetarianism, for the Manicheans believed that the Divine light was contained in plants in a greater proportion than any other substance in this world, and in some plants more than others (which is still a popular belief in Iran); and they consumed lettuce in large quantities. But lettuce poses a special problem; the evil of the lettuce may be nothing more than a folk warning of the ancient vegetarian cults regarding a plant which any well-informed modern traveller in the East also avoids religiously, just as he or she drinks tea rather than unboiled water.

The Yazīdī's more important heterodoxies have cost them innumerable persecutions and struggles. They are closely related to similar Gnostic sects like the Ahl-i Ḥaqq. *See* AHL-I ḤAQQ; MANICHEISM.

Yemen (from an Arabic root meaning "felicity"). The region in the south of the Arabian peninsula, which was called Arabia Felix by the Romans, is today divided into two separate countries: the Republic of Yemen with its capital at Sana'a', and the People's Democratic Republic of Yemen with its capital at Aden. In 1990 the two countries were formally united as the Republic of Yemen, population 13,483,178. The Yemen receives the monsoon rains from the Indian Ocean, is fertile and agriculturally very rich. It was the seat of numerous civilisations in pre-Islamic times, notably the Sabaean, Minaean and Himyaritic.

Until the time of Constantine the Great, when cremation in the Roman Empire was replaced by the practice of burial, the economic basis of the Yemen was the export of frankincense used as incense, and myrrh used for cosmetics, both from indigenous trees. Many religions in turn played an important role in the Yemen: Judaism was the religion of one of the kings in the Yemen named Dhū Nuwāṣ, who was overthrown by the Christian Negus of Ethiopia acting on behalf of the Byzantine Emperor who had called for the punishment of Dhū Nuwāṣ because of the destruction of the Christian community of Najrān (AD 523) in South Arabia.

Christianity spread widely in the Yemen as a result of Abyssinian suzerainty, until, when the Yemen became a Persian satrapy (around AD 575), Zoroastrianism was introduced.

In the first century of the Hijrah, the Yemen was converted to Islam. Today, 40% of the population of the Republic of Yemen, mostly tribesmen in the mountains, are Zaydī Shī'ites. (The most recent Imām of these Shī'ites died in exile in London after the declaration of the republic.) The rest are Sunnīs of the Shāfi'ī School of Law. There are also small minorities of different branches of Ismā'īlism, remnants of once larger communities.

Yemenis from the Hadhramaut were noted seafarers in the age of the dhows, and in the age of steamships they became stokers famed for their ability to withstand great heat. They have migrated near and far, to India and particularly to Indonesia where there is a large community of Indonesians of Yemeni descent.

Yezidis, *see* YAZĪDĪS.

Yemen, Breath of the. It was a saying of the Prophet that "there is a wind which comes from the Yemen which brings me comfort". The saying is also well-known in India as: "There is a wind from India ..."

Yūnus. The Jonah of the Bible. He is also called *Dhū-n-Nūn* ("he of the fish"). Yūnus was a Divine Messenger (*rasūl*), who was swallowed by a fish, praised God nevertheless, and was delivered. The Arabic letter *nūn* (with the ancient meaning of fish) is a semi-circle, open at the top, with a point in its center. It has been interpreted to symbolize a vessel, or ark, which carries the point, the germ of future manifestations, across the gulf that separates one cycle from another. (This interpretation comes from the same source that used the symbol of a half-moon as a boat carrying a particle of light pictured as a star.) This transition between worlds must be made in darkness and the preservation of the immortal soul or, macrocosmically speaking, the continuity between cycles, is symbolized by Yūnus' trials. His message is salvation through complete resignation to God.

Yūnus Emre (d. *725*/1325?). An Anatolian Turkish poet who composed Gnostic poetry in the vernacular. He is very popular with Turkish Sufis and his poetry has often been set to mystic songs. It is very likely that he is an apocryphal figure, a name around which a genre and a popular corpus of anonymous poetry has collected. Humanism is one of his themes:

Here or in India or in Africa
All things resemble each other.
We feel the same love for grains.
Before death we tremble together.

I am Job: I have found all his patience
I am St. George: I died a thousand times."

The sentiments are very close to Rūmī:

Whoever has one drop of love
Possesses God's existence.

and he is essentially Gnostic, the ideas resembling those of al-Ḥallāj, who was also very popular in Turkey:

If you don't identify Man as God,
All your learning is of no use at all.

The universe is the oneness of Deity
The true man is he who knows this unity.

You better seek Him in yourself
you and He aren't apart — you're one.
The image of the Godhead is a mirror:
The man who looks sees his own face in there.

Death should give you no fear at all
Fear not, your life is eternal.

He is God Himself — human are His images.
See for yourself: God is man, that is what He is.

Yurt. A round dwelling, made of wood and felt, used by Mongolian and Turkic nomads in the regions around Central Asia. This style of nomad dwelling is completely different from the famous "black tents" of the Arabs, made of twisted goat's hair. Yurt, as well as meaning the home, also means a home territory. The yurt and the tent are respectively symbols of the two great nomadic cultures each with a different origin and filiation in the dim past. *See* MONGOLS; YASA.

Yūsuf. The Joseph of the Bible, his story is told with concise beauty in the Sūrah Yusūf (the "Chapter of Joseph") of the Koran. The favorite son of Jacob (*Ya'qūb*), he was sold into slavery by his jealous brothers, and taken to Egypt; there he was taken as a slave into the household of Fitfir (Potiphar; also misread as "Qitfir" in some manuscripts), a great man of the country. He was so handsome that when the women of Egypt saw him, in their distraction, they cut their hands with their serving knives. This proverbial beauty is said to be one of the rewards of paradise, where all men are as beautiful as Yūsuf.

The wife of Fitfir made advances to Yūsuf. He resisted them and tried to escape, and his innocence was proven by the fact that his shirt was torn at the back. He was, nevertheless, put into prison, and released only after many years for correctly interpreting Pharaoh's dreams. His brothers came to him to ask for food in time of famine. His shirt sent to his father restored the sight Ya'qub had lost from weeping for the loss of Yūsuf.

Z

Zabūr. The Arabic name of the Psalms of David (*Dāwūd*). The word echoes the Hebrew *Zamīr* ("song") and *Mizmōr* ("melody"), both of which are used to designate the Psalms of David. The *Zabūr* is described in the Koran as having been given to David by God: "and to David We gave the Psalms (*Zabūr*)" (4:163). This means that the Psalms are accepted in Islam as being revealed scripture, along with the Pentateuch and the Gospels. *See* BIBLE.

Zāhid (from *zahida*, "to abstain", and cognate with zuhd, "abstinence"). An ascetic. *See* ZUHD.

Ẓāhir (lit. "outward"). *Aẓ-Ẓāhir* is a Divine Name ("The Outward"), which is complementary to *al-Bāṭin* ("The Inward"). To these are joined in the Koran the Divine Names *al-Awwal* ("The First") and *al-Ākhir* ("The Last"). "He is the First and the Last, the Outward and the Inward, and He is All-knowing of all things" (57:3).

The words *ẓāhir* and *bāṭin* are also used to mean "exoteric" and "esoteric". The theologians and legal scholars representing an exoteric point of view are sometimes termed the *'ulamā' aẓ-ẓāhir* (the "savants of the exterior") by the mystics who are called the *'ulamā' al-bāṭin*. The Koran makes the statement quoted above in the context of verses relating to manifested creation; the "First and the Last" refer to time and the "Outward and the Inward" to space; quite clearly any scholarly perspective that attempts to exclude the outward in favor of the inward, or vice versa, is partial. The true Sufis have never failed to make this point clear and to aim at a realisation of the Totality.

Ẓāhirī. A school of law which never gained a significant acceptance and is now extinct. It was begun by disciples of Dāwūd ibn Khalaf al-Iṣfahānī, called *aẓ-Ẓāhirī* ("the literalist"; *204-241*/819-855 or *297*/910).

He had been himself a disciple of ash-Shāfi'ī but he rejected completely the doctrine of analogy (*qiyās*), and the opinions of any but the closest of the Companions, and insisted upon a strictly literal interpretation of the Koran and Sunnah. The objection to analogy went so far as even to forbid *searching* for the reasons for a religious law.

Ibn Ḥazm in Spain was a Ẓāhirī, as were a number of Sufis including Ibn 'Arabī. This surprising fact leads one to conclude that the literalism of the Ẓāhirīs was not simply a desire for simple solutions. Their literalism did not stop at the letter, but rather took it as a point of departure, as an intensification of the apprehension of the Divine Reality. It is Dāwūd ibn Khalaf who reports the Ḥadīth: "he who loves with unrequited love and remains chaste, dies a martyr." This ambiance of heroic lyricism seems an aspect of the absoluteness of the Ẓāhirī stand. It breathes the same kind of certainty which comes from the Koran itself for, in the words of the Ẓāhirīs: "We describe God as He describes Himself."

Zā'ir (lit. "visitor"). A name for a person visiting the tomb of the Prophet. Such visits are called *ziyārah*; the term is transposed for visits in search of blessing made to Saint's tombs. In some countries the visiting of Saint's tombs is a very important part of religious life, despite the fact that there are Ḥadīth which discourage this.

Zakāh (Taken to mean "purification" from the verb *zakā* which signifies "to thrive", "to be wholesome", "to be pure"). The giving up of a portion of the wealth one may possess, in excess of what is needed for sustenance, to "purify" or legitimize what one retains. *Zakāh* is one of the Five Pillars and is in effect a tax on one's possessions. It may be paid directly to the poor as alms, or to travelers, or to the state. *Zakāh* may be used for the upkeep of the poor, for those who own less than that prescribed for the paying of *zakāh* and who have no earning capacity; for the destitute; Muslims in debt through pressing circumstances; travelers in need; those serving the cause of Islam, and fighting in the way of God (*al-muqātilūn fī sabīl Allāh*); for slaves to buy themselves out of bondage; for benevolent works. Those who collect tax on behalf of the state for disbursement are also allowed to take the needs of their livelihood from it.

The amount due varies according to different kinds of properties. A contribution in kind, whose minimum schedule is called a *nisbah*, is specified on numbers of livestock according to species but only on those which are freely pastured and not used for the immediate needs of the household or as work animals. On land it is the *'ushr*, or tenth, of its produce, although further refinements exist in regard to different grains, irrigated and non-irrigated lands, etc. On gold and silver, that is, liquid assets, to which are also assimilated merchandise, financial instruments, stocks and bonds, beyond an untaxed franchise of "200 dinars", the *nisbah* is 2.5% of that value which has been held for one year. On the other hand, alms need not be limited to the legal minimums; what is paid over the legal minimum is *sadaqah*; while benevolent, it is also recommended as a pious and expiatory act.

The classical rates of *zakāh* assumed that wealth was held in the form of cattle and land rather than financial instruments or paper. The rates of *zakāh* on cattle and land production are much higher than those on monetary possessions. Therefore, some modern Muslim scholars are studying ways on how rates of *zakāh* may be equitably adjusted to contemporary modes of wealth, so that the religious tax falls between 5-10% of income in excess of essential need.

The person liable for *zakāh* must be Muslim and not indebted to the value of the worth upon which the tax is due. Tithe is not due upon personal dwellings. It is also not assessed on basic necessities, personal possessions, furniture, tools and instruments, riding and draft animals etc.

The *zakāh al-fiṭr*, more commonly known as *fitrah*, is considered by most to be non-obligatory alms, but almost always paid by the pious, roughly equivalent to a quart of grain per person in a household, paid directly to the needy at the end of Ramaḍān. *See* FIVE PILLARS; KHARĀJ; SADAQAH; 'USHR.

Zakariyyā. The father of Yaḥyā (John the Baptist). In the Koran he was a guardian of the Blessed Virgin while she kept vigil in a *miḥrāb* (prayer niche), which is symbolically assimilated to the Holy of Holies. When Zakariyyā came to see her he found that she received sustenance directly from God and required no food (3:37).

Zakariyyā in his old age had petitioned God for a son and was granted Yaḥyā (3:38). As a sign of God's favor Zakariyyā was struck dumb for three days.

Zakāt, *see* ZAKĀH

Zamakhsharī, Abū-l-Qāsim Maḥmūd ibn 'Umar (*467-538*/1075-1144). A Persian who was a great authority on the Arabic language. He wrote studies of grammar and literature (*Asās al-Balāghah*, "Foundations of Rhetoric"), but is best known for his commentary on the Koran, *al-Kashshāf 'an Ḥaqā'iq at-Tanzīl* ("The Unveiler of the Truths of Revelation"). While this book maintains the Mu'tazilite, or "rationalist", point of view, and affirms the createdness of the Koran, it was much studied because it extols the literary beauty of the text.

Zamzam. The name of the well near the Ka'bah. It is located 20m/60ft southeast of the Black Stone corner of the Ka'bah, near the Station of Abraham (*Maqām Ibrāhīm*), within the Grand Mosque of Mecca. The spring of Zamzam appeared when Hagar and her son Ismā'īl (Ishmael), abandoned in the desert, had exhausted the water in the goatskin given them by Abraham. Then Hagar cast herself to and fro in desperation, but God heard Ismā'īl (Ismā'īl/Ishmael; the name means "God hears") and the water gushed forth, making the sound *zam, zam*.

The site of the well was later forgotten for a time, for it had been filled up with stones and treasure trove by the Jurhumites who inhabited Mecca before the Quraysh. Its site was rediscovered by the uncle of the Prophet, 'Abd al-Muṭṭalib.

To drink the water of Zamzam is a rite of both the lesser and the greater pilgrimages. Today the well is not open at the surface; instead the water is led off to underground galleries reached by a flight of steps where numerous faucets supply the water to scores of people a time.

The well itself is 31m/100ft deep and is lined by masonry stones to approximately a third of its depth. The circumference of the opening is approximately 1.80m/5ft. Today the water is passed under ultraviolet lights for bacterial control. The water supply is extremely copious, enough for thousands of people daily. The well is fed by several springs, the largest of which enters the well at a third of the distance from the surface. Contrary to descriptions once current in the West, the taste of Zamzam is agreeable and refreshing, and it can be drunk in vast quantities.

The water is carried by pilgrims back to all parts of the Islamic world where it is drunk as water filled with blessing and given to the sick. The well of Zamzam is mentioned in Psalm 84: "How amiable are thy tabernacles, O Lord of hosts! Blessed are they that dwell in Thy house... who passing through the valley of Baca [Bakkah is the ancient name of Mecca] make it a well..." *See* MECCA; KA'BAH.

Zananah. The name of the women's quarters in an Indian Muslim household, equivalent to the Turkish *haramlik.*

Zands. A short-lived (*1163-1209*/1750-1794) series of monarchs in Persia who seized power during the lengthy period of instability after the reign of Nādir Shāh (*see* AFSHĀRIDS). The most able of the Zands was Muḥammad Karīm who ruled as the representative (*wakil*) of a nominal Ṣafavid Shah, Ismā'īl III. The Zands were supplanted by the Qājārs but they provided a lull in the internecine wars and a period of comparative peace and piety.

Zanj. The name given by the Arabs to the black tribes inhabiting the coastal regions of East Africa (whence "Zanzibar"), which were a source of slaves for the Muslim Empire. In the decade around *257*/870 a group of 'Irāqi farm slaves rose in rebellion ("the revolt of the Zanj") against the 'Abbāsids, and maintained control over much of the Shaṭṭ al-'Arab. They sacked Baṣrah before they were finally put down by the Caliph's troops. The revolt eventually involved whites, Beduins and peasants. The leader called himself 'Alī ibn Muḥammad and used the title of Mahdī. He may have been Persian. Massignon guessed that the revolt had been fomented by Manicheans and it seems to have been the prelude to the Qarmaṭī revolution. However, Ḥamdān Qarmaṭ met with the Zanj leader to propose cooperation and apparently decided there was no common ground. The Zanj adopted Kharijite slogans (Koran 9:111 was inscribed on their flag) and practices, praising the first two Caliphs and ignoring 'Uthmān and 'Alī. But the leader also claimed descent from 'Alī (disputed by many), so the practice was not consistent. Although it was a slave revolt and a class war, the Zanj themselves acquired slaves.

Zayd ibn al-Ḥārith (d. *8*/630). A slave given to the Prophet by Khadījah, the Prophet's first wife; when Zayd's father found him and tried to free him, Zayd refused to leave the Prophet, who himself freed him and made him an adopted son.

The Prophet once entered the house of Zayd and, looking upon his wife Zaynab, was enchanted by her beauty; there was some embarrassment, after which Zayd divorced Zaynab and the Prophet married her. A revelation later treated of the legality of marrying the wife of an adopted son (33:37). Some modern Muslims are shocked by the idea of the Prophet being attracted to Zaynab, and interpret the marriage as having been motivated purely by the desire to create a legal precedent. Zayd was a noted warrior and died in battle.

Zaydīs (Ar. *Zaydiyyah*). A branch of Shī'ism, also called "Fivers", found in the Yemen. Upon the death in *95*/713 of the fourth Shī'ite Imām 'Alī Zayn al-'Ābidīn, the Zaydīs diverged from the other Shī'ites (who went on to become the Twelve-Imām majority) in that they chose to follow Zayd (d. *122*/740) as Imām, rather than his brother Muḥammad al-Baqīr. They rallied to Zayd's more vigorous resistance to the Umayyads.

Today the Zaydīs are the most moderate of all Shī'ite groups and the closest to the Sunnīs, although they have their own school of law (*madhhab*). Their Shī'ism is a political preference for the rule and authority of 'Alī and his descendants, and it has little or none of the ascription of supernatural powers, supernal knowledge and the function of intermediary between man and God that is found among the Twelve-Imām Shī'ites. The affinity of the Yemen with Shī'ism arises because it was periodically ruled by Persia before Islamic times and was historically a place of refuge for political and religious refugees from the Sāssānīds who brought to it the same religious concepts that later gave rise to Shī'ism in Islam. Notably various splinter groups of the Ismā'īlīs continue to exist in the Yemen. A Zaydī state also existed near the Caspian Sea among the Daylamites from *250*/864, with interruptions, until *520*/1126.

From the beginning of the *4th*/10th century the Zaydīs have been established in the Yemen, first at Sa'ādah and later at Sanā'a' and today comprise about 40% of the population of the Yemen Arab Republic. The rest of the Yemenis are Sunnīs of the Shāfi'ī School of Law. In the Zaydī theory of the Imāmate any descendant of 'Alī can be Imām; there can be more than one, or indeed, none at all. The claim is established by a demonstrated capacity for rule — that is, by taking power — and confirmed by learning. But there are no overtones of supernatural knowledge, miraculous powers, and prerogatives such as those which hedge the concept of the Imāmate among the Twelvers. The Zaydīs accept the Caliphates of Abū Bakr and 'Umar, and are split over 'Uthmān, some accepting his Caliphate as being legitimate only for the first years. The Zaydīs do not admit *mut'ah* (temporary marriages), as do the Twelve-Imām Shī'ites. They were historically much influenced by the Mu'tazilites, or rationalists.

The Zaydī kingdom of the Rassī dynasty was founded by Yaḥyā ibn Ḥusayn ar-Rassī. The dynasty ruled in Sanā'a', with many wars and interruptions, from the *4th*/10th century until 1962, when it was overthrown by Colonel 'Abd Allāh as-Sallāl. Internal fighting between Republicans and Royalists continued until 1972, but the Imām had gone into exile in London before that and has since died.

Zaynab bint 'Alī. A daughter of 'Alī and Fāṭimah. Her tomb is in Damascus and is a place of Shī'ite pilgrimage.

Zaynab bint Jaḥsh. A wife of the Prophet. She had been the wife of his adopted son Zayd. Zayd divorced her so that the Prophet could marry her. *See* WIVES of the PROPHET.

Zaynab bint Khuzaymah. A wife of the Prophet and a widow of 'Ubayd, a Muslim slain at Badr. She died not long after her marriage to the Prophet. For her kind nature she was called the "mother of the poor", *Umm al-masākīn. See* WIVES of the PROPHET.

Zaynab bint Muḥammad. A daughter of the Prophet and Khadījah. Her husband Abū-l-'Āṣ was an unbeliever; she left him to join her father in Medinah. Abū-l-'Āṣ was taken prisoner by the Muslims at the Battle of Badr and ransomed by Zaynab. He returned to Mecca and was later taken prisoner again and freed by Zaynab a second time before he finally entered Islam.

Zāwiyah (lit. "a corner"). In North Africa the word means an oratory or small mosque, a place of religious retreat, or in particular, a meeting place of Sufis for prayer and the invocation of the Name of God (*dhikr*). A *zāwiyah* may be small or large, even a mausoleum of a Saint associated with a religious order. It is the equivalent of what is called a *khānaqah* in the East, or a *tekke* or *durgah* in Turkey. It can also be that part of a home that is set aside for prayer.

Zikr, *see* DHIKR.

"Zikrism". A modern Soviet name for the Qadiriyyah Sufi ṭarīqah. The term is inexact since all Sufi orders practice some form of invocation or dhikr ("zikr"). *See* DHIKR.

Zīna'. Fornication or sexual relations which are illicit in Islamic law, a sin and socially considered a crime, for which the Koran mentions different degrees of punishment, from mild to severe. Stoning, however, is not one of them; this existed among the Jews (*see* Deuteronomy 22:21-24). Zealous stories to the contrary do exist which intend to show that stoning was a punishment for zīna' in early Islam, but they carry the marks of apocrypha.

Conviction for zīna' in a court of law requires four eye witnesses (thus apocryphal stories typically have the guilty spontaneously confessing). The witnesses can themselves be liable for equal punishment for false accusation, and since even confessions need to be made four separate times and can be retracted, it is in practice something which Islamic law has put beyond the scope of society's punishment. On the folk level of mob justice, however, stoning has taken place in recent times and in Arab societies it is not uncommon for men to murder a female of their family, with relative impunity, who is considered to have "shamed" the family.

Islam's approach to the problem of applying some of its harsher laws is analogous to the situation prevailing in Judaism which, in the case of similar laws, has imposed so many conditions to their being carried out, that extreme sentences are never imposed for moral crimes. In the past Islamic courts have been so reluctant to impose sanctions in such cases that even a child out of wedlock need not be taken to be a proof. For this there came into existence the stratagem of the "Sleeping Foetus". (As one Muslim Judge in the Gulf recently said "What would we have to have done with the Virgin Mary?") *See* SLEEPING FOETUS.

Zindīq (from Persian *zand*, "free interpretation" meaning "heresy" or, which Browne thought more probable, a Persian form of the Aramaic *Saddiqai*, "faithful" a higher grade of Manichean whence also the Arabic *Ṣiddiq*, and among Kabbalists, *Tsadik*). A freethinker, atheist, or heretic. Originally *zindīq* meant dualist; thus one could speak of a "Christian zindīq". In the West the term was sometimes translated as "materialist" because dualists make matter equivalent to God, or rather, two gods. If matter is considered to exist independently of a higher principle then limitation is also an absolute, and an anti-god which means "a god of evil", is an inevitable consequence. This can be seen in physics which, when it concludes that matter (rather than a principle of God is reality), also concludes that creation begins with matter and antimatter. If matter is "divine" or reality itself, then so is the individual, hence dualist and freethinker are associated concepts.

Zindīq was a term used in Persia in the reign of Bahram I (Varahran 273-276) when the Sāssānīds tried to expel from their empire all "Ahrimanic" beliefs and practices, notably the Manicheans. It is in this sense that the term zindīq was also used by the Muslims. Manicheans were present in great numbers among the clerks employed by the 'Abbāsids in 'Irāq and Persia, among them Ibn al-Muqaffā', the author of *Kalīlah wa Dimnah.*

For a time Manicheism threatened to become the dominant religion of the educated classes, but from *162*/779 to *169*/786 there was a wave of persecution of Manicheans in the 'Abbāsid Empire. The Caliph al-Mahdī had Manicheans crucified in Aleppo, and in the last two years of his reign a systematic attack was begun which sought to extirpate them. The Manicheans were sought out, brought before an officer called the *'Arīf* ("expert"), and punished, often by crucifixion. A history of the time says:

> 'Tolerance is laudable,' the Spiller [the Caliph Abū-l-'Abbās] had once said, 'except in matters dangerous to religious belief, or to the Sovereign's dignity.'
>
> Mahdī [d. *169*/785] persecuted Freethinkers, and executed them in large numbers. He was the first Caliph to order the composition of polemical works in refutation of Freethinkers and other heretics; and for years he tried to exterminate them absolutely, hunting them down throughout all provinces and putting accused persons to death on mere suspicion.
>
> "Hast thou any doubt at all in thy mind," runs a catechism of these times, "that the Koran was brought down to the Prophet of God by the faithful spirit Gabriel; that in that Book God has declared what is lawful and what is unlawful, and ordained His rules, and established His observances; and has expounded the history of what has been and what is to be to the end of time?"
>
> "I have no doubt," the catechumen shall reply.
>
> "Hast thou any doubt at all in thy mind that..."
>
> "I have no doubt."

This hunt after Manicheans continued under al-Hādī, who died suddenly, and suspiciously, and then declined under Hārūn ar-Rashīd (except for his suppression of
the Barmakids), and into the Caliphate of al-Ma'mu^n (d. *218*/833), but by this time most Manicheans had gone underground, disguising themselves as Muslims, and many were to metamorphose into the Seveners. Indeed, in the time of al-Ma'mun *zindiqs* had an easy time: Browne says that "according to von Kremer it was fashionable to pose as a heretic, and we find a poet remonstrating in the following lines with one of these sheep dressed in wolf's clothing: 'O Ibn Ziyād, father of Ja'far! Thou professest outwardly another creed than that which thou hidest in they heart. Outwardly, according to thy words, thou art a *Zindiq*, But inwardly thou art a respectable Muslim. Thou art no *Zindiq*, but thou desirest to be regarded in the fashion!'" This period was a rare exception, however. The last great attack on *zindiqs* came in the time of al-Muqtadir (908-932) when as many as ten thousand were sentenced to death. The most celebrated among them, and the one whose execution triggered the others, was al-Ḥallāj. This last persecution was instigated by Shī'ites who were set about exterminating their Gnostic rivals (which, when Shī'ism became the state religion in Iran, was also carried out against many Sufi groups). In his *Fihrist*, an-Nadīm (d. *385*/995) gives several lists of theologians and writers whom he says were really Dualists in disguise. Others were being uncovered at the time. Manicheism is now called *al-Manawiyyah* in Arabic. (*See* SEVENERS.)

After the early period, with some notable exceptions, the practice in Islam in regard to atheism or various forms of heresy, had been more and more one of tolerance as long as it is a private matter. However, heresy and atheism expressed in public may well be considered a scandal and a menace to society; in some societies they are punishable, at least to the extent that the perpetrator is silenced. In particular, blasphemy against God and insulting the Prophet are major crimes. There is a document called the "Letter of the Three Imposters" which was the most scandalous free-thinking treatise of its time which was attributed to 'Ubayd Allāh the Fāṭimid and which found its way into Europe. *See* ANTINOMIANISM; ARCHEGOS; HIGHEST INITIATION, BOOK of the; MADA'IN; MANICHEISM; THREE IMPOSTERS.

Ziryāb (*173-243*/789-857). A famous singer and musician in Baghdad, a pupil of Ibrāhīm al-Mawṣilī, or his son Isḥāq, Ziryāb left 'Irāq and came to Cordova where he was well received by the Umayyad ruler 'Abd ar-Raḥmān II (d. *237*/852). Ziryāb's real name was Abū-l-Ḥasan 'Alī ibn Nāfī and it is said he was a Kurd from Mosul. He brought to Spain a new musical form from Baghdad of which he was the master. (But the musical tradition from which it sprang could well have been brought to Iran by Gypsies [az-Zutt] in the 5th century.) He also improved the instrument *al-'ūd* ("lute") by adding a fifth string. The resulting new style flourished in Spain and became classical "Andalusian" music which is still played today, particularly by the Arab orchestras of Morocco. Ziryāb became the arbiter of fashion at Cordova and introduced other cultural refinements of the East of his day, including fine cuisine, another tradition which has survived in Morocco.

Ziyārah (lit. "visit"). A visit to the tomb of the Prophet and to the holy places of Medinah in general. Traditions have grown up about the order in which various stations in the Prophet's Mosque (*al-Masjid ash-sharīf*) are to be visited, and what recitations should be made in each place. The program of visits also includes other mosques in Medinah, the battlefield of Uhud, and the al-Baqī' cemetery.

The word is also used for the visits to the tombs of Saints or Shī'ite Imāms. The practice is in fact forbidden in Islam by Ḥadīth, but the *ijmā'* ("consensus") of the Islamic community has made it otherwise. The interdiction is upheld by the Wahhābīs, who have nevertheless been obliged to tolerate the visiting of the tomb of the Prophet.

It was, and still is, a common Sufi practice to visit the tombs of Saints as places appropriate for meditation and seeking God's grace. There are innumerable such pilgrimage Saint's tombs from Morocco to Indonesia, and many renowned as great gathering places of Sufis, particularly at times of festive commemoration. Some are renowned in different ways; the Shaykh al-Būzīdī advised the seeker who could not find a true spiritual master to go and pray at the tomb of Abū Madyān in Algeria.

The visiting of tombs of Shī'ite Imāms and their relatives is an important religious activity for Twelve-Iman Shī'ites. Such places include Medinah, Mashhad, Kerbala, Najaf, Kāzimayn, and Qumm. Shī'ite manuals of pious visitations are called *ziyarat-nama*. *See* MOSQUE of the PROPHET.

Zoroastrianism. A renewal of the original Indo-European tradition as transmitted to the Iranian peoples. The Koran calls the Zoroastrians *Mājūs*, (but in usage afterwards the term became very non-specific and could refer to any Iranian religion). Muslim authorities, going back to the Caliph 'Umar, accept Zoroastrians as a "People of the Scripture", with a revealed religion, and thus qualified for the protection of the Islamic state. Known in Iran as *Zardushtis*, Zoroastrians had the status of *dhimmis*, who could not be compelled to enter Islam. *See* AHL al-KITĀB.

Zoroastrianism is extremely ancient; its Prophet, Zoroaster lived some time between 1400 and 1200 BC or even earlier, and was the first to proclaim that salvation is possible for all, the humble of mankind as well as the heroes of legend. He composed hymns called *Gāthās* to glorify the Creator, to which were later added the writings known as *Avesta*. Among his teachings are doctrines of a resurrection after death as the assembly of the bones and their reunion with a heavenly body, the existence of the soul (*urvan*), the existence of heaven and hell, (and an intermediate state, or limbo between the two), the end of time and the world (*frasho-kereti* "the perfection of time or *frashegird*") after a struggle between the forces of good and evil (sometimes defined as that between the Saoshyant, the world saviour, and Azhi Dahhaka, a kind of demon, not destroyed by an early mythic hero and chained inside in Mount Demavend), and a universal Last Judgement. These concepts, of course, reappear in Christianity and Islam. Zoroastrian metaphysics provides the prototype for the doctrine of the Logos (the *Amesha Spenta*) and that of the Angels. Michael and Satan in particular, are considered by many scholars of religion as the transformed assimilation into Semitic religions of the figures of Ahura Mazda (later called Ohrmazd) and Angra Maiynu (later called Ahriman). Thus, many of the teachings of Zoroaster are found in post-exile Judaism.

The conquest of Babylon by Cyrus in 539 BC and thereafter Egypt by his son Cambyses in 529 BC brought Zoroastrian doctrines to all the classical world. The Indo-European peoples have demonstrated an intellectual propensity to think metaphorically, to idealize, to take the concrete and turn it into the abstract. The Semitic peoples have a marked propensity to concretize. When these two dynamics of consciousness came in contact with each other during the Iranian expansion into the Semitic world, being diametrically opposed to each other, a reaction took place which could be termed alchemical, a reaction which is still going on to this day. Semitic religious elements combined with Zoroastrian ones to produce new religions. Notably numerous Gnosticisms, and then Christianity and Islam appeared on the Semitic side of the equation. These appeared not only through Judaism, but through the action of Zoroastrianism directly upon the Abrahamic monotheism of the Arabs, and on other religious traditions of Mesopotamia. Zoroastrianism also felt the effect of Semitic consciousness, and this produced Mithraism (evidently strongly influenced by Hellenism as well), but especially Zurvanism, and Manicheism on the Iranian side of the equation. In religious terms, the collision of worlds formed the spiritual, intellectual, and psychological ambience for the revelation of Christianity and Islam.

Zoroaster taught the coming of a world saviour (*Saoshyant*), and Zoroastrian myth recounts, moreover, that the seed of Zoroaster was preserved in a lake and that a virgin bathing in that lake would conceive the saviour. The story of the Magi, or Zoroastrian priests, bringing gifts and following a star (perhaps the "astra" of Zoroaster, as it was once interpreted) is the mythic element used to confirm to the intended audience, which at the time of the New Testament was familiar with Zoroastrian prophecies, that here indeed, was the prophesied Saoshyant or world saviour. (Probably also influencing the Magi story was the journey of a Zoroastrian King Tiridates of Armenia, a vassal, who came to Rome to swear fealty to Nero). In Christianity, besides the Zoroastrian elements which are its bedrock, the Canaanite myth of Tammuz, the vegetation god who dies and returns to life, obviously provides the other critical element, along with the soteriology of the Osiris and Dionysian cults, Pythagorianism, and the crucible of the Essenes.

It is worthy to note that the Arabic word for Paradise, *firdaws*, is originally from Persian *pardes* through the Greek, revealing the origin of the concept. Besides the great metaphysical and eschatological context that Zoroastrianism contributes to Islam, one can point to the five daily prayers, also found among the Zoroastrians, the use of water for sacralisation before prayer and as a great purification (ablutions and *barashnom*), and an emphasis on ritual purity. (In Zoroastrianism water has the power to return the priest to the state of unfallen man for the performance of rituals; this becomes ritual ablution among the Essenes and the Mandaeans, Baptism for the Christians, and ritual ablution in Islam.)

The importance of intention in Islam, in Arabic *niyyah*, would seem to derive from the Zoroastrian "good thought". Besides Iranian influences upon the Arabs for many centuries before Islam, afterwards there followed many centuries where innumerable Muslim theologians of Persian origin brought their cultural background into the new religion. Many other originally Zoroastrian details have been incorporated into Muslim doctrine and practice such as the idea, familiar to most Muslims, of the soul crossing the "bridge" after death (this is the Zoroastrian *chinvat*; no reference to a bridge exists in the Koran), and the widespread injunction among Muslims, attributed to Ḥadīth, of not breathing into fire as, for example, in not blowing out a candle with the breath. (Zoroastrians regard fire as sacred, and the maintenance of perpetual flames, some today which have existed without interruption for two thousand years, form a central element of ritual worship.) The Muslim belief that the dead can hear for three days probably originates with the Zoroastrian idea that the dead soul lingers for three days before departing for the other world. (Whence also the three days interval between Good Friday and the Sunday of resurrection.) The dialogue between God and Satan as found in the Koran (and also in Goethe's *Faust*), is prefigured by a similar exchange between Ahura Mazda and Ahriman in Yasna 30/40 (*Zand Akasih*) and in the *Bundahishn*. The assembly of the bones, found in

Ezekiel, and in the Koran as part of the resurrection of dead, is in the Zoroastrian *Zodsperad.* In Zoroastrianism there is a primordial tree in the first world whose leaves contained the cure for all the diseases that entered the world after it was attacked by Ahriman. There is a widely repeated saying in Islam, usually presented as a Ḥadīth, that "for every illness there is a cure."

Despite appearance, Zoroastrianism is fundamentally non-dualist in that the principle of evil, Angra Mainyu, while "uncreated" (but rather a "byproduct" of creation), is not symmetrical with the Creator and the principle of good, Ahura Mazda. Angra Maiynu cannot attack Ahura Mazda Himself (unlike Manicheism where the principle of evil attacks the principle of good). Angra Maiynu attacks instead the creation of Ahura Mazda after a period of thousands of years. Nor can Angra Maiynu even corrupt *all* of the creation of Ahura Mazda. He can only corrupt the lowest part of the creation, the *getik*, or material plane which is vulnerable to the principle of evil, while the creation in itself is thoroughly good. (In Manicheism the physical world itself is a mixture of the two principles.) Nor can Angra Maiynu corrupt the world forever; there comes a time when it is restored to its original state. Indeed, in virtue of this non-dualism Zoroastrianism calls itself *behdin*, "the Good Religion".

Zoroastrian Cosmic history is divided into three "times". The first is that of primordial integrity (*bundahishn*), before manifestation is corrupted by the principle of evil. In the first world there is no death or disease, the seas are not salt, and fire has no smoke. The middle "time" is the mixture of good and evil, (*gumeshisn*) on the lower material planes of creation. Angra Maiynu swoops upon the world, rather the way he does in *Paradise Lost*, bringing death and disease, and plunges into the oceans making them salty. This middle time is familiar to us all. But then after the end of the world, after the eschatological separation, there is a third new world (*wizarishn*) which is again good, like the first.

The fall of man idea derives from this Zoroastrian idea of the corruption of the original perfect world. The story in Genesis of the garden of Eden is of Iranian origin. But the descent of the heavenly Jerusalem in the New Testament, or restoration of a perfect world in the *Apocatastatis*, is the restoration which Zoroastrianism called the third time. Because Zoroastrianism was the first religion to speak of the end of the world, apocalyptic ideas appeared in the Biblical world after the conquest of Babylon by Cyrus. They were met with incredulity {"we are only destroyed by time") and so they were at first transmitted as "secret" doctrines to the initiated. The first mysticism or esoterism are these Zoroastrian apocalyptic doctrines which were openly expounded within Zoroastrianism, but which became mysterious secrets when they reached new peoples. Thus when the Book of Revelation speaks of the chaining of Satan for a thousand years, Persian folklore tells that he is Azhi Dahakka chained inside Mount Demavend near Teheran, put there by the holy blacksmith Kavi, founder of the legendary dynasty, the Kavianeh, whose legendary leather apron studded with precious stones, the Drafshi Kavianeh, pops up in history and was used by the Persians as a battle flag, captured by the Arabs at the Battle of Qadisiyah. But at the end of time the chains which hold Azhi Dahhaka also break loose, along with chaos. (The "bottomless pit" of Revelations was also known among the pre-Islamic Arabs, and is probably the mysterious term *hawiyah* of Koran 101:9.)

Zoroastrianism, therefore, accords with Islam in that Satan is given the latitude to corrupt creation, but not the heavens. Satan himself disappears into "non-existence" when the world disappears, or even when the consciousness capable of conceiving nothingness refuses to fall into the metaphysical error of attributing a substance to nothingness, for Satan's "existence", or power to subvert the believer, depends upon the believer's free-will and responsibility.

However, after the late 5th century BC, that is, after the Iranians swept the Middle East, there appeared the consequences within Zoroastrianism of the effect of contact with the diametrically opposing world view of the Semitic peoples. This reaction emerged as a powerful heresy among the Parthians known as Zurvanism. In Zurvanism, Ahura Mazda as Ohrmazd and Ahriman as Angra Mainyu became the "twin sons" of a higher principle called Zurvan ("Time"), who thus included both within himself. In this way the development of monotheism which begins with Zoroastrianism took a detour. The principles of good and evil were brought into a symmetry which is dualist where original (and subsequent) Zoroastrianism was not. Zurvanism became the dominant state doctrine under the Sāssānīds who ruled Persia at the time of the revelation of Islam. As Zurvanism became dominant it was accompanied by the emergence of other radically dualistic doctrines in Persia. Interestingly, along with Zurvanism (which was to disappear from Zoroastrianism proper with the Islamic conquest) the Sāssānīds also raised to prominence a Persian form of the Babylonian goddess Ishtar, who as Anahid (or Anahita), became the patron of the dynasty. But this detour which Monotheism took in Zurvanism also led to Manicheism, in which Zurvan, Ohrmazd and Ahriman, became simply two abstract principles, virtually devoid of personality, defined only by their opposition to each other; and this abstraction of two principles mathematically opposed to each other triggered the rectification brought by Islam which presented mankind with a dramatically more transcendent understanding of Reality in a single God beyond personality: Allāh.

For the Arabs, the term *Mājūs* covered all the Iranian religions, dualist and non-dualist according to case. It is perhaps for this reason that the Koran is ambiguous in its inclusion of the *Mājūs* among the "People of the Book", rather than categorical, as it is in regards to Christians and Jews. The inclusion of the Zoroastrians was decided as a matter of interpretation; in its ambiguity the Koran left the matter open to be determined at the proper time when direct experience shed the necessary light for adequate discernment, and when the Muslims were in a position to discriminate between the different currents that actually made up the Iranian religions.

There are today some 30,000 Zoroastrians left in Iran, mostly in Teheran and Yazd, where they have a distinguished reputation for honesty and uprightness, and a population of some 130,000 in India, in Bombay and the Gujerat, where they are known as Parsees.

The Zoroastrians worship light, and eternal fires (origin of our "eternal flames") are kept burning by priests who performed ceremonies with them five times a day. Some fires which still exist today have been kept going for thousands of years without interruption. The three most important of these fire altars (*ādur*) were the *ādur-farnbāgh*, the protective fire of the priests, in the district of Kabul, the *ādur-gushnāsp*, the royal fire between Urmia and Hamadhān, and *ādur-burzenmihr*, the fire of the farmers in the Rēvand mountains, northeast of Nishāpūr.

Important figures of the Zoroastrian pantheon, some of which also are the names of months, are *fravardīn* (the *fravashi*, guardian angels); *urdvahisht*, the archangel *Asha*, "upright law"; *khvardād*, "integrity" one of the *Amesha Spenta* or "immortal holy ones"; *tīr* (*Tishtrya*, Sirius, the dog-star); *amurdād* ("immortality", another of the *Amesha Spenta*); shahrēvar (the archangel of the "kingdom"); *mihr* (Mithra); ābān (the "waters"); represented by the goddess *Anāhita*, of whom the Sāssānid kings were hereditary priests; *ādur* (fire); *dadhv* (the Creator, Ahura Mazda); *vahman* ("good thought") an *Amesha Spenta*; and *spandarmad* ("holy submission",) a protective archangel symbolizing the earth.

The Greeks had much contact with the Persians. Heraclitus' doctrines were doubtless influenced by them, and in Plato's *Symposium* the discussion of love being spheres looking for their lost halves is Zoroastrian in origin. One of Plato's students was a Persian. It is recorded that while Plato was dying, a "Chaldean" (a Zoroastrian priest who was Plato's house guest) played a flute with soothing mystical melodies to calm his fever and a Thracian sang magical songs. *See* AHL al-KITĀB.

Zubayr ibn al-'Awwām (d. *36*/656). A famous Companion, one of the "Ten Well-Betided Ones" who were assured of paradise by the Prophet, and the fifth convert to Islam, having adopted Islam while still a child. He was a grandson of *'Abd al-Muṭṭalib* on his mother's side and so a cousin to the Prophet, who called him al-ḥawārī (the "disciple") because of his military and personal services to him. The word is used by the Koran for the disciples of Jesus. He was married to Asmān, a daughter of Abū Bakr.

Zubayr was given dispensation to wear silk clothes because of illness (garments made *wholly* of silk are forbidden to men, but not garments partly of silk, that is, with stripes of alternating materials).

During the Caliphate of 'Alī, Zubayr joined the rebellion of Ṭalḥāḥ and 'Ā'ishah and was killed in the Battle of the Camel fighting against 'Alī's army. One of his sons, 'Abd Allāh ibn Zubayr, revolted against the Umayyads, declared himself Caliph, and seized control of Mecca for a time before being finally defeated.

Zubaydah bint Ja'far ibn al-Manṣūr. Granddaughter of the Caliph Manṣūr, the favorite wife of Hārūn ar-Rashīd, and mother of the Caliph Amīn. She built a road for the use of pilgrims from Baghdad to

Mecca. Cisterns to provide water supply still stand along the way which is called the *Darb Zubaydah* ("Zubaydah's Road"). She was known for her generosity, keeping a lavish court, and for the building of mosques.

Zuhd (lit. "asceticism"). The renunciation of ease and comfort in the name of religious discipline in order to detach the soul from the world. An ascetic is called a *zāhid.* This is, above all, a mystical attitude which finds its example in the Prophet himself, who practiced frequent fasts and long hours of application in prayer in the middle of the night. But it is not an indispensable aspect of mysticism, at least insofar as hardship is concerned. The widespread school of Imām ash-Shādhilī, for example, prescribed a detachment which is inward rather than outward, without of course admitting indulgence, or love of creature comfort, but also without pursuing mortification for itself.

Ibn al-'Arīf said:

> Asceticism is for the common run of people, since it consists in making the concupiscent appetite abstain from pleasures, in renouncing the temptation to return again to that from which one is separated, in dropping the search for what one has lost, in depriving oneself of superfluous desires, in thwarting the goad of the passions, in neglecting all which does not concern the soul. But this is an imperfection as regards the path of the elect, for it presupposes an importance attached to the things of this world, an abstention from their use, an outward mortification in depriving oneself of things here, while inwardly an attachment is felt for them
>
> To make an issue of the world amounts to turning thyself toward thyself: it is to pass thy time struggling with thyself; it is to take account of thy feelings and to remain with thyself against thy concupiscence...
>
> In all truth, asceticism is the ardent aspiration of the heart towards Him alone; it is to place in Him the aspiration and desires of the soul; to be preoccupied uniquely with Him, without any preoccupation, in order that He (to Whom be praise!) may remove from thee the mass of these causes.

Or, as al-Ḥujwīrī said: "The poor man is not he whose hand is empty of provisions, but he whose nature is empty of desires."

Zurkhāneh, *see* FUTUWWAH.

Wa'Llāhu a'lam

And God knows best.

There is an obviously apocryphal Ḥadīth well known to Sufis in Morocco:
"*Badā al-Islām gharībān fasi'aūdu gharibān kama badā; faṭaoba' li'lghuraba'i.*"
Islam began in the wilderness and will return to the wilderness; may God have mercy on the wilderness.

الحَمدُ لِلّٰهِ

THANKS BE TO GOD

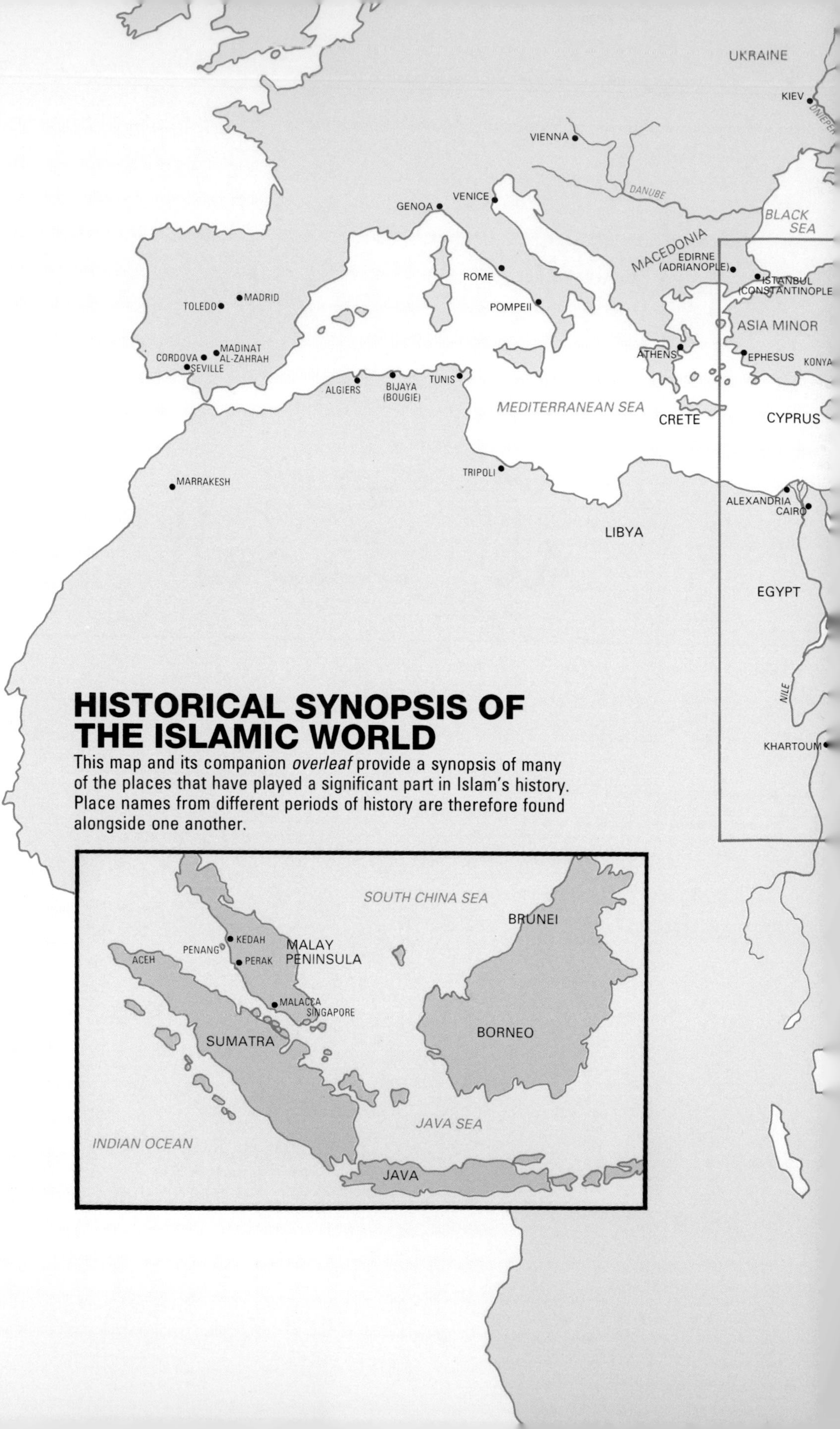

HISTORICAL SYNOPSIS OF THE ISLAMIC WORLD

This map and its companion *overleaf* provide a synopsis of many of the places that have played a significant part in Islam's history. Place names from different periods of history are therefore found alongside one another.

NOVGOROD
KAZAN
RUSSIA
MONGOLIA
KARAKORUM
SARATOV
VOLGA
DON
URAL
KIRGIZ STEPPE
IRTYSH
SARAI
UIGHURS
ASTRAKHAN
TURKESTAN
LAKE BALKASH
SOLDAIA (SUDAK)
ARAL SEA
SYR-DARYA (JAXARTES)
GOBI DESERT
HAMI
CAUCASUS MTS
DAGHESTAN
CASPIAN SEA
SOGDIANA
TURFAN
TOMAK
KHARASHAHR
KHWARIZM
TRANSOXIANA
KUCHA
TUN-HUANG
KHIVA
URGANJ
ARMENIA
TAKLA MAKAN
BUKHARA
SAMARKAND
BADAKHSHAN
YARKAND
CHERCHEN
URFA (EDESSA)
AZERBAIJAN
TABRIZ
ARDABIL
AMU-DARYA (OXUS)
NIYA
SINKIANG
QAZVIN
DAYLAM
MAZAR-I SHARIF
KHOTAN
MESHED (MASHHAD)
ANTIOCH
ALEPPO
BIG ZAB
TEHRAN
PARTHIA
BACTRIA
DASHT-E KAVIR (SALT DESERT)
LITTLE ZAB
KHORASAN
KABUL
BEIRUT
IRAQ
BAGHDAD
PERSIA (IRAN)
QUHISTAN
HERAT
GAZNI
DAMASCUS
TUN
TIBET
ACRE
BABYLON
TIGRIS
ISFAHAN
DASHT-E LUT
SIJISTAN
LAHORE
AMRITSAR
HIMALAYA MOUNTAINS
JERUSALEM
EUPHRATES
SUSA
YAZD
SISTAN
AFGHANISTAN
PUNJAB
SIMLA
AL BASRAH
KERMAN
KANDAHAR
MULTAN
SHIRAZ
INDUS
DELHI
NEPAL
BRAHMAPUTRA
PERSIAN GULF
FARS
ORMUZ
AGRA
JAIPUR
CAWNPORE
SIND
GANGES
AL-HASA
PATNA
KARACHI
MEDINA
YAMAMA
OMAN
MUSCAT
GUJERAT
BARODA
BENGAL
ARABIA
ARABIAN SEA
UJJAIN
JEDDAH
MECCA
INDIA
RUB' AL KHALI
BAY OF BENGAL
RED SEA
HYDERABAD
YEMEN
ADEN
See enlargement overleaf
NELLORE
MADRAS
INDIAN OCEAN
CEYLON
MALDIVE ISLANDS
625 miles
1000 kms

HISTORICAL SYNOPSIS OF THE MIDDLE EAST

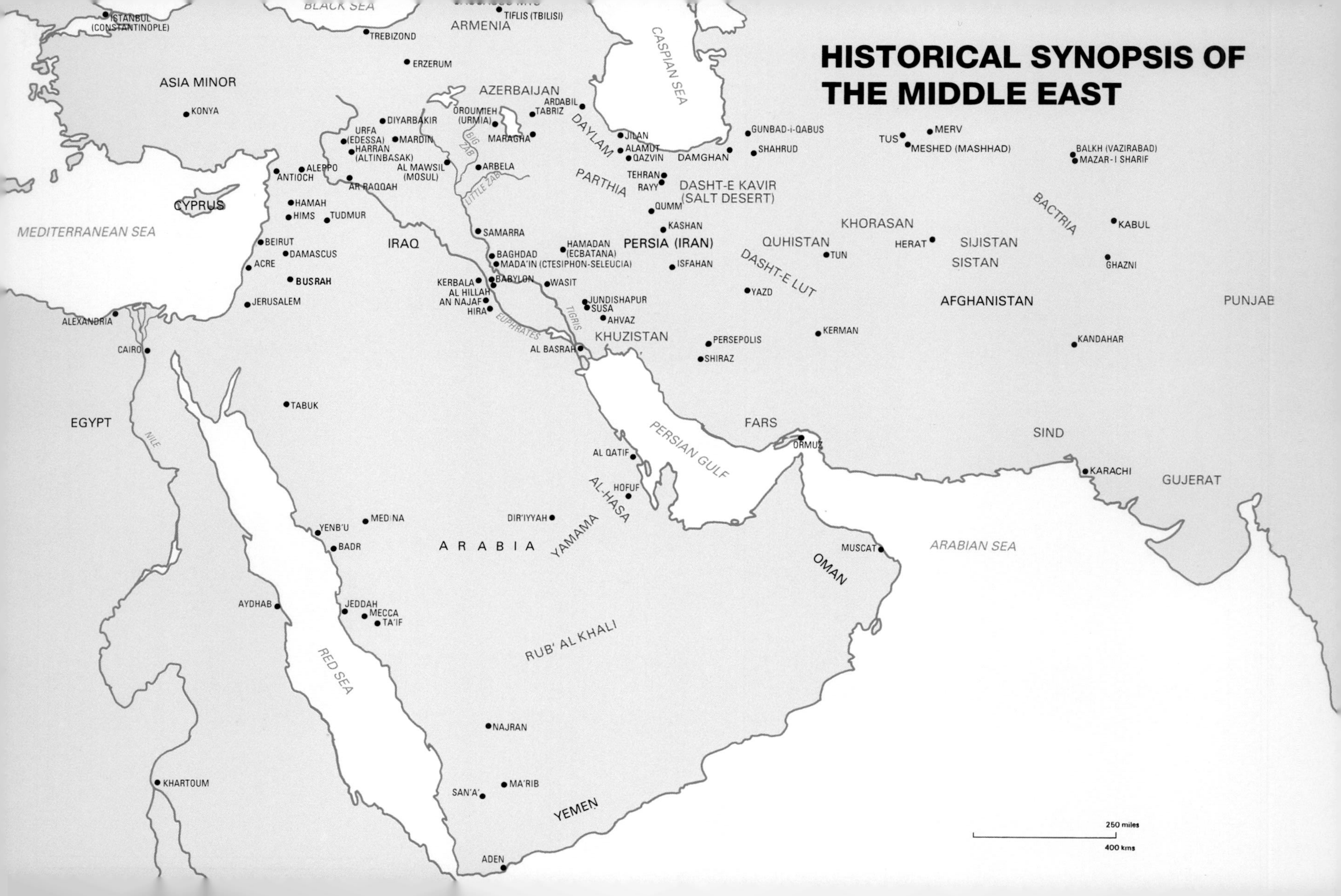

ARABIA AND ITS NEIGHBORS AT THE TIME OF THE PROPHET'S BIRTH

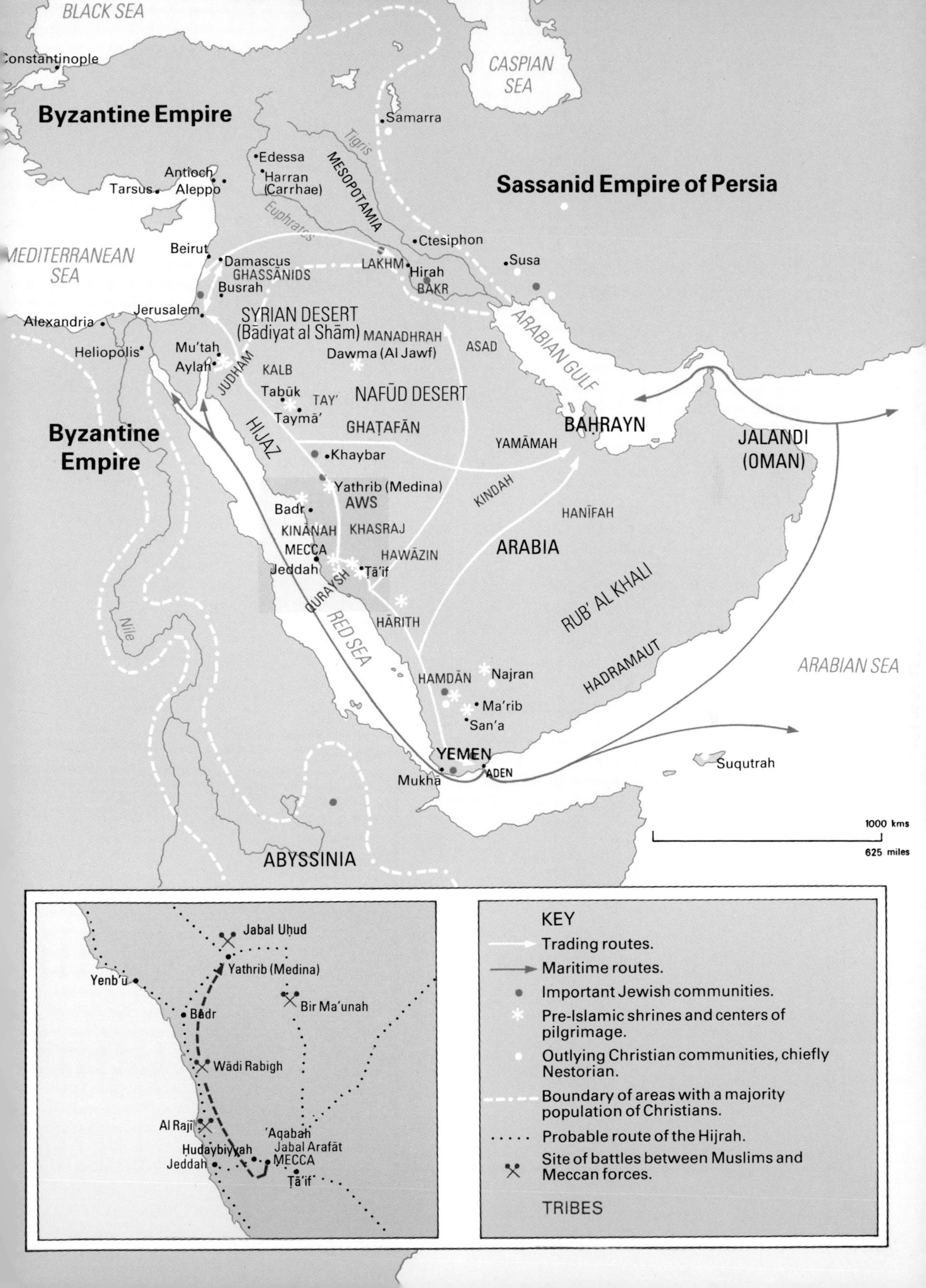

BLACK SEA
Constantinople
CASPIAN SEA
Byzantine Empire
Samarra
Tigris
MESOPOTAMIA
Edessa
Harran (Carrhae)
Antioch
Tarsus
Aleppo
Sassanid Empire of Persia
Euphrates
Ctesiphon
Beirut
Damascus
MEDITERRANEAN SEA
GHASSĀNIDS
LAKHM
Hirah
Susa
Busrah
BAKR
Jerusalem
Alexandria
SYRIAN DESERT (Bādiyat al Shām)
MANADHRAH
ASAD
ARABIAN GULF
Heliopolis
Mu'tah
Aylah
Dawma (Al Jawf)
JUDHAM
KALB
Tabūk
TAY'
NAFŪD DESERT
Taymā'
HIJAZ
GHAṬAFĀN
BAHRAYN
Byzantine Empire
YAMĀMAH
JALANDI (OMAN)
Khaybar
Yathrib (Medina)
AWS
KINDAH
HANĪFAH
Badr
KINĀNAH
KHASRAJ
ARABIA
MECCA
HAWĀZIN
Jeddah
Ṭā'if
QURAYSH
RUB' AL KHALI
RED SEA
Nile
HĀRITH
ARABIAN SEA
HAMDĀN
Najran
HADRAMAUT
Ma'rib
San'a
YEMEN
ADEN
Mukhā
Suqutrah
1000 kms
625 miles
ABYSSINIA
Jabal Uḥud
Yathrib (Medina)
Yenb'u
Bir Ma'unah
Badr
Wādi Rabigh
Al Rajī
'Aqabah
Ḥudaybiyyah
Jabal Arafāt
MECCA
Jeddah
Ṭā'if
KEY
Trading routes.
Maritime routes.
Important Jewish communities.
Pre-Islamic shrines and centers of pilgrimage.
Outlying Christian communities, chiefly Nestorian.
Boundary of areas with a majority population of Christians.
Probable route of the Hijrah.
Site of battles between Muslims and Meccan forces.
TRIBES

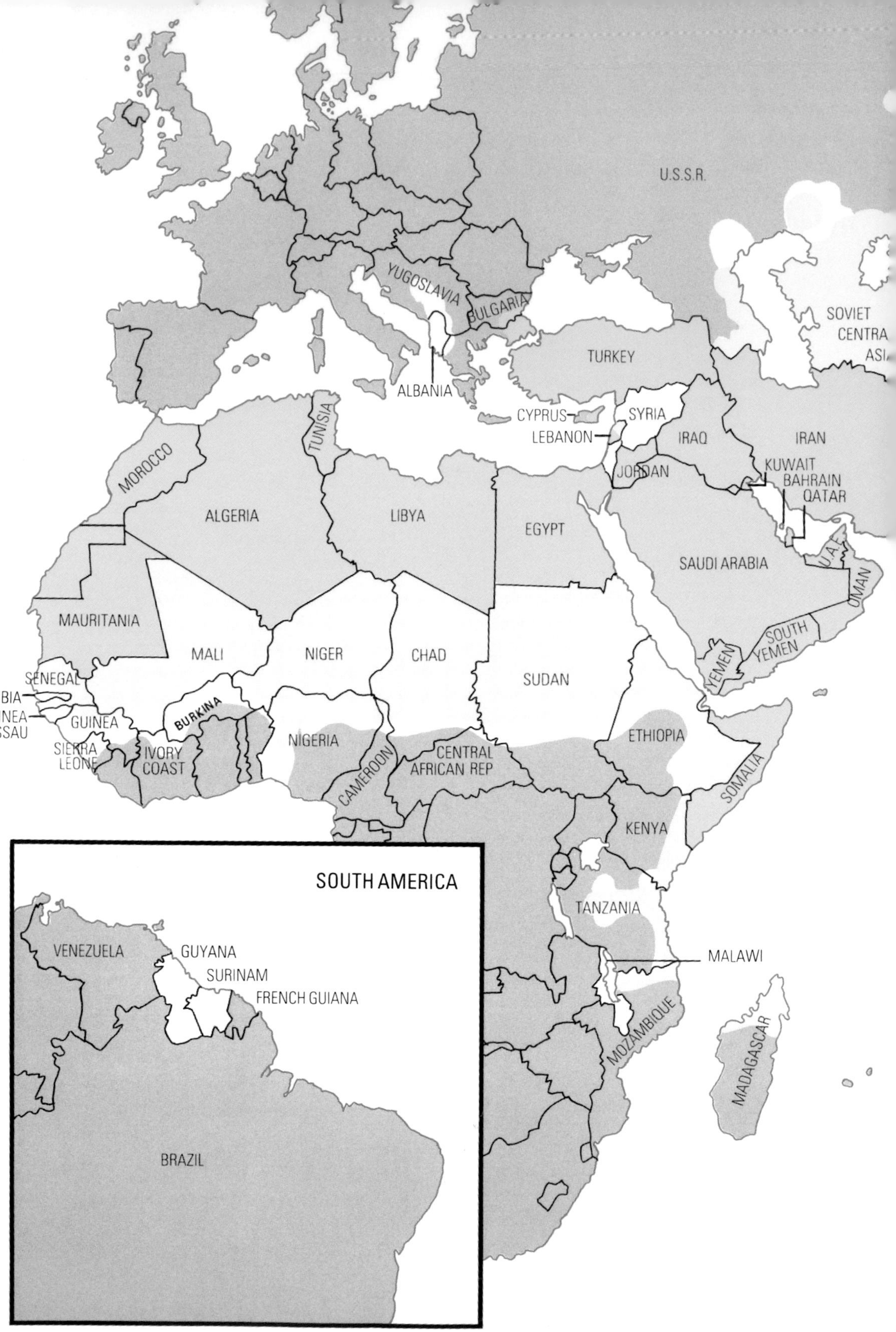
U.S.S.R.
SOVIET CENTRA ASI
YUGOSLAVIA
BULGARIA
ALBANIA
TURKEY
CYPRUS
SYRIA
LEBANON
IRAQ
IRAN
JORDAN
KUWAIT
BAHRAIN
QATAR
U.A.E.
OMAN
SAUDI ARABIA
YEMEN
SOUTH YEMEN
MOROCCO
TUNISIA
ALGERIA
LIBYA
EGYPT
MAURITANIA
MALI
NIGER
CHAD
SUDAN
SENEGAL
GAMBIA
GUINEA BISSAU
GUINEA
SIERRA LEONE
BURKINA
IVORY COAST
NIGERIA
CAMEROON
CENTRAL AFRICAN REP
ETHIOPIA
SOMALIA
KENYA
TANZANIA
MALAWI
MOZAMBIQUE
MADAGASCAR
SOUTH AMERICA
VENEZUELA
GUYANA
SURINAM
FRENCH GUIANA
BRAZIL

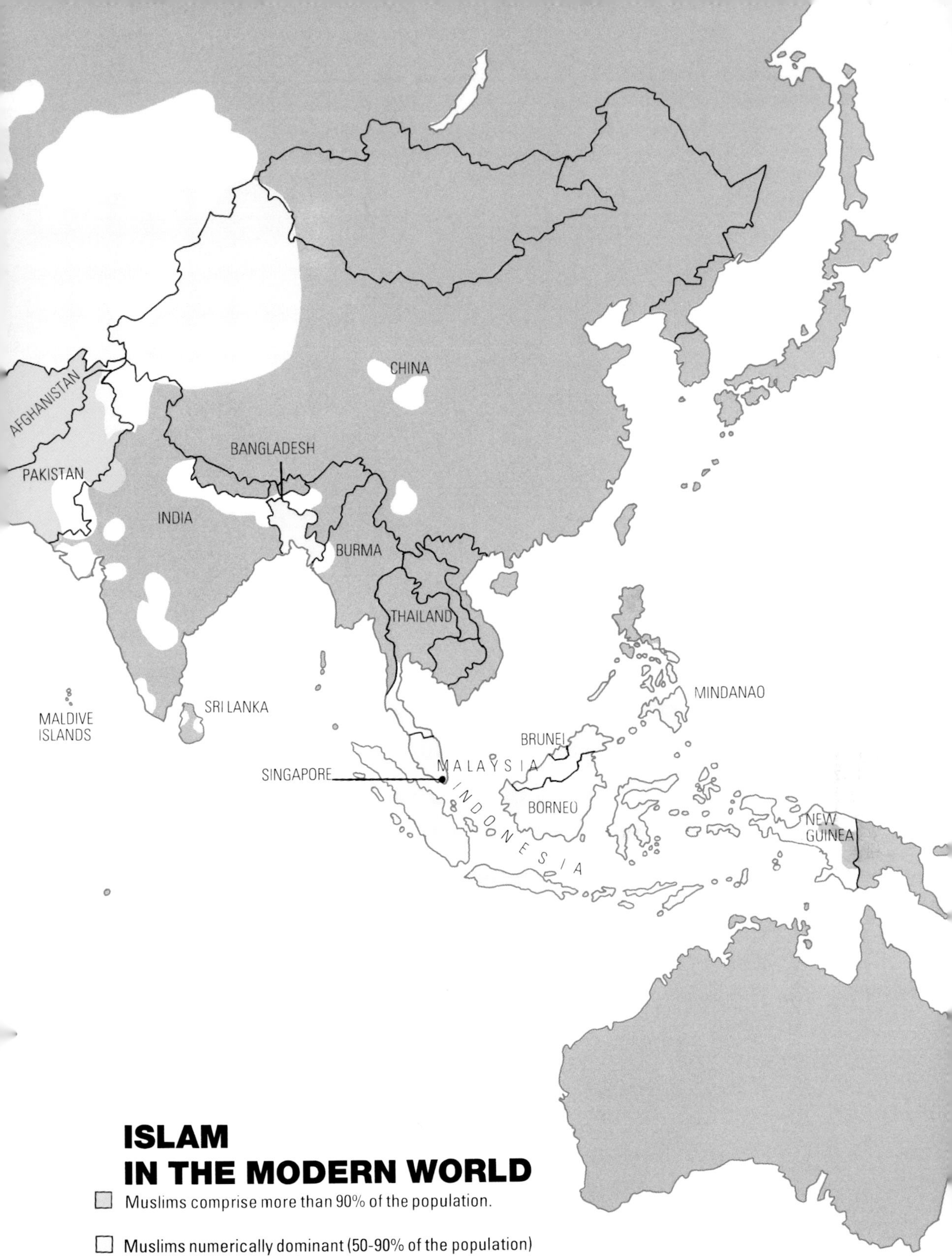

ISLAM IN THE MODERN WORLD

- Muslims comprise more than 90% of the population.
- Muslims numerically dominant (50-90% of the population)
- Muslims a substantial minority (10-50% of the population).

THE ḤAJJ the pilgrimage to Mecca

Before arrival in Mecca the pilgrim puts on *iḥrām* (consecration and pilgrim clothing) at one of the *mawāqīt* (see box below), or before, even at the point of departure, and the appropriate intentions (*an-niyyāt*) are formulated.

Note: a day runs from sunset to sunset

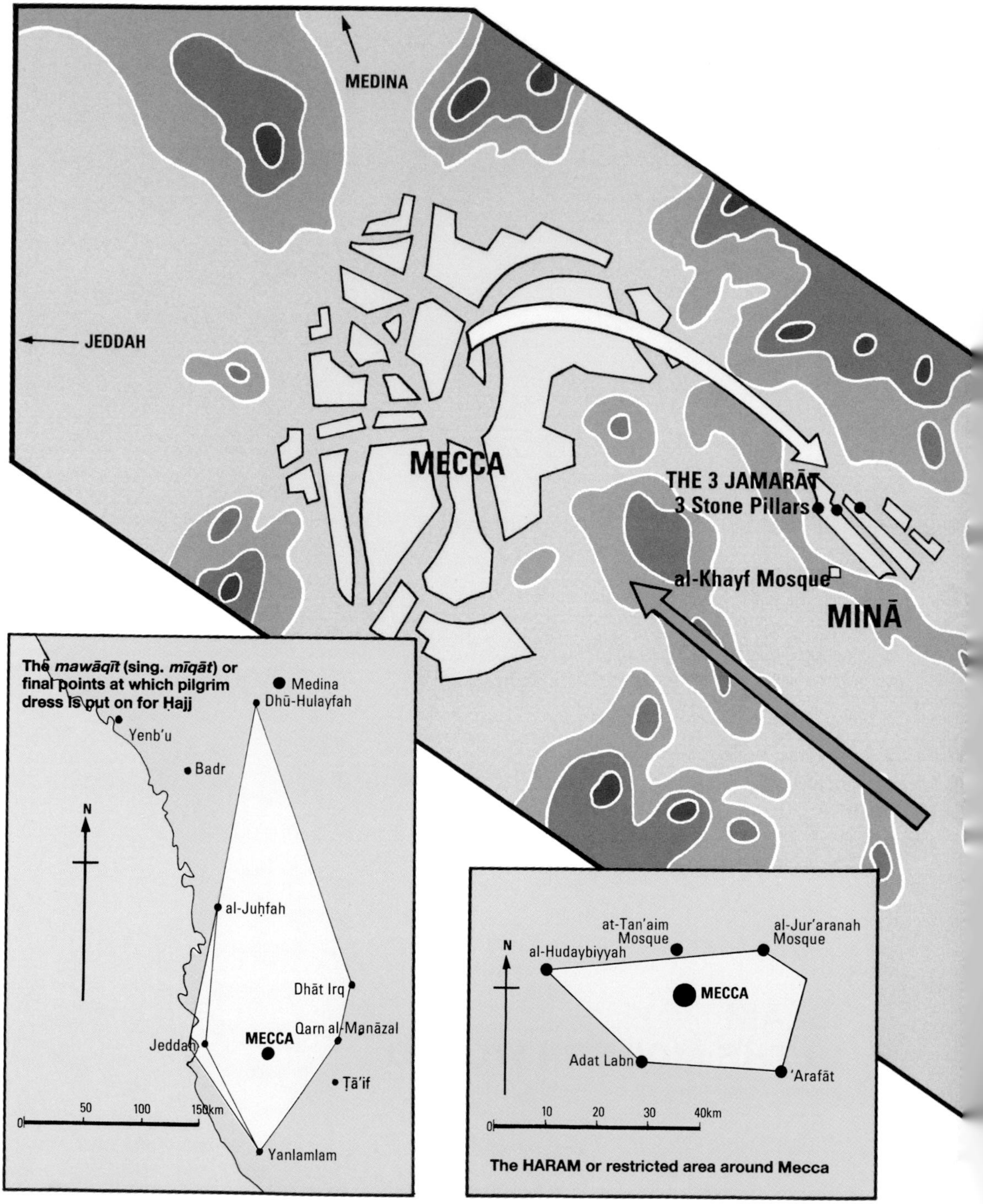

'ALIDS

Those held to be the Imāms by Twelve-Imām Shīʻism are numbered accordingly (see SHĪʻISM.)

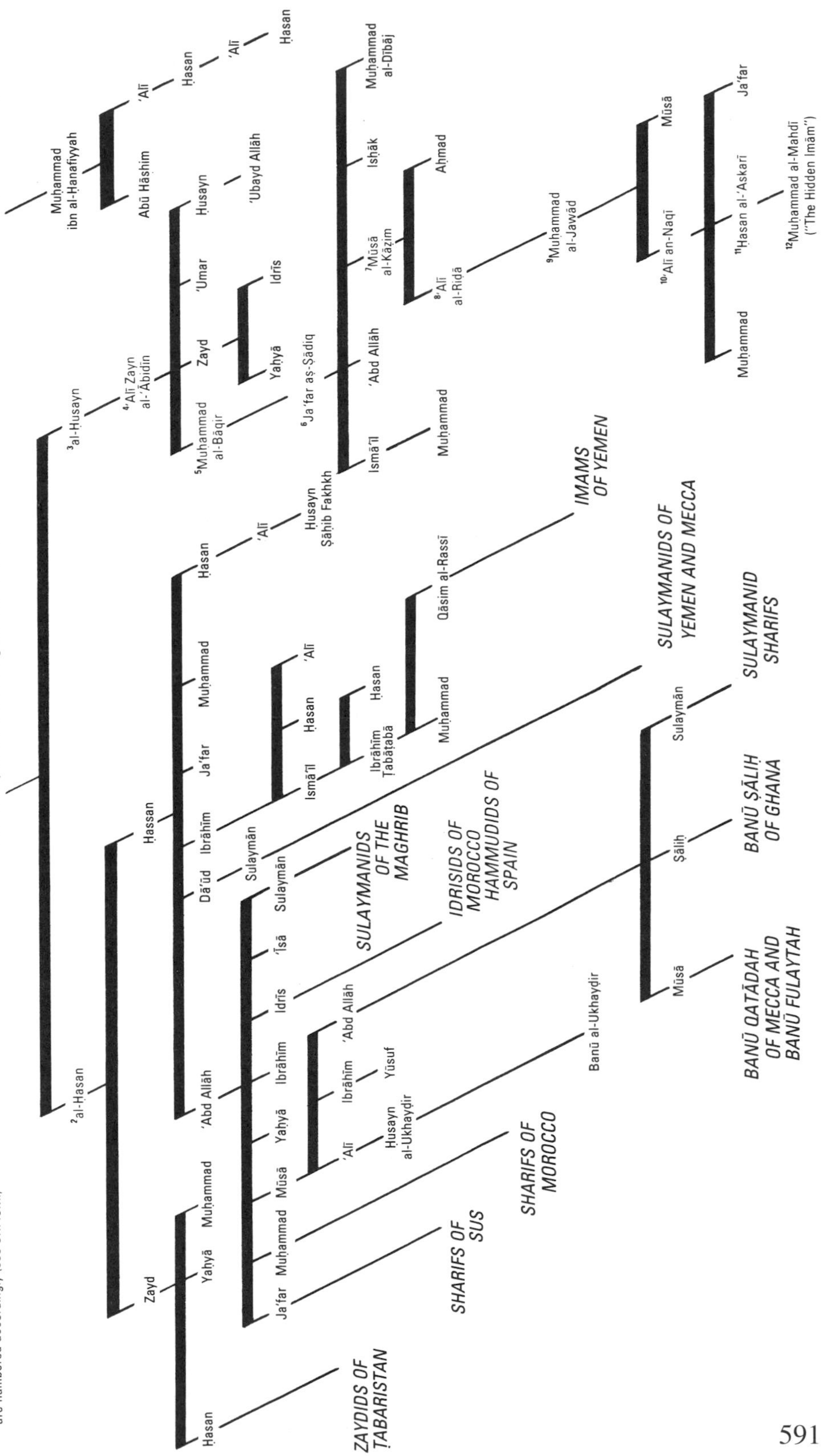

CHRONOLOGY

The Millennia before Muhammad:
One to two million years ago: the movement of Homo Erectus out of Africa.

The spread of Homo Sapiens around the globe beginning 100,000 years ago and reaching every continent 60,000 years ago, and the appearance of boats and rafts. After 12,000 BC, according to a theory which is contested among linguists, there was once a hypothetical language called Nostratic which split into Indo-European (which became Sanskrit, Persian, and most European languages), Dravidian, Kartvellian (languages of the Caucasus), Uralic (Finnish, Estonian, Hungarian), Altaic (Turkic and Mongolian languages), and Afro-Asiatic which includes the Semitic languages.

10,000 BC

The first known outbreaks of smallpox occur among agricultural settlements in Northeastern Africa; the domestication of the wolf as a dog in Western Asia, followed by the boar as a pig in Turkey around 8400 BC and then the goat, sheep, and cattle (from the aurochs), the chicken from a jungle fowl, Gallus, Gallus, Gallus, probably in the area of Thailand before 6000 BC. Also, the horse is domesticated in Central Asia 4000 BC and the donkey and the dromedary camel in Arabia and the Bactrian camel in Central Asia in 3000 BC. (In South America the Llama and Alpaca were domesticated in 4000 BC.) The Introduction of agriculture in the Middle East 10,000 years ago. Weaving of cloth begins about 7000 BC. Between 5400 to 5000 BC wine is made at Hajji Firuz Tepe, in the northern Zagros mountains near the present town of Urmia. Between 4000 and 2000 BC an expansion of people began in the area of the southwest Russian steppes, where the domestication of the horse took place, bringing the Indo-European peoples to Europe, Iran, and India.

3200 BC

The first wheels which were solid wood disks probably used on four wheel carts to transport goods.

Writing appears in Sumeria and Egypt. A roll of papyrus is sealed in a tomb in Egypt in 3000 BC.

2870 BC

Tin is mined 100 km north of Tarsus (Turkey.) Smelted in small crucibles with blowpipes and mixed in proportions of 5-10% with copper it makes bronze. Tin was also probably brought from Afghanistan. Bronze is easier to cast into molds than copper and almost as strong as steel. It was used to make a variety of things from axes and awls to hammers, sickles and weapons. The Bronze age is set from 3000 BC to 1100 BC.

2600 BC

A ruler of the Sumerian city of Uruk may be the inspiration of the Epic of Gilgamesh written down on clay tablets one thousand years later. There are parallels between the Gilgamesh and Noah accounts of a flood. Geological evidence has been found for a catastrophic flood of the Black Sea in which the sea's surface rose as much as 30 cm (a foot) a day for a hundred days at the height of the flood. For that to occur water would have poured into the Black Sea through the Bosphorus at a rate 400 times that of Niagara Falls. Beginning 12,000 years ago the world recovered from an iceage and went through a thousand year arid period in which the Black Sea level dropped. Then 7,500 years ago the Black Sea rose quickly four hundred feet (as seen from beaches underwater near Varna, Bulgaria.) The greatest loss of dry land would have been on the western and northern coasts of the Black Sea. As people left the Black Sea area, farming developed elsewhere. (*NYT* Dec 12-17, 1996)

2500 BC

The Sphinx built by Pharaoh Khafre in Egypt. Some have contended that it was built as early as 7000 BC.

In the Indus valley ceramic ownership seals with a kind of writing appear.

2000 BC

or earlier, Mesopotamian religious epics from Uruk: the "Tammuz Lamentations" (Inanna's or Ishtar's descent to the Netherworld); the Babylonian creation story *Enuma Elish* ("When on high...") and the theory that the primeval ocean, personified by the goddess Nammu, alone had begotten a male sky and a female earth; their union was En-Lil who separated the sky from the earth and with the latter had engendered all living creatures. It is adopted in Sumer, Babylon, and Assyria.

Early chariot wheels appear on the steppes of Russia with eight or twelve spokes.

c.1950 BC

Law code of Bilalama. This code written in Akkadian, was discovered during excavations in Tell Harmal, now a suburb of Baghdad. It already substitutes the literal interpretation of "an eye for an eye a tooth for a tooth" in some cases by milder fines.

c.1850 BC

Abraham and his family come from Ur in Sumer to Harran in northern Mesopotamia (in Roman times called Carrhae, today Altinbasak in southern Turkey, near Urfa, classical Edessa). Harran was the ancient Harranu (Biblical Haran) of Sumerian times. It lay north of the Euphrates on the safer of two roads, which avoided the deserts of the nomadic Amorites, from Ur and Babylon to the Mediterranean. Sin (the Semitic name of the Sumerian Nanna) the god of the moon had an important and famous temple in Harran (cf. Koran 6:76-88). Shamash the sun god (Sumerian Utu or Babar, the "resplendent") probably also had a temple. Particularly interesting from the point of view of later developments, Nusku, a god of light, the son of Sin was also venerated in Harran. Later an Iranian royal road leads from Susa, crossing the Tigris below Arbela, passing by Harran and ending at Sardis (and thence to Ephesus.) It was in Harran that Abraham's father Terah (in Arabic Azar) died; it was there that Abraham was commanded to go into Canaan by God in the Old Testament; it was there that Isaac married Rebekah, and Jacob labored for Laban. It was the center of the Biblical land of Padan-Aram. Padam-Aram was occupied by the Amorites until 1100 BC and thereafter by the Aramaeans until they lost their national identity with their conquest by the Assyrians in 732 BC. The adoption by the Aramaeans of the Canaanite alphabet (based upon cuneiform) from Ugarit (Ras Shamra), instead of the cuneiform script itself, made their language into the *lingua franca* of the Near East.

Four spoked chariot wheels depicted on seals found in Anatolia.

1792-1750 BC

Reign of Hammurabi, King of Babylon. The descendant of a Shaykh of the Amorites, a Semitic people of the deserts between Mesopotamia and the Syrian coast, he made Marduk, formerly a degree below the gods Anu and En-il, the principle deity of the Sumero-Akkadian pantheon, unified the Mesopotamian kingdoms as far north as Diyarbakr (but not Elam and coastal Syria) under Babylonian rule, and, in the tradition of new rulers, promulgated *mesharum*, "justice". The Code of Hammurabi sets down measures to protect women and children from arbitrary treatment; it sets down severe penalties for infractions but allows for mitigating circumstances and forgiveness, provides for compensation through the bride-gift in case of divorce, gives certain rights of property to women, and protects the rights of wives against those of concubines. (Under the Code of Hammurabi, Sarah and her children would have had guarantees of rights such that Sarah need not have been incited to cause Hagar to be set into the desert.) The epilogue of the code says that "the strong may not injure the weak, and that the widow and orphan might receive justice. Let the oppressed citizen who is involved in a lawsuit come before my image as king of justice, let him have my inscription read out to him, and let him hear my precious words. Let this monument throw light upon his case, and may he discover his rights and his heart be made glad."

c.1700 BC

Date of a surviving Sumerian text from Nippur with the theme of the great Flood and a hero called Ziusudra; a later Babylonian Flood text calls the hero Atrahasis; both are forerunners of the Gilgamesh version written at Nineveh in the 7th century BC with the hero Ut-Napishtem.

c.1700-1500 BC

At the beginning of the Bronze Age among the Iranian peoples, the religion of the ancient gods of contracts and oaths, Mithra and Varuna, decays, and non-ethical deities arise such as Indra, indifferent to truth or the good, who only give power – not justice – to their devotees. There is social disorder and robber bands become rife, and war chariots are invented. At this juncture there appears Zoroaster and Zoroastrianism. It is the first religion to speak of the end of the world, a universal judgement with a paradise accessible to everyone; the immortal soul; and the prophecy of a universal saviour, the Saoshyant. Zoroastrian myth says that the seed of Zoroaster went into a lake; a virgin bathing in that lake will one day conceive the world saviour. The latest plausible date for Zoroaster is 1200 BC according to Mary Boyce.

1500-1200 BC

In China, during the Shang dynasty, oracle inscriptions are made on the underside of turtle shells and on ox bones.

1350 BC

First recorded smallpox epidemic during the Egyptian-Hittite war.

c.1275 BC

Chariot wheel reaches a height of development.

c.1250 BC

Moses. Exodus of the Jews from Egypt across Sinai, followed by the period of Judges.

c.1200 BC

The appearance of the alphabet at Ugarit among a Canaanite people in northern coastal Syria. This alphabet, the first, is an adaptation of the Sumerian cuneiform but the symbols stand for sounds rather than words.

1157 bc

Pharaoh Ramses V dies as a young man, possibly of smallpox.

c.1025 BC

The Aryans descend down the valley of the Ganges. The Rig-Veda in India.

c.1010-955 BC

David, the greatest expansion of the kingdom of Israel and Jerusalem its capital. In the Bible David is depicted as a superb military leader who captured Jerusalem and made it his capital and united the kingdoms of Judah and Israel ushering in a glorious era. This view is now challenged as not historical.

c. 955-935 BC

Solomon, son of David, who built the Temple and embellished the prestige of Jerusalem and whose influence extended from Egypt to the Euphrates.

Thereafter the separation of the Northern Kingdom, called Israel, made up of ten tribes, and the southern Kingdom, Judah, made up of two tribes, Judah and Benjamin, and a small number of the tribe of Levi.

753 BC

According to Varro, the founding of Rome.

747 BC

February 26. "The Chaldean Era"; this date is used as a timepoint for the dating of events by Ptolemy before the Seleucid era in 312 BC

732 BC

The independence of Judah, the southern kingdom, by the payment of tribute to Assyria.

721 BC

The conquest of Israel, the Northern of the two Kingdoms, by the Assyrians. The ten "lost" tribes disappear, that is, they are absorbed into other populations, including a group that maintains something of a Jewish identity, the Samaritans. The "lost tribes" are declared by the Talmud to "have no share in the world to come". The kingdom of Judah survives as a vassal first of the Assyrians, then the Egyptians, but the worship of Yahweh becomes triumphant among the surviving Jews.

660 BC

Byzantium founded. In this century the cult of Isis and Osiris appears in Syria, spreading rapidly after 333 BC having begun in Egypt almost a thousand years earlier. It had a Eucharist of bread and Isis' milk, and instituted the cult of the savior-God, later transformed into the Dionysus and Demeter cults of the Hellenic world. The Dionysian Bacchantes also practiced omophagia, the eating of living victims, including children, which was transformed into a higher form in the Eleusinian and Demeter mysteries and of course in Christianity.

621 BC

In Judah, Josiah reads Deuteronomy to the people. This, compiled by the Levites of Judah probably during the reign of Manassah, a pagan king who suppressed the worship of Yahweh, is the first book of the Jewish Bible to appear, and is a response to the crisis brought on by the assimilation of the Ten Northern tribes. It is a novel approach to preserve the political authority of Yahweh by making him, rather than the foreign gods whose authority was hitherto not contested as valid within their own territories, and demonstrated by political ascendancy, and towards whom the Israelites assimilated, the authour of the defeats and afflictions which Israel and Judah underwent, with threats of worse. The curse in Deuteronomy 21:23 against all who are hanged on a tree could have been directed against the crucified priests of the Attis cult. "This idea had become so deeply rooted in pagan consciousness that it was almost an obsession: the god-man must die and rise from the grave so that his devotees might also be resurrected into life immortal. However, as advancing civilisation softened the manners of all races, this ceremony became an innocuous scene in a passion-play. And finally the living priest was simulated by a lifeless figure which was first impaled and then laid in his sacred tomb." (Larson: *The Religion of the Occident.*)

The Books of Moses, which refer to an earlier past, are written down in the fifth century BC but continue to be revised down to the fourth century BC and perhaps after that. The books of the Prophets appear between the fourth and second century BC, although Daniel (in Aramaic) is probably even later, followed by the minor writings. The Hebrew Bible as a whole becomes fixed by a Rabbinic Council held in Jamnia in Palestine in AD 100 The oldest available manuscript of a substantial part of the Old Testament in Hebrew, a codex of the Prophets in Cairo, dates from AD 987 and another in St Petersburg, Russia is dated AD 916 The oldest manuscript of the entire Hebrew Bible is dated AD 1008 and is known as the Leningrad Codex.

612 BC

Nineveh destroyed by the Medes. In three years after this, Judah is subjected to Egypt, and after 605 BC, subjection to Babylonia which had defeated Egypt.

610 BC

The Spartan state is "reformed" – the *Eunomia* –as a military totalitarianism of masters and slaves, the helots. The reorganisation, similar to other states run by and for elites, is attributed to a ninth century BC lawgiver, Lycurgus. The Soviet Minister of Foreign Affairs Andrei Gromyko once made the observation to an American diplomat that the Soviet Union was the re-establishment of the Spartan state.

598 BC

The capture of Jerusalem by Nebuchadnezzar and the first deportation of Jews to Babylonia.

593 BC

The prophetic call of Ezekiel. Following the Babylonian exile, Judaism comes into contact with Iranian religions. From contacts between the Jews and Persians eschatological ideas ("the gathering of the bones") – proto mysticism – appear among the Jews; the Jewish tradition begins to cast a shadow, or devolve into exoterist and esoterist tendencies. The first esoterisms are apocalyptic, a knowledge of final ends. These will become the Heikhalot or Merkava schools of mysticism in which the adept, possessing a knowledge of divine Names and sacred signs, ascends through palaces or the seven heavens.

587 BC

The destruction of Jerusalem and second deportation of Jews.

586-538 BC

The period of the Jewish Exile from Judah.

585 BC

May 28; A battle between Lydians and Assyrians broken off by an eclipse of the sun which was predicted by Thales.

585 BC

The Medes conquer Anatolia as far as the river Halis.

582 BC

Pythagoras born at Samos. He established a secret society, influenced by the Orphics, taught transmigration of souls, rites of purification, that all things are numbers, and that numbers set a limit to the unlimited. The Orphics also taught transmigration, purification and the divine origin of the soul.

Pythagoras created in Croton in Italy a political religious organisation which consisted "of celibate brotherhoods, *thiasoi* whose objective was their own moral regeneration through a communistic reorganisation of society". This movement survived as a religious cult which influenced many philosophers such as Plato, and Justin Martyr, and movements such as the Essenes through which it left a decisive stamp upon Christianity.

According to myth Pythagoras sojourned in hell for seven years where he saw Homer and Hesiod suffering tortures. Pythagoras absorbed elements from many religions, including India, and the soteriology of Osiris and Zagreus-Dionysus. His teachings because central to all mystery and esoteric cults of the ancient world. "Pythagoras was said to have remembered all his previous reincarnations." In the 4th century BC Heraclides of Pontus launched the fiction that Pythagoras studied with Zoroaster in Babylon, which is historically impossible, but this was taken up by Aristoxenus and incorporated in the general chronology developed by Appolodorus in the 2nd century BC. Thence it was adopted by the Magi as the dating of Zoroaster, incorrectly, as 258 years before Alexander the Great.

581 BC

A third deportation of Jews to Babylonia.

c.563-483 BC

The life of Siddhartha and the preaching of Buddhism. After his final *nirvana*, the "First Council" of Buddhism takes place in Rajagadha in Bihar (see AD 120).

559 BC

Astyages the Mede is deposed by the Achaemenian Persian king, Cyrus II.

539 BC

Babylon captured by Cyrus II, the Great (rules 559-530 BC).

539-332 BC

Phoenicia under Persian rule.

538 BC

The edict of Cyrus permitting the Jews to return to Jerusalem. 40,000 under the leadership of Zerubabel do so, while the majority prefer to remain where they are, and indeed emigrate elsewhere. II Isaiah:

"...that saith of Cyrus, He is my shepherd, and shall perform my pleasure: even saying to Jerusalem, Thou shalt be built; and to the temple, Thy foundation shall be laid.

"Thus saith the Lord to his anointed, to Cyrus, whose right hand I have holden,

"to subdue nations before him...

"I will go before thee, and make the crooked places straight." (44-45)

535 BC

Heraclitus born in Ephesus, d. 475. He taught that all things carried within themselves their opposites and that Being and Non-Being were part of every whole, and that permanence is an illusion of mind. *Panta rhei kai uden minei* – "everything flows and nothing remains" – all is becoming. He also said a "person sleeping participates in the work of the cosmos". His philosophy carries distinct traces of contact with Dualism.

530-522 BC

The rule of Cambyses II, son of Cyrus who had the title "King of Babylon".

525 BC

Persian conquest of Egypt. Further Persian influence throughout the ancient Near East. A projected campaign against Carthage is not undertaken because the Phoenicians refuse to war against a sister colony.

521-486 BC

Rule of Darius I, a "confirmed" Zoroastrian (there was nothing to prove to historians that Cyrus was a Zoroastrian; and nothing to disprove it either), after putting to death, "the false Gaumata or Bardiya" the Magian, a pretender who claimed to be a brother (named Gaumata or Bardiya) of Cambyses (who had himself been supposedly put to death by Cambyses). Gaumata had achieved successful acceptance in Iran during Cambyses' absence by remitting taxes for three years. The putting down of revolts and the overthrow of the "false" Gaumata is recorded by Darius at Naqshi-Rustam on the road between Kermanshah and Hamadhan. The story of Darius putting down the false Gaumata was a scandal of classic times; there are some who say that Gaumata was a true brother of Cambyses and that Darius usurped the throne; Darius' story is carved in stone; and to prevent anyone effacing it he had the steps leading up to the inscription cut away to prevent access to the rock carvings.

Good roads with stations for royal messengers foster communications throughout the empire, and thereby, spread of ideas. The Persian empire is extended beyond the Indus. The Zoroastrian "lake" reaches from India to Egypt. Darius makes Susa his capital. (Cyrus had also used Susa as a capital although he also resided at Ecbatana (the Median capital meaning "Place of Assembly") and Babylon. He left as his main residence Pasargadae (possibly meaning "the camp of the Persians" where he is buried and where the Achaemenid kings were crowned. When Darius' palace at Susa was complete he continued building at Persepolis.

5th Cent. BC

Lao Tzu in China and the Tao teh Ching.

516 BC

Temple in Jerusalem rebuilt.

510 BC

The founding of the Roman republic.

495 BC

Birth of Empedocles, Greek philosopher born in Sicily d. 435. He declared the atmosphere to be a substance, not a mere void, and explained motion as the action of harmony and discord. In other words, he posited two principles, sometimes translated as love and hate.

490 BC

Battle of Marathon; Persian invading force routed by the Greeks.

480-479 BC

Xerxes' expedition into Greece turned back at Plataea and the fleet routed at Thermopylae. For this expedition Xerxes ordered a canal to be built a mile and a quarter long through a Greek Peninsula because a fleet had been destroyed there, near Mount Athos, by a storm twelve years earlier. The canal was 100 feet wide at the surface, 50 feet at the bottom and 45 feet deep. The canal ran from the Sea of Ierissou to the Sea of Agiou Orous near Salonika. The archeological site was recently discovered.

Death of Confucius in China (551-479? BC.); the doctrine that the proper relationships in the Cosmic order are truth.

444-432 BC

The administration of Nehemiah as royal governor.

412 BC

Alkibiades flies to the Persian Satrap Tissaphernes.

400 BC

A Greek army revolting against Xerxes II under Xenophon is defeated at Cunaxa; "the retreat of the 10,000".

397-395 BC

Agesilaos, King of Sparta campaigns against the Persians in Asia Minor.

399 BC

Socrates is put to death at Athens for heretical teaching.

397 BC

The arrival of Ezra the Scribe, viewed by many as the true founder of Judaism, combining the emphasis on the Torah, and its exposition and teaching in the Synagogue, and the meticulous obedience of the rules in daily conduct.

347 BC

Death of Plato (b. 427 BC). When he was dying, a Chaldean (i.e. a Persian Magus), who was a house guest sang certain magical songs to allay his fever while a Thracian played soothing music on a flute for him (according to Neanthes, after Philippos in K. Gaiser, Philodems Academica).

336-323 BC

Alexander the Great conquers the Persian Empire through the battles of Granicus (334), Isus (333, where Alexander captures the Persian Queen and her children), and Gaugamela ("the pasturage of Camels" near Arbela in the foothills of the Assyrian mountains, 331).

Darius III is murdered in 331 BC

At the temple of Ammon in Egypt the god had announced that Alexander was his son and foretold that he would dominate the world. When Alexander is at Persepolis a fire breaks out and the city is destroyed.

329 BC

Alexander adopts Persian dress and court etiquette, and marries the Persian princess Roxana, daughter of an important chief whom Alexander made satrap of Bactria. He introduces the *proskynos* to himself, or prostration towards the "King of Kings" which was required of the Persians by the court etiquette of the Achaemenids.

326 BC

Alexander wins victories in India near the Indus, but his army refuses to go farther. Alexander turns back.

323 BC

Alexander dies at Babylon.

322 BC

Death of Aristotle (b. 384 BC).

312 BC

1 October. The Seleucid era in Syria and a system of computation of time; later used as a universal time reference by the Jews, called the "Dating of Records" (*Minyan Shetaroth*) and by the Arabs, called the age of Alexander (*li-l-Iskandar*). (For the Babylonians and above all their astronomers the Seleucid era began on April 3, 311 BC – Kugler, *Sterndienst und Sternkunde in Babel.*)

301 BC

After the Battle of Ipsus, the political organisation of Alexander's empire is stabilized into a division among a Macedonian monarchy in Europe, a Ptolemaic monarchy in Egypt, and a Seleucid monarchy in Asia. Seleucus married Apama, a noble Persian woman and created a dynasty which united Macedonian and Iranian blood. He founded Antioch on the Orontes and Seleucia on the Tigris which became his capital. (Ctesiphon was later built by the Parthians facing Seleucia and the two were called Mada'in by the Arabs).

300 BC

Great Wall of China begun by Qin Shih-huang-ti which will run 2,400 km from north of Peking to the Yellow Sea. It will be extensively rebuilt in the 15th and 16th centuries with the Ming adding 3,000 watchtowers.

Epicurus, exhibiting that freedom from priest-ridden society that characterized the Classical Greeks, declares that there is no providence nor life after death. Among the Jews *apikoros* becomes the epithet of a freethinker, or one who does not submit to the Rabbis.

300-250 BC

In Mesoamerica the Mayans, Olmecs, and Zapotecs develop writing.

Although tradition says that Ananda, a disciple of the Buddha brought Buddhism to Gandhara (Northern Pakistan and neighboring Afghanistan) only fifty years after Sakyamuni's death, the historic presence of Buddhism appears in Gandhara after the Maurya Empire (350-150 BC).

285 BC

A first red sea canal is dug by the Ptolemies.

275 BC

First account of the Flood in a European language written in Greek by Berossus, a priest of the god Marduk (or Bel) in Babylon. His history, *Babylonaica* or *Chaldaica* was dedicated to King Antiochus I and related history from the beginning of the world to the time of Alexander. The work exists in quoted fragments.

264 BC

Death of Zeno (b. 336 BC), founder of the Stoic school.

268-267 BC

Consecration of the Emperor Asoka in India. Asoka was a Buddhist and regretted the suffering he had cause during wars. Inspired perhaps by the Achaemenids, Asoka had rocks and pillars inscribed in Kharosthi characters and Greek and Aramaic, with his edicts and exploits, including his remorse. His capital was Patna (Pataliputra) and he ruled northern and Central India. Although a Buddhist he upheld all religions. By tradition around 250 BC monks set out on missions, one of which was led by Mahinda, a son of Asoka, and brought Buddhism to Ceylon (Shri Lanka), the first Buddhist state.

c 240 BC

Arsaces I and his brother Tiridates found the kingdom of the Parthians in the Caspian region between the domains of the Seleucids and Bactria. Tiridates is crowned at the temple of Anahita at Arsak; Ecbatana becomes the Parthian summer capital. The Parthians may have been a people of Scythian origin who spoke Pahlavi and had Persian culture.

c. 200 BC
Ecclesiastes; humanism appears in the Bible.

By this time the Septuagint translation of the Hebrew Bible into Greek, begun perhaps one hundred years earlier by Jews in Alexandria, is complete. As far as is known this is the first translation.

200 BC - 100 AD
Jewish and then Christian Apocalyptic writings. (Iranian influences are also very strong upon Buddhism in Central Asia, but can also be assumed in South India where Iranians make contacts through trade. Iranian influences would account for the appearance in Mahayana Buddhism of divinities of light in the first centuries AD)

190 BC
The Seleucid, Antiochus III, the Great defeated by Rome at the Battle of Magnesia in Asia Minor. The Seleucids lose control of Bactria and their rule is reduced to Syria.

The making of parchment, which began in Pergamom, from the skin of sheep is perfected.

171-138 BC
Parthia is ruled by Mithridates I; the Parthian empire is enlarged and Ctesiphon is founded as the Parthian capital, a round city, facing Seleucia.

168 BC
Revolt of Judas Maccabeus and his brothers against the Seleucids. The Temple of Jerusalem is appropriated by Antiochus IV to the worship of Olympian Zeus for a period of four years.

162 BC
In what is now south east Turkey, not far from Harran, in the former Seleucid province of Commagene, made into an independent kingdom in 162 BC by a governor named Ptolemy, an Iranian prince named Mithridates I establishes himself. His family, the Orontids, originally ruled in Armenia at the time of Darius.

The kingdom of Commagene becomes the Westernernmost Zoroastrian country, which unlike Zoroastrianism elsewhere depicts its divinities in the form of Hellenistic statues. (See 109 BC) Their gods had both Persian and Greek names such as Apollo-Mithras and Zeus-Oromasdes. In Commagene wine is used liturgically. It was a border kingdom between the Persian and Roman empires. The capital was Samosata. The Kingdom endures until AD 72 when its ruling dynasty is wiped out by Vespasian in the course of the Jewish war.

142-63 BC
Jerusalem is liberated and Simon Maccabeus establishes the Hasmonean dynasty whose successor will be John Hyrcanus. The names Hasmonean and Hyrcanus (Hyrcania) suggest connections with Persia which have not been explained. From 134 to 129 BC the Seleucids exact tribute but allow independence. At the end the Pharisees petition Pompey to abolish the Hasmonean monarchy.

According to Josephus three distinct groups had been fully developed in the Jewish population: they were the Essenes, the Pharisees, and the Saducees, of whom the last represented the wealthy upper-class Jews, who had embraced Epicureanism as their philosophy. For a time the Pharisees entertained the ideas of the Pythagorean saviour cults, but eventually abandoned them, returning to Hebraic concepts. (Josephus expounds a Pythagorean theory of the soul to his soldiers at Jotopata.) The Essenes however, absorbed from Zoroastrianism, the "intensely personal and vivid concepts of hell and heaven; the use of water for baptism and spiritual purification; the saviour born of a true virgin-mother; the belief in demons who make human beings impure and must be exorcised; the Messiah of moral justice; the universal judgement, based upon good and evil works; the personal immortality and the single life of every human soul; the apocalyptic vision and prophecy; and the final tribulation before the Parousia."

c.130 BC
Beginning of the Qumran community. Gnostic sects revealing strong elements of Zoroastrian ideas appear in Judaism; some sects consciously strive to produce a Messiah.

c. 125 BC
Mithridates II extends the Parthian frontier to the Oxus and wards off the Sakae, the Scythians. The Parthian empire consolidated.

109 BC
The earliest horoscope in history shows that Antiochus was crowned King of Commagene (see 162 BC) at 7:30 pm on 14 July. King Antiochus raised some of the greatest statuary which survives on Nemrut Dag.

c. 100 BC
The South Arabian kingdom of Saba subdues Ma'in.

"Persistent persecution of the Essenes, partly because of doctrinal deviations but perhaps even more because of their condemnations of the Jewish authorities, who frequently invaded neighboring territories and forced people there to accept Judaism and circumcision on pain of death... under Alexander Jannaeus who ruled from 103-78 BC this hostility and persecution intensified... Josephus relates that Jannaeus, who had at first espoused the Pharisees, later went over to the Sadducees; and when the former were accused of conspiring with the Syrians to subvert the government, Jannaeus had 800 leading Rabbis crucified at one time; and as they hung on their 'trees' or crosses, he had his soldiers cut the throats of their wives and children as he himself feasted at a great banquet with his concubines and his favorites. This had been doubted by many until the fact was confirmed by the publication of a Dead Sea Scroll fragment which related precisely the same facts." (Larson.)

70 or 69 BC

"The climactic event in Essene history... the Teacher of Righteousness – that is the Essene leader – went boldly into Jerusalem and there, in the very temple itself, he proclaimed and condemned the lawless corruption and aggressions of the priests and authorities who ruled in Israel. He was therefore seized and executed, by what means is not certain, but some scholars believe that he was crucified."

"Shortly thereafter, the persuasion developed among his followers – until it became an actual dogma – that he was the Most High God of the Universe Himself who had appeared for a time as a man among men; that he died a sacrificial death for the redemption of sinners; that he had risen from the grave on the third day; that he had returned to his throne in heaven; and that before the end of the then-existing generation, he would send a representative to the earth. This representative would in due course be invested with unlimited power and would terminate the present dispensation, conduct the last judgement, and establish the communal kingdom of the saints on earth, who would then come into possession of all the property of the wicked, who would, thereafter suffer infinite and eternal agonies in hell."

"Except for a few original documents written after 69 BC and the final interpolations added to the *Testaments of the Twelve Patriarchs* at the same time, the cult seems at this point to have considered its corpus of literature and revelation complete. The members studied their scriptures in the various communes scattered about Palestine. Those destined for a special type of leadership were sent to the headquarters at Qumran near the Dead Sea where they multiplied their holy writings in a scriptorium, where members underwent ritual baptisms daily, and where, dressed in white robes, they partook of sacramental meals in an upper chamber every day." (Larson, *Whatever Happened to the Dead Sea Scrolls?*)

64 BC

Pompey annexes Syria; end of the Seleucids. In 63 BC the Romans annex Judaea; Hyrcanus II remains as high priest and later as ethnarch.

53 BC

The Parthian army of Orodes defeats the Romans at the Battle of Carrhae (Harran). 1,000 camels loaded with spare arrows accompany the mounted Parthian archers. The head and arm of Crassus are brought to Orodes, according to tradition, as he is watching the Bacchae of Euripedes. This defeat obliges the Romans to add cavalry to their armies.

48 BC

Smallpox appears in China.

37 BC

End of the Hasmonean dynasty; Herod the Great is appointed king of Judaea by the Roman senate.

30 BC

Death of Cleopatra, last of the Ptolemies of Egypt, as Egypt falls to the Romans.

24 BC

Augustus sends an army under Aelius Gallus, governor of Egypt to invade South Arabia. He lands at Leuke Kome (Yanbu'), marches to Marib, and breaks off his siege after six days.

4 BC

or earlier, religious scholars place the birth of Jesus. The mythic elements in the story of the birth of the Messiah include the visit of the Magi in which the priests of Zoroastrianism come to pay homage. The Magi enter the picture because they "recognize" Jesus to be the Saoshyant or world saviour prophesied by Zoroastrianism; but it also means that Christianity thereby acknowledges a confluence with Zoroastrian currents along with the more evident Canaanite one, namely that of the dying and resurrected vegetation god, Tammuz.

Also, the Jesus story will incorporate the Osiris Soteriology, particularly in its Greek Dionysian and mystery religions adaptations, the Eucharists that these Soteriologies developed, the Pythagorean concepts of the salvation of the Elect, especially as elaborated by the Essenes, the world renunciation of Buddhism, with the general framework of Zoroastrianism.

AD ERA BEGINS

6 AD

Beginning of the administration of Palestine by Roman procurators.

7 AD

"Judas the Gaulonite, the originator of the fourth Jewish sect the Zealots 'whose doctrines infected the nation to an incredible degree' leads a revolt which is crushed. The activities of the Zealots are supplemented by those of the Sicarii, a secret society of Assassins who mingled with the multitudes in the crowded streets especially during the feast and holy days, and struck down their victims with daggers. The High Priest Jonathan was one of the first to fall."

8 AD

29 August. In the Ethiopian calendar the beginning of the "Incarnation Era".

c. 25 AD

Appearance of John the Baptist, "a voice crying in the wilderness, make straight the way for the Lord".

30

The Crucifixion.

35

Saul goes to Damascus to refute the Christians, who appear to be one more Gnostic heresy within Judaism;, on his way he loses his sight as, perhaps, he works in his mind the arguments he will use to unmask the Christians; arguments which necessarily extinguish themselves in the evidence of the Christian doctrine creating a momentary blank, the blindness or a vision of a void, which, like samadhi, is an existential recognition. Ananias places his hands upon him and his vision returns. Paul is converted. According to Shahrastani, "Paul introduced philosophy into the religion of Peter."

37

Birth of Josephus, an aristocratic Pharisee, who was a neophyte for three years among the Essenes. In 66 he was appointed by the Sanhedrin a joint governor of Galilee. After being caught up in events he settled in Rome where he was given citizenship and a pension. He wrote a history of the Roman war which was rewritten and translated into Greek by collaborators, and he wrote in Greek himself a history of the Jews to the year 66.

40

Philo Judaeus, a Jewish Hellenist from Alexandria, born around 20 BC, goes to Rome at the head of a Jewish embassy to persuade the Emperor Gaius to abstain from demanding that Jews honour the Emperor as a god. They are the only people in the empire exempted from this requirement which helps to draw converts to Judaism. Philo embodied ideas from Plato, the Pythagoreans, and the Stoics, and could be thought of as a Greek philosopher, but he upheld the spiritual supremacy of the Jews and Mosaic revelation, which, however, he interpreted allegorically, particularly the book of Genesis.

c. 50

Simon Magus in Samaria.

50-64

The writing of Paul's Epistles, the earliest Christian documents extant. Gnosticising tendencies appear in Corinth and other communities; Letter to the Corinthians. Around the year 64, Paul, Peter, and James, the so-called "brother" of Jesus, die.

64

The conflagration of Rome. Ten fourteenths of the city burns; Tacitus implicates Nero. But a new theory by Gerhard Baudy indicates that the Christians were actually to blame. They fomented apocalyptic prophecies of the destruction of the city and these centered on the rising of the star Sirius, a prophecy known throughout the Mediterranean. In the year 64, Sirius rose on July 19, the date of the fire and an anniversary of an earlier fire in Rome four hundred years earlier. Nero was at Antium and rushed to the city to direct the fire fighters, who numbered 7,000 since the time of Augustus. One of Nero's own palaces burned. It may be that Nero, far from persecuting Christians and looking for a scapegoat, was actually punishing them for arson according to the laws of Rome.

65

First historical record of Buddhist acts of piety performed by a Chinese prince. Perhaps from this came the legend, which is not historically true, that the Han Emperor Ming (ruled 58-75) had a dream in which a divine "golden image" appeared to him. He sent envoys to India who returned seven years later with Buddhist teachers, among them Kasyapmatanga, a White Horse, and the *Sutra in Forty Two Sections.* For the teachers the Emperor was said to have founded the White Horse Monastery in Lo-yang, which historically exists from the 3rd century. Buddhism actually entered China through the Silk Road, Central Asia, and Parthia, the Kushan empire in what is today northern Pakistan, and into Shantung by sea.

66 (or 63)

Tiridates, brother of the Parthian Vologases I becomes King of Armenia and travels to Rome to be crowned by Nero; according to Tacitus he refused to go by sea for fear of "polluting the water" a Zoroastrian tenet. The divinity which symbolized the water was Anahita. His tent, a historian says, was decorated with stars. Some believe that the text of the Avesta was compiled in the reign of Vologases I, and that the journey of Tiridates is the basis for the story of the Three Magi, although that story stands on its own by virtue of its symbolism, the acknowledgment of the Zoroastrian elements of the Christ story.

The Jewish rebellion against Rome.

70

The Destruction of the Temple by Titus and the deportation of many Jews. On the eve of the fall of Jerusalem Rabbi Yohannan ben Zakkai makes a concordat with the Roman military authorities who allow him to move unmolested from Jerusalem to Jamnia to establish there his school of Rabbinic research.

According to Larson, The Book of Revelation is composed between January and September 70, because it says that "the holy city shall they tread under foot for forty and two months". The siege by the Roman army lasted eight months, which Larson takes to mean that the book was written before the siege ended, otherwise such a gross error could not have occurred, nor would the destruction of the city and the Temple been left unrecorded. Larson calls the Book of Revelation "an expression of Jewish Gnostic Christianity, which was actuated by the bitterest hostility not only toward its Hellenic counterpart, but also toward Judaism. The Jesus of Revelation was a human being of the line of David; but the supernational Christ was simply the Word, the Power, the Wisdom of the Supreme God. Whoever the author of Revelation may have been, his Christology was Cerinthian; and it is not hard to understand why so many of the Fathers rejected the document... the writer was not concerned over the persecution of Gentile Christians by Nero; what aroused in him such frenetic wrath was the Roman attack on Judaea, supplemented by popular and bloody assaults upon the Jewish communities in cities throughout the Middle East, which occurred simultaneously. Antichrist is Vespasian... he is deeply outraged by 'blasphemy of them which say they are Jews, but are not, but are of the synagogue of Satan.' These and similar denunciations point to Paul and his school, against whom the Jewish Christians were embittered to a degree which passes all comprehension."

Masada, a fort in the Judaean desert near the Dead Sea, made into a citadel by Herod the Great, becomes a Zealot stronghold which holds out against the Romans after the destruction of the Temple, until the one thousand defenders kill each other. The event is described at length by the historian Josephus.

70-150

The Gospels are written, beginning with the Gospel of Mark, perhaps in 60-67. The Greek Matthew may be a recension of an earlier Aramaic version perhaps older than Mark. The Gospel of Luke claims to be only a written rendition of common belief and tradition. Luke and Matthew contain material from the *Sayings of Jesus.* The Gospel of John cannot be before 120, and was written to retain Greek converts. There existed at one time Jewish Gospels known as the Gospel According to the Hebrews and the Gospel According to the Ebionites.

72

The kingdom of Commagene is wiped out by Vespasian in the course of the Jewish war. Vespasian incorporates Commagene into the province of Syria. (See 162 BC and 109 BC).

c. 80

Beginning of orthodox Judaism.

85

Birth of Marcion in Sinope. As a Hellenist Gnostic he was called the "Wolf of the Pontus" by Eusebius. Tertullian called him "more repellent than the Scythian, more erratic than the Hamaxoban, more inhuman than the Massagete, more outrageous than the Amazon, darker than the cloud, colder than winter, flimsier than ice, more perfid than the Hister, more precipitous than the Caucasus".

New Testament texts appear: The Gospels of Matthew and Luke, and the Acts.

c. 95

New Testament texts: Hebrews, I Peter and the Pastoral letters.

c. 100

Elchasai (Elkhasaios), founder of a baptizing sect, in Syria. Mani will be born into this sect, many of whose tenets are direct forerunners of statements in the Koran. Related to the Elkhasites are the Ebionites, from Aramaic, "the poor ones". See 200.

Jewish Merkava esoterism.

A Rabbinic Council held at Jamnia in Palestine gives final approval for the Hebrew Scripture. The first book to have been published, given an outward form, or in this case, actually composed, is Deuteronomy in 621 BC which is a response on the part of the Levites of Judah to the crisis of the assimilation of the "Ten Lost Tribes" and the disappearance of the northern Kingdom of Israel. The Books of Moses refer to an earlier past but were written partly in the fifth century BC and acquire an authoritative form only around four hundred BC. The next two centuries produce the books of the Prophets, although Daniel comes even later, as do the minor writings. After the council, the Hebrew Bible is thereafter no longer altered, but a body of oral traditions develops as an "Oral Law" and is codified in written form in the third century and is called the Mishnah. A mass of commentary and debate results in two compilations each known as the Talmud, one in Palestine in the fourth century and the other in Babylonia in the fifth.

Justin Martyr, Christian apologist, is born a pagan in Flavia Neapolis, ancient Sichem, what today is Nablus, Palestine.

105
The first papermaker, according to tradition was Ts'ai Lun who created paper from hemp, tree bark, rags, and fishnets. Papermaking eventually came to Baghdad through Samarkand. The Maya made a writing surface from mulberry bark. The Egyptians made papyrus by pressing layers of the sedge plant that grows along the Nile.

106
Trajan annexes Petra.

110-130
Proliferation of Christian and non-Christian Gnostic texts.

116
Trajan brings southern Mesopotamia under Roman control and some Baptist sects look upon events as presaging the end of the world.

c. 120
According to tradition, the Buddhist canon, the Tripitaka, is written down in Sanskrit, under the auspices of the Kushan Emperor Kanishka (78-144) in Kashmir. Tradition calls this "the Fourth Buddhist Council". (The traditional "First Council" is considered to have taken place in Rajagadha (Rajgir in Bihar) after the death of the Buddha, and the second at Vaisali, also in Bihar a century later; only the first two councils or "communal readings" are recognized by all schools of Buddhism. The First Council was presided by Maha Kashyapa, the senior monk alive, to create the first canon by questioning monks of what they remembered – "Thus have I heard" – of what the Buddha said. Upali expounded the *Vinaya Pitaka* – "the discipline", and Ananda, the Buddha's personal attendant, the *Sutra Pitaka* – the Basket of religious discourses. In the same epoch as the Council of Kanishka, the Pali Tibetan Canon is written down in Ceylon by Theravadin monks (and printed for the first time in its entirety in 1893 by order of King Chulalongkorn of Siam). The oldest dated Mahayana Buddhist monument, from the year five of Kanishka, is a statue of the Buddha at Gandhara flanked by two Bodhisattvas, Maitreya and Vajrapani.

New Testament texts appear (up to 150): Gospel of John and letters of John; Jude and II Peter.

Pausanias declares "The Eleusinian mysteries and the Olympian Games seem to exhibit more than anything else the divine purpose."

132-135
Revolt of Bar Kochbah against Hadrian.

140
Marcion and Valentinus (Gnostic leaders) in Rome. The spread of Valentinian Gnosticism.

Marcion sought the answer to the question "Unde Malum? – whence does evil come from. Marcion says that according to the parable in Luke 6:43 there were two trees, one bearing good fruit and one evil. Marcion teaches, according to Couliano, not two principles, but nine; the good God whose residence is in the third heaven. "But in order to have a residence he needs Space to dwell in and heavenly Matter to build his mansion. These are three principles. The fourth is the Saviour, Christ, who proclaims in the lower world the existence of the good God. The fifth is the Demiurge; the sixth, the Space of his residence; the seventh, worldly matter; the eigth, the malignant Opponent; and the ninth is the Messiah of the Jews announced by the Demiurge. This Messiah has nothing to do with Christ; the latter became manifest, the former is still to come (and will)."

150
The virgin birth of Jesus becomes an established Christian doctrine. The Ebionites, when Jesus was baptized, read the event thus: "Thou art my beloved Son, in whom I am well pleased; and again: This day I have begotten thee." These words and ideas – maintained by the Marcionites and in some degree by the Manicheans – were expunged from the Christian texts and replaced with the virgin birth of the Saviour idea from other Hellenist cults.

Formation of Poimandres (the Hermetic Corpus).

Claudius Ptolemy, Hellenist astronomer and cosmologist: the Ptolemaic system and the *Almagest.*

Jewish Heikhalot esoterism.

c. 150-211
Clement of Alexandria.

154
The Edessan dualist philosopher Bardesanes is born.

162
Galen settles in Rome.

168
Bardesanes receives his "revelation".

170
Birth of Flavius Philostratus of Lemnos who, agreeing with classical writers generally, declared that "the Jews have long been in revolt not only against the Romans but against humanity and that they are a race apart and irreconcilable, that cannot share with the rest of mankind

in the pleasures of the table nor join in their libations or prayers and sacrifices, separated from ourselves by a greater gulf than divides us from Susa or Bactra or the more distant Indies..." in *Apollonius of Tyana.*

172

The prophetic movement of Montanes reaches its height in Asia and comes to Rome. Montanus was a desexed priest of Cybele in Phrygia who converted to Christianity about 155. With two prophetesses, Priscilla and Maximilla, he declared that the Holy Ghost had been revealed to them as the Paraclete. Prophecy returned to the Church and the Parousia or Second Coming was probably announced several times or considered immanent.

180

Tatian, a pupil of Justin Martyr, writes the *Diatessaron,* a combination of the gospels, which is used by Mani. The *Diatessaron* contains almost all of the Gospel of John, but only half of Mark; the genealogies are omitted, but the Virgin birth is intact. Tatian was an Encratite, opposed to wine, sex, marriage, and meat.

c.180-222

Activity of Bardesanes (also Bardaisan or Daisan, Daysan) of Edessa (near Harran) northern Syria, today southern Turkey. This Gnostic teacher, along with Marcion, will be considered a direct forerunner of Mani. (Ephrem Syrus: "The Babylonian Mani went through the door that Bardesanes opened").

185-254

Origin, learned Alexandrian eunuch, remembered for *Contra Celsum* and *De Principiis,* developed "a Trinitarian concept designed to refute the Marcionites and the Sabellians. The three Persons are co-eternal and consubstantial but not co-equal. In answer to an accusation by Celsus that the Christians made Jesus greater then God Himself, Origen declared: 'The Son is not mightier than the Father, but inferior to Him.' He made the Persons co-eternal and called them *hypostases.*" Despite his good intentions he became considered a universal heretic and was officially anathemized. Origen enunciated the very important idea that evil is not an essence, not a substance, but the absence of good.

200

One historian estimated that for a population of one Million in Rome at this time, there were 80 thousand Jews, 20 to 30 thousand adepts of Egyptian cults, the same number of adepts of Syrian cults, 20 thousand Christians, and 10 thousand adepts of Mithra.

The Ebionites (perhaps arising from the Essenes) appear as distinct from the Christians. From Aramaic, "the poor ones", also known as Nazarenes (not the same as the early Christians) these are Christian-Jews. "According to the Ebionites, the Jews were the chosen people under the new covenant as under the old, and the Gentile proselytes were like whining dogs receiving crumbs from the table of their Lord. Jesus, born of Mary and Joseph, was of the line of David, and destined to occupy the throne of Israel... according to the Ebionites the Mosaic Law had not been reduced by Jesus, but made more refined and severe..."

The Ebionites have daily ritual baths, a initiatory baptism, and yearly Christian-like mysteries. In these secret rituals they use an unleavened bread and pure water. They say that God established two natures, Jesus and the Devil; the first has power over the coming age, and the second over the present. They say Jesus came from human seed but chose and was chosen to be son of God, the Christ nature having come upon him in the form of a dove (that is, at the Baptism). He was not born of God the Father but was created, like an Archangel, but greater. Jesus was a Prophet like Adam and Moses; he came to put an end to sacrifices. Like the Elkhasites they used the term *yawm ad-Din* for the Day of Judgement. According to M.P. Roncaglia ("Elements Ébionites et Elkésaïtes dans le Coran") the Ebionite-Elkhasites are the Mughtasila out of whom Mani arose, according to an-Nadim in the *Fihrist.* In the tenth century they were living between the Tigris and the Euphrates, and are also the Sabians of the Koran, considered to be a Divinely revealed religion. They were also called the Baptizing sect and Christians of "St John". Adversaries of the Prophet Muhammad accused him of being one of these Sabians (a fact recorded by Wellhausen), which, given the large Manichean content of Koranic doctrine, is quite understandable.

Most of the books now included in the New Testament are from this time accepted as Scripture in Rome according to the Muratorian Fragment, with the Canon fully settled in 367 by the Bishop Athanasius of Alexandria in a public letter which lists the twenty-seven books held authoritative ever since.

Activity of Tertullian, a married Church presbyter of Carthage who formulated the early doctrine of the Trinity, and fought numerous heresies. He "coined the term Monarchian to describe those who sought to establish Christianity as an uncompromising monotheism without in any way reducing the divinity of Christ". Foreshadowing the Dark Ages brought on by Christianity, Tertullian asked the question echoed by other Church Fathers, "What does Athens have to do with Jerusalem?"

Gnostic *Acts of Peter* written which are the source of the legend that Peter went to Rome and was crucified there.

205-270

Plotinus. Creation through emanation; a provisional pantheism which is, in the end, rectified when creation is equated with nothingness and the One with the One.

216
April 14; (8 Nisan-Farmuthi 527) the birth of Mani in Babylonia into the Elchasite sect which his father Pattik had joined while his wife was pregnant with Mani. Mani's mother is called Maryam. On both sides, by legend, he is descended from Parthian princely blood related to the Arsacids.

220
A prelate in the Roman Church named Sabellius develops a Monarchian Trinity; the persons are modalities of activity assuming various functions successively; similar to the doctrine of Patripassianism.

224-641
End of the Parthian Arsacids and the beginning of rule by the Sassanid Dynasty. The victory of Ardashir the Sassanid over Artaban V, the Parthian Arsacid. Sasan the grandfather of Ardashir I had been a superintendent of a Zoroastrian fire dedicated to the goddess Anahita at Istakhr near Persepolis (Takht-i Jamshyd and Naqsh-i Rustam.) Resurgence of Zoroastrianism with Zurvanite (radical dualist) tendencies. Zurvanism may have arisen from the influences upon Zoroastrianism from the Semitic tradition through mutual contact, just as Semitic religion evolved radically into Gnosticism, Christianity, and Islam from the profound effects of Zoroastrianism.

In Zurvanism Ahriman is a twin brother of Ahuramazda, and is thus made into an equal of Ahuramazda; both are considered sons of Zurvan, or Endless Time, whereas in orthodox Zoroastrianism Ahuramazda has no brother, no equal, and Ahriman's corrupting activity is limited to the lowest levels of Ahuramazda's creation. Ahriman is not *essentially comparable* to Ahuramazda, and there is no Zurvan.

Along with the accession of the new dynasty, a goddess named Anahita (Ishtar, also sometimes equated with Artemis and even Athena) appears in Persian wall carvings commemorating Sassanid coronations. The priestly castes of Zoroastrianism develop and take on considerable temporal power. In later Shi'ite legends a Sassanid princess, Shahrbanu ("the Lady of the Land") captured at the Battle of Qadisiyyah, becomes the mother of the Shi'ite Imams by being married to Husayn (there are no historic records of such an event taking place; it is a mythological extrapolation on the part of Shi'ism). The name of this legendary princess is one of the names of Anahita. There was a current prophecy in Persia that one thousand years after Zoroaster (his dates were commonly mistaken into very recent times) the faith founded by him and the Persian Empire would fall together.

The Sassanids learned – erroneously – from the Babylonians that Zoroaster had lived three hundred years before Alexander the Great (in reality Zoroaster lived considerably before 1000 BC). Thus, according to a prophecy current at the time and the defective Babylonian chronology, the Sassanid dynasty could hope to continue only for some 150 years. To cheat prophecy and extend the duration of the dynasty, Ardashir created the official fiction that only 266 years separated the Sassanids from Alexander, whereas in fact there were some 550 years. Arab and Persian historians maintained the false chronological interval as 266 years. This falsification was explained by Mas'udi in the *Kitabu'-t-Tanbih wa'l-Ishraf* as a "political and theological secret". The dynasty ran for 434 years until Yazdigerd III was murdered in 651-2.

228
First vision or revelation of Mani (January 4; 8 Nisan-Farmuthi 539); his "Twin" (*syzygy*) alter ego, or in later teaching, an emanation of the "Jesus of Light" an emanation of the *Nous*, manifests in Mani's thirteenth year.

240
Mani's call to be "Apostle of Light". In his twenty-fourth year (April 18/19, shortly after the Naw Ruz; 8 Nisan-Farmuthi 551) the syzygy-angel "Tawm" (in the Coptic text Mani's heavenly twin is called the *saish* "double" and also called the Paraclete) manifests himself again and commands Mani to act. This is Mani's birth "according to the spirit". The Angel says to Mani: "Peace unto thee Mani from me and from the Lord who sent me to thee and who has selected thee for his apostleship. He bids thee now to call the peoples to the truth and to proclaim from him the good message of the truth and to dedicate thyself to this task. The time is now come for thee to stand forth openly and to preach thy teaching." In a superbly audacious act of imposture, Mani will go on, in effect, to accuse all the religions of being false copies of his own.

241
Mani's journey to India, the valley of the Indus, probably to the port of Deb, on a merchant ship of a certain Oggias, perhaps an early convert. This was in the last years of the reign of Ardashir, when the Persian conquest of the King of the Kushans, Vasudeva, had not yet passed Seistan or contemporaneously with the conquest of the Indus by Shahpur, then co-regent. If so, then Mani was taking an opportunity to show what his religion could do and how useful it could be to the new empire. On this journey of Mani is attributed the conversion of "the King of Turan" (according to Klimkeit, this is in Baluchistan) to Manicheism.

Shahpur I succeeds his father Ardashir as the King of Kings.

242-243
Shahpur leads a campaign against Gordien III of

Rome. It is possible that Mani accompanied him in this campaign (or, alternately, the campaign of 256-260 against Valerian.) If indeed this campaign, then Mani was present on the field with the Persian army while Plotinus was present with the Roman.

243

Mani's audience with Shapur I (September 4), after Mani's return from India, the Indus valley, and Baluchistan where he converted the Turan Shah and established a community. He returned by way of Babylon, and Mesene, on the lower reaches of the Tigris, where Mani converts the ruler, and by way of Susiana. Mani, who is lame in the right foot, tells the king that he is a "healer from the land of Babel"; in offering the King a religion which claims to supersede Christianity, Zoroastrianism, and Buddhism, Mani provides him with a vehicle which appears to promise a unified basis of the empire. His missionaries establish cells within the other religions as well as their own temples. The religion is spread to India, Central Asia, Syria and Egypt. Mani is a friend to Peroz, governor of Khorasan (and brother of Shapur), which will help in the mission to that region. Manicheism will appear in Spain and Rome. Mani's missionaries will use icons attributed to Mani. *Nagar-Khani* and *Nagarestan*, "House of Pictures" are terms which will be used of Manichean temples in later Persian. Such "Houses of Pictures" will also be called the "House of Mani"). An important characteristic of Manichean art is calligraphy with very small letters. Concurrently, or because of Mani, there develops Christian iconography, and Christian icons in general, and the Christian use of nimbus or haloes in pictures. Mani also uses codices or bound books, particularly very small books, to spread his teachings. These are easily carried, in preference to scrolls which are bulky. Combined with the small writing, Mani can be said to be the inventor of the pocketbook, a book which is easily concealed.

The Manichean doctrine of the three times will appear in pseudo-Buddhism in China as the "Sutra of the Three Moments"; (as also the apocryphal inscription on a statue of Isis at Sais: "I am the past, the present, the future; no mortal has ever looked under my veil.") Later Manicheism will be seen as an empire within an empire and be persecuted by the Christians and the Sassanids.

After meeting with Shapur, Mani sends a deputation to the west under Adda and Patik (Pattig), a deputation which had previously been in "Rome" – probably meaning the Eastern Roman Empire.)

250?

Death of Nagarjuna, Indian master of Buddhism who wrote the "Great Treatise of the Perfection of Wisdom" which is preserved in the Chinese translation made by Kumarajiva. Nagarjuna identified Samsara with Nirvana, and took the existence of any contradiction as proof of error.

250-275

Composition of the Manichean Psalms of Thomas. One of the dominant characteristics of Manichean manuscripts is that they are written in very small characters with the letters close together.

Around this time there took place a debate between Mani and a Christian Bishop named Archelaus in the city of Harran, in northern Mesopotamia, now southern Turkey, north of Syria, near Edessa. This theological debate is recorded in the "Acta Archelai". It describes Mani dressed in a variegated cloak (according to Puech, sky blue), wide trousers one leg of which was red, and the other leek green (also described as yellow by Puech), his appearance was that of a military commander, or, an old Persian artificer, (that is, Magus or Chaldean, or as Puech says, a Mithraic priest). Mani also has an ebony staff, long plaited beard, a Babylonian book under his left arm. He wears platform shoes (*trisolium*). He was lame or club footed. His followers attribute feats of levitation to him; other followers studiously deny miracles.

250-300

Redaction of the Mandaean ritual book (Qolasta).

260

Shapur I takes the Roman Emperor Valerian captive near Edessa (Carrhae or Harran) along with 70,000 legionaries who are resettled in Iran (many at Jundishapur) and employed in public works in Khuzistan. The Emperor dies in captivity.

hu Shih-hsing, the first Chinese Buddhist pilgrim to go west in search of Buddhist texts. He went to Khotan and was followed by travelers to India. Fa-Hsien traveled in 399-413; Hsüan-Tsang who traveled 630-644; I-tsing traveled 671-695.

Adda (also known to Christians as Adimantis and polemicised by Augustine) and Abzakya bring Manicheism to Bet Garmai on the Little Zab in Mesopotamia. According to Soghdian texts, Adda also converted a woman called Nafsha by curing her of an illness by invoking the name of Jesus and the laying on of hands. Her sister was a Queen whose husband held the title of Caesar. It is highly probable that this sister was Zenobia of Palmyra. Either before, in the year 244, or after this, Adda and Patik (or Pattig, but not the father of Mani) were on a mission to the Eastern Roman empire; Adda would have gone to Alexandria where he was not the first Manichean missionary; according to Alexander of Lycopolis (Assiut in Egypt) that was someone called Pappos. Other missionaries were Akouas and Thomas, and Mar Ammo, who went to Central Asia.

267

The imperial husband of Zenobia is murdered in a family feud and she takes over the reins of government.

272

Aurelian routs the Palmyrene army at Emesa (Homs); he destroys Palmyra (Tadmir) thus ending the greatest instance up until that time, under the Queen Zenobia, of Arab political expansion. Soon thereafter the Persians install the Lakhmids as rulers of a buffer state centered at Hirah (near today's Najaf and Kufah). The Romans will follow by sponsoring the Syrian Ghassanids between Damascus and Petra.

273

Manicheism in Syria and Palestine. According to Epiphanius of Salamis, the first person to bring Manicheism to Eleutheropolis in Palestine was Akouas, whence the Manicheans were called Akouanitans. Akouas is identified as Mar Zaku, a second generation Manichean leader. He is called *veteranus* and may have been a soldier who came in contact with Manicheism as a prisoner. However, he is also revered by Manicheans in the East along with other leaders such as Pattig and Adda.

274 (or 276)

Kartir, the Grand Mobad of Sassanid Zoroastrianism, convinces the King Vahram that Mani is a harmful figure. Mani arrives on January 21 at Bet Laphat (Jundishapur). He is imprisoned for 26 days on January 31 (or, by other reckoning January 19) and dies on February 26 (or February 14 – the fourth day of Shahrevr). During his imprisonment the sister of Vahram is taken ill and dies, and Mani is brought to the King in chains to answer questions as to the whereabouts of her soul.

Although Mani dies of exhaustion and the heavy chains (25 kilos each three at the hands, three at the feet, one at the neck), his death is called in Manichean texts a crucifixion and martyrdom (*stavrosis* or *dargirdeh*). At his death three women disciples close his open eyes and flee. (Mar Ammo who bought Manicheism to Khorasan, and encountered a resistance on the part of local divinities at Nishapur, had left several days before.) The authorities pass a torch over Mani's body to prove that he is really dead. The body is cut up, his head is exposed at the city gates and the remains are thrown in a rubbish heap.

The term of Mani's imprisonment becomes a Manichean month of fasting ending in February or March with the principle Manichean ceremony, the night feast of the Bema, celebrated on the 30th day of the fast (several days after the anniversary of the death), in front of an empty chair, the chair of the resurrected Mani, who returns in the invisible to "live forever" (the meaning in Aramaic of "Mani Hayy" – or Manicheism.) The return of Mani on the empty throne is called his "Pari-nirvana". This anniversary of the death of Mani will influence the identification of the night of the revelation of the Koran, "the Night of Destiny" as being the 27th Ramadan, the Muslim month of fasting. (Canonic Muslim sources do not specify which night of Ramadan is that night; they only say one of the last ten nights.)

281/282

After an interregnum in the Manichean church, Sisinios becomes the recognized head, or Archegos (also called Sardar, and in Arab sources, later, Imam), but as Manicheans are persecuted, many flee beyond the Oxus and Khorasan becomes the center of activity.

284

29 August. In the Coptic calendar the beginning of the "Era of Martyrs" with the reign of Diocletian.

291(or 292 or 286)

The successor of Mani as head of the Manichean church, the *Princeps Magistrorum* or *archegos*, his disciple Sisinnios undergoes "martyrdom" which is actually death by a sword in the reign of Vahram II. (A Sisinnios is also a Saint in the Byzantine Calendar who wards against the "infant stealing witch of childbirth", Lilith.) His successor, later also martyred, is called Innaios, had been an envoy to India.

293

'Amr ibn Adi, Lakhmid King of Hirah (near present day Najaf and Kufah), is a protector of Manicheism (270-300). 'Amr sent Innaios, one of the Manicheans in Hirah named as his emissary to the Sassanid Great King Narses to plead against the persecution of Manicheism. The Manicheans may have had a role in an uprising in Egypt against the Romans, and this may have softened the attitude of Narses who was cited as an enemy of the Manicheans. In Hirah (which later becomes Kufah), a center of Arab Manicheism, a system of writing Arabic was also developed for the purpose of spreading Mani's works; but it served instead for writing the Koran. Ibn Rosteh, around 905 in the *Kitab al-Al'aq an-Nafisa* will report that Manicheans had come to Mecca from Hirah before Islam. Hirah was also on the route from Mecca to Mada'in, the Persian capital. Thus trading Arabs from Mecca could have observed the Bema ceremony, the central rite of Manicheism which commemorates the return of the martyred Mani as an invisible presence seated upon an apparently empty chair before which is spread a feast. Meccan encounter with the Bema feast is perhaps recorded in this "picture" in the Koran: "Think not of those, who are slain in the way of Allah, as dead. Nay, they are living. *With their Lord they have provision.* (*'inda Rabbihim razzaquna*)" (Koran: 2:154 and 3:169).

296
A Roman army under the General Galerius is routed near Carrhae (Harran) by the Persians. The Persian presence in northern Mesopotamia and Northwestern Iran spawns what has been called a "Sethian" Gnosis from that region.

297
The Persians are defeated by the Roman Galerius and peace is made. The Roman Emperor Diocletian issues an edict against the Manicheans which is addressed to the Roman Proconsul of Africa, Julian, instructing him to extirpate the religion of "monsters" from the enemy kingdom of the Persians. Diocletian prescribed death for the leaders and the authors of their scriptures.

298
After the defeat of the Persians by the Romans in the reign of Diocletian, the Lakhmids under Imru'-l-Qays I go over to the Romans and overrun North and Central Arabia even laying siege to Najran, then held by Shammar Yuhar'ish III of Himyar.

c. 300
Anti-Manichean treatise by a Neoplatonist Church figure, Alexander of Lycopolis (Assiut) in Egypt. Alexander was a pagan who became a Manichean and then a Christian and claimed to have learned Manicheism from someone close to Mani. The time of Hegemonius, the presumed author who recorded the "Acta Archelai". In this work, Mani is depicted as having participated in a debate with Archelaus, a Christian Bishop of Karkhar, a city of Mesopotamia, commonly identified with Harran (Carrhae). Archelaus is thought to have died in 278. Archelaus says that Mani dressed in a blue cloak with yellow trousers, which was the costume of a Mithraic priest, a kind of "guru suit" of its time. (See 250-275).composition of the Pistis Sophia.

The rise of Himyar; Shammar Yuhar'ish III defeats Saba and later overthrows Hadhramaut, ruling all of South Arabia.

301
St Gregory the Illuminator converts King Tiridates III of Armenia to Christianity. The Armenian Church, which is monophysite, does not accept the Council of Chalcedon's definition of the nature of Christ in 451.

A Sogdian text tells of Manichean missionary activities by a disciple called Gabryab. The King of Erevan was won, briefly, to the teachings of Mani, against the objections of Christians at the court, by the healing of his wife's daughter through invocation of the name of Jesus (a common theme in Manichean conversion stories).

302
Edict of the Emperor Diocletian against the Manicheans.

c. 305
Death of Porphyry, Neo-Platonic philosopher, author of the *Isagoge*.

312
Constantine the Great defeats the General Maxentius near Rome.

313
Constantine proclaims equal rights for all religions in the Empire and promulgates the Edict of Milan restoring confiscated property to the Christians. He later bans gladiatorial combats.

321
Emperor Constantine issues a law on the seventh of March making Sunday the day of rest: "All judges and city people and the craftsmen shall rest upon the venerable Day of the Sun. Country people, however, may freely attend to the cultivation of the fields because it frequently happens that no other days are better adapted for planting the grain in the furrows or the vines in the trenches. So that the advantage given by heavenly providence may not for the occasion of a short time perish." The Emperor Antoninus Pius had already noted that Christians observed Sunday as a day of rest or as the sabbath. Justin Martyr and others had advocated Sunday as a sabbath day to distance themselves from Jews and it was already a common Christian practice when Constantine passed a civil law in this respect, but the use of Sunday as the Christian sabbath nevertheless originates from Mithraism.

325
The First Ecumenical Council called at Nicaea to decide on the Arian position that Jesus was neither man nor God but something in between (or not of the same substance as God, *hetero-ousia*). The Bishop Alexander, succeeded in 328 by Athanasius, supports *homoousia*, "consubstantiality" between the nature of Jesus and God, a doctrine which is adopted. The council placed the passion of Christ on March 22-25, and settled the date on which Easter is still celebrated (a date taken from Mithraism.)

326
Equal rights for all religions is rescinded as regards Manicheism. Constantine issues an edict against the Manicheans.

330

May 11. Constantine dedicates his capital Constantinople, on the site of Byzantium.

c. 350

The Nag Hammadi codices are written in Egypt.

The Himyar king is converted to Christianity; Christianisation of Abyssinia and churches are established at Zafar and Aden.

Around this time, the monk Eusebius Hieronymus, Saint Jerome, at the behest of Pope Damasus, working for twenty five years in a cell in Bethlehem, using all the written sources at his disposal and oral information, translates the Bible from Hebrew and Greek into Latin. His renderings such as "salvation" "sermon" "sacrament" "predestination" become part of the ecclesiastical vocabulary.

Mummification of the dead wanes in Egypt when Antony and Athanasius assure their followers that at the resurrection Christ will give them celestial bodies even if their earthly ones had been consumed by worms.

354-430

The great architect of Western Christianity, St Augustine, a Berber born in North Africa, and Bishop of Hippo. He spent nine years as a Manichean. He became a Roman magistrate in Milan, appointed by a pagan who hoped that, as a Manichean, and not a Christian, Augustine would be tolerant of other religions and not agitate for the suppression of Pagan rites. Unfortunately, Augustine was thereupon Baptized by Ambrose at Milan in 386.

"The Gospel Jesus and Paul teach predestination and election by grace; and in the former original sin is implied. It is extraordinary that in hundreds of books composed by the Greek and Latin Fathers not even one ever noticed this doctrine; all proclaimed the congenital freedom of the will." A British monk named Pelagius seeking to defeat the Manicheans arrived in Rome... "for centuries the theory of free will as well as the contradictory doctrine of human depravity had been proclaimed by the Church. Pelagius compelled it to choose between the two... in 410... he declared that each soul is a new creation endowed with pristine purity, and that infants who die without sin attain paradise without baptism; that human nature, being the creation of God, is basically good; that the will possesses an inalienable freedom which cannot be destroyed even by the force of habit; that the grace of Christ is universal; that Jesus was the teacher and exemplar rather than a sacrifice or an atonement; that man can attain perfection through the practice of the Gospel ethics as well as through faith; and that salvation, therefore, is within the power of the human will and can be attained by practical works. Although Pelagius was himself a celibate, who declared that we must obey the command of Christ to renounce all material possessions and confer these upon the poor, he and his followers always held marriage and all normal human appetites in the highest esteem."

The rationalist Pelagius went to Palestine, and Augustine took it upon himself to set these errors straight rationally, but was thereby driven to drop his previous libertarianism, affirm predestinarianism, the crushing primacy of original sin, and the necessity and trumping efficacy of baptism. (Constantine waited until his deathbed to be baptized so he could be absolved from all sins at the last moment.) Augustine thus also accepted Manicheism's anti-cosmic, evil-creation ideas along with the sinfulness of the flesh and carnal relations, which are the work of the devil and which transmit original sin. To counter this he posited reliance upon the capricious mystery of grace for some, and the lack of it for others. In private Augustine may have believed in Traducianism, that a child's soul is generated by its parents.

In fighting Donatism, Augustine declared that the rites are effective even if the performers are defective, that is, reprobates. The Donatists complained that when they expelled someone for moral turpitude, he was immediately given equal rank by the Catholics. Augustine's argument was interesting in that if the Donatists were right, and Baptism performed by the unworthy was ineffective, then nobody could claim to be a Christian.

In opposing the "heresies" which he felt compelled to do, Augustine backed into doctrines which he supposedly had repudiated and upheld a totalitarianism of the Church, advocating revolt against the civil government. "Throughout, Augustine assumes that Catholic violence constitutes the tenderest love and affection." He was accused by many of being a de facto Manichean, without the doctrinal supports.

"Augustine formulated many of the administrative and political theories which still govern the Catholic Church... first, the unity and universality of the Church; second, the impossibility of separating the good from the bad in this world; third the nature of baptism and other sacraments; fourth, the necessity of coercion and persecution; and fifth, the use and purpose of secular power."

However, to his eternal credit, Augustine put forward the concept of another thinker, one who was admittedly, anathemized, namely Origen: that evil does not have an essence, but is rather an absence of good, which is the quintessential repudiation of Manicheism.

358

The Mithraeum of Alexandria destroyed by the Arian George, and after his accession in 379 Theodosius took extreme measures to extirpate this widespread Persian religion, which had temples in Germany and Scotland, as well as throughout the Roman world. The adoption of Sunday as the Christian Sabbath, the 25th of December (birth of Mithra) as the birth of Jesus reflect how much Christianity owes to Mithraism. The rays of sun coming out of the head of the Statue of Liberty in New York also recall the *sol invictus* or "invincible sun" of Mithraism.

363
Titus of Bostra and the polemic against the Manicheans: Adversus Manicheos.

372
Edict of Valentinian I against the Manichees.

373-382
Augustine is a Manichee "hearer" – a novice or low-level follower – in North Africa.

375
Marcus Diaconus in his biography of Porphyrius of Gaza said of the Manicheans: "Outwardly they were sheep and inwardly ravenous wolves and venomous beasts, for hypocrisy marks all their works and deeds."

381
"The Ecumenical council of Constantinople; reaffirmed the Nicene or *homoousian* Creed, condemned Macedonius and the Pneumatomachi (fighters against the spirit), adopted the *Filioque* theology, and formally elevated the Holy Ghost to equality in the Trinity."

386
Kumarajiva, the Indian Buddhist scholar, comes to China.

Priscillian, a Catholic Bishop in Spain, is executed for Manicheism. Priscillian also appeared naked in the middle of the congregation during mass. Ioan P. Couliano ("Tree of Gnosis") thinks it is possible that the tomb of Santiago in Compostella may actually be the tomb of Priscillian.

379-395
Manicheism legally ranks as a crime and sacrilege in the Roman Empire. Appointment of Inquisitors.

380
Theodosius the Great makes Christianity the religion of the Roman Empire.

381
Theodosius issues a decree against the Manicheans.

388-399
Augustine, having become a Christian, writes anti-Manichean Treatises.

390
Bishop Theophilus, with the help of the Emperor Theodosius, razed the Serapeum of Alexandria, the most imposing temple in the city, built during the Ptolemaic dynasty. Serapis was a combination of Osiris and Apis, the bull. This was the Hellenized form of Osiris worship and soteriology. In the fourth century the Egyptians believed that if Serapis were offended the Nile would not overflow. Before the advent of the Christian Priest-State many cults existed side by side and people could choose what they believed. The destruction of this classical civilisation by the new religion brings on the Dark Ages in Europe.

394
Theodosius the Great (d. 395) bans pagan rites and the Olympic games. Theodosius also abolished the Eleusinian mysteries, the mystic festivals of Demeter and her daughter Persephone held outside of Athens in the autumn and the spring. Originally limited to the residents of Attica, they became open to all Greeks and later to Romans as well. The Emperors Hadrian and Marcus Aurelius were initiates. Virtually all citizens of Athens were initiated. The mysteries promised joys to the good after death and punishment to the bad and were judged thereby to have a beneficial moral effect on the population. When the Emperor Valentinus put an end to religious celebrations at night the Eleusinian mysteries were excepted. There were many acts of devotion to be performed at Eleusis and on the road there, in addition to the solemn ceremonies (which included a fertility scene with a giant phallus and yoni). But the road to Eleusis also included merriment and banter. The mysteries were in the hereditary hands of two priestly families, the Eumolpidae and the Kerykes. "The Hymn to Demeter declares: 'Happy is he among mortals who has beheld these things! and he that is initiate, and hath no lot in them, hath never equal lot in death beneath the murky gloom.' Pindar, writing in the fifth century [BC], declared that the happy survival of the soul is possible only for those who have by 'good fortune, culled the fruit of the rite that released from toil,' that is, the Eleusinian, concerning which he continues: 'Blessed is he who hath seen these things before he goeth beneath the hollow earth; for he understandeth the end of mortal life, and the beginning of a new life given of god.' Isocrates, 436-338 [BC], declared that Demeter enabled mankind to rise above the status of beasts by conferring 'the fruits of earth;' and that she instituted 'the holy rite which inspires in those who partake of it sweeter hopes regarding both the end of life and all eternity.'" (Larson, *Religion of the Occident.*) In 396 Christian monks accompanying the Arian Alaric destroyed the shrine, but the spirit of the Eleusinian mysteries had already been incorporated into Christianity through the Gospel of John.

399-414
Chinese Buddhist scholar and pilgrim Fa-Hsien (317-420) goes to India through Central Asia and returns by Sea. He visited India for six years, left an invaluable account of his travels, and translated Buddhist works into Chinese.

c. 400
Coptic Manichean texts from Medinat Madi (Fayyum).

Abukarib As'ad, king of Himyar controls much of the Arabian peninsula and installs the Kinda clan as governors of North-East Arabia. He builds the "Elephant Road" of the Yemen from Zafar to Taif. The Persians are driven from the Arabian coast of the Gulf.

402
Kumarajiva arrives at Ch'ang-an, the capital of a Buddhist ruling house of Tibetan origin. The state sponsors translations of Buddhist texts, both Mahayana and Hinayana into Chinese and the Madhyamak philosophy is introduced into China.

410
A bishop of the church of Hirah is mentioned as attending a Synod of the Mesopotamian Church. The Christians of Hirah (or Hertha), which was to become the center of the Lakhmid kingdom, were called *'Ibad.*

421-38
Reign in Iran of Vahram V, after the death of Yazdagird I who emerges victorious from a dynastic struggle owing to the help of an Arab prince of Hirah. Vahram, who was raised among the Arabs, is one of the most renowned of the Sassanids, known as a hunter, poet, and musician.

438
The Roman Emperor Theodosius II issues the Theodosian code which further restricts pagans.

431
(Third Ecumenical) Council of Ephesus. Cyril of Alexandria, supports a doctrine of the coherence of human and divine natures in Jesus. He has Nestorius, Bishop of Constantinople anathemized. Nestorius held that Jesus was two persons one with a divine nature, and the other with a human. The Council affirms that Mary may be called *Theotokos*, "Mother of God". Nestorius is banished and goes to Arabia and then to the East; beginning of Nestorianism.

449
"The Robber Synod" at Ephesus. It made the Monophysitism of Eutyches and Dioscurus briefly the official Christology of the Church. (*See* 451)

450-519
Relaxing of the Antimanichean Edict.

451
The ecumenical Council of Chalcedon, reversed the decision of the Robber Synod in 449 and condemned Monophysitism. Instead, the thoroughly Aristotelian definition of Jesus as being "true man and true God". The council also further anathemized all vestigies of Nestorianism.

455
Rome sacked by the Vandals under Gaiseric.

459-484
Firuz, King of Persia, doubtless out of strategic considerations to cultivate a Christian group within his borders, gives royal support to the Nestorians; dyophysitism (Nestorianism) becomes the official Christian doctrine within the Persian Empire.

468
Birth of the grandfather of Muhammad, 'Abd al-Muttallib (based on his death taking place at the age of 110 years when the Prophet was eight years old.)

484
A Persian army led by Firuz (Peroz) to support their allies the Chionitae in Soghdiana is destroyed by Hephtalites or White Huns. Trade declines in the Silk Road until the early sixth century.

488
Accession of Kavad to the Sassanid throne after a brief reign of four years by Balash.

489
The Nestorian college driven out of Edessa by the Byzantine Emperor Zeno and set up in Nisibis by Bar-Soma. The Nestorians, now definitively established in Iran, soon abolish celibacy of the Priesthood perhaps in response to the pressure of Zoroastrian practice.

Iran is in social upheaval; in that rigid class society there is a disaffected movement among the common people calling for social equality and the redistribution of property which is to be held in common as are women. This is a revolutionary materialistic movement associated with Manicheism led by a leader called Mazdak. It can very fairly be called communism. Kavad at first champions the movement and introduces a number of laws to do with the status of women. He is deposed as the result of a plot, his life is spared, he escapes to the Hephtalite court where he spent his youth.

490
The War of al-Basus among the Arabs; the rise of pre-Islamic poets follows.

491
Armenia repudiates the Council of Chalcedon.

494-524
The social revolutionary movement of the Mazdakites in Persia. The Mazdakites loot property, abduct women, and expropriate land.

499
Kavad returns to Iran with a Hepthalite army, deposes his brother Zamasp and regains his throne. Now he is much less well disposed to the Mazdakites who include a number of converted noblemen. When they oppose the succession of his son Chosroes he breaks with them. The Mazdakites are opposed by the Christian and Zoroastrian clergy; eventually they are overthrown, their books are burnt, and their property is confiscated. Many Mazdakite Jews and Persians flee to Azerbaijan. Fifty years later a similar revolt erupts in Bokhara.

504-554
The height of the Lakhmid dynasty in Iraq under the King Mundhir III and the Persian suzerainty of Kabad and Chosroes I. Mundhir III is said to have made human sacrifices to al-'Uzza, among them Christian nuns. One of his wives however, Hind bint Nu'man, was a Christian, the daughter of a Ghassanid prince. She founded a Christian convent in Hirah, whose dedicatory inscription is handed down by Yaqut. Her son, 'Amr b. Mundhir, a professed Christian, became the succeeding Lakhmid ruler after 554 and until 569. His successors appear not to have been Christian since Nu'man the Lakhmid also made human sacrifices to al-'Uzza.

513(or 515)
The Synod of Tyre (not an ecumenical council, that is, accepted by all); rejection of the Chalcedonian formula due to the influence of the Monophysite Patriarch of Antioch, Severus who is eventually driven from his see. However, the continued resistance on the part of Monophysitism will lead Justinian to move towards some accommodation with it.

516
Dhu Nuwas (Yusuf As'ar), King of the Yemen.

523
Massacre of the Christians of Najran in southern Arabia by Dhu Nuwas (Yusuf As'ar), a Judaizing ruler in South Arabia who compelled people to become Jews. The Christian martyrs of Najran are mentioned in the Koran (85: 4-11). Those who refuse to convert to Judaism, the religion of Dhu Nuwas, are thrown into a burning pit. A survivor of the massacre escapes to Byzantium, and holding up a gospel, calls upon the Emperor to avenge the martyrs.

525
The Monophysite Christian Abyssinians, under the Negus Ella Asbeha (Hellestheaios), at the request of Justin I, Emperor of Byzantium, send an army to punish Dhu Nuwas and conquer the Yemen. Dhu Nuwas, last of the Himyar kings, "rides his horse into the sea". The Abyssinians make San'a the capital and appoint Sumyafa', a Christian Arab, viceroy of the Yemen.

Harith of Kinda, grandfather of the poet Imru'-l-Qays, is killed along with 48 other members of the tribe by Mundhir III the Lakhmid king of Hirah. In the turmoil following, some members of the Kinda rejoin the Yemen division of the tribe. The father of Imru'-l-Qays, the Amir over the Asad, is assassinated. Imru'-l-Qays unsuccessfully tries to avenge his father's death, and ends up in exile guarding five coats of mail and his family. Later he is called to Constantinople but dies at what is Ankara today, perhaps poisoned by the Byzantines after having been appointed by them as head of the Arab armies of the Ghassanis.

529
Al-Harith ibn Jabala (in Greek Aretas) of the Jafnid branch of the Ghassanis is made *Phylarch*, or prince of the Ghassanis by the Byzantine emperor. He also has the title of *Patrikios*.

529
The Byzantine Emperor Justinian, as part of the suppression of paganism, closes the Neoplatonic Academy of Athens. This gives impetus to other schools such as that of the Nestorians in Jundishapur, Persia and that of Harran. Around this time the Codex Justianus is also published, part of the codification and reform of Roman Law, as a result of a commission headed by a Jurist named Tribonius. These codices add to the prestige of Roman Law and eventually influence the formation of the Islamic *shari'ah*.

531
Beginning of the reign of the Sassanid Chosroes I (Anushirwan) in Persia, and a resurgence of Zoroastrianism, following the suppression of the Mazdakites. The Mazdakites, who practiced a form of communism, are usually considered to be a school of Manicheism. The Mazdakite period is remembered with horror in Iranian history, when confusion reigned and "children did not know their fathers". Similar revolts and movements reappear in later Iranian history, notably the Qarmati revolt, and the Mazdakites are recalled as a

warning by Nizam al-Mulk during the height of the Assassin period. Gibbon said of Anushirwan: "A disciple of Plato was seated on the throne of Persia."

535
Abrahah, a Christian Ethiopian soldier of fortune overthrows the viceroy of the Abyssinians in the Yemen.

537
The Church of the Holy Wisdom, the Hagiah Sophia, is built in Byzantium by Anthemios of Tralles and Isidorus of Miletus.

c. 540
Death of Imru'-l-Qays (called al-Malik ad-Dillil) at Ankara, after his departure from Constantinople. The first and perhaps greatest of the pre-Islamic poets, author of one of the *qasidas* known as the *mu'allaqat*, the "hung" or "consecrated" odes.

542
Justinian consents to the appointment of two independent Monophysite bishops for lands on the Arabian frontier, the first so recognized: Jacobus Baradaeus and Theodore.

554
The Lakhmid king Mundhir III falls in battle with Harith ibn Jabala of the Ghassanis. Mundhir is succeeded by his son 'Amr ibn Hind (until 569).

565
Justinian closes the Academy of Aristotle.

569
al-Mundhir succeeds his father al-Harith ibn Jabala as Phylarch of the Ghassanis. Later he is suspected of double dealing with the Persians and taken prisoner by the Byzantines after having been invited to attend the dedication of a church. Other Jafnids head the Ghassanis.

570
"The Year of the Elephant", traditional year for the attack on Mecca by Abrahah (although some modern scholars say this must have taken place earlier in 547 for example). This is the traditional year for the birth of the Prophet.

570-575
Chosroes I of Persia conquers the Yemen under the general Wahriz, and Abrahah is killed. Saif of Yazan, a Himyar nobleman is made viceroy of the Persians.

T'ien T'ai school of Buddhism founded in China as a Confucian reaction to the development of the Ch'an Sect (later in Japan, Zen), and the development of the Amitabha (O-mi-t'o, "Buddha of the Boundless Light", later in Japan, Amida) school of the Happy Western Paradise (*Sukhavati*). It has been suggested that the Amitabha idea originates in Persia, perhaps in Balkh, where Buddhism was strongly implanted. It is possible that Amitabha is a syncretistic assimilation of Ahura Mazda. Popularity of "the path to perfection" in the Lotus Sutra (*Saddharmapundarika* Sutra).

578
Death of 'Abd al-Muttallib, reportadly at the age of 110 years, grandfather of Muhammad who then was eight years old.

579
Anushirwan (Chosroes) succeeded by Hormazd IV in Persia. Sometime before his accession a wall is built at Derbend south of the Caspian Sea to stop marauders from the East. After Islam this Sassanid wall becomes known as "the wall of Alexander".

551
Council of Constantinople II (ecumenical). Origen, long dead, anathemized in detail. Nestorianism again condemned.

c.580
Collapse of the dam of Ma'rib signals to the desert Arabs the symbolic end of the great age of South Arabian Kingdoms.

Ghassanis devastate Hirah, capital of the Lakhmids, near present day Najaf and Kufah.

A Yemeni merchant come to Mecca is cheated by a member of the tribe of Quraysh. Having no ally he stands upon the slopes of Abu Qubays and calls for redress; a group of Meccans band to stand together as one man to jointly aid the oppressed; this is called the "Oath of Chivalry" (*Hilf al-Fudul*). At that time the head of the Hashim clan is the Prophet's uncle Zubayr who, as one of the founders of the pact, takes Muhammad to participate in the oath.

581
Ghassanid dynasty abolished by the Byzantines over religious quarrels.

580-585
War of Fijar; the Quraysh war with the Beduin tribes of the Hawazin over the perfume trade of the Yemen against the background of Persian and Byzantine economic politics; they breach the traditional period of yearly truce and fight during the month of Ramadan, whence the name, which means "The Sacrilegious War". The War is a series of incidents stemming from various quarrels.

589-628
Reign of Chosroes II in Persia.

590
'Uthman ibn Huwayrith attempts to create an alliance with Byzantium and rule Mecca.

595
The Prophet marries his first wife, Khadijah. He is noted as an archer, and is known to the Meccans as *Amin*, "the trusty one" for his probity and honesty. He has very sharp vision and can discern twelve stars in the constellation of the Pleiades.

600
The death of Mar Shad Ohrmizd leader of the eastern branch of Manicheism. He may have been buried in Mazar-i Sharif (Balkh, Afghanistan). A tomb, probably his, is later protected during Islamic rule by being called the tomb of 'Ali, the fourth Caliph. In Central Asia, the Manicheans followed the model of Buddhism and founded monasteries. When they went to China these monasteries did not include living quarters, but did have spaces for common meals and place to tend to the sick.

Around this time a group of Jewish savants known as the Masoretes devise a system of vowel signs which record the pronunciations and thereby fix the meanings of the Hebrew Bible according to what at that time was deemed to be correct, but thereby introduce variations in the text of the Council of Jamnia of 100 AD.

602
The last Lakhmid king, Nu'man III, quarrels with the Persian Chosroes II Parviz over the Persian's request for marriage to his daughter. Nu'man is put to death by being trampled by an elephant. The Persians install a Persian governor in Hirah over the Arabs.

605
A Chinese visitor to Soghdiana writes "An Account of the Western Barbarians" (Hsi-fan chi). Wei Chieh says that it was predominantly a Zoroastrian region, and gives a description of Zoroastrian rites in Samarkand. But Manicheism is strong in the regions south and in the early Middle Ages the existence of a Manichean monastery in Samarkand is attested by the *Hudud al-'Alam.*

608
The Ka'bah in Mecca is rebuilt. The Prophet, before his mission, is chosen by the Quraysh to put the Black Stone back into the new Ka'bah.

THE MISSION OF THE PROPHET:

610
The beginning of the Prophet's mission; according to reports in Bukhari, the Prophet already had prophetic dreams which were "like the breaking of the light of dawn". Now the revelation of the Koran descends upon him in a cave at the summit of a mountain outside Mecca during the month of Ramadan.

Accession of Heraclius as Emperor of Byzantium.

611
The Battle of Dhu Qar in which an Arab tribe, the Bani Bakr, defeat a Persian army. (Also put at 605)

613
Public preaching of Islam begins.

614
The Persians capture Damascus. The Persians are thus again in Syria; this probably marks the end of the Ghassanid dynasty.

615
The first emigration of Muslims to Abyssinia to escape Meccan persecution. They are received by the Negus and allowed to remain despite attempts by the Meccans to turn the Abyssinians against the emigrants.

Chosroes II Parviz, spurred by the assassination of the Byzantine Emperor Maurice in 602 fought wars with Byzantium beginning in 608; now the Persians sack Jerusalem and take the "True Cross" to Ctesiphon.

616-618
Conversion of 'Umar. The Prophet is continually satirized and insulted by the pagan Quraysh. The Quraysh declare a ban on the clan of the Bani Hashim because of the Prophet's preaching. The ban is lifted two years later through growing opposition to it by Meccan sympathizers to the Hashimites.

617
Civil war at Yathrib (which will become Medinah); the fourth battle of that conflict, the inconclusive Battle of Bu'ath, between the tribes of Aws and Khazraj.

619
"The Year of Sadness": Death of Khadijah, the Prophet's first wife, and the death of Abu Talib, his uncle and protector, head of the Bani Hashim clan.

Constantinople under siege from an alliance of the Persians and the Avars.

620

The Prophet goes to Ta'if to seek haven and converts, and is successful in neither. On the return journey from Ta'if the Prophet recites the Koran at night in Nakhlah; seven passing Jinn stop and listen.

Isra' and *Mi'raj*, or "Night Journey". The Prophet is taken in one night from Mecca to Jerusalem mounted on the Buraq brought by the Angel Gabriel. From the Temple Mount, the *al-Aqsa*, the Prophet, carried by Gabriel, ascends into the Divine Presence in heaven.

In the pilgrimage of that year, six men of the tribe of Khazraj of Yathrib (Medinah) enter Islam at the hand of the Prophet.

621

The First 'Aqabah covenant with twelve men of Khazraj and Aws of Yathrib (Medinah).

622

Second 'Aqabah covenant. The converted Medinans pledge to defend the Prophet.

In the Byzantine-Persian wars, the tide turns in favor of the Byzantines. Heraclius undertakes successful campaigns against the Persians.

Hsüan Tsang, born in Lo-yang in 602, receives at Ch'eng-tu the complement of the Buddhist monastic rules. He leaves Ssu-ch'uan and goes to the capital of the new T'ang dynasty Ch'ang-an, in the province of Shensi. This was the Rome of ancient China and one of the first centers of Buddhism in the Far East. Missionaries from India and Kashgaria had arrived there five centuries earlier and set about translating from Sanskrit into Chinese the literature of the, now two, Buddhist Vehicles, split into sects with many discrepancies. Hsüan Tsang's sympathies lie with the school of mysticism known as Vij_2avada or Yogachara. This vies with Hinayana and its rules of monasticism for the monks and charity for the laymen, with Mahayana and its theory of universal salvation and metaphysic, and with the Madyamika, or Middle Path, with its theory of the void and a system of pietism. Hsüan Tsang wishes to find the roots and resolves to undertake a journey to the sources.

THE HIJRAH

In the Christian year 622, the 1st day of Muharram, the first month of the Arab year, fell on July 15/16. This became the first year of the Islamic era when in September of that year the Prophet entered Medinah and the Islamic state was born. The usage of dating the Islamic era – year one – from the year in which the Hijrah took place was officially instituted by the Caliph 'Umar sixteen years later. That New Year's Day of that Arab year became, in retrospect, the beginning of year one in the Arab (and later Islamic) calendar year (already in progress) when the Hijrah took place a few months later.20 or 27 September, the Hijrah, the Prophet arrives in Medinah, having fled Mecca some two weeks earlier, and narrowly escaped a joint attempt by the leaders of several clans to assassinate him.

As one of his first acts, in the house of Anas ibn Malik he establishes brotherhood (*akha*) between the Medinans (*Ansar*) and the Refugees (*Muhajirun*); each adopts another; they are declared to belong to a Muslim community (*ummah*).

623

The Prophet concludes the marriage with 'A'ishah which had been contracted earlier in Mecca. (After the death of Khadijah he had already married a widow, Sawdah. The marriage to 'A'ishah is concluded, in accordance with Semitic custom, when she reaches the biological age of marriage, which is puberty.)

Second year of the Hijrah = 5 July 623

Heraclius, who had taken the Byzantine throne in 610, undertook a campaign against the Persians with success. The next year, 624 Heraclius enters into Atropatene (Azerbaijan) and destroys the great fire-temple.

624

(*Rajab AH 2*); Muslim raid by 'Abd Allah ibn Jahsh to Nakhlah. He captures a Meccan caravan in the last day of Rajab, a sacred month in which fighting was prohibited by customary law. The verse is revealed: "They question you about the sacred month and fighting therein. Say: to fight therein is a grave offence; but barring men from God's path and sacrilege against Him and the holy mosque and driving out His people therefrom are graver with God. And torturing is graver than killing..." (Koran 2: 217).

February? (*Sha'ban*? *AH 2*); the direction of prayer changed from Jerusalem to Mecca (according to Bell: *Rabi' al-awwal AH 2*; December, 623)17 March (*19 Ramadan AH 2*); an outnumbered Muslim army defeats a Meccan force at Badr.(*15 Shawwal AH 2*); Muslim attack on the Jewish tribe of the Bani Qaynuqa'.(*Dhu al-Hijjah AH 2*; April 624) Meccan raid on Medinah.

3rd year of the Hijrah = 24 June 624

625

March (*7 Shawwal AH 3*); Muslims defeated at Jabal Uhud outside of Medinah.

4th year of the Hijrah = 13 June 625

625

(*Rabi' al-Awwal* or *al-Akhir AH 4*; September); Muslim campaign against the Jewish tribe of Bani Nadir, who are expelled.(*Dhu al-Hijjah*) Prophet's marriage with Zaynab.

5th year of the Hijrah = 2 June 626

626

4 September. Li Shih-min deposes his father and become the Chinese Caesar, the second T'ang Emperor, T'ai-tsung. Shortly China expands to include Mongolia.

627

April (*Dhu al-Qa'dah AH 5*); Medinah besieged by a combined Meccan and Beduin army – Battle of the Trench (*khandaq*); this is also called the "War of the Confederates –" *al-ahzab*). The Battle is followed by the destruction of the treacherous Bani Qurayzah. Later tradition projects back onto Salman al-Farsi, a probably apocryphal figure, the credit for the advice to build the trench (an ancient Sumerian defensive trench existed around a city near the later Samarra' and the Persians had built a trench in Iraq, maintained by the Lakhmids, against the Arabs); the Prophet is pictured as saying to Salman "you are of the people of the House" (*anta minna ahl al-bayt*) which becomes a formula of investiture in the initial 'Abbasid conspiracy along with the propaganda slogan: "Felicity [or "the anointed one"] [will come] from the People of the House." The "People of the House" is a formula with a double meaning; one for the Arabs, and another for the adherents of Iranian religions.

Heraclius carries his campaign against the Persians into the Tigris provinces.

6th year of the Hijrah = 23 May 627

627

(*Sha'ban AH 6*; December); Muslim campaign against the Bani Mustaliq; 'A'ishah's misadventure.

628

March-April (*Dhu al-Qa'dah* or *al-Hijjah AH* 6); The Prophet, having received a Koranic revelation that he will pray in Mecca, undertakes a pilgrimage with approximately 1,000 unarmed men; the caravan is stopped at Hudaybiyyah, a short distance from Mecca. In a moment of great danger when 'Uthman who has gone to Mecca to parley does not return promptly, the Prophet, in a state like that of his revelations, suddenly has the Muslims who are waiting for the news and fearing a massacre, take a new oath of fealty to him. This oath will be called the *bay'at ar-ridwan* ("the Pact of Felicity"), according to the words of the Koran which says God was "well pleased" (cf. Gr. *eudokia*) with those who renewed their commitment to struggle in the "way of God with their lives and with their property". Then the Meccan representatives come and negotiate the Treaty of Hudaybiyyah which will allow the Muslims to perform the pilgrimage unhindered the next year; in so doing the pagan Meccans have been brought to compromise with the Muslims. This will strongly advance the Prophet's prestige among the undecided Arabs.(*6* or *7 AH*); According to tradition, Messengers sent to the Muqawqis, ruler of Egypt, Chosroes II Parviz of Persia, Heraclius of Byzantium, the rulers of the Yemen, and to others, calling them to Islam before they would be conquered and subjugated. The Muqawqis sent gifts by way of return, the Persian Shah Kavad II (Siroes) who had succeeded Chosroe II in the meantime, tore up the letter. Badhan, *Qa'il*, or ruler, of the Yemen, saw certain prophecies made by the Prophet fulfilled regarding the death of Chosroes II in Persia, revolted against the Persian suzerainty, and entered Islam. (Chosroes II was a reprehensible ruler, mean and given to empty pomp.) The gifts of the Egyptian viceroy to the Prophet were a riding mule and two coptic concubines. One of these, Maria, is the mother of the Prophet's son Ibrahim, who dies in infancy. (The sending of the messengers may be an apocryphal back projection of historic events). According to traditional accounts, the sending of the messengers followed a vision which took place during the digging of the trench to defend Medinah. Tradition relates that the Prophet split a large stone and three flashes of light emerged; the first illuminated for the Prophet the castles of the Yemen, the second the castles of Syria, and the third the palace of Kisra' (Chosroes) at Mada'in (Ctesiphon-Seleucia). This is understood to be a sign that God was opening, for the conquest of Islam from Arabia, the South, the West, and the East.

7th year of the Hijrah = 11 May 628

(*Jumada al-Awla AH 7*; according to Bell, this took place in *Muharram*); The Jewish citadels of Khaybar conquered. Growing strength of the Muslims becomes apparent.

According to a weak tradition, Ka'b ibn Malik marks the points of the sacred boundary (*haram*) declared around Medinah.

Siroes (Kabad II) of Persia makes peace with Heraclius and returns the "True Cross".

629

March-April (*Dhu al-Qa'dah AH 7*); the Muslim pilgrimage to Mecca (*'umratu al-qadiyyah*) which was agreed by the Treaty of Hudaybiyyah; Bilal calls the prayer from the top of the Ka'bah – the *shahadah* echoes in the valley of Mecca, while the Quraysh watch and listen from the hill of Abu Qubays.

8th year of the Hijrah = 1 May 629

(*Jumada al-Awla AH 8*; September); The Byzantines repulse a Muslim excursion at Mu'tah; the first time that Khalid ibn Walid takes command of Muslim armies. Prophet sees the events in a vision and calls Khalid the "Sword of God".

Death of Siroes (Kavadh II) in Persia and beginning of a period of anarchy. He is succeeded by daughters of Chosroes II Parviz, Purandukht and Azarmidukht, (Boran) and then by various pretenders.

630

January (*20 Ramadan AH 8*); The conquest of Mecca. The Ka'bah purified of idols.

Battle of Hunayn; attack on Ta'if.

9th year of the Hijrah = 20 April 630

9th year of Hijrah – the "Year of Deputations", tribes from all over Arabia come to accept Islam. In *Muharram*/April messengers are sent over Arabia to collect the poor-tax from converted tribes.

October to December (*Rajab*). The Prophet leads a military expedition to Tabuk in north Arabia.

The Chinese Buddhist pilgrim Hsüan Tsang (Xūanzang) visits Balkh and reports that the monastery of Naw Bahar was at some distance from a large group of Hinayana monasteries and that *Naw Bahar* (which he called *Nava Sangharama*, recognizable as Naw Bahar from Soghdian Buddhist texts) was reserved for the exclusive use of monks from "north of the great snowy mountains". The separation from the Hinayana monasteries and the use of the name Nava Vihara ("new monastery") which in Persian is Naw Bahar and means "new spring" suggests that it and the other Buddhist monasteries of the same name west and north of Balkh were doctrinally different from traditional Buddhism. It was from Naw Bahar in Balkh that the Barmakids came, who rose mysteriously and quickly to become the ministers of the 'Abbasids. If the name Nava Vihara-Naw Bahar-New Spring was an intentional pun it would fit the pattern of deliberate plays on meaning such as *Dar al-Hijrah* ("House of Refuge" – the Qarmatians), and *al-Qahirah al-Mu'izz li-Dini-Llah* ("The Victorious City of the Exalter of the Religion of God" the Fatimids), a pattern which corresponds to Manicheism.

On his way to Balkh and India to seek the origins of Buddhism, Hsüan Tsang had left China without the permission of the T'ang Emperor. In Turfan, called by the Chinese Kao-ch'ang, however, he found official support, letters of introduction, and an escort to continue his journey. Turfan, within two hundred years to become a Uighur Turkish Manichean kingdom, at this time was Indo-European, whose language, Tokharian is closely related to Italo-Celtic. The German scholar-explorer von Le Coq called this culture one of "belated antiquities" and Grousset as "lost in space". It was a mixture of Persian, Indian, and Hellenist with Buddhism as its religion, and the most easterly occurrence of Hellenic figures of Gandharan Buddhas. Indo-Europeans in a Turco-Mongol ocean, Tokharian art demonstrates a longing and nostalgia for its cultural kindred.

631

(*Ramadan*) 'Ali sent on a mission to Yemen.

The pilgrimage of that year is conducted by Abu Bakr. Idolators are prohibited from making the pilgrimage to Mecca from then on.

The destruction of Pagan temples in Arabia begins; Jarir ibn 'Abd Allah is sent to destroy Dhu-l-Khalasah in the northern Yemen. It is defended by its custodians and three hundred are killed. Later Dhu-l-Khalasah, a quartz crystal, was made into the doorstep of the mosque of Tabalah. Khalid ibn Walid was sent to destroy the sanctuary of al-'Uzza at Nakhlah.

10th year of the Hijrah = 9 April 631

632

The periodic intercalation of extra months to bring the lunar year in line with the solar is prohibited by the Koran; the Muslims return to a purely lunar calendar.27 January; Death of the Prophet's son Ibrahim.

March (*Dhu al-Hijjah AH 10*); The "Farewell Pilgrimage". While preaching at 'Arafat to the multitude the Prophet receives the final revelation of the Koran (V:3).

March 16 (*18 Dhu al-Hijjah AH 10*); Returning from the pilgrimage, the Prophet joins with a Muslim army led by 'Ali at Ghadir Khumm. 'Ali's command had been criticised for excessive severity. The Prophet defends 'Ali against criticism. The event and the statements made there are later taken by Shi'ites (but not by Sunnis) to be a designation of 'Ali as the successor to the Prophet.

In China, Nestorian Christians receive official permission to propagate their religion from the T'ang dynasty.

AFTER THE DEATH OF THE PROPHET: The First Caliphs

11th year of the Hijrah = 29 March 632

June 8 (*12 Rabi' al-Awwal AH* 11); The Prophet dies. He is succeeded by Abu Bakr as head of the community, *khalifah*, the "one who is left behind", the Caliph.

Some Beduin tribes repudiate Islam and repulse the collectors of the poor-tax; false prophets arise: the *Hurub ar-Riddah* or "wars of apostasy". Already before the death of the Prophet, a false messiah in the Yemen, al-Aswad, also called *Dhu-l-Himar*, the "Man of the Donkey" and *Dhu-l-Khimar*, the "Veiled One", is captured and put to death. Abu Bakr refuses to turn Usama aside from a campaign to Syria which the Prophet had ordered and instead himself takes the field against the apostates.

In Iran, a prince of the royal blood, the grandson of Chosroes II Parviz is brought out of hiding in Istakhr and is crowned. Yazdagird III becomes the last Sassanid King. (Kavadh II, who had killed his father Chosroes II in 628 was himself killed several months later, and rule passed to a general Shahrbaraz and a daughter of Chosroes II, Baran.)

633

The end of the "Wars of Apostasy" (*Hurub ar-Riddah*). The false prophet Musaylamah killed by Wahshi in a battle fought by a Muslim army led by Khalid ibn al-Walid.

Southern Mesopotamia conquered.

634

Byzantines defeated by Muslims at Battle of Ajnadayn in Palestine.

Abu Bakr dies having designated 'Umar as his successor.

635

Conquest of Syria. Damascus taken.

Jews and Christians are expelled from Arabia.

636

The Persian Sassanids are defeated at the Battle of Qadisiyyah. (According to many sources this is in 637.) Ibn Khaldun cites that there the Persian concentration amounted to 120,000, who with their retainers amounted to 200,000. However, he further cites that according to 'A'ishah and az-Zuhri, the troop concentration with which the Persian general Rustum advanced against Sa'd was only 60,000, all of whom had their retainers.

637

Byzantines are defeated at Yarmuk River (according to other sources this is in August 636/15). In this battle Khalid ibn al-Walid orders the veterans of Badr, some one hundred men in all, not to fight but instead to stand on the sidelines and perform the ritual prayer.

The Caliph 'Umar formalizes the convention of dating the Islamic era from the Hijrah and the foundation of the Islamic state.

Founding of Kufah as a garrison town.

Conquest of Jerusalem. (According to *Islamologie* this is in 638/17.) 'Umar leaves Medinah in the charge of 'Ali, and visits Jerusalem. He orders the clearing of the Temple Mount left in disorder in accordance with Jesus' prophecies concerning the destruction of Jerusalem after the Temple's destruction by the Romans.

638

The Byzantines (who held the orthodox Christian doctrine of Jesus as having two natures, human and Divine, in one person), find the Monophysite Christians of Syria (who believe that Jesus is one nature in one person who was entirely Divine) allying themselves with the Muslims. To win back the support of the Monophysites, the Byzantines offer the compromise formula of *monothelitism* (that although he had two natures, a human and divine, emphasis is placed on the will of Jesus which is identified as one with the Divine will). This compromise, the *Ecthesis*, does not win back the support of the Monophysite Ghassani Christians, but is the origin of the Maronites.

640

'Amr ibn al-'Asi begins conquest of Egypt.

Kufah and Basrah founded as garrison towns (*amsar*). Kufah is near Hirah, the former Lakhmid capital, and Kufah will supplant this city and absorb its population.

641

'Amr ibn al-'Asi founds Fustat (outskirts of present day Cairo).

End of the reign of Heraclius as Emperor of Byzantium.

642
Definitive defeat of the Persians at Nihawand.

644
'Umar assassinated by a slave. 'Uthman is elected Caliph.

645
Death of the poetess al-Khansa' a nickname for Tumadir bint 'Amr, who was famous for the elegies of her sons and brothers killed in battle for Islam.

Hsüan-tsang returns to China from pilgrimage to India; translation of Buddhist books into Chinese; establishment in China of the scholasticism of Vasubandhu; rise of the Pure Land Schools in China; development of Taoism as a religion.

649
Cyprus conquered by Arabs.

650
The Koran is collected and edited in the canonical recension.

Anosch bar Danqa, head of the Mandaeans, effects the protection of the community under Islam.

651
Yazdagird III, last Sassanid Emperor is assassinated near Merv.'Uthman "loses the ring of the Prophet in a well in Medinah"; beginning of discord.

656
'Uthman assassinated by the son of Abu Bakr and his compatriots amidst general insurrection in Medinah. 'Ali becomes Caliph. Revolt of Talhah, Zubayr, and 'A'ishah against the Caliph. They are defeated at the Battle of the Camel. Talhah and Zubayr are killed, 'A'ishah is sent back to Medinah. 'Ali settles at the military camp-city of Kufah; evidently he seeks alliance with the former Lakhmids against Mu'awiyah and the Ghassanis.

657
Battle of Siffin. Mu'awiyah, under pretext of revenge for 'Uthman's death, attacks 'Ali's army. Stalemate between the armies; offers of negotiation accepted. Departure of the Kharijites from 'Ali's army.

658
Mu'awiyah declared Caliph by treachery of negotiators at Adhruh; outcome repudiated by 'Ali.'Ali crushes Kharijites at the Battle of Nahrawan.

THE UMAYYAD DYNASTY

661
'Ali assassinated by a Kharijite, Ibn Muljam. Brief Caliphate of Hasan, son of 'Ali, who cedes his title to Mu'awiyah. Beginning of the Umayyad dynasty.

662-675
Ziyad "ibn Abihi" ("son of his father"; he had been acknowledged by Mu'awiyah as the extra-marital son of Abu Sufyan) is Umayyad governor in Iraq.

667
Arab armies reach Central Asia.

668
And again in 705, a Taoist book called the *Sutra on the Conversion of Barbarians* (*Hua-hu-ching*) is proscribed in China. This is a polemic in the form of back dated prophecies which seeks to make Mani and the Buddha into avatars of Lao Tzu. Its purpose is to subordinate Buddhism, but it also elevates Manicheism. In it Lao-Tzu who does not die, goes through the Western Pass, and becomes reborn as Mani in Syria (which for the Chinese was the whole Middle East.) The book also says that "450 years after Mani, the metallic vapor, (or vital force) will rise and my teaching will prosper. As a sign, holy images of Mani will come from the Western regions into the Middle Kingdom... This will be a sign of realisation. The two vapors, yellow and white, will coalesce and the Three Schools will be united together and return to me."

669
The Companion Abu Ayyub dies at the walls of Constantinople in an unsuccessful Muslim attack.

670
Hasan, son of 'Ali, dies.

Kairouan/Qayrawan is founded and 'Uqbah ibn Nafi' is militarily successful in North Africa although he sends back the message, speaking of the Berbers: "We have met our match." 'Uqbah rides his horse into the Atlantic Ocean with his sword unsheathed and says: "Lord, you are my witness that I can go no farther."

674-679
Constantinople unsuccessfully besieged by Muslim armies. In 677 the Byzantines destroy an Arab fleet at Syllaeum, for the first time using Greek fire. Kallinikos of Heliopolis builds the fire spouting ships which use a mixture of naphta and a secret ingredient, probably saltpeter. Thereafter the Arabs and Byzantines make a thirty year peace.

678

'A'ishah dies.

680-683

Reign of the Caliph Yazid I.

680

10 Oct (*10 Muharram AH 61*); Martyrdom of Husayn, son of 'Ali, killed by Yazid's troops at Kerbala in Iraq. This event is the "passion" and historic tragedy of Twelve-Imam Shi'ism. The placing of the event on the tenth of Muharram, which was already a day of religious observance in Islam, was certainly deliberate and after the fact; the actual day was probably not recorded. Yazid died in the same year; but he apologized to Muhammad ibn al-Hanifiyyah, head of the 'Alid clan, paid him a large sum of money as an indemnity, and expressed sorrow for the killing of Husayn.

Schism of the Ibadites from the Kharijites.

Council at Constantinople III (ecumenical). Condemned Monothelitism (*see* 638; i.e. The *Ecthesis* had not brought the hoped for results.)

683

Medinah is sacked by Umayyads because of uprisings.

683-692

'Abd Allah ibn az-Zubayr declares himself Caliph and holds Mecca in defiance of the Umayyads. ('Abd Allah ibn az-Zubayr claimed to be the first Muslim child born in Medinah after the Hijrah.)

683

During a siege of Mecca the Ka'bah catches fire from a flaming arrow (*AH 64*). Because of this fire the Black Stone cracks into three pieces. (It is today seven and splinters, into which it was deliberately broken by the Qarmatis when they stole the stone in the 10th century.) The Ka'bah is rebuilt on a larger scale by 'Abd Allah ibn az-Zubayr, who upon examination of the foundations, concludes that the Ka'bah had once been larger before rebuildings by the Quraysh.

At Marj Rahit north of Damascus the Kalb who support the Umayyads are victorious over the Qays who support 'Abd Allah ibn Zubayr.

684-704

Reign of the Empress Wu in China; she received a Manichean Bishop, Mihr Ohrmuzd (Mi-we-mo-ssu), who presents the "Sutra of the Two Principles". Mihr Ohrmuzd is the pupil of an earlier missionary, a Mozak or priest of high rank (in the reign of the Emperor Kao-Tsang 650-683, from which time Chinese Manicheism traditionally dated itself), and predecessor of another in 719. In 705 the short-lived Chou dynasty comes to an end and the T'ang are restored.

685-687

The appearance of the Tawwabun in Kufah, the "repentants" who offer themselves in sacrifice for the death of Husayn. There were 16,000 men enrolled in the Diwan of Sulayman ibn Surad al-Khuza'i, leader of the Tawwabun. 4,000 appeared at the mustering place to form an expedition to fight against the Umayyads. 1,000 actually walked out of Kufah and were annihilated at 'Ayn al-Wardah (Ra's al-'Ayn) in the Jazirah during three days 4-6 January 685. They were a group without military experience and were instead bent on martyrdom. Within a year, but in a continuation of this movement, Mukhtar, promoting Muhammad ibn al-Hanafiyyah, a son of 'Ali by a woman from the Bani Hanif tribe, as the Mahdi, leads a more war-like but ultimately unsuccessful revolt in Iraq. He celebrates a victory in which 'Ubayd Allah Ibn Ziyad, who had Husayn killed, is himself killed, by a mysterious ceremony in front of an empty chair which he calls "the throne of 'Ali". This revolt known as the Kaysaniyyah or Mukhtariyyah is the introduction of the Mahdi idea into Islam. (The idea of a "Mahdi" does not appear in collections of *Hadith* until after Bukhari and Muslim.) The notion of changes in God's Will is also introduced by Mukhtar which becomes later a fundamental tenet of Shi'ism. Shahrastani will say that the propagandist of the 'Abbasids, Abu Muslim, was a Kaysani; this means that the 'Abbasid struggle harnesses the same elements as Mukhtar. Mukhtar is killed on April 4, 687 at Kufah.

Muhammad ibn Hanafiyyah, a son of 'Ali and secret figurehead of the Mukhtariyyah/Kaysaniyyah revolt in Iraq, is thrown into prison in Mecca along with his cousin the 'Abassid, 'Abd Allah ibn 'Abbas by 'Abd Allah ibn Zubayr because they refuse to support him in his revolt against the Umayyads. They wish to remain aloof from political struggles, in appearance at least. Muhammad ibn al-Hanafiyyah sends a letter to Mukhtar in Kufah, with a reproach for their failure to aid Husayn, who sends 2,000 horsemen to free the 'Alids and 'Abassids. This may be the first instance in which the 'Abassids learn of the Kufah connection between the 'Alids and a shadowy political, religious, and military organisation, doubtless the relic of the Manichean Lakhmids, in Iraq. It is in any case the occasion where they witness its efficacy. This organisation in Iraq later becomes the support of the 'Abbasid revolution.

686

After this incident Muhammad ibn Hanifiyyah went to live in Aylah (today's Eilat) to avoid further clashes with 'Abd Allah ibn Zubayr. 'Abd Allah ibn 'Abbas remained in Mecca.

687
After the death of Mukhtar and the collapse of his revolt, Muhammad ibn Hanifiyyah and 'Abd Allah ibn 'Abbās go to live in Ta'if which is the dwelling place of Mukhtar's tribe, the Thaqif, probably because they feel more secure there. There 'Abd Allah ibn 'Abbas dies at the age of 72, by tradition having instructed his family to go to Syria and swear allegiance to the Umayyad 'Abd al-Malik, on family grounds, since they are related through 'Abd Manaf.

691
The Dome of the Rock sanctuary and the al-Aqsa' mosque are built in Jerusalem.

694
A Manichean dignitary (electus) appears at the Chinese imperial court. Manicheism is spread by Soghdian merchants and Soghdian (an Eastern Iranian language) has become the principal language of Eastern Manicheism.

692
Al-Hajjaj ibn Yusuf captures Mecca; 'Abd Allah ibn az-Zubayr is killed (*AH 73*), putting an end to what the Umayyads call the *fitnah*, or revolt of the old conservative, non-'Alid, opposition to the Umayyads. Al-Hajjaj pulls down the new, larger Ka'bah rebuilt by 'Abd Allah ibn az-Zubayr after a fire caused by a previous siege, and rebuilds it on the previous scale.

693
The Umayyad 'Abd al-Malik begins minting the first coins of the Islamic state in Damascus; in this he is followed by al-Hajjaj ibn Yusuf in Iraq. In *77*/696 a gold dinar is created on the Byzantine aureus model which until then had predominated among the Arabs. (Baghdad maintained a ratio of gold to silver of 7/1 until *656*/1258. In the Christian countries it was 12/1; after 1204 in the Christian West the ratio fluctuated until it became 10/1 in 1492 and thereafter, in Spain went to 13.3/1 in 1546, 14.8/1 in 1641 and more.) As the Arabs begin their own gold coinage, at the same time Arabic is made the official language of accounts which until then had been kept in Greek in Syria and Persian in Iraq. The officials had been entirely non-Arab, so their languages had until then, remained the official languages until this change.

700
(or 703 or 705). The death of Muhammad ibn Hanafiyyah, a son of 'Ali, but not by Fatimah. He was the figurehead for the Mukhtariyyah (Kaysaniyyah) revolt in Iraq. The title of Mahdi had originally been invented for him. He was the head of both the clan of the 'Alids and the 'Abbasids while he was alive when both he and 'Abd Allah ibn 'Abbas were in Ta'if, avoiding conflicts with the Umayyads, after the collapse of the Mukhtariyyah.

After the death of Muhammad ibn al-Hanafiyyah, the 'Abbasids under the leadership of the youngest adult male 'Ali ibn 'Abd Allah ibn 'Abbas purchase a village, Humaymah, in the mountains of the Sharat, southeast of the Dead Sea, northeast of 'Aqabah on the route from Aylah to Petra, and on the route from the Hejaz to Damascus, where they settle, although they also spend much time at Damascus at the court.

701
Death of the poet Jamil, author of *ghazals* that exemplified a languishing from hopeless love of the style called *'Udhrite* from the name of his tribe.

703
Hajjaj founds the city of al-Wasit on the ancient course of the Tigris (since changed) across from the city of Kashkar which it will supplant. The 8th century Nestorian Bishop of Kashkar in Bet Aramaie, Theodore Bar Konai, will write the *Book of Scholia* which will preserve extracts from an unknown Manichean work, among them the names of Manichean deities and demons. Al-Wasit in the 10th century will become a Qarmati center. Legend says that King Solomon had founded a town near Wasit called Zandaward, and Solomon's Jinn fashioned for this town five iron gates. These gates were recuperated by Hajjaj and re-used in Wasit. Tabari states that these gates were taken up by Mansur and used in Baghdad, and could still be seen in his time.

705
The Great Umayyad Mosque of Damascus is built.

707
Arab conquest of Balkh. This brings to an end the Persian resistance; in 661 the dihqans of Tokharistan put on the throne for a short period Peroz the son of Yazdagird III; Peroz later fled to China, where his son Narseh was also forced to seek refuge. After the fall of Balkh these attempts to hang on to Persian sovereignty came to an end. The patriarch of the Barmakid family thereafter went from Balkh to Damascus to investigate the new superpower. There he represented himself as a philosopher, astrologer, and physician from the east, and perhaps made the first contact with the 'Abbasid family which was to become a strategic alliance during the 'Abbasid revolution.

710
Abu Hashim, son of Muhammad ibn al-Hanifiyyah, and the senior head of all three major branches of the

'Alids is taken from Medinah to Damascus where he is cast into prison. He was accused by Zayd ibn Hasan, the elder of the Hasani 'Alid branch, in the presence of the Caliph, of having a *shi'ah*, a partisan faction in Kufah made up of survivors from the Mukhtariyyah. 'Ali ibn Husayn (known later as Zayn al-'Abidin, considered by Twelve Imam Shi'ites to be an Imam, later in time) head of the Husayni 'Alid branch in Mecca comes to his aid in Damascus, intercedes, and Abu Hashim is released from prison. He remains in Damascus until one day in 715, after the death of Walid, he announces his intention to return to Medinah with a Caravan bound there. His real intention is to go Humaymah, the 'Abbasid headquarters, southeast of the Dead Sea, with his cousin the 'Abbasid, Muhammad ibn 'Ali.

711

Tariq ibn Ziyad, a Berber under the Arab general Musa ibn Nusayr, begins invasion of Spain. (The name Gibraltar comes from *Jabal Tariq*, the "mountain of Tariq" which displaced the Roman name of Mons Calpe.) Battle of Wadi Bakkah.

711-712

Muslim armies make conquests in Transoxiana and Sindh in India.

713

Death of 'Ali Zayn al-'Abidin, Shi'ite Imam; some Shi'ites follow his son Zayd (instead of his older brother Muhammad al-Baqir). Zayd takes up military resistance against the Umayyads. Beginning of Zaydi ("Fiver") Shi'ism. The year 712-713 (94 H.) was known as the *sanat al-fuqaha'* because of the many religious scholars who died in it.

714

The Arabs reach Kashgar.

715

Abu Hashim, head of the 'Alids leaves Damascus for Humaymah with the 'Abassid, Muhammad ibn 'Ali. (See 710.)

716

Abu Hashim, head of the 'Alids dies in Humaymah (the 'Abbasid headquarters, southeast of the Dead Sea, 50km southwest of Ma'an, Jordan) but passes on to the 'Abassids the *'ilm*, the knowledge of how to deal with the secret partisan cells in Kufah who supported Muhammad ibn Hanafiyyah during the Mukhtariyyah (Kaysaniyyah) revolt (and presumably pretended to support Husayn, and probably had supported 'Ali.) With Abu Hashim were a few members of the clandestine organisation in Kufah. But notably Salamah ibn Bujayr, leader of the Shi'ah in Kufah since the collapse of Mukhtar's revolt, had remained in Damascus. In Humaymah were 1. Abu Riyah Maysarah an-Nabbal ("the arrow maker"); 2. Abu 'Amr Yaqtin al-Bazzar ("seed and corn chandler") 3. Muhammad ibn Khunays; 4. Abu Bistam Masqalah at-Tahhan ("miller"); 5. Hayyan al-'Attar ("perfumer and spice dealer"); 6. Ibrahim ibn Salamah. They were not inclined to recognize the transfer and wanted to leave. But Muhammad ibn 'Ali persuaded them to stay a while until their leader arrived from Damascus. When Salamah ibn Bujayr arrived he knew of the arrangement to transfer the Hashimiyyah to the 'Abbasids and complied. He gave them the list, the *diwan* of some members of the conspiracy in Kufah. It included Abu Salamah al-Khallal ("the vinegar seller"). The emphasis on trade names proving the craft or "worker" affiliation was a feature of several revolts including ones in Europe.

717-718

Unsuccessful Muslim siege of Constantinople.

717

Muslim raids across the Pyrenees.

100 H. = 3 August 718

718

Resistance to Muslim rule begins in the Asturias in Spain.

719

Capture of Narbonne in France by the Muslims.

The King of Kazanistan and Tocharistan sends a Manichean priest of the highest rank (magister), a Mozak (Mu-che or Mukhi) as an envoy to the T'ang court. Building of a Manichean Church in Peking.

720

Death of the Qurayshi Meccan poet 'Umar ibn Abu Rabi'a, author of the love lyrics called *ghazals* which came after the odes or *qasidas*.

721

Muhammad ibn 'Ali ibn 'Abd Allah ibn al-'Abbas sends an emissary to Khorasan to look for support for a revolution to bring the family of 'Abbas to power.

724-738

According to an-Nadim writing in 987, a schism occurs among the Manicheans under Muslim rule. The followers of Mihr, "Master of Masters" oppose Miqlas, the abbot of a monastery of *siqqidut* or the "true electi". The controversy centers over the question of relations policy (*wisalat*) with the new rulers the Muslims, the importance of social programmes over political ones, the validity of a leader of the church who does not reside in the traditional center, Mada'in (Ctesiphon), near Baghdad. A similar break had already taken place earlier, when those who fled Sassanid persecution established an independent sect, the Dinawariyyah, in Transoxiana under the leadership in the 5th or sixth century of Mar Shad Ormizd. (The name Dinawariyyah is either from a place name, Dinawar, in Khorasan, or relates to the sense of *din*, religion, for in Chinese texts the sect is called *tien-na-wu.*)

The Manicheans at this time are under the protection of an Umayyad governor in Iraq, Khalid ibn 'Abd Allah al-Qasri (who has a Christian mother), who gives a mule to Mihr, puts on his finger a silver ring, and gives him a robe of honour.

728

The great Sufi, Hasan of Basrah, dies.

Spread of Mu'tazilite or rationalist doctrines.

732

Muslim advance into France checked by Charles Martel in a battle between Tours and Poitiers.

After a report on Manichean beliefs known as the "Compendium" is made by a Manichaean priest in China upon order of the government, an edict is issued by the Chinese emperor which says that "the doctrine of Mo-mo-ni (Mar Mani) is through and through a perverted creed. Falsely it takes the name of Buddhism and deceives the people. This must be formally prohibited. But since it is the indigenous faith of the western barbarians and other people, it shall not be accounted a crime for them to practice it on their own behalf." The T'ang however, do not enforce the decree thoroughly and in 762 Soghdian Manichean priests welcome the Uighurs who liberate Loyang and thereafter, in 763, the Uighur ruler is converted to Manicheism.

733

Death of the poet al-Farazdaq, who had satirical contests (*naqa'id*) with another poet, Jarir.

The struggle with the Iconoclasts in the Byzantine empire; St. John of Damascus, in the employ of the Umayyads, defends church use of images.

734

A revolt of the Rawandiyyah in Khorasan lasts into 737. These are supporters of the 'Abbasids.

735

Death of Dhu ar-Rumma, called "the last of the poets", of the Iraqi school, his poems were devoted to descriptions of desert life.

738

Kharijite revolts in Iraq.

740

Death of Zayd ibn 'Ali ibn Husayn ibn 'Ali ibn Abi Talib, Imam of the Zaydi Shi'ites, in Kufah; end of the Zaydi revolt in Iraq. There were later Zaydi revolts in Khorasan (Zayd's son Yahya was crucified there by the governor Nasr ibn Sayyar in 743) and especially in Daylam. That year, 125 H. marks the definitive transformation of the Shi'ite movement of Khorasan to 'Abbasid allegiance from 'Alid. It was reported that every male child born in Khorasan that year was named Yahya or Zayd by reason of the grief which descended upon the people. It is probably then that the banners of the 'Abbasids appear as black as a sign of mourning for Zayd and his son. The Zaydi movement survives today in Yemen.

Muslims are established on the West Coast of Africa at Kilwa.

According to the Khazarist theory put forward by Aurther Koestler, based on the works of the American historian J.D.M. Dunlop, the Khazar king Bulan is converted to Judaism at this time, leading to the conversion of his people. (Although Koestler is the best known name associated with the Khazars, before Koestler a number of Polish historians spoke of the Khazar origins of Polish Jews.) The Khazar kingdom lay north of the Caspian and the Black Sea and between them. (The Crimea has sometimes been called "Little Khazaria" and the Caspian is called the "Khazar Sea" in the Islamic world). Underpinning this theory is the putative, forged or not, correspondence between Hasdai Ibn Shaprut, a Jewish Minister at the Court of the Caliph of Cordova and the Jewish scribe of the Khazar King Joseph in the 10th century. Ibn Shaprut refers to the Khazar country as Ashkenaz, the original Biblical Hebrew name for a region near the Caspian (before it was transferred to Germany and Eastern Europe). The Cordovan Jew seeks to determine the nature of the Jewishness of the Khazars and learns of a miraculous conversion two hundred years earlier. The Khazars were a Turkic people. If they adopted Judaism it would seem to have been a political gesture of neutrality between Christian Byzantium and the Islamic empire, and that this Judaism would have been Karaite, that is, non-Talmudic and non-Rabbinic, at least until some reforms introduced by a later king called Obadiah after the year 800. This Judaism would have been only of the ruling classes, introduced by Karaite missionaries from Persia. It was not the religion of the general population but could account for the appearance of Karaite Judaism in the Crimea and as far north as Poland and Lithuania. This could have been spread by Khazars and Turkic Cumans who migrated westward and fought alongside joint Polish-Lithuanian forces against the troops of the Teutonic Order in 1410 at the Battle of Tannenberg. Such Turkish speaking regiments of Karaite soldiers were imported from the Crimea by Alexander Vytautus, known as Witold, Grand Duke of Lithuania to his capital at Troki in 1398. Other such groups of Turkish speaking Karaites and Muslims, broadly known as Tatars, appeared in Hungary and Poland. Some of these Karaites could have been assimilated into Western Jewry and adopted the obligatory ethnic fiction of rabbinical Judaism at a time of gradual and long term German migrations towards the East and similar Turkic migrations towards the West. Ibrahim ibn Ya'qub said that the Khazars at one point spoke a Slavic language. (The Bulgarians today are Slavicized Turks). A linguistic analysis of Yiddish by Paul Wexler shows it is a Slavic language which was "relexified" by German over time; that is, the original Slavic words were replaced by German ones in those cases where the German words were compatible with the Slavic structures; where they were not, the words were relexified from Hebrew. Yiddish is today 80 to 85% German (from High German) and the rest is Hebrew, Russian and Polish. A modern example of a relexification is the modern Hebrew word 'bevakashem' which is built on the Russian 'pozhaluista' meaning "please" or 'you are welcome'; the Russian elements have been replaced by Hebrew ones. Wexler also suggests that Yiddish is above all a language of converts to Judaism.

743

Khalid ibn 'Abd Allah al-Qasri (see 724-738) is tortured and put to death by his successor.

745

Activity of a Khorasanian religious leader named Bihafrid. His doctrines are obscure; he may have been a Mazdean reformer who claimed to receive revelations. He proclaimed five or seven daily prayers, without prosternations, towards the sun or "in the direction of the sun's source", the west. He had gone to China whence he brought back a "very thin green cloak and shirt". Other cryptic references to his prophecies and actions are found in an-Nadim, al-Biruni, and Shahrastani. He may have been the exponent of a heretical Zoroastrian movement since the Zoroastrian priests in particular were his enemies. He seems to have been put to death by troops of Abu Muslim, but his teachings had an influence in northern Iran for several centuries after his death.

746

Rebellions of the Kalb in Syria and the Kharijites in Iraq.

747

The 'Abbasids mount the theological tiger of Persia to ride to power (see 758 and 827). Abu Muslim unfurls the black flag of the 'Abbasids in Khorasan with the motto "Felicity [or the "anointed one"] will come from the People of the House." The term "People of the House" could be a translation of a Manichean Buddhist term *Buddhagotra* which means "family" or "house" of the Buddha, from Sanskrit gotra, house or family. (Balkh in Khorasan was a center of Manichean Buddhism.) This Manichean term was given to the light suffering in this world, the "Living Soul" – *viva anima* in Augustine, a designation which can be traced back to 1 Corinthians 15:45 "The first man Adam, became a living soul." (Asmussen p. 47 *Manichean Literature.*)

The 'Abbasid revolt is declared before the end of Ramadan. (The breaking of a fast is symbolically the pronouncing of a secret). The Manicheans, who were widespread in Khorasan, have a month of fasting on whose 27th day their founder Mani died. On the 30th they celebrate a feast which is the anniversary of the apotheosis or "pari-nirvana" of Mani. The death of Mani on the 27th day of the month of fasting has been transposed to the Muslim month of fasting – Ramadan. The 27th of Ramadan has become established as the night traditionally assumed by Muslims to be the night of the revelation of the Koran; otherwise the night is not specified in any Islamic Canonic source. The litterateur al-Jahiz called the 'Abbasids "a foreign Khorasanian dynasty" (*dawlah ajami khorasani*).

"On the night of 25 Ramadan 129 (10 June 747), the inhabitants of Safidhanj, a village on the outskirts of Merv, witnessed a remarkable spectacle, part religious convocation and part political demonstration. The Khuza'i shaykh of the village, Sulayman ibn Kathir, led a group of men dressed completely in black to a place of assemblage near his residence. There they proceeded to raise two large black banners, one which they named 'the shadow' on a pole fourteen cubits long and another, called 'the clouds,' on a pole thirteen cubits long. As they did so, a newcomer in the village known as Abu Muslim chanted a verse from the Koran: 'Leave is given to those who fight because they were wronged; surely God is able to help them' (22:39). They then kindled bonfires, and in response, men from surrounding villages, also robed in black, left their homes to join their comrades in Safidhanj."

Padma Sambhava ("the Lotus born one") coming from India (or Afghanistan) converts the King of Tibet to tantric Buddhism, the *Vajrayana.* (Padma Sambhava is considered an incarnation of the Sakyamuni Buddha; the Buddha of course precisely does *not* incarnate on the one hand; on the other, Mani readily called himself the apostle of the Buddha.) Part of the doctrine is that of *terma* ("treasures") or texts which were hidden treasures in caves that were transmitted in secret until the fifth century when they were made known. They were propagated in India by the school of the "84 Perfect Ones" who include Naropa, Krishnacharya, and Saraha. In the Tibetan mantra *Om Mani Padma Hum* the Mani means "Jewel" in Sanskrit and the prayer wheel is called *Mani chos ekhor* where Mani means "precious". Padma Sambhava is mandalized as a rainbow. Padma Sambhava is pictured with a scepter called the *khatvṯnga*. Literally the word means a "body on a couch" (and a derived meaning of bedpost). Here the body is a yogi or a god who in the teachings rises symbolically to heaven as the stretched surface of the cot or couch, assimilated to a drum, is rhythmically struck along with the intonation of the mantra.

The 'Abbasid Imam Ibrahim, who is the momentary figurehead of the 'Abbasid revolution, is arrested by the Umayyads and perishes in prison.

748
The Umayyad governor of Khorasan defeated by Qahtabah.

THE 'ABBASID DYNASTY

750
The Umayyad Caliph Marwan is defeated at the Battle of the Greater Zab river. Marwan dies in Egypt. The 'Abbasid dynasty founded by Abu-l-'Abbas as-Saffah.

751
First Ibadite Imam.

Battle of Atlakh at the Talas (also written as Taras) River between victorious Muslim forces and T'ang Chinese in Central Asia. The first confrontation between the two expanding empires establishes a boundary. The 'Abbasid forces were commanded by Ziyad ibn Salih al-Khuza'i, a subaltern of Abu Muslim; 20,000 prisoners were taken. Use of paper is introduced among the Arabs, when a paper factory is established in Samarkand by the Chinese who were taken prisoner. Muslim supremacy in Central Asia definitively displaced Chinese influence.

754
Al-Mansur becomes Caliph until 775; An-Nadim says that at this time the Archegos, or head of the Manichean religion in Ctesiphon is Abu Hilal ad-Dayhuri from North Africa. There is an important Manichean colony in the region of Algeria and Tunisia.

Conciliabulum in Constantinople. "Under the direction of Constantine V, this synod condemned the use of all relics, images, and statues of saints and especially those pertaining to or depicting God, the Virgin, or Jesus Christ. It also denounced monachism and many other practices which had developed in the Church since Apostolic times." *See* 787; This council was utterly reversed.

755
'Abd ar-Rahman I ad-Dakhil becomes Emir of Cordoba, having escaped from the 'Abbasids in the East. He founds the Umayyad dynasty of Spain. First construction of the great Mosque of Cordoba.

The capitals of the T'ang dynasty are conquered by An Lu-shan, and the government escapes to the mountains.

Abu Muslim, who has secretly told his followers that he is divine, is executed by the 'Abbasids. Shahrastani writes later that Abu Muslim was a Kaysani. (See 685-687). A pardon (*aman*) is extended to the partisans of the Umayyads. Revolt of Sinbad (Sondpadh) in the name of Abu Muslim.

757
Execution of Ibn al-Muqaffa', translator of the political allegory of *Kalilah and Dimnah*. Apparently a Manichean, he expressed rationalist opinions regarding the Prophet and the Koran while at the same time recommending to the Caliph that he allow himself to be divinized. After his execution a limb of Ibn Muqaffa' is thrown into a fire as a sign he will be condemned to hell.

758
A group of six hundred members of a sect which had brought the 'Abbasids to power, and followers of Abu Muslim (who had claimed divinity for himself), the Rawandis, surround the residence of the Caliph al-Mansur at Hashimiyyah and "ask for food and drink" (presumably they are asking for the Manichean Bema ceremony). They demand that the Caliph declare himself God. He has many of them killed. This throws light on the nature of the propaganda of Abu Muslim in Khorasan in favor of the 'Abbasids, a propaganda which the 'Abbasids used to obtain power, and then disavowed. The 'Abbasid support of Mu'tazilitism is a relic of their concessions to Persian religious movements. A Persian scholar, Zabih Bihruz, has claimed that al-Mansur was, in secret, a Manichean.

759
Death of Wasil ibn 'Ata', a founder of Mu'tazilitism. (Abu Hudhaifa) Wasil b. 'Ata' (al-Ghazzal) was a *mawla*, a client convert. He had an "amazing ingenuity" for, although he could not pronounce the sound "r", and avoided words containing that sound (he

would have had a lot of difficulty saying the fundamental Islamic formula "Bismi Llahi ar-Rahman Rahim" and very significantly could thereby only pronounce half the shahadah), he could say anything he wished in beautiful Arabic. (The report of the defect is probably meant precisely to convey reservations about his inner convictions.) He was apparently the head of a secret organisation for a writer said: "Beyond the Pass of China, on every frontier to far distant Sus and beyond the Berbers, he has preachers. A tyrant's jest, an intriguer's craft does not break their determination. If he says 'Go' in winter, they obey; in summer they fear not the month of burning heat" (Jahiz, *Bayan* I,37). There is a folk Hadith which says: "The Mu'tazila are the *Majus* (adherents of Iranian religion); do not follow one in prayer, nor join in carrying his bier when he is dead."

762

'Abbasids found Baghdad, following Astrological calculations, under the sign of Leo with Sagittarius rising on the horizon. Baghdad is near the old Persian capital of Ctesiphon. Unlike the Umayyads who called themselves the "Khalifahs (viceregents) of the Messenger of God", the 'Abbasids will style themselves "Khalifahs of God".

Death of Isma'il, son of Ja'far as-Sadiq (sixth Shi'ite Imam). Using Isma'il as a cover, Iranian dualist religions penetrate Islam and the Sevener Movement emerges which produces the Qarmatis and Fatimids. The creation of the Shi'ite *Nur Muhammadi* doctrine which is attributed to Ja'far. This, modified, works its way into Sufism by the 12th century, as in the "Prayer of Ibn Mashish". The *Nur Muhammadi* doctrine, as put into the mouth of Ja'far as-Sadiq, speaks of a creation by emanation. In this doctrine "God became particles of light" which are concentrated in 'Ali and his descendents, who are the intermediaries between man and God. This bears an unmistakable resemblance to the Manichean creation myth.

A Zaydi revolt fails when Muhammad ibn 'Abd Allah an-Nafs az-Zakiyyah, descended from Hasan, is killed. He had claimed the Imamate; some followers held that he did not die (a typical assertion of Shi'ite sects regarding the death of the Imam claiming it was only an illusion, as in effect, was the death of Mani, or indeed the Manichean version of the Crucifixion of Jesus). Other followers transferred their allegiance to a descendant of Husayn, Muhammad Ibn Qasim in Talaqan. This was followed by other Zaydi revolts in Tabaristan and Daylam.

A Uighur army liberates Lo-yang, the T'ang capital, and the Uighurs become protectors of Manicheism.

763

Manicheism, because of the conversion of a "Qaghan", or chief, becomes the state religion among the Central Asian Uighurs, although many are Buddhist, or Buddhist-Manichean. The Qaghan Mo-Yu (Būögū Qan, reigned 759-780) is converted in Loyang. His predecessors were Külü Bilgä (744-747) and Bilgä Qaghan (747-759). This ruler, and perhaps his successors such as Qutlugh Bilgä Qaghan (790-795), were known as *Zahag-i Mani* to the envoys of the Archegos from Mada'in (Baghdad). The story of the conversion is told on an inscription at Karabalghasun on the river Orkhon (erected in the reign of the Qaghan who ruled 808-821 honouring the four founding Qaghans). In this inscription Manicheism is praised as a civilizing influence because it turned the Uighurs from a people who practiced the "abnormal customs of blood sacrifices – [or drinking hot blood] into a people of vegetarians [eaters of a bowl of rice], from a state which indulged in excessive killing, to a nation which exhorts reighteousness". At first the Uighur empire was centered at Karabalghasun on the river Orkhon in Mongolia near lake Baikal, but after the destruction of the empire by the Kirghiz in 840, many Uighurs went to Qocho (Kao-Ch'ang), east of Turfan in the Tarim river basin, and this became the center (850-1250). This center was visited by the Sufi al-Hallaj around 866. Among the Uighurs Mani was venerated as *kün ai tängri*, 'sun-moon' god. (See 821 and 840.)

The *Isagoge* of Plotinus' pupil Porphyry is translated into Arabic.

765

Death of Ja'far as-Sadiq, scholar and, for the Shi'ites, the "sixth Imam". Ja'far as-Sadiq was also a teacher of Malik ibn Anas and Abu Hanifah, founders of Sunni schools of Law. (His alleged Shi'ism apparently did not rub off on them.)

767

Death of Abu Hanifah, founder of the Hanafi School of Law.

768

Upon the demands of the Uighurs, chinese decrees authorize the establishment of Manichean temples; such decrees also appear in 771. This came at a time of weakness for the T'ang dynasty and when Taoism gained over Buddhism while foreign ideas in art, science and religion penetrated China.

774

Death of Abu Mikhnaf, traditionalist, and al-Awza'i, jurist.

775-932

Measures are taken by the 'Abbasids against zindiqs

(Manicheans), particularly in the reign of al-Mahdi and Harun ar-Rashid. The son of a vizier of al-Mahdi, Abu 'Ubayd, is denounced as a Manichean and confesses. In Mada'in (Ctesiphon) Manicheans are chained and paraded in the streets. One method of abjuration was to invite the suspect to profane a portrait of Mani, (which happened to the poet Abu Nuwas, although the humorous account says he was drunk and actually vomited on the picture), and to eat a bird (meat being forbidden for Manicheans).

778
Charlemagne leads a campaign in Spain.

780
End of the revolt of al-Muqanna', "the veiled one". His name was Hashim; he had been a secretary of Abu Muslim and appeared in the entourage of al-Mansur. He went on to claim to be the new incarnation of God after Abu Muslim; he appeared before his followers wearing a gold-embroidered veil. After having succeeded in establishing control over a wide area in Transoxiana he was cornered in the fortress of Sanam near Kesh; he had fire set to the fortress destroying himself, his wives, and his followers.

An expert (*'Arif*) is named in Aleppo to expose Manicheans posing as Muslims.

783
After the death of Muhammad ibn 'Isa Hamdawayh, a new inquisitor of the Manicheans, or *sahib az-zanadiqa* is named, Muhammad al-Kalwadi.

784
Death of Bashhar ibn Burd, the first major poet in Arabic of non-Arab (Iranian) origin. Proponent of the "new style" which embellished verses by the use of tropes and antitheses, conceits which exploit the possiblities of Arabic morphology; these were called *al-badi'*, or "innovations". Burd is called by many a Manichean.

785
The great Mosque of Cordova expanded under the Spanish Umayyad Caliph al-Hadi.

787
Council of Nicaea (ecumenical). "Reversed the Conciliabulum of 754 utterly and established the Catholic Church as it continued through the Middle Ages." By default, as a result of the rise of Islam, the Bishop of Rome becomes the universal head of the Church; Constantine VI of Constantinople throws in the towel and writes that to "Hadran, pope of old Rome, belongs the dignity of the chief priesthood". Shortly thereafter, the Churches of East and West become divided politically, and then schismatically.

789
Foundation of the city of Fez by Idriss I in Morocco.

791
Death of the Grammarian Khalil ibn Ahmad from Oman. He worked out complex metrical theories about Arab poetry (inspired it is said by listening to the rhythms of the coppersmiths beating plates in the market) and compiled the first dictionary (*Kitab al-'Ayn*) using a phonetic scheme according to the origins of sound of use to poets and possibly influenced by Indian ideas.

Theodore Bar Koni, a Nestorian bishop of Kashkar (al-Wasit) in Bet Aramaie writes in Syriac the *Book of Scholia* which contains extracts of a Manichean book thus providing an important document for the study of Manicheism and for Mandaeism.

793
Death of Sibawaih, a Persian philologist, student of Khalil ibn Ahmad. Sibawaih, which means "little apple" is the author of "the Book" which determined the principles of Arabic grammar.

795
Death of Malik ibn Anas, founder of Maliki School of Law.

796
Death of Saif ibn 'Umar, collector of the tribal traditions of the Tamim.

798
Death of Muhammad ibn Ishaq, grandson of a Mesopotamian convert, compiler of the first "Biography of the Prophet" later edited by Ibn Hisham (d. 833).

Death of Abu Yusuf, Hanafi jurist. As chief judge for Harun ar-Rashid, Abu Yusuf wrote the "Book of the Land-Tax" which broadly covers civil administration.

800
Aghlabids in Tunisia; Arab merchants arrive in Canton by sea.

Around this time paper is manufactured in Baghdad, on the model of a paper factory which already existed in Samarqand.

801
Death of the famous female Sufi, Rabi'ah al-'Adawiyyah.

803
Fall of the Barmecides, the family who were viziers to Harun ar-Rashid. The Barmecides were originally "Buddhist" priests in Balkh; an-Nadim calls them

Manicheans. Ibn Khaldun says "The reason for the destruction of the Barmecides was their attempt to gain control over the dynasty and their retention of the tax revenue."

When the Uighurs come to the Chinese court they bring Manichean clerics with them.

805
Death of Muhammad ash-Shaybani, Hanafi jurist.

806
Rafi' ibn Layth uprising in Samarkand against the 'Abbasid rule.

Plato's *Timaeus* translated into Arabic.

807
Death of 'Abbas ibn al-Ahnaf, creator of the courtly *ghazal*, or short poem on themes of chivalrous love.

808
Foundation of a second town on the river Fez by Idris II in Morocco.

809
Death of the Caliph Harun ar-Rashid. He saw the golden age of the 'Abbasids; under him the Hanafi school of law gained ascendancy. His son al-Amin by Zubayda becomes Caliph; but Huran's covenant calls for al-Ma'mun, a son by a Persian mother to succeed al-Amin, and then another brother, al-Musta'sim to succeed al-Ma'mun.

810
Death of the poet Abu Nuwas (possibly also in 803).

Tahir ibn al-Husayn comes to prominence as al-Ma'mun's general in the war against al-Ma'mun's brother al-Amin. Tahir is later appointed governor of Baghdad, then rules Khorasan. In the civil war between the brothers, the Round City of Mansur in Baghdad is destroyed; in the turmoil there is an 'Alid revolt in Kufah led by "Ibn Taba Taba", Mecca is despoiled by a free booter named Abu Saraya, after whose death the people of Mecca name another 'Alid, Muhammad ibn Ja'far as-Sadiq as Caliph, but eventually al-Ma'mun affirms his authority.

813
Al-Ma'mun becomes Caliph; flowering of scholarship, translation of Greek works into Arabic.

200 H. = 11 August 815

814
An inscription in three languages is made at Karabalghasun on the river Orkhon which declares the conversion of the Uighurs to Manicheism. The Chinese term there used is Mingjiao, or "religion of light". (*See* 763.)

817
Uprising against the Spanish Umayyad Caliph al-Hakam I in Cordoba. Part of the population emigrates to Fez creating the city's "Andalusian quarter" to be followed a few years later by emigrants from Kairouan in Tunisia, creating the "Kairouan" quarter.

The 'Abbasid dynasty came to power by exploiting the religious ideas of the people of Khorasan; al-Ma'mun, more than his predecessors, finds himself riding a theological tiger and is obliged to begin making more and more concessions to his Persian constituents; he names the 'Alid figure, 'Ali ar-Rida, 8th Shi'ite Imam, as his successor and marries his daughter to the Imam. But Baghdad resists this cleaving to the forces of Shi'ism by acclaiming Ibrahim, a son of al-Mahdi, as Caliph in Baghdad while al-Ma'mun rules in Merv. Later, after putting down Ibrahim, eliminating 'Ali ar-Rida, and moving to Baghdad, al-Ma'mun will deem it necessary to again concede to the nativist Persian forces by imposing Mu'tazilite doctrines by force.

818
Al-Ma'mun, under pressure from Arab and Sunni elements in Baghdad, renounces some of his Shi'ite overtures; 'Ali ar-Rida dies in Nagaun near Tus, presumably poisoned. He is buried next to Harun ar-Rashid, the father of al-Ma'mun. The shrine, which is today's city of Meshhed (after the Safavids come to power), will displace Tus as the town of the region.

819
Ahmad ibn Asad ibn Saman is appointed governor of Farghana by al-Ma'mun; his brothers become governors of Samarkand, Shash, and Herat. Beginning of Samanid rule in Transoxiana which will last until 1005 when their territory is divided between Karakhanids and Ghaznavids.

820
Death of ash-Shafi'i, founder of the Shafi' School of Law, author of the *Risala* ("the Treatise"). Ash-Shafi'i laid down the principle that accepted or "reliable" traditional opinion, as embodied in the corpus of Hadith, be a cornerstone of Islamic law.

Death of Shankara, exponent of the most important school of Vedanta, *Advaita.*

821
Al-Ma'mun names his general Tahir Ibn al-Husayn (Dhu'l-Yaminayn) governor of Khurasan. A year later

Tahir makes signs of independence in Merv and dies the next day. The Caliph is suspected, but the rule passes to Tahir's son Talha. His son rules in Khorasan from Nishapur first in the name of the 'Abbasids, then virtually independently, with the Samanids of Transoxiana as vassals. Tahirids rule until 873, then lose control to Samanids and Saffarids. But this hereditary nomination is considered the first post-Islamic Persian dynasty and may be considered the beginning of the dissolution of the 'Abbasid empire.

Around this time there is a traveller or an envoy who visits the ruler of the Uighurs, the Tughuzghuz (Uighurs of the Tien Shan), who is a Manichean. The exact date is unknown and could have been as late as 866. Minorsky surmised the envoy could have been from Rafi' ibn Layth, a rebel in Samarkand (revolt 806-809). He could also have been an envoy of the Archegos in Mada'in (Baghdad), leader of the Manicheans. The traveller, Tamim ibn Bahr Mutawwi'i (Massignon says this means: "volunteer for the faith") leaves a short geographical description of his travels but not the substance of them. (See 763 and 840).

822
The musician Ziryab arrives in Cordoba and establishes a grand style and high degree of elegance in the arts of living.

823
Death of al-Waqidi, author of a large work on the *maghazi*, or campaigns of the Prophet.

825
Death of Abu 'Ubayda, perhaps of Mesopotamian Jewish origin, literary scholar of the Basrah school, described by Abu Nuwas as "a skin stuffed with knowledge" about history. He was a proponent of *shu'ubiyyah* or ethnic resurgence against Arab domination. He also produced the first collected work of exegesis on the Koran.

826
Death of the Arab poet Abu al-'Atahiya, who wrote didactic and moral verse and could be called "the father of Arabic religious poetry".

827
Caliph al-Ma'mun, appeasing the theological expectations of his Persian power base, adopts Mu'tazilite doctrines and proclaims that the Koran is created.

828
Two Venetian Merchants steal the corpse of St Mark from Alexandria and bring it to Venice.

830
The *Bayt al-Hikmah*, an academy for the sciences and for the translation of Greek works into Arabic is founded in Baghdad by the Caliph al-Ma'mun.

831
Palermo taken by the Arabs.

Death of al-Asma'i, poetic critic of the Basrah school.

833
Caliph al-Ma'mun institutes the *mihnah* (inquisition) to determine the adherence to Mu'tazilite doctrines on the part of Judges and scholars.

Al-Ma'mun dies, al-Mu'tasim becomes Caliph and introduces the use of Turkish mercenaries.

Death of Ibn Hisham, the editor of Ibn Ishaq's biography of the Prophet.

836
'Abbasids leave their residence in Baghdad and make the military camp-city of Samarra' their capital. At this time they also surrounded themselves with a Turkish slave guard, instead of the traditional Iranian military supporters.

837
The revolt of Babak in Azerbaijan is put down by Afshin, a general of the 'Abbasids. Afshin, a descendant of Shurushna princes, will himself be put to death in 840 on accusations of heresy. The revolt of Babak is one of a series of many movements in Khorasan which in the opinion of Muslim historians sought to bring back some Iranian religion. Afshin, the general who put down Babak was himself implicated in another such revolt, that of Mazyar in 839.

839
Diplomatic exchanges between Cordoba and Constantinople.

Revolt of Mazyar in Khorasan. He was a prince of Tabaristan (Mazandaran) with an Iranian religion. It was discovered that Haidar Afshin, the Turkish general who had captured Babak, was in league with Mazyar and their goal was to return Khorasan to another Iranian religion. Mazyar was executed in Samarra' and Afshin, who was from Ushrushana, died in prison. It became clear that in the army there were many sympathizers to such Iranian religions.

840
The Kirghiz ravage Karabalghasun which is near Lake Baikal on the Orkhon river and shatter the empire of the Uighurs. The Arab writer Jahiz thought that the

Uighurs lost their military prowess because of their conversion to Manicheism. With the fall of the first Uighur Empire, the Uighurs moved south to Turfan in the Tarim basin; other Manicheans remained behind to proselytize the Kirghiz. The second Uighur Empire flourished from 850-1250 at Qocho (Kao-ch'ang), which is Turfan, also as a Manichean kingdom, at least as far as the ruling elite were concerned. The three Manichean works in Chinese in the Cave of the Thousand Buddhas in Dun Huang on the Silk Road may date from this period, as well as the many Manichean fragments which have been found at Turfan. The Manichean ruler of Qocho, the Idiqut, was visited by the Sufi al-Hallaj around 866.

Books IV-VI of the *Enneads* by Plotinus are translated from Syriac into Arabic by a Christian and circulate under the name The *Theology of Aristotle*, which is in reality a manual of Neoplatonism.

843

Iconoclasm is defeated in the Byzantine Empire. The Emperor affirms the veneration of sacred images.

After the fall of the first Uighur kingdom, the T'ang no longer look to them for protection against foreign invaders and Manicheism is prohibited in China, although it will re-emerge in South China. Manichees are persecuted and priests were even massacred and dressed to look like Buddhists in death, with their heads shaved, like Buddhists, to remove traces of the religion (as well as to humiliate the Manicheans). After two centuries during which foreign ideas entered China in art and especially religion, China turns in upon itself. There is an ascendancy of Taoism and even Buddhist temples, as Buddhism is seen as a foreign religion, are restricted without being prohibited altogether.

844

Death of the mathematician al-Khwarizmi who introduced the use of decimal Arabic numerals, the zero, and after whom the word algorithm (mathematical procedure) is named.

Ibn Khurdadhbih, postmaster of Samarra', compiles the first list of post-roads.

845

Death of Muhammad Ibn Sa'd, secretary of Waqidi, author of a large biographical dictionary, and histories of cities.

Death of Habib ibn Aws at-Ta'i Abu Tammam, son of a Christian wine merchant of Damascus, poet panegyrist of Cairo and Baghdad; collector of an anthology of ancient poetry.

847

Mihnah ("inquisition", or forced imposition of Mu'tazilite tenets) is ended; the doctrines of the *ahl al-hadith* prevail over the Mu'tazilites; this orthodox reaction entails persecution of Shi'ites. In this year takes place one of a series of conjunctions of Jupiter and Saturn around which the Isma'ilis will spread prophecies and then create events tailored to fit.

850-860

Abu 'Isa al-Warraq, cited by an-Nadim, attains notoriety as a crypto-Manichean. Possibly, his disciple and brother-in-law, Ibn ar-Rawandi is also one. They are combatted in the Book of Triumph (*Kitab al-Intisar*) of al-Khayyat (d. 912).

850

"The Chain of Histories", traveler's tales about India, Africa, and China.

Around this time, conversion to Islam passes 50% in the Islamic empire.

855

Death of Ibn Hanbal, founder of the Hanbali School of Law.

"The Book of Religion and Empire" about the beliefs of other religions, by 'Ali Ibn Rabban at-Tabari, a convert from Christianity.

859

Death of Ibn Masawaih, physician who expanded on the work of Galen.

861

Death of al-Mutawakkil, first Caliph to be murdered by his Turkish troops. In that year al-Mutawakkil had ordered that the sacred cypress of Kishnar be cut down. According to tradition, this tree had been planted by Zoroaster. It was located near the Zoroastrian sacred fire of Adur Burzen Mihr in Khorasan. The Caliph died before the tree could be brought to Iraq.

863

Manicheism is banned in China but despite all persecutions persists; traces are still to be found in Chinese secret societies, and two of Mani's books were even included in the Taoist pantheon.

864

Spread of Zaydi Shi'ism in Daylam on the Caspian coast near Azerbaijan; Zaydi state founded by Hasan ibn Zayd. Sporadic existence of Zaydi type Shi'ism in the region until 1126.

865

The Caliph Musta'in makes an unsuccessful attempt

to escape from the tyranny of the Turkish guard by fleeing to Baghdad from Samarra'. There follows a second siege of Baghdad (the first was during the War of the Brothers which destroyed the Round City) in the name of a rival Caliph Mu'tazz whom the captain of the Turkish guard sets up in the place of Musta'in. The city is defended by Muhammad ibn 'Abd Allah, a grandson of the Tahir who besieged it in the time of Ma'mun. After a year's siege Musta'in is forced to abdicate and is then killed. The three northern quarters of East Baghdad, Rusafah, Shammasiyah, and Mukharim never fully recover from the siege.

866

al-Hallaj visits Pu-ku-ts'un (865-900), the Idiqut, or Uighur Manichean ruler in Qocho (Kao Ch'ang 40 kilometers east of today's Turfan), in what is now Chinese Turkestan, or Xinjiang.

869

Death of al-Jahiz ("the goggle eyed"), Arab litterateur. Grandson of a Negro slave, al-Jahiz wrote theological tracts, a large work on rhetoric, forty treatises and a collection of the essays called "The Book of Animals". (A pseudo-work is also called "The Book of Beauties and Antithesis".

Death of Abu 'Abd Allah Muhammad ibn Karram, founder of the Karramiyyah, a heretic sect which gave God a material substance. The sect had an influence upon Sabuktagin of Ghaznah, and was strong in Khorasan and particularly in Nayshabur where there was an open conflict with Sunni Hanafis and Shafi'is in the year 1095. The sect became extinct with the Mongol invasions.

869-883

Revolt of the Zanj (slaves from East Africa), in Iraq. 'Ali ibn Muhammad founds a kingdom of Negro slaves in Basrah. The Zanj revolt is influenced by the Qarmatis and led by a Persian, Bihbud. The Zanj themselves had slaves.

867-879

The first of the Saffarids, Ya'qub as-Saffar ("the Coppersmith") rules Sistan, then in 873 seizes Nishapur from the Tahirids and rules much of Persia under 'Abbasid suzerainty. In 911 and 913 the Saffarid dynasty suffered setbacks from the Samanids of Transoxiana, and again from Mahmud of Ghaznah in 1003. But they continued as a power in Sistan, often under vassalage, until 1495.

870

Conquest of Malta.

Death of al-Bukhari, author of the *Sahih*, one of the great collections of Hadith, or sayings of the Prophet.

Approx. death of al-Kindi, "the Philosopher of the Arabs", first Arab student of the Greeks to make an independent name for himself, credited with 265 treatises on ethics, metaphysics, logic, medicine, music, astronomy, mathematics.

The Caliph Mu'tamid accedes to the Caliphate and moves the capital back to Baghdad from Samarra'.

872

Migration of the dualist Paulicians from Asia Minor to Thrace. This is probably the cause of the rise of the Cathares in Europe.

873

Death of the eleventh Shi'ite Imam at the age of twenty-eight. Twelve Imam Shi'ites are without an Imam; they believe the eleventh Imam (who had no wife) had a son with a concubine, herself the daughter of a Byzantine emperor; they believe this son, who would be the twelfth Imam, disappeared into hiding upon the death of his father by entering the *sardib* or cellar of the family house. This "Hidden Imam" was represented in the world by chosen deputies called *wakils* until 940. The period 873-940 is called "the Lesser Occultation". After 940 begins the "Greater Occultation" in which there are no representatives who know his whereabouts. This "Greater Occultation" continues today and will last until the coming of the Mahdi, which for Shi'ites is the return of this Imam.

Death of Abu-l-Husayn Muslim (also put at 875), compiler of one of the two collections of Hadith called the *Sahihayn*.

Plato's *Republic* translated into Arabic.

Death of Hunayn ibn Ishaq, translator of Plato and Galen.

874

Isma'ili propagandist Muhammad ibn Nusayr agitates in the Levant. His sect specializes in bringing Christians into a pseudo-Christian halfway sect on their way to becoming Dualists. Later pseudo-Islam is also added to the mix at which point the original goal becomes lost and the sect acquires its own identity although recognizing an affinity with related "conduit" sects.

Death of Abu Yazid al-Bistami, first of the so-called "drunken Sufis". Bistami's doctrinal teacher is Abu 'Ali as-Sindhi (from India, who is not Muslim for it is Bistami – also non-Muslim to begin with but of an "Iranian" religion – who teaches Sindhi the prayers of Islam; in other words Bistami taught Sindhi how to be a Muslim, and Sindhi taught Bistami what they really believed in, their own doctrine. Bistami introduces the phrase *Ibn al-Wuqt*, "son of the moment", originally meaning perhaps, "son of the times".

Death of 'Abd Allah the Elder (al-Akbar) who had taken over from his father (whom Ibn Rizam says is Maymun al-Qaddah) the running of affairs of the Isma'ilis in Salamiyyah in Syria.

Birth of 'Ubayd Allah al-Mahdi future first Fatimid, grandson of 'Abd Allah the Elder, in 'Askar Mukram in Khuzistan on 31 July 874 (*12 Shawwal 260*).

875
The Samanid Nasr ibn Ahmad receives the governorship of all of Transoxiana from al-Mu'tamid.

877
Building of the Ibn Tulun mosque in Cairo.

881
The Da'i Ibn Hawshab (Mansur al-Yemen) comes to Yemen from Kufah disguised as a cotton merchant and lands at Aden. He then proceeds to build several fortresses. The one at Bayt Rayb he calls a *Dar al-Hijrah* ("House of Refuge" – from Islam –) others are also established in Iraq and Tazrut in North Africa, and in al-Ahsa'.

882
The Governor of Kufah, Ahmad ibn Muhammad at-Ta'i, informs the authorities in Baghdad that there are people grouping in southern Iraq who have a non-Islamic religion; these are prepared to fight the Community of Muhammad with the sword and impose their own religion; but no-one listens to him. (Tabari III 2127)'Ubayd Allah, the future Mahdi and Fatimid Caliph as a boy comes from Khuzistan, where he was born, to Salamiyyah which has already been his family's new headquarters (retracing, apparently – or allegorically – himself his grandfather's previous emigration).

883
Death of Dawud ibn Khalaf, founder of the Zahiri School of Law.

Isma'ili missionaries sent from the Yemen to Sindh.

884
Death of Bihbud, the Persian leader of the Zanj revolt.

886
Death of Abu Ma'shar of Balkh, philosopher and student of al-Kindi, and known as Albumasar in the West.

Isma'ili Da'i Hamdan Qarmat sends Abu Sa'id al-Jannabi to Bahrayn to organize affairs there.

889
Death of Ibn Qutaybah of Merv, leading figure of a new school in Arabic literature which blended the secretarial style with traditional art-language and argumentative prose of the philologists into a medium for factual, imaginative and abstract subjects. He wrote a literary thesaurus called "The Fountains of Story" which are essays on sovereignty, war, friendship, asceticism, with quotations from tradition and literary and historical sources. He also wrote "the Book of Subjects of Knowledge", a summary of the early traditions of the Arabs and Persians, and biographies of the chief figures in Islamic history, "the Book of Poetry and Kings". Although a Persian, he defended the Arabs against the attacks of the *Shu'ubiyyah*.

890
The Arabs settle in Provence and carry out raids as far north as Switzerland. Rural population declines in the Islamic empire and cities grow. Between 800 and 915, tax income declines from 520 million dirhams a year to 217.

Rise of the populist revolutionary sect, the Qarmatis, an offshoot of the Isma'ilis, or "Seveners" but without "Imams". The Qarmati leader, Hamdan Qarmat establishes his center, which he calls the "Abode of Exile or Emigration" or "House of Refuge" (*Dar al-Hijrah*) in southern Iraq at a village called Mahtamabad in the district of al-Furat in the Sawad of Kufah, around 890. According to the *Fihrist*, "Qarmat had read in the stars that the Iranians were about to regain control of the Arab empire." (The Iranians reckoned conjunctions of Saturn and Jupiter as indicative of the change of dynasties.) The division between Qarmati and Fatimid Isma'ilis will assert itself in India as well. According to Arab dictionaries Qarmat is Aramaic for the "man with the two red eyes" (i.e. "a teacher of secret doctrine") but the word also acquires the meaning "to write with a minuscule script", which is a characteristic of Manichean writing. The Qarmatis have an evolved social programme of equality and property in common (*ulfah*), and very strict commercial laws.

891
Death of the historian al-Ya'qubi, author of a chronological universal history from a Shi'ite point of view.

892
Muhammad at-Tirmidhi, historian, dies.

Death of al-Baladhuri, historian, author of *The Genealogies of the Nobles* and the *History of the Conquests.*

Al-Mu'tadid restores the Capital of the Caliphate to Baghdad. He settles in East Baghdad building a complex of palaces on the Tigris below the Mukharrim Quarter, forming the Harim or Precinct which was afterwards known as the Dar-al-Khilafah.

893

Death of Taifur, author of the *History of Baghdad.*

An Isma'ili missionary from Sana'a in the Yemen named Abu 'Abd Allah ash-Shi'i, but originally from Kufah, arrives in Ifriqiya, or North Africa. He has joined the Isma'ili movement in southern Iraq and worked under the tutelage of a Fatimid Da'i in the Yemen, Ibn Hawshab ("Mansur al-Yemen", himself also originally from Kufah). Having made contact with pilgrims to Mecca from Tunisia the year before, Abu 'Abd Allah calls the Berbers of Ifriqiya (Tunisia), whom Ibn Khaldun later says already belonged to a Batini (secret Gnostic) sect, to accept among them as leader a figure calling himself "the Mahdi" who will come from the East. The legend says that the Berbers were introduced to "Isma'ilism" by missionaries in the time of Ja'far as-Sadiq. Around that time a North African, Abu Hilal ad-Dayhuri went to Baghdad and became the Archegos or head of the Manichean religion. The propagandist Abu 'Abd Allah spreads a fabricated Hadith which says that "in the third century of the Hijrah, the sun will rise in the West". (Cf Koran 2:258: "Bethink thee of him who had an argument with Abraham about his Lord, because Allah had given him the kingdom; how, when Abraham said: My Lord is He who giveth life, and causeth death, he answered: I give life and cause death. Abraham answered : 'Lo! Allah causeth the sun to rise in the East, so do thou cause it to come up from the West.' Thus was the disbeliever abashed. And Allah guideth not wrong-doing folk." This fabrication of the Hadith, is an example of the infiltration of antinomialism; it also points to the willingness on the part of the Berbers to directly challenge the tenets of Islam, in fact to challenge the God of the Koran; and it means that they were not Muslims but adherents of a rival religion. The purpose of the establishment of the Mahdi was to end the era of Islam, and bring about the *qiyamah*, or "resurrection", the resurrection of something which had been engulfed by Islam: the Batini religion of which Ibn Khaldun wrote. Abu 'Abd Allah began his organizing work among the Banu Saktan in Ikjan, and lesser Kabylia in Algeria, where he apparently encountered some resistance whereupon he then transferred his headquarters to Tazrut among the Banu Ghashman where he founded a *Dar al-Hijrah*, an "abode of refuge, or emigration", as the Qarmatis had founded in Wasit.

March or April (*Muharram 280*) is given as the birth of 'Abd ar-Rahman, the Qa'im, son of 'Ubayd Allah (at this point 19 years old himself) and Abu Shalaghlagh's daughter. Presumably Abu Shalaghlagh ('Ubayd Allah's uncle) dies soon after having designated his nephew as his successor to whatever role he has been claiming for himself by informing the *Da'is* of the *jaza'ir* or "islands". (This designation 'Ubayd Allah will call an act of "spiritual adoption" in his *Letter to the Yemenite Community.*) Presumably this is initially taken by the Da'is that 'Ubayd Allah is merely a new *Hujjah*, or "Bishop". But the following reveals the true nature of events:According to the *Sirat Ja'far*, the *Da'i* Abu-l-'Abbas, brother of Abu 'Abd Allah as-Shi'i asked Fayruz, *Da'i-l-du'at* and *bab al-abwab*, that he be allowed to make his Isma'ili vow of allegiance to the "head" of the organisation in Salamiyyah. This was done behind a curtain; then the curtain was drawn away revealing the "Imam" (Abu Shalaghlagh) the Mahdi ('Ubayd Allah) and the Qa'im. Up until then Abu Shalaghlagh was considered to be a *Hujjah*, or Bishop, probably one of twelve, representing the leader whose identity was secret. This act was a change in the party line; Abu Shalaghlagh previously claimed to represent the leader, now he claimed to be the leader. The secret leader may well have existed (if only as the head of the twelve Bishops, for example) and this was an attempt to take over the leadership from him, since a number of Da'is refused to follow Salamiyyah from that point on, eventually even going so far as to attack the Mahdi with the intention of destroying him. If these Da'is were following only Salamiyyah up until then and no one else, such a radical rejection of a former leader considered to be supreme would be hard to explain. If they saw this as an attempt on the part of one leader to usurp the role from someone else or from a larger organisation, the nature of their resistance is more clear. It has been interpreted that the supreme leader was only mythical, which is certainly true in one or more senses, but if the leader was the Archegos in Ctesiphon-Baghdad, who was soon to flee Baghdad (and who was himself in any case a stand-in for Mani, the real mythical leader) then events make sense. Fayruz himself abandoned the Mahdi when he fled to Egypt.

896

Death of Sahl at-Tustari, the teacher of al-Hallaj. Tustari believed that God is "particles of light". He also speaks of *'umud an-nur* ("columns of light") but in his school he insists that his followers base themselves *upon the Koran* when formulating ideas. (Such an insistence would not be necessary to impress upon Muslims; which means that his followers are not actually Muslims). Tustari expresses the idea of the "redemption of Satan" which will be taken up by Hallaj, Ibn 'Arabi, and 'Abd al-Karim Jili. Tustari, a so-called "drunken Sufi" introduces ideas into Sufism regarding a union with God in the "secret" of the innermost being (*sirr*).

897
The Governor of Kufah first undertakes a raid against Isma'ili villages of the Sawad and sends a series of Qarmatis in chains to Baghdad, where it emerges that a state secretary (*katib*) has been in correspondence with them, who is arrested.

898
A Zaydi Shi'ite state is established in the Yemen by the Imam al-Hadi Yahya ibn al-Husayn ar-Rassi.

Death of Hakim at-Tirmidhi, biographer of Sufis.

899
Baghdad chroniclers record the appearance of Abu Sa'id al-Hasan al-Jannabi at the head of a force of Beduin warriors; Abu Sa'id (killed by a slave in *301*/913-914), originally a missionary, occupies the city of al-Qatif. He founds a *Dar al-Hijrah* and an independent Qarmati state centered at al-Ahsa in Arabia on the Persian Gulf which survives to *470*/1077-1078, whereupon rapprochement takes place with the Fatimids. After Abu Sa'id his son Abu-l-Qasim Sa'id (*301-311*/913-923) ruled and then Abu Tahir Sulayman (d. *332*/943-944). They had a council called al-'Iqdaniyyah.

Probable date of parting of the ways between the Fatimid Isma'ilis and the Qarmatis under Hamdan Qarmat and his brother-in-law 'Abdan. Historians of the time put the Qarmatis at 100,000 concentrated in the Sawad (the "Black Earth" agricultural region) of Kufah, and the Yemen, and Yamamah.

According to Ibn Rizam, whose account on this point is accepted by those who otherwise see him as a polemicist not worthy of belief, a conflict broke out between the leader in Salamiyyah and the Da'i Hamdan Qarmat: "Qarmat used to correspond with the man in Salamiyyah... Now when that one died who had been there during his time, and his son succeeded him, he [the son] wrote to Hamdan Qarmat. But when Hamdan received the letter, he wanted nothing to do with what it contained, for it seemed to him that certain expressions to which he was accustomed had now been changed; to him this was suspicious." The Qarmati leader 'Abdan went to Salamiyyah to find that the Isma'ili leader was dead, that 'Ubayd Allah was the new leader, and there was a new doctrine. The Isma'ili movement had operated in the name of a secret leader; the code word for this leader was "Muhammad ibn Isma'il". 'Ubayd Allah claimed he and his descendants (and ascendants) were what the code word had stood for. 'Ubayd Allah went from being *Hujjah*, (or rather, *Hujjah* designate, being the nephew of Abu Shalaghlagh who probably was *Hujjah*, or Bishop of the movement, considered as representative of the Imam or secret leader) to being Imam or secret leader himself. Sources say that there twelve *Hujjahs*. That would mean that one Bishop and his family were now claiming leadership of the whole movement, and saying that they had been that unique leadership all along. Hamdan Qarmat went to Kalwadha whence he was never heard from again. (However, some Isma'ilis believe he reappears later under a different name as a loyal Fatimid Da'i in Egypt.) Then, a mysterious messenger appeared from Taleqan (in Daylam rather than Taleqan in Khorasan) in Iraq looking for Qarmat; not finding Qarmat he went to 'Abdan to recall him to 'Ubayd Allah. Ibn Rizam: "'Abdan let him know that they had discontinued the *da'wah* or propaganda because *his father* [this has led some to belief that the messenger was 'Ubayd Allah's brother] had deceived them. He had claimed a false pedigree for himself, and had made propaganda for the Mahdi Muhammad ibn Isma'il , and we did likewise. But when it became clear to us that none of this meant anything... and it was only your father behind the affair, we turned in repentance to God. It is enough for us that your father made us into unbelievers, do you now wish to make us into unbelievers once again? Vanish, and go back to whence you came". The messenger did manage to bring one Iraqi Da'i to the Fatimid side: Zikrawaih ibn Mihrawaih. So, 'Abdan was murdered at the instigation of Zikrawaih ibn Mihrawaih, Da'i of western Iraq (whose father 'Abdan had recruited). However, Abu Sa'id al-Jannabi, the Qarmati, had the Da'i Abu Zakariyya' ad-Dammami, who sided with 'Ubayd Allah, killed. Zikrawaih went into hiding.

In Western Persia and Rayy the Isma'ilis do not join with the Fatimid 'Ubayd Allah al-Mahdi and remain dissident until after 934, or perhaps until the time of the fourth Fatimid Caliph al-Mu'izz (953-975). The Musafirids of Azerbaijan also side against the Fatimids. In Khorasan some Da'is side with the Fatimids. Yemen first sides with the Fatimids, then in *291*/903 one Da'i, Ibn al-Fadl edges towards independence and in *299*/911, after reoccupying San'a' himself claims to be the Mahdi. The *Da'i* Ibn Hawshab, an architect of the Ifriqiya policy of preparing the Berbers for an emigration of the leadership to North Africa, sides with 'Ubayd Allah the Fatimid. He dies in *302*/914.

900
Qarmati raids in the neighborhood of Basrah.

Abu Sa'id al-Jannabi besieges Hajar, the fortified capital of the Bahrayn oases, two miles from Hofuf in al-Ahsa'; for the first time the Caliph al-Mu'tadid sends 2,000 troops against the Qarmatis, who defeat the Caliph's forces.

901
Zikrawaih ibn Mihrawaih (also called Zakaroye ibn

Mihroye) sends his son Husayn to the tribe of the Kalb in Palmyrene Syria "to pose as a descendant of Muhammad ibn Isma'il ibn Ja'far and to proselytize among them for the Imam from among his progeny..." It would appear that taking the identity of Muhammad ibn Isma'il for the purpose of propaganda was a common practice for a certain level of leader in the organisation; what the Qarmatis resented was that someone, 'Ubayd Allah, took the identity permanently for his own use.

902
Husayn succeeds in recruiting many of the Kalb; the messenger who is presumed to be the brother of 'Ubayd Allah the Mahdi appears again, seeks out Zikrawaih who sends the mysterious messenger, depicted as "son of the *Hujjah*" to Husayn. Husayn presents this man to the tribes as the true chief (*sahib al-amr*) of their movement (rather than 'Ubayd Allah, which in the past led to speculation regarding 'Ubayd Allah's true identity).

Zikrawayh ibn Mihrawayh organizes Qarmati revolts between *289-295*/902-908 in Iraq and Syria. One of the Qarmati groups, the Banu'l Asbagh clan of the Kalb, adopt the name *al-Fatimiyyun*, which is later adopted by 'Ubayd Allah himself. 'Ubayd Allah leaves Salamiyyah warned by carrier pigeons from Baghdad that the 'Abbasid authorities have learned his identity and have taken measures to arrest him. Women of the family are left behind, including the 'Ubayd Allah's mother and the ten-year-old Qa'im's "childwife". 'Ubayd Allah goes to ar-Ramla in Palestine where it is recorded he watched a meteor shower with the Governor on the roof of the Governor's house (the Governor was an Isma'ili initiate). The meteor shower took place on 28 October 902. He said the meteor shower was a miraculous sign of his identity. He hid in Ramla and then he went to Egypt in *291*/903.

Abu 'Abd Allah's followers (the "Friends of God" *awlia Allah*) in North Africa occupy Mila – the Roman Mileve or Mileu which makes the Emir of Kairouan aware of the danger growing in the West. Pilgrims carry messages between the Mahdi and Abu Abd Allah; but the Qayrawan *Jund* beats back Abu 'Abd Allah who is obliged to abandon Tazrut and reestablish the *Dar al-Hijrah* in Ikjan.

The Aghlabid Ibrahim II conquers Taormina, the last Christian stronghold in Sicily, and crosses the straits of Messina to Calabria but dies of dysentery before Cosenza.

903
Abu-l-Qasim Yahya ibn Zikrawaih, son of Zikrawaih ibn Mihrawayh, having successfully gathered Beduins from the Syrian desert, threatens Damascus from December 902 to July 903 but dies in the siege perhaps incinerated by a naphta projectile. The Qarmatis do not take the city but are otherwise victorious. Abu-l-Qasim Yahya ibn Zikrawaih was known as the "Master of the Camel" (*Sahib an-Naqa*); Ivanow cites an Isma'ili pseudo-Hadith apparently preserved orally in India that "the Prophet once saw God [sic] wearing a red cloak riding on a camel at 'Arafat" (the root of 'Arafat means to "recognize" or "to know"). Yahya may also have let himself be taken to be the Mahdi or "Muhammad ibn 'Abd Allah ibn Muhammad ibn Isma'il ibn Ja'far as-Sadiq", the secret leader of the whole movement, as well. Yahyah's brother Husayn takes over leadership. Husayn, known as *Sahib ash-Shama* ("the man with the birthmark") and *Sahib al-Khal* captures Salamiyyah. *Just before*, Abu Muhammad, the brother of 'Ubayd Allah died in Salamiyyah. Husayn also captures Hamah, Baalbak and forces Damascus to come to terms, and seems to set up a state expecting a Mahdi, presumably 'Ubayd Allah, to come and take control; but in a battle near Ma'arrat al-Nu'man with an 'Abbasid Baghdad army under Muhammad ibn Sulayman, the Fatimid army is catastrophically defeated. Thereupon Husayn in Salamiyyah orders a massacre of the inhabitants of Salamiyyah, the destruction of the residence of 'Ubayd Allah and the members of the Mahdi's household left behind. Was he disappointed with 'Ubayd Allah or was he all along seeking his own interest? This, as so many details, is not clear. The coalition supporting Husayn breaks up. Husayn is captured near Salihiyye or Doura Europos, and brought to Raqqa' before the Caliph al-Muqtafi, whence the captives are brought to Baghdad. In Northern Syria Isma'ilis are hunted down. Several Da'i's present themselves to the authorities asking for pardon. Husayn is executed early in 904/*291* in Baghdad along with hundreds of others, after receiving two hundred lashes his body is exposed for a year. Another son of Zikrawaih, Abu-l-Fadl tried to lead Qarmati revolts in Syria. In this connection Tabari, III 2226 (Goeje 51) tells the story of a woman whose son had joined the Qarmatis; she went looking for him. When she found him, he said to her "What is your religion?" She was surprised at this question; then he said "Everything that we knew before was folly; the true religion is what we practice now." Tabari's account of the Qarmatis is based upon the interrogation of an Isma'ili captive related to Zikrawaih ibn Mihrawaih by an 'Abbasid, Muhammad ibn Da'ud al-Jarrah.'Ubayd Allah the Mahdi goes to Egypt.

In Isfahan, Ibn Rustah writes the *al-'Alaq an-Nafisah*, a geographical work in which he says that some Qurayshis had brought Manicheism to Mecca from Hirah before Islam. Ibn Qutaibah also says that *zandaqa*, or Manicheism was brought from Hirah to Mecca.

Abu Sa'id al-Hasan al-Jannabi, originally a missionary of Qarmat, subjugates the Yamamah in Arabia and invades Oman. His son Abu Tahir Sulayman lays waste to southern Iraq; he attacks the pilgrim routes.

Internal struggles among the Aghlabids allow Abu 'Abd Allah in North Africa to reconquer Mila and take Satif as well.

904
'Ubayd Allah spends a year in Egypt, until November 904, under the protection of one of his initiates in al-Fustat, while his chamberlain Ja'far undergoes "light" torture at the hands of the authorities in Egypt.

905
When Egypt, which had been under the independent Tulunids is taken under direct 'Abbasid rule by the War Minister Muhammad ibn Sulayman (who had wrecked the son of Zikrawaih), 'Ubayd Allah is abandoned by one of his Da'is named Firuz (who goes to Yemen and joins opponents). Thereupon 'Ubayd Allah does not himself go to Yemen from Egypt as was planned but instead goes first to Tripoli in North Africa and then to Sijilmassa in south Morocco. En route to Morocco, a library of books of his is captured in Egypt. Halfway between Alexandria and Cyrenaica the caravan is attacked by Berber robbers, and his books are lost; this library is much lamented; one of the books is prophecies of the future, an echo of the legendary "Kitab al-Ja'far", or mythical book of the 'Alids. Years later these books are regained by 'Ubayd's son, the Qa'im.

In Sijilmassa, after several years in hiding, 'Ubayd Allah is arrested and imprisoned by the Midrarid *amir*, who is a Kharijite and totally independent of Baghdad, but who is nevertheless presumably acting on the advice of the 'Abbasids or the Aghlabids or in any case in their interest.

Before 'Ubayd Allah leaves Egypt he sends Ja'far the Chamberlain back to Salamiyyah to recover hidden money left in the ruined family house; earlier he had sent a servant back to Salimiyyah to curse him and encourage the people to destroy what was left of the house in such a way as to preserve hidden treasure which had earlier been collected as part of the religious tithe from Iraq and Syria. Ja'far was to use the recuperated money to buy several camel-loads of cotton to disguise his activities. Upon 'Ubayd's departure the Da'i Abu 'Ali (in whom some see Hamdan Qarmat as having improbably resurfaced under a new name) remains in Egypt as the contact for the only Isma'ili community which is on 'Ubayd Allah's side, namely one Da'i in the Yemen (and the struggling faction in North Africa). However, in the same Yemen and nearby, another former Da'i has turned against 'Ubayd Allah and heads a rival community.

906
Mutineers against the Aghlabids free Abu-l-'Abbas (brother of Abu 'Abd Allah) from prison in Qayrawan. Abu 'Abd Allah captures the city of Tubna with Roman war methods. Here he applies Islamic principles of taxation, but strictly and orthodoxly.

One of Zikrawaih's Da'is named Abu Ghanim, a school teacher from an area south of Babylon takes the name Nasr (victory), collects remnants of Fatimid tribes and makes war in the direction of Damascus falling back upon Tiberias. After attacks by government troops he is killed by his own.

In October another Da'i of Zikrawaih's, al-Qasim ibn Ahmad attacks Kufah on the 'Id al-Adha under white banners of the Shi'ah shouting "Vengeance for Husayn". The attackers wreak havoc but are driven off. While it can be interpreted that these attacks are in support of the Fatimid Mahdi, they fit into a pattern of desperate acts of a religious movement which has created, over a long period of political preparation, millenial expectations of the triumph of its cause which is the restoration of its religion, Manicheism, to an ascendancy which has been, in their minds, wrongly supplanted by Islam.

907
Zikrawaih who had been in hiding near Qadisiyyah, meets his forces in October 906, "Beduins, Non-Arab Muslims (*mawali*), Aramaean peasants (*nabati*)". Removed from the view of his forces, concealed, he is addressed as "Lord" (*sayyid*) while al-Qasim proceeds to the outermost edge of the region watered by the Euphrates around the province of Kufah where he predicts that the population will rise up and join them. On the 12th of October he is engaged by several thousand government troops and beats them off successfully. He pillages the second of three pilgrim caravans on its way from Mecca to Baghdad, seizing treasures of the Tulunids of Egypt who had been exiled to Baghdad.

907
10 January (22 Rabi' I *294*) A government army sent from Baghdad battles Zikrawaih in the Wadi Dhi Qar, "near the ruins of Iram" for two days. Zikrawaih is wounded, captured by the 'Abbasids, and dies two days later having failed to create a Qarmati state in Iraq and Syria. His corpse is preserved and exposed to view in Baghdad. Another Da'i, "The Smith" (*al-haddad*), and others surrender in Baghdad. Remnants of his followers, joined by Persians, continue limited activities under the name of the Baqliyyah, or "Vegetarians" under the leadership of Abu Hatim az-Zutti and others until they are absorbed into the Qarmatis of Bahrayn around 932.

Oleg, the Viking leader of Kievan Russia, attacks Constantinople and exacts agreements.

THE RISE of the FATIMIDS in NORTH AFRICA

908

Probable date of the departure of the Archegos, the head of the Manichean church from the "land of Babel" [Bab-El, "Gate of El"], that is, Mada'in (Ctesiphon), in the vicinity of Baghdad (according to an-Nadim who says he left in the reign of Muqtadir.) Massignon, however, says that the year 296 H (30 September 908-20 September 909) was "*precisely*" the year in which the Archegos left, but does not give his reasons. However, the logic of his statement is self-evident: the Archegos' departure may be connected with these other events which took place in that year:

Death of the Caliph al-Muktafi, accession of al-Muqtadir through intrigue, followed by a palace revolt and accession of Ibn al-Mu'tazz as Caliph, followed by the deposition and death of Ibn al-Mu'tazz and the restoration of al-Muqtadir.

After the death of the Caliph al-Muktafi a power struggle which had been building behind the scenes for a long time came to a head. Until then, the powers around the throne were Sunnis and state administration was carried out through Sunni secretaries. In reality however, these so-called Sunni secretaries were crypto-Manichean families. As Brockelmann says "Manicheism, particularly in Iraq, still exercised a great influence... and very nearly became the religion of the educated classes." (p. 112, H.I.P.) In addition, more crypto-Manicheans were brought into the government by the Barmakids who had helped the 'Abbasids to power in the first place. The Barmakids themselves were destroyed by Harun ar-Rashid in 805, but their administrative proteges remained, still in control of the mechanism of government because they were in control of the bureaucracy. In 908, a shift was about to take place. The political influence of Twelve Imam Shi'ites had increased to a tipping point. At the death of al-Muktafi, Shi'ite bankers and functionaries put the 13 year old al-Muqtadir on the Caliphal throne as their puppet. Several months later the "Sunnis" struck back and on the 17th of December Ibn al-Mu'tazz was put on the throne in Baghdad while the reigning Caliph, al-Muqtadir, was removed. But this Caliphate lasted for one day only and ended with his assassination.

Ibn al-Mu'tazz, the grandson of the Caliph al-Mutawakkil, was the son of the Caliph al-Mu'tazz who himself had been put on the throne in 866 until 869 by the Turkish Guards of Samarra' when the Caliph al-Musta'in fled from them to Baghdad. A poet, he wrote "The Epistles", a miniature epic of 450 iambic couplets celebrating the reign of his cousin the Caliph al-Mu'tadid, and works on poetics influenced by Aristotle's *Rhetoric* which had recently been translated into Arabic. He had led a life away from politics extolling the pure Arabic of the Beduins while occupying himself with literary criticism. But he was opposed to Twelve Imam Shi'ites. The day after the child Caliph al-Muqtadir had been deposed, the Shi'ites successfully countered and Ibn al-Mu'tazz, "The Caliph for a Day", was executed. This was a decisive shift of state power into the hands of Shi'ites who had thus prevailed in the attempt to restore the status quo ante. The Shi'ites, as direct rivals, were more aggressive against Manicheans than the authentic Sunnis, and above all knew who the Manicheans were when the real Sunnis generally did not have a clue. The Manicheans who until then were usually disguised as Sunnis (but thereafter increasingly as Twelve Imam Shi'ites) were now out of power and under serious threat. This would have signaled the time for the Archegos to depart. These events were followed by the execution of al-Hallaj in 924, an event long time coming, preceded by years of imprisonment on charges of crypto-Manicheism, and thereafter by the executions of thousands throughout the empire whom Massignon calls Hallajians and whom others call Isma'ilis.

In any case, according to an-Nadim (d. 385/995) in "the Catalog" (*al-Fihrist*), this removal of the center of Manicheism took place in the reign of the Caliph al-Muqtadir (908-932). Because many Manicheans fled to Khorasan, it is often assumed that the Archegos went to Samarkand, which, along with Ifriqiya (Tunisia and Algeria), was a center of Manichean activity; however, there is no trace of his appearance in Central Asia. An-Nadim says the Manicheans were split; that there had existed a sect among them in Transoxiana called the *Dinawariyyah* (possibly from Dinawar, the name of several places, one of which is in Khorasan), and the contention had been over the question whether the Imam of the sect could have validity if he resided outside of Ctesiphon. This division had disappeared and then apparently a new division took place into the *Miqlasiyyah* and *Mihriyyah*; with the contention being over rules "of social relationships", one of the two groups being dedicated to programmes of social evolution and revolution (like the Mazdakites) and the other to peaceful coexistence or non-revolutionary development with the existing powers. And an-Nadim observes, that in 987, there seemed to be only a handful of Manicheans left in Baghdad in his day, whereas before there had been hundreds. An-Nadim does not explain why, but the reason is that most of them, had evolved; or as Ibn Hazm (d. 1094) had observed of the Fatimids: "I see that Mazdak has become a Shi'ite."

Conjunction of Jupiter and Saturn in the constellation of Aries on the 13th of March 908. The Isma'ilis used the conjunctions of these two planets, with astrological implications of dynasty and rulership, as propaganda to create expectations of historical changes of cosmic proportions (see 895 and 928). In coming to North Africa 'Ubayd Allah was attacked by bandits and his arcane books were stolen. The first expedition of his son al-Qa'im to Egypt brought no other results than the recovery of the books which made 'Ubayd Allah exclaim that this in itself was a great victory. The declaration of the Fatimid Caliphate in 910 is the fulfillment of the meaning of the propaganda which stated the "sun would rise in the West" (see 895), that is, the movement to North Africa of a leader who had originally been in the East, and in the sense of the Koran 2:258, a direct and successful challenge to Islam on the part of a rival religion.

909

26 August (6 *Dhu-l-Hijjah 296*) 'Ubayd Allah and his son (or adopted son) the Qa'im, are freed from detention in Sijilmassa, Morocco by Abu 'Abd Allah and are presented to the Kutama army and Da'is; the Fatimids take this to be his enthronement as Caliph. 'Ubayd Allah, who had lived in Sijilmassa from 905 to 909, was at the end, before the arrival of the Ketama Berber troops, placed under house arrest by the Midrarid Amir, while his servants were tortured to determine their true identities and purposes. On the way to Tunis 'Ubayd Allah, now called al-Mahdi saw for the first and last time the *Dar al-Hijrah* from which his propaganda had been initiated in Ikjan. Al-Mahdi ordered that all the treasure which had heretofore been collected should be turned over to him.

910

In Rabi' II *297*/Friday 5 January 910, having been freed from imprisonment by Abu 'Abd Allah ash-Shi'i, in Sijilmassa, Morocco, 'Ubayd Allah al-Mahdi made his triumphant entry into Raqqada, the royal suburb of Qayrawan, where he was publicly proclaimed Caliph and his name read in the Friday sermon as Caliph. He is established as "the Mahdi" among the Ketama Berbers of Ifriqiya (Tunisia). This is the founding of the Fatimid dynasty, which, calling itself a Caliphate, will claim authority over the leadership of the Islamic world. 'Ubayd Allah takes the title al-Mahdi Bi'Llah. A new genealogy is put forth claiming descent from Isma'il the son of Ja'far as-Sadiq; originally descent had been claimed from another son, 'Abd Allah al-Aftah; who was known to have no sons; this is abandoned and replaced by a genealogy claiming descent from Muhammad ibn Isma'il ibn Ja'far. Ibn Hazm in Spain remarks of all this: "I see that Mazdak has become a Shi'ite." Later, al-Mu'izz is depicted as answering questions in Egypt about his ancestry "he drew his sword from its sheath and replied: 'This is my pedigree!' and, throwing gold pieces to the assembly, he added, 'And here is my noble ancestry..." With this event the period of concealment (*dawr al-satr*) and of the hidden Imams in the history of early Isma'ilism, had come to an end, being followed by a period of unveiling or manifestation (dawr al-kashf), "when the Isma'ili Imam appeared publicly at the head of his community" (Daftary).

'Ubayd Allah was an Isma'ili coming from Iraq or Persia and claiming a descent from the Prophet. When the family still lived in Basrah, his ancestor 'Abd Allah the Elder claimed to be descended from 'Aqil ibn Abi Talib; when 'Ubayd Allah made claims to leadership of the Isma'ilis in 899 he also claimed to be descended from Ja'far as-Sadiq and thus from 'Aqil's brother 'Ali ibn Abi Talib. These claims were later vehemently refuted by 'Alid descendants (who also asserted that the dynasty is descended from Daysan, that is Bardesanes, who along with Marcion was considered a forerunner of Mani),The Mahdi is reunited with his mother, his daughters, his nieces, and his son's wife who had been brought from Tripoli by the slave Su'luk who years earlier had been sent to Salimiyyah to recover them. The expectations about his role, which are of course unrealizable, are transferred to his son who acquires the title al-Qa'im and the full name of the Prophet, Abu-l-Qasim Muhammad ibn 'Abd Allah.

In describing the doctrines of the Isma'ilis, Hollister says in *The Shi'a of India* (p. 251) that "salvation lies in recognizing the Imam of the Age... the soul of a disciple... is then drawn at physical death... to a Lower Paradise... they receive the final touch of the 'knowledge of the Imam,' and when the Imam dies he 'combines himself all the pure souls' of his period and carries them to the Tenth Intelligence... The bodies of the faithful are absorbed by the Sun and the Moon and there purified, after which they are absorbed into plants and animals and serve as nourishment for the Imam. The souls of unbelievers, those who have failed to recognize the Imam, 'find no rest and wander to and fro' in darkness. 'They struggle towards subtlety but are set back.' After a long period these darkened souls again assume human form and have a new opportunity to recognize the Imam of the Age. The substance of the bodies of the believers passes through different stages of animal, vegetable and mineral worlds until it too is purified."

Later that year, doubts arise in the Ketama Berbers and Abu 'Abd Allah regarding the Mahdi's authenticity. From circles opposed to him reports say there was dismay over his appearance and demeanor: "They found [around him] silk and brocade clothing, gold and silver vessels, Greek eunuchs, and indications of the use of alcohol. [Wine is also prohibited in Manicheism.] In their Berber simplicity they disapproved of all this..." The spokesman of the Ketama confronts the Mahdi before his throne and tells him to his face: "We have doubts as to your affair! Perform a miracle for us if you really are the Mahdi, as you have maintained." Al-Mahdi reacted with indignation and recalled that the miracle of Muhammad was the Koran. But the Batinis maintain that the Koran has another, "true" albeit very different meaning from what is obvious if taken at face value. The decoding (*ta'wil*) of this alternate meaning was the putative "miracle of Muhammad's successors", and al-Mahdi's ancestor. This actually brilliantly sums up the nature of the Isma'ili movement which was to turn Islam into a receptacle for the "Religion of Truth" by reinterpreting Islam to have a hidden sense.

Death of the Sufi al-Junayd. Junayd had become the spokesman of "orthodox" Sufism and "sobriety", which is a reproach directed at the "Drunken Sufis" or those "mystics" such as al-Bistami, Abu Sa'id Ibn Abi-l-Khayr, and al-Hallaj, who claim to be God.

911
February: The first Fatimid Caliph has Abu Abd Allah, who prepared his arrival among the Ketama Berbers, and his brother Abu-l-'Abbas murdered. Al-Mahdi has already created a secret police (*diwan al-kashf*). There is also a purge of leaders of the Ketama Berbers who, nevertheless, retain primacy in the new alliances. Having laid the claim to ruling the Islamic world forces the Fatimid Isma'ilis to adopt a new attitude towards the institution, the Caliphate, which they had previously tried to destroy, and towards Islam which they claimed to nullify and replace. Instead of the expected New Age a different kind of new age will take place in which there will be ever repeated cycles of seven Imams succeeding each other until the last *natiq* (speaker-prophet) appears.

Towards the end of the year, after *The Letter to the Yemenite Community* detailing the supposed family tree which al-Mahdi thought would unite Yemen and his North African armies in Egypt, the Da'i 'Ali ibn al-Fadl expresses his discord with al-Mahdi and declares war on Ibn Hawshab (*Mansur al-Yaman*) besieging him for eight months. Then al-Fadl himself declares the Millennium by abolition of the Islamic religious law, the *shari'ah.*

300 H.- 18 August 912

912
With the new Hijrah century, the Fatimids adopt what had been an imperial privilege exercised by Baghdad and Byzantium: they coin a gold Fatimid dinar. The Umayyads of Spain will follow their example in *324*/935.

913
Abu Sa'id, chief of the Qarmatis, is assassinated in his palace at al-Hasa'. His son Abu-l-Qasim Sa'id takes over the leadership of the Bahrayn Qarmatis.

914
Ibn Hawshab, the *Mansur al-Yaman*, dies on 31 December (11 Jumada II 302) in his *Dar al-Hijrah*; next year his adversary 'Ali ibn al-Fadl also dies and is succeeded by his son. Ibn Hawshab entrusts the leadership of the *Da'wah* to his son Abu-l-Hasan al-Mansur and an experienced Da'i named ash-Shawiri. Ash-Shawiri asks 'Ubayd Allah to confirm him which he does. Abu-l-Hasan goes to North Africa to ask to be confirmed as chief Da'i of the Yemen but is refused whereupon he returns to Islam and begins persecuting Isma'ilis effectively reducing Fatimid influence and leaving mainly Qarmatis in the Yemen. His brother Ja'far ibn Mansur al-Yaman remains loyal to the Fatimids and writes the *Kitab al-Kashf* and the "Wise Man and the Boy" but keeps out of politics. Ibn Hawshab's northern Yemeni "island" (*jazirah* or jurisdiction) still exists.

915
28 October (15 Rabi' II 303) 'Ali ibn al-Fadl, rival to Ibn Hawshab dies in Mudhaykhira (legend says poisoned by physicians sent by the Mahdi). In January 916 Yu'fir As'ad attacks the Isma'ili fortresses in the vicinity of Mudhaykhira and Ibn al-Fadl's two sons and three daughters are taken prisoner and then the sons are beheaded; Baghdad Caliphal authority is restored.

921
The Fatimid al-Mahdi and his court enter into al-Mahdiyya, the new capital whose construction began in 916, replacing the original capital Raqqada (Qayrawan). When the fortress of al-Mahdiyya becomes the only refuge of the Fatimids during the Berber revolt of 944-947 the legend circulates that al-Mahdi prophesied that the fortress was created to serve its role (by providing him safety) for "only for one hour of one single day" during which the Berbers partly gained access to the fortress itself. The son of al-Mahdi returns from his second unsuccessful Egyptian campaign to this new capital.

The conversion of the Volga Bulgars to Islam.

Embassy of Ibn Fadlan, sent by the Caliph al-Muqtadir, to the Bulgar Khanate and to Russia. It lasts two years.

922
Execution of al-Hallaj, in Baghdad. Husayn ibn Mansur al-Hallaj, a Persian, son of a Majusi, or follower of an Iranian religion, claimed to be God by saying *Ana al-Haqq* ("I am the Reality"). This was not merely a theoretical idea because he was accused of letting himself be actually worshiped using as justification a verse of the Koran "He is God in Heaven and

He is God in earth" with himself as the God on earth. In his youth he visited India and Central Asia. He is described as performing "miracles" which were challenged as fraud already in his lifetime (and are obviously magician's tricks). He had many followers who looked upon him as a mystical teacher but in his own lifetime he was extremely controversial having also frequently been accused of being a *zindiq*, or dualist (Manichean). This, *zandaqa*, or crypto-Manicheism, was indeed the actual charge brought against him in his trial, but also against many others. According to Massignon, 10,000 "Hallajians", were also imprisoned or put to death, both before his trial and for as long as sixteen years afterwards (the case of Shalmaghani), not only in Baghdad, but elsewhere in the empire. The party which instigated this persecution were Shi'ites who were the backers of the Sunni Caliph al-Muqtadir, and who were becoming increasingly influential. Indeed, the "Hidden" (and mythical) Twelfth Imam of the Shi'ites sentenced Hallaj to death through his representative the *wakil* several years before the Caliphal court reached its verdict. In the years immediately after the trial and execution of Hallaj overt Manicheans fled Baghdad, where they had been numerous, for Khorasan, where they were also persecuted, and thereafter all went underground dissimulating their true religion. It was, however, Shi'ite rivalry apart, Hallaj's and his co-religionists association with the revolutionary movements of the Isma'ilis which made him seem dangerous to the court at a time of growing political and social unrest as rival Isma'ili factions, the Qarmatis and Fatimids, threatened the empire with rebellion. When Hallaj was arrested there was found in his house a quantity of manuscripts written on Chinese silk in a very fine hand with very small letters (a characteristic of Manichean writing); these were instructions to agents on how to indoctrinate new disciples and lead them on degree by degree. He was condemned by the theologians of Baghdad and a majority of Sufis including al-Junayd. A few of the Sufis who had condemned him, professed, thirty and forty years later, doubt regarding their condemnations of him, namely that perhaps he had been a legitimate Sufi after all. Above all, some one hundred years after his death, a propaganda began from Central Asia which depicted al-Hallaj as a sacrificial victim and martyr who exemplified "esoterism" suffering at the hands of uncomprehending "exoterism". In other words, it was all a misunderstanding of al-Hallaj's words "*ana al-Haqq*" ("I am the Divine Reality").

923

Death of at-Tabari, the historian, author of the *Annals* and the great Koranic commentary, *Jami' al-Bayan*. He expressly forbade adding anything to his great Chronicle. His final years were spent blockaded in his house by hostile theological partisans.

Ibn al-Jawzi of the 12th century recounts that in this year fourteen sacks of books confiscated from Manicheans were burned in Baghdad. Because of Manichean book illumination techniques, streams of melted gold and silver emerged from the pyre (F. Déroche, *Le Livre Manuscrit Arabe*).

924

According to Ibn al-Jawzi (Goeje, *Memoire sur les Carmathes* p. 177), in this year a prisoner of battle who becomes a slave of the Qarmatis in Eastern Arabia (al-Ahsa', al-Hasa, Lahsa) hears from his Qarmati owner that while the Prophet Muhammad was someone "who knew how to rule", all the Caliphs were reprehensible; *including 'Ali* whom the Qarmati calls "an imposter". From this it appears that Islam (and Shi'ism) is only a cover for the Qarmatis who have a secret religion and a secret ritual called "the Night of the Imam". Nasir-i Khusraw, a Fatimid Isma'ili from Central Asia who visited the Qarmatis in 1051, says that most of the legal prescriptions of Islam were abolished for those among them "who knew the *truth*". The religion of the Qarmatis has been described as "a cult of reason" but with a readiness to accept deification of their leaders. The word *qarmata* took on the meaning to "write in small letters with the lines close together" (which was a hallmark of Manichean writing.)

The Qarmatis raid a caravan returning to Baghdad from the pilgrimage to Mecca and the Caliph's parasol, the *Khamsah*, is captured.

925

Death of Abu Bakr Muhammad ar-Razi, famous physician and alchemist who extols a religion of reason and knowledge (and is thereby associated with the materialist dualists).

A Baghdad chronicler reports that "Between Kufah and Baghdad there came forward a man who purported to be Muhammad ibn Ismail..." Troops of the Baghdad government, 500 horse and 1,000 foot, are sent out to put down the revolt; several rebels are taken prisoner.

The police arrest thirty Qarmatis who used to gather for teaching sessions in a mosque in Baratha, a suburb of Baghdad. The prisoners were found to be carrying white tinted seals, bearing the motto; Muhammad ibn Isma'il, al-Imam al-Mahdi, the friend of God. Their leader, a certain al-Ka'ki, escaped but his deputy was sentenced to 300 lashes and led around the city on a camel exposed to public view. The jurisconsults confirmed that this group served "unbelief and the disunity of the believers".

928

In this year the Isma'ilis predicted the dawn of a new

world order and the abolition of Islam because of the conjunction of Jupiter and Saturn; according al-Biruni and to the *Fihrist* of an-Nadim, the Qarmatis awaited with this "seventh conjunction" of the two planets now taking place in the fire sign of Sagittarius, the inauguration of the era of the "true religion". (The first conjunction of a series in which this would be the seventh took place in the year 809; other conjunction years were 829, 848, 868, 888, 908. Following were 948 and 967.) Al-Mas'udi reports that the Caliph al-Mansur let himself be guided by astrological predictions. At this time astrology was much followed in Baghdad. (Mani had written treatises on astrology.) Nasir-i Khusraw will write in his *Diwan* about the decline of Khorasan: "the spheres themselves have somehow gone awry... Balkh, the house of wisdom... turned upon its head...") Leading up to this conjunction Abu Tahir the Qarmati chief intensified attacks upon the 'Abbasids, without, however, capturing Baghdad. He then turned to a more symbolic act in 930, by attacking Mecca, massacring residents and pilgrims, and carrying off the Black Stone. See 930.

929

'Abd ar-Rahman III, the Umayyad ruler of Spain takes the title of Caliph (apparently following the example of the Fatimids).

Death of the Harranian mathematician and astronomer al-Battani.

930

The Qarmatis of Abu Tahir raid Mecca and take the Black Stone from the Ka'bah (*17 Dhu al-Hijjah 317*/Jan 21) to al-Hasa' (al-Ahsa') in eastern Arabia, or to Bahrayn. For several days the Qarmatis under Abu Tahir massacred residents of Mecca and Pilgrims, desecrated the Grand Mosque, and finally carried off the Black Stone (See 928.) Perhaps this event was a substitution for the overthrow of the 'Abbasids which was hoped for in the year 928 but could not be pulled off at the appropriate time. Despite great difficulties, the Fatimids had succeeded in declaring a Caliphate in 910, close to the conjunction of Jupiter and Saturn of 908. Many Isma'ili philosophers spoke of the end of the era of Islam, and the emergence of the "true religion", often saying that it had already come. Stealing the Black Stone was one way of symbolizing this. The Fatimids, however, now part of the establishment, could not publicly approve such a stance, and the Fatimid Caliph al-Mahdi eventually wrote to Abu Tahir to reprimand him.

931

Abu Tahir recognizes in Ramadan 319 a young Persian from Isfahan as the Mahdi in the Qarmati state, which at this point included Arabia and Oman. The timing coincided with what was believed to be the passing of 1,500 years after Zoroaster or the year 1242 of the "era of Alexander" (the Seleucid era which began in 312 BC). (The Sassanids, not knowing the true epoch of Zoroaster consulted the Babylonians about the questions of dates. The Babylonians confused Cyrus with Zoroaster and since then until modern times, when archaeology and scholarship have shown the true epoch of Zoroaster to be 1,200 BC or even hundreds of years earlier, it has been commonly, but erroneously, believed that Zoroaster existed in the sixth century BC. Many modern books perpetuate this error.) These prophecies, which were probably invented as propaganda a century or so earlier by the Isma'ilis for the purpose of destabilizing the 'Abbasid rule, predicted the restoration of the reign of the "Magians". The Isfahani Mahdi whose name may have been Zakariyya' instituted the cursing of Muhammad, the burning of religious books, "the worship of fire "...and began to execute Qarmati nobles. Eventually, Abu Tahir changed his mind and had him killed. (*See* 928).

THE BUYID SUZERAINTY in BAGHDAD

932

The Buyid Mu'izz ad-Dawlah assumes control as "Prince of Princes" and makes the 'Abbasid Caliph into a figurehead.

933

Because the Qarmatis are trying to bring about a paradise on earth and instead bring widespread terrorism, the pilgrimage to Mecca is severely curtailed from Iraq and is not led by Baghdadi officials as usual. But in this year as-Sijistani, the Da'i who will succeed an-Nasafi, and reach rapprochement with the Fatimids, decides to go to Mecca.

934

The 'Abbasid Caliph al-Qahir is deposed. A cruel ruler, he is himself blinded and reduced to begging in Baghdad for another sixteen years before his death.

The 'Abbasid Caliph ar-Radi is so weak that during his reign, until 940, the pilgrimage to Mecca is suspended because of Qarmati unrest in the Hejaz.

Abu Hatim ar-Razi, the Da'i of Rayy, goes to Azerbaijan where he dies. Ar-Razi, a Qarmati Isma'ili who does not follow the Fatimid party line, and does not recognize the Fatimids as Imams, teaches that the Isma'ili communities are leaderless after the "disappearance of the seventh Imam Muhammad ibn Isma'il". From that disappearance, according to him, there are no more "Imams" and in this interval (*fatrah*) the communities are instead led by twelve adjutants (*lahiq*), or, one could say, Bishops, all equal in rights. But he does recognize that one of them – who may not be a descendant of the prophet – (thereby repudiating Fatimid claims) – may be an arbiter or deputy (*khalifa*) of the Imam, thereby recognizing the Fatimid as a *primus inter pares* – while nevertheless rejecting the essence of their claims. This is as much as to say that the Manichean Archegos has disappeared and only the twelve Bishops remain, but one of them, in his disguise as Caliph has indeed achieved a pre-eminent role.

935
Death of the great theologian al-Ash'ari who began the movement which extinguished the Mu'tazilites, and devised a theology which upheld the absoluteness of God.

The Umayyads of Spain, again following the example of the Fatimids, coin a gold Cordovan dinar, exercising what had been an imperial privilege of Baghdad and Byzantium.

936
The royal city of Medinat az-Zahrah is founded at Cordoba.

939
Death of Muhammad ibn Ya'qub al-Kulayni, Shi'ite theologian, author of the "Compendium of the Science of Religion" (*al-Kafi fi 'Ilm ad-Din*). His work is a collection of 16,000 Hadith, one of the most important to Shi'ites among whom he is called the *Thiqat al-Islam* ("The Trustworthy of Islam").'Abd ar-Rahman of Cordova defeated by Ramiro of Leon at Simancas.

940
The Fourth *wakil* (representative) of the "Hidden Imam" refuses to name a successor as he dies, saying: "the matter now rests with God". The "Greater Occultation" begins for the Twelve-Imam Shi'ites which will last until the return of the Twelfth Imam from the invisible as the Mahdi. (They do not accept the Sevener or Isma'ili version of the Mahdi doctrine). (See 873.)

Death of the Persian poet Rudaki, in Samarkand. One of the first to compose in new Persian, he is an Isma'ili, or, more old school, simply a Manichean.

942
Death of Saadia Gaon, Jewish philosopher born in Egypt. He was the head of a Jewish academy in Sura, Babylonia; he wrote on Hebrew grammar and on philosophy, the *Book of Beliefs and Opinions*. He translated the Old Testament into Arabic.

Death of al-Jahshiyari, author of "The History of the Viziers".

943
The Samanid rulers of Bukhara execute an-Nasafi, the Isma'ili Da'i of Khorasan, and others. An-Nasafi had succeeded in making many converts to Isma'ilism among the Samanids of Bukhara including the ruler Nasr ibn Ahmad. The Turkish guard grew uneasy and attempted a coup which did not succeed but brought to power the son of Nasr, Nuh who proceeded to liquidate the Isma'ilis. An-Nasafi (Nakhshabi) incorporated Neoplatonic philosophy into Isma'ili cosmology against the opposition of Abu Hatim; but as these eastern Isma'ili leaders did not yet recognize the Imamate of the Fatimids, Fatimid cosmology did not incorporate these new developments until as-Sijistani recognized the Fatimid al-Mu'izz, probably after the conquest of Egypt. Persecutions of Isma'ilis in Khorasan continue.

948
The third Fatimid al-Mansur has a royal and Isma'ili city built outside Kairouan. This city is round like the original Round City of Baghdad with the Imams palace in the center.

949
Sunni-Shi'ite rivalries grow in Baghdad after the steady ascent of Twelve Imam Shi'ite influence. This first appeared in the reign of the Caliph al-Muqtadir who was supported by Shi'ite bankers.

950
Death of the philosopher al-Farabi, known as the "second teacher" after Aristotle who adapted the Organon giving Aristotelian logic an Islamicised vocabulary.

Activity of the Bogomils in Bulgaria. The Bogomils believed that the Trinity only existed for thirty-three years while Jesus was in the world and was pictured as "that of a human faced Father with the Son to his right and the Spirit to his left represented as beams emanated through his eyes".

Islam reaches Khotan in Turkestan via Kashgar. The ruler of Khotan becomes Muslim. Buddhism soon vanishes in the region.

"The Wonders of India" written by a Persian ship captain from Ramhurmuz.

951
In Iraq, the mysterious Brotherhood of Purity. (*Ikhwan as-Safa'*, the name is taken from a group of animals in the fables of *Kalila wa Dimna*, who band together to free themselves from a trap into which they have fallen). The Brotherhood of Purity, who are Isma'ilis, compile an encyclopedia of universal knowledge. This group of Isma'ilis uphold the idea of an Imam (unlike the Qarmati Isma'ilis) but do not recognize the Fatimids as their leaders).

The Qarmatis return the Black Stone to Mecca by tossing it in a sack into the Friday Mosque of Kufah, with a note "By Command we took it, and by Command we return it." According to the historian Ibn al-Athir they did *not* accept a ransom for the stone (and no-one has claimed to have paid ransom.) It is apparently at this time that the stone was broken into the seven pieces in which it is today. (Musabbihi and Abu-l-Mahasin say it was deliberately broken by the Qarmatis. It was, until then, in three pieces).

953
John of Görtz sent to Cordoba as Otto I's ambassador.

956
Death of al-Mas'udi, historian. A Shi'ite, he wrote vast encyclopedias which survive in the summary called "the Meadows of Gold". He also wrote "The Summary of Marvels", a compendium on travels, legendary history, and geography.

958
Multan in Sindh goes over to the Fatimid cause, during the reign of the Fatimid al-Mu'izz (953-975); around this time the Isma'ili *jazirah* of Northern Iran which is based in Rayy also goes over to the Fatimids.

960
Conversion of the Turkic Qarakhanids to Islam.

961
Extension of the great Mosque of Cordoba by al-Hakam II.

962
The Buyid ruler al-Mu'izz ad-Dawlah institutes the observance of the 'Id al-Ghadir as a day of celebration, and the public mourning of the death of Husayn on the tenth of Muharram, both Shi'ite holy days. (Later in Persia, on this day the Muezzins will cry out from the minarets before the call to prayer: "This day the corpse of Husayn lies naked in the desert!") The 'Id al-Ghadir, which is a celebration of the events of Ghadir Khumm which the Shi'ites believe was the designation of 'Ali as successor to Prophet Muhammad, as traditionally celebrated in Persia, has a certain "carnevalesque" character that suggests an older religion, obscured or prohibited by the new religion, manifesting itself in acts of controlled or sanctioned rebellion, similar to Mardi Gras in the Catholic world, or the "Eve of Saint John" in the Russian Orthodox. Cakes filled with honey which represent the first three Caliphs are made; these cakes are bitten into as a symbolical devouring of what are taken to be the spiritual imposters of an alien religion.

965
Death of al-Mutannabi, the poet, of the tribe of Ju'fi. He was born in the "Shi'ite" quarter of the Kinda in the city of Kufah. His early days were with the Qarmatis of the desert.

In Multan the khutba is read in the name of the Fatimid al-Mu'izz. This state lasts until 1006 when it is taken over by Mahmud of Ghaznah.

967
Death of Abu-l-Faraj, a Qurayshi descended from Marwan the Umayyad, born in Isfahan, who spent much time at the court of Saif ad-Dawla in Aleppo. He wrote the *Kitab al-Aghani* or "Book of Songs" about Arab songs, singers, and ancient customs.

969
The Fatimid general Jawhar conquers Egypt and founds Cairo, near pre-existing towns. Al-Jawzi reports that Jawhar's soldiers on expedition to Syria destroyed the "tabernacle", used in rituals by the Qarmatis. Perhaps this "tabernacle" was the "empty chair" that Mukhtar the Kaysani leader also used in ceremonies, calling it "the throne of 'Ali".

Death of the vizier Abu-l-Fadl Ibn al-'Amid who wrote his court correspondence in saj', or rhymed prose.

971
The governor of Sistan, Khalaf ibn Ahmad, puts to death the Isma'ili Da'i Abu Ya'qub as-Sijistani.

972
Founding of al-Azhar university; first a school for the preparation of Isma'ili propagandists, later one of the most renowned Muslim universities.

974
Death of al-Qadi an-Nu'man, Chief Judge of the Faṭimids and Da'i ad-Du'at. Both of his sons and grandson also become Chief Da'i.

976
The Spanish Umayyad al-Hakam II dies; he is succeeded by Hisham II but the real power behind the throne is the *hajib*, or chamberlain, known as al-Mansur Bi'Llah.

977
High point of Qarmati influence at Kufah; when the news of the death of Abu Yusuf Ya'qub, Qarmati chief, arrives in Kufah, shops are closed for three days in sign of mourning.

Ibn Hawqal expands an earlier work by al-Istakhri (written 951) on travel.

984

A Qarmati army advances near Baghdad and is appeased by concessions. But in the next year, after several victories near Kufah, they are so completely defeated that their power shows clear decline.

Death of Ibn Nubata, the court preacher of Saif ad-Dawla; he wrote his sermons in *saj'*, or rhymed prose.

985

Al-Mansur conducts campaigns in Spain and captures Coimbra in Portugal.

Ibn Khaldun gives this date as the end of Qarmati influence in Bahrayn. They will soon lose al-Qatif in Eastern Arabia.

987

Al-Mansur extends the great Mosque of Cordoba.

An-Nadim observes, writing in the *Fihrist*, that "today the Manicheans are no longer numerous in Muslim countries. In Baghdad, under Mu'izz ad-Dawlah (945-967), I used to know of three hundred; today you could not even find five in the capital. They are called *ajari*; they live in the vicinity of Samarkand, the villages of Sogdiana, and especially in Navikat (Farghana above Badakshan)."

988

Al-Maqdisi revises his accounts of customs, beliefs, practices of the peoples of foreign lands.

990

A college founded at Baghdad contains a library of 10,400 books; the great library of the Fatimid Caliph al-'Aziz contains 120,000; and the library of al-Hakim at Cordova even more.

991

Death of Muhammad ibn Babawayh. Also known by the alternate names Ibn Babuya, as-Saduq, or al-Qummi. He is one of the principal early Shi'ite theologians, the author of a large number of books of which the most famous is *Man la yahduruhu-l-faqih* ("When no theologian is present").

995

Death of Ibn 'Abbad, known as "the Sahib" who popularized the use of *saj'* for composition.

1005Death of Abu Hilal al-'Askari, author of a critical analysis of poetry and prose in terms of structure, rhetorical devices, and figures of speech.

1006

Mahmud of Ghaznah invades Multan and destroys the pro-Fatimid Isma'ili state.

1008

Death of al-Hamadhani at Herat, a Belle-Lettrist known as the *Badi' az-Zaman* ("The Wonder of the Age") for his prodigious memory and spectacular facility with poetry and composition, and creator of the genre known as the *Maqamat*, short anecdotes designed to exhibit literary ability structured around a picaresque and eloquent figure named Abu-l-Fatah and his narrator-companion, Ibn Hasham.

The date of the oldest complete manuscript of the Hebrew Bible, the Leningrad Codex. Partial texts, the codex of the Prophets in Cairo, date from 897.

400 H. = 25 August 1009

1009

Destruction of the Church of the Holy Sepulchre in Jerusalem by the Fatimid ruler al-Hakim, one of the events leading to the Crusades.

1010

The King of Gao (in Africa) converts to Islam.

Firdawsi writes the *Shah-Nameh.*

Mahmud of Ghaznah massacres Isma'ilis in Multan.

1011

The Sharifs, or descendents of the Prophet, in Baghdad, along with Jurists, issue a manifesto which refutes the Fatimid claims to be descended from the Prophet. Instead, they assert the Fatimids are descendants of Daysan, or Bardesanes, a Gnostic philosopher of Edessa, who along with Marcion was considered by the Muslims to be the direct forerunner of Mani.

1013

The Fatimid al-Hakim makes a cousin of his, 'Abd ar-Rahim, heir to the Caliphate. His name is stamped on coins. This would have been a considerable innovation, but when a son, the future az-Zahir is born to al-Hakim the designation is rescinded. When al-Hafiz, a cousin of al-Amir became Caliph, this precedent was cited, but with the explanation that since the Isma'ili Imam knows the past and the future, al-Hakim knew that the cousin would not take the throne, made the designation to allay anxieties, but also to create a precedent for the day when a cousin was obliged or destined to succeed in what was until then considered an inviolable father to son transmission. In modern times the successor to the Aga Khan III was his grandson, not the son, Aly Khan, who was passed over.

1015

The Sharif ar-Radi dies, the most noted poet of his day, author of the *Nahj al-Balaghah*, or discourses attributed to 'Ali.

1020
Death of Firdawsi, author of the *Shah-Nameh*.

1021
Death of al-Hakim, Fatimid ruler. As the Isma'ili Imam, he is considered in secret to be God himself; this secret was proclaimed publicly among the Isma'ilis of Syria and Palestine, some of whom become the Druze sect who hold al-Hakim, to be God, now alive in the invisible.

1030
Death of Mahmud of Ghaznah in Afghanistan. Mahmud did not formally take the title of Sultan but allowed himself to be called that (i.e. a ruler independent of the Caliph).

1031
Decline of the Caliphate of Cordova. Muslim Spain breaks up into the "Reyes de las Taifas", or petty kingdoms.

The Seljuqs establish themselves in Merv. Tughril Beg mints coins with the title Sultan, Shahinshah and a symbol, an early *tughra*, perhaps symbolizing a bow and arrow.

1035
The Cave of the Thousand Buddhas is sealed in Dun Huang, in Chinese Turkestan. The cave was discovered in the course of repair work by a Taoist priest at the beginning of the 20th century and then excavated by Sir Aurel Stein and later Paul Pelliot and then by the Chinese. Along with numerous Buddhist texts, the cave contained three texts about Manicheism in Chinese.

1036
Death of al-'Utbi, court official of the Buyids, who wrote a rhymed-prose monograph "The Book of Yamin ad-Dawla" which praised his patrons. By calling the ruler "the shadow of God on earth" he created a widely used precedent for justifying extreme submission to the temporal power.

1037
Death of the philosopher and physician Ibn Sina (Avicenna).

Death of Abu Mansur al-Baghdadi, author of the major description of the sects of Islam, *Farq bayn al-Firaq*.

1038
Death of ath-Tha'alibi, philologist and writer, author of a history of the early kings of Persia.

1048
Death of al-Biruni, great scientist, philosopher, scholar, translator of works into and out of Sanskrit, author of a unique Muslim study of the civilisation of India, the *Kitab al-Hind*.

Birth of mathematician, poet, philosopher 'Umar al-Khayyam.

1050
Nasir-i Khusraw visits the remaining Qarmatis in al-Hasa, in eastern Arabia. The doctrine remained influential there into the time of Ibn Batutah (d. 1378). Today the region is Twelve Imam Shi'ite.

The appearance of the Qabbalah in southern France.

In the Rhineland, Ashkenaz Hasside introduce the 4th or 5th century mystical book of the *Sefer Yetsirah* into European Judaism with citations of sources from an "Aaron of Baghdad" through Samuel Kalonymides. One of their ideas is that of a *kavod* or "field" of manifestation to explain how God could be seen by the Prophets. The *kavod* concept may be derived from the Koran where it appears in a different but related sense: "We verily created man in an atmosphere (*kabad*)" (90:4).

The Arab tribe of the Bani Hilal arrive in North Africa.

Indicative of the power struggle between Isma'ilis and Sunnis in Egypt, a Sunni, Hasan ibn 'Ali al-Yazuri becomes chief Qadi and then da'i ad-du'at in Egypt.

1051
In Sindh the Isma'ili Sumras revolt against the Ghaznavids and establish a dynasty ruling from Thatta. They persist for three centuries.

1054
The Schism between the Western Christian Church led by Rome and the Eastern Christian Church led by Constantinople, and later Moscow, becomes permanent.

Patarenes (Cathari) spread in North Italy and southern France in the wake of the schism of the Christian church.

THE SELJUQ SUZERAINTY

1055
The Seljuq Toghrul Beg enters Baghdad, and rules in the name of the 'Abbasids, taking the title of Sultan. The Seljuqs were a family of Oguz (Ghuzz) Turks claiming descent from a certain Seljuq ibn Dukak who entered Islamic lands in the late 10th century and set-

tled in the neighborhood of Bukhara where they began becoming Muslims.

1058

Death of the poet Abu-l-'Ala al-Ma'arri. His close friend and possibly teacher was Mu'ayyad of Shiraz, an Isma'ili *Da'i*, himself the author of *Majalis* which are close in spirit to al-Ma'arri's *Luzumiyat* and the *Risalat al-Ghufran*. The two correspond about "vegetarianism"; al-Ma'arri was a vegetarian, like traditional Manicheans. al-Ma'arri wrote: "They all err – Muslim, Christian, Jew, and Magian; two make Humanity's universal sect: one man intelligent without religion, and one religious without intellect..."

While the Seljuq Tughril goes to Western Persia to put down a revolt, a Turkish rebel named Arslan al-Basasiri briefly seizes Baghdad and the Friday prayers are said in the name of the Fatimid Caliph. The Fatimids are also acknowledged a year earlier in Mawsil, and also in Kufah and Wasit. The Fatimid chief Da'i Mu'ayyad al-Shirazi is instrumental in bringing this about by supplying al-Basasiri with money and arms from Cairo. The Fatimids will make the claim that in this year the insignia of the Caliphate were taken from Baghdad to Cairo. The 'Abbasid Caliph al-Qa'im, left under the protection of the 'Uqaylid Quraysh, is freed in 1059 by Tughril, and al-Basasiri, abandoned by the Fatimids, is killed near Kufah.

Death of the Jurist and political scientist al-Mawardi, author of the *al-Ahkam as-Sultaniyyah* ("The Ordinances of Government").

1062

Almoravids under Yusuf ibn Tashfin conquer Morocco.

1063

Founding of Marrakesh by the Almoravids.

1064

Death of the philosopher, theologian, and poet, Ibn Hazm. He wrote an anatomy of chivalrous love, "The Necklace of the Dove", many attacks on theological opponents, and a work on comparative religion "The Book of Religious and Philosophical Sects".

1065

The Vizier Nizam al-Mulk founds the Nizamiyyah madrasah, under Shafi' tenets, in Baghdad. Although the Shafi's had been supporters of the Seljuqs (while the Hanbalis of Nishapur had supported the Ghaznavids), the Seljuqs themselves, when al-Kunduri, originally a Shafi' protégé, was vizier of Tughril Beg and Alp Arslan, had persecuted the Shafi'i leaders. With Nizam al-Mulk as Vizier of the Seljuqs this policy was reversed; the Shafi's came to the fore and Ash'arism became the ideological line of defense against the Fatimid propaganda. With the creation of schools by Nizam al-Mulk followed the institutionalisation of the *'ulama'* or religious scholar class.

1069

The Sharif of Mecca accedes to Alp Arslan and the khutbah is no longer read in the name of the Fatimids (except for a brief return to Fatimid allegiance in 1074-1081) but instead in the name of the 'Abbasids.

1071

The Byzantines of the Emperor Romanus IV Diogenes defeated at the Battle of Manzikert on 26 August by the Seljuq Alp Arslan. The Emperor is captured. The defeat is a contributory cause of the Crusades. Most of Asia Minor conquered by Seljuqs.

Death of Ibn Zaydun of Cordova, ranked as the greatest of the Spanish poets. He is noted for his romantic life and his attachment to an Umayyad princess, Wallada.

Death of al-Qushayri, author of the *Risalah* on Sufism, and another more pantheistic and antinomian work.

Death of al-Mu'ayyad fi'd-Din ash-Shirazi, Isma'ili propagandist in Syria who eventually became the Chief Da'i.

1072

Death of Alp Arslan on campaign against the Qarakhanids in Transoxiana; Malik Shah becomes Sultan. A poet composed an epitaph: "Thou has seen Alp Arslan's head in pride exalted to the sky; Come to Merv, and see how lowly in the dust that head doth lie."

1074

A dyke below the Qurij Canal bursts in Baghdad inundating the whole of the eastern city.

1075

Death of the great Spanish historian, Ibn Hayyan.

1077

Death of the Sufi authority al-Hujwiri in Lahore.

1078

'Abd al-Qahir al-Jurjani, dies, the most perspicacious of the literary critics. He applied psychological and logical analysis which examined the ideas expressed as well as their form.

1081

Harran is occupied by the Beduin Sharaf ad-Dawlah, an ally of the Seljuq Turks. According to Ibn Shaddad,

Sharaf's governor, Yahya ibn ash-Shatir destroys Harran's temple to the Moon God Sin which the Muslim conqueror of the city Ibn Ghanam in the 7th century allowed the "Sabians" to build when he turned their original temple into a Friday Mosque.

1083
Alfonso VI of Castile defeats al-Mu'tamid of Seville.

1085
Toledo is taken from the Muslims by Alfonso VI.

1086
Yusuf ibn Tashfin comes to the help of Muslim princes in Spain and defeats the Christians at Battle of az-Zallaqah.

1088
The Grand mosque of Isfahan is built by the Seljuqs.

1090
Hasan-i as-Sabbah seizes Alamut fortress in Northern Persia; beginning of the Nizari branch of Isma'ilis who will be called the "Assassin" sect by the Crusaders.

Third Almoravid landing in Spain; King of Granada deposed by Yusuf ibn Tashfin.

A Chinese text mentions the Arab use of compasses. (Astrolabes made in Harran have already been in use.)

1092
Nizam al-Mulk murdered by Nizari "Assassins".

1094
Capture of Valencia by al-Cid.

1095
Pope Urban calls for the first Crusade.

Armed conflict in Nayshabur between the heretical Karramiyyah and Sunni Hanafis and Shafi'is.

1097
Konya becomes capital of the Seljuqs of Rum.

1098
The Crusaders capture Antioch.

The former king of Seville, al-Mu'tamid, for whom "the most trivial and transient events of life clothed themselves in a poetic form", dies south of Marrakesh in the exile imposed upon him by the Almoravid conquest of Spain.

1099
15 July; Jerusalem captured by Crusaders.

1100
Baldwin becomes King of the Latin Kingdom of Jerusalem.

500 H. = 2 September 1106

1106
Yusuf ibn Tashfin, Almoravid ruler, dies.

1111
Death of al-Ghazali, theologian, jurist, mystic considered by many to be the *Mujaddid*, or "Renewer" of the age.

Almoravids capture Santarem, Badajoz, Porto, Evora, and Lisbon.

1118
The Knights Templar, so called because their headquarters is on the Dome of the Rock, are founded in Jerusalem.

1118-35
Reign of 'Abbasid Caliph al-Mustarshid, the first since the Buyids to again have a personal army, who tries unsuccessfully to assert himself as a temporal ruler by attempting to take control of Hilla militarily. (He is assassinated by Nizaris).

1120
Antimanichean edict in China. Outbreak of the Fang La rebellion in Chekiang which is joined by Manicheans from the prefecture of T'ai. Consequently persecution against all religious societies is intensified and Manicheans are singled out. (Sung Dynasty 1126-1279). Manichean temples in applying for licences in China described themselves as Taoist temples.

1121
Beginning of Almohad movement in Morocco. Its founder Ibn Tumart was called al-Mahdi. Ibn Khaldun says of him: "al-Mahdi's power did not depend exclusively on his Fatimid descent... [which]... had become obscured and knowledge of it disappeared from among the people, although it remained alive in him and his family through tradition".

1122
Death of al-Hariri of Basrah, author of the very popular collection of stories called the *Maqamat*, noted for their literary and linguistic qualities. The dramatic anecdotes of Hariri's *Maqamat* center around an eloquent character named Abu Zayd of Seruj and his narrator companion Harith ibn Hammam. The choice of names,

which is as nondescript as possible, is understandable from this Hadith of the Prophet: "Every one of you (Arabs) is a *Harith* [one who acquires gain by trade] and everyone of you a *Hammam* [one who is subject to cares and anxieties].

1124
Death of Hasan-i as-Sabbah, the chief of the Assassins. Hasan having killed two of his sons, he is succeeded by his lieutenant Kiya Buzurg-Ummid.

1126
Birth of the philosopher and physician Ibn Rushd (Averroes).

1130
Death of Ibn Tumart, the founder of the Almohad movement. Al-Amir bi-Ahkam Allah, tenth Fatimid Caliph and twentieth imam of the Musta'lian Isma'ilis is assassinated by a group of Nizari *fida'is*. Fatimid rule passes into steep decline. A few months before his death, al-Amir allegedly had a son, Tayyib, born Rabi' II, AD 524, who is the subject of an epistle sent to the Sulayhid Queen of Yemen, al-Malika as-Sayyida. The reports of Tayyib are contradictory; on the one hand, Tayyib's existence was concealed from members of the court, and on the other he was immediately designated heir to al-Amir. In any case, Tayyib disappears. From this stems a group of Musta'li Isma'ilis who believe that Tayyib disappeared into a *ghaybah* or supernatural concealment from the world, from which he will return. It is during this period that the Nizaris consolidate their power in Persia and Syria. Although al-Amir's cousin immediately takes the throne as Regent, after a few days he is displaced for a year and ten days by Abu 'Ali Kutayfat, a son of the late vizier and power broker al-Afdal ibn Badr al-Jamali. Kutayfat had not been killed in the earlier power struggles because he was considered sickly. When he took over the government first as Vizier, raised up by the army two weeks after al-Amir's death, he then had al-Hafiz (at that time a Regent under the name 'Abd al-Majiīd) deposed. Kutayfat instituted Twelve Imam Shi'ite doctrine and political practice, having the khutbah read in the name of the Twelver Hidden Imam. He also issued coins in the name of the Twelfth Imam, and made himself his representative, or na'ib. In December 1131 Kutayfat was overthrown and killed, and 'Abd al-Majīd, previously a Regent, became a Fatimid Caliph-Imam named al-Hafiz li-Din Allah.

1131
Death of the poet, philosopher, mathematician 'Umar al-Khayyam.

1132
An inscription placed in the Ibn Tulun mosque in this year calls the Fatimids a "prophetic state" (*ad-dawlah an-nabawiyyah*) and the rule of *al-Hafiz al-khilafa al-'alawiyyah al-Hafiziyyah.*

1135
Birth of Maimonides in Cordoba.

1136
Completion of a shrine in Mazar-i Sharif, near Balkh. A report reaches Balkh "from India" that the tomb of Hazrat 'Ali, the fourth Caliph, is located nearby. ('Ali was killed in Kufah in faraway Iraq; his burial place was unknown; tradition has placed his grave, *discovered by a vision* of Harun ar-Rashid while hunting, in Najaf, in Iraq near to Kufah, today the major site of Shi'ite pilgrimage.)

The report of 'Ali's miraculous burial place in Afghanistan, thousands of miles from Iraq, is at first denied by a Mulla of the place who then has a dream (that is, the sense of the idea becomes clear to him) in which 'Ali appears and confirms that he is indeed buried there. The shrine is built by Sultan Sanjar and later destroyed by Jenghiz Khan. In 1481 it is rebuilt by Husayn Baikara and becomes an important pilgrimage center replacing Balkh altogether as a city.

It is not 'Ali who is buried there. It may be the tomb of Mar Shad Ormizd, a leader in the 5th or 6th century of the Manichean Dinawariyyah sect, or even Mar Ammo, who brought Manicheism to Khorasan. By pretending that the tomb was that of 'Ali, the Manicheans thus preserved the tomb of one of their own which otherwise would have been despised by the orthodox Muslims. Its destruction by Jenghiz Khan was characteristic; the Mongols attacked a number of Manichean and otherwise Dualist sites, including Alamut and Harran, while sparing Sunni and Shi'ite ones because Shi'ite advisors pointed the Mongols towards their particular rivals in order to eliminate them. After the Mongols, Manicheans and Isma'ilis were so submerged that they only began to reappear in the Islamic consciousness in the 19th century and only in the shape of Isma'ilis.

Third siege of Baghdad (following the War of the Brothers, and the siege of the Turkish Guard in 866). In the reign of ar-Rashid, Baghdad was besieged by an army under the command of Sultan Mas'ud the Seljuq. After a blockade of fifty days, and insurrection in Baghdad, the Caliph flies to Mosul where he abdicates and his uncle Muhammad Muqtafi is set up in his place. Sultan Mas'ud retires eastward.

1137
Death of Ramanuja (b. 1017), exponent of qualified non-dualism, or *vashishta-vedanta.*

1138
Death of Kiya Buzurg-Ummid, head of the Assassins at Alamut. He is succeeded by his son Muhammad ibn Buzurg Ummid.

1143

Death of Zamakhshari of Khwarizm; author of a handbook of grammar, *al-Mufassal*, and a noted commentary on the Koran which was expunged of its Mu'tazilite traits and made more acceptable in its edition by al-Baidawi (d. 1286).

The first translation of the Koran into a Western language, Latin, is made by Robertus Retenensis and Hermannus Dalmata, under the patronage of Peter the Venerable, Abbot of Cluny. Peter the Venerable had visited Spain in 1141-1143 and had been a friend of Bernard of Clairvaux, who called for the Crusades. The translation, according to Sale, is full of errors and omissions. It was published in Basel in 1543 and later again in Zuerich in 1560.

1145

End of Almoravid rule in Spain.

1146

The Almohads capture Fez.

1147

Second Crusade led by Conrad II and Louis VII.

1149

Another Fatimid becomes Caliph in Egypt, az-Zafir; followed by al-Fa'iz, and al-'Adid; Fatimid rule definitively ends in 1171 when Saladin has the Khutbah read in the name of the reigning 'Abbasid, al-Mustadi'.

1153

Al-Idrissi makes a famous world map for Roger of Sicily.

Death of Shahrastani, Persian scholar of religions and author of the *Kitab al-Millal wa Nihal*, "Book of Religious and Philosophical Sects".

1154

The Turkic Ghuzz, who paid a yearly tribute of 24,000 sheep to Sultan Sanjar rebel against an increase in tribute. Sanjar takes the field against them, and despite their attempt to make recompense and amends, attacks them. Desperate, they defeat Sanjar, take him captive, and proceed to pillage Merv and Nishapur and throughout Khorasan except for Herat which holds out against them. The tribulations are described in Anwari's (d. 587/1191?) poem "Tears of Khorasan". The head of Husayn which had been preserved in Damascus for a time and then in Ascalon, is moved to Cairo by the Fatimid Vizier Tala'i' ibn Ruzzik, out of the way of the advancing Franks.

1157

Death of the Seljuq Sultan Sanjar and decline of Seljuq rule.

The Almohads capture Granada and Almeria.

The Archbishop of Rheims discovers a hotbed of Catharism when a village girl repulses the advances of a cleric.

Fourth siege of Baghdad (after 1136, 865, and 810) by Sultan Muhammad, the nephew of Seljuq Sultan Mas'ud who besieged Baghdad in 136. After two months the siege is repulsed by Caliph Muqtafi.

1159

Death of Ibn Quzman, Spanish Muslim troubadour, who wrote *zajals* ("melody") from court to court.

1162

Accession of Hasan II called *'Ala Dhikri-hi as-Salam* (literally "blessings upon his memory") in Alamut. Hasan II is the son of Muhammad son of Buzurg-Ummid, who was Sabbah's lieutenant and successor. Since Hasan-i Sabbah promulgated the doctrine that he who proclaims the function of Imam is the Imam, and Muhammad Buzurg-Ummid was already being treated as Imam in substance, the legend arises that Hasan II is not the son of Muhammad but a substitute, in reality a descendant of Nizar, son of the Fatimid Caliph al-Mustansir who died in 1094. At his death, in a coup, Nizar was imprisoned and died in 1095 while his brother al-Musta'li was placed on the throne. Through the stratagem of a pregnant concubine escaping from the political events in Cairo and bringing a descendant to Alamut, the progeny reappears in the form of Hasan-i Sabbah's lieutenant's grandson, substituted at birth.

Meanwhile, Rashid ad-Din Sinan, a school master from Basrah, leaves Alamut, where he was being indoctrinated, to go to Syria where he becomes the most celebrated of Syrian Nizari leaders.

1163

The term Cathare (the "pure ones" from the Greek) is used for the first time in a trial of "Christian" Manicheans in Cologne. The trial is followed by an autodafé.

1164

Hasan II, the Assassin chief in Alamut, assumes the function of Isma'ili Imam and declares the advent of the *Qiyamah* ("the Resurrection"), that is, the dropping of the protective pretense of being Muslims (an end to the preceding period of the so-called "veiling" called the *satr*) and with it the abandonment of the hated "cover" of the Islamic law (*shari'ah*). The "resurrection" is the beginning of open reversion to Manicheism, up until then their secret and disguised religion. This change in policy proves to be temporary because it is unsustainable for political reasons, those which caused the dissimulation in the first place, the overwhelming presence of a hostile orthodox majority surrounding the "islands" of Manicheism isolated by the "flood" of ignorance represented by Islam. The change in policy was marked by a cryptic ceremony held in the presence of representatives from various regions and was called the "Feast of the Resurrection" and was treated as a cosmic event taking place in the open courtyard of the fortress of Alamut. This episode has naturally caught the imagination of many modern proponents of mysticism and given birth to much deep and erroneous speculation.

The "Feast of the Resurrection" (*'Id al-Qiyamah*) took place on the 17th of Ramadan in the Hijri year 559 (8 August 1164) on one of the days listed as the anniversary of the death of 'Ali (the stand-in for Mani). A pulpit, *minbar*, was erected in the courtyard of Alamut facing, in Juwayni's account, a direction opposite that of the Muslim *minbar*, four banners in the colours white, red, yellow, and green were fixed to the pillars of the pulpit, and Nizari representatives from various regions were placed around the pulpit. The leader, Hasan, wearing a white gown and a white turban, came down from the castle and ascended the pulpit, greeted the assembly, sat down, and after some time got up, holding his sword, delivered in a loud voice the message which was being transmitted to him in that moment from the Imam in the invisible, rather the way that Mani was addressed and responded from the invisible in the ceremony of the Bema. The lifting of the Shari'ah was declared, the command to obedience was made, and an address in Arabic which was translated into Persian. Juwayni notes that the language of this address was "for the most part, broken, corrupt and full of gross mistakes and confused expressions" – perhaps not Arabic at all but an attempt at Aramaic, the classical language of Manicheism. And then the feasting began (during the day, which is not done during Ramadan; it should be noted that for the Isma'ilis the common interpretation of fasting Ramadan is "keeping the secret"; thus breaking the fast is making the secret known. The proclamation of the Resurrection is made elsewhere and also in Syria, where it does not entail any significant consequence.

After 1210 the Resurrection was revoked by Jalal ad-Din, called the "New Muslim" and a rapprochement began with the Sunnis whereby the Isma'ili leader was accepted as a prince among princes by the 'Abbasids.

1166

Death of 'Abd al-Qadir al-Jilani, famous Sufi.

Hasan II of Alamut is stabbed to death the castle of Lamasar by a brother-in-law who belonged to a local Buwayhid family who opposed his Resurrectionist policies. Hasan is succeeded by his 19 year old son, Nur ad-Din Muhammad II, who continues the Resurrection doctrine.

1167

The great Almohad mosque of Seville is built, which is today its cathedral.

1171

Salah ad-Din (Saladin) takes control of Egypt; the beginning of the Ayyubid dynasty and the end of the Fatimids.

Death of the Spanish philosopher Ibn Tufayl.

1175

Formalisation of Gnostic Buddhism in Japan. The first Amidist "Pure Land Sect" (*Jodo*) founded in Japan by Genku (Honen Shonin (1133-1212). See 575, 1224 and 1253.

1176

Death of Ibn 'Asakir, the historian of Damascus.

1180-1225

Reign of Caliph an-Nasir, the last significant 'Abbasid. He (and his two successors) has an army and attempting to build a power structure around himself he becomes the head of various "chivalric orders", the *futuwwah* which now rise to the fore having existed as such since the 10th century.

1187

4 July; Salah ad-Din (Saladin) defeats Crusaders at the Battle of the Horn of Hattin and later captures Jerusalem.

1188

Death of Usama ibn Munqidh, who wrote an autobiography of an Arab knight in the Crusades.

1189

Third Crusade led by Frederick Barbarossa, and Richard the Lion Heart.

1190

In a chronicle of the Crusaders, the name "Turkey" appears for the first time applied to new Turkish lands in Asia Minor.

1191

Death of Shihab ad-Din Suhrawardi (al-Maqtul), founder of the *Ishraqi* or "illuminationist" school, executed for heresy in Aleppo.

1192
In Tyre, in April, the Syrian Isma'ilis assassinate the Marquis Conrad of Montferrat, the newly elected Frankish King of Jerusalem. The act is carried out by two Fida'is disguised as Christian monks.

Death of Rashid ad-Din Sinan, the *Shaykh al-Jabal*, called the "Old man of the Mountain" by the Crusaders, the leader of the Assassins in Syria, in his castle of Kahf. The Assassins, or Nizari Isma'ilis descended from the Fatimids, had become established in what had been Qarmati territory by "converting" the Seljuq prince of Aleppo, Ridwan ibn Tutush (d. 1113).

Rashid ad-Din Sinan is succeeded by a Persian Da'i called Abu Mansur ibn Muhammad, or, simply, Nasr al-'Ajami. After Jalal ad-Din's rapprochement with the Sunnis in Alamut following the year 1211, the Syrian Nizari relations also improved with the Ayyubids. They continued to assassinate Crusaders.

1193
Death of Salah ad-Din (Saladin) and the division of the Ayyubid Empire.

Ghurids take Delhi and put an end to the Kanauj empire.

1195
The Almohad al-Mansur defeats the Castillian Spanish at the Battle of Alarcos.

1197
Death of Mawlana Burhan ad-Din Marghinani of Transoxiana, authour of "The Guidance" (*al-Hidaya*), a compendium of earlier works on Hanafi law. This compendium will enjoy wide usage in India.

1198
Death of Ibn Rushd (Avveroes), the last great Muslim Aristotelian philosopher. Averroes wrote a refutation of al-Ghazali's attack on the philosophers. With Averroes the development and even study of philosophy dies away in Islam to be replaced by a great development of Sufism among all classes of society; but in the Christian West, Muslim philosophy, which is an adaptation of Hellenistic philosophy in a Monotheist structure, is taken over part and parcel and becomes the basis for Western intellectual renewal.

1200
Death of the Persian poet 'Attar.

Beginning of the Islamisation of Indonesia.

Death of Ibn al-Jawzi, Hanbali preacher who introduced a new type of homiletic *adab*, and satirized the Sufis in "Deceits of the Devil" (*Talbis Iblis*).

Death of al-Qadi al-Fadil, Saladin's chief secretary, a noted literary stylist.

1201
Death of 'Imad ad-Din, "the secretary from Isfahan" to Saladin who wrote on the Saljuqs and on Saladin.

600 H. 10 September 1203

1203
Death of the Persian poet Nizami.

1204
Fourth Crusade; the Doge Dandolo of Venice leads the Crusaders to sack Constantinople. The Mandelion disappears from Constantinople.

Death of Maimonides.

1206
Temujin, having taken the name Jenghiz Khan ("oceanic", or universal ruler), becomes the leader of the united Mongol tribes at a *quriltai* (assembly) in Qaraqorum.

Beginning of the Delhi Sultanate.

1209
The Albigensian crusade launched against the Cathares in France.

1210
Death of Nur ad-Din Muhammad II at Alamut, possibly of poison, and accession of Jalal ad-Din Hasan III. The new Master of Alamut and Chief of the Assassins, called the *Naw Musulman* ("The New Muslim") draws forward again the curtain which was drawn back by Hasan in 1164, resumes observance of the Islamic religious law, and professes to be a Sunni Muslim. Juwayni describes Jalal ad-Din as hostile to his father. End of the "Resurrection" (*al-Qiyamah*) and the resumption of the "Veiling" (*Satr*). Rapprochement with Sunnis, first recognizing the suzerainty of the Khwarazm-Shah, after which Jalal ad-Din is accepted as a prince by the 'Abbasids and actually becomes an ally of the Caliph an-Nasir, and, in accordance with the Caliph's policy, turns against the Khwarazm-Shah. Later, at the request of the Caliph, Jalal ad-Din has one of the Caliph's rebels, Ighlamish assassinated in 1217. One of the first to recognize the threat of the Mongols, Jalal ad-Din sent secret couriers to Jenghiz Khan pledging his submission to them after the Mongols crossed the Oxus. At the time of Jalal ad-Din, Syrian-Isma'ili relations also improved with the Ayyubids.

1211
In the largest single autodafé in France, 400 Cathares

("Christian" Manicheans) are burned at the stake in Lavaur (Tarn).

1212
The Almohads are defeated in Spain at the Battle of las Navas de Tolosa.

1213
Syrian Isma'ilis assassinate Raymond, son of Bohemond IV of Antioch in the Cathedral of Tartus.

1217
Death of Ibn Jubair of Valencia, who, during a pilgrimage made between 1183 and 1185, kept a journal which was published after his return to Granada.

Death of Yehuda of Worms son of Samuel ben Kalonymus of Speyer, of a family that came to the Rhineland from Italy and brought with them a mystical trend in Judaism attributed to an "Aaron of Baghdad".

1218
Fifth Crusade.

At the Otrar river, a Khwarazmian governour massacres one hundred Mongol emissaries as spies. Beginning of Mongol attacks against Muslim countries.

1220
Khwarazm-Shahis defeated by Mongols under Jenghiz Khan.

Death of Najm ad-Din Kobra, Persian theosopher of Khwarizm. His school of thought, strongly influenced by Manichean ideas (*see Man of Light* by Corbin), becomes the *Kubrawiyyah* or, in India, the "Firdawsi silsilah" or mystical line which competes in the figure of Najm ad-Din Sughra, the *Marde Buzurg Sahib-i Wilayat* ("Sacred Man, Lord of Sanctity") with the Chishtis at the time of the Delhi Sultanate.

1221
Jalal ad-Din Hasan III dies in Alamut of dysentery. His sister and Sunni wives are accused of poisoning him and disposed of. He is succeeded by his son 'Ala ad-Din Muhammad III, aged 9, who slowly drops the trappings of Islam and resumes the policy of the Resurrection (see 1164). Juwayni says that 'Ala ad-Din received no education, since being the Imam, it was thought he was not in need of any and this caused the falling away from the pretense of Islam. A few years later, this lack of education joined with a malady turned "the witless 'Ala ad-Din into a madman fit only to be kept in bonds and chains". (*See 1255*).

1224
The "True Pure Land" sect founded in Japan by Shinran Shonen, a disciple of Honen. The Amidist sect (Amitabha or Amida Buddha, of presumed Iranian origin) introduces marriage of the priests, emphasis on *nembutsu* (invocation of the Name of the now deified Buddha), and part of the *samsara* (from which the orthodox Buddhist seeks to escape into Nirvana) is sanitized as a paradise (the "pure land") for devotees of the sect. This precedes the innovation of Nichiren (see 1253) and will become the most widespread of all Japanese sects, with Zen close behind.

1226
Yaqut writes his *Great Geographical Dictionary* which LeStrange calls the "greatest storehouse of geographical facts compiled by any one man during the Middle Ages".

1227
Death of Jenghiz Khan. Division of the empire among his sons and grandson.

1227
Frederick II of Germany, who is also the King of Sicily and titular King of Jerusalem, goes on Crusade to the Holy Land. His envoys bring gifts of 80,000 dinars to Majd ad-Din, the Syrian Isma'ili Chief. The Hospitallers are displeased and make the Isma'ilis their tributaries in turn, as do the Templars.

1229
Death of Yaqut, by birth an Anatolian Greek. Enslaved as a youth he made a number of journeys as a traveling clerk. He established himself in Merv but fled the advancing Mongols to Aleppo. He wrote the *Geographical Dictionary*, and *Dictionary of Men of Letters*. (See 1226.)

1230
End of Almohad rule in Spain. Rise of the Merinids in Morocco, Zijanids in Tlemcen, Hafsids of Tunis, Beni Hud in Spain.

1231
Death of 'Abd Latif of Baghdad, a physician and authour who wrote the *Description of Egypt*.

1234
Death of Ibn Athir (also given as 1223), authour of the "History of the Atabegs of Mosul" (1211) and *al-Kamil* ("The Complete"), a universal history of Islam, and biographical work, "Lions of the Thicket", describing 7,500 companions of the Prophet.

Death of Baha' ad-Din of Mosul, a military Judge who wrote a biography of Saladin.

1235

Death in Egypt of the Sufi poet Sharaf ad-Din Abu-l-Qasim 'Umar ibn 'Ali Ibn al-Farid, authour of the *Khamriyyah*, or "Wine-ode".

Death of Qutb ad-Din Bakhtiari, Indian Sufi, who dies, it is reported, after a four day ecstasy upon hearing the couplet: "For those slain by the dagger of belief, there is new life, every time, from the unseen." This is comparable to the Koran 2:154 and 3:169 that "those who are killed in the way of Allah are not dead but are alive in the unseen where they have a sustenance from their Lord" which itself may very well have its origin in the Manichean doctrine that those who die as martyrs are really alive, as Mani is himself is alive, joining in the nourishment of the Bema feast. This also relates to the words attributed to al-Hallaj on his way to the gibbet that "this is the end of drink with the seven headed dragon in July (Tammuz)". Tammuz is Adonis, the god who dies and returns to life.

1236

Death of Mu'in ad-Din Muhammad Chishti (which is "Sijzi", i.e. from Sijistan, b. 1142). Chishti dies in Ajmeer in India.

Pope Gregory IX (1227-1241) writes a letter to his representatives in the Holy Land condemning the *close relations* between the Isma'ilis and the Hospitallers and the Templars.

1240

Death of Ibn 'Arabi in Damascus, proponent of the Sufi school of *Wahdat al-Wujud*, the "Unity of Being", a form of Monism.

1243

Near Köse Dag in Eastern Turkey, a Mongol detachment overwhelms the army of the Sultan of Rum.

1244

After a year-long siege, the principle castle of the Cathares (Manicheans) of southern France, Montsegur is captured, and its defenders, the "perfected ones", are burnt at the stake.

1248

Death of al-Qifti, who wrote biographical dictionaries of men of science.

1249

Seventh Crusade. Saint Louis at Damietta.

1250

Mamluk dynasty arises in Egypt.

Saint Louis, the French King visits Acre. The Isma'ilis negotiate with him. Reginald de Vichier, Grand Master of the Hospitallers, and William de Chateauneuf, Grand Master of the Templars intervene to forestall relations between their tributaries, the Isma'ilis, and the French King. But an Arabic speaking monk, Yves le Breton, meets the current "Old Man of the Mountain", as the Franks call the Shaykh al-Jabal, the Nizari leader, in Masyaf or one of the other Nizari strongholds for an exchange of theological views.

1253

Establishment of radical dualism in Japanese Buddhism. Nichiren (1222-1282) sect is founded in Japan. Worshiping the Lotus (Hokke) Sutra, with a doctrine of the "unity of person and law", following in the steps of the "pure land", or a "relative" re-divinisation of creation, it is an "esoteric" absolutisation, or divinisation, of the individual. After World War II, as Sokka Gokkai, the sect spreads to America and Europe.

1254

Isma'ili Assassins are dispatched to Mongolia to kill Möngke, unsuccessfully, in reprisal for his anti-Nizari operations.

1255

The Isma'ili leader of Alamut, 'Ala ad-Din Muhammad III, "who had always been fond of sheepherding, was found murdered in a hut, adjoining his sheepfold, in Shirkuh near Alamut". (*See 1221*). He is succeeded by his son Rukn ad-Din Khurshah who is 15 years old. Nizaris are now instructed to adhere to Islamic law; that is, the "Resurrection" is again replaced by the "Veil", or *Satr* as the Mongols close in.

1256

Hülagu Khan, with Nestorian and Shi'ite advisors in his entourage, conquers the Assassin fortress of Maymundiz with mangonels and Rukn ad-Din Khurshah, upon the advice of Nasir ad-Din Tusi, surrenders himself on November 19. In December Alamut is taken and al-Juwayni, secretary to Hülagu selects books from its library for himself; Lamasar holds out for another year. Girdkuh holds out for 13 more years. The last Grand Master Rukn ad-Din is sent to Qaraqorum amusing himself with camel fights on the way. There Möngke refuses to see him and he is put to death in 1257. As Juwayni says: "and of him and his stock no trace was left, and he and his kindred became but a tale on men's lips and a tradition in the world". Beginning of the Mongol dynasty in Persia, the Il-Khanids.

THE FALL of BAGHDAD to the MONGOLS

1258

After a fifty day siege which begins in January, with

part of the Mongol army crossing the Tigris at Takrit in order to attack Baghdad from the West, Hülagu Khan sacks Baghdad for forty days; his attack is aided by Shi'ites within the city; many inhabitants are butchered; a conflagration destroys the Mosque of the Caliph, the Shrine of Musa al-Kazim and the tombs of the Caliphs at Rusafah; end of the 'Abbasids in Baghdad, but figurehead 'Abbasids will continue in Cairo under the Mamluks. The Mongol invasions bring to an end the grand age of Islamic development and mark its completion; they also purify Islam of the active influence of the most radical heretical sects, originating in pre-Islamic religions, which played a catalytic role in that development. Some of these sects such as the Karramiyyah are exterminated, while others are reduced to a latent state. Twelve Imam Shi'ites, on the other hand, increase their influence under the Mongols.

Death of Baha' ad-Din Zuhair 'of Egypt' a court poet.

1260

March: Ket-Buqa in charge of the advance Mongol army makes a triumphal entry into Damascus after the surrender of Aleppo and Hamah, and the surrender of Isma'ili fortresses including Masyaf.

Possible date for the translation into Spanish of an account of the Ascension of the Prophet to heaven (the "Night Journey or *mi'raj*) by a Jewish Physician named Abraham at the court of Alfonso X ("the Wise") of Castile. This account was shortly thereafter translated into French as *Le Livre de l'Eschiele Mahomet* (preserved at the Bodleian library at Oxford) and Latin (at Paris and Rome) and may have been known to Dante and thus influenced his *Divine Comedy.* Other references to the Night Journey abounded in Spain, such as in the codex *Uncastillo* of Aragon dated to 1222. The Ascension also formed the basis for a literary work by Abu-l-'Ala al-Ma'arri. But both Dante and al-Ma'arri were even more influenced by the Zoroastrian *Book of Arda Viraz,* paraphrased in Ptolemy, as were elaborate Islamic accounts of the ascension itself.

Revival of Buddhism takes place in Merv.

1260

3 Sept.; Mamluks led by Qutuz and his lieutenant Baybars defeat the Mongols at the Battle of 'Ayn Jalut (Goliath's Well). The Mongol Ket-Buqa is put to death. Baybars who led the vanguard, murders Qutuz and becomes Sultan.

Kubilai declared Great Khan by his army, founds the Mongol Yūan dynasty in China.

1264

Kubilai founds Khanbaliq (Peking) as his capital.

1265

Death of Hülagu Khan.

Death of Farid ad-Din, key figure in the Chishti line; his disciple was Nizam ad-Din Awliya (buried in Delhi) who is the high point of the Chishtis during the Delhi Sultanate; the Chishti line goes on to become important in the Punjab and through Muhammad Gesudaraz becomes important in the Deccan.

1269

The Merinids establish themselves at Marrakesh.

Death of the Arab philosopher Ibn Sab'in (a Monist: "There is nothing but God") who corresponded with Frederick II Hohenstaufen.

1270

Death of Ibn Abu Usaibi'a, biographer of men of science.

1271

Journey of Marco Polo to China.

Unsuccessful attempt by Syrian Isma'ilis to assassinate Baybars leads him to reduce all Nizari fortresses. On the other hand Baybars uses the Isma'ilis to threaten the Count of Tripoli in 1271, murder Philip of Montfort, lord of Tyre, in 1270, and attempt the life of prince Edward of England in 1272.

1273

Death of the Sufi Jalal ad-Din ar-Rumi, whose father came from Balkh, (formerly a Manichean and later Isma'ili stronghold), where he faced persecution, to Konya, where he was welcomed by the Turkic rulers. Rumi created a mythology around an imaginary teacher, Shamsi Tabrizi, who like Mani, is put to death for his radical esoterism. Shamsi is present at the meetings of the Mevlevis, sitting on an empty sheepskin, a feature which was adopted by many Turkish Sufi groups. (Isma'ilis rightly consider Rumi to be one of them. The empty sheepskin is a variant of "the empty throne", or Bema.)

1274

Death of Ibn Sa'id, Andalusian man of letters.

1275

The Nestorian patriarch of Baghdad creates a Bishopric in Peking.

Death of Thomas Aquinas, ("The Angelic Doctor").

1276

Death of Madhva (b. 1197) exponent of "dualist" or *dvaita vedanta.*

1279

Death of Nasir ad-Din Tusi, Isma'ili theologian and mathematician-astronomer who established the Maragha observatory for the Mongols.

1280

Moses of Léon writes the *Zohar*, attributing it to Shimon Bar Yohai. The *Zohar* speaks of "Allah of the shining pearl".

1282

Death of Ibn Khallikan, of Syrian birth but claiming descent from the Barmakids. He wrote a biographical dictionary "The Obituaries of Eminent Men" (which leaves out the first and second generations of Muslims, and the Caliphs).

1290

Jews expelled from England.

1291

Last Crusader stronghold falls to Mamluks.

Death of the Persian poet Sa'di.

1292

Marco Polo and his uncle Maffeo visit Ch'ūan-chou in Southern China which he calls Zaitun. A "wise Saracen" tells them of a sect which no-one can identify. After several visits Marco Polo discovers they have a psalter and concludes they are Christians. Marco Polo had stumbled on a large group of Manicheans; he estimated these "Christians" to be 700,000 families. Two members of this sect arrive before Kublai Khan who asked them if they wanted to be classified as Christians or as Buddhists. They chose to be classified as Christians and this obliged the Nestorians to be their advocates. As Chinese Buddhists had been the most active anti-Manicheans it was in the Manichean's interest to be under the Christian wing. In 1957 a Manichean shrine on Hua-piao hill was identified in this area of former Zaitun, now called Quanzhou, in Fujian province.

1294

Marco Polo returns to Italy.

c.1297

Establishment of small Islamic states in the north of Sumatra.

1299

The Mongols under Ghazan defeat the Mamluks under an-Nasir Muhammad at Hims and loot Damascus. Ibn Taymiyya is active in seeking defense for Damascus whose siege is reported by Ibn Kathir. A second occupation by the Mongols is repulsed.

700 H. = 16 September 1300

1300

The Venetians copy the art of making decorative glassware from Damascus, and after 1401, when Timur had destroyed the Damascene glass furnaces, Venice surpasses the Islamic world in making glass.

1304

First firearms invented in the Islamic world using a bamboo tube to propel an arrow by black gunpowder. Although black gunpowder was used in China by the 10th century for fireworks, it may have been actually invented by Arabs. By the 14th century firearms are being used in Europe and begin deciding battles in the 16th. (*See 1387*)

1307

Friday, thirteenth of October, every Knight Templar in France is arrested on Phillipe le Bel's orders.

1309

In England the Knights Templar are also arrested, but having three months warning, many have gone underground. The English King Edward II had received orders from the Pope earlier to arrest the Templars but had ignored them until an official Bull was issued.

1311

Death of Ibn Mansur who composed the dictionary of Arabic called the *Lisan al-'Arab* in twenty volumes.

1312

After a prosecution begun by the King Philippe le Bel of France, the order of the Knights Templar is abolished by the Synod of Vienna; its property is transferred to the Hospitallers except in France where it is confiscated by the Crown. The Templars, as a secret organisation, had close contacts with the Assassins, or Isma'ilis, in Syria, another secret organisation. (Pope Gregory IX had condemned the Knight's close relations with the Isma'ilis in 1236.) Both groups had beliefs and practices contrary to those of the Christian and Muslim mainstream around them which put them into the position of being able to deal more openly with each other as secret lodges with mutual interests and an analogous freedom of belief and action in regards to the religions within which they operated. It is probably through these contacts between the two underground groups that Isma'ili traditions (particularly in their Druze forms) and the Qarmati craft guild structures, the basis of their social programme to create a new society, flow into Europe in the form of Freemasons.

The King of France, seeing the danger to himself in this creation of an international empire within an empire, moves against the Templars destroying the military and political superstructure; the guilds remain and the legend arises within Free-Masonry that the last Grand Master of the Templars, Jacques de Molay, cursed seven generations of the Kings of France, escaped the destruction and went to Scotland to become the Grand Master of the Masonic Scottish Rite.

1316

Death of Uljaytu, Il-Khanid ruler who converted to Islam as Muhammad Khudabanda.

1317

Execution of the historian and Il-Khanid Vizier Rashid ad-Din at-Tabib, author of a monumental universal history.

1325

Traditional date of death of Yunus Emre, Turkish gnostic poet, himself probably a literary creation.

Death of 'Allamah Hilli (Mansur Hasan ibn Yusuf ibn 'Ali al-Hilli), Shi'ite theologian, a student of Nasir ad-Din Tusi, an Isma'ili mathematician and scholar.

1326

Ottoman Turks under Orkhan capture Bursa.

1328

Death of Ibn Taymiyyah, traditionalist theologian.

1331

Death of the Sultan of Hamah, Abu'l-Fida, who had made abridgements of the history of Ibn Athir.

Ottomans seize Nicaea (Iznik).

1336

Death of 'Ala ad-Dawlah Semnani, Persian theosopher.

Death of the Ilkhan Abu Sa'id followed by the break-up of Mongol dominions in the Middle East. With this, small Mongol or Turkish ruled principalities appear in Persia, Mesopotamia, and Anatolia.

1337

The Byzantines repulse an attack by the Ottoman chief Orkhan, but Nicomedia (Izmit) is captured. By 1340 practically all the Byzantine territory in Asia Minor is taken by the Turks apart from the coastal fortresses facing and adjoining Constantinople itself.

Beginning of the Hundred Year's War in Europe.

Shaykh Hasan Buzurg, chief of the line of Jalayrids who succeeded the Il-Khan makes Baghdad his residence.

1342

Jews are banished from some parts of Italy.

1345

At the request of the Byzantine Emperor John VI Cantacuzenus, Ottoman forces cross into Europe to help him in his struggle with his rival John V Palaeologus.

In Anatolia, the Ottomans capture Ankara.

1346-1349

The Black Plague in Europe. Kipchak Mongols who are besieging a Genoese trading center in the Crimea, begin dying in large numbers from an infectious disease. They catapult their dead into the city. Genoese sailors coming to Messina in Italy spread the plague there, and from ships's rats to other ports in Europe.

At the Battle of Crécy, fifteen hundred armored French noblemen fall to the English longbow (from Wales) wielded by peasants.

1348

Death of adh-Dhahabi, author of a *History of Islam.*

1349

A Madrasah or university theological school is founded at Granada.

1351

The plague in Europe causes an increase in the income of peasants and craftsmen because of the decline in population. The English parliament passes a Statute of Laborers in an attempt to hold down wages.

1361

The Ottomans capture Adrianople (Edirne).

1362

The Sultan Hasan Madrasah built at Cairo.

The English courts change the language for court proceedings from French to English.

1368

In China, an insurgent monk, a leader of the "Maitreya Society" with a red scarf for its insignia, drives the Mongols from Peking and founds the Ming ("Light") Dynasty. In 1370 he enacts laws of suppression against the Manicheans ("soldiers and civilians who impersonate divinities") who are accused of usurping the title of the Ming Dynasty (*Ming Chao*) by their name of "Religion of Light" (*Ming Chiao*).

1369
Timur (Tamerlane) conquers Khorasan and Transoxiana.

1378
Death of Ibn Batutah, a Moroccan, the greatest world traveler.

1380
Timur begins his conquest of Iran.

1381
Peasant's revolt in England. The leader of the revolt is named Walter the Tyler (Wat Tyler's Revolt). The Knights Hospitaller of St John, now known as the Knights of Malta, who had received much of the confiscated property of the Knights Templar are singled out for destruction by the revolt. The revolt is directed by a group based in London called "the Great Society (*magnas societas*)". The revolt seeks the end of serfdom and attacks monasteries and abbeys and cuts off the head of the Archbishop of Canterbury. The revolt followed the suppression of the Knights Templar in Europe. The arrest of the Templars in England followed that of those in Europe by several months, giving them a chance to go underground.

1385
Ottoman conquests in the Balkans (Rumelia).

1387
Firearms appear in Iran where they are known as *radd-andaz*, "give a push"; at the end of the 15th century primitive cannons are being produced at Herat. (*See 1304*).

1389
The Ottomans defeat the Serbs at Kosovo Polye ("the Field of Blackbirds"). The Serb King Lazar and the Turkish Sultan Murad are both killed, but Turkish expansion in Europe is assured. Bayezid I, called *Yildirim*, "the Thunderbolt" becomes the fourth Ottoman ruler.

Death of the Persian poet Hafiz and the theologian Taftazani.

1391
First Ottoman siege of Constantinople.

1393
Timur occupies Baghdad for several months, now mostly in ruins, and gives instructions to his lieutenant Mirza Abu Bakr to rebuild the city.

1394
The Ottoman ruler Bayezid I requests the title "Sultan of Rum" (a title of the former Seljuqs of Konya) from the figurehead Caliph (who is under the tutelage of the Mamluk Sultan) in Cairo.

Timur begins first attacks on eastern Asia Minor.

Expulsion orders against Jews in France.

1395
The Ottomans besiege Constantinople; Bayezid is distracted by a Western incursion which he defeats at Nicopolis in 1396.

800 H. 24 September 1397

1398
Birth of Kabir, a syncretist, in India.

1399
Timur (Tamerlane) sacks Delhi.

1400
The *Ornament of Chevaliers and Banner of Gallants* by Ibn Hudhail of Granada.

1402
Timur (Tamerlane) captures the Ottoman Sultan Bayezid in a battle on a plain near Ankara; Bayezid commits suicide eight months later. Timur also occupies Damascus and deports artisans to Samarkand.

1405
Death of Timur (Tamerlane).

A Chinese Muslim, Zheng He, who rose to power as a military commander of the Emperor, commands a fleet which is said to have included 28,000 sailors on 300 ships, the longest of which was 400 feet (130m) long and 160 feet (50m) wide. In 1405 he begins the first of seven major naval expeditions of exploration which bring him to Africa and to Calicut in India. His expeditions continue until 1433. From Africa he brings back giraffes to China. It is believed that one of his ships wrecked on the island of Pate off Kenya and his sailors remained there, blending into the population. After the death of the Yongle Emperor in 1424 quietist Confucianist reaction in China leads to a dismantling of the fleet and the eventual prohibition of building a boat with two masts by 1500.

1406
Death of the historian Ibn Khaldun in Cairo.

1408
Kara Koyunlu victory over Miran Shah.

1410
Prince Musa, son of Bayezid, after consolidating Ot-

toman losses in Rumelia or Europe, and regaining Thrace, Thessaly, Serbia and raiding into Austria, lays siege to Constantinople.

1411
The Kara Koyunlu occupy Baghdad.

1413
Ottomans: Musa is defeated near Sofia by his brother Mehmet who has rallied forces in Anatolia and made an alliance with the Byzantine Emperor and a Serbian Prince. Musa is captured after taking flight and strangled.

1414
Death of Fairuzabadi, compiler of the dictionary of Arabic called the *Qamus.*

1416
Chinese Muslim colonies founded in Java.

Venetian fleet defeats the Turks at Gallipoli.

Mehmet the Ottoman faces a revolt led by Qadi Bedreddin, former chief military judge, who stirs up revolt teaching a mixture of mysticism, religious communism, and interconfessional universalism.

A Sayyid Radi of Lahijan in Daylam invites several thousand Daylamis to the banks of the Safid Rud and then has them massacred along with their chiefs.

1418
Death of al-Qalqashandi, author of a manual for secretaries with discourses on the geography and political administration of foreign lands, with information about them, and with specimens of official correspondence.

1421
The Ottoman Murad II takes power and resumes territorial expansion of the empire winning victories against Greeks, Serbs, Hungarians.(*See 1405*) The Ming Emperor of China sends a "treasure fleet" under Admiral Zheng He, a Muslim also known as Sin Bao, to explore the world. Sailing west, following the routes of Arab traders, the fleet may have reached Kenya. Seven ships returned in 1423, whereupon China abandoned its explorations.

1422
Murad the Ottoman lays a premature siege to Constantinople which is soon abandoned.

1425
In Egypt and Syria the *Ashrafi* Dinar is coined which is equivalent to the Venetian sequin.

1429
The observatory of Ulugh Beg is built at Samarkand.

1430
Murad completes conquest of Macedonia by taking Salonika which the Greeks had sold to the Venetians. Institution of the *devshirme* or "boy levy" among the Christian populations of the Balkans for state service. Development of the Ottoman historical tradition linking the Ottomans with Turkish tribal legend and earlier states, and development of a civil service class.

1440
Turks abandon a siege of Belgrade because of resistance by the Hungarians.

1442
Death of al-Maqrizi, author of a topographical description of Egypt (*Khitat*); a history of the Fatimids (*I'tibar*), and a history of the Mamluk and Ayyubid dynasties (*Suluk*).

1443
Birth of Sayyid Muhammad of Jawnpore who will lead an Indian Mahdist movement.

1444
Murad signs a ten-year truce with the Hungarians at Szeged and retires to Bursa abdicating in favor of his twelve year old son, Mehmet II. The Hungarians are tempted to break the truce and cross the Danube to Bulgaria; Murad assembles his forces and defeats the Hungarian King Ladislas at Varna.

1448
Turks defeat Hungarians at second battle of Kosovo.

1449
Death of the historian Ibn Hajar, who compiled centennial dictionaries of those who lived in the time.

1450
Death of Ibn 'Arabshah, secretary to the Ottoman Sultan at Adrianople, author of a biography of Timur entitled the *Marvels of Destiny*, and the *Entertainment of Caliphs* (north Persian stories).

Cessation of "Balkan dualism" (Bogomils).

THE OTTOMANS CAPTURE CONSTANTINOPLE

1453
April- 29 May: Ottoman siege and fall of Constantinople.

1456
The Turks besiege Belgrade.

1469
Birth of Nanak, founder of Sikhism, in India.

Uzun Hasan defeats the Timurid Abu Sa'id.

The Ak Koyunlu dispossess the Kara Koyunlu of Baghdad.

1478
Pope Sixtus IV authorizes the creation of the Inquisition.

1479
Mosque of Demak, oldest in Indonesia.

The Italian painter Gentile Bellini sojourns in Istabul and paints a famous portrait of Mehmet II, which is much copied and becomes in vogue in Europe.

1481
The Timurid Husayn Baikara rebuilds the shrine of Mazar-i Sherif.

1483
A Latin translation of Avicenna's *al-Kanun fi Tibb* ("Canon of Medicine") is published in Venice.

1484
A medical treatise of Ibn Rushd is published in Venice, which has become a publishing center in Europe and a conduit of Islamic arts, crafts, and science.

1485
Birth of Chaitanya in India.

1487
Bartolomeu Diaz rounds "The Cape of Storms" which is renamed by the Portuguese King "The Cape of Good Hope".

1489
Ibn Majid of the Najd composes manuals for navigators in the Indian Ocean in verse (to aid memorisation) and prose.

1492
Granada and its dependencies, the last Muslim Kingdom in Spain, falls on January 2 to the "Catholic Kings" Ferdinand and Isabella. In March, the Jews are ordered to leave Spain by July.

Columbus lands in the New World. (In Portugal and Spain part of the costs of the voyages of discovery is financed by the Knights of Christ, successor orders to the Templars.)

Death of the Persian poet Jami.

900 H. =2 October 1494

1496
Jews are ordered to leave Portugal but in the next year feigned conversions to Christianity are officially sanctioned and many remain.

1497
The Moghul founder Babur captures Samarkand.

Death of as-Sakhawi, author of a centennial or epochal dictionary in twelve volumes, one of which is devoted to noted women.

1498
Vasco Da Gama, with Ibn Majid as navigator, reaches India and lands at Goa.

1501
Isma'il I and the beginning of the Safavid dynasty in Persia. Twelve-Imam Shi'ism becomes the state religion in Persia.

Death of the Uzbek poet Mir 'Ali-Shir Neva'i.

1503-1523
An Arabic edition of the Koran is said to have been published at Venice of which all copies were destroyed by order of the Pope.

1505
Death of Jalal ad-Din as-Suyuti, prolific author. Among his works, the *Itqan*, a commentary on the Koran, and a *History of the Caliphs*, and the *Kitab al-Muzhir*, based upon earlier works, about the theoretical aspects of the Arabic language, such as the total number of roots and possible words, etc.

1507
The Portuguese under d'Albuquerque establish strongholds in Persian Gulf.

1508
Shah Isma'il I of Persia takes Baghdad from the Ak Koyunlu Turkomans.

1511
D'Albuquerque conquers Malacca.

1514
Turks acquire knowledge of the maps of Christopher Columbus; the Turkish Admiral Piri-Re'is.

At the Battle of Chaldiran on August 23, the Ottomans under Selim defeat the armies of the Shah Isma'il of Iran and occupy Tabriz. Shi'ite expansion contained. After the battle, it is said that Isma'il never smiled again.

1517
The Ottoman Sultan Selim Yavuz ("the Grim") defeats the Mamluks and conquers Egypt.

1519
Beginning of the Celali ("Jelali") Revolts in Anatolia against the Ottoman Empire which last into the next century.

1519
Following expulsions of Jews from Arles (1493) Tarascon (1496) Provence (1500) and Pfefferkorn's demands that the Talmud be confiscated for anti-Christian teachings, Jews are expelled from Regensburg. After 1550, aside from crypto-Jews, the only important Jewish communities for a time in German lands are in Worms and Frankfurt.

1520
Reign of Süleyman the Magnificent, who calls himself the *Padishah-i Islam*, the "Emperor of Islam".

One person accompanying the Spanish conquistador Hernando Cortés carries smallpox to America.

1521
Ottomans capture Belgrade.

1525
Death of Behzad of Herat, miniaturist. Having worked at Tabriz earlier (1506), Behzad, who uses gold as his background, founds a miniaturist school which marks a departure from Mongol styles which, through Tabriz, brought back the art form which had originally flourished in Basrah and Baghdad and had been used for book illustrations such as *Kalila wa Dimna*, and *Hariri's Maqamat*. From Herat the tradition will be taken to India by Humayun.

The tradition of Persian miniatures (as well as Christian icons and Tibetan Tankas) probably also draws directly upon precedents in Manichean art and the notion of Divine light trapped in matter. The use of gold and silver probably dates from their depiction of the divinity of "purified" or "true" substance. Gnostic halos signify a radiation of divinity on the part of the person; halos in Christian icons, a receptivity to the Holy Spirit.

1526
The Ottoman victory at Mohacs opens way to Hungary. Louis of Hungary dies at the Battle.

The Battle of Panipat in India, Moghul conquest; Babur makes Delhi and Agra his capital.

1528
The Ottomans take Buda in Hungary.

1529
Unsuccessful Ottoman siege of Vienna.

1534
A general of Sülayman the Magnificent takes Baghdad from the Persians.

1535
The Capitulations between France and the Ottomans.

1537
The Ottomans take Venetian possessions in the Aegean.

The enterprising Paganini brothers make the first printed Koran in Venice, but it is not a commercial success in the Islamic world which prefers handwritten Korans.

1538
The Ottomans attack Corfou.

1539
Death of Guru Nanak, founder of Sikhism in the Punjab. The movement, with its scripture, the Adi Granth, while seemingly incorporating elements of Islam and Hinduism, is neither. Like the Kabirpanth which precedes it, it is rather a rejection of the two religions.

1540
A narrative of the struggles between Muslims and Christians in Abyssinia written by a Somali Arab named Arabfaqih.

1543
The Latin translation of the Koran made under the order of Peter the Venerable in the 12th century is published in Basel at the request of Luther by the Zwinglian Bibliander (Buchmann). It is again published in 1560 in Zuerich along with refutations by Philip Melancthon, Nicholas of Cusa, Savanarola and others. This translation is, needless to say, full of errors and omissions.

1546
Peri-Re'is takes Aden; the Ottomans establish themselves in the Yemen.

Death of Martin Luther (b. 1483), who will be considered in some theological circles, particularly among Catholics, as a Neo-Catharist or Manichean.

1547
An Italian translation of the Koran by Andrea Arrivabene, (*L'Alcorano di Macometto*), probably an adap-

tation of the existing Latin translation is published in Venice.

1550

The architect Sinan builds the Süleymaniye mosque in Istanbul.

Rise of the Muslim Kingdom of Atjeh in Sumatra. Expansion of Islam in Java, the Moluccas, and Borneo.

A "Description of Africa and the Noteworthy Features found therein" in Italian by Leo Africanus is published in Venice. Leo Africanus was al-Hasan ibn Muhammad al-Bassan az-Zayyati al-Fasi born in Granada in 1489; he was educated in Marrakesh. A traveler, he was captured by pirates and sold as a slave to the Pope, Leo X Medici. The Pope having found him remarkable, christened him after himself with the name Leo Giovanni in 1520. Leo Africanus taught Arabic at Bologna, wrote several works in Italian, and returned to the Islamic world in Tunis in 1528 where his trace disappears.

1551

The Ottoman Admiral Piri-Re'is takes Musqat.

1552-1556

Ivan the Terrible conquers Kazan and Astrakhan from the Tatars, leading to Russian control of the entire Volga.

1556

Death of Sülayman the Magnificent.

1560

Death of Tashk"pruzade, author of a dictionary of Turkish savants.

Pronounced provincial unrest in the Ottoman Empire known as the Celali ("Jelali") revolts reach a high point.

1565

The Ottomans besiege Malta.

Death of ash-Sha'rani, author of Sufi biography.

1568

Alpujarra uprising of the Moriscos in Spain.

1570

Death of the Kabbalist Moses Cordovero (b. 1522) in Safad, teacher of Isaac Luria. He was a disciple of the mystic poet Solomon Alkabez and the codifier Joseph Caro. He was called the founder of the Kabbalistic school in Safed.

1571

The Ottomans defeated at the naval Battle of Lepanto by Don John of Austria; end of Turkish dominance in the Mediterranean. A larger Ottoman naval force is defeated by the Catholic Holy League of Habsburgs, Papal States, Venitian Republic, and Genoa in the Gulf of Corinth. The Venetians however, pay the Ottomans indemnities to preserve their special trading position.

1572

Death of the Kabbalist Isaac Luria of Safad at the age of 38; a clear case of Neo-Manicheism, he speaks of the "particles of light" in vessels which will be broken, the gathering of the particles of light and the light liberated by the Messiah, a theme which reappears again in later Hassidism and Kabbalism.

1573

The Ottomans take Cyprus.

1574

The Ottomans occupy Tunis.

1578

The Battle of the Three Kings at Qsar al-Kabir in Morocco. King Sebastian of Portugal killed.

1579

The *Mazhar* ("Declaration") in Moghul India that the Emperor Akbar is the arbiter of religious questions. This is preceded by two pilgrimages on the part of Akbar to the tomb of Chishti. (The *Mujtahid* status of the Emperor is supposed to be restricted within those areas not already prescribed by the *Shari'ah*.) This is followed by the enunciation of the *Din-i-Llahi* ("Divine Religion") in 1582, an eclectic syncretism practiced in the court, and the establishment of the *'Ibadat-khana*, or "Hall of Worship" in Fatehpur Sikri, where the representatives of the religions were encouraged to tear themselves apart in disputations while Akbar sat on a high pillar. (*See 1605*).

1588-1628

Reign of the Safavid Shah Abbas I.

1000 H. =19 October 1591

1591

Musta'li Isma'ilis split into Sulaymanis and Daudis.

1595

Sultan Mehmet III succeeds to the Ottoman throne and orders the execution of his nineteen brothers; it is the last royal massacre, a way of eliminating rivals to the throne practiced amongst the Turco-Mongols from early times and formalized among the Ottomans by a declaration of Mehmet the Conqueror: "To whichever of my sons the Sultanate may be vouchsafed, it is proper for him to put his brothers to death, to preserve the order of the world." When Mehmed III died in 1603 he left two young sons, Ahmet and Mustafa. When Ahmet I died in 1617, his younger brother, Mustafa I, succeeded him. But as the law of fratricide came to and end, so did the practice of princely apprenticeships as provincial governors, and the princes instead grew up in a life of gilded imprisonment in an extension of the Harem from which they emerged only to die or to reign. This led to a degeneration in the royal line until the end of the 18th century when the *Kafes* (cage) system of raising the royal heirs was relaxed.

At the same time, until 1610, brigands terrorize Anatolia. They arise from an unpaid body of troops released from service. They had been created for, and trained in, the use of muskets. These troops had been known as Sekbans.

1596

Following in the steps of the Portuguese, the first Dutchman to double the Cape of Good Hope, Cornelius Houtman, reaches Sumatra and Bantam. The Dutch begin to establish factories in India, Ceylon, Sumatra and the Red Sea and dominate the Indian trade in Europe.

1600

The Moghul Emperor Akbar tries to conquer the Deccan.

Death of the Ottoman Turkish poet Baki (born 1526) who wrote a famous elegy for the Sultan Süleyman.

1602

Shah 'Abbas captures Bahrayn from the Portuguese.

Dutch East India company formed out of an amalgam of trading companies by the States-General of the United Provinces.

1603

Abu-l Fazl 'Allami (b. 1551 in Agra), Akbar's propagandist for his "Universalist" movement (the *Din-i Llahi*) is assassinated by a Rajput at the behest of Jahangir. He wrote the "Institutes of Akbar" (*A'in-i Akbari*). He exalted the *Padishah* or ruler.

1605

The Moghul Emperor Akbar dies. Twenty men in Akbar's palace had followed a secret religion with Akbar as its head and drawing upon a power they believed to come to them from the sun. Akbar's secret Sunni opponent, 'Abd al-Qadir Bada'uni, documented the religious deviation of the Akbar period in the *Muntakhab at-Tawarikh* ("Selected Histories"). (*See 1579*)

1609

Expulsion of Moriscos (Muslims forced to convert outwardly to Catholicism) from Spain.

1611

The King James Version of the Bible is published, the work of more than fifty scholars over three years. Because of the impact of this work on the English language and literature, and Protestantism which emphasizes reading scripture, only in English is the Bible so commonly familiar and widely quoted by the literate public. In second place would be German because of the Luther translation. In other Christian languages, even after its translation into the vernaculars, the Bible is much less well known by the general public. An interesting contrast are the Islamic countries where the entire Koran is known by heart by thousands upon thousands of otherwise little educated people. However, although they can repeat it from memory, not even all Arabic speakers are aware of the meaning of most of the words.

1612

The Shah Mosque of Isfahan is built.

1616

A German translation of the Koran (*Der Türken Alcoran*) by Schweigger, probably an adaptation of the Italian adaptation of 1547, is published in Nuremberg.

1619

Batavia is founded in Java by the Dutch to be the seat of the supreme government of their trading possessions in the East Indies.

1623

Under Shah Abbas the Persians take Baghdad from the Ottomans. They are driven out by the Turks in 1638.

1624

Death of Ahmad al-Faruqi Sirhindi, Indian religious leader, a Naqshbandi, who drew upon precedents set by Sayyid Muhammad of Jawnpore. Sirhindi was called the *Mujaddid al-Alf ath-thani*, "the Renewer of the Second Millennium (of Islam)". He attacked the exponents of *Wahdat al-Wujud* (Monism) and advanced instead *Wahdat ash-Shuhud* (the "Unity of Consciousness"; that is, that it is *awareness*, and not Being that overlaps or is the point of contact between man and God.)

Death of Muhammad Amin, one of the founders of the Shi'ite Akhbari school.

1627

Death of Ahmad Baba of Timbuktu, author of a centennial or epochal dictionary, a historical work.

1635
The Dutch conquer Formosa.

1638
Turkish Sultan Murad IV reconquers Baghdad from the Persians. It remains the residence of the Turkish Pasha of Mesopotamia until the British take over Iraq after the end of WW II, in the words of the British general "liberating it to bring democracy".

1640
Death of Mulla Sadra, Persian theologian and philosopher.

Great age of Sufism in Atjeh in Sumatra; Ibn 'Arabi, 'Abd al-Karim al-Jili, and Ibn 'Ata'Allah studied.

1641
A Dutch translation of the Koran, from the German of 1616, in Hamburg. The Dutch also take Malacca from the Portuguese, having also driven the English out of the East Indies after the massacre of Amboyna in 1623, which forces the English to retire to India and concentrate on their efforts there.

1642
Death of 'Abd al-Haqq ad-Dihlawi al-Bukhari (b. 1551 in Delhi). A Sunni, he advocated the study of Hadith in Moghul India and wrote "The Perfection of Faith".

1647
The Taj Mahal is built in Agra. André du Ryer, former French Consul in Egypt publishes an inaccurate but new translation of the Koran in French. It is translated into English in 1688 and Dutch in 1698, later into German and is reprinted in French until 1770.

1652
The Dutch found a colony at the Cape of Good Hope as a half-way station to the East.

1653
Papal Bull against Jensenites, *Cum Occasione*. Cornelius Otto Jensen (Jansenius) 1585-1638 in his study of Augustine *Augustinus* said that every good work brought grace infallibly. The work was attacked for being Calvinist, that is, removing all reality from the will. Port Royal was a nunnery with aristocratic support where the ideas of Jansenism were harbored; Blaise Pascal was a follower.

1655-1667
Under the Pope Alexander VII the council of Roman censors forbids Catholics to publish or translate the Koran, but an unpublished translation into Latin is made by a Franciscan, Germain of Silesia which exists in manuscript in Montpellier and the Escorial.

1656
An account of the Songhay kingdom written by as-Sa'di of Timbuktu.

1657
Death of Hajji Khalifa (Katib Chelebi), secretary to the War Department of the Sublime Porte in Istanbul and author of a bibliography called the *Kashf az-Zunun* ("Remover of Doubts") of Arabic, Persian, and Turkish works.

1658
The Dutch drive the Portuguese out of Ceylon and by 1664 wrest the Malabar coast from them. But their of policy of brutal domination for the purposes of trade monopoly prevents them from establishing themselves more deeply and their empire begins to crumble when Clive attacks the Dutch in Chinsura in Bengal in 1758.

1659
Death of Dara Shikoh, son of Shah Jahan. Shikoh was a Qadiri "Universalist" and Monist.

1661
Charles II of England receives Bombay (Port. "Bom Bahia") from the Portuguese as part of Catherine of Braganza's dowry.

1676
Death of Sabbatai Zevi, around whom had developed a Messianic movement in Judaism. Zevi, born in 1625 into a Spanish Jewish family in Smyrna, entered into states in which he advocated breaking Jewish religious laws. He had a large following in Europe, and many came to him in Turkey; the Turks obliged Zevi to convert to Islam, which he did while preserving his own new religion in secret. Those Jews who converted with him became known in Turkey as *D'nmeh* or false converts who kept a secret Sabbatian cult under the cover of Islam. Many Turks today believe that the *D'nmeh* came to power in Turkey first as the "Young Turk" revolt and then as the Kemalist movement, which severely limited public expression of Islam in Turkey. After the "conversion" of Sabbatai Zevi, the annals of the Jews of Italy for the Zevi years were destroyed to expunge all record of him. Those who had taken part in the movement later concealed their connections with it. Sabbatianism rationalized apostasy as a function of Messiahship for subsequent movements in Judaism, such as Frankism, which was a direct successor to Sabbatianism.

1677
First Russo-Ottoman war.

1679
Death of the Turkish traveller Evliya Chelebi who wrote an account of his journeys.

1683

The Ottomans unsuccessfully besiege Vienna; they are routed by the King of Poland, Jan Sobieski, who, in a dawn attack after morning mass, swoops down on the encircling Turkish army from the Kahlenberg above Vienna.

1686

The Ottomans lose Hungary to Austrians.

1687

Turkish defeat at Mohacs.

Death of ash-Shirbini, Egyptian satirist.

Isaac Newton publishes the Philosophiae Naturalis Principia Mathematica.

1100 H. = 26 October 1688

1688

The Austrians take Belgrade.

Alexander Ross translates du Ryer's French translation of the Koran into English.

1689

Mustafa Köprülü becomes grand Vizier in Istanbul.

1690

The Turks retake Belgrade.

1694

An Arabic edition of the Koran, called Alcoranus is published in Hamburg by Hinckelmann as the work of a "pseudo-prophet".

1696

Peter the Great of Russia takes the Turkish fortress of Azov.

Antoine Galland (who first translated the *Thousand and One Nights*) publishes the *Bibliothèque Orientale ou Dictionnaire universel contenant généralement tout ce qui regarde la connaisance des peuples de l'orient.* This is the first Encyclopedia of the Islamic world. The work was begun by Barthélemy d'Herbelot.

1698

Ludovic Maracci (1612-1700), confessor of Pope Innocent XI, translates the Koran into Latin with commentaries intended to "disprove" it. The work is published in Padua, along with the Arabic text, notes and refutations (which were already published in Rome in 1691), is entitled *Rufutatio Alcorani*; his polemical translation is used as the basis for many others, including Sale's version into English in 1734.

1700

Catholicizing of the last Paulicians in Bulgaria.

Birth of Israel Baal Shem Tov ("Master of the Holy Name") near Podolia (also the birthplace of Jacob Frank), who will found modern Hassidism. Hassidism, a pietistic and Gnostic mixture of mainstream Judaism and Kabbala, will, according to David Bakan, incorporate latent Sabbatian elements. He calls this synthesis of rabbinism and mysticism "a new form of Judaism". "The early Sabbatianism which became transformed into the Jewish reform movement and liberalism opened the way for the passage of Jews from the ghetto and shtetl world into the wider currents of Western civilisation... it was achieved by a rapid and dramatic severance of Jews from their ancient traditions and from their Jewish identification... with Chassidism the passage was slower and more even... Chassidism emphasized the pleasurable aspects of life, albeit in a religious context. Chassidism thawed the medieval Jewish mind by opening new possibilities for happiness and satisfaction as contrasted with the old resignation and deprivation... Chassidism runs a close parallel to Romanticism as a way of bringing medieval Man into the modern world." (*Sigmund Freud and the Jewish Mystical Tradition.*) Smallpox kills 400,000 Europeans a year from all levels of society including King Louis XV of France.

1702

Death of Munajjim Bashi, Turkish chronicler.

1707

Death of 'Alamgir (Awrangzeb), "last of the Great Moghuls".

1708

Death of Guru Gobind Singh (b. 1666), Sikh leader who, following a policy of open hostility to Muslims, created the military community of Sikhism, the *Khalsa*, which took the vow to observe the five emblems (beginning with 'Ks'): the beard, comb, loincloth, steel bangle, and short sword.

1710-1711

Russo-Ottoman war.

1716

First Russian translation of the Koran, made by Pyotr Posnikov according to Du Ryer's translation, upon the orders of Peter the Great.

1726

The Turkish poet Ahmed Nedim and the "Century of Tulips", a period from 1718 to 1730 when Western styles were fashionable in Turkey; printing presses are used.

1730
Nadir Shah of Persia drives out Afghans.

1731
Death of 'Abd al-Ghani of Nablus, author of a mystical travel literature.

1734
Translation of the Koran from Arabic into English by George Sale. (See 1698).

1739
Nadir Shah sacks Delhi.

1740
The Latin Church represented by France is given rights in the Holy Land by treaty of capitulations with the Ottomans. Rivalry which broke out between the French (Catholics) and the Russians (Orthodox) in 1850 over privileges in the Holy Places of Christianity became a cause leading to the Crimean War of 1854-1856.

1743
Under the designs of Nadir Shah, an English adventurer, John Elton who "took the turban" and the name of Jamal Beg, builds ships on the Caspian sea; in the Persian gulf a flotilla of twenty vessels is formed. The Persian Navy never plays any significant role.

1745
Muhammad 'Abd al-Wahhab is received in Dir'iyyah by Muhammad ibn Sa'ud.

1746
Translation into German of Sale's English translation of the Koran.

1750
Karim Khan Zand founds the short lived Zand dynasty which provides a lull of peace and piety amidst internecine wars. This is the first dynasty of Iranian stock after an interval of nearly one thousand years of Turkish rulers. From the very first, Karim Khan declares himself regent on behalf of a hypothetical grandchild of the Safavid Shah Sultan Husayn, and never evinced any desire to assume the royal title of Shah. His rule is considered a happy time. His main concern was to bring back order and prosperity to the impoverished provinces. He also attempted to revive the arts and crafts by creating workshops for producing pottery and glass, and reduced the tax burden on the peasants by limiting the arbitrary powers of the landowners. He succeeded in partially restoring the irrigation system, especially in Fars and southern Iran. In Shiraz he put up a number of beautiful buildings; the Vakil mosque, the Caravanserai, and the Mausoleums of the great Shirazi poets, Sa'di and Hafiz.

1757
Part of the rivalry between the French and the British, the Battle of Plassey in Bengal, in which Clive defeated a young local Muslim ruler who had taken the side of the French in Chandernagore, is taken as the date of the beginning of the British Empire in India.

The Wahhabis take al-Hasa.

1761
The French colony of Pondicherry in India capitulates to the British, ending French involvement.

1762
Death of Shah Wali Allah, Indian religious leader from an 'ulama' family, who called himself the *Qa'im az-Zaman* ("The foundation of the age"). Claiming the quality of *Mujtahid*, or original authority in himself, but grounded in al-Ghazali, he translated the Koran into Persian; his sons translated it into Urdu. While rejecting Shi'ite claims he nevertheless accorded "Hazrat 'Ali" ('Ali ibn Abu Talib) a special veneration. Denouncing a descent into disbelief in India he wrote to Nadir Shah of Persia calling him to come to India to purify Islam. He had taken the initiations of the Qadiris, Naqshabandis, Chishtis, the major Indian Sufi orders; this is as much as to say that his role was that of a synthesis but based upon what he called the reliable foundation, *al-wathiq*.

1768-1774
Russo-Ottoman war. Peace of Kuchuk Kaynarja; the Ottomans advance the claim to be the successors to the Caliphate.

1770
French translation of Sale's English translation of the Koran.

1772
The first German translation of the Koran directly out of the Arabic by D. F. Megerlin (*Die Türkische Bible*). This translation is studied by Goethe.

1773
A German translation of the Koran is made by Fr. Eb. Boysen.

1782
New French translation of the Koran by Claude Savary.

1783
Russia conquers the Crimea.

1200 H. = 4 November 1785

1785
Muslim revolt against Chinese Emperor by Shi San.

1787-1792
Russo-Ottoman War.

An Arabic Koran for Muslims in the Russian Empire, since called the "Mawlay Usman" edition, is published at St. Petersburg by order of Catherine II; it is followed by others, in particular the edition of Kazan in 1803.

1789
Efforts at modernisation of the Ottoman Empire under Selim III.

1790
Death of Murtada az-Zabidi, compiler of the dictionary of Arabic called the *Taj al-Arus*, based upon the *Qamus*.

A Russian translation of Du Ryer's French translation of the Koran is made by M. E. Verevkin and published in St. Petersburg.

1791
Death of Ma (Muhammad) Ming-hsin, founder of the "New Sect" in China, a militant Chinese Muslim movement directed against the Manchus.

Death of Jacob Frank (born 1726). Frank, from a Sabbatian family in the Austro-Hungarian Empire, was the leader of another Jewish Messianic movement. This movement had a trinity made of Zevi as God (see 1676), a female counterpart (there was a male-female concept of divinity) – the Shekinah or Matronita, and Frank as Messiah. He led a large number of Jews into a fraudulent mass conversion into Catholicism; was later imprisoned by the Church for heresy and libertinism but released under royal patronage whereupon he assumed the title of Baron of Offenbach. A characteristic that Frank introduced into Sabbatianism was the idea of sanctification through sin. Freud (who will "heal", as the Cathari healed, by the elimination of guilt) will come from a family of Hassidic, but it is also alleged, Frankist, antecedents.

France adopts a decree which makes Jews (at that time 40,000, mainly in Alsace) full citizens but the decree is not made effective.

1792
Death of Vahid Bihbahani, a Mulla who forced the Akhbari school of Shi'ism out of Iran by declaring them unbelievers and using force against them, thus definitively establishing the ascendancy of the Usuli school and opening the way for a spectacular growth in the power of the religious authorities in Iran. Because the Usulis allow the higher religious authorities to apply entirely unprecedented rulings (*ijtihad*), the number of such Mullas called *Mujtahids*, originally a handful, expanded to the hundreds, which led to the foremost amongst them to distinguish themselves with the title *Hujjat al-Islam*. Further growth in numbers took place and the elite of the elite then took the title *Ayatallah*. Akhbaris, who insist on no new rulings since the disappearance of the Imams, are still to be found in Iraq, Bahrayn, and India. They are sometimes called "Ja'fari Shi'ites".

Sale's English translation of the Koran is translated into Russian by Aleksei Kolmakov and published in St. Petersburg.

1796
Edward Jenner injects a boy with the first smallpox vaccination, made from a dairy maid's cowpox lesion. Later the vaccine is made from another bovine smallpox called vaccinia.

1798
Napoleon's victory at the Battle of the Pyramids in Cairo, but Nelson destroys a French Fleet at Aboukir. Accompanying Napoleon to Egypt was a scientific commission of scholars, artists and archaeologists who remained when he left in 1799. They collect scientific information and publish the monumental work of science and scholarship called the "Description of Egypt". They also collect and find such artifacts as the Rosetta stone, which are ceded to the British government at the capitulation of Alexandria in 1801.

1799
Napoleon, anticipating the conquest of Acre, prepares a proclamation of something like a Jewish homeland in Palestine, but his military campaign is thwarted by the British. The proclamation also calls forth more resistance in France than it confounds the British.

1800
Russia annexes Georgia.

1806
Napoleon makes a decree giving Jews citizenship in France. A congress of Jewish representatives held in Paris is called the Sanhedrin after the council which ruled the Jews from 106 BC to AD 72 At this council Napoleon asks the Sanhedrin if they consider themselves French or an alien nation within France. Naturally, they answer that they are French.

1811
War between Russia and Persia.

1812
Treaty of Gulistan; Persia loses its Caucasus possessions to Russia.

1801
Wahhabis raid Kerbala, destroying the shrine and killing about 2,000.

1803
Wahhabis capture Mecca and Medinah.

1804
Muhammad 'Ali viceroy of Egypt.

1806-1812
Russo-Ottoman War.

1809
Founding of the Sokoto Caliphate in Nigeria by Usumanu dan Fodio.

The Persian Mulla Shaikh Ja'far (d. 1812/1227) writes the *Kashif al-Ghita'* ("removal of the Husk") which declares that in absence of "the Hidden Imam" the Mujtahids, or more precisely the best of them (*afdal*), can declare Holy War, which in Shi'ite Islam until then, was the prerogative of the Imam. This will lead Fath 'Ali Shah to declare Holy War against Russia for its incursions into the Caucasus, which will end in the peace of Torkamanchai in 1828.

1810
Death of Rabbi Nachman of Bratslav, born in 1772, "The Dead Hassid" who left no successor. An empty seat is carried by his followers in a yearly processional signifying his living presence in the invisible. He said: "Wherever I go, I go to the land of Israel."

English missionary Henry Martyn (d. 1812) finishes his translations of the New Testament into Urdu, Hindi, and Persian. He dies before he can make a translation into Arabic.

1811
Massacre of the Mamluks by Muhammad 'Ali.

1816
Printing press introduced into Persia at Tabriz by 'Abbas Mirza, the Crown Prince.

1817
Shah Khalil Allah, Nizari Isma'ili Imam (albeit with a Ni'mat Allahi name), son of Sayyid Abu-l-Hasan Khan (who had been governor of Kirman under the Zands, and upon his dismissal had retired to the surroundings of Qum, the Mahallat), is killed by an uprising in Yezd. His son receives the title Aga Khan from the Qajar, Fath 'Ali Shah, who punishes the perpetrators and gives one of his daughters in marriage to him (Fath 'Ali Shah had two thousand children and grand-children) and makes him governor of Qum and the surrounding districts, the Mahallat, whence he acquires the name Aga Khan Mahallati.

1818
Muhammad 'Ali's son Ibrahim Pasha conducts campaign against Wahhabis; Dir'iyyah destroyed.

1820-1840
The high-point of the Fara'izi movement in Bengal. Dudu Miyan, son of the first leader Hajj Shari'atullah, takes up insurrection against the British and militates for affirmation of Islamic practices amongst Bengali Muslims.

1821
Muslim revolt in Sinkiang, China.

1821-1830
The Greek War of Independence. When the news of the Greek revolt reaches Istanbul the Turks hang the Greek patriarch and the chief Greek translator at the Sublime Porte, putting an end to the influence of the Phanariot Greeks. These were Greeks who lived in a certain quarter of Istanbul and had functioned as translators to the Turkish government. Foreign ambassadors worked through these translators and thus this group, who were loyal to the Porte, enjoyed considerable power and prestige. Thereafter, Turks, rather than Greeks, were trained in foreign languages.

1822
Mullah Hajj Taqi Borjani of Kazvin makes a declaration of *takfir* (unbelief) against Shaikh Ahmad Ahsai, founder of the Shaikhis who upheld individual revelation through dreams and contact with the Prophet and the Imams. The "Declaration of Unbelief" exists only amongst the Shi'ites, and is a possibility which was developed in the 19th century.

Jean-Fran$_7$ois Champollion deciphers hieroglyphs from the Rosetta stone.

1823
Death of Mulay-l-'Arabi Darqawi, Sufi in Morocco, considered to be a *mujaddid*, or renewer. He began a revival of Sufism in North Africa whose influence still continues today.

1826
Revolt of the Janissaries and their suppression. Once the Janissaries were out of the way, Mahmud II removed

the Shaykh al-Islam from temporal power, but in return he was given more than consultative power, in the form of judicial authority in religious matters, a power which itself was taken away from the Grand Vizier. The Grand Mufti or Shaykh al-Islam now presided over a government department, installed in the former residence of the Agha of the Janissaries; the bureaucratisation of the 'Ulama'. Schools were taken away from the 'Ulama' and placed under the Ministry of Education; legal responsibilities went to the Ministry of Justice. The *Waqf* or pious foundations left by legacy for the upkeep of religion were transferred to state control.

The office of the Grand Vizier or *Sadrazam* was transformed into Ministries of Foreign and Civil Affairs (later the Ministry of the Interior). The office of the *Defertdar* (treasurer) was renamed the Ministry of Finance. The Council of Ministers (Privy Council) was created. A Census was made of the male population of Rumelia and Anatolia (except the Arab provinces), and a land survey was made to register all land holdings.

The concept of *adalet* or civil justice was introduced, earning Mahmud the name "Adli". This was a body of legislation separate from that of God and the ruler, i.e. *shari'ah* and 3. Legal proceedings were laid down for the punishment of bribery.

Death of Ahmad al-Ahsa'i, founder of the Shaykhis in Persia. His follower Sayyid Kazim of Resht (d. *1249*/1843) becomes the leader of the Shaikhis.

War between Russia and Persia.

1827

Triple Alliance against Turkey. Naval Battle of Navarino.

Against a background of North African pirate incursions against Europe and European shipping, a dispute arises between France and the Turkish government of Algeria. The dispute concerns French debts contracted to two Algerian Jews who supplied wheat to the French government during the Directory. The Turkish Dey of Algiers, Hussein, slaps the French consul across the face with his fly whisk. This begins a series of incidents which leads to the attachment of Algeria to France, beginning with the French blockade of Algiers.

1828

A lithographed edition of the Koran is published at Tabriz (sometimes the date is given as 1833) followed by others published in India and Turkey. (Wood block printings of the Koran were made earlier, perhaps as early as the tenth century.)

Fath 'Ali Shah of Iran, having suffered several defeats at the hands of the Russians, signs the treaty of Torkamanchai with Russia, which brings Azerbaijan into the Russian Empire.

An new adaptation by Wahl in Halle of the Boysen German translation of the Koran of 1773.

1828-1829

Russo-Ottoman War.

1829

A Persian Mullah, Ahmad Naraqi (*1185-1245*/1771-1829), collects historical materials and Hadith regarding political authority in a document called the *'Awa'id al-Ayyam.* He quotes what he believes to be an inspired tradition which concludes that while "The kings have authority over the people, the religious scholars have authority over the kings." This is a direct predecessor of Khomeini's *Vilayat-i Faqih*, or "Government of the Jurisprudent".

A.S. Griboyedov, Russian writer and Ambassador to Tehran is murdered along with the entire embassy staff and guard, except one aide who was absent from the legation. Among the articles of the treaty of Torkamanchai was the return of prisoners; on this basis Griboyedov had his Cossacks search homes in search of Armenian and Georgian women who were taken for questioning. It was rumored that two such Georgian women, who had embraced Islam and borne children to a notable named Asaf ad-Dawla, were being forced against their will to renounce Islam and made known their situation by reciting the Koran so loudly that they could be heard outside the embassy. This led to rioting; the women were released but the riots continued; the Cossack guard fired on the mob and in the end the legation was sacked.

A French ship, *La Provence*, carrying a truce flag is fired upon in the harbor of Algiers. The French resolve to land troops.

1830

French begin to occupy Algeria, a process which is not completed until the beginning of the 20th century. John Darby, an English Clergyman begins to popularize the "Rapture" doctrine in which believers are taken out of the world before the beginning of final tribulations. This idea, new to modern Christianity, was a common feature of ancient Gnostic cults. Darby's doctrines are known as Dispensationalism. He makes several visits to America. Darby's writings become in the 20th century the basis for "Scofield's Reference Bible" published by Oxford University Press. It is a King James Bible with highly tendentious glosses. Revised and augmented since Scofield's death, this book is the cornerstone of the proliferation of Christian Zionists in America. Scofield was himself sponsored by a wealthy Zionist, Samuel Untermyer of New York.

1831

Ibrahim Pasha conquers Syria.

1832

The creation of the Sultanate of Zanzibar.

1833

Was Hat Muhammad aus dem Judenthume Aufgenommen ("What did Muhammad take from Judaism") by Abraham Geiger is published in Bonn (published in English in Delhi in 1898 and as *Judaism* and *Islam* by Ktav, 1970). An extremely misleading work since much of what it alleges "Muhammad took from Judaism", Judaism itself took from Zoroastrianism and Mesopotamian tradition.

1834

Fluegel's first Arabic edition of the Koran published in Leipzig, later to be reprinted. It becomes the basis of much work by European Orientalists, but its numbering of the verses is different from that used in the Islamic world.

Succession of Muhammad Shah in Persia marked by intervention by both Britain and Russia in Iranian politics.

1835

'Abd al-Qadir defeats the French at Macta.

1837

Order of the Sanusiyyah founded.

1838-1842

First Anglo-Afghan war; British invade to thwart Russian influence; Afghans under Dost Muhammad are victorious and the retreating British are massacred.

1839

Beginning of the Tanzimat proclamations: November 3: *Hatt-i-Sharif Gülhane.* The earliest modern constitutional document in any Islamic country since the agreements between the Prophet and the People of Medinah sometimes called "the Constitution of Medinah". The *Hatt-i Sharif* guaranteed freedom and security of life, honour, and property; a regular method of assessing and collecting taxes and the abolition of tax farming; an equally regular method of levying and recruiting the armed forces and fixing the duration of their service; fair public trial under the law, and no punishment without legal sentence.

The Sultan's appointed councils of deliberation were given quasi-legislative powers, and enlarged to include ministers and other notables of the Empire. Supreme among these was the Council of Justice, organized in 1840. Members of the councils were free to express their opinions, and the Sultan bound himself to approve their majority decisions. In his decrees he would follow and refrain from abrogating laws laid down by the charter.

Most radical would have been the treatment of Christians, who would thus be legally equal and liable for military service. In practice, their military service continued to be replaced by a new poll-tax called an exemption tax; however, they continued to be allowed to serve in the Navy as before. Ultimately many goals of the Tanzimat were frustrated.

1840

Damascus Affair: A capuchin friar named Thomas and his Muslim servant Ibrahim disappeared in Syria on February 5th. The French Consul Count Ratti-Menton supported accusations by local Christians that Jews were responsible for the murder of the pair to obtain blood to make matzoth. Several prominent Jews of Damascus were arrested and tortured. In March Jews of Istanbul, alarmed by the blood libel of Damascus and a similar libel in Rhodes, alerted western Jewish leaders. An international campaign, with great publicity, was mounted led by Moses Montefiore of England and Isaac Mo$_3$se (Alphonse) Crémieux of France, with interventions by Queen Victoria, Lord Henry Palmerston, the American Secretary of State John Forsyth, and Klemens von Metternich of Austria to obtain a release of the victims. Montefiore and Crémieux went to Syria, and in August won release of the imprisoned Jews. The Sultan of Turkey Abd al-Majid issued a Firman on 6 November denouncing the blood libel saying that "charges made against them and their religion are nothing but pure calumny" with promises that would be written into the Hatt-i Sharif of Gülhane that "the Jewish nation shall possess the same advantages and enjoy the same privileges as are granted to the numerous other nations who submit to our authority. The Jewish nation shall be protected and defended. However, incidents of blood libel continued; there were nine more by 1900 in Damascus, and elsewhere as well including one in Iran.

Formation of the Ottoman Bank with a guaranteed government subsidy; treasury bonds were introduced with a fluctuating rate of interest.

Kazimirsky's (Albin de Biberstein-Kazimirski) translation of the Koran into French from the Arabic, and in Germany, a translation by Ullman. Kazimirski revises and improves his translation in the next year.

Emancipation law in Germany removes restrictions on Jews and gives them full rights.

Aga Khan I (Hasan 'Ali Shah 1804-1881), who had been made Governor of Kirman (or so he claimed) in 1835, revolted against the Shah in 1837 and occupied the citadel of Bam (destroyed by an earthquake in 2003). He was obliged to surrender to Qajar authorities, was sent to Teheran, escaped or was allowed to return to Qum and his residence, Mahallat. Now he sends his family and possessions to Kerbala by way of Baghdad, and then proceeds to revolt again but is defeated in the second of two skirmishes.

1841

Having unsuccessfully revolted against the Shah of Iran, the Aga Khan I (see 1817) with one hundred horsemen goes to Kandahar to seek asylum with the British by offering them his services. When the British leave Kandahar in 1842 he follows them to Quetta, then Sindh which he helps the British to subjugate, and after more peregrinations in India, settles in Bombay in 1848, where he died in 1881.

1843

Kerbala as a holy city had become a place of refuge for thieves and brigands from Iran and Iran, among them Ibrahim Zafa'rani, a luti or brigand of Iranian origin, who gained control of the town. To restore government control the Ottoman Najib Pasha entered the town with a Sunni army. The inhabitants resisted and a massacre ensued in which the number killed ranged from 4,000 up. The incident brought Iran and Turkey close to war.

Sanusiyyah Brotherhood mother-*zawiyah* founded in Libya.

1844

May 23: Beginning of Babi sect in Persia. Sayyid Mirza 'Ali Muhammad of Shiraz (born 1819) declared the year before, in 1843, that the Hidden Imam would reappear in Kerbala in the Hijrah year *1261*/1845. Now, 1,000 lunar years after the disappearance of the Hidden Imam (1844 is the Hijri year *1260* and the Hidden Imam disappeared in the Hijri year *259* or Gregorian 873) Sayyid Mirza 'Ali Muhammad goes to Bushireh on the Gulf coast and declares himself to be the *Bab* namely, the "Door" or "Gate", to the Hidden Imam. A Mulla of Shiraz, Muhammad Sadiq (or 'Ali Akbar Ardistani), appends to the call to prayer from the Aga Qasim mosque: "I testify that 'Ali Muhammad [the "Bab"] is the remnant (*baqiya*) of God." The *Bab* is arrested by the governor of Fars, and taken to Shiraz to face a commission of inquiry. Among the questions put to him were to describe the circumference of the earth, questions of Arabic grammar and syntax, and signs of the coming the Hidden Imam. Then he is imprisoned in Azerbaijan. In 1847 the Bab declares himself the Hidden Imam. He is taken to Tabriz where he faces a new commission of inquiry. Many Mujtahids made declarations of *Takfir* (unbelief) against him and his followers. The *Babis* or followers of the *Bab* will eventually mutate into the Baha'is. (*See* 1850, 1852, 1863.)

Reform of the Ottoman currency on European models; the Mejidiyye coinage based on a gold pound was introduced to stabilize the currency, which in the past was allowed to depreciate to meet deficits thus creating a climate of corruption among salaried officials whose standard of living was always being eroded.

The Sultan of Morocco allies himself with the Emir 'Abd al-Qadir in Algeria and is defeated by the French at the Battle of Isly.

The First Rabbinical Conference in Brunswick, Germany unanimously decides to take all measures to remove the "Kol Nidre" ceremony. The Kol Nidre, which means "All vows" has been a source of controvery with Christianity since the Middle Ages. This ceremony, performed on the eve of Yom Kippur says: "All vows we are likely to make, all oaths and pledges we are likely to take between this and the next Yom Kippur, we publicly renounce... let them all be null and void... and not be considered neither vows nor pledges." The recommendation by the Rabbis to abolish this secret reservation freeing one from all oaths is not brought to pass except by the Reformed movement which nevertheless reinstated the Kol Nidre as before in 1945.

1847

Two Khoja (Nizari Isma'ili) women in Bombay sue in court to receive inheritance according to Islamic law and not their father's will which excludes them. Sir Erskine Perry rules that their community customs, rather than Islamic law, prevail in this case, recognizing the Khojas, or one group of Indian Nizari Isma'ilis, as a community apart from the Muslim community. (*See* also 1866 and 1905.)

Beginning of secular Nizamiyyah courts in Turkey: these are mixed civil and criminal courts. This was the first formal recognition in Turkey – as already in certain other Islamic states – of a legal system independent of the 'Ulama'.

1850

Execution of the *Bab* in Persia on July 8. After the first volley of a firing squad a disciple of the *Bab* was killed but the bullets cut the rope which suspended the *Bab* himself. He ran away, was suspended again, and shot by a second firing squad. The body was first buried in a shrine outside of Teheran by Mirza Yahya, Subh-i Azal. Eighteen years later the body was removed and hidden by Baha'is.

The execution of the *Bab* leads to uprisings of Babis and their massacre; some Babis follow a new leader, Subh-i Azal and then another leader: Baha' Allah. Beginning of Baha'is (Azalis eventually disappear).

Reform movement of Khayr ad-Din Pasha in Tunisia.

Opening of the first secular institution of higher learning, the "House of Science" (*Dar al-Funun*) in Isfahan in Iran. The Shah, Nasir ad-Din, made three journeys to Europe during his reign (1848-1896), and under his minister Mirza Taqi Khan Amir Kabir (1848-1851), a programme of modernisation was undertaken.

Reform of the commercial code along Western lines in Turkey. Foreigners, who through capitulations had the right to be tried by their own consular courts in civil and criminal cases, now could take commercial cases to Turkish courts. This led to an expansion in trade and saw the establishment of modern commercial companies, banks, and insurance companies in Turkey. The urban populations tripled and quadrupled in size within a generation, and the economic shift saw the decline of the peasantry and artisans. In the business centers there was an influx of foreign and Levantine populations causing resentment. Foreign commercial companies take on an importance inside the Ottoman Empire.

Prince Louis Napoleon of France, aspiring to be emperor, and looking for support from Catholicism, instructs his ambassador to the Sublime Porte for restitution of the rights granted to the Latin Church by a treaty with the Ottomans of 1740, rights which had been revoked by a *Firman* or proclamation many years earlier and given to the Russians and the Orthodox Church. The practical question comes down to whether Latin monks, having the right to the grotto in the Church of Bethlehem, should possess the key to the chief door, which is in the hands of the Russians, and one of the keys to the other two doors of the manger. It also involved the restitution in the sanctuary of a silver star with the coat of arms of France that had been removed, and rights at Gethsemane "to a cupboard and a lamp in the tomb of the Virgin". The silver star was replaced, and the keys were given to the Latin Patriarch in an official ceremony at Christmas. Thus the Orthodox were divested of rights in the Holy Land that they had previously acquired. This was a contributing cause to the Crimean War of 1854-1856.

1851

A revised penal code is promulgated in Turkey.

1852

Militant Babism in Persia culminates in an attempt on the life of Nasir ad-Din Shah. Twenty-eight Babis, including the poetess Qurratu'l-'Ayn are tortured and put to death.

1853

Spread of the Tijani tariqah in West Africa.

The Crimean War: after a build up of warships and armies on the part of the Russians, the Ottomans declare war on Russia 4 October 1853. After the bombardment of the Turkish port of Sinope by the Russians, the French and British come to the aid of the Turks.

1854

In early Christianity the Isis and Demeter component was displaced out of the picture. In Mark 3:33 Jesus would not speak to his mother and said "who is my mother". But with the Gospel of John around 120 Mary appeared at the crucifixion, was addressed reverentially by Jesus; she became a serious force with the Council of Ephesus in 431 which approved the idea of Theotokos or "Mother of God" and anathemized Nestorius who opposed it. In 1854 the Catholic Church made the Immaculate Conception of Mary official doctrine.

1855

Muslim revolt in Yunnan, China.

1856

The Treaty of Paris ends the Crimean War; the Black Sea is neutralized and opened to all merchant vessels; the Dardenelles and Bosphorus are closed to warships; the Russians cede Southern Bessarabia to Moldavia, and the delta of the Danube. Russia makes commitments to respect the territorial integrity of the Ottoman Empire.

Modernizing Tanzimat reforms in Turkey: *Hatt-i Hümayun.*

1857

Alexandria-Cairo railroad completed.

In Northern India a series of revolts known as the Sepoy Mutiny break out and continue for several months. The loss of British life is small but the massacre of 211 British women and children in Cawnpore creates bitterness and mistrust.

1858

End of the Moghul dynasty; the last Moghul is exiled to Rangoon. The British Government takes control of the East India Company and all its territory becomes known as British India governed by a Vice-roy.

Growing dependence of the Ottomans upon foreign loans.

1859

Imam Shamil captured by Russian troops, marking the end of Muslim resistance in the Caucuses which began in 1834.

A concordance of the Koran is published in St. Petersburg by Kazem Bek.

1860

Construction of the Suez Canal begins.

Formation of the Alliance Israélite Universelle dedicated to the modernisation of Jewish communities in North Africa and the Near East.

1861

The so-called "*Faramushkhana*", a Masonic or pseudo-Masonic lodge in Teheran, founded by Mirza Malkum Khan, is dissolved by royal decree. "Faramushkhana" is often mis-translated literally as "house of forgetfulness". Actually it meant "House of the Freemasons". Freemasons are called *fara-mason*, or plural *fara-mush*, which in Persian also means "forgetting", hence the common mis-translation. Malkum Khan, who had studied chemistry in Paris, performed simple chemical experiments at the lodge and proposed that the Shah should be nominal Grand Master.

1863

The Afghans expel the Persians from Herat.

Isma'il becomes Pasha of Egypt until 1880. Because of the American Civil War, Egyptian cotton becomes the major export.

At the request of the Persians the Ottomans imprison the Baha'i and Azali leaders first in Edirne and then in Palestine. (*See* 1844, 1850, 1852.)

1864

Kazimirsky's translation of the Koran into French (1840) is translated into Russian and published by K. Nikolaev.

Death of Murtada Ansari who consolidated the supremacy of the Shi'ite Usuli school. After the death of his teacher Shaykh Muhammad Hasan Najafi, Murtada Ansari became the first universally recognized Shi'ite *Marja'i-taqlid*, accepted by Iranian, Arab, Turkish and Indian Usuli Shi'ites. (Until then there had been more than one *Marja'i* each recognized by different Shi'ite groups.) The dominance of the Usuli school leads to the power of the Mullas in Iran in the next century. After the death of Murtada Ansari, gradually Mirza Hasan Shirazi (d. *1312*/1895) emerged as the new *Marja'i Taqlid.*

Britain's need for better communications with India following the Indian Mutiny leads to the introduction of the telegraph into Persia, followed by extensions in 1870 and 1872.

Maurice Joly writes the satire "Dialogues in Hell between Machiavelli and Montesquieu" which will be adapted as the "Protocols of the Elders of Zion".

1865

The founding of the *Yeni Osmanlilar*, or "Young Ottomans" seeking reform through Turkish nationalism under the slogan *Hürriyet* – "Liberty".

The Indo-European telegraph, across Iran, begun in 1862, becomes operational.

1866

The "Aga Khan case"; some Khojas (Nizari Isma'ilis in India) dispute the Imam's personal right to their property. The case is tried before Sir Joseph Arnould in the Bombay High Court. The Judge rules in favor of the Aga Khan I and makes an analogy that the Sunnis are like Catholics and the Isma'ilis like Protestants. Testimony is heard regarding the divinity of the Aga Khan. He first claims to be able to perform miracles and then later disclaims this saying that miracles are performed by Prophets, and if he were to perform miracles then faith would be unnecessary because the people would have certainty. The English Judge's decision leads to a consolidation of the Aga Khan I's hold over the Khojas of India giving him an absolute right over their communal property and to a portion of their income. It also refutes the contention of some of the Khojas that they are in reality Sunni Muslims. (*See* also 1847 and 1905.)

Isma'il of Egypt assumes the Persian title of Khedive and has the Turkish Sultan agree to succession in Egypt from father to son, rather than succession to the oldest brother of the previous ruler as before in Turkish governments.

1867

The founding of the Deoband Religious School in India which is set into the perspective of Shah Wali Allah.

1869

Suez canal opened.

The University of Istanbul founded.

1870

Isaac Moïse Cremieux (known as Alphonse, but also as Albert and Adolphe), French minister of Justice, makes the Jews of Algeria (but not the Arabs) citizens of France. The law also extends French citizenship to European Jews and Christians who are willing to settle on occupied Arab lands or towns.

Baron Julius de Reuter is given exclusive rights to develop Iranian mineral resources, create a bank, exploit rail and telegraph. Strong objections are made on the part of Russia and the concessions are annulled.

1873
The Dutch attack the Muslim kingdom of Atjeh in Sumatra and capture the Sultan.

1874
Founding in India of the Aligarh school, later university, by Sir Sayyid Ahmed Khan.

1875
Introduction of a mixed civil and *shari'ah* legal system in Egypt.

1876
The *Majalla*, a uniform compilation of the laws of obligation based upon the Hanafi school begun in 1869 is completed.

The first Arab daily newspaper, *al-Ahram* in Cairo.

Rodwell's translation of the Koran into English.

1877
The Koran, translated into Russian from the Arabic by G. S. Sabliukov (1804-1880), is published in Kazan. This, until the end of the 20th century the only complete translation into Russian from Arabic (other Russian translations were from French), was, until perestroika, last published in 1907 with a parallel text in Arabic.

A lithographed Koran is published in Istanbul.

1878
At the end of his stay in Cairo, al-Afghani became the Grand Master of the Kawkab ash-Sharq ("Eastern Star") Masonic Lodge. His sojourn in Cairo began in 1871 after he left Istanbul, where he had arrived in 1869 from Afghanistan and India. He also set up a secret organisation called *Majami' al-'Urwa* in Egypt and North Africa with Muhammad 'Abduh. In 1879 al-Afghani was exiled from Egypt and went to India, and in 1883 to Paris.

1878-1879
The Second Anglo-Afghan war, again to counter Russian expansion; Britain retains control of foreign policy after the treaty of Gandomak.

Creation of the Persian Cossack Brigade, trained by Russian officers, as a Royal Guard. In 1921 its commander, Reza Shah will found the Pahlevi dynasty. This brigade was the first successful attempt to modernize the Iranian army which until then depended upon feudal levies.

1880
English translation of the Koran by E. H. Palmer, published in the Wisdom of the East series.

1881
French Occupy Tunisia; British occupy Egypt; Rise of the Mahdi of the Sudan.

1300 H. = 12 November 1882

1883
Jamal ad-Din al-Afghani publishes a response to a lecture of Ernest Renan's at the Sorbonne in which Renan characterized Islam "as the heaviest chain ever borne by humanity". Afghani's answer in the *Journal des Débats* (May 18, 1883) was the following: "Muslim society has still not freed itself from the tutelage of religion... I cannot prevent myself from hoping that Muhammadan society will one day succeed in breaking its bonds..." This is in strong contrast to what he would write in the *al-'Urwa al-Wuthqa*, in which he said, "I wish the monarch of all the Muslims to be the Koran, and the focus of their unity, their faith." Al-Afghani was born in the village of Asadabad in Iran in 1839. He was an agitator who sought his own self advancement by posing as an advocate of whatever ideology would serve his purpose at any one time. That he himself was indifferent to the ideas he advocated, except expediency and therefore modernism, is clear from his career which can be described as that of a political confidence man. He had the ability to charm audiences. He attached himself to such people as Muhammad 'Abduh and Sa'd Zaghlul, as he attached himself to any means which advanced his influence.

1884
Muhammad 'Abduh and Jamal ad-Din al-Afghani publish a magazine in Paris for Islamic reform called *al-Urwa al-Wuthqa* concerned with analyzing the internal and external situation of the Islamic world and proposing remedies for its problems.

1885
Khartoum seized by the Mahdi's forces; General Gordon killed; the Mahdi of the Sudan dies shortly thereafter.

1886
Jamal ad-Din al-Afghani goes back to Iran where he shocks Nasir ad-Din Shah in their first encounter and has himself put under surveillance. In 1887 al-Afghani leaves for Russia, but returns to Iran in 1890. After this stay he is expelled, moreover becoming the first known case of someone forced by the government from the refuge mosque (*bast*) of 'Abd al-'Aziz outside Teheran where he had repaired.

1887
Michelson-Morley experiment to demonstrate the existence of the "ether". A light wave is split into two beams, reflected back and measured for interference to

see if there is an "ether drag". The experimenters decide that there is no "ether drag" and that the ether does not exist. Until then it was assumed that light is propagated in an medium called the "ether". The importance of this experiment for religion is that until then, Western science assumed the same metaphysical hypothesis as that of Middle Ages Christianity; a hypothesis exactly similar to the "Five Divine Presences" (because both are derived from Zoroastrian ideas about the nature of reality.) This hypothesis, originated in Zoroastrianism but became the metaphysics of Islam, (scholastic) Christianity, and Buddhism. It says that there is a physical world, surrounded by a subtle world ("the ether"), which is surrounded by a spiritual world ("the world of angels") and that the spiritual world is contained in Being. The experiment reduced this hypothesis to the existence of a physical world only, making only matter real. It was this change in concepts which led to absolute materialism and laid the groundwork for the adoption of a "big bang theory". This experiment marks the adoption by science of a theory of metaphysical dualism. (Later experiments by Michelson led him to conclude that there was a "slight" ether drag; these were ignored by science. But in any case, the ether was a construct between material reality, and a non-material reality; the bridge between the two was abandoned after this experiment, without much philosophic reflection.) For Isaac Newton, religion and science were one; after this experiment God was banished from science, but with Him went the need for intellectual coherence.

1888

Ghulam Mirza Ahmad and the beginning of the Ahmadiyyah in India.

1889

Nasir ad-Din Shah of Iran leaves for his third visit to Europe in whose wake followed a number of foreign concessions and monopolies, among them, soon to be revoked, a concession for a national lottery. (Games of chance are forbidden in Islam.)

Britain and Russia create separate banks in Iran.

1891-92

Revolt in Iran against the tobacco concession of 1890 which awarded high profits and monopoly to a foreign company. The 'Ulama' led by Mirza Hasan Shirazi (the *Marja'i Taqlid*) mount a radical protest; the concession was revoked but the non-performance clause led to high Iranian foreign debts.

First major waves of Jewish immigration to Palestine in response to persecution in Eastern Europe and Russia.

Uprising of the Ahl-Haqq in Daylam led by a Sayyid Muhammad.

1893

The Durand line divides British India and Afghanistan, which today splits the Pashtuns between Afghanistan and Pakistan.

1896

Kitchener defeats Mahdists at Umdurman.

Nasir ad-Din Shah of Iran is assassinated by Mirza Rida Kirmani. a follower of Jamal ad-Din al-Afghani.

1897

First World Zionist Congress, Basel, Switzerland convened by Theodore Herzl, who wrote: "In Basel I created the Jewish State. In five years, perhaps, certainly in fifty, everyone will see it." (The idea of Zionism came to Herzl when he was watching a Wagnerian opera *Tannhäuser.*)

1898

The Fashoda incident. A conflict between French and British colonial interests in Africa in which the French seized a fortress in the Sudan and the British had to fight their way from Egypt to the fortress. The question was resolved through negotiation.

1900

The first manuscript of the *Umm al-Kitab*, in Persian, is found in Central Asia and brought to the Asiatic Museum of the Imperial Russian Academy. Further copies are found in 1906, 1914, and 1918. The greater part of the content of the book was probably originally written in Arabic in Kufah around the *2nd*/8th century, and is early Islamic Gnosis directed at co-opting nascent Islam.

Germany and the Ottoman Turks begin construction of the Hejaz railway; the Damascus to Medinah spur is completed in 1908.

1901

'Abd al-'Aziz (Ibn Sa'ud) takes Riyad.

German translations of the Koran by Grigull in Halle and by Max Henning in Leipzig.

1902

From 1902-1914, in four expeditions to Central Asia, Albert von le Coq and Albert Grünwedel bring back 1,000 fragments of Manichean texts in fourteen languages from the ruined Manichean monastery of Turfan, in Sinkiang.

1903

After the sixth Zionist Congress in Basel, the World Zionist Conference engages the London law firm of Lloyd George, Roberts & Co. to represent their interests. Lloyd George became Prime Minister during

WW I and issued the Balfour Declaration. Arthur Balfour, Foreign Minister in the latter part of WW I, was himself the Prime Minister in 1903.

1905

Beginning of the Salafiyyah movement.

Sir Aurel Stein excavates some Chinese Manichean texts amidst thousands of Buddhist texts in the Cave of the Thousand Buddhas at Dun Huang.

A legal case is brought in Bombay against the Aga Khan III by Hajji Bibi, a widow and sister of the Aga Khan's wife, Shahzadi. The sisters were daughters of Aga Jungi Shah who was killed in Jeddah along with his son while returning from pilgrimage in 1896. Jungi Shah was an uncle of the Aga Khan. The case proposed that the family, and not solely the Aga Khan, had rights to the property and income of the Aga Khan. The case was ruled against them, and in favor of the Aga Khan III, by the Judge Louis Pitman Russel in 1908, also further defining the sect as distinct from the Sunnis and the Twelve Imam Shi'ahs. (*See* also 1847 and 1866.)

Kaiser Wilhelm II visits Tangier and makes political waves with statements in favor of a free Morocco, at a time when Morocco is being gathered into the French orbit through loans that require the gradual surrender of sovereignty.

1906

The Conference of Algeciras prepares the way for the French Protectorate of Morocco.

The Dinshaway affair in Egypt: a British officer out hunting is killed by villagers; the harshness of British reprisals causes a scandal and Lord Cromer resigns.

French invasion of Morocco, using a riot in Casablanca as a pretext.

Arthur Balfour's first meeting with Chaim Weizman.

Muslims in India form a pro-independence organisation called the Muslim League separating from the Hindu dominated Indian National Congress.

December 30: A constitution is promulgated in Iran.

1907

Paul Pelliot goes to Dun Huang and brings backs texts which he edits along with Edouard Chavannes. Other texts are taken to Peking; Russian expeditions also bring some texts to Saint Petersburg

1909

The first Kibbutz or collective farm is founded at Deganiah in the Jordan Valley by Aaron David Gordon (1856-1922) and Russian Jews.

1911

The "Agadir Incident" in which a German gunboat the "Panther" was sent to Agadir to challenge French influence in Morocco.

1912

Muhammadiyyah, modernist reform movement in Indonesia.

A Balkan war by Serbs, Bulgarians, Montenegrins and Greeks to drive Turkey out of the peninsula.

The Sultan of Morocco signs the Treaty of the French Protectorate. The state had been undergoing a disintegration; in 1911 the Sultan, Moulay Hafiz, was obliged to call in French troops to put down an uprising of the tribes around Fez, and a pretender from Mauritania, al-Hiba had proclaimed himself Sultan in Tiznit and had taken Marrakesh. Spain gains control of the Rif after Spanish miners had been attacked.

1913

A second Balkan war centered on fighting between Serbs and Bulgarians after their defeat of Turkey the previous year.

Italian translations of the Koran by Fracassi published in Milan and one by Branchi published in Rome; also a Swedish translation by Zettersteen in Stockholm.

First Arab National Congress held in Paris demands recognition of Arabs as a nation within the Ottoman empire.

1914

Formation of secret Arab nationalist societies in the Ottoman Empire.

A report by a commission sent by The Carnegie Endowment for International Peace to study the reports of cruelty in the two Balkan wars is published on the eve of the outbreak of WW I. The report notes that in regions liberated from the Turks there is some sentiment which regrets their absence.

Outbreak of World War I; Turkey enters on the side of Germany because of an alliance fashioned by Enver Pasha, Minister of War.

Egypt, under British military occupation since 1882, becomes a British protectorate.

1915

May 7: The British liner *Lusitania* travelling from New

York to Liverpool is struck off the Irish coast by a single German torpedo; it is apparently carrying a cargo of munitions because the ship explodes; 1,200 lives are lost including 128 Americans. Strong American reaction but Americans are not instructed to travel on ships bearing non-belligerant flags.

The Turkish Governor of Syria, Jemal Pasha, has Zionist leaders arrested and deported from Palestine, among them David Ben Gurion and Yitzhak Ben Zvi, along with 12,000 Jews who are not Turkish citizens. He approves a decree which reads: "The Sublime Porte in its resentment of the provoking element which is planning to create in the Palestinian territory of the Ottoman Empire a Jewish government under the name of 'Zionism'... orders the confiscation of all Zionist stamps, flags, and cheques of the Anglo-Palestine Company... and orders all the Zionist societies and organisations to disband."

August 19: British steamer the *Arabic* is sunk off Ireland with the loss of two American lives. Germans apologize and offer compensation.

Arthur Balfour's second meeting with Chaim Weizman (the first was in 1906) in which he says: "You know, I was thinking of that conversation of ours, and I believe that after the guns stop firing you may get your Jerusalem."

1916

March 24: A British channel steamer the Sussex is sunk (purportedly, as it has been claimed that this was invented) with some loss of American life. Germany agrees to restrictions on submarine warfare.

In an account prepared in 1944 by Mr James A. Malcolm, one time Armenian advisor to the British Government on eastern affairs, he said he visited Sir Mark Sykes in the summer of 1916 and found him glum because of the bleak situation for Britain as a result of the War. Sir Mark Sykes complained of not being able to enlist the "substantial" Jewish influence in America to bring about American intervention on the side of Britain. "Reports from America revealed a very pro-German tendency among wealthy American-Jewish bankers and bond houses, nearly all of German origin, and among them Jewish journalists who took their cue from them... I inquired what special argument of consideration the Allies put forward to win over American Jewry... Sir Mark replied that he made use of the same argument as used elsewhere, viz., that we shall eventually win and it was better to be on the winning side...

"I informed him that there was a way to make American Jewry thoroughly pro-Ally, and make them conscious that only an Allied victory could be of permanent benefit to Jewry all over the world... I said to him, 'You are going the wrong way about it... do you know of the Zionist Movement?'... Sir Mark admitted ignorance of the movement and I told him something about it and concluded by saying, 'you can win the sympathy of the Jews everywhere in one way only, and that way is by offering to try and secure Palestine for them'... Sir Mark was taken aback. He confessed that what I had told him was something quite new and most impressive...

"He [Sykes] told me that Lord Milner was greatly interested to learn of the Jewish Nationalist movement but could not see any possibility of promising Palestine to the Jews... I replied that seemed to be the only way to acheive the desired result, and mentioned that one of President Wilson's most intimate friends, for whose humanitarian views he has the greatest respect, was Justice Brandeis of the Supreme Court, who was a convinced Zionist...

"If he could obtain from the War Cabinet an assurance that help would be given to securing Palestine for the Jews, it was certain that Jews in all neutral contries would become pro-British and pro-Ally... I said I thought it would be sufficient if I were personally convinced of the sincerity of the Cabinet's intentions so that I could go to the Zionists and say, 'If you help the Allies, you will have the support of the British in securing Palestine for the Jews'...

"A day or two later, he informed me that the Cabinet had agreed to my suggestion and authorized me to open negotiations with the Zionists... A wealthy and influential anti-Zionist banker... was shown the telegram announcing the provisional promise of Palestine to the Jews... he was very much moved and said, 'How can a Jew refuse such a gift?'

"All these steps were taken with the full knowledge and approval of Justice Brandeis, between whom and Dr. Weizmann there was an active interchange of cables..." Mr Malcolm, an Oxford educated Armenian, had actually been charged by the Armenian Church Prelate with wresting Eastern Turkey as a homeland for the Armenians, instead succeeded in wresting Palestine as a homeland for Jews. Despite James Malcolm's account, which he doubtless believed to be the first suggestion of a British government contract with Zionism, it is clear that other members of the British government had contacts and were cognizant of the possibilities before Malcolm. The decision to turn to the Zionists was signaled by the change in British government which took place in December 1916 but was already in process; the law firm of Lloyd George had been engaged by the Zionist Conference in 1903 to represent their interests.

Arab revolt against the Turks. Husayn, the Sharif of Mecca (1854-1931) who reigned in Mecca from 1908 to 1916, and then declared himself King of Hejaz until he was conquered by 'Abd al-'Aziz ibn Sa'ud in 1925, with his two sons, 'Abd Allah and Faisal, opens warfare on the colonial power, the Turks. T. E. Lawrence leads attacks on the Hejaz railway.

Sykes-Picot Agreement (which is secret) agrees to divide the Arab territories of the Turkish empire into French and British zones of influence after the war.

October: Jews of German origin in America, such as the wealthy lawyer Samuel Untermyer, and his friend Supreme Court Justice Louis Brandeis, up until this time, supported Germany in the war; but in anticipation of the Balfour Declaration apparently broached in secret discussions at this time they abruptly changed sides for the British, and threw their support for America's entry into the war against Germany. Brandeis advised Wilson that the Sussex sinking justified declaring war on Germany. The *Hilfsverein der deutschen Jueden*, located in Berlin transfers its loyalty from Germany to the Allies.

Woodrow Wilson was re-elected to a second term as US president with the slogan "He kept us out of war." Wilson was attempting to bring an end to the war without victory for either side. In December, Herbert Asquith, Prime Minister in Britain since 1908 was forced to resign; a new war cabinet was formed with Lloyd George as Prime Minister and Arthur Balfour as Foreign Minister. On December 18, the US ambassador to Britain conveyed an "offer of peace" to Britain on the part of the Central Powers. On the following day in his first speech to Parliament as Prime Minister Lloyd George heaped scorn on the proposal and vowed that Britain and its allies would fight on to final victory.

1917

January 9: The German government makes the decision to begin unrestricted submarine warfare on February 1.

January 16: Zimmermann Note sent, encoded from Berlin to the German ambassador in Washington by several routes, including through the US Embassy in Berlin via Copenhagen and Britain, which monitored American diplomatic traffic. The Zimmermann note is a rather preposterous contingency plan, proposed to Zimmerman, German Minister of Foreign Affairs by Herr von Kemnitz, an East Asia expert in the German foreign office, of what to do if America entered the War because of the declaration of unrestricted submarine warfare around Britain. In such a case, the German ambassador in Mexico was instructed to offer an alliance inviting Mexico to attack the United States with German support with the prospect of regaining territories lost to the U.S. such as Texas, Arizona and New Mexico! Many believe the idea was thought up in Britain and insinuated to the Germans through British agents with the intention of creating the incident which actually followed.

January 19: Zimmermann Note forwarded, encoded, from the German Embassy in Washington to the German legation in Mexico by Western Union telegram.

January 20: Presumed date when the Zimmermann note is decoded by the British.

Late January: Chaim Weizmann is introduced to Mark Sykes and submits to him a memorandum entitled "Outline of Program for the Jewish resettlement of Palestine in accordance with the aspirations of the Zionist movement."

January 31: Germany announces unrestricted submarine warfare against Britain, to begin the following day.

February 3: U.S. breaks off diplomatic relations with Germany. The German ambassador, Count von Bernstorff, is given his passport and told to leave the U.S.

February 7: Sykes meets with Weizmann and other Zionist leaders.

February 14: Count von Bernstorff leaves New York on the Danish steamer Friedrich VIII bound for Copenhagen with safe conduct from the British on condition that the ship stop at Halifax, Nova Scotia, for inspection. Bernstorff at the time of the sinking of the Lusitania almost single-handedly prevented war between Germany and the U.S.

February 16: The ship Friedrich VIII enters Halifax and is held there without communication for almost two weeks.

February 17: Conference among leading Zionists in Britain leading to the Balfour Declaration.

February 26: The U.S. State Department receives a telegram from London containing an English translation of the Zimmermann Note purportedly decoded by the British. The American ambassador in London, Walter Page, had received a copy of the Zimmerman note supposedly obtained by the British in Mexico, from the version sent from the German Embassy in Washington to Mexico in an old code through Western Union. But that text actually matched the text transmitted from Berlin to Washington in a new code which was supposedly not yet broken.

February 27: Friedrich VIII permitted to sail from Halifax.

March 1st: Text of the Zimmermann Note published in the U.S. Greeted with great tumult by Congress and the press.

Woodrow Wilson describes the February Russian Revolution as "wonderful and heartening things that have been happening in Russia."

March 27: Trotsky leaves New York with 250 revolutionaries for Russia with a large amount of money in cash and more waiting in Sweden; his ship stops in Halifax, Canada, where the British, knowing that this is a danger, Russia could withdraw from the war, attempt to prevent him from going to Russia, but are obliged, by pressure from the US, to let him go. Trotsky arrives in Russia on May 17.

April 3: Lenin arrives in Petrograd from Switzerland with fifty exiled Bolsheviks. He also picks up money in Sweden. The Germans had cultivated the revolutionaries and now sent them in a "sealed" train through Germany in order to foment more trouble in Russia which is an important British ally, despite the earlier Revolution.

April 6: The U.S. declares war on Germany.

April 16: Chaim Weizmann is dismayed to learn of the secret Sykes-Picot agreement to divide Turkish territories between the British and French. The agreement is modified to keep part of northern Palestine not with French controlled Syria but within British controlled Palestine.

October 1: Faysal and the Arabs occupy Damascus.

November 2: The British government "issues", in the form of a letter from Arthur Balfour to Lord Walter Rothschild, head of the organisation of British Zionists, the Balfour Declaration in which Britain endorses the establishment in Palestine of "a national home for the Jewish people" on the understanding that "nothing shall be done which may prejudice the civil and religious rights of existing non-Jewish communities in Palestine". Because of a remark by Lloyd George ("acetone converted me to Zionism") it was often said that the Declaration was a "reward" to the Chemist Chaim Weizmann for his development of an alternative process to make acetone which was necessary to manufacture explosives such as nitrocellulose and cordite in England when these materials could not be obtained from Germany. In addition to an undisputed desire to assure high explosives for the War, it is also said that Lloyd George was motivated by Christian piety. However, in 1937 to a commission on Palestine he said it was done in order to secure international Jewish support for the war. And, as Churchill said in Parliament shortly after the war, "it is not as if we got nothing for the Balfour declaration". Chaim Weizmann received 10,000 pounds sterling for his chemical work from the British government. Within days of the Balfour Declaration, another remarkable event takes place:November: The Bolshevik coup d'état takes over the Russian revolution. The Germans had implemented their own plan which was to sow chaos in Russia by sending Lenin with many revolutionaries into Russia. Under Lenin, Russia soon withdrew from the War. Churchill would write in 1920: "The struggle which is now beginning between the Zionist and Bolshevik Jews is little less than a struggle for the soul of the Jewish people." Weizmann had a brother who was a Communist. Weizmann quotes his own mother as saying if the Communist revolutionary son was proved right she would be content to live in Communist Russia, but if the Zionist revolution triumphed she would be happy in Palestine. She lived in Russia until 1948 and then ended her days in Israel.

December 11: Allenby enters Jerusalem.

Translation of the Koran into English by Mawlana Muhammad Ali. This translation and its commentary reflects the point of view of the Ahmadiyyah sect.

1918

Armistice with the Ottomans on 30 October. World War I ends 11 November.

Zaghlul and the *wafd* movement in Egypt.

Manichean manuscript found in a cave near Tebessa (Theveste) in Algeria.

1919

Third Anglo-Afghan War; Afghan army attacks British troops in India; Britain gives up its interest in Afghanistan which becomes a fully independent state.

1920

Britain is granted League of Nations mandate at the San Remo conference to govern Palestine, which is defined as lands on both sides of the Jordan River. France is given a mandate in Syria from which Lebanon will be created. The British general occupying Baghdad declares that Britain is bringing democracy to Iraq.

"Great Iraqi Revolt", Sunnis, Shi'ites, and Kurds together revolt against the British in Iraq.

A "passionate" Zionist, Sir Herbert Samuel is made High Commissioner for Palestine 1920-1925. Sir Herbert had been involved in the initial negotiationes regarding the Balfour Declaration. Avi Schlaim writes that the British government "could not have chosen a more suitable man for the post". The Chief Administrative officer asked him to sign a receipt: "Received from Major General Sir Louis Bols, KCB – One Palestine, complete." Sir Samuel is faulted by others for being too conciliatory towards the Arabs of Palestine and actually trying to slow down Jewish immigration as being too distabilizing.

Treaty of Sèvres reduces Ottoman Empire to Anatolia.

1921

The sons of Husayn, the Sharif of Mecca, 'Abd Allah and Faysal, are made Kings of Transjordan and Iraq, respectively.

Afghanistan signs treaties of friendship with Turkey, Italy, Persia, and Russia.

1921-1926

The revolt of 'Abd al-Karim against colonial rule in Moroccan Rif; declaration of "the Republic of the Rif".

1922

Egypt becomes independent of British control.

Mustafa Kemal, who, many Turks claim is from a *D'nmeh* family (see 1676) on his father's side, abolishes the Turkish Sultanate.

1923

Chinese scholars take notice of a shrine in southern Fukien presumed to be dedicated to Mu-ni thought to be Sakyamuni, the Buddha. Further research by a local archeologist shows that it is actually dedicated to Mo Mo-Ni (Mar Mani), and the site is a Manichean pseudo-Buddhist temple from the 14th century. But scholars then overlook the temple which is not identified again until 1957.

Treaty of Lausanne signed with Turkey creating modern Turkey's borders.

Transjordan is split from Palestine but remains under British mandate until 1946.

Zionist leader Vladimir Jabotinsky writes in the "Iron Will" that a people have never submitted willingly to a colonisation of their homeland and the Arabs in Palestine would not be the first.

1924

The Turkish Caliphate abolished. Husayn of Mecca declares himself Caliph in Amman.

The typeset "Royal Egyptian Koran" called the *mushaf al-malik* is published in Cairo at the order of Fu'ad I. Using the reading of Hafs as transmitted by 'Asim, it becomes a standard edition.

Revolt of Uzun Haji in Daghestan against Soviet power.

According to W. J. M. Childs, in Harold W.V. Temperley, ed., *A History of the Peace Conference of Paris*, the reason for the Balfour declaration lay in the state of Russia at the time [1916]: "Russian Jews had been secretly active on behalf of the Central Powers from the first; they had been the chief agents of German pacifist propaganda; by 1917 they had done much in preparation for that general disintegration of Russian national life, later recognized as the revolution. It was believed that if Great Britain declared for the fulfillment of Zionist aspirations in Palestine under its own pledge, one effect would be to bring Russian Jewry to the cause of the Entente... it was believed further, that it would greatly influence American opinion in favor of the Allies. Such were the chief considerations, which during the later part of 1916 and the next ten months of 1917, impelled the British Government towards making a contract with Jewry. But when the matter came before the British Cabinet... Jewish influence within and without the Cabinet is understood to have exerted itself strenuously and pertinaciously against the proposed Declaration. Under the pressure of Allied needs the objections of the anti-Zionists were either overruled or the causes of the objection removed, and the Balfour Declaration was published to the world on 2nd November 1917. That it is in purpose a definite contract with Jewry is beyond question." The objections were those of old English Jewish families such as that of Edwin Montagu, Secretary for India, who felt their identity as loyal British citizens would be compromised by Zionism. Weizmann's view of Jewish identity was expressed in his famous address to the First Jewish Congress: "There are no English, French, German, or American Jews, but only Jews living in England, in France, in Germany, or in America."

1925

King 'Abd al-'Aziz conquers Mecca and Medinah. Union of the Kingdom of the Najd and Hejaz.

Reza Khan seizes government in Iran and establishes Pahlavi dynasty.

1926

King of the Najd 'Abd al-'Aziz (Ibn Sa'ud) takes title of "King of Najd and Hejaz."

1927

Death of the Egyptian nationalist leader Zaghlul.

1928

Turkey declared a secular state. The Arab alphabet is replaced with the Latin.

Hasan al-Banna founds the Muslim Brotherhood.

Secular code and new court system adopted in Iran.

Nazira Zayn ad-Din calls the women's Islamic veil: "A veil of cloth, a veil of ignorance, a veil of hypocrisy, and a veil of stagnation". (cited by Fuad Ajami in "Dream Palaces of the Arabs".

1929

Abdication of Amir Amanullah in Afghanistan following resistance and backlash from social reforms which he introduced starting in 1923.

Italian translation of the Koran by Bonelli, Milan; a new but inaccurate French translation by Montet.

1930

Muhammad Marmaduke Pickthall's translation of the Koran into English, the first reliable one, appears. It is still the most reliable complete translation for the religious sense. Pickthall followed the major traditional commentaries and was himself a Muslim who understood the Koran. Pickthall had turned to the al-Azhar for advice; this caused a debate to rage whether or not the Koran should be translated at all. In fact, there can be little doubt that throughout its history the Koran has been translated to aid its study by those who were not Arabic speakers. In the 18th century well-known translations were made into Persian and Urdu.

1932

Turkish women receive equal political rights.

Saudi Arabia adopts the name of "Kingdom of Hejaz and Nejd."

Iraq is recognized as an independent monarchy.

1933

The Eastern Turkestan Islamic Republic is declared in Kashgar, in the Uighur region which is Chinese Xinjiang. This is short-lived and a decade later Uighurs found another republic further north in Yili and govern a semi-autonomous area there under Kuomintang control until Communists take over in 1949.

1934

War between King 'Abd al-'Aziz and Imam Yahya of the Yemen; Peace treaty of Ta'if. 'Asir becomes part of Saudi Arabia.

Death of Ahmad al-'Alawi in Algeria, a Darqawi Sufi Shaykh who had 200,000 disciples in the Islamic world.

A translation of the Koran into English is made by 'Abd Allah Yusuf 'Ali, a Bohora Isma'ili. The translation and commentary reflect the views of his sect.

New surge of Jewish immigration to Palestine with the persecution of Jews by the Third Reich.

1935

Iran becomes the official name of Persia.

1936

A member of Weizmann's circle, Samuel Landman, publishes a pamphlet entitled *Great Britain, the Jews, and Palestine* in which he complains that in 1916 there was a "gentlemen's agreement" between the Zionists and the British Goverment; the Zionists rôle was to "induce the American president to come into the War on the British side". The Zionists had fulfilled their side (and that their wartime service accounted in "no small measure" for Nazi anti-semitism) while the British had not delivered a Jewish state in Palestine.

French translation of the Koran by Pesle and Tidjani.

The Jewish defense force in Palestine, the Haganah, numbers 25,000, while "Tower and Stockade" settlements are built on land bought by the Jewish National Fund which by 1948 had bought 231,000 acres, and established 83,000 agricultural settlers in 233 settlements.

Between 1936 and 1939 the British suppress an Arab Revolt in Palestine, an action which Shlomo Ben-Ami writing in 2006 credited with determining Zionist success in 1948.

Afghanistan signs mutual trade agreement with the USSR and a treaty of friendship with the USA.

1937

Richard Bell's translation of the Koran into English. It assumes that where there is a shift of subject or tone "an editorial change" has taken place in the text. These places are marked; the format and the frame of mind it creates destroys it as a translation for someone interested in the spirituality of the Koran as understood by Muslims, although it has evident scholarly value.

Atatürk dies and is succeeded as President of Turkey by Ismet Inönü.

1939-1945

World War II.

1940

Muslim League demands partition of India.

The King of Morocco, Mohammad V, refuses to cooperate with Vichy measures against Jews. He says "There are no Jews in Morocco, only Moroccan subjects."
Iran is pro-German. The Soviet Union invades Iran from the north and the British from the south to force Reza Shah to abdicate in favor of his son Mohammad Reza Shah.

Lebanon declares independence from France.

1941

All the mosques in Algiers on one day preach sermons calling upon Muslims not to cooperate with Vichy anti-Jewish measures.

1944

The Arab League founded.

Lord Moyne, British Colonial Secretary and cabinet minister for Palestine, who thought that making it a "homeland for Jews" would end disastrously, is assassinated in Cairo by Zionists.

1945

Some 100,000 Jews arrive in Palestine during and just after the war, many running a British blockade.

The Ba'th party founded by Michel Aflaq and Salah ad-Din Bitar.

1946

January 22, Qazi Muhammad proclaims a Kurdish republic in the Mahabad region of Iran. The army of this republic is led by Mulla Mustafa Barzani and his brother Shaykh Ahmad from Iraq. At the end of the year the Iranian army retakes Mahabad without a fight; Qazi Muhammad is hanged and the Barzanis return to Iraq and then fight their way through Turkey and northern Iran to the Soviet Union where they live as refugees for a decade.

US and British government reports say that "very large numbers of Jews, almost amounting to a second Exodus, have been migrating from Eastern Europe to the American zones of Germany and Austria with the intention in the majority of cases of making their way to Palestine... part of a carefully organized plan financed by special groups in the United States." Dr Chaim Weizmann demanded the resignation of General Morgan for publicly calling attention to this mass movement of people in otherwise occupied Europe. The subject later became part of documentaries frequently shown on National Public Television in America.

1947

August 14: Partition of India and Pakistan.

October: A rebellion breaks out in Kashmir. Pakistan sends in troops. The Hindu Maharajah signs an agreement to join India in exchange for military support.
November 27: United Nations partition plan of Palestine, by a vote of 33 to 13 with 10 abstentions and one absent. At the age of 24, Shimon Peres is manpower chief of the Haganah, the fledgling Jewish military. The Soviet Union assists with military equipment. Czechoslovakia becomes an arms supplier to Israel into the early fifties, when that role is taken over by the U.S.

December 18: Under Plan Gimmel to expand Jewish settlements in Arab areas, Palmach troops of the underground Haganah army attacked the Palestinian village of Khissas in northern Galilee.

1948

India and Pakistan go to war over Kashmir. The fighting continues until 1949 when the UN arranges a cease-fire.

April 10: Massacre of 254 Arab men, women, and children at Deir Yassin by the Irgun, one of whose leaders was Menachem Begin, later Prime Minister of Israel. Begin was also wanted for murder in Britain, which he never visited, for the death of four British soldiers.

May 14: end of the British Mandate of Palestine and establishment of the State of Israel. Thirty-seven men attend a meeting in Tel Aviv, which declares the independence of Israel as "a natural and historic right". Of the thirty-seven participants, one was born in Palestine, one in Yemen, and thirty-five in Europe. Arab armies enter Palestine on May 15 in response to the attacks begun on Arab villages in December and conquest of areas of Palestine outside of what was defined by the UN Arab-Israel war. The Five Arab armies which entered Palestine totaled 13,876; the Israeli troops were 27,400 and were better armed. At the end of the war Israel expands to 77.4% of Palestine from 56.47% at the beginning.

September 17: Count Folke Bernadotte assassinated by the Stern Gang, one of whose leaders was Yitzhak Shamir, later Prime Minister of Israel. Bernadotte was attempting to negotiate an armistice between Jews and Arabs. He had prepared a report, not yet made public, that the Negev, which had been seized, should be returned to the Arabs and that Jerusalem should be made an international city. Also killed with Bernadotte was a French colonel named Serot. A French news agency received a letter expressing regret about the Frenchman because the intended victim was a Swedish general named Lündstrom, also in the car, who was "also an Anti-Semite" (that is, like "Bernadotte".) Bernadotte had negotiated with Himmler to save ten thousand Jews but aspersions had been cast on his sympathies, although Bernadotte thought his work had earned him goodwill. It is said that the murderers had fled to Czechoslovakia.

Transjordan renamed Arab Hashimite Kingdom of Jordan.

1949

Assassination of Hasan al-Banna.

Regis Blachère publishes a new French translation of the Koran: *Le Coran, Traduction Nouvelle.*

James Forrestal, US Secretary of Defense, commits suicide. He had become identified with opposition to United Nations policy on Palestine. He had said that the "decision was fraught with great danger for the future security of this country" and had tried to remove the question from the political agendas of both parties, by mutual agreement between Democrats and Republicans, as an issue not in the US interest.

Israel signs an armistice with Egypt in February, Lebanon in March, Jordan in April, Syria in July.

In Syria the civilian government of Shukri al-Quwatli is overthrown by Colonel Husni Za'im in March. Za'im is overthrown by Colonel al-Hinnawi in August, and replaced by Colonel Adib Shishakli in December.

1950

Menderes becomes Prime Minister in Turkey.

Mohammed Ali Jinnah, the founder of Pakistan, dies of tuberculosis. Terrorist attacks on Jews in Baghdad, including an attack on the Shem-Tov synagogue in which three people die. These were later revealed in Israel to be Zionist attempts to force a reluctant Jewish population to immigrate. (*Ha-Olam Hazeh*, 20 April and 1 June 1966; Ilan Halevi.)

1951

Libyan independence.

Mossadegh becomes Prime Minister in Iran. Iranian oil is nationalized.

King Abdullah of Jordan assassinated in Jerusalem, while his grandson Hussein, who was at his side, is unhurt.

1952

King Faruq of Egypt forced to abdicate.

Hussein becomes King of Jordan, replacing his father Talal who is declared mentally unfit.

1953

Four Irgun men, wounded at the Deir Yassin massacre, claim compensation from the Israeli government, which first rejects their claims as stemming from an "unauthorized" attack, whereupon they produce a letter from a military headquarters in Jerusalem authorizing the action.

Colonel Ariel Sharon leads a "reprisal" raid against the Jordanian town of Qibya, blowing up 45 houses and killing every living soul, 69 Arab villagers, the majority of them women and children. He said later he had thought the houses were empty.

Shimon Peres is Director General of Israeli Defense Ministry; sets up electronics and aircraft industries and persuades France to supply Israel with a nuclear reactor. In the U.S. he works to obtain desired military supplies.

July 17: Israel attempted to buy Jet warplanes starting in 1948 but only succeeded in buying German WW II Messerschmits. Finally Britain was the first to sell Israel such aircraft and on this date the first British Gloucestor Meteor Jets arrive at Ramat Aviv airbase.

August. The Shah dismisses Mossadegh; there are riots and the Shah flees Iran; after American orchestrated counter demonstrations in favor of the Shah he returns and Mossadegh is placed under arrest. Mossadegh falls in a coup d'etat afterwards.

In November, a foundation stone is laid in the expansion of the Prophet's mosque in Medinah.

King 'Abd al-'Aziz, founder of the Kingdom of the Saudi Arabia, dies and is succeeded by his son Sa'ud. General Mohammad Daoud becomes Prime Minister in Afghanistan and turns to the Soviet Union for economic and military aid after the US declines to help.

1954

The government of Shishakli in Syria is removed by the army.

October 26; the Muslim Brotherhood attempts to assassinate Nasser.

Algerian revolution against France begins.

The Pope crowns Mary "Queen of Heaven" in an elaborate ceremony at the Basilica of St. Peter.

1955

A. J. Arberry's translation, *The Koran Interpreted* is published.

February: beginning of Baghdad Pact with Turkish-Iraqi agreement, Britain, Pakistan, and Iran join in several months.

April: Non-aligned conference at Bandung.

1956

End of French Protectorate in Morocco.

Tunisian independence.

J. H. Kramer's translation of the Koran into Dutch.

March 23: Pakistan is proclaimed an Islamic republic.

July. Nassar nationalizes Suez Canal.

October 29. Israel invades Sinai.

November 5: Anglo-French force invades the Suez Canal Zone.

December 22: Anglo-French force in Canal Zone replaced by UN troops.

1957

Bey of Tunisia deposed; Bourguiba becomes president.

The Chinese Manichean shrine of Quanzhou, Fujian is located by an archeologist named Wu Wen-liang.

1958

February 1: United Arab Republic created by Egypt and Syria.

U.S. Marines in Lebanon from July to October.

The King of Iraq is overthrown by a revolt led by Colonel Qasim.

1959

Shimon Peres is first elected to Parliament; he is appointed Deputy Defense Minister.

1961

English translation of the Koran by N. J. Dawood.

Syria leaves the United Arab Republic.

Pakistan "closes" its border with Afghanistan (the Khyber Pass) to discourage Pashtun efforts at reunification with the Pashtun in Afghanistan.

1962

July 5: Independence of Algeria from France after the beginning of a war of liberation in

Death of Ahmad, the Zaydi Imam of the Yemen; he is succeeded by Crown Prince Badr who takes the name Imam Mansur Bi-Llah Muhammad. Shortly thereafter civil war begins with Egypt and the Soviet Union supports Republican forces, and Saudi Arabia supports Loyalists. Although the Republicans were victorious, the influence of Saudi Arabia reasserted itself in the country during the 1970s.

September 8: In Algeria, a constitution is adopted making it a one-party state under a President and the National Liberation Front.

September 15, Ahmed Ben Bella is elected President-Foundation of the Islamic League (*Rabita*).

1963

Feb. Ba'th party comes to power in Syria.

Kratchkovsky's Russian translation of the Koran is published posthumously.

Riots in Iran against the government of the Shah. Khomeini plays a leading role.

Yasser Arafat founds the al-Fatah Palestinian organisation.

Iranian women are given the right to vote.

Mohammad Daoud forced to resign as Prime Minister in Afghanistan following border disputes with Pakistan.

1964

The beginning of the Ogaden conflicts which last until 1988. Somalia attempted unsuccessfully to occupy Ethiopia's Ogaden area, home to an ethnic Somali majority.

Khomeini is exiled from Iran.

April 14: In Algeria, first wave of nationalisations starts.

May 28: The PLO is formed in Jerusalem and draws up a Palestine National Charter as its framework.

June 15: In Algeria, French army pulls out last units.

A constitution is adopted in Afghanistan in view of democracy but King Zahir Shah and the legislature fail to agree on reforms.

1965

Malcolm X assassinated.

June 19: Revolutionary council led by Houari Boumediene takes power in Algeria. Ben Bella arrested.

September: The issue of Kashmir flares into war between Pakistan and India. New UN cease-fire brokered by the Soviet Union as the Tashkent declaration.

Mehdi Ben Barka, a prominent Moroccan nationalist and opposition figure is kidnapped in Paris and never seen again.

1966

A new German translation of the Koran by Rudi Paret.

1967

June 5: Israeli airstrikes on Egypt and Syria begin the "Six Day War".

June 8: Israeli Jets attempt to sink the U.S. observer ship *Liberty* which appears at the moment that Israel plans to invade Syria, an action discouraged by the U.S. and while an alleged massacre was taking place of Egyptian prisoners. In repeated attacks by Israeli aircraft and torpedo boats 34 Americans are killed and 171 wounded from a 295 man crew. U.S. planes from an American Carrier launched to defend the Liberty were twice recalled in the air by Washington. The U.S. government covered up the incident and even prevented survivors from the ship from creating a monument, citing Israel's contention that the attack was an accident. However, the National Security Agency had a Navy plane overhead which recorded conversations by the Israeli pilots showing that they were fully aware of what they were doing and that the attack was deliberate. (*NYT* April 23, 2001).

July 28: Israel annexes old Jerusalem.

November 4: Coup in the Yemen by 'Abd ar-Rahman al-Iryani against 'Abdullah Sallal.

UN resolution 242 which calls upon Israel to withdraw from lands conquered in the six day war and affirms a right for Israel's security within its pre-1967 borders.

November 30: British troops leave Aden, which will become South Yemen or the People's Democratic Republic of Yemen until unification with the Arab Republic of Yemen (San'a) in 1990.

1968

Completion of expansion of the Grand Mosque of Mecca which was begun in 1957. 142,200 sq. meters of space added; the *sa'y* and *tawaf* may be performed on two levels. The capacities of the new mosque are: 15,000 persons may perform the *sa'y* at one time or .6 million per day; 28,000 can perform *tawaf* at one time; 124,000 can pray at one time under normal conditions, and under the conditions of hajj 275,000 have been accommodated at one time with another 100,000 outside around the mosque.

Following a proclamation of freedom of worship in Spain the year before, the first new synagogue is opened in Spain since the expulsion of Jews in 1492.

The charter of the PLO is revised stating that "armed struggle is the sole means for liberating Palestine".

July 17: Coup in Iraq; Ahmad Hasan al-Bakr becomes President.

July 23: El-Al airliner hijacked to Algeria.

October 26: General Hafiz al-Asad overthrows the government in Syria in a bloodless coup which he calls the "corrective movement".

December 26: Attack on El-Al airliner in Athens.

1969

February 3: Yasser Arafat is acknowledged leader of the Palestine Liberation Organisation.

February 18: Attack on an Israeli airliner – General Hafiz al-Asad takes direct control of Syrian government.

July 1: Israel moves its government offices from Tel Aviv to Jerusalem.

August: Israel attacks villages in Lebanon which it says are Palestinian bases.

August 21: a mentally disturbed American Jew sets fire to the al-Aqsa mosque in Jerusalem.

August 29: TWA airliner hijacked by Palestinians.

September 1: King Idris of Libya ousted in a coup led by Colonel Qaddafi.

A Lebanese Shi'ite Shaykh from Lebanon, 'Abd al-Monem az-Zein, trained in Najaf, arrives in Dakar, Senegal and begins proselytizing Shi'ism.

1970

A cyclone and tidal wave strike East Pakistan, killing 266,000 people. East Pakistan accuses the government in West Pakistan of delaying relief supplies. In Pakistan the military junta rejects in "East Pakistan" or Bengal, the election of Shaykh Mujiber Rahman's Awami League and arrests Mujiber Rahman. This leads to civil war and the break-up of Pakistan and the creation of Bangladesh as the Indian army intervenes.

July: Completion of Aswan High Dam.

July: Qabus bin Sa'id overthrows his father and takes control of the Sultanate of Oman.

PFLP hijack Swiss and American airliners and blow them up releasing passengers.

"Black September". King Hussein of Jordan attacks armed Palestinian formations in his country. The struggle began a year earlier and will end the following year with the elimination of a Palestinian military presence in Jordan.

Syria sent tanks into Jordan to support the Palestinians; these were repulsed by Jordanian air attacks and in the disarray which followed Hafez al-Asad consolidates his power.

September 28: Nasser dies and Anwar as-Sadat becomes President of Egypt.

December Zulfikar Ali Bhutto's Pakistan People's Party wins in Pakistan.

1971

April: Establishment of Bangladesh, formerly East Pakistan.7 May: Soviet-Egyptian Treaty of Friendship signed.

A celebration of twenty-five centuries of Iranian rule is held by the Shah at Persepolis; this identification with Achaemenid Iran contributes to the alienation of the religious classes. It perhaps also symbolizes the resurgence of an ancient struggle between the principle of royal rule and that of rule by priests. The event is followed by the growth of clandestine organisations amongst religious students dedicated to a radical restoration of Islam.

A poet of Syrian Alawi origin, 'Ali Ahmad Said, famous in the Arabic speaking world under the pen name Adonis, publishes a poem named "The Funeral of New York" in which a nameless narrator wanders through the financial district and Harlem looking in vain for Walt Whitman's ghost and angrily imagining "an eastern wind uprooting skyscrapers, a cloud necklaced with fire" and "people melting like tears".

December: After the secession of East Pakistan or Bangladesh, a third war which lasts two weeks over Kashmir between India and Pakistan.

1972

Formation of the Islamic Conference.

April: Soviet-Iraqi treaty of Friendship signed.

May 30: Three Japanese kill 26 persons at Lod Airport in Tel Aviv.

July 18: President Anwar as-Sadat orders Soviet advisors to leave Egypt.

July: Peace agreement between India and Pakistan calls for peaceful Kashmiri negotiations.

September 5: Palestinian attack on Israeli Olympic team in Munich; 11 Israelis killed.

Repairs on the Great Mosque of Sana'a in Yemen reveal a "paper grave", like the Genizah in Egypt, between two roofs; this was a place to preserve old religious texts which could not be thrown away. Fragments of very old Korans are found among the documents, which still have to be thoroughly studied.

1973

February 21: Israel shoots down Libyan airliner over Sinai.

April 10: Three Palestinian leaders, including the head of FATAH are killed in Beirut by Israeli commandos.

July: King Zahir Shah of Afghanistan overthrown. He goes into exile in Rome. The coup leader, Mohammad Daoud, proclaims a republic but rules in an authoritarian fashion.

August: Pakistan adopts a Constitution providing for a president as head of state and a Prime Minister as chief executive. Bhutto becomes prime minister.

October 6: The Yom Kippur War. Egypt and Syria attack Israel; The Soviet Union gives aid to the Arabs and on October 14 the U.S. begins re-supplying Israel.

October 16: After a vast tank battle in the Sinai, the Israelis cross the Suez canal.

October 23: UN Security Council resolution 339 which repeats resolution 338 calling for a cease-fire; accepted by warring nations. On October 28 negotiations begin between Egypt and Israel at kilometer 101 on the Suez-Cairo road.

November 5: The Organisation of Arab Oil Exporting Countries announces an embargo of oil to the United States and the Netherlands.

1974

Pakistan extends recognition to Bangladesh, former East Pakistan.

The Turkish Prime Minister, Bulent Ecevit seeks support of Milli Sulamit, the National Salvation Party, an Islamic Fundamentalist group.

After Golda Meir resigns as Prime Minister, Shimon Peres loses contest for party leadership to Yitzhak Rabin; Peres becomes Defense Minister and rebuilds military.

March 18: Arab oil embargo of the United States lifted.

October 28: The Arab League meeting in Rabat recognizes the PLO as the sole legitimate representative of the people of Palestine.

November 13: Yassir 'Arafat addresses the United Nations General Assembly.

1975

Secretary of State Henry Kissinger signs a "memorandum of understanding" which obligates the US to maintain a strategic reserve for, and to ship oil, to Israel, even if there are US shortages, in times of crisis, in US tankers. It costs the US about 3 billion a year. (Observer, 4/20/2003).

March 7: Agreement between Iraq and Iran regarding Khuzistan.

March 25: King Faysal of Saudi Arabia is assassinated by a deranged nephew of his at a *majlis* or open reception.

Elijah Muhammad dies; Wallace Warith Deen Muhammad becomes leader of the "Nation of Islam" among Blacks in the United States; the movement shifts to Islamic orthodoxy, and the name is changed to American Muslim Mission.

Civil War in Lebanon.

June 5: The Suez Canal reopens after eight years closure.

The Shah proclaims one-party rule in Iran.

November 9: 350,000 Moroccans respond to a call by King Hassan and march across the border into Spanish Sahara, claiming the region as Moroccan territory, since, during the Almoravid dynasty, it was ruled as a single entity. After the withdrawal of the Spanish a war will ensue between Morocco and the Algerian backed Polisario in the Sahara for the next ten years until the issue is put to a United Nations supervised plebescite.

November 10: United Nations General Assembly resolution declares that "Zionism is a form of Racism". This is rescinded in 1991.

In Algeria, nationalisation of last French companies.

November 21: President Anwar as-Sadat of Egypt comes to Israel to address the Knesset.

1976

February: Policemen and Muslims battle each other over several weeks after a judge's ruling temporarily overturns the ban on Jews venturing up onto Haram ash-Sharif, the top of the Temple Mount, to pray. (Orthodox Jewish law prohibits Jews from entering the Temple Mount because they could walk on the Holy of Holies which was permitted only to the High Priest.) Jews had long been restricted to an area at the base of the compound's western wall.

The Shah introduces a new calendar; in Iran the Islamic year 1355 of the Hijrah becomes the year 2535 of "the era of the King of Kings". The obligatory official use of what is perceived to be a neo-pagan calendar increases the consternation of the Islamic opposition.

The "World of Islam Festival" is held in London.

Israeli rescue raid on Entebbe airport, Uganda to release hostages of hijacked airliner.

December 10: Boumedienne wins "99%" of the vote in presidential elections.

1977

Shimon Peres temporarily becomes Prime Minister when Yitzhak Rabin resigns over his wife's illegal bank account, but loses election to Menachem Begin of the Likud party.

July: General Mohammad Zia al-Haq removes Bhutto from office and declares martial law in Pakistan. Bhutto is tried for abetting the murder of a political opponent and is hanged in 1979.

October: Smallpox is eradicated from the earth with the last known case of smallpox on earth, in Somalia, not far from where it is believed to have appeared; but samples of the variola virus are preserved by both Russia and the U.S.

1978

April: The leader of Afghanistan, Daoud, is killed in a coup. The People's Democratic Party of Afghanistan forms a pro-Soviet Government led by Nur Mohammad Taraki.

Imam Musa Sadr, the religious leader of the Lebanese Twelve Imam Shi'ites, a Mulla from Iran who contributed greatly to a resurgence of the Shi'ites in Lebanon and to the foundation of the organisation *Amal*, disappears on a trip to Libya, and is apparently assassinated.

Israel invades Lebanon.

September 18: Camp David agreement between President Anwar as-Sadat of Egypt and Prime Minister Menahem Begin of Israel thanks to intensive mediating by President Carter. The agreement calls for more negotiations to determine the future of the West Bank and the Gaza strip. Prime Minister Begin agrees to "recognize the legitimate rights of the Palestinians", and not to build any more settlements on the West Bank while the negotiations are held. The agreement calls for a peace treaty between the two countries and withdrawal of the Israelis from the Sinai.

October: Iraq expels Ayatollah Khomeini. The request of one hundred Iranian Mullas prevails upon President D'Estaing of France to "accord the necessary respect and honour" to Khomeini and to give him asylum.

Khomeini publishes the *Vilayat-i Faqih*, "The Government of the Jurisprudent" which proposes that in the absence of the Hidden Imam competent Jurists are mandated by the Hidden Imam to govern in his place. In theory this resolves the tension of Shi'ite political practice which otherwise assumes all government other than that of the Hidden Imam to be illegitimate.

November: A copy of *The Rubaiyat of Omar Khayyam* which had been acquired by the University of Cambridge is found to be a forgery. It was one of a number of such manuscripts which began to appear with increasing frequency, having originated, apparently, in Teheran.

December: President Anwar as-Sadat and Prime Minister Menahem Begin share the Nobel Peace Prize.

In Algeria, Houari Boumedienne dies.

1979

January 2: Menahem Begin in Cairo; he becomes the first Israeli Prime Minister to visit an Arab country.

After several years of growing unrest, the Shah leaves Iran on January 16 for exile in Egypt; end of Pahlavi dynasty, followed by the declaration of the Islamic Republic of Iran.

February 7: Col. Chadli Benjedid elected president in Algeria.

A peace treaty is signed between Egypt and Israel. President Carter signs the agreement as a witness. Eighteen Arab countries cut diplomatic and economic relations with Cairo.'Ali Bhutto, former leader of Pakistan, is hanged. Convicted of trying to murder a political opponent in 1974, many world leaders ask Zia al-Haqq for clemency for Bhutto. Nevertheless, and despite internal unrest, the sentence is carried out.

June: reacting to rule in Syria by the Alawi sect of Hafez al-Asad, the secret Muslim Brotherhood, a Sunni organisation, massacres 50 Alawi cadets in the dining room of a military academy in Aleppo.

July: Algeria frees Ahmad Ben Bella, a key leader in Algeria's struggle for independence from France. Ben Bella was president of Algeria and had been deposed by Houari Boumedienne in 1965 and placed under house arrest.

November 4: Iranian students seize the U.S. embassy in Teheran and take 49 hostages. Later in the month women and black hostages are released. The others remain in captivity.

September 16: In Afghanistan, President Taraki is killed in a coup. Amin Hafizullah takes over.

September 22: Israel and South Africa jointly test a 2-3 kiloton nuclear bomb in the south Indian Ocean.

September 24: The Arab League relocates to Tunis from Cairo in rebuke for the Egyptian-Israeli peace treaty.

1400 H. = 21 November 1979

1979

On *1 Muharram AH 1400*/21 November, the first day of the fifteenth Islamic century, revolutionary fanatics led by a group of student conspirators from the theological university of Medinah attempt to promote one of their group as Mahdi and fulfill certain Hadith reported by Abu Dawud. They seize the Grand Mosque of Mecca and hold it against the army for two weeks. The Hadith in question says: "A man of the people of Medinah will go forth, fleeing to Mecca, and some of the people of Mecca will come to him and against his will they will lead him forth and swear fealty to him between the *rukn* [Black Stone corner of the Ka'bah] and the Maqam Ibrahim." Of the 300 who took part in the seizure of the Mosque, 117 rebels were killed and 143 captured. 63 conspirators will be put to death. Government losses are put at 127 dead and 417 wounded.

The Soviets fly 5,000 troops into Afghanistan. The number quickly rises to 40,000 and finally to 100,000. President Amin Hafizullah is shot and Babrak Karmal, who was Taraki's Vice President, returns from Moscow and is installed as a Soviet puppet.

1980

January: 63 members of the Meccan rebellion who were captured are beheaded. 41 are Saudis, 10 Egyptian, 5 Kuwaiti, and the rest from Iraq, Sudan and Yemen. According to Saudi authorities more than 700 were involved.

February 17: Israeli diplomats open an embassy in Cairo, the first Israeli embassy in the Arab world.

March: Afghan War. Soviet and Afghan troops begin attacks on Mujahidin strongholds.

April 28: An effort by the United States to rescue American hostages in Iran fails. Eight helicopters with commandos had been dispatched to Iran. Three had technical failures and turned back. The remaining helicopters landed in the desert in Iran to re-fuel Eight soldiers were killed when a helicopter collided with a transport plane, and the mission turns into a fiasco and is aborted.

July 27: The Shah of Iran, Mohamed Reza Pahlevi dies in Egypt.

September 20: Teheran calls up reserves after Iraq invades Iran, seeking to wrest away Khuzistan, an Arab speaking and oil rich province of Iran. Khuzistan had been jointly run by Iraq and Iran since a 1975 treaty which is now abrogated by Iraq. Khomeini spurns peace offers and vows to fight until the end.

Muhammad Asad's translation of the Koran into English.

1981

January 20: 52 American hostages in Iran are liberated as Ronald Reagan is sworn to office as President. This was purportedly the fruit of what became called the "October Surprise", a deal with Iran just before the U.S. presidential elections. Soon afterwards, in a secret reversal of American policy, a flow of U.S. arms to Iran begins with authorisations given to Israel to sell U.S. military equipment. No U.S. rationale for the arms sales to Iran could be established; however, Israel's interest was in keeping the Iran-Iraq war going. Agreements made between Secretary of State Alexander M. Haig Jr and Prime Minister Menachem Begin in 1981 regarding sales of arms to Iran were rescinded in the spring of 1982, but continued as an "oral agreement" for at least 18 months after that, reported the *International Herald Tribune*, December 9, 1991.

October 6. During a military parade in Cairo, President Anwar as-Sadat is assassinated by a group of soldiers who are taking part in the parade, apparently in revenge for measures taken by as-Sadat against Islamic fundamentalists.

1982

February: Uprising in Hamah against the Alawi regime of Hafez al-Asad; Baath party officials are killed and broadcasts are made calling for a nation-wide insurrection. Syrian troops kill ten thousand in the city of Hamah and level half the town.

March: "The Reagan administration had secretly changed policy toward Iran shortly after taking office in 1981, allowing the Israelis, bitter foes of Mr Saddam, to ship American arms valued at several billion dollars to Tehran... By late March 1982, US Intelligence was reporting that Iraq was on the verge of collapse, creating fears in Washington and the region that Iran's fundamentalist government would dominate the Gulf and its huge oil reserves... The Reagan administration secretly decided to provide highly classified intelligence to Iraq – more than two years earlier than previously disclosed – while also permitting the sale of American-made arms to Baghdad in a successful effort to help President Saddam Hussein avert defeat in the war with Iran." (*International Herald Tribune*, January 27, 1992.)

April 11: An American-born Israeli soldier slips into the Dome of the Rock with a machine gun, kills 2 Arabs and wounds 11.

April 25: Israel returns the Sinai to Egypt in accordance with the Camp David agreements.

May 24: After Iran begins its *Basij* campaign of using waves of suicide adolescents with a plastic key to paradise around their necks and no weapons other than those they find on the battlefield to storm Iraqi positions, Iran recaptures Khurramshahr, major port city which had been almost surrounded by Iraq. 30,000 Iraqis are taken prisoner.

June 6. Israel invades Lebanon with 20,000 troops. Although the main opponents are Palestinians and Syrians, the war will result in 30,000 Shi'ite casualties and radicalize the Shi'ite population of Lebanon against Israel.

July 27: Israel bombs West Beirut killing 120 civilians. Israel admits the use of cluster bombs, but, against U.S. assertions, denies that their use is in violation of treaties with the U.S.

August 23: Thousands of Palestinians evacuate Beirut for South Yemen. 35,000 Israeli troops are now in Lebanon; there are also 30,000 Syrians. As of August, 20,000 are reported killed in Lebanon as a result of the Israeli Invasion.

August 31: After leaving Beirut, where they had been since 1971, 'Arafat establishes PLO headquarters in Tunisia.

September 18: Massacre in Sabra and Shatila refugee camps in West Beirut carried out by hundreds of Christian militia men belonging to Major Saad Haddad. The Phalangists are allowed to enter the camps by the Israelis; they had declined an earlier invitation by the Israelis to raid the camps. After the assassination of Lebanese President Bashir Gemayel, the Phalangists took the Israeli offer. Ariel Sharon, who was behind the events, claimed that he never "thought" the Phalangists would kill people. An official inquiry placed the number of dead men, women and children at 800; Palestinians claim 7,000. Time magazine reported that Ariel Sharon incited the Phalangists; he sued for libel; a court decided that the statements were defamatory but not libellous (Reported by MSNBC Nov 20, 2001.)

September 25: Hundreds of thousands demonstrate in Tel Aviv because of the Israeli involvement in the Sabra and Shatila massacres.

October: U.S. Marines are in Lebanon as part of a peacekeeping force which includes France and Italy.

The taking of U.S. hostages in Lebanon begins by Hizbollah and by Islamic Jihad. David Dodge, acting president of the American University of Beirut is kidnapped and released a year later.

1983

'Arafat's personal advisor, Issam Sartawi, who supports dialogue with Israel, is killed in Portugal by the Abu Nidal group, which is not part of the PLO.

February: An investigation led by the chief justice of Israel's Supreme Court finds that Ariel Sharon as defense minister, was "indirectly responsible" for the massacre of hundreds of Palestinian civilians, many of them women and children, by Christian militiamen five months earlier in Beirut.

April 18: Suicide car bomb attack on U.S. embassy in Beirut. 63 are killed. Palestinian and Lebanese Shi'ite groups claim responsibility.

October 23: A Mercedes truck loaded with over 1,100 kilos of explosives penetrates a U.S. military compound in Beirut. 216 U.S. Marines are killed. Minutes later another truck with bombs kills 58 at a French military compound. Several groups claim responsibility of which the Shi'ites are the most likely to be responsible.

November 24: Six Israeli prisoners are released by the PLO in return for 5,000 Palestinian prisoners held by Israel.

December 20: Yassir 'Arafat and 4,000 Palestinians evacuate on French ships from Tripoli, Lebanon where they had been surrounded by Syrian troops and rival Palestinians.

1984

January 3: An American Navy pilot who had been shot down over Lebanon is released by Syrians after a private mission to Damascus by Rev. Jesse Jackson.

January 13: Chadli Benjedid re-elected in Algeria.

February: Beginning with Frank Regier, five Americans in Lebanon are abducted in the course of this year.

February 26: 1,400 U.S. Marines complete withdrawal from Beirut; failure of President Reagan's Middle East policy.

April 17: During a protest outside a Libyan embassy in London, gunmen on the embassy roof kill a British Policewoman and wound 10 others. Qaddafi refuses to allow British police to enter the embassy, and a week later the Libyans are allowed to leave the country. Britain breaks diplomatic relations with Libya.

May: Iran and Iraq attack oil shipping in the Persian Gulf. Iran is warned by the Arab League about neutral shipping, although Iraq is no less involved.

September 20: A car bomb kills 40 at the U.S. Embassy in Beirut. The embassy had been moved to a site in northeast Beirut after previous attacks on the embassy in West Beirut. After a deadlocked election in Israel, Shimon Peres becomes Prime Minister in a Labor-Likud unity government; he is widely praised for bringing troops out of Lebanon and slashing runaway inflation.

1985

March 16: Terry A. Anderson, Beirut bureau chief for the Associated Press, is kidnapped by Hizbollah, the pro-Iranian militant organisation. He will become the longest held hostage in Lebanon.

March 17: Iran in heavy fighting takes the highway linking Baghdad and Basrah.

August 17: Kharg Island, through which 90% of the oil produced in Iran passes, is bombed by the Iraqis as part of their aerial campaign against Iranian cities.

October 1: Israeli air raid on PLO headquarters in Tunis. More than 170 Palestinians and Tunisians are killed. Yassir 'Arafat narrowly escapes death.

October 27. Italian Cruise ship the "Achille Lauro" is hijacked in the Mediterranean by heavily armed Palestinians. An American Jewish tourist, Leon Klinghoffer, is murdered. The hijackers demand release of prisoners held by the Israelis. The hijackers surrender after being offered free passage by Egypt. The plane carrying the hijackers is intercepted by U.S. Navy jets and is forced to land in Sicily. However, the hijackers are allowed to leave by Italian authorities.

November: Oliver L. North, of the White House, helped by Duane R. Claridge of the CIA, arrange for a shipment of missiles to Iran from Israel. For such clandestine shipments of weapons, Iran would influence Hizbollah in Lebanon to release Western hostages. At the release of two such hostages, Benjamin Weir and Father Lawrence Jenko, the Church of England envoy Terry Waite, later a hostage himself, was in attendance throwing off any surmises as to the reason for their release.

December 30: Palestinian terrorists of Abu Nidal co-ordinate attacks at El Al counters at Rome and Vienna airports.

1986

In a previously agreed switch, Shimon Peres becomes Foreign Minister in a unity government, under Prime Minister Yitzhak Shamir of the Likud.

April 15: 18 U.S. Air Force F-111's bomb Benghazi and Tripoli in Libya in retaliation for Libya's role in the bombing of a discotheque earlier that month in Berlin in which 2 U.S. servicemen and a Turk were killed, and 50 U.S. servicemen injured, along with 200 others. In the raid on Libya 100 people are killed in Tripoli and 30 in Benghazi, including an adopted daughter of Col. Qaddafi. In November 1997 five people go on trial in Berlin for the bombing of the discotheque, two Palestinians, a Libyan, and two Germans who are accused of acting on orders from Libyan intelligence.

March: Jonathan Jay Pollard, an American Jew, is sentenced to life imprisonment in America for spying for Israel.

May: In Afghanistan, Babrak Karmal is replaced by Najibullah, chief of the Afghan secret service. Fighting intensifies toward the end of the year when the Muslim guerrillas, based in Pakistan, receive weapons from the United States.

September: British newspapers publicize Israeli nuclear technician Mordechai Vanunu's revelations about Israel's nuclear programme in Dimona which show that at the time Israel had enough material for two hundred nuclear devices. Vanunu, a Moroccan Jew recently converted to Christianity, is lured to Rome by Mossad, kidnapped to Israel, tried for espionage, and sentenced to 18 years in prison, most of it in solitary confinement, being released in 2004.

November: Iran-Contra affair disclosures. U.S. sales of arms to Iran through Israeli intermediaries come to light. The implications include offers of arms to Iran for Western hostages held in Lebanon. Profits from the arms sales were used to supply Contra guerrillas in Central America. The affair will reverberate in U.S. politics for years to come.

1987

Najibullah announces a programme of national reconciliation to draw the resistance into a powersharing deal. The rebels refuse.

May: an Iraqi plane mistakenly attacks a U.S. frigate, the U.S.S. Stark in the Persian Gulf. 37 American sailors are killed when the ship is hit by an Exocet missile. Attacks on Tankers in the Gulf lead many Western navies to station warships in the Gulf.

July: 402 die in Mecca during the pilgrimage as a result of a riot caused by an Iranian political demonstration. Responding to an exhortation made earlier by Khomeini that the pilgrims should carry out "a disavowal of the pagans" some Iranian pilgrims began demonstrating and shouting anti-Saudi and anti-American slogans while waving pictures of Khomeini. The police intervened and a stampede followed in which 275 Iranians, many of them, women, were killed. The dead also included 85 Saudi policemen, and 42 pilgrims of other nationalities. 649 persons, of them 302 Iranians, were admitted to hospitals. The event leads to tensions between Saudi Arabia and Iran; a number of Saudi Embassies and Saudia Airlines offices are attacked by terrorists.

As a result of the "Tanker War", attacks by Iraqis and Iranians, the latter especially using "suicide" speedboats, on oil shipping in the Gulf, the U.S. convoys Kuwaiti tankers through the Gulf which are reflagged with the U.S. flag.

December 9: Beginning of the Intifida, the Palestinian uprising in the occupied West Bank.

1988

January 15: Israeli policemen firing tear gas confront Palestinian protestors near the mosques of the Temple Mount and injure at least 70.

January: Shimon Peres narrowly loses an election to Yitzhak Shamir but becomes Finance Minister in a unity government.

Death of 'Abd al-Ghaffur Khan, Pathan leader.

February to October. The Iraqi government carries out a military operation code named "Anfal" against its Kurdish population in which over 100,000 Kurds disappear, presumed dead. Kurdish towns, including Halabja, are attacked with chemical weapons. These are mustard gas and three kinds of nerve gas. They cause genetic mutations and damage and the population continues to suffer ten years later as a result of these gas attacks.

April: Afghanistan and Pakistan sign an accord clearing the way for the Soviet Army's departure but the guerillas go on fighting.

April 16: Abu Jihad, the head of FATAH, is killed in Tunis in an Israeli commando attack.

July 3: The cruiser U.S.S. Vincennes shoots down an Iranian Airbus A-300 on a scheduled flight between Bandar Abbas and Dubai because the flight is mistakenly identified as hostile. 290 die.

A riot erupts in Jerusalem after the Israeli authorities begin excavating a tunnel under the Temple Mount and the al-Aqsa Mosque. Arabs express fear that Jewish extreme right groups will use the area for terrorism.

July 18: Iran accepts the United Nations ceasefire plan in the Iran-Iraq war. Until now, Khomeini has continuously demanded the ouster of Saddam Hussein as a condition for the end of the war which has claimed 1,000,000 victims, and in 1988 saw Teheran hit by large numbers of Iraqi Scud missiles. August: Zia al-Haq of Pakistan is killed in an air crash. He is succeeded by Ghulam Ishaq Khan.

October 5: Riots in Algiers and other cities.

November 15: The Palestine National Council in exile in Algiers proclaims the creation of the independent Palestinian state and accepts UN security council resolution 242 implicitly recognizing the existence of the state of Israel. The council rejects all forms of terrorism.

December: Panam flight 103 explodes over Lockerbie, Scotland. 270 people are killed.

December 9: As the Intifada enters the third year, 615 Palestinians killed by Israelis, 15,000 to 20,000 Palestinians are wounded, 50,000 Palestians are arrested, and 100 Israelis have been killed by Palestinians.

December 22: Chadli Benjedid re-elected in Algeria.

Benazir Bhutto becomes Prime Minister in Pakistan.

1989

January: U.S. Navy planes shoot down two Libyan jets over the Mediterranean because the Libyans approach U.S. naval vessels in a zone which Qaddafi has declared an exclusive Libyan security zone in violation of international agreements.

February 14: Khomeini urges the execution of Salman Rushdie, Indian born British author of a book called the Satanic Verses. The book, which describes the wives of the Prophet of Islam as prostitutes, and the Prophet himself as a contemptuous scoundrel, is universally viewed by Muslims as blasphemy, a view supported by some Christian and Jewish religious leaders. Many in the West however, defend Rushdie, who is forced to go into hiding, as a victim of the suppression of free speech.

February 15: The last of 15,000 soldiers, the Soviet 40th Army withdraws from Afghanistan.

February 23: New Constitution approved in Algeria.

July 9: Two bombs explode in Mecca. One person died and 16 were wounded. The Saudi authorities blame Iranian inspired terrorists.

July 28: Israelis kidnap Shi'ite leader Shaikh 'Abd al-Karim Obeid from a village in Lebanon. Shortly thereafter, following threats, a Lebanese terrorist group delivers a videotape of the hanging of Marine Lieutenant Colonel William Higgins. It is suggested that the death of Higgins, who was a UN observer kidnapped in Lebanon and held hostage as a spy, actually took place several months earlier. The Israelis offer to send Shaikh Obeid to the United States for "trial".

A Koran, known as the "Holy Koran of Othman", originally from the Mosque of Hajj Akhrar in Samarkand, and later kept in the Russian Imperial Library, then in Taskhent, is returned to the care of the Muslim authorities of Central Asia by the Soviet government. After the Russian revolution this copy of the Koran, according to a decision made by Lenin in 1917 following a request by Muslim commissars, was transferred from what had become the State Public Library to the Kraeovogo Musul'manskogo S'ezda Petrogradskogo Natsional'nogo Okruga and then to the keeping of the national soviet in Tashkent. This Koran was deliberately prepared with bloodstains on the pages before binding, deduced from the fact that the stains move from the inner edge of the pages to the middle and are symmetric throughout, apparently a kind of medieval forgery. Because of the bloodstains and its apparent age it became known as the actual Koran held by the Caliph Othman when he was assassinated. However, it has been dated by scholarly examination as being from the first quarter of the eight century – not from the sixth. The text is in a frame of 50x44 cm; the size of the pages is 68x53 cm, of which 353 are parchment and 69, which replace original missing pages, are paper.

The Prophet's Mosque in Medinah is enlarged under King Fahd.

Death of Khomeini.

September: Fundamentalists set up the Islamic Salvation Front in Algeria. Mouloud Hamrouche named Prime Minister.

Insurgency in Kashmir after election irregularities and a government by Dr Farooq Abdallah, regarded as an Indian puppet.

1990

The Grand Mosque of Mecca is enlarged by King Fahd. The capacity of the Grand Mosque is now 695,000 worshipers, up from 313,000 and that of the Prophet's Mosque is now 98,500 up from 16,500.

May: North and South Yemen unite to form one country. North Yemen (Yemen Arab Republic, with its capital at Sana'a) was a republic since 1962 when the Imam was deposed. South Yemen (People's Democratic Republic of Yemen with its capital at Aden) gained independence from Britain in 1967. With democratic change sweeping the Soviet Union, an earlier timetable for unification was hastened. The new president is 'Ali 'Abdullah Saleh of North Yemen. The joint capital is Sana'a. June: In a move to distance himself from his Marxist past, Najibullah makes constitutional reforms.

June 12: Municipal elections in Algeria give fundamentalists control in more than half of Algeria's cities and towns.

July 2: During the Pilgrimage to Mecca 1,426 pilgrims are killed in a stampede in a pedestrian underpass at Mina, one of the Pilgrimage sites.

August: Saddam Hussein of Iraq invades and annexes Kuwait making it a province of Iraq. Saddam had consulted the U.S. ambassador before the invasion; the ambassador said she and the U.S. had no objections to a matter which did not concern them.

October 8. Israeli Police kill 19 and wound 100 in Jerusalem. The incident is touched off by a militant procession of the "The Temple Mount Faithful" a Jewish group dedicated to ousting the Mosques from the Temple Mount, among which are two principal historic sanctuaries, the al-Aqsa Mosque and the Dome of the Rock. The first claims of the authorities that the Police had to defend Jews praying at the Wall from rocks thrown from above are shown in a subsequent court investigation to be untrue, and the actual cause of the massacre is found to be the actions of the police themselves.

Chechen independence movement led by Jakar Dudayev calls for sovereignty.

1991

January: Coalition forces begin aerial bombardments of Iraq leading to 100 hours of ground fighting in which Iraqi forces are routed and Iraq is forced to give up Kuwait. Retreating Iraqis blow up oil wells in Kuwait leaving them burning. The war engages 541,000 Americans as well as British, French, Saudi, Moroccan, Egyptian, and forces of other countries. It costs 61 thousand million dollars of which 7 thousand million are paid by the United States and the rest by allies. 146 Americans were killed, and 467 wounded. Iraqi casualties, at first placed in the hundreds of thousands, are later estimated at 10,000. During the war Iraq fired more than 80 Scud missiles killing 28 Americans and 2 Israelis.

March: Kurds in Iraq rebel and seize key towns in the north of Iraq. The Iraqi army, which by the cease-fire agreement is allowed to fly its helicopters, responds forcefully and more than a million Kurds flee into the hills and into Turkey and Iran. March: The U.S. Congress passes a resolution, which is signed into law by President George Bush Sr (H.J. Res. 104, Public Law 102-14) which states that the "Seven Noahide Laws" "are the bedrock of society from the dawn of civilisation... and that the Lubavitch movement [a Jewish Hasidic group] has fostered and promoted these ethical values and principles throughout the world... and that March 26, 1991, the start of the 90th year of Rabbi Menachem Mendel Schneerson, leader of the worldwide Lubavitch movement, is designated Education Day, USA..."

The so-called "laws of Noah" are actually a declaration of Jewish sovereignty over non-Jews. They are a Talmudic prescription for non-Jews as a second class category of being, without real humanity or free will, but who, by following these laws become "righteous gentiles", and *ger toshav*, which, according to some Jewish authorities, are "semi-converts", (the latter interpretation Chabad Lubavitchers do not accept, however). Although of little practical consequence, the symbolic importance of this act of the U.S. government is enormous. It became controversial when it was more widely learned that according to these "Noahide Laws" in their Talmudic context, not only Hinduism, or Native American Religion, but also Christianity is considered a form of idolatry which can be punished by decapitation. The Lubavitchers carry on a low level but sincere campaign to convince Christians that Christmas is an "illegal" holiday; according to the full ramifications of the binding "Noahide laws", Christians, and others, are not allowed to "invent" religious holidays for themselves on pain of death. The followers of Schneerson, who promote these laws and the concept behind them as compulsory for non-Jews consider him to be the Messiah, and, in his words, "the goal of this generation is to go out to the final war... to conquer and purify all the gentile countries... Even in the future, the nations [*goyim*] will continue to exist, to serve and help the Jewish people."

April 3: Chadli Benjedid in Algeria calls first multiparty legislative elections for June 27.

April: After a decade of fighting, Afghan guerillas capture the southern city of Khost handing the government of Najibullah its greatest military setback.

The Security Council passes Resolution 688, calling on Iraq not to repress its minorities, the Shi'ites in the south and the Kurds in the north. The U.S., France, and Britain offer protection to the Kurds in the north. Iraq is prohibited from operating aircraft north of the 36th parallel.

May: United Nations Secretary General Perez de Cuellar announces a peace plan for Afghanistan.

June: Islamic fundamentalists clash with security forces in Algiers. The Algerian President proclaims a state of siege, dismisses Hamrouche Government and postpones elections.

The war between the Moroccan government and the Polisario in the Western Sahara comes to a standstill awaiting a UN sponsored referendum.

August: The last prime minister of Iran under Shah Reza Pahlevi, Shahpur Bakhtiar is strangled in his house in southern Paris while police officers stand guard outside.

September: The United States and the Soviet Union agree to end all military aid to the two sides in the Afghan civil war by the end of the year.

September 29: State of siege lifted in Algeria.

October 27: Without recognition from Moscow Dudayev is elected president of Chechnya. In the following year opposition to Dudayev will grow in Chechnya.

October 30: Middle East peace talks start in Madrid as U.S. Secretary of State James Baker says, within the framework of UN resolutions 242 and 338. Israel refuses PLO participation, but does not object to consultation between the Palestinian delegates and the PLO. November: the last oil well fires are extinguished in Kuwait, years before originally predicted.

U.S. government charges two agents of Libyan intelligence with the bombing of Panam flight 103 over Lockerbie Scotland in December 1988. The U.S. claims that the bomb was in a suitcase directed towards the flight in question from Malta, and connected with the flight in Frankfurt. Minuscule fragments of a computer chip of a type bought by Libya were found in the wreckage. Many, including Israel, receive the announcement with scepticism on the basis that others had a greater interest in the bombing.

November 18: Church of England envoy, Terry Waite, who had been taken hostage in Lebanon while on mission for the Archbishop of Canterbury to secure release of other hostages in Lebanon, is released from captivity along with the American Thomas M. Sutherland.

November 24: Presidential elections in Tajikistan which test the influence of democratic, Islamic, and Communist parties.

November 20: Hizbollah spokesman 'Abbas Massawi announces a new policy which delinks the release of Western hostages with Israeli release of Arab prisoners, and promises release of all hostages by the end of the year.

In a break with deeply engrained habits of self-idealisation, a play opens in Cairo, entitled "In Plain Arabic" (after a Koranic quotation) which is critical of Arabs' ways of seeing and not seeing themselves.

December 2: Release of Joseph Cicippio, Western hostage in Lebanon, followed by Alan Steen and Terry Anderson, last American hostage in Lebanon.

December 9: As of the fourth anniversary of the Intifada, B'Tselem, an Israeli human rights group, reports 1,400 deaths to date.

December: The United Nations General Assembly votes to rescind the resolution which named Zionism a form of racism.

In Burma, many Muslims flee to Bangladesh from militant Buddhists.

December 26: In Algeria, Islamic Front wins 188 seats in first round of elections.

A special state security court in Egypt sentences a writer, Alaa Hamed, and his publisher to eight years in prison for what it calls "blasphemy" in a novel called "A Distance in a Man's Mind". In the novel the hero meets prophets of the past and challenges them in bawdy and frivolous language to prove their miracles. It concludes with an imaginary trial in which the protagonist disproves religion with rational arguments and is condemned to death.

The Soviet Union is replaced by the Commonwealth of Independent States.

1992

Shimon Peres loses Labor party leadership to Yitzhak Rabin in a national primary; becomes Foreign Minister after Labor wins elections.

Pakistan cuts off military aid to the Afghan rebels and endorses the United Nations peace inititative.

January 12: Algeria's High Security Council invalidates the nation's first multiparty election because Islamic Fundamentalists receive a commanding lead in the initial round of parliamentary voting. President Chadli Benjedid resigns. Runoff election is canceled.

January 16: Mohammad Boudiaf, former Algerian National Liberation Front dissident, returns from 27 years of exile to be sworn in as head of presidential council. Clashes continue.

A committee of clerics from the al-Azhar university confiscates eight books on religious topics at the Cairo book fair. One person involved is Said Ashmawy, himself a chief judge in the court which condemned Alaa Hamed. Ashmawy was the author of five of the works; one of them, *Political Islam* critically examined assumptions about the Islamic state.

Scandal in France because Georges Habash, is admitted to a Paris hospital for medical treatment.

February: The Israeli military gives an order which allows soldiers to immediately shoot to kill any Arab who is seen carrying arms.

In Algeria, after the leaders of Islamic Fundamentalists are jailed by the military government, confrontations continue between the police and Fundamentalist guerrilas.

The former Soviet republics of Kazakhstan, Kyrgyztan, Uzbekistan sign agreements of cooperation with Turkey.

February 16: Israeli jets ambush and kill Hizbollah leader 'Abbas Mussawi in Lebanon.

February 29: As Yugoslavia breaks up, Bosnia and Herzogovina declares independence and Bosnian Serbs declare a separate state. Fighting spreads. Sarajevo surrounded soon after.

March 17: Israeli Embassy in Buenos Aires is bombed; responsibility is claimed by Islamic Jihad, which is associated with Hizbollah.

March 18: Najibullah offers to transfer power to an interim government in Afghanistan.

April: Civil rights groups in Israel report that undercover army agents systematically assassinate selected Palestinians in the process of accosting them.

April 10: The new Secretary General of the UN Boutros Boutros Ghali says warring parties in Afghanistan have agreed to form a "pre-transition" council that will hand over power to an interim government.

April 15: UN sanctions are introduced against Libya.

April 16: Najibullah is ousted from power in Afghanistan.

April 20: The beginning of classes is announced for Bir Zeit university closed by Israeli military order in January 1988. Five other Palestinian universities closed at the same time have already been reopened.

April 21: An Algerian fundamentalist newspaper advocates violence against the government.

April 25: Amidst a struggle between the warlords Ahmad Shah Massoud and Gulbeddin Hekmatyar, a religious leader, Sibgatullah Mojadedi, arrives in Kabul to preside over the council of government.

May 17: A crowd of 200,00 overflows in St. Peter's square as Pope John Paul II beatifies the Spanish founder of the conservative Opus Dei religious movement. Monsignor Josémaria Escriv· de Balaguer was raised to this status only 17 years after his death. Some have labeled Opus Dei a sinister and powerful force. The beatification was the culmination of a bitter argument regarding Monsignor Escriv·'s qualifications, who has been called vain, bad-tempered and anti-Semitic by former members of Opus Dei which they call a secretive cult with undue influence. Before the ceremonies, Monsignor Escriv·'s body was moved from a crypt in the organisation's Rome headquarters to the alter of its chapel so that believers could venerate him. A Sudanese nun, Guiseppina Bakhita was also beatified.

In an effort at unity, Kurds in Iraq elect a government in May and set up a parliament in Erbil, trying to establish a semi-autonomous state.
June: Mojadedi replaced in Afghanistan; Burhanuddin Rabbani, an ethnic Tajik is proclaimed President, while rival factions continue to fight.

June 29: President Boudiaf of Algeria is assassinated in Annaba.

July 3: International relief airlift begins to Sarajevo.

August: U.S. coalition imposes no-flight zone on Iraq's warplanes in the south, below the 32 parallel, to protect Shi'ite minorities from attack.

December 6: The Congress Government in New Delhi promised, and failed, to prevent a Hindu nationalist mob from destroying a 16th century mosque, the Babri Masjid built by the first Mogul Emperor Babur in Ayodhya in North India. The Mosque had been built on the site of an earlier Hindu temple.

December: U.S. F-16 shoots down an Iraqi MiG-25 in the southern no-flight zone.

1993

January 2: Cyrus R. Vance of the United Nations and Lord Owen of the European Community announce a peace proposal to divide Bosnia into ten provinces.

January 13: Another Iraqi plane is shot down by the U.S., and Iraq moves surface-to-air missiles into the south and refuses to remove them. The U.S., Britain, and France strike four missile-radar sites and two missile sites.

January 19: The 1986 law forbidding those living within Israeli jurisdication to have any contact with terrorist organisations is abolished. But Israel continues to consider the PLO a terrorist organisation.

January 21: Yassir 'Arafat speaks on Israeli television live from from Tunis by telephone.

March 1: American planes begin air drops of food over Bosnia.

April 9: Faisal Husseini, a journalist who is close to 'Arafat is accepted by as the Israelis as a member of the Palestinian delegation to talks.

April 12: NATO jets enforce a no-flight zone over Bosnia.

August 12: Mr Husseini maintains that the negotiators are "clearly representatives of the PLO in the peace talks".

August 29: Israel announces an agreement with the PLO on autonomy for the Gaza strip and Jericho.
April 30: The Bosnian Serb leader Radovan Karadzic signs the Vance-Owen plan, but the Bosnian Serb assembly rejects it on May 6.

June 26: President Clinton orders a cruise missile strike against Baghdad to retaliate for a reported plot to kill former President Bush in Kuwait. Some twenty cruise missiles are launched to strike at night at government buildings. (In 2006, one of the charges in the first trial of Saddam Hussein is that he attacked a village because of an assassination attempt on his life.)

July 12: Mortar shell kills 12 at communal water tap in Dobrinja suburb of Sarajevo.

September 13: "Declaration of Principles" agreement signed in Washington for partial Palestinian autonomy. Yassir 'Arafat and Israeli Prime Minister Yitzhak Rabin shake hands on the White House lawn.

Nawaz Sharif is charged with corruption and dismissed by Ishaq Khan. The government is restored by the supreme court but Sharif resigns and Benazir Bhutto is elected back into power.

1994

January 12: NATO threatens airstrikes on Serbs if the airport of Sarajevo is not opened.

January 19: another round of talks collapses in Geneva as the Muslim led government of Bosnia rejects a proposed division of Bosnia.

Serbia and Croatia sign a diplomatic pact.

January 22: Shelling kills six children in Sarajevo.

February 4: Mortar attack kills ten people in Sarajevo.

February 5: Mortar shell kills over 60 and wounds 200 in Sarajevo.

February 9: After meeting in Davos, Switzerland, Yassir 'Arafat and Shimon Peres sign a partial agreement that focuses on security procedures at border crossings of the self-rule areas of Palestine.

February 22: NATO reluctantly sets this date as the deadline for Bosian Serbs to pull back artillery around Sarajevo or face air attacks. Bosnian Serbs comply and new settlement negotiations begin.

February 25: 29 Palestinians at prayer in the Hebron mosque in which the Prophet Abraham is believed to be buried are massacred by Dr. Baruch Goldstein, a Jewish immigrant settler from Brooklyn living in Qiryat Arbaa. The Israeli-PLO peace negotiations are broken off and riots break out throughout the occupied territories triggering more deaths of Israelis and Palestinians.

April 5: After the resumption of negotiations, an Arab car bomb explodes in Afula, Israel killing 7. Israel excludes Arabs from the occupied territories from working in Israel.

April: Israel attacks a United Nations run refugee camp in southern Lebanon at Qana. More than 100 are killed. Israel insists that the attack was a mistake but a UN report published in May, made by European military experts says the attack was deliberate.

March 31: Israel agrees to the deployment of an international observer force in Hebron. Israeli-PLO talks resume.

April 13: The target date set for completing the Israeli troop withdrawal from Gaza and Jericho passes with substantial numbers of troops remaining.

April 28: 'Arafat and Peres meeting in Cairo set May 4 as a date for signing a final agreement after Israel accedes to some of the PLO's requests that it be allowed to use "symbols of statehood" in the future autonomous areas.'Arafat and Rabin sign a self-rule agreement in Cairo. They defer a final decision on the boundaries of Jericho and on a uniformed Palestinian security presence at the Allenby bridge and Rafah border border crossings.

An Aramaic stele is found which speaks of the conquest of "Bet David" by an Aramaean King. This is the first (and so far only) reference to King David outside of the Bible.

Israel and the PLO sign an agreement in Cairo on an Israeli withdrawal from the Gaza strip and Jericho. May: Fighting erupts between the two main Kurdish factions in northern Iraq. The Patriotic Union of Kurdistan seizes Erbil, including the parliament, from the Kurdistan Democratic party.

May 23: At least 207 died during a stampede at Mina during the casting of the stones at the pilgrimage to Mecca. A stampede in 1990 killed 1,426 pilgrims.

In Turkey 37 writers and intellectuals were burned to death after Islamic Fundamentalists attacked and set fire to a hotel where they were attending a conference because the man who translated Salman Rushdie's controversial book "The Satanic Verses" was one of the conference speakers.

Taslima Nasrin: a second arrest warrant is issued in Dhaka for her because of a book of essays she wrote in 1992. She had gone into hiding after June 4 because a court in Chatak ordered her arrest for allegedly hurting religious sensibilities. A number of factors led to this, one of which was an interview in which she said that the Koran should be revised. This book of 88 pages is the second of her twenty works to be attacked after her 1993 novel "Lajja" or "Shame" spurred Islamic groups to march in Dhaka demanding her execution; in August she fled to Sweden. "Lajja" was banned in Bangladesh; it concerned the plight of a Hindu family in Bangladesh following the demolition of a mosque by Hindu fundamentalists in India. Over 2,000 Hindus were killed in Bangladesh following the mosque destruction, where Hindu temples, shops and homes were also burned. The book was pirated in India and sold as propaganda. At the end of 1993 one religious authority offered $1,500 for her assassination. Miss Nasrin is 32 yrs old and was trained as a physician. In 1991 she received a literary prize in Calcutta after writing about sexual oppression; her prize was ignored in Bangladesh.

June 20: A bomb in a prayer hall in Meshhed kills 25 and injures 70; a caller claimed that the bomb was set off to mark the founding on June 20, 1981, of the People's Mujahedeen, an Iraq based opposition group; but Mujahedeen spokesmen in Paris denied the accusation and condemned the bombing.

July 1: 'Arafat makes a triumphant return to Gaza.

September: A skirmish in Afghanistan at Spinbaldak near the Pakistan border involving the Taliban and other Afghan forces. It brings the Taliban 800 truckloads of arms and ammunition that had been stored in caves since the Soviet occupation, making them the best supplied faction in Afghanistan. The Taliban also gain the support of Nasirullah Babar, Pakistan's Interior Minister. After they take control of Kandahar he sees them as the means to an economic alliance with the states of Central Asia who need a way to the sea.

October 19: A Hamas militant sets off a bomb on a Tel Aviv Bus. 23 are killed.

November 11: Islamic Holy War detonates a bomb near an Israeli military position in Gaza.

November 30: Grand Ayatollah Ali Araki died in Teheran at an age estimated to be 106 years. He was considered by some to the Marja' at-Taqlid, or the Usuli Shi'ite "reference of emulation". Ayatollah 'Ali Khamenei is considered by some to have succeeded Araki to this position.

December 11: After several skirmishes Russian troops launch a full-scale invasion of Chechnya taking control of the capital Grozny.

Shimon Peres shares the Nobel Peace Prize with Yitzhak Rabin and Yassir 'Arafat.

Jordan signs a peace agreement with Israel.

1995

Two members of Islamic Jihad blow themselves up amidst a group of Israeli soldiers near Netanya. 21 are killed.

May 12: Two fires destroy the town of Charar-i-Sharif and the tomb of Nureddin Wali in Kashmir. Inhabitants accuse the Indian army of setting the fires. Kashmir, the only Muslim majority state in India, has seen an insurgency that up to this date had claimed 20,000 lives.

April 9: An Islamic Jihad suicide bomber attacks an Israeli military convoy in Gaza. 8 dead.

July 24: A suicide bomb on a bus near Tel Aviv. 6 dead.

August 21: A bomb in a Jerusalem bus. 5 dead.

September 28: Israel and the PLO sign an agreement in Washington extending Palestinian self-rule to wide areas of the West Bank.

October: A Palestinian, Fathi Shikaki, a leader of a terrorst organisation known as Jihad, is shot outside his hotel in Malta.

Kabbalists in Israel perform the "Pulsa Dinura" ceremony to curse Yitzhak Rabin, and call for his death.

October 25: Israeli troops begin withdrawing from six Palestinian cities in the West Bank. A withdrawal from most of Hebron, the last city under Israeli occupation is set for March.

November 4: Yitzhak Rabin assassinated by Israeli rightist; Shimon Peres becomes Prime Minister.

November: A bomb kills five Americans at the Saudi National Guard offices in Riyad, Saudi Arabia.

1996

The population of Iran almost doubles to 60 million from 35 million in 1979 when the Ayatollahs dropped the legal age of marriage to 9 and everyone was exhorted to make babies for the revolution. Today 45 percent of the population is under 17. As a result, Ayatollah 'Ali Khamenei issues an edict that lists the withdrawal method, condoms, and vasectomies as acceptable methods of birth control, adding: "When wisdom dictates that you do not need more children, a vasectomy is permissible." Historically among the Sunnis, Islamic law opinions have not been unanimous, but nevertheless favored acceptance of birth control and permitted abortion. (One of the first Hadith in most of the standard and basic collections reiterates the Aristotelian position that the soul attaches to the body ninety days after conception. This was, until recently, also the position of the Catholic Church.)

January 5: A bomb inside a cellular telephone kills Palestinian bombmaker Yahya Ayyash, called "the engineer". This assasination by the Israeli intelligence Shin Beth sets off a wave of suicide bombings inside Israel which begins on February 25 and which kills 61 people in 1996.

January 20: Palestinians in the West Bank and Gaza Strip go the polls for the first time electing 'Arafat head of the Palestinian Authority and choosing a legislative council.

February 25: Two suicide attacks in Israel, one on a bus in Jerusalem. 26 dead.

March 3: Suicide bomber on a bus in Jerusalem and a bomber on a shopping street in Tel Aviv. 32 dead.

April: In Chechnya, Dudayev is killed in a Russian bombing raid.

May 12: On CBS' "60 Minutes" Lesly Stahl asks US Secretary of State Madeleine Albright about the sanctions instituted against Iraq in 1991: "We have heard that half a million children died, I mean that's more than children than died in Hiroshima. Is the price worth it?" Albright responds "I think this is a very hard choice but it is a price we have to be prepared to pay; we think the price is worth it."

May 29: Benjamin Netanyahu narrowly defeats Shimon Peres in Israeli elections. An opponent of the Rabin-Peres deals with the Arabs, Netanyahu's government lifts curbs on expansion of Jewish settlements imposed by the previous Labor government. 'Arafat accuses the Israelis of violating the self-rule accords.

June 25: A truck bomb in front of U.S. military housing in Dhahran, Saudi Arabia kills nineteen and wounds hundreds.

June 26: Necmettin Erbakan of the Welfare Party becomes Prime Minister in Turkey, the first time that an Islamic party has come to power since Turkey was made a secular state by Mustafa Kemal in 1928.

July: The "Institute for Advanced Strategic and Political Studies", an Israeli think tank, publishes a paper entitled "A Clean break: A New Strategy for Securing the Realm. It urges Israelis and the new right wing Israeli leader Benjamin Netanyahu to seek the downfall of Syria, Iraq, and Iran. Specifically it suggests that Israel work with Jordan and Turkey to bring about the downfall of Saddam Hussein, abandon the Oslo accords, and "land for peace", encourage a policy of preemptive strikes, reserving a right to invade the West Bank and Gaza in the name of self-defence, and a "renewal of Zionism". (The Israeli strategy of breaking Iraq into three countries, Kurdish, Sunni, and Shi'ite, actually predates the "Clean Break" by many years.) What is different here is the policy is enunciated from America. The chief author is Richard Perle of the "American Enterprise Institute", along with James Colbert, Charles Fairbanks, Jr., Douglas Feith, Robert Lowenberg, Jonathon Troop, David Wurmser, and Meyrav Wurmser. Some of the authors have or acquire positions within the U.S. government and Department of Defense, and pursue this policy from within the American government pushing for an invasion of Iraq by America. These calls are resisted by the Pentagon until 9/11. (*Washington Times*, 10/7/03)

Iranian troops push into northern Iraq, purportedly in pursuit of Iranian Kurdish rebels, but causing the Democratic party to fear an Iranian effort to aid its rival.

Russian head of national security Aleksandr Lebed signs a peace agreement in Grozny, Chechnya. Thereafter, the Chechens take control of the country and Russian presences diminishes. Shari'ah law is partly insituted in Chechnya which is now called Ichkeria.

August 22: According to the Iranian Deputy Prime Minister Tariq Aziz, Massoud Barzani, head of the Kurdish Democratic Party wrote a letter seeking the Iraq government to intervene in the factional fighting between Kurds in Northern Iraq. Peace talks between the two factions are held in the American embassy in London but on August 31 the Iraqi army seizes Erbil routing the Patriotic Union.

September 4: After months of delay Netyanyahu meets 'Arafat, and the two leaders proceed with negotiations on Hebron and other aspects of the self-rule accords.

September: Massoud Barzani, leader of one Kurdish faction in the Kurdish Democratic Party invites the Iraqi army into the northern Iraq "safe haven" established after the Gulf War in order to use the army to attack a rival Kurdish leader, Jalal Talabani. Talabani, of the Patriotic Union of Kurdistan seeks the support of Iran. Because of the violation of the safe haven, the U.S. fires cruise missiles at Iraqi targets and reinforces its soldiers in Kuwait.

September 25: Frustration over the non-implementation of treaty agreements over self-rule for Palestinians by the Netanyahu government flares into violence. More than 70 people are killed in three days of violent Palestinian protests and gun battles between Israeli and Palestinian forces across the West Bank and Gaza Strip. The protests are sparked by the opening of a new entrance to an archeological tunnel under the Temple Mount and the al-Aqsa Mosque. Formerly the only entrance was from the Western Wall. An opening at the northern end, at the Muslim quarter, was made in July 1988 but closed over protests. In April of 1996 the Rabin government had made an agreement with the Muslim authorities in which Muslims would be allowed to worship in an underground complex called Solomon's stables under the Mount through a gate which would be controlled by Palestinians. In exchange, the Muslims would not oppose the opening of the new entrance, which the Muslims claim would compromise the Muslim nature of the quarter. The Muslim gate was never made.

September 27: Violence continues with Palestinian policemen firing at Israeli soldiers. Muslim youth hurl stones into the Plaza below the Temple Mount. Israelis police charge, killing three and wounding fifty. Five Israeli police are wounded.

September 27: The Taliban, a fundamentalist military grouping in Afghanistan meaning "scholars" but designating rather illiterate youths raised in exile in refugee camps in Pakistan, capture Kabul. Their leader is named Mullah Omar. The government of Burhannudin Rabbani is deposed as his troops flee northward. The Taliban hang Muhammad Najibullah who headed the Soviet backed government during the Afghan war and his brother Shahpur Ahmadzai and on September 28 they hang two more such leaders, Turkhi and Jafzar. They institute harsh measures in the name of Fundamentalism prohibiting woman physicians from practicing medicine and making children caught foraging for food stand in the street with their faces smeared with ordure as a punishment for theft short of amputation because they are minors. A backlash ensues against the Taliban, and the Tajik General Massoud's troops make the Pathan Taliban retreat from positions north of Kabul.

October: Violence continues in Israel and Palestine. President Clinton calls Arabs and Israelis to Washington for talks.

The U.S. Congress passes a law prohibiting female genital cutting making it punishable by up to five years in prison. The new law requires U.S. representatives to the World Bank to oppose loans to 28 African countries where the practice exists but which do not have educational programmes to oppose it. This follows the case of Fauziya Kassindja, a young woman who fled Togo to avoid having her genitals cut, and sought asylum in the U.S.

November 5: Ms Benazir Bhutto, prime minister of Pakistan is put under house arrest on charges of corruption, abuse of power, intimidation of the judiciary, and breakdown of law and order. President Farook Leghari promises new elections in February.

Dr Farooq Abdullah again at the head of government in Kashmir.

1997

January 1: An Israeli soldier fires into a market at Hebron wounding six Arabs to stall the signing of an agreement regarding Hebron.

January 13: Israel agrees to pull out of part of Hebron.

January 28: Chechens elect Aslan Maskhadov as their new president.

February 10: Chinese authorities impose a curfew on a town in the restive northwestern Xinjiang region after at least ten pople were killed in a riot. About 1,000 Muslim separatists of the Uighur ethnic minority rampaged through the town. Ethnic Chinese make up 38 percent of the population and the Turkic speaking Uighurs are in the majority. The riot began after a Chinese policeman tried to arrest a Uighur who resisted. The Police fired tear gas into the crowd. Xinjiang has a long history of separatist clashes.

Nawaz Sharif elected in Pakistan.

March: Bands of Buddhist monks vandalize mosques in Mandalay and Rangoon. Burma is 90% Buddhist and 4% Muslim.

March 13: A deranged Jordanian soldier shoots a group of Israeli schoolgirls on a field trip in Bakura, Jordan. 7 dead.

The Israelis begin building at a site in East Jerusalem touching off Palestinian unrest.

March 21: A suicide bomb at a sidewalk cafe in Tel Aviv. 3 dead.

April 15: A fire sweeps through a pilgrim encampment at Mina. The death toll was put at over 217 with more than 1,290 people injured, most of them in a panic that followed. Some 70,000 tents were destroyed in the blaze which began after cooking gas canisters exploded. Most of the victims were from the Indian subcontinent.

In Arabia the number of schools to train Imams rises above 600; many of these schools are not licensed by the state as prescribed by law; tension rises over this issue.

May: Taliban capture north Afghanistan.

May 12: Yeltsin and Maskhadov sign a peace treaty.

After the Palestinian Authority announces that Arabs who sell land to Jews will be tried and executed, several killings by persons unknown take place of Palestinians who had sold land to Jews.

The rebel leader in Tajikistan, Sa'id Abdullah Nuri and President Emomali Rakhmonov sign a pact in Moscow, presided over by President Boris N. Yeltsin, ending five years of civil war.

June: Prime Minister Erbakan of Turkey is forced to resign under pressure from the military.

The Grand Shaikh of the al-Azhar in Egypt announces that he will allow his body organs to be donated after his death.

A lower court in Egypt annuls a law banning genital cutting. The Government announces it will appeal to a higher court.

July: Mr Hanafi, a professor at Cairo University is denounced for writing scornfully of Islam. In 1995 another professor, Abu Zeid, was forced by a court to divorce his Muslim wife because his statements were taken to mean that he had left Islam.

July 30: Two Arab suicide bombers attack a Jerusalem market. 15 dead.

August: Two Arab suicide bombers cause many deaths and injuries in a Jerusalem market. Israel institutes measures of collective punishment against the Palestinians. September 4: Three Arab suicide bombers on a shopping street in Jerusalem. 4 dead.

September 5: 9 Israeli Commandos killed in a raid in Southern Lebanon.

Opposition forces drive the Taliban back to Kabul.

Hundreds of villagers are massacred in Algeria in a number of separate incidents by Islamic militant revolutionaries while security forces do not intervene.

October 1: At the request of Jordan, the ailing Hamas leader Shaikh Ahmad Yassin was freed by Israel and taken to Amman, with the expectation that he would be allowed to return to Gaza. This was done in return for the release of Israeli Mossad agents seized in Amman, who, posing as Canadian tourists, attempted to murder another Hamas leader, Khaled Mashaal earlier in the week.

October 29: Iraq orders all American arms inspectors to leave within a week. This begins a crisis which lasts into November.

Taliban agree to enforce a world ban on opium trade.

November 17: 58 European tourists are massacred by Islamic militants in Luxor, Egypt.

Crisis over Iraq's refusal to allow Americans to participate in UN arms inspection teams.

December 29: Egypt's highest court upholds a ban on genital cutting of girls. The ban had been overturned by a lower court. The ban had been imposed by the Egyptian ministry of health.

1998

Ahmad Chalabi in an interview with the Jerusalem Post suggests that if the Iraqi National Congress (at the time an expatriate resistance organisation sponsored by the US government) is successful in its efforts to topple Saddam Hussein, the new government will restore the oil pipeline from Kirkuk to Haifa which has been inoperative since the state of Israel was established in 1948. (*New Yorker*, 6/7/2004)

The "Project for the New American Century" (PNAC) publishes a letter to President Clinton urging war against Iraq and the removal of Saddam Hussein because he is a "hazard" to a "significant portion of the world's supply of oil". The letter calls for the US to go to war alone, and attacks the United Nations. It says the US should not be "crippled by a misguided insistence on unanimity in the the UN security Council". Ten of the eighteen signatories later join the Bush II administration, including Secretary of Defense Donald Rumsfeld, Assistant Defense Secretary Paul Wolfowitz, Assistant Secretary of State Richard Armitage, Undersecretaries of State John Bolton and Paula Dobriansky, presidential advisor for the Middle East Elliot Abrams, and Zalmay Khalilzad who becomes Bush's envoy to Iraq. At the time of the Invasion of Iraq, newspapers will speak of a mysterious "cabal" forgetting this early declaration of its existence, before Bush II is elected. (*NYT* 3/22/03.)

Massacres of villagers by Islamic militants continue in Algeria. The death toll in the war since 1991 is estimated at 76,000.

March: A U.S. court, in a secret decision whose details are hidden even from the lawyers of the defendants, rules to extradite to Iraq several Iraqis who worked for the CIA as members of opposition groups to Saddam Hussein.

March 29: Muhyiaddin ash-Sharif, a suspected Hamas bombmaker is killed in Ramallah the West Bank. He was found near a car that had exploded. The Palestinian authority says that he was killed in an internal feud, not by Israelis.

April 9: A stampede in Mina during the pilgrimage to Mecca kills over 100 pilgrims.

May 11-13: India explodes five atomic bombs. At the head of the project is an Indian Muslim scientist, Avul Pakir Jainulabdeen Abdul Kalam. Shortly thereafter Pakistan explodes its atomic bomb which can be delivered by missile or by F-16.

After increasingly violent student demonstrations in Indonesia, Suharto steps down as head of state, leaving the government to the Vice-President Habibie.

Mayor Ehud Olmert of Jerusalem signs a demolition order for several new houses built in Arab Jerusalem after violent clashes over the construction.

May 28: Pakistan detonates five atomic devices and puts the country into a "state of emergency". The Pakistani scientist credited with the Pakistani bomb is Abdul Qadeer Khan.

June: Fighting breaks out between Muslim separatists in Kosovo and Yugoslav police and army.

In Iraq the UN Commission discovers traces of VX nerve gas in Iraqi missile war heads.

July: The Taliban prohibit television sets, VCRs and Satellite dishes. Russia and Iran provide aid to the northern coalition opposing the Taliban, Ahmad Shah Massoud and Uzbekistan send aid to Abdul Rashid Dostum. The Northern Coalition receives materièl from Tajikistan by air. Saudi Arabia and Pakistan aid the Taliban. Iran also aids Hizb-i-Wahdat, an Afghan Shi'ite group. Both sides are armed with Russian Tanks and Migs. Unocal Oil of Russia and Bridas of Argentina vie for influence over future oil exploitation; Usama Bin Ladin keeps his mountain stronghold with several hundred fighters and threatens terrorism in the U.S.

August: The Taliban seize towns in north Afghanistan, including Mazar-i Sharif.

Terrorists explodes bombs in U.S. embassies in Kenya and Tanzania on the same day, August 7. The U.S. suspects Usama Bin Ladin.

Saddam Hussein's army moved into Kurdish held areas in northern Iraq and crushed the Iraqi National Congress, a CIA backed umbrella group for Kurds and other anti-Hussein dissidents. The U.S. allowed 5,000 Kurds and other Iraqis to resettle in the U.S.

On August 20 the U.S. attacks Usama Bin Ladin's training camps in Afghanistan with cruise missiles and also a pharmaceutical factory in Khartoum, Sudan which it claims was used in the manufacture of VX nerve poison gas. The Cruise missiles are in retaliation for the attacks on U.S. embassies earlier in the month. The attack on the Sudanese pharmaceutical plant was later criticised on several points. The CIA had taken one sample only of soil outside the plant and the analysis of the soil, according to the CIA, showed traces of Empta, a chemical used in making VX by the "Iraqi method". However, critics point out, one sample is not convincing and Empta is chemically similar to many commercially available pesticides and weed-killers, "Round-Up", a brand name, among them. Also, account was not taken of the fact that the plant, Shifaa, did indeed produce the majority of the pharmaceuticals used in Sudan. European engineers who had set up the plant said that in their opinion the plant could not have been used for nerve gas production. Others pointed out that there were a number of targets in Sudan that were much more clearly military and strategic than the pharmaceutical factory. Also, the alleged Bin Ladin or Iraqi financing for the plant was not demonstrated by the U.S. authorities.

August 21: The Grand Mufti of Daghestan, Sa'id Muhammad Hajji Abubakarov was killed when a bomb destroyed his car near the Jam'a Mosque in Mahachkala, the capital of Daghestan. The bombing was attributed to "Wahhabi", that is, fundamentalist activists in the region against whom the Mufti had spoken out at the state council. Other bombs and attacks had also been attributed to these fundamentalists.

Nawaz Sharif of Pakistan announces that he wants to make Koranic law, the law of Pakistan. Many say that this would only exacerbate communal strife, and that this is only a political move to buttress his own position. The Constitution of Pakistan already prohibits any legislation which contradicts Koranic law or Koranic injunctions. In other words, in the opinions of numerous Islamic scholars in Pakistan itself, the government of the country is already as Islamic as any government can be. Addressing one problem of Islamic taxation, Nawaz Sharif spoke of making zakat taxes compulsary; but such an action itself would be in contradiction with Islamic custom. (For this reason taxes collected by the 'Abbasid government in the tenth century were largely on the basis of *kharaj*, which was a fiction that pretended that land holdings belonged to non-Muslims, which was no longer the case at that time.)

September: Iran protests to the Taliban the killing of eight Iranian government agents during the Taliban's takeover of Mazar-i Sharif, and deploys troops along the border.

The Iranian government closes down an underground Baha'i university begun in 1987. The Baha'i Institute of Higher Education had graduated 145 bachelor's degrees but existed clandestinely.

October 23: Arafat and Netanyhahu sign a pact in Washington, the "Wye Plantation Memorandum". The Palestinian Charter will remove a call for the destruction of Israel. Palestinians will step up efforts to combat terrorism – and the CIA will coordinate intelligence between Israel and Palestine. Israel will withdraw troops from an additional 13 percent of the West Bank over the next twelve weeks. A joint Israel-Palestinian committee will discuss additional Israel troop withdrawals. Corridors of safe passage will be provided for Palestinians travelling between Gaza and the West Bank. Israel will release 750 jailed Palestinians. The Palestinians will be permitted to construct an airport in Gaza.

When Netyanyahyu returns to Israel he faces demonstrations by right-wingers and refuses to ratify or implement the agreement upon the pretext of non-presentation of a security plan on the part of the Palestinians before the plan is due.

October 29: The U.S. government decides to provide more support to factions working for the overthrow of Saddam Hussein by voting a bill of 97 million dollars to that end.

In Bangladesh, feminist author Taslima Nasrin, who fled Bangladesh in 1994 but returned to be at the side of her dying mother, is forced to go into hiding by demonstrations calling for "death to the apostate". Taslima Nasrin was quoted in a Calcutta newspaper saying that the "Koran should be thoroughly revised". She has said that every religion opresses women and that shari'ah laws should be abolished. In 1993 she wrote a novel "Shame" that depicted a murderous rampage by Bangladeshi Muslims against the Hindu minority but it is her shrill comments which inflamed opinions against her. In November a group offers a reward for information to her whereabouts.

Saddam Hussein's government refuses to cooperate with UN inspection teams looking for weapons of mass destruction in Iraq.

November: Turkish Kurdish separatist Abdullah Ocalan asks Russia for political asylum. He is the leader of the Kurdistan Workers Party (PKK) whose guerillas are fighting for self-rule in southeast Turkey. Later, he appears in Italy and is arrested in Rome, where renouncing terrorism, he seeks asylum while Turkey asks for his extradition. He is also wanted in Germany which remains neutral on the matter.

The Taliban criticize a five million dollar reward offered by the U.S. for information leading to the arrest of Usama Bin Ladin, who is accused of organizing the bombings of U.S. embassies.

Rebel forces led by Mahmud Khudoberdiyev fighting the government in northern Tajikistan around Khodzhant threaten to bomb a dam in Kayrakum which could flood the region. The army succeeds in driving off his forces.

November 6: Suicide car bomb in Jerusalem kills 2 and injures 21. Hamas is blamed. Netanyahu says this is the reason why the pact with the Palestinians is not ratified.

November 12: The Israeli Cabinet narrowly ratifies Wye accord with the Palestinians after a two-week delay but adds new stipulations. For example, Netanyahu says that the entire Palestinian National Council must meet and vote by a majority to strike clauses from the Palestinian covenant calling for the destruction of Israel. These new stipulations are seen by the Palestinians as leading to new conflicts. Shortly thereafter the process halts as new elections are called in Israel.

November 15: Saddam Hussein vows to cooperate with UN inspectors and a strike against Iraq by U.S. and British military is called off as it begins.

November 22: In Iran, Dariush Foruhar, leader of the Iran Nation Party, an opposition group tolerated by the government, is found stabbed along with his wife. Afterwards three other dissidents are killed in mysterious circumstances and other political activists are missing.

The trial of Ibrahim Anwar, former Prime Minister of Malaysia continues.

Palestinian airport at Gaza opens.

December 9: The severed heads of four foreigners are found in Chechnya. They were employees of a telephone company who had been kidnapped by two dozen armed men in Grozny on October 3, probably for ransom.

December: U.S. bombs Iraq to "degrade" its ability to make weapons of mass destruction after a UN inspection team pulls out because of non-cooperation.

December 24: Hizbollah guerillas fire Katyusha rockets into Northern Israel in revenge for Israeli attacks in Southern Lebanon.

1999

January 4: 15 Shi'ites are massacred in a mosque in Pakistan by Sunni vigilantes.

Iraqi fighters engage U.S. planes in the no-fly zone in Iraq in many incidents.

Senegal prohibits female genital cutting.

Religious rioting in Indonesia claims 45 lives. 1,300 miles northeast of Maluku province on the Island of Ambon, four days of rioting between Christians and Muslims.

King Hussein returns to Jordan from months of cancer treatment in the U.S. He names his son Abdullah as Crown Prince, replacing his brother Hassan, and returns to the U.S. for further treatment.

U.S. jets fire missiles at Basrah, hitting civilian targets by mistake, in return for targeting by Iraqi anti-aircraft sites.

February: King Hussein of Jordan dies.

David Wurmser (see "A Clean Break" in 1996), urges the US to support an insurgency against Saddam Hussein as part of a broad policy to defeat pan-Arabism in Iraq. (David Wurmser, "Tyranny's Ally, America's failure to defeat Saddam Hussein".)

Iraq threatens its neighbors, in particular Turkey, for allowing its airbases to be used by the U.S. in its attacks on Iraq.

The Kurdish leader Ocalan is apprehended in Kenya by Turkey and incarcerated on an island in the sea of Marmara. Violent demonstrations begin in Europe by Kurds against Greek embassies in the belief that the Greeks, in whose protective custody Ocalan found himself, were involved in Ocalan's capture; in fact the U.S. provides information to Turkey about Ocalan's whereabouts.

Ayatollah Mohammed Sadeq as-Sadr is assassinated in Najaf along with his two sons. He is the third Shi'ite cleric to be killed in Iraq in less than a year. Although he followed the Iraq government line, which is Sunni dominated, he had issued a fatwa that called upon Iraqis to attend Friday prayer in mosques rather than by watching television at home; the government is opposed to large gatherings.

Turkish Prime Minister Bulent Ecevit makes allusions to possible accommodation with Kurdish demands if Kurds lay down their arms; the Turkish army begins operations against Kurdish resistance. Turkey cracks down on Islamists in the country.

March: U.S. air attacks on Iraq become more intense.

An Israeli general is killed by Hizbollah in south Lebanon.

Bomb explodes in Vladikavkaz, the capital of the North Ossetia region thirty miles from Chechnya killing more than fifty people.

Bomb explodes in Grozny, capital of Chechnya near the motorcade of Aslan Maskhadov.

Thirteen Jews of Shiraz and eight Muslims are arrested in Iran and accused of spying.

March 20: Saddam Hussein sends Iraqi pilgrims on Hajj; the Saudis offer to pay expenses but Hussein demands that Saudi Arabia pay expenses out of frozen funds which is refused, and eighteen thousand Iraqi pilgrims return to Iraq with numerous recriminations after refusing to enter camps set up for them in Mecca.

March 24: After continuing massacres of ethnic Albanians by the Serb military in Kosovo, and the breakdown of talks in France, Nato attacks Serbia to force Slobodan Milosevic to accept terms regarding the province whose population is 90% Albanian Muslims.

April 1: Religious riots spread in Indonesia.

As bombing of Serbia continues, Serbs drive half a million ethnic Albanians out of Kosovo destroying their passports, documents, and automobile licence plates to deprive them of their identities. One hundred thousand ethnic Albanian men disappear and hundreds of thousands flee into hiding within Kosovo while killings, rapes, and atrocities multiply.

April 14: The politically motivated trial of Ibrahim Anwar, former Prime Minister of Malaysia, ends in his conviction and sentencing to six years in prisons. Demonstrations break out in Kuala Lumpur.

April 16: A Pakistani court convicts former Prime Minister Benazir Bhutto of taking kickbacks while she was in office in the 1990's. She is sentenced to five years in prison and is barred from office. Her husband Asif Ali Zardari is also sentenced for corruption.

A court in Egypt sentences six members of Jihad to death in absentia, and others are also sentenced.

After other political candidates withdraw saying that the elections in Algeria are rigged, the sole candidate remaining, 'Abdelaziz Bouteflika, the 62 year old former foreign minister returned from an absence of twenty years in Switzerland, is elected president of the republic in an election denounced as un-democratic.

May: Turkey: a female member of the Turkish Islamic Virtue Party, Merve Kavakci is prevented from taking her seat in the Parliament because she wears a head scarf. When it is discovered that shortly before she took American citizenship, she loses her Turkish citizenship by decree, because, "although Turkey allows dual citizenship, she did not ask for permission". Several hundred women take to demonstrations in the streets of Istanbul in protest. The head of the Virtue Party, Recai Kutan estimated that there were twenty cases of dual citizenship in the parliament. Earlier Ms Kavakci left medical school in Turkey because she was not allowed to sit examinations in a head scarf. Her father headed an Islamic organisation in Texas, USA, where she earned a degree in computer science.

"Strategic Assessment 1999" a policy document prepared for the US Joint Chiefs of Staff and the Secretary of Defense confirms US readiness to fight a war for oil. (*Sydney Morning Herald* 5/20/03).

President Khatami of Iran visits Saudi Arabia, the first such visit since the Iranian revolution.

Saudi Mufti Shaikh Bin Baz dies; he is replaced by Shaikh Abd al-'Aziz bin 'Abdullah ash-Shaikh. Bin Baz was the highest religious authority in Saudi Arabia, known for his literalist fundamentalism and also for supporting the Saudi monarchy.

Ehud Barak wins elections in Israel. 'Ali Akbar Nateq-Nouri, a leading hard liner, is elected to a fourth term as speaker of the Iranian parliament.

In a war in the mountains of Jammu and Kashmir, Pakistan shoots down two Indian jets; a surviving pilot is shortly therafter returned to India.

On the first day of his trial in Turkey, 'Abdullah Ocalan surprises observers by admitting all acts of terrorism and asks for freedom for himself to lead a political party to reconcile Kurds and Turks.

Iran and Egypt plan to introduce Sara and Laila, dolls for children, which represent Islamic values and modesty.

June: Indonesia votes in its first free democratic election which is carried out without coercion. Former President Suharto casts a vote.

The 2,500 strong Israeli backed "South Lebanon Army, a Christian militia begins pulling out of Jezzin in South Lebanon. Many of them have sent their families to Marjayoun in the Israeli occupied zone.

The Kashmir war between India and Pakistan continues at the highest level in thirty years.

Fundamentalist attacks take place again in Algeria.

Former Deputy Prime Minister Anwar Ibrahim of Malaysia, after being sentenced to six years in prison on corruption charges goes on trial again this time charged with sodomy in what is widely regarded as a staged political vendetta.

Taliban forces go on the offensive in northern Afghanistan.

Serb forces complete withdrawal from Kosovo on the 15th in keeping with an agreement reached with Nato as Nato forces occupy Kosovo. The Serb orthodox church calls for Milosevic to resign.

Hizbollah guerrillas in Lebanon fire rockets into northern Israel and Israel bombs Lebanon including a power station in Beirut.

A Court in Turkey sentences the Kurdish leader Ocalan to death.

July: Student demonstrations in Iran calling for more democracy are violently opposed by vigilantes controlled by the government and are followed by a pro-government demonstration which is sponsored by the government itself.

July 23: King Hassan of Morocco dies. He is succeeded by one of his sons, Muhammad. King Hassan succeeded in retaining virtually absolute power while appearing to be a modern and contemporary leader forging alliances with Israel and the United States. In the case of the United States, Morocco's ties go back to the beginning: it was the first country to recognize the U.S. when it declared independence and made a gift of land in Tangier for one of the earliest American foreign legations.

President Abdelaziz Bouteflika of Algeria, having made in September a peace accord with a main rebel faction, the Islamic Salvation Army, calls for an amnesty for those who participated in the uprisings against the government, except for those who committed murder. The Algerian civil war has killed 100,000 since 1992.

In Iran, a special Court for Clergy orders a five year ban on the country's leading pro-reform newspaper, *Salam* and suspends its editor Muhammad Moussavi-Khoeiniha from journalism for three years.

August:Rabbi Ovadia Yosef, former chief Sephardic Rabbi of Israel, and leader of the Shas Party, creates an uproar when he says that Jewish Holocaust victims were "reincarnations of the souls of sinners, people who transgressed and did all sorts of things that should not be done. They had been reincarnated in order to atone."

War resumes for Russia in the Caucasus. Several thousand Islamic Fundamentalist fighters cross from Chechnya into Dagestan with the intention of creating a united Islamic republic in the two Caucasus countries independent of Russia. Leading the Chechens is Shamil Basayev, who led a raid in Budyonnovsk in Russia, and Khattab, a Saudi or Jordanian guerrilla fighter who arrived in the region in 1995. Dagestan is a mountainous region with a population of two million but thirty-four different ethnic nationalities. Dagestan is important to Russia because of its port, Mahachkala on the Caspian and pipelines to Azerbaijan.

In Israel new schoolbooks are adopted which admit that after the founding of the state of Israel "On nearly every front and in nearly every battle, the Jewish side had the advantage over the Arabs in terms of planning, organisation, operation of equipment and also in the number of trained fighters who participated in the battle" and that "the expulsion of the [Arab] residents of Ramie and Lod received the authorisation of the political leadership". In the past the propaganda line was that Jews were the underdog and that Arabs fled because they wanted to take over everything after the expected success of the Arab armies.

War continues for Iraq with British and American planes having fired more than 1,100 missiles against 359 targets in Iraq in retaliation for Iraqi targeting of planes over Iraqi no-fly zones.

September: After the Russians drive the Chechens out of Dagestan, a bomb explodes near Russian officer's quarters in Dagestan killing 64 as Chechen fighters return to Dagestan in their thousands, and a number of bombs explode in Moscow destroying apartment houses.

Israel and the Palestinian Authority sign a new agreement regarding troop withdrawal as two car bombs explode in Israel.

The neo-conservative think tank "Project for a New American Century" (which wrote the letter to Clinton in 1998 urging him to invade Iraq) writes a blueprint for the creation of "a global pax Americana". The report calls for the political control of the Internet, the subversion for the growth in power of even close allies and regime change in China, North Korea, Libya, Syria, Iran and other countries. It mentions that advanced forms of biological warfare can target specific genotypes and may transform biological warfare from terrorism to a useful political tool. The report complains that desired changes may take a long time "absent some catastrophic and catalyzing event – like a new Pearl Harbor."

The Israel High Court prohibits the use of torture by the security organisations. It does so, in the commentary of a Judge, reluctantly. In 1996 the Israel High Court not only upheld torture but the State attorney

Shal Nitzan defended Shin Bet saying "no enlightened nation would agree that hundreds of people should lose their lives because of a rule saying torture is forbidden under any circumstances." Justice Cheshin turned on a lawyer, Rosenthal, who demurred to say that torture was justified to "save lives" calling that "the most immoral and extreme position I have ever heard in my life... a thousand people are about to be killed and you propose that we don't do anything". The torture was carried out in secret sometimes on totally innocent people.

September 28: Israeli General Ariel Sharon makes a visit to the Temple Mount in Jerusalem (which, as site of the Holy of Holies is forbidden to visits by Jews by the Rabbinate of Israel). This visit is highly criticized by the government of Ehud Barak on political grounds. The visit is intended to send the message of Israel's hard right to the Palestinians regarding their expectations of a Palestinian state – that it is not to be – and the next day the second Palestinian Intifida begins, and shortly thereafter Ariel Sharon becomes Prime Minister in the new elections.

October: After bombing Grozny and other towns in Chechnya the Russian army occupies the northern third of Chechnya to the Terek river.

Israel ends a policy by which the Interior Ministry stripped Arabs from East Jerusalem of their right to live in East Jerusalem if they temporarily left to work elsewhere. Since 1967 about 5,400 Palestinians lost rights to enter the city and their Israeli health benefits and social security.

October 12: General Pervez Musharraf, having been relieved as Chief of Staff over his aggressive handling of the border fighting with India over Kashmir, carries out a coup d'état in Pakistan and puts P.M. Nawaz Sharif under house arrest.

Zein al-Abidine al-Mihdar, an Islamic militant leader, is executed in Yemen, along with others, after being convicted of kidnapping sixteen Western tourists, four of whom died in an attempt to rescue them in December of 1998.

October 25: A "safe passage" road link is opened between the Gaza Strip and the Palestinian West Bank.

2001

April: Rabbi Ovadia Yosef, former chief Sephardic Rabbi of Israel, and leader of the Shas Party, in a Passover sermon, calls for the annihilation of Arabs. "It is forbidden to be merciful to them. You must send missiles to them and annihilate them. They are evil and damnable."

September 9: Ahmad Shah Massoud, a leader of the Northern Alliance, is wounded in an assassination attempt. Al-Qaeda, sending assassins posing as reporters, explode a bomb inside a camera. Massaoud, a Tajik, dies several days later.

September 11: Two planes hijacked by terrorists trained or coordinated by al-Qaeda crash into the Twin Towers of the World Trade Center. A third plane crashes into the Pentagon, and another crashes without a target because the passengers overpowered the hijackers. 19 Hijackers are involved: Muhammad Atta, the leader is an Egyptian; 15 are Saudi; 2 UAE; 1 Lebanese. The overall planner may have been originally in Hamburg, Germany. Later, a person is charged as having been an intended 20th hijacker.

October 7: The U.S. begins bombing Afghanistan and Usama Bin Ladin releases a taped message through the Qatar television network al-Jazeerah calling for Holy War against America. Shortly after, President Bush says that the U.S. has always supported the creation of a Palestinian state.

Oct 17: Rehavam Zeevi, an Israeli minister of Tourism, and General who supported the annexation of the Palestinian West Bank to Israel is assassinated by Palestinian terrorists sparking Israeli reprisals. Zeevi proposed ethnic cleansing by deporting the Palestinians from the West Bank and Gaza and said that Israel should lay claim to the Kingdom of Jordan because the tribes of Gad, Reuven and Menashe had lived – which is to say, as nomads wandered there – over two thousand years ago. Zeevi referred to the Palestinians working in Israel as "lice" who must be stopped: "a cancer spreading among us". He also advocated that Arabs who were Israeli citizens should not be allowed to vote. He had just resigned from the government of Ariel Sharon because Sharon was being too soft, along with Avigdot Lieberman who advocated bombing the Aswan dam in Egypt. Zeevi had founded the Moledat or Homeland Party.

Oct 19: The Israelis begin occupying positions in West Bank cities.

Oct 21: Several Pakistani gunmen belonging to an extremist organisation gun down sixteen Christians at a church in south central Pakistan. (Christians are less than 2% of the population.)

October 25: Abdul Haq, a Pashtun of the Ahmadzai tribe and former guerrilla commander is captured and executed by the Taliban. He had entered Afghanistan from Peshawar hoping to rally anti-Taliban forces. Requests for help from the U.S. forces went unanswered according to official sources, although the Taliban say that a plane and helicopters came to his aid. Abdul Haq had been in exile in Dubai and was a supporter of the 87 year old former King Zahir Shah who lives in exile in Rome.

November 11; the Northern Alliance captures Mazar-i Sharif and Taloqan.

November 13; Northern Alliance takes Kabul.

November 26; Russia sends a hospital team to Kabul.

November 20: Amnesty international and other groups accuse Israel of continuing to use torture. In Geneva, Israel's representative answered that the practices of the security forces's methods did not amount to torture under the 1987 Convention against Torture. "A 'careful reading' of the convention, Mr Levy said, 'clearly suggests that pain and suffering, in themselves, do not necessarily constitute torture.'" (*NYT*)

November 27: A conference about the future government of Afghanistan begins in Bonn, Germany. In Jalalabad, Noor Muhammad said: "I am very hopeful about this meeting in Germany. We have to be. The Afghan crisis has left our neighbors and the whole world in crisis. This is a world in which each nation is a house; our house was on fire. Now the United States is on fire. The Taliban are finished but the bombing goes on. We need a government." (*NYT*) The conference names Hamid Karzai interim head of government.

December: After mounting Palestinian suicide attacks in Israel, Israel begins attacking Palestinian Authority targets in earnest.

December 8: Kandahar passes under effective control of the anti-Taliban forces. War focuses on the mountain cave strongholds of Tora Bora in the search for Bin Ladin. Most intelligence services believe that Bin Ladin died of ill health in this month in Tora Bora.

December 11: the FBI arrests the leader of the Jewish Defence League in a conspiracy to blow up Mosques and Islamic centers in California. This leads to added surveillance of such Jewish terrorist groups as Kahane Chai.

December 13: Five armed men attack the Indian parliament in New Delhi; fourteen people die including the attackers. The terrorists are presumed to be members of Lashkar-i Tayyiba or Jaish-i Muhammad, organisations based in Pakistan. Tensions rise between India and Pakistan as India makes the same kinds of demands on Pakistan that the U.S. made on Afghanistan and Israel upon the Palestinians.

2002

January 2: As war tensions increase between India and Pakistan, President Musharraf places new limitations on mujahidin organisations based in Pakistan.

March 6: The Belgian Court of Appeals agrees to hear the case that Ariel Sharon and other Israelis are war criminals because of their involvement in the massacres of Sabra and Shatila.

March 12: *NYT* reports that in the struggles between Palestinians and Israelis in the 1980's twenty five Palestinians were killed for each Israeli, whereas today it is one Israeli to 3 Palestinians.

June 10: The Loya Jirga opens in Afghanistan.

Ariel Sharon comes to Washington and tells President Bush that Israel wants peace, Israel is committed to peace, but now is not the right time for peace. (Reminiscent of Henry Kissinger who said in the 80's that America should do nothing about Israel and the Palestinians for ten years.)

It is revealed that an American citizen, Jose Padilla is being held in prison as a foreign combatant because he was planning to explode a radioactive bomb.

June: Israel begins building a fence on the occupied territories; Ariel Sharon opposes an interim Palestinian state.

July: Israel attacks a neighborhood in Gaza with a missile fired from a plane. They kill a leader of Hamas but also many civilians. When criticised they say they had no choice. It also turns out that the attack was carried out despite an agreement with Fatah to call the Palestinians to a cease fire.

Ariel Sharon votes yes to legislation liberating religious students from military service.

Gideon Ezra, Israel's Deputy Interior Minister, says, "The *more aggressive* the attack [on Iraq] is, the more it will help Israel against the Palestinians. The understanding would be that what is good to do in Iraq, is also good for here." He also says that a US invasion of Iraq would "undoubtedly deal a psychological blow" to the Palestinians. Yuval Steinitz, a Likud party member of the Knesset's Foreign Affairs and Defense Committee suggests that the imposition of a pro-American regime in Baghdad would ease Israel's discomfort with Syria. "After Iraq is taken by US troops and we see a new regime installed in Afghanistan, and Iraqi bases become American bases, it will be very easy to pressure Syria... if this happens we will really see a new Middle East." (*Christian Science Monitor*, 8/30/02).

Large scale demonstrations in Iran against the government.

Because of the large number of runaway girls in Iran, and rising prostitution, the government proposes creating "Chastity Houses" or, in reality, brothels where temporary marriage certificates (sigheh) are given to couples. The practice of temporary marriage has always existed in Shi'ism but under this plan it would be institutionalized in a systematic way that has raised outcry in the country.

July 29: The BBC reports that 40% of the West Bank – occupied Palestinian territory – is in the control of Israeli settlers and that Arabs are prevented from cultivating land that they own near these settlements. A similar situation exists in the Gaza strip.

2003

The head of the al-Azhar, Shaikh Tantawi, affirms that Jihad is licit self defense or resistance.

March 20th: U.S. invades Iraq. Paul Wolfowitz: "For bureaucratic reasons we settled on one issue, weapons of mass destruction, because it was the one reason we could all agree on." (*Washington Times* 5/30/03).

"For more than a half-century, American foreign policy involving oil has been cloaked in intrigue and deception, from the overthrow of the Premier of Iran in 1953 to the arming of Afghan rebels throught the 1980's, from the permanent establishment of a military presence in the Persian Gulf to the early support of Saddam Hussein in Iraq. If Iraq is now handled openly – meaning the war really was about liberating Iraq from a dictator and the rest of the world from a security threat, as the Bush administration asserts, and not about gaining control of oil reserves, as much of the world believes – it will be a historic first. The yardstick to measure US intentions will be 1950's Iran... Before the US-inspired overthrow of the Iranian government, American oil companies had no presence in that country. After the coup, five US oil companies moved in and produced oil for the next 25 years. More dependent on imports than ever before, the US today is seeking to diversify its sources. Iraq is the only country capable of flooding the world with cheap oil on the scale of Saudi Arabia... the fact is that oil – who has it, who produces it, who fixes its price – governs everything of significance in the Persian Gulf and affects economies everywhere. While the Bush Administration has repeatedly asserted that Iraq's oil belongs to its citizens – 'We'll make sure that Iraq's natural resources are used for the benefit of their owners, the Iraqi people," the president said – the stakes go far beyond Iraq. The amount of oil that Iraq brings to market will not just determine the living standards of Iraqis but affect everything from the Russian economy to the price Americans pay for gasoline, from the stability of Saudi Arabia to Iran's future." – *Time* magazine 5/10/03).

The Boston Globe wrote: "A powerful corollary of the strategy is that a pro-US Iraq would make the region safer for Israel and, indeed, its staunchest proponents are ardent supporters of the Israeli right-wing. Administration officials, meanwhile have increasingly argued that the onset of an Iraq allied to the US would give the administration more sway in bringing about a settlement to the Israeli-Palestinian conflict, though Cheney and others have offered few details on precisely how." (*Boston Globe* 9/10/02).

In October 2002 Deutsche Bank published a report entitled "Baghdad Bazaar Big Oil in Iraq" which analyzed the large stakes that certain countries and oil companies have in the United State's conflict with Iraq. It notes that the removal of Saddam Hussein would benefit US and British companies, while Russian, French, and Chinese companies would benefit from a peaceful outcome.

US forces destroy the tomb of Michel Aflaq, founder of the Ba'th party, in Baghdad.

2004

January: Afghan Loya Jirga approves new constitution.

March: Interim constitution approved in Iraq.

March 11: 202 killed and 1,400 wounded when four commuter trains are bombed in Madrid.

Shaykh Yassin, spiritual leader of Hamas, and seven others, are hit by an Israeli missle in Gaza.

August. Four Christian churches attacked in Iraq.

Two Russian passenger planes in Russia are destroyed by bombs on board carried on by women.

September: Chechen insurgents take 1,200 hostages in a school in Beslan. 340 die as a school is stormed by security forces.

2005

Rabbi Ovadia Yosef, former chief Sephardic Rabbi of Israel, and leader of the Shas Party, invokes a curse over Sharon's plan to withdraw from the Gaza Strip. "The Holy One wants us all to return to the Torah, and then He will strike him with one blow and he will die. He will sleep and never wake up," the BBC reports him as "saying this in an apparent reference to Ariel Sharon". Rabbi Ovadia caused uproar before by calling Jewish Holocaust victims sinners who were reincarnated in order to atone, and by calling for the annihilation of Arabs by missiles.

July 7: British Pakistanis carry out suicide bomb attacks on public transport in London. 56 victims are killed and many more are wounded.

Israel withdraws from the Gaza strip while five Israeli West Bank settlements are confirmed to remain under direct Israeli control. Israel continues building the security wall on the West Bank. In July, a group of Kabbalists in Rosh Pina recite the "Pulsa Dinura" ceremony to curse Ariel Sharon.

2006

Feb. The Golden Mosque of the Shi'ites in Samarra is destroyed and civil war begins.

Many fabrications emerge as part of the buildup to the Iraq war including the assertion that 9/11 terrorist Atta had a meeting with Iraqis in the Iraq embassy in Prague (which did not occur), and a tape which Colin Powell played showing an Iraqi general concerned about traces of chemicals; the tape did not prove they had such weapons, as asserted, but rather that they had destroyed them.

June. Three inmates of the Guantanamo "detention center" commit suicide. The commandant calls this "assymetrical warfare".

July. Hamas from Gaza abducts an Israeli soldier with French citizenship and offers to exchange him for Palestinian women and children in Israeli prisons. Israel holds the Palestinian government responsible, destroys a U.S. built power plant in Gaza and attacks Gaza with rockets and artillery. Then Hizbollah in Lebanon kills several Israelis on the Lebanese side of the border, but south of the "Blue Line" and abducts two soldiers offering to exchange them for some of the 9,400 prisoners held in Israel. Israel calls this an act of war on the part of Lebanon, bombs the Beirut airport, destroys bridges and roads, bombs villages, Foreign Embassies evacuate, 700,000 refugees flee, and four UN observers are killed (after repeated telephone warnings that their position was under attack). U.S. Secretary of State Condoleeza Rice repeats that it is too early to call for a cease fire; President Bush affirms Israel's right to defend itself. Ehud Olmert says that the bombing of Lebanese civilians is intended to reduce popular support for Hizbollah and General Halutz says: "For every [Hizbollah] rocket we shall destroy ten high rise buildings in Beirut."

After 33 days of neutralizing Hizbollah's capacities, Israel agrees to a UN enforced ceasefire. The UN censures Israel for its heavy use of cluster bombs in residential neighborhoods during the last three days of fighting when ceasefire agreements are being made, leaving an estimated 1,00,000 unexploded bomblets in the cities of Lebanon. Three explosions take place every day in Lebanon as a result of these bomblets. The UN also censures Hizbollah for sending rockets into Israel.

September 12: Pope Benedict XVI delivers a lecture at the University of Regensburg in which he cites an "erudite" Byzantine Emperor, Manuel II Paleologus who says to a learned Persian in 1394-1402:

"Show me just what Mohammed brought that was new, and there you will find things only evil and inhuman, such as his command to spread by the sword the faith that he preached."

An uproar breaks out in the Islamic world. The Pope disingenuously replies that this is not his opinion.

French television reports a leak from French Intelligence which says that Usama Bin Ladin died in August 2006 of Typhoid fever. Most informed observers, such as President Musharraf of Pakistan, believe that Bin Ladin died of ill health in December 2001 in Tora Bora.

The Vatican's International Theological Commission continues to work on a document to abolish the concept of "Limbo".

The Civilian death toll due to the Iraq war is over 600,000 according to a study by Johns Hopkins, the Columbia School of Nursing, and al-Mustansiriya Hospital in Baghdad.

2007

January: The Ethiopean army drives out the "United Islamic Courts" in Somalia and re-installs the War Lords, renamed as the interim government, into power. The U.S. bombs targets in Somalia claiming they are al-Qaeda strongholds. The U.S. raids the Iranian consulate in Erbil, Iraq. The U.S. army and the Iraqis carry out an operation in Najaf against a dissident Shi'ite faction which had planned to attack Shi'ite pilgrims and demonstrators during the Ashura and to assassinate Shi'ite leaders such as Ayatollah Sistani. Fighting intensifies between Fatah and Hamas in Gaza.

February: Former US Undersecretary of Defense Douglas J. Feith is accused by investigators of manipulating intelligence reports to support the invasion of Iraq.

The British announce they will withdraw large numbers of troops from Basrah, which already is largely run by Shi'ite militias. These militias, however, may be quite different from Muqtada as-Sadr's Mahdi army, because the Shi'ites of Basrah are a different sect, Akhbaris and not, like Sadr Usulis. Although they have in recent times been little aware of these differences, circumstances may bring about a greater distance between the two groups in Iraq. The Shi'ites gained in power after the Mongol invasions and they gain further after the American one.

March: An Egyptian Blogger is sentenced to four years in prison for "insulting Islam, the Prophet Muhammad, and Egyptian President Mubarak".

April: The Iranians capture British Soldiers on patrol in the Shatt al-Arab who Iran claims were in Iranian waters; the soldiers are released after confessions are aired on television.

Pope Benedict XVI waived in 2005 the five year waiting period before beatification could begin in the process of making Jean Paul II a saint. Now a miracle is recorded in which a nun was cured of Parkinson's disease (after the death of Jean-Paul II) by praying to Jean Paul II. (Jean Paul himself had Parkinson's which was not cured.)

Suicide bombing spreads and reaches new heights. See MARTYRS; TAWWABUN.

BASED, IN PART, UPON:

A.J. Arberry (*Arabic Poetry*);
Mary Boyce (*The Zoroastrians*);
Brockelmann (*History of the Islamic Peoples*);
The Dartmouth Bible;
Freeman-Grenville (*The Muslim and Christian Calendars*);
Facts on File;
Heinz Halm (*Das Reich des Mahdi*);
H.A.R. Gibb (*Introduction to Arabic Literature*);
M. Hodgeson (*The Venture of Islam; The Order of the Assassins*);
Norman Itzkowitz (*Ottoman Empire and Islamic Tradition*);
Martin A. Larson (*The Religion of the Occident*);
The New York Times;
Hollister (*The Shia of India*);
Samuel Lieu (*Manichaeism*);
Martin Lings (*Muhammad*);
Kurt Rudolf (*Gnosis*);
George Roux (*Ancient Iraq*).
Other sources are numerous.

BIBLIOGRAPHY

Koranic passages are from the translation by A. J. Arberry, *The Koran Interpreted*, Oxford University Press, 1964. Hujwīrī's *Kashf al-Mahjūb*, Niffarī, Imru'-l-Qays, al-Hallāj and reports of him, the end of Yazdagird, the letter to the Muqawqīs, the Kharijite Sermon, the Creed of al-Ash'arī, the Sermon on Jihād, some Koran verses, and some selected stories, are from Eric Schroeder's *Muhammad's People*. Additional passages from the Koran are from Muhammad Marmaduke Pickthall, *The Glorious Koran*. The quotations from Ibn 'Atā'illāh are from Victor Danner's *Ibn 'Atā'illāh's Sufi Aphorisms*. Excerpts from the *Khamriyyah* are from *The Mystical Poems of Ibn al-Farid* by A.J. Arberry, Abū Sa'id on love is from his translation of the *Book of Truthfulness*, Ḥasan Basrī on the world and the conversion of al-Ghazālī is from his *Sufism*. Quotations of Muslim thinkers are also taken from Whitall N. Perry's *The Treasury of Traditional Wisdom*. The *Burdah* of Ka'b is from *The Life of Muhammad* translated by A. Guillaume. The Chinese description of the Arabs in *Ta Shih* is from Bretschneider, *Ancient Chinese Knowledge of Arabs* quoted in Broomhall, *Islam in China*. The writings of the Shaykh ad-Darqawi are from *Letters of a Sufi Master*, and the *Salāt al-Mashīshiyyah* is from the *Prayer of Ibn Mashish*, both translated by Titus Burkhardt. Ibn al-'Arif on *istridrāj* is from the translation of the *Maḥāsin al-Majālis* by Elliot and Abdulla. The Chinese *Three Character Rhymed Classic of the Ka'bah* was translated by J. Peter Hobson. *The Book of the Highest Initiation* is from Stern, Isma'ili Studies.

In addition, the following books were principally consulted:

Addas, Claude. *Ibn 'Arabî ou la quête du Soufre Rouge*. Paris: Éditions Gallimard, 1989.

Agha, Said Saleh. *The Revolution which Toppled the Umayyads (Neither Arab nor 'Abbasid)*. Leiden: Brill, 2003.

Akademia Nauk SSSR. *Islam: Entsiklopedicheskii Slovar'*. Moscow: Nauka, 1991.

Amabe, Fukuzo. *The Emergence of the 'Abbasid Autocracy*. Kyoto: Kyoto University Press, 1995.

Amabe, Fukuzo. *State-Building and Autonomy in 'Abbasid Frontiers*. Nihon Tosho Center. Tokyo, 2005.

Anawati, Georges C. *Études de Philosophie Musumane*. Paris: Librairie Philosophique J. Vrin, 1974.

Andrae, Tor. *Mohamed, the Man and his Faith*. New York: Charles Scribner's Sons, 1936.

Andrae, Tor. *In the Garden of the Myrtles*. Albany: State University of New York Press, 1987.

Arberry, A.J. *The Book of Truthfulness* (trans. of the *Kitab as-Sidq*, by Abu Sa'id al-Kharraz). London: Oxford University Press, 1937.

Arberry, A.J. *Muslim Saints and Mystics*. London: Routledge and Kegan Paul, 1966.

Arberry, A.J. *The Mystical Poems of Ibn al-Farid*. Dublin: Emery Walker (Ireland) Ltd., 1956

Arberry, A.J. *Sufism*. London: George Allen and Unwin, 1950.

Arjomand, Said Amir. *The Shadow of God and the Hidden Imam*. Chicago: University of Chicago Press, 1984.

al-Ash'ari, Abu'l-Hasan 'Ali Ibn Isma'il. *Al-Ibanah 'an Usul ad-Diyanah: The Elucidation of Islam's Foundation*. A translation with Introduction and notes by Walter Conrad Klein. New Haven, American Oriental Society, 1940.

Austin, R.J.W. *Sufis of Andalusia*. London: George Allen and Unwin, 1971.

Awn, Peter. *Satan's Tragedy and Redemption: Iblis in Sufi Psychology*. Leiden: E.J. Brill, 1983.

Baerlein, Henry. *The Diwan of Abu'l-Ala*. London: John Murray, 1908.

al-Baghdadi, Abu Mansur 'Abd al-Qahir ibn Tahir. *Moslem Schisms and Sects: al-Farq bayn al-Firaq* (Part I), translated by Kate Chambers Seelye. New York; Columbia University Press, 1920.

al-Baghdadi, Abu Mansur 'Abd al-Qahir ibn Tahir. *Moslem Schisms and Sects: al-Farq bayn al-Firaq*, (Part II), translated by Abraham S. Halkin. Tel-Aviv: 1935.

Barthold, W. *Turkestan down to the Mongol Invasion*. (Translated from the Russian by Mrs. T. Minorsky.) London: Luzac, 1968.

Bausani, Alessandro. *The Persians*. London: Elek Books; 1971.

Behruz, Zabih. *Taqvim va Tarikh Dar Iran az Rasd Zardusht ta Rasd Khayyam, Zaman Mihr va Mani*. Tehran: Iran Koudah 1952.

Bell, Richard, and Watt, W. Montgomery. *Introduction to the Qur'an*. Edinburgh: Edinburgh University Press, 1972.

Bell, Richard. *The Origin of Islam in its Christian Environment*. London: Frank Cass & Co. Ltd. 1968 (reprint).

Al-Biruni. *The Chronology of Ancient Nations*. Translated by C. Edward Sachau. London: W.H. Allen & Co., 1870.

Al-Biruni. *Alberuni's India*. Translated by Edward C. Sachau. Delhi: S. Chand & Co., 1964. (Reprint).

Al-Biruni. *The Book of Instruction in the Elements of the Art of Astrology*. Translated by R. Ramsay Wright. London: Luzac & Co.; 1934

Blachère, Régis. *Introduction au Coran*. Paris: G.-P. Maissoneuve et Larose, 1977.

Bleeker, C. Jouco and Widengren, Geo. *Historia Religionum*. Leiden: E. J. Brill, 1971.

Boewering, Gerhard. *The Mystical Vision of Existence in Classical Islam: The Qur'anic Hermeneutics of the Sufi Sahl at-Tustari*. Berlin: Walter de Gruyter, 1980.

Bosworth, C.E. *The Islamic Dynasties*. Edinburgh: Edinburgh University Press, 1980.

Bouhdiba, Abdelwahab. *Sexuality in Islam*. London: Routledge and Kegan Paul, 1985.

Boyce, Mary. *A History of Zoroastrianism*. Leiden: E.J. Brill, 1975-1991.

Boyce, Mary. *Zoroastrians*. London: Routledge and Kegan Paul, 1979.

Boyle, J.A. *The History of the World Conqueror* (by 'Ata-Malik Juvaini). Manchester: Manchester University Press, 1958.

Boyle, J.A. *The Successors of Genghiz Khan* (the History of Rashīd ad-Dīn aṭ-Ṭabīb). New York and London: Columbia University Press, 1971.

Brett, Michael. *The Rise of the Fatimids*. Leiden: Brill, 2001.

Brocklemann, Carl. *History of the Islamic Peoples*. London: Routledge and Kegan Paul, 1948.

Brown, John P. *The Darvishes or Oriental Spiritualism*. London: Oxford University Press, 1927.

Burckhardt, Titus. *Art of Islam*. London: World of Islam Festival, 1976.

Burckhardt, Titus. *Fez, Stadt des Islam*. Olten: Urs Graf Verlag. 1960.

Burckhardt, Titus. *Introduction to Sufi Doctrine*. Wellingborough: Thorson's Publishers, 1976.

Burckhardt, Titus. *Letters of a Sufi Master*. London: Perennial Books, 1973.

Burckhardt, Titus. *Moorish Culture in Spain*. London: George Allen and Unwin Ltd., 1972.

Burckhardt, Titus. *The Prayer of Ibn Mashish*. Studies in Comparative Religion, Winter-Spring 1978, Pates Manor, Bedfont, Middlesex.

Burton, Sir Richard. *Personal Narrative of a Pilgrimage to al-Madinah and Meccah*. London: Tyleston and Edwards, 1893.

Carlsen, Robin Woodsworth. *The Imam and His Islamic Revolution*. Victoria, British Columbia: The Snow Man Press, 1982.

Corbin, Henry. *Avicenne et le Récit Visionnaire*. Paris and Teheran: Librairie D'Amérique et D'Orient Adrien-Maisonneuve, 1954.

Corbin, Henry. *Cyclical Time and Isma'ili Gnosis*. London: Kegan Paul International, 1983.

Corbin, Henry. *The Dramatic Element Common to the Gnostic Comogonies of the Religions of the Book*. Studies in Comparative Religion, Summer-Autumn, 1980. Pates Manor, Bedfont, Middlesex.

Coulson, N.J. *A History of Islamic Law*. Edinburgh: Edinburgh University Press, 1964.

Daftary, Farhad. *The Isma'ilis, Their History and Doctrines*. Cambridge: Cambridge University Press, 1990.

Daiber, Hans. *Wasil Ibn 'Ata' als Prediger und Theologe*. Leiden: E.J. Brill, 1988.

Daniel, Elton L. *The Political and Social History of Khurasan under 'Abbasid Rule*. Minneapolis and Chicago: Bibliotheca Islamica, 1979.

Danner, Victor. *Ibn 'Ata'illah's Sufi Aphorisms.* Leiden: E.J. Brill,. 1973.

Danziger, Raphael. *Abd al-Qadir and the Algerians.* New York: Holmes and Meier, 1977.

Davis, F. Hadland. *Jami.* Lahore: Sh. Muhammad Ashraf, 1968.

Decret, François. *Mani et la Tradition Manichéene.* Paris: Editions de Seuil, 1974.

Denferr, Ahmad von. *'Ulum al-Qur'an.* London: The Islamic Foundation, 1983.

Dermenghem, Emile. *Vies des Saints Musulmans.* Alger: Éditions Baconnier.

Donaldson, Dwight M. *The Shi'ite Religion.* London: Luzac and Company, 1933.

Doniach, N.S. *The Oxford English-Arabic Dictionary.* Oxford: The Clarendon Press, 1962.

Eban, Abba. *Heritage: Civilization and the Jews.* New York: Summit Books, 1984.

Elder, Edgar Earl. *A Commentary on the Creed of Islam: Sa'd al-Din al-Taftazani on the Creed of Najm al-Din Nasafi.* New York: Columbia University Press, 1950.

Elliot, William and Abdulla, Adnan K. *Mahasin al-Majalis* by Ibn al-'Arif. Avebury, 1980.

Encyclopedia of Islam. Leiden: E.J. Brill, 1st Ed. 1913-1939; 2nd Ed. 1960-.

His Majesty King Abdul Aziz Project for The Extension and Construction of Haram Sharif. Associated Consulting Engineers (ACE) Ltd., Karachi, Pakistan and Mecca Mukarramah.

Filippani-Ronconi, Pio. *Ummu'l-Kitâb.* Naples: Istituto Universitario Orientali di Napoli; 1966.

Filoramo, Giovanni. *A History of Gnosticism.* Cambridge: Basil Blackwell, 1990.

Firo, Kais M. *A History of the Druzes.* Leiden: E.J. Brill, 1992.

Foerster, Werner. *Gnosis.* London: Oxford at the Clarendon Press, 1972.

Freeman-Grenville, G. S. P. *The Muslim and Christian Calendars.* London: Oxford University Press, 1963.

Friedlander, Ira. *The Whirling Dervishes.* New York, Macmillan, 1975.

Friedlander, Shems, with al-Hajj Shaikh, Muzaffareddin. *Ninety-Nine Names of Allah.* New York: Harper and Row, 1978.

Frye, Richard N. *The Golden Age of Persia.* London: Weidenfeld and Nicolson, 1975.

Frye, Richard N. *The Heritage of Central Asia.* Princeton: Markus Wiener Publishers, 1996.

Fu-ch'u, Ma. *The Three-Character Rhymed Classic on the Ka'bah (the Cube of Heaven)*; Translated by J. Peter Hobson. Studies in Comparative Religion, Summer-Autumn, 1980. Pates Manor, Bedfont, Middlesex.

Fyzee, Asaf A.A. *The Book of Faith (The Da'a'im al-Islam of al-Qadi al-Nu'man).* Bombay: Nachiketa Publications Ltd, 1974.

Gätje, Helmut. *Koran und Koranexegese.* Zuerich: Artemis Verlag, 1971.

Gaudefroy-Demombynes, Maurice. *Muslim Institutions.* London: George Allen and Unwin, 1950.

Geiger, Abraham. *Judaism and Islam* (Was Hat Mohammad aus dem Judenthume Aufgenommen). New York: Ktav Publishing House, Inc., 1970.

Geijbels, M. *An Introduction to Islam.* Rawalpindi: Pakistan Committee for Theological Education, 1977.

Ghazali, Abu Hamid Muhammad, *The Mysteries of the Human Soul (Al-Madnun bihi 'ala ghairi ahlihi).* Translated by Abdul Qayyum "Shafaq" Hazarvi. Lahore: Sh. Muhaamad Ashraf, 1981.

Ghirshman, R. *L'Iran des origines* à l'Islam. Paris: Payot, 1951.

Gibb, H.A.R. *Arabic Literature.* Oxford: Oxford University Press, 1963.

de Goeje, M. J. *Mémoire sur les Carmathes du Bahrain et les Fatimides.* Leiden: E.J. Brill, 1886.

Goldziher, Ignaz. *Études sur la Tradition Islamique*, traduites par Léon Bercher. Paris: Adrien-Maisonneuve, 1952.

Goldziher, Ignaz. *Streitshrift des Gazali gegen die Batinijja-Sekte.* Leiden: E.J. Brill, 1956.

Goodman, Lenn Evan. *The Case of the Animals versus*

Man before the King of the Jinn (Risa'il al-Ikhwan as-Safa). Boston: Twayne Publishers, 1978.

Gramlich, Richard. *Islamische Mystik*. Stuttgart: Kohlhammer, 1992.

Green, Tamara M. *The City of the Moon God*. Leiden: E.J. Brill, 1992.

Grousset, René. *Conqueror of the World*. New York, The Orion Press, 1966

Grousset, René. *The Empire of the Steppes*. New Brunswick, New Jersey: Rutgers University Press, 1970.

von Grunebaum, Gustave, Ed. *Unity and Variety in Muslim Civilization*. Chicago: University of Chicago Press, 1955.

Guerdan, René. Byzantium: Its Triumphs and Tragedy. London: George Allen and Unwin, 1956.

Guillaume, A. *The Life of Muhammad* (Ibn Ishaq's *Sirat Rasul Allah*). Karachi: Oxford University Press, 1970.

Halm, Heinz. *Das Reich des Mahdi; Der Aufstieg der Fatimiden*. Munich: C.H. Beck, 1991.

Halm, Heinz. Die Islamische Gnosis. Zuerich: Artemis Verlag, 1982.

Halm, Heinz. *Die Schia*. Darmstadt: Wissenchaftliche Buchgesselschaft, 1988.

Halm, Heinz. *Kosmologie und Heilslehre der Fruehen Isma'iliya*. Wiesbaden: Deutsche Morgenlandische Gesellschaft (Kommissionsverlag Franz Steiner GMBH), 1978.

Halm Heinz. *Shi'a Islam: From Religion to Revolution*. Princeton: Markus Wiener Publishers, 1997.

Halman, Talât Sait. *The Humanist Poetry of Yunus Emre*. Istanbul: Publications of the R.C.D. Cultural Institute. No Date.

al-Hamdani, Husayn F. *On the Geneology of the Fatimid Caliphs*. Cairo: American University at Cairo, 1958.

Hamilton, Charles, trans. *The Hedaya*. Delhi: The Islamic Book Trust, 1982.

Hamidullah, Muhammad. *The Battlefields of the Prophet Muhammad*. Hyderabad-Deccan, 1973.

Harmatta, J. Ed. *From Hecataeus to al-Huwarizmi*. Budapest: Akadémiai Kiado, 1984.

Hazard, Harry W. *Atlas of Islamic History*. Second Edition; Princeton: Princeton University Press, 1952.

Hollister, John Norman. *The Shi'a of India*. London: Luzac and Company, Ltd., 1953.

Hodgson, Marshall G.S. *The Order of the Assassins*. 'S-Gravenhage: Mouton & Co., 1955.

Hodgson, Marshall G.S. *The Venture of Islam*. Chicago: The University of Chicago Press, 1974.

Hourani, George Fadlo. *Arab Seafaring*. Beirut: Khayats, 1963.

Howard, I.K.A. *Kitab al-Irshad*, (The Book of Guidance by Shaykh al-Mufid). Qum: Ansariyan Publications.

Howarth, David. *The Desert King*. New York: McGraw-Hill, 1964.

Hughes, Thomas Patrick. *A Dictionary of Islam*. W.H. Allen and Unwin, 1885.

Ibn 'Arabi, Muhyiddin. *La Sagesse des Prophètes* (Fusus al-Hikam), translated by Titus Burckhardt. Paris: Editions Albin Michel, 1955.

Ibn al-Jawzi. *The Devil's Delusion* (Talbis Iblis) (translated by D.S. Margoliouth.) Hyderabad: Islamic Culture, 1935-1946.

Ibn al-Jawzi. *La Pensee Vigile* (Sayd al-Khatir) (translated by Daniel Reig.) Paris: Sindbad, 1986.

Ibn al-Kalbi, Hisham. *The Book of Idols*, translated by Nabih Amin Faris. Princeton, Princeton University Press, 1952.

Ibn Khaldun. *The Muqadimmah* (translated by Franz Rosenthal). Princeton, New Jersey: The Princeton University Press (for the Bollingen Foundation), 1958.

Ibn Rusteh. *Les Autours Precieux (Kitab al-A'lak an-Nafīsa)*. Traduction de Gaston Wiet. Cairo: Publications de la Société de Géographie d'Égypte, 1955.

Ibn Sa'd. *Kitab al-Tabaqat al-Kabir*. Karachi: Pakistan Historical Society.

Itzkowitz, Norman. *Ottoman Empire and Islamic Tradition*. Chicago: University of Chicago Press, 1972.

Ivanow, W. *The Alleged Founder of Isma'ilism*. Bombay: The Ismaili Society, 1946.

Ivanow. W. *The Rise of the Fatimids*. London: Oxford University Press: Islamic Research Association Series No.10. 1942.

Ivanow. W. *Studies in Early Persian Ismailism*. Bombay: The Ismaili Society Series, 1955.

Ivanow. W. *The Rawdatu't-Taslim, commonly called Tasawwurat* by Nasiru'd-din Tusi. Leiden: E.J. Brill, for the Ismaili Society, 1950.

Jafri, S. Husain M. *Origins and Early Development of Shi'ism*. London: Longman, Librairie du Liban, 1979.

Jeffery, Arthur. *A Reader on Islam*. 'S-Gravenhage: Mouton & Co., 1962.

Jeffery, Arthur. *Islam: Muhammad and His Religion*. Indianapolis: Bobbs-Merrill Company, Inc. 1958.

Kaidi, Hamza with Najm ad-Din Bammate and al-Hashimi Tijani. *Mecca and Medina Today*. Paris: Les Editions Jeune-Afrique, 1980.

Kassis, Hanna E. *A Concordance of the Qur'an*. Berkeley: University of California Press, 1983.

Kastein, Josef. *The History of the Jews*. New York: Garden City Publishing, 1933.

Khalidi, Tarif. *Islamic Historiography*. Albany: State of New York University Press, 1975.

Klein, F.A. *The Religion of Islam*. Reprint of the 1906 edition; New Delhi; Cosmo Publications, 1978.

Klimovich, L. I. *Kniga o Korane*. Moscow: Izdatel'stvo Politicheskoi Literaturi, 1986.

Kreiser, Klaus; Diem, Werner; Majer, Hans Georg, editors. *Lexikon der Islamischen Welt*. Stuttgart: Verlag W. Kohlhammer GmbH, 1974.

Kriss, Rudolf and Hubert Kriss-Heinrich. *Volksglaube im Bereich des Islam*. Wiesbaden: Harrasowitz, 1962.

Kritzeck, James. *Anthology of Islamic Literature*. Middlesex: Penguin, 1964.

Lane-Poole, Stanley. *Essay on the Brotherhood of Purity*. Lahore: Muhammad Ashraf; 1954 (Reprint).

Larson, Martin A. *The Religion of the Occident*. Paterson, New Jersey: Littlefield, Adams and Co. (Student Outline Series), 1961.

Lassner, Jacob. *The Shaping of 'Abbasid Rule*. Princeton: Princeton University Press, 1980.

Lawrence, Bruce B. *Shahrastani on the Indian Religion*. The Hague: Mouton, 1976.

Le Strange, Guy. *Baghdad and the Abbasid Caliphate*. Oxford: Clarendon Press, 1900.

Les Grandes Dates de l'Isam. Paris: Librairie Larousse, 1990.

Lewis, Bernard. *The Assassins*. New York: Basic Books.

Lewis, Bernard. *Istanbul and the Civilization of the Ottoman Empire*. Norman: University of Oklahoma Press, 1963.

Lewis, Bernard. *The Origins of Isma'ilism*. Cambridge: W. Heffer and Sons Ltd., 1940.

Lichtenstadter, Ilse. *Introduction to Classical Arabic Literature*. New York: Schocken Books, 1976.

Lieu, Samuel N.C. *Manichaeism*. Manchester: Manchester University Press, 1985.

Lings, Martin. *A Sufi Saint of the Twentieth Century*. London: George Allen and Unwin, 1971.

Lings, Martin. *Muhammad*. London: George Allen and Unwin, Islamic Texts Society, 1983.

Lory, Pierre. *Les Commentaires Ésotériques du Coran d'après 'Abd ar-Razzaq al-Qashani*. Paris: Les Deux Océans, 1980.

Lubis, Hajj Muhammad Bukhari. *Qasidahs in Honor of the Prophet*. Malaysia: Penerbit Universiti Kebansaan Malaysia, 1983.

MacDonald, Duncan Black. *Development of Muslim Theology, Jurisprudence and Constitutional Theory*. Lahore: Premier Book House, 1963 (first published 1903)

Madelung, Wilferd. *Religious and Ethnic Movements in Medieval Islam*. Hampshire: Variorum, 1992.

Madelung, Wilferd. *Religious Schools and Sects in Medieval Islam*. London Variorum Reprints, 1985.

Madelung, Wilfred. *Religious Trends in Early Islamic Iran*. Albany: Bibliotheca Persica, 1988.

Margouliouth, D.S. *The Table-Talk of a Mesopotamian Judge*. London: The Royal Asiatic Society, 1922.

Marsh, Clifton E. *From Black Muslims to Muslims: The Transition from Separatism to Islam, 1930-1980.* Metuchen, New Jersey, and London: The Scarecrow Press, 1988.

Massignon, Louis. *Akhbar al-Hallaj.* Paris: Librairie Philosophique J. Vrin, 1957.

Massignon, Louis. *Al-Hallaj, Martyr Mystique de L'Islam.* Paris: Librairie Orientaliste Paul Geuthner, 1921.

Massignon, Louis. *Essai Sur les Origines du Lexique Technique de la Mystique Musulmane.* Paris: Librairie Orientaliste Paul Geuthner, 1922.

Massignon, Louis. *Opera Minora.* Beirut: Dar al-Maaref, 1963.

Al-Mas'udi. *Les Prairies d'Or.* Traduction française de Barbier de Maynard et Paret de Courteille. Revue et corrigée par Charles Pellat. Paris: Societé Asiatique, 1962.

Mez, Adam. *The Renaissance of Islam.* Translated by Salahuddin Khuda Bakhsh and D.S. Margoliouth. Delhi: Idarah-i Adabiyat-i Delli, 1937, reprinted 1979.

Minorsky, V. *Hudud al-'Alam.* Translated and explained, edited by C.E. Bosworth. London: Luzac and Company, 1970.

Momen, Moojan. *An Introduction to Shi'i Islam.* New Haven and London: Yale University Press, 1985.

Monnot, Guy. *Penseurs Musulmans et Religions Iraniennes.* Paris: Librairie Philosophique J. Vrin, 1974.

Moosa, Matti. *Extremist Shiites.* Syracuse, New York: Syracuse University Press, 1988.

Mottahedeh, Roy. *The Mantle of the Prophet.* New York: Simon and Schuster. 1985.

Ibn-Munqidh, Usamah. *An Arab-Syrian Gentleman and Warrior.* Translated by Philip K. Hitti. New York: Columbia University Press, 1929.

Musallam, B.F. *Sex and Society in Islam.* Cambridge: Cambridge University Press, 1983.

An-Nadim, Muhammad ibn Ishaq. *The Fihrist of al-Nadim*, translated by Bayard Dodge. New York: Columbia University Press, 1970.

Nasir, Jamal J. *The Islamic Law of Personal Status.* London: Graham and Trotman, 1986.

Nasr, Seyyed Hossein, and Hamid Dabashi and Seyyed Vali Reza Nasr; Editors. *Expectations of the Millennium: Shi'ism in History.* Albany: State University of New York Press, 1989.

Nasr, Seyyid Hossein. *Ideals and Realities of Islam.* London: George Allen and Unwin Ltd. 1966.

Nasr, Seyyid Hossein. *An Introduction to Islamic Cosmological Doctrines.* Cambridge, Massachusetts: The Belknap Press, 1960.

Nasr, Seyyed Hossein. *Islamic Science.* London: World of Islam Festival, 1976.

Nasr, Seyyid Hossein. *Three Muslim Sages.* Cambridge, Massachusets: Harvard University Press, 1963.

Nawawi, Mahiudin Abu Zakaria. Minhaj-et-Talibin: *A Manual of Muhammadan Law according to the school of Shaf'i.* (translated from the French of L.W.C. Van Den Berg by E.C. Howard; reprint of the 1914 edition.) Lahore: Law Publishing Company, 1977.

Nawawi. *The Forty Hadith* (translated by Ezzeddin Ibrahim and Denys Johnson-Davies). Beirut: Holy Koran Publishing House, 1976.

Nelson, Kristina. *The Art of Reciting the Qur'an.* Austin: University of Texas Press, 1985.

Netton, Ian Richard. *Muslim Neoplatonists.* London: Geroge Allen and Unwin, 1982.

Nicholson, Reynold A. *The Kashf al-Mahjub of al-Hujwiri.* London, Luzac and Co., 1936.

Nicholson, Reynold A. *A Literary History of the Arabs.* London: Cambridge University Press, 1966 (originally published 1907).

Nicholson, Reynold A. *Studies in Islamic Mysticism.* Cambridge: Cambridge University Press, 1921

Nyberg, H.S. (Editor). *Le Livre du Triomphe et de la Réfutation d'Ibn er-Rawendi l'Hérétique par Abou'l-Hosein Abderrahim Ibn Mohammed Ibn Osman el-Khayyat.* (Kitab al-Intisar). Cairo, Imprimerie de la Bibliotheque Égyptienne, 1925.

Padwick, Constance E. *Muslim Devotions.* London S.P.C.K., 1961.

Pareja, F.M. with L. Hertling, A. Bausani, Th. Bois. *Islamologie.* Beirut: Imprimerie Catholique, 1957-1963.

Pellat, Charles. *Arabische Geisteswelt*. Zuerich: Artemis Verlag, 1967.

Perry, Whitall. *A Treasury of Traditional Wisdom*. London: George Allen and Unwin, 1971.

Pesle, O. *La Femme Musulmane dans le Droit, la Religion, et les Moeurs*. Rabat: Editions de la Porte, 1946.

Peters, F.E. *Aristotle and the Arabs*. New York: New York University Press, 1968.

Pickthall, Muhammad Marmaduke. *The Glorious Koran*. London: George Allen and Unwin, 1976.

Pritchard, James B., Editor. *Ancient Near Eastern Texts*. Princeton: Princeton University Press; 1969.

Al-Qayrawani, Ibn Abi Ziyad. *La Risala*, translated by Léon Bercher. Alger: Editions Populaires de l'Armee, 1975.

Rahman, Fazlur. *Health and Medicine in the Islamic Tradition*. New York: Crossroad, 1987.

Rahman, Fazlur. *Major Themes of the Qur'an*. Chicago: Bibliotheca Islamica, 1980.

Rahman, Fazlur. *Prophecy in Islam*. London: George Allen and Unwin, 1955.

Rahman, Fazlur. *Selected Letters of Sirhindi*. Karachi, Iqbal Academy.

Ralli, Augustus. *Christians at Mecca*. London: William Heinemann, 1909.

Renz, Alfred. *Geschichte und Stätten des Islam*. Munich: Prestel Verlag, 1977.

Rippin, Andrew, Editor. *Approaches to the History of Interpretation of the Qur'an*. Oxford: Clarendon Press, 1988.

Ritter, Hellmut. *Das Meer der Seele Mensch, Welt und Gott in den Geschichten der Fariduddin 'Attar*. Leiden: E.J. Brill, 1955.

Rizvi, Saiyid Athar Abbas. *A History of Sufism in India*. New Delhi: Mushiram Manoharlal Publishers Pvt. Ltd, 1983.

Robson, Dr. James. Trans. *Mishkat al-Masabih*. Lahore: Sh. Muhammad Ashraf, 1970.

Ronart, Stephan and Nandy. *Concise Encyclopedia of Arabic Civilization*. Amsterdam and Djakarta: Djambatan, 1959.

Ronart, Stephan and Nandy. *Lexikon der Arabischen Welt* (revision of The Concise Encyclopaedia of Arabic Civilization). Zuerich: Artemis Verlag, 1972.

Roux, George. *Ancient Iraq*. London: George Allen and Unwin, 1980 (Second Edition).

Sadighi, Gholam Hossein. *Les Mouvements Religieux Iraniens au IIe et au IIIe siècle de l'hégire*. Paris: Les Presses Modernes, 1938.

Schimmel, Annemarie. *As Through a Veil, Mystical Poetry in Islam*. New York: Columbia University Press, 1982.

Schroeder, Eric. *Muhammad's People*. Portland, Maine: Bond Wheelwright, 1955.

Schuon, Frithjof. *Understanding Islam*. London: George Allen and Unwin Ltd., 1963.

Shacht, Joseph. *An Introduction to Islamic Law*. Oxford: Oxford University Press, 1964.

Shacht, Joseph, and Bosworth, C.E. *The Legacy of Islam*. Oxford: At the Clarendon Press, 1974.

Shafi'i', Muhammad ibn Idris. *Al-Risala fi usul al-Fiqh*, translated by Majid Khadduri, 2nd Edition. Cambridge: The Islamic Texts Society, 1987.

Shahrastani, Muhammad ben 'Abd al-Karim. *Kitab al-Milal, Les Dissidences de l'Islam*, translated by Jean-Claude Vadet. Paris: Librairie Orientaliste Paul Geuthner S.A., 1984.

Shahrastani, Muhammad ibn 'Abd al-Karim. *The Summa Philosophiae of al-Shahrastânî: Kitâb Nihâyatu'l-Iqdam fî 'Ilmi'l-Kalâm*. Translated by Alfred Guillaume. London; Oxford University Press, 1934.

Shahrastani, Muhammad ibn `Abd al-Karim. *Muslim Sects and Divisions*, translated by A.K. Kazi and J.G. Flynn. London: Kegan Paul International, 1984.

Sharif, M.M. (Editor). *A History of Muslim Philosophy*. Wiesbaden: Otto Harrasowitz, 1963.

Sharon, M. *Black Banners from the East*. Jerusalem: The Magnes Press, The Hebrew University and Leiden: E. J. Brill, 1983.

Sharon, M. *Revolt: The Social and Military Aspects of the 'Abbasid Revolution*. Jerusalem: The Hebrew University, 1990.

Le Shi'isme Imamite. Colloque de Strasbourg. Various authors. Paris: Presses Universitaires de France, 1970.

Smith, Margaret. *An Early Mystic of Baghdad*, A Study of the Life and Teaching of Harith B. Asad al-Muhasibi. London: Sheldon Press (Reprinted), 1977.

Smith, W. Robertson. *The Religion of the Semites*. Meridian Books, New York, 1956.

Sourdel, Dominique and Janine. *Dictionnaire historique de l'Islam*. Paris: Presses Universitaire de France, 1996.

Spuler, Bertold. *The Mongol Period*. Princeon: Markus Wiener Publishers, 1994.

Stern, S.M. *Studies in Early Isma'ilism*. Jerusalem and Leiden: The Magnes Press — Hebrew University — E.J. Brill, 1983.

Stern, S. M.; Hourani, Albert, and Brown Vivian; Editors. *Islamic Philosophy and the Classical Tradition*. Columbia, South Carolina: University of South Carolina Press; 1973.

Stoyanov, Yuri. *The Hidden Tradition in Europe*. London: Penguin Arkana, 1994.

Tabari, 'Ali. *The Book of Religion and Empire*. Translated by A. Mingana. Lahore: Law Publishing Company. No Date.

Tabari. *The History of al-Tabari*. Albany: State University of New York Press, 1989.

Trimingham, J. Spencer. *The Sufi Orders in Islam*. London: Oxford University Press, 1971.

Tuetey, Charles Greville. *Imrulkais of Kinda, Poet*. London: Diploma Press, 1977.

Vajda, Georges. *Les Zindiqs au pays d'islam au début de la période abbaside*. RSO XVII, 1938.

Van den Bergh, Simon. *Averroes' Tahafut al-Tahafut*. London: Luzac and Co., 1954.

Vatikiotis, Panayiotis J. *The Fatimid Theory of State*. Lahore: Orientalia Publishers. ND.

Waldmann, Helmut. *Der Kommagenische Mazdaismus*. Tuebingen: Ernst Wasmuth Verlag, 1991.

Watt, W. Montgomery, and Cachia, Pierre. *A History of Islamic Spain*. Edinburgh: Edinburgh University Press, 1965.

Watt, M. Montgomery. *Islamic Political Thought*. Edinburgh: Edinburgh University Press, 1968.

Watt, W. Montgomery. *The Influence of Islam on Medieval Europe*. Edinburgh: Edinburgh University Press, 1972.

Watt, W. Montgomery. *Islamic Philosophy and Theology*. Edinburgh: Edinburgh University Press, 1962.

Watt, W. Montgomery. *A Companion to the Qur'an*. London: George Allen and Unwin Ltd., 1967.

Wehr, Hans. *Arabic English Dictionary*, edited by J.M. Cowan. Ithaca, New York: Cornell University Press, 1960.

Wellhausen, Julius. *The Arab Kingdom and its Fall*, translated by Margaret Graham Weir. Beirut: Khayats, 1963. (Originally published in English 1927.)

Widengren, Geo. *Muhammad, the Apostle of God and His Ascension*. Uppsala: Uppsala Universitets Arsskrift, 1955:1.

Wilson, Peter Lamborn and Pourjavady, Nasrollah. *Isma'ilis and Ni'matullahis* (Studia Islamica Fasciculo XLI) Paris: G.-P. Maisonneuve-Larose, 1975.

Wolfson, Harry Austryn. *The Philosophy of the Kalam*. Cambridge, Massachusetts: Harvard University Press, 1976.

Wunderli, Peter. *Etudes sur le livre de l'Eschiele Mahomet*. Winterthur: Editions P.G. Keller, 1965.

Zaehner, R.C. *Hindu and Muslim Mysticism*. New York: Schocken, 1969.

Zakariya, Mohamed U. *The Calligraphy of Islam*. Washington D.C.: Center for Contemporary Arab Studies, Georgetown University, 1979.

Zambaur, E. de. *Manuel de Généalogie et de Chronologie pour l'Histoire de l'Islam*. Orientbuchhandlung Heinz Lafaire, 1955.

Ziadeh, Nicola. *Sanusiyah*. Leiden: E.J. Brill, 1958.